NICHOL

D0714150

LONDON
STREET ATLAS

CONTENTS

Key to Map Pages 2-3

Key to Map Symbols 4-5

Central London Maps 6-21

Main London Maps 22-104

Theatres and Cinemas Map 105

Shopping Map 105

Bus Map.. 106

Index to Places of Interest 107-108

Index to Place Names 109-110

Index to Street Names 111

 Nicholson
An *Imprint* of HarperCollins*Publishers*

First published 1994
© Nicholson 1994

Generated from the Bartholomew London Digital Database.

The Ordnance Survey is not responsible for the accuracy of the National Grid in this publication.

London Underground Map by permission of London Regional Transport LRT Registered User Number 94/1496

Printed in Hong Kong.

ISBN 0 7028 1906 9

Nicholson
HarperCollins*Publishers*
77-85 Fulham Palace Road
London W6 8JB

Great care has been taken throughout this atlas to be accurate but the publishers cannot accept responsibility for any errors which appear or their consequences. Queries or information regarding the London Street Atlas should be addressed to the Publishing Director at the above address.

F/J 6373   LNB

KEY TO MAP PAGES

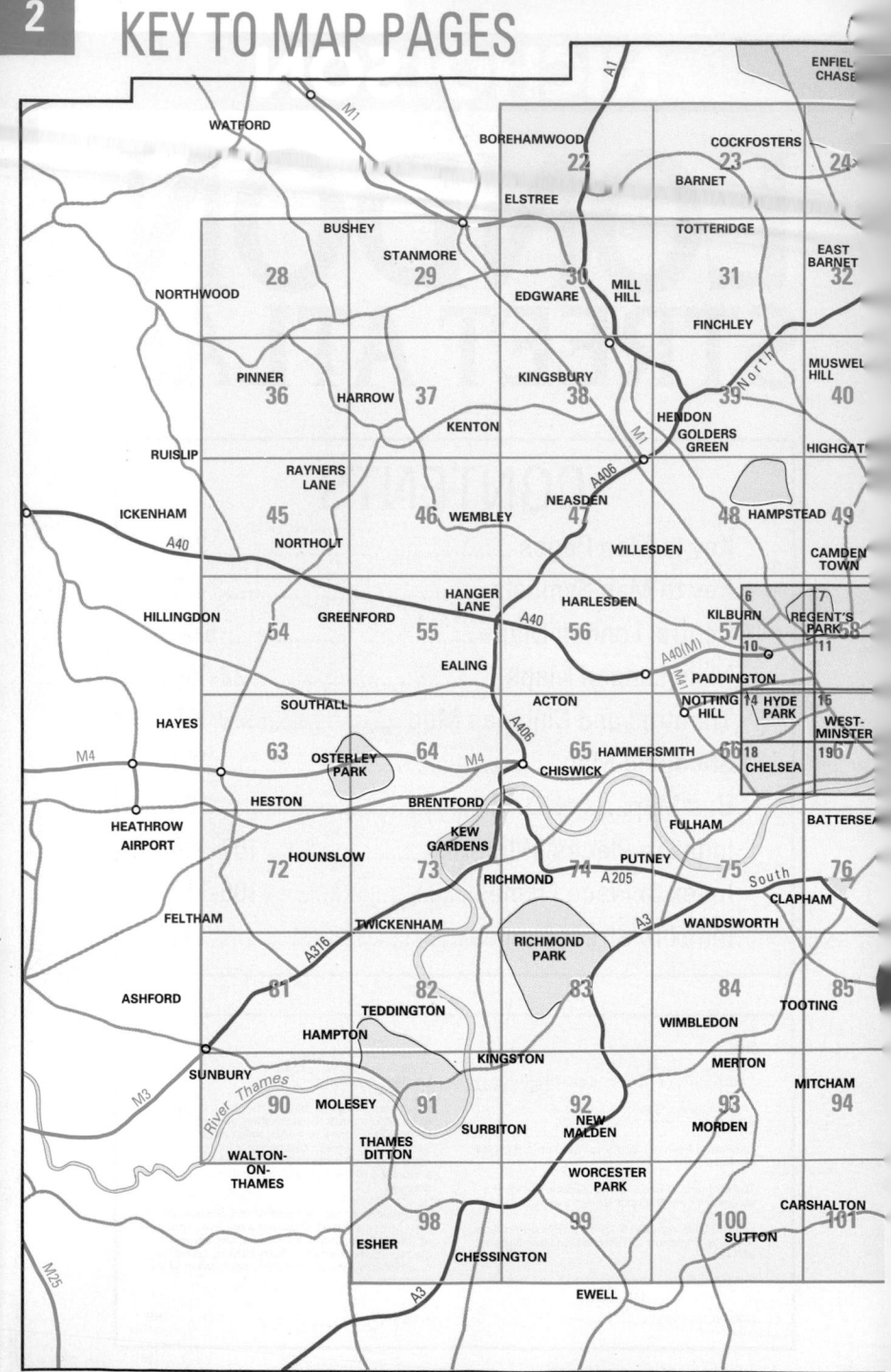

ENFIELD CHASE

WATFORD

BOREHAMWOOD 22

COCKFOSTERS 23

BARNET

24

ELSTREE

BUSHEY

STANMORE 29

TOTTERIDGE

EAST BARNET 32

NORTHWOOD 28

30 MILL HILL

31

EDGWARE

FINCHLEY

PINNER 36

HARROW 37

KINGSBURY 38

39

MUSWELL HILL 40

RUISLIP

KENTON

HENDON

GOLDERS GREEN

HIGHGATE

RAYNERS LANE

NEASDEN 47

HAMPSTEAD 49

ICKENHAM 45

46 WEMBLEY

48

NORTHOLT

WILLESDEN

CAMDEN TOWN

HILLINGDON

GREENFORD 54

HANGER LANE 55

HARLESDEN 56

KILBURN 57

6

REGENT'S PARK 58

EALING

10

11

PADDINGTON

SOUTHALL

ACTON

NOTTING HILL 14

HYDE PARK 15

HAYES

63

64

65 HAMMERSMITH 66

18 CHELSEA

WEST-MINSTER 19 67

OSTERLEY PARK

CHISWICK

HESTON

BRENTFORD

HEATHROW AIRPORT

KEW GARDENS

FULHAM

BATTERSEA

HOUNSLOW 72

73

PUTNEY 74 75

RICHMOND

FELTHAM

TWICKENHAM

WANDSWORTH

CLAPHAM

76

ASHFORD

81

82

RICHMOND PARK 83

84

TOOTING 85

TEDDINGTON

WIMBLEDON

HAMPTON

KINGSTON

SUNBURY

90 MOLESEY

91

MERTON

MITCHAM 94

SURBITON

92 NEW MALDEN

93 MORDEN

WALTON-ON-THAMES

THAMES DITTON

WORCESTER PARK

CARSHALTON 101

98

99

100 SUTTON

ESHER

CHESSINGTON

EWELL

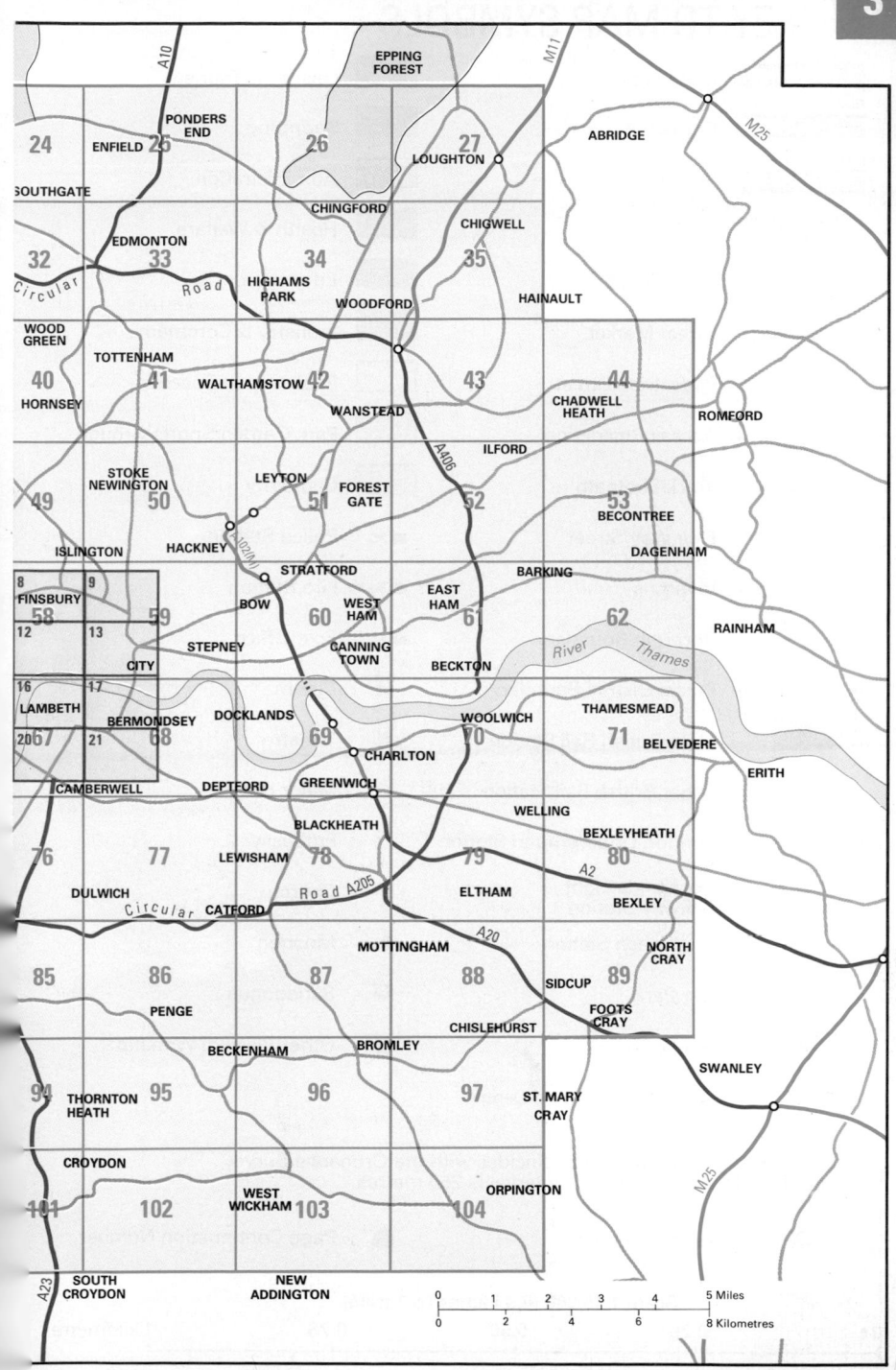

KEY TO MAP SYMBOLS

A40(M)	Motorway		Leisure & Tourism
Dual **A4**	Primary Route		Shopping
Dual **A40**	'A' Road		Administration
B504	'B' Road		Health & Welfare
	Other Road		Education
	Street Market		Industry & Commerce
	Pedestrian Street		Public Open Space
•————•	Access Restriction		Park/Garden/Sports Ground
═══════ -------	Track/Footpath	† † †	Cemetery
→	One Way Street	▬ *POL*	Police Station
– – – – – – –	Riverbus	▬ Fire Sta	Fire Station
CITY	Borough Boundary	▬ *PO*	Post Office
EC2	Postal District Boundary	🎥	Cinema
⟶≢⟵	Main British Rail Station	⛉	Theatre
⟶⊛⟵	Other British Rail Station	⊠	Major Hotel
⊖	London Underground Station	⊐	Embassy
⟶⊝⟵	Docklands Light Railway Station	+	Church
⬤	Bus/Coach Station	☾	Mosque
🅿	Car Park	✡	Synagogue
🚾	Public Toilet	Mormon ▪	Other Place of Worship
i	Tourist Information Centre		

The reference grid on this atlas coincides with the Ordnance Survey National Grid System. The grid interval is 250 metres.

A	Grid Reference	▲8	Page Continuation Number

Scale 1:10,000 (6.3 inches to 1 mile)

0	0.25	0.50	0.75	1 kilometre
0	¼		½ mile	

M41	Motorway			Leisure & Tourism
Dual **A4**	Primary Route		USA	Administration & Law Embassy
Dual **A40**	'A' Road			Health & Welfare
B504	'B' Road			Education
	Other Road			Industry & Commerce
	Toll			Cemetery
	Street Market			Golf Course
	Pedestrian Street			Public Open Space/ Allotments
	Cycle Path			Park/Garden/Sports Ground
------	Track/Footpath			Wood/Forest
→	One Way Street		Pol	Police Station
--P--	Pedestrian Ferry		Fire Sta	Fire Station
--V--	Vehicle Ferry		PO	Post Office
	County/Borough Boundary		Lib	Library
	Postal District Boundary		▲	Youth Hostel
	Main British Rail Station		□	Tower Block
	Other British Rail Station		ℹ	Tourist Information Centre
	London Underground Station		⊕	Heliport
	Docklands Light Railway Station		⚕	Windmill
	Bus/Coach Station		+	Church
P	Car Park		☾	Mosque
WC	Public Toilet		✡	Synagogue

The reference grid on this atlas coincides with the Ordnance Survey National Grid System. The grid interval is 500 metres.

A	Grid Reference	24	Page Continuation Number

Scale 1:20,000 (3.2 inches to 1 mile)

| 25 | OS National Grid Kilometre Square | |

0	0.25	0.50	0.75	1 kilometre

0	¼	½ mile

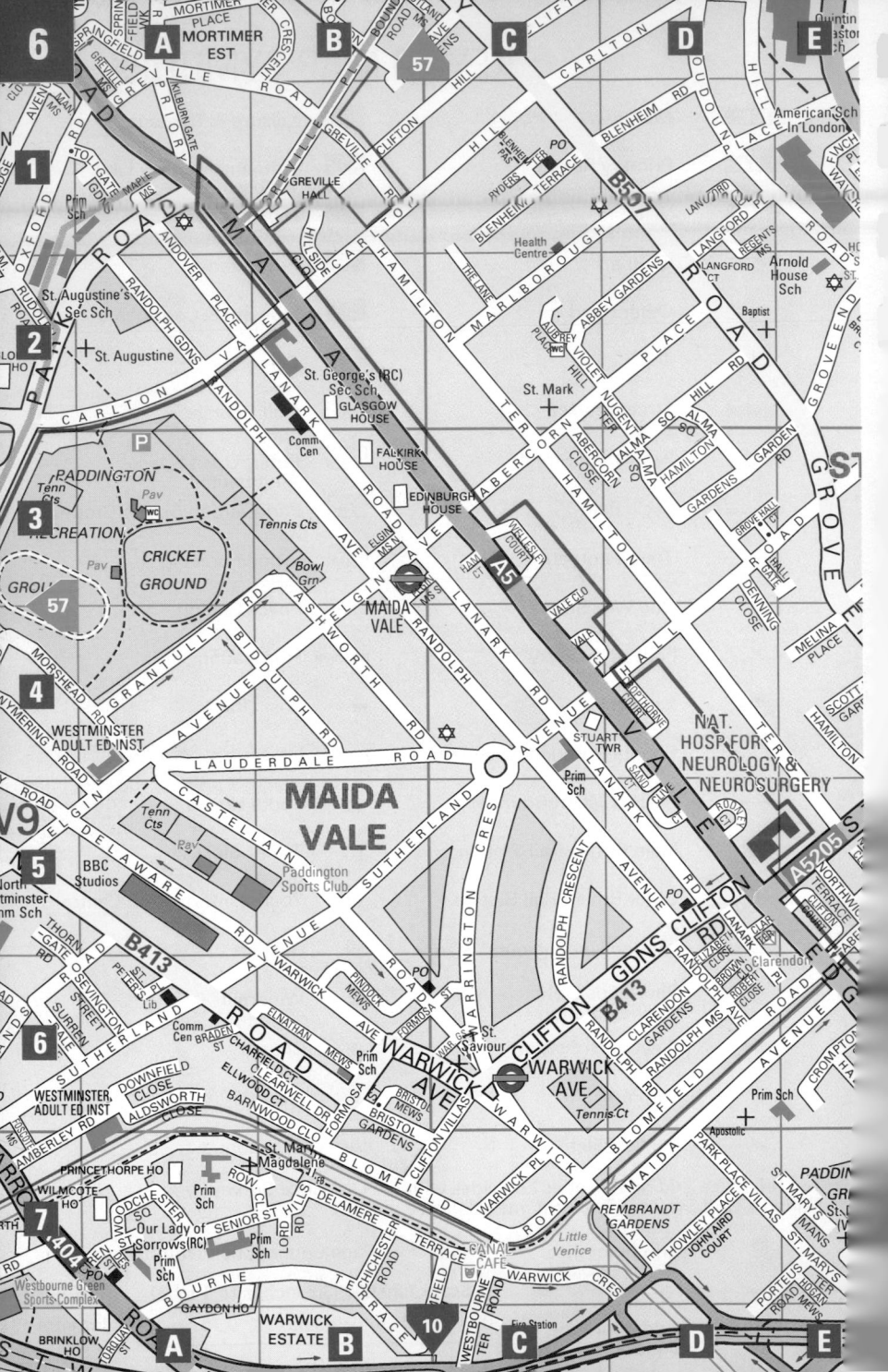

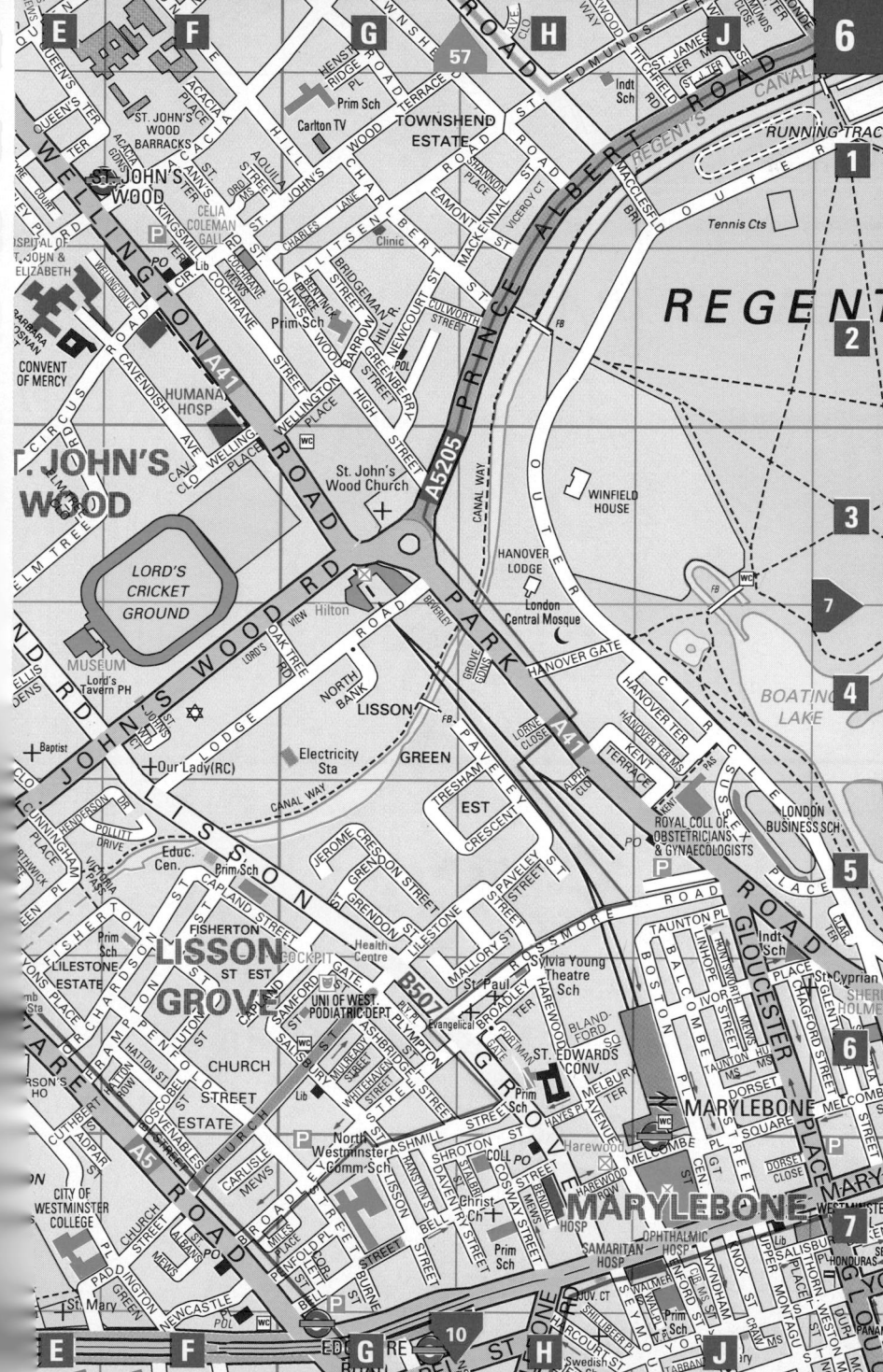

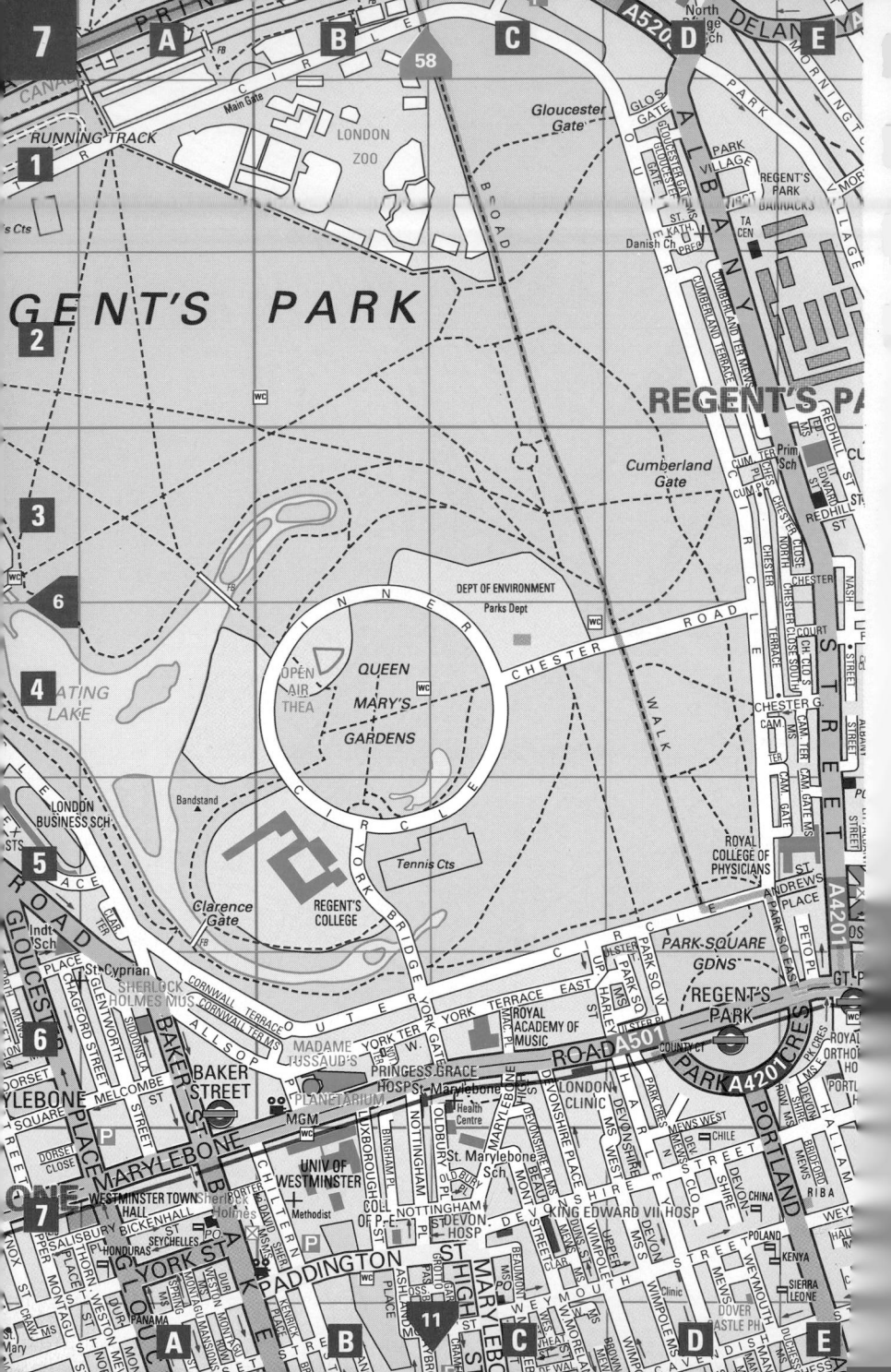

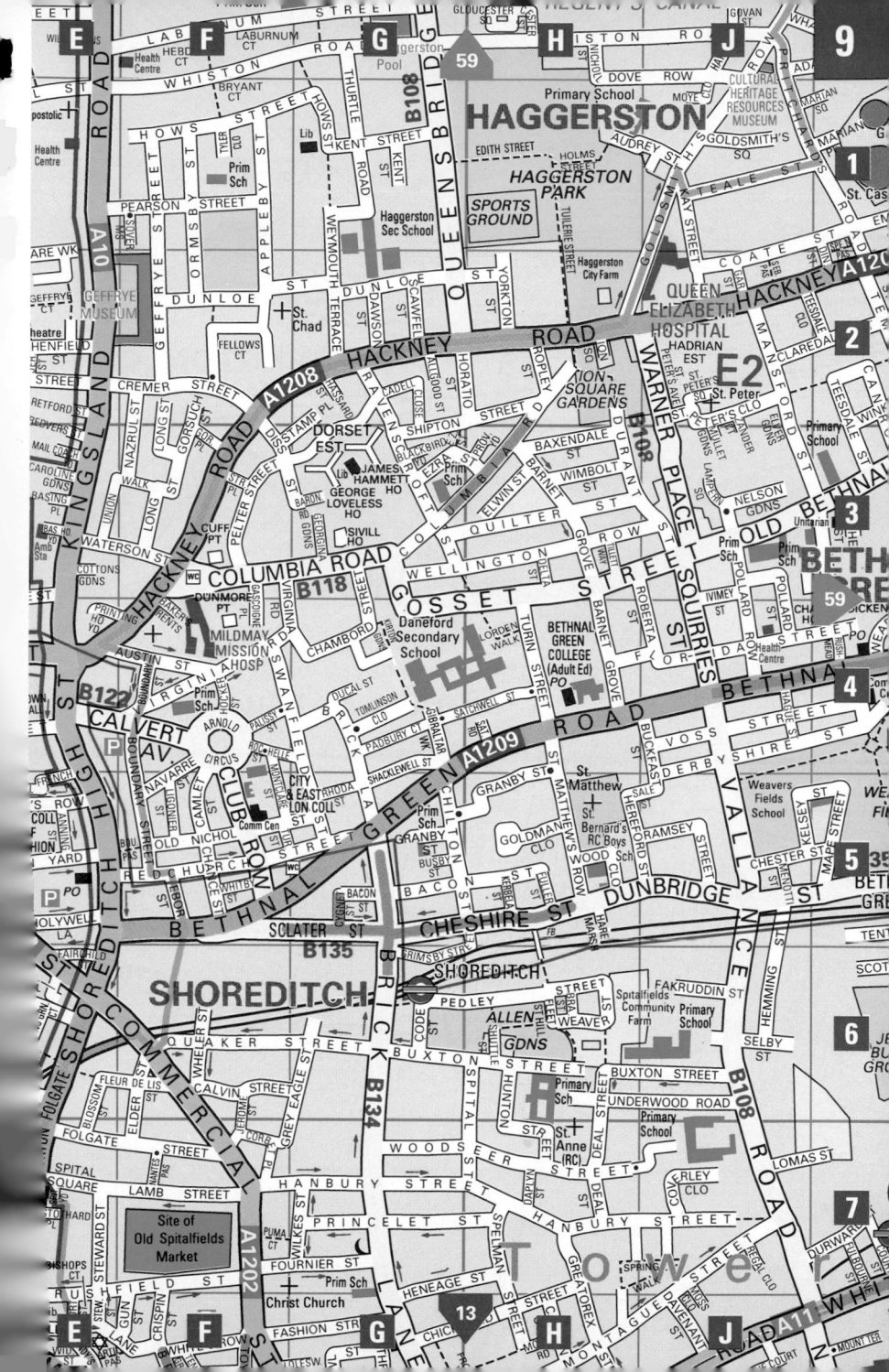

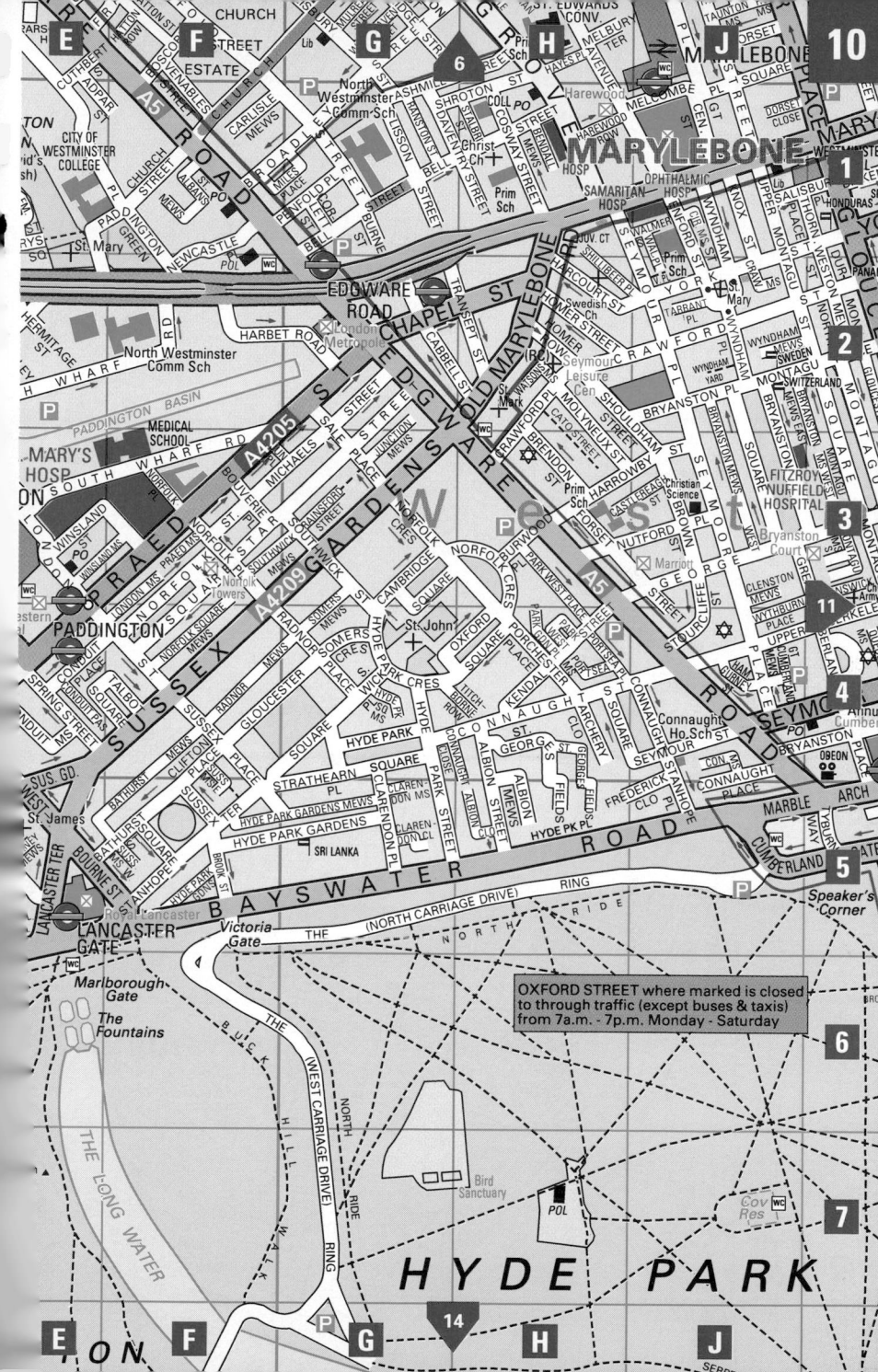

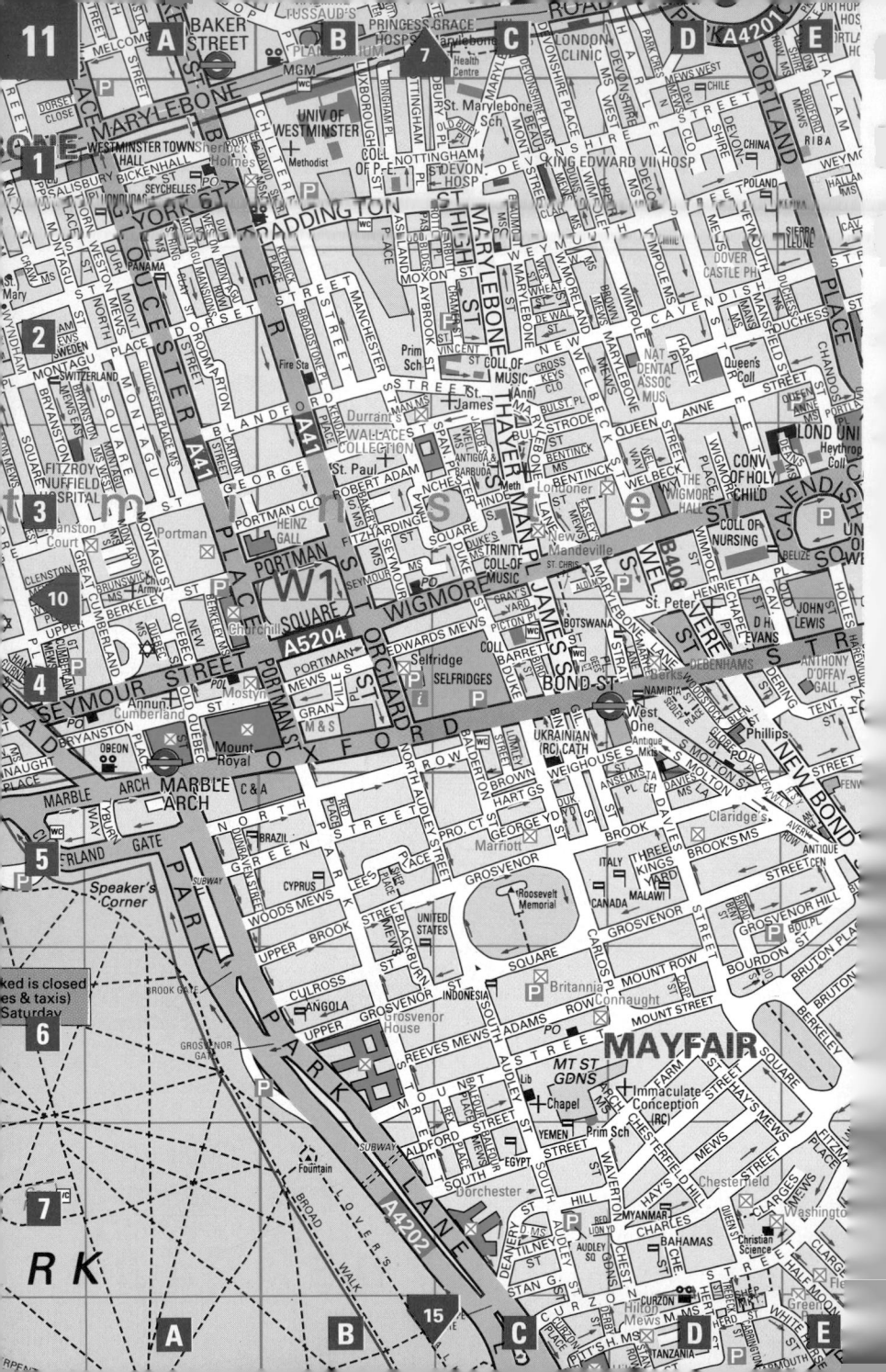

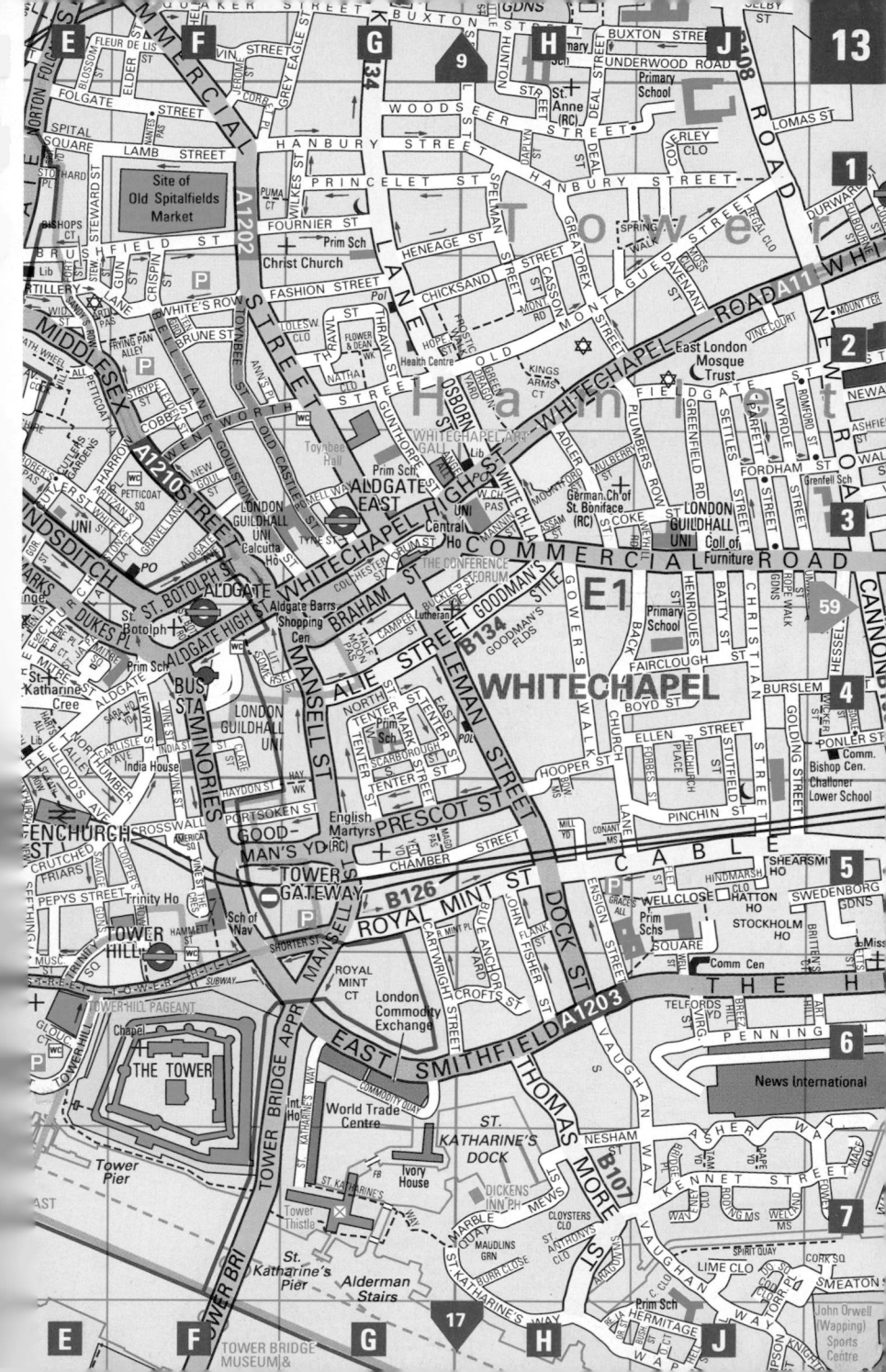

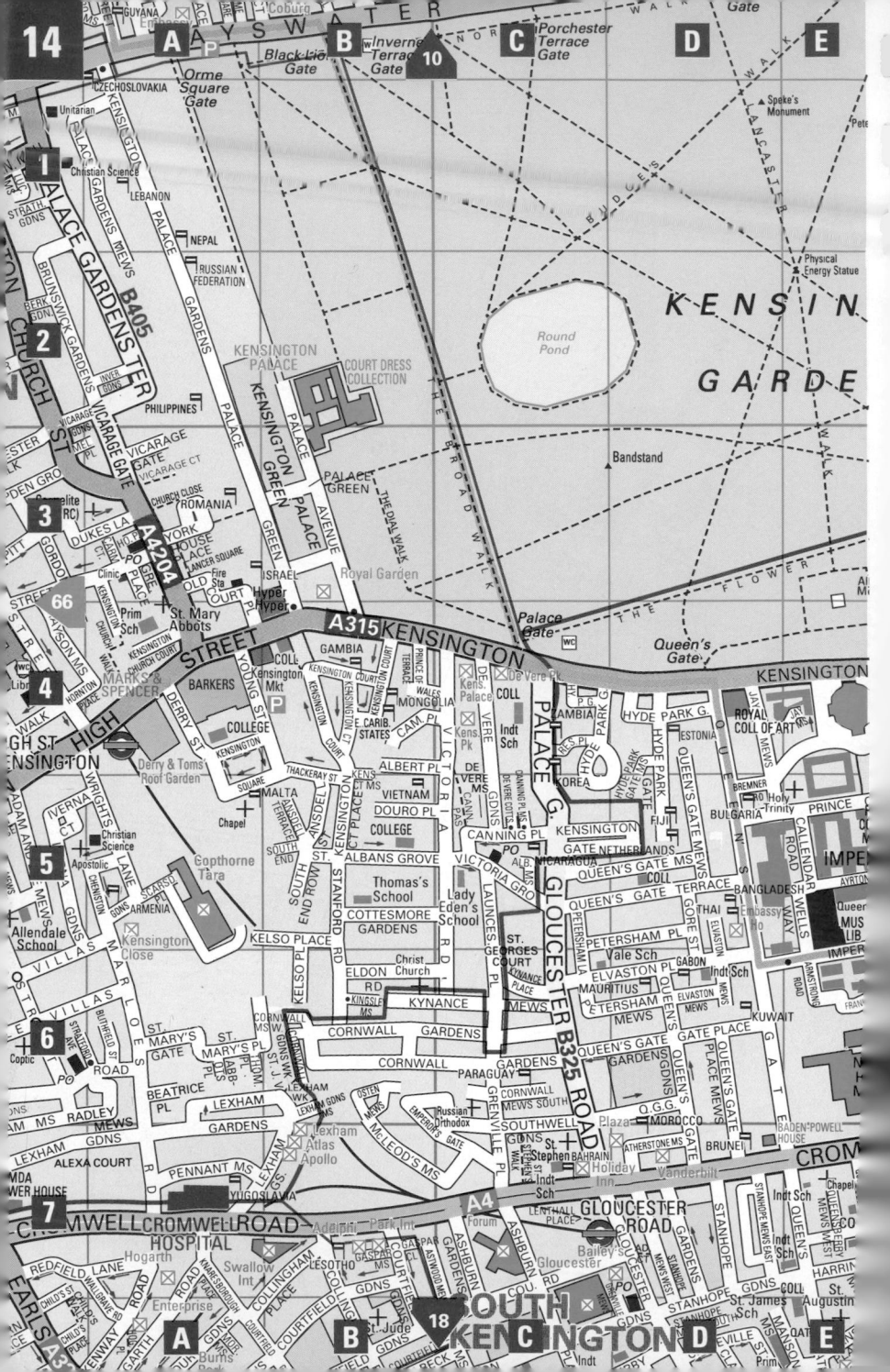

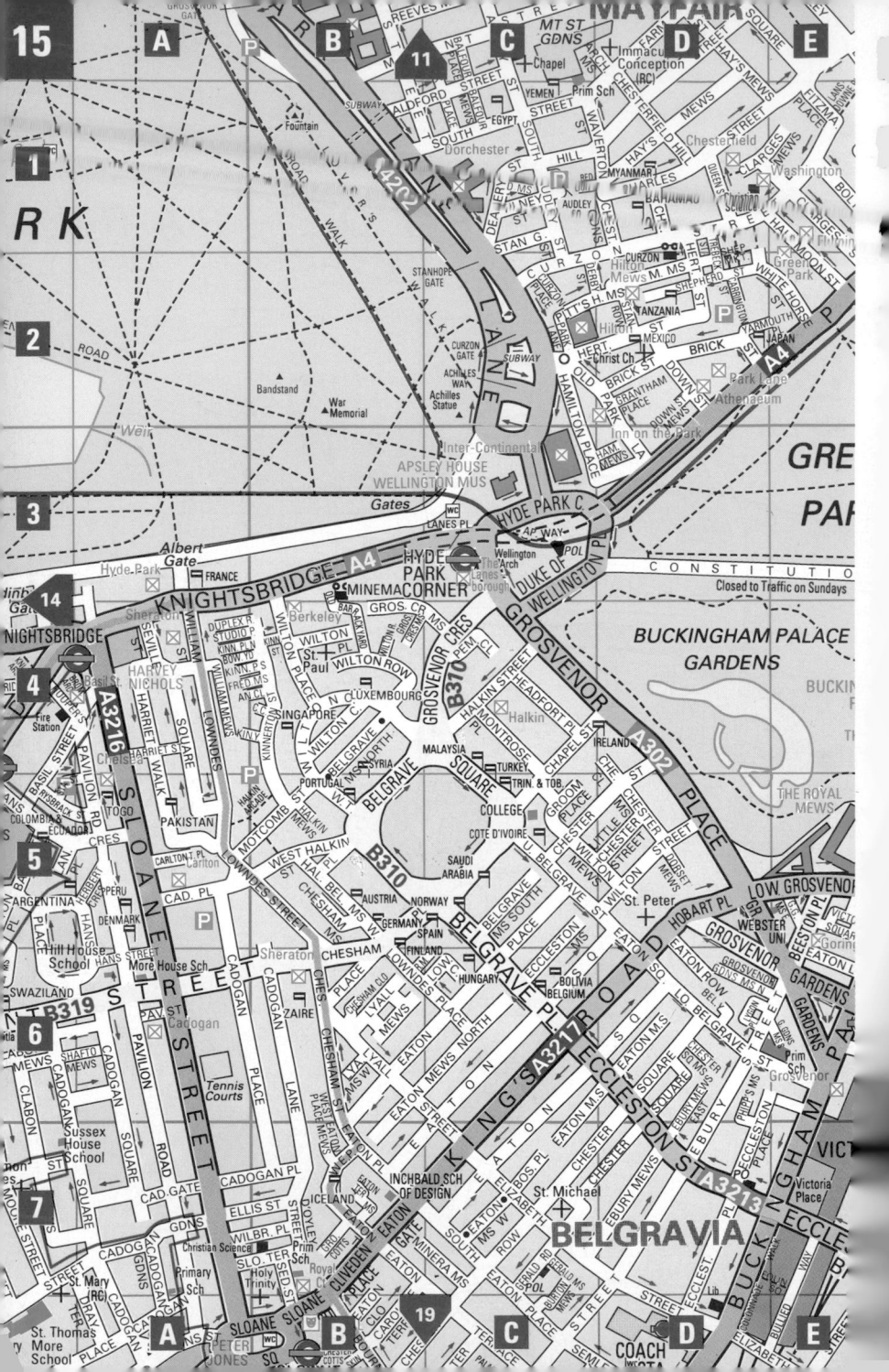

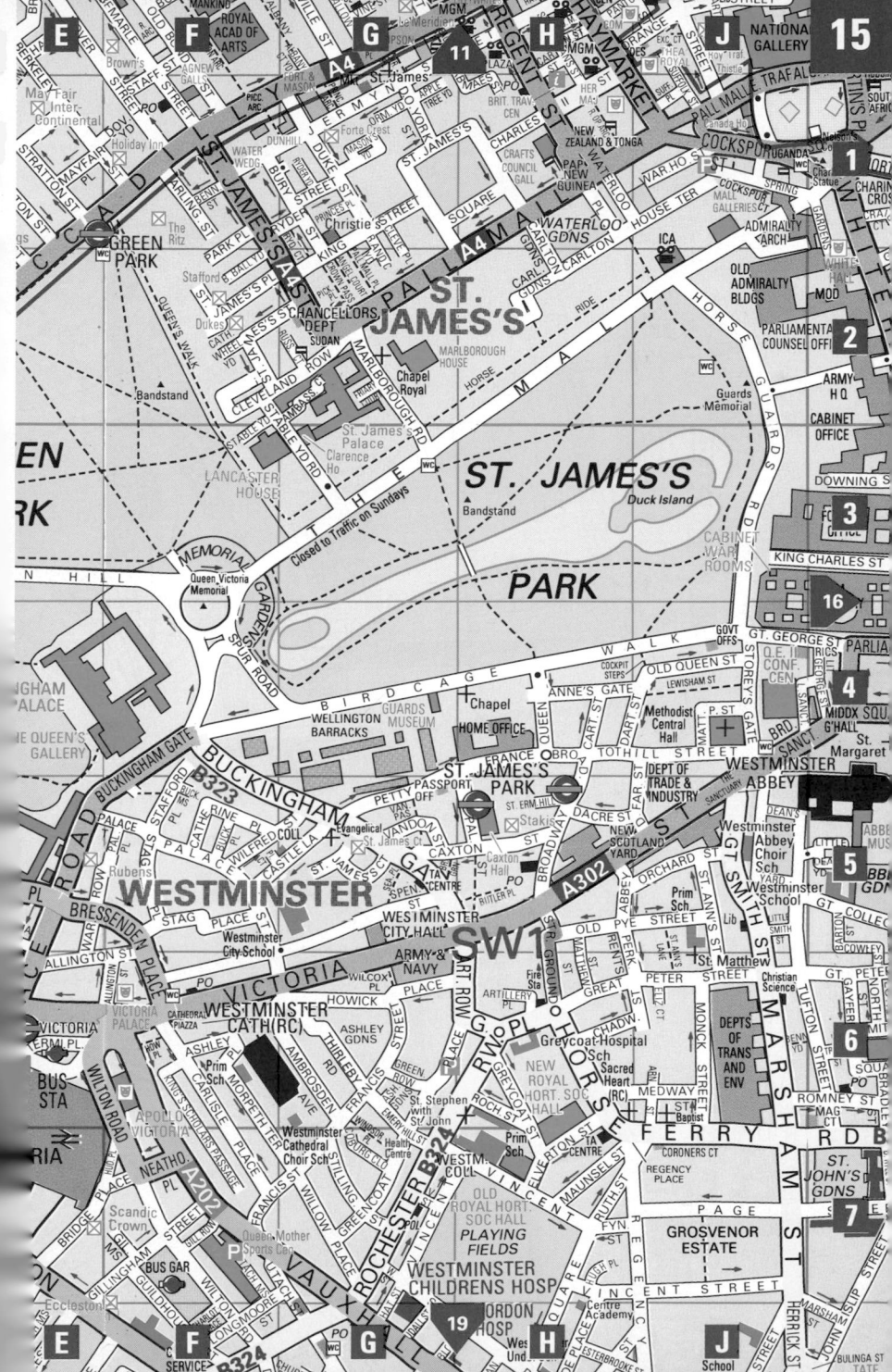

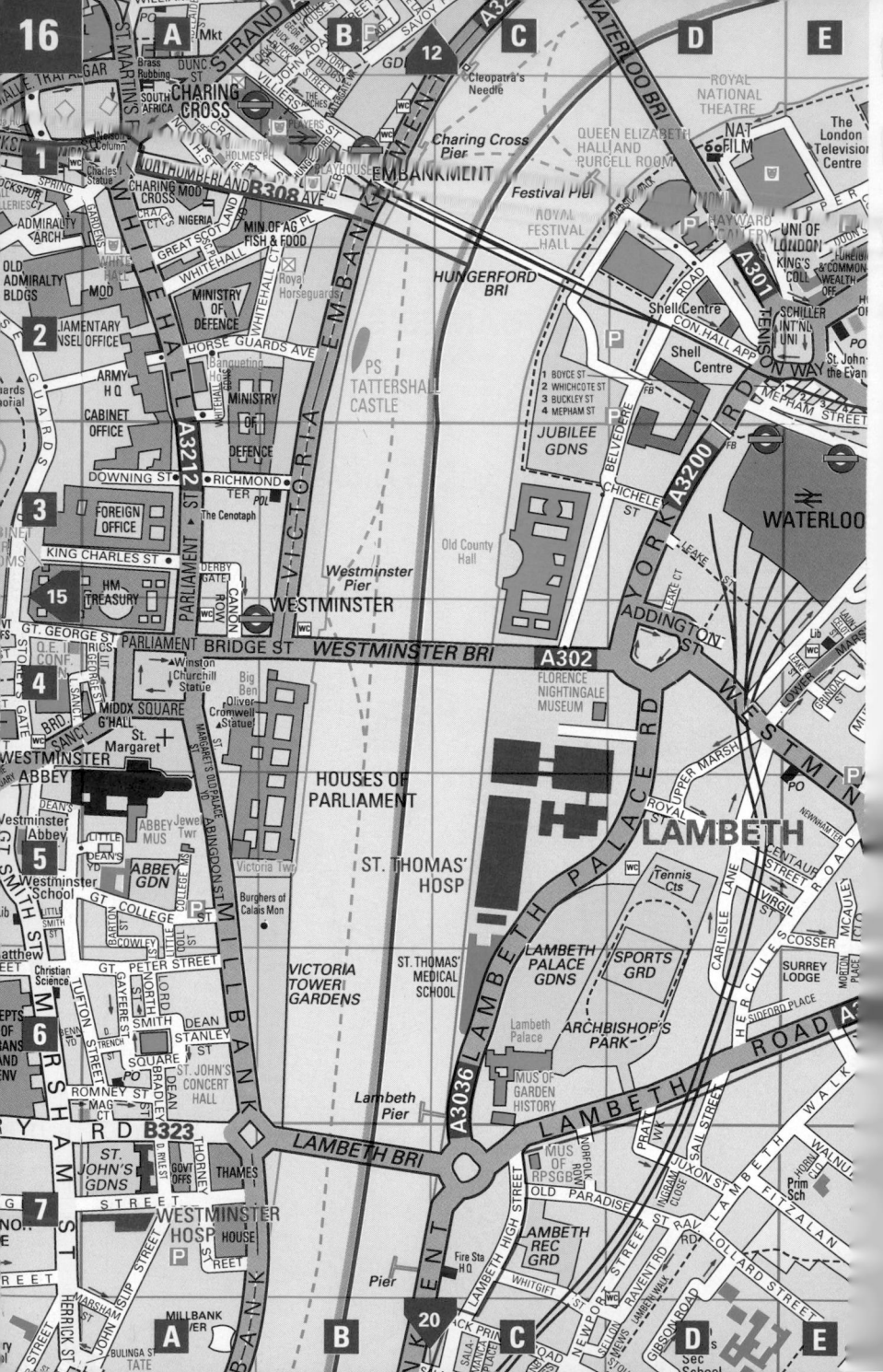

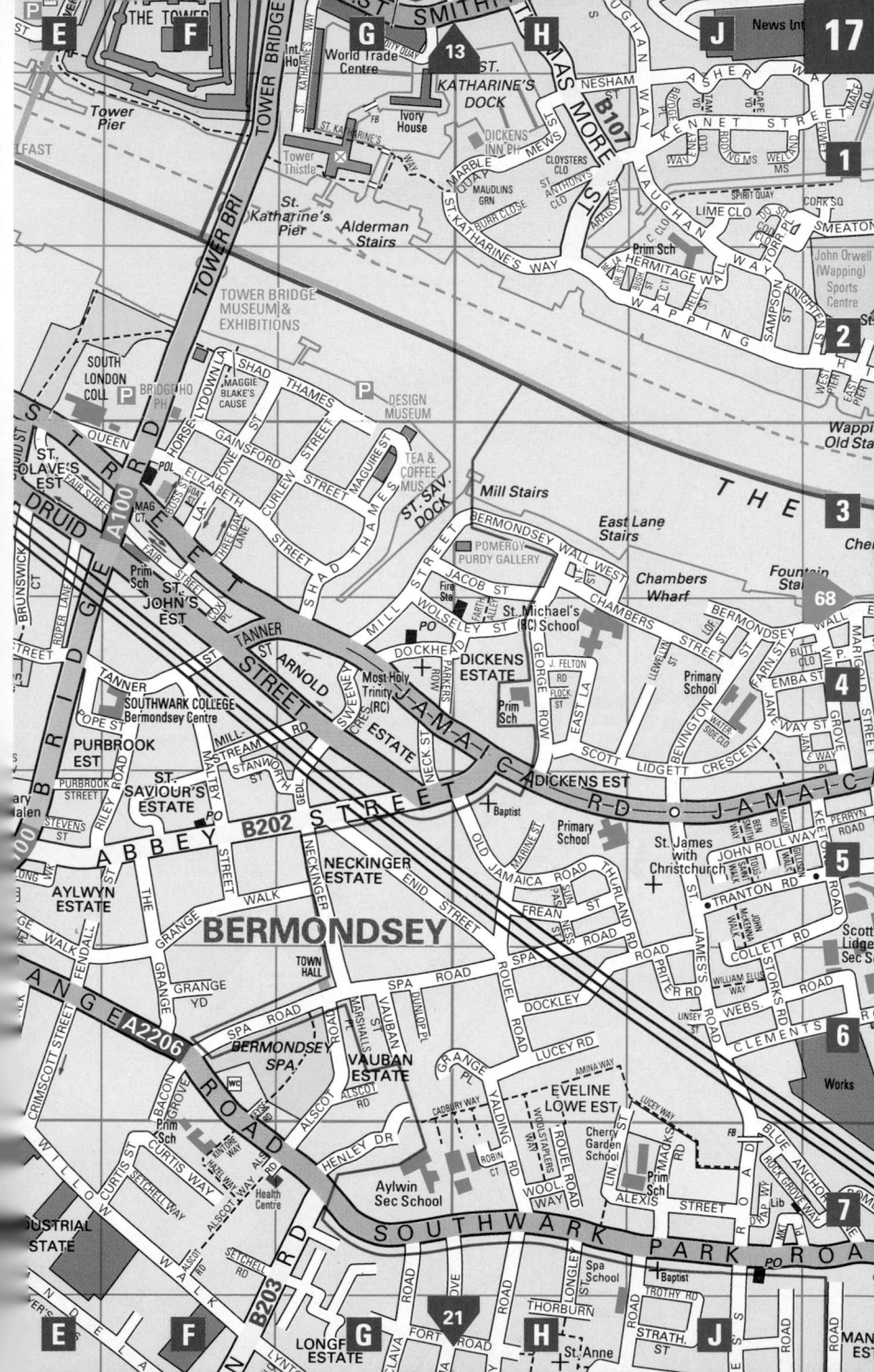

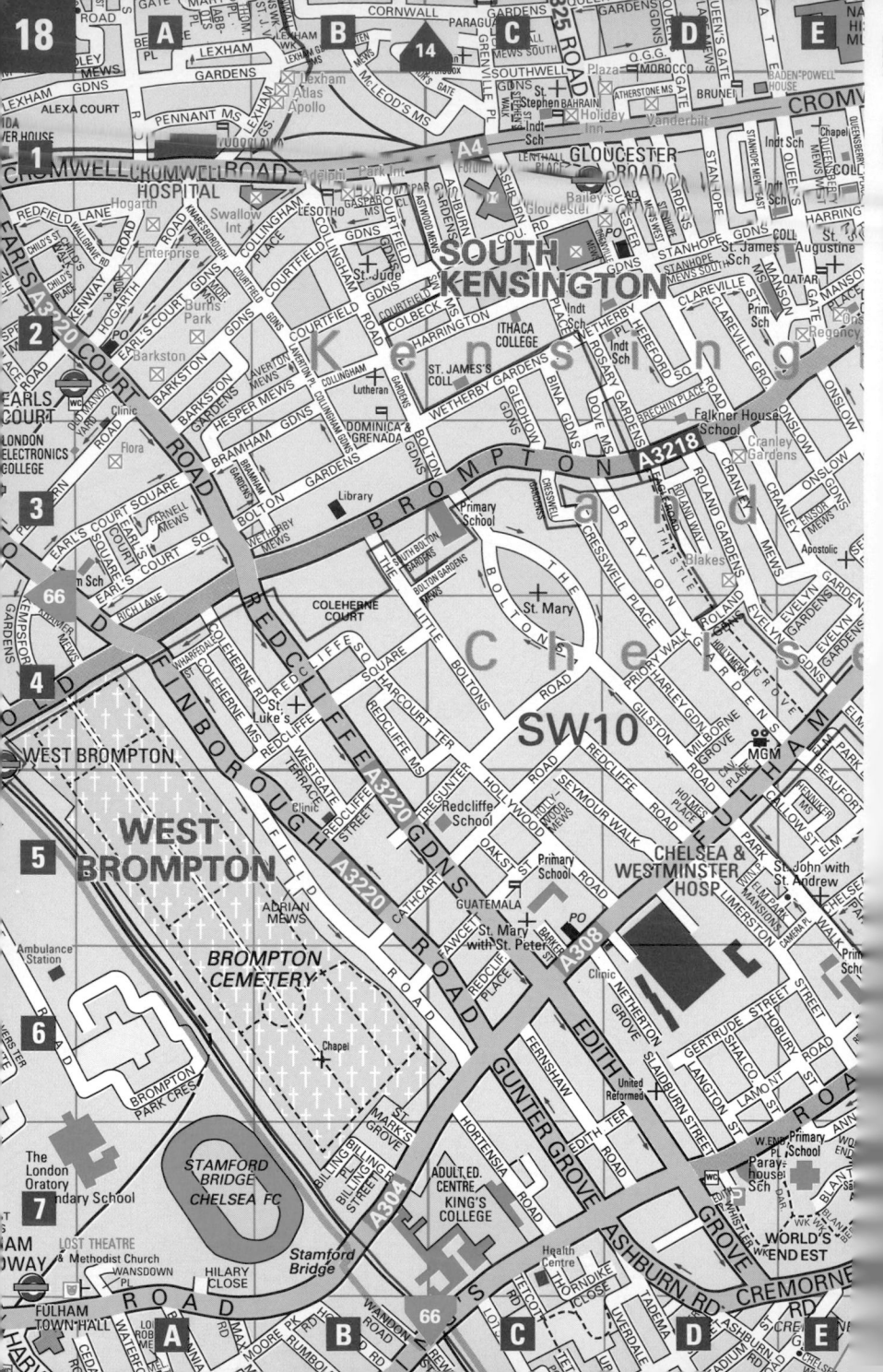

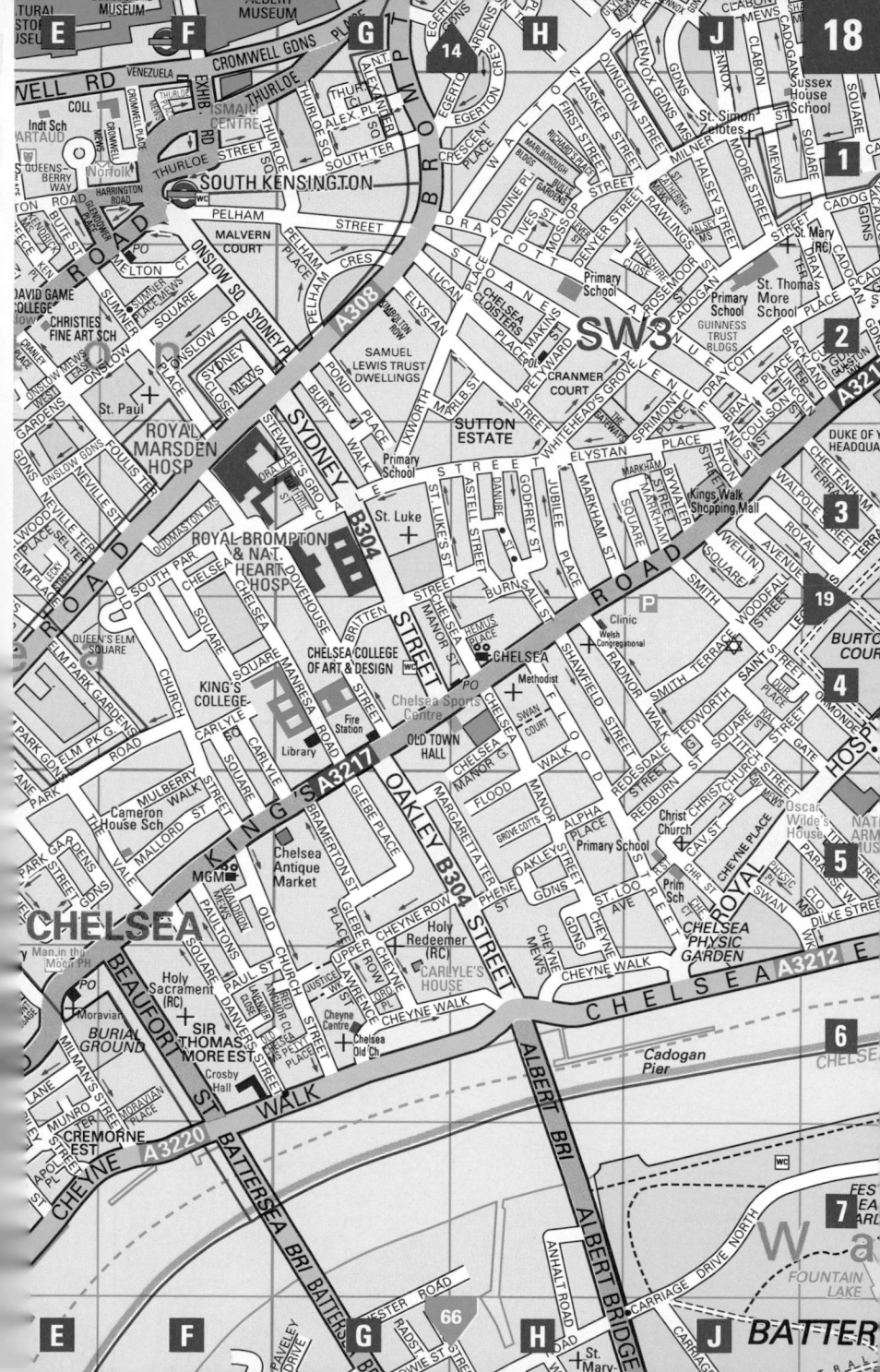

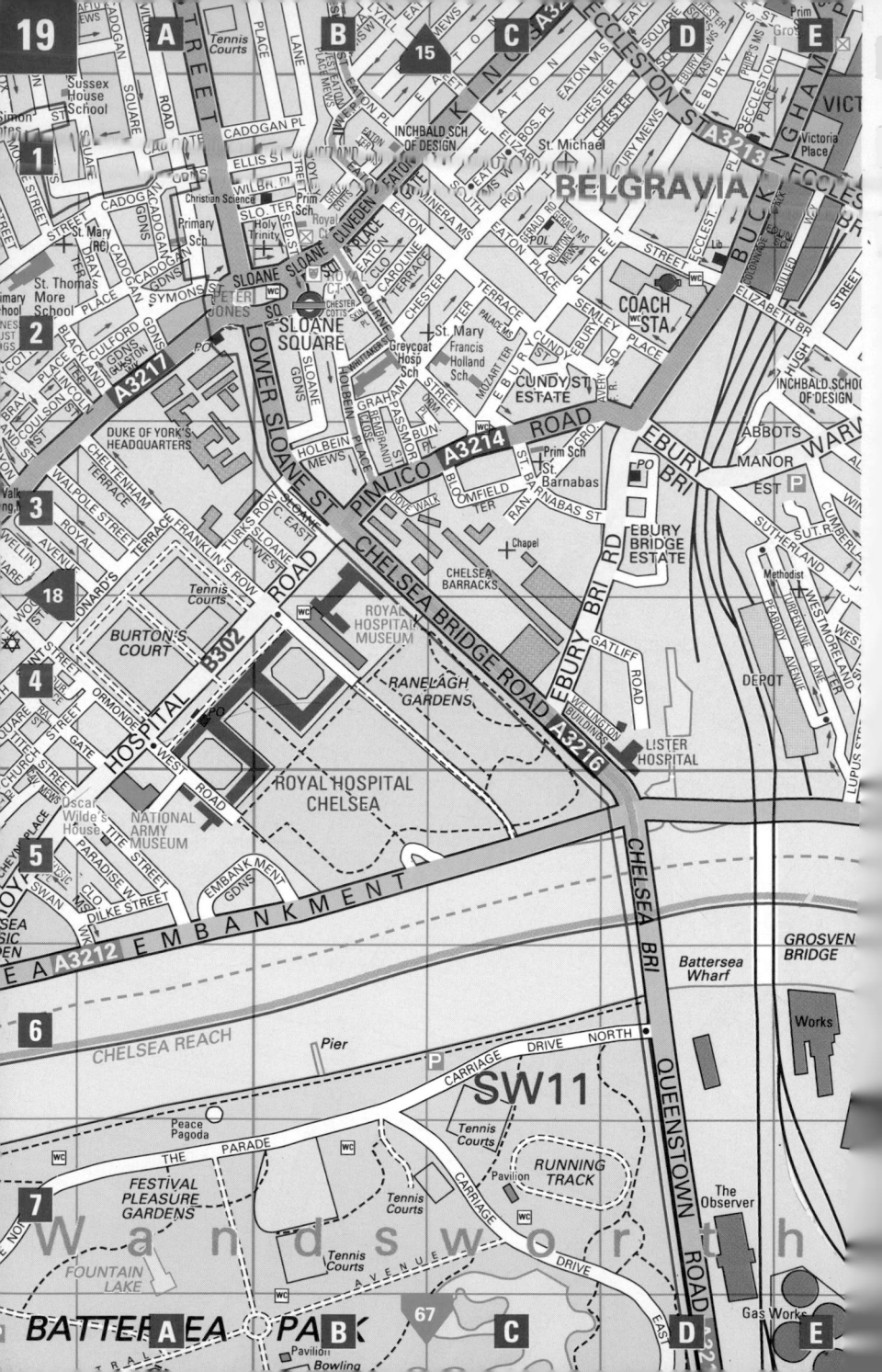

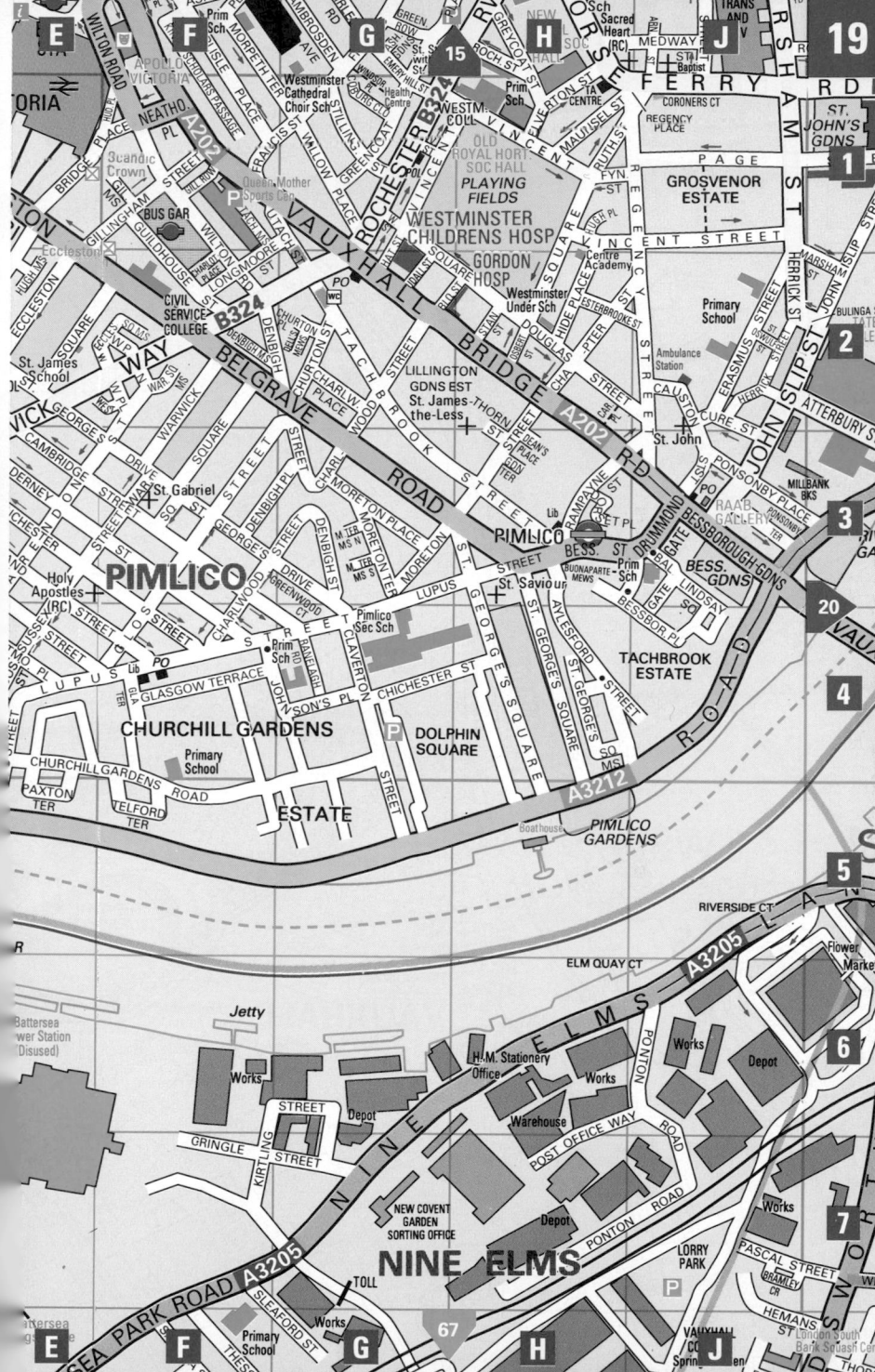

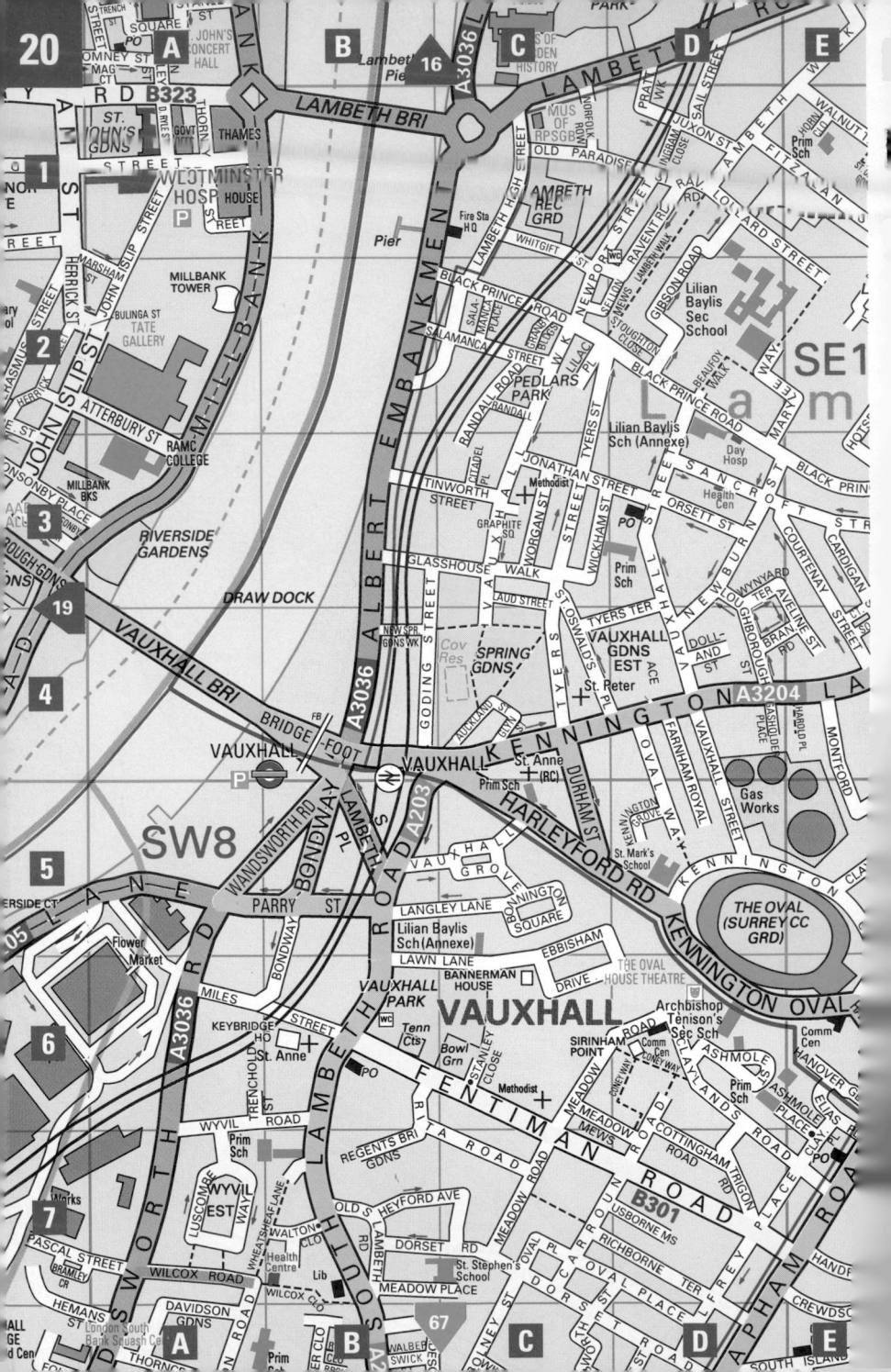

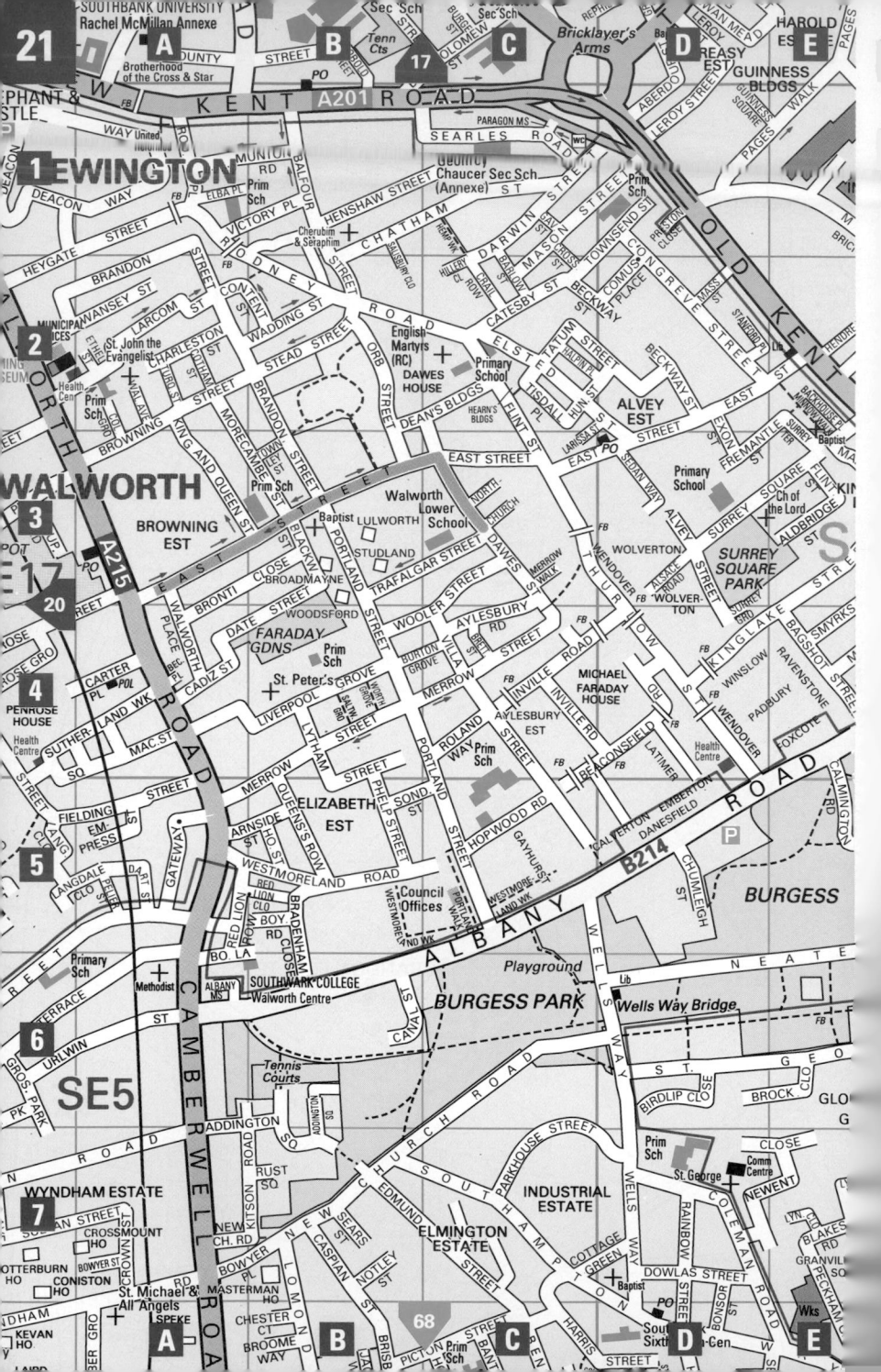

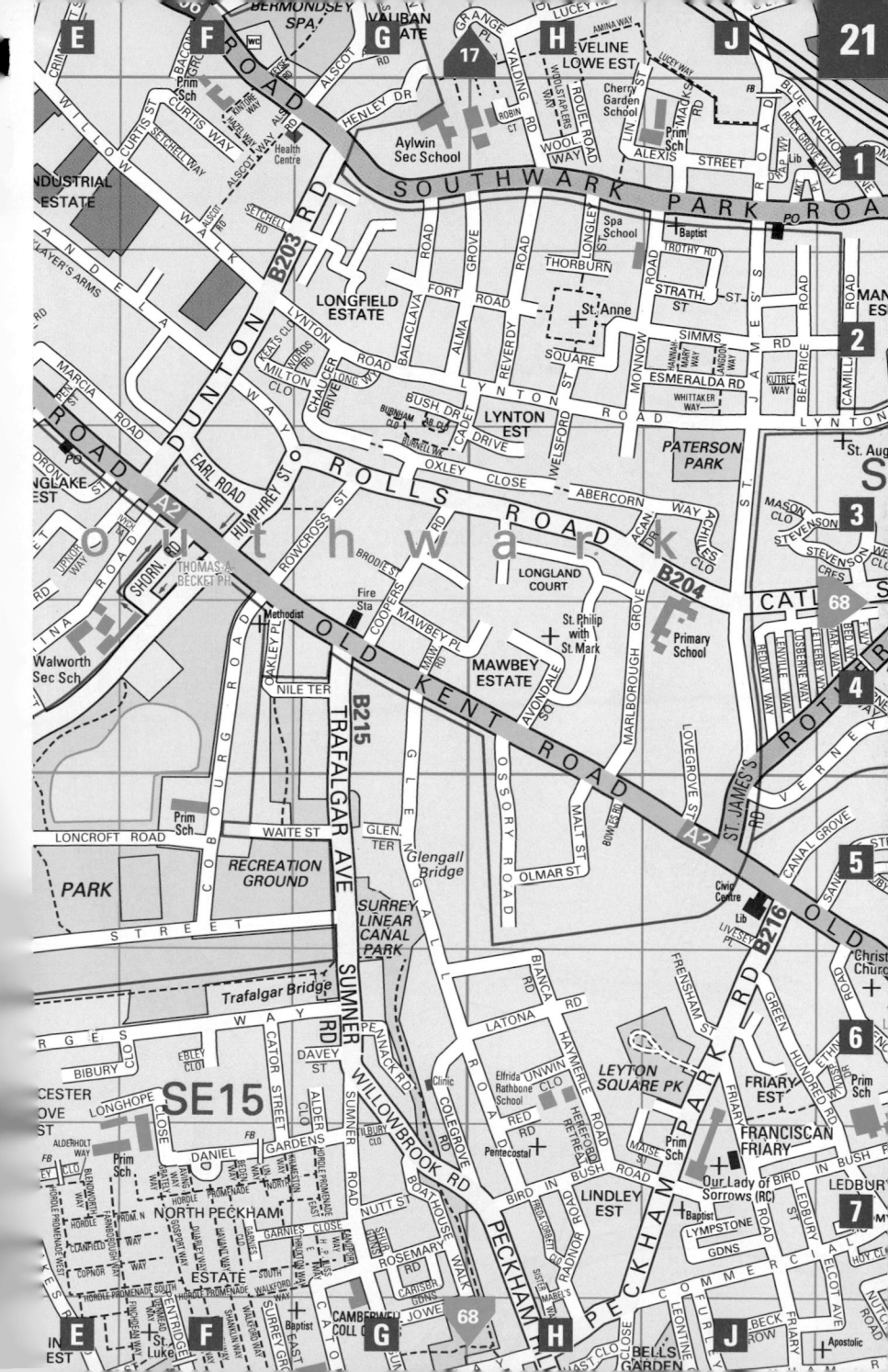

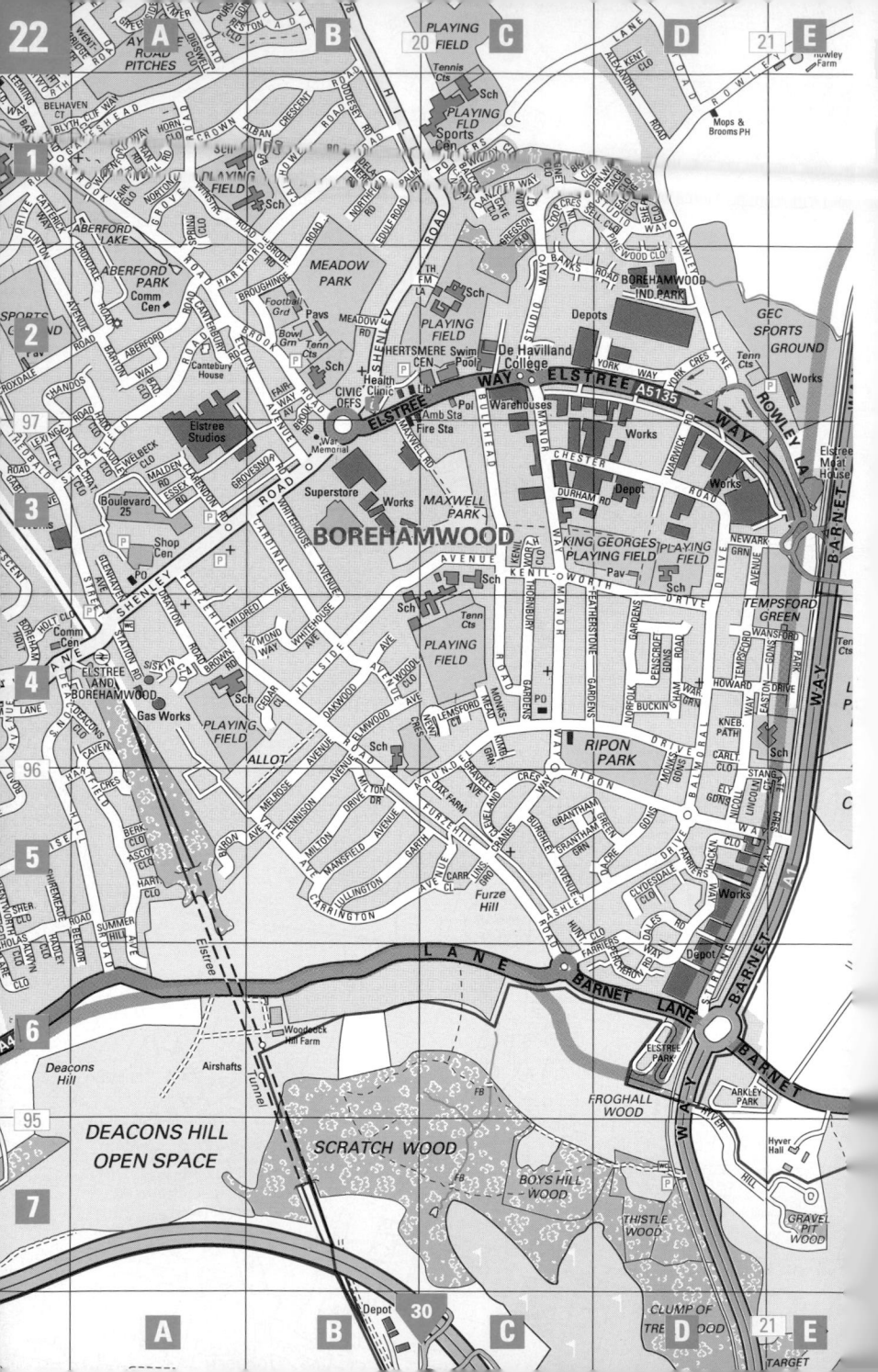

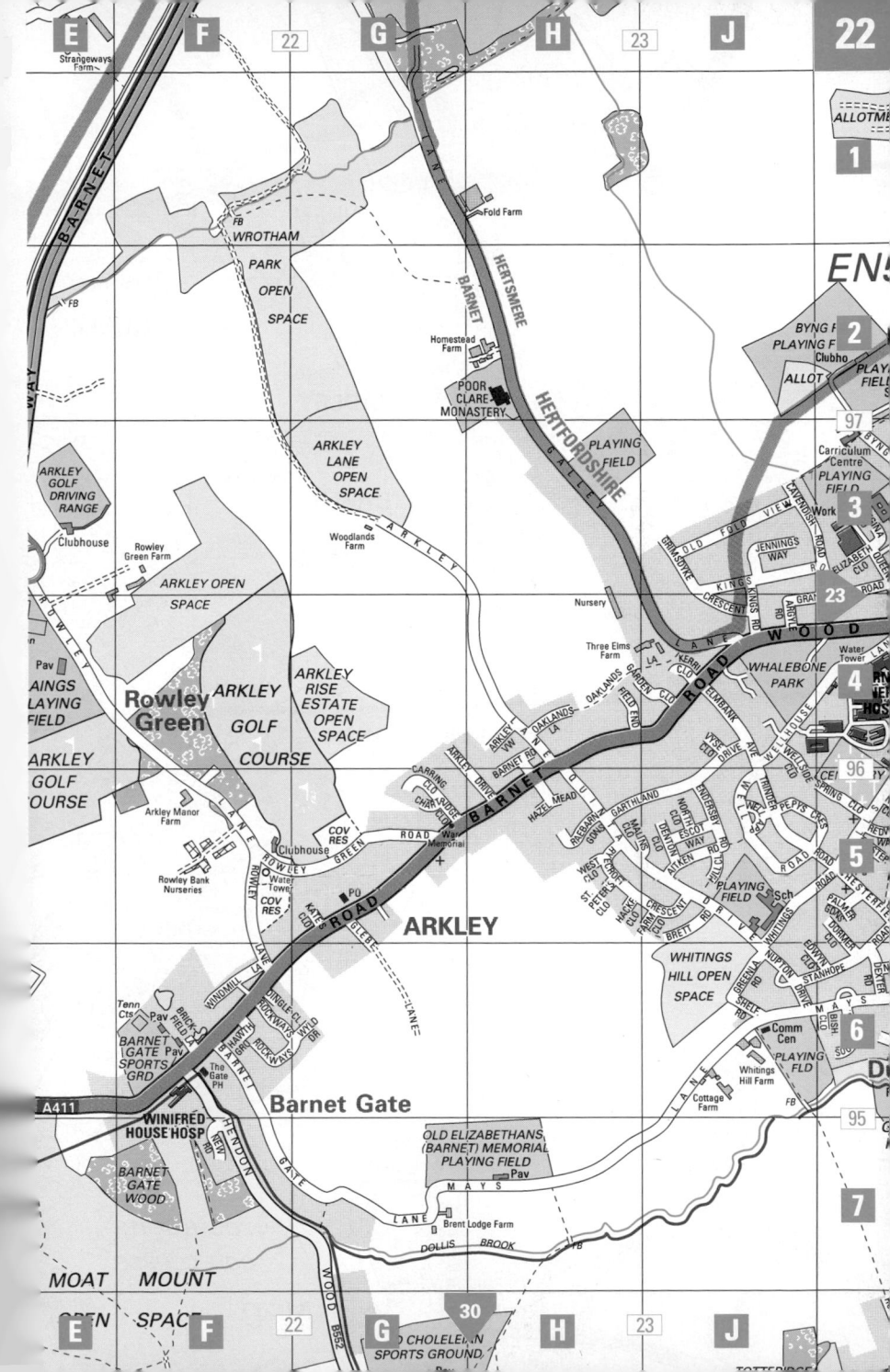

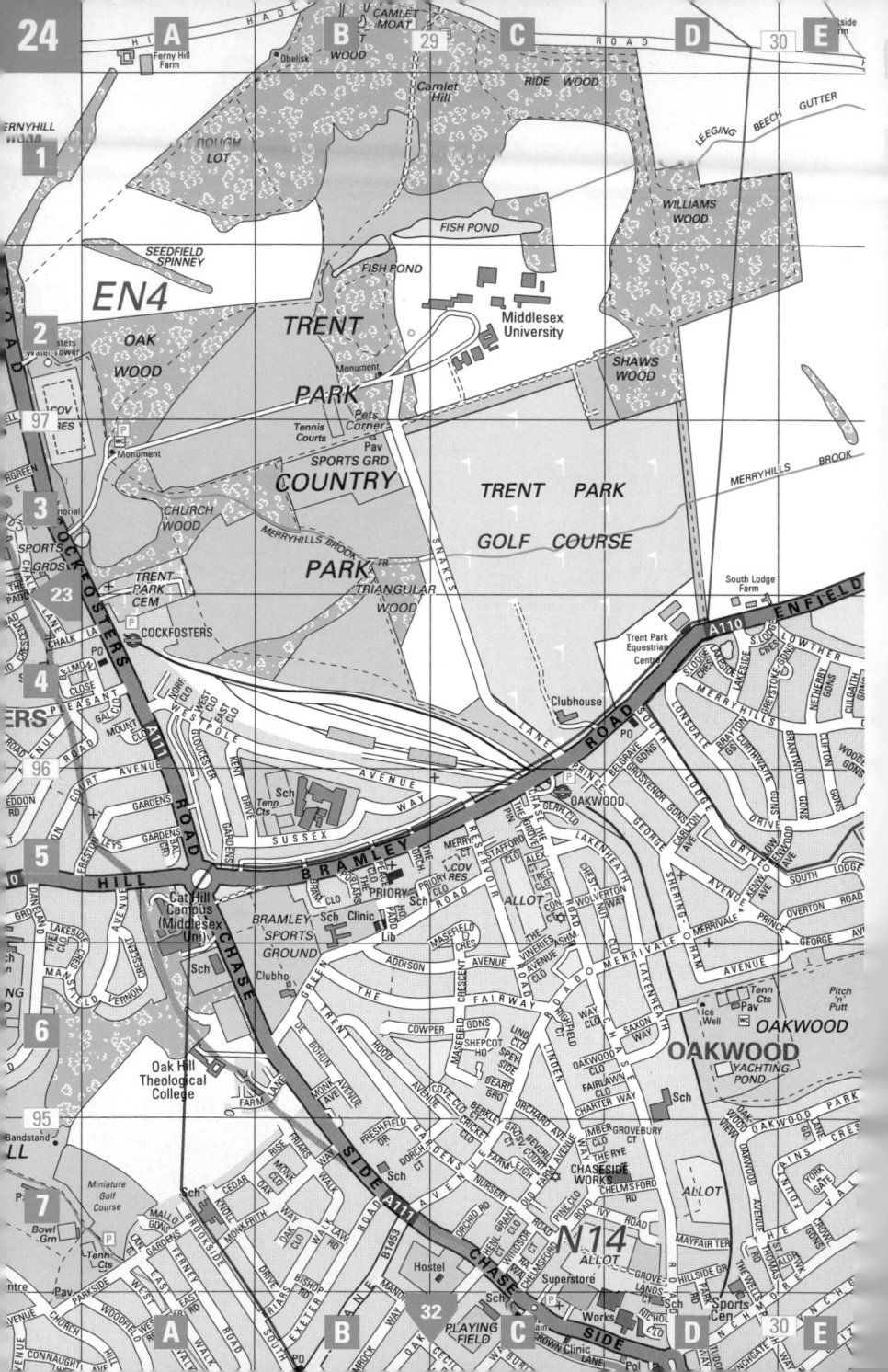

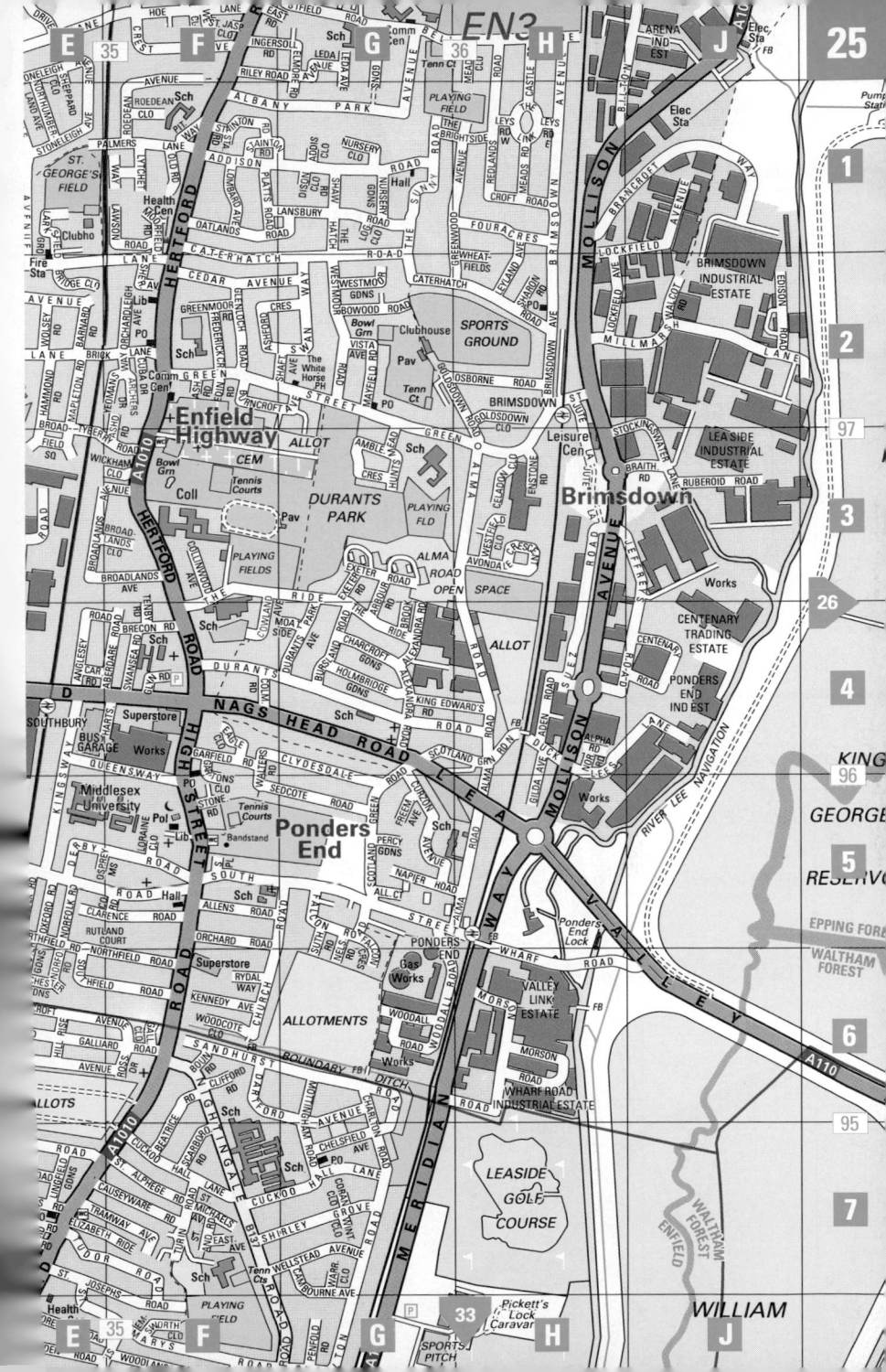

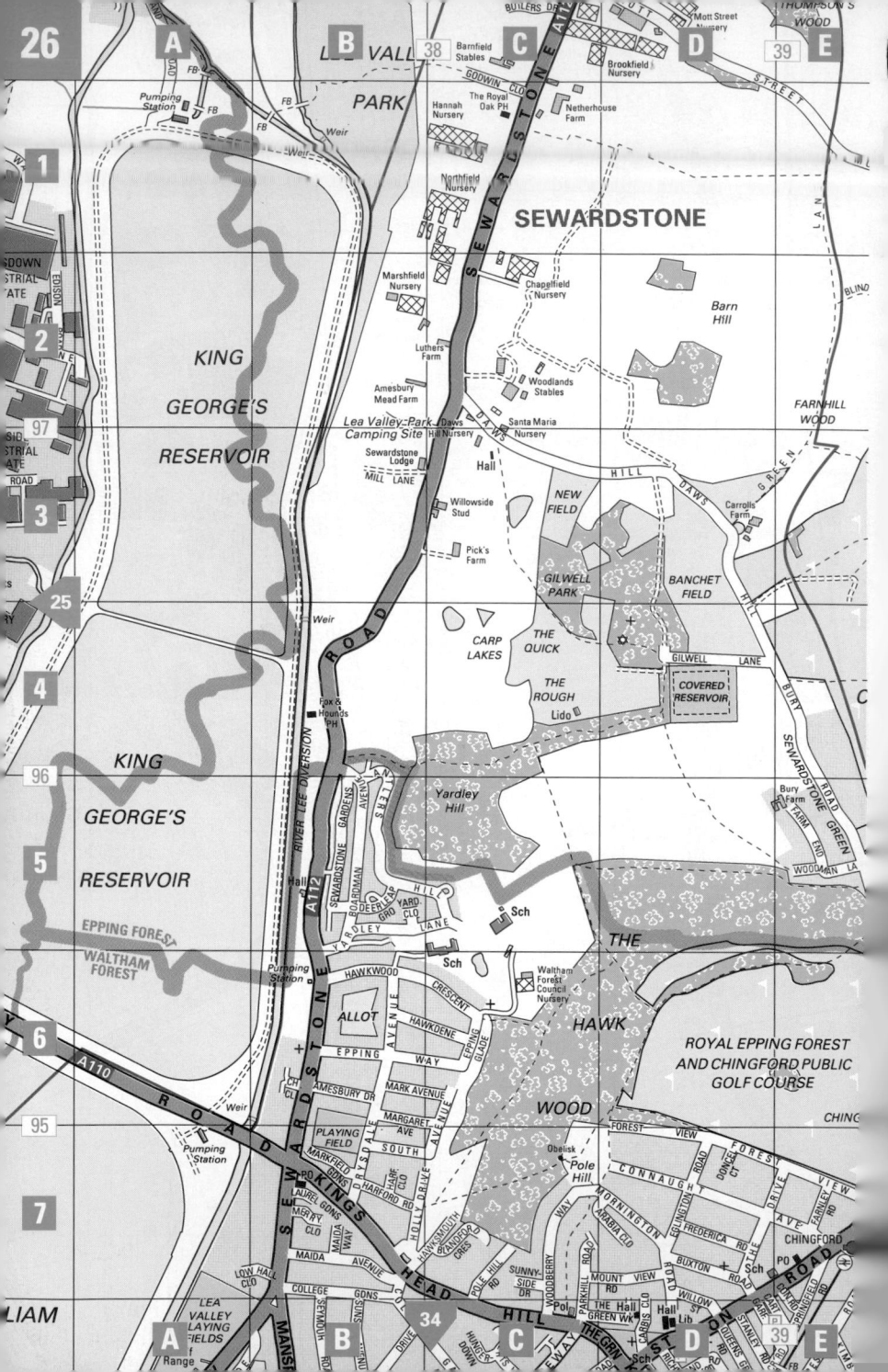

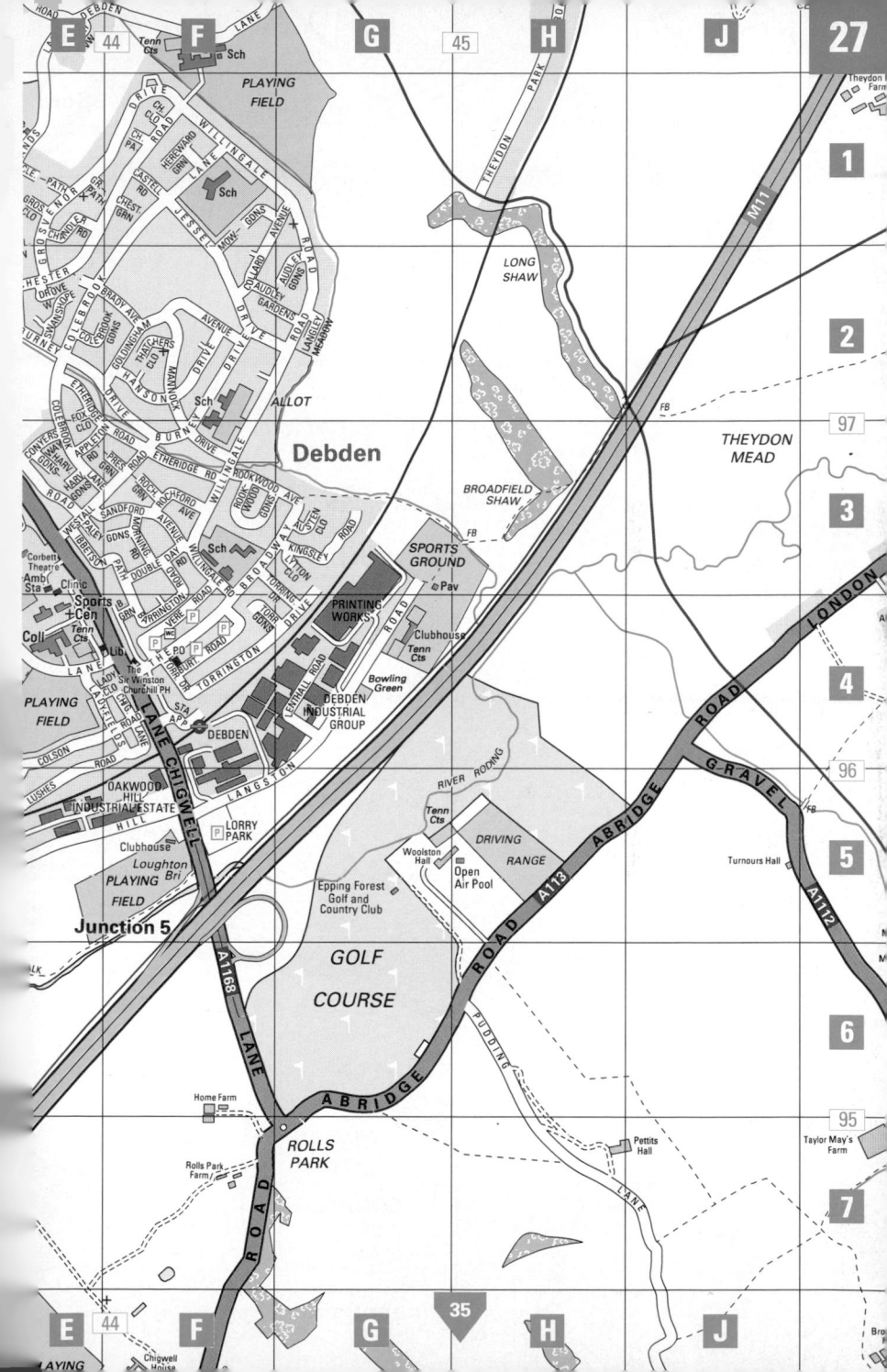

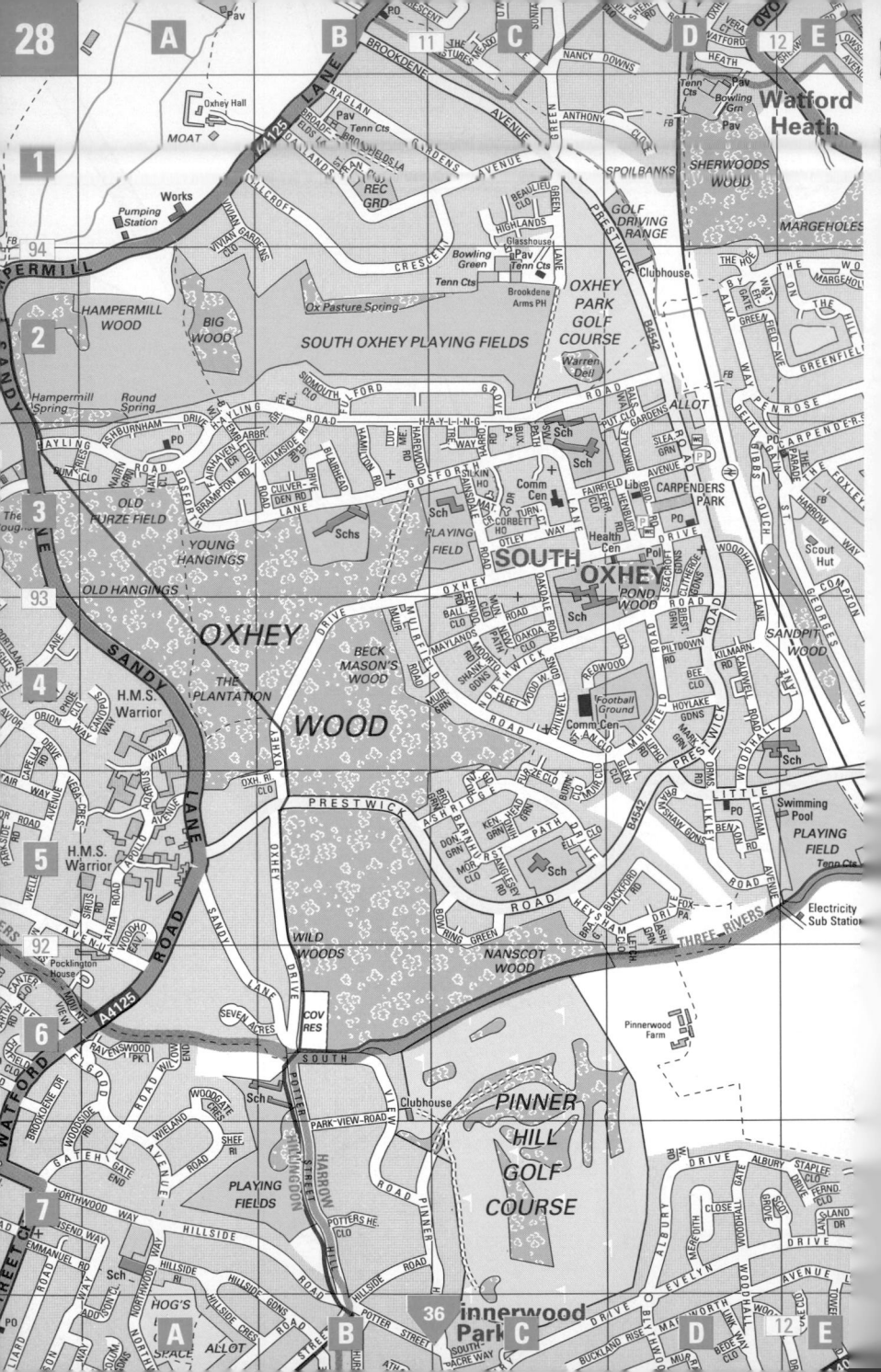

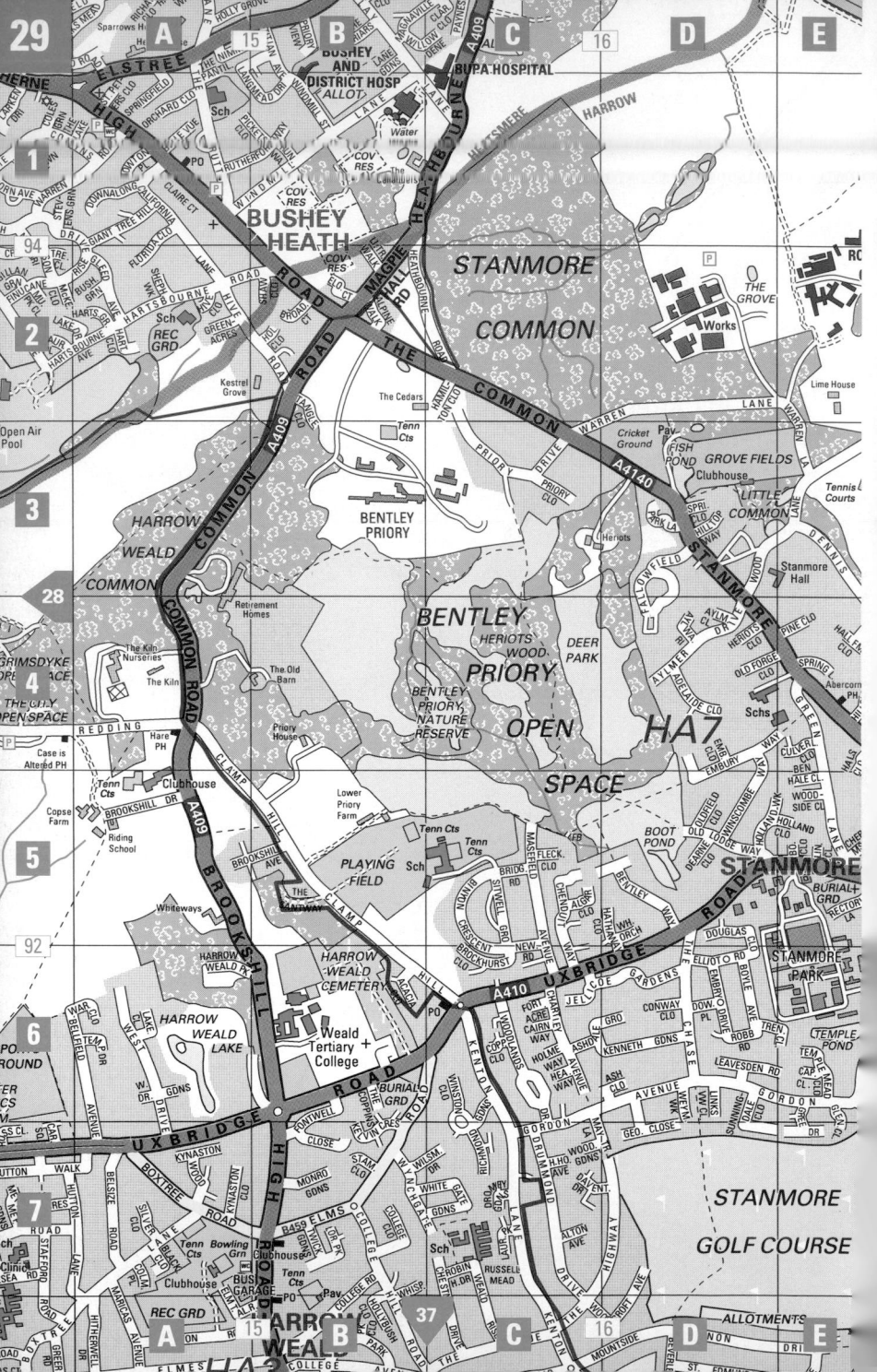

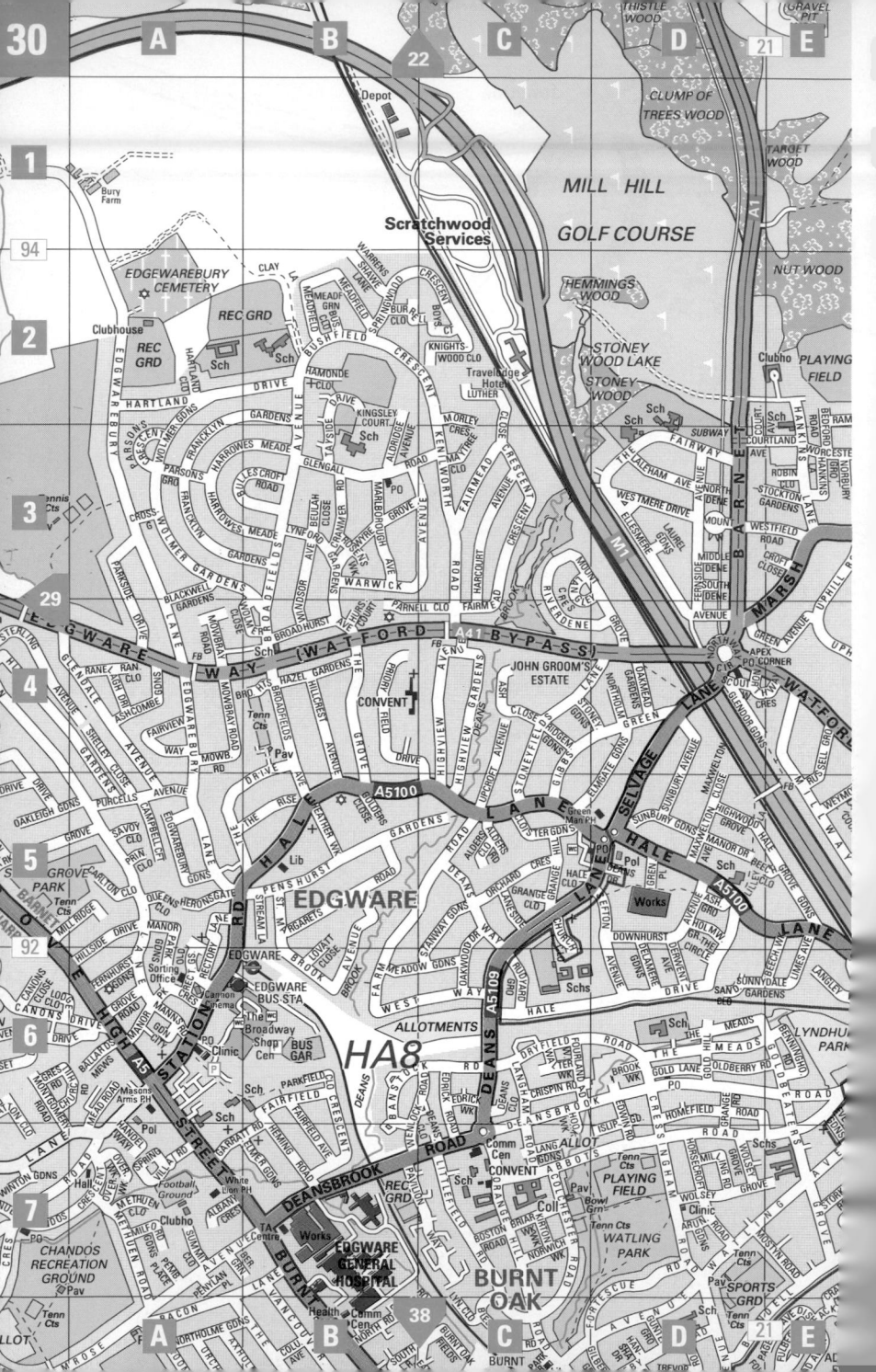

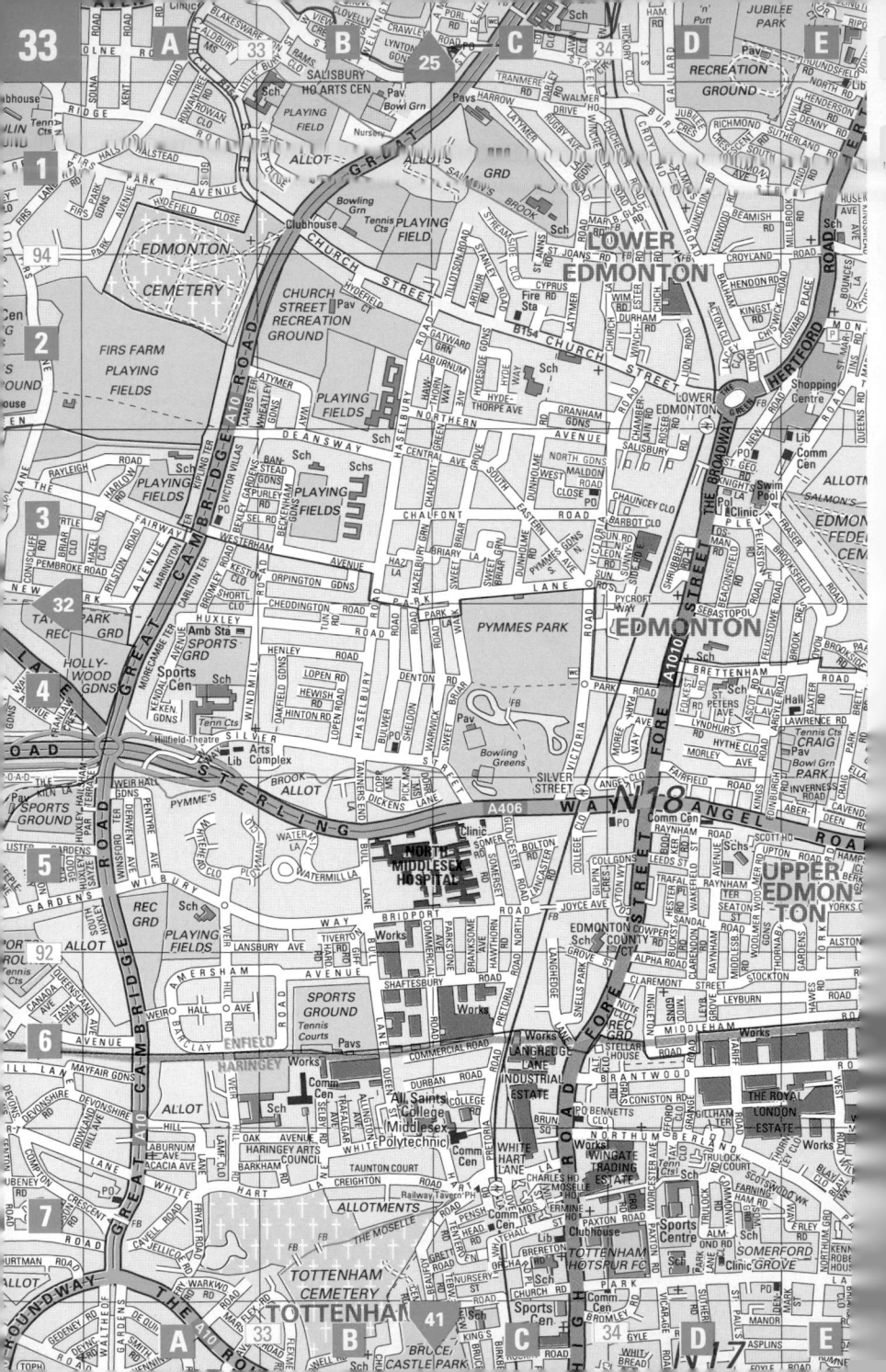

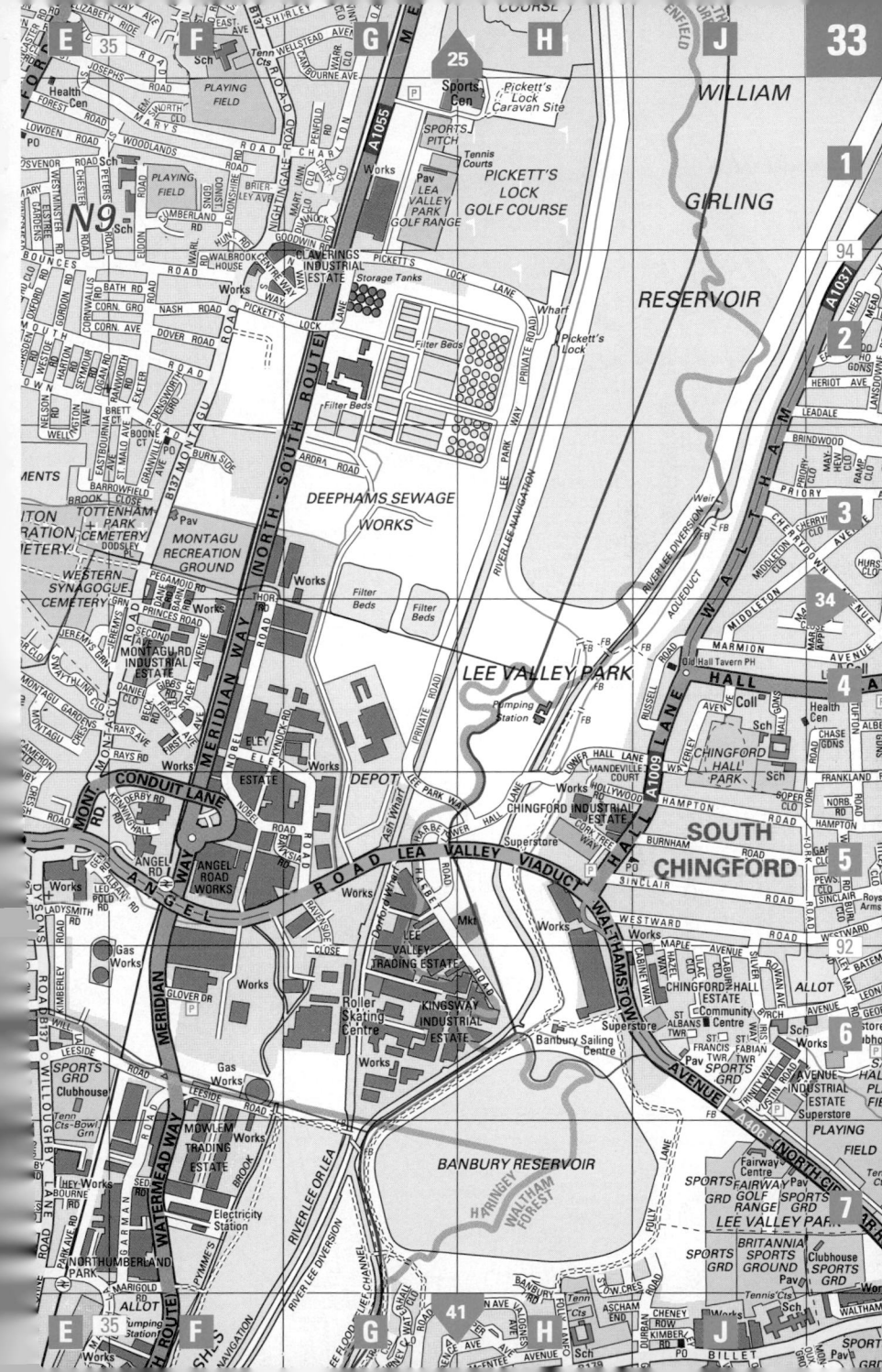

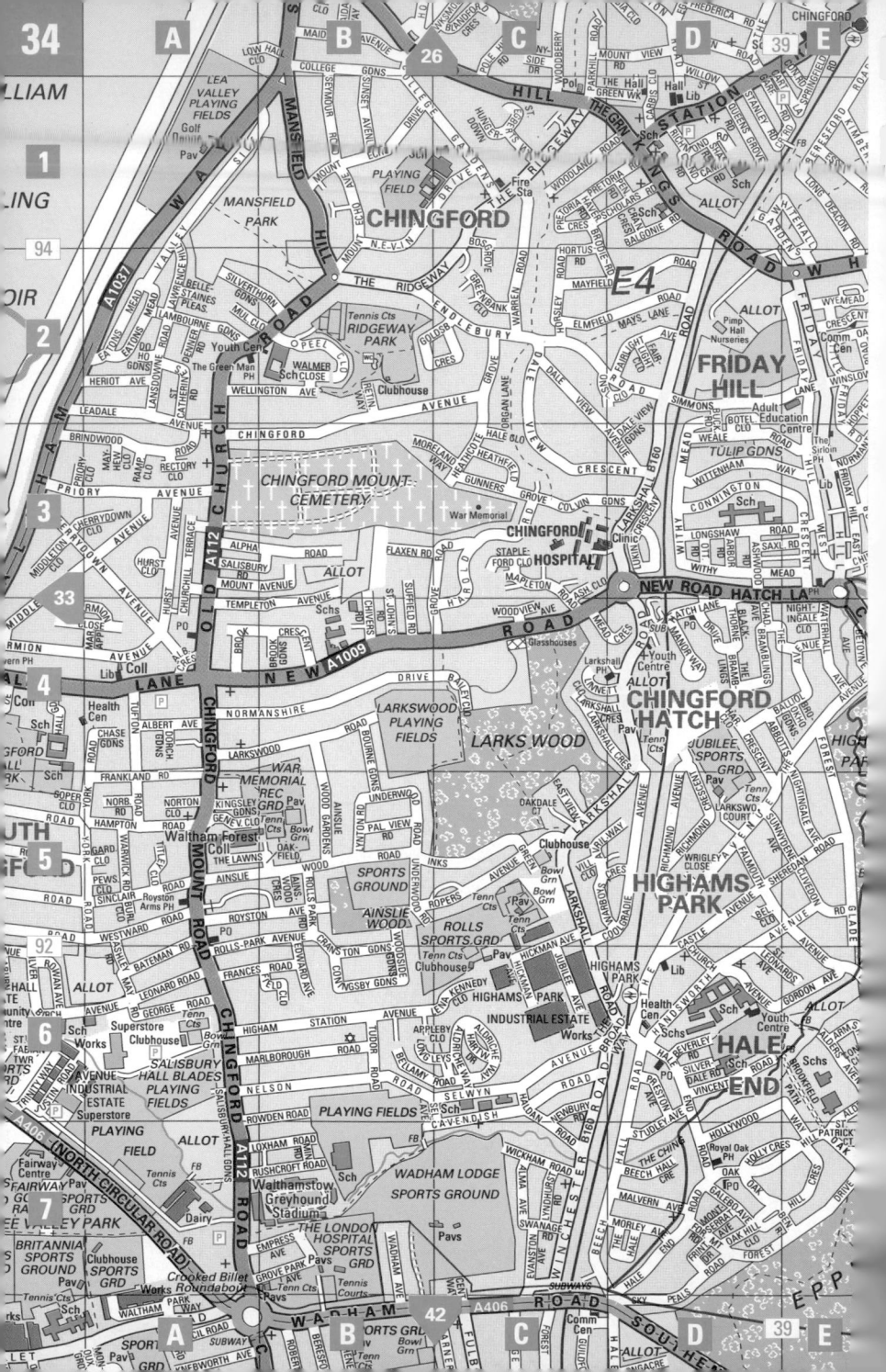

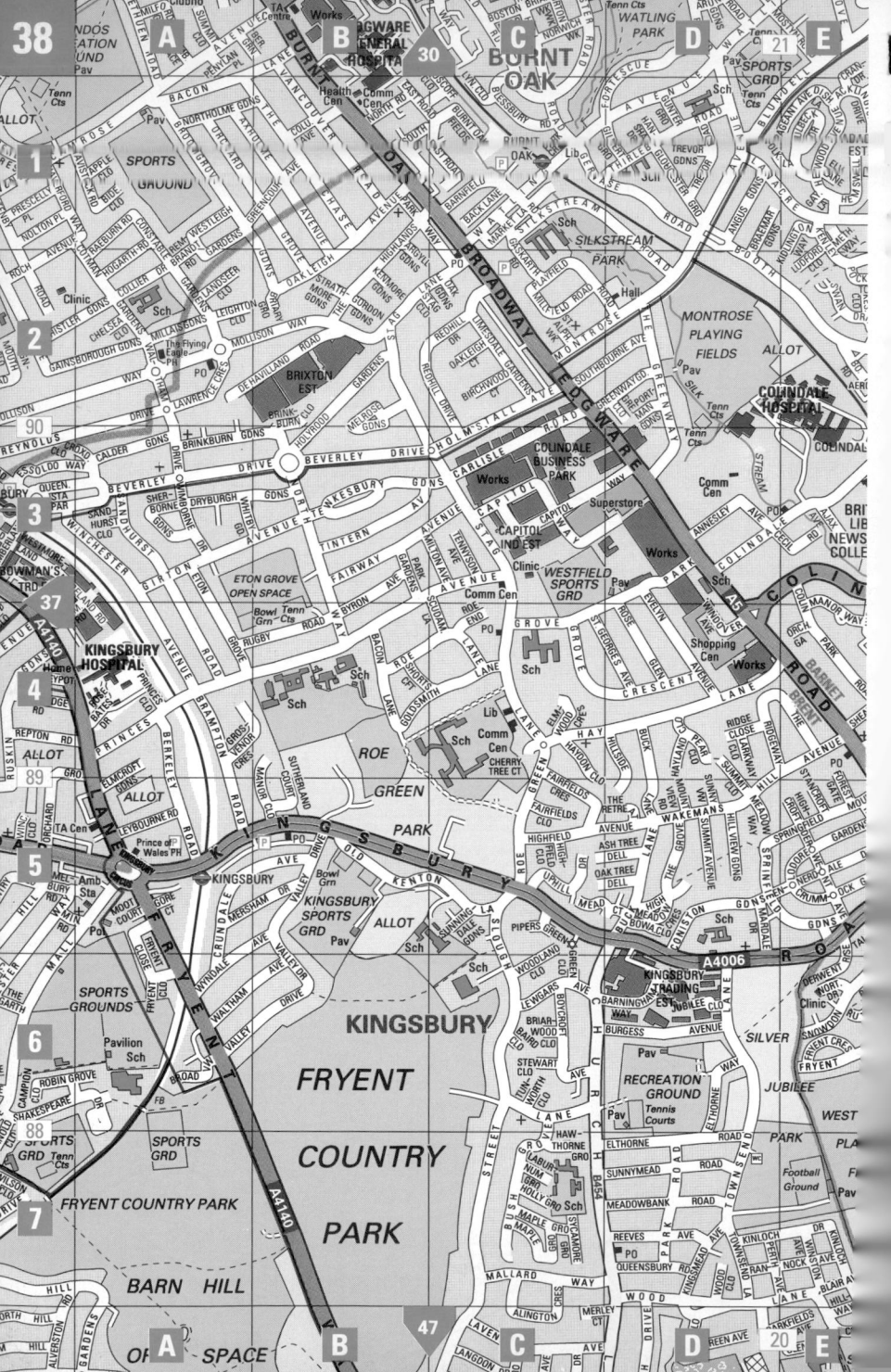

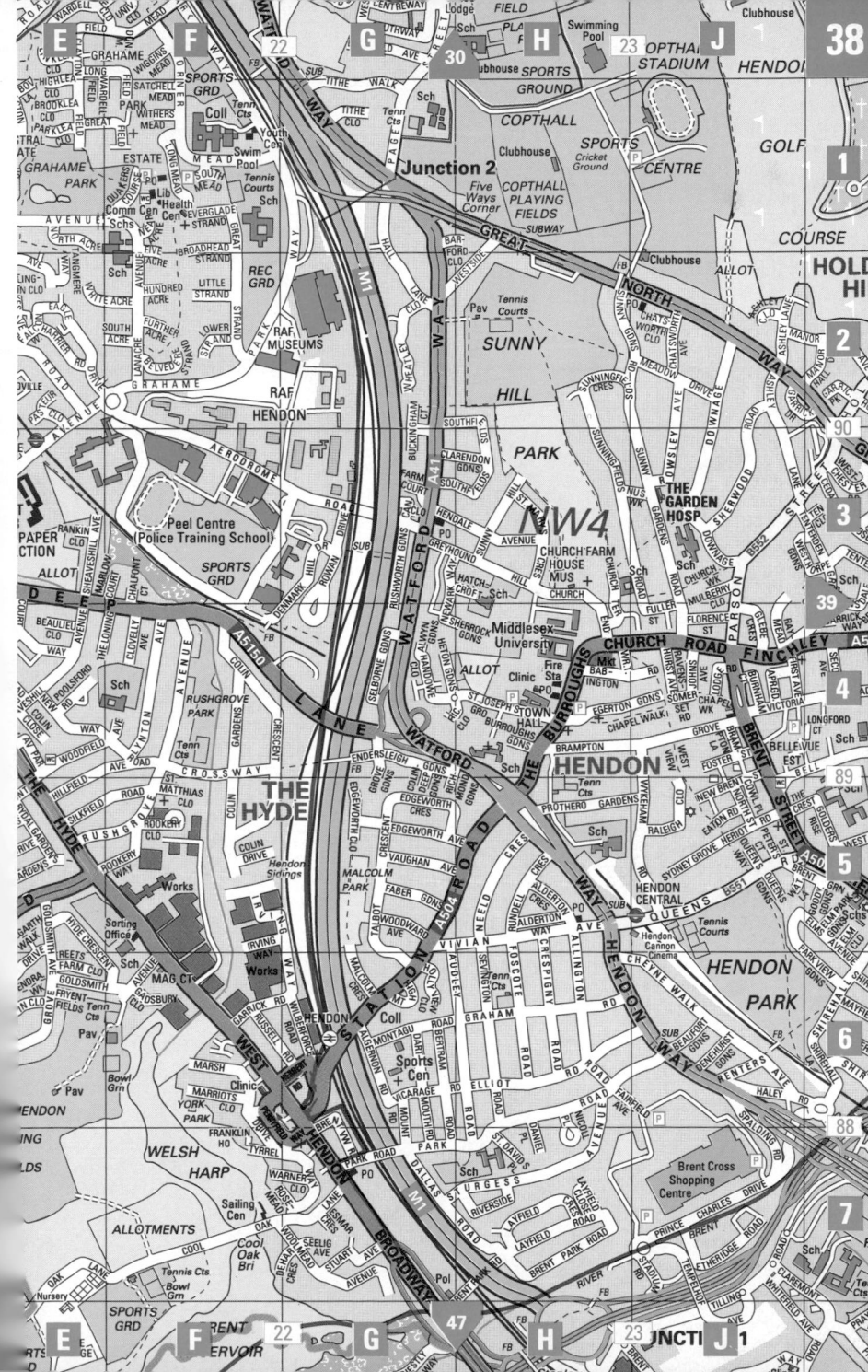

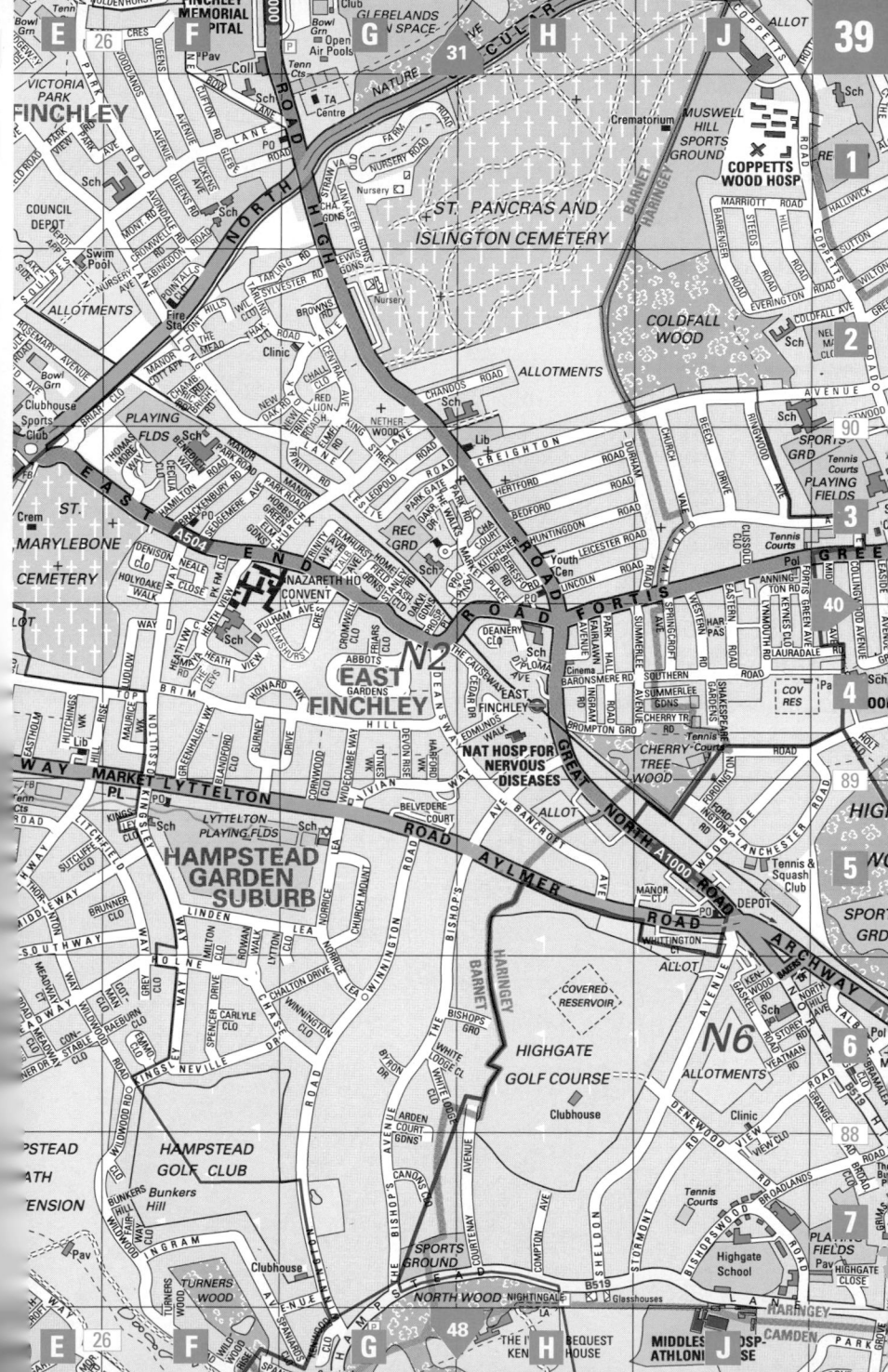

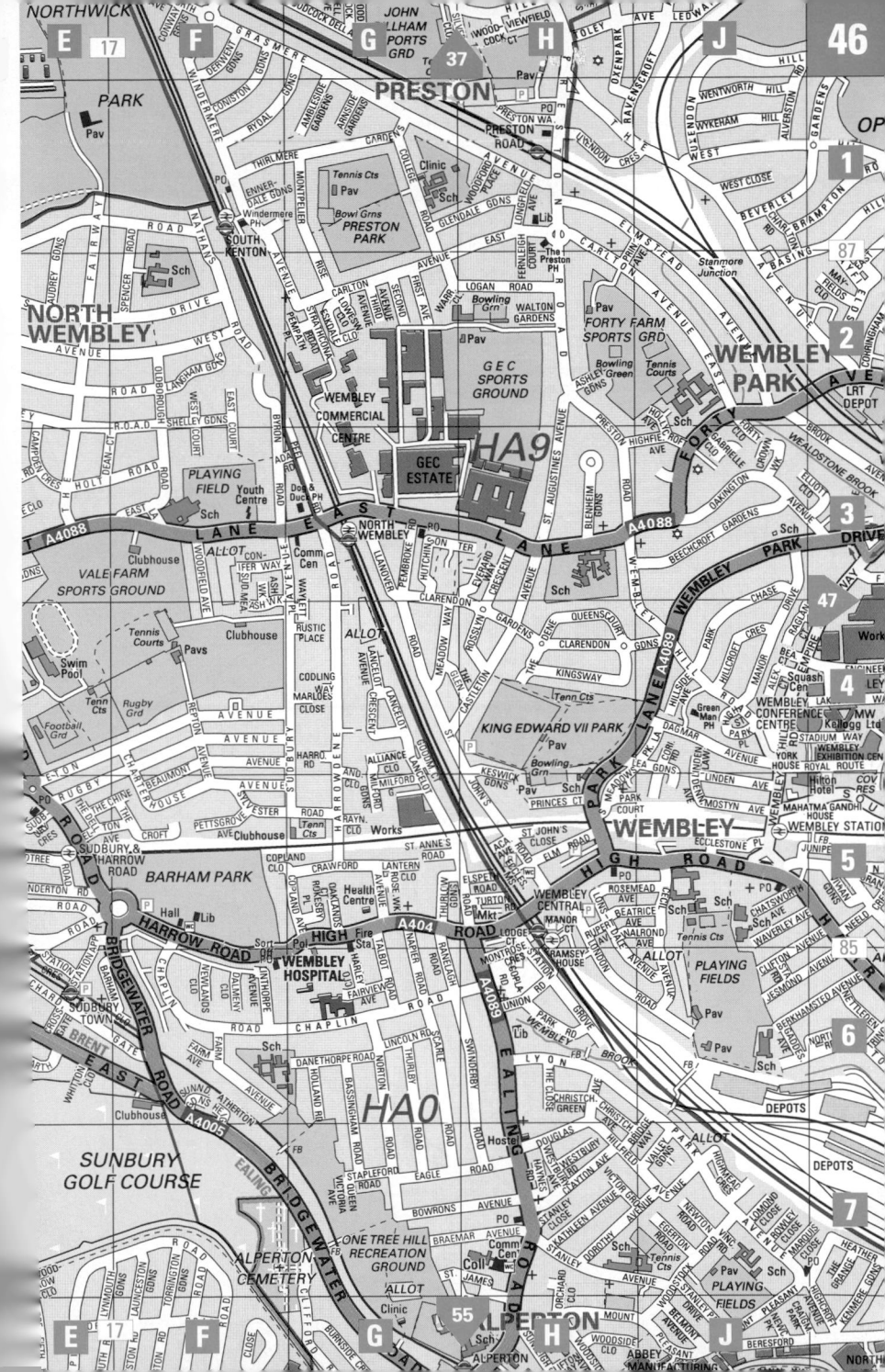

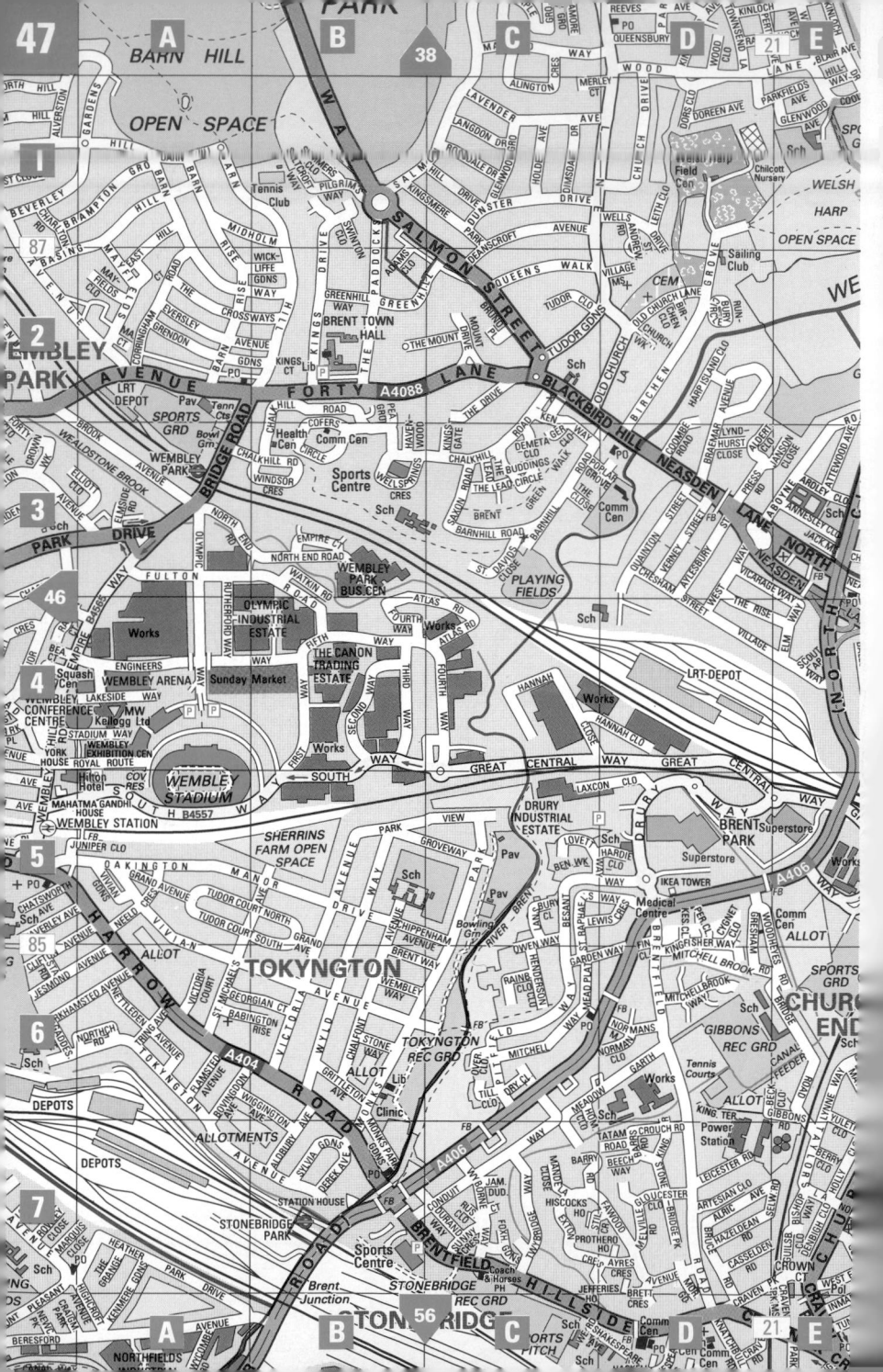

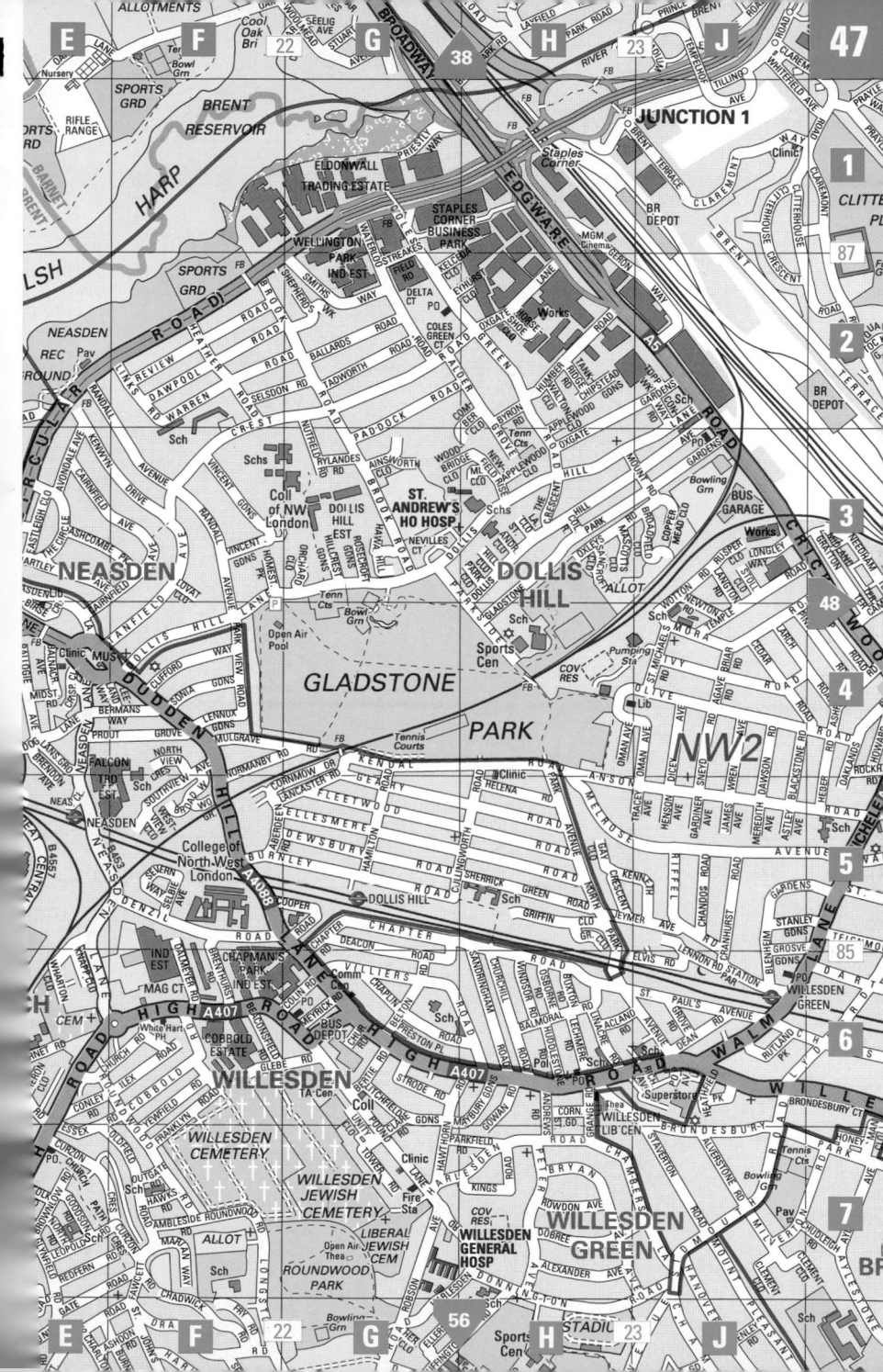

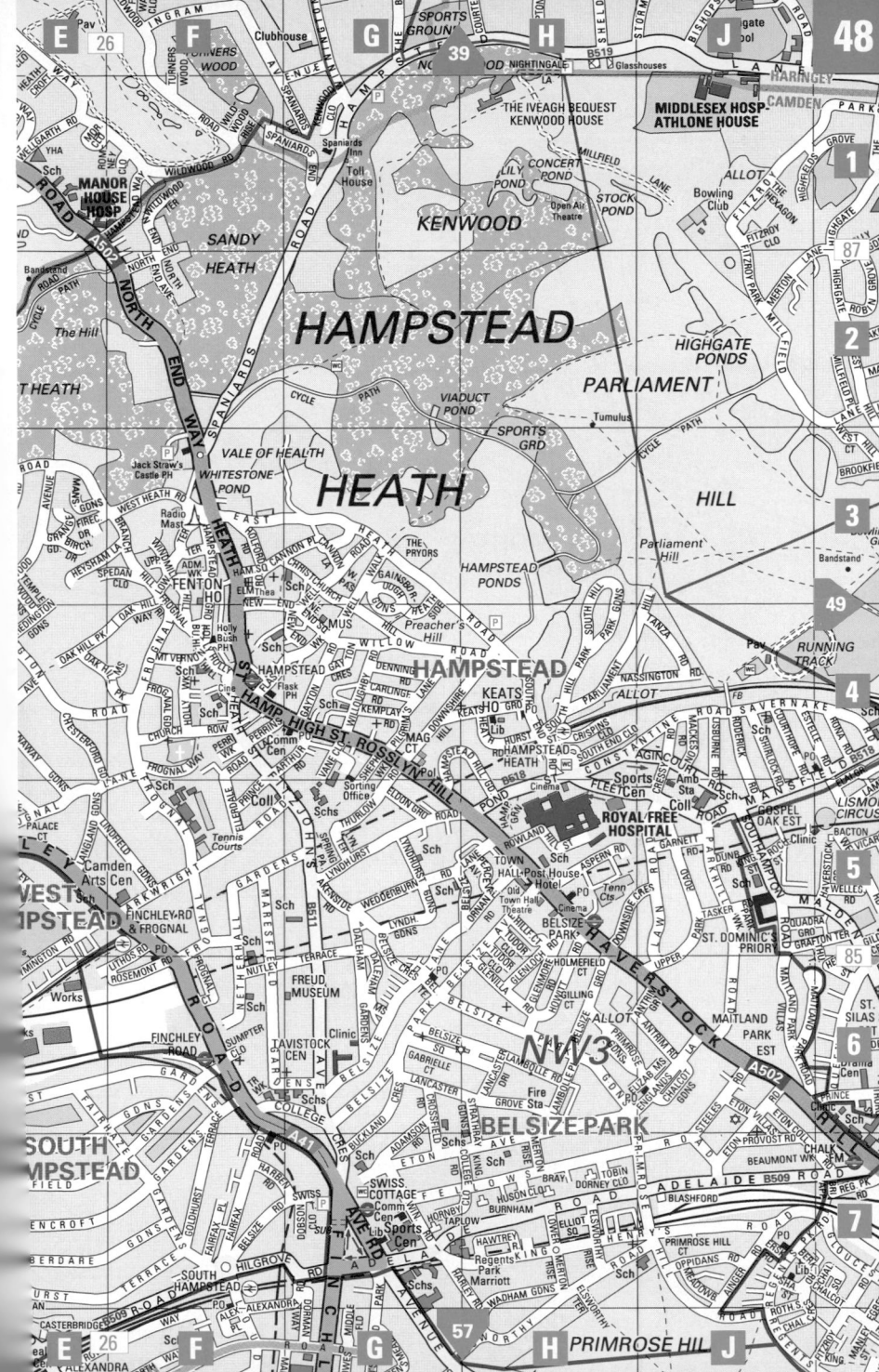

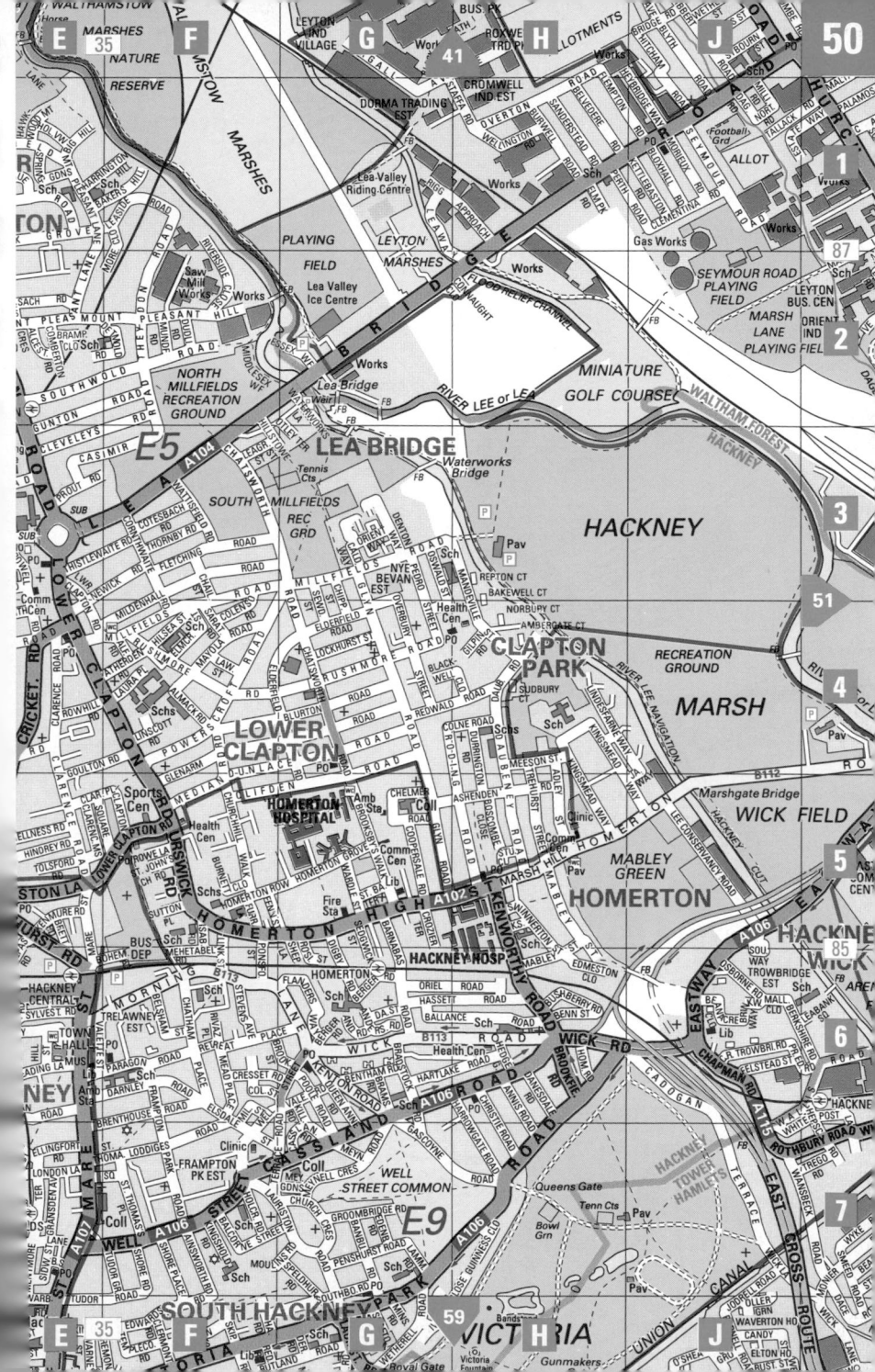

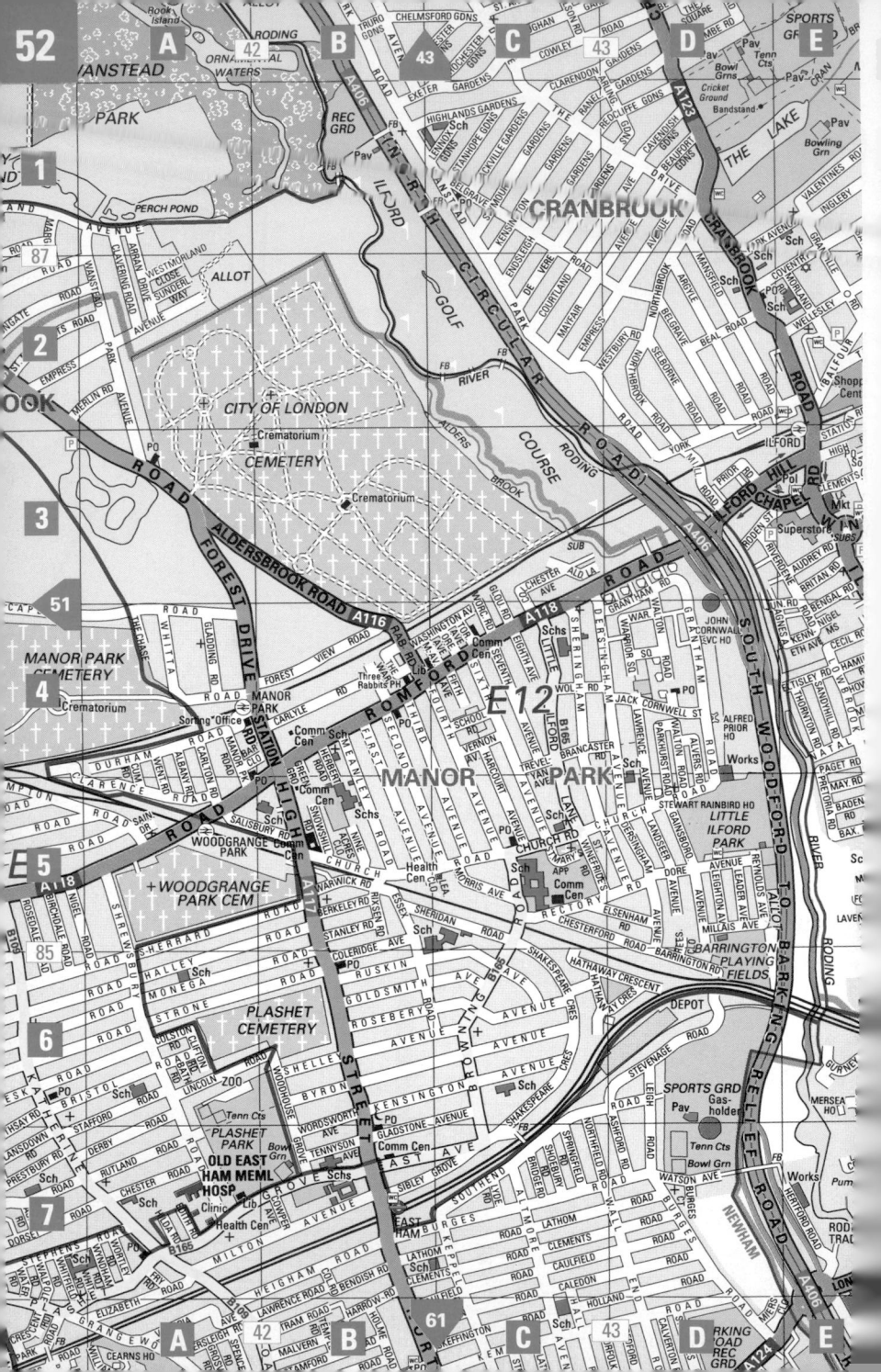

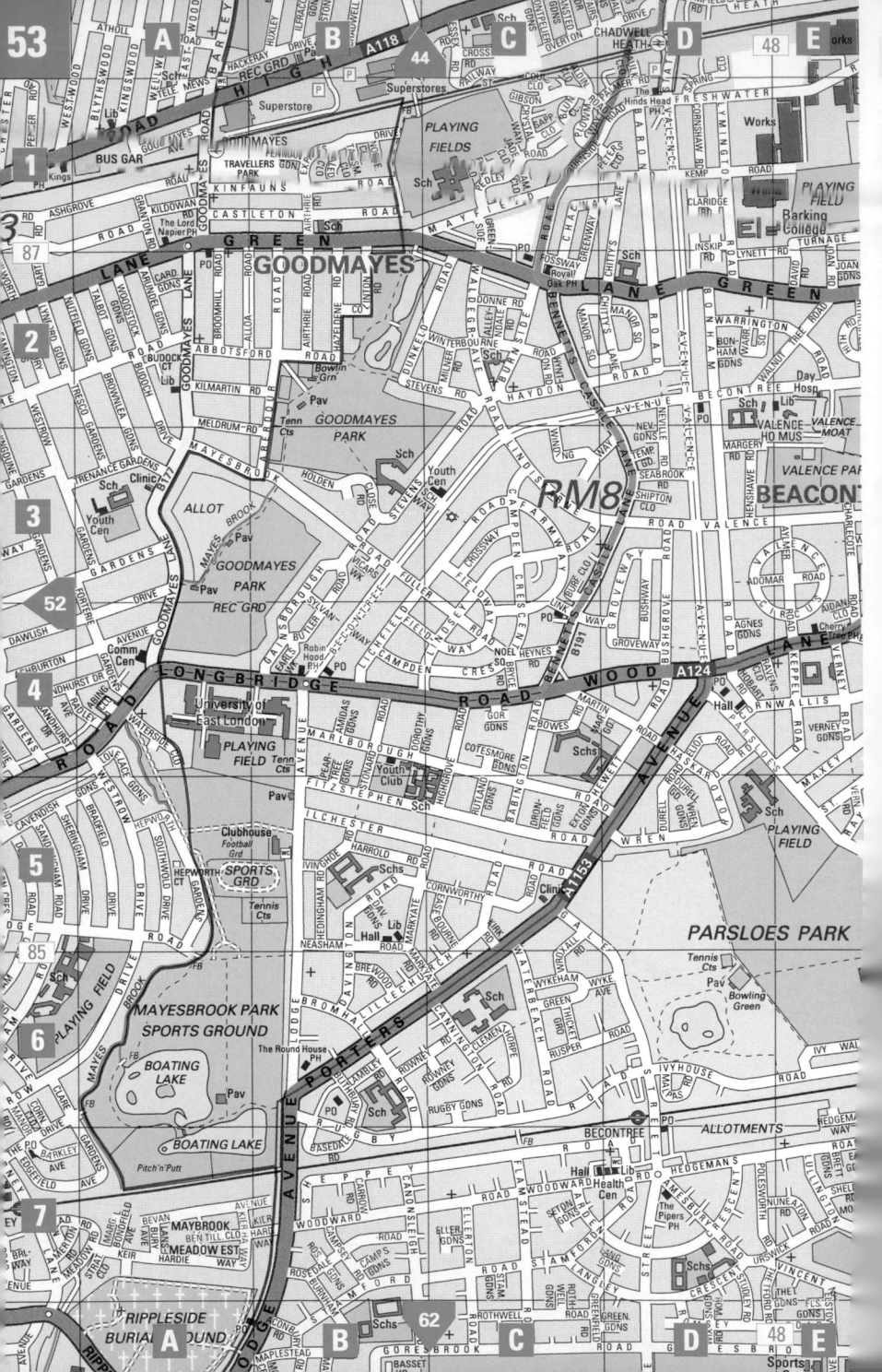

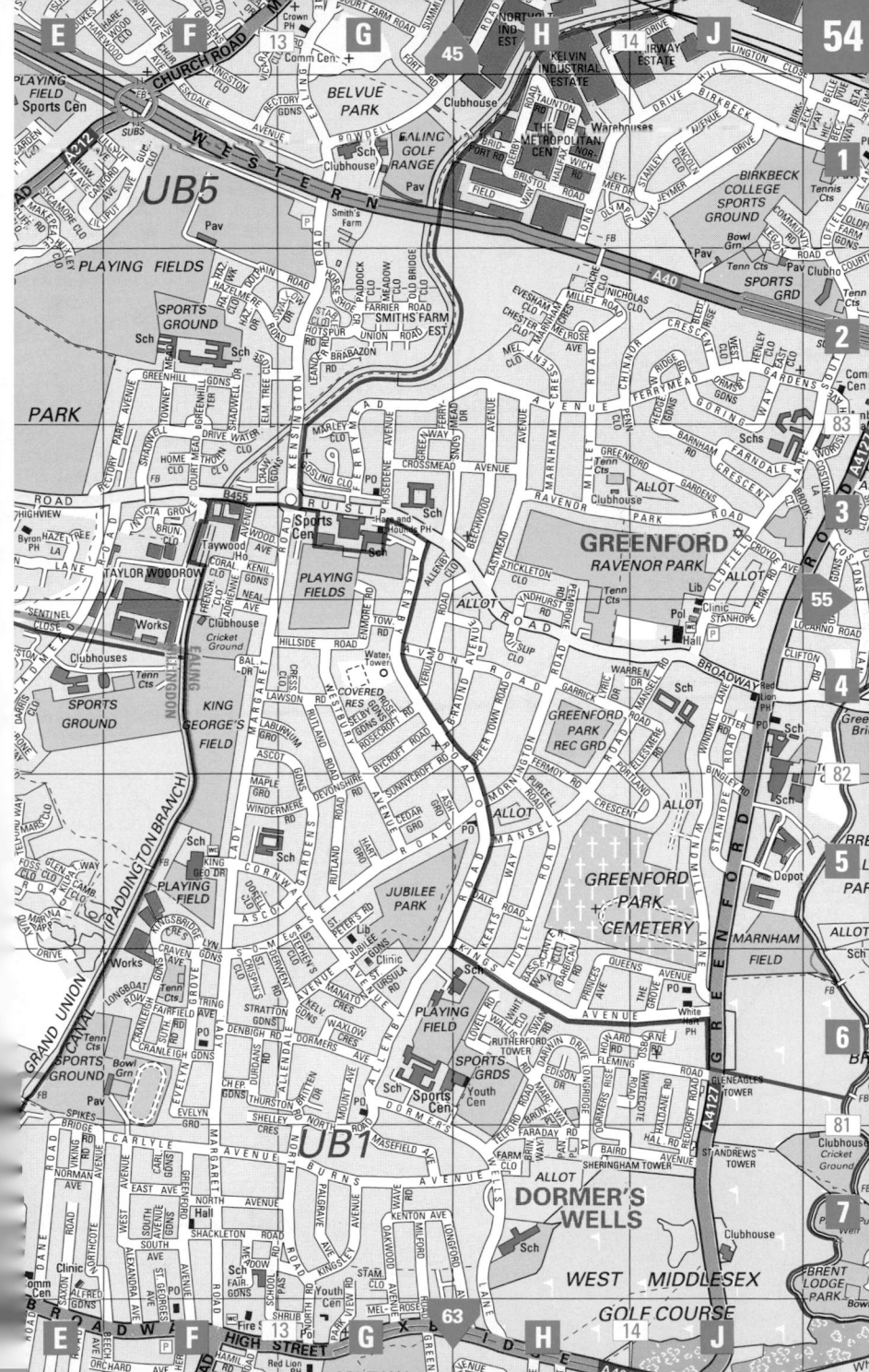

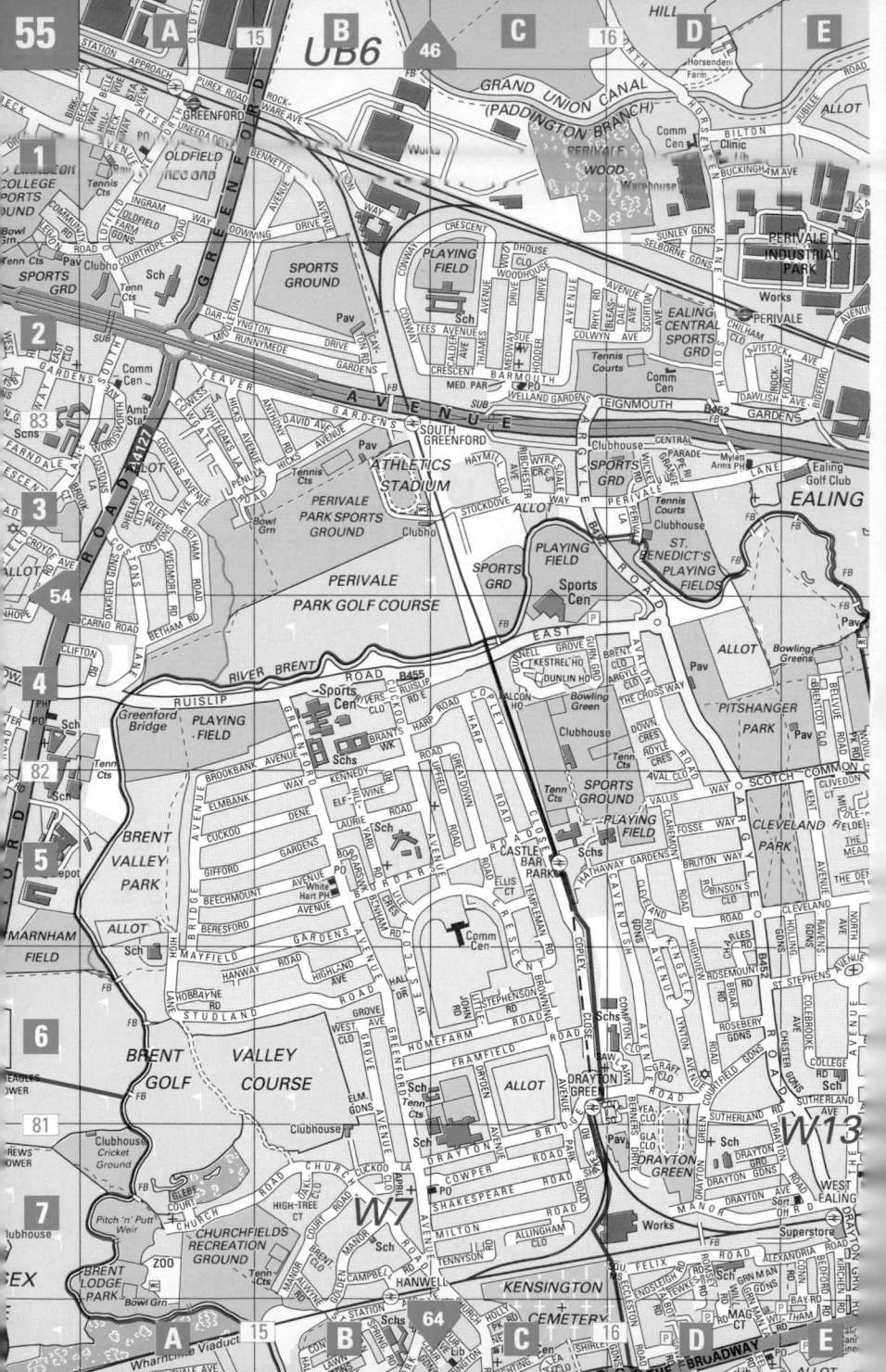

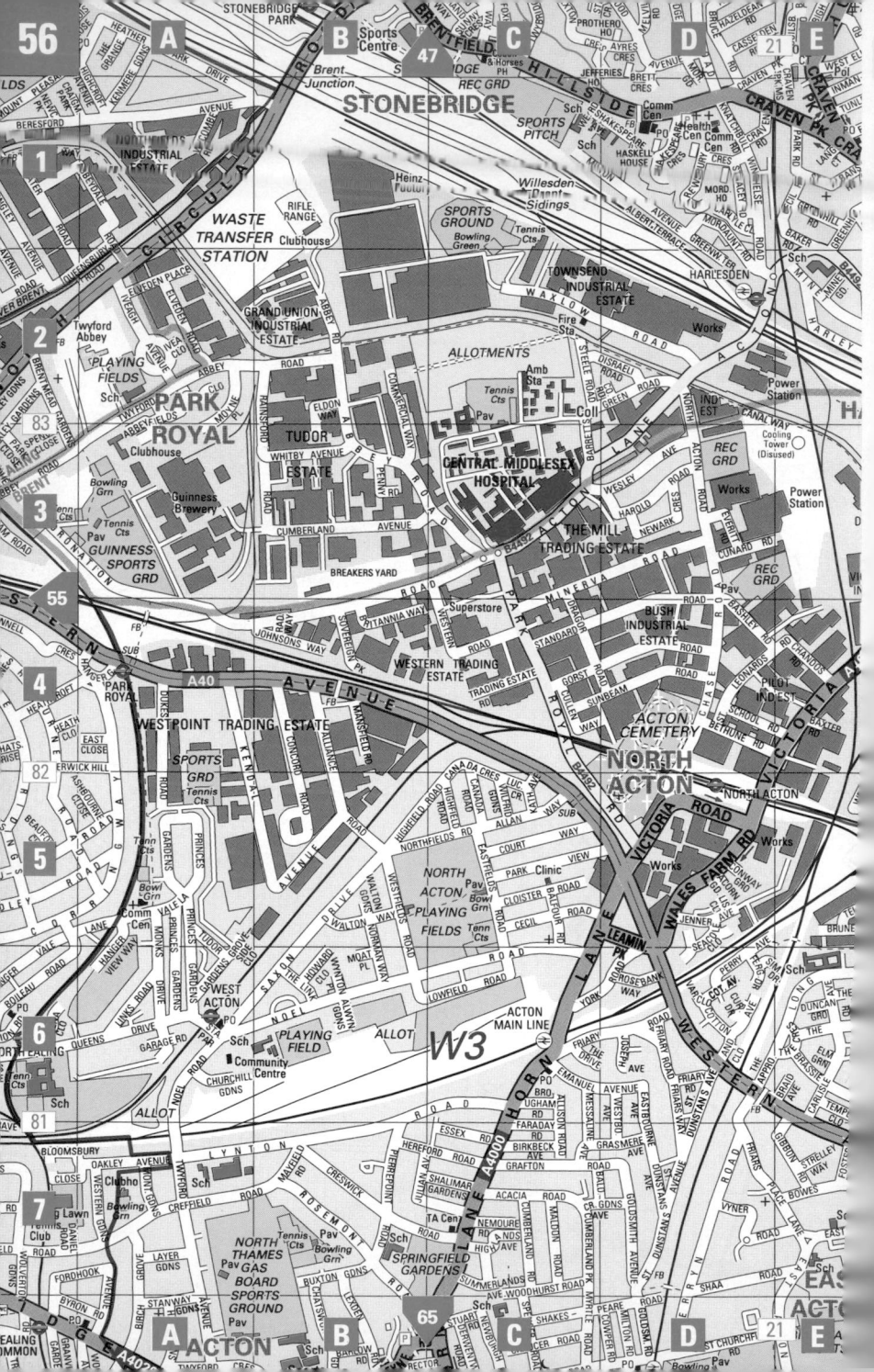

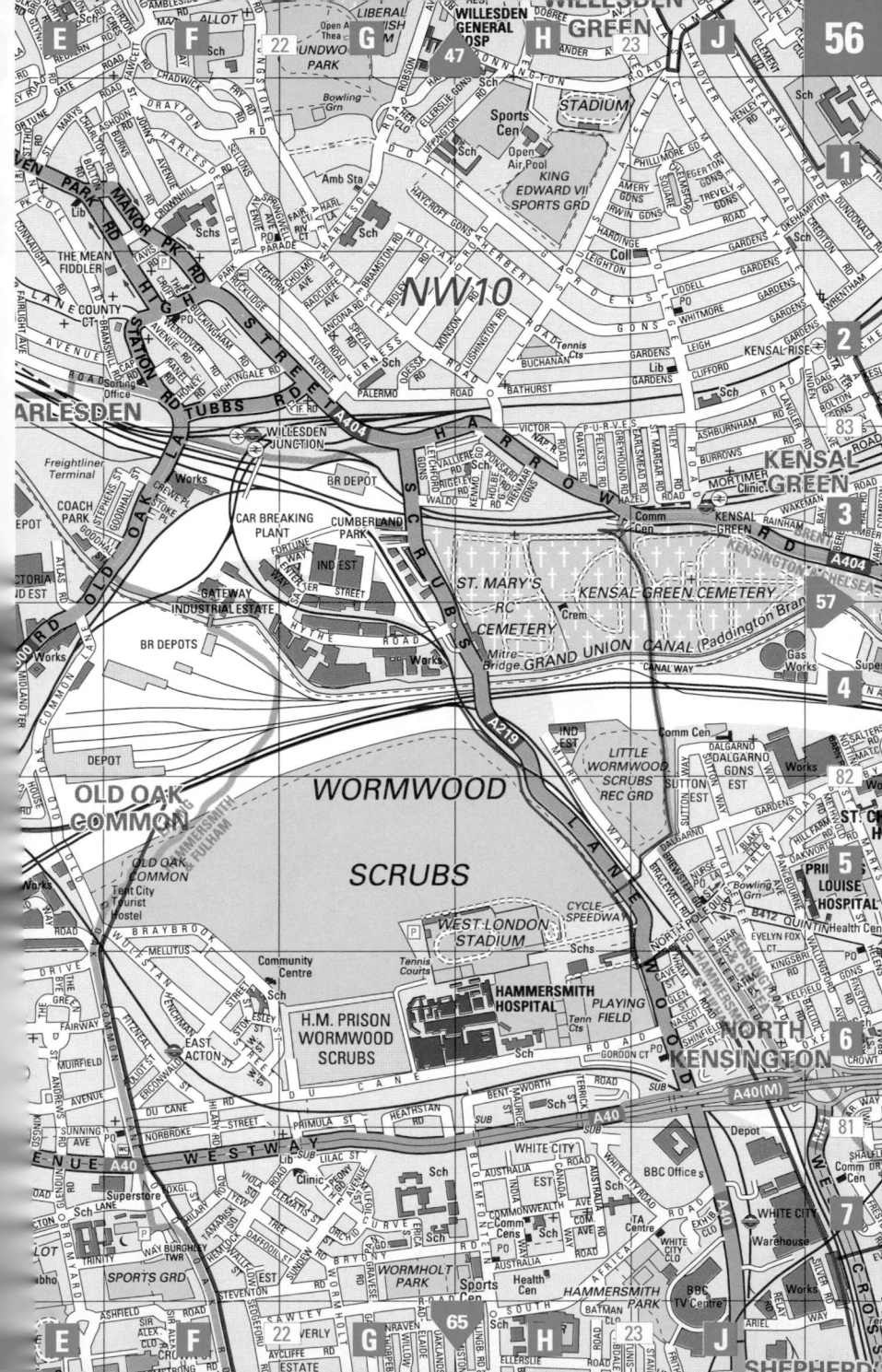

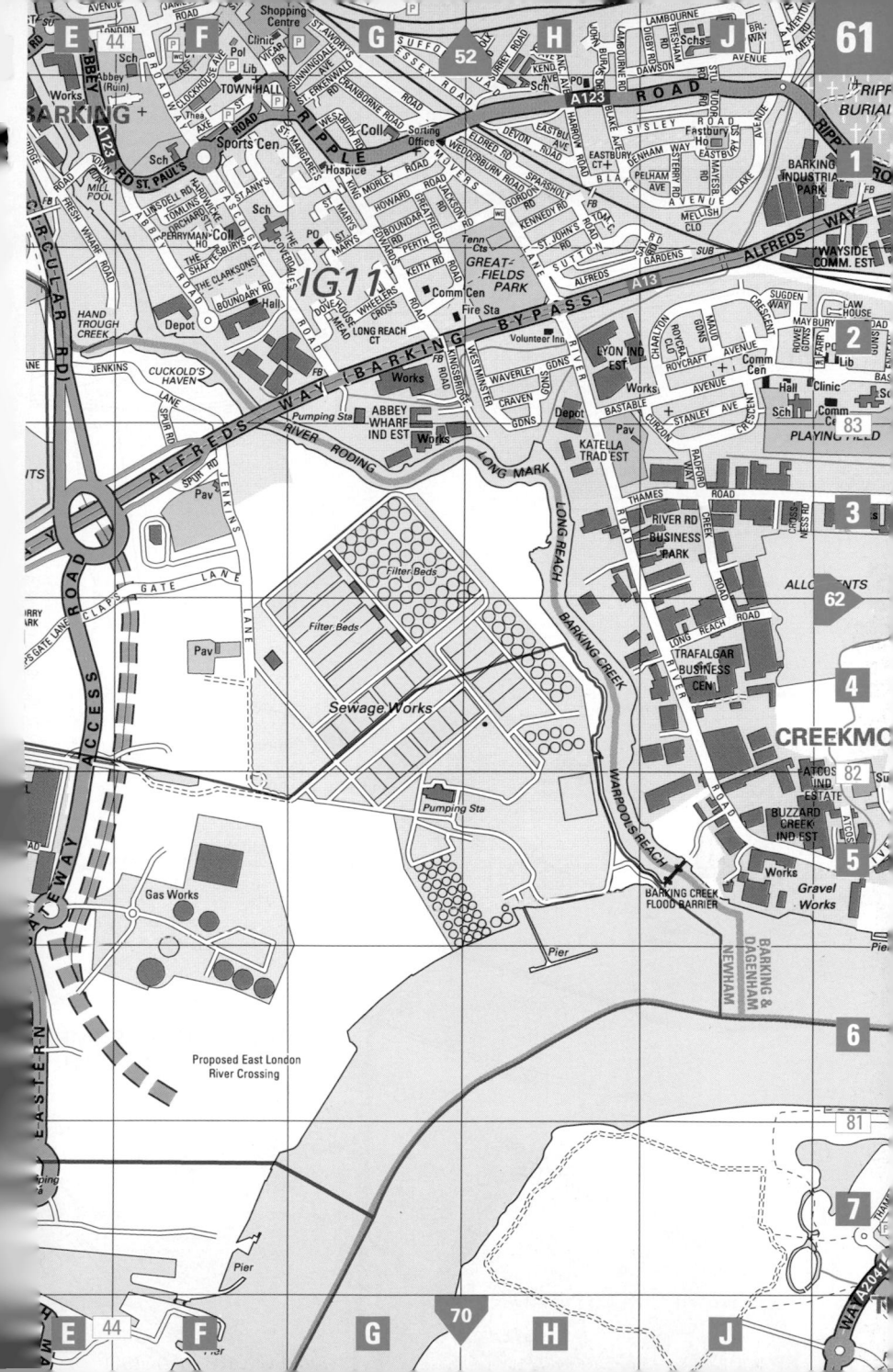

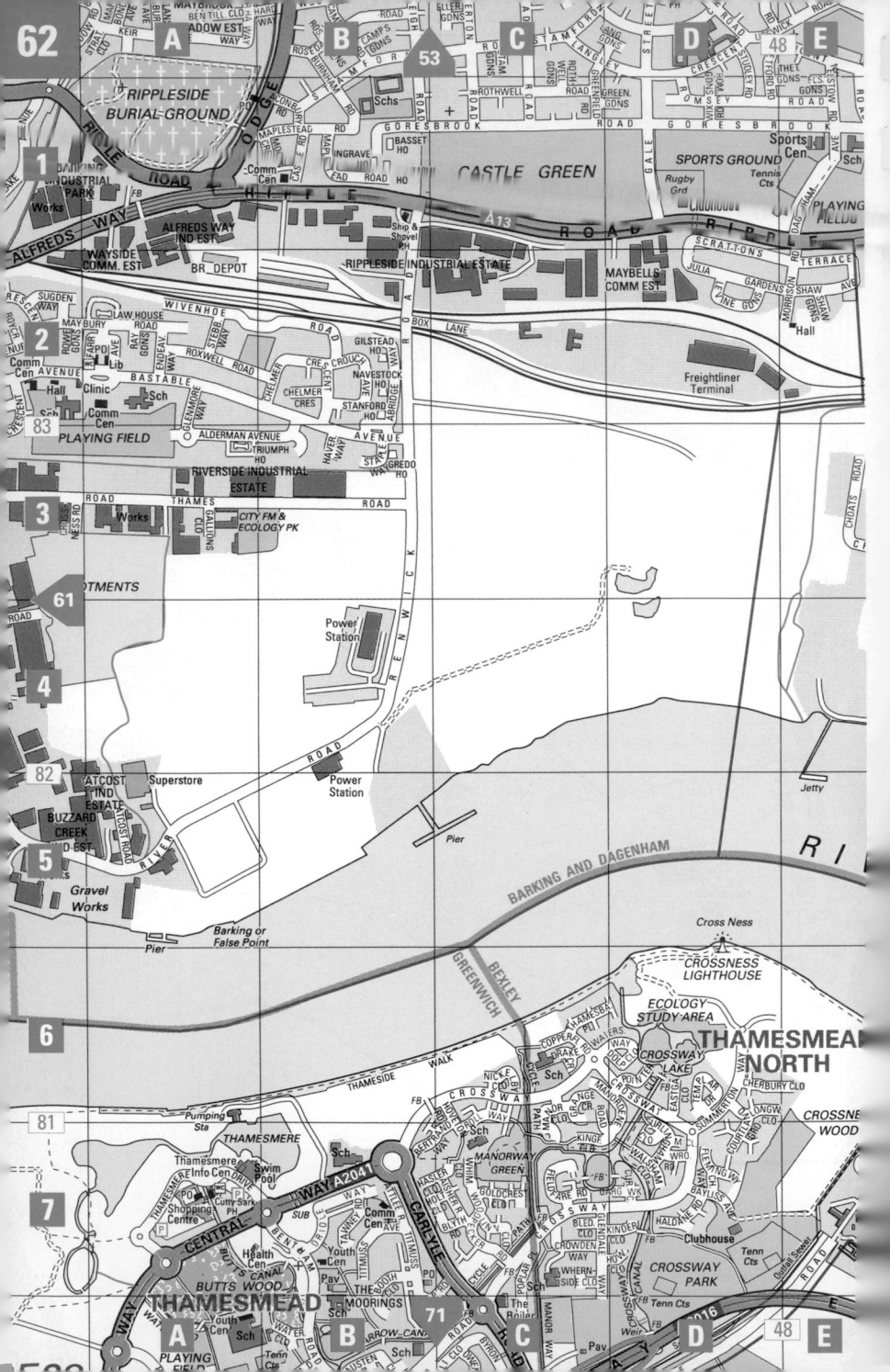

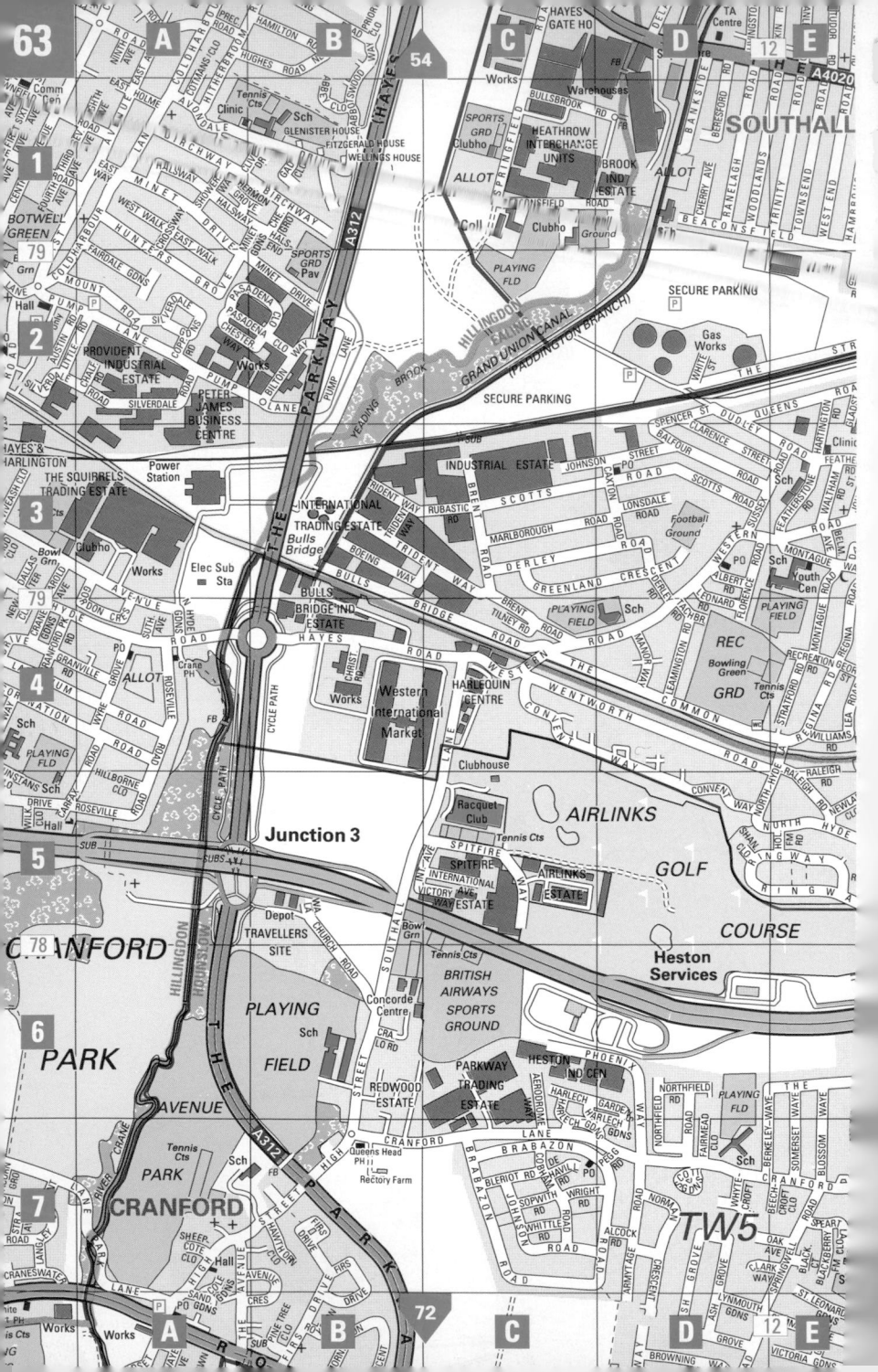

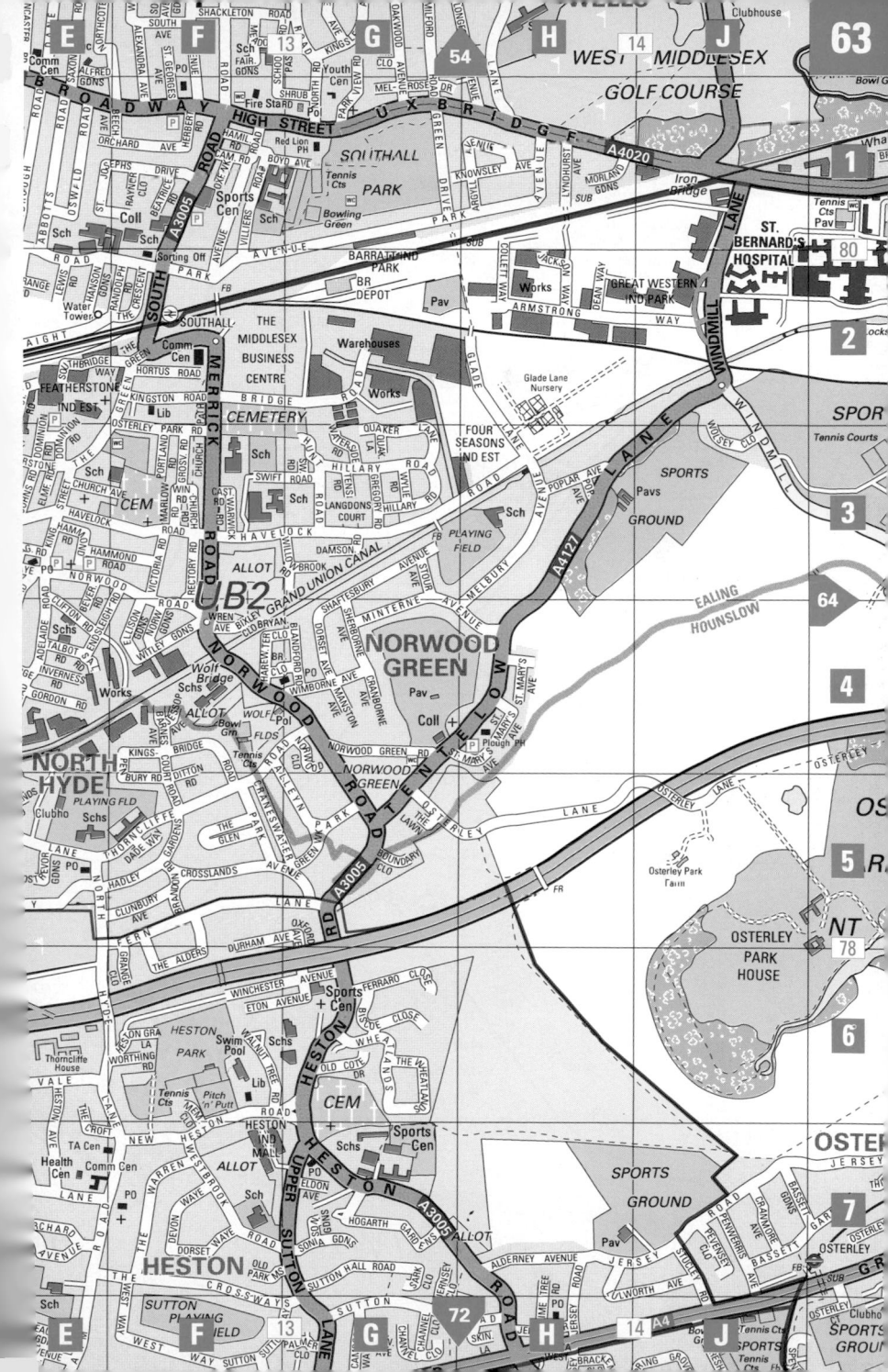

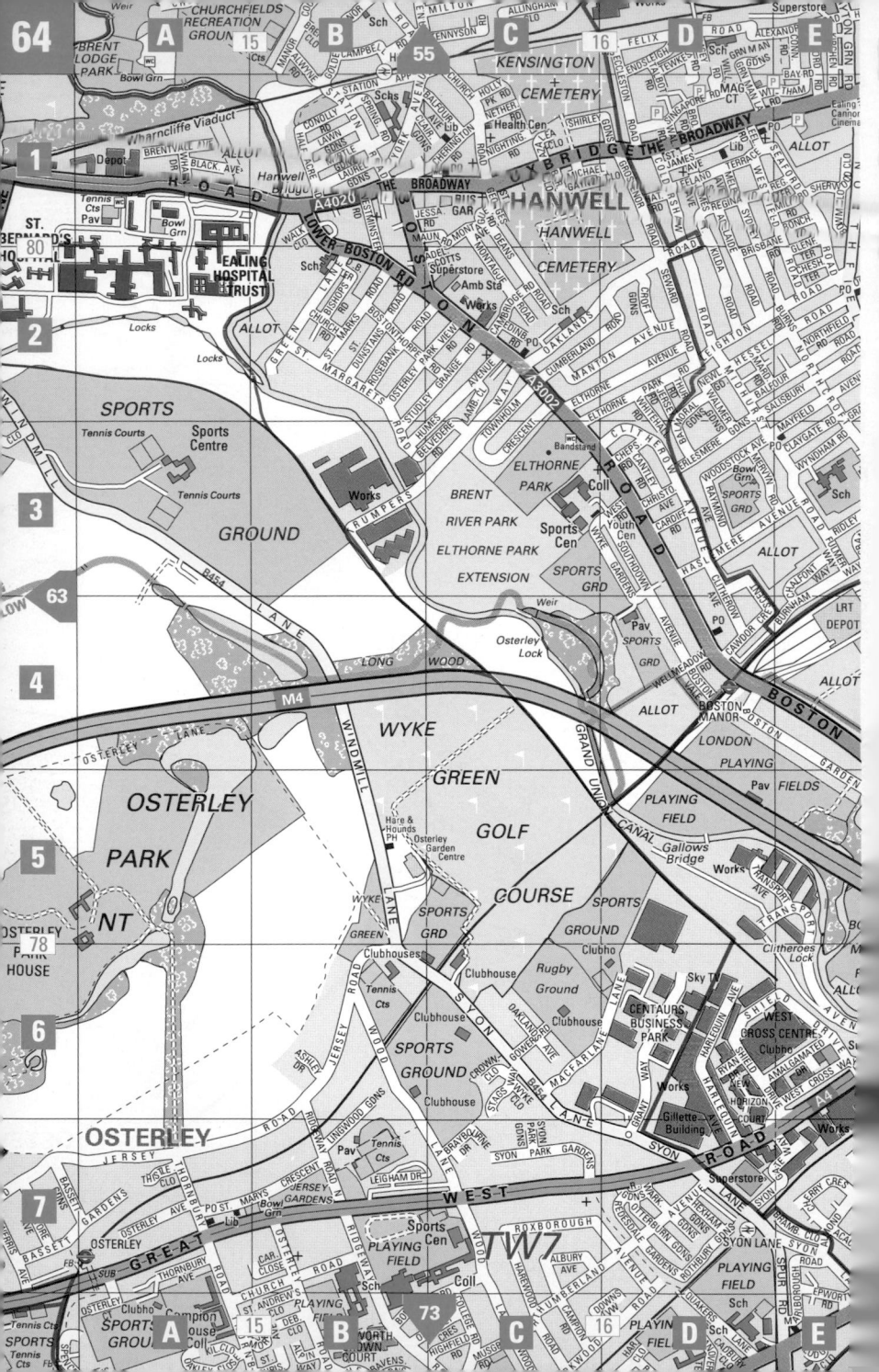

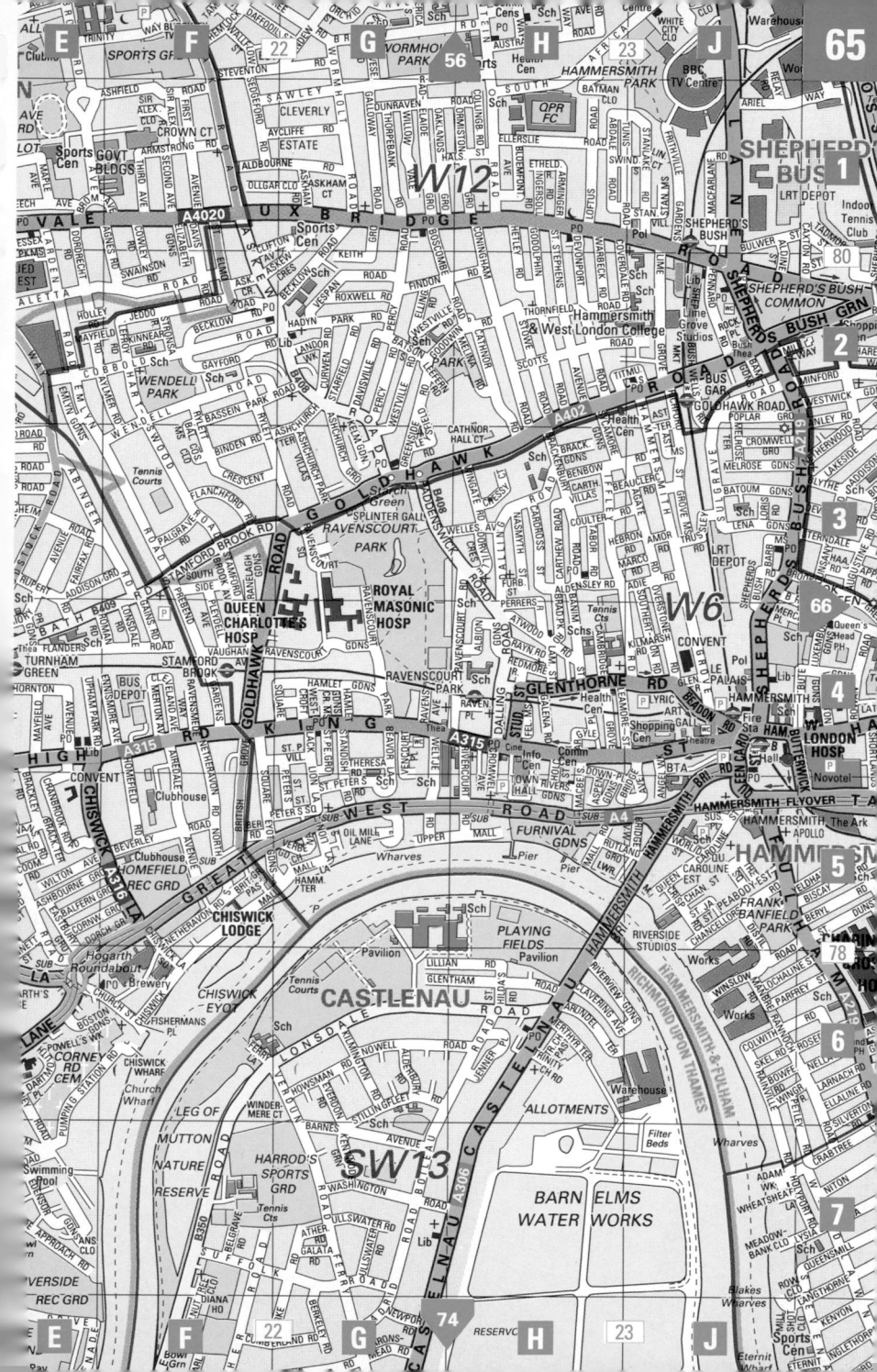

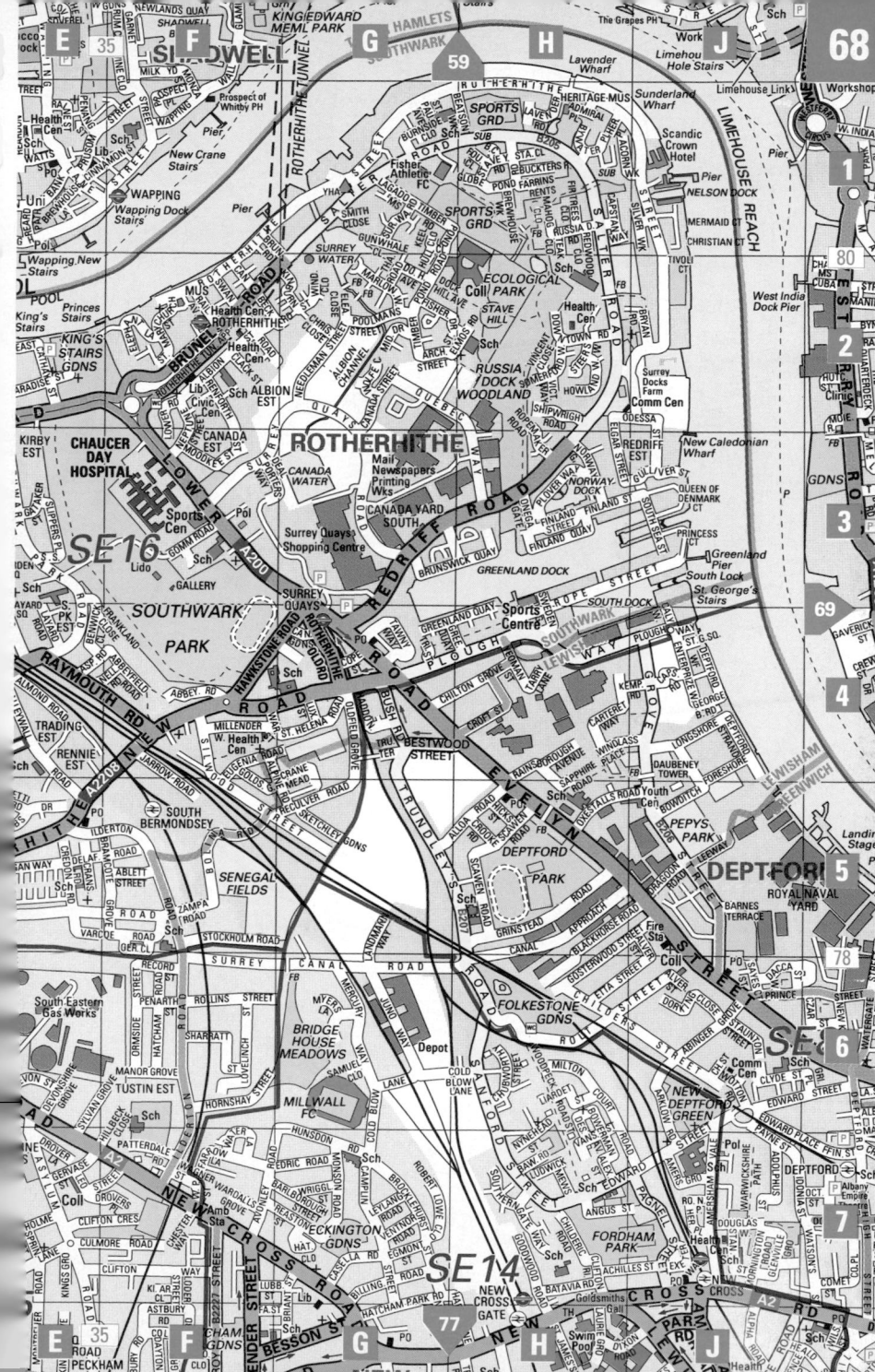

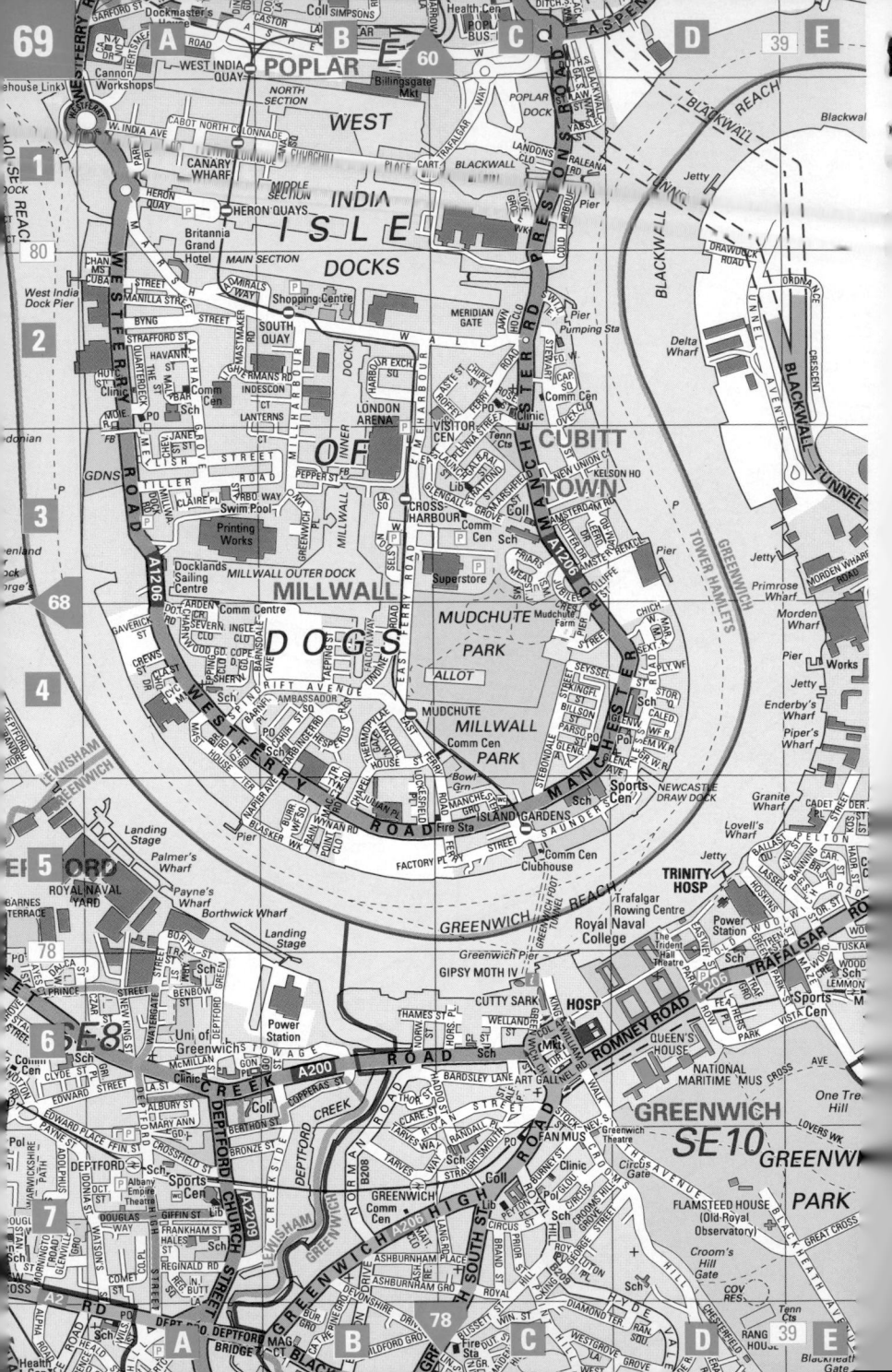

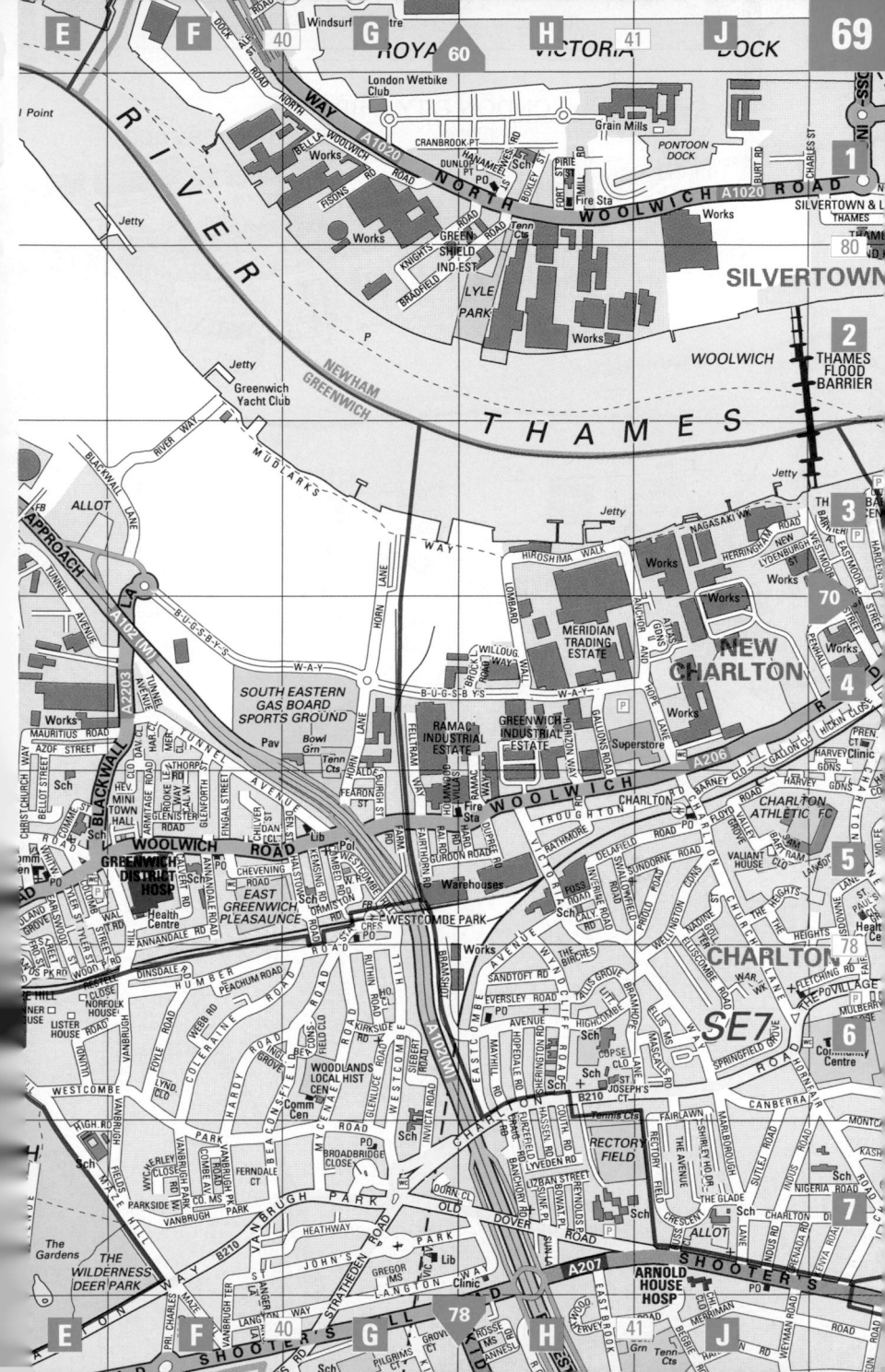

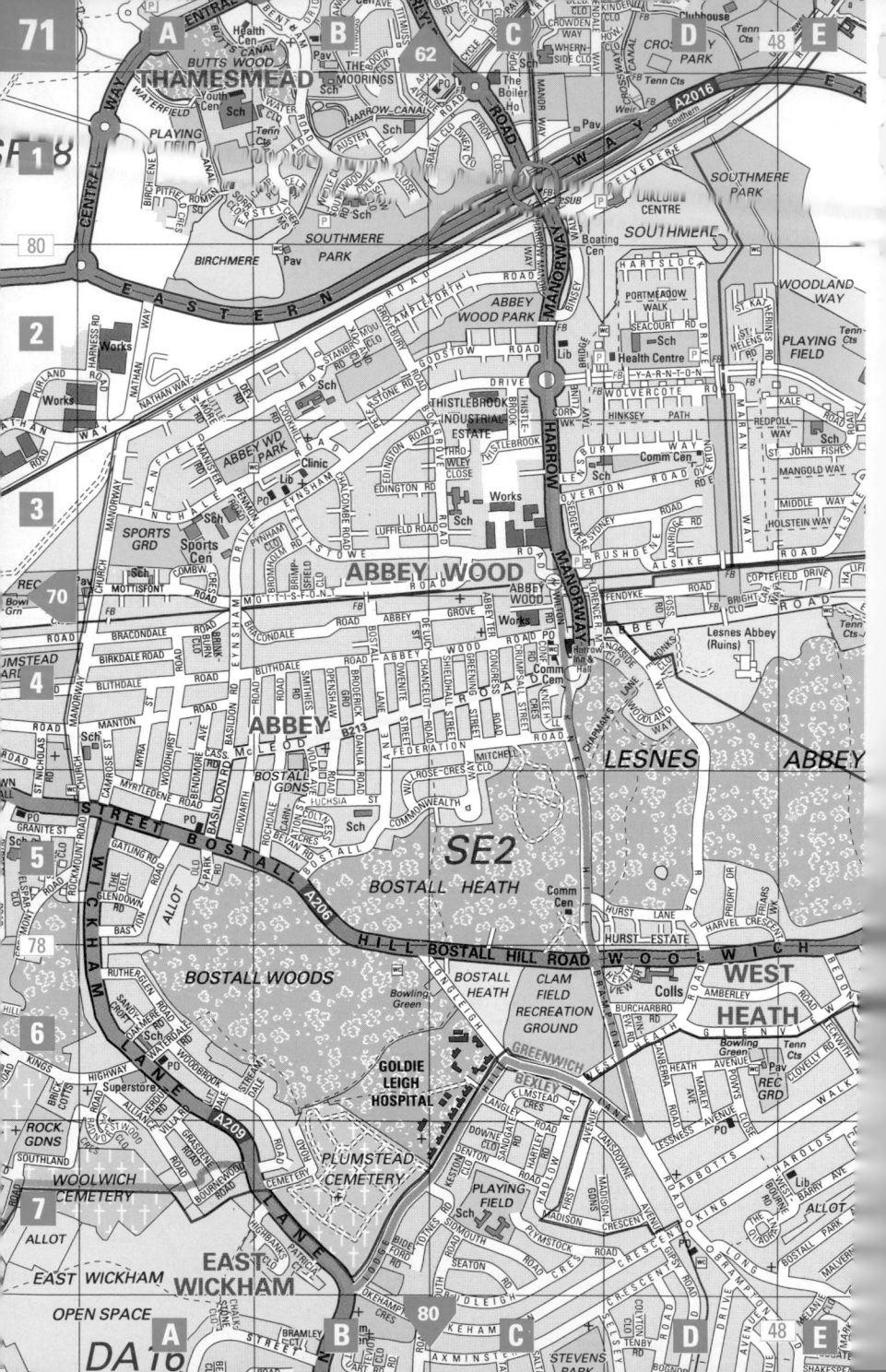

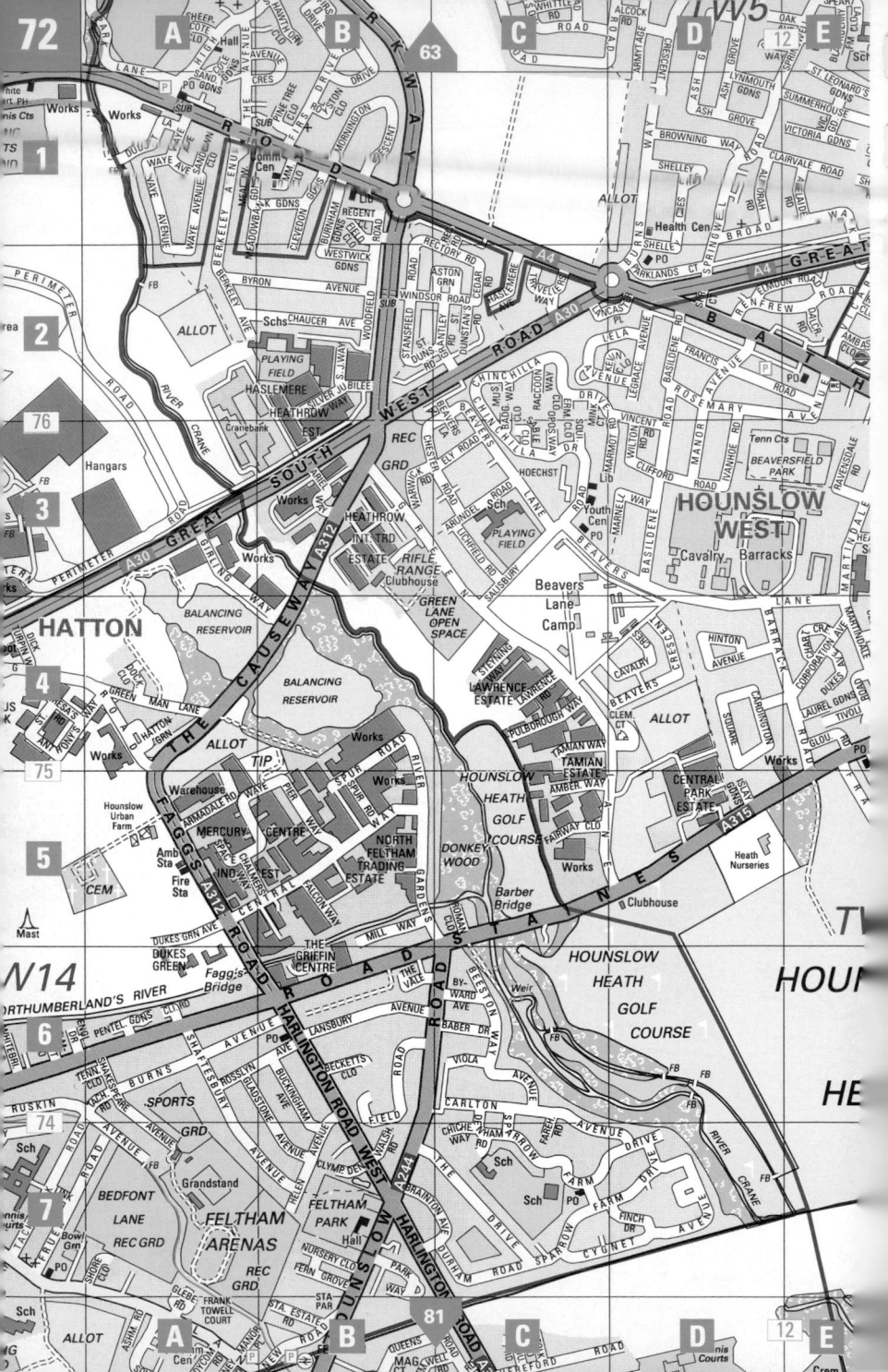

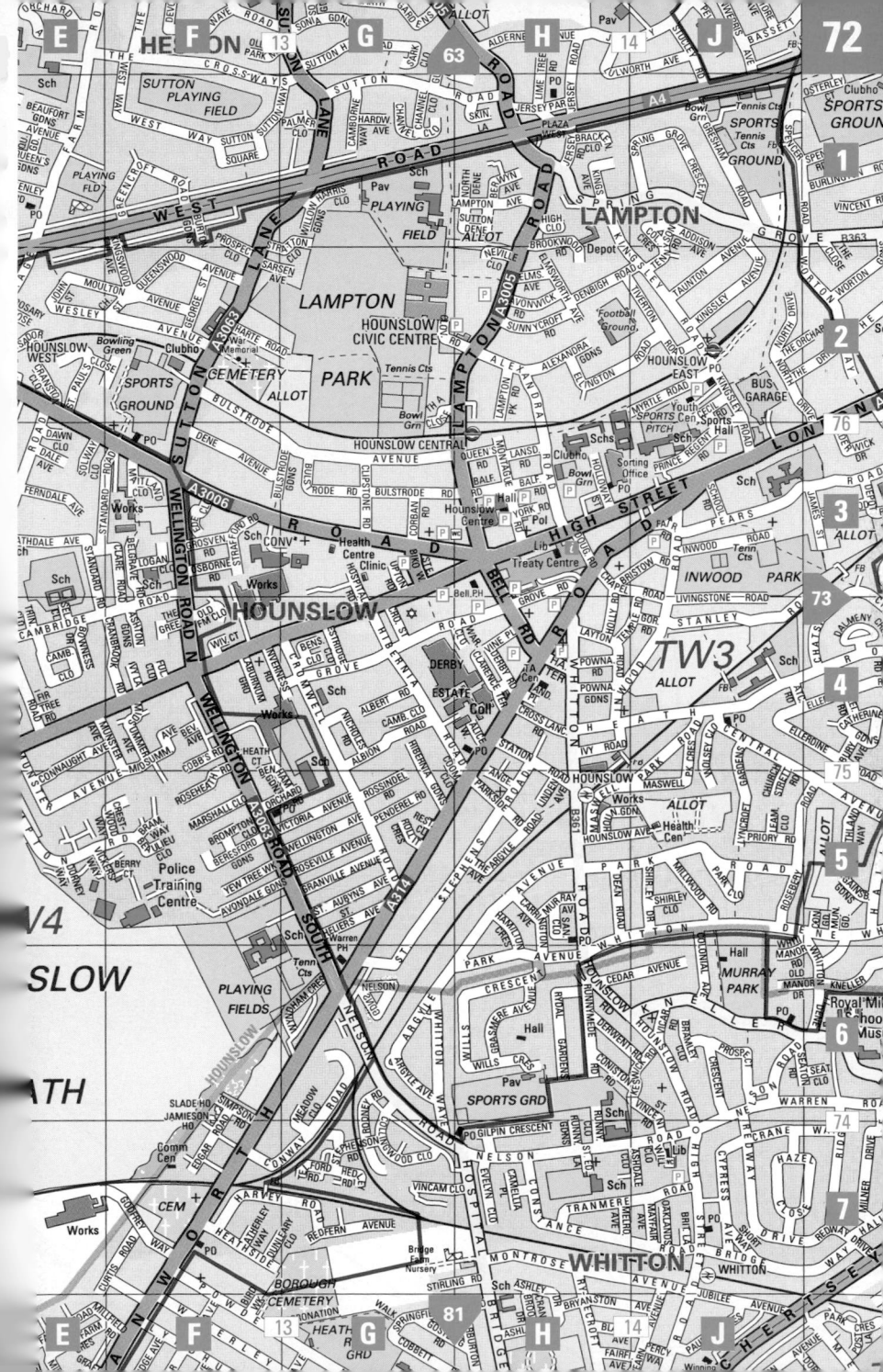

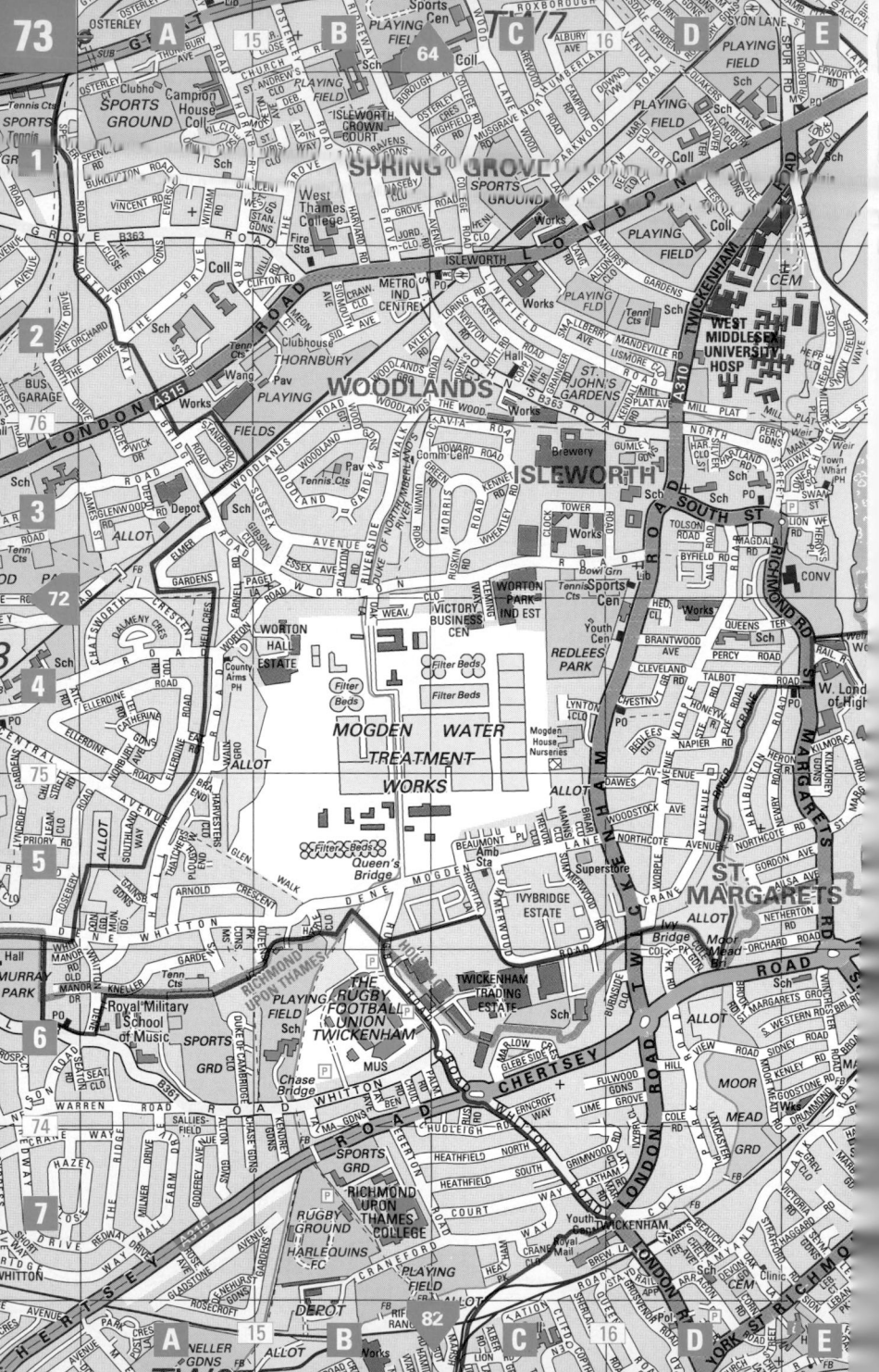

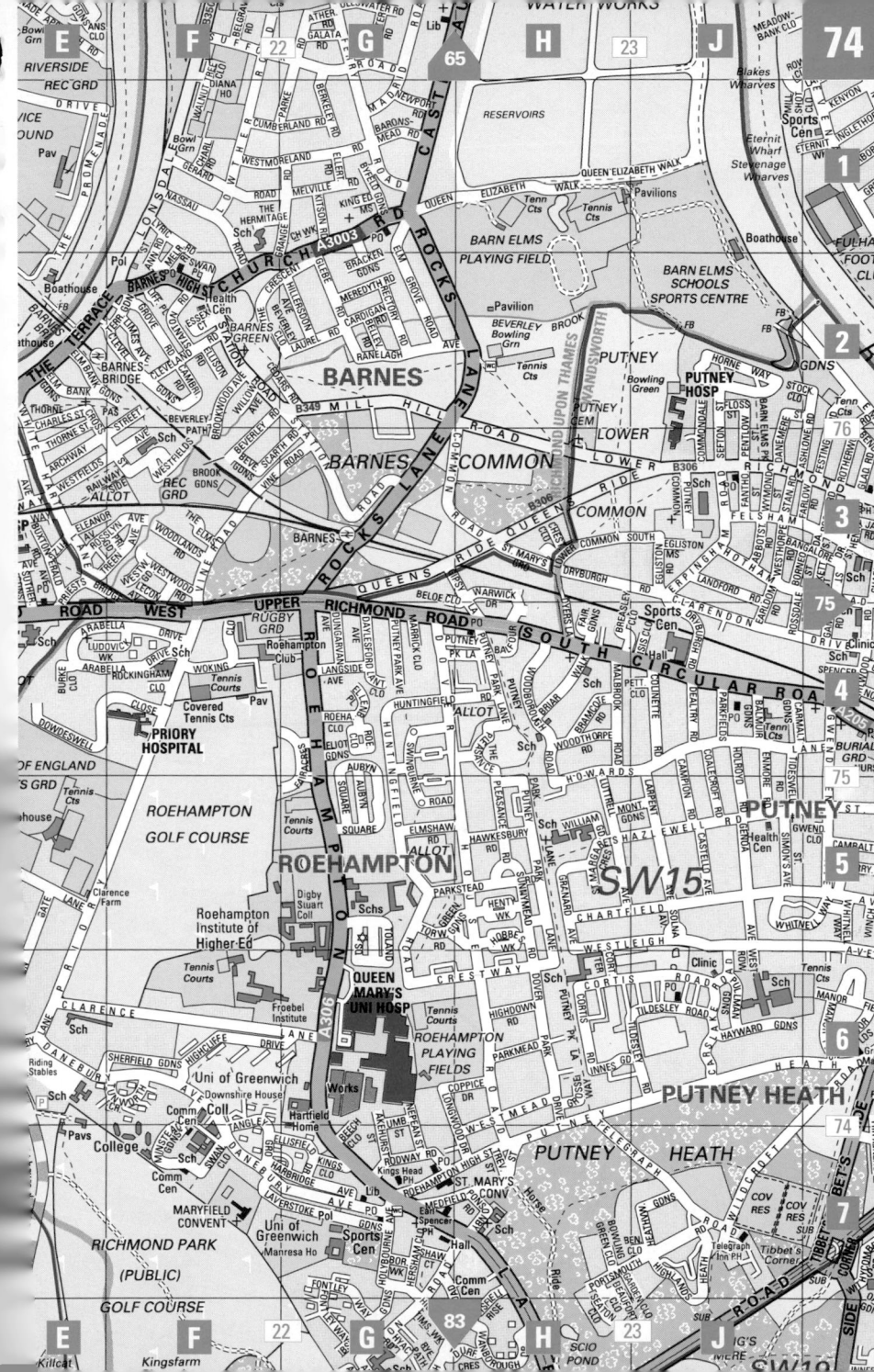

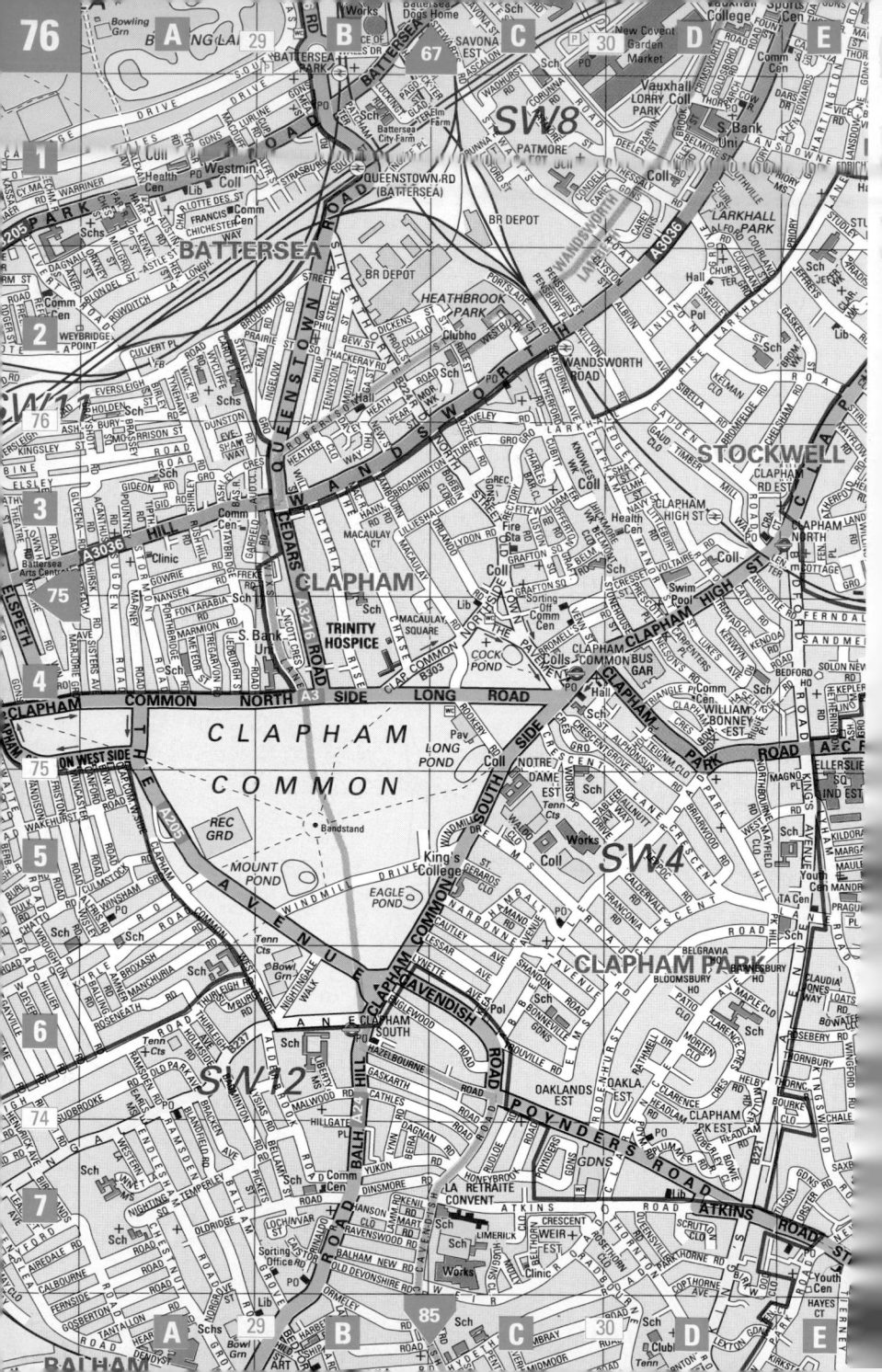

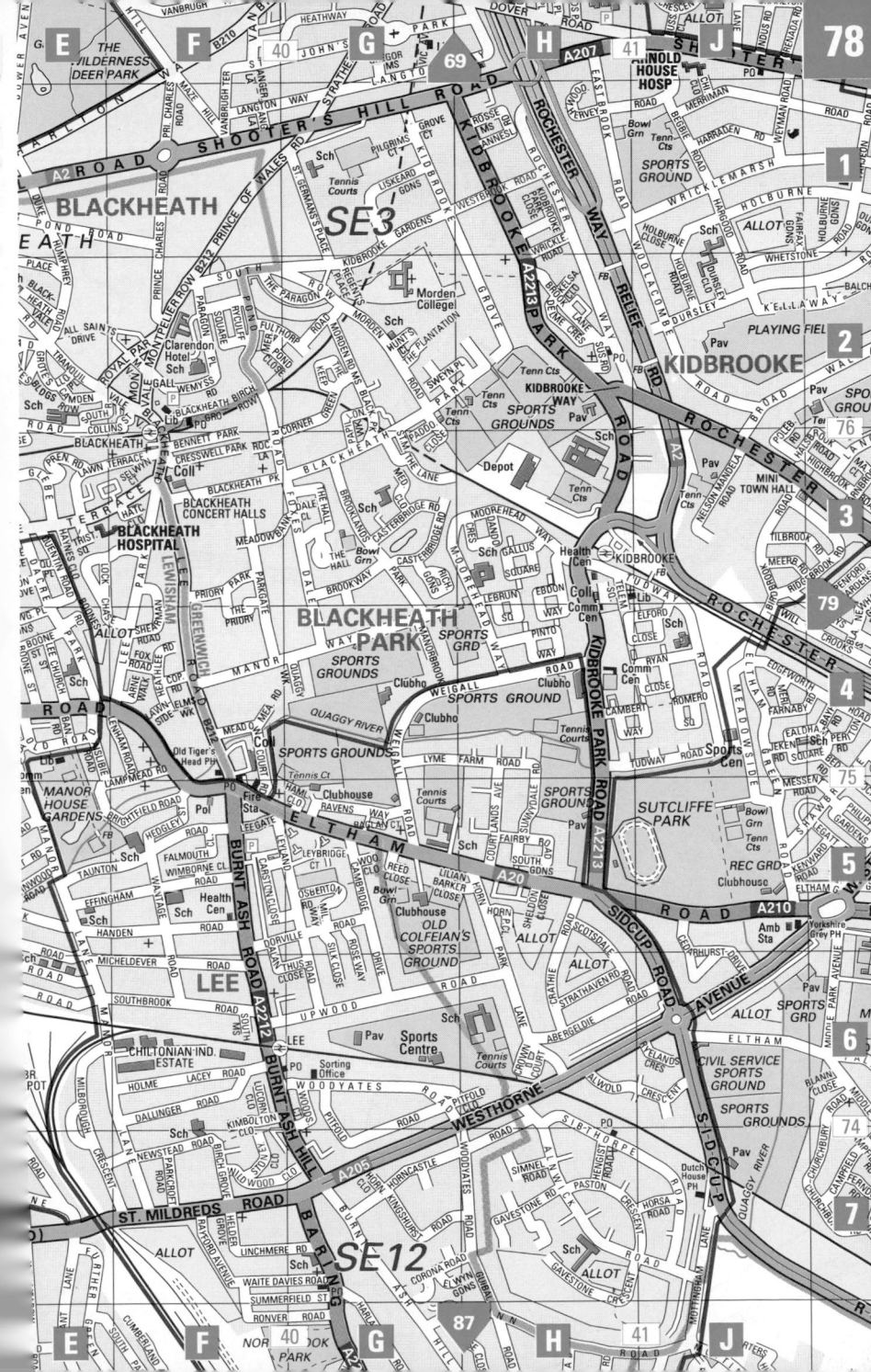

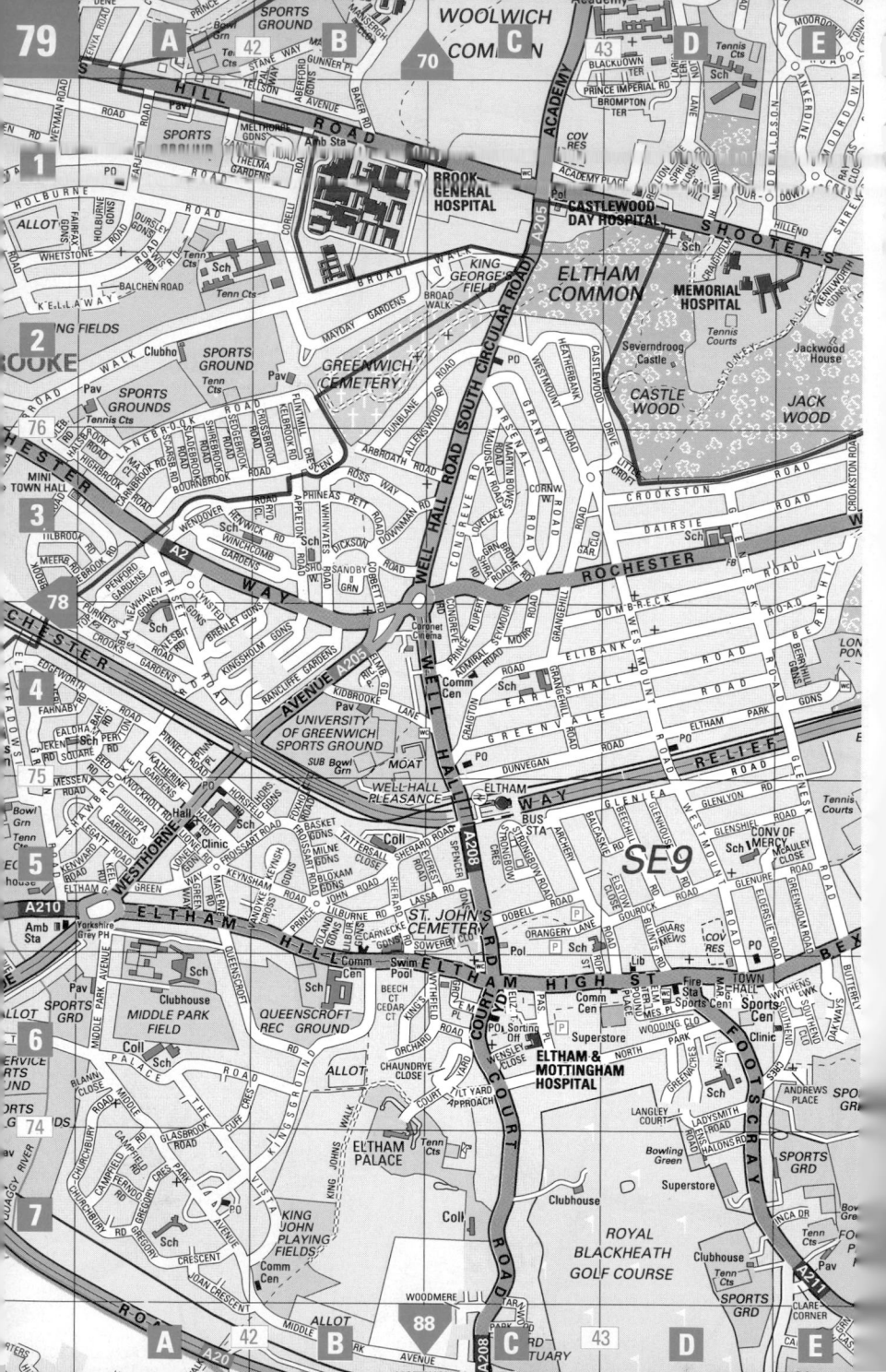

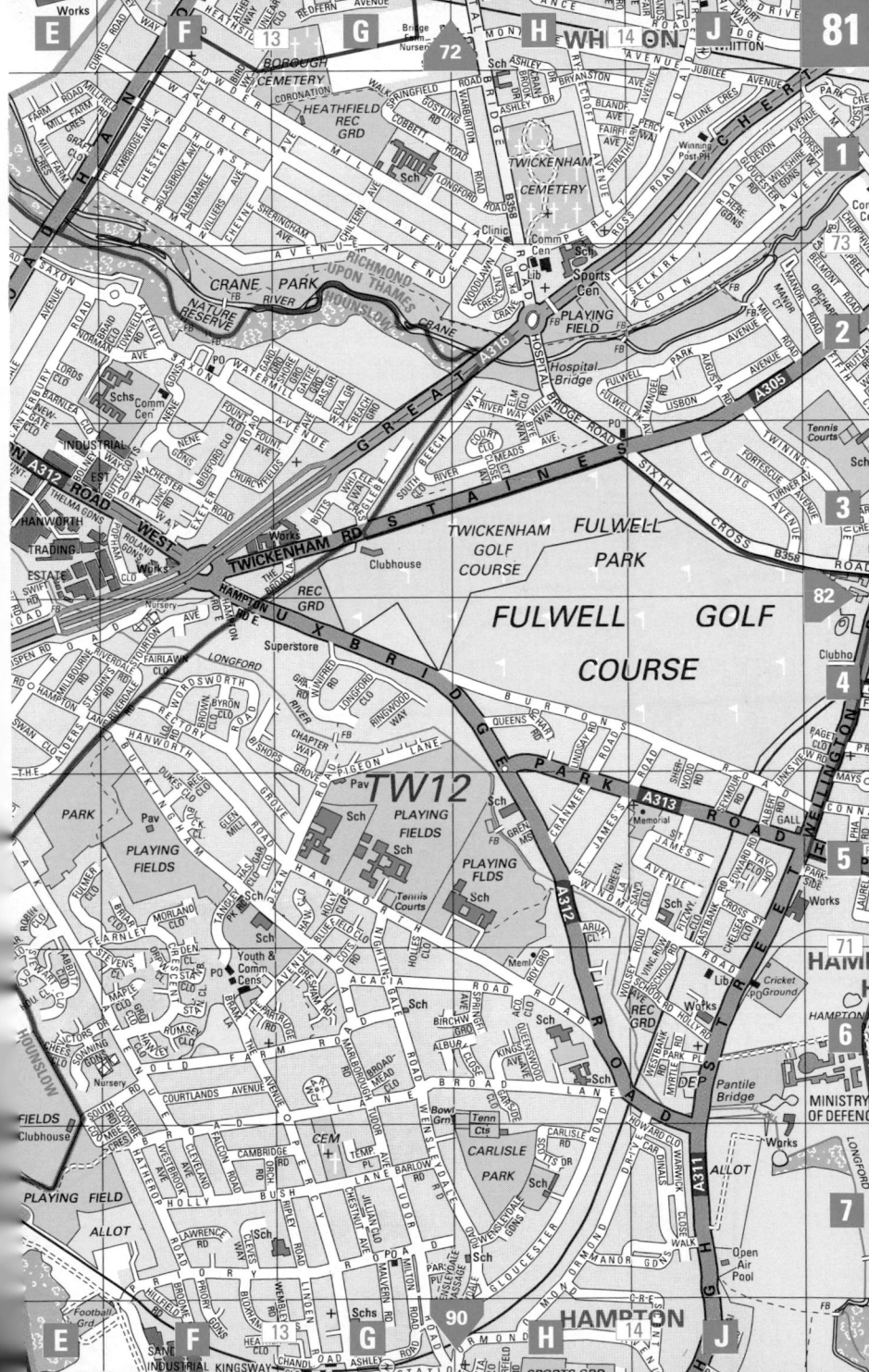

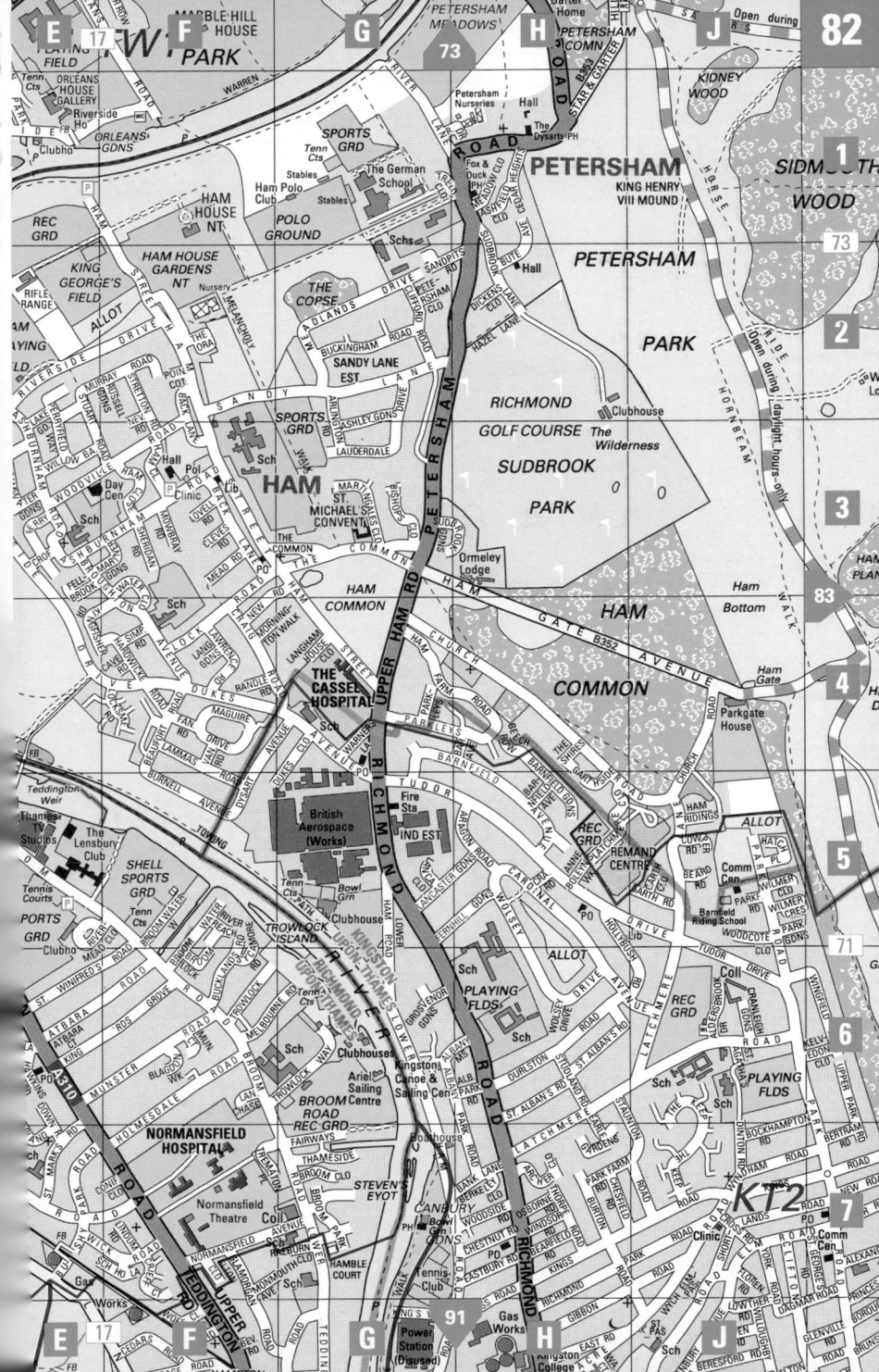

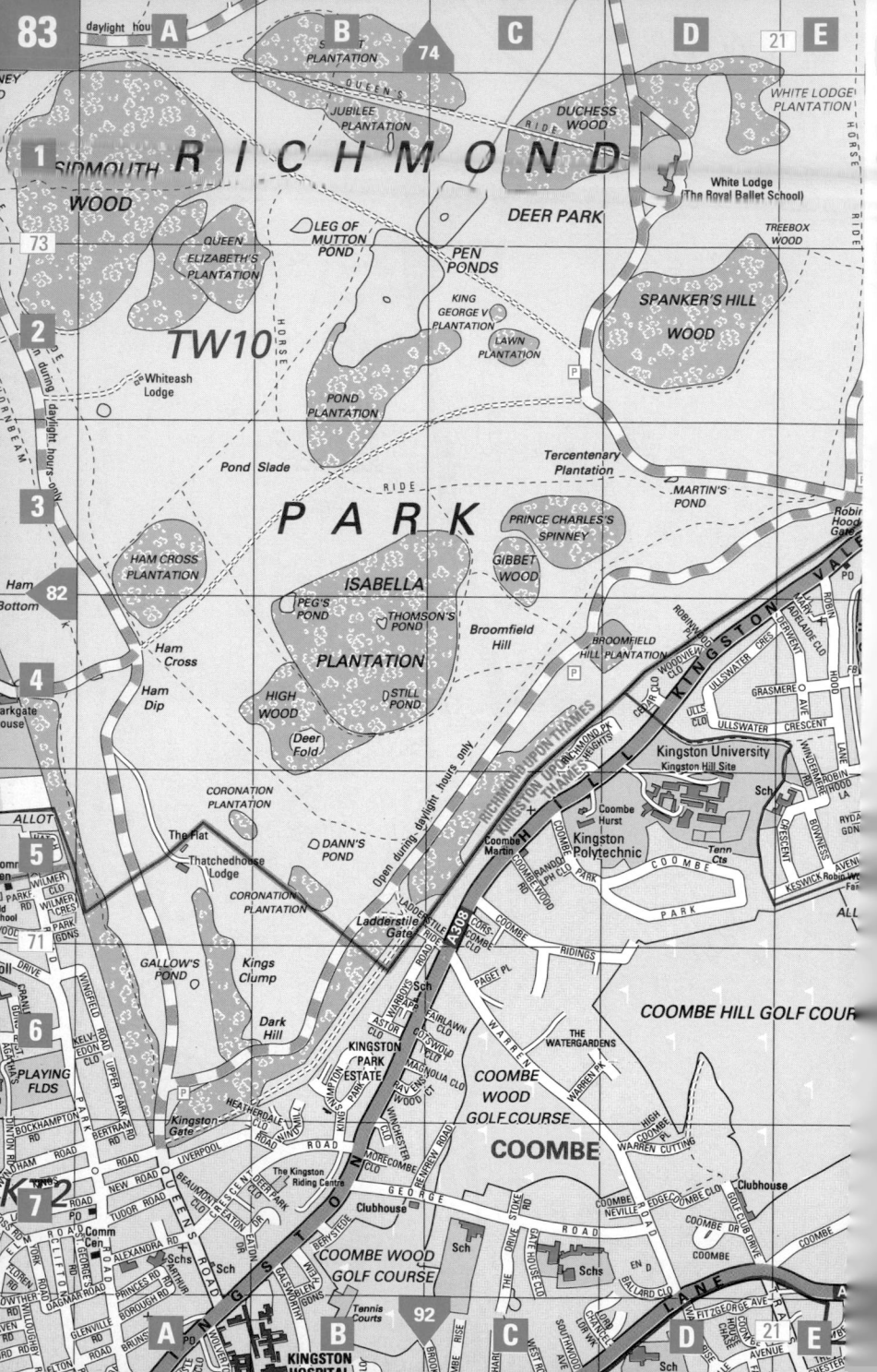

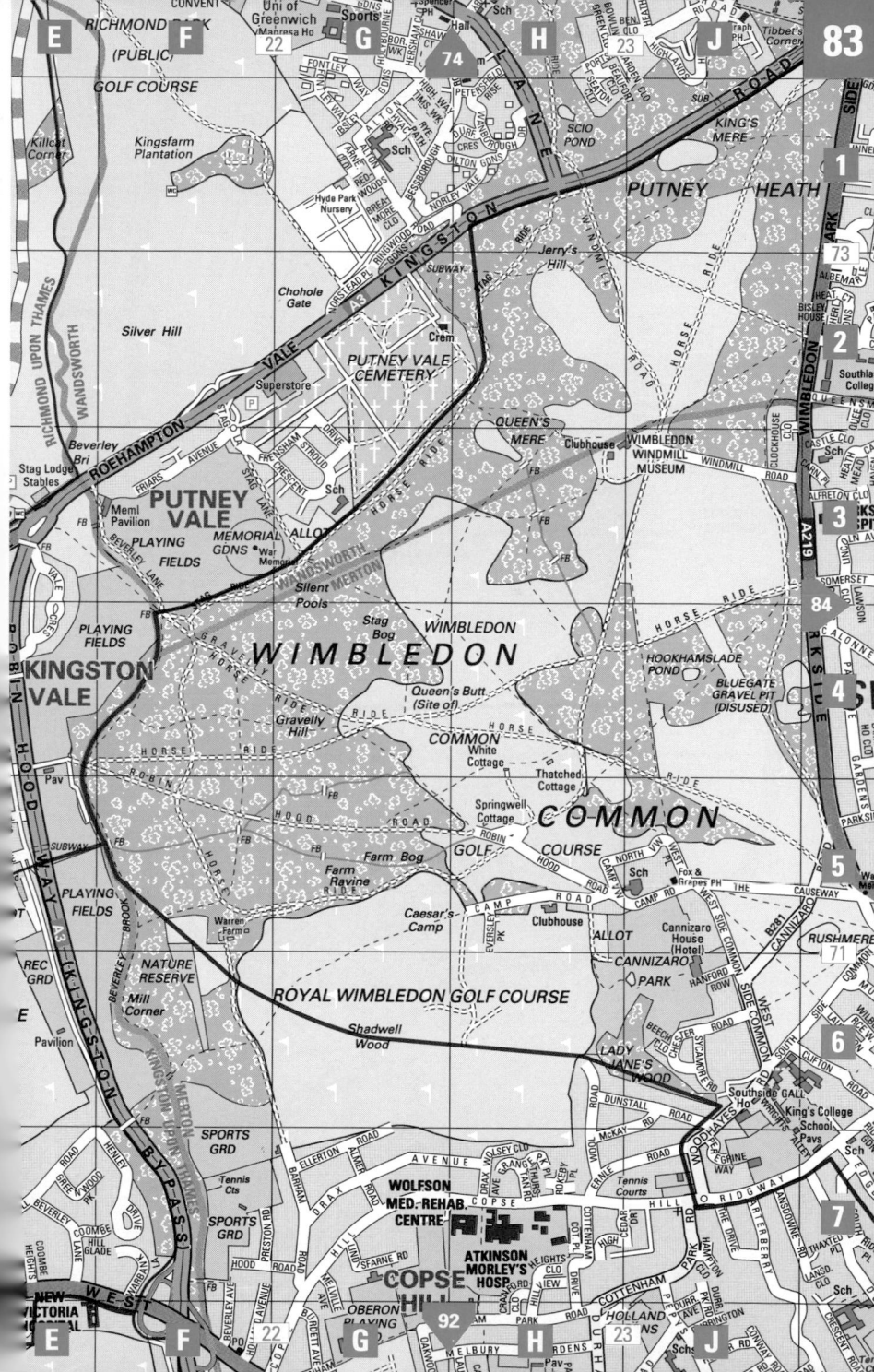

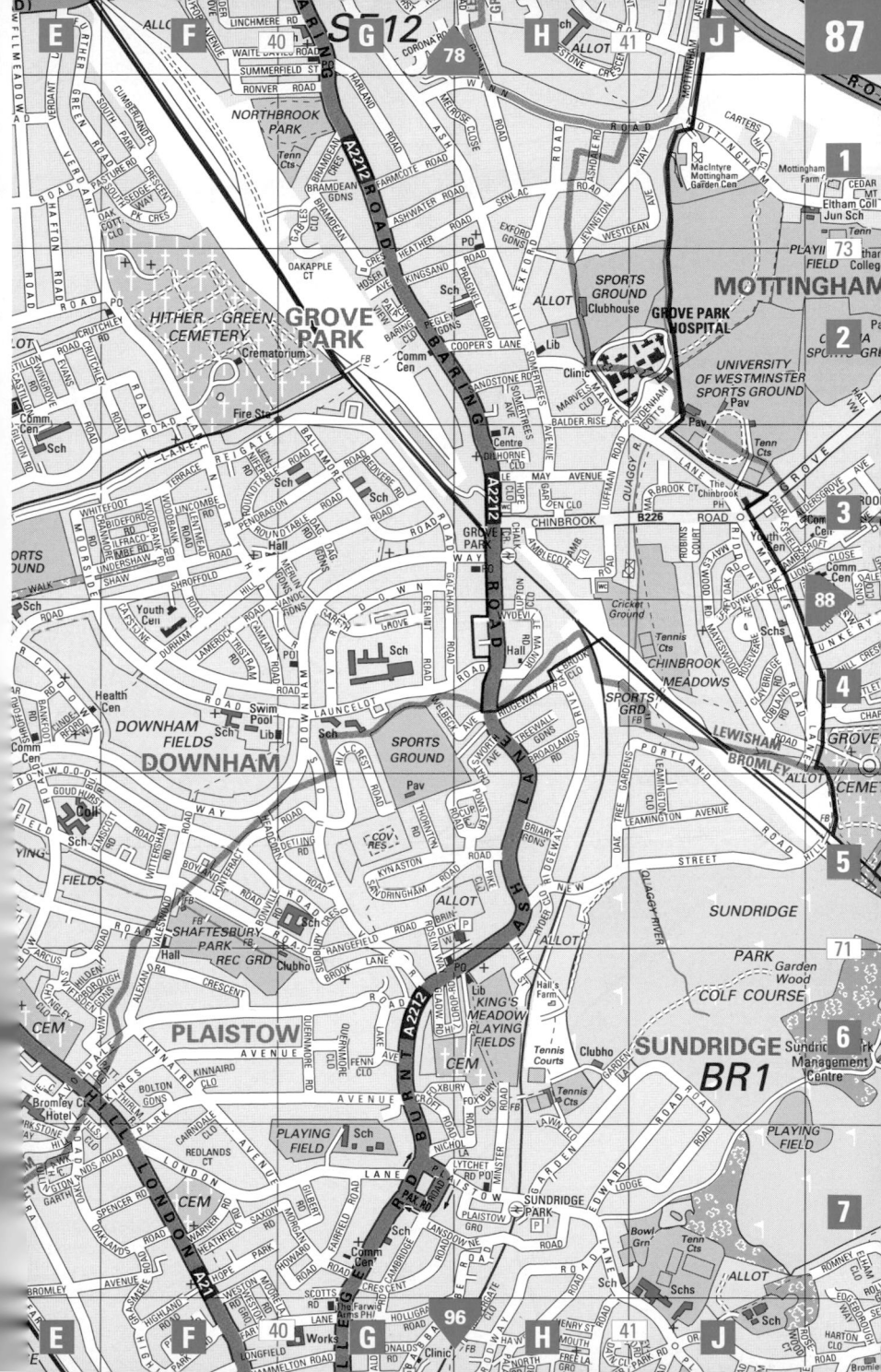

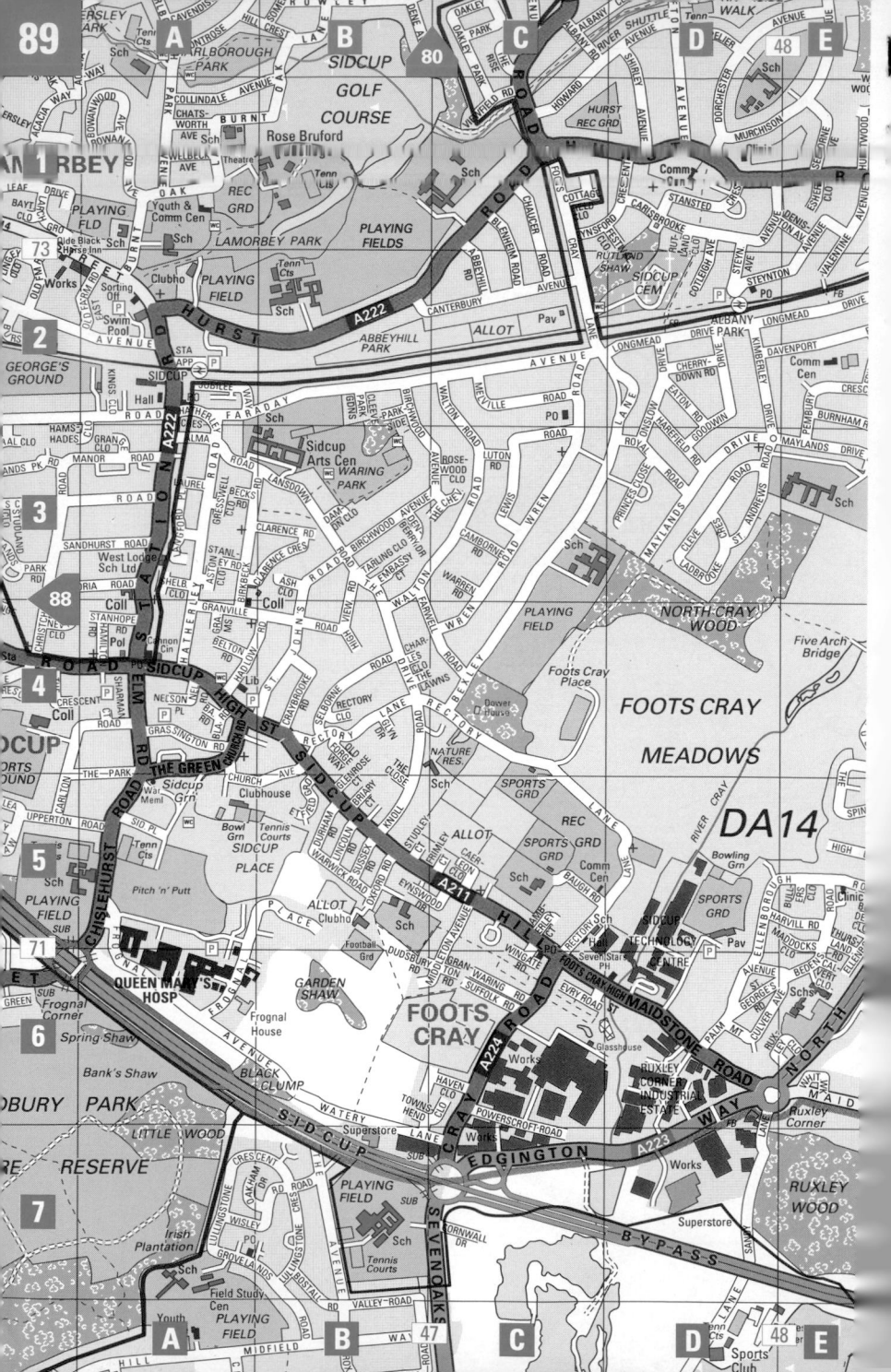

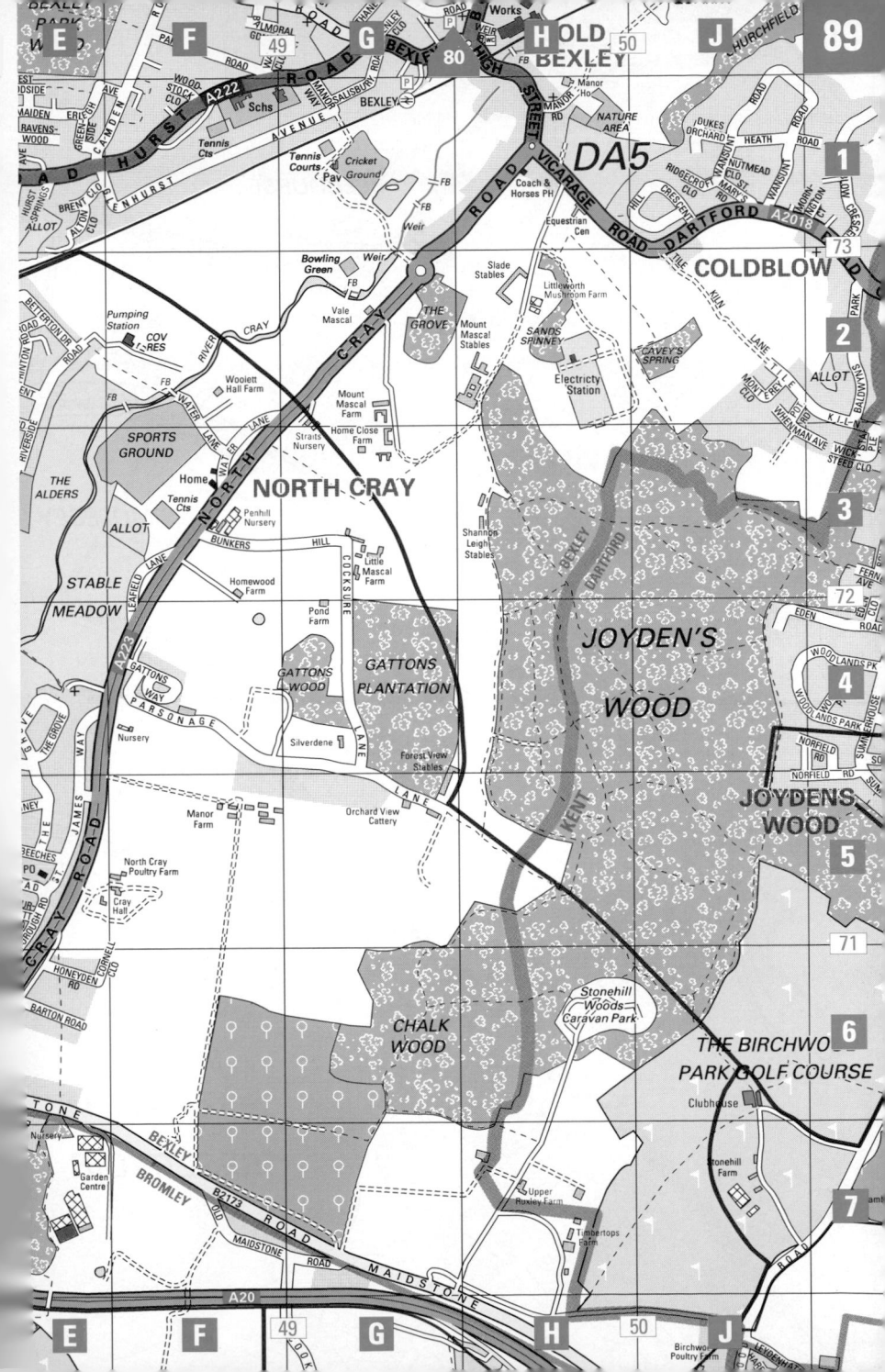

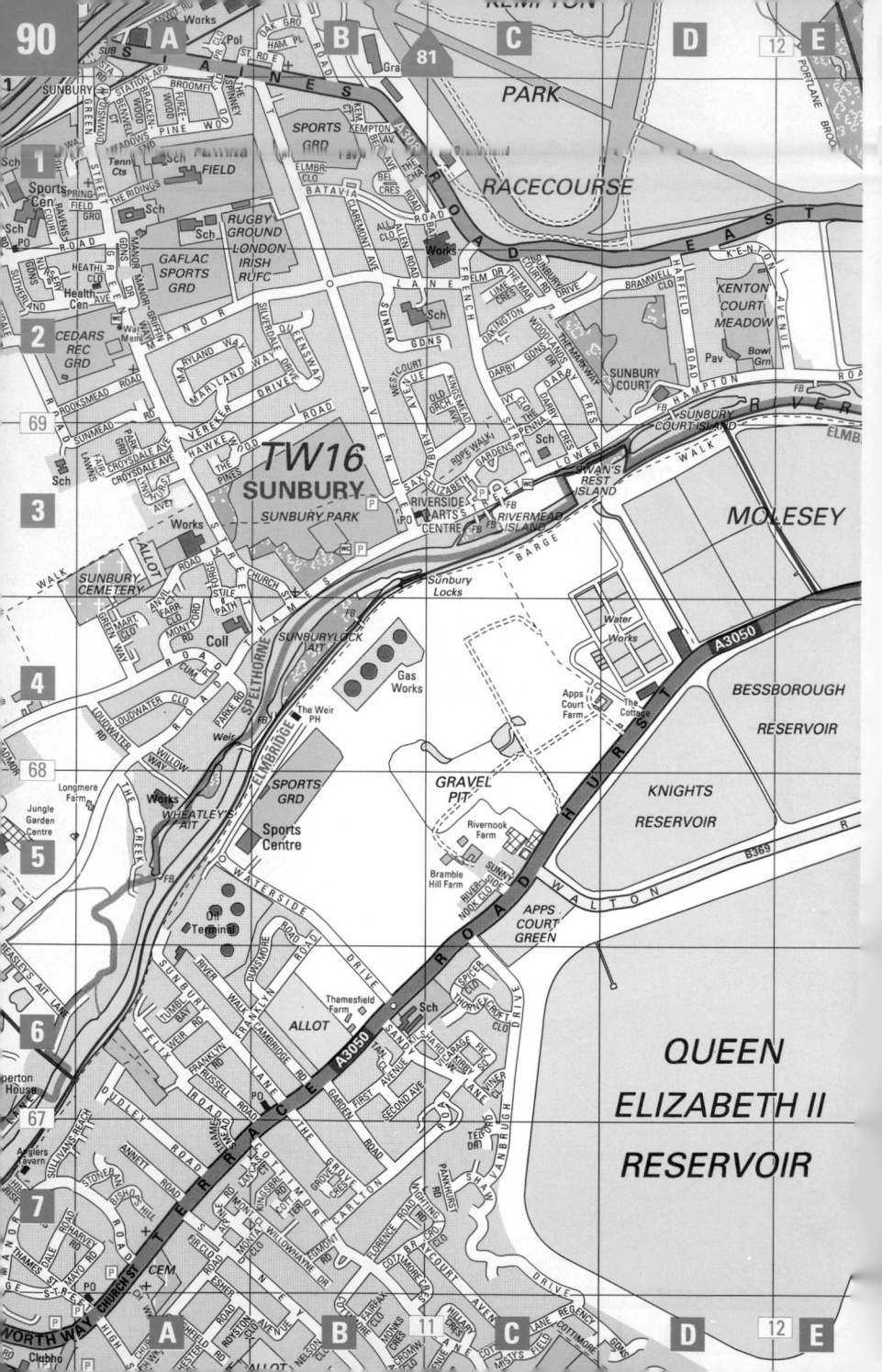

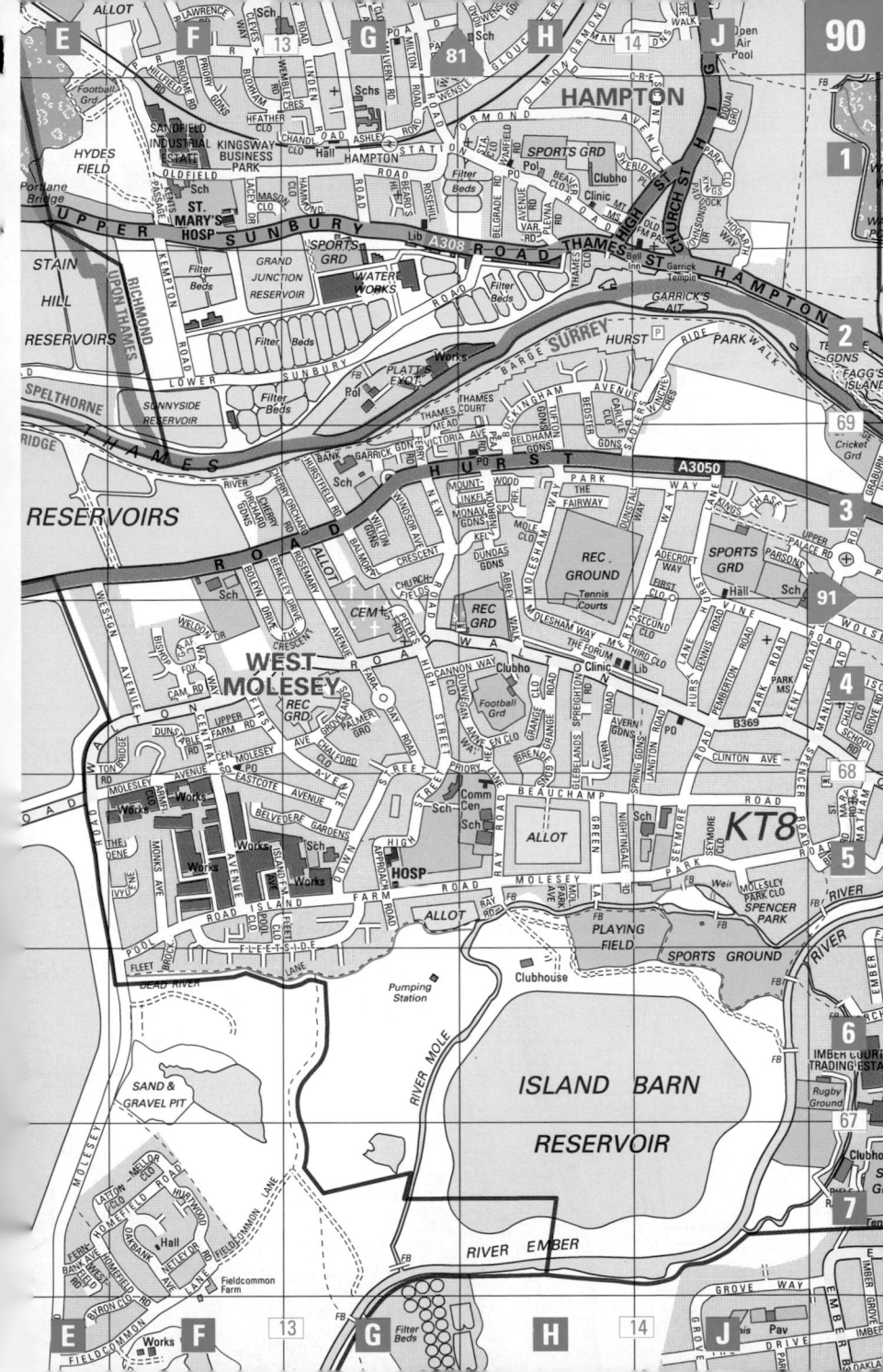

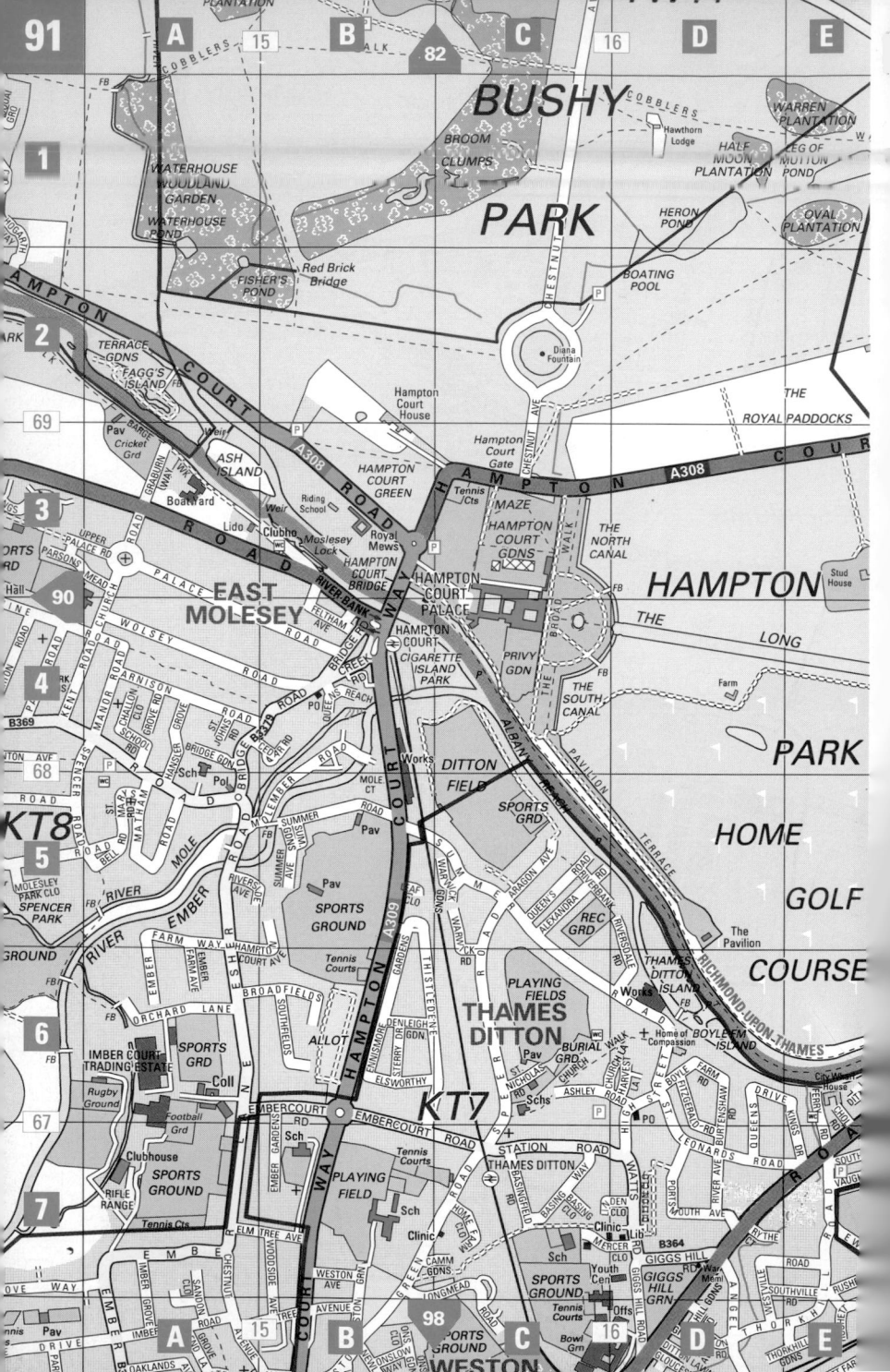

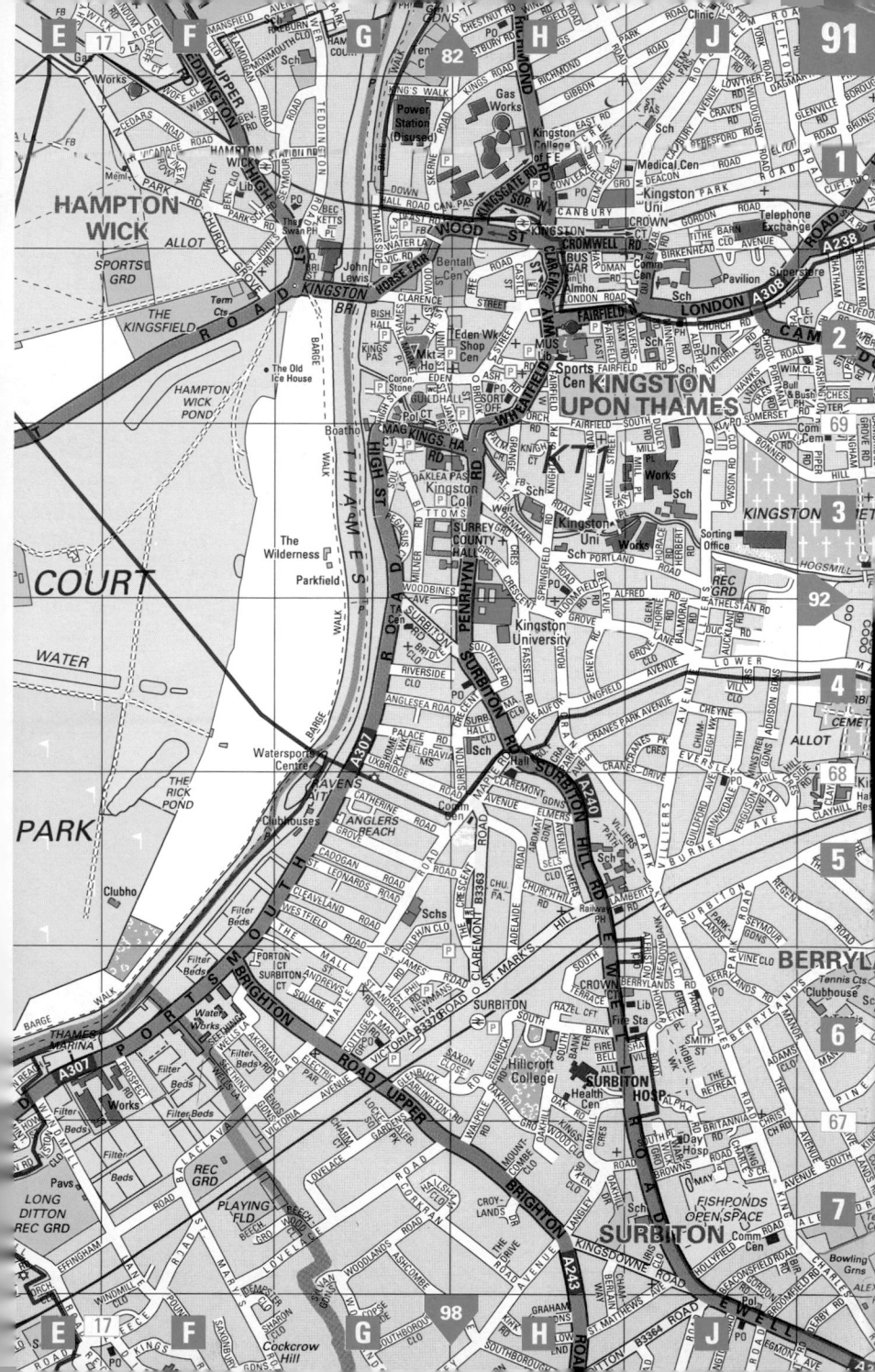

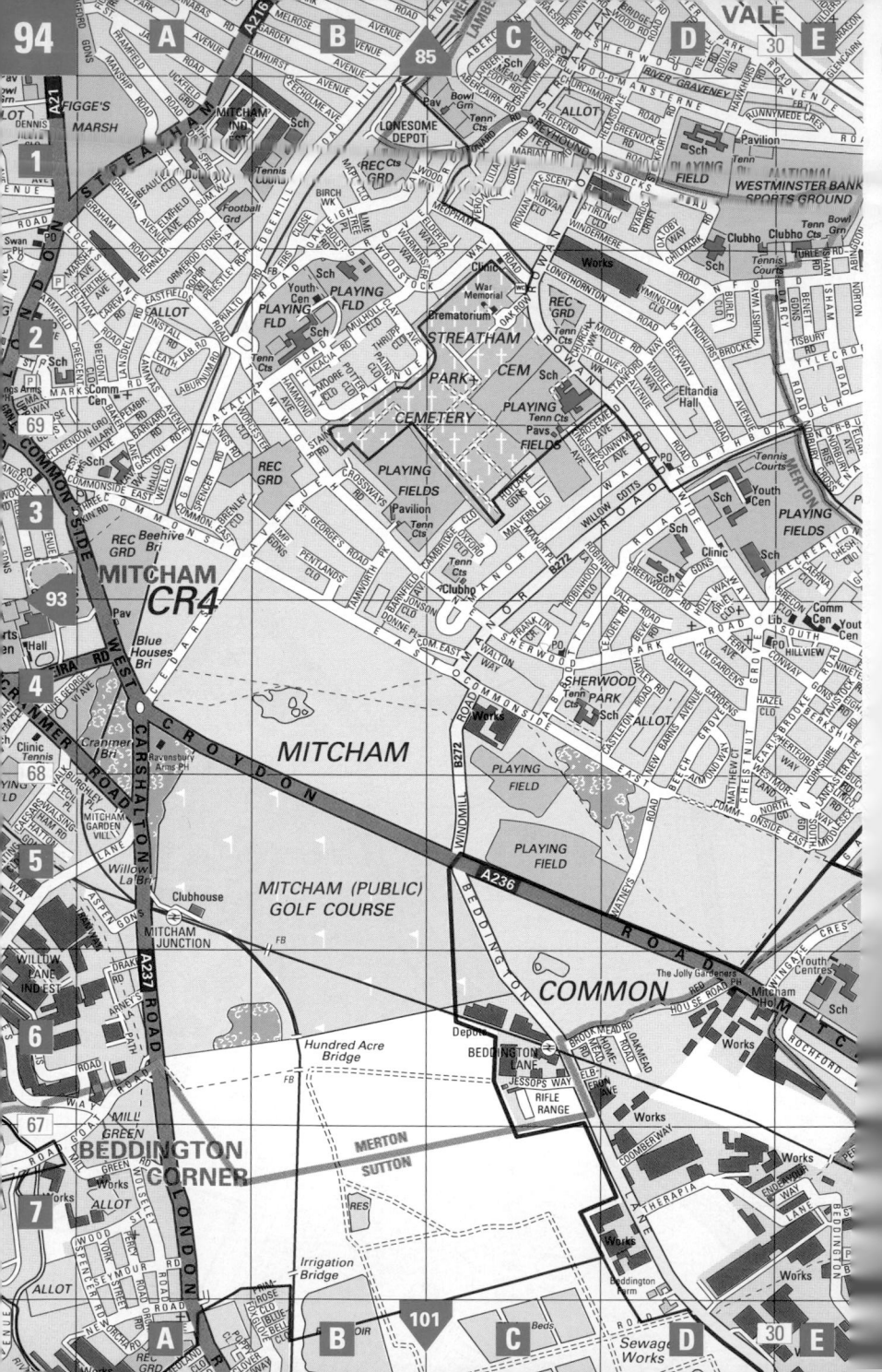

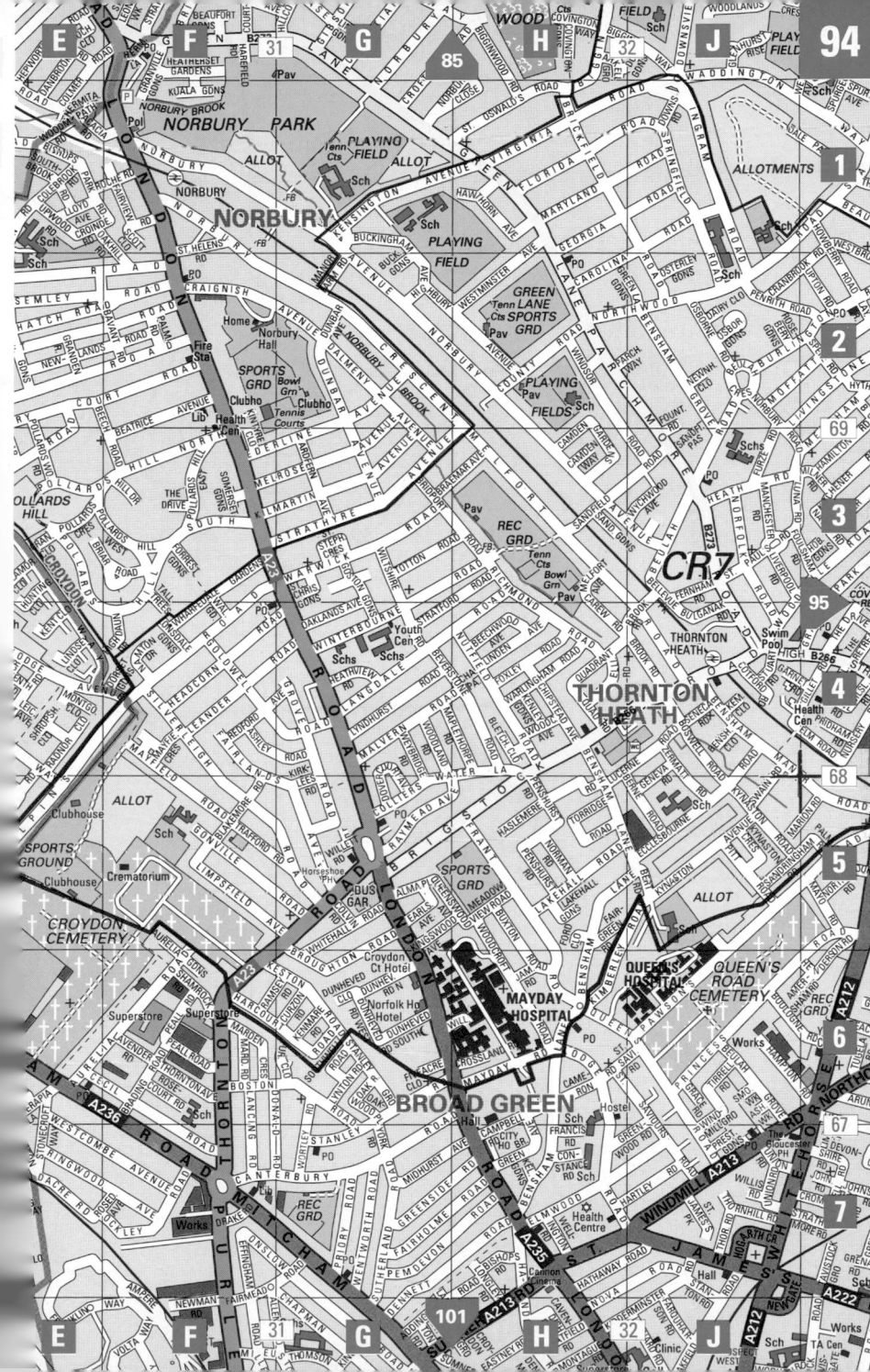

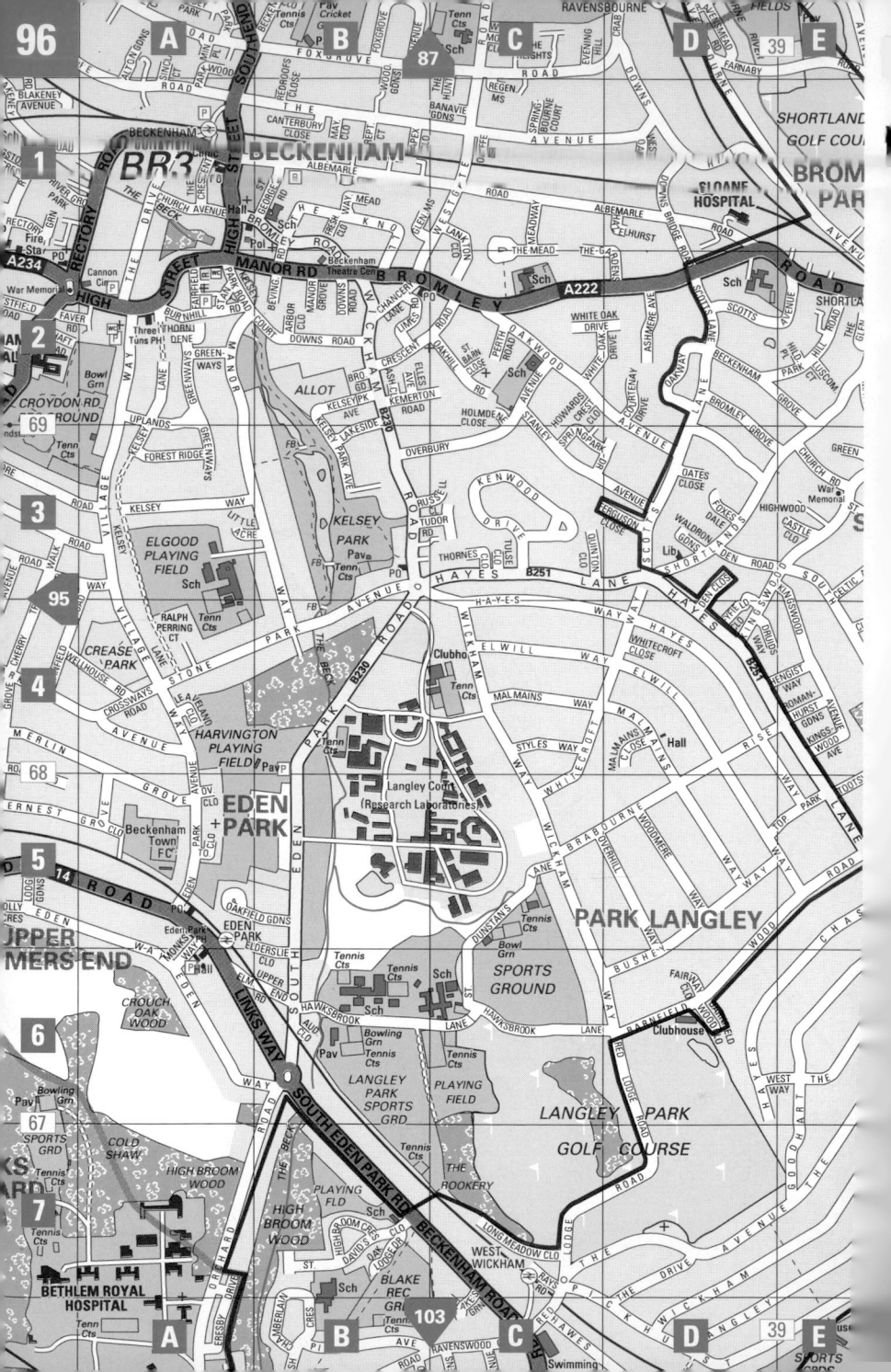

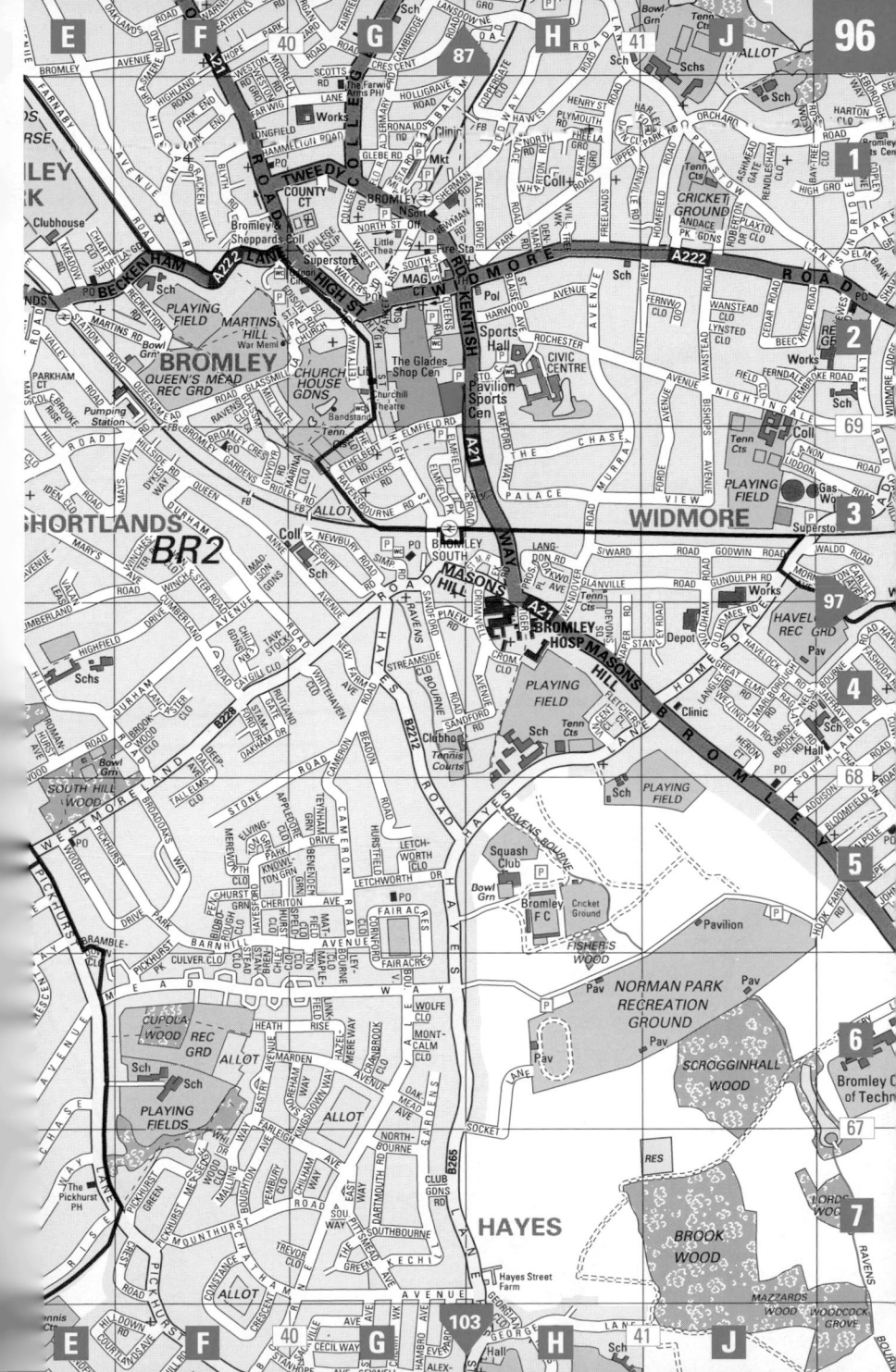

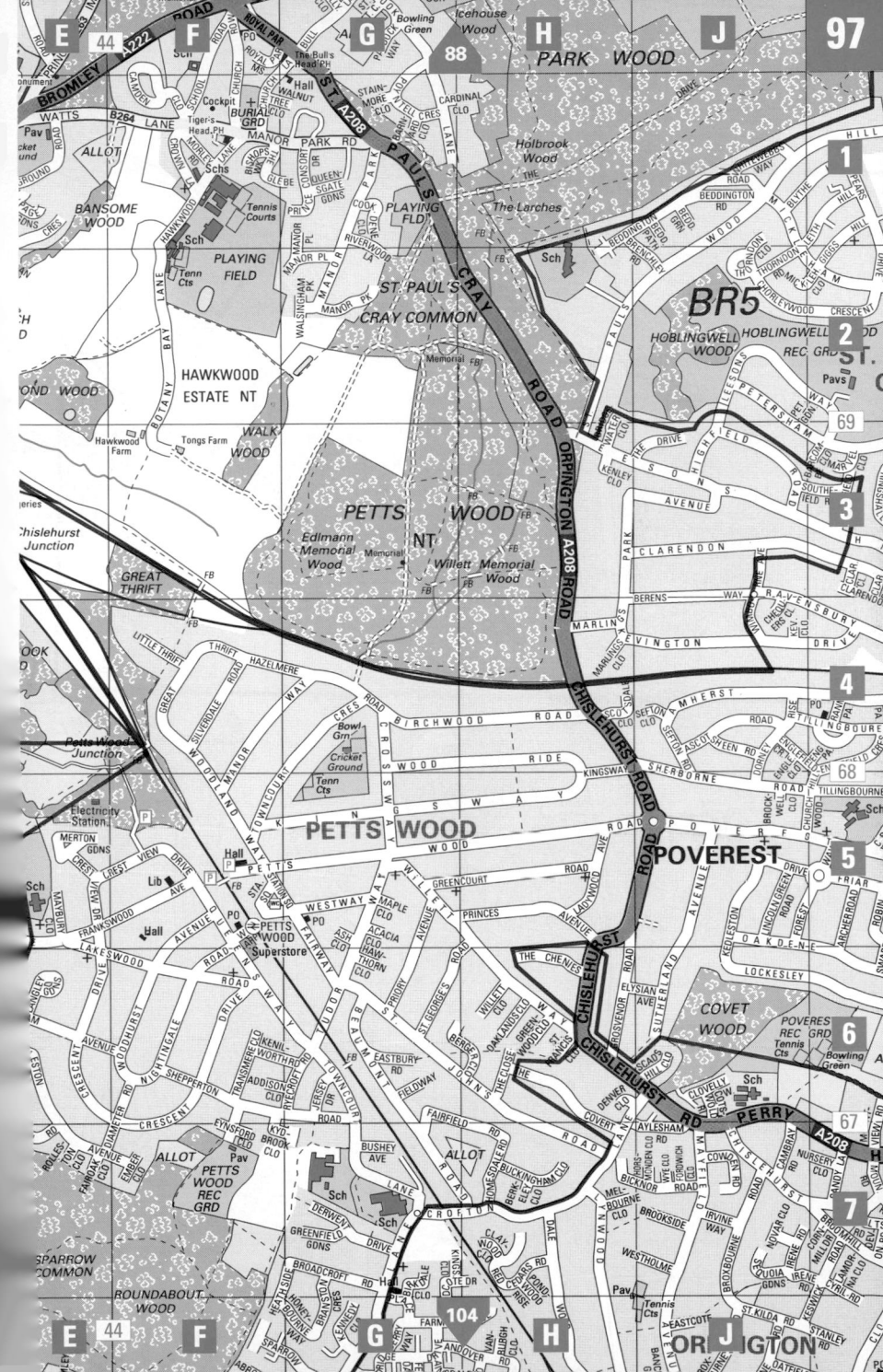

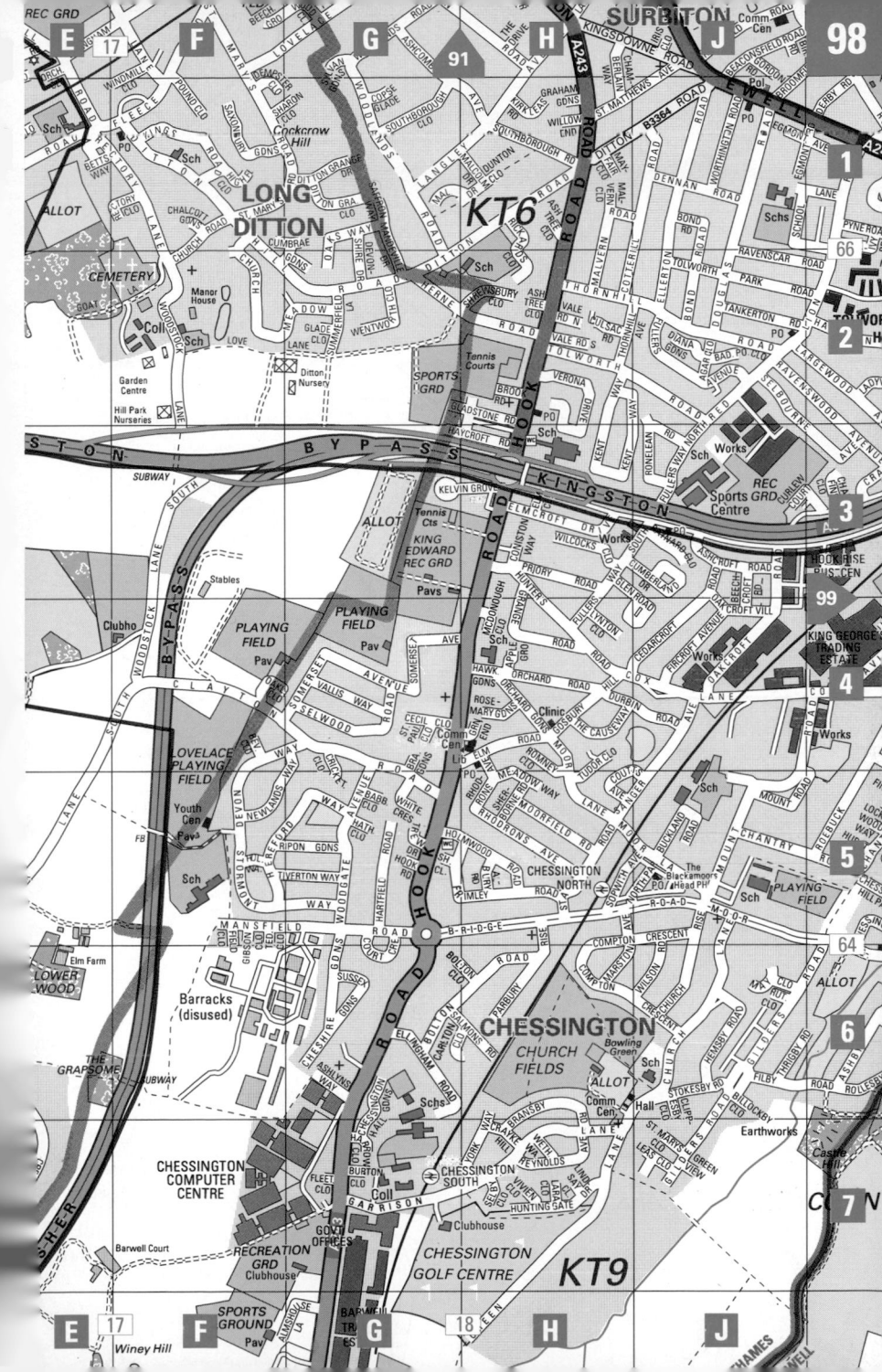

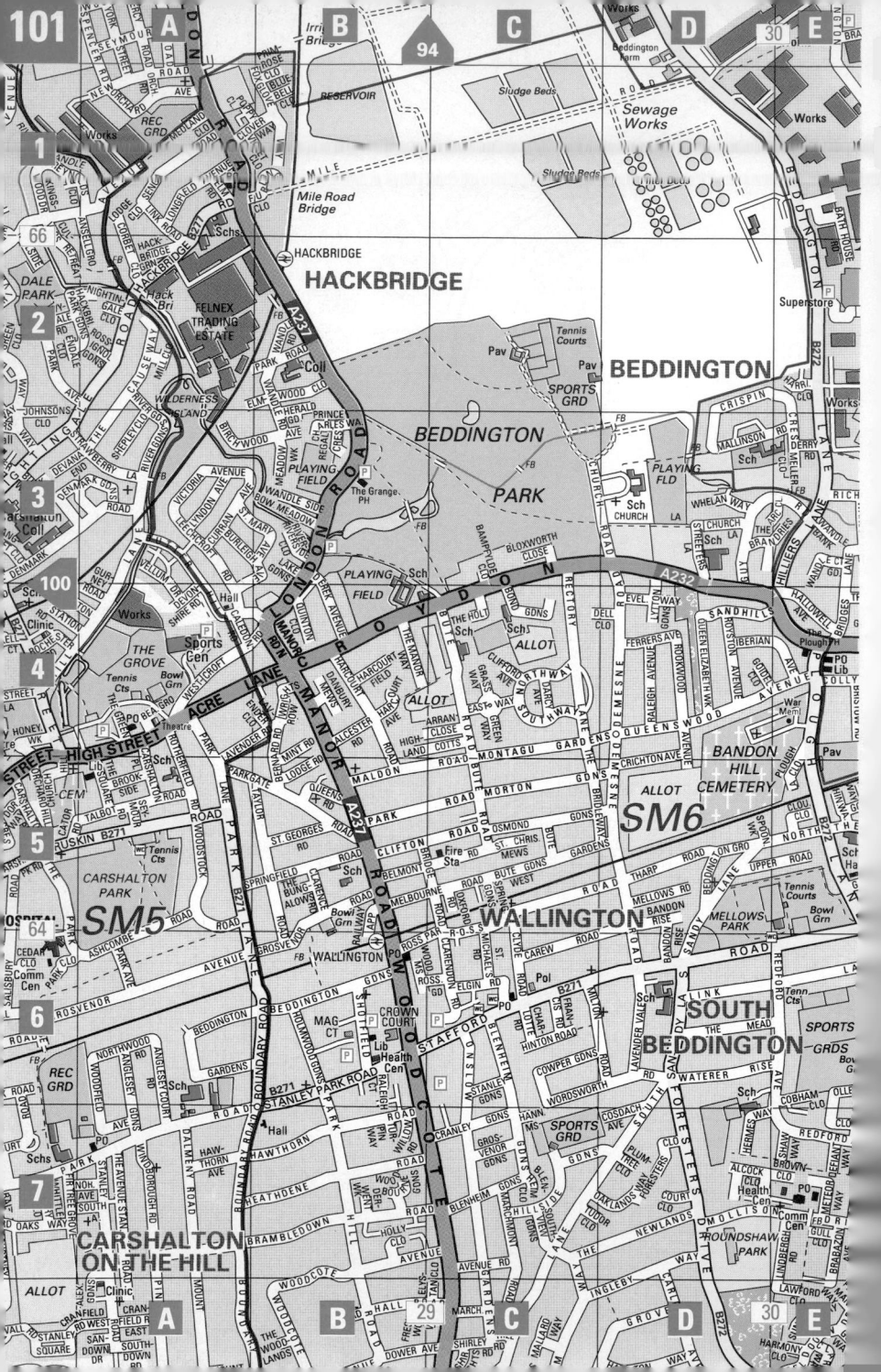

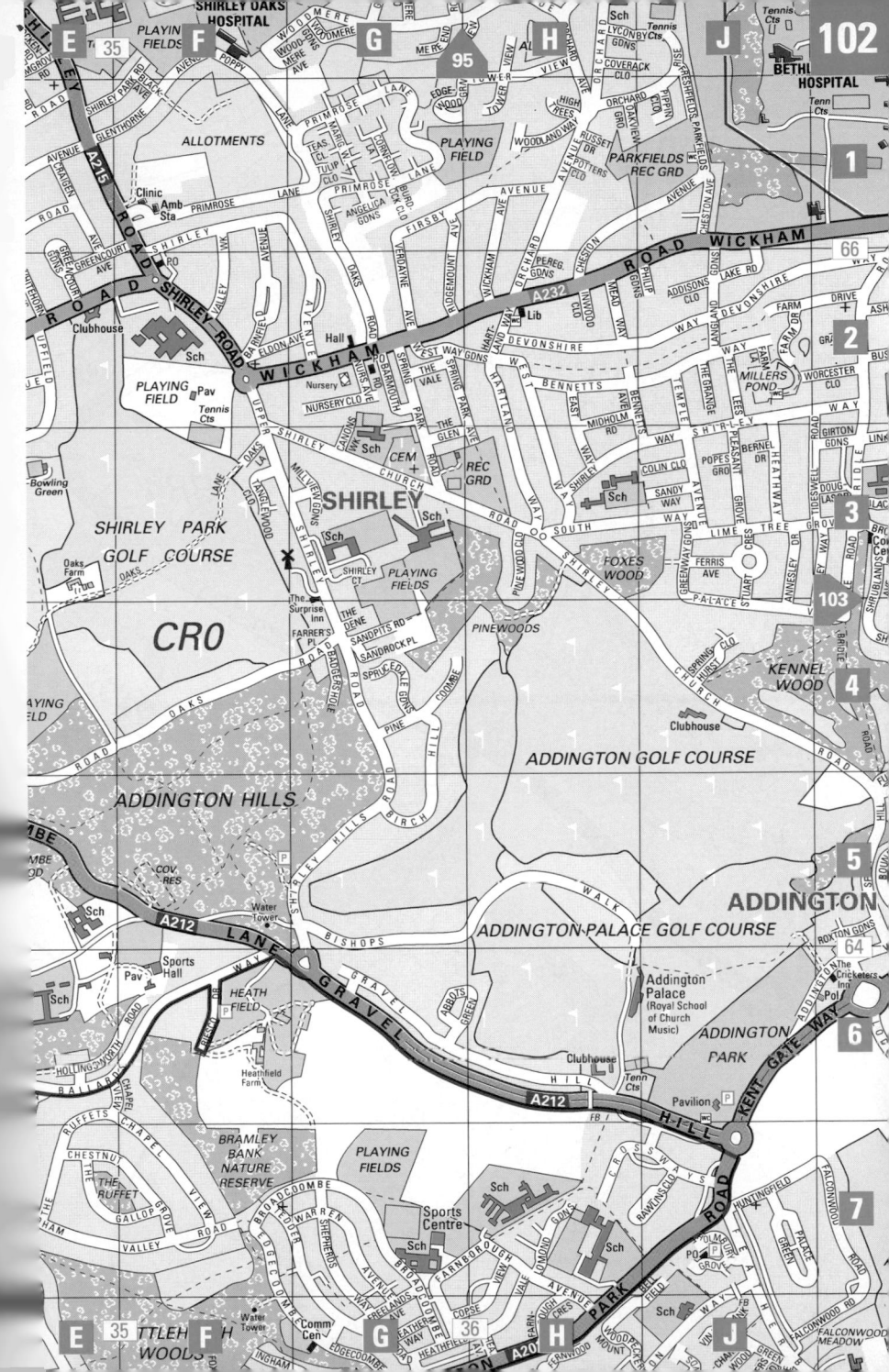

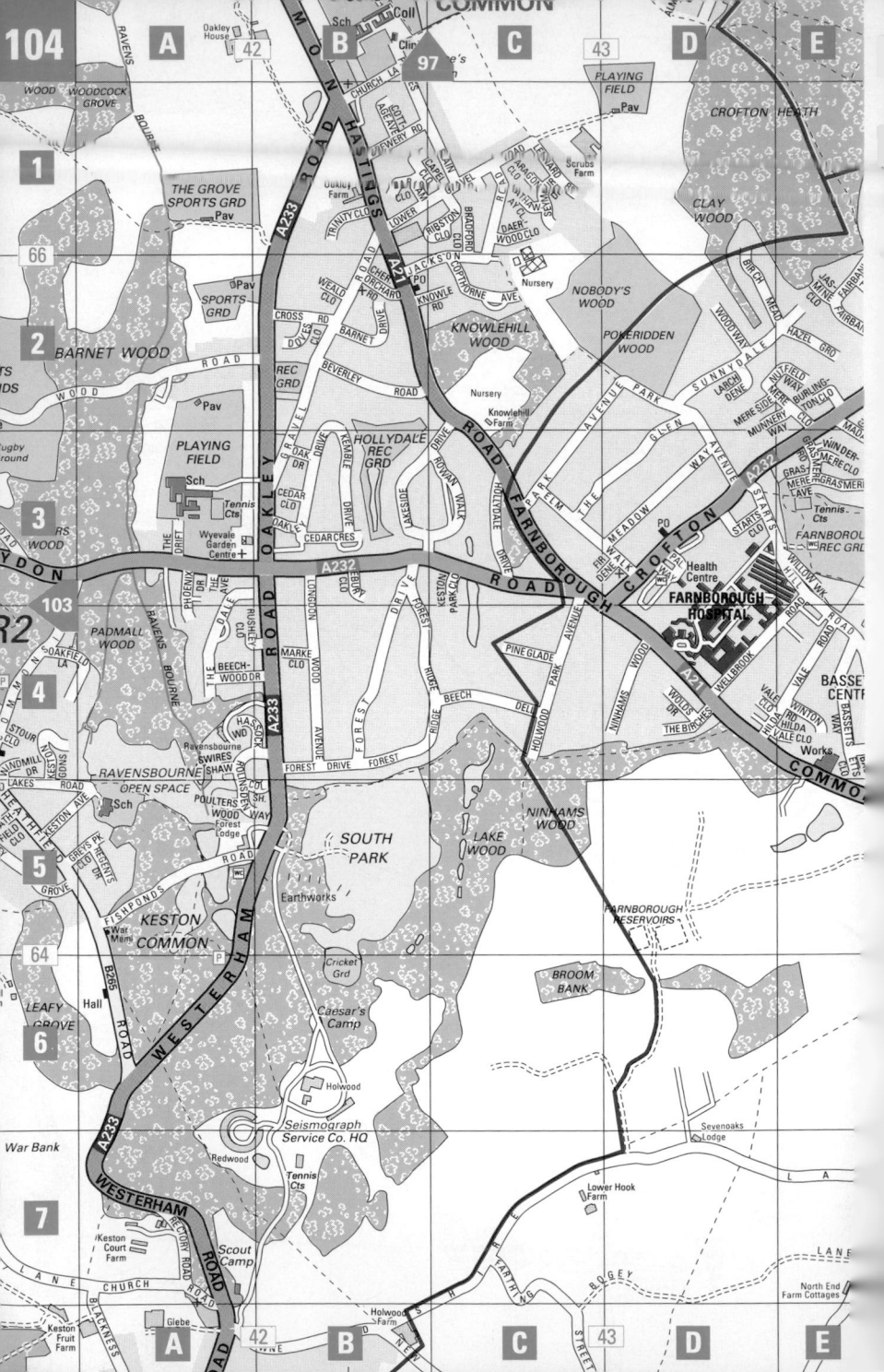

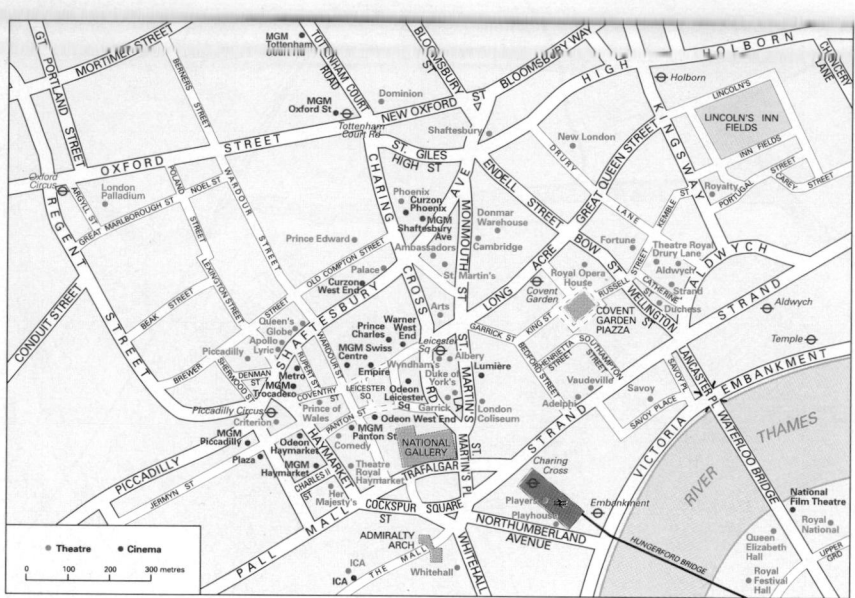

THEATRES

Adelphi 071 334 0055
Albery 071 867 1115
Aldwych 071 836 6404
Ambassadors 071 836 1171
Apollo 071 494 5070
Arts 071 836 2132
Cambridge 071 379 5299
Comedy 071 867 1045
Criterion 071 839 4488
Dominion 071 580 9562
Donmar Warehouse
    071 867 1150
Duchess 071 494 5075
Duke of York's 071 836 5122
Fortune 071 836 2238
Garrick 071 494 5085
Globe 071 494 5065
Her Majesty's 071 494 5400
ICA 071 930 3647
London Coliseum
    071 836 3161
London Palladium
    071 494 5020
Lyric 071 494 5045
New London 071 405 0072
Palace 071 434 0909
Phoenix 071 867 1044
Piccadilly 071 867 1118
Players 071 839 1134
Playhouse 071 839 4401

Prince Edward 071 734 8951
Prince of Wales
    071 839 5987
Queen Elizabeth Hall
    071 928 3002
Queen's 071 494 5040
Royal Festival Hall
    071 928 8800
Royal National 071 928 2252
Royal Opera House
    071 240 1066
Royalty 071 494 5090
St. Martin's 071 836 1443
Savoy 071 836 8888
Shaftesbury 071 379 5399
Strand 071 930 8800
Theatre Royal, Drury Lane
    071 494 5000
Theatre Royal, Haymarket
    071 930 8800
Vaudeville 071 836 9987
Whitehall 071 867 1119
Wyndham's 071 867 1116

CINEMAS

Curzon Phoenix 071 240 9661
Curzon West End 071 439 4805
Empire 071 437 1234

ICA 071 930 3647
Lumière 071 836 0691
Metro 071 437 0757
MGM Haymarket
    071 839 1527
MGM Oxford St
    071 636 0310
MGM Panton St 071 930 0631
MGM Piccadilly 071 437 3561
MGM Shaftesbury Avenue
    071 836 6279
MGM Swiss Centre
    071 439 4470
MGM Tottenham Court Rd
    071 636 6148
MGM Trocadero 071 434 0031
National Film Theatre
    071 633 0274
Odeon Haymarket
    0426 915343
Odeon Leicester Sq
    0426 915683
Odeon Mezzanine
    (Odeon Leicester Sq)
    0426 915683
Odeon West End 0426 915574
Plaza 071 437 1234
Prince Charles 071 437 8181
Warner West End
    071 437 4343

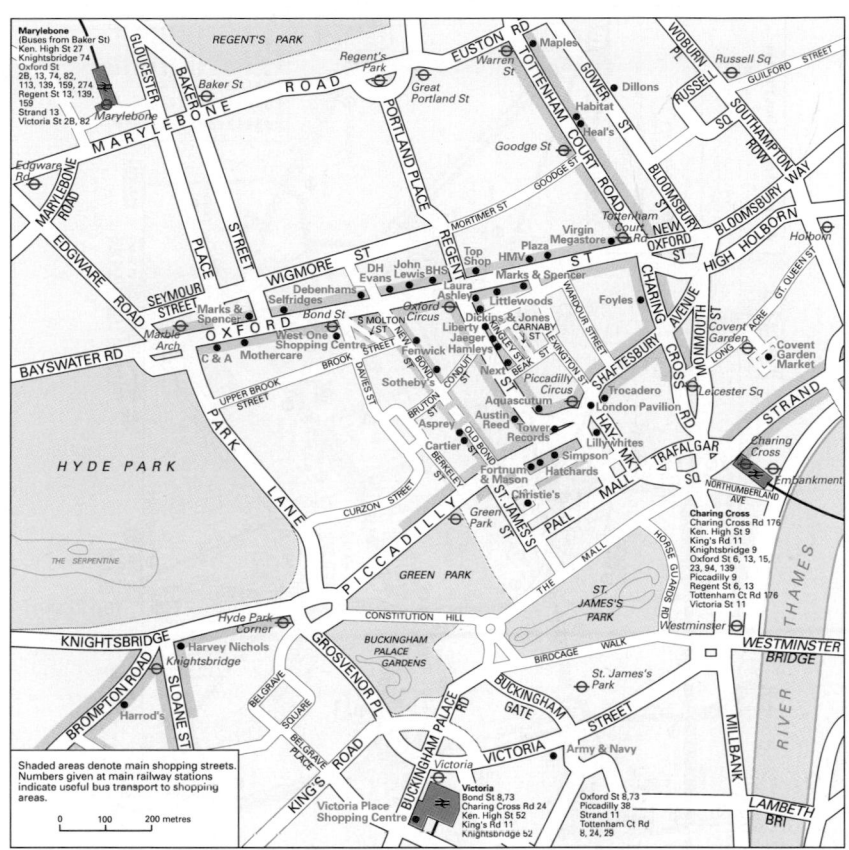

SHOPS

Aquascutum *071 734 6090*
Army & Navy *071 834 1234*
Asprey *071 493 6767*
Austin Reed *071 734 6789*
BHS(Oxford St) *071 629 2011*
C & A *071 629 7272*
Cartier *071 793 3962*
Christie's *071 839 9060*
Covent Garden Market
  071 836 9137
DH Evans *071 629 8800*
Debenhams *071 580 3000*
Dickins & Jones *071 734 7070*
Dillons *071 636 1577*
Fenwick *071 629 9161*
Fortnum & Mason
  071 734 8040
Foyles *071 437 5660*

Habitat (Tottenham Court Rd)
  071 631 3880
Hamleys *071 734 3161*
Harrod's *071 730 1234*
Harvey Nichols
  071 235 5000
Hatchards *071 439 9921*
Heal's *071 636 1666*
HMV *071 631 3423*
Jaeger *071 734 8211*
John Lewis *071 629 7711*
Laura Ashley (Regent St)
  071 437 9760
Liberty *071 734 1234*
Lillywhites *071 930 3181*
Littlewoods *071 434 4301*
London Pavilion
  071 437 1838

Maples *071 387 7000*
Marks & Spencer
  (Marble Arch) *071 935 7954*
Marks & Spencer (Oxford St)
  071 437 7722
Mothercare *071 629 6621*
Next (Regent St) *071 434 2515*
Plaza on Oxford St
  071 637 8811
Selfridges *071 629 1234*
Simpson *071 734 2002*
Sotheby's *071 493 8080*
Top Shop *071 636 7700*
Tower Records *071 439 2500*
Trocadero *071 439 1791*
Victoria Place Shopping
  Centre *071 931 8811*
Virgin Megastore *071 631 1234*

WEST END & CITY BUS ROUTES

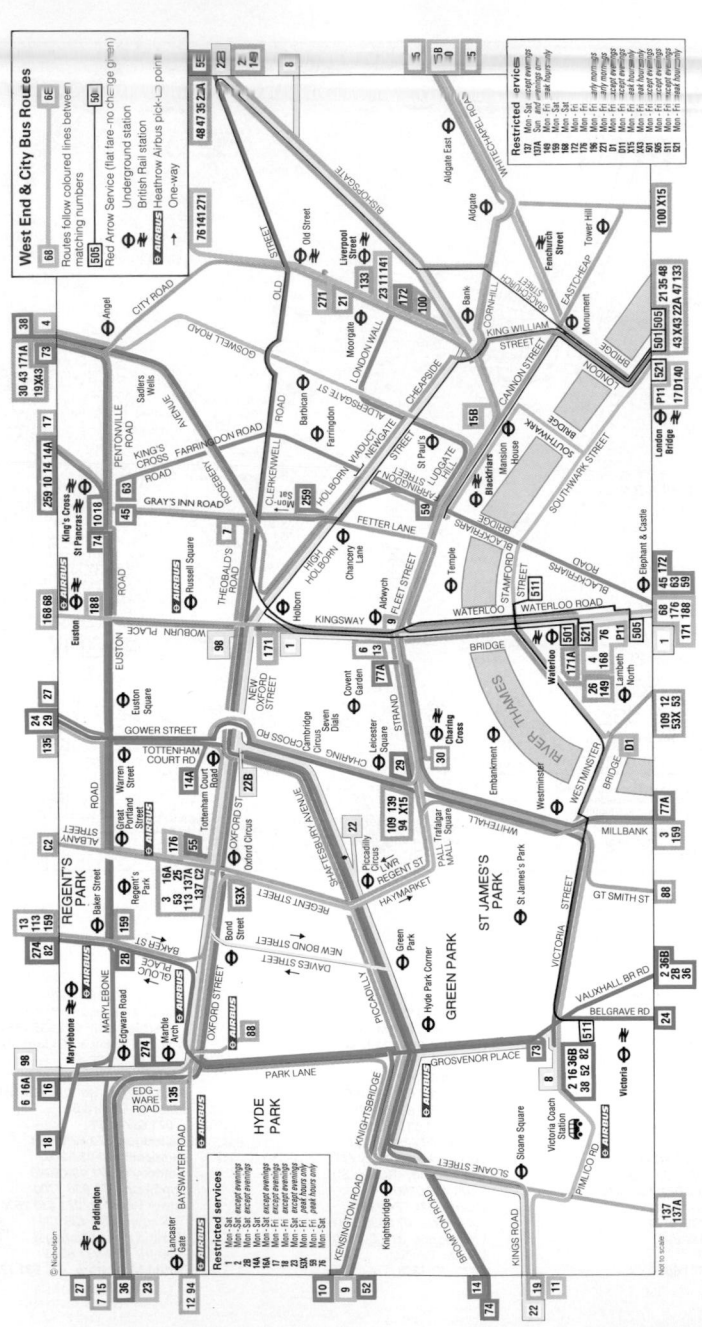

Admiralty Arch	15	J1
Agnew Galleries	15	F1
Albert Memorial	14	E3
Alexandra Palace	40	D3
Angel Centre, The	8	F2
Angel Information Centre	58	H1
Anthony d'Offay Gallery	11	E4
Apollo Victoria	15	F6
Apothecaries' Hall	12	G4
Apsley House,	15	C3
Wellington Museum		
Armourers' and Brasiers' Hall	13	B2
Arsenal Football Club	49	H4
Ashby Windmill	76	E6
Avery Hill Park, Eltham	79	F6
Baden Powell House	18	D1
Baker Street	7	A6
Bank of England	13	B4
Bank of England Museum	13	C4
Bankside Gallery	12	H6
Banqueting House	16	A2
Barbican Arts and	13	A1
Conference Centre		
Barnes Common	74	G3
Battersea Park	66	J7
Bentley Priory, Harrow	29	B3
Bermondsey Market	17	D4
Bethnal Green Museum of	59	F3
Childhood		
Big Ben	16	B4
Billingsgate Fish Market	69	B1
Blackheath	78	D1
Bloomsbury Square	12	B2
Borough Market	17	B2
Brentford Football Club	64	G6
British Dental Association	11	D2
Museum, Wimpole St.		
British Library	12	A2
British Medical Association	7	J5
British Museum	12	A2
British Travel Centre	15	H1
Broadgate Ice and Arena	13	D2
Brockwell Park	76	H6
Brompton Oratory,	14	G6
Brompton Rd.		
Bruce Castle Museum,	41	B1
Tottenham		
Brunel Engine House,	68	F2
Railway Ave.		
Buckingham Palace	15	E4
Burlington Arcade,	11	F6
Burlington Gdns.		
Bushy Park	91	C1
Business Design Centre	58	G1
Cabaret Mechanical Theatre,	12	B5
Covent Garden Market		
Cabinet Office	16	A3
Cabinet War Rooms	15	J3
Camden Lock (Waterbuses)	49	B7
Camden Lock Market	49	B7
Camley Street Natural Park	8	A1
Carlyle's House	18	G6
Carnaby Street	11	F4
Caxton Hall	15	H5
Cenotaph, The	16	A3
Central Criminal Court	12	H3
(Old Bailey)		
Centrepoint	11	J3
Charing Cross Road	11	J4
Charlton Athletic	69	J5
Football Club		
Charterhouse	12	H1
Chelsea Antique Market	18	G5
Chelsea Flower Show,	19	B5
Royal Hospital Grounds		
Chelsea Football Club	18	A7
Chelsea Old Town Hall	18	G4
Chelsea Physic Garden	18	J5
Chinatown, Gerrard Street	11	J5
Chiswick House	65	E6
Church Farm House	38	H3
Museum, Hendon		
City University	8	G4
Clapham Common	76	A4
Clarence House	15	G3
Cleopatra's Needle	12	C6
Clissold Park	50	A2
Clothworkers' Hall	13	E5
Coliseum, The	12	A6
College of Arms	12	J5
Conference Forum, The	13	G3
Court Dress Collection,	14	B2
Kensington Palace		
Courtauld Institute Galleries	12	C5
Covent Garden	12	B5
Crafts Council Gallery,	15	H1
Waterloo Pl.		
Crystal Palace Football Club	95	B4
Crystal Palace National	86	D6
Sport Centre		
Crystal Palace Park	86	C5
Cuming Museum	20	J2
Custom House	13	D6
Cutty Sark	69	C6
Danson Park, Welling	80	C4
Department of Trade	15	J5
and Industry		
Department of Transport		
and Environment	15	J6
Design Centre	11	H6
Design Museum	17	G3
Dickens House, Doughty St.	8	D6
Doctor Johnson's House,	12	F3
Gough Sq.		
Dominion	11	J3
Downing Street	16	A3
Drapers' Hall	13	C3
Dulwich College Picture	77	B7
Gallery		
Dulwich Park	77	C7
Ealing Common	64	H1
Earls Court Exhibition	66	D5
Centre		
Eel Pie Island	82	D1
Eltham Palace	79	B7
Epping Forest	26	J1
Eros	11	H6
Faraday Museum	11	F6
(The Royal Institution),		
Albemarle St.		
Fenton House, Hampstead	48	F3
Festival Pleasure Gardens,	19	B7
Battersea Park		
Finsbury Park	40	H7
Fishmongers' Hall	13	C6
Fitzroy Square	7	F6
Flamstead House Museum,	69	D7
Greenwich		
Fleet Street	12	F4
Florence Nightingale	16	C4
Museum		
Flower Market	20	A5
Foreign Office	16	A3
Fortnum and Mason	15	G1
Freightliners City Farm	49	G6
Freud Museum,	48	G6
Maresfield Gdns.		
Fulham Football Club	75	A1
Fulham Palace	75	B2
Geological Museum	14	F6
George Inn,	17	B2
Borough High St.		
Gipsy Moth IV	69	C6
Golders Hill Park	48	D2
Goldsmiths' Hall	12	J3
Gray's Inn	12	D1
Green Park	15	E3
Greenwich Park	69	D7
Greenwich Pier	69	C6
Grocers' Hall	13	B4
Guildhall	13	B3
Gunnersbury Park, Ealing	64	J4
H.M. Treasury	16	A3
H.M.S. 'Belfast'	17	E1
H.M.S. 'President'	12	F5
Haberdashers' Hall	13	A3
Hackney Marshes	50	J4
Haggerston City Farm	9	H2
Ham House	82	F1
Hamleys	11	F5
Hammersmith Palais	65	J4
Hampstead Heath	48	G2
Hampton Court Palace	91	B3
Harrods	14	J5
Harrow School	46	B1
Hay's Galleria	17	D1
Hayward Gallery	16	D1
Heinz Gallery, R.I.B.A.	11	B3
Hogarths House,	65	E6
Hogarth La.		
Holland Park	66	C2
Home Office	15	H4
Horniman Museum	86	E1
Horse Guards Parade	16	A2
Hospital Museum,	19	B4
Chelsea Royal Hospital		
Hounslow Heath	72	E6
Houses of Parliament	16	B4
Hyde Park	14	G1
Hyde Park Corner	15	C3
Imperial College,	14	E5
University of London		
Imperial War Museum	16	F6
Institute of Contemporary	15	J2
Arts		
Ironmongers' Hall	12	J2
Ismaili Centre	18	F1
Jack Straw's Castle P.H.	48	F3
Jewel Tower,	16	A5
Houses of Parliament		
Jewish Museum	7	J5
Jubilee Gardens	16	C3
Keats House, Hampstead	48	H4
Kempton Park Racecourse	81	C7
Kensington Gardens	14	D2
Kensington Palace	14	B2
Kenwood House,	48	H1
Hampstead		
Kew Bridge Steam Museum	64	H3
Kew Gardens	64	G5
Kew Observatory	73	E3
Kings Road, Chelsea	18	F5
Lambeth Palace	16	C6
Lancaster House	15	F3
Leadenhall Market	13	D4
Leicester Square	11	J6
Leighton House,	66	C3
Holland Park Rd.		
Lesnes Abbey (ruins)	71	D4
Leyton Orient Football Club	51	B3
Liberty	11	F4
Lincoln's Inn	12	D3
Linley Sambourne House,	66	D2
Stafford Ter.		
Little Venice (Waterbuses)	10	C1
Livesey Museum	68	E6
Lloyds of London	13	D4
London Brass Rubbing	12	A6
Centre, St. Martin-in-the-		
Fields Church		
London Bridge	17	C1
London Central Mosque	6	H4
London College of Printing	16	H6
London Diamond Centre	11	E4
London Dungeon	17	C2
London Palladium	11	F4
London Peace Pagoda,	19	A6
Battersea Park		
London Silver Vaults	12	E2
London Stone	13	B5
London Toy and Model	10	D5
Museum, Craven Hill		
London Transport Museum,	12	B5
Covent Gdn.		
London Zoo	7	B1
Lord's Cricket Ground	6	F3
and Museum		
Madame Tussaud's	7	B6
Mall Galleries	15	J1
Mansion House	13	B4
Marble Arch	11	A5
Marble Hill House,	73	F7
Twickenham		
Marlborough House	15	G2
Master Mariners' Hall,	12	E6
H.Q.S. 'Wellington'		
Mercers' Hall	13	B4
Merchant Taylors' Hall	13	C4
Methodist Central Hall	15	J4
Middlesex Guildhall	16	A4
Millbank Tower	20	A2
Millwall Football Club	68	G6
Ministry of Agriculture,	16	B1
Fisheries and Food		

Ministry of Defence	16	A2
Monument, The	13	QE
Morden College	78	G2
Museum of Garden History	16	C6
Museum of Instruments,	14	E5
Royal College of Music		
Museum of London	12	J2
Museum of Mankind,	11	F6
Burlington Gdns.		
Museum of the	16	D1
Moving Image (M.O.M.I.)		
Museum of the Royal	16	C6
Pharmaceutical Society of		
Great Britain (R.P.S.G.B.)		
Music Information Centre	11	C4
Musical Museum, High St.,	64	H6
Brentford		
National Army Museum	19	A5
National Gallery	11	J6
National Maritime Museum	69	D6
National Portrait Gallery	11	J6
National Postal Museum	12	H3
National Westminster Tower	13	D3
Natural History Museum	14	E6
Nelson's Column	16	A1
New Covent Garden Market	67	D7
New Scotland Yard	15	H5
North Woolwich Station	70	D2
Museum		
Northern Ireland	15	E1
Tourist Board		
Notting Hill Carnival,	57	B6
Ladbroke Gro.		
Old Admiralty Buildings	15	J2
(M.o.D.)		
Old County Hall	16	C3
Old Curiosity Shop	12	C4
Old Deer Park, Richmond	73	G3
Olympia	66	B3
Operating Theatre Museum	17	C2
Orleans House Gallery,	82	E1
Twickenham		
Oscar Wilde's House	19	A5
Osterley Park House	63	J5
Oval, The (Cricket Ground)	20	D5
Oxford Circus	11	F4
Oxford Street	11	A4
P.S. 'Tattershall Castle'	16	B2
Pall Mall	15	G2
Passmore Edwards Museum	51	F6
Passport Office	15	G5
Patent Office	12	E3
Percival David Foundation	7	J6
of Chinese Art, Gordon Sq.		
Peter Pan Statue	14	E1
Petticoat Lane (Market)	13	E2
Petts Wood	97	G3
Photographers' Gallery,	11	J5
Great Newport Street		
Piccadilly Circus	11	H6
Planetarium	7	B6
Pollock's Toy Museum	11	G1
Pomeroy Purdy Gallery	17	H3
Primrose Hill	57	J1
Prince Henry's Room	12	E4
Public Record Office	12	E3
Public Record Office	12	E4
Museum		
Q.P.R. Football Club	65	H1
Queen Elizabeth Hall and	16	D1
Purcell Room		
Queen Elizabeth II	15	J4
Conference Centre		
Queen Elizabeth's Hunting	26	F7
Lodge, Epping Forest		
Queen Victoria Memorial	15	F4
Queen's Gallery	15	E4
Queen's Ice Rink	10	B6
Queen's Tower	14	E5
Queens Club	66	B5
(Tennis Centre)		
R.A.A.B. Gallery	19	J3
R.A.F. Museum, Hendon	38	F2
Regent Street	11	E3
Regent's Park	6	J2
Richmond Palace (remains)	73	F5
Richmond Park	83	A1
Roman Bath, Strand	12	D5

Rotunda Museum of	70	C5
Artillery, Woolwich		
Royal Academy of Arts	11	F6
Royal Academy of	11	H1
Dramatic Art (R.A.D.A.)		
Royal Academy of Music	7	C6
Royal Albert Hall	14	E4
Royal Botanic Gardens	64	G5
Royal College of Art	14	E4
Royal College of Music	14	E5
Royal College of Surgeons	12	D3
Royal Courts of Justice	12	D4
Royal Exchange (L.I.F.F.E.)	13	C4
Royal Festival Hall	16	D2
Royal Geographical Society	14	F4
Royal Horticultural Society	15	H6
(New Hall)		
Royal Horticultural Society	19	H1
(Old Hall)		
Royal Mews	15	E5
Royal National Theatre	16	D1
Royal Naval College	69	D6
Royal Opera House	12	B4
Saatchi Collection	57	E1
St. Bartholomew-the-Great	12	H2
Church, Cloth Fair		
St. Bride's Church and Crypt	12	G4
Museum		
St. Bride's Printing Library,	12	G4
Bride La.		
St. Clement Danes Church,	12	D4
Strand		
St. James's Palace	15	G2
St. James's Park	15	H3
St. John's Gate and	8	G6
Museum of the Order of		
St. John		
St. Katharine's Dock	17	H1
St. Lawrence Jewry Church,	13	A3
Gresham St.		
St. Martin-in-the-Fields	12	A6
Church, Trafalgar Square		
St. Mary at Hill Church,	13	D5
Lovat La.		
St. Mary-le-Bow Church	13	A4
St. Paul's Cathedral	12	J4
Salters' Hall	13	A2
Salvation Army International	12	J5
Headquarters,		
Queen Victoria St.		
Schooner Kathleen and May	17	B1
Science Museum	14	F6
Science Reference Library	12	E2
Scottish Tourist Board	15	J1
Selfridges	11	C4
Serpentine Gallery	14	F2
Serpentine, The	14	G2
Shakespeare Globe Museum	16	J1
Shell Centre	16	D2
Sherlock Holmes Museum	7	A6
Sir John Soane's Museum,	12	C3
Lincoln's Inn Fields		
Skinners' Hall, Dowgate Hill	13	B5
Smithfield Central Market	12	G2
Soho	11	H5
Somerset House	12	C5
Sotheby's	11	E5
South Bank	16	D1
South London Art Gallery,	77	B1
Peckham Rd.		
Southwark Cathedral	17	B1
Southwark Park	68	F4
Speaker's Corner	11	A5
Spitalfields Community Farm	9	H6
Stepping Stones Farm	59	G5
Stock Exchange	13	C4
Story of Telecommunications	12	H5
Strand, The	16	A1
Surrey Docks Farm	68	J2
Syon House, Brentford	73	F1
Tate Gallery	20	A2
Telecom Tower	11	F1
Temple Bar	12	E4
Temple of Mithras,	13	A4
Victoria St.		
Temple, The	12	E5
Thames Flood Barrier	70	A2
Thames House	20	A1

Theatre Museum,	12	B5
Tavistock Street		
Theatre Royal, Drury La.	12	B4
Tottenham Hotspur	33	C7
Football Club		
Tower Bridge Museum and	17	F2
Exhibitions		
Tower Hill	13	F6
Tower Pier	17	E1
Tower of London	13	F6
Toynbee Hall	13	G3
Trafalgar Square	16	A1
Trent Park, Enfield	24	B2
Trinity House	13	F5
Trocadero	11	H6
Twickenham Rugby Ground	73	B6
University College London	7	H5
University of London	7	J6
Victoria Coach Station	19	D2
Victoria Embankment	16	B1
Gardens		
Victoria Park	59	H1
Victoria Tower,	16	A5
Houses of Parliament		
Victoria and Albert Museum	14	F6
Vintners' Hall	13	A5
Wallace Collection	11	C3
Walworth City Farm	20	H4
Waterlow Park, Highgate	49	B1
Wellington Arch	15	C3
Wellington Museum	15	C3
Wembley Conference Centre	46	J4
Wembley Stadium	47	A5
Wesley's House	9	C5
West Ham United	61	A2
Football Club		
Westminster Abbey	16	A5
Westminster Abbey Museum	16	A5
Westminster Cathedral	15	F6
Westminster City Hall	15	G5
Westminster Pier	16	B3
Whitbread Brewery	13	A1
Whitbread Shire Horse	9	A5
Stables, Garrett St.		
Whitechapel Art Gallery	13	G3
Whitehall	16	A2
William Morris Gallery,	42	A3
Lloyd Park		
Wimbledon	84	B4
(All England Tennis Club)		
Wimbledon Common	83	F4
Wimbledon Football Club	84	E4
Woolwich Common	70	C7
World Trade Centre	13	G6
Y.H.A., Carter Lane	12	H4
Y.H.A., Earl's Court	18	A3
Y.H.A., Holland House	66	C2
Y.H.A., Oxford Street	11	G4
Y.M.C.A.	11	J3
Y.W.C.A.	11	J3
Zamana Gallery,	18	F1
Ismaili Centre		

Abbey Wood SE2 71 B3
Acton W3 65 A1
Addington, Croy. 102 J5
Addiscombe, Croy. 102 C1
Aldborough Hatch, Ilf. 43 H3
Aldersbrook E12 51 H2
Alperton, Wem. 55 H1
Anerley SE20 95 E2
Arkley, Barn. 22 G5
Avery Hill SE9 79 F6
Balham SW12 84 J1
Banstead, Bans. 93 E2
Barbican EC2 **13** **A2**
Barking, Bark. 61 E1
Barkingside, Ilf. 43 E3
Barnes SW13 74 G2
Barnet, Barn. 23 C3
Barnet Gate, Barn. 22 F6
Barnsbury N1 49 G6
Battersea SW11 76 A2
Bayswater W2 **10** **C4**
Bayswater W2 57 E6
Beacontree, Dag. 53 D3
Beacontree Heath, Dag. 53 G1
Beckenham, Beck. 96 B1
Beckton E6 61 D5
Beddington, Wall. 101 D2
Beddington Corner, Mitch. 94 A7
Bedford Park W4 65 D3
Belgravia SW1 **19** **C1**
Belgravia SW1 67 A3
Bell Green SE6 86 J3
Bellingham SE6 87 A3
Belmont, Har. 37 D2
Belsize Park NW3 48 H6
Belvedere, Belv. 71 H4
Benhilton, Sutt. 100 E2
Bermondsey SE1 **17** **F5**
Bermondsey SE1 68 C3
Berrylands, Surb. 91 J6
Bethnal Green E2 59 D2
Bexley, Bex. 80 G6
Bexleyheath, Bexh. 80 F5
Bickley, Brom. 97 C3
Blackfen, Sid. 79 J7
Blackheath SE3 78 E1
Blackheath Park SE3 78 G4
Bloomsbury WC1 **12** **A1**
Bloomsbury WC1 58 D5
Borehamwood, Borwd. 22 B3
Borough, The SE1 **16** **J4**
Borough, The SE1 67 J2
Bow E3 59 J2
Bowes Park N22 32 E6
Brentford, Brent. 64 F6
Brimsdown, Enf. 25 H3
Brixton SW2 76 E4
Broad Green, Croy. 94 G6
Broadgate EC2 **13** **C1**
Brockley SE4 77 H5
Bromley E3 60 B4
Bromley, Brom. 96 F2
Bromley Common, Brom. 97 C7
Bromley Park, Brom. 96 E1
Brompton SW3 **14** **G6**
Brompton SW3 66 H3
Brondesbury NW2 48 A6
Brondesbury Park NW6 48 A7
Brunswick Park N11 31 J2
Buckhurst Hill, Buck.H. 26 H7
Burnt Oak, Edg. 30 C7
Bush Hill Park, Enf. 25 B5
Bushey Heath, Herts. 29 B1
Bushey Mead SW20 93 A3
Camberwell SE5 67 J7
Camden Town NW1 58 C1
Canning Town E16 60 G6
Canons Park, Edg. 29 H7
Carpenters Park, Wat. 28 F2
Carshalton, Cars. 100 H5
Carshalton on the Hill, Cars. 101 A7
Castelnau SW13 65 G6
Catford SE6 87 B1
Chadwell Heath, Rom. 44 D6
Charlton SE7 69 J6
Cheam, Sutt. 100 A6
Chelsea SW3 **18** **E5**
Chelsea SW3 66 G6
Chessington, Chess. 98 H6
Chigwell, Chig. 35 E3
Childs Hill NW2 48 D2

Chingford E4 34 B1
Chingford Green E4 34 F1
Chingford Hatch E4 34 D4
Chipping Barnet, Barn. 23 B4
Chislehurst, Chis. 88 D7
Chislehurst West, Chis. 88 D5
Chiswick W4 65 D6
Church End N3 39 C1
Church End NW10 47 E6
Clapham SW4 76 B3
Clapham Park SW4 76 C6
Claygate, Esher 98 B7
Clayhall, Ilf. 43 C2
Clerkenwell EC1 **8** **G6**
Clerkenwell EC1 58 H4
Cockfosters, Barn. 23 H4
Coldblow, Bex. 89 J2
Collier Row, Rom. 44 G1
Collier's Wood SW19 84 G7
Coombe, Kings.T. 83 C7
Copse Hill SW20 83 G7
Cottenham Park SW20 92 G1
Cranbrook, Ilf. 52 C1
Cranford, Houns. 63 A7
Cricklewood NW2 48 A3
Crouch End N8 40 C6
Croydon, Croy. 102 A2
Cubitt Town E14 69 C3
Custom House E16 61 A6
Dagenham, Dag. 53 G6
Dalston E8 50 B7
Dartmouth Park NW5 49 B3
Debden, Loug. 27 G3
Deptford SE8 68 J5
Dollis Hill NW2 47 H3
Dormer's Wells, Sthl. 54 H7
Downham, Brom. 87 F4
Ducks Island, Barn. 23 A6
Dulwich SE21 77 B7
Ealing W5 55 F7
Earls Court SW5 66 C5
Earlsfield SW18 84 F1
East Acton W3 56 E7
East Barnet, Barn. 23 H6
East Dulwich SE22 77 D6
East Finchley N2 39 G4
East Ham E6 61 B2
East Molesey, E.Mol. 91 A3
East Sheen SW14 74 D4
East Wickham, Well. 89 A3
Eastcote, Pnr. 36 C6
Eastcote Village, Pnr. 36 B5
Eden Park, Beck. 96 A5
Edgware, Edg. 30 B5
Edmonton N9 33 D4
Elmers End, Beck. 95 G3
Elmstead, Chis. 88 A5
Eltham SE9 79 A6
Enfield, Enf. 25 C3
Enfield Highway, Enf. 25 F2
Enfield Town, Enf. 25 A2
Epsom, Epsom 83 C7
Falconwood, Well. 79 G3
Farnborough, Orp. 104 E5
Feltham, Felt. 81 A2
Finchley N3 39 E1
Finsbury EC1 **8** **F3**
Finsbury EC1 58 H3
Finsbury Park N4 49 G1
Forest Gate E7 51 G5
Forest Hill SE23 86 G1
Friday Hill E4 34 D2
Friern Barnet N11 31 H4
Fullwell Cross, Ilf. 43 G1
Furzedown SW17 85 A5
Gants Hill, Ilf. 43 D5
Golders Green NW11 39 D7
Goodmayes, Ilf. 53 B2
Gospel Oak NW5 49 A4
Grange Hill, Chig. 35 G6
Grange Park N21 24 H5
Greenford, Grnf. 54 H3
Greenwich SE10 69 D6
Grove Park SE12 87 G2
Grove Park W4 65 C7
Gunnersbury W4 65 B4
Hackbridge, Wall. 101 B2
Hackney E8 50 E6
Hackney Wick E9 50 J5
Hadley, Barn. 23 C2
Haggerston E2 **9** **H1**

Haggerston E2 59 C2
Hainault, Chig. 35 J4
Hale End E4 34 D6
Ham, Rich. 82 F3
Hammersmith W6 65 J5
Hampstead NW3 48 G4
Hampstead Garden Suburb N2 39 F5
Hampton, Hmptn. 90 H1
Hampton Hill, Hmptn. 82 A6
Hampton Wick, Kings.T. 91 E1
Hanwell W7 64 C1
Hanworth, Felt. 81 D4
Harlesden NW10 56 E2
Harringay N8 40 G5
Harrow, Har. 37 A7
Harrow on the Hill, Har. 46 B1
Harrow Weald, Har. 37 B1
Hatch End, Pnr. 28 E7
Hayes, Brom. 96 H7
Headstone, Har. 36 J4
Hendon NW4 38 H4
Herne Hill SE24 76 J5
Heston, Houns. 63 F7
High Barnet, Barn. 23 A2
High Beach, Loug. 26 G1
Higham Hill E17 41 H2
Highams Park E4 34 D5
Highbury N5 49 H5
Highgate N6 40 B7
Highwood Hill NW7 30 G2
Hinchley Wood, Esher 98 C3
Hither Green SE13 78 E6
Holborn WC2 **12** **C3**
Holborn WC2 58 F6
Holders Hill NW4 39 A2
Holloway N7 49 E4
Homerton E9 50 H5
Honor Oak SE23 77 F6
Honor Oak Park SE4 77 J6
Hornsey N8 40 F4
Hounslow, Houns. 72 F4
Hounslow, West Houns. 72 D3
Hoxton N1 **9** **D2**
Hoxton N1 59 A4
Hyde, The NW9 38 F5
Ilford, Ilf. 52 F3
Isleworth, Islw. 73 C3
Islington N1 58 G1
Joydens Wood, Bex. 89 J5
Kennington SE11 **20** **E6**
Kennington SE11 67 G6
Kensal Green NW10 56 J3
Kensal Rise NW6 57 A2
Kensal Town W10 57 A4
Kensington W8 66 C1
Kentish Town NW5 49 C6
Kenton, Har. 37 E5
Kew, Rich. 65 A6
Kidbrooke SE3 78 J2
Kilburn NW6 57 C2
King's Cross N1 58 D1
Kingsbury NW9 38 B6
Kingston upon Thames, Kings.T. 91 H2
Kingston Vale SW15 74 E6
Ladywell SE13 78 A5
Lambeth SE1 **16** **D5**
Lambeth SE1 67 F3
Lamorbey, Sid. 88 J1
Lampton, Houns. 72 H1
Lea Bridge E5 50 G3
Lee SE12 78 F6
Lessness Heath, Belv. 71 H5
Lewisham SE13 78 B3
Leyton E11 51 B1
Leytonstone E11 42 D7
Limehouse E14 59 H7
Lisson Grove NW8 **6** **F5**
Little Ealing W5 64 C4
Long Ditton, Surb. 98 F1
Longlands, Chis. 88 F3
Loughton, Loug. 27 C5
Lower Clapton E5 50 F4
Lower Edmonton N9 33 C1
Lower Holloway N7 49 E4
Lower Sydenham SE26 86 G4
Loxford, Ilf. 52 F5
Maida Hill W9 57 C4
Maida Vale W9 **6** **B5**
Maida Vale W9 57 E4

Place	Page	Grid
Manor Park E12	52	B5
Mark's Gate, Rom.	44	E2
Marylebone NW1	**10**	**H1**
Marylebone NW1	57	H4
Mayfair W1	**11**	**D6**
Mayfair W1	58	A6
Merry Hill, Wat.	28	H1
Merton SW19	93	D1
Merton Park SW19	93	D2
Mile End E1	59	H3
Mill Hill NW7	30	G5
Millwall E14	69	B3
Mitcham, Mitch.	94	A3
Monken Hadley, Barn.	23	C1
Monks Orchard, Croy.	95	J7
Morden, Mord.	93	D3
Morden Park, Mord.	93	B6
Mortlake SW14	74	C3
Motspur Park, N.Mal.	92	G6
Mottingham SE9	87	J2
Muswell Hill N10	40	B3
Neasden NW2	47	E3
New Barnet, Barn.	23	E4
New Beckenham, Beck.	86	J6
New Charlton SE7	69	J4
New Cross SE14	77	H1
New Cross Gate SE14	77	G1
New Eltham SE9	88	D2
New Malden, N.Mal.	92	D3
New Southgate N11	32	D4
Newbury Park, Ilf.	43	G5
Newington SE17	**20**	**J1**
Newington SE17	67	J3
Nine Elms SW8	**19**	**G7**
Noel Park N22	40	G2
Norbiton, Kings.T.	92	B2
Norbury SW16	94	F1
Nork, Bans.	93	A1
North Acton W3	56	D4
North Cheam, Sutt.	100	A3
North Cray, Sid.	89	F3
North Finchley N12	31	G5
North Harrow, Har.	36	G6
North Hyde, Sthl.	63	E4
North Kensington W10	56	J6
North Sheen, Rich.	74	A2
North Wembley, Wem.	46	E2
North Woolwich E16	70	B2
Northolt, Nthlt.	45	E7
Northumberland Heath, Erith	71	J7
Norwood Green, Sthl.	63	G4
Norwood New Town SE19	85	J6
Notting Hill W11	57	B6
Nunhead SE15	77	F3
Oakleigh Park N20	31	G1
Oakwood N14	24	D6
Old Bexley, Bex.	80	H7
Old Ford E3	59	J1
Old Malden, Wor.Pk.	99	D1
Old Oak Common NW10	56	E5
Orpington, Orp.	104	J1
Osidge N14	32	B1
Osterley, Islw.	64	A7
Paddington W2	**10**	**C2**
Paddington W2	57	E5
Palmers Green N13	32	G3
Park Langley, Beck.	96	C5
Park Royal NW10	56	A2
Parsons Green SW6	75	C1
Peckham SE15	68	C7
Penge SE20	86	F7
Pentonville N1	**8**	**E2**
Pentonville N1	58	G2
Perivale, Grnf.	55	F1
Petersham, Rich.	82	H1
Petts Wood, Orp.	97	G5
Pimlico SW1	**19**	**F3**
Pimlico SW1	67	B5
Pinner, Pnr.	36	E4
Pinner Green, Pnr.	36	C2
Pinnerwood Park, Pnr.	36	C1
Plaistow E13	60	H3
Plaistow, Brom.	87	F6
Plumstead SE18	70	H5
Ponders End, Enf.	25	G5
Poplar E14	60	B7
Poverest, Orp.	97	J5
Preston, Wem.	46	G1
Primrose Hill NW8	57	J1
Putney SW15	74	J5
Putney Heath SW15	74	J6
Putney Vale SW15	83	F3
Queensbury, Har.	37	G3
Rayners Lane, Har.	16	F1
Raynes Park SW20	92	H3
Redbridge, Ilf.	43	C6
Regent's Park NW1	**7**	**D2**
Regent's Park NW1	58	B3
Richmond, Rich.	73	H6
Roehampton SW15	74	G5
Rosehill, Sutt.	100	E1
Rotherhithe SE16	68	G3
Rowley Green, Barn.	22	F4
Roxeth, Har.	46	A2
Ruislip Manor, Ruis.	45	A2
Rush Green, Rom.	44	J7
St. Helier, Cars.	93	G7
St. James's SW1	**15**	**G2**
St. James's SW1	67	C1
St. John's SE8	78	A2
St. John's Wood NW8	**6**	**E3**
St. John's Wood NW8	57	F2
St. Luke's EC1	**9**	**A5**
St. Luke's EC1	58	J4
St. Margarets, Twick.	73	D5
St. Pancras WC1	**8**	**A4**
St. Pancras WC1	58	E3
Sands End SW6	75	F1
Selhurst SE25	95	B6
Seven Kings, Ilf.	43	H7
Sewardstone E4	26	C1
Sewardstonebury E4	26	E4
Shacklewell N16	50	C4
Shadwell E1	59	F7
Shepherd's Bush W12	65	J1
Shirley, Croy.	102	G3
Shooter's Hill SE18	79	F1
Shoreditch E1	**9**	**F6**
Shoreditch E1	59	C4
Shortlands, Brom.	96	E3
Sidcup, Sid.	88	J4
Silvertown E16	69	J2
Snaresbrook E11	42	E5
Soho W1	**11**	**H5**
Soho W1	58	C6
Somers Town NW1	**7**	**A2**
Somers Town NW1	58	D3
South Acton W3	65	B3
South Beddington, Wall.	101	D6
South Chingford E4	33	J5
South Croydon, S.Croy.	101	J6
South Hackney E9	59	F1
South Hampstead NW6	48	E7
South Harrow, Har.	45	H3
South Kensington SW7	**18**	**C2**
South Kensington SW7	66	E3
South Lambeth SW8	76	E1
South Norwood SE25	95	C3
South Oxhey, Wat.	28	C3
South Ruislip, Ruis.	45	C4
South Tottenham N15	41	B5
South Wimbledon SW19	84	D7
South Woodford E18	42	F2
Southall, Sthl.	63	D1
Southborough, Brom.	97	C6
Southend SE6	87	C4
Southfields SW18	84	D1
Southgate N14	32	C2
Southwark SE1	**16**	**H2**
Southwark SE1	67	H1
Spring Grove, Islw.	73	B2
Stamford Hill N16	50	C1
Stanmore, Stan.	29	D5
Stepney E1	59	F5
Stockwell SW9	76	D3
Stoke Newington N16	50	B2
Stonebridge NW10	56	B1
Stoneleigh, Epsom	99	G5
Strand WC2	**12**	**A5**
Strand WC2	58	E7
Stratford E15	51	C6
Strawberry Hill, Twick.	82	B3
Streatham SW16	85	E4
Streatham Hill SW2	85	F1
Streatham Park SW16	85	C4
Streatham Vale SW16	85	D7
Stroud Green N8	40	F6
Sudbury, Wem.	46	D5
Summerstown SW17	84	E4
Sunbury, Sun.	90	B3
Sundridge, Brom.	87	J6
Surbiton, Surb.	91	H7
Sutton, Sutt.	100	D7
Sydenham SE26	86	E5
Teddington, Tedd.	92	D6
Thames Ditton, T.Ditt.	91	D7
Thamesmead SE28	71	A1
Thamesmead North SE28	62	D6
Thamesmead West SE18	70	F3
Thornton Heath, Th.Hth.	94	H4
Tokyngton, Wem.	47	B6
Tolworth, Surb.	99	A2
Tooting Graveney SW17	84	H6
Tottenham N17	41	B1
Tottenham Hale N17	41	D3
Totteridge N20	31	B1
Tufnell Park N7	49	D4
Tulse Hill SE21	85	J1
Twickenham, Twick.	82	D2
Underhill, Barn.	23	D5
Upper Clapton E5	50	E1
Upper Edmonton N18	33	D5
Upper Elmers End Beck.	95	J5
Upper Holloway N19	49	C3
Upper Norwood SE19	86	A7
Upper Sydenham SE26	86	D4
Upper Tooting SW17	84	H3
Upper Walthamstow E17	42	C4
Upton E7	51	H7
Upton Park E6	60	J1
Vauxhall SW8	**20**	**C6**
Vauxhall SW8	67	D6
Waddon, Croy.	101	G2
Walham Green SW6	66	E7
Wallington, Wall.	101	C5
Walthamstow E17	42	B2
Walworth SE17	**20**	**J3**
Walworth SE17	68	A5
Wandsworth SW18	75	C5
Wanstead E11	42	G7
Wapping E1	68	D1
Watford Heath, Wat.	28	D1
Wealdstone, Har.	37	C3
Welling, Well.	80	A3
Wembley, Wem.	46	H5
Wembley Park, Wem.	46	J2
West Barnes, N.Mal.	92	H4
West Brompton SW10	**18**	**A5**
West Brompton SW10	66	D6
West Dulwich SE21	86	A3
West Ewell, Epsom	99	E7
West Green N15	40	J4
West Ham E15	51	F7
West Hampstead NW6	48	E5
West Harrow, Har.	36	J7
West Heath SE2	71	D6
West Kilburn W9	57	C3
West Molesey, W.Mol.	90	F4
West Norwood SE27	85	J3
West Wickham, W.Wick.	103	C2
Westbourne Green W2	57	D5
Westminster SW1	**15**	**F5**
Westminster SW1	67	C3
Weston Green, T.Ditt.	98	C1
Whetstone N20	31	E2
Whitechapel E1	**13**	**H4**
Whitechapel E1	59	D6
Whitton, Twick.	72	H7
Widmore, Brom.	96	J3
Willesden NW10	47	F6
Willesden Green NW10	47	H7
Wimbledon SW19	84	B6
Wimbledon Park SW19	84	C3
Winchmore Hill N21	24	F7
Wood Green N22	40	E1
Woodford, Wdf.Grn.	34	H6
Woodford Bridge, Wdf.Grn.	35	C7
Woodford Green, Wdf.Grn.	34	G5
Woodford Wells, Wdf.Grn.	34	H3
Woodlands, Islw.	73	B2
Woodmansterne, Bans.	93	H1
Woodside, Croy.	95	C6
Woolwich SE18	70	C5
Worcester Park, Wor.Pk.	99	F2
World's End, Enf.	24	G3
Wrythe, The, Cars.	100	H2
Yeading, Hayes	54	B3

General Abbreviations

All	Alley	Embk	Embankment	Pas	Passage
Allot	Allotments	Est	Estate	Pav	Pavilion
Amb	Ambulance	Ex	Exchange	Pk	Park
App	Approach	FB	Footbridge	Pl	Place
Arc	Arcade	FC	Football Club	Prec	Precinct
Ave	Avenue	Fld	Field	Prom	Promenade
Bdy	Broadway	Flds	Fields	Quad	Quadrant
Bldgs	Buildings	Fm	Farm	Pt	Point
Bowl	Bowling	Gall	Gallery	RC	Roman Catholic
Bri	Bridge	Gar	Garage	Rd	Road
C of E	Church of England	Gdn	Garden	Rds	Roads
Cath	Cathedral	Gdns	Gardens	Rec	Recreation
Cem	Cemetery	Govt	Government	Res	Reservoir
Cen	Central, Centre	Gra	Grange	Ri	Rise
Cft	Croft	Grd	Ground	S	South
Ch	Church	Grds	Grounds	Sch	School
Chyd	Churchyard	Grn	Green	Shop	Shopping
Cin	Cinema	Gro	Grove	Sq	Square
Circ	Circus	Gros	Groves	St	Street
Clo	Close	Ho	House	St.	Saint
Co	County	Hos	Houses	Sta	Station
Coll	College	Hosp	Hospital	SUB	Subway
Comm	Community	Ind	Industrial	Swim	Swimming
Conv	Convent	Junct	Junction	TA	Territorial Army
Cor	Corner	La	Lane	Tenn	Tennis
Cors	Corners	Las	Lanes	Ter	Terrace
Coron	Coroners	Lo	Lodge	Thea	Theatre
Cotts	Cottages	Lwr	Lower	Trd	Trading
Cov	Covered	Mag	Magistrates	Twr	Tower
Crem	Crematorium	Mans	Mansions	Twrs	Towers
Cres	Crescent	Meml	Memorial	Vill	Villas
Ct	Court	Mkt	Market	Vw	View
Ctyd	Courtyard	Mkts	Markets	W	West
Dep	Depot	Ms	Mews	Wd	Wood
Dr	Drive	Mt	Mount	Wds	Woods
Dws	Dwellings	Mus	Museum	Wf	Wharf
E	East	N	North	Wk	Walk
Ed	Education	PH	Public House	Wks	Works
Elec	Electricity	Par	Parade	Yd	Yard

Abbreviations of District Names

Ash.	Ashtead	Grnf.	Greenford	Sid.	Sidcup
Bark.	Barking	Har.	Harrow	Sthl.	Southall
Barn.	Barnet	Hmptn.	Hampton	Stan.	Stanmore
Beck.	Beckenham	Houns.	Hounslow	Sun.	Sunbury-on-Thames
Belv.	Belvedere	Ilf.	Ilford	Surb.	Surbiton
Bex.	Bexley	Islw.	Isleworth	Sutt.	Sutton
Bexh.	Bexleyheath	Kes.	Keston	T.Ditt.	Thames Ditton
Borwd.	Borehamwood	Kings.T.	Kingston upon Thames	Tedd.	Teddington
Brent.	Brentford	Loug.	Loughton	Th.Hth.	Thornton Heath
Brom.	Bromley	Mitch.	Mitcham	Twick.	Twickenham
Buck.H.	Buckhurst Hill	Mord.	Morden	Uxb.	Uxbridge
Cars.	Carshalton	N.Mal.	New Malden	W.Mol.	West Molesey
Chess.	Chessington	Nthlt.	Northolt	W.Wick	West Wickham
Chig.	Chigwell	Nthwd.	Northwood	Wall.	Wallington
Chis.	Chislehurst	Orp.	Orpington	Walt.	Walton-on-Thames
Croy.	Croydon	Pnr.	Pinner	Wat.	Watford
Dag.	Dagenham	Pot.B.	Potters Bar	Wdf.Grn.	Woodford Green
Dart.	Dartford	Rain.	Rainham	Well.	Welling
E.Mol.	East Molesey	Rich.	Richmond	Wem.	Wembley
Edg.	Edgware	Rom.	Romford	Wey.	Weybridge
Enf.	Enfield	Ruis.	Ruislip	Wor.Pk.	Worcester Park
Epp.	Epping	S.Croy.	South Croydon		
Felt.	Feltham	Sev.	Sevenoaks		

NOTES

This index contains some street names in standard text which are followed by another street named in italics. In these cases the street in standard text does not actually appear on the map due to insufficient space but can be located close to the street named in italics.

Abbess Clo. E6 61 B5
Oliver Gdns.
Abbess Clo. SW2 85 G1
Abbeville Rd. N8 40 D4
Barrington Rd.
Abbeville Rd. SW4 76 C6
Abbey Ave., Wem. 55 H2
Abbey Clo., Hayes 63 B1
Abbey Clo., Nthlt 54 F3
Invicta Gro.
Abbey Clo., Pnr. 36 B3
Abbey Cres., Bark. 71 G4
Abbey Dr. SW17 85 A5
Church La.
Abbey Gdns. NW8 6 C2
Abbey Gdns. NW8 57 F2
Abbey Gdns. W6 66 B6
Abbey Gro. SE2 71 B4
Abbey La. E15 60 C2
Abbey La., Beck. 87 A7
Abbey Manufacturing 55 J1
Est., Wem.
Abbey Orchard St. 15 J5
SW1
Abbey Orchard St. 67 D3
SW1
Abbey Par. W5 55 J3
Hanger La.
Abbey Pk., Beck. 87 A7
Abbey Rd. E15 60 D2
Abbey Rd. NW6 48 E7
Abbey Rd. NW8 57 E1
Abbey Rd. NW10 56 B2
Abbey Rd. SE2 71 D4
Abbey Rd. SW19 84 F7
Abbey Rd., Bark. 52 E7
Abbey Rd., Belv. 71 D4
Abbey Rd., Bexh. 80 E4
Abbey Rd., Croy. 101 H3
Abbey Rd., Enf. 25 B5
Abbey Rd., Ilf. 43 G5
Abbey Rd. Est. NW8 57 E1
Abbey St. E13 60 G4
Abbey St. SE1 17 E5
Abbey St. SE1 68 C3
Abbey Ter. NW10 55 J2
Abbey Ter. SE2 71 C4
Abbey Vw. NW7 30 F3
Abbey Wk., W.Mol. 90 H3
Abbey Way SE2 71 D2
Wolvercote Rd.
Abbey Wf. Ind. Est., 61 G2
Bark.
Abbey Wd. Rd. SE2 71 B4
Abbeydale Rd., Wem. 56 A1
Abbeyfield Rd. SE16 68 F4
Abbeyfields Clo. 56 A2
NW10
Abbeyhill Rd., Sid. 89 C2
Abbot St. E8 50 C6
Abbots Clo. N1 49 J6
Alwyne Rd.
Abbots Clo., Orp. 104 F1
Abbots Clo., Ruis. 45 D3
Abbots Cres., Enf. 24 H2
Abbots Dr., Har. 45 G2
Abbots Gdns. N2 39 G4
Abbots Grn., Croy. 102 G6
Abbots La. SE1 17 E2
Abbots Manor Est. 19 D3
SW1
Abbots Pk. SW2 85 G1
Abbot's Pl. NW6 57 E1
Abbot's Rd. E6 61 A1
Abbots Rd., Edg. 30 C7
Abbots Ter. N8 40 E6
Abbots Way, Beck. 95 H5
Abbotsbury Clo. E15 60 C2
Abbotsbury Clo. W14 66 C2
Abbotsbury Rd.
Abbotsbury Gdns., 36 C6
Pnr.
Abbotsbury Rd. 66 B2
W14
Abbotsbury Rd., 103 F2
Brom.
Abbotsbury Rd., 93 E5
Mord.
Abbotsford Ave. N15 40 J4
Abbotsford Gdns., 34 G7
Wdf.Grn.
Abbotsford Rd., Ilf. 53 A2
Abbotshall Ave. N14 32 C3
Abbotshall Rd. SE6 87 D1
Abbotsleigh Clo., 100 E7
Sutt.
Abbotsleigh Rd. 85 C4
SW16
Abbotsmede Clo., 82 C2
Twick.
Abbotstone Rd. 74 J3
SW15
Abbotswell Rd. SE4 77 J5

Abbotswood Clo., 71 E3
Belv.
Coptefield Dr.
Abbotswood Gdns., 43 C3
Ilf.
Abbotswood Rd. 85 D3
SW16
Abbotswood Way, 63 B1
Hayes
Abbott Ave. SW20 93 A1
Abbott Clo., Hmptn. 81 E6
Abbott Clo., Nthlt. 45 F6
Abbott Rd. E14 60 C6
Abbotts Clo., Rom. 44 H3
Abbotts Cres. E4 34 D4
Abbotts Dr., Wem. 46 E2
Abbotts Pk. Rd. E10 42 C7
Abbotts Rd., Barn. 23 E4
Abbotts Rd., Mitch. 94 C4
Abbotts Rd., Sthl. 63 E1
Abbotts Rd., Sutt. 100 B4
Abbotts Wk., Bexh. 71 D7
Abchurch La. EC4 13 C5
Abchurch La. EC4 59 A7
Abchurch Yd. EC4 13 B5
Abdale Rd. W12 65 H1
Aberavon Rd. E3 59 H3
Abercairn Rd. SW16 85 C7
Aberconway Rd., 93 E3
Mord.
Abercorn Clo. NW7 31 B7
Abercorn Clo. NW8 6 C3
Abercorn Clo. NW8 57 F3
Abercorn Cres., Har. 45 H2
Abercorn Gdns., Har. 37 G7
Abercorn Gdns., 44 B6
Rom.
Abercorn Pl. NW8 6 C3
Abercorn Rd. NW7 31 B7
Abercorn Rd. NW7 31 B7
Abercorn Way SE1 21 H3
Abercorn Way SE1 68 D5
Abercrombie St. 75 H2
SW11
Aberdare Clo., 103 C2
W.Wick.
Aberdare Gdns. NW6 48 E7
Aberdare Gdns. NW7 31 A7
Aberdare Rd., Enf. 25 F4
Aberdeen La. N5 49 H5
Aberdeen Par. N18 33 E5
Angel Rd.
Aberdeen Pk. N5 49 J5
Aberdeen Pk. Ms. N5 49 J4
Aberdeen Pl. NW8 6 E5
Aberdeen Rd. N5 49 H4
Aberdeen Rd. N18 33 E5
Aberdeen Rd. NW10 47 F5
Aberdeen Rd., Croy. 101 J4
Aberdeen Rd., Har. 37 C2
Aberdeen Ter. SE3 78 D2
Aberdour Rd., Ilf. 53 B3
Aberdour St. SE1 21 D1
Aberdour St. SE1 68 B4
Aberfeldy St. E14 60 C6
Aberford Gdns. SE18 79 B1
Aberford Rd., Borwd. 22 A2
Aberfoyle Rd. SW16 85 D6
Abergeldie Rd. SE12 78 H6
Abernethy Rd. SE13 78 E4
Abersham Rd. E8 50 C5
Abery St. SE18 70 H4
Abingdon Clo. NW1 49 D6
Camden Sq.
Abingdon Clo. SE1 21 G2
Abingdon Clo. SW19 84 F6
Abingdon Rd. N3 39 F2
Abingdon Rd. SW16 94 E2
Abingdon Rd. W8 66 D3
Abingdon St. SW1 16 A5
Abingdon St. SW1 67 D3
Abingdon Vill. W8 66 D3
Abinger Clo., Brom. 97 B3
Abinger Clo., Ilf. 53 A4
Abinger Clo., Wall. 101 E5
Abinger Gdns., Islw. 73 B3
Sussex Ave.
Abinger Gro. SE8 68 J6
Abinger Ms. W9 57 D4
Warlock Rd.
Abinger Rd. W4 65 E7
Ablett St. SE16 68 F5
Abney Gdns. N16 50 C2
Stoke Newington
High St.
Aboyne Dr. SW20 92 G2
Aboyne Est. SW17 84 G3
Aboyne Rd. NW10 47 E3
Aboyne Rd. SW17 84 G3
Abridge Rd., Chig. 27 G6
Abridge Way, Bark. 62 B2

Abyssinia Clo. SW11 75 H4
Cairns Rd.
Acacia Ave. N17 33 A7
Acacia Ave., Brent. 64 E7
Acacia Ave., Mitch. 94 B2
Acacia Ave., Ruis. 45 A1
Acacia Ave., Wem. 55 H2
Acacia Clo. SE20 95 D2
Selby Rd.
Acacia Clo., Orp. 97 G5
Acacia Clo., Stan. 29 B6
Acacia Dr., Sutt. 100 C1
Acacia Gdns. NW8 6 F1
Acacia Gdns., 103 C2
W.Wick.
Acacia Gro. SE21 86 A2
Acacia Gro., N.Mal. 92 E3
Acacia Pl. NW8 6 F1
Acacia Pl. NW8 57 G2
Acacia Rd. E11 51 E2
Acacia Rd. E17 41 H6
Acacia Rd. N22 40 G1
Acacia Rd. NW8 6 F1
Acacia Rd. NW8 57 G2
Acacia Rd. SW16 94 E1
Acacia Rd. W3 56 C7
Acacia Rd., Beck. 95 J3
Acacia Rd., Enf. 25 A1
Acacia Rd., Hmptn. 81 G6
Acacia Rd., Mitch. 94 A2
Acacia Way, Sid. 88 J1
Academy Gdns., 102 C1
Croy.
Academy Gdns., 54 D2
Nthlt.
Academy Pl. SE18 79 C1
Academy Rd. SE18 79 C1
Acanthus Dr. SE1 21 H3
Acanthus Dr. SE1 68 D5
Acanthus Rd. SW11 76 A3
Accommodation Rd. 39 C7
NW11
Acfold Rd. SW6 75 E1
Achilles Clo. SE1 21 J3
Achilles Clo. SE1 68 D5
Achilles Rd. NW6 48 D5
Achilles St. SE14 68 H7
Achilles Way W1 15 C2
Acklington Dr. NW9 38 E1
Ackmar Rd. SW6 75 D1
Ackroyd Dr. E3 59 J5
Ackroyd Rd. SE23 77 G7
Ackworth Clo. N9 25 F7
Acland Cres. SE5 77 A4
Acland Rd. NW2 47 H6
Acol Cres., Ruis. 45 B5
Acol Rd. NW6 48 D7
Aconbury Rd., Dag. 62 H1
Acorn Clo. E4 34 B5
The Lawns
Acorn Clo., Chis. 88 F5
Acorn Clo., Enf. 24 H1
Acorn Clo., Stan. 29 E7
Acorn Ct., Ilf. 43 H6
Acorn Gdns. SE19 95 C1
Acorn Gdns. W3 56 D5
Acorn Par. SE15 68 E7
Carlton Gro.
Acorn Wk. SE16 68 H1
Acorn Way SE23 86 G3
Acorn Way, Orp. 104 E4
Acorns, The, Chig. 35 H4
Acorns Clo., Hmptn. 81 H6
Acre La. SW2 76 E4
Acre La., Cars. 101 A4
Acre La., Wall. 101 A4
Acre Rd. SW19 84 G6
Acre Rd., Dag. 53 H7
Acre Rd., Kings.T. 91 H1
Acris St. SW18 75 F5
Acton Clo. N9 33 D2
Acton La. NW10 56 C3
Acton La. W3 65 C2
Acton La. W4 65 C4
Acton Ms. E8 50 C1
Acton Pk. Ind. Est. W3 65 D2
Acton St. WC1 8 C4
Acton St. WC1 58 F3
Acuba Rd. SW18 84 E1
Acworth Clo. N9 25 F7
Turin Rd.
Ada Gdns. E14 60 D6
Ada Gdns. E15 60 F1
Ada Pl. E2 59 D1
Ada Rd. SE5 68 B7
Ada Rd., Wem. 46 F3
Ada St. E8 59 E1
Ada St. SE25 95 E3
Adair Rd. W10 57 B4
Adair Twr. W10 57 B4
Appleford Rd.

Adam & Eve Ct. W1 11 G3
Adam & Eve Ms. W8 66 D3
Adam Ct. SW7 18 D1
High St.
Adam St. WC2 12 B6
Adam St. WC2 59 E7
Adam Wk. SW6 65 J7
Adams Clo. N3 31 D7
Falkland Ave.
Adams Clo. NW9 47 B2
Adams Clo., Surb. 91 J6
Adams Ct. EC2 13 C3
Adams Gdns. Est. 68 F2
SE16
St. Marychurch St.
Adams Pl. E14 69 B1
North Colonnade
Adams Pl. N7 49 F5
Georges Rd.
Adams Rd. N17 41 A2
Adams Rd., Beck. 95 H5
Adams Row W1 11 C6
Adams Row W1 58 A7
Adams Sq., Bexh. 80 E3
Regency Way
Adams Way, Croy. 95 C6
Adamson Rd. E16 60 G6
Adamson Rd. NW3 48 G7
Adamsrill Clo., Enf. 25 A5
Adamsrill Rd. SE26 86 H4
Adare Wk. SW16 85 F3
Adastral Est. NW9 38 E1
Adcock Wk., Orp. 104 J4
Borkwood Pk.
Adderley Gdns. SE9 88 D4
Adderley Gro. SW11 76 A5
Culmstock Rd.
Adderley Rd., Har. 37 C1
Adderley St. E14 60 C6
Addington Ct. SW14 74 D3
Addington Dr. N12 31 F6
Addington Gro. SE26 86 H4
Addington Rd. E3 60 A3
Addington Rd. E16 60 E4
Addington Rd. N4 40 G6
Addington Rd., 101 G1
Croy.
Addington Rd., 103 C4
W.Wick.
Addington Sq. SE5 21 A7
Addington Sq. SE5 68 A6
Addington St. SE1 16 D4
Addington Village 102 J6
Rd., Croy.
Addis Clo., Enf. 25 G1
Addiscombe Ave., 95 D7
Croy.
Addiscombe Ct. Rd., 102 B1
Croy.
Addiscombe Gro., 102 B2
Croy.
Addiscombe Rd., 102 B2
Croy.
Addison Ave. N14 24 B6
Addison Ave. W11 66 B1
Addison Ave., Houns. 72 J1
Addison Bri. Pl. W14 66 C4
Addison Clo., Nthwd. 36 A1
Addison Clo., Orp. 97 F6
Addison Cres. W14 66 B3
Addison Dr. SE12 78 H5
Eltham Rd.
Addison Gdns. W14 66 A3
Addison Gdns., 91 J4
Surb.
Addison Gro. W4 65 E3
Addison Pl. W11 66 B1
Addison Pl., Sthl. 54 G7
Longford Ave.
Addison Rd. E11 42 G6
Addison Rd. E17 42 B5
Addison Rd. SE25 95 D4
Addison Rd. W14 66 B3
Addison Rd., Brom. 96 J5
Addison Rd., Enf. 25 F1
Addison Rd., Ilf. 43 F1
Addison Rd., Tedd. 82 E6
Addison Way NW11 39 C4
Addison Way, Hayes 54 A6
Addisons Clo., Croy. 102 J2
Addle Hill EC4 12 H4
Addle St. EC2 13 A2
Adecroft Way, 90 J3
W.Mol.
Adela Ave., N.Mal. 92 H5
Adela St. W10 57 B4
Kensal Rd.
Adelaide Ave. SE4 77 J4
Adelaide Clo., Stan. 29 D4
Adelaide Cotts. W7 64 C2

Name	Pg	Grid
Adelaide Gdns., Rom.	44	E5
Adelaide Gro. W12	65	G1
Adelaide Rd. E10	51	C3
Adelaide Rd. NW3	48	G7
Adelaide Rd. W13	64	D1
Adelaide Rd., Chis.	88	E5
Adelaide Rd., Houns.	72	E1
Adelaide Rd., Ilf.	52	E2
Adelaide Rd., Rich.	73	J4
Adelaide Rd., Sthl.	63	E4
Adelaide Rd., Surb.	91	H5
Adelaide Rd., Tedd.	82	C6
Adelaide St. WC2	12	A6
Adelaide Ter., Brent.	64	G5
Adelaide Wk. SW9	76	G4
Sussex Wk.		
Adelina Gro. E1	59	F5
Adelina Ms. SW12	85	D1
Kings Ave.		
Adeline Pl. WC1	11	J2
Adeline Pl. WC1	58	D5
Adelphi Ter. WC2	12	B6
Adelphi Ter. WC2	58	E7
Aden Gro. N16	50	A4
Aden Rd., Enf.	25	H4
Aden Rd., Ilf.	43	E7
Aden Ter. N16	50	A4
Adeney Clo. W6	66	A6
Adenmore Rd. SE6	78	A7
Adie Rd. W6	65	J3
Adine Rd. E13	60	H4
Adler St. E1	13	H3
Adler St. E1	59	D6
Adley St. E5	50	H4
Admaston Rd. SE18	70	F6
Admiral Pl. SE16	68	H1
Admiral Seymour Rd. SE9	79	C4
Admiral Sq. SW10	75	F1
Admiral St. SE8	78	A1
Admirals Clo. E18	42	H4
Admirals Wk. NW3	48	F3
Admirals Way E14	69	A2
Admiralty Rd., Tedd.	82	C6
Adolf St. SE6	87	B4
Adolphus Rd. N4	49	H1
Adolphus St. SE8	68	J7
Adomar Rd., Dag.	53	D3
Adpar St. W2	10	E1
Adpar St. W2	57	G5
Adrian Ave. NW2	47	H1
North Circular Rd.		
Adrian Ms. SW10	18	B5
Adrian Ms. SW10	66	E6
Adrienne Ave., Sthl.	54	F3
Adys Rd. SE15	77	C3
Aerodrome Rd. NW4	38	G3
Aerodrome Rd. NW9	38	F3
Aerodrome Way, Houns.	63	C6
Aeroville NW9	38	E2
Affleck St. N1	8	D2
Afghan Rd. SW11	75	H2
Agamemnon Rd. NW6	48	C5
Agar Clo., Surb.	98	J7
Agar Gro. NW1	49	C7
Agar Gro. Est. NW1	49	C7
Agar Pl. NW1	49	C7
Agar St. WC2	12	A6
Agar St. WC2	58	E7
Agate Rd. E16	61	A6
Agate Rd. W6	65	J3
Agatha Clo. E1	68	E1
Penang St.		
Agaton Rd. SE9	88	F2
Agave Rd. NW2	47	J4
Agdon St. EC1	8	G5
Agdon St. EC1	58	H4
Agincourt Rd. NW3	48	J4
Agnes Ave., Ilf.	52	E4
Agnes Clo. E6	61	D7
Agnes Gdns., Dag.	53	D4
Agnes Rd. W3	65	F1
Agnes St. E14	59	J6
Agnew Rd. SE23	77	G7
Agricola Pl., Enf.	25	C5
Aidan Clo., Dag.	53	E4
Aileen Wk. E15	51	F7
Devenay Rd.		
Ailsa Ave., Twick.	73	D5
Ailsa Rd., Twick.	73	E5
Ailsa St. E14	60	C5
Ainger Ms. NW3	48	J7
Ainger Rd.		
Ainger Rd. NW3	48	J7
Ainsdale Clo., Orp.	96	H4
Ainsdale Cres., Pnr.	36	G3
Ainsdale Rd. W5	55	G4
Ainsdale Rd., Wat.	28	C3
Ainsley Ave., Rom.	44	H6
Ainsley Clo. N9	33	B1
Ainsley St. E2	59	E3
Ainslie Wk. SW12	76	B7
Balham Gro.		
Ainslie Wd. Cres. E4	34	B5
Ainslie Wd. Gdns. E4	34	B5
Ainslie Wd. Rd. E4	34	A5
Ainsworth Clo. NW2	47	G3
Ainsworth Rd. E9	50	F7
Ainsworth Rd., Croy.	101	H2
Ainsworth Way NW8	57	F1
Aintree Ave. E6	61	B1
Aintree Cres., Ilf.	43	F2
Aintree Est. SW6	66	B7
Dawes Rd.		
Aintree Rd., Grnf.	55	E2
Aintree St. SW6	66	B7
Air St. W1	11	G6
Air St. W1	58	C7
Airdrie Clo. N1	49	F7
Airdrie Clo., Hayes	54	E5
Glencoe Rd.		
Airedale Ave. W4	65	F4
Airedale Ave. S. W4	65	F5
Netheravon Rd. S.		
Airedale Rd. SW12	75	J7
Airedale Rd. W5	64	F3
Airlie Gdns. W8	66	D1
Campden Hill Rd.		
Airlie Gdns., Ilf.	52	E1
Airlinks Est., Houns.	63	C5
Airthrie Rd., Ilf.	53	B2
Aisgill Ave. W14	66	C5
Aisher Rd. SE28	62	C7
Aislibie Rd. SE12	78	E4
Aitken Clo. E8	59	D1
Pownall Rd.		
Aitken Rd. SE6	87	B2
Aitken Rd., Barn.	22	J5
Ajax Ave. NW9	38	E3
Ajax Rd. NW6	48	C5
Akehurst St. SW15	74	G6
Akenside Rd. NW3	48	G5
Akerman Rd. SW9	76	H2
Akerman Rd., Surb.	91	F6
Alabama St. SE18	70	G7
Alacross Rd. W5	64	G2
Alan Dr., Barn.	23	B6
Alan Gdns., Rom.	44	G7
Alan Rd. SW19	84	B5
Alandale Dr., Pnr.	36	B2
Alanthus Clo. SE12	78	F5
Alaska St. SE1	16	E2
Alba Clo., Hayes	54	D4
Ramulis Dr.		
Alba Gdns. NW11	39	B6
Alba Pl. W11	57	C6
Portobello Rd.		
Albacore Cres. SE13	78	B6
Alban Cres., Borwd.	22	A1
Albany, The W1	11	F6
Albany, The, Wdf.Grn.	34	F4
Albany Clo. N15	40	H4
Albany Clo. SW14	74	B4
Albany Clo., Bex.	80	C7
Albany Ct. E4	26	B6
Chelwood Clo.		
Albany Ctyd. W1	11	G6
Albany Cres., Edg.	30	A7
Albany Cres., Esher	98	B6
Albany Mans. SW11	66	H7
Albert Bri. Rd.		
Albany Ms. SE5	21	A6
Albany Ms., Kings.T.	82	G6
Albany Pk. Ave., Enf.	25	F1
Albany Pk. Rd., Kings.T.	82	G6
Albany Pas., Rich.	73	J5
Albany Pl. N7	49	G4
Benwell Rd.		
Albany Rd., Brent.	64	H6
Albany Rd. E10	42	A7
Albany Rd. E12	52	A4
Albany Rd. E17	41	H6
Albany Rd. N4	40	F6
Albany Rd. N18	33	F5
Albany Rd. SE5	21	B6
Albany Rd. SE5	68	A6
Albany Rd. SW19	84	E5
Albany Rd. W13	55	F7
Albany Rd., Belv.	71	F6
Albany Rd., Bex.	80	G6
Albany Rd., Brent.	64	G6
Albany Rd., Chis.	88	E5
Albany Rd., N.Mal.	92	D4
Albany Rd., Rich.	73	J5
Albert Rd.		
Albany Rd., Rom.	44	F6
Albany St. NW1	7	D1
Albany St. NW1	58	B2
Albany Vw., Buck.H.	34	G1
Albatross St. SE18	70	H7
Albatross Way SE16	68	G2
Needleman St.		
Albemarle SW19	84	A2
Albemarle App., Ilf.	43	E6
Albemarle Gdns., Ilf.	43	E6
Albemarle Gdns., N.Mal.	92	D4
Albemarle Pk., Stan.	29	F5
Albemarle Rd., Barn.	23	H7
Albemarle Rd., Beck.	96	B1
Albemarle St. W1	11	F6
Albemarle St. W1	58	B7
Albemarle Way EC1	8	G5
Albermarle Ave., Twick.	81	F1
Alberon Gdns. NW11	39	C4
Albert Ave. E4	34	A4
Albert Ave. SW8	67	F7
Albert Bri. SW3	18	H6
Albert Bri. SW3	66	H6
Albert Bri. SW11	18	H7
Albert Bri. SW11	66	H7
Albert Bri. Rd. SW11	18	H7
Albert Bri. Rd. SW11	66	H7
Albert Carr Gdns. SW16	85	E5
Albert Clo. E9	59	E1
Northiam St.		
Albert Clo. N22	40	D1
Albert Ct. SW7	14	E4
Albert Ct. SW7	66	G2
Albert Cres. E4	34	A4
Albert Dr. SW19	84	B2
Albert Embk. SE1	20	B4
Albert Embk. SE1	67	E5
Albert Gdns. E1	59	G6
Albert Gro. SW20	93	A1
Albert Hall Mans. SW7	14	E4
Albert Mans. SW11	75	J1
Albert Bri. Rd.		
Albert Ms. W8	14	C5
Albert Pl. N3	39	D1
Albert Pl. N17	41	C3
High Rd.		
Albert Pl. W8	14	B4
Albert Pl. W8	66	E2
Albert Rd. E10	51	C2
Albert Rd. E16	70	B3
Albert Rd. E17	42	A5
Albert Rd. E18	42	H3
Albert Rd. N4	49	F1
Albert Rd. N15	41	B6
Albert Rd. N22	40	C1
Albert Rd. NW4	39	A4
Albert Rd. NW6	57	C2
Albert Rd. NW7	30	F5
Albert Rd. SE9	88	B3
Albert Rd. SE20	86	G6
Albert Rd. SE25	95	D4
Albert Rd. W5	55	E4
Albert Rd., Barn.	23	G4
Albert Rd., Belv.	71	F5
Albert Rd., Bex.	80	G6
Albert Rd., Brom.	97	A5
Albert Rd., Buck.H.	35	A2
Albert Rd., Dag.	53	G1
Albert Rd., Hmptn.	81	J5
Albert Rd., Har.	36	J3
Albert Rd., Houns.	72	G4
Albert Rd., Ilf.	52	E3
Albert Rd., Kings.T.	91	J2
Albert Rd., Mitch.	93	J3
Albert Rd., N.Mal.	92	F4
Albert Rd., Rich.	73	H5
Albert Rd., Sthl.	63	D3
Albert Rd., Sutt.	100	G5
Albert Rd., Tedd.	82	C6
Albert Rd., Twick.	82	C1
Albert Rd. Est., Belv.	71	F5
Albert Sq. E15	51	E5
Albert Sq. SW8	67	F7
Albert St. N12	31	F5
Albert St. NW1	58	B1
Albert Ter. NW1	58	A1
Albert Ter. NW10	56	D1
Albert Ter., Buck.H.	35	A2
Albert Ter. Ms. NW1	58	A1
Regents Pk. Rd.		
Albert Wk. E16	70	D2
Pier Rd.		
Alberta Ave., Sutt.	100	B4
Alberta Est. SE17	20	H3
Alberta Est. SE17	67	H6
Alberta Rd., Enf.	25	D6
Alberta Rd., Erith	80	J1
Alberta St. SE17	20	G3
Alberta St. SE17	67	H5
Albion Ave. N10	40	A1
Albion Ave. SW8	76	D2
Albion Clo. W2	10	H5
Albion Dr. E8	50	C7
Albion Est. SE16	68	F2
Albion Gdns. W6	65	H4
Albion Gro. N16	50	B4
Albion Hill, Loug.	26	J5
Albion Ms. N1	49	G7
Albion Ms. NW6	48	C7
Kilburn High Rd.		
Albion Ms. W2	10	H5
Albion Ms. W2	57	H6
Albion Pk., Loug.	27	A5
Albion Pl. EC1	12	G1
Albion Pl. EC1	58	H5
Albion Pl. EC2	13	C2
Albion Rd. E17	42	C3
Albion Rd. N16	50	A4
Albion Rd. N17	41	D2
Albion Rd., Bexh.	80	F4
Albion Rd., Houns.	72	G4
Albion Rd., Kings.T.	92	C1
Albion Rd., Sutt.	100	G6
Albion Rd., Twick.	82	B1
Albion Sq. E8	50	C7
Albion St. SE16	68	F2
Albion St. W2	10	H4
Albion St. W2	57	H6
Albion St., Croy.	101	H1
Albion Ter. E8	50	C7
Albion Vill. Rd. SE26	86	F3
Albion Way EC1	12	J2
Albion Way SE13	78	C4
Albion Way, Wem.	47	B3
North End Rd.		
Albrighton Rd. SE22	77	B3
Albuhera Clo., Enf.	24	G1
Albury Ave., Bexh.	80	E2
Albury Ave., Islw.	64	C7
Albury Clo., Hmptn.	81	G6
Albury Dr., Pnr.	36	C1
Albury Ms. E12	51	J1
Albury Rd., Chess.	98	H5
Albury St. SE8	69	A6
Albyfield, Brom.	97	C3
Albyn Rd. SE8	78	A1
Alcester Cres. E5	50	E2
Alcester Rd., Wall.	101	B4
Alcock Clo., Wall.	101	D7
Alcock Rd., Houns.	63	D7
Alconbury Rd. E5	50	D2
Alcorn Clo., Surb.	100	D2
Alcott Clo. W7	55	C5
Westcott Cres.		
Alcuin Ct., Stan.	29	F6
Aldborough Rd., Dag.	53	J6
Aldborough Rd. N., Ilf.	43	J5
Aldborough Rd. S., Ilf.	52	H1
Aldbourne Rd. W12	65	F1
Aldbridge St. SE17	21	E3
Aldbridge St. SE17	68	B5
Aldburgh Ms. W1	11	C3
Aldbury Ave., Wem.	47	B7
Aldbury Ms. N9	25	A7
Aldebert Ter. SW8	67	E7
Aldeburgh Clo. E5	50	E2
Southwold Rd.		
Aldeburgh Pl., Wdf.Grn.	34	G4
Aldeburgh St. SE10	69	G5
Alden Ave. E15	60	F4
Aldenham St. NW1	7	D1
Aldensley Rd. W6	65	H3
Alder Clo. SE15	21	G6
Alder Clo. SE15	68	C6
Alder Gro. NW2	47	G2
Alder Ms. N19	49	C2
Bredgar Rd.		
Alder Rd. SW14	74	D3
Alder Rd., Sid.	88	J3
Alderbrook Rd. SW12	76	B6
Alderbury Rd. SW13	65	G6
Aldergrove Gdns., Houns.	72	E2
Bath Rd.		
Alderholt Way SE15	21	E7
Alderman Ave., Bark.	62	A3
Alderman Judge Mall, Kings.T.	91	H2
Eden St.		
Aldermanbury EC2	13	A3
Aldermanbury EC2	58	J6
Aldermanbury Sq. EC2	13	A2
Aldermans Hill N13	32	E4
Alderman's Wk. EC2	13	D2
Aldermary Rd., Brom.	96	G1
Aldermoor Rd. SE6	86	J3
Alderney Ave., Houns.	63	H7
Alderney Gdns., Nthlt.	45	F7

Alderney Rd. E1 59 G4
Alderney St. SW1 19 E3
Alderney St. SW1 67 B4
Alders, The N21 24 G6
Alders, The, Felt. 81 E4
Alders, The, Houns. 63 F6
Alders, The, W.Wick. 103 H3
Alders Ave., Wdf.Grn. 34 E6
Alders Clo. E11 51 H2
Aldersbrook Rd.
Alders Clo. W5 64 G3
Alders Clo., Edg. 30 C5
Alders Gro., E.Mol. 90 H4
Esher Rd.
Alders Rd., Edg. 30 C5
Aldersbrook Ave., 25 B2
Enf.
Aldersbrook Dr., 82 J6
Kings.T.
Aldersbrook La. E12 52 C3
Aldersbrook Rd. E11 51 H2
Aldersbrook Rd. E12 51 H2
Aldersey Gdns., 52 G6
Bark.
Aldersford Clo. SE4 77 G5
Aldersgate St. EC1 12 J1
Aldersgate St. EC1 58 J5
Aldersgrove Ave. 87 J3
SE9
Aldershot Rd. NW6 57 C1
Aldersmead Ave., 95 G6
Croy.
Aldersmead Rd., 86 H7
Beck.
Alderson St. W10 57 B4
Kensal Rd.
Alderton Clo. NW10 47 D3
Alderton Clo., Loug. 27 D4
Alderton Cres. NW4 38 H5
Alderton Hall La., 27 D4
Loug.
Alderton Hill, Loug. 27 B5
Alderton Ri., Loug. 27 D4
Alderton Rd. SE24 76 J3
Alderton Rd., Croy. 95 C7
Alderton Way NW4 38 H5
Alderton Way, Loug. 27 C5
Alderville Rd. SW6 75 C2
Alderwick Dr., 73 A3
Houns.
Alderwood Rd. SE9 79 G6
Aldford St. W1 15 B1
Aldford St. W1 67 A1
Aldgate EC3 13 F4
Aldgate EC3 59 B6
Aldgate Ave. E1 13 F4
Aldgate High St. EC3 13 F4
Aldgate High St. EC3 59 C6
Aldine Ct. W12 65 J1
Aldine Pl.
Aldine Pl. W12 65 J1
Uxbridge Rd.
Aldine St. W12 65 J1
Aldington Clo., Dag. 44 C7
Aldington Rd. SE18 70 A3
Aldis Ms. SW17 84 H5
Aldis St. SW17
Aldis St. SW17 84 H5
Aldred Rd. NW6 48 D5
Aldren Rd. SW17 84 F3
Aldrich Ter. SW18 84 F2
Lidiard Rd.
Aldriche Way E4 34 C6
Aldridge Ave., Edg. 30 B3
Aldridge Ave., Ruis. 45 D2
Aldridge Ave., Stan. 37 H1
Aldridge Ri., N.Mal. 92 E7
Aldridge Rd. Vill. 55 C7
W11
Aldridge Wk. N14 24 E7
Aldrington Rd. SW16 85 C4
Aldsworth Clo. W9 6 A6
Aldsworth Clo. W9 57 E4
Aldwick Clo. SE9 88 G3
Aldwick Rd., Croy. 101 F3
Aldworth Gro. SE13 78 C6
Aldworth Rd. E15 51 E7
Aldwych WC2 12 C5
Aldwych WC2 58 F7
Aldwych Ave., Ilf. 43 F4
Alers Rd., Bexh. 80 D5
Aleston Beck Rd. E16 61 A6
Fulmer Rd.
Alexa Ct. W8 66 D4
Lexham Gdns.
Alexander Ave. 47 H7
NW10
Alexander Clo., Barn. 23 G4
Alexander Clo., 103 G1
Brom.
Alexander Clo., Sid. 79 H6
Alexander Clo., 82 C2
Twick.

Alexander Ms. W2 10 A3
Alexander Pl. SW7 18 G1
Alexander Pl. SW7 66 H4
Alexander Rd. N19 49 E3
Alexander Rd., Bexh. 80 D2
Alexander Rd., Chis. 88 E5
Alexander Sq. SW7 18 G1
Alexander Sq. SW3 66 H4
Alexander St. W2 57 D6
Alexandra Ave. N22 40 D1
Victoria Rd.
Alexandra Ave. SW11 76 A1
Alexandra Ave. W4 65 D7
Alexandra Ave., Har. 45 F1
Alexandra Ave., Sthl. 54 F7
Alexandra Ave., 100 D3
Sutt.
Alexandra Clo., Har. 45 G3
Alexandra Cotts. 77 J1
SE14
Alexandra Ct. N14 24 C5
Alexandra Ct., Wem. 46 J4
Alexandra Cres., 87 F6
Brom.
Alexandra Dr. SE19 86 B5
Alexandra Dr., Surb. 92 A7
Alexandra Est. NW8 57 E1
Alexandra Gdns. N10 40 B4
Alexandra Gdns. W4 65 E7
Alexandra Gdns., 72 H2
Houns.
Alexandra Gro. N4 49 H1
Alexandra Gro. N12 31 E5
Alexandra Ms. N2 39 J3
Fortis Grn.
Alexandra Pk. Rd. 40 B2
N10
Alexandra Pk. Rd. 40 C1
N22
Alexandra Pl. NW8 57 F1
Alexandra Pl. SE25 95 A5
Alexandra Pl., Croy. 102 B1
Alexandra Rd.
Alexandra Rd. E6 61 D3
Alexandra Rd. E10 51 C3
Alexandra Rd. E17 41 J6
Alexandra Rd. E18 42 H3
Alexandra Rd. N8 40 G3
Alexandra Rd. N9 25 E7
Alexandra Rd. N10 40 B1
Alexandra Rd. N15 41 A5
Alexandra Rd. NW4 39 A4
Alexandra Rd. NW8 48 F7
Alexandra Rd. SE26 86 G6
Alexandra Rd. SW14 74 D3
Alexandra Rd. SW19 84 C6
Alexandra Rd. W4 65 D2
Alexandra Rd., 64 G6
Brent.
Alexandra Rd., Croy. 102 B1
Alexandra Rd., Enf. 25 G4
Alexandra Rd., 72 H2
Houns.
Alexandra Rd., 83 A7
Kings.T.
Alexandra Rd., Mitch. 84 H7
Alexandra Rd., Rich. 73 J2
Alexandra Rd. 44 D6
(Chadwell Heath),
Rom.
Alexandra Rd., T.Ditt. 91 C5
Alexandra Rd., Twick. 73 F6
Alexandra Sq., Mord. 93 D5
Alexandra St. E16 60 G5
Alexandra St. SE14 68 H7
Alexandra Wk. SE19 86 B5
Alexandria Rd. W13 55 D7
Alexis St. SE16 21 J1
Alexis St. SE16 68 D4
Alfearn Rd. E5 50 F4
Alford Grn., Croy. 103 D6
Alford Pl. N1 12 A2
Alford Rd. SW8 76 D1
Alford Rd., Erith 71 J5
Alfoxton Ave. N15 40 H4
Alfred Gdns., Sthl. 54 C7
Alfred Ms. W1 11 H1
Alfred Ms. W1 58 D5
Alfred Pl. WC1 11 H1
Alfred Pl. WC1 58 D5
Alfred Prior Ho. E12 52 D5
Alfred Rd. E15 51 F5
Alfred Rd. SE25 95 D5
Alfred Rd. W2 57 D5
Alfred Rd. W3 65 C1
Alfred Rd., Belv. 71 F5
Alfred Rd., Buck.H. 35 A2
Alfred Rd., Felt. 81 C2
Alfred Rd., Kings.T. 91 H3
Alfred Rd., Sutt. 100 F5
Alfred St. E3 59 J3
Alfred St. E16 60 F7

Alfreda St. SW11 76 B1
Alfreds Gdns., Bark. 61 H2
Alfreds Way, Bark. 61 F3
Alfreds Way Ind. Est., 62 A1
Bark.
Alfreton Clo. SW19 84 A3
Alfriston Ave., Croy. 94 E7
Alfriston Ave., Har. 36 G6
Alfriston Clo., Surb. 91 J5
Alfriston Rd. SW11 76 H5
Algar Clo., Islw. 73 D3
Algar Rd.
Algar Clo., Stan. 29 C5
Algar Rd., Islw. 73 D3
Algarve Rd. SW18 84 E1
Algernon Rd. NW4 38 G6
Algernon Rd. NW6 57 D1
Algernon Rd. SE13 78 B3
Algers Clo., Loug. 27 A5
Algers Mead, Loug. 27 A5
Algers Rd., Loug. 27 A5
Algiers Rd. SE13 78 A4
Alibon Gdns., Dag. 53 G5
Alibon Rd., Dag. 53 F5
Alice Gilliatt Ct. W14 66 C5
Alice Ms., Tedd. 82 C5
Luther Rd.
Alice St. SE1 17 D6
Alice St. SE1 68 B3
Alice Way, Houns. 72 H4
Alicia Ave., Har. 37 E4
Alicia Clo., Har. 37 F4
Alicia Gdns., Har. 37 E4
Alie St. E1 13 G4
Alie St. E1 59 C6
Alington Cres. NW9 47 C1
Alison Clo. E6 61 D6
Alison Clo., Croy. 102 G1
Shirley Oaks Rd.
Aliwal Rd. SW11 75 H4
Alkerden Rd. W4 65 E5
Alkham Rd. N16 50 C1
All Hallows Rd. N17 41 B1
All Saints Clo. N9 33 D2
All Saints Dr. SE3 78 E2
All Saints Ms., Stan. 29 B6
Uxbridge Rd.
All Saints Pas. SW18 75 E5
Wandsworth High St.
All Saints Rd. SW19 84 F7
All Saints Rd. W3 65 C3
All Saints Rd. W11 57 C6
All Saints Rd., Sutt. 100 E3
All Saints St. N1 8 C1
All Saints St. N1 58 D2
All Saints Twr. E10 42 B7
All Souls Ave. NW10 56 H2
All Souls Pl. W1 11 E2
Allan Barclay Clo. 41 C6
N15
High Rd.
Allan Way W3 56 C5
Allandale Ave. N3 39 B3
Allard Cres. 28 J1
(Bushey), Wat.
Allardyce St. SW4 76 F4
Allbrook Clo., Tedd. 82 B5
Allcroft Rd. NW5 49 A5
Allen Clo., Sun. 90 B1
Allen Clo., Mitch. 46 C5
Allen Edwards Dr. 76 E1
SW8
Allen Pl., Twick. 82 D1
Church St.
Allen Rd. E3 59 J1
Allen Rd. N16 50 B4
Allen Rd., Beck. 95 G2
Allen Rd., Croy. 101 F1
Allen Rd., Sun. 90 B1
Allen St. W8 66 D3
Allenby Clo., Grnf. 54 G2
Allenby Rd. SE23 86 H3
Allenby Rd., Sthl. 54 G3
Allendale Ave., Sthl. 54 G6
Allendale Clo. SE5 77 A1
Love Wk.
Allendale Clo. SE26 86 G5
Allendale Rd., Grnf. 46 E6
Allens Rd., Enf. 25 F5
Allensbury Pl. NW1 49 D7
Allenswood Rd. SE9 79 B3
Allerford Ct., Har. 36 H5
Allerford Rd. SE6 87 B3
Allerton Rd. N16 49 J2
Allerton Wk. N7 49 F2
Durham Rd.
Alestree Rd. SW6 66 B7
Alleyn Cres. SE21 86 A2
Alleyn Pk. SE21 86 A2
Alleyn Pk., Sthl. 63 G5
Alleyn Rd. SE21 86 A3

Alleyndale Rd., Dag. 53 C2
Allfarthing La. SW18 75 E6
Allgood Clo., Mord. 93 A6
Allgood St. E2 9 G2
Allgood St. E2 59 C2
Allhallows La. EC4 13 B6
Allhallows Rd. E6 61 B5
Alliance Clo., Wem. 46 G4
Milford Gdns.
Alliance Rd. E13 60 J4
Alliance Rd. SE18 71 A6
Alliance Rd. W3 56 B4
Allied Ind. Est. W3 65 E2
Allied Way W3 65 E2
Larden Rd.
Allingham Clo. W7 55 C7
Allingham St. N1 8 J1
Allingham St. N1 58 J2
Allington Ave. N17 33 B6
Allington Clo., Grnf. 45 J7
Allington Ct. SW19 84 A5
High St.
Allington Ct., Enf. 25 G5
Allington Rd. NW4 38 H5
Allington Rd. W10 57 B2
Allington Rd., Har. 36 J5
Allington Rd., Orp. 104 G2
Allington St. SW1 15 E6
Allington St. SW1 67 B3
Allison Clo. SE10 78 C1
Dartmouth Hill
Allison Gro. SE21 86 B1
Allison Rd. N8 40 G5
Allison Rd. W3 56 C6
Allitsen Rd. NW8 6 G2
Allitsen Rd. NW8 57 H2
Allnutt Way SW4 76 D5
Alloa Rd. SE8 68 H5
Alloa Rd., Ilf. 53 A2
Allonby Gdns., Wem. 46 F1
Windermere Ave.
Alloway Rd. E3 59 H3
Allsop Pl. NW1 7 A6
Allsop Pl. NW1 57 J4
Allum Way N20 31 F1
Allwood Clo. SE26 86 G4
Alma Ave. E4 34 C7
Alma Cres., Sutt. 100 B5
Alma Gro. SE1 21 G2
Alma Gro. SE1 68 C4
Alma Pl. NW10 56 H3
Harrow Rd.
Alma Pl. SE19 86 C7
Church Rd.
Alma Pl., Th.Hth. 94 G5
Alma Rd. N10 32 B7
Alma Rd. SW18 75 F4
Alma Rd., Cars. 100 H5
Alma Rd., Enf. 25 H3
Alma Rd., Esher 98 B1
Alma Rd., Sid. 89 A3
Alma Rd., Sthl. 54 E7
Alma Row, Har. 37 A1
Alma Sq. NW8 6 D3
Alma Sq. NW8 57 F3
Alma St. E15 51 D6
Alma St. NW5 49 B6
Alma Ter. SW18 75 G7
Almack Rd. E5 50 F4
Almeida St. N1 49 H7
Almer Rd. SW20 83 G7
Almeric Rd. SW11 75 J4
Almington St. N4 49 E1
Almond Ave. W5 64 H3
Almond Ave., Cars. 100 J2
Almond Clo. SE15 77 D2
Almond Clo., Brom. 97 D7
Almond Clo., Brent. 64 E7
Almond Rd. N17 33 D7
Almond Rd. SE16 68 E4
Almond Way, Borwd. 22 B4
Almond Way, Brom. 97 D7
Almond Way, Har. 36 H2
Almond Way, Mitch. 94 D5
Almonds Ave., 34 G2
Buck.H.
Almorah Rd. N1 50 A7
Almorah Rd., Houns. 72 D1
Alnwick Gro., Mord. 93 E4
Bordesley Rd.
Alnwick Rd. E16 60 J1
Alnwick Rd. SE12 78 H7
Alperton La., Grnf. 55 G2
Alperton La., Wem. 55 G2
Alperton St. W10 57 B4
Alpha Clo. NW1 6 H4
Alpha Gro. E14 69 A2
Alpha Pl. NW6 57 A2
Alpha Pl. SW3 18 H5
Alpha Pl. SW3 66 H6
Alpha Rd. E4 34 A3
Alpha Rd. N18 33 D6
Alpha Rd. SE14 77 J1

Alpha Rd., Croy. 102 B1
Alpha Rd., Enf. 25 H4
Alpha Rd., Surb. 91 J6
Alpha Rd., Tedd. 82 A5
Alpha St. SE15 77 D2
Alphea Clo. SW19 84 H7
Courtney Rd.
Alpine Ave., Surb. 99 C2
Alpine Clo., Croy. 102 B3
Alpine Copse, Brom. 97 D2
Alpine Rd. SE16 68 F4
Alpine Rd., Walt. 90 A7
Alpine Vw., Sutt. 100 H5
Alpine Wk., Stan. 29 B2
Alpine Way E6 61 D5
Alric Ave. NW10 47 D7
Alric Ave., N.Mal. 92 E3
Alroy Rd. N4 40 G7
Alsace Rd. SE17 21 D3
Alscot Rd. SE1 21 G1
Alscot Rd. SE1 68 C4
Alscot Way SE1 21 F1
Alscot Way SE1 68 C4
Alsike Rd. SE2 71 D3
Alsike Rd., Erith 71 E3
Alsom Ave., Wor.Pk. 99 F4
Alston Clo., Surb. 91 E7
Alston Rd. N18 33 E5
Alston Rd. SW17 84 G4
Alston Rd., Barn. 23 B3
Alt Gro. SW19 84 C7
St. George's Rd.
Altair Clo. N17 33 C6
Altash Way SE9 88 C2
Altenburg Ave. W13 64 E3
Altenburg Gdns. 75 J4
SW11
Altham Rd., Pnr. 28 E7
Althea St. SW6 75 E2
Althorne Gdns. E18 42 F4
Althorne Way, Dag. 53 G2
Althorp Rd. SW17 84 J1
Althorpe Ms. SW11 75 G1
Westbridge Rd.
Althorpe Rd., Har. 36 J5
Altmore Ave. E6 52 C7
Alton Ave., Stan. 29 C7
Alton Clo., Bex. 89 E1
Alton Clo., Islw. 73 C2
Alton Gdns., Beck. 87 A7
Alton Gdns., Twick. 73 A6
Alton Rd. N17 41 A3
Alton Rd. SW15 83 G1
Alton Rd., Croy. 101 G3
Alton Rd., Rich. 73 H4
Alton St. E14 60 B5
Altyre Clo., Beck. 95 J5
Altyre Rd., Croy. 102 A2
Altyre Way, Beck. 95 J6
Alva Way, Wat. 28 D2
Alvanley Gdns. NW6 48 E5
Alverston Gdns. 95 B5
SE25
Alverstone Ave. 84 D2
SW19
Alverstone Ave., 23 H7
Barn.
Alverstone Gdns. 88 F1
SE9
Alverstone Rd. E12 52 D4
Alverstone Rd. NW2 47 J7
Alverstone Rd., 92 F4
N.Mal.
Alverstone Rd., Wem. 46 J1
Alverton St. SE8 68 J5
Alveston Ave., Har. 37 E3
Alvey Est. SE17 21 D2
Alvey St. SE17 21 D3
Alvey St. SE17 68 B5
Alvia Gdns., Sutt. 100 F4
Alvington Cres. E8 50 C5
Alway Ave., Epsom 99 C5
Alwold Cres. SE12 78 H6
Alwyn Ave. W4 65 D5
Alwyn Clo., Croy. 103 B7
Alwyn Gdns. NW4 38 G4
Alwyn Gdns. W3 56 B6
Alwyne La. N1 49 H7
Canonbury Rd.
Alwyne Pl. N1 49 J6
Alwyne Rd. N1 49 J7
Alwyne Rd. SW19 84 C6
Alwyne Rd. W7 55 B7
Alwyne Sq. N1 49 J6
Alwyne Vill. N1 49 H7
Alyth Gdns. NW11 39 D6
Alzette Ho. E2 59 G2
Mace St.
Amalgamated Dr., 64 D6
Brent.
Amanda Clo., Ilf. 35 G6
Amazon St. E1 59 E6
Hessel St.

Ambassador Clo., 72 E2
Houns.
Ambassador Gdns. 61 C5
E6
Ambassador Sq. E14 69 B4
Cahir St.
Ambassador's Ct. 15 G2
SW1
Amber Ave. E17 41 H1
Amer St. E15 51 D6
Salway Rd.
Amberden Ave. N3 39 D3
Ambergate Ct. E5 50 H4
Ambergate St. SE17 20 H3
Ambergate St. SE17 67 H5
Amberley Clo., Orp. 104 J5
Warnford Rd.
Amberley Clo., Pnr. 36 F3
Amberley Ct., Sid. 89 C5
Amberley Gdns., Enf. 25 B7
Amberley Gdns., 99 F4
Epsom
Amberley Gro. SE26 86 E5
Amberley Gro., Croy. 95 C7
Amberley Rd. E10 42 A7
Amberley Rd. N13 32 F2
Amberley Rd. SE2 71 D6
Amberley Rd. W9 57 D5
Amberley Rd., 34 J1
Buck.H.
Amberley Rd., Enf. 25 C7
Amberley Way, 72 C5
Houns.
Amberley Way, Mord. 93 C7
Amberley Way, Rom. 44 H4
Amberwood Ri., 92 E6
N.Mal.
Amblecote Clo. SE12 87 H3
Amblecote Rd. SE12 87 H3
Ambler Rd. N4 49 H3
Ambleside, Brom. 90 D5
Ambleside Ave. 85 D4
SW16
Ambleside Ave., 95 H5
Beck.
Ambleside Clo. E9 50 F5
Churchill Wk.
Ambleside Cres., Enf. 25 G3
Ambleside Gdns., 43 B4
Ilf.
Ambleside Gdns., 100 F6
Sutt.
Ambleside Gdns., 46 G1
Wem.
Ambleside Rd. NW10 47 F7
Ambleside Rd., Bexh. 80 G2
Ambrooke Rd., Belv. 71 G3
Ambrosden Ave. 15 G6
SW1
Ambrosden Ave. 67 C3
SW1
Ambrose Ave. NW11 39 B7
Ambrose Clo. E6 61 B5
Lovage App.
Ambrose Clo., Orp. 104 J3
Stapleton Rd.
Ambrose Ms. SW11 75 J2
Abercrombie St.
Ambrose St. SE16 68 E4
Ambrose Wk. E3 60 A2
Malmesbury St.
Amelia St. SE17 20 J3
Amelia St. SE17 67 H5
Amen Cor. EC4 12 H4
Amen Cor. SW17 84 J6
Amen Ct. EC4 12 H3
America Sq. EC3 13 F5
America St. SE1 16 J2
Amerland Rd. SW18 75 C5
Amersham Ave. N18 33 A6
Amersham Gro. SE14 68 J7
Amersham Rd. SE14 77 J1
Amersham Rd., Croy. 94 J6
Amersham Vale SE14 68 J7
Amery Gdns. NW10 56 H1
Amery Rd., Har. 46 D2
Amesbury Ave. SW2 85 E2
Amesbury Clo., 99 J1
Wor.Pk.
Amesbury Dr. E4 26 B6
Amesbury Rd., Brom. 97 A3
Amesbury Rd., Dag. 53 D7
Amesbury Rd., Felt. 81 D2
Amethyst Rd. E15 51 D4
Amherst Ave. W13 55 F6
Amherst Dr., Orp. 93 H4
Amherst Rd. W13 55 F6
Amhurst Gdns., Islw. 73 C1
Amhurst Pk. N16 41 A7
Amhurst Pas. E8 50 D5
Amhurst Rd. E8 50 E5
Amhurst Rd. N16 50 C4
Amhurst Ter. E8 50 D4

Amhurst Wk. SE28 71 A1
Pitfield Cres.
Amidas Gdns., Dag. 53 B4
Amiel St. E1 59 F4
Amies St. SW11 75 J3
Amina Way SE16 17 H6
Amis Ave., Epsom 99 A6
Amity Gro. SW20 92 J1
Amity Rd. E15 60 F1
Ammanford Gdn. 38 E6
NW9
Ruthin Clo.
Amner Rd. SW11 76 A6
Amoco Ho. W5 55 H3
Amor Rd. W6 65 J3
Amott Rd. SE15 77 D3
Amoy Pl. E14 60 A6
Ampere Way, Croy. 94 F7
Ampleforth Rd. SE2 71 B2
Ampthill Sq. Est. NW1 7 G2
Ampton Pl. WC1 8 C4
Ampton St. WC1 8 F3
Ampton St. WC1 8 C4
Amroth Clo. SE23 86 F1
Amroth Clo. SE23 69 C3
Amsterdam Rd. E14 69 C3
Amwell Clo., Enf. 25 A6
Amwell Ct. Est. N4 49 J1
Amwell St. EC1 8 E3
Amwell St. EC1 58 G3
Amyand Cotts., 73 E6
Twick.
Amyand Pk. Rd.
Amyand La., Twick. 73 E7
Marble Hill Gdns.
Amyand Pk. Gdns., 73 E7
Twick.
Amyand Pk. Rd.
Amyand Pk. Rd., 73 D7
Twick.
Amyruth Rd. SE4 78 A5
Anatola Rd. N19 49 B2
Dartmouth Pk. Hill
Ancaster Cres., 92 G6
N.Mal.
Ancaster Rd., Beck. 95 G3
Ancaster St. SE18 70 H7
Anchor & Hope La. 69 J4
SE7
Anchor Ms. SW12 76 B6
Hazelbourne Rd.
Anchor St. SE16 68 E4
Anchor Yd. EC1 9 A5
Anchorage Clo. 84 D5
SW19
Ancill Clo. W6 66 B6
Ancona Rd. NW10 56 G2
Ancona Rd. SE18 70 G5
Andace Pk. Gdns., 96 J1
Brom.
Andalus Rd. SW9 76 E3
Ander Clo., Wem. 46 G4
Anderson Clo. W3 56 D6
Anderson Ho., Bark. 61 G2
The Coverdales
Anderson Pl., Houns. 72 H4
Anderson Rd. E9 50 G6
Anderson Rd., 43 A3
Wdf.Grn.
Anderson St. SW3 18 J3
Anderson St. SW3 66 H5
Anderson Way, Belv. 71 H2
Anderton Clo. SE5 77 A3
Andover Clo., Grnf. 54 H4
Ruislip Rd.
Andover Pl. NW6 6 A1
Andover Rd. N7 49 F2
Andover Rd., Orp. 100 H4
Andover Rd., Twick. 82 A1
Andre St. E8 50 D5
Andrew Borde St. 11 J3
WC2
Andrew Clo., Ilf. 35 G6
Andrew Pl. SW8 76 D1
Cowthorpe Rd.
Andrew St. E14 60 C6
Andrews Clo. E6 61 B6
Linton Gdns.
Andrews Clo., 34 J2
Buck.H.
Andrews Clo., Har. 37 A7
Bessborough Rd.
Andrews Clo., 99 J2
Wor.Pk.
Andrews Crosse WC2 12 E4
Andrews Pl. SE9 79 E6
Andrew's Rd. E8 59 E1
Andrews Wk. SE17 20 H6
Andwell Clo. SE2 71 B2
Anerley Gro. SE19 86 C6
Anerley Hill SE19 86 C6
Anerley Pk. SE20 86 D7

Anerley Pk. Rd. SE20 86 E7
Anerley Rd. SE19 86 D7
Anerley Rd. SE20 86 D7
Anerley Sta. Rd. 95 E1
SE20
Anerley St. SW11 75 J2
Anerley Vale SE19 86 C7
Anfield Clo. SW12 76 C7
Belthorn Cres.
Angel All. E1 13 G3
Angel Clo. N18 33 C5
Angel Ct. EC2 13 C3
Angel Ct. SW1 15 G2
Angel Ct. SW17 84 J4
Angel Hill, Sutt. 100 E3
Sutton Common Rd.
Angel Hill Dr., Sutt. 100 E3
Angel La. E15 51 D6
Angel Ms. N1 8 F2
Angel Ms. N1 58 G2
Angel Pas. EC4 13 B6
Angel Pl. N18 33 D5
Angel Clo.
Angel Pl. SE1 17 B3
Angel Rd. N18 33 D5
Angel Rd., Har. 37 B6
Angel Rd., T.Ditt. 91 D7
Angel Rd. Wks. N18 33 F5
Angel St. EC1 12 J3
Angel St. EC1 58 J6
Angel Wk. W6 65 J5
Angelfield, Houns. 72 H4
Angelica Gdns., 102 G1
Croy.
Angell Pk. Gdns. 76 G3
SW9
Angell Rd. SW9 76 G3
Angerstein La. SE3 78 F1
Angle Grn., Dag. 53 C1
Burnside Rd.
Anglers Clo., Rich. 82 F4
Locksmeade Rd.
Angler's La. NW5 49 B6
Angles Rd. SW16 85 E4
Anglesea Ave. SE18 70 E4
Anglesea Rd. SE18 70 E4
Anglesea Rd., 91 G4
Kings.T.
Anglesey Ct. Rd., 101 A6
Cars.
Anglesey Gdns., 101 A6
Cars.
Anglesey Rd., Enf. 25 H4
Anglesey Rd., Wat. 28 C5
Anglesmede Cres., 36 E3
Pnr.
Anglesmede Way, 36 E3
Pnr.
Anglia Ho. E14 59 H6
Anglo Rd. E3 59 J2
Angrave Ct. E8 59 C1
Angrave Pas. E8 59 C1
Haggerston Rd.
Angus Clo., Chess. 99 A5
Angus Dr., Ruis. 45 C4
Angus Gdns. NW9 38 D1
Angus Rd. E13 60 J3
Angus St. SE14 68 H7
Anhalt Rd. SW11 18 H7
Anhalt Rd. SW11 66 H7
Ankerdine Cres. 79 E1
Anlaby Rd., Tedd. 82 B5
Anley Rd. W14 66 A2
Anmersh Gro., Stan. 37 G1
Ann La. SW10 18 E7
Ann La. SW10 66 G7
Ann St. SE18 70 F5
Anna Clo. E8 59 C1
Anna Neagle Clo. E7 51 G4
Dames Rd.
Annabel Clo. E14 60 B6
Annandale Rd. SE10 69 F5
Annandale Rd. W4 65 E5
Annandale Rd., 102 G5
Croy.
Annandale Rd., Sid. 79 H7
Anne Boleyn's Wk., 82 H5
Kings.T.
Anne Boleyn's Wk., 100 A7
Sutt.
Anne Case Ms., 92 D3
N.Mal.
Sycamore Gro.
Anne St. E13 60 G4
Anne Way, Ilf. 35 F6
Anne Way, W.Mol. 90 H4
Annesley Ave. NW9 38 D3
Annesley Clo. NW10 47 E3
Annesley Dr., Croy. 102 J4
Annesley Rd. SE3 78 H1
Annesley Wk. N19 49 C2
Macdonald Rd.
Annett Rd., Walt. 90 A7

Annette Clo., Har. 37 B2
Spencer Rd.
Annette Cres. N1 49 J7
Essex Rd.
Annette Rd. N7 49 F3
Annie Besant Clo. E3 59 J1
Anning St. EC2 9 E5
Annington Rd. N2 39 J3
Annis Rd. E9 50 H6
Ann's Clo. SW1 15 A4
Ann's Pl. E1 13 F2
Annsworthy Ave., 95 A3
Th.Hth.
Grange Pk. Rd.
Ansdell Rd. SE15 77 F2
Ansdell St. W8 14 B5
Ansdell St. SE18 66 E3
Ansdell Ter. W8 14 B5
Ansell Gro., Cars. 101 A1
Ansell Rd. SW17 84 H3
Anselm Clo., Croy. 102 C3
Park Hill Ri.
Anselm Rd., SW6 66 D6
Anselm Rd., Pnr. 28 F7
Ansford Rd., Brom. 87 C5
Ansleigh Pl. W11 57 A7
Anson Clo., Rom. 44 H2
Anson Rd. N7 49 C4
Anson Rd. NW2 47 H5
Anstey Rd. SE15 77 D3
Anstey Wk. N8 40 H4
Anstice Clo. W4 65 E7
Anstridge Path SE9 79 G6
Anstridge Rd.
Anstridge Rd. SE9 79 G6
Antelope Rd. SE18 70 C3
Anthony Clo. NW7 30 E4
Anthony Clo., Wat. 28 C1
Anthony Rd. SE25 95 D6
Anthony Rd., Grnf. 55 B2
Anthony Rd., Well. 80 A1
Anthony St. E1 59 E6
Antigua Clo. SE19 86 A5
Salters Hill
Antill Rd. E3 59 H3
Antill Rd. N15 41 D4
Antill Ter. E1 59 G6
Antlers Hill E4 26 B4
Anton Cres., Sutt. 100 D3
Anton St. E8 50 D5
Antoneys Clo., Pnr. 36 D2
Antrim Gro. NW3 48 J6
Antrim Mans. NW3 48 J6
Antrim Rd.
Antrim Rd. NW3 48 J6
Antrobus Clo., Sutt. 100 C5
Antrobus Rd. W4 65 C4
Anvil Rd., Sun. 90 A4
Anworth Clo., 34 H6
Wdf.Grn.
Apex Clo., Beck. 96 B1
Apex Twr., N.Mal. 92 E3
Aplin Way, Islw. 73 B1
Apollo Ave., Brom. 96 H1
Rodway Rd.
Apollo Clo., Nthwd. 28 A5
Apollo Pl. SW10 18 E7
Apollo Way SE28 70 G3
Broadwater Rd.
Apothecary St. EC4 12 G4
Appach Rd. SW2 76 G5
Apple Garth, Brent. 64 G4
Apple Gro., Chess. 98 H4
Apple Gro., Enf. 25 B3
Apple Mkt., Kings.T. 91 G2
Eden St.
Apple Tree Yd. SW1 15 G1
Appleby Clo. E4 34 B6
Appleby Clo. N15 41 A5
Appleby Clo., Twick. 82 A2
Appleby Rd. E8 50 D7
Appleby Rd. E16 60 F6
Appleby St. E2 9 F2
Appleby St. E2 59 C2
Appledore Ave., 80 J1
Bexh.
Appledore Ave., Ruis. 45 C3
Appledore Clo. SW17 84 J2
Appledore Clo., 96 F5
Brom.
Appledore Clo., Edg. 38 A1
Appledore Cres., 88 H3
Sid.
Appleford Rd. W10 57 B4
Applegarth, Croy. 103 B7
Applegarth, Esher 98 C5
Applegarth Dr., Ilf. 43 J4
Applegarth Rd. SE28 71 B1
Applegarth Rd. W14 66 A3
Appleton Gdns., 92 G6
N.Mal.
Appleton Rd. SE9 79 B3
Appleton Rd., Loug. 27 E3

Appleton Sq., Mitch. 93 H1
Appletree Gdns., 23 H4
Barn.
Applewood Clo. N20 31 H1
Applewood Clo. NW2 47 H3
Appold St. EC2 9 D1
Appold St. EC2 59 B5
Apprentice Way E5 50 E1
Clarence Rd.
Approach, The NW4 39 A5
Approach, The W3 56 D6
Approach, The, Enf. 25 E2
Approach, The, Orp. 104 J2
Approach Rd. E2 59 F2
Approach Rd. SW20 92 J2
Approach Rd., Barn. 23 F4
Approach Rd., W.Mol. 90 G5
Aprey Gdns. NW4 38 J4
April Clo. W7 55 B7
April Clo., Felt. 81 H3
April Clo., Orp. 104 J5
Briarswood Way
April Glen SE23 86 C3
April St. E8 50 C4
Apsley Clo., Har. 36 J5
Apsley Rd. SE25 95 E4
Apsley Rd., N.Mal. 92 C3
Apsley Way W1 15 C3
Aquarius Way, 28 A5
Nthwd.
Aquila St. NW8 6 F1
Aquila St. NW8 57 G2
Aquinas St. SE1 16 F2
Arabella Dr. SW15 74 E4
Arabia Clo. E4 26 C7
Arabin Rd. SE4 77 H4
Aragon Ave., T.Ditt. 91 C5
Aragon Clo., Brom. 104 C1
Seymour Dr.
Aragon Dr., Ilf. 35 F7
Aragon Dr., Ruis. 45 D1
Aragon Ms. E1 17 H1
Aragon Rd., Kings.T. 82 H5
Aragon Rd., Mord. 93 A6
Aran Dr., Stan. 29 F4
Arandora Cres., Rom. 44 B7
Arbery Rd. E3 59 H3
Arbor Clo., Beck. 96 B2
Arbor Rd. E4 34 D3
Arbour Rd., Enf. 25 G4
Arbour Sq. E1 59 G6
Arbroath Grn., Wat. 28 A3
Arbroath Rd. SE9 79 B3
Arbury Ter. SE26 86 E3
Oaksford Ave.
Arbuthnot La., Bex. 80 E6
Arbuthnot Rd. SE14 77 G2
Arbutus St. E8 59 C1
Arcade, The EC2 13 D2
Arcadia Ave. N3 39 D1
Arcadia St. E14 60 A6
Arcadian Ave., Bex. 80 E6
Arcadian Clo., Bex. 80 E6
Arcadian Gdns. N22 32 F7
Arcadian Rd., Bex. 80 E6
Arch St. SE1 16 J6
Arch St. SE1 67 J3
Archbishops Pl. SW2 76 F6
Archdale Rd. SE22 77 C5
Archel Rd. W14 66 D6
Archer Clo., Kings.T. 82 H7
Archer Ho. SW11 75 G1
Vicarage Cres.
Archer St. SE25 95 E4
Archer St. W1 11 H5
Archers Dr., Enf. 25 F2
Archers Wk. SE15 77 C1
Exeter Rd.
Archery Clo. W2 10 H4
Archery Clo. W2 57 H6
Archery Clo., Har. 37 C3
Archery Rd. SE9 79 C5
Arches, The SW6 75 C2
Munster Rd.
Arches, The WC2 16 B1
Arches, The, Har. 45 H2
Archibald Ms. W1 11 D6
Archibald Ms. W1 58 G2
Archibald Rd. N7 49 D4
Archibald St. E3 60 A3
Archway Clo. N19 49 C2
St. Johns Way
Archway Clo. SW19 84 E4
Archway Clo., Wall. 101 D3
Archway Mall N19 49 C2
Magdala Ave.
Archway Rd. N6 39 J5
Archway Rd. N19 49 C1
Archway St. SW13 74 E3
Arcola St. E8 50 C5
Arctic St. NW5 49 A5
Gillies St.

Arcus Rd., Brom. 87 E6
Ardbeg Rd. SE24 77 A5
Arden Clo., Har. 46 A3
Arden Ct. Gdns. N2 39 G6
Arden Cres. E14 69 A4
Arden Cres., Dag. 53 C7
Arden Est. N1 9 D2
Arden Est. N1 59 B2
Arden Gro., Orp. 104 F4
Arden Mhor, Pnr. 36 B4
Arden Rd. N3 39 B3
Arden Rd. W13 55 F7
Ardent Clo. SE25 95 B3
Ardfern Ave. SW16 94 G3
Ardfillan Rd. SE6 87 D1
Ardgowan Rd. SE6 78 E7
Ardilaun Rd. N5 49 J4
Ardleigh Gdns., Sutt. 93 D7
Ardleigh Ho., Bark. 61 F1
St. Ann's
Ardleigh Ms., Ilf. 52 E3
Bengal Rd.
Ardleigh Rd. E17 41 J1
Ardleigh Rd. N1 50 B6
Ardleigh Ter. E17 41 J1
Ardley Clo. NW10 47 E3
Ardley Clo. SE6 86 H3
Ardlui Rd. SE27 85 J2
Ardmay Gdns., Surb. 91 H5
Ardmere Rd. SE13 78 D6
Ardmore La., Buck.H. 26 H7
Ardoch Rd. SE6 87 D2
Ardra Rd. N9 33 G3
Ardrossan Gdns., 99 G3
Wor.Pk.
Ardshiel Clo. SW15 75 A3
Bemish Rd.
Ardwell Ave., Ilf. 43 F5
Ardwell Rd. SW2 85 E2
Ardwick Rd. NW2 48 D4
Argall Ave. E10 41 G7
Argent St. SE1 16 H3
Argon Ms. SW6 66 D7
Argus Clo., Rom. 44 H1
Argus Way W3 65 B3
Argus Way, Nthlt. 54 E3
Argyle Ave., Houns. 72 G6
Argyle Clo. W13 55 D4
Argyle Pas. N17 41 C1
Argyle Rd.
Argyle Pl. W6 65 H4
Argyle Rd. E1 59 G4
Argyle Rd. E15 51 E5
Argyle Rd. E16 60 H6
Argyle Rd. N12 31 D5
Argyle Rd. N17 41 D1
Argyle Rd. N18 33 D4
Argyle Rd. W13 55 D5
Argyle Rd., Barn. 22 J4
Argyle Rd., Grnf. 55 C3
Argyle Rd., Har. 36 H6
Argyle Rd., Houns. 72 H5
Argyle Rd., Ilf. 52 D2
Argyle Rd., Tedd. 82 B5
Argyle Sq. WC1 8 B3
Argyle St. WC1 8 A3
Argyle St. WC1 58 E3
Argyle Wk. WC1 8 A4
Argyll Ave., Sthl. 63 H1
Argyll Clo. SW9 76 F3
Dalyell Rd.
Argyll Gdns., Edg. 38 B2
Argyll Rd. W8 66 D2
Argyll St. W1 11 F4
Argyll St. W1 58 C6
Arica Rd. SE4 77 H4
Ariel Rd. NW6 48 D6
Ariel Way W12 65 J1
Aristotle Rd. SW4 76 D3
Arkell Gro. SE19 85 H7
Arkindale Rd. SE6 87 C3
Arkley Cres. E17 41 J5
Arkley Dr., Barn. 22 G4
Arkley La., Barn. 22 G3
Arkley Rd. E17 41 J5
Arkley Vw., Barn. 22 H4
Arklow Rd. SE14 68 J6
Arkwright Rd. NW3 48 F5
Arlesford Rd. SW9 76 E3
Arlesley Clo. SW15 75 B6
Lytton Gro.
Arlingford Rd. SW2 76 G5
Arlington N12 31 D3
Arlington Ave. N1 9 A1
Arlington Ave. N1 58 J1
Arlington Clo., Sid. 79 H7
Arlington Clo., Sutt. 100 D2
Arlington Clo., Twick. 73 F6
Arlington Dr., Cars. 100 J2
Arlington Gdns. W4 65 C5
Arlington Gdns., Ilf. 52 D1
Arlington Lo. SW2 76 F4

Arlington Ms., Twick. 73 E6
Arlington Rd.
Arlington Rd. N14 32 B2
Arlington Rd. NW1 58 B1
Arlington Rd. W13 55 E6
Arlington Rd., Rich. 92 G2
Arlington Rd., Surb. 91 G6
Arlington Rd., Tedd. 82 C4
Arlington Rd., Twick. 73 F6
Arlington Sq. N1 58 J1
Arlington St. SW1 15 F1
Arlington St. SW1 67 C1
Arlington Way EC1 8 F3
Arlington Way EC1 58 G3
Arliss Way, Nthlt. 54 C1
Arlow Rd. N21 32 G1
Armada Ct. SE8 69 A6
Watergate St.
Armada St. SE8 69 A6
Armadale Clo. N17 41 E4
Armadale Rd. SW6 66 D7
Armadale Rd., Felt. 72 A5
Armagh Rd. E3 59 J1
Armfield Clo., W.Mol. 90 F5
Armfield Cres., Mitch. 93 J2
Armfield Rd., Enf. 25 A1
Arminger Rd. W12 65 H1
Armitage Rd. NW11 48 B1
Armitage Rd. SE10 69 F5
Armour Clo. N7 49 F6
Roman Way
Armoury Way SW18 75 D5
Armstead Wk., Dag. 53 G7
Armstrong Ave., 34 E6
Wdf.Grn.
Armstrong Clo. E6 61 C6
Porter Rd.
Armstrong Clo., Dag. 53 D1
Palmer Rd.
Armstrong Clo., Pnr. 36 A6
Armstrong Cres., 23 G3
Barn.
Armstrong Rd. SW7 14 E6
Armstrong Rd. SW7 66 G3
Armstrong Rd. W3 65 F1
Armstrong Rd., Felt. 81 E5
Armstrong Way, 63 H2
Sthl.
Armytage Rd., 63 D7
Houns.
Arnal Cres. SW18 75 B7
Arndale Cen., The 75 E6
SW18
Arndale Wk. SW18 75 E5
Garratt La.
Arne Gro., Orp. 104 J3
Arne St. WC2 12 B4
Arne Wk. SE3 78 F4
Arneway St. SW1 15 J6
Arneways Ave., Rom. 44 D4
Arnewood Clo. SW15 83 G1
Arney's La., Mitch. 94 A6
Arngask Rd. SE6 78 D7
Arnhem Way SE22 77 B5
East Dulwich Gro.
Arnison Rd., E.Mol. 91 A4
Arnold Circ. E2 9 F4
Arnold Circ. E2 59 C3
Arnold Clo., Har. 37 J7
Arnold Cres., Islw. 73 A5
Arnold Est. SE1 17 G4
Arnold Est. SE1 68 C2
Arnold Gdns. N13 32 H5
Arnold Rd. E3 60 A3
Arnold Rd. N15 41 C3
Arnold Rd. SW17 84 J7
Arnold Rd., Dag. 53 F7
Arnold Rd., Nthlt. 45 D6
Arnos Gro. N14 32 D4
Arnos Rd. N11 32 C5
Arnott Clo. SE28 62 C7
Applegarth Rd.
Arnott Clo. W4 65 D4
Fishers La.
Arnould Ave. SE5 77 A4
Arnsberg Way, Bexh. 80 G4
Arnside Gdns., Wem. 46 G1
Arnside Rd., Bexh. 80 G1
Arnside St. SE17 21 A5
Arnside St. SE17 67 J6
Arnulf St. SE6 87 D4
Arodene Rd. SW16 85 G6
Arodene Rd. SW2 76 F6
Arragon Gdns. SW16 85 E7
Arragon Gdns., 103 B3
W.Wick.
Arragon Rd. E6 61 A1
Arragon Rd., Twick. 73 D7
Arran Clo., Wall. 101 C4
Arran Dr. E12 52 A1

Arran Ms. W5 64 J1
Arran Rd. SE6 87 B2
Arran Wk. N1 49 J7
Arras Ave., Mord. 93 F5
Arrol Rd., Beck. 95 F3
Arrow Rd. E3 60 B3
Arrowscout Wk., 54 E3
  Nthlt.
  Argus Way
Arrowsmith Clo., 35 J5
  Chig.
Arrowsmith Path, 35 H5
  Chig.
Arrowsmith Rd., 35 H5
  Chig.
Arrowsmith Rd., 27 B3
  Loug.
Arsenal Rd. SE9 79 C2
Arterberry Rd. SW20 83 J7
Artesian Clo. NW10 47 D7
Artesian Rd. W2 57 D6
Arthingworth St. 60 E1
  E15
Arthur Ct. W2 10 A3
Arthur Gro. SE18 70 F4
Arthur Henderson 75 C2
  Ho. SW6
Arthur Rd. E6 61 C2
Arthur Rd. N7 49 F4
Arthur Rd. N9 33 C2
Arthur Rd. SW19 84 B5
Arthur Rd., Kings.T. 83 A7
Arthur Rd., N.Mal. 92 H5
Arthur Rd., Rom. 44 D6
Arthur St. EC4 13 C5
Arthurdon Rd. SE4 78 A5
Artichoke Hill E1 59 E7
  Pennington St.
Artichoke Pl. SE5 77 A1
Artillery Clo., Ilf. 43 F6
  Horns Rd.
Artillery La. E1 13 E2
Artillery La. E1 59 B5
Artillery Pas. E1 13 E2
Artillery Pl. SE18 70 C4
Artillery Pl. SW1 15 H6
Artillery Row SW1 15 H6
Artillery Row SW1 67 D3
Artington Clo., Orp. 104 F4
Artizan St. E1 13 E3
Arundel Ave., Mord. 93 C4
Arundel Clo. E15 51 E4
Arundel Clo. SW11 75 H5
  Chivalry Rd.
Arundel Clo., Bex. 80 F6
Arundel Clo., Croy. 101 H3
Arundel Clo., Hmptn. 81 H5
Arundel Ct. N12 31 H6
Arundel Ct., Har. 45 G4
Arundel Dr., Borwd. 22 B5
Arundel Dr., Har. 45 F4
Arundel Dr., Wdf.Grn. 34 G7
Arundel Gdns. N21 32 G1
Arundel Gdns. W11 57 C7
Arundel Gdns., Edg. 30 D7
Arundel Gdns., Ilf. 53 A2
Arundel Great Ct. 12 D5
  WC2
Arundel Gro. N16 50 B5
Arundel Pl. N1 49 G6
Arundel Rd., Barn. 23 H3
Arundel Rd., Croy. 95 A6
Arundel Rd., Houns. 72 C3
Arundel Rd., Kings.T. 92 B2
Arundel Rd., Sutt. 100 B7
Arundel Sq. N7 49 G6
Arundel St. WC2 12 D5
Arundel St. WC2 58 F7
Arundel Ter. SW13 65 H6
Arvon Rd. N5 49 G5
Ascalon St. SW8 67 C7
  Rushcroft Rd.
Ascham Dr. E4 34 B7
Ascham End E17 41 H1
Ascham St. NW5 49 C5
Aschurch Rd., Croy. 95 C7
Ascot Clo., Borwd. 22 A5
Ascot Clo., Ilf. 35 H6
Ascot Clo., Nthlt. 45 G6
Ascot Gdns., Sthl. 54 F4
Ascot Rd. E6 61 C3
Ascot Rd. N15 41 A5
Ascot Rd. N18 33 D4
Ascot Rd. SW17 85 A6
Ascot Rd., Orp. 97 J4
Ascott Ave. W5 64 H2
Ash Clo. SE20 95 F2
Ash Clo., Cars. 100 J2
Ash Clo., Edg. 30 C4
Ash Clo., N.Mal. 92 D2
Ash Clo., Orp. 97 G5
Ash Clo., Sid. 89 B3
Ash Clo., Stan. 29 D6

Ash Ct., Epsom 99 C4
Ash Gro. E8 59 E1
Ash Gro. N13 32 J3
Ash Gro. NW2 48 A4
Ash Gro. SE20 95 F2
Ash Gro. W5 64 H2
Ash Gro., Enf. 25 B7
Ash Gro., Houns. 72 D1
Ash Gro., Sthl. 54 G5
Ash Gro., Wem. 46 D4
Ash Gro., W.Wick. 103 C2
Ash Hill Clo. 28 H1
  (Bushey), Wat.
Ash Hill Dr., Pnr. 36 C3
Ash Island, E.Mol. 91 A3
Ash La., Croy. 101 H4
Ash Rd. E15 51 E5
Ash Rd., Croy. 103 A2
Ash Rd., Orp. 104 J7
Ash Rd., Sutt. 98 B7
Ash Row, Brom. 97 D7
Ash Tree Clo., Croy. 95 H6
Ash Tree Clo., Surb. 98 H1
Ash Tree Dell NW9 38 D5
Ash Tree Way, Croy. 95 H5
Ash Wk. SW2 85 F1
Ash Wk., Wem. 46 F3
Ashbourne Ave. E18 42 H4
Ashbourne Ave. N20 31 J2
Ashbourne Ave. 39 C5
  NW11
Ashbourne Ave., 71 E7
  Bexh.
Ashbourne Ave., Har. 46 A2
Ashbourne Clo. N12 31 H4
Ashbourne Clo. W5 56 A5
Ashbourne Ct. E5 50 H4
  Daubeney Rd.
Ashbourne Gro. NW7 30 D5
Ashbourne Gro. SE22 77 C5
Ashbourne Gro. W4 65 E5
Ashbourne Ri., Orp. 104 G4
Ashbourne Rd. W5 55 J4
Ashbourne Rd., 85 A6
  Mitch.
Ashbourne Ter. 84 D7
  SW19
Ashbourne Way 39 C5
  NW11
  Ashbourne Ave.
Ashbridge Rd. E11 42 E7
Ashbridge St. NW8 6 G6
Ashbridge St. NW8 57 H4
Ashbrook Rd. N19 49 D1
Ashbrook Rd., Dag. 53 H3
Ashburn Gdns. SW7 18 C1
Ashburn Gdns. SW7 66 F4
Ashburn Pl. SW7 18 C1
Ashburn Pl. SW7 66 F4
Ashburnham Ave., 37 C6
  Har.
Ashburnham Clo. N2 39 G3
Ashburnham Clo., 28 A3
  Wat.
  Ashburnham Dr.
Ashburnham Dr., 28 A3
  Wat.
Ashburnham Gdns., 37 C7
  Har.
Ashburnham Gro. 69 B7
  SE10
Ashburnham Pl. SE10 69 B7
Ashburnham Retreat 69 B7
  SE10
Ashburnham Rd. 56 J3
  NW10
Ashburnham Rd. 18 D7
  SW10
Ashburnham Rd. 66 F7
  SW10
Ashburnham Rd., 71 J4
  Belv.
Ashburnham Rd., 82 E2
  Rich.
Ashburton Ave., 102 E1
  Croy.
Ashburton Ave., Ilf. 52 H4
Ashburton Clo., 102 D1
  Croy.
Ashburton Ct., Pnr. 36 D3
Ashburton Gdns., 102 D2
  Croy.
Ashburton Gro. N7 49 G4
Ashburton Rd. E16 60 G6
Ashburton Rd., 102 D2
  Croy.
Ashburton Rd., Ruis. 45 A2
Ashburton Ter. E13 60 G2
  Grasmere Rd.
Ashbury Gdns., Rom. 44 D5
Ashbury Rd. SW11 75 J3
Ashby Ave., Chess. 99 A6
Ashby Gro. N1 49 J7

Ashby Ms. SE4 77 J2
Ashby Rd. N15 41 D5
Ashby Rd. SE4 77 J2
Ashby St. EC1 8 H4
Ashby Wk., Croy. 94 J6
Ashchurch Gro. W12 65 G3
Ashchurch Pk. Vill. 65 G3
  W12
Ashchurch Ter. W12 65 G3
Ashcombe Ave., 91 G7
  Surb.
Ashcombe Gdns., 30 A4
  Edg.
Ashcombe Pk. NW2 47 E3
Ashcombe Rd. SW19 84 D5
Ashcombe Rd., Cars. 101 A6
Ashcombe Sq., 92 C3
  N.Mal.
Ashcombe St. SW6 75 E2
Ashcroft, Pnr. 28 G6
Ashcroft Ave., Sid. 80 A6
Ashcroft Cres., Sid. 80 A6
Ashcroft Rd. E3 59 H3
Ashcroft Rd., Chess. 98 J3
Ashcroft Sq. W6 65 J4
  King St.
Ashdale Clo., Twick. 72 J7
Ashdale Gro., Stan. 29 C6
Ashdale Rd. SE12 87 H1
Ashdale Way, Twick. 72 J7
  Ashdale Clo.
Ashdene SE15 77 E1
  Carlton Gro.
Ashdene, Pnr. 36 C3
Ashdon Clo., 34 H6
  Wdf.Grn.
Ashdon Rd. NW10 56 F1
Ashdown Clo., Beck. 96 B2
Ashdown Cres. NW5 49 A5
  Queens Cres.
Ashdown Rd., Enf. 25 F3
Ashdown Rd., 91 H2
  Kings.T.
Ashdown Wk. E14 69 A4
  Charnwood Gdns.
Ashdown Wk., Rom. 44 H2
Ashdown Way SW17 85 A2
Ashen Gro. SW19 84 D3
Ashenden Rd. E5 50 H5
Asher Way E1 17 J1
Asher Way E1 51 D6
Ashfield Ave., Felt. 81 B1
Ashfield Clo., Rich. 82 H1
Ashfield La., Chis. 88 F6
Ashfield Par. N14 32 D1
Ashfield Rd. N4 40 J6
Ashfield Rd. N14 32 C3
Ashfield Rd. W3 65 F1
Ashfield St. E1 59 E5
Ashfields, Loug. 27 C2
Ashford Ave. N8 40 E4
Ashford Ave., Hayes 54 D6
Ashford Clo. E17 41 J6
Ashford Cres., Enf. 25 F2
Ashford Grn., Wat. 28 D5
Ashford Rd. E6 52 D6
Ashford Rd. E18 42 H2
Ashford Rd. NW2 48 A4
Ashford St. N1 9 D3
Ashgrove Rd., Brom. 87 D6
Ashgrove Rd., Ilf. 52 J1
Ashingdon Clo. E4 34 C3
Ashington Rd. SW6 75 C2
Ashlake Rd. SW16 85 E4
Ashland Pl. W1 11 B1
Ashland Pl. W1 58 A5
Ashlar Pl. SE18 70 E4
  Masons Hill
Ashleigh Gdns., 100 E2
  Sutt.
Ashleigh Rd. SE20 95 F3
Ashleigh Rd. SW14 74 E3
Ashley Ave., Ilf. 43 E2
Ashley Ave., Mord. 93 D5
  Chalgrove Ave.
Ashley Clo. NW4 38 J2
Ashley Clo., Pnr. 36 B2
Ashley Cres. N22 40 G2
Ashley Cres. SW11 76 A3
Ashley Dr., Borwd. 22 C5
Ashley Dr., Islw. 64 B6
Ashley Dr., Twick. 81 H1
Ashley Gdns. N13 32 J4
Ashley Gdns. SW1 15 G6
Ashley Gdns., Orp. 104 H5
Ashley Gdns., Rich. 82 G2
Ashley Gdns., Wem. 46 H2
Ashley Gro., Loug. 27 B3
  Staples Rd.
Ashley La. NW4 38 J2
Ashley La., Croy. 101 H4
Ashley Pl. SW1 15 F6
Ashley Pl. SW1 67 C3

Ashley Rd. E4 34 A5
Ashley Rd. E7 51 J7
Ashley Rd. N17 41 D3
Ashley Rd. N19 49 E1
Ashley Rd. SW19 84 E6
Ashley Rd., Enf. 25 F2
Ashley Rd., Hmptn. 90 G1
Ashley Rd., Rich. 73 H3
  Jocelyn Rd.
Ashley Rd., T.Ditt. 91 C6
Ashley Rd., Th.Hth. 94 F4
Ashley Wk. NW7 30 J7
Ashlin Rd. E15 51 D4
Ashling Rd., Croy. 102 D1
Ashlone Rd. SW15 74 J3
Ashlyns Way, Chess. 98 A6
Ashmead N14 24 C5
Ashmead Gate, Brom. 96 A1
Ashmead Rd. SE8 78 A2
Ashmead Rd., Felt. 81 A1
Ashmere Ave., Beck. 96 D2
Ashmere Clo., Sutt. 99 J5
Ashmere Gro. SW2 76 E4
Ashmill St. NW1 10 G1
Ashmill St. NW1 57 H5
Ashmole Pl. SW8 20 D6
Ashmole Pl. SW8 77 F6
Ashmole St. SW8 20 D6
Ashmole St. SW8 77 F6
Ashmore Ct., Houns. 63 G6
  Wheatlands
Ashmore Gro., Well. 79 G3
Ashmore Rd. W9 57 C2
Ashmount Rd. N15 41 C5
Ashmount Rd. N19 40 C7
Ashmount Ter. W5 64 G4
  Murray Rd.
Ashneal Gdns., Har. 46 A3
Ashness Gdns., Grnf. 46 E6
Ashness Rd. SW11 75 J5
Ashridge Clo., Har. 37 F6
Ashridge Cres. SE18 70 F7
Ashridge Dr., Wat. 28 B5
Ashridge Gdns. N13 32 D5
Ashridge Gdns., Pnr. 36 E4
Ashridge Way, Mord. 93 C3
Ashridge Way, Sun. 81 A6
Ashtead Rd. E5 41 D7
Ashton Clo., Sutt. 100 D4
Ashton Gdns., 72 F4
  Houns.
Ashton Gdns., Rom. 44 E6
Ashton Rd. E15 51 D5
Ashton St. E14 60 C7
Ashtree Ave., Mitch. 93 G2
Ashurst Clo. SE20 95 E1
Ashurst Dr., Ilf. 43 E6
Ashurst Rd. N12 31 H5
Ashurst Rd., Barn. 23 J5
Ashurst Wk., Croy. 102 E2
Ashvale Rd. SW17 84 J5
Ashville Rd. E11 51 D2
Ashwater Rd. SE12 87 G1
Ashwell Clo. E6 61 B6
  Northumberland Rd.
Ashwin St. E8 50 C6
Ashwood Gdns., 103 B6
  Croy.
Ashwood Rd. E4 34 D3
Ashworth Clo. SE5 77 A2
  Denmark Hill
Ashworth Rd. W9 6 B4
Ashworth Rd. W9 57 E3
Aske St. N1 9 D3
Askern Clo., Bexh. 80 D4
Askew Cres. W12 65 F2
Askew Rd. W12 65 G1
Askham Ct. W12 65 G1
Askham Rd. W12 65 G1
Askill Dr. SW15 75 B5
  Keswick Rd.
Asland Rd. E15 60 D1
Aslett St. SW18 75 F7
Asmara Rd. NW2 48 B5
Asmuns Hill NW11 39 C5
Asmuns Pl. NW11 39 C5
Aspen Clo. N19 49 C2
  Hargrave Pk.
Aspen Clo. W5 64 J2
Aspen Copse, Brom. 97 C2
Aspen Dr., Wem. 46 D6
Aspen Gdns. W6 65 H5
Aspen Gdns., Mitch. 94 A5
Aspen Grn., Erith 71 F3
Aspen La., Nthlt. 54 C7
Aspen Way E14 60 C7
Aspen Way, Felt. 81 B3
Aspenlea Rd. W6 66 A6
Aspern Rd. NW3 48 H5
Aspinall Rd. SE4 77 F3
Aspinden Rd. SE16 68 E4
Aspley Rd. SW18 75 E5
Asplins Rd. N17 41 D1

Asquith Clo., Dag. 53 C1
Crystal Way
Ass Ho. La., Har. 28 H4
Assam St. E1 13 H3
Assembly Pas. E1 59 F5
Assembly Wk., Cars. 100 H7
Assurance Cotts., Belv. 71 F5
Heron Hill
Astall Clo., Har. 37 B1
Sefton Ave.
Astbury Rd. SE15 77 F1
Aste St. E14 69 C2
Astell St. SW3 18 H3
Astell St. SW3 66 H5
Asteys Row N1 49 H7
River Pl.
Asthall Gdns., Ilf. 43 F4
Astle St. SW11 76 A2
Astley Ave. NW2 47 J5
Aston Ave., Har. 37 F7
Aston Clo., Sid. 89 A3
Aston Grn., Houns. 72 C2
Aston Ms., Rom. 44 C7
Reynolds Ave.
Aston Rd. SW20 92 J2
Aston Rd. W5 55 G6
Aston Rd., Esher 98 B5
Aston St. E14 59 H6
Astonville St. SW18 84 D1
Astor Ave., Rom. 44 J6
Astor Clo., Kings.T. 83 B6
Astoria Wk. SW9 76 G3
Astrop Ms. W6 65 J3
Astrop Ter. W6 65 J2
Astwood Ms. SW7 18 B1
Astwood Ms. SW7 66 E4
Asylum Rd. SE15 68 E7
Atalanta St. SW6 75 A1
Atbara Ct., Tedd. 82 E6
Atbara Rd., Tedd. 82 E6
Atcham Rd., Houns. 72 J4
Atcost Rd., Bark. 62 A5
Atheldene Rd. SW18 75 F7
Athelney St. SE6 87 A3
Athelstan Rd., Kings.T. 91 J4
Athelstane Gro. E3 59 J2
Athelstone Rd., Har. 37 A2
Athena Clo., Har. 46 B2
Byron Hill Rd.
Athenaeum Pl. N10 40 B3
Fortis Grn. Rd.
Athenaeum Rd. N20 31 F1
Athenlay Rd. SE15 77 G5
Athens Gdns. W9 57 D4
Elgin Ave.
Atherden Rd. E5 50 F4
Atherfold Rd. SW9 76 E3
Atherley Way, Houns. 72 F7
Atherstone Ms. SW7 18 D1
Atherstone Ms. SW7 66 F4
Atherton Dr. SW19 84 A4
Atherton Heights, Wem. 46 F6
Atherton Ms. E7 51 F6
Atherton Pl., Har. 37 A3
Atherton Pl., Sthl. 54 H7
Longford Ave.
Atherton Rd. E7 51 F6
Atherton Rd. SW13 65 G7
Atherton Rd., Ilf. 43 B2
Atherton St. SW11 75 H2
Athlon Rd., Wem. 55 G2
Athlone, Esher 98 B6
Athlone Clo. E5 50 E4
Goulton Rd.
Athlone Rd. SW2 76 F7
Athlone St. NW5 49 A6
Athol Clo., Pnr. 36 B1
Athol Gdns., Pnr. 36 B1
Athol Rd., Erith 71 J5
Athol Sq. E14 60 C6
Athole Gdns., Enf. 25 B5
Atholl Rd., Ilf. 44 A7
Atkins Dr., W.Wick. 103 D2
Atkins Rd. E10 42 B6
Atkins Rd. SW12 76 D7
Atkinson Rd. E16 60 J5
Atlantic Rd. SW9 76 G4
Atlas Gdns. SE7 69 J4
Atlas Ms. E8 50 C6
Tyssen St.
Atlas Ms. N7 49 F6
Atlas Rd. E13 60 G2
Atlas Rd. NW10 56 E3
Atlas Rd., Wem. 47 C4
Atley Rd. E3 60 A1
Atney Rd. SW15 75 B4
Atria Rd., Nthwd. 28 A5
Atterbury Rd. N4 40 G6
Atterbury St. SW1 20 A2
Atterbury St. SW1 67 E4
Attewood Ave. NW10 47 E3
Attewood Rd., Nthlt. 45 E6
Attfield Clo. N20 31 G2
Attlee Clo., Hayes 54 B3
Attlee Rd. SE28 62 B7
Attlee Rd., Hayes 54 A3
Attlee Ter. E17 42 B4
Attneave St. WC1 8 E4
Atwater Clo. SW2 85 G1
Atwell Clo. E10 42 B6
Belmont Pk. Rd.
Atwell Rd. SE15 77 D2
Rye La.
Atwood Ave., Rich. 74 A2
Atwood Rd. W6 65 H4
Aubert Pk. N5 49 G4
Aubert Rd. N5 49 H4
Aubrey Pl. NW8 6 C2
Aubrey Rd. E17 42 A3
Aubrey Rd. N8 40 E5
Aubrey Rd. W8 66 C1
Aubrey Wk. W8 66 C1
Aubyn Hill SE27 85 J4
Aubyn Sq. SW15 74 G4
Auckland Clo. SE19 95 C1
Auckland Gdns. SE19 95 B1
Auckland Hill SE27 85 J4
Auckland Ri. SE19 95 B1
Auckland Rd. E10 51 B3
Auckland Rd. SE19 95 C1
Auckland Rd. SW11 75 H4
Auckland Rd., Ilf. 52 E1
Auckland Rd., Kings.T. 91 J4
Auckland St. SE11 20 C4
Auden Pl. NW1 58 A1
Audleigh Pl., Chig. 35 D6
Audley Clo. SW11 76 A3
Audley Clo., Borwd. 22 A3
Audley Ct. E18 42 F4
Audley Ct., Pnr. 36 C2
Audley Gdns., Ilf. 52 J2
Audley Gdns., Loug. 27 F2
Audley Pl., Sutt. 100 E7
Audley Rd. NW4 38 G6
Audley Rd. W5 55 J5
Audley Rd., Enf. 24 H2
Audley Rd., Rich. 73 J5
Audley Sq. W1 15 C1
Audrey Clo., Beck. 96 B6
Audrey Gdns., Wem. 46 E2
Audrey Rd., Ilf. 52 E3
Audrey St. E2 9 J1
Audrey St. E2 59 D2
Audric Clo., Kings.T. 92 A1
Augurs La. E13 60 H3
Augusta Rd., Twick. 81 J2
Augusta St. E14 60 B6
Augustine Rd. W14 66 A3
Augustine Rd., Har. 36 H1
Augustus Clo., Brent. 64 G7
Augustus Rd. SW19 84 A1
Augustus St. NW1 7 E2
Augustus St. NW1 58 B2
Aulton Pl. SE11 20 F4
Aultone Way, Cars. 100 J3
Aultone Way, Sutt. 100 E2
Aurelia Gdns., Croy. 94 F5
Aurelia Rd., Croy. 94 E6
Auriga Ms. N16 50 A5
Auriol Clo., Wor.Pk. 99 E3
Auriol Pk. Rd.
Auriol Dr., Grnf. 46 A7
Auriol Pk. Rd., Wor.Pk. 99 E3
Auriol Rd. W14 66 B4
Austell Gdns. NW7 30 E3
Austen Clo. SE28 71 B1
Austen Clo., Loug. 27 G3
Austen Ho. NW6 57 D3
Austen Rd., Har. 45 H2
Austin Ave., Brom. 97 B5
Austin Clo. SE23 77 J7
Austin Clo., Twick. 73 F5
Austin Ct. E6 60 J1
Kings Rd.
Austin Friars EC2 13 C3
Austin Friars EC2 59 A6
Austin Friars Pas. EC2 13 C3
Austin Friars Sq. EC2 13 C3
Austin Rd. SW11 76 A1
Austin St. E2 9 F4
Austin St. E2 59 C3
Austral Clo., Sid. 88 J3
Austral St. SE11 20 G1
Austral St. SE11 67 H4
Australia Rd. W12 56 H7
Austyn Gdns., Surb. 99 B1
Autumn Clo., Enf. 25 D1
Autumn St. E3 60 A1
Avalon Clo. W13 55 D5
Avalon Clo., Enf. 24 G2
Avalon Rd. SW6 75 E1
Avalon Rd. W13 55 D4
Avard Gdns., Orp. 104 F4
Avarn Rd. SW17 84 J6
Ave Maria La. EC4 12 H4
Ave Maria La. EC4 58 H6
Avebury Ct. N1 59 A1
Poole St.
Avebury Pk., Surb. 91 G7
Avebury Rd. E11 51 D1
Southwest Rd.
Avebury Rd. SW19 93 C1
Avebury Rd., Orp. 104 G3
Avebury St. N1 59 A1
Poole St.
Aveline St. SE11 20 E4
Aveline St. SE11 67 G5
Aveling Pk. Rd. E17 42 A2
Avenell Rd. N5 49 H3
Avening Rd. SW18 75 D7
Brathway Rd.
Avening Ter. SW18 75 D6
Avenons Rd. E13 60 G4
Avenue, The E4 34 D6
Avenue, The E11 42 H6
Avenue, The N3 39 D2
Sylvan Ave.
Avenue, The N8 40 G3
Avenue, The N10 40 C2
Avenue, The N11 32 B5
Avenue, The N17 41 B2
Avenue, The NW6 57 A1
Avenue, The SE7 69 J7
Avenue, The SE10 69 D7
Avenue, The SW4 76 A5
Avenue, The SW11 75 J7
Bellevue Rd.
Avenue, The SW18 75 H7
Avenue, The W4 65 E3
Avenue, The W13 55 E7
Avenue, The, Barn. 23 B3
Avenue, The, Beck. 96 B1
Avenue, The, Bex. 80 D6
Avenue, The, Brom. 97 A3
Avenue, The, Cars. 101 A7
Avenue, The, Croy. 102 B3
Avenue, The, Epsom 99 H7
Avenue, The, Esher 98 B6
Avenue, The, Hmptn. 81 F6
Avenue, The, Har. 37 C1
Avenue, The, Houns. 72 H5
Avenue, The (Cranford), Houns. 72 A1
Avenue, The, Kes. 104 A3
Avenue, The, Loug. 27 A6
Avenue, The, Orp. 104 J2
Avenue, The, Orp. (St. Paul's Cray) 89 B7
Avenue, The (Church Ave.), Pnr. 36 F6
Avenue, The, Pnr. (Royston Parke Rd.) 28 F6
Avenue, The, Rich. 73 J2
Avenue, The, Sun. 90 B1
Avenue, The, Surb. 91 J6
Avenue, The (Cheam), Sutt. 99 J7
Avenue, The, Twick. 73 E5
Avenue, The, Wem. 46 H1
Avenue, The, W.Wick. 96 C7
Avenue, The, Wor.Pk. 99 F2
Avenue Clo. N14 24 C6
Avenue Clo. NW8 57 H1
Avenue Clo., Houns. 72 A1
The Ave.
Avenue Cres. W3 65 B2
Avenue Cres., Houns. 63 B7
Avenue Elmers, Surb. 91 H5
Avenue Gdns. SE25 95 D3
Avenue Gdns. SW14 74 E3
Avenue Gdns. W3 65 B2
Avenue Gdns., Houns. 63 A7
The Ave.
Avenue Gdns., Tedd. 82 C7
Avenue Ind. Est. E4 33 J6
Avenue Ms. N10 40 B3
Avenue Pk. Rd. SE27 85 H2
Avenue Rd. E7 51 H4
Avenue Rd. N6 40 C7
Avenue Rd. N12 31 F4
Avenue Rd. N14 24 B7
Avenue Rd. N15 41 A5
Avenue Rd. NW3 48 G7
Avenue Rd. NW8 48 G7
Avenue Rd. NW10 56 F2
Avenue Rd. SE20 95 F1
Avenue Rd. SE25 95 C2
Avenue Rd. SW16 94 D2
Avenue Rd. SW20 92 H2
Avenue Rd. W3 65 B2
Avenue Rd., Beck. 95 G1
Avenue Rd., Belv. 71 J4
Avenue Rd., Bexh. 80 E4
Avenue Rd., Brent. 64 F5
Avenue Rd., Erith 71 J7
Avenue Rd., Hmptn. 90 H1
Avenue Rd., Islw. 73 C1
Avenue Rd., Kings.T. 91 H3
Avenue Rd., N.Mal. 92 E4
Avenue Rd., Pnr. 36 E3
Avenue Rd., Rom. (Chadwell Heath) 53 D1
Avenue Rd., Sthl. 63 F2
Avenue Rd., Tedd. 82 D7
Avenue Rd., Wall. 101 C7
Avenue Rd., Wdf.Grn. 34 J6
Avenue S., The, Surb. 91 J7
Avenue Ter., N.Mal. 92 C3
Kingston Rd.
Averil Gro. SW16 85 H6
Averill St. W6 66 A6
Avern Gdns., W.Mol. 90 H4
Avern Rd., W.Mol. 90 H4
Avery Fm. Row SW1 19 D2
Avery Gdns., Ilf. 43 C5
Avery Hill Rd. SE9 79 G6
Avery Row W1 11 E5
Avery Row W1 58 B7
Aviary Clo. E16 60 F5
Aviemore Clo., Beck. 95 J5
Aviemore Way, Beck. 95 H5
Avignon Rd. SE4 77 G3
Avington Gro. SE20 86 F7
Avington Way SE15 21 F7
Avis Sq. E1 59 G6
Avoca Rd. SW17 85 A4
Avocet Ms. SE28 70 G3
Avon Clo., Hayes 54 C4
Avon Clo., Sutt. 100 F4
Avon Clo., Wor.Pk. 99 G2
Avon Ct., Grnf. 54 H4
Braund Ave.
Avon Ms., Pnr. 36 F1
Avon Path, S.Croy. 101 J6
Avon Pl. SE1 17 A4
Avon Rd. E17 42 D3
Avon Rd. SE4 78 A3
Avon Rd., Grnf. 54 G4
Avon Way E18 42 G3
Avondale Ave. N12 31 E5
Avondale Ave. NW2 47 E3
Avondale Ave., Barn. 31 J1
Avondale Ave., Esher 98 D3
Avondale Ave., Wor.Pk. 99 F1
Avondale Clo., Loug. 27 C7
Avondale Ct. E11 51 E1
Avondale Ct. E16 60 E5
Avondale Rd.
Avondale Ct. E18 42 H1
Avondale Cres., Enf. 25 H3
Avondale Cres., Ilf. 43 A5
Avondale Dr., Hayes 63 A1
Avondale Dr., Loug. 27 C7
Avondale Gdns., Houns. 72 F5
Avondale Ms., Brom. 87 G6
Avondale Rd.
Avondale Pk. Gdns. W11 57 B7
Avondale Pk. Rd. W11 57 B7
Avondale Ri. SE15 77 C3
Avondale Rd. E16 60 E5
Avondale Rd. E17 42 A7
Avondale Rd. N3 39 F1
Avondale Rd. N13 32 G2
Avondale Rd. N15 40 H5
Avondale Rd. SE9 88 B2
Avondale Rd. SW14 74 D3
Avondale Rd. SW19 84 E5
Avondale Rd., Brom. 87 E6
Avondale Rd., Har. 37 C3
Avondale Rd., S.Croy. 101 J7
Avondale Rd., Well. 80 C2
Avondale Sq. SE1 21 H4
Avondale Sq. SE1 68 D5
Avonley Rd. SE14 68 F7
Avonmore Pl. W14 66 B4
Avonmore Rd.
Avonmore Rd. W14 66 B4
Avonmouth St. SE1 16 J5
Avonmouth St. SE1 67 J3
Avonwick Rd., Houns. 72 H2
Avril Way E4 34 C5

Avro Way, Wall.	101	E7
Awlfield Ave. N17	41	A1
Awliscombe Rd.,	79	J2
Well.		
Axe St., Bark.	61	F1
Axholme Ave., Edg.	38	A1
Axminster Cres.,	80	C1
Well.		
Axminster Rd. N7	49	E3
Aybrook St. W1	**11**	**B2**
Aybrook St. W1	58	A5
Aycliffe Clo., Brom.	97	C4
Aycliffe Rd. W12	65	F1
Ayles Rd., Hayes	54	B3
Aylesbury Clo. E7	51	F6
Atherton Rd.		
Aylesbury Est. SE17	**21**	**C4**
Aylesbury Rd. SE17	**21**	**C4**
Aylesbury Rd. SE17	68	A5
Aylesbury Rd., Brom.	96	G3
Aylesbury St. EC1	**8**	**G6**
Aylesbury St. EC1	58	H4
Aylesbury St. NW10	47	D3
Aylesford Ave., Beck.	95	H5
Aylesford St. SW1	**19**	**H4**
Aylesford St. SW1	67	D5
Aylesham Rd., Orp.	97	J7
Aylestone Ave. NW6	48	A7
Aylett Rd. SE25	95	E4
Belfast Rd.		
Aylett Rd., Islw.	73	B2
Ayley Cft., Enf.	25	D5
Aylmer Clo., Stan.	29	D4
Aylmer Dr., Stan.	29	D4
Aylmer Rd. E11	51	F1
Aylmer Rd. N2	39	H5
Aylmer Rd. W12	65	F2
Aylmer Rd., Dag.	53	E3
Ayloffe Rd., Dag.	53	F6
Aylton Est. SE16	68	F2
Renforth St.		
Aylward Rd. SE23	86	G2
Aylward Rd. SW20	93	C2
Aylward St. E1	59	F6
Aylwards Ri., Stan.	29	D4
Aylwyn Est. SE1	**17**	**E5**
Aylwyn Est. SE1	68	B3
Aynhoe Rd. W14	66	A4
Aynscombe La.	74	C3
SW14		
Aynscombe Path	74	C2
SW14		
Thames Bank		
Ayr Ct. W3	56	A5
Monks Dr.		
Ayres Clo. E13	60	G3
Ayres Cres. NW10	47	D7
Ayres St. SE1	**17**	**J3**
Ayres St. SE1	67	J2
Aysrome Rd. N16	50	B3
Ayrton Rd. SW7	**14**	**E5**
Aysgarth Rd. SE21	77	B6
Aytoun Pl. SW9	76	F2
Aytoun Rd. SW9	76	F2
Azalea Clo. W7	64	C1
Azalea Wk., Pnr.	36	B5
Azenby Rd. SE15	77	C2
Azile Everitt Ho.	70	F5
SE18		
Vicarage Pk.		
Azof St. SE10	69	E4
B		
Baalbec Rd. N5	49	H5
Babbacombe Clo.,	98	G5
Chess.		
Babbacombe Gdns.,	43	B4
Ilf.		
Babbacombe Rd.,	96	G1
Brom.		
Baber Dr., Felt.	72	C6
Babington Ri., Wem.	47	A6
Babington Rd. NW4	38	H4
Babington Rd. SW16	85	D5
Babington Rd., Dag.	53	C5
Babmaes St. SW1	**15**	**I11**
Bacchus Wk. N1	**9**	**D2**
Baches St. N1	**9**	**C4**
Baches St. N1	59	A3
Back Ch. La. E1	**13**	**J4**
Back Ch. La. E1	59	D7
Back Hill EC1	**8**	**E6**
Back Hill EC1	58	G4
Back La. N8	40	E5
Back La. NW3	48	F4
Heath St.		
Back La., Bex.	80	G7
Back La., Brent.	64	G6
Back La., Edg.	38	C1
Back La., Rich.	82	F3
Back La., Rom.	44	E7
St. Chads Rd.		
Back Rd., Sid.	89	A4
Back St. W3	65	B1
Steyne Rd.		
Backhouse Pl. SE17	**21**	**E2**
Bacon Gro. SE1	**17**	**F6**
Bacon Gro. SE1	68	C3
Bacon La. NW9	38	B4
Bacon La., Edg.	38	A1
Bacon St. E1	**9**	**G5**
Bacon St. E1	59	C4
Bacon St. E2	**9**	**G5**
Bacon St. E2	59	C4
Bacons La. N6	49	A1
Bacton NW5	49	A5
Bacton St. E2	59	F3
Digby St.		
Baddow Clo., Dag.	62	G1
Baddow Clo.,	35	A6
Wdf.Grn.		
Baden Pl. SE1	**17**	**B3**
Baden Powell Clo.,	98	J2
Surb.		
Baden Rd. N8	40	D4
Baden Rd., Ilf.	52	E5
Badger Clo., Felt.	81	A3
Sycamore Clo.		
Badger Clo., Houns.	72	C3
Badgers Clo., Enf.	24	H3
Badgers Clo., Har.	37	A6
Badgers Copse, Orp.	104	J2
Badgers Copse,	99	F2
Wor.Pk.		
Badgers Cft. N20	31	B1
Badgers Cft. SE9	88	D3
Badgers Hole, Croy.	102	G4
Badgers Wk., N.Mal.	92	E2
Badlis Rd. E17	42	A2
Badminton Clo.,	22	A2
Borwd.		
Badminton Clo., Har.	37	B4
Badminton Clo.,	45	G7
Nthlt.		
Badminton Rd. SW12	76	A6
Badsworth Rd. SE5	76	J1
Bagley's La. SW6	75	E1
Bagleys Spring, Rom.	44	E4
Bagshot Ct. SE18	79	D1
Prince Imperial Rd.		
Bagshot Rd., Enf.	25	C7
Bagshot St. SE17	**21**	**E4**
Bagshot St. SE17	68	B5
Baildon St. SE8	69	A7
Watson's St.		
Bailey Clo. E4	34	C4
Bailey Pl. SE26	86	G6
Baillies Wk. W5	64	G2
Liverpool Rd.		
Bainbridge Rd., Dag.	53	F4
Bainbridge St. WC1	**11**	**J3**
Bainbridge St. WC1	58	B3
Baird Ave., Sthl.	54	H7
Baird Clo. NW9	38	C6
Baird Gdns. SE19	86	B4
Baird Rd., Enf.	25	E4
Baird St. EC1	**9**	**A5**
Baizdon Rd. SE3	78	E2
Baker La., Mitch.	94	A2
Baker Pas. NW10	56	E1
Acton La.		
Baker Rd. NW10	50	E1
Baker Rd. SE18	79	B1
Baker St. NW1	**7**	**A6**
Baker St. W1	**11**	**A1**
Baker St. W1	57	J5
Baker St., Enf.	25	A3
Bakers Ave. E17	42	B6
Bakers Ct. SE25	95	B3
Bakers End SW20	93	B2
Bakers Fld. N7	49	D4
Crayford Rd.		
Bakers Hill E5	50	E1
Bakers Hill, Barn.	23	F2
Bakers La. N6	39	.J6
Baker's Ms. W1	**11**	**B3**
Bakers Ms., Orp.	104	J6
Bakers Pas. NW3	48	F4
Heath St.		
Baker's Rents E2	**9**	**F4**
Bakers Row E15	60	E2
Baker's Row EC1	**8**	**E6**
Baker's Row EC1	58	G4
Bakery Pl. SW11	75	J4
Altenburg Gdns.		
Bakewell Ct. E5	50	H3
Mandeville St.		
Bakewell Way, N.Mal.	92	E2
Bala Gdn. NW9	38	E6
Snowdon Dr.		
Balaam St. E13	60	G4
Balaams La. N14	32	D2
Balaclava Rd. SE1	**21**	**G2**
Balaclava Rd. SE1	68	C4
Balaclava Rd., Surb.	91	F7
Balben Path E9	50	G7
Speldhurst Rd.		
Balcaskie Rd. SE9	79	C5
Balchen Rd. SE3	79	A2
Balchier Rd. SE22	77	E6
Balcombe St. NW1	**6**	**J5**
Balcombe St. NW1	57	J4
Balcon Way, Borwd.	22	C1
Balcorne St. E9	50	F7
Balder Ri. SE12	87	H2
Balderton St. W1	**11**	**C4**
Balderton St. W1	58	A6
Baldock St. E3	60	B2
Baldry Gdns. SW16	85	E6
Baldwin Cres. SE5	76	J1
Baldwin St. EC1	**9**	**B4**
Baldwin Ter. N1	**8**	**J1**
Baldwin Ter. N1	58	J2
Baldwin's Gdns. EC1	**12**	**E1**
Baldwin's Gdns. EC1	58	G5
Baldwins Hill, Loug.	27	C2
Baldwyn Gdns. W3	56	D7
Balfe St. N1	**8**	**B2**
Balfe St. N1	58	E2
Balfern Gro. W4	65	E5
Balfern St. SW11	75	H2
Balfour Ave. W7	64	C1
Balfour Gro. N20	31	J3
Balfour Ho. W10	57	A5
St. Charles Sq.		
Balfour Ms. N9	33	D3
Fore St.		
Balfour Ms. W1	**15**	**C1**
Balfour Pl. SW15	74	H4
Balfour Pl. W1	**11**	**C6**
Balfour Rd. N5	49	J4
Balfour Rd. SE25	95	D5
Balfour Rd. SW19	84	E7
Balfour Rd. W3	56	C5
Balfour Rd. W13	64	D2
Balfour Rd., Brom.	97	A5
Balfour Rd., Cars.	100	J7
Balfour Rd., Har.	37	A5
Balfour Rd., Houns.	72	H3
Balfour Rd., Ilf.	52	E2
Balfour Rd., Sthl.	63	D3
Balfour St. SE17	**21**	**B1**
Balfour St. SE17	68	A4
Balgonie Rd. E4	34	D1
Balgowan Clo.,	92	E4
N.Mal.		
Balgowan Rd., Beck.	95	H3
Balgowan St. SE18	70	J4
Balham Gro. SW12	76	A7
Balham High Rd.	85	A1
SW12		
Balham High Rd.	85	A3
SW17		
Balham Hill SW12	76	B7
Balham New Rd.	76	B7
SW12		
Balham Pk. Rd.	84	.I1
SW12		
Balham Rd. N9	33	D2
Balham Sta. Rd.	85	B1
SW12		
Balkan Wk. E1	59	E7
Pennington St.		
Ballamore Rd., Brom.	87	G3
Ballance Rd. E9	50	G6
Ballantine St. SW18	75	F4
Ballard Clo., Kings.T.	83	D7
Ballards Clo., Dag.	62	H1
Ballards Fm. Rd.,	102	D6
Croy.		
Ballards Fm. Rd.,	102	D6
S.Croy.		
Ballards La. N3	39	D1
Ballards La. N12	31	F6
Ballards Ms., Edg.	30	A6
Ballards Ri., S.Croy.	102	D6
Ballards Rd. NW2	47	G2
Ballards Rd., Dag.	62	H2
Ballards Way, Croy.	102	E6
Ballards Way,	102	D6
S.Croy.		
Ballast Quay SE10	69	D5
Ballater Clo., Wat.	28	C4
Ballater Rd. SW2	76	E4
Ballater Rd., S.Croy.	102	C5
Ballina St. SE23	77	G7
Ballingdon Rd. SW11	76	A6
Ballinger Pt. E3	60	B3
Bromley High St.		
Balliol Ave. E4	34	E4
Balliol Rd. N17	41	B1
Balliol Rd. W10	56	J6
Balliol Rd., Well.	80	B2
Balloch Rd. SE6	87	D1
Ballogie Ave. NW10	47	E4
Ballow Clo. SE5	68	B7
Harris St.		
Balls Pond Pl. N1	50	A6
Balls Pond Rd.		
Balls Pond Rd. N1	50	A6
Balmain Clo. W5	64	G1
Balmer Rd. E3	59	J2
Balmes Rd. N1	59	A1
Balmoral Ave., Beck.	95	H4
Balmoral Clo. SW15	75	A6
Westleigh Ave.		
Balmoral Cres.,	90	G3
W.Mol.		
Balmoral Dr., Borwd.	22	D5
Balmoral Dr., Sthl.	54	F4
Balmoral Gdns. W13	64	D3
Balmoral Gdns., Bex.	80	F7
Balmoral Gdns., Ilf.	52	J1
Balmoral Gro. N7	49	F6
Balmoral Ms. W12	65	F3
Balmoral Rd. E7	51	J4
Balmoral Rd. E10	51	B2
Balmoral Rd. NW2	47	H6
Balmoral Rd., Har.	45	G4
Balmoral Rd.,	91	J4
Kings.T.		
Balmoral Rd.,	99	H3
Wor.Pk.		
Balmore Cres., Barn.	24	A5
Balmore St. N19	49	B2
Balmuir Gdns. SW15	74	J4
Balnacraig Ave.	47	E4
NW10		
Balniel Gate SW1	**19**	**J3**
Balniel Gate SW1	67	D5
Baltic Clo. SW19	84	G7
Baltic Ct. SE16	68	G2
Timber Pond Rd.		
Baltic St. EC1	**8**	**J6**
Baltic St. EC1	58	J4
Baltimore Pl., Well.	79	J2
Balvernie Gro. SW18	75	C7
Bamber Ho., Bark.	61	F1
St. Margarets		
Bamborough Gdns.	65	J2
W12		
Bamford Ave., Wem.	55	J1
Bamford Ct. E15	51	B5
Clays La.		
Bamford Rd., Bark.	52	F6
Bamford Rd., Brom.	87	C5
Bampfylde Clo.,	101	C3
Wall.		
Bampton Rd. SE28	86	G3
Banavie Gdns., Beck.	96	C1
Banbury Ct. WC2	**12**	**A5**
Banbury Ct., Sutt.	100	D7
Banbury Enterprise	101	H2
Cen., Croy.		
Factory La.		
Banbury Rd. E9	50	G7
Banbury Rd. E17	33	H7
Banbury Rd. SW11	75	H2
Banchory Rd. SE3	69	H7
Bancroft Ave. N2	39	H5
Bancroft Ave.,	34	G2
Buck.H.		
Bancroft Ct., Nthlt.	36	J1
Bancroft Gdns., Har.	36	J1
Bancroft Gdns., Orp.	104	J1
Bancroft Rd. E1	59	G3
Bancroft Rd., Har.	36	J1
Bandon Ri., Wall.	101	D5
Bangalore St. SW15	74	J3
Bangor Clo., Nthlt.	45	H5
Banim St. W6	65	H4
Banister Rd. W10	57	A3
Bank, The N6	48	B1
Highgate High St.		
Bank, The N19	49	D1
Cholmeley Pk.		
Bank Ave., Mitch.	93	G2
Bank End SE1	**17**	**A1**
Bank End SE1	67	J1
Bank La. SW15	74	E5
Bank La., Kings.T.	82	H7
Bankfoot Rd., Brom.	87	E4
Bankhurst Rd. SE6	77	J7
Banks La., Bexh.	80	F4
Banks Rd., Borwd.	22	C2
Banksia Rd. N18	33	F5
Banksian Wk., Islw.	73	B1
The Gro.		
Bankside SE1	**12**	**J6**
Bankside SE1	58	H7
Bankside, Enf.	24	H1
Bankside, S.Croy.	102	C6
Bankside, Sthl.	63	D1
Bankside Ave., Nthlt.	54	A2
Townson Ave.		
Bankside Clo., Cars.	100	H6
Bankside Dr., T.Ditt.	98	E1
Bankside Way SE19	86	B6
Lunham Rd.		
Bankton Rd. SW2	76	G4

Bankwell Rd. SE13 78 E4
Banner St. EC1 9 A6
Banner St. EC1 58 J4
Bannerman Ho. SW8 20 C6
Bannerman Ho. SW8 67 F6
Banning St. SE10 [illegible]
Bannister Clo. SW2 85 G1
Ewen Cres.
Bannister Clo., Grnf. 46 A5
Bannister Ho. E9 50 G5
Homerton High St.
Bannockburn Rd. SE18 70 H4
Banstead Gdns. N9 33 B3
Banstead St. SE15 77 F3
Banstead Way, Wall. 101 E5
Banstock Rd., Edg. 30 B6
Banton Clo., Enf. 25 E2
Central Ave.
Bantry St. SE5 68 A7
Banwell Rd., Bex. 80 D6
Woodside La.
Banyard Rd. SE16 68 E3
Southwark Pk. Rd.
Baptist Gdns. NW5 49 A6
Queens Cres.
Barandon Wk. W11 57 A7
Whitchurch Rd.
Barb Ms. W6 65 J3
Barbara Brosnan Ct. NW8 6 E2
Barbauld Rd. N16 50 B3
Barber Clo. N21 24 G7
Barber's All. E13 60 H3
Barbers Rd. E15 60 B2
Barbican, The EC2 12 J1
Barbican, The EC2 58 J5
Barbican Rd., Grnf. 54 H6
Barbon Clo. WC1 12 B1
Barbot Clo. N9 33 D3
Barchard St. SW18 75 E5
Barchester Clo. W7 64 C1
Barchester Rd., Har. 37 A2
Barchester St. E14 60 B5
Barclay Clo. SW6 66 D7
Barclay Oval, Wdf.Grn. 34 G4
Barclay Rd. E11 51 E1
Barclay Rd. E13 60 J4
Barclay Rd. E17 42 C5
Barclay Rd. N18 33 A6
Barclay Rd. SW6 66 D7
Barclay Rd., Croy. 102 A3
Barclay Way SE22 77 D7
Lordship La.
Barcombe Ave. SW2 85 E2
Bard Rd. W10 57 A7
Barden St. SE18 70 H7
Bardfield Ave., Rom. 44 D3
Bardney Rd., Mord. 93 E4
Bardolph Rd. N7 49 E4
Bardolph Rd., Rich. 73 J3
St. Georges Rd.
Bardsey Pl. E1 59 F5
Bardsey Wk. N1 49 J6
Marquess Est.
Bardsley Clo., Croy. 102 C3
Bardsley La. SE10 69 C6
Barfett St. W10 57 C4
Barfield Ave. N20 31 J2
Barfield Rd. E11 51 F1
Barfield Rd., Brom. 97 D3
Barfields, Loug. 27 D4
Barfields Gdns., Loug. 27 D4
Barfields
Barfields Path, Loug. 27 D4
Barford Clo. NW4 38 G1
Barford St. N1 58 G1
Barforth Rd. SE15 77 E3
Barfreston Way SE20 95 E1
Bargate Clo. SE18 70 J5
Bargate Clo., N.Mal. 92 G7
Barge Ho. Rd. E16 70 E2
Barge Ho. St. SE1 16 F1
Barge Wk., E.Mol. 91 G2
Barge Wk., Kings.T. 91 G2
Barge Wk., Walt. 90 C3
Bargery Rd. SE6 87 B1
Bargrove Clo. SE20 86 D7
Bargrove Cres. SE6 86 J2
Elm La.
Barham Clo., Brom. 104 B1
Barham Clo., Chis. 88 E5
Barham Clo., Rom. 44 H2
Barham Clo., Wem. 46 E6
Barham Rd. SW20 83 G7
Barham Rd., Chis. 88 E5
Barham Rd., S.Croy. 101 J4
Baring Clo. SE12 87 G2
Baring Rd. SE12 78 G7
Baring Rd., Barn. 23 G4
Baring Rd., Croy. 102 D1

Baring St. N1 59 A1
Bark Pl. W2 10 A5
Bark Pl. W2 57 E7
Barker Dr. NW1 49 C7
Barker St. SW10 18 C5
Barker St. SW10 66 F6
[illegible] Way SE22 86 D1
Dulwich [illegible]
Barkham Rd. N17 [illegible]
Barking Ind. Pk., Bark. 61 J1
Barking Rd. E6 61 A2
Barking Rd. E13 60 G4
Barking Rd. E16 60 E5
Barkis Way SE16 68 E5
Egan Way
Barkston Gdns. SW5 18 A2
Barkston Gdns. SW5 66 E4
Barkway Ct. N4 49 J3
Queens Dr.
Barkwood Clo., Rom. 44 J5
Barlborough St. SE14 68 G7
Barlby Gdns. W10 57 A4
Barlby Rd. W10 56 J5
Barley La., Ilf. 44 A7
Barley La., Rom. 44 B4
Barley Mow Pas. EC1 12 H2
Barley Mow Pas. W4 65 D5
Heathfield Ter.
Barleycorn Way E14 59 J7
Barleyfields Clo., Rom. 44 B6
Barlow Clo., Wall. 101 E6
Cobham Clo.
Barlow Pl. W1 11 E6
Barlow Rd. NW6 48 C6
Barlow Rd. W3 65 B1
Barlow Rd., Hmptn. 81 G7
Barlow St. SE17 21 C2
Barmeston Rd. SE6 87 B2
Barmor Clo., Har. 36 H2
Barmouth Ave., Grnf. 55 C2
Barmouth Rd. SW18 75 F6
Barmouth Rd., Croy. 102 G2
Barn Clo., Nthlt. 54 C2
Barn Cres., Stan. 29 F6
Barn Elms Pk. SW15 74 J2
Barn Hill, Wem. 47 A1
Barn Ms., Har. 45 G3
Barn Ri., Wem. 47 A1
Barn St. N16 50 B3
Stoke Newington Ch. St.
Barn Way, Wem. 47 A1
Barnabas Ct. N21 24 G5
Cheyne Wk.
Barnabas Rd. E9 50 G5
Barnaby Clo., Har. 45 J2
Barnaby Way, Chig. 35 D3
Barnard Clo. SE18 70 D3
Barnard Clo., Chis. 97 G1
Barnard Clo., Sun. 81 B7
Oak Gro.
Barnard Clo., Wall. 101 D7
Alcock Clo.
Barnard Gdns., Hayes 54 B4
Barnard Gdns., N.Mal. 92 G4
Barnard Gro. E15 51 F7
Vicarage La.
Barnard Hill N10 40 B1
Barnard Ms. SW11 75 H4
Barnard Rd. SW11 75 H4
Barnard Rd., Enf. 25 E2
Barnard Rd., Mitch. 94 A3
Barnardo St. E1 59 G6
Devonport St.
Barnard's Inn EC1 12 E3
Barnby St. E15 60 E1
Barnby St. NW1 7 G3
Barnby St. NW1 58 C3
Barncroft Clo., Loug. 27 C5
Barncroft Grn., Loug. 27 D5
Barncroft Rd., Loug. 27 D5
Barnehurst Ave., Bexh. 80 J1
Barnehurst Ave., Erith 80 J1
Barnehurst Clo., Erith 80 J1
Barnehurst Rd., Bexh. 80 J2
Barnes All., Hmptn. 90 J2
Hampton Ct. Rd.
Barnes Ave. SW13 65 G7
Barnes Ave., Sthl. 63 F4
Barnes Bri. SW13 74 E2
Barnes Bri. W4 74 E2
Barnes Clo. E12 52 A4
Barnes Ct. E16 60 J5
Ridgewell Rd.
Barnes Ct., Wdf.Grn. 35 A5
Barnes End, N.Mal. 92 G5

Barnes High St. SW13 74 F2
Barnes Ho., Bark. 61 G1
St. Marys
Barnes Rd. N18 33 F4
Barnes Rd., Ilf. 52 F5
Barnes St. E14 59 H6
Barnes Ter. SE8 68 J5
Barnesbury Ho. SW4 76 D6
Barnet [illegible], Barn. 22 E1
Barnet Dr., Brom. [illegible]
Barnet Gate La., Barn. 22 [illegible]
Barnet Gro. E2 9 H3
Barnet Gro. E2 59 D3
Barnet Hill, Barn. 23 C4
Barnet Ho. N20 31 F2
Barnet La. N20 31 C1
Barnet La., Barn. 23 D6
Barnet Rd. (Arkley), Barn. 22 D6
Barnet Trd. Est., Barn. 23 C3
Barnet Way NW7 30 D3
Barnet Wd. Rd., Brom. 103 H2
Barnett St. E1 59 E6
Kinder St.
Barney Clo. SE7 69 J5
Barnfield, N.Mal. 92 E6
Barnfield Ave., Croy. 102 F2
Barnfield Ave., Kings.T. 82 H5
Barnfield Ave., Mitch. 94 B4
Barnfield Clo. N4 40 E7
Crouch Hill
Barnfield Gdns. SE18 70 E6
Plumstead Common Rd.
Barnfield Gdns., Kings.T. 82 H5
Barnfield Pl. E14 69 A4
Barnfield Rd. SE18 70 E6
Barnfield Rd. W5 55 F4
Barnfield Rd., Edg. 38 C1
Barnfield Wd. Clo., Beck. 96 D6
Barnfield Wd. Rd., Beck. 96 D6
Barnham Rd., Grnf. 54 J3
Barnham St. SE1 17 E3
Barnham St. SE1 68 B2
Barnhill, Pnr. 36 C5
Barnhill Ave., Brom. 96 F5
Barnhill La., Hayes 54 B4
Barnhill Rd., Hayes 54 B4
Barnhill Rd., Wem. 47 C3
Barnhurst Path, Wat. 28 C5
Barningham Way NW9 38 D6
Barnlea Clo., Felt. 81 E2
Barnmead Gdns., Dag. 53 F5
Barnmead Rd., Beck. 95 H1
Barnmead Rd., Dag. 53 F5
Barnsbury Clo., N.Mal. 92 C4
Barnsbury Cres., Surb. 99 B1
Barnsbury Gro. N7 49 F6
Barnsbury La., Surb. 99 B2
Barnsbury Pk. N1 49 G7
Barnsbury Rd. N1 8 E1
Barnsbury Rd. N1 58 G2
Barnsbury Sq. N1 49 G7
Barnsbury St. N1 49 G7
Barnsbury Ter. N1 49 F7
Barnscroft SW20 92 H3
Barnsdale Ave. E14 69 B4
Barnsdale Rd. W9 57 C4
Barnsley St. E1 59 E4
Barnstaple Rd., Ruis. 45 C3
Barnston Wk. N1 58 J1
Popham St.
Barnwell Rd. SW2 76 G5
Barnwood Clo. W9 6 A6
Barnwood Clo. W9 57 E4
Barnwood Ct. E16 69 G1
North Woolwich Rd.
Baron Gdns., Ilf. 43 F3
Baron Gro., Mitch. 93 H4
Baron Rd., Dag. 53 D1
Baron St. N1 8 E2
Baron St. N1 58 G2
Baron Wk. E16 60 F5
Star La.
Baron Wk., Mitch. 93 H4
Baroness Rd. E2 9 G3
Baronet Gro. N17 41 D1
St. Paul's Rd.
Baronet Rd. N17 41 D1
Barons, The, Twick. 73 E6
Barons Ct. Rd. W14 66 B5
Barons Gate, Barn. 23 H6
Barons Keep W14 66 B5

Barons Mead, Har. 37 B4
Barons Pl. SE1 16 F4
Barons Pl. SE1 67 G2
Barons Wk., Croy. 95 H6
Baronsfield Rd., Twick. 73 E6
Baronsmead Rd. SW13 74 G1
Baronsmede W5 64 J2
Baronsmere Rd. N2 39 H4
Barque Ms. SE8 69 A6
Watergate St.
Barrack Rd., [illegible] 72 D4
Barracks La., Barn. [illegible]
High St.
Barratt Ave. N22 40 F2
Barratt Ind. Pk., Sthl. 63 G2
Barratt Way, Har. 37 A3
Tudor Rd.
Barrenger Rd. N10 39 J1
Barrett Rd. E17 42 C4
Barrett St. W1 11 C4
Barrett St. W1 58 A6
Barretts Grn. Rd. NW10 56 C3
Barretts Gro. N16 50 B5
Barrhill Rd. SW2 85 E2
Barrie Est. W2 10 E5
Barrie Twr. W3 65 C2
Barriedale SE14 77 H2
Barrier App. SE7 70 A3
Barringer Sq. SW17 85 A4
Barrington Clo. NW5 49 A5
Grafton Rd.
Barrington Clo., Ilf. 43 C1
Hurstleigh Gdns.
Barrington Clo., Loug. 27 F4
Barrington Rd.
Barrington Grn., Loug. 27 F4
Barrington Rd. E12 52 D6
Barrington Rd. N8 40 D5
Barrington Rd. SW9 76 H3
Barrington Rd., Bexh. 80 D2
Barrington Rd., Loug. 27 F4
Barrington Rd., Sutt. 100 D1
Barrington Vill. SE18 79 D1
Barrow Ave., Cars. 100 J7
Barrow Clo. N21 32 H3
Barrow Hedges Clo., Cars. 100 H7
Barrow Hedges Way, Cars. 100 H7
Barrow Hill, Wor.Pk. 99 E2
Barrow Hill Clo., Wor.Pk. 99 E2
Barrow Hill
Barrow Hill Rd. NW8 6 G2
Barrow Hill Rd. NW8 57 H2
Barrow Pt. Ave., Pnr. 36 E2
Barrow Pt. La., Pnr. 36 E2
Barrow Rd. SW16 85 D6
Barrow Rd., Croy. 101 G5
Barrow Wk., Brent. 64 F5
Glenhurst Rd.
Barrow Way N7 49 F3
Barrowdene Clo., Pnr. 36 E2
Paines La.
Barrowell Grn. N21 32 H2
Barrowfield Clo. N9 33 E3
Barrowgate Rd. W4 65 C5
Barrs Rd. NW10 47 D7
Barry Ave. N15 41 C6
Craven Pk. Rd.
Barry Ave., Bexh. 71 E7
Barry Clo., Orp. 104 H3
Barry Rd. E6 61 B6
Barry Rd. NW10 47 C7
Barry Rd. SE22 77 D6
Barset Rd. SE15 77 F3
Barson Clo. SE20 86 F7
Barston Rd. SE27 85 J2
Barstow Cres. SW2 85 F1
Barter St. WC1 12 B2
Barter St. WC1 58 E5
Barters Wk., Pnr. 36 E3
High St.
Barth Rd. SE18 70 H4
Bartholomew Clo. EC1 12 J2
Bartholomew Clo. EC1 58 J5
Bartholomew Clo. SW18 75 F4
Bartholomew La. EC2 13 C4
Bartholomew Pl. EC1 12 J2
Bartholomew Rd. NW5 49 C6
Bartholomew Sq. E1 59 E4
Coventry Rd.
Bartholomew Sq. EC1 9 A5
Bartholomew Sq. EC1 58 J4

Bartholomew St. SE1 17 C6
Bartholomew St. SE1 68 A3
Bartholomew Vill. 49 C6
 NW5
Bartle Ave. E6 61 B2
Bartle Rd. W11 57 B6
Bartlett Clo. E14 60 A6
Bartlett Ct. EC4 12 F3
Bartlett St., S.Croy. 102 A5
Barton Ave., Rom. 53 H1
Barton Clo. E6 61 C6
 Brandreth Rd.
Barton Clo. E9 50 F5
 Churchill Wk.
Barton Clo. SE15 77 E3
 Kirkwood Rd.
Barton Clo., Bexh. 80 E5
Barton Clo., Chig. 35 F2
Barton Grn., N.Mal. 92 D2
Barton Meadows, Ilf. 43 E4
Barton Rd. W14 66 B5
Barton Rd., Sid. 89 E6
Barton St. SW1 16 A5
Barton Way, Borwd. 22 A2
Bartram Rd. SE4 77 H5
Barwick Rd. E7 51 H4
Barwood Ave., 103 B1
 W.Wick.
Basden Gro., Felt. 81 G2
Basedale Rd., Dag. 53 B7
Baseing Clo. E6 61 D7
Bashley Rd. NW10 56 D4
Basil Ave. E6 61 B2
Basil Gdns., Croy. 102 G1
 Primrose La.
Basil St. SW3 14 J5
Basil St. SW3 66 J3
Basildene Rd., Houns. 72 D3
Basildon Ave., Ilf. 43 D1
Basildon Rd. SE2 71 A5
Basildon Rd., Bexh. 80 E2
Basing Clo., T.Ditt. 91 C7
Basing Ct. SE15 77 C1
Basing Dr., Bex. 80 F6
Basing Hill NW11 48 C1
Basing Hill, Wem. 46 J2
Basing Ho., Bark. 61 G1
 St. Margarets
Basing Ho. Yd. E2 9 E3
Basing Pl. E2 9 E3
Basing St. W11 57 C6
Basing Way N3 39 D3
Basing Way, T.Ditt. 91 C7
Basingdon Way SE5 77 A4
Basingfield Rd., T.Ditt. 91 C7
Basinghall Ave. EC2 13 B2
Basinghall Ave. EC2 59 A5
Basinghall St. EC2 13 B3
Basinghall St. EC2 58 J5
Basire St. N1 58 J1
Baskerville Rd. SW18 75 H7
Basket Gdns. SE9 79 B5
Baslow Clo., Har. 37 A1
Baslow Wk. E5 50 G4
 Overbury Rd.
Basnett Rd. SW11 76 A3
Bassano St. SE22 77 C5
Bassant Rd. SE18 70 J6
Bassein Pk. Rd. W12 65 F2
Basset Ho., Dag. 02 B1
Bassett Gdns., Islw. 63 J7
Bassett Rd. W10 57 A6
Bassett St. NW5 49 A6
Bassett Way, Grnf. 54 H6
Bassetts Clo., Orp. 104 E3
Bassetts Way, Orp. 104 E4
Bassingham Rd. 75 F7
 SW18
Bassingham Rd., 46 G6
 Wem.
Basswood Clo. SE15 77 E3
 Linden Gro.
Bastable Ave., Bark. 61 H2
Bastion Rd. SE2 71 A6
Baston Manor Rd., 103 H3
 Brom.
Baston Rd., Brom. 103 H1
Bastwick St. EC1 8 J5
Bastwick St. EC1 58 J4
Basuto Rd. SW6 75 D1
Batavia Clo., Sun. 90 C1
Batavia Ms. SE14 68 H7
 Clifton Ri.
Batavia Rd. SE14 68 H7
Batavia Rd., Sun. 90 B1
Batchelor St. N1 8 F1
Batchelor St. N1 58 G2
Bate St. E14 59 J7
 Three Colt St.
Bateman Clo., Bark. 52 F6
 Glenny Rd.
Bateman Ho. SE17 20 G6
Bateman Rd. E4 34 A6

Bateman St. W1 11 H4
Bateman's Bldgs. W1 11 H4
Bateman's Row EC2 9 E5
Bateman's Row EC2 59 B4
Bates Cres. SW16 85 C7
Bates Cres., Croy. 101 G5
Bath Clo. SE15 68 E7
 Asylum Rd.
Bath Ct. EC1 8 E6
Bath Ho. Rd., Croy. 101 E1
Bath Pas., Kings.T. 91 G2
 St. James's Rd.
Bath Pl., Barn. 23 C3
Bath Rd. E7 52 A6
Bath Rd. N9 33 E2
Bath Rd. W4 65 E4
Bath Rd., Houns. 72 D2
Bath Rd., Mitch. 93 G3
Bath Rd., Rom. 44 E6
Bath St. EC1 9 A4
Bath St. EC1 58 J3
Bath Ter. SE1 16 J6
Bath Ter. SE1 67 J3
Bathgate Rd. SW19 84 A3
Baths Rd., Brom. 97 A4
Bathurst Ave. SW19 93 E1
 Brisbane Ave.
Bathurst Gdns. NW10 56 H2
Bathurst Ms. W2 10 F5
Bathurst Rd., Ilf. 52 E1
Bathurst St. W2 10 F5
Bathurst St. W2 57 G7
Bathway SE18 70 D4
Batley Pl. N16 50 C3
Batley Rd. N16 50 C3
 Stoke Newington
 High St.
Batley Rd., Enf. 25 A1
Batman Clo. W12 65 H1
Batoum Gdns. W6 65 J3
Batson St. W12 65 G2
Batsworth Rd., Mitch. 93 G3
Batten Clo. E6 61 C6
 Savage Gdns.
Batten St. SW11 75 H3
Battenburg Wk. SE19 86 B5
 Brabourne Gro.
Battersby Rd. SE6 87 D2
Battersea Bri. SW3 18 F7
Battersea Bri. SW3 66 G7
Battersea Bri. SW11 18 G7
Battersea Bri. SW11 66 H7
Battersea Bri. Rd. 66 H7
 SW11
Battersea Ch. Rd. 75 G1
 SW11
Battersea High St. 75 G1
 SW11
Battersea Pk. SW11 66 J7
Battersea Pk. Rd. 76 B1
 SW8
Battersea Ri. SW11 75 H2
 SW11
Battersea Ri. SW11 75 G5
Battery Rd. SE28 70 H2
Battishill St. N1 49 H7
 Waterloo Ter.
Battle Bri. La. SE1 17 D2
Battle Bri. La. SE1 68 B1
Battle Bri. Rd. NW1 8 A2
Battle Bri. Rd. NW1 58 E2
Battle Clo. SW19 84 F6
 North Rd.
Battle Rd., Belv. 71 J4
Battle Rd., Erith 71 J4
Battledean Rd. N5 49 H5
Batty St. E1 13 J3
Batty St. E1 59 D6
Baudwin Rd. SE6 87 E2
Baugh Rd., Sid. 89 C5
Baulk, The SW18 75 D7
Bavant Rd. SW16 94 F2
Davaria Rd. N19 49 E2
Bavent Rd. SE5 76 J2
Bawdale Rd. SE22 77 C5
Bawdsey Ave., Ilf. 43 J4
Bawtree Rd. SE14 68 H7
Bawtry Rd. N20 31 J3
Baxendale St. E2 9 H3
Baxendale St. E2 59 D3
Baxter Rd. E16 60 J6
Baxter Rd. N1 50 A6
Baxter Rd. N18 33 E4
Baxter Rd. NW10 56 E4
Baxter Rd., Ilf. 62 E7
Bay Ct. W5 64 H3
 Popes La.
Bay Tree Clo., Brom. 96 J1
Bayes Clo. SE26 86 F5
Bayfield Rd. SE9 79 A4
Bayford Ms. E8 50 E7
 Bayford St.

Bayford Rd. NW10 57 A3
Bayford St. E8 50 E7
Bayham Pl. NW1 58 C1
Bayham Rd. W4 65 D3
Bayham Rd. W13 55 E7
Bayham Rd., Mord. 93 E4
Bayham St. NW1 58 C1
Bayley St. WC1 11 H2
Bayley St. WC1 58 D5
Bayley Wk. SE2 71 E5
 Woolwich Rd.
Baylis Rd. SE1 16 E4
Baylis Rd. SE1 67 G2
Bayliss Ave. SE28 62 D7
Bayne Clo. E6 61 C6
 Savage Gdns.
Baynes Clo., Enf. 25 D1
Baynes Ms. NW3 48 G6
 Belsize La.
Baynes St. NW1 49 C7
Baynham Clo., Bex. 80 F6
Bayonne Rd. W6 66 B6
Bayston Rd. N16 50 C3
Bayswater Rd. W2 10 A6
Bayswater Rd. W2 57 E7
Baythorne St. E3 59 J5
Baytree Clo., Sid. 88 J1
Baytree Rd. SW2 76 F4
Bazalgette Clo., 92 D5
 N.Mal.
Bazalgette Gdns., 92 D5
 N.Mal.
Bazely St. E14 60 C7
Bazile Rd. N21 24 G6
Beach Gro., Felt. 81 G2
Beacham Clo. SE7 70 A5
Beachborough Rd., 87 C4
 Brom.
Beachcroft Rd. E11 51 E3
Beachcroft Way N19 49 D1
Beachy Rd. E3 51 A7
Beacon Gro., Cars. 101 A4
Beacon Hill N7 49 E5
Beacon Rd. SE13 78 D6
Beacons Clo. E6 61 B5
 Oliver Gdns.
Beaconsfield Clo. N11 32 A5
Beaconsfield Clo. 69 G6
 SE3
Beaconsfield Clo. W4 65 C5
Beaconsfield Rd. E10 51 C2
Beaconsfield Rd. E16 60 F4
Beaconsfield Rd. E17 41 J6
Beaconsfield Rd. N9 33 D3
Beaconsfield Rd. N11 32 A3
Beaconsfield Rd. N15 41 B4
Beaconsfield Rd. 47 F6
 NW10
Beaconsfield Rd. SE3 69 F7
Beaconsfield Rd. SE9 88 B2
Beaconsfield Rd. 21 C4
 SE17
Beaconsfield Rd. 68 A6
 SE17
Beaconsfield Rd. W4 65 D3
Beaconsfield Rd. W5 64 F2
Beaconsfield Rd., 97 A3
 Drum.
Beaconsfield Rd., 95 A6
 Croy.
Beaconsfield Rd., 98 B7
 Esher
Beaconsfield Rd., 63 C1
 Hayes
Beaconsfield Rd., 92 D2
 N.Mal.
Beaconsfield Rd., 63 D1
 Sthl.
Beaconsfield Rd., 91 J7
 Surb.
Beaconsfield Rd., 73 E6
 Twick.
Beaconsfield Ter., 44 D6
 Rom.
Beaconsfield Ter. Rd. 66 B3
 W14
Beaconsfield Wk. E6 61 D6
 East Ham Manor Way
Beaconsfield Wk. 75 C1
 SW6
 Parsons Grn. La.
Beacontree Ave. E17 42 D1
Beacontree Rd. E11 42 F7
Beadlow Clo., Cars. 93 G6
 Olveston Wk.
Beadman St. SE27 85 H4
Beadnell Rd. SE23 86 G1
Beadon Rd. W6 65 J4
Beadon Rd., Brom. 96 G4
Beaford Gro. SW20 93 B3
Beagle Clo., Felt. 81 B4
Beak St. W1 11 G5
Beak St. W1 58 C7

Beal Clo., Well. 80 A1
Beal Rd., Ilf. 52 D2
Beale Clo. N13 32 H5
Beale Pl. E3 59 J2
Beale Rd. E3 59 J1
Beam Ave., Dag. 62 H1
Beaminster Gdns., Ilf. 43 E2
Beamish Dr. 28 J1
 (Bushey), Wat.
Beamish Rd. N9 33 D1
Bean Rd., Bexh. 80 D4
Beanacre Clo. E9 50 J6
Beanshaw SE9 88 D4
Beansland Gro., Rom. 44 E2
Bear All. EC4 12 G3
Bear Gdns. SE1 16 J1
Bear Gdns. SE1 67 J1
Bear La. SE1 16 H2
Bear La. SE1 67 H1
Bear Rd., Felt. 81 D5
Bear St. WC2 17 J5
Beard Rd., Kings.T. 82 J5
Beardell St. SE19 86 C6
Beardow Gro. N14 24 C6
Beard's Hill, Hmptn. 90 G1
Beard's Hill Clo., 90 G1
 Hmptn.
 Beard's Hill
Beardsfield E13 60 G1
 Valetta Gro.
Beardsley Way W3 65 D2
Beardsley Rd., 82 H7
 Kings.T.
Bearstead Ri. SE4 77 J5
Beatrice Ave. SW16 94 F2
Beatrice Ave., Wem. 46 H5
Beatrice Clo. E13 60 G4
 Chargeable La.
Beatrice Clo., Pnr. 36 A4
 Reid Clo.
Beatrice Ct., Buck.H. 35 A2
Beatrice Ct., Wem. 46 J4
Beatrice Pl. W8 14 A6
Beatrice Pl. W8 66 E3
Beatrice Rd. E17 42 A5
Beatrice Rd. N4 40 G7
Beatrice Rd. N9 25 F7
Beatrice Rd. SE1 21 J2
Beatrice Rd. SE1 68 D4
Beatrice Rd., Rich. 73 J5
 Albert Rd.
Beatrice Rd., Sthl. 63 F1
Beatson Wk. SE16 68 H1
Beattock Ri. N10 40 B4
Beatty Rd. N16 50 B4
Beatty Rd., Stan. 29 F6
Beatty St. NW1 7 F1
Beatty St. NW1 58 C2
Beattyville Gdns., Ilf. 43 D3
Beauchamp Clo. W4 65 C3
 Church Path
Beauchamp Pl. SW3 14 H5
Beauchamp Pl. SW3 66 H3
Beauchamp Rd. E7 51 H7
Beauchamp Rd. SE19 95 A1
Beauchamp Rd. 75 H4
 SW11
Beauchamp Rd., 90 H5
 E.Mol.
Beauchamp Rd., 100 D3
 Sutt.
Beauchamp Rd., 73 D7
 Twick.
Beauchamp Rd., 90 H5
 W.Mol.
Beauchamp Ter. 74 H3
 SW15
 Dryburgh Rd.
Beauclerc Rd. W6 65 H3
Beauclerk Clo., Felt. 81 B1
 Florence Rd.
Beaufort Ave., Har. 37 D4
Beaufort Clo. E4 34 B6
 Higham Sta. Ave.
Beaufort Clo. SW15 74 H7
Beaufort Clo. W5 55 H5
Beaufort Clo., Rom. 44 J4
Beaufort Clo., Rich. 82 F4
 Beaufort Rd.
Beaufort Dr. NW11 39 D4
Beaufort Gdns. NW4 38 U3
Beaufort Gdns. SW3 14 H5
Beaufort Gdns. SW3 66 H3
Beaufort Gdns. SW16 85 F7
Beaufort Gdns., 72 E1
 Houns.
Beaufort Gdns., Ilf. 52 D1
Beaufort Gdns. SW6 66 C6
 Lillie Rd.
Beaufort Pk. NW11 39 D4
Beaufort Rd. W5 55 J5
Beaufort Rd., Kings.T. 91 H4
Beaufort Rd., Rich. 82 F4

Beaufort Rd., Twick. 73 F7
Beaufort St. SW3 18 F6
Beaufort St. SW3 66 G6
Beaufort Way, Epsom 99 G7
Beaufoy Rd. N17 33 B7
Beaufoy, Wlk. SE11 20 D2
Beaufoy Wk. SE11 67 F4
Beaulieu Ave. SE26 86 E4
Beaulieu Clo. NW9 38 E3
Beaulieu Clo. SE5 77 A3
Beaulieu Clo., 72 F5
Houns.
Beaulieu Clo., Mitch. 94 A1
Beaulieu Clo., Twick. 73 G6
Beaulieu Clo., Wat. 28 C1
Beaulieu Dr., Pnr. 36 D6
Beaulieu Gdns. N21 24 J7
Beaumanor Gdns. 88 D4
SE9
Beanshaw
Beaumaris Dr., 35 A7
Wdf.Grn.
Beaumont Ave. W14 66 C5
Beaumont Ave., Har. 36 H6
Beaumont Ave., Rich. 73 J3
Beaumont Ave., 46 F5
Wem.
Beaumont Clo., 83 A7
Kings.T.
Beaumont Cres. W14 66 C5
Beaumont Gdns. 48 D3
NW3
Beaumont Gro. E1 59 G4
Beaumont Ms. W1 11 C1
Beaumont Pl. W1 7 G5
Beaumont Pl. W1 58 C4
Beaumont Pl., Barn. 23 C1
Beaumont Pl., Islw. 73 C5
Beaumont Ri. N19 40 D7
Beaumont Rd. E10 42 B7
Beaumont Rd. E13 60 H3
Beaumont Rd. SE19 85 J6
Beaumont Rd. SW19 75 B7
Beaumont Rd. W4 65 C3
Beaumont Rd., Orp. 97 G6
Beaumont Sq. E1 59 G4
Beaumont St. W1 11 C1
Beaumont St. W1 58 A5
Beaumont Wk. NW3 48 J7
Beauvais Ter., Nthlt. 54 D3
Beauval Rd. SE22 77 C6
Beaver Clo. SE26 86 D7
Lullington Rd.
Beaver Clo., Hmptn. 90 H1
Beaver Gro., Nthlt. 54 E3
Jetstar Way
Beaverbank Rd. SE9 88 G1
Beavers Cres., 72 D4
Houns.
Beavers La., Houns. 72 C2
Beaverwood Rd., 88 H6
Chis.
Beavor La. W6 65 G4
Bebbington Rd. SE18 70 H4
Bebletts Clo., Orp. 104 J5
Bec Clo., Ruis. 45 D3
Beccles Dr., Bark. 52 H6
Beccles St. E14 59 J7
Beck Clo. SE13 78 B1
Beck Ct., Beck. 95 G3
Beck La., Beck. 95 G3
Beck Rd. E8 59 E1
Beck Way, Beck. 95 J3
Beckenham Gdns. N9 33 B3
Beckenham Gro., 96 D2
Brom.
Beckenham Hill Rd. 87 C5
SE6
Beckenham Hill Rd., 87 B6
Beck.
Beckenham La., 96 E2
Brom.
Beckenham Pl. Pk., 87 B7
Beck.
Beckenham Rd., 95 G1
Beck.
Beckenham Rd., 96 B7
W.Wick.
Beckers, The N16 50 D3
Rectory Rd.
Becket Ave. E6 61 D3
Becket Clo. SE25 95 D6
Becket Fold, Har. 37 C5
Courtfield Cres.
Becket Rd. N18 33 F4
Becket St. SE1 17 B5
Beckett Clo. NW10 47 D6
Beckett Clo. SW16 85 D2
Beckett Clo., Belv. 71 E3
Tunstock Way
Beckett Wk., Beck. 86 H6
Beckets Clo., Felt. 72 B6
Becketts Clo., Orp. 104 J3

Becketts Pl., Kings.T. 91 G1
Beckford Rd., Croy. 95 C6
Becklow Gdns. W12 65 G2
Becklow Rd.
Becklow Rd. W12 65 F2
Becks Rd., Sid. 89 A3
Beckton Retail Pk. E6 61 D5
Beckton Rd. E16 59 E5
Beckway Rd. SW16 94 D2
Beckway St. SE17 21 D2
Beckway St. SE17 66 A1
Beckwith Rd. SE24 77 A6
Beclands Rd. SW17 85 A6
Becmead Ave. SW16 85 D4
Becmead Ave., Har. 37 E5
Becondale Rd. SE19 86 B5
Becontree Ave., Dag. 53 B4
Bective Pl. SW15 75 C4
Bective Rd.
Bective Rd. E7 51 G4
Bective Rd. SW15 75 B4
Becton Pl., Erith 71 H7
Bedale St. SE1 17 B2
Bedale St. SE1 68 A1
Beddington Fm. Rd., 94 E7
Croy.
Beddington Gdns., 101 A6
Cars.
Beddington Gdns., 101 B6
Wall.
Beddington Grn., 97 J1
Orp.
Beddington Gro., 101 D5
Wall.
Beddington La., 94 C5
Croy.
Beddington Path, 97 J1
Orp.
Beddington Rd., Ilf. 43 J7
Beddington Rd., Orp. 97 H1
Bede Clo., Pnr. 36 D1
Bede Rd., Rom. 44 C6
Bedenham Way SE15 21 F7
Bedens Rd., Sid. 89 E6
Bedfont Clo., Mitch. 94 A2
Bedford Ave. WC1 11 J2
Bedford Ave. WC1 58 D5
Bedford Ave., Barn. 23 C5
Bedford Ave., Hayes 54 B6
Bedford Clo. N10 32 A7
Bedford Cor. W4 65 E4
The Ave.
Bedford Ct. WC2 12 A6
Bedford Gdns. W8 66 D1
Bedford Hill SW12 85 B1
Bedford Ho. SW4 76 E4
Bedford Pk., Croy. 101 J1
Bedford Pl. WC1 12 A1
Bedford Pl. WC1 58 E5
Bedford Pl., Croy. 102 A1
Bedford Rd. E6 61 D1
Bedford Rd. E17 42 A2
Bedford Rd. E18 42 G2
Bedford Rd. N2 39 H3
Bedford Rd. N8 40 D6
Bedford Rd. N9 25 E7
Bedford Rd. N15 41 B4
Bedford Rd. N22 40 E1
Bedford Rd. NW7 30 E2
Bedford Rd. SW4 76 E3
Bedford Rd. W4 65 D3
Bedford Rd. W13 55 E7
Bedford Rd., Har. 36 A3
Bedford Rd., Ilf. 52 E3
Bedford Rd., Sid. 88 H3
Bedford Rd., Twick. 82 A3
Bedford Rd., Wor.Pk. 99 J2
Bedford Row WC1 12 D1
Bedford Row WC1 58 F5
Bedford Sq. WC1 11 J2
Bedford Sq. WC1 58 D5
Bedford St. WC2 12 A5
Bedford St. WC2 58 E7
Bedford Way WC1 7 J6
Bedford Way WC1 58 D4
Bedfordbury WC2 12 A6
Bedgebury Gdns. 84 B2
SW19
Bedgebury Rd. SE9 79 A4
Bedivere Rd., Brom. 87 G3
Bedlow Way, Croy. 101 F4
Bedonwell Rd. SE2 71 E6
Bedonwell Rd., Belv. 71 E6
Bedonwell Rd., 80 F1
Bexh.
Bedser Dr., Grnf. 46 A3
Bedster Gdns., 90 H2
W.Mol.
Bedwardine Rd. SE19 86 B7
Bedwell Rd. N17 41 B1
Bedwell Rd., Belv. 71 G5
Bedwin Way SE16 68 E5
Catlin St.

Beeby Rd. E16 60 H5
Beech Ave. N20 31 H1
Beech Ave. W3 65 E1
Beech Ave., Brent. 64 E7
Beech Ave., Buck.H. 34 H2
Beech Ave., Ruis. 45 B1
Beech Ave., Sid. 80 A7
Beech Clo. N9 25 D6
Beech Clo. SE9 68 J6
Clyde St.
Beech Clo. SW15 74 G7
Beech Clo. SW19 83 I6
Beech Clo., Cars. 100 J2
Beech Clo., Sun. 90 D2
Harfield Rd.
Beech Copse, Brom. 97 C2
Beech Copse, 102 B5
S.Croy.
Beech Ct. E17 42 D3
Beech Ct. SE9 79 B6
Beech Ct., Ilf. 52 D3
Riverdene Rd.
Beech Dell, Kes. 104 C4
Beech Dr. N2 39 J2
Beech Gdns. W5 64 H2
Beech Gdns., Dag. 53 H7
Beech Gro., Ilf. 35 H6
Beech Gro., Mitch. 94 D5
Beech Gro., N.Mal. 92 D3
Beech Hall Cres. E4 34 D7
Beech Hall Rd. E4 34 C7
Beech Hill, Barn. 23 F1
Beech Hill Ave., 23 F1
Barn.
Beech Ho., Croy. 103 B6
Beech Ho. Rd., Croy. 102 A3
Beech La., Buck.H. 34 H2
Beech Lawns N12 31 G5
Beech Rd. N11 32 E6
Beech Rd. SW16 94 E2
Beech Row, Rich. 82 H4
Beech St. EC2 12 J1
Beech St. EC2 58 J5
Beech St., Rom. 44 J4
Beech Tree Glade E4 34 F1
Forest Side
Beech Wk. NW7 30 E6
Beech Way NW10 47 D7
Beech Way, Twick. 81 G3
Beechcroft, Chis. 88 D7
Beechcroft Ave. 39 C7
NW11
Beechcroft Ave., Har. 36 G7
Beechcroft Ave., 92 C1
N.Mal.
Beechcroft Ave., Sthl. 63 E7
Beechcroft Clo., 63 E7
Houns.
Beechcroft Clo., Orp. 104 G4
Beechcroft Gdns., 46 D3
Wem.
Beechcroft Rd. E18 42 H2
Beechcroft Rd. SW14 74 C3
Elm Rd.
Beechcroft Rd. SW17 84 H2
Beechcroft Rd., 98 J4
Chess.
Beechcroft Rd., Orp. 104 G4
Beechdale N21 32 F2
Beechdale Rd. SW2 76 F6
Beechen Cliff Way, 73 C1
Islw.
Henley Clo.
Beechen Gro., Pnr. 36 F3
Beeches Ave., The, 100 H7
Cars.
Beeches Clo. SE20 95 F1
Genoa Rd.
Beeches Rd. SW17 84 H3
Beeches Rd., Sutt. 100 B1
Beechfield Cotts., 96 J2
Brom.
Beechfield Gdns., 44 J7
Rom.
Beechfield Rd. N4 40 J6
Beechfield Rd. SE6 86 J1
Beechfield Rd., 96 J2
Brom.
Beechhill Rd. SE9 79 D5
Beechmont Clo., 87 E5
Brom.
Beechmore Gdns., 100 A2
Sutt.
Beechmore Rd. SW11 75 J1
Beechmount Ave. W7 55 A5
Beecholme Ave., 94 B1
Mitch.
Beecholme Est. E5 50 E3
Prout Rd.
Beechtree Clo., Stan. 29 F5
Beechtree Pl., Sutt. 100 E5
St. Nicholas Way

Beechvale Clo. N12 31 H5
Beechway, Bex. 80 D6
Beechwood Ave. N3 39 C3
Beechwood Ave., 54 H3
Grnf.
Beechwood Ave., 45 H3
Har.
Beechwood Ave., 104 H5
Orp.
Beechwood Ave., 74 A1
Rich.
Beechwood Ave., 81 A6
Sun.
Beechwood Ave., 94 H4
Th.Hth.
Beechwood Clo. NW7 30 D5
Beechwood Clo., 91 G7
Surb.
Beechwood Ct., Sun. 81 A6
Beechwood Cres., 80 D3
Bexh.
Beechwood Dr., Kes. 104 A4
Beechwood Dr., 34 F5
Wdf.Grn.
Beechwood Gdns. 55 J3
NW10
North Circular Rd.
Beechwood Gdns., 45 H3
Har.
Beechwood Gdns., 43 C5
Ilf.
Beechwood Gro., 91 F7
Surb.
Beechwood Ms. N9 33 D2
Winchester Rd.
Beechwood Pk. E18 42 G3
Beechwood Ri., Chis. 88 E4
Beechwood Rd. E8 50 C6
Beechwood Rd. N8 40 D4
Beechwoods Ct. 86 C5
SE19
Crystal Palace Par.
Beechworth Clo. 48 D2
NW3
Beecroft Rd. SE4 77 H5
Beehive La., Ilf. 43 C5
Beehive Pas. EC3 13 D4
Beehive Pl. SW9 76 G3
Beeleigh Rd., Mord. 93 E4
Beeston Clo. E8 50 D5
Ferncliff Rd.
Beeston Clo., Wat. 28 D4
Beeston Pl. SW1 15 E6
Beeston Rd., Barn. 23 G6
Beeston Way, Felt. 72 C6
Beethoven St. W10 57 B3
Beeton Clo., Pnr. 28 G7
Begbie Rd. SE3 78 J1
Beggars Roost La., 100 D6
Sutt.
Begonia Pl., Hmptn. 81 G6
Gresham Rd.
Begonia Wk. W12 56 F6
Du Cane Rd.
Beira St. SW12 76 B7
Bekesbourne St. E14 59 H6
Ratcliffe La.
Belcroft Clo., Brom. 87 F7
Hope Pk.
Beldham Gdns., 90 H3
W.Mol.
Belfairs Dr., Rom. 44 C7
Belfairs Grn., Wat. 28 D5
Heysham Dr.
Belfast Rd. N16 50 C2
Belfast Rd. SE25 95 E4
Belfont Wk. N7 49 E4
Belford Gro. SE18 70 D4
Belfort Rd. SE15 77 F2
Belgrade Rd. N16 50 B4
Belgrade Rd., Hmptn. 90 H1
Belgrave Clo. N14 24 C5
Prince George Ave.
Belgrave Clo. W3 65 C2
Avenue Rd.
Belgrave Cres., Sun. 90 B1
Belgrave Gdns. N14 24 D5
Belgrave Gdns. NW8 57 E1
Belgrave Gdns., Stan. 29 F5
Copley Rd.
Belgrave Ms. N. SW1 15 B4
Belgrave Ms. N. SW1 67 A3
Belgrave Ms. S. SW1 15 C5
Belgrave Ms. S. SW1 67 A3
Belgrave Ms. W. SW1 15 B5
Belgrave Ms. W. SW1 67 A3
Belgrave Pl. SW1 15 C5
Belgrave Pl. SW1 67 A3
Belgrave Rd. E10 51 C1
Belgrave Rd. E11 51 G2
Belgrave Rd. E13 60 J3
Belgrave Rd. E17 42 A5

Belgrave Rd. SE25 95 D4
Belgrave Rd. SW1 19 F2
Belgrave Rd. SW1 67 B4
Belgrave Rd. SW13 65 F7
Belgrave Rd., Houns. 72 F3
Belgrave Rd., Ilf. 52 C1
Belgrave Rd., Mitch. 93 G3
Belgrave Rd., Sun. 90 B1
Belgrave Sq. SW1 15 B5
Belgrave Sq. SW1 67 A3
Belgrave St. E1 59 G5
Belgrave Ter., Wdf.Grn. 34 G3
Belgrave Wk., Mitch. 93 G3
Belgrave Yd. SW1 15 D6
Belgravia Gdns., Brom. 87 E6
Belgravia Ho. SW4 76 D6
Belgravia Ms., Kings.T. 91 G4
Belgrove St. WC1 8 B3
Belgrove St. WC1 58 E3
Belham Wk. SE5 77 A1
D'Eynsford Rd.
Belinda Rd. SW9 76 H3
Belitha Vill. N1 49 F7
Bell Clo., Pnr. 36 C2
Bell Ct., Surb. 99 B2
Barnsbury La.
Bell Dr. SW18 75 B7
Bell Fm. Ave., Dag. 53 J3
Bell Grn. SE26 86 J3
Bell Grn. La. SE26 86 J5
Bell Ho. Rd., Rom. 53 J1
Bell Inn Yd. EC3 13 C4
Bell La. E1 13 F2
Bell La. E1 59 C5
Bell La. E16 69 G1
Bell La. NW4 38 J4
Bell La., Twick. 82 D1
Bell Meadow SE19 86 B4
Dulwich Wd. Ave.
Bell Rd., E.Mol. 91 A5
Bell Rd., Enf. 25 A1
Bell Rd., Houns. 72 H3
Bell St. NW1 10 G1
Bell St. NW1 57 H5
Bell Water Gate SE18 70 D3
Bell Yd. WC2 12 E4
Bell Yd. WC2 58 G6
Bellamy Clo. W14 66 C5
Aisgill Ave.
Bellamy Dr., Stan. 37 E1
Bellamy Rd. E4 34 B6
Bellamy Rd., Enf. 25 A2
Bellamy St. SW12 76 B7
Bellasis Ave. SW2 85 E2
Belle Staines Pleasaunce E4 34 A2
Belle Vue, Grnf. 55 A1
Belle Vue Est. NW4 38 J4
Belle Vue La. (Bushey), Wat. 29 A1
Belle Vue Rd. E17 42 D2
Bellefields Rd. SW9 76 F3
Bellegrove Clo., Well. 79 J2
Bellegrove Rd., Well. 79 H2
Bellenden Rd. SE15 77 C3
Belleville Rd. SW11 75 H5
Bellevue Ms. N11 32 A5
Bellevue Rd.
Bellevue Pk., Th.Hth. 94 J3
Bellevue Pl. E1 59 F4
Cleveland Way
Bellevue Rd. N11 32 A4
Bellevue Rd. SW13 74 G2
Bellevue Rd. SW17 84 H1
Bellevue Rd. W13 55 E4
Bellevue Rd., Bexh. 80 F5
Bellevue Rd., Kings.T. 91 H3
Bellew St. SW17 84 F3
Bellfield, Croy. 102 J7
Bellfield Ave., Har. 29 A5
Bellflower Clo. E6 61 B5
Sorrell Gdns.
Bellgate Ms. NW5 49 B3
York Ri.
Bellingham Grn. SE6 87 A3
Bellingham Rd. SE6 87 C3
Bellot St. SE10 69 E5
Bellring Clo., Belv. 71 G6
Bells All. SW6 75 D2
Bells Gdn. Est. SE15 68 D7
Buller Clo.
Bells Hill, Barn. 23 A5
Belltrees Gro. SW16 85 F5
Bellwood Rd. SE15 77 G4
Belmarsh Rd. SE28 70 H2
Western Way
Belmont Ave. N9 33 D1
Belmont Ave. N13 32 E5
Belmont Ave. N17 40 J3
Belmont Ave., Barn. 23 J5
Belmont Ave., N.Mal. 92 G5
Belmont Ave., Sthl. 63 E3
Belmont Ave., Well. 79 H2
Belmont Ave., Wem. 55 J1
Belmont Circle, Har. 37 E2
Kenton La.
Belmont Clo. E4 34 D5
Belmont Clo. N20 31 E1
Belmont Clo. SW4 76 C3
Belmont Clo., Barn. 23 J4
Belmont Clo., Wdf.Grn. 34 H4
Belmont Ct. NW11 39 C5
Belmont Gro. SE13 78 D3
Belmont Hall Ct. SE13 78 D3
Belmont Gro.
Belmont Hill SE13 78 C3
Belmont La., Chis. 88 F5
Belmont La., Stan. 29 F7
Belmont Pk. SE13 78 D4
Belmont Pk. Clo. SE13 78 D4
Belmont Pk.
Belmont Pk. Rd. E10 42 B6
Belmont Ri., Sutt. 100 C7
Belmont Rd. N15 40 J4
Belmont Rd. N17 40 J3
Belmont Rd. SE25 95 E5
Belmont Rd. SW4 76 C3
Belmont Rd. W4 65 D4
Belmont Rd., Beck. 95 J2
Belmont Rd., Chis. 88 E5
Belmont Rd., Erith 71 G7
Belmont Rd., Har. 37 C3
Belmont Rd., Ilf. 52 F3
Belmont Rd., Twick. 82 A2
Belmont Rd., Wall. 101 B5
Belmont St. NW1 49 A7
Belmont Ter. W4 65 D4
Belmont Rd.
Belmor, Borwd. 22 A5
Belmore Ave., Hayes 54 A6
Belmore La. N7 49 D5
Belmore St. SW8 76 D1
Beloe Clo. SW15 74 G3
Belper Ct. E5 50 G4
Pedro St.
Belsham St. E9 50 F6
Belsize Ave. N13 32 F6
Belsize Ave. NW3 48 G6
Belsize Ave. W13 64 E3
Belsize Cres. NW3 48 G5
Belsize Gdns., Sutt. 100 E4
Belsize Gro. NW3 48 H6
Belsize La. NW3 48 G6
Belsize Pk. NW3 48 G6
Belsize Pk. Gdns. NW3 48 H6
Belsize Pk. Ms. NW3 48 G6
Belsize La.
Belsize Pl. NW3 48 G6
Belsize La.
Belsize Rd. NW6 57 E1
Belsize Rd., Har. 29 A7
Belsize Sq. NW3 48 G6
Belsize Ter. NW3 48 G6
Belson Rd. SE18 70 C4
Beltane Dr. SW19 84 A3
Belthorn Cres. SW12 76 C7
Belton Rd. E7 51 H7
Belton Rd. E11 51 E4
Belton Rd. N17 41 B3
Belton Rd. NW2 47 G6
Belton Rd., Sid. 89 A4
Belton Way E3 60 A5
Beltran Rd. SW6 75 E2
Beltwood Rd., Belv. 71 J4
Belvedere Ave. SW19 84 B5
Belvedere Ave., Ilf. 43 E2
Belvedere Bldgs. SE1 16 H4
Belvedere Clo., Tedd. 82 B5
Belvedere Ct. N2 39 G5
Belvedere Dr. SW19 84 B5
Belvedere Gdns., W.Mol. 90 F5
Belvedere Gro. SW19 84 B5
Belvedere Ho., Felt. 81 A1
Belvedere Ind. Est., Belv. 71 J3
Belvedere Pl. SE1 16 H4
Belvedere Rd. E10 50 H1
Belvedere Rd. SE1 16 D3
Belvedere Rd. SE1 67 F2
Belvedere Rd. SE2 71 D1
Belvedere Rd. SE19 86 C7
Belvedere Rd. W7 64 B3
Belvedere Rd., Bexh. 80 F3
Belvedere Sq. SW19 84 B5
Belvedere Strand NW9 38 F2
Belvedere Way, Har. 37 H6
Belvoir Clo. SE9 88 B3
Belvoir Rd. SE22 77 D7
Belvue Clo., Nthlt. 45 G7
Belvue Rd., Nthlt. 45 G7
Bembridge Clo. NW6 48 B7
Bemerton Est. N1 49 E7
Bemerton St. N1 58 F1
Bemish Rd. SW15 75 A3
Bempton Dr., Ruis. 45 B2
Bemsted Rd. E17 41 J3
Ben Hale Clo., Stan. 29 E4
Ben Jonson Rd. E1 59 G5
Ben Smith Way SE16 17 J5
Ben Tillet Clo., Bark. 53 A7
Benares Rd. SE18 70 J4
Benbow Rd. W6 65 H3
Benbow St. SE8 69 A6
Benbury Clo., Brom. 87 C5
Bench Fld., S.Croy. 102 C6
Bencroft Rd. SW16 85 C7
Bencurtis Pk., W.Wick. 103 D3
Bendall Ms. NW1 10 H1
Bendemeer Rd. SW15 75 A3
Bendish Rd. E6 52 B7
Bendmore Ave. SE2 71 A5
Bendon Valley SW18 75 E7
Benedict Clo., Belv. 71 E3
Tunstock Way
Benedict Clo., Orp. 104 H3
Benedict Rd. SW9 76 F3
Benedict Rd., Mitch. 93 G3
Benedict Way N2 39 F3
Benenden Grn., Brom. 96 F5
Benett Gdns. SW16 94 E2
Benfleet Clo., Sutt. 100 F3
Bengal Rd., Ilf. 52 E4
Bengarth Dr., Har. 37 A2
Bengarth Rd., Nthlt. 54 D1
Bengeworth Rd. SE5 76 J3
Bengeworth Rd., Har. 46 D4
Benham Clo. SW11 75 G3
Benham Gdns., Houns. 72 F4
Benham Rd. W7 55 B5
Benhams Pl. NW3 48 F4
Holly Wk.
Benhill Ave., Sutt. 100 E4
Benhill Rd. SE5 68 A7
Benhill Rd., Sutt. 100 F3
Benhill Wd. Rd., Sutt. 100 F4
Benhilton Gdns., Sutt. 100 E3
Benhurst Ct. SW16 85 G5
Benhurst La. SW16 85 G5
Benin St. SE13 78 D7
Benjafield Clo. N18 33 E4
Brettenham Rd.
Benjamin Clo. E8 59 D1
Benjamin St. EC1 12 G1
Benjamin St. EC1 58 H5
Benledi St. E14 60 D6
Benn St. E9 50 H6
Bennerley Rd. SW11 75 H5
Bennets Copse, Chis. 88 B6
Bennet's Hill EC4 12 H5
Bennett Clo., Kings.T. 91 F1
Bennett Clo., Well. 80 A2
Bennett Gro. SE13 78 B1
Bennett Pk. SE3 78 F3
Bennett Rd. E13 60 J4
Bennett Rd. N16 50 B4
Bennett Rd., Rom. 44 E6
Bennett St. SW1 15 F1
Bennett St. W4 65 E6
Bennetts Ave., Croy. 102 H2
Bennetts Ave., Grnf. 55 B1
Bennetts Castle La., Dag. 53 C4
Bennetts Clo. N17 33 C6
Bennetts Way, Croy. 102 H2
Bennetts Yd. SW1 15 J6
Benningholme Rd., Edg. 30 E6
Bennington Rd. N17 41 B1
Bennington Rd., Wdf.Grn. 34 E7
Benn's Wk., Rich. 73 H4
Rosedale Rd.
Benrek Clo., Ilf. 43 F1
Bensbury Clo. SW15 74 J7
Bensham Clo., Th.Hth. 94 J4
Bensham Gro., Th.Hth. 94 J2
Bensham La., Croy. 94 H7
Bensham La., Th.Hth. 94 H4
Bensham Manor Rd., Th.Hth. 94 J4
Bensley Clo. N11 31 J5
Benson Ave. E6 60 J2
Benson Clo., Houns. 72 G4
Benson Quay E1 59 F7
Garnet St.
Benson Rd. SE23 86 F1
Benson Rd., Croy. 101 G3
Bentfield Gdns. SE9 87 J3
Aldersgrove Ave.
Benthal Rd. N16 50 D2
Bentham Rd. E9 50 G6
Bentham Rd. SE28 62 B7
Bentham Wk. NW10 47 C5
Bentinck Ms. W1 11 C3
Bentinck Pl. NW8 6 G2
Bentinck St. W1 11 C3
Bentinck St. W1 58 A6
Bentley Dr., Ilf. 43 F6
Bentley Rd. N1 50 B6
Tottenham Rd.
Bentley Way, Stan. 29 D5
Bentley Way, Wdf.Grn. 34 G3
Benton Rd., Ilf. 52 G1
Benton Rd., Wat. 28 D5
Bentons La. SE27 85 J4
Bentons Ri. SE27 86 A5
Bentry Clo., Dag. 53 E2
Bentry Rd., Dag. 53 E2
Bentworth Rd. W12 56 H6
Benwell Ct., Sun. 90 A1
Benwell Rd. N7 49 G4
Benwick Clo. SE16 68 E4
Benworth St. E3 59 J3
Benyon Rd. N1 59 A1
Southgate Rd.
Berber Rd. SW11 75 J5
Bercta Rd. SE9 88 F2
Bere St. E1 59 G7
Cranford St.
Berenger Wk. SW10 18 E7
Berens Rd. NW10 57 A3
Berens Way, Chis. 97 J4
Beresford Ave. N20 31 J2
Beresford Ave. W7 55 A5
Beresford Ave., Surb. 99 B1
Beresford Ave., Twick. 73 F6
Beresford Ave., Wem. 55 J1
Beresford Dr., Brom. 97 B3
Beresford Dr., Wdf.Grn. 34 J4
Beresford Gdns., Enf. 25 B4
Beresford Gdns., Houns. 72 F5
Beresford Gdns., Rom. 44 E5
Beresford Rd. E4 34 E1
Beresford Rd. E17 42 B1
Beresford Rd. N2 39 H3
Beresford Rd. N5 50 A5
Beresford Rd. N8 40 G5
Beresford Rd., Har. 37 A5
Beresford Rd., Kings.T. 91 J1
Beresford Rd., N.Mal. 92 C4
Beresford Rd., Sthl. 63 D1
Beresford Rd., Sutt. 100 C7
Beresford Sq. SE18 70 E4
Beresford St. SE18 70 E3
Beresford Ter. N5 49 J5
Berestede Rd. W6 65 F5
Bergen Sq. SE16 68 H3
Norway Gate
Berger Clo., Orp. 97 G6
Berger Rd. E9 50 G6
Berghem Ms. W14 66 A3
Blythe Rd.
Bergholt Ave., Ilf. 43 B5
Bergholt Cres. N16 41 B7
Bergholt Ms. NW1 49 C7
Rossendale Way
Bering Wk. E16 61 A6
Berkeley Ave., Bexh. 80 D1
Berkeley Ave., Grnf. 46 A6
Berkeley Ave., Houns. 72 A1
Berkeley Ave., Ilf. 43 D2
Berkeley Clo., Borwd. 22 A5
Berkeley Clo., Kings.T. 82 H7
Berkeley Clo., Orp. 97 H7
Berkeley Clo., Ruis. 45 A3
Berkeley Ct. N14 24 C6
Berkeley Cres., Barn. 23 G5
Berkeley Gdns. N21 25 A7
Berkeley Gdns. W8 66 D1
Brunswick Gdns.
Berkeley Gdns., Esher 98 D6
Berkeley Ho. E3 60 A3
Wellington Way
Berkeley Ms. W1 11 A4

Berkeley Pl. SW19 84 A6
Berkeley Rd. E12 52 B5
Berkeley Rd. N8 40 D5
Berkeley Rd. N15 41 A3
Berkeley Rd. NW9 38 A4
Berkeley Rd. NW12 74 G1
Berkeley Sq. W1 11 E0
Berkeley Sq. W1 58 B7
Berkeley St. W1 11 F1
Berkeley St. W1 67 B1
Berkeley Wk. N7 49 F2
Durham Rd.
Berkeley Waye, 63 D7
Houns.
Berkhampstead Rd., 71 G5
Belv.
Berkhamsted Ave., 46 J6
Wem.
Berkley Dr., W.Mol. 90 F3
Berkley Gro. NW1 48 J7
Berkley Rd.
Berkley Rd. NW1 48 J7
Berkshire Gdns. N13 32 G6
Berkshire Gdns. N18 33 E5
Berkshire Rd. E9 50 J6
Berkshire Way, 94 E4
Mitch.
Bermans Way NW10 47 E4
Bermondsey Sq. SE1 17 E5
Bermondsey St. SE1 17 D2
Bermondsey St. SE1 68 B2
Bermondsey Wall E. 17 J4
SE16
Bermondsey Wall E. 68 D2
SE16
Bermondsey Wall W. 17 H3
SE16
Bermondsey Wall W. 68 D2
SE16
Bernal Clo. SE28 62 D7
Haldane Rd.
Bernard Ave. W13 64 E3
Bernard Cassidy St. 60 F5
E16
Bernard Gdns. SW19 84 C5
Bernard Rd. N15 41 C5
Bernard Rd., Rom. 44 J7
Bernard Rd., Wall. 101 B5
Bernard St. WC1 8 A6
Bernard St. WC1 58 E4
Bernards Clo., Ilf. 35 F7
Bernays Clo., Stan. 29 F6
Bernays Gro. SW9 76 F4
Berne Rd., Th.Hth. 94 H5
Bernel Dr., Croy. 102 J3
Berners Dr. W13 55 D6
Berners Ms. W1 11 G2
Berners Ms. W1 58 C5
Berners Pl. W1 11 G3
Berners Pl. W1 58 C6
Berners Rd. N1 58 G1
Berners Rd. N22 40 G1
Berners St. W1 11 G2
Berners St. W1 58 C5
Berners Rd., Croy. 95 A7
Bernville Way, Har. 37 J5
Kenton Rd.
Bernwell Rd. E4 34 E3
Berridge Grn., Edg. 30 B7
Berridge Rd. SE19 86 B5
Berriman Rd. N7 49 F3
Berriton Rd., Har. 45 F1
Berry Clo. N21 32 H1
Berry Clo. 47 E7
NW10
Berry Ct., Houns. 72 F5
Berry Hill, Stan. 29 G4
Berry La. SE21 86 A4
Berry Pl. EC1 8 H4
Berry St. EC1 8 H5
Berry St. EC1 58 H4
Berry Way W5 64 H3
Berrybank Clo. E4 34 C2
Greenbank Clo.
Berrydale Rd., Hayes 54 E4
Berryfield Clo. E17 42 B4
Berryfield Clo., Brom. 97 B1
Berryfield Rd. SE17 20 H3
Berryfield Rd. SE17 67 H5
Berryhill SE9 79 E4
Berryhill Gdns. SE9 79 E4
Berrylands SW20 92 J3
Berrylands, Surb. 91 J6
Berrylands Rd., Surb. 91 J6
Berryman Clo., Dag. 53 C3
Bennetts Castle La.
Berrymans La. SE26 86 G4
Berrymead Gdns. W3 65 C2
Berrymede Rd. W4 65 D3
Berryhill SE9 79 E4
Bert Rd., Th.Hth. 94 J5
Bert Way, Enf. 25 C4
Bertal Rd. SW17 84 G4
Berthon St. SE8 69 A7
Bertie Rd. NW10 47 G6

Bertie Rd. SE26 86 G6
Bertram Cotts. SW19 84 D7
Hartfield Rd.
Bertram Rd. NW4 38 G6
Bertram Rd., Enf. 25 D4
Bertram Rd., Kings.T. 83 A7
Durtram St. N19 49 B2
Bertram Way, Enf. 25 C4
Bertrand St. SE13 78 B3
Bertund Way SE28 62 B7
Berwick Ave., Hayes 94 D6
Berwick Clo., Stan. 29 C7
Gordon Ave.
Berwick Cres., Sid. 79 H6
Berwick Rd. E16 60 H6
Berwick Rd. N22 40 H1
Berwick Rd., Well. 80 B1
Berwick St. W1 11 G3
Berwick St. W1 58 C6
Berwyn Ave., Houns. 72 H1
Berwyn Rd. SE24 85 H1
Berwyn Rd., Rich. 74 B4
Beryl Ave. E6 61 B5
Beryl Rd. W6 66 A5
Berystede, Kings.T. 83 B7
Besant Ct. N1 50 A5
Mildmay Gro.
Besant Rd. NW2 48 B4
Besant Wk. N7 49 F2
Newington Barrow
Way
Besant Way NW10 47 C5
Besley St. SW16 85 C7
Bessborough Gdns. 19 J3
SW1
Bessborough Gdns. 67 D5
SW1
Bessborough Pl. SW1 19 H3
Bessborough Pl. SW1 67 D5
Bessborough Rd. 83 G1
SW15
Bessborough Rd., 46 A1
Har.
Bessborough St. SW1 19 H3
Bessborough St. SW1 67 D5
Bessemer Rd. SE5 76 J2
Bessie Lansbury Clo. 61 D6
E6
Bessingby Rd., Ruis. 45 B2
Bessingham Wk. SE4 77 G4
Frendsbury Rd.
Besson St. SE14 77 F1
Bessy St. E2 59 F3
Roman Rd.
Bestwood St. SE8 68 G4
Beswick Ms. NW6 48 E6
Lymington Rd.
Betchworth Clo., 100 G5
Sutt.
Turnpike La.
Betchworth Rd., Ilf. 52 H2
Betham Rd., Grnf. 55 A3
Bethecar Rd., Har. 37 B5
Bethell Rd., Well. 80 C3
Bethell Ave. E16 60 F4
Bethell Ave., Ilf. 43 D7
Bethersden Clo., 86 J7
Beck.
Bethnal Grn. Rd. E1 9 F5
Bethnal Grn. Rd. E1 59 C4
Bethnal Grn. Rd. E2 9 A4
Bethnal Grn. Rd. E2 59 C4
Bethune Ave. N11 31 J4
Bethune Rd. N16 41 A7
Bethune Rd. NW10 56 D4
Bethwin Rd. SE5 20 H7
Bethwin Rd. SE5 67 H7
Betjeman Clo., Pnr. 36 G4
Betony Clo., Croy. 102 G1
Primrose La.
Betoyne Ave. E4 34 E4
Betstyle Rd. N11 32 B4
Betterton Dr., Sid. 89 E2
Betterton St. WC2 12 A4
Betterton St. WC2 58 E6
Bettons Pk. E15 60 E1
Bettridge Rd. SW6 75 C2
Betts Clo., Beck. 95 H2
Kendall Rd.
Betts Rd. E16 60 H7
Victoria Dock Rd.
Betts St. E1 59 E7
The Highway
Betts Way SE20 95 E1
Betts Way, Surb. 98 E1
Beulah Ave., Th.Hth. 94 F4
Beulah Rd.
Beulah Clo., Edg. 30 B3
Beulah Cres., Th.Hth. 94 J2
Beulah Gro., Croy. 94 J6
Beulah Hill SE19 85 H6
Beulah Path E17 42 B5
Addison Rd.

Beulah Rd. E17 42 B5
Beulah Rd. SW19 84 C7
Beulah Rd., Sutt. 100 D4
Beulah Rd., Th.Hth. 94 J3
Bev Callender Clo. 76 B3
SW8
Daley Thompson Way
Bevan Ave., Bark. 53 A7
Duvan Ct., Croy. 101 G5
Bevan Rd. SE2 11 B6
Bevan Rd., Barn. 23 J4
Bevan St. N1 58 J1
Bevenden St. N1 9 C3
Bevenden St. N1 59 A3
Bevercote Wk., Belv. 71 F6
Osborne Rd.
Beveridge Rd. NW10 47 E7
Curzon Cres.
Beverley NW8 6 G4
Beverley Ave. SW20 92 F1
Beverley Ave., 72 F1
Houns.
Beverley Ave., Sid. 77 J7
Beverley Clo. N21 32 J1
Beverley Clo. SW11 75 G4
Maysoule Rd.
Beverley Clo. SW13 74 F2
Beverley Clo., Chess. 98 F4
Beverley Clo., Enf. 25 B6
Beverley Ct. N14 24 C7
Beverley Ct. SE4 77 J3
Beverley Cres., 42 H1
Wdf.Grn.
Beverley Dr., Edg. 38 A3
Beverley Gdns. NW11 39 B7
Beverley Gdns. SW13 74 F3
Beverley Gdns., Stan. 37 D1
Beverley Gdns., 46 J1
Wem.
Beverley Gdns., 99 G1
Wor.Pk.
Green La.
Beverley La. SW15 83 F3
Beverley La., 83 E7
Kings.T.
Beverley Path SW13 74 F2
Beverley Rd. E4 34 D6
Beverley Rd. E6 61 A3
Beverley Rd. SE20 95 E2
Beverley Rd. SW13 74 F3
Beverley Rd. W4 65 F5
Beverley Rd., Bexh. 80 D2
Beverley Rd., Brom. 104 B2
Beverley Rd., Dag. 53 E4
Beverley Rd., 91 F1
Kings.T.
Beverley Rd., Mitch. 94 D4
Beverley Rd., N.Mal. 92 G4
Beverley Rd., Ruis. 45 A2
Beverley Rd., Sthl. 63 E4
Beverley Rd., Wor.Pk. 99 J2
Beverley Way SW20 92 F1
Beverley Way, N.Mal. 92 F1
Beversbrook Rd. N19 49 D3
Beverstone Rd. SW2 76 F5
Beverstone Rd., 94 G4
Th.Hth.
Bevill Allen Clo. 84 J5
SW17
Bevin Clo. SE16 68 H1
Bevin Rd., Hayes 54 A3
Bevin Way WC1 8 E3
Bevington Rd. W10 57 B5
Bevington Rd., Beck. 96 B2
Bevington St. SE16 17 J4
Bevington St. SE16 68 D2
Bevis Marks EC3 13 E3
Bevis Marks EC3 59 B6
Bewcastle Gdns., Enf. 24 E4
Bewdley St. N1 49 G7
Bewick St. SW8 76 B2
Bewley Rd. SE27 85 H5
Bewley La., Sid. 89 C4
Bexhill Clo., Felt. 81 E2
Bexhill Rd. N11 32 D5
Bexhill Rd. SE4 77 J6
Bexhill Rd. SW14 74 C3
Bexhill Wk. E15 60 E2
Mitre Rd.
Bexley Gdns. N9 33 A3
Bexley High St., Bex. 80 G7
Bexley La., Sid. 89 C4
Bexley Rd. SE9 79 E5
Bexley Rd., Erith 71 J7
Beynon Rd., Cars. 100 J5
Bianca Rd. SE15 21 H6
Bianca Rd. SE15 68 C6
Bibsworth Rd. N3 30 C2
Bibury Clo. SE15 21 E6
Bibury Clo. SE15 68 B6
Bicester Rd., Rich. 74 A3
Bickenhall St. W1 11 A1
Bickenhall St. W1 57 J5

Bickersteth Rd. SW17 84 J6
Bickerton Rd. N19 49 C2
Bickley Cres., Brom. 97 B4
Bickley Pk. Rd., Brom. 97 B3
Bickley Rd. E10 42 B7
Bickley Rd., Brom. 97 A2
Bickley St. SW17 84 H5
Bicknell Rd. SE5 76 J3
Bicknoller Rd., Enf. 25 B1
Bicknor Rd., Orp. 97 H7
Bidborough Clo. 96 F5
Brom.
Bidborough St. WC1 8 A4
Bidborough St. WC1 58 E3
Biddenden Way SE9 88 D4
Bidder St. E16 60 G5
Biddestone Rd. N7 49 F4
Biddulph Rd. W9 6 A4
Biddulph Rd. W9 57 E3
Bideford Ave., Grnf. 55 E2
Bideford Clo., Edg. 38 A1
Bideford Clo., Felt. 81 F3
Bideford Gdns., Enf. 25 B7
Bideford Rd., Brom. 87 F3
Bideford Rd., Ruis. 45 B3
Bideford Rd., Well. 71 B7
Bidwell Gdns. N11 32 C7
Bidwell St. SE15 77 E1
Big Hill E5 50 E1
Bigbury Rd. N17 33 B7
Barkham Rd.
Biggerstaff Rd. E15 60 C1
Biggerstaff St. N4 49 G2
Biggin Ave., Mitch. 93 J1
Biggin Hill SE19 94 H1
Biggin Way SE19 85 H7
Bigginwood Rd. 85 H7
SW16
Biggs Row SW15 75 A3
Felsham Rd.
Bigland St. E1 59 E6
Bignell Rd. SE18 70 E5
Bignold Rd. E7 51 G4
Bigwood Rd. NW11 39 E5
Bill Hamling Clo. SE9 88 C2
Billet Clo., Rom. 44 D3
Billet Rd. E17 41 G1
Billet Rd., Rom. 44 B4
Billing Pl. SW10 18 B7
Billing Pl. SW10 66 E7
Billing Rd. SW10 18 B7
Billing Rd. SW10 66 E7
Billing St. SW10 18 B7
Billing St. SW10 66 E7
Billing Way SW5 18 C2
Billingford Clo. SE4 77 G4
Billington Rd. SE14 68 G7
Billiter Sq. EC3 13 E4
Billiter St. EC3 13 E4
Billiter St. EC3 59 B6
Billockby Clo., Chess. 98 J6
Billson St. E14 69 C4
Bilsby Gro. SE9 88 A4
Bilton Rd., Grnf. 55 D1
Bilton Way, Enf. 25 H1
Bilton Way, Hayes 63 B2
Bina Gdns. SW5 18 C2
Bina Gdns. SW5 66 F4
Bincote Rd., Enf. 24 F3
Binden Rd. W12 65 F3
Bindon Grn., Mord. 93 E4
Bayham Rd.
Binfield Rd. SW4 76 E1
Binfield Rd., S.Croy. 102 C5
Bingfield St. N1 58 E1
Bingham Pl. W1 11 B1
Bingham Rd., Croy. 102 D1
Bingham St. N1 50 A6
Bingley Rd. E16 60 J6
Bingley Rd., Grnf. 54 J4
Bingley Rd., Sun. 81 A7
Binney St. W1 11 C4
Binney St. W1 58 A6
Binney St. E5 65 E5
Binns Rd. W4 65 E5
Binsey Wk. SE2 71 C2
Binyon Cres., Stan. 29 C5
Birbeck Gdns., 34 F2
Wdf.Grn.
Birbetts Rd. SE9 88 C2
Birch Av. N13 32 J3
Birch Clo. E16 60 E5
Birch Clo. N19 49 C2
Hargrave Pk.
Birch Clo. SE15 77 D2
Birch Clo., Brent. 64 E7
Birch Clo., Buck.H. 35 A3
Birch Clo., Rom. 44 H3
Birch Clo., Tedd. 82 D5
Birch Clo., Dag. 53 J3
Birch Grn. NW9 30 E7
Clayton Fld.
Birch Gro. SE12 78 F7
Birch Gro. W3 65 A1
Birch Gro., Well. 80 A4

Birch Hill, Croy.	102	G5
Birch Mead, Orp.	104	D2
Birch Pk., Har.	28	J7
Birch Rd., Felt.	81	D5
Birch Rd., Rom.	44	H3
Birch Row, Brom.	97	D7
Birch Tree Ave.,	103	F5
W.Wick.		
Birch Tree Way,	102	E2
Croy.		
Birch Wk., Borwd.	22	A1
Grove Rd.		
Birch Wk., Erith	71	J6
Birch Wk., Mitch.	94	B1
Bircham Path SE4	77	G4
St. Norbert Rd.		
Birchanger Rd. SE25	95	D5
Birchdale Gdns.,	44	D7
Rom.		
Birchdale Rd. E7	51	J5
Birchdene Dr. SE28	71	A1
Birchen Clo. NW9	47	D2
Birchen Gro. NW9	47	D2
Birchend Clo.,	102	A6
S.Croy.		
Sussex Rd.		
Birches, The N21	24	F6
Birches, The SE7	69	H6
Birches, The, Orp.	104	D4
Birches Clo., Mitch.	93	J3
Birches Clo., Pnr.	36	E5
Birchfield St. E14	60	A7
Birchin La. EC3	**13**	**C4**
Birchin La. EC3	59	A6
Birchington Clo.,	80	H1
Bexh.		
Birchington Rd. N8	40	D6
Birchington Rd. NW6	57	D1
Birchington Rd.,	91	J7
Surb.		
Birchlands Ave.	75	J7
SW12		
Birchmead Ave., Pnr.	36	C4
Birchmere Row SE3	78	F2
Birchmore Wk. N5	49	J3
Highbury Quad.		
Birchville Ct.	29	B1
(Bushey), Wat.		
Heathbourne Rd.		
Birchway, Hayes	63	A1
Birchwood Ave. N10	40	A3
Birchwood Ave.,	95	J4
Beck.		
Birchwood Ave., Sid.	89	B2
Birchwood Ave.,	101	A3
Wall.		
Birchwood Clo.,	93	E4
Mord.		
Birchwood Ct. N13	32	H5
Birchwood Clo., Edg.	38	C2
Birchwood Dr. NW3	48	E3
Birchwood Gro.,	81	G6
Hmptn.		
Birchwood Rd. SW17	85	B5
Birchwood Rd., Orp.	97	G4
Bird in Bush Rd.	**21**	**H7**
SE15		
Bird in Bush Rd. SE15	68	D7
Bird St. W1	**11**	**C4**
Bird Wk., Twick.	81	F1
Bird-in-hand La.	97	A2
Brom.		
Bird-in-hand Pas.	86	F2
SE23		
Dartmouth Rd.		
Birdbrook Clo., Dag.	53	J7
Birdbrook Rd. SE3	78	J3
Birdcage Wk. SW1	**15**	**G4**
Birdcage Wk. SW1	67	C2
Birdham Clo., Brom.	97	B5
Birdhurst Ave.,	102	A4
S.Croy.		
Birdhurst Gdns.,	102	A4
S.Croy.		
Birdhurst Ri.,	102	B5
S.Croy.		
Birdhurst Rd. SW18	75	F4
Birdhurst Rd. SW19	84	H6
Birdhurst Rd.,	102	B5
S.Croy.		
Birdlip Clo. SE15	**21**	**D6**
Birdlip Clo. SE15	68	B6
Birds Fm. Ave., Rom.	44	H1
Birdsfield La. E3	59	J1
Birdwood Clo., Tedd.	82	B4
Birkbeck Ave. W3	56	D7
Birkbeck Gdns., Grnf.	54	J1
Wdf.Grn.		
Birkbeck Gro. W3	75	J2
Birkbeck Hill SE21	85	H2
Birkbeck Ms. E8	50	C5
Sandringham Rd.		
Birkbeck Pl. SE21	85	J1
Birkbeck Rd. E8	50	C5
Birkbeck Rd. N8	40	E4
Birkbeck Rd. N12	31	F5
Birkbeck Rd. N17	41	C1
Birkbeck Rd. NW7	30	F5
Birkbeck Rd. SW19	84	E5
Birkbeck Rd. W3	65	D1
Birkbeck Rd. W5	64	F4
Birkbeck Rd., Beck.	95	F2
Birkbeck Rd., Enf.	25	A1
Birkbeck Rd., Ilf.	43	G5
Birkbeck Rd., Sid.	89	A3
Birkbeck St. E2	59	E3
Cambridge Heath Rd.		
Birkbeck Way, Grnf.	54	J1
Birkdale Ave., Pnr.	36	G3
Birkdale Clo., Orp.	97	G7
Birkdale Gdns., Wat.	28	D3
Birkdale Rd. SE2	71	A4
Birkdale Rd. W5	55	H4
Birkenhead Ave.,	91	J2
Kings.T.		
Birkenhead St. WC1	**8**	**B3**
Birkenhead St. WC1	58	E3
Birkhall Rd. SE6	87	D1
Birkwood Clo. SW12	76	D7
Birley Rd. N20	31	F2
Birley St. SW11	76	A2
Birnam Rd. N4	49	F2
Birse Cres. NW10	47	E4
Birstall Grn., Wat.	28	D4
Birstall Rd. N15	41	B5
Biscay Rd. W6	66	A5
Biscoe Clo., Houns.	63	G6
Biscoe Way SE13	78	D3
Bisenden Rd., Croy.	102	B2
Bisham Clo., Cars.	93	J7
Bisham Gdns. N6	49	A1
Bishop Fox Way,	90	F4
E.Mol.		
Bishop Ken Rd., Har.	37	C2
Bishop Kings Rd.	66	B4
W14		
Bishop Rd. N14	24	B7
Bishop St. N1	58	J1
Bishop Way NW10	47	E7
Bishop's Ave. E13	60	H1
Bishops Ave. SW6	75	A2
Bishops Ave., Brom.	96	J2
Bishops Ave., Rom.	44	C6
Bishops Ave., The	39	G7
N2		
Bishops Bri. W2	**10**	**D3**
Bishops Bri. W2	57	F5
Bishops Bri. Rd. W2	**10**	**B3**
Bishops Bri. Rd. W2	57	E6
Bishops Clo. E17	42	B4
Bishops Clo. SE9	88	F2
Bishops Clo., Barn.	23	A6
Bishops Clo., Enf.	25	E2
Central Ave.		
Bishops Clo., Rich.	82	G3
Bishops Clo., Sutt.	100	D3
Bishop's Ct. EC4	**12**	**G3**
Bishop's Ct. WC2	**12**	**E3**
Bishops Gro. N2	39	G6
Bishops Gro., Hmptn.	81	F4
Bishop's Hall,	91	G2
Kings.T.		
Bishops Hill, Walt.	90	A7
Bishop's Pk. Rd. SW6	75	A2
Bishops Pk. Rd.	94	E1
SW16		
Bishops Rd. N6	40	A6
Bishops Rd. SW6	75	B1
Bishops Rd. W7	64	B2
Bishops Rd., Croy.	94	H7
Bishops Ter. SE11	**20**	**F1**
Bishops Ter. SE11	67	G4
Bishops Wk., Chis.	91	F1
Bishops Wk., Croy.	102	G6
Bishop's Wk., Pnr.	36	E3
High St.		
Bishops Way E2	59	E2
Bishopsford Rd.,	93	F7
Mord.		
Bishopsgate EC2	**13**	**E2**
Bishopsgate EC2	59	B6
Bishopsgate Chyd.	**13**	**D3**
EC2		
Bishopsthorpe Rd.	86	G4
SE26		
Bishopswood Rd. N6	39	J7
Bisley Clo., Wor.Pk.	99	J1
Bispham Rd. NW10	55	J3
Bisson Rd. E15	60	C2
Bisterne Ave. E17	42	D3
Bittacy Clo. NW7	31	A6
Bittacy Hill NW7	31	A6
Bittacy Pk. Ave. NW7	31	A6
Bittacy Ri. NW7	30	J6
Bittacy Rd. NW7	31	A6
Bittern St. SE1	**16**	**J4**
Bittoms, The,	91	G3
Kings.T.		
Bixley Clo., Sthl.	63	F4
Black Boy La. N15	40	J5
Black Fan Clo., Enf.	24	J1
Black Friars Ct. EC4	**12**	**G5**
Black Friars La. EC4	**12**	**G5**
Black Friars La. EC4	58	H6
Black Gates, Pnr.	36	F3
Church La.		
Black Horse Ct. SE1	**17**	**C5**
Black Lion La. W6	65	G4
Black Path E10	41	G7
Black Prince Rd. SE1	**20**	**B2**
Black Prince Rd. SE1	67	F4
Black Prince Rd. SE11	**20**	**D2**
Black Prince Rd. SE11	67	F4
Black Swan Yd. SE1	**17**	**D3**
Blackall St. EC2	**9**	**D5**
Blackberry Fm. Clo.,	63	E7
Houns.		
Blackbird Hill NW9	47	C2
Blackbird Yd. E2	**9**	**G3**
Blackborne Rd., Dag.	53	G6
Blackbrook La.,	97	D3
Brom.		
Blackburn Rd. NW6	48	E6
Blackburne's Ms. W1	**11**	**B5**
Blackburne's Ms. W1	58	A7
Blackbush Ave.,	44	D5
Rom.		
Blackbush Clo., Sutt.	100	E7
Blackdown Ter. SE18	70	C7
Blackett St. SW15	75	A3
Blackfen Rd., Sid.	79	H6
Blackford Rd., Wat.	28	D5
Blackford's Path	74	G7
SW15		
Roehampton High St.		
Blackfriars Bri. EC4	**12**	**G6**
Blackfriars Bri. EC4	58	H7
Blackfriars Bri. SE1	**12**	**G6**
Blackfriars Bri. SE1	58	H7
Blackfriars Pas. EC4	**12**	**G5**
Blackfriars Rd. SE1	**16**	**G1**
Blackfriars Rd. SE1	67	H1
Blackheath Ave.	69	D7
SE10		
Blackheath Gro. SE3	78	F2
Blackheath Hill SE10	78	C1
Blackheath Pk. SE3	78	F3
Blackheath Ri. SE13	78	C2
Blackheath Rd. SE10	78	B1
Blackheath Vale SE3	78	E2
Blackheath Village	78	F2
SE3		
Blackhorse La. E17	41	G4
Blackhorse La., Croy.	95	D7
Blackhorse Rd. E17	41	G4
Blackhorse Rd. SE8	68	H5
Blackhorse Rd., Sid.	89	A4
Blackland Ter. SW3	**18**	**J2**
Blackland Ter. SW3	66	J4
Blacklands Rd. SE6	87	C4
Blackmore Ave., Sthl.	64	A1
Blackmore Rd.,	27	B7
Buck.H.		
Blackmores Gro.,	82	D6
Tedd.		
Blackness La., Kes.	104	A7
Blackpool Rd. SE15	77	E2
Blacks Rd. W6	65	J4
Queen Caroline St.		
Blackshaw Pl. N1	50	B7
Hertford Rd.		
Blackshaw Rd. SW17	84	F4
Blacksmiths Clo.,	44	C6
Rom.		
Blackstock Ms. N4	49	H2
Blackstock Rd		
Blackstock Rd. N4	49	H2
Blackstock Rd. N5	49	H2
Blackstone Est. E8	50	D7
Blackstone Rd. NW2	47	J5
Blackthorn Ct.,	63	E7
Houns.		
Blackthorn Gro.,	80	E3
Bexh.		
Blackthorn St. E3	60	A4
Blackthorne Ave.,	102	F1
Croy.		
Blackthorne Dr. E4	34	D4
Blacktree Ms. SW9	76	G3
Blackwall La. SE10	69	E5
Blackwall Tunnel	69	D1
E14		
Blackwall Tunnel	69	E2
App. SE10		
Blackwall Tunnel	60	A2
Northern App. E3		
Blackwall Tunnel	60	C4
Northern App. E14		
Blackwall Way E14	60	C7
Blackwater Rd., Sutt.	100	E4
High St.		
Blackwater St. SE22	77	C5
Blackwell Clo. E5	50	H4
Blackwell Clo., Har.	29	A7
Blackwell Gdns., Edg.	30	A3
Blackwood St. SE17	**21**	**B3**
Blackwood St. SE17	68	A5
Blade Ms. SW15	75	C4
Deodar Rd.		
Bladindon Dr., Bex.	80	C7
Bladon Gdns., Har.	36	H6
Blagdens Clo. N14	32	C2
Blagdens La. N14	32	D2
Blagdon Rd. SE13	78	B6
Blagdon Rd., N.Mal.	92	F4
Blagdon Wk., Tedd.	82	F6
Blagrove Rd. W10	57	B5
Blair Ave. NW9	38	E7
Blair Clo. N1	49	J6
Blair Clo., Sid.	79	H5
Blair St. E14	60	C6
Blairderry Rd. SW2	85	E2
Blairhead Rd., Wat.	28	B3
Blake Ave., Bark.	61	H1
Blake Clo. W10	56	J5
Blake Clo., Well.	79	H1
Blake Gdns. SW6	75	E1
Blake Hall Cres. E11	51	G1
Blake Hall Rd. E11	42	G7
Blake Ho., Beck.	87	A6
Blake Rd. E16	60	F4
Blake Rd. N11	32	C7
Blake Rd., Croy.	102	B2
Blake Rd., Mitch.	93	H3
Blake St. SE8	69	A6
Watergate St.		
Blakeden Dr., Esher	98	C6
Blakehall Rd., Cars.	100	J6
Blakemore Rd. SW16	85	E3
Blakemore Rd.,	94	F5
Th.Hth.		
Blakemore Way, Belv.	71	E3
Blakeney Ave.,	95	J1
Beck.		
Blakeney Clo. E8	50	D5
Ferncliff Rd.		
Blakeney Clo. N20	31	F1
Blakeney Clo. NW1	49	D7
Rossendale Way		
Blakeney Rd., Beck.	95	J1
Blakenham Rd. SW17	84	J4
Blaker Ct. SE7	69	J7
Fairlawn		
Blaker Rd. E15	60	C1
Blakes Ave., N.Mal.	92	F5
Blake's Grn.,	103	C1
W.Wick.		
Blakes La., N.Mal.	92	F5
Blakes Rd. SE15	**21**	**E7**
Blakes Ter., N.Mal.	92	G5
Blakesley Ave. W5	55	F6
Blakesley Wk. SW20	93	C2
Blakesware Gdns. N9	25	C2
Blakewood Clo., Felt.	81	C4
Blanch Clo. SE15	68	F7
Clifton Way		
Blanchard Clo. SE9	88	B3
Blanchard Way E8	50	D6
Blanche St. E16	60	F4
Blanchedowne SE5	77	A4
Blanchland Rd.,	93	E5
Mord.		
Bland St. SE9	79	A4
Blandfield Rd. SW12	76	A6
Blandford Ave., Beck.	95	H2
Blandford Ave.,	81	H1
Twick.		
Blandford Clo. N2	39	F5
Blandford Clo.,	101	E3
Croy.		
Wandle Rd.		
Blandford Cres. E4	26	C7
Blandford Rd. W4	58	A3
Blandford Rd. W5	64	G2
Blandford Rd., Beck.	95	F2
Blandford Rd., Sthl.	63	G4
Blandford Rd., Tedd.	82	A5
Blandford Sq. NW1	**6**	**H6**
Blandford Sq. NW1	57	H4
Blandford St. W1	**11**	**A3**
Blandford St. W1	57	J6
Blandford Waye,	54	C6
Hayes		
Blaney Cres. E6	61	F3
Blanmerle Rd. SE9	88	E1
Blann Clo. SE9	79	A6
Blantyre St. SW10	**18**	**E7**
Blantyre St. SW10	66	G7
Blantyre Wk. SW10	**18**	**E7**

Blashford NW3 48 J7
Blashford St. SE13 78 D7
Blasker Wk. E14 69 A5
Blawith Rd., Har. 37 B4
Blaydon Clo. N17 33 E7
Blaydon Wk. N17 33 F7
Bleak Hill La. SE18 70 J6
Blean Gro. SE20 86 F7
Bleasdale Ave., Grnf. 55 [illegible]
Blechynden St. W10 57 A7
Bramley Rd.
Blechynden St. W11 57 A7
Bramley Rd.
Bleddyn Clo., Sid. 80 C6
Bledlow Clo. SE28 62 C7
Bledlow Ri., Grnf. 54 J2
Bleeding Heart Yd. EC1 12 F2
Blegborough Rd. SW16 85 C6
Blendon Dr., Bex. 80 D6
Blendon Path, Brom. 87 F7
Hope Pk.
Blendon Rd., Bex. 80 C6
Blendon Ter. SE18 70 F5
Blendworth Way SE15 21 E7
Blenheim Ave., Ilf. 43 D6
Blenheim Clo. N21 32 J1
Elm Pk. Rd.
Blenheim Clo. SW20 92 J3
Blenheim Clo., Grnf. 55 A2
Leaver Gdns.
Blenheim Clo., Rom. 44 J4
Blenheim Clo., Wall. 101 C7
Blenheim Ct. N19 49 E2
Marlborough Rd.
Blenheim Ct., Sid. 88 G3
Blenheim Cres. W11 57 B7
Blenheim Cres., S.Croy. 101 J7
Blenheim Dr., Well. 79 J1
Blenheim Gdns. NW2 47 J6
Blenheim Gdns. SW2 76 F6
Blenheim Gdns., Kings.T. 83 B7
Blenheim Gdns., Wall. 101 C6
Blenheim Gdns., Wem. 46 H3
Blenheim Gro. SE15 77 D2
Blenheim Pas. NW8 6 C1
Blenheim Ri. N15 41 C4
Talbot Rd.
Blenheim Rd. E6 61 A3
Blenheim Rd. E15 51 E4
Blenheim Rd. E17 41 G3
Blenheim Rd. NW8 6 D1
Blenheim Rd. NW8 57 F2
Blenheim Rd. SE20 86 F7
Maple Rd.
Blenheim Rd. SW20 92 J3
Blenheim Rd. W4 65 E3
Blenheim Rd., Barn. 23 A3
Blenheim Rd., Brom. 97 B4
Blenheim Rd., Har. 36 H6
Blenheim Rd., Nthlt. 45 H6
Blenheim Rd., Sid. 89 C1
Blenheim Rd., Sutt. 100 D3
Blenheim St. W1 11 D4
Blenheim Ter. NW8 6 C1
Blenheim Ter. NW8 57 F2
Blenkarne Rd. SW11 75 J6
Bleriot Rd., Houns. 63 C7
Blessbury Rd., Edg. 38 C1
Blessington Clo. SE13 78 D3
Blessington Rd. SE13 78 D4
Bletchingley Clo., Th.Hth. 94 H4
Bletchley Ct. N1 9 B2
Bletchley St. N1 9 A2
Bletchley St. N1 58 J2
Bletsoe Wk. N1 9 A1
Blincoe Clo. SW19 84 A2
Blind La., Loug. 26 E2
Bliss Cres. SE13 78 B2
Coldbath St.
Blissett St. SE10 78 C1
Blisworth Clo., Hayes 54 E4
Braunston Dr.
Blithbury Rd., Dag. 53 B6
Blithdale Rd. SE2 71 A4
Blithfield St. W8 14 A6
Blithfield St. W8 66 E3
Blockley Rd., Wem. 46 E2
Bloemfontein Ave. W12 65 H1
Bloemfontein Rd. W12 56 H7
Blomfield Rd. W9 10 B1
Blomfield Rd. W9 57 E5
Blomfield St. EC2 13 C2
Blomfield St. EC2 59 A5
Blomfield Vill. W2 10 B2
Blomfield Vill. W2 57 E5
Blomville Rd., Dag. 53 E3
Blondel St. SW11 76 A2
Blondin Ave. W5 64 F4
Blondin St. E3 60 A2
Bloom Gro. SE27 85 H3
Bloom Pk. Rd. SW6 66 C7
Bloomburg St. SW1 19 G2
Bloomfield Cres., Ilf. 43 E6
Bloomfield Pl. W1 11 E5
Bloomfield Rd. N6 40 A6
Bloomfield Rd. SE18 70 E5
Bloomfield Rd., Brom. 97 A5
Bloomfield Rd., Kings.T. 91 H4
Bloomfield Ter. SW1 19 C3
Bloomfield Ter. SW1 67 A5
Bloomhall Rd. SE19 86 A5
Bloomsbury Clo. W5 55 J7
Bloomsbury Ct. WC1 12 B2
Bloomsbury Ct., Pnr. 36 F3
Bloomsbury Ho. SW4 76 D6
Bloomsbury Pl. SW18 75 F5
Fullerton Rd.
Bloomsbury Pl. WC1 12 B1
Bloomsbury Sq. WC1 12 B2
Bloomsbury Sq. WC1 58 E5
Bloomsbury St. WC1 11 J2
Bloomsbury St. WC1 58 D5
Bloomsbury Way WC1 12 A3
Bloomsbury Way WC1 58 E5
Blore Clo. SW8 76 D1
Thessaly Rd.
Blore Ct. W1 11 H5
Blossom Clo. W5 64 H2
Almond Ave.
Blossom Clo., Dag. 62 F1
Blossom Clo., S.Croy. 102 C5
Melville Ave.
Blossom La., Enf. 24 J1
Blossom St. E1 9 E6
Blossom St. E1 59 B4
Blossom Waye, Houns. 63 E7
Blount St. E14 59 H5
Bloxam Gdns. SE9 79 B5
Bloxhall Rd. E10 50 J1
Bloxham Cres., Hmptn. 81 F7
Bloxworth Clo., Wall. 101 C3
Blucher Rd. SE5 67 J7
Blue Anchor All., Rich. 73 H4
Kew Rd.
Blue Anchor La. SE16 21 J1
Blue Anchor La. SE16 68 D4
Blue Anchor Yd. E1 13 H5
Blue Anchor Yd. E1 59 D7
Blue Ball Yd. SW1 15 F2
Bluebell Clo. SE26 86 C4
Bluebell Clo., Orp. 104 F2
Bluebell Clo., Wall. 101 B1
Bluefield Clo., Hmptn. 81 G5
Bluegates, Epsom 99 G7
Bluehouse Rd. E4 34 E3
Blundell Rd., Edg. 38 D1
Blundell St. N7 49 E7
Blunden Clo., Dag. 53 C1
Blunts Rd. SE9 79 D5
Blurton Rd. E5 50 F4
Blyth Clo. E14 69 D4
Saunders Ness Rd.
Blyth Rd. E17 41 J7
Blyth Rd. SE28 62 C7
Blyth Rd., Brom. 96 F1
Blythe Clo. SE6 77 J7
Blythe Clo., Twick. 73 C7
Grimwood Rd.
Blythe Hill SE6 77 J7
Blythe Hill, Orp. 97 J1
Blythe Hill La. SE6 77 J7
Blythe Rd. W14 66 A3
Blythe St. E2 59 E3
Blythe Vale SE6 86 J1
Blythswood Rd., Ilf. 53 A1
Blythwood Rd. N4 40 E7
Blythwood Rd., Pnr. 36 D1
Boadicea St. N1 58 F1
Copenhagen St.
Boardman Ave. E4 26 B5
Boar's Head Yd., Brent. 64 G7
Brent Way
Boathouse Wk. SE15 21 G7
Boathouse Wk. SE15 68 C7
Boathouse Wk., Rich. 73 G1
Kew Rd.
Bob Anker Clo. E13 60 G3
Chesterton Rd.
Bob Marley Way SE24 76 G4
Marcus Garvey Way
Bobbin Clo. SW4 76 C3
Bockhampton Rd., [illegible] 82 J7
Bocking St. E8 59 E1
Boddicott Clo. SW19 84 B2
Bodia Rd. SW1[illegible] 84 J6
Bodiam Clo., Enf. 25 A2
Bodiam Rd. SW16 85 D7
Bodley Clo., N.Mal. 92 E5
Bodley Manor Way SW2 76 G7
Papworth Way
Bodley Rd., N.Mal. 92 D6
Bodmin Clo., Har. 45 F3
Bodmin Gro., Mord. 93 E4
Bodmin St. SW18 84 D1
Bodnant Gdns. SW20 92 H3
Bodney Rd. E8 50 E5
Boeing Way, Sthl. 63 B3
Boevey Path, Belv. 71 F5
Orchard Ave.
Bogey La., Orp. 104 C7
Bognor Gdns., Wat. 28 C5
Bowring Grn.
Bognor Rd., Well. 80 D1
Bohemia Pl. E8 50 F6
Bohun Gro., Barn. 23 H6
Boileau Rd. SW13 65 G7
Boileau Rd. W5 55 J6
Bolden St. SE8 78 B2
Bolderwood Way, W.Wick. 103 B2
Boldmere Rd., Pnr. 36 C7
Boleyn Ave., Enf. 25 E1
Boleyn Clo. E17 42 A4
Boleyn Ct., Buck.H. 34 G1
Boleyn Dr., Ruis. 45 D2
Boleyn Dr., W.Mol. 90 F3
Boleyn Gdns., Dag. 53 J7
Boleyn Gdns., W.Wick. 103 B2
Boleyn Gro., W.Wick. 103 C2
Boleyn Rd. E6 61 A2
Boleyn Rd. E7 51 G7
Boleyn Rd. N16 50 B5
Boleyn Way, Barn. 23 F3
Boleyn Way, Ilf. 35 F6
Bolina Rd. SE16 68 F5
Bolingbroke Gro. SW11 75 J6
Bolingbroke Rd. W14 66 A3
Bolingbroke Wk. SW11 75 G1
Bolliger Ct. NW10 56 C4
Park Royal Rd.
Bollo Bri. Rd. W3 65 B3
Bollo La. W3 65 B2
Bollo La. W4 65 C4
Bolney St. SW8 67 F7
Bolney Way, Felt. 81 E3
Bolsover St. W1 7 E6
Bolsover St. W1 58 B4
Bolstead Rd., Mitch. 94 B1
Bolt Ct. EC4 12 F4
Boltmore Clo. NW4 39 A3
Bolton Clo. SE20 95 D2
Selby Rd.
Bolton Clo., Chess. 98 G6
Bolton Cres. SE5 20 F7
Bolton Cres. SE5 67 H6
Bolton Gdns. NW10 57 A2
Bolton Gdns. SW5 18 A3
Bolton Gdns. SW5 66 E5
Bolton Gdns., Brom. 87 F6
Bolton Gdns., Tedd. 82 D6
Bolton Gdns. Ms. SW10 18 B3
Bolton Gdns. Ms. SW10 66 E5
Bolton Rd. E15 51 F6
Bolton Rd. N18 33 C5
Bolton Rd. NW8 57 E1
Bolton Rd. NW10 56 E1
Bolton Rd. W4 65 C7
Bolton Rd., Chess. 98 G6
Bolton Rd., Har. 36 J4
Bolton St. W1 15 E1
Bolton St. W1 67 B1
Bolton Wk. N7 49 F2
Durham Rd.
Boltons, The SW10 18 C3
Boltons, The SW10 66 F5
Boltons, The, Wem. 46 C4
Boltons, The, Wdf.Grn. 34 G4
Bombay St. SE16 68 E4
Bomore Rd. W11 57 B7
Bon Marche Ter. SE27 86 B4
Gipsy Rd.
Bonar Pl., Chis. 88 B7
Bonar Rd. SE15 68 D7
Bonchester Clo., Chis. 88 D7
Bonchurch Clo., Sutt. 100 E7
Bonchurch Rd. W10 57 [illegible]
Bonchurch Rd. W13 64 E1
Bond Ct. EC4 13 B4
Bond Gdns., Wall. 101 C4
Bond Rd., Mitch. 93 H2
Bond Rd., Surb. 98 J1
Bond St. E15 51 E5
Bond St. W4 65 E4
Chiswick Common Rd.
Bond St. W5 55 G7
Bondfield Rd. E6 61 B5
Lovage App.
Bondfield Rd., Hayes 54 A3
Bonding Yd. Wk. SE16 68 H2
Finland St.
Bondway SW8 20 B5
Bondway SW8 67 E6
Boneta Rd. SE18 70 C3
Bonfield Rd. SE13 78 C4
Bonham Gdns., Dag. 53 D2
Bonham Rd. SW2 76 F5
Bonham Rd., Dag. 53 D2
Bonheur Rd. W4 65 D2
Bonhill St. EC2 9 C6
Bonhill St. EC2 59 A4
Boniface Gdns., Har. 28 H7
Boniface Wk., Har. 28 H7
Bonner Hill Rd., Kings.T. 91 J3
Bonner Rd. E2 59 F2
Bonner St. E2 59 F2
Bonnersfield Clo., Har. 37 C6
Bonnersfield La., Har. 37 C6
Bonneville Gdns. SW4 76 C6
Bonnington Sq. SW8 20 C5
Bonnington Sq. SW8 67 F6
Bonnington Twr., Brom. 97 B6
Bonny St. NW1 49 C7
Bonser Rd., Twick. 82 C2
Bonsor St. SE5 68 B7
Bonville Gdns. NW4 38 G4
Handowe Clo.
Bonville Rd., Brom. 87 F5
Book Ms. WC2 11 J4
Booker Clo. E14 59 J5
Wallwood St.
Booker Rd. N18 33 D5
Boone Ct. N9 33 F3
Boone St. SE13 78 E4
Boones Rd. SE13 78 E4
Boord St. SE10 69 E3
Boot St. N1 9 D4
Boot St. N1 59 B3
Booth Clo. SE28 62 B7
Booth Rd. NW9 38 D2
Booth Rd., Croy. 101 H2
Waddon New Rd.
Boothby Rd. N19 49 D2
Booth's Pl. W1 11 G2
Bordars Rd. W7 55 B5
Bordars Wk. W7 55 B5
Borden Ave., Enf. 25 A6
Border Cres. SE26 86 E5
Border Gdns., Croy. 103 B4
Border Rd. SE26 86 E5
Bordergate, Mitch. 93 J1
Borders La., Loug. 27 D4
Bordesley Rd., Mord. 93 E4
Bordon Wk. SW15 74 G7
Boreas Wk. N1 8 H2
Boreham Ave. E16 60 G6
Boreham Clo. E11 51 C1
Hainault Rd.
Boreham Rd. N22 40 J2
Borehamwood Ind. Pk., Borwd. 22 D2
Borer's Pas. E1 13 E3
Borgard Rd. SE18 70 C4
Borkwood Pk., Orp. 104 J4
Borkwood Way, Orp. 104 H4
Borland Rd. SE15 77 F4
Borland Rd., Tedd. 82 E6
Borneo St. SW15 74 J3
Borough High St. SE1 17 A4
Borough High St. SE1 67 J2
Borough Hill, Croy. 101 H3
Borough Rd. SE1 16 H5

Borough Rd. SE1 67 H3
Borough Rd., Islw. 73 B1
Borough Rd., 92 A1
Kings.T.
Borough Rd., Mitch. 93 H2
Borough Sq. SE1 16 J4
Borrett Clo. SE17 20 J4
Borrodaile Rd. SW18 75 E6
Borrowdale Ave., 37 D2
Har.
Borrowdale Clo., Ilf. 43 B4
Borrowdale Ct., Enf. 24 J1
Borthwick Ms. E15 51 E4
Borthwick Rd.
Borthwick Rd. E15 51 E4
Borthwick Rd. NW9 38 F6
West Hendon Bdy.
Borthwick St. SE8 69 A5
Borwick Ave. E17 41 J3
Bosbury Rd. SE6 87 C3
Boscastle Rd. NW5 49 B3
Boscobel Pl. SW1 19 C1
Boscobel Pl. SW1 67 A4
Boscobel St. NW8 6 F6
Boscobel St. NW8 57 G4
Boscombe Ave. E10 42 D7
Boscombe Clo. E5 50 H5
Boscombe Gdns. 85 E6
SW16
Boscombe Rd. SW17 85 A6
Boscombe Rd. SW19 93 D1
Boscombe Rd. W12 65 G1
Boscombe Rd., 99 J1
Wor.Pk.
Bosgrove E4 34 C1
Boss St. SE1 17 F3
Bostal Row, Bexh. 80 F3
Harlington Rd.
Bostall Hill SE2 71 A5
Bostall Hill Rd. SE2 71 C6
Bostall La. SE2 71 B5
Bostall Manorway 71 B4
SE2
Bostall La.
Bostall Pk. Ave., 71 E7
Bexh.
Bostall Rd., Orp. 89 B7
Boston Gdns. W4 65 E6
Boston Gdns., Brent. 64 D4
Boston Manor Rd., 64 E4
Brent.
Boston Pk. Rd., Brent. 64 F5
Boston Pl. NW1 6 J6
Boston Pl. NW1 57 J4
Boston Rd. E6 61 B3
Boston Rd. E17 42 A6
Boston Rd. W7 64 B1
Boston Rd., Croy. 94 F6
Boston Rd., Edg. 30 C7
Boston Vale W7 64 D4
Bostonthorpe Rd. W7 64 B2
Boswell Ct. WC1 12 B1
Boswell Rd., 94 J4
Th.Hth.
Boswell St. WC1 12 B1
Boswell St. WC1 58 E5
Bosworth Clo. E17 41 J1
Bosworth Rd. N11 32 D6
Bosworth Rd. W10 57 B4
Bosworth Rd., Barn. 23 D3
Bosworth Rd., Dag. 53 G3
Botany Bay La., Chis. 97 F2
Boteley Clo. E4 34 D2
Botha Rd. E13 60 H5
Botham Clo., Edg. 30 C7
Pavilion Way
Bothwell Clo. E16 60 F5
Bothwell St. W6 66 A6
Delorme St.
Botolph All. EC3 13 D5
Botolph La. EC3 13 D5
Botsford Rd. SW20 93 B2
Botts Ms. W2 57 D6
Chepstow Rd.
Botts Pas. W2 57 D6
Chepstow Rd.
Boucher Clo., Tedd. 82 C5
Boughton Ave., 96 F7
Brom.
Boughton Rd. SE28 70 H3
Boulcott St. E1 59 G6
Boulevard, The, Pnr. 36 G4
Pinner Rd.
Boulogne Rd., Croy. 94 J6
Boulton Ho., Brent. 64 H5
Boulton Rd., Dag. 53 E3
Boultwood Rd. E6 61 C6
Bounces La. N9 33 E2
Bounces Rd. N9 33 E2
Boundaries Rd. SW12 84 J2
Boundaries Rd., Felt. 81 C1
Boundary Clo. SE20 95 D2
Haysleigh Gdns.

Boundary Clo., Ilf. 52 H4
Loxford La.
Boundary Clo., 92 B3
Kings.T.
Boundary Clo., Sthl. 63 G5
Boundary La. SE17 21 A6
Boundary La. E13 61 A3
Boundary La. SE17 67 J6
Boundary Par. N8 40 E6
Boundary Pas. E2 9 F5
Boundary Rd. E13 60 J2
Boundary Rd. E17 41 J7
Boundary Rd. N9 25 F6
Boundary Rd. N22 40 H3
Boundary Rd. NW8 57 E1
Boundary Rd. SW19 84 G6
Boundary Rd., Bark. 61 G1
Boundary Rd., Cars. 101 A7
Boundary Rd., Pnr. 36 D7
Boundary Rd., Sid. 79 H5
Boundary Rd., Wall. 101 B6
Boundary Row SE1 16 G3
Boundary St. E2 9 F4
Boundary St. E2 59 C4
Boundary Way, 103 A5
Croy.
Boundfield Rd. SE6 87 E3
Bounds Grn. Rd. N11 32 C6
Bounds Grn. Rd. N22 32 E7
Bourchier St. W1 11 H5
Bourdon Pl. W1 11 E5
Bourdon Rd. SE20 95 F2
Bourdon St. W1 11 D6
Bourdon St. W1 58 B7
Bourke Clo. NW10 47 E6
Mayo Rd.
Bourke Clo. SW4 76 E6
Bourlet Clo. W1 11 F2
Bourn Ave. N15 41 A4
Bourn Ave., Barn. 23 G5
Bournbrook Rd. SE3 79 A3
Bourne, The N14 32 D1
Bourne Ave. N14 32 E2
Bourne Ave., Ruis. 45 C5
Bourne Ct., Ruis. 45 B5
Bourne Dr., Mitch. 93 G2
Bourne Est. EC1 12 E1
Bourne Est. EC1 58 G5
Bourne Gdns. E4 34 B4
Bourne Hill N13 32 F2
Bourne Hill Clo. N13 32 F2
Bourne Hill
Bourne Mead, Bex. 80 J5
Bourne Pl. W4 65 D5
Dukes Ave.
Bourne Rd. E7 51 F3
Bourne Rd. N8 40 E6
Bourne Rd., Bex. 80 H7
Bourne Rd., Brom. 97 A4
Bourne St. SW1 19 B2
Bourne St. SW1 67 A4
Bourne St., Croy. 101 H2
Waddon New Rd.
Bourne Ter. W2 10 A1
Bourne Ter. W2 58 D5
Bourne Vale, Brom. 103 F1
Bourne Vw., Grnf. 46 C4
Bourne Way, Brom. 103 E2
Bourne Way, Epsom 99 C4
Bourne Way, Sutt. 100 C5
Bournemead Ave., 54 A2
Nthlt.
Bournemead Clo., 54 A3
Nthlt.
Bournemead Way, 54 B2
Nthlt.
Bournemouth Rd. 77 D2
SE15
Bournemouth Rd. 93 D1
SW19
Bournside Cres. N14 32 D1
Bournside Gdns. 87 C5
SE6
Bournevale Rd. SW16 85 E4
Bournewood Rd. 71 A7
SE18
Bournville Rd. SE6 78 A7
Bournwell Clo., Barn. 23 J3
Bourton Clo., Hayes 63 A1
Avondale Dr.
Bousfield Rd. SE14 77 G2
Boutflower Rd. SW11 75 H4
Bouverie Gdns., Har. 37 G6
Bouverie Ms. N16 50 B2
Bouverie Rd.
Bouverie Pl. W2 10 F3
Bouverie Pl. W2 57 G6
Bouverie Rd. N16 50 B1
Bouverie Rd., Har. 36 J6
Bouverie St. EC4 12 F4
Bouverie St. EC4 58 G6
Boveney Rd. SE23 77 G7
Bovill Rd. SE23 77 G7

Bovingdon Ave., 47 A6
Wem.
Bovingdon La. NW9 38 E1
Bovingdon Rd. SW6 75 E1
Bow Bri. Est. E3 60 B2
Bow Chyd. EC4 13 A4
Bow Common La. E3 59 H4
Bow Ind. Est. E15 51 B7
Bow La. EC4 13 A4
Bow La. EC4 58 J6
Bow La. N12 31 F7
Bow La., Mord. 93 B6
Bow Rd. E3 59 J3
Bow St. E15 51 E5
Bow St. WC2 12 B4
Bow St. WC2 58 E6
Bowater Clo. NW9 38 D5
Bowater Clo. SW2 76 E6
Bowater Pl. SE3 69 H7
Bowater Rd. SE18 70 A3
Bowden Dr. SE21 86 B3
Bowden Rd., Har. 36 J7
Bowen St. E14 60 B6
Bower Ave. SE10 78 E1
Bower Clo., Nthlt. 54 C2
Bower St. E1 59 G6
Bowerdean St. SW6 75 E1
Bowerman Ave. SE14 68 H6
Bowers Wk. E6 61 C6
Northumberland Rd.
Bowes Clo., Sid. 80 B6
Bowes Rd. N11 32 B5
Bowes Rd. N13 32 E5
Bowes Rd. W3 56 E7
Bowes Rd., Dag. 53 C4
Bowfell Rd. W6 65 J6
Bowford Ave., Bexh. 80 E1
Bowhill Clo. SW9 20 F7
Bowhill Clo. SW9 67 G7
Bowie Clo. SW4 76 D7
Bowland Rd. SW4 76 D4
Bowland Rd., 34 J6
Wdf.Grn.
Bowland Yd. SW1 15 A4
Bowles Rd. SE1 21 H5
Bowley La. SE19 86 C5
Bowley Rd. SE19 86 C5
Farquhar Rd.
Bowling Grn. Clo. 74 H7
SW15
Bowling Grn. Ct. EC2 9 E6
Bowling Grn. Ct. SE2 59 B4
Bowling Grn. La. EC1 8 F5
Bowling Grn. La. EC1 58 G4
Bowling Grn. Pl. SE1 17 B3
Bowling Grn. Pl. SE1 68 A2
Bowling Grn. Row 70 C3
SE18
Samuel St.
Bowling Grn. St. 20 E5
SE11
Bowling Grn. St. 67 G6
SE11
Bowling Grn. Wk. N1 9 D3
Bowls, The, Chig. 35 H4
Bowls Clo., Stan. 29 E5
Bowman Ave. E16 60 F7
Bowman Ms. SW18 84 C1
Bowmans Clo. W13 64 E1
Bowmans Lea SE23 77 F7
Bowmans Meadow, 101 B3
Wall.
Bowmans Ms. E1 13 H5
Bowmans Ms. N7 49 E3
Seven Sisters Rd.
Bowmans Pl. N7 49 E3
Hercules St.
Bowman's Trd. Est. 37 J3
NW9
Bowmead SE9 88 C2
Bowmore Wk. NW1 49 D7
Agar Gro.
Bowness Clo. E8 50 C6
Beechwood Rd.
Bowness Cres. SW15 83 E5
Bowness Dr., Houns. 72 E4
Bowness Rd. SE6 78 B7
Bowness Rd., Bexh. 80 H2
Bowood Rd. SW11 76 A5
Bowood Rd., Enf. 25 G2
Bowring Grn., Wat. 28 C5
Bowrons Ave., Wem. 46 G7
Bowyer Clo. E6 61 C5
Bowyer Pl. SE5 21 A7
Bowyer Pl. SE5 67 J7
Bowyer St. SE5 21 A7
Bowyer St. SE5 67 J7
Box La., Bark. 62 B2
Boxall Rd. SE21 77 B6

Boxgrove Rd. SE2 71 B2
Boxley Rd., Mord. 93 F4
Boxley St. E16 69 H1
Boxmoor Rd., Har. 37 E4
Boxoll Rd., Dag. 53 F4
Boxted Clo., Buck.H. 35 B1
Boxtree La., Har. 36 J1
Boxtree Rd., Har. 29 A7
Boxworth Gro. N1 58 F1
Richmond Ave.
Boyard Rd. SE18 70 E5
Boyce St. SE1 16 E2
Boyce Way E13 60 G4
Boycroft Ave. NW9 38 C6
Boyd Ave., Sthl. 63 F1
Boyd Clo., Kings.T. 83 A7
Crescent Rd.
Boyd Rd. SW19 84 G6
Boyd St. E1 13 J4
Boyd St. E1 59 D6
Boydell Ct. NW8 48 G7
St. John's Wd. Pk.
Boyfield St. SE1 16 H4
Boyfield St. SE1 67 H2
Boyland Rd., Brom. 87 F5
Boyle Ave., Stan. 29 D6
Boyle Fm. Rd., T.Ditt. 91 D6
Boyle St. W1 11 F5
Boyne Ave. NW4 39 A4
Boyne Rd. SE13 78 C3
Boyne Rd., Dag. 53 G3
Boyne Ter. Ms. W11 66 C1
Boyseland Ct., Edg. 30 C2
Boyson Rd. SE17 21 B5
Boyson Rd. SE17 68 A6
Boythorn Way SE16 68 E5
Credon Rd.
Boyton Clo. E1 59 G4
Stayners Rd.
Boyton Clo. N8 40 E3
Boyton Rd. N8 40 E3
Brabant Ct. EC3 13 D5
Brabant Rd. N22 40 F2
Brabazon Ave., Wall. 101 E7
Brabazon Rd., 63 C7
Houns.
Brabazon Rd., Nthlt. 54 G2
Brabazon St. E14 60 B6
Brabourn Gro. SE15 77 F2
Brabourne Clo. SE19 86 B5
Brabourne Cres., 71 F6
Bexh.
Brabourne Heights 30 E3
NW7
Brabourne Ri., Beck. 96 C5
Bracewell Ave., Grnf. 46 D6
Bracewell Rd. W10 56 J5
Bracewood Gdns., 102 C3
Croy.
Bracey St. N4 49 E2
Bracken Ave. SW12 76 A6
Bracken Ave., Croy. 103 A3
Bracken Clo. E6 61 C5
Bracken Clo., Twick. 72 G7
Hedley Rd.
Bracken Dr., Chig. 35 E6
Bracken End, Islw. 73 A5
Bracken Gdns. SW13 74 G2
Bracken Hill Clo., 96 F1
Brom.
Bracken Hill La.
Bracken Hill La., 96 F1
Brom.
Bracken Ind. Est., Ilf. 35 J7
Bracken Ms., Rom. 44 H6
Brackenbridge Dr., 45 D3
Ruis.
Brackenbury Gdns. 65 H3
W6
Brackenbury Rd. N2 39 F3
Brackenbury Rd. W6 65 H3
Brackendale N21 32 F2
Brackendale Clo., 72 H1
Houns.
Brackenfield Clo. E5 50 E4
Tiger Way
Brackens, The, Enf. 25 B7
Brackenwood, Sun. 90 A1
Brackley Clo., Wall. 101 E7
Brackley Rd. W4 65 E5
Brackley Rd., Beck. 86 J7
Brackley Sq., 35 A7
Wdf.Grn.
Brackley St. EC1 13 A1
Brackley Ter. W4 65 E5
Bracklyn Ct. N1 9 B1
Bracklyn St. N1 9 B1
Bracklyn St. N1 59 A2
Bracknell Clo. N22 40 G1
Bracknell Gdns. NW3 48 E4
Bracknell Way NW3 48 E4
Bracondale Rd. SE2 71 A4

Brad St. SE1	16 F2	Bramah Grn. SW9 76 G1	Bramwell Clo., Sun. 90 D2	Braybrooke Gdns. 86 C7

Brad St. SE1 16 F2
Bradbourne Rd., Bex. 80 G7
Bradbourne St. SW6 75 D2
Bradbury Clo., 22 B1
 Borwd.
Bradbury Pl., Sthl. 63 F4
Bradbury St. N16 50 B5
Braddon Rd., Rich. 73 J3
Braddyll St. SE10 69 E5
Braden St. W9 6 A6
Bradenham Ave., 80 A4
 Well.
Bradenham Clo. SE17 21 B5
Bradenham Clo. SE17 68 A6
Bradenham Rd., Har. 37 E4
Bradfield Dr., Bark. 53 A5
Bradfield Rd. E16 69 G2
Bradfield Rd., Ruis. 45 E5
Bradford Clo. SE26 86 E4
 Coombe Rd.
Bradford Clo., Brom. 104 C1
Bradford Dr., Epsom 99 F6
Bradford Rd. W3 65 E2
 Warple Way
Bradford Rd., Ilf. 52 G1
Bradgate Rd. SE6 78 A6
Brading Cres. E11 51 H2
Brading Rd. SW2 76 F7
Brading Rd., Croy. 94 F6
Bradiston Rd. W9 57 C3
Bradley Clo. N1 8 F1
Bradley Clo. N7 49 F6
 Sutterton St.
Bradley Gdns. W13 55 E6
Bradley Ms. SW17 84 J1
 Bellevue Rd.
Bradley Rd. N22 40 F2
Bradley Rd. SE19 85 J6
Bradman Row, Edg. 30 C7
 Pavilion Way
Bradmead SW8 67 B7
Bradmore Ho. E1 59 F5
 Jamaica St.
Bradmore Pk. Rd. W6 65 H4
Bradshaws Clo. SE25 95 D3
Bradstock Rd. E9 50 G6
Bradstock Rd., 99 G5
 Epsom
Bradwell Ave., Dag. 53 G2
Bradwell Clo. E18 42 F4
Bradwell Ms. N18 33 D4
 Lyndhurst Rd.
Bradwell Rd., Buck.H. 35 B1
Bradwell St. E1 59 G3
Brady Ave., Loug. 27 F2
Brady St. E1 59 E4
Braemar Ave. N22 40 E1
Braemar Ave. NW10 47 D3
Braemar Ave. SW19 84 D2
Braemar Ave., Bexh. 80 J4
Braemar Ave., 94 G3
 Th.Hth.
Braemar Ave., Wem. 46 G7
Braemar Gdns. NW9 38 D1
Braemar Gdns., Sid. 88 G3
Braemar Gdns., 103 C1
 W.Wick.
Braemar Rd. E13 60 F4
Braemar Rd. N15 41 B5
Braemar Rd., Brent. 64 G6
Braemar Rd., 99 H3
 Wor.Pk.
Braes St. N1 49 H7
Braeside, Beck. 87 A5
Braeside Ave. SW19 93 B1
Braeside Clo., Pnr. 28 G7
 The Ave.
Braeside Cres., Bexh. 80 J4
Braeside Rd. SW16 85 C7
Braesyde Clo., Belv. 71 F4
Brafferton Rd., 101 J4
 Croy.
Braganza St. SE17 20 G4
Braganza St. SE17 67 H5
Braham St. E1 13 G4
Braham St. E1 59 C6
Braid Ave. W3 56 E6
Braid Clo., Felt. 81 F2
Braidwood Rd. SE6 87 D1
Braidwood St. SE1 17 D2
Brailsford Clo. SW19 84 H7
 Mitch.
Brailsford Rd. SW2 76 G5
Brainton Ave., Felt. 72 B7
Braintree Ave., Ilf. 43 B4
Braintree Rd., Dag. 53 G3
Braintree Rd., Ruis. 45 B4
Braintree St. E2 59 F4
Braithwaite Ave., 44 G7
 Rom.
Braithwaite Gdns., 37 F1
 Stan.
Braithwaite Rd., Enf. 25 J3

Bramah Grn. SW9 76 G1
Bramalea Clo. N6 40 A6
Bramall Clo. E15 51 F5
 Idmiston Rd.
Bramber Ct. W5 64 H4
 Sterling Pl.
Bramber Rd. N12 31 H5
Bramber Rd. W14 66 C6
Bramble Acres Clo., 100 D7
 Sutt.
Bramble Clo., Croy. 103 A4
Bramble Clo., Stan. 29 G7
Bramble Cft., Erith 71 J4
Bramble Gdns. W12 56 F7
 Wallflower St.
Bramble La., Hmptn. 81 F6
Bramblebury Rd. 70 F5
 SE18
Brambledown Clo., 96 E5
 W.Wick.
Brambledown Rd., 101 A7
 Cars.
Brambledown Rd., 102 B7
 S.Croy.
Brambledown Rd., 101 B7
 Wall.
Brambles, The, Chig. 35 F6
Brambles Clo., Islw. 64 E7
Bramblewood Clo., 100 J1
 Cars.
Bramblings, The E4 34 D4
Bramcote Ave., 93 J4
 Mitch.
Bramcote Gro. SE16 68 F5
Bramcote Rd. SW15 74 H4
Bramdean Cres. 87 G1
 SE12
Bramdean Gdns. 87 G1
 SE12
Bramerton Rd., 95 J3
 Beck.
Bramerton St. SW3 18 G5
Bramerton St. SW3 66 H6
Bramfield Ct. N4 49 J2
 Queens Dr.
Bramfield Rd. SW11 75 H6
Bramford Ct. N14 32 D2
Bramford Rd. SW18 75 F4
Bramham Gdns. SW5 18 A3
Bramham Gdns. SW5 66 E5
Bramham Gdns., 98 G4
 Chess.
Bramhope La. SE7 69 H6
Bramlands Clo. SW11 75 H3
Bramley Clo. E17 41 H2
Bramley Clo. N14 24 B5
Bramley Clo., Hayes 54 A7
 Orchard Rd.
Bramley Clo., Orp. 104 E1
Bramley Clo., 101 H5
 S.Croy.
Bramley Clo., Twick. 72 J6
Bramley Ct., Well. 80 B1
Bramley Cres. SW8 19 J7
Bramley Cres., Ilf. 43 D6
Bramley Gdns., Wat. 28 C5
Bramley Hill, 101 H5
 S.Croy.
Bramley Rd. N14 24 B5
Bramley Rd. W5 64 F7
Bramley Rd. W10 57 A7
Bramley Rd., Sutt. 100 G5
Bramley St. W10 57 A6
Bramley Way, Houns. 72 F5
Bramley Way, 103 B2
 W.Wick.
Brampton Clo. E5 50 E2
Brampton Gdns. N15 40 J5
 Brampton Rd.
Brampton Gro. NW4 38 H4
Brampton Gro., Har. 37 D4
Brampton Gro., Wem. 46 J1
Brampton La. NW4 38 J4
Brampton Pk. Rd. N8 40 G3
Brampton Rd. E6 61 A4
Brampton Rd. N15 40 J5
Brampton Rd. NW9 38 A4
Brampton Rd. SE2 71 C6
Brampton Rd., Bexh. 80 D3
Brampton Rd., Croy. 95 C7
Brampton Rd., Wat. 28 A3
Bramsham Gdns., 28 D5
 Wat.
Bramshaw Ri., N.Mal. 92 E6
Bramshaw Rd. E9 50 G6
Bramshill Clo., Chig. 35 H5
 Tine Rd.
Bramshill Gdns. NW5 49 B3
Bramshill Rd. NW10 56 E2
Bramshot Ave. SE7 69 G6
Bramshot Way, Wat. 28 A2
Bramston Clo., Ilf. 35 J6
Bramston Rd. NW10 56 G2

Bramwell Clo., Sun. 90 D2
Brancaster Rd. E12 52 C4
Brancaster Rd. SW16 85 E3
Brancaster Rd., Ilf. 43 G6
Brancepeth Gdns., 34 G2
 Buck.H.
Branch Hill NW3 48 F3
Branch Pl. N1 50 A1
Branch Rd. E14 59 H7
Brancker Clo., Wall. 101 E7
 Brown Clo.
Brancker Rd., Har. 37 G3
Brancroft Way, Enf. 25 H1
Brand St. SE10 69 C7
Brandlehow Rd. 75 C4
 SW15
Brandon Est. SE17 20 H6
Brandon Est. SE17 67 H6
Brandon Rd. E17 42 C3
Brandon Rd. N7 49 E7
Brandon Rd., Sthl. 63 F5
Brandon Rd., Sutt. 100 E4
Brandon St. SE17 21 A2
Brandon St. SE17 67 J4
Brandram Rd. SE13 78 E3
Brandreth Rd. E6 61 C6
Brandreth Rd. SW17 85 B2
Brandries, The, 101 D3
 Wall.
Brandville Gdns., Ilf. 43 E4
Brandy Way, Sutt. 100 D7
Brangbourne Rd., 87 C5
 Brom.
Brangton Rd. SE11 20 D4
Brangton Rd. SE11 67 F5
Brangwyn Cres. SW19 93 F2
Branksea St. SW6 66 B7
Branksome Ave. N18 33 C6
Branksome Rd. SW2 76 E4
Branksome Rd. SW19 93 D1
Branksome Way, Har. 37 H6
Branksome Way, 92 C1
 N.Mal.
Bransby Rd., Chess. 98 H7
Branscombe Gdns. 24 G7
 N21
Branscombe St. SE13 78 B3
Bransdale Clo. NW6 57 E1
 West End La.
Bransgrove Rd., Edg. 29 J7
 Merlin Cres.
Branston Cres., Orp. 104 G1
Branstone Rd., Rich. 73 J1
Brants Wk. W7 55 B4
Brantwood Ave., 71 J7
 Erith
Brantwood Ave., 73 D4
 Islw.
Brantwood Clo. E17 42 B3
Brantwood Gdns., 24 E4
 Enf.
Brantwood Gdns., 43 B4
 Ilf.
Brantwood Rd. N17 33 C6
Brantwood Rd. SE24 76 J5
Brantwood Rd., 80 H2
 Bexh.
Brasher Clo., Grnf. 46 A5
 Lilian Board Way
Brass Tally All. SE16 68 G2
 Archangel St.
Brassey Rd. NW6 48 C6
Brassey Sq. SW11 76 A3
Brassie Ave. W3 56 E6
Brasted Clo. SE26 86 F4
Brasted Clo., Bexh. 80 D5
Brathway Rd. SW18 75 D7
Braund Ave., Grnf. 54 H4
Braundton Ave., 88 J1
 Sid.
Braunston Dr., 54 E4
 Hayes
Bravington Pl. W9 57 C4
 Bravington Rd.
Bravington Rd. W9 57 C3
Brawne Ho. SE17 20 H6
Braxfield Rd. SE4 77 H4
Braxted Pk. SW16 85 F6
Bray NW3 48 H7
Bray Clo., Borwd. 22 C1
Bray Cres. SE16 68 G2
 Marlow Way
Bray Dr. E16 60 F7
 Bowman Ave.
Bray Pas. E16 60 F7
 Bowman Ave.
Bray Pl. SW3 18 J2
Bray Pl. SW3 66 J4
Bray Rd. NW7 31 A6
Brayards Rd. SE15 77 E2
Braybourne Dr., Islw. 64 C7
Braybrook St. W12 56 F5

Braybrooke Gdns. 86 C7
 SE19
 Fox Hill
Brayburne Ave. SW4 76 C2
Braycourt Ave., 90 B7
 Walt.
Braydon Rd. N16 41 D7
Brayfield Ter. N1 49 G7
 Lofting Rd.
Brayford Sq. E1 59 H6
 Summercourt Rd.
Brayton Gdns., Enf. 24 D4
Braywood Rd. SE9 79 G4
Brazil Clo., Croy. 94 E7
Breach La., Dag. 62 G3
Bread St. EC4 13 A5
Bread St. EC4 58 J7
Breakspears Rd. SE4 77 J3
Bream Gdns. E6 61 D3
Bream St. E3 51 A7
Breamore Clo. SW15 83 G1
Breamore Rd., Ilf. 52 J2
Bream's Bldgs. EC4 12 E3
Bream's Bldgs. EC4 58 G6
Breamwater Gdns., 82 E3
 Rich.
Brearley Clo., Edg. 30 C7
 Pavilion Way
Breasley Clo. SW15 74 H4
Brechin Pl. SW7 18 D2
Brecknock Rd. N7 49 D5
Brecknock Rd. N19 49 C4
Brecknock Rd. Est. 49 C4
 N7
Brecon Clo., Mitch. 94 E3
Brecon Clo., Wor.Pk. 99 J2
 Cotswold Way
Brecon Rd. W6 66 B6
Brecon Rd., Enf. 25 F4
Brede Clo. E6 61 D3
Bredgar Rd. N19 49 C2
Bredhurst Clo. SE20 86 F6
Bredon Rd. SE5 76 J3
Bredon Rd., Croy. 95 C7
Breer St. SW6 75 E3
Breezers Hill E1 13 J6
Brember Rd., Har. 45 J2
Bremner Rd. SW7 14 D5
Brenchley Clo., Brom. 96 F6
Brenchley Clo., Chis. 97 D1
Brenchley Gdns. 77 F6
 SE23
Brenchley Rd., Orp. 97 H1
Brenda Rd. SW17 84 J2
Brende Gdns., 90 H4
 W.Mol.
Brendon Ave. NW10 47 E4
Brendon Gdns., Har. 45 H4
Brendon Gdns., Ilf. 43 H5
Brendon Rd. SE9 88 G2
Brendon Rd., Dag. 53 F1
Brendon St. W1 15 H3
Brendon St. W1 57 H6
Brendon Way, Enf. 25 B7
Brenley Clo., Mitch. 94 A3
Brenley Gdns. SE9 79 A4
Brent Clo., Bex. 89 E1
Brent Cres. NW10 55 J2
Brent Cross Shop. 38 J7
 Cen. NW4
Brent Grn. NW4 38 J5
Brent Grn. Wk., Wem. 47 C3
Brent Lea, Brent. 64 F7
Brent Pk. NW10 47 F7
Brent Pk. Rd. NW4 38 H7
Brent Pl., Barn. 23 D5
Brent Rd. E16 60 G5
Brent Rd. SE18 70 E7
Brent Rd., Brent. 64 F6
Brent Rd., Sthl. 63 C3
Brent St. NW4 38 J4
Brent Ter. NW2 38 J1
Brent Vw. Rd. NW9 38 G6
Brent Way N3 31 D6
Brent Way, Brent. 64 G7
Brent Way, Wem. 47 B6
Brentcot Clo. W13 55 E4
Brentfield NW10 47 B7
Brentfield Clo. NW10 47 D6
 Normans Mead
Brentfield Gdns. 39 A7
 NW2
 Hendon Way
Brentfield Rd. NW10 47 D6
Brentford Business 64 F7
 Cen., Brent.
Brentford Clo., Hayes 54 D4
Brentham Way W5 55 G4
Brenthouse Rd. E9 50 F6
Brenthurst Rd. NW10 47 F6
Brentmead Clo. W7 55 B7
Brentmead Gdns. 55 J2
 NW10

Brentmead Pl. NW11 39 A6
North Circular Rd.
Brenton St. E14 59 H6
Brentside, Brent. 64 F6
Brentside Clo. W13 55 D4
Brentside Executive Cen., Brent. 64 E6
Brentvale Ave., Sthl. 64 A1
Brentvale Ave., Wem. 55 J1
Brentwick Gdns., Brent. 64 H4
Brentwood Clo. SE9 88 F1
Brentwood Ho. SE18 70 A7
Shooter's Hill Rd.
Brereton Rd. N17 33 C7
Bressenden Pl. SW1 15 E5
Bressenden Pl. SW1 67 B3
Bressey Gro. E18 42 F2
Brett Clo. N16 50 B2
Yoakley Rd.
Brett Clo., Nthlt. 54 D3
Broomcroft Ave.
Brett Ct. N9 33 F2
Brett Cres. NW10 47 D7
Brett Gdns., Dag. 53 E7
Brett Ho. Clo. SW15 75 A6
Putney Heath La.
Brett Pas. E8 50 E5
Kenmure Rd.
Brett Rd. E8 50 E5
Brettell St. SE17 21 C4
Brettenham Ave. E17 42 A1
Penrhyn Ave.
Brettenham Rd. E17 42 A2
Brettenham Rd. N18 33 D4
Brewer St. W1 11 G5
Brewer St. W1 58 C7
Brewer's Grn. SW1 15 G5
Brewers La., Rich. 73 G5
George St.
Brewery Clo., Wem. 46 D5
Brewery La., Twick. 73 C7
Brewery Rd. N7 49 E7
Brewery Rd. SE18 70 G5
Brewery Rd., Brom. 104 B1
Brewhouse La. E1 68 E1
Brewhouse Rd. SE18 70 C4
Brewhouse St. SW15 75 B3
Brewhouse Wk. SE16 68 H1
Brewhouse Yd. EC1 8 G5
Brewood Rd., Dag. 53 B6
Brewster Gdns. W10 56 J5
Brewster Ho. E14 59 J7
Brewster Rd. E10 51 B1
Brian Rd., Rom. 44 C5
Briant St. SE14 77 G1
Briants Clo., Pnr. 36 F2
Briar Ave. SW16 85 F7
Briar Clo. N2 39 E2
Briar Clo. N13 32 J3
Briar Clo., Buck.H. 35 A2
Briar Clo., Hmptn. 81 F5
Briar Clo., Islw. 73 C5
Briar Ct., Sutt. 99 J4
Briar Cres., Nthlt. 45 H6
Briar Gdns., Brom. 103 F1
Briar La., Croy. 103 B4
Briar Pas. SW16 94 E3
Pollards Cres.
Briar Pl. SW16 94 F3
Briar Rd.
Briar Rd. NW2 47 J4
Briar Rd. SW16 94 E3
Briar Rd., Har. 37 F5
Briar Rd., Twick. 82 B1
Briar Wk. SW15 74 H4
Briar Wk. W10 57 B4
Droop St.
Briar Wk., Edg. 30 C7
Briarbank Rd. W13 55 D6
Briardale Gdns. NW3 48 D3
Briarfield Ave. N3 39 E2
Briars Clo. N17 33 E7
Briarswood Way, Orp. 104 J5
Briarwood Clo. NW9 38 C6
Briarwood Dr., Nthwd. 36 A2
Briarwood Rd. SW4 76 D5
Briarwood Rd., Epsom 99 G6
Briary Clo. NW3 48 H7
Fellows Rd.
Briary Ct., Sid. 89 B5
Briary Gdns., Brom. 87 H5
Briary Gro., Edg. 38 B2
Briary La. N9 33 C3
Brick Ct. EC4 12 E4
Brick Fm. Clo., Rich. 74 B1
Brick La. E1 9 G4
Brick La. E1 59 C4
Brick La. E2 9 G6
Brick La. E2 59 C3
Brick La., Enf. 25 E2
Brick La., Stan. 29 G7
Honeypot La.
Brick St. W1 15 D2
Brick St. W1 67 B1
Brickfield Clo., Brent. 64 F7
Brickfield Cotts. SE18 70 J6
Brickfield La., Barn. 22 F6
Brickfield Rd. E3 60 B4
Brickfield Rd. SW19 84 E4
Brickfield Rd., Th.Hth. 94 H1
Brickfields, Har. 46 A2
Bricklayer's Arms SE1 21 E1
Brickwood Clo. SE26 86 E3
Brickwood Rd., Croy. 102 B2
Bride Ct. EC4 12 G4
Bride La. EC4 12 G4
Bride Pl., Croy. 102 A1
Bride St. N7 49 F6
Bridewell Pl. E1 68 E1
Brewhouse La.
Bridewell Pl. EC4 12 G4
Bridford Ms. W1 11 E1
Bridge, The, Har. 37 C4
Bridge App. NW1 49 A7
Bridge Ave. W6 65 H5
Bridge Ave. W7 55 A5
Bridge Clo., Enf. 25 E2
Bridge End E17 42 C1
Bridge Gdns., E.Mol. 91 A4
Bridge Gate N21 24 J7
Bridge Ho. Quay E14 69 C1
Prestons Rd.
Bridge La. NW11 39 B4
Bridge La. SW11 75 H1
Bridge Pk. SW18 75 D5
Bridge Pl. SW1 19 E1
Bridge Pl. SW1 67 B4
Bridge Pl., Croy. 102 A1
Bridge Rd. E6 52 C7
Bridge Rd. E15 60 D1
Bridge Rd. E17 41 J7
Bridge Rd. N9 33 D3
Fore St.
Bridge Rd. N22 40 E1
Bridge Rd. NW10 47 E6
Bridge Rd., Beck. 86 J7
Bridge Rd., Bexh. 80 E2
Bridge Rd., Chess. 98 G5
Bridge Rd., Croy. 101 J3
Duppas Hill Rd.
Bridge Rd., E.Mol. 91 A5
Bridge Rd., Houns. 73 A3
Bridge Rd., Islw. 73 A3
Bridge Rd., Sthl. 63 F2
Bridge Rd., Sutt. 100 E6
Bridge Rd., Twick. 73 E6
Bridge Rd., Wall. 101 B5
Bridge Rd., Wem. 47 A3
Bridge Row, Croy. 102 A1
Cross Rd.
Bridge St. SW1 16 A4
Bridge St. SW1 67 E2
Bridge St. W4 65 D4
Bridge St., Pnr. 36 E3
Bridge St., Rich. 73 G5
Bridge Ter. E15 51 D7
Bridge Vw. W6 65 J5
Bridge Way N13 32 F4
Bridge Way NW11 39 C5
Bridge Way, Twick. 72 J7
Bridge Way, Wem. 46 H7
Bridge Wf. Rd., Islw. 73 E3
Church St.
Bridge Wks. Ind. Est., Uxb. 54 E4
Bridge Yd. SE1 17 C1
Bridgefield Rd., Sutt. 100 D6
Bridgefoot SE1 20 B4
Bridgefoot SE1 67 E5
Bridgeford St. SW18 84 F3
Bridgeland Rd. E16 60 G7
Bridgeman Rd. N1 49 F7
Bridgeman Rd. W4 65 C3
Bridgeman Rd., Tedd. 82 D6
Bridgeman St. NW8 6 G2
Bridgeman St. NW8 57 H2
Bridgen Rd., Bex. 80 E6
Bridgend Rd. SW18 75 F4
Bridgenhall Rd., Enf. 25 C1
Bridgeport Pl. E1 17 J1
Bridgeport Pl. E1 68 D1
Bridges Ct. SW11 75 G3
Bridges La., Croy. 101 E4
Bridges Pl. SW6 75 C1
Bridges Rd. SW19 84 E6
Bridges Rd., Stan. 29 C5
Bridges Rd. Ms. SW19 84 E6
Bridges Rd.
Bridgetown Clo. SE19 86 B5
St. Kitts Ter.
Bridgeview Ct., Ilf. 35 G6
Bridgewater Clo., Chis. 97 H3
Bridgewater Gdns., Edg. 37 J2
Bridgewater Rd., Ruis. 45 A4
Bridgewater Rd., Wem. 46 F6
Bridgewater Sq. EC2 12 J1
Bridgewater St. EC2 12 J1
Bridgeway, Bark. 52 J7
Bridgeway St. NW1 7 G2
Bridgeway St. NW1 58 C2
Bridgewood Clo. SE20 86 E7
Bridgewood Rd. SW16 85 D7
Bridgewood Rd., Wor.Pk. 99 G3
Bridgwater Rd. E15 60 C1
Bridle Clo., Epsom 99 D5
Bridle Clo., Kings.T. 91 G4
Bridle La. W1 11 G5
Bridle Path, Croy. 101 E3
Bridle Path, Wdf.Grn. 34 E7
Bridle Rd., Croy. 103 A3
Bridle Rd., Esher 98 E6
Bridle Rd., Pnr. 36 C6
Bridle Way, Croy. 103 A5
Bridle Way, Orp. 104 F4
Bridle Way, The, Wall. 101 C4
Bridlington Rd. N9 25 E7
Bridlington Rd., Wat. 28 D3
Bridport Ave., Rom. 44 H6
Bridport Pl. N1 9 C1
Bridport Pl. N1 59 A1
Bridport Rd. N18 33 B5
Bridport Rd., Grnf. 54 H1
Bridport Rd., Th.Hth. 94 G3
Bridport Ter. SW8 76 D1
Wandsworth Rd.
Bridstow Pl. W2 57 D6
Talbot Rd.
Brief St. SE5 76 H1
Brierley, Croy. 103 B6
Brierley Ave. N9 33 F1
Brierley Clo. SE25 95 D4
Brierley Rd. E11 51 D4
Brierley Rd. SW12 85 C2
Brierly Gdns. E2 59 F2
Royston St.
Brig Ms. SE8 69 A6
Watergate St.
Brigade Clo., Har. 46 A2
Brigade St. SE3 78 F2
Royal Par.
Briggeford Clo. E5 50 D2
Geldeston Rd.
Bright Clo., Belv. 71 D4
Bright St. E14 60 B6
Brightfield Rd. SE12 78 F5
Brightling Rd. SE4 77 J6
Brightlingsea Pl. E14 59 J7
Brightman Rd. SW18 84 G1
Brighton Ave. E17 41 J5
Brighton Dr., Nthlt. 45 G6
Brighton Gro. SE14 77 H1
New Cross Rd.
Brighton Rd. E6 61 D3
Brighton Rd. N2 39 F2
Brighton Rd. N16 50 B4
Brighton Rd., S.Croy. 101 J5
Brighton Rd., Surb. 91 F6
Brighton Ter. SW9 76 F4
Brightside, The, Enf. 25 G1
Brightside Rd. SE13 78 D6
Brightwell Cres. SW17 84 J5
Brigstock Rd., Belv. 71 H4
Brigstock Rd., Th.Hth. 94 G5
Brill Pl. NW1 7 J2
Brill Pl. NW1 58 D2
Brim Hill N2 39 F4
Brimpsfield Clo. SE2 71 B3
Brimsdown Ave., Enf. 25 H2
Brimsdown Ind. Est., Enf. 25 J2
Brindle Gate, Sid. 88 H1
Pinewood Ave.
Brindley St. SE14 77 J1
Brindley Way, Brom. 87 G5
Brindley Way, Sthl. 54 H7
Brindwood Rd. E4 33 J3
Brinkburn Clo. SE2 71 A4
Brinkburn Clo., Edg. 38 B2
Brinkburn Gdns., Edg. 38 A3
Brinkley Rd., Wor.Pk. 99 H2
Brinklow Cres. SE18 70 E7
Brinklow Ho. W2 57 E5
Brinkworth Rd., Ilf. 43 B3
Brinkworth Way E9 50 J6
Brinsdale Rd. NW4 39 A3
Brinsley Rd., Har. 37 A2
Brinsley St. E1 59 E6
Watney St.
Brinsworth Clo., Twick. 82 A1
Brinton Wk. SE1 16 G2
Brion Pl. E14 60 C5
Brisbane Ave. SW19 93 E1
Brisbane Rd. E10 51 B2
Brisbane Rd. W13 64 D2
Brisbane Rd., Ilf. 43 E7
Brisbane St. SE5 68 A7
Briscoe Clo. E11 51 F2
Briscoe Rd. SW19 84 G6
Briset Rd. SE9 79 A3
Briset St. EC1 12 G1
Briset Way N7 49 F2
Bristol Gdns. W9 6 B6
Bristol Gdns. W9 57 E4
Bristol Ms. W9 6 B6
Bristol Pk. Rd. E17 41 H4
Hervey Pk. Rd.
Bristol Rd. E7 51 J6
Bristol Rd., Grnf. 54 H1
Bristol Rd., Mord. 93 F5
Briston Gro. N8 40 E6
Bristow Rd. SE19 86 B5
Bristow Rd., Bexh. 80 E1
Bristow Rd., Croy. 101 E4
Bristow Rd., Houns. 72 H3
Britannia Clo. SW4 76 D4
Clapham Cres.
Britannia Clo., Nthlt. 54 D3
Britannia La., Twick. 72 J7
Britannia Rd. E14 69 A4
Britannia Rd. N12 31 F3
Britannia Rd. SW6 66 E7
Britannia Rd., Ilf. 52 E3
Britannia Rd., Surb. 91 J7
Britannia Row N1 58 H1
Britannia St. WC1 8 C3
Britannia St. WC1 58 F3
Britannia Wk. N1 9 B3
Britannia Way NW10 56 B4
Britannia Way SW6 75 E1
Britannia Rd.
British Gro. W4 65 F5
British Gro. Pas. W4 65 F5
British Gro. S. W4 65 F5
British Gro. Pas.
British Legion Rd. E4 34 F2
British St. E3 59 J3
Brittain Rd., Dag. 53 E3
Britten Clo. NW11 48 E1
Britten Dr., Sthl. 54 G6
Britten St. SW3 18 G4
Britten St. SW3 66 H5
Brittenden Clo., Orp. 104 H6
Britten's Ct. E1 59 E7
The Highway
Britton St. EC1 8 G6
Britton St. EC1 58 H4
Brixham Cres., Ruis. 45 A1
Brixham Gdns., Ilf. 52 H5
Brixham Rd., Well. 80 D1
Brixham St. E16 70 C1
Brixton Est., Edg. 38 B2
Brixton Hill SW2 76 E7
Brixton Hill Pl. SW2 76 E7
Brixton Hill
Brixton Oval SW2 76 G4
Brixton Rd. SW9 76 G3
Brixton Sta. Rd. SW9 76 G3
Brixton Water La. SW2 76 G5
Broad Ct. WC2 12 B4
Broad Grn. Ave., Croy. 94 H7
Broad La. EC2 13 D2
Broad La. EC2 59 B5
Broad La. N8 40 F5
Tottenham La.
Broad La. N15 41 C4
Broad La., Hmptn. 81 F7
Broad Lawn SE9 88 D2
Broad Oak, Wdf.Grn. 34 H5
Broad Oak Clo. E4 34 A5
Royston Ave.
Broad Sanctuary SW1 15 J4
Broad Sanctuary SW1 67 D2
Broad St., Dag. 53 G7
Broad St., Tedd. 82 C6
Broad St. Ave. EC2 13 D2
Broad St. Pl. EC2 13 C2
Broad Vw. NW9 38 A6

Broad Wk. N21 32 F2
Broad Wk. NW1 7 C1
Broad Wk. NW1 58 A1
Outer Circle
Broad Wk. SE3 78 J2
Broad Wk. NW1 15 B1
Broad Wk. W1 67 A1
Broad Wk., Houns. 72 D1
Broad Wk., Rich. 84 I7
Broad Wk., The W8 14 C3
Broad Wk., The W8 66 F1
Broad Wk., The, 91 C4
E.Mol.
Broad Wk. La. NW11 39 C7
Broad Yd. EC1 8 G6
Broadbent Clo. N6 49 B1
Broadbent St. W1 11 D5
Broadberry Ct. N18 33 E6
Broadbridge Clo. 69 G7
SE3
Broadcoombe, 102 F7
S.Croy.
Broadcroft Ave., 37 G2
Stan.
Broadcroft Rd., Orp. 97 G7
Broadfield Clo. NW2 47 J3
Broadfield Ct. 29 B2
(Bushey), Wat.
Broadfield Heights, 30 B4
Edg.
Broadfield La. NW1 49 E7
Broadfield Rd. SE6 78 E7
Broadfield Sq., Enf. 25 E2
Broadfield Way, 34 J3
Buck.H.
Broadfields, E.Mol. 91 A6
Broadfields, Har. 36 H1
Broadfields Ave. 24 G7
N21
Broadfields Ave., 30 B4
Edg.
Broadfields La., Wat. 28 B1
Broadfields Way 47 F5
NW10
Broadgate E13 60 J2
Broadgate Circle EC2 13 D1
Broadgate Rd. E16 61 A6
Fulmer Rd.
Broadgates Ave., 23 E1
Barn.
Broadhead Strand 38 F1
NW9
Broadheath Dr., Chis. 88 C5
Broadhinton Rd. SW4 76 B3
Broadhurst Ave., 30 B4
Edg.
Broadhurst Ave., Ilf. 52 J4
Broadhurst Clo. NW6 48 F6
Broadhurst Gdns.
Broadhurst Clo., 73 J5
Rich.
Lwr. Gro. Rd.
Broadhurst Gdns. 48 E6
NW6
Broadhurst Gdns., 35 F4
Chig.
Broadhurst Gdns., 45 C2
Ruis.
Broadlands, The, 81 F3
Felt.
Broadlands Ave. 85 E2
SW16
Broadlands Ave., 25 E3
Enf.
Broadlands Clo. N6 40 A7
Broadlands Clo. 85 E2
SW16
Broadlands Clo., Enf. 25 F3
Broadlands Rd. N6 39 J7
Broadlands Rd., 87 H4
Brom.
Broadlands Way, 92 F6
N.Mal.
Broadlawns Ct., Har. 37 C1
Broadley St. NW8 10 F1
Broadley St. NW8 57 G5
Broadley Ter. NW1 6 H6
Broadley Ter. NW1 57 H4
Broadmayne SE17 21 B3
Broadmead SE6 87 A3
Broadmead Ave., 92 G7
Wor.Pk.
Broadmead Clo., 81 G6
Hmptn.
Broadmead Clo., Pnr. 28 E7
Broadmead Est., 34 J7
Wdf.Grn.
Broadmead Rd., 54 E4
Hayes
Broadmead Rd., 54 E4
Nthlt.
Broadmead Rd., 34 G6
Wdf.Grn.

Broadoaks, Surb. 99 B1
Broadoaks Way, 96 F5
Brom.
Broadstone Pl. W1 11 B2
Broadview Rd. SW16 85 D7
Broadwalk E18 42 F3
Broadwalk, Har. 36 G5
Broadwall SE1 16 H1
Broadwall SE1 67 G1
Broadwater Gdns., 101 F4
Orp.
Broadwater Rd. N17 41 B1
Broadwater Rd. SE28 70 F3
Broadwater Rd. 84 H4
SW17
Broadway E15 51 D7
Broadway N20 31 F2
Broadway SW1 15 H5
Broadway SW1 67 D3
Broadway, Bark. 52 F7
Broadway, Bexh. 80 E4
Broadway, Grnf. 54 J4
Broadway, Surb. 99 B1
Broadway, The E4 34 C6
Broadway, The E13 60 H2
Broadway, The N8 40 E6
Broadway, The N9 33 D3
Broadway, The N22 40 G2
Broadway, The NW7 30 E5
Broadway, The SW19 84 D7
Broadway, The W5 55 G7
Broadway, The W7 64 B1
Broadway, The W13 64 D1
Broadway, The, Dag. 53 F2
Whalebone La. S.
Broadway, The, 99 G5
Epsom
Broadway, The, Har. 37 B2
Broadway, The, 27 F7
Loug.
Broadway, The, Pnr. 28 F7
Broadway, The, Sthl. 54 D7
Broadway, The, Stan. 29 F5
Broadway, The, 100 B6
Sutt.
Broadway, The, 98 B1
T.Ditt.
Hampton Ct. Way
Broadway, The, Wem. 46 H3
East La.
Broadway, The, 34 H6
Wdf.Grn.
Broadway Ave. 95 A5
Croy.
Broadway Ave. 73 E6
Twick.
Broadway Clo., 34 H6
Wdf.Grn.
Broadway Ct. SW19 84 D6
The Bdy.
Broadway Gdns., 93 H4
Mitch.
Broadway Mkt. E8 59 E1
Broadway Ms. E5 41 C7
Broadwick St. W1 11 G5
Broadwick St. W1 58 C6
Brocas Clo. NW3 48 H7
Fellows Rd.
Brock Pl. E3 60 B4
Brock Rd. E13 60 H5
Brock St. SE15 77 E3
Evelina Rd.
Brockdish Ave., Bark. 52 J5
Brockenhurst, W.Mol. 90 F6
Brockenhurst Ave., 99 E1
Wor.Pk.
Brockenhurst Gdns. 30 E6
NW7
Brockenhurst Gdns., 52 F5
Ilf.
Brockenhurst Rd., 95 E7
Croy.
Brockenhurst Way 94 D2
SW16
Brocket Clo., Chig. 35 J5
Brocket Way, Chig. 35 H5
Brockham Clo. SW19 84 C5
Brockham Cres., 103 D7
Croy.
Brockham Dr. SW2 76 F7
Fairview Pl.
Brockham Dr., Ilf. 53 E6
Brockham St. SE1 17 A5
Brockham St. SE1 67 J3
Brockhurst Clo., Stan. 29 C6
Brockill Cres. SE4 77 H4
Brocklebank Rd. SE7 69 H4
Brocklebank Rd. 75 F7
SW18
Brocklehurst St. SE14 68 G7
Brocklesby Rd. SE25 95 E4
Brockley Ave., Stan. 29 H3
Brockley Clo., Stan. 29 H4

Brockley Cross SE4 77 H3
Endwell Rd.
Brockley Footpath 77 F4
SE15
Brockley Gdns. SE4 77 J2
Brockley Gro. SE4 77 J5
Brockley Hall Rd. SE4 77 H5
Brockley Ms. SE4 29 F1
Brockley Ms. SE4 77 H6
Brockley Pk. SE23 77 H7
Brockley Ri. SE23 77 H7
Brockley Rd. SE4 77 J3
Brockley Vw. SE23 77 H7
Brockley Way SE4 77 G5
Brockleyside, Stan. 29 H4
Brockman Ri., Brom. 87 D4
Brocks Dr., Sutt. 100 B3
Brockshot Clo., 64 G5
Brent.
Brockway Clo. E11 51 E2
Brockwell Clo., Orp. 97 J4
Brockwell Pk. Gdns. 76 G7
SE24
Brockworth Clo. 21 E6
SE15
Brockworth Clo. 68 B6
SE15
Broderick Gro. SE2 71 B4
Brodewater Rd., 22 B2
Borwd.
Brodia Rd. N16 50 B3
Brodie Rd. E4 34 C1
Brodie St. SE1 21 G3
Brodlove La. E1 59 G7
Brodrick Rd. SW17 84 H2
Brograve Gdns., 96 B2
Beck.
Broke Wk. E8 59 D1
Marlborough Ave.
Broken Wf. EC4 12 J5
Brokesley St. E3 59 J3
Bromar Rd. SE5 77 B3
Bromborough Gro., 28 C5
Wat.
Brome Rd. SE9 79 C3
Bromefield, Stan. 37 F1
Bromehead St. E1 59 F6
Commercial Rd.
Bromell's Rd. SW4 76 C4
Bromfelde Rd. SW4 76 D3
Bromfelde Wk. SW4 76 E2
Bromfield St. N1 8 F1
Bromfield St. N1 58 G2
Bromhall Rd., Dag. 53 B6
Bromhedge SE9 88 C3
Bromholm Rd. SE2 71 B3
Bromley Ave., Brom. 87 E7
Bromley Common, 96 J4
Brom.
Bromley Cres., Brom. 96 F3
Bromley Gdns., 96 F3
Brom.
Bromley Gro., Brom. 96 D2
Bromley Hall Rd. E14 60 C5
Bromley High St. E3 60 B3
Bromley Hill, Brom. 87 E6
Bromley La., Chis. 88 F7
Bromley Pl. W1 11 F1
Bromley Rd. E10 42 B6
Bromley Rd. E17 42 A2
Bromley Rd. N17 41 C1
Bromley Rd. N18 33 A3
Bromley Rd. SE6 87 B2
Bromley Rd., Beck. 96 B2
Bromley Rd. (BR1), 87 D4
Brom.
Bromley Rd. (BR2), 96 H3
Brom.
Bromley Rd., Chis. 97 E1
Bromley St. E1 59 G5
Brompton Arc. SW3 14 J4
Brompton Clo. SE20 95 D2
Selby Rd.
Brompton Clo., 72 F5
Houns.
Brompton Gro. N2 39 H4
Brompton Pk. Cres. 18 A6
SW6
Brompton Pk. Cres. 66 E6
SW6
Brompton Pl. SW3 14 H5
Brompton Pl. SW3 66 H3
Brompton Rd. SW1 14 J4
Brompton Rd. SW1 66 J2
Brompton Rd. SW3 18 G1
Brompton Rd. SW3 66 H3
Brompton Rd. SW7 14 G6
Brompton Rd. SW7 66 H3
Brompton Sq. SW3 14 G5
Brompton Ter. SE18 79 D1
Bromwich Ave. N6 49 A2
Bromyard Ave. W3 56 E7

Bromyard Ho. SE15 68 E7
Commercial Way
Brondesbury Ct. NW2 48 A6
Brondesbury Ms. 48 D7
NW6
Willesden La.
Brondesbury Pk. 47 J7
NW2
Brondesbury Pk. 48 A7
NW6
Brondesbury Rd. 57 C2
NW6
Brondesbury Vill. 57 C2
NW6
Bronsart Rd. SW6 66 B7
Bronson Rd. SW20 93 A2
Bronte Clo. E7 51 G4
Bective Rd.
Bronte Clo., Ilf. 43 D4
Bronte Ho. NW6 57 D3
Bronti Clo. SE17 21 A5
Bronti Clo. SE17 67 J5
Bronze St. SE8 69 A7
Brook Ave., Dag. 53 H7
Brook Ave., Edg. 30 B6
Brook Ave., Wem. 47 A3
Brook Clo. SW20 92 H3
Brook Clo., Chis. 79 D1
Brook Cres. E4 34 A4
Brook Cres. N9 33 E4
Brook Dr. SE11 16 F6
Brook Dr. SE11 67 G3
Brook Dr., Har. 36 J4
Brook Gdns. E4 34 B4
Brook Gdns. SW13 74 F3
Brook Gdns., 92 C1
Kings.T.
Brook Gate W1 11 A6
Brook Grn. W6 65 J3
Brook Ind. Est., 63 D1
Hayes
Brook La. SE3 78 H2
Brook La., Bex. 80 D6
Brook La., Brom. 87 G6
Brook La. N., Brent. 64 G5
Brook Mead, Epsom 99 E6
Brook Meadow N12 31 E3
Brook Ms. N. W2 10 D5
Brook Par., Chig. 35 E3
High Rd.
Brook Pl., Barn. 23 D5
Brook Ri., Chig. 35 D3
Brook Rd. N8 40 E4
Brook Rd. N22 40 F2
Brook Rd. NW2 47 F2
Brook Rd., Borwd. 22 A1
Brook Rd., Buck.H. 34 G2
Brook Rd., Ilf. 43 H6
Brook Rd., Loug. 27 B4
Brook Rd., Surb. 98 H2
Brook Rd., Th.Hth. 94 J4
Brook Rd., Twick. 73 D6
Brook Rd. S., Brent. 64 G6
Brook St. N17 41 C2
High Rd.
Brook St. W1 11 D5
Brook St. W1 58 A7
Brook St. W2 10 F5
Brook St. W2 57 G7
Brook St., Belv. 71 H5
Brook St., Erith 71 H6
Brook St., Kings.T. 91 H2
Brook Wk. N2 39 G1
Old Fm. Rd.
Brook Wk., Edg. 30 D6
Brook Way, Chig. 35 D3
Brookbank Ave. W7 55 A5
Brookbank Rd. SE13 78 A3
Brookdale N11 32 C4
Brookdale Rd. E17 42 A3
Brookdale Rd. SE6 78 B6
Brookdale Rd., Bex. 80 E6
Brookdene Rd. SE18 70 J4
Brooke Ave., Har. 45 J3
Brooke Rd. E5 50 D3
Brooke Rd. E17 42 C4
Brooke Rd. N16 50 C3
Brooke St. EC1 12 E2
Brooke St. EC1 58 G5
Brookehowse Rd. 87 A2
SE6
Brookend Rd., Sid. 88 H1
Brooke's Ct. EC1 12 E1
Brookfield N6 49 A3
Brookfield Ave. E17 42 C4
Brookfield Ave. NW7 30 H6
Brookfield Ave. W5 55 G4
Brookfield Ave., 100 H4
Sutt.
Brookfield Clo. NW7 30 H6
Brookfield Ct., Grnf. 54 J3
Brookfield Ct., Har. 37 G5
Brookfield Cres. NW7 30 H6

Name	Page	Grid
Brookfield Cres., Har.	37	H5
Brookfield Gdns., Esher	98	C6
Brookfield Pk. NW5	49	B3
Brookfield Path, Wdf.Grn.	34	E6
Brookfield Rd. E9	50	H6
Brookfield Rd. N9	33	D3
Brookfield Rd. W4	65	D2
Brookfields, Enf.	25	G4
Brookfields Ave., Mitch.	93	H5
Brookhill Clo. SE18	70	E5
Brookhill Clo., Barn.	23	H5
Brookhill Rd. SE18	70	E4
Brookhill Rd., Barn.	23	H5
Brookhouse Gdns. E4	34	E4
Brooking Rd. E7	51	G5
Brookland Clo. NW11	39	E4
Brookland Garth NW11	39	E4
Brookland Hill NW11	39	E4
Brookland Ri. NW11	39	D4
Brooklands Ave. SW19	84	E2
Brooklands Ave., Sid.	88	G2
Brooklands Dr., Grnf.	55	F1
Brooklands Pk. SE3	78	G3
Brooklands Rd., T.Ditt.	98	C1
Brooklands St. SW8	76	D1
Brooklea Clo. NW9	38	E1
Brooklyn Ave. SE25	95	E4
Brooklyn Ave., Loug.	27	B4
Brooklyn Clo., Cars.	100	H2
Brooklyn Gro. SE25	95	E4
Brooklyn Rd. SE25	95	E4
Brooklyn Rd., Brom.	97	A5
Brookmead Ave., Brom.	97	C5
Brookmead Rd., Croy.	94	C6
Brookmill Rd. SE8	78	A1
Brooks Ave. E6	61	C4
Brooks Clo. SE9	88	D2
Brooks Ct. E15	51	B5
Clays La.		
Brooks La. W4	65	A6
Brook's Ms. W1	**11**	**D5**
Brook's Ms. W1	58	B7
Brooks Rd. E13	60	G1
Brooks Rd. W4	65	A5
Brooksbank St. E9	50	F6
Brooksby Ms. N1	49	G7
Brooksby St.		
Brooksby St. N1	49	G7
Brooksby's Wk. E9	50	G5
Brookscroft Rd. E17	42	B1
Brookshill, Har.	29	A5
Brookshill Ave., Har.	29	A5
Brookshill Dr., Har.	29	A5
Brookside N21	24	F6
Brookside, Barn.	23	H6
Brookside, Cars.	101	A5
Brookside, Ilf.	35	F6
Brookside, Orp.	97	J7
Brookside Clo., Barn.	23	B6
Brookside Clo., Felt.	81	A3
Sycamore Clo.		
Brookside Clo., Har.	37	G5
Brookside Clo. (Kenton), Har.	45	E4
Brookside Cres., Wor.Pk.	99	G1
Green La.		
Brookside Rd. N9	33	E4
Brookside Rd. N19	49	C2
Junction Rd.		
Brookside Rd. NW11	39	B6
Brookside Rd., Hayes	54	C7
Brookside S., Barn.	24	A7
Brookside Wk. N3	39	A3
Brookside Wk. N12	31	D6
Brookside Wk. N14	39	B4
Brookside Wk. NW11	39	B4
Brookside Way, Croy.	95	G6
Brooksville Ave. NW6	57	B1
Brookvale, Erith	80	H1
Brookview Rd. SW16	85	C5
Brookville Rd. SW6	66	C7
Brookway SE3	78	G3
Brookwood Ave. SW13	74	F3
Brookwood Clo., Brom.	96	F4
Brookwood Rd. SW18	84	C1
Brookwood Rd., Houns.	72	H1
Broom Clo., Brom.	97	B6
Broom Clo., Tedd.	82	G7
Broom Gdns., Croy.	103	A3
Broom Lock, Tedd.	82	F6
Broom Mead, Bexh.	80	G5
Broom Pk., Tedd.	82	G7
Broom Rd., Croy.	103	A3
Broom Rd., Tedd.	82	E4
Broom Water, Tedd.	82	F6
Broom Water W., Tedd.	82	F5
Broomcroft Ave., Nthlt.	54	C3
Broome Rd., Hmptn.	81	F7
Broome Way SE5	67	J7
Broomfield E17	41	J7
Broomfield, Sun.	90	A1
Broomfield Ave. N13	32	F5
Broomfield Ave., Loug.	27	C6
Broomfield La. N13	32	E4
Broomfield Pl. W13	64	E1
Broomfield Rd.		
Broomfield Rd. N13	32	E5
Broomfield Rd. W13	64	E1
Broomfield Rd., Beck.	95	H4
Broomfield Rd., Bexh.	80	G5
Broomfield Rd., Rich.	73	J1
Broomfield Rd., Rom.	44	D7
Broomfield Rd., Surb.	98	J5
Broomfield Rd., Tedd.	82	F6
Melbourne Rd.		
Broomfield St. E14	60	A5
Broomgrove Gdns., Edg.	38	A1
Broomgrove Rd. SW9	76	F2
Broomhill Ri., Bexh.	80	G5
Broomhill Rd. SW18	75	D5
Broomhill Rd., Ilf.	53	J2
Broomhill Rd., Wdf.Grn.	34	G6
Broomhill Wk., Wdf.Grn.	34	F7
Broomhouse La. SW6	75	D2
Broomhouse Rd. SW6	75	D2
Broomloan La., Sutt.	100	D2
Broomsleigh St. NW6	48	C5
Broomwood Rd. SW11	75	J6
Broseley Gro. SE26	86	H5
Broster Gdns. SE25	95	C3
Brough Clo. SW8	67	E7
Kenchester Clo.		
Brougham Rd. E8	59	D1
Brougham Rd. W3	56	C6
Broughinge Rd., Borwd.	22	A2
Broughton Ave. N3	39	B3
Broughton Ave., Rich.	82	E3
Broughton Dr. SW9	76	G4
Broughton Gdns. N6	40	C6
Broughton Rd. SW6	75	E2
Broughton Rd. W13	55	E7
Broughton Rd., Orp.	104	G2
Broughton Rd., Th.Hth.	94	G6
Broughton St. SW8	76	A2
Brouncker Rd. W3	65	C2
Browells La., Felt.	81	B2
Brown Clo., Wall.	101	E7
Brown Hart Gdns. W1	**11**	**C5**
Brown Hart Gdns. W1	58	A7
Brown St. W1	**10**	**J3**
Brown St. W1	57	J6
Brownfield St. E14	60	B6
Brownhill Rd. SE6	78	B7
Browning Ave. W7	55	C6
Browning Ave., Sutt.	100	H4
Browning Ave., Wor.Pk.	99	H1
Browning Clo. W9	**6**	**D6**
Browning Clo., Hmptn.	81	F4
Browning Clo., Well.	79	H1
Browning Est. SE17	**21**	**A3**
Browning Est. SE17	67	J5
Browning Ho. W12	56	J6
Wood La.		
Browning Ms. W1	**11**	**C2**
Browning Rd. E11	42	F7
Browning Rd. E12	52	C6
Browning St. SE17	**21**	**A3**
Browning St. SE17	67	J5
Browning Way, Hoúns.	72	D1
Brownlea Gdns., Ilf.	53	A2
Brownlow Ms. WC1	**8**	**D6**
Brownlow Ms. WC1	58	F4
Brownlow Rd. E7	51	H4
Woodford Rd.		
Brownlow Rd. E8	59	C1
Brownlow Rd. N3	31	E7
Brownlow Rd. N11	32	E6
Brownlow Rd. NW10	47	F7
Brownlow Rd. W13	64	D1
Brownlow Rd., Borwd.	22	A4
Brownlow Rd., Croy.	102	B4
Brownlow St. WC1	**12**	**D2**
Brown's Bldgs. EC3	**13**	**E4**
Browns La. NW5	49	B5
Browns Rd. E17	42	A3
Browns Rd., Surb.	91	J7
Brownspring Dr. SE9	88	E4
Brownswell Rd. N2	39	G2
Brownswood Rd. N4	49	H3
Broxash Rd. SW11	76	A6
Broxbourne Ave. E18	42	H4
Broxbourne Rd. E7	51	G3
Broxbourne Rd., Orp.	104	J1
Broxholm Rd. SE27	85	G3
Broxted Rd. SE6	86	J2
Broxwood Way NW8	57	H1
Bruce Castle Rd. N17	41	C1
Bruce Clo. W10	57	B5
Ladbroke Gro.		
Bruce Clo., Well.	80	B1
Bruce Gdns. N20	31	J3
Balfour Gro.		
Bruce Gro. N17	41	B1
Bruce Hall Ms. SW17	85	A4
Brudenell Rd.		
Bruce Rd. E3	60	B3
Bruce Rd. NW10	47	D7
Bruce Rd. SE25	95	A4
Bruce Rd., Barn.	23	B3
St. Albans Rd.		
Bruce Rd., Har.	37	B2
Bruce Rd., Mitch.	85	A7
Bruckner St. W10	57	C3
Brudenell Rd. SW17	84	J3
Bruffs Meadow, Nthlt.	45	E6
Bruges Pl. NW1	49	C7
Randolph St.		
Brumfield Rd., Epsom	99	C5
Brummell Clo., Bexh.	80	J3
Brundley Way, Brom.	87	G5
Brune St. E1	**13**	**F2**
Brune St. E1	59	C5
Brunel Clo. SE19	86	C6
Brunel Clo., Nthlt.	54	F3
Brunel Est. W2	57	D5
Brunel Pl., Sthl.	54	H6
Brunel Rd. SE16	68	F2
Brunel Rd. W3	56	E5
Brunel Rd., Wdf.Grn.	35	C5
Brunel St. E16	60	F6
Victoria Dock Rd.		
Brunel Wk. N15	41	B4
Brunel Wk., Twick.	72	G7
Stephenson Rd.		
Brunner Clo. NW11	39	E5
Brunner Rd. E17	41	H5
Brunner Rd. W5	55	G4
Bruno Pl., Wem.	47	C2
Brunswick Ave. N11	32	A3
Brunswick Cen. WC1	**8**	**A5**
Brunswick Clo., Bexh.	80	D4
Brunswick Clo., Pnr.	36	E6
Brunswick Clo., T.Ditt.	98	C1
Brunswick Clo., Twick.	82	A3
Brunswick Ct. SE1	**17**	**E3**
Brunswick Ct. SE1	68	B2
Brunswick Ct., Barn.	23	G5
Henry Rd.		
Brunswick Cres. N11	32	A3
Brunswick Gdns. W5	55	H4
Brunswick Gdns. W8	66	D1
Brunswick Gdns., Ilf.	35	F7
Brunswick Gro. N11	32	A3
Brunswick Ind. Pk. N11	32	B4
Brunswick Ms. SW16	85	D6
Potters La.		
Brunswick Ms. W1	**11**	**A3**
Brunswick Pk. SE5	77	A1
Brunswick Pk. Gdns. N11	32	A2
Brunswick Pk. Rd. N11	32	A2
Brunswick Pl. N1	**9**	**C4**
Brunswick Pl. N1	59	A3
Brunswick Pl. SE19	86	D7
Brunswick Quay SE16	68	G3
Brunswick Rd. E10	51	C1
Brunswick Rd. E14	60	C6
Brunswick Rd. N15	41	B4
Brunswick Rd. W5	55	G4
Brunswick Rd., Bexh.	80	D4
Brunswick Rd., Kings.T.	92	A1
Brunswick Rd., Sutt.	100	E4
Brunswick Sq. N17	33	C6
Brunswick Sq. WC1	**8**	**B5**
Brunswick Sq. WC1	58	E4
Brunswick St. E17	42	C5
Brunswick Vill. SE5	77	B1
Brunswick Way N11	32	B4
Brunton Pl. E14	59	H6
Brushfield St. E1	**13**	**E1**
Brushfield St. E1	59	B5
Brussels Rd. SW11	75	G4
Bruton Clo., Chis.	88	C7
Bullers Wd. Dr.		
Bruton La. W1	**11**	**E6**
Bruton La. W1	58	B7
Bruton Pl. W1	**11**	**E6**
Bruton Pl. W1	58	B7
Bruton Rd., Mord.	93	F4
Bruton St. W1	**11**	**E6**
Bruton St. W1	58	B7
Bruton Way W13	55	D5
Bryan Ave. NW10	47	H7
Bryan Clo., Sun.	81	A7
Bryan Rd. SE16	68	J2
Bryanston Ave., Twick.	81	H1
Bryanston Clo., Sthl.	63	F4
Bryanston Ms. E. W1	**10**	**J2**
Bryanston Ms. W. W1	**10**	**J2**
Bryanston Pl. W1	57	J5
Bryanston Pl. W1	**10**	**J2**
Bryanston Sq. W1	**10**	**J2**
Bryanston Sq. W1	57	J5
Bryanston St. W1	**10**	**J4**
Bryanston St. W1	57	J6
Bryanstone Rd. N8	40	D5
Bryant Clo., Barn.	23	C5
Bryant Ct. E2	**9**	**F1**
Bryant Rd., Nthlt.	54	C3
Bryant St. E15	51	D7
Bryantwood Rd. N7	49	G5
Bryce Rd., Dag.	52	C4
Brycedale Cres. N14	32	C4
Bryden Clo. SE26	86	H5
Brydges Pl. WC2	**12**	**A6**
Brydges Rd. E15	51	D5
Brydon Wk. N1	58	E1
Outram Pl.		
Bryett Rd. N7	49	E3
Brymay Clo. E3	60	A3
Bryn-y-Mawr Rd., Enf.	25	C4
Brynmaer Rd. SW11	75	J1
Bryony Rd. W12	56	G7
Buchan Rd. SE15	77	F3
Buchanan Ct., Borwd.	22	C2
Banks Rd.		
Buchanan Gdns. NW10	56	H2
Bucharest Rd. SW18	75	F7
Buck Hill Wk. W2	**10**	**F6**
Buck La. NW9	38	D4
Buck St. NW1	49	B7
Buck Wk. E17	42	D4
Foresters Dr.		
Buckden Clo. SE12	78	H6
Upwood Rd.		
Buckfast Rd., Mord.	93	E4
Buckfast St. E2	**9**	**J4**
Buckfast St. E2	59	D3
Buckhold Rd. SW18	75	D6
Buckhurst Ave., Cars.	100	H1
Buckhurst St. E1	59	E4
Buckhurst Way, Buck.H.	35	A4
Buckingham Arc. WC2	**12**	**B6**
Buckingham Ave. N20	23	F7
Buckingham Ave. Felt.	72	B6
Buckingham Ave., Grnf.	55	D1
Buckingham Ave., Th.Hth.	94	G1
Buckingham Ave., Well.	79	H4
Buckingham Ave., W.Mol.	90	H3
Buckingham Clo. W5	55	F5
Buckingham Clo., Enf.	25	B2
Buckingham Clo., Hmptn.	81	E5
Buckingham Clo., Orp.	97	H7
Buckingham Ct. NW4	38	G3
Buckingham Dr., Chis.	88	E5
Buckingham Gdns., Edg.	29	H7

Buckingham Gdns., 94 G2
Th.Hth.
Buckingham Gdns., 90 H2
W.Mol.
Buckingham Ave.
Buckingham Gate 15 F4
SW1
Buckingham Gate 67 B3
SW1
Buckingham La. SE23 77 H7
Buckingham Ms. 56 F2
NW10
Buckingham Rd.
Buckingham Ms. 15 F5
SW1
Buckingham Palace 19 D2
Rd. SW1
Buckingham Palace 67 B4
Rd. SW1
Buckingham Pl. SW1 15 F5
Buckingham Rd. E10 51 B3
Buckingham Rd. E11 42 J5
Buckingham Rd. E15 51 F5
Buckingham Rd. E18 42 F1
Buckingham Rd. N1 50 B6
Buckingham Rd. N22 40 E1
Buckingham Rd. 56 F2
NW10
Buckingham Rd., 22 D4
Borwd.
Buckingham Rd., 29 J7
Edg.
Buckingham Rd., 81 F4
Hmptn.
Buckingham Rd., Har. 37 A5
Buckingham Rd., Ilf. 52 G2
Buckingham Rd., 91 J4
Kings.T.
Buckingham Rd., 94 E5
Mitch.
Buckingham Rd., 82 G2
Rich.
Buckingham St. WC2 12 B6
Buckland Cres. NW3 48 G7
Buckland Ri., Pnr. 36 C1
Buckland Rd. E10 51 J4
Buckland Rd., Chess. 98 J5
Buckland Rd., Orp. 104 H4
Buckland St. N1 9 C2
Buckland St. N1 59 A2
Buckland Wk., Mord. 93 F4
Buckland Way, 99 J1
Wor.Pk.
Bucklands Ri., Tedd. 82 F6
Buckle St. E1 13 G3
Buckleigh Ave. SW20 93 C3
Buckleigh Rd. SW16 85 D6
Buckleigh Way SE19 95 C1
Buckler Gdns. SE8 88 C3
Southold Ri.
Bucklers All. SW6 66 D6
Haldane Rd.
Bucklers Way, Cars. 100 J3
Bucklersbury EC4 13 B4
Bucklersbury EC4 59 A6
Buckles Ct., Belv. 71 D3
Fendyke Rd.
Buckley Rd. NW6 48 C7
Buckley St. SE1 16 E2
Buckmaster Rd. 75 H4
SW11
Bucknall St. WC2 11 J3
Bucknall St. WC2 58 D6
Bucknell Clo. SW2 76 F4
Buckner Rd. SW2 76 F4
Buckrell Rd. E4 34 D2
Buckstone Clo. SE23 77 F6
Buckstone Rd. N18 33 D5
Buckters Rents SE16 68 H1
Buckthorne Rd. SE4 77 H6
Budd Clo. N12 31 E4
Buddings Circ., Wem. 47 C3
Budd's All., Twick. 73 F5
Arlington Rd.
Budge Row EC4 13 B5
Budge's Wk. W2 14 C1
Budge's Wk. W2 57 G7
Budich Ct., Ilf. 53 A2
Budleigh Cres., Well. 80 C1
Budoch Dr., Ilf. 53 A2
Buer Rd. SW6 75 B2
Bugsby's Way SE7 69 G4
Bugsby's Way SE10 69 F4
Bulganak Rd., Th.Hth. 94 J4
Bulinga St. SW1 20 A2
Bulinga St. SW1 67 D4
Bull All., Well. 80 B3
Welling High St.
Bull Inn Ct. WC2 12 B6
Bull La. N18 33 B5
Bull La., Chis. 88 G7
Bull La., Dag. 53 H3
Bull Rd. E15 60 F2

Bull Wf. La. EC4 13 A5
Bull Yd. SE15 77 D1
Peckham High St.
Bullards Pl. E2 59 G3
Bullbanks Rd., Belv. 71 J4
Bullen St. SW11 75 H2
Buller Clo. SE15 68 D7
Buller Rd. N17 41 D2
Buller Rd. N22 40 G2
Buller Rd. NW10 67 A2
Chamberlayne Rd.
Buller Rd., Bark. 52 H7
Buller Rd., Th.Hth. 95 A2
Bullers Clo., Sid. 89 E5
Bullers Wd. Dr., Chis. 88 C7
Bullescroft Rd., Edg. 30 A3
Bullhead Rd., Borwd. 22 C2
Bullied Way SW1 19 E2
Bullivant St. E14 60 C6
Bull's All. SW14 74 D2
Bulls Bri. Ind. Est., 63 B3
Sthl.
Bulls Bri. Rd., Sthl. 63 B3
Bulls Gdns. SW3 18 H1
Bull's Head Pas. EC3 13 D4
Bullsbrook Rd., 63 C1
Hayes
Bulmer Gdns., Har. 37 G7
Bulmer Ms. W11 57 D7
Kensington Pk. Rd.
Bulmer Pl. W11 66 D1
Bulow Ct. SW6 75 E2
Bulstrode Ave., 72 F2
Houns.
Bulstrode Gdns., 72 F3
Houns.
Bulstrode Pl. W1 11 C2
Bulstrode Rd., Houns. 72 G3
Bulstrode St. W1 11 C3
Bulstrode St. W1 58 A6
Bulwer Ct. Rd. E11 51 D1
Bulwer Gdns., Barn. 23 F4
Bulwer Rd.
Bulwer Rd. E11 42 D7
Bulwer Rd. N18 33 B4
Bulwer Rd., Barn. 23 E4
Bulwer St. W12 65 J1
Bunces La., Wdf.Grn. 34 F7
Bungalow Rd. SE25 95 B4
Bungalows, The 85 B7
SW16
Bungalows, The, 101 B5
Wall.
Bunhill Row EC1 9 B5
Bunhill Row EC1 59 A4
Bunhouse Pl. SW1 19 B3
Bunhouse Pl. SW1 67 A5
Bunkers Hill NW11 39 F7
Bunkers Hill, Belv. 71 G4
Bunkers Hill, Sid. 88 J7
Bunning Way N7 49 E7
Bunns La. NW7 30 E6
Bunsen St. E3 59 H2
Kenilworth Rd.
Bunting Clo., Mitch. 93 J5
Buntingbridge Rd., 43 G5
Ilf.
Bunton St. SE18 70 D3
Creton St.
Bunyan Rd. E17 41 H3
Buonaparte Ms. SW1 19 H3
Burbage Clo. SE1 17 B6
Burbage Clo. SE1 68 A3
Burbage Rd. SE21 77 A7
Burbage Rd. SE24 76 J6
Burberry Clo., N.Mal. 92 E2
Burbridge Way N17 41 C2
Burcham St. E14 60 B6
Burcharbro Rd. SE2 71 D6
Burchell Rd. E10 51 B1
Burchell Rd. SE15 77 E1
Burcote Rd. SW18 75 G7
Burden Clo., Brent. 64 F5
Burden Way E11 51 H2
Brading Cres.
Burdenshott Ave., 74 B4
Rich.
Burder Clo. N1 50 B6
Burder Rd. N1 50 B6
Balls Pond Rd.
Burdett Ave. SW20 92 G1
Burdett Clo., Sid. 89 E5
Burdett Ms. W2 10 A3
Burdett Ms. W2 58 B3
Burdett Rd. E3 59 H4
Burdett Rd. E14 59 J5
Burdett Rd., Croy. 95 A6
Burdett Rd., Rich. 73 J2
Burdett St. SE1 16 E5
Burdetts Rd., Dag. 62 F1
Burdock Clo., Croy. 102 G1
Burdock Rd. N17 41 D3
Burdon La., Sutt. 100 B7

Burfield Clo. SW17 84 G4
Burford Clo., Dag. 53 C3
Burford Clo., Ilf. 43 F4
Burford Gdns. N13 32 F3
Burford Rd. E6 61 B3
Burford Rd. E15 51 D7
Burford Rd. SE6 86 J2
Burford Rd., Brent. 81 H5
Burford Rd., Brom. 97 B4
Burford Rd., Sutt. 100 D2
Burford Rd., Wor.Pk. 92 F7
Burford Wk. SW6 66 E7
Cambria St.
Burford Way, Croy. 103 C6
Burge St. SE1 17 C6
Burges Ct. E6 52 D7
Burges Rd. E6 52 B7
Burgess Ave. NW9 38 D6
Burgess Clo., Felt. 81 E4
Burgess Hill NW2 48 D4
Burgess Rd. E15 51 E4
Burgess Rd., Sutt. 100 E4
Burgess St. E14 60 A5
Burgh St. N1 8 H11
Burgh St. N1 58 H2
Burghill Rd. SE26 86 H4
Burghley Ave., 22 C5
Borwd.
Burghley Ave., N.Mal. 92 D1
Burghley Pl., Mitch. 93 J5
Burghley Rd. E11 51 E1
Burghley Rd. N8 40 G3
Burghley Rd. NW5 49 B4
Burghley Rd. SW19 84 A4
Burghley Twr. W3 56 F7
Burgon St. EC4 12 H4
Burgos Gro. SE10 78 B1
Burgoyne Rd. N4 40 H6
Burgoyne Rd. SE25 95 C4
Burgoyne Rd. SW9 76 F3
Burham Clo. SE20 86 F7
Maple Rd.
Burhill Gro., Pnr. 36 E2
Burke Clo. SW15 74 E4
Burke St. E16 60 F6
Burland Rd. SW11 75 J5
Burleigh Ave., Sid. 79 J5
Burleigh Ave., Wall. 101 A3
Burleigh Gdns. N14 32 C1
Burleigh Ho. W10 57 A5
St. Charles Sq.
Burleigh Pl. SW15 75 A6
Burleigh Pl., Mitch 93 J5
Burleigh Rd., Enf. 25 B4
Burleigh Rd., Sutt. 100 B1
Burleigh St. WC2 12 C3
Burleigh Wk. SE6 87 C1
Muirkirk Rd.
Burley Clo. E4 34 A5
Burley Clo. SW16 94 D2
Burley Rd. E16 60 J5
Burlington Arc. W1 11 F6
Burlington Ave., Rich. 74 A1
Burlington Ave., 44 H6
Rom.
Burlington Clo. E6 61 B6
Northumberland Rd.
Burlington Clo. W9 57 C4
Burlington Clo., 104 E2
Orp.
Burlington Gdns. W1 11 F6
Burlington Gdns. W1 58 C7
Burlington Gdns. W3 65 C5
Burlington Gdns. W4 65 C5
Burlington Gdns., 44 E7
Rom.
Burlington La. W4 65 C7
Burlington Ms. W3 65 C1
Burlington Pl. SW6 75 B2
Burlington Rd.
Burlington Pl., 24 H3
Wdf.Grn.
Burlington Ri., Barn. 31 H1
Burlington Rd. N10 40 A2
Tetherdown
Burlington Rd. N17 41 D1
Burlington Rd. SW6 75 B2
Burlington Rd. W4 65 C5
Burlington Rd., Enf. 25 A1
Burlington Rd., Islw. 73 A1
Burlington Rd., 92 F4
N.Mal.
Burlington Rd., 94 J2
Th.Hth.
Burma Ms. N16 50 A4
Burma Rd. N16 50 A4
Burmester Rd. SW17 84 F3
Burn Side N9 33 F3
Burnaby Cres. W4 65 C6
Burnaby Gdns. W4 65 B6
Burnaby St. SW10 66 F7
Burnbrae Clo. N12 31 E6
Burnbury Rd. SW12 85 C1

Burncroft Ave., Enf. 25 F2
Burne Jones Ho. W14 66 C4
Burne St. NW1 10 G1
Burne St. NW1 57 H5
Burnell Ave., Rich. 82 F5
Burnell Ave., Well. 80 A2
Burnell Gdns., Stan. 37 G1
Burnell Rd., Sutt. 100 E4
Burnell Wk. SE1 21 G5
Burnels Ave. E6 61 D3
Burnett Clo. N7 49 F6
Roman Way
Burnett Clo. E9 50 F5
Burney Ave., Surb. 91 J5
Burney Dr., Loug. 27 E2
Burney St. SE10 69 C7
Burnfoot Ave. SW6 75 B1
Burnham NW3 48 H7
Burnham Clo. SE1 21 G2
Burnham Ct. NW4 38 J4
Burnham Cres. E11 42 J4
Burnham Dr., 100 A2
Wor.Pk.
Burnham Gdns., 95 C7
Croy.
Burnham Gdns., 72 B1
Houns.
Burnham Rd. E4 33 J5
Burnham Rd., Dag. 53 B7
Burnham Rd., Mord. 93 E5
Burnham Rd., Sid. 89 E2
Burnham St. E2 59 F3
Burnham St., 92 A1
Kings.T.
Burnham Way W13 64 E4
Burnhill Rd., Beck. 96 A2
Burnley Clo., Wat. 28 C5
Burnley Rd. NW10 47 F5
Burnley Rd. SW9 76 F2
Burns Ave., Felt. 72 A6
Burns Ave., Sid. 80 A6
Burns Ave., Sthl. 54 G7
Burns Clo. SW19 84 G6
North Rd.
Burns Clo., Well. 79 J1
Burns Rd. NW10 56 F1
Burns Rd. SW11 75 J2
Burns Rd. W13 64 E2
Burns Rd., Wem. 55 H2
Burns Way, Houns. 72 D2
Burnsall St. SW3 18 H3
Burnsall St. SW3 66 H5
Burnside Clo. SE16 68 G1
Burnside Clo., Barn. 23 D3
Burnside Clo., 73 D6
Twick.
Burnside Cres., Wem. 55 G1
Burnside Rd., Dag. 53 C2
Burnt Ash Hill SE12 78 F6
Burnt Ash La., 87 G7
Brom.
Burnt Ash Rd. SE12 78 F5
Burnt Oak Bdy., Edg. 30 B7
Burnt Oak Flds., Edg. 38 C1
Burnt Oak La., Sid. 89 A2
Burnthwaite Rd. SW6 66 C7
Burntwood Clo. 84 G1
SW18
Burntwood Gra. Rd. 84 G1
SW18
Burntwood La. SW17 84 F3
Buross St. E1 59 E6
Commercial Rd.
Burr Clo. E1 17 H1
Burr Clo., Bexh. 80 F3
Burr Rd. SW18 84 D1
Burrage Gro. SE18 70 F4
Burrage Pl. SE18 70 E5
Burrage Rd. SE18 70 F4
Burrard Rd. E16 60 H6
Burrard Rd. NW6 48 D5
Burrell Clo., Croy. 95 H6
Burrell Clo., Edg. 30 B2
Burrell Row, Beck. 96 A2
High St.
Burrell St. SE1 16 G1
Burrell St. SE1 67 H1
Burrell Twr. E10 42 A7
Burrells Wf. Sq. E14 69 B5
Burritt Rd., Kings.T. 92 A2
Burroughs, The NW4 38 H4
Burroughs Gdns. 38 H4
NW4
Burrow Clo., Chig. 35 J5
Burrow Rd.
Burrow Grn., Chig. 35 J5
Burrow Rd., Chig. 35 J5
Burrow Rd. SE22 76 J7
Rosendale Rd.
Burrows Ms. SE1 16 G3
Burrows Rd. NW10 56 J3
Bursdon Clo., Sid. 88 J2
Bursland Rd., Enf. 25 G4

Burslem St. E1 13 J4
Burslem St. E1 59 D6
Burstock Rd. SW15 75 B4
Burston Rd. SW15 75 A5
Burstow Rd. SW20 93 B1
Burt Rd. E16 69 J1
Burtenshaw Rd., 91 D7
  T.Ditt.
Burtley Clo. N4 49 J1
Burton Clo. NW7 31 A4
Burton Clo., Chess. 98 G7
Burton Gdns., Houns. 72 F1
Burton Gro. SE17 21 B4
Burton La. SW9 76 G2
Burton Ms. SW1 19 C2
Burton Pl. WC1 7 J4
Burton Rd. E18 42 H3
Burton Rd. NW6 48 C7
Burton Rd. SW9 76 H2
Burton Rd., Kings.T. 82 H7
Burton Rd., Loug. 27 F4
Burton St. WC1 7 J4
Burton St. WC1 58 D3
Burtonhole La. NW7 30 J5
Burtons Rd., Hmptn. 81 H4
Burtwell La. SE27 86 A4
Burwash Ho. SE1 17 C4
Burwash Rd. SE18 70 G5
Burwell Ave., Grnf. 46 B6
Burwell Clo. E1 59 E6
  Bigland St.
Burwell Rd. E10 50 H1
Burwell Wk. E3 60 A4
Burwood Ave., Brom. 103 H2
Burwood Ave., Pnr. 36 B5
Burwood Clo., Surb. 99 A1
Burwood Pl. W2 10 H3
Burwood Pl. W2 57 H6
Bury Clo. SE16 68 G1
  Rotherhithe St.
Bury Ct. EC3 13 E3
Bury Gro., Mord. 93 E5
Bury Pl. WC1 12 A2
Bury Pl. WC1 58 E5
Bury Rd. E4 26 E4
Bury Rd. N22 40 G3
Bury Rd., Dag. 53 H5
Bury St. EC3 13 E4
Bury St. EC3 59 B6
Bury St. N9 25 A7
Bury St. SW1 15 G1
Bury St. SW1 67 C1
Bury St. W. N9 25 A7
Bury Wk. SW3 18 G2
Bury Wk. SW3 66 H4
Busbridge Ho. E14 60 A5
  Brabazon St.
Busby Ms. NW5 49 D6
Busby Pl. NW5 49 D6
Busby St. E2 9 G5
Bush Clo., Ilf. 43 G5
Bush Cotts. SW18 75 D5
  Putney Bri. Rd.
Bush Ct. W12 66 A2
Bush Gro. NW9 38 C7
Bush Gro., Stan. 29 G7
Bush Hill N21 24 J7
Bush Hill Rd. N21 25 A6
Bush Hill Rd., Har. 37 J6
Bush Ind. Est. NW10 56 D4
Bush La. EC4 13 B5
Bush Rd. E8 59 E1
Bush Rd. E11 42 F7
Bush Rd. SE8 68 G4
Bush Rd., Buck.H. 35 A4
Bush Rd., Rich. 64 J6
Bushbaby Clo. SE1 17 D6
Bushberry Rd. E9 50 H6
Bushell Clo. SW2 85 F2
Bushell Grn. 29 A2
  (Bushey), Wat.
Bushell St. E1 17 J2
Bushell Way, Chis. 88 D5
Bushey Ave. E18 42 F3
Bushey Ave., Orp. 97 G7
Bushey Ct. SW20 92 H3
Bushey Hill Rd. SE5 77 B1
Bushey La., Sutt. 100 D3
Bushey Lees, Sid. 79 J6
  Fen Gro.
Bushey Rd. E13 60 J2
Bushey Rd. N15 41 B6
Bushey Rd. SW20 92 H3
Bushey Rd., Croy. 103 A2
Bushey Rd., Sutt. 100 D3
Bushey Way, Beck. 96 D6
Bushfield Clo., Edg. 30 B2
Bushfield Cres., 30 B2
  Edg.
Bushfields, Loug. 27 D5
Bushgrove Rd., Dag. 53 D4
Bushmoor Cres. SE18 70 F7
Bushnell Rd. SW17 85 B2

Bushway, Dag. 53 D4
Bushwood E11 51 F1
Bushwood Dr. SE1 21 G2
Bushwood Rd. SE1 68 C4
Bushwood Rd., Rich. 65 A6
Bushy Pk. Gdns., 82 A5
  Tedd.
Bushy Pk. Rd., Tedd. 82 E7
Bushy Rd., Tedd. 82 C6
Butcher Row E1 59 G7
Butcher Row E14 59 G7
Butchers Rd. E16 60 G6
Bute Ave., Rich. 82 H2
Bute Ct., Wall. 101 C5
  Bute Rd.
Bute Gdns. W6 66 A4
Bute Gdns., Wall. 101 C5
Bute Gdns. W., Wall. 101 C5
Bute Rd., Croy. 101 G1
Bute Rd., Ilf. 43 E5
Bute Rd., Wall. 101 C4
Bute St. SW7 18 E1
Bute St. SW7 66 G4
Bute Wk. N1 50 A6
  Marquess Rd.
Butler Ave., Har. 37 A7
Butler Pl. SW1 15 H5
Butler Rd. NW10 47 F7
  Curzon Cres.
Butler Rd., Dag. 53 B4
Butler Rd., Har. 36 J7
Butler St. E2 59 F3
  Digby St.
Butter Hill, Cars. 101 A3
Butter Hill, Wall. 101 A3
Butterfield Clo. SE16 68 E2
  Wilson Gro.
Butterfield Clo., 73 C6
  Twick.
  Rugby Rd.
Butterfield Sq. E6 61 C6
  Guildford Rd.
Butterfields E17 42 C5
Butterfly La. SE9 79 E6
Butteridges Clo., Dag. 62 F1
Buttermere Clo., 93 A6
  Mord.
Buttermere Dr. 75 B5
  SW15
Buttermere Wk. E8 50 C6
Butterwick W6 65 J4
Butterworth Gdns., 34 G5
  Wdf.Grn.
  Harts Gro.
Buttesland St. N1 9 C3
Buttesland St. N1 59 A3
Buttfield Clo., Dag. 53 H6
Buttmarsh Clo. SE18 70 E5
Butts, The, Brent. 64 F6
Butts, The, Sun. 90 C3
  Elizabeth Gdns.
Butts Cotts., Felt. 81 F3
Butts Cres., Felt. 81 G3
Butts Piece, Nthlt. 54 B2
  Longhook Gdns.
Butts Rd., Brom. 87 E3
Buttsbury Rd., Ilf. 67 F5
Buxted Clo. E8 50 C7
Buxted Rd. N12 31 H5
Buxted Rd., Wdf.Grn. 35 A6
Buxton Ct. N1 9 A3
Buxton Cres., Sutt. 100 B4
Buxton Dr. E11 42 E4
Buxton Dr., N.Mal. 92 D2
Buxton Gdns. W3 56 B7
Buxton Path, Wat. 28 C3
Buxton Rd. E4 26 D7
Buxton Rd. E6 61 B3
Buxton Rd. E15 51 E5
Buxton Rd. E17 41 H4
Buxton Rd. N19 49 D1
Buxton Rd. NW2 47 H6
Buxton Rd. SW14 74 E3
Buxton Rd., Ilf. 43 H6
Buxton Rd., Th.Hth. 44 H5
Buxton St. E1 9 G6
Buxton St. E1 59 C4
Buzzard Creek Ind. 61 J5
  Est., Bark.
By the Wd., Wat. 28 D2
Byam St. SW6 75 F2
Byards Cft. SW16 94 D1
Byatt Wk., Hmptn. 81 E6
  Victors Dr.
Bycroft Rd., Sthl. 54 G4
Bycroft St. SE20 86 G7
  Parish La.
Bycullah Ave., Enf. 24 H3
Bycullah Rd., Enf. 24 H2
Bye, The W3 56 E6
Bye Way, The, Har. 37 C1
Bye Ways, Twick. 81 H3
Byegrove Rd. SW19 84 G6

Byeway, The SW14 74 C3
Byeway, The, Epsom 99 F4
Byeways, The, Surb. 92 A5
Byfeld Gdns. SW13 74 G1
Byfield Rd., Islw. 73 D3
Byford Clo. E15 51 E7
Bygrove, Croy. 103 B6
Bygrove St. E14 60 B6
Byland Clo. N21 24 F7
Bylands Clo. SE2 71 B3
  Finchale Rd.
Bylands Clo. SE16 68 G1
  Rotherhithe St.
Byne Rd. SE26 86 F6
Byne Rd., Cars. 100 H2
Bynes Rd., S.Croy. 102 A7
Byng Pl. WC1 7 H6
Byng Pl. WC1 58 D4
Byng Rd., Barn. 23 A3
Byng St. E14 69 A2
Bynon Ave., Bexh. 80 F3
Byre, The N14 24 B6
  Farm La.
Byre Rd. N14 24 A6
  Farm La.
Byrne Rd. SW12 85 B1
Byron Ave. E12 52 B6
Byron Ave. E18 42 F3
Byron Ave. NW9 38 B4
Byron Ave., Borwd. 22 A5
Byron Ave., Houns. 72 B1
Byron Ave., N.Mal. 92 G5
Byron Ave., Sutt. 100 G4
Byron Ave. E., Sutt. 100 G4
Byron Clo. E8 59 D1
Byron Clo. SE28 71 C1
Byron Clo., Hmptn. 81 F4
Byron Ct. W9 57 D4
  Lanhill Rd.
Byron Ct., Enf. 24 H2
  Bycullah Rd.
Byron Dr. N2 39 G6
Byron Gdns., Sutt. 100 G4
Byron Hill Rd., Har. 46 A1
Byron Ho., Beck. 87 B6
Byron Ms. W9 57 D4
  Shirland Rd.
Byron Rd. E10 51 B1
Byron Rd. E17 42 A3
Byron Rd. NW2 47 H2
Byron Rd. NW7 30 G5
Byron Rd. W5 64 J1
Byron Rd., Har. 37 C2
Byron Rd. 37 B6
  (Wealdstone), Har.
Byron Rd., Wem. 46 F2
Byron St. E14 60 C6
  St. Leonards Rd.
Byron Way, Nthlt. 54 E3
Bysouth Clo., Ilf. 43 E1
Bythorn St. SW9 76 F4
Byton Rd. SW17 84 A6
Byward Ave., Felt. 72 C6
Byward St. EC3 13 E6
Byward St. EC3 59 B7
Bywater Pl. SE16 68 H1
Bywater St. SW3 18 J3
Bywater St. SW3 66 H5
Bywell Pl. W1 11 F2
Bywood Ave., Croy. 95 F6
Byworth Wk. N19 49 D1
  Courtauld Rd.

C

C.I. Twr., N.Mal. 92 E3
Cabbell St. NW1 10 G2
Cabbell St. NW1 57 H5
Cabinet Way E4 33 J6
Cable Pl. SE10 78 C1
  Diamond Ter.
Cable St. E1 13 J5
Cable St. E1 59 D7
Cabot Sq. E14 69 A1
Cabot Way E6 61 A1
  Parr Rd.
Cabul Rd. SW11 75 H2
Cactus Wk. W12 56 F7
  Du Cane Rd.
Cadbury Clo., Islw. 73 D1
Cadbury Way SE16 17 G6
Caddington Clo., 23 H5
  Barn.
Caddington Rd. NW2 48 B3
Caddis Clo., Stan. 29 C7
  Daventer Dr.
Cade Rd. SE10 78 D1
Cadell Clo. E2 9 G2
Cader Rd. SW18 75 F6
Cadet Dr. SE1 21 G3
Cadet Pl. SE10 69 E5
Cadiz Rd., Dag. 53 J7
  York Pl.

Cadiz St. SE17 21 A4
Cadiz St. SE17 67 J5
Cadley Ter. SE23 86 F2
Cadmer Clo., N.Mal. 92 E4
Cadogan Clo., Beck. 96 D1
  Albemarle Rd.
Cadogan Clo., Har. 45 H4
Cadogan Clo., Tedd. 82 B5
Cadogan Ct., Sutt. 100 E6
Cadogan Gdns. E18 42 H3
Cadogan Gdns. N3 39 E1
Cadogan Gdns. N21 24 G5
Cadogan Gdns. SW3 19 A1
Cadogan Gdns. SW3 66 J4
Cadogan Gate SW1 19 A1
Cadogan Gate SW1 66 J4
Cadogan La. SW1 15 B6
Cadogan La. SW1 67 A3
Cadogan Pl. SW1 15 A5
Cadogan Pl. SW1 66 J3
Cadogan Pl., Surb. 91 G5
Cadogan Sq. SW1 15 A6
Cadogan Sq. SW1 66 J3
Cadogan St. SW3 18 J2
Cadogan St. SW3 66 J4
Cadogan Ter. E9 50 J6
Cadoxton Ave. N15 41 C6
Cadwallon Rd. SE9 88 E2
Caedmon Rd. N7 49 F4
Caerleon Clo., Sid. 89 C5
Caerleon Ter. SE2 71 B4
  Blithdale Rd.
Caernarvon Clo., 94 E3
  Mitch.
Caernarvon Dr., Ilf. 43 D1
Caesars Wk., Mitch. 93 J5
Cage Rd. E16 60 E5
  Malmesbury Rd.
Cahill St. EC1 9 A6
Cahir St. E14 69 B4
Caird St. W10 57 B3
Cairn Ave. W5 64 G1
Cairn Way, Stan. 29 C6
Cairndale Clo., Brom. 87 F7
Cairnfield Ave. NW2 47 E3
Cairngorm Clo., 82 D5
  Tedd.
  Vicarage Rd.
Cairns Ave., Wdf.Grn. 35 B6
Cairns Rd. SW11 75 H5
Cairo New Rd., Croy. 101 H2
Cairo Rd. E17 42 A4
Caishowe Rd., 22 B1
  Borwd.
Caistor Ms. SW12 76 B7
  Caistor Rd.
Caistor Pk. Rd. E15 60 F1
Caistor Rd. SW12 76 B7
Caithness Gdns., Sid. 79 J6
Caithness Rd. W14 66 A3
Caithness Rd., Mitch. 85 B7
Calabria Rd. N5 49 H6
Calais Gate SE5 76 H1
  Calais St.
Calais St. SE5 76 H1
Calbourne Rd. SW12 75 J7
Calcott Wk. SE9 88 B4
Caldbeck Ave., 99 G2
  Wor.Pk.
Caldecot Rd. SE5 76 J2
Caldecott Way E5 50 G3
Calder Ave., Grnf. 55 C2
Calder Clo., Enf. 25 B3
Calder Gdns., Edg. 38 A3
Calder Rd., Mord. 93 F5
Calderon Pl. W10 56 J5
  St. Quintin Gdns.
Calderon Rd. E11 51 C4
Caldervale Rd. SW4 75 D5
Calderwood St. SE18 70 D4
Caldicot Grn. NW9 38 E6
  Snowdon Dr.
Caldwell Rd., Wat. 28 D4
Caldwell St. SW9 67 F7
Caldy Rd., Belv. 71 H3
Caldy Wk. N1 49 J7
  Marquess Est.
Cale St. SW3 18 G3
Cale St. SW3 66 H5
Caleb St. SE1 16 J3
Caledon Rd. E6 61 B1
Caledon Rd., Wall. 101 A4
Caledonia St. N1 8 B2
Caledonia St. N1 58 E2
Caledonian Clo., Ilf. 53 E1
Caledonian Rd. N1 8 B2
Caledonian Rd. N1 58 E2
Caledonian Rd. N7 49 F4
Caledonian Wf. Rd. 69 D4
  E14
Caletock Way SE10 69 F5
Calico Row SW11 75 F3
  York Pl.

Calidore Clo. SW2 76 F6
Endymion Rd.
California La. 29 A1
(Bushey), Wat.
California Rd., N.Mal. 92 C3
Callaby Ter. N1 50 A6
Wakeham St.
Callaghan Clo. SE13 78 E4
Clinton Rd.
Callander Rd. SE6 87 B2
Callard Ave. N13 32 H5
Callcott Rd. NW6 48 C7
Callcott St. W8 66 D1
Hillgate Pl.
Callendar Rd. SW7 14 E5
Callendar Rd. SW7 66 G3
Callingham Clo. E14 59 J5
Wallwood St.
Callis Rd. E17 41 J6
Callow St. SW3 18 D5
Callow St. SW3 66 G6
Calmington Rd. SE5 21 E4
Calmington Rd. SE5 68 B5
Calmont Rd., Brom. 87 D6
Calne Ave., Ilf. 43 E1
Calonne Rd. SW19 84 A4
Calshot St. N1 8 C1
Calshot St. N1 58 F2
Calshot Way, Enf. 24 H3
Calthorpe Gdns., Edg. 29 H5
Jesmond Way
Calthorpe Gdns., 100 F3
Sutt.
Calthorpe St. WC1 8 D5
Calthorpe St. WC1 58 F4
Calton Ave. SE21 77 B6
Calton Rd., Barn. 23 F6
Calverley Clo., Beck. 87 B6
Calverley Cres., Dag. 53 G2
Calverley Gdns., Har. 37 G7
Calverley Gro. N19 49 D1
Calverley Rd., Epsom 99 G6
Calvert Ave. E2 9 E4
Calvert Ave. E2 59 B3
Calvert Clo., Belv. 71 G4
Calvert Clo., Sid. 89 E6
Calvert Rd. SE10 69 F5
Calvert Rd., Barn. 23 A2
Calvert St. NW1 58 A1
Chalcot Rd.
Calverton SE5 21 D5
Calverton Rd. E6 61 D1
Calvert's Bldgs. SE1 17 B2
Calvin St. E1 9 F6
Calvin St. E1 59 C4
Calydon Rd. SE7 69 H5
Calypso Way SE16 68 J4
Cam Rd. E15 60 D1
Camac Rd., Twick. 82 A1
Cambalt Rd. SW15 75 A5
Camberley Ave. 92 H2
SW20
Camberley Ave., Enf. 25 B4
Camberley Clo., Sutt. 100 A3
Cambert Way SE3 78 H4
Camberwell Ch. St. 77 A1
SE5
Camberwell Glebe 77 B1
SE5
Camberwell Grn. SE5 77 A1
Camberwell Gro. SE5 77 A1
Camberwell New Rd. 20 F7
SE5
Camberwell New Rd. 67 G6
SE5
Camberwell Pas. SE5 76 J1
Camberwell Rd.
Camberwell Rd. SE5 21 A6
Camberwell Rd. SE5 67 J6
Camberwell Sta. Rd. 76 J1
SE5
Cambeys Rd., Dag. 53 H5
Camborne Ave. W13 64 E2
Camborne Ms. W11 57 B6
St. Marks Rd.
Camborne Rd. SW18 75 D7
Camborne Rd., Croy. 95 D7
Camborne Rd., Mord. 93 A5
Camborne Rd., Sid. 89 C3
Camborne Rd., Sutt. 100 D7
Camborne Rd., Well. 79 J2
Camborne Way, 72 G1
Houns.
Cambourne Ave. N9 25 G7
Cambray Rd. SW12 85 C1
Cambray Rd., Orp. 97 J7
Cambria Clo., Houns. 72 G4
Cambria Clo., Sid. 88 G1
Cambria Ct., Felt. 72 B7
Hounslow Rd.
Cambria Rd. SE5 76 J3
Cambria St. SW6 66 E7
Cambrian Ave., Ilf. 43 H5

Cambrian Clo. SE27 85 H3
Cambrian Rd. E10 42 A7
Cambrian Rd., Rich. 73 J6
Cambridge Ave. NW6 57 D2
Cambridge Ave., 46 C5
Grnf.
Cambridge Ave., 92 E2
N.Mal.
Cambridge Ave., 79 J4
Well.
Cambridge Barracks 70 C4
Rd. SE18
Cambridge Circ. WC2 11 J4
Cambridge Circ. WC2 58 D6
Cambridge Clo. 92 H1
SW20
Cambridge Clo., 72 E4
Houns.
Cambridge Cotts., 65 A6
Rich.
Cambridge Cres. E2 59 E2
Cambridge Cres., 82 D5
Tedd.
Cambridge Dr. SE12 78 G5
Cambridge Dr., Ruis. 45 D2
Cambridge Gdns. 40 A1
N10
Cambridge Gdns. 33 A7
N17
Great Cambridge Rd.
Cambridge Gdns. 25 A7
N21
Cambridge Gdns. 32 G5
N21
Cambridge Gdns. 57 D2
NW6
Cambridge Gdns. 57 A6
W10
Cambridge Gdns., 25 D2
Enf.
Cambridge Gdns., 92 A2
Kings.T.
Cambridge Gate NW1 7 E5
Cambridge Gate Ms. 7 E5
NW1
Cambridge Grn. SE9 88 E1
Cambridge Gro. SE20 95 E1
Cambridge Gro. W6 65 H4
Cambridge Gro. Rd., 92 A3
Kings.T.
Cambridge Heath Rd. 59 E4
E1
Cambridge Heath Rd. 59 F4
E2
Cambridge Mans. 75 J1
SW11
Cambridge Rd.
Cambridge Par., Enf. 25 D1
Great Cambridge Rd.
Cambridge Pk. E11 42 G7
Cambridge Pk., 73 F6
Twick.
Cambridge Pk. Rd. 42 F7
E11
Cambridge Pl. W8 14 B4
Cambridge Pl. W8 66 E2
Cambridge Rd. E4 34 D1
Cambridge Rd. E11 42 F6
Cambridge Rd. NW6 57 D3
Cambridge Rd. SE20 95 E3
Cambridge Rd. SW11 75 J1
Cambridge Rd. SW13 74 F2
Cambridge Rd. SW20 92 H1
Cambridge Rd. W7 64 C2
Cambridge Rd., Bark. 52 F7
Cambridge Rd., 87 G7
Brom.
Cambridge Rd., Cars. 100 H6
Cambridge Rd., 87 G7
Hmptn.
Cambridge Rd., Har. 36 G5
Cambridge Rd., 72 E4
Houns.
Cambridge Rd., Ilf. 52 H1
Cambridge Rd., 92 A2
Kings.T.
Cambridge Rd., 94 B3
Mitch.
Cambridge Rd., 92 D4
N.Mal.
Cambridge Rd., Rich. 65 A7
Cambridge Rd., Sid. 88 H4
Cambridge Rd., Sthl. 63 F1
Cambridge Rd., Tedd. 82 C4
Cambridge Rd., 73 G6
Twick.
Cambridge Rd., Walt. 90 B6
Cambridge Rd., 90 F4
W.Mol.
Cambridge Rd. Est., 92 A2
Kings.T.
Cambridge Rd. N. 65 B5
W4

Cambridge Row 70 E5
SE18
Cambridge Sq. W2 10 G3
Cambridge Sq. W2 57 H6
Cambridge St. SW1 19 E3
Cambridge St. SW1 67 B4
Cambridge Ter. N13 32 G5
Cambridge Ter. NW1 7 D4
Cambridge Ter. Ms. 7 E4
NW1
Cambus Clo., Hayes 54 C3
Cambus Rd. E16 60 G5
Camdale Rd. SE18 70 J7
Camden Ave., Felt. 81 C2
Camden Clo., Chis. 97 F1
Camden Est. SE15 77 C1
Camden Gdns. NW1 49 B7
Kentish Town Rd.
Camden Gdns., Sutt. 100 E5
Camden Gdns., 94 H3
Th.Hth.
Camden Gro., Chis. 88 E6
Camden High St. 58 B1
NW1
Camden Hill Rd. 86 B6
SE19
Camden La. N7 49 D6
Camden Lock Pl. 49 B7
NW1
Chalk Fm. Rd.
Camden Ms. NW1 49 C7
Camden Pk. Rd. NW1 49 D6
Camden Pk. Rd., 88 C7
Chis.
Camden Pas. N1 58 H1
Camden Rd. E11 42 H6
Camden Rd. E17 41 J6
Camden Rd. N7 49 E4
Camden Rd. NW1 49 C7
Camden Rd., Bex. 89 E1
Camden Rd., Cars. 100 J4
Camden Rd., Sutt. 100 D5
Camden Row SE3 78 E2
Camden Sq. NW1 49 D6
Camden Sq. SE15 77 C1
Exeter Rd.
Camden St. NW1 49 C7
Camden Ter. NW1 49 D6
North Vill.
Camden Wk. N1 58 H1
Camden Way, Chis. 88 C7
Camden Way, Th.Hth. 94 H3
Camdenhurst St. E14 59 H6
Camel Rd. E16 70 A1
Camelford Wk. W11 57 B6
Lancaster Rd.
Camellia Pl., Twick. 72 H7
Camellia St. SW8 67 E7
Camelot Clo. SE28 70 G2
Camelot Clo. SW19 84 D4
Camelot St. SE15 68 E7
Green Hundred Rd.
Camera Pl. SW10 18 E5
Camera Pl. SW10 66 G6
Cameron Clo. N18 33 E4
Cameron Clo. N20 31 H2
Myddelton Pk.
Cameron Pl. E1 59 E6
Varden St.
Cameron Rd. SE6 86 J2
Cameron Rd., Brom. 96 G4
Cameron Rd., Croy. 94 H6
Cameron Rd., Ilf. 52 H1
Cameron Sq., Mitch. 93 H1
Camerton Clo. E8 50 C6
Buttermere Wk.
Camilla Rd. SE16 68 E4
Camille Clo. SE25 95 D3
Camlan Rd., Brom. 87 F4
Camlet St. E2 9 F5
Camlet St. E2 59 C4
Camlet Way, Barn. 23 D2
Camley St. NW1 7 J1
Camley St. NW1 49 D7
Kings.T.
Church Rd.
Camomile St. EC3 13 D3
Camomile St. EC3 59 B6
Camp Rd. SW19 83 H5
Camp Vw. SW19 83 H5
Campana Rd. SW6 75 D1
Campbell Ave., Ilf. 43 E4
Campbell Clo. SE18 79 D1
Moordown
Campbell Clo. SW16 85 D5
Campbell Clo., Ruis. 36 A6
Campbell Clo., Twick. 82 A2
Campbell Ct. N17 41 C1

Campbell Cft., Edg. 30 A5
Campbell Rd. E3 60 A3
Campbell Rd. E6 61 B1
Campbell Rd. E15 51 F4
Trevelyan Rd.
Campbell Rd. E17 41 J4
Campbell Rd. N17 41 C1
Campbell Rd. W7 55 B7
Campbell Rd., Croy. 94 H7
Campbell Rd., E.Mol. 91 C3
Hampton Ct. Rd.
Campbell Rd., Twick. 82 A1
Campbell Wk. N1 58 E1
Outram Pl.
Campdale Rd. N7 49 D3
Campden Cres., Dag. 53 B4
Campden Cres., 46 E3
Wem.
Campden Gro. W8 66 D2
Campden Hill W8 66 D2
Campden Hill Gdns. 66 D1
W8
Campden Hill Pl. W11 66 C1
Holland Pk. Ave.
Campden Hill Rd. W8 66 D1
Campden Hill Sq. W8 66 C1
Campden Ho. Clo. 66 D2
W8
Hornton St.
Campden Rd., 102 B5
S.Croy.
Campden St. W8 66 D1
Campen Clo. SW19 84 B2
Queensmere Rd.
Camperdown St. E1 13 G4
Campfield Rd. SE9 79 A7
Campion Clo. E6 61 C7
Campion Clo., Croy. 102 B4
Campion Clo., Har. 37 J6
Campion Pl. SE28 71 B1
Campion Rd. SW15 74 J4
Campion Rd., Islw. 73 C1
Campion Ter. NW2 48 A4
Camplin Rd., Har. 37 H5
Camplin St. SE14 68 G7
Campsbourne, The 40 E4
N8
Rectory Gdns.
Campsbourne Rd. N8 40 E3
Campsey Gdns., Dag. 53 B7
Campsey Rd., Dag. 53 B7
Campsfield Rd. N8 40 E3
Campsbourne Rd.
Campshill Pl. SE13 78 C5
Campshill Rd.
Campshill Rd. SE13 78 C5
Campus Rd. E17 41 J6
Camrose Ave., Edg. 37 J2
Camrose Ave., Erith 71 H6
Camrose Ave., Felt. 81 B4
Camrose Clo., Croy. 95 H7
Camrose Clo., Mord. 93 D4
Camrose St. SE2 71 A5
Canada Ave. N18 32 J6
Canada Cres. W3 56 C4
Canada Est. SE16 68 F3
Canada Gdns. SE13 78 C5
Monument Gdns.
Canada Rd. W3 56 C5
Canada Sq. E14 69 B1
Canada St. SE16 68 G3
Canada Way W12 56 H7
Canada Yd. S. SE16 68 G3
Canadian Ave. SE6 87 B1
Canal App. SE8 68 H5
Canal Clo. E1 59 H4
Canal Gro. SE15 21 J5
Canal Gro. SE15 68 D6
Canal Head SE15 77 D1
Peckham High St.
Canal St. SE5 21 B6
Canal St. SE5 68 A6
Canal Wk. N1 59 A1
Canal Wk. SE26 86 F5
Canal Way NW1 58 A1
Regents Pk. Rd.
Canal Way NW10 56 D2
Canal Way W10 57 A4
Canal Way, Wem. 55 J1
Canal Way, W.10 57 B4
Kensal Rd.
Canary Wf. E14 69 A1
Canberra Clo. NW4 38 G3
Canberra Dr., Nthlt. 54 C3
Canberra Rd. E6 61 C1
Barking Rd.
Canberra Rd. SE7 69 J6
Canberra Rd., Bexh. 71 D6
Canbury Ave., 91 J1
Kings.T.
Canbury Ms. SE26 86 D3
Wells Pk. Rd.

Canbury Pk. Rd., 91 H1
Kings.T.
Canbury Pas., 91 G1
Kings.T.
Cancell Rd. SW9 76 G1
Candahar Rd. SW11 75 H2
Candler St. N15 41 A6
Candover St. W1 11 F2
Candy St. E3 59 J1
Cane Clo., Wall. 101 E7
Kingsford Ave.
Caney Ms. NW2 48 A2
Claremont Rd.
Canfield Rd., Ruis. 45 B5
Canfield Gdns. NW6 48 E7
Canfield Pl. NW6 48 F6
Canfield Gdns.
Canfield Rd., 35 B7
Wdf.Grn.
Canford Ave., Nthlt. 54 E1
Canford Clo., Enf. 24 G2
Canford Gdns., 92 E6
N.Mal.
Canford Rd. SW11 76 A5
Canham Rd. SE25 95 B3
Canham Rd. W3 65 E2
Canmore Gdns. 85 C7
SW16
Cann Hall Rd. E11 51 E4
Canning Cres. N22 40 F1
Canning Cross SE5 77 B2
Canning Pas. W8 14 C5
Canning Pl. W8 14 C5
Canning Pl. W8 66 F3
Canning Pl. Ms. W8 14 C5
Canning Rd. E15 60 E2
Canning Rd. E17 41 H4
Canning Rd. N5 49 H3
Canning Rd., Croy. 102 C2
Canning Rd., Har. 37 B3
Cannington Rd., Dag. 53 C6
Cannizaro Rd. SW19 83 J5
Cannon Clo. SW20 92 J3
Cannon Clo., Hmptn. 81 H6
Hanworth Rd.
Cannon Dr. E14 60 A7
Cannon Hill N14 32 D3
Cannon Hill NW6 48 D5
Cannon Hill La. 93 B3
SW20
Cannon La. NW3 48 G3
Cannon La., Pnr. 36 C5
Cannon Pl. NW3 48 F3
Cannon Pl. SE7 70 B5
Cannon Rd. N14 32 E3
Cannon Rd., Bexh. 80 E1
Cannon St. EC4 12 J4
Cannon St. EC4 58 J2
Cannon Way, W.Mol. 90 E4
Cannonbury Ave., 36 D6
Pnr.
Canon Ave., Rom. 44 C5
Canon Beck Rd. SE16 68 G2
Canon Mohan Clo. 24 B6
N14
Farm La.
Canon Rd., Brom. 96 J3
Canon Row SW1 16 A3
Canon Row SW1 67 E2
Canon St. N1 59 J2
Canon Trd. Est., 47 B4
The, Wem.
Canonbie Rd. SE23 77 F7
Canonbury Cres. N1 49 J7
Canonbury Gro. N1 49 J7
Canonbury La. N1 49 H7
Canonbury Pk. N. N1 49 J6
Canonbury Pk. S. N1 49 J6
Canonbury Pl. N1 49 H6
Canonbury Rd. N1 49 H6
Canonbury Rd., Enf. 25 B1
Canonbury Sq. N1 49 H7
Canonbury St. N1 49 J7
Canonbury Vill. N1 49 H7
Canonbury Yd. N1 58 J1
New N. Rd.
Canons Clo. N2 39 G7
Canons Clo., Edg. 29 J6
Canons Cor., Edg. 29 H4
Canons Dr., Edg. 29 H4
Canons Wk., Croy. 102 G3
Canonsleigh Rd., 52 H7
Dag.
Canopus Way, Nthwd.28 A4
Canrobert St. E2 59 E3
Cantelowes Rd. NW1 49 D6
Canterbury Ave., Ilf. 43 B7
Canterbury Ave., Sid. 89 C2
Canterbury Clo. E6 61 C6
Harper Rd.
Canterbury Clo., 96 B1
Beck.

Canterbury Clo., 35 J3
Chig.
Canterbury Clo., 54 H6
Grnf.
Canterbury Cres. 76 G3
SW9
Canterbury Gro. 85 G4
SE27
Canterbury Pl. SE17 20 H2
Canterbury Pl. SE17 67 H4
Canterbury Rd. E10 42 C7
Canterbury Rd. NW6 57 C2
Canterbury Rd., 22 A2
Borwd.
Canterbury Rd., Croy. 94 G7
Canterbury Rd., Felt. 81 E3
Canterbury Rd., Har. 36 H5
Canterbury Rd., 93 E7
Mord.
Canterbury Ter. NW6 57 D2
Cantley Gdns. SE19 95 C1
Cantley Gdns., Ilf. 43 F6
Cantley Rd. W7 64 D3
Canton St. E14 60 A6
Cantrell Rd. E3 59 J4
Cantwell Rd. SE18 70 E7
Canute Gdns. SE16 68 G4
Canvey St. SE1 16 H1
Cape Clo., Bark. 52 F6
North St.
Cape Rd. N17 41 D3
High Cross Rd.
Cape Yd. E1 17 J1
Capel Ave., Wall. 101 F5
Capel Clo. N20 31 F3
Capel Clo., Brom. 104 C1
Capel Ct. EC2 13 C4
Capel Ct. SE20 95 F1
Melvin Rd.
Capel Gdns., Ilf. 52 J4
Capel Gdns., Pnr. 36 F4
Capel Pt. E7 51 H4
Capel Rd. E7 51 H4
Capel Rd. E12 52 A4
Capel Rd., Barn. 23 H6
Capener's Clo. SW1 15 B4
Capern Rd. SW18 84 F1
Cargill Rd.
Capital Interchange 65 A5
Way, Brent.
Capitol Ind. Est. NW9 38 C3
Capitol Way NW9 38 C3
Capland St. NW8 6 F5
Capland St. NW8 57 G4
Caple Rd. NW10 56 F2
Capper St. WC1 7 G6
Capper St. WC1 58 C4
Caprea Clo., Hayes 54 D5
Triandra Way
Capri Rd., Croy. 102 C1
Capstan Clo., Rom. 44 B6
Capstan Ride, Enf. 24 G2
Crofton Way
Capstan Rd. SE8 68 J4
Capstan Sq. E14 69 C2
Capstan Way SE16 68 H1
Capstone Rd., Brom. 07 F4
Capthorne Ave., Har. 45 E1
Capuchin Clo., Stan. 29 E6
Capworth St. E10 51 A1
Caradoc Clo. W2 57 D6
Caradoc St. SE10 69 E5
Caradon Way N15 41 A4
Caravel Ms. SE8 69 A6
Watergate St.
Carberry Rd. SE19 86 B6
Carbery Ave. W3 64 J2
Carbis Clo. E4 34 D1
Carbis Rd. E14 59 J6
Carbuncle Pas. Way 40 E7
N17
Carburton St. W1 11 E1
Carburton St. W1 58 B5
Cardale St. E14 69 C3
Plevna St.
Carden Rd. SE15 77 E3
Cardiff Rd. W7 64 D3
Cardiff Rd., Enf. 25 B4
Cardiff St. SE18 70 H7
Cardigan Gdns., Ilf. 53 H2
Cardigan Rd. E3 59 J2
Cardigan Rd. SW13 74 G2
Cardigan Rd. SW19 84 F6
Cardigan Rd., Rich. 73 H6
Cardigan St. SE11 20 E3
Cardigan St. SE11 67 G5
Cardigan Wk. N1 49 J7
Ashby Gro.
Cardinal Ave., 22 B3
Borwd.

Cardinal Ave., 82 H5
Kings.T.
Cardinal Ave., Mord. 93 B6
Cardinal Bourne St. 17 C6
SE1
Cardinal Bourne St. 68 A3
SE1
Cardinal Clo., Chis. 97 G1
Cardinal Clo., Mord. 93 B6
Cardinal Clo., 99 G4
Wor.Pk.
Cardinal Cres., 92 C2
N.Mal.
Cardinal Dr., Ilf. 35 F6
Cardinal Pl. SW15 75 A4
Cardinal Rd., Felt. 81 B1
Cardinal Rd., Ruis. 45 D1
Cardinal Way, Har. 37 B3
Wolseley Rd.
Cardinals Wk., 81 J7
Hmptn.
Cardinals Way N19 49 D1
Cardine Ms. SE15 68 E7
Cardington Sq., 72 D4
Houns.
Cardington St. NW1 7 G3
Cardington St. NW1 58 C3
Cardozo Rd. N7 49 E5
Cardrew Ave. N12 31 G5
Cardrew Clo. N12 31 G5
Cardross St. W6 65 H3
Cardwell Rd. N7 49 E4
Cardwell Rd. SE18 70 C4
Carew Clo. N7 49 F2
Carew Rd. N17 41 D2
Carew Rd. W13 64 F2
Carew Rd., Mitch. 94 A2
Carew Rd., Th.Hth. 94 H3
Carew Rd., Wall. 101 C6
Carew St. SE5 76 J2
Carey Ct., Bexh. 80 H5
Carey Gdns. SW8 76 C1
Carey La. EC2 12 J3
Carey Pl. SW1 19 H2
Carey Rd., Dag. 53 E4
Carey St. WC2 12 D4
Carey St. WC2 58 F6
Carey Way, Wem. 47 C4
Fourth Way
Carfax Pl. SW4 76 D4
Holwood St.
Carfree Clo. N1 49 G7
Bewdley St.
Cargill Rd. SW18 84 E1
Cargreen Rd. SE25 95 C4
Carholme Rd. SE23 86 J1
Carisbrook Clo., 37 G2
Stan.
Carisbrooke Ave., 89 D1
Bex.
Carisbrooke Clo., Enf. 25 C1
Carisbrooke Gdns. 21 G7
SE15
Carisbrooke Rd. E17 41 H4
Carisbrooke Rd., 96 J4
Brom.
Carisbrooke Rd., 94 D4
Mitch.
Carker's La. NW5 49 B5
Carleton Ave., Wall. 101 D7
Carleton Clo., Esher 98 A1
Carleton Rd. N7 49 D5
Carlile Clo. E3 59 J2
Carlingford Gdns., 84 J7
Mitch.
Carlingford Rd. N15 40 H3
Carlingford Rd. NW3 48 G4
Carlingford Rd., 93 A6
Mord.
Carlisle Ave. EC3 13 F4
Carlisle Ave. W3 56 E6
Carlisle Clo., Kings.T. 92 A1
Carlisle Gdns., Har. 37 G7
Carlisle Gdns., Ilf. 43 B6
Carlisle La. SE1 16 D6
Carlisle La. SE1 67 F3
Carlisle Ms. NW8 10 F1
Carlisle Pl. N11 32 B4
Carlisle Pl. SW1 15 F6
Carlisle Pl. SW1 67 C3
Carlisle Rd. E10 51 A1
Carlisle Rd. N4 40 G7
Carlisle Rd. NW6 57 B1
Carlisle Rd. NW9 38 C3
Carlisle Rd., 81 H7
Hmptn.
Carlisle Rd., Sutt. 100 C5
Carlisle St. W1 11 H4
Carlisle Wk. E8 50 C6
Laurel St.
Carlisle Way SW17 85 A5
Carlos Pl. W1 11 C5

Carlos Pl. W1 58 A7
Carlow St. NW1 7 F1
Carlton Ave. N14 24 D5
Carlton Ave., Felt. 72 C6
Carlton Ave., Har. 37 E5
Carlton Ave., S.Croy.102 B7
Carlton Ave. E., 46 G2
Wem.
Carlton Ave. W., 46 E2
Wem.
Carlton Clo. NW3 48 D2
Carlton Clo., Borwd. 22 D4
Carlton Clo., Chess. 98 G6
Carlton Clo., Edg. 30 A5
Carlton Ct. SW9 76 H1
Carlton Ct., Ilf. 43 G3
Carlton Cres., Sutt. 100 B4
Carlton Dr. SW15 75 A5
Carlton Dr., Ilf. 43 G3
Carlton Gdns. SW1 15 H2
Carlton Gdns. SW1 67 D3
Carlton Gdns. W5 55 F6
Carlton Gro. SE15 77 E1
Carlton Hill NW8 6 B1
Carlton Hill NW8 57 E2
Carlton Ho. Ter. SW1 15 H2
Carlton Ho. Ter. SW1 67 D1
Carlton Pk. Ave. 93 A2
SW20
Carlton Rd. E11 51 F1
Carlton Rd. E12 52 A4
Carlton Rd. E17 41 H1
Carlton Rd. N4 40 G7
Carlton Rd. N11 32 A5
Carlton Rd. SW14 74 C3
Carlton Rd. W4 65 D2
Carlton Rd. W5 55 F7
Carlton Rd., Erith 71 H6
Carlton Rd., N.Mal. 82 E2
Carlton Rd., Sid. 88 J5
Carlton Rd., S.Croy. 102 A6
Carlton Rd., Walt. 90 B7
Carlton Rd., Well. 80 B3
Carlton Sq. E1 59 G4
Argyle Rd.
Carlton St. SW1 11 H6
Carlton St. E11 42 H5
Carlton Ter. N18 33 A3
Carlton Ter. SE26 86 F3
Carlton Twr. Pl. SW1 15 A5
Carlton Twr. Pl. SW1 66 J3
Carlton Vale NW6 72 D2
Carlwell St. SW17 84 H5
Carlyle Ave., Brom. 97 A3
Carlyle Ave., Sthl. 54 F7
Carlyle Clo. N2 39 F6
Carlyle Clo., W.Mol. 56 D1
Carlyle Clo., W.Mol. 90 H2
Carlyle Gdns., Sthl. 54 F7
Carlyle Pl. SW15 75 A4
Carlyle Rd. E12 52 B4
Carlyle Rd. SE28 62 B7
Carlyle Rd. W5 64 F4
Carlyle Rd., Croy. 102 D2
Carlyle Sq. SW3 18 F4
Carlyle Sq. SW3 66 G6
Carlyon Ave., Har. 55 H1
Carlyon Clo., Wem. 55 H1
Carlyon Rd., Hayes 54 B5
Carlyon Rd., Wem. 55 H2
Carmalt Gdns. SW15 74 J4
Carmarthen Gdn. 38 E6
NW9
Snowdon Dr.
Carmel Ct. W8 14 A3
Carmel Ct., Har. 36 J1
Carmelite Rd.
Carmelite Rd., Har. 36 J1
Carmelite St. EC4 12 F5
Carmelite St. EC4 58 G7
Carmelite Wk., Har. 36 J1
Carmelite Way, Har. 36 J2
Hampden Rd.
Carmen St. E14 60 B6
Carmichael Clo. 75 G3
SW11
Darien Rd.
Carmichael Clo., 45 A4
Ruis.
Carmichael Rd. SE25 95 D4
Carminia Rd. SW17 85 B2
Carnaby St. W1 11 F4
Carnaby St. W1 58 C6
Carnac St. SE27 86 H4
Carnanton Rd. E17 42 D1
Carnarvon Ave., Enf. 25 C6
Carnarvon Rd. E10 42 C6
Carnarvon Rd. E15 51 H6
Carnarvon Rd. E18 42 F2
Carnarvon Rd., Barn. 23 B2
Carnation St. SE2 71 B5
Carnbrook Rd. SE3 79 A3
Carnecke Gdns. SE9 79 B5

Carnegie Clo., Surb. 98 J2
Fullers Ave.
Carnegie Pl. SW19 84 A3
Carnegie St. N1 58 F1
Carnforth Clo., 99 B6
Enam.
Carnforth Rd. SW16 80 D7
Carnie Lo. SW17 85 B3
Manville Rd.
Carnoustie Dr. N1 49 F7
Carnwath Rd. SW6 75 D3
Carol St. NW1 58 C1
Carolina Rd., Th.Hth. 94 H2
Caroline Clo. N10 40 B2
Alexandra Pk. Rd.
Caroline Clo. SW16 85 F4
Caroline Clo. W2 10 B6
Caroline Clo., Croy. 102 B4
Brownlow Rd.
Caroline Clo., Islw. 64 B7
Caroline Ct., Stan. 29 D6
The Chase
Caroline Gdns. E2 9 E3
Caroline Gdns. SE15 68 E7
Caroline Pl. SW11 76 A2
Caroline Pl. W2 10 B5
Caroline Pl. W2 10 B6
Caroline Pl. Ms. W2 10 B6
Caroline Rd. SW19 84 C7
Caroline St. E1 59 G6
Caroline Ter. SW1 19 B2
Caroline Ter. SW1 67 A4
Caroline Wk. W6 66 B6
Laundry Rd.
Carpenders Ave. 28 E3
Wat.
Carpenter Gdns. N21 32 H2
Carpenter St. W1 11 D6
Carpenters Ct., 82 B2
Twick.
Carpenters Pl. SW4 76 D4
Carpenters Rd. E15 51 A6
Carr Rd. E17 41 J2
Carr Rd., Nthlt. 45 G6
Carr St. E14 59 H5
Carrara Wk. SW9 76 G4
Somerleyton Rd.
Carriage Dr. E. SW11 19 C7
Carriage Dr. E. SW11 67 A7
Carriage Dr. N. SW11 19 C6
Carriage Dr. N. SW11 66 J7
Carriage Dr. S. SW11 75 J1
Carriage Dr. W. 66 J7
SW11
Carrick Dr., Ilf. 43 F1
Carrick Gdns. N17 33 B7
Flexmere Rd.
Carrick Ms. SE8 69 A6
Watergate St.
Carrill Way, Belv. 71 D4
Borwd.
Carrington Ave., 22 B5
Borwd.
Carrington Ave., 72 H5
Houns.
Carrington Clo., Barn. 22 G5
Carrington Clo., 22 C5
Borwd.
Carrington Clo., 95 H7
Croy.
Carrington Gdns. E7 51 H4
Woodford Rd.
Carrington Rd., Rich. 74 A4
Carrington Sq., Har. 28 J7
Carrington St. W1 15 D2
Carrol Clo. NW5 49 B4
Carroll Clo. E15 51 F5
Carroll Hill, Loug. 27 C3
Carron Clo. E14 60 B6
Carronade Pl. SE28 70 F3
Carroun Rd. SW8 20 C7
Carroun Rd. SW8 67 F7
Carrow Rd., Dag. 53 B7
Carroway La., Grnf. 55 A3
Cowgate Rd.
Carrs La. N21 24 J5
Carshalton Gro., 100 G4
Sutt.
Carshalton Pk. Rd., 100 J6
Cars.
Carshalton Pl., Cars. 101 A4
Carshalton Rd., 100 H5
Cars.
Carshalton Rd., 94 A4
Mitch.
Carshalton Rd., Sutt. 100 F5
Carslake Rd. SW15 74 J6
Carson Rd. E16 60 G4
Carson Rd. SE21 85 J2
Carson Rd., Barn. 23 J4
Carstairs Rd. SE6 87 C3
Carston Clo. SE12 78 F5
Carswell Clo., Ilf. 43 A4
Roding La. S.

Carswell Rd. SE6 78 C7
Cart La. E4 26 D7
Carter La. EC4 12 H4
Carter La. EC4 58 H6
Carter Pl. SE17 21 A4
Carter Pl. SE17 67 J5
Carter Rd. E13 61 J1
Carter Rd. SW19 84 G6
Carter St. SE17 20 J5
Carter St. SE17 67 J6
Carteret St. SW1 15 H4
Carteret St. SW1 67 D2
Carteret Way SE8 68 H4
Carterhatch Rd., Enf. 25 F1
Carters Clo., 100 A2
Wor.Pk.
Carters Hill Clo. SE9 87 J1
Carters La. SE23 86 H2
Carters Yd. SW18 75 D5
Wandsworth High St.
Carthew Rd. W6 65 H3
Carthew Vill. W6 65 H3
Carthusian St. EC1 12 J1
Carthusian St. EC1 58 E6
Cartier Circle E14 69 B1
Carting La. WC2 12 B6
Carting La. WC2 58 E7
Cartmel Clo. N17 33 E7
Heybourne Rd.
Cartmel Rd., Bexh. 80 G1
Cartmell Gdns., 93 F5
Mord.
Carton St. W1 11 A3
Cartwright Gdns. 8 A4
WC1
Cartwright Gdns. 58 E3
WC1
Cartwright Rd., Dag. 53 E7
Cartwright St. E1 13 G6
Cartwright St. E1 59 C7
Carver Rd. SE24 76 J6
Carville Cres., Brent. 64 H4
Cary Rd. E11 51 E4
Carysfort Rd. N8 40 D5
Carysfort Rd. N16 50 A3
Cascade Ave. N10 40 C4
Cascade Clo., Buck.H. 35 J2
Cascade Rd.
Cascade Rd., Buck.H. 35 A2
Casella Rd. SE14 68 G7
Casewick Rd. SE27 85 G5
Casimir Rd. E5 50 E3
Casino Ave. SE24 77 A5
Caspian St. SE5 21 B7
Caspian St. SE5 68 A7
Caspian Wk. E16 61 A6
King George Ave.
Casselden Rd. NW10 47 D7
Cassidy Rd. SW6 66 D7
Cassilda Rd. SE2 71 A4
Cassilis Rd., Twick. 73 E5
Cassiobury Rd. E17 41 H5
Cassland Rd. E9 50 G7
Cassland Rd., 95 A4
Th.Hth.
Casslee Rd. SE6 77 J7
Casson St. E1 13 H2
Casson St. E1 59 D5
Castalia Sq. E14 69 C2
Plevna St.
Castell Rd., Loug. 27 F1
Castellain Rd. W9 6 A5
Castellain Rd. W9 57 E4
Castellane Clo., Stan. 29 C7
Daventer Dr.
Castello Ave. SW15 74 J5
Castelnau SW13 74 G1
Castelnau Pl. SW13 65 H6
Castelnau
Castelnau Row SW13 65 H6
Lonsdale Rd.
Casterbridge NW6 57 E1
Casterbridge Rd. SE3 78 G3
Casterton St. E8 50 E6
Wilton Way
Castile Rd. SE18 70 D4
Castillon Rd. SE6 87 E2
Castlands Rd. SE6 86 J2
Castle Ave. E4 34 D5
Castle Baynard St. 12 H5
EC4
Castle Clo. E9 50 H5
Swinnerton St.
Castle Clo. SW19 84 A3
Castle Clo., Brom. 96 E3
Castle Ct. EC3 13 C4
Castle Dr., Ilf. 43 B6
Castle La. SW1 15 F5
Castle La. SW1 67 C3
Castle Ms. N12 31 F5
Castle Rd.
Castle Ms. NW1 49 B6
Castle Rd.

Castle Par., Epsom 99 G7
Ewell Bypass
Castle Pl. NW1 49 B6
Castle Rd.
Castle Pl. W4 65 E4
Windmill Rd.
Castle Pt. E6 60 J2
Castle Rd. N12 31 F5
Castle Rd. NW1 49 B6
Castle Rd., Dag. 00 D1
Castle Rd., Enf. 25 H1
Castle Rd., Islw. 73 C2
Castle Rd., Nthlt. 45 H6
Castle Rd., Sthl. 63 F3
Castle St. E6 60 J2
Castle St., Kings.T. 91 H2
Castle Wk., Sun. 90 C3
Elizabeth Gdns.
Castle Way SW19 84 A3
Castle Way, Felt. 81 C4
Castle Yd. N6 40 A7
North Rd.
Castle Yd. SE1 16 H1
Castle Yd., Rich. 73 G5
Hill St.
Castlebar Hill W5 55 E5
Castlebar Ms. W5 55 F5
Castlebar Pk. W5 55 E4
Castlebar Rd. W5 55 F6
Castlecombe Dr. 75 A7
SW19
Castlecombe Rd. SE9 88 B4
Castledine Rd. SE20 86 E7
Castleford Ave. SE9 88 E1
Castlegate, Rich. 73 J3
Castlehaven Rd. NW1 49 B7
Castleleigh Ct., Enf. 25 A5
Castlemaine Ave., 102 C5
S.Croy.
Castlemaine Twr. 75 J2
SW11
Castlereagh St. W1 10 H3
Castleton Ave., Wem. 46 H4
Castleton Rd. E17 42 D2
Castleton Rd. SE9 88 A4
Castleton Rd., Ilf. 53 A1
Castleton Rd., Mitch. 94 D4
Castleton Rd., Ruis. 45 D1
Castletown Rd. W14 66 B5
Castleview Gdns., 43 B6
Ilf.
Castlewood Dr. SE9 79 C2
Castlewood Rd. N15 41 D6
Castlewood Rd. N16 41 D7
Barn.
Castor La. E14 60 B7
Cat Hill, Barn. 23 J5
Caterham Ave., Ilf. 43 C2
Caterham Rd. SE13 78 C3
Catesby St. SE17 21 C2
Catesby St. SE17 68 A4
Catford Bdy. SE6 78 B7
Catford Hill SE6 86 J1
Catford Ms. SE6 78 B7
Holbeach Rd.
Catford Rd. SE6 78 A7
Cathall Rd. E11 51 D2
Cathay St. SE16 68 E2
Cathcart Dr., Orp. 104 H2
Cathcart Hill N19 49 C3
Cathcart Rd. SW10 18 B5
Cathcart Rd. SW10 66 E6
Cathcart St. NW5 49 B6
Cathedral Pl. EC4 12 J4
Cathedral St. SE1 17 B1
Cathedral St. SE1 68 A1
Catherall Rd. N5 49 J3
Catherine Ct. N14 24 C5
Conisbee Rd.
Catherine Gdns. 73 A4
Houns.
Catherine Griffiths 8 F5
Ct. EC1
Catherine Pl. SW1 15 F5
Catherine Pl. SW1 67 C3
Catherine Rd., Surb. 91 G5
Catherine St. WC2 12 C5
Catherine St. WC2 58 F7
Catherine Wheel All. 13 E2
E1
Catherine Wheel 64 G7
Rd., Brent.
Catherine Wheel Yd. 15 F2
SW1
Cathles Rd. SW12 76 B6
Cathnor Hill Ct. W12 65 H3
Cathnor Rd. W12 65 H2
Catlin St. SE16 21 J4
Catlin St. SE16 68 D5
Catling Clo. SE23 86 F3
Catlins La., Pnr. 36 B3

Cato Rd. SW4 76 D3
Cato St. W1 10 H2
Cator La., Beck. 95 J1
Rectory Grn.
Cator Rd. SE26 86 G6
Cator Rd., Cars. 100 J5
Cator St. SE15 68 C6
Cator St. SE15 00 D6
Catton St. WC1 12 C2
Catton St. WC1 58 E5
Caulfield Rd. E6 61 B1
Caulfield Rd. SE15 77 E2
Causeway, The N2 39 H4
Causeway, The 75 E5
SW18
Causeway, The 83 J5
SW19
Causeway, The 101 A3
Cars.
Causeway, The 98 H4
Chess.
Causeway, The 98 C7
Esher
Causeway, The, Felt. 72 A4
Tedd.
Causeway, The, Felt. 82 C6
Broad St.
Causeyware Rd. N9 25 E7
Causton Rd. N6 40 B7
Causton St. SW1 19 J2
Causton St. SW1 67 D4
Cautley Ave. SW4 76 C5
Cavalier Clo., Rom. 44 D4
Cavalry Cres., 72 D4
Houns.
Cavalry Gdns. SW15 75 C5
Upper Richmond Rd.
Cavaye Pl. SW10 18 D4
Cave Rd. E13 60 H2
Cave Rd., Rich. 82 F4
Cavell Dr., Enf. 24 G2
Cavell Rd. N17 33 A7
Cavell St. E1 59 E5
Cavendish Ave. N3 39 D2
Cavendish Ave. NW8 6 F2
Cavendish Ave. NW8 57 G2
Cavendish Ave. W13 55 D5
Cavendish Ave., 71 J7
Erith
Cavendish Ave., Har. 46 A4
Cavendish Ave., 92 G5
N.Mal.
Cavendish Ave., 45 B5
Ruis.
Cavendish Ave., Sid. 80 A7
Cavendish Ave., 79 J3
Well.
Cavendish Ave., 42 H1
Wdf.Grn.
Cavendish Clo. N18 33 E5
Cavendish Rd.
Cavendish Clo. NW6 48 C7
Cavendish Rd.
Cavendish Clo. NW8 6 F3
Cavendish Clo. NW8 57 G3
Cavendish Ct. EC3 13 E3
Cavendish Cres., 22 A4
Borwd.
Cavendish Dr. E11 51 D1
Cavendish Dr., Edg. 29 J6
Cavendish Dr., Esher 98 B5
Cavendish Gdns., 52 H3
Bark.
Cavendish Gdns., Ilf. 52 D1
Cavendish Gdns., 44 E5
Rom.
Cavendish Ms. N. W1 11 E1
Cavendish Ms. S. W1 11 E2
Cavendish Pl. W1 11 E3
Cavendish Pl. W1 58 B6
Cavendish Rd. E4 34 C7
Cavendish Rd. N4 40 G6
Cavendish Rd. N18 33 E5
Cavendish Rd. NW6 48 B7
Cavendish Rd. SW12 76 B6
Cavendish Rd. SW19 84 G7
Cavendish Rd. W4 74 C1
Cavendish Rd., Barn. 22 J3
Cavendish Rd., 101 H1
Croy.
Cavendish Rd., 92 E5
N.Mal.
Cavendish Rd., Sutt. 100 F7
Cavendish Sq. W1 11 E3
Cavendish Sq. W1 58 B6
Cavendish St. N1 9 B2
Cavendish St. N1 59 A2
Cavendish Ter., Felt. 81 A2
High St.
Cavendish Way, 103 B1
W.Wick.
Cavenham Gdns., 52 G3
Ilf.

Caverleigh Way, Wor.Pk.	99	G1
Caversham Ave. N13	32	G3
Caversham Ave., Sutt.	100	B2
Caversham Ms. SW3	18	J5
Caversham Rd. N15	40	J4
Caversham Rd. NW5	49	C6
Caversham Rd., Kings.T.	91	J2
Caversham St. SW3	18	J5
Caversham St. SW3	66	J6
Caverswall St. W12	56	J6
Caveside Clo., Chis.	97	D1
Cawdor Cres. W7	64	D4
Cawnpore St. SE19	86	B5
Caxton Gro. E3	60	A3
Caxton Ms., Brent.	64	G6
The Butts		
Caxton Rd. N22	40	F2
Caxton Rd. SW19	84	F5
Caxton Rd. W12	66	A1
Caxton Rd., Sthl.	63	D3
Caxton St. SW1	15	G5
Caxton St. SW1	67	C3
Caxton St. N. E16	60	F7
Victoria Dock Rd.		
Caygill Clo., Brom.	96	F4
Cayley Clo., Wall.	101	E7
Brabazon Ave.		
Cayton Pl. EC1	9	B4
Cayton Rd., Grnf.	55	B2
Cayton St. EC1	9	B4
Cazenove Rd. E17	42	A1
Cazenove Rd. N16	50	C2
Cearns Ho. E6	61	A1
Cecil Ave., Bark.	52	G7
Cecil Ave., Enf.	25	C4
Cecil Ave., Wem.	46	J5
Cecil Clo., Chess.	98	G4
Cecil Ct. WC2	12	A6
Cecil Ct., Barn.	23	A3
Cecil Pk., Pnr.	36	E4
Cecil Pl., Mitch.	93	J5
Cecil Rd. E11	51	E3
Cecil Rd. E13	60	G1
Cecil Rd. E17	42	A1
Cecil Rd. N10	40	B2
Cecil Rd. N14	32	C1
Cecil Rd. NW9	38	D3
Cecil Rd. NW10	56	E1
Cecil Rd. SW19	84	E7
Cecil Rd. W3	56	C5
Cecil Rd., Croy.	94	E6
Cecil Rd., Enf.	24	J4
Cecil Rd., Har.	37	B3
Cecil Rd., Houns.	72	J2
Cecil Rd., Ilf.	52	E4
Cecil Rd., Rom.	44	D7
Cecil Rd., Sutt.	100	C4
Cecil Way, Brom.	103	G1
Cecile Pk. N8	40	E6
Cecilia Clo. N2	39	F3
Cecilia Rd. E8	50	C5
Cedar Ave., Barn.	23	H7
Cedar Ave., Enf.	25	F2
Cedar Ave., Hayes	54	A6
Acacia Ave.		
Cedar Ave., Rom.	44	E5
Cedar Ave., Ruis.	45	C6
Cedar Ave., Sid.	80	A7
Cedar Ave., Twick.	72	H6
Cedar Clo. SE21	85	J1
Cedar Clo. SW15	83	D4
Cedar Clo., Borwd.	22	B4
Cedar Clo., Brom.	104	B3
Cedar Clo., Buck.H.	35	A2
Cedar Clo., Cars.	100	J6
Cedar Clo., E.Mol.	91	B4
Cedar Rd.		
Cedar Clo., Rom.	44	J4
Cedar Copse, Brom.	97	C2
Cedar Ct. E8	50	C7
Cedar Ct. N1	49	J7
Essex Rd.		
Cedar Ct. SE9	79	B6
Cedar Ct. SW19	84	A3
Cedar Cres., Brom.	104	B3
Cedar Dr. N2	39	H4
Cedar Dr., Pnr.	28	G7
Cedar Gdns., Sutt.	100	F6
Cedar Gro. W5	64	H3
Cedar Gro., Bex.	80	C6
Cedar Gro., Sthl.	55	A3
Cedar Heights, Rich.	82	H1
Cedar Ho., Croy.	103	B6
Cedar Lawn Ave., Barn.	23	B5
Cedar Mt. SE9	88	A1
Cedar Pk. Gdns., Rom.	44	D7
Cedar Ri. N14	24	A7
Cedar Rd. N17	41	C1
Cedar Rd. NW2	47	J4
Cedar Rd., Brom.	96	J2
Cedar Rd., Croy.	102	A2
Cedar Rd., E.Mol.	91	B4
Cedar Rd., Houns.	72	C2
Cedar Rd., Rom.	44	J4
Cedar Rd., Sutt.	100	F6
Cedar Rd., Tedd.	82	D5
Cedar Ter., Rich.	73	H4
Cedar Tree Gro. SE27	85	H5
Cedar Vista, Rich.	73	H1
Kew Rd.		
Cedar Way NW1	49	D7
Cedarcroft Rd., Chess.	98	J4
Cedarhurst Dr. SE9	78	J5
Cedarne Rd. SW6	66	E7
Cedars, The, Buck.H.	34	G1
Cedars, The, Tedd.	82	C6
Adelaide Rd.		
Cedars Ave. E17	42	A5
Cedars Ave., Mitch.	94	A4
Cedars Clo. NW4	39	A3
Cedars Ct. N9	33	B2
Church St.		
Cedars Ms. SW4	76	B4
Cedars Rd. E15	51	E6
Cedars Rd. N9	33	D2
Church St.		
Cedars Rd. N21	32	H2
Cedars Rd. SW4	76	B3
Cedars Rd. SW13	74	F2
Cedars Rd. W4	65	C6
Cedars Rd., Beck.	95	H3
Cedars Rd., Croy.	101	E3
Cedars Rd., Kings.T.	91	F1
Cedars Rd., Mord.	93	D4
Cedarville Gdns. SW16	85	F6
Cedra Ct. N16	50	D1
Cedric Rd. SE9	88	F3
Celadon Clo., Enf.	25	H3
Celandine Clo. E14	60	A5
Celandine Dr. SE28	71	B1
Celandine Way E15	60	E3
Celbridge Ms. W2	10	B3
Celestial Gdns. SE13	78	D4
Celia Rd. N19	48	E3
Celtic Ave., Brom.	96	E3
Celtic St. E14	60	B5
Cemetery La. SE7	70	B6
Cemetery Rd. E7	51	F4
Cemetery Rd. N17	33	B7
Cemetery Rd. SE2	71	B7
Cenacle Clo. NW3	48	D3
Centaur St. SE1	16	D5
Centaur St. SE1	67	F3
Centaurs Business Pk., Islw.	64	D6
Centenary Rd., Enf.	25	J4
Centenary Trd. Est., Enf.	25	J4
Central Ave. E11	51	D2
Central Ave. N2	39	G2
Central Ave. N9	33	B3
Central Ave. SW11	67	A7
Central Ave., Enf.	25	E2
Central Ave., Houns.	72	J4
Central Ave., Pnr.	36	F6
Central Ave., Wall.	101	E5
Central Ave., Well.	79	J2
Central Ave., W.Mol.	90	F4
Central Gdns., Mord.	93	F5
Central Hill SE19	86	A5
Central Mkts. EC1	12	H2
Central Mkts. EC1	58	J5
Central Pk. Ave., Dag.	53	H3
Central Pk. Est., Houns.	72	D5
Central Pk. Rd. E6	61	A2
Central Pl. SE25	95	E4
Portland Rd.		
Central Rd., Mord.	93	D6
Central Rd., Wem.	46	E5
Central Rd., Wor.Pk.	99	G1
Central Sq. NW11	39	D5
Central Sq., W.Mol.	90	F4
Central St. EC1	8	J3
Central St. EC1	58	J3
Central Way SE28	71	A1
Central Way, Cars.	100	H7
Central Way, Felt.	72	A5
Lavender Vale		
Centre Ave. E11	51	G2
Centre Ave. W3	65	D1
Centre Ave. W10	56	J3
Harrow Rd.		
Centre Common Rd., Chis.	88	F6
Centre Rd. E7	51	G2
Centre Rd. E11	51	G2
Centre Rd., Dag.	62	H2
Centre St. E2	59	E2
Centre Way E17	34	C7
Centre Way N9	33	F2
Centreway NW7	30	G7
Centreway, Ilf.	52	F2
Centric Clo. NW1	58	B1
Oval Rd.		
Centurion Clo. N7	49	F7
Centurion Way, Erith	71	G3
Century Rd. E17	41	H3
Cephas Ave. E1	59	F4
Cephas St. E1	59	F4
Ceres Rd. SE18	70	J4
Cerise Rd. SE15	77	D1
Cerne Clo., Hayes	54	C7
Cerne Rd., Mord.	93	F6
Cerney Ms. W2	10	E5
Cervantes Ct. W2	10	B4
Cester St. E2	59	D1
Whiston Rd.		
Ceylon Rd. W14	66	A3
Chadacre Ave., Ilf.	43	C3
Chadacre Rd., Epsom	99	H6
Chadbourn St. E14	60	B5
Chadd Dr., Brom.	97	B3
Chadd Grn. E13	60	G1
Chadville Gdns., Rom.	44	D5
Chadway, Dag.	53	C1
Chadwell Ave., Rom.	44	B7
Chadwell Heath La., Rom.	44	B4
Chadwell St. EC1	8	F3
Chadwell St. EC1	58	G3
Chadwick Ave. E4	34	D4
Chadwick Clo., Tedd.	82	D6
Chadwick Rd. E11	42	E7
Chadwick Rd. NW10	56	F1
Chadwick Rd. SE15	77	C2
Chadwick Rd., Ilf.	52	E3
Chadwick St. SW1	15	H6
Chadwick St. SW1	67	D3
Chadwick Way SE28	62	D7
Chadwin Ms. E13	60	H5
Chadwin Rd. E13	60	H5
Chadworth Way, Esher	98	A5
Chaffinch Av., Croy.	95	G6
Chaffinch Clo. N9	33	G1
Chaffinch Clo., Croy.	95	G5
Chaffinch Clo., Surb.	99	A3
Chaffinch Rd., Beck.	95	H1
Chafford Way, Rom.	44	C4
Chagford St. NW1	6	J6
Chagford St. NW1	57	J4
Chailey Ave., Enf.	25	C2
Chailey Clo., Houns.	72	D1
Springwell Rd.		
Chailey St. E5	50	F3
Chalcombe Rd. SE2	71	B3
Chalcot Clo., Sutt.	100	D7
Chalcot Cres. NW1	57	J1
Chalcot Gdns. NW3	48	J6
Chalcot Rd. NW1	49	A7
Chalcot Sq. NW1	49	A7
Chalcott Gdns., Surb.	98	F1
Chalcroft Rd. SE13	78	E5
Chaldon Path, Th.Hth.	94	H4
Chaldon Rd. SW6	66	B7
Chale Rd. SW2	76	E6
Chalet St. NW7	30	G4
Chalfont Ave., Wem.	47	B6
Chalfont Ct. NW9	38	F3
Chalfont Grn. N9	33	B3
Chalfont Rd. N9	33	B3
Chalfont Rd. SE25	95	C3
Chalfont Rd., Hayes	63	A2
Chalfont Way W13	61	E3
Chalford Clo., W.Mol.	90	G4
Chalford Rd. SE21	86	A3
Chalford Wk., Wdf.Grn.	43	A1
Chalgrove Ave., Mord.	93	D5
Chalgrove Cres., Ilf.	43	B2
Chalgrove Gdns. N3	39	B3
Chalgrove Rd. E9	50	F6
Morning La.		
Chalgrove Rd. N17	41	E1
Chalgrove Rd., Sutt.	100	G7
Chalice Clo., Wall.	101	D6
Lavender Vale		
Chalk Cres. SE12	87	H3
Chalk Frm. Rd. NW1	49	A7
Chalk Hill Rd. W6	66	A4
Shortlands		
Chalk La., Barn.	23	J3
Chalk Pit Way, Sutt.	100	F5
Chalk Rd. E13	60	H5
Chalkenden Clo. SE20	86	E7
Chalkhill Rd., Wem.	47	A3
Chalklands, The, Wem.	47	C3
The Leadings		
Chalkstone Clo., Well.	80	A1
Chalkwell Pk. Ave., Enf.	25	B4
Challice Way SW2	85	F1
Challin St. SE20	95	F1
Challis Rd., Brent.	64	G5
Challoner Clo. N2	39	G2
Challoner Cres. W14	66	C5
Challoner St.		
Challoner St. W14	66	C5
Challoners Clo., E.Mol.	91	A4
Chalmers Wk. SE17	20	H6
Chalmers Way, Felt.	72	A5
Chalsey Rd. SE4	77	J4
Chalton Dr. N2	39	F6
Chalton St. NW1	7	G1
Chalton St. NW1	58	C2
Chamber St. E1	13	G5
Chamber St. E1	59	C7
Chamberlain Clo. SE28	70	G3
Broadwater Rd.		
Chamberlain Cotts. SE5	77	A1
Camberwell Gro.		
Chamberlain Cres., W.Wick.	103	B1
Chamberlain La., Pnr.	36	A4
Chamberlain Rd. N2	39	F2
Chamberlain Rd. N9	33	D3
Chamberlain Rd. W13	64	D2
Midhurst Rd.		
Chamberlain St. NW1	48	J7
Regents Pk. Rd.		
Chamberlain Wk., Felt.	81	E4
Burgess Clo.		
Chamberlain Way, Pnr.	36	B3
Chamberlain Way, Surb.	91	H7
Chamberlayne Rd. NW10	56	J1
Chambers Gdns. N2	39	G3
Chambers La. NW10	47	H7
Chambers Rd. N7	49	E4
Chambers St. SE16	17	H4
Chambers St. SE16	68	D2
Chambord St. E2	9	G4
Chambord St. E2	59	C3
Champion Cres. SE26	86	H4
Champion Gro. SE5	77	A3
Champion Hill SE5	77	A3
Champion Hill Est. SE5	77	B3
Champion Pk. SE5	77	A2
Champion Rd. SE26	86	H4
Champness Clo. SE27	86	A4
Rommany Rd.		
Champneys Clo., Sutt.	100	C7
Chance St. E1	9	F5
Chance St. E1	59	C4
Chance St. E2	59	C4
Chancel St. SE1	16	G2
Chancel St. SE1	67	H1
Chancellor Gro. SE21	85	J2
Chancellor Pas. E14	69	A1
South Colonnade		
Chancellors Rd. W6	65	J5
Chancellors St. W6	65	J5
Chancelot Rd. SE2	71	B4
Chancery La. WC2	12	E3
Chancery La. WC2	58	G6
Chancery La., Beck.	96	B2
Chanctonbury Clo. SE9	88	E3
Chanctonbury Gdns., Sutt.	100	E7
Chanctonbury Way N12	31	D4
Chandler Ave. E16	60	G5
Chandler Clo., Hmptn.	90	G1
Chandler Rd., Loug.	27	E1
Chandler St. E1	68	E1
Wapping La.		
Chandlers Ms. E14	69	A4
Chandlers Way SW2	76	G7
Chandos Ave. E17	42	A2
Chandos Ave. N14	32	C3
Chandos Ave. N20	31	F1
Chandos Ave. W5	64	G4
Chandos Clo., Buck.H.	34	H2
Chandos Cres., Edg.	29	J7

Chandos Pl. WC2 12 A6
Chandos Pl. WC2 58 E7
Chandos Rd. E15 51 D5
Chandos Rd. N2 39 G2
Chandos Rd. N17 41 B2
Chandos Rd. NW2 47 J5
Chandos Rd. NW10 56 E4
Chandos Rd., Har. 36 J5
Chandos Rd., Pnr. 22 D7
Chandos St. W1 11 E2
Chandos St. W1 58 B5
Chandos Way NW11 48 E1
Change All. EC3 13 C4
Channel Clo., Houns. 72 G1
Channelsea Rd. E15 60 D1
Chant Sq. E.15 51 D7
Chant St. E15 51 D7
Chantrey Rd. SW9 76 F3
Chantry Clo., Har. 37 J5
Chantry Clo., Sid. 89 E5
Ellenborough Rd.
Chantry La., Brom. 97 A5
Bromley Common
Chantry Pl., Har. 36 H1
Chantry Pt. W9 57 C4
Chantry Rd., Chess. 98 J5
Chantry Rd., Har. 36 H1
Chantry St. N1 58 H1
Chapel Ct. N2 39 H3
Chapel Ct. SE1 17 B3
Chapel Fm. Rd. SE9 88 J3
Chapel Ho. St. E14 69 B5
Chapel La., Chig. 35 J3
Chapel La., Pnr. 36 D3
Chapel La., Rom. 44 D7
Chapel Mkt. N1 8 E1
Chapel Mkt. N1 58 G2
Chapel Path E11 42 H6
Chapel Pl. EC2 9 D4
Chapel Pl. N1 8 F1
Chapel Pl. N17 33 C7
White Hart La.
Chapel Pl. W1 11 D4
Chapel Pl. W1 58 B6
Chapel Rd. SE27 85 H4
Chapel Rd. W13 64 E1
Chapel Rd., Bexh. 80 G4
Chapel Rd., Houns. 72 H3
Chapel Rd., Ilf. 52 D3
Chapel Rd., Twick. 73 E7
Orleans Rd.
Chapel Side W2 10 A5
Chapel Side W2 57 E7
Chapel Stones N17 41 C1
Kings Rd.
Chapel St. E15 51 D7
Chapel St. NW1 10 G2
Chapel St. NW1 57 H5
Chapel St. SW1 15 C4
Chapel St. SW1 67 A3
Chapel St., Enf. 25 A3
Chapel Ter., Loug. 27 B4
Forest Rd.
Chapel Vw., S.Croy. 102 F6
Chapel Wk. NW4 38 H4
Chapel Wk., Croy. 101 J2
Wellesley Rd.
Chapel Way N7 49 F3
Sussex Way
Chapelmount Rd., 35 C6
Wdf.Grn.
Chaplin Clo. SE1 16 F3
Chaplin Clo. SE1 67 G2
Chaplin Rd. E15 60 E1
Chaplin Rd. N17 41 C3
Chaplin Rd. NW2 47 G6
Chaplin Rd., Dag. 53 E7
Chaplin Rd., Wem. 46 F6
Chapman Cres., Har. 37 H5
Chapman Rd. E9 50 J6
Chapman Rd., Belv. 71 G5
Chapman Rd., Croy. 101 G1
Chapman St. E1 59 E7
Chapman's La. SE2 71 C4
Chapmans La., Belv. 71 D4
Chapmans Pk. Ind. 47 F6
Est. NW10
Chapone Pl. W1 11 H4
Chapter Clo. W4 65 C3
Beaumont Rd.
Chapter Ho. Ct. EC4 12 H4
Chapter Rd. NW2 47 G5
Chapter Rd. SE17 20 H4
Chapter Rd. SE17 67 H4
Chapter St. SW1 19 H2
Chapter St. SW1 67 D4
Chapter Way, 81 G4
Hmptn.
Chara Pl. W4 65 D6
Charcroft Gdns., Enf. 25 G4
Chardin Rd. W4 65 E4
Elliott Rd.
Chardmore Rd. N16 50 D1

Chardwell Clo. E6 61 B6
Northumberland Rd.
Charecroft Way W12 66 A2
Charfield Ct. W9 6 A6
Charford Rd. E16 60 G5
Chargeable La. E13 60 F4
Chargeable St. E16 60 F3
Chargrove Clo. SE16 68 G2
Marlow Way
Charing Clo., Orp. 104 J4
Charing Cross WC2 16 A1
Charing Cross Rd. 11 J4
WC2
Charing Cross Rd. 58 D6
WC2
Charlbert St. NW8 6 G1
Charlbert St. NW8 57 H2
Charlbury Ave., Stan. 29 G5
Charlbury Gdns., Ilf. 52 J2
Charlbury Gro. W5 55 F6
Charldane Rd. SE9 88 E3
Charlecote Gro. 86 E3
SE26
Charlecote Rd., Dag. 53 E3
Charlemont Rd. E6 61 C3
Charles Barry Clo. 76 C3
SW4
Charles Burton Ct. 50 H5
E5
Ashenden Rd.
Charles Clo., Sid. 89 B4
Charles Cres., Har. 37 A7
Charles Dickens Ho. 59 E3
E2
Charles Grinling Wk. 70 D4
SE18
Charles Ho. N17 33 C7
Charles La. NW8 6 G1
Charles Pl. NW1 7 G4
Charles Rd. E7 51 J7
Lens Rd.
Charles Rd. SW19 93 D1
Charles Rd. W13 55 D6
Charles Rd., Rom. 44 D7
Charles II St. SW1 15 H1
Charles II St. SW1 67 D1
Charles Sevright Dr. 31 A5
NW7
Charles Sq. N1 9 C4
Charles St. E16 70 A1
Charles St. SW13 74 E2
Charles St. W1 15 D1
Charles St. W1 67 B1
Charles St., Croy. 101 J3
Charles St., Enf. 25 C5
Charles St., Houns. 72 E2
Charlesfield SE9 87 J3
Charleston Clo., Felt. 81 A3
Charleston St. SE17 21 A2
Charleston St. SE17 67 J4
Charleville Circ. SE26 86 D5
Charleville Rd. W14 66 B5
Charlieville Rd., Erith 71 J7
Northumberland Pk.
Charlmont Rd. SW17 84 J6
Charlotte Despard 76 A1
Ave. SW11
Charlotte Ms. W1 11 G1
Charlotte Ms. W14 66 B4
Munden St.
Charlotte Pl. NW9 38 C5
Charlotte Pl. SW1 19 F2
Charlotte Pl. W1 11 G2
Charlotte Rd. EC2 9 D4
Charlotte Rd. EC2 59 B4
Charlotte Rd. SW13 74 F1
Charlotte Rd., Dag. 53 H6
Charlotte Rd., Wall. 101 C6
Charlotte Row SW4 76 C3
North St.
Charlotte Sq., Rich. 73 J6
Greville Rd.
Charlotte St. W1 11 G1
Charlotte St. W1 58 C5
Charlotte Ter. N1 58 F1
Charlton Ch. La. SE7 69 J5
Charlton Cres., Bark. 61 J2
Charlton Dene SE7 69 J7
Charlton Kings Rd. 49 D5
NW5
Charlton La. SE7 70 A5
Charlton Pk. La. SE7 70 A7
Charlton Pk. Rd. SE7 70 A6
Charlton Pl. N1 8 G1
Charlton Pl. N1 58 H2
Charlton Rd. N9 33 G1
Charlton Rd. NW10 56 E1
Charlton Rd. SE3 69 H7
Charlton Rd. SE7 69 J5
Charlton Rd., Har. 37 G5
Charlton Rd., Wem. 46 J1
Charlton Way SE3 78 E1

Charlwood Clo., Har. 29 B7
Kelvin Cres.
Charlwood Pl. SW1 19 G2
Charlwood Pl. SW1 67 C4
Charlwood Rd. SW15 75 A4
Charlwood Sq., 93 G3
Mitch.
Charlwood St. SW1 19 G3
Charlwood St. SW1 67 C5
Charlwood Ter. 75 A4
SW15
Cardinal Pl.
Charmian Ave., Stan. 37 G3
Charminster Ave. 93 D2
SW19
Charminster Ct., 91 G6
Surb.
Charminster Rd. SE9 88 A4
Charminster Rd., 100 A1
Wor.Pk.
Charmouth Rd., Well. 80 B1
Charnock Rd. E5 50 E3
Charnwood Ave. 93 D2
SW19
Charnwood Clo., 92 E4
N.Mal.
Charnwood Dr. E18 42 H3
Charnwood Gdns., 69 A4
E14
Charnwood Pl. N20 31 F3
Charnwood Rd. SE25 95 A5
Charnwood St. E5 50 E2
Charrington Rd., 101 H2
Croy.
Drayton Rd.
Charrington St. NW1 7 H1
Charrington St. NW1 58 D2
Charsley Rd. SE6 87 B2
Chart Clo., Brom. 96 E1
Chart Clo., Croy. 95 F6
Stockbury Rd.
Chart St. N1 9 C3
Chart St. N1 59 A3
Charter Ave., Ilf. 52 G1
Charter Ct., N.Mal. 92 E3
Charter Cres., Houns. 72 E4
Charter Dr., Bex. 80 E7
Charter Rd., Kings.T. 92 B3
Charter Rd., The, 34 E6
Wdf.Grn.
Charter Sq., Kings.T. 92 B2
Charter Way N3 39 C4
Regents Pk. Rd.
Charter Way N14 24 C6
Charterhouse Ave., 46 F4
Wem.
Charterhouse Bldgs. 8 H6
EC1
Charterhouse Sq. 12 H1
EC1
Charterhouse Sq. 58 H5
EC1
Charterhouse St. 12 G2
EC1
Charterhouse St. 58 G5
EC1
Charteris Rd. N4 49 G1
Charteris Rd. NW6 57 C1
Charteris Rd., 34 H7
Wdf.Grn.
Charters Clo. SE19 86 B5
Chartfield Ave. SW15 74 H5
Chartfield Sq. SW15 75 A5
Chartfield Ave.
Chartham Gro. SE27 85 G3
Royal Circ.
Chartham Rd. SE25 95 E3
Chartley Ave. NW2 47 E3
Chartley Ave., Stan. 29 C6
Charton Clo., Belv. 71 F6
Chartridge Clo., Barn. 22 G5
Chartwell Clo. SE9 88 F2
Chartwell Dr., Orp. 104 G5
Chartwell Pl., Sutt. 100 C3
Chartwell Way SE20 95 E1
Charwood SW16 85 G4
Chase, The E12 52 A4
Chase, The SW4 76 B3
Chase, The SW16 85 F7
Chase, The SW20 93 B1
Chase, The, Bexh. 96 H3
Chase, The, Brom. 96 H3
Chase, The, Chig. 35 E4
Chase, The, Edg. 38 B1
Chase, The, Pnr. 36 E4
Chase, The 36 C6
(Eastcote), Pnr.
Chase, The, Rom. 44 E6
(Chadwell Heath)
Chase, The, Stan. 29 D5
Chase, The, Sun. 90 B1
Chase, The, Wall. 101 E5
Chase Ct. Gdns., Enf. 24 J3

Chase Gdns. E4 34 A4
Chase Gdns., Twick. 73 A6
Chase Grn., Enf. 24 J3
Chase Grn. Ave., Enf. 24 H2
Chase Hill, Enf. 24 J3
Chase La., Ilf. 43 G5
Chase Ridings, Enf. 24 G2
Chase Rd. N14 24 C5
Chase Rd. NW10 56 D4
Chase Rd. N3 56 D4
Chase Side N14 24 A5
Chase Side, Enf. 24 J3
Chase Side Ave. 93 B2
SW20
Chase Side Ave., Enf. 24 J2
Chase Side Cres., 24 J1
Enf.
Chase Way N14 32 B2
Chasefield Rd. SW17 84 J4
Chaseley Dr. W4 74 B3
Wellesley Rd.
Chaseley St. E14 59 H6
Chasemore Gdns., 101 H5
Croy.
Thorneloe Gdns.
Chaseville Pk. Rd. 24 E5
N21
Chasewood Ave., 24 H2
Enf.
Chatfield Rd. SW11 75 F3
Chatfield Rd., Croy. 101 H1
Chatham Ave., Brom. 96 F7
Chatham Clo. NW11 39 D5
Chatham Clo., Sutt. 93 C7
Chatham Pl. E9 50 F6
Chatham Rd. E17 41 H3
Chatham Rd. E18 42 F2
Grove Hill
Chatham Rd. SW11 75 J6
Chatham Rd., 92 A2
Kings.T.
Chatham Rd., Orp. 104 F5
Chatham St. SE17 21 B1
Chatham St. SE17 68 A4
Chatsfield Pl. W5 55 H6
Chatsworth Ave. 38 J2
NW4
Chatsworth Ave. 93 B1
SW20
Chatsworth Ave., 87 H5
Brom.
Chatsworth Ave., 89 A1
Sid.
Chatsworth Ave., 46 J5
Wem.
Chatsworth Clo. NW4 38 J2
Chatsworth Clo., 22 A3
Borwd.
Chatsworth Clo., 103 F2
W.Wick.
Chatsworth Ct. W8 66 D4
Pembroke Rd.
Chatsworth Cres., 73 A4
Houns.
Chatsworth Dr., Enf. 25 D7
Chatsworth Est. E5 50 G4
Elderfield Rd.
Chatsworth Gdns. W3 65 B1
Chatsworth Gdns., 45 H1
Har.
Chatsworth Gdns., 92 F5
N.Mal.
Chatsworth Pl., 93 J3
Mitch.
Chatsworth Pl., Tedd. 82 D4
Chatsworth Ri. W5 55 J4
Chatsworth Rd. E5 50 F3
Chatsworth Rd. E15 51 F5
Chatsworth Rd. NW2 48 A6
Chatsworth Rd. W4 65 C6
Chatsworth Rd. W5 55 J4
Chatsworth Rd., 102 A4
Croy.
Chatsworth Rd., 54 B4
Hayes
Chatsworth Rd., 100 A5
Sutt.
Chatsworth Way 85 H3
SE27
Chatterton Rd. N4 49 H3
Chatterton Rd., 97 A4
Brom.
Chatto Rd. SW11 75 J5
Chaucer Ave., Hayes 54 A5
Chaucer Ave., Houns. 72 B2
Chaucer Ave., Rich. 74 A3
Chaucer Clo. N11 32 C5
Chaucer Dr. SE1 21 G2
Chaucer Dr. SE1 68 C4
Chaucer Gdns., 100 D3
Sutt.
Chaucer Grn., Croy. 95 F7

Chaucer Rd. E7 51 G6
Chaucer Rd. E11 42 G6
Chaucer Rd. E17 42 C2
Chaucer Rd. SE24 76 G5
Chaucer Rd. W3 65 C1
Chaucer Rd., Sid. 89 C1
Chaucer Rd., Sutt. 100 D4
Chaucer Rd., Well. 79 J1
Chaucer Way SW19 84 G6
Chauncey Clo. N9 33 D3
Chaundrye Clo. SE9 79 B6
Chauntler Rd. E16 60 H7
Victoria Dock Rd.
Cheam Common Rd., Wor.Pk. 99 H2
Cheam Mans., Sutt. 100 B7
Cheam Pk. Way, Sutt. 100 B6
Cheam Rd. (SM1), Sutt. 100 C6
Cheam St. SE15 77 E3
Evelina Rd.
Cheapside EC2 12 J4
Cheapside EC2 58 J6
Cheddar Waye, Hayes 54 B6
Cheddington Rd. N18 33 B3
Chedworth Clo. E16 60 F6
Hallsville Rd.
Cheeseman Clo., Hmptn. 81 E6
Cheesemans Ter. W14 66 C5
Chelford Rd., Brom. 87 D5
Chelmer Cres., Bark. 62 B2
Chelmer Rd. E9 50 G5
Chelmsford Clo. E6 61 C6
Guildford Rd.
Chelmsford Clo. W6 66 A6
Chelmsford Gdns., Ilf. 43 B7
Chelmsford Rd. E11 51 D1
Chelmsford Rd. E17 42 A6
Chelmsford Rd. E18 42 F1
Chelmsford Rd. N14 24 C7
Chelmsford Sq. NW10 56 J1
Chelsea Bri. SW1 19 D5
Chelsea Bri. SW1 67 B6
Chelsea Bri. SW8 19 D5
Chelsea Bri. SW8 67 B6
Chelsea Bri. Rd. SW1 19 B3
Chelsea Bri. Rd. SW1 67 A5
Chelsea Cloisters SW3 18 H2
Chelsea Clo. NW10 56 D1
Winchelsea Rd.
Chelsea Clo., Edg. 38 A2
Chelsea Clo., Hmptn. 81 J6
Chelsea Embk. SW3 18 H6
Chelsea Embk. SW3 66 H6
Chelsea Gdns., Sutt. 100 B4
Chelsea Harbour Dr. SW10 75 F1
Chelsea Manor Gdns. SW3 18 H4
Chelsea Manor Gdns. SW3 66 H5
Chelsea Manor St. SW3 18 H4
Chelsea Manor St. SW3 66 H5
Chelsea Pk. Gdns. SW3 18 E5
Chelsea Pk. Gdns. SW3 66 G6
Chelsea Sq. SW3 18 F3
Chelsea Sq. SW3 66 G5
Chelsea Wf. SW10 66 G7
Lots Rd.
Chelsfield Ave. N9 25 G7
Chelsfield Gdns. SE26 86 F3
Chelsham Rd. SW4 76 D3
Chelsham Rd., S.Croy. 102 A6
Chelston App., Ruis. 45 A2
Chelston Rd., Ruis. 45 A1
Chelsworth Dr. SE18 70 G6
Cheltenham Ave., Twick. 73 D7
Cheltenham Clo., N.Mal. 92 C3
Northcote Rd.
Cheltenham Clo., Nthlt. 45 H6
Cheltenham Gdns. E6 61 B2
Cheltenham Gdns., Loug. 27 B6
Cheltenham Pl. W3 65 B1
Cheltenham Pl., Har. 37 H4
Cheltenham Rd. E10 42 C6
Cheltenham Rd. SE15 77 F4
Cheltenham Ter. SW3 19 A3
Cheltenham Ter. SW3 66 J5
Chelverton Rd. SW15 75 A4
Chelwood Clo. E4 26 B6
Chelwood Gdns., Rich. 74 A2
Chelwood Wk. SE4 77 H4
Chenappa Clo. E13 60 G3
Chenduit Way, Stan. 29 C5
Cheney Rd. NW1 8 A2
Cheney Rd. NW1 58 E2
Cheney Row E17 41 J1
Cheney St., Pnr. 36 C5
Cheneys Rd. E11 51 E3
Chenies, The, Orp. 97 H6
Chenies Ms. WC1 7 H6
Chenies Pl. NW1 7 J1
Chenies Pl. NW1 58 D2
Chenies St. WC1 11 H1
Chenies St. WC1 58 D5
Cheniston Gdns. W8 14 A5
Cheniston Gdns. W8 66 E3
Chepstow Clo. SW15 75 B6
Lytton Gro.
Chepstow Cres. W11 57 D7
Chepstow Cres., Ilf. 43 H6
Chepstow Gdns., Sthl. 54 F6
Chepstow Pl. W2 57 D6
Chepstow Ri., Croy. 102 B3
Chepstow Rd. W2 57 D6
Chepstow Rd. W7 64 D3
Chepstow Rd., Croy. 102 B3
Chepstow Vill. W11 57 C7
Chepstow Way SE15 68 C7
Exeter Rd.
Chequer St. EC1 9 A6
Chequers Clo., Orp. 97 J4
Chequers Gdns. N13 32 H5
Chequers La., Dag. 62 F5
Chequers Rd., Loug. 27 D5
Chequers Way N13 32 H5
Cherbury Clo. SE28 62 D6
Cherbury St. N1 9 C2
Cherbury St. N1 59 A2
Cherchefelle Ms., Stan. 29 E5
Cherimoya Gdns., W.Mol. 90 H3
Kelvinbrook
Cherington Rd. W7 64 C1
Cheriton Ave., Brom. 96 F5
Cheriton Ave., Ilf. 43 C2
Cheriton Clo. W5 55 F5
Cheriton Dr. SE18 70 G7
Cheriton Sq. SW17 85 A2
Cherry Ave., Sthl. 63 D1
Cherry Clo. SW2 76 G7
Tulse Hill
Cherry Clo. W5 64 G3
Cherry Clo., Cars. 100 J2
Cherry Clo., Mord. 93 B4
Cherry Cres., Brent. 64 E7
Cherry Gdn. St. SE16 68 E2
Cherry Gdns., Dag. 53 F5
Cherry Garth, Brent. 64 G5
Cherry Gro., Hayes 63 B1
Cherry Hill, Barn. 23 E6
Cherry Hill Gdns., Croy. 101 F4
Cherry Laurel Wk. SW2 76 F6
Beechdale Rd.
Cherry Orchard Gdns., Croy. 102 A2
Oval Rd.
Cherry Orchard Gdns., W.Mol. 90 F3
Cherry Orchard Rd., Brom. 104 B2
Cherry Orchard Rd., Croy. 102 A2
Cherry Orchard Rd., W.Mol. 90 F3
Cherry Tree Clo., Wem. 46 C4
Cherry Tree Ct. NW9 38 C4
Cherry Tree Dr. SW16 85 E3
Cherry Tree Ri., Buck.H. 34 J4
Cherry Tree Rd. E15 51 E4
Wingfield Rd.
Cherry Tree Rd. N2 39 J4
Cherry Tree Wk., Beck. 95 J4
Cherry Tree Wk., W.Wick. 103 F4
Cherry Tree Way, Stan. 29 E6
Cherry Wk., Brom. 103 G1
Cherry Way, Epsom 99 D6
Cherry Wd. Way W5 56 A5
Hanger Vale La.
Cherrycot Hill, Orp. 104 G4
Cherrycot Ri., Orp. 104 F4
Cherrycroft Gdns., Pnr. 28 F7
Westfield Pk.
Cherrydown Ave. E4 33 J3
Cherrydown Clo. E4 33 J3
Cherrydown Rd., Sid. 89 D2
Cherrydown Wk., Rom. 44 H2
Cherrywood Clo., Kings.T. 83 A7
Cherrywood Dr. SW15 75 A5
Cherrywood La., Mord. 93 B4
Cherston Gdns., Loug. 27 D4
Cherston Rd.
Cherston Rd., Loug. 27 D4
Chertsey Dr., Sutt. 100 B2
Chertsey Rd. E11 51 D2
Chertsey Rd., Ilf. 52 G4
Chertsey Rd., Twick. 73 C6
Chertsey St. SW17 85 A5
Chervil Clo., Felt. 81 A3
Chervil Ms. SE28 71 B1
Cherwell Ct., Epsom 99 C4
Cheryls Clo. SW6 75 E1
Cheseman St. SE26 86 E3
Chesfield Rd., Kings.T. 82 H7
Chesham Ave., Orp. 97 E6
Chesham Clo. SW1 15 B6
Chesham Cres. SE20 95 F2
Chesham Ms. SW1 15 B5
Chesham Ms. SW1 67 A3
Chesham Pl. SW1 15 B6
Chesham Pl. SW1 67 A3
Chesham Rd. SE20 95 F2
Chesham Rd. SW19 84 G5
Chesham Rd., Kings.T. 92 A2
Chesham St. NW10 47 D3
Chesham St. SW1 15 B6
Chesham St. SW1 67 A3
Chesham Ter. W13 64 E2
Cheshire Clo. SE4 77 J2
Cheshire Clo., Mitch. 94 E3
Cheshire Gdns., Chess. 98 G6
Cheshire Rd. N22 32 F6
Cheshire St. E2 9 G5
Cheshire St. E2 59 C4
Chesholm Rd. N16 50 B3
Cheshunt Rd. E7 51 H6
Cheshunt Rd., Belv. 71 G5
Chesilton Rd. SW6 75 C1
Chesley Gdns. E6 61 A2
Chesney Cres., Croy. 103 C7
Chesney St. SW11 76 A1
Chesnut Est. N17 41 C3
Chesnut Rd.
Chesnut Gro. N17 41 C3
Chesnut Rd.
Chesnut Rd. N17 41 C3
Chessington Ave. N3 39 B3
Chessington Ave., Bexh. 71 E7
Chessington Clo., Epsom 99 C6
Chessington Ct., Pnr. 36 F4
Chessington Hall Gdns., Chess. 98 G7
Chessington Hill Pk., Chess. 99 A5
Chessington Lo. N3 39 C3
Chessington Rd., Epsom 99 B6
Chessington Way, W.Wick. 103 B2
Chesson Rd. W14 66 C6
Chesswood Way, Pnr. 36 D2
Chester Ave., Rich. 73 J6
Chester Ave., Twick. 81 F1
Chester Clo. SW1 15 D4
Chester Clo. SW1 67 B2
Chester Clo. SW13 74 H3
Chester Clo., Loug. 27 F1
Chester Clo., Sutt. 100 D2
Broomloan La.
Chester Clo. N. NW1 7 E3
Chester Clo. S. NW1 7 E4
Chester Cotts. SW1 19 B2
Chester Ct. NW1 7 E3
Chester Ct. SE5 68 A7
Chester Cres. E8 50 C6
Ridley Rd.
Chester Dr., Har. 36 F6
Chester Gdns. W13 55 E6
Chester Gdns., Enf. 25 E6
Chester Gdns., Mord. 93 F6
Chester Gate NW1 7 D4
Chester Gate NW1 58 B3
Chester Grn., Loug. 27 F1
Chester Ms. SW1 15 D5
Chester Ms. SW1 67 B3
Chester Path, Loug. 27 F1
Chester Pl. NW1 7 D3
Chester Rd. E7 52 A7
Chester Rd. E11 42 H6
Chester Rd. E16 60 E4
Chester Rd. E17 41 G5
Chester Rd. N9 33 E1
Chester Rd. N17 41 A3
Chester Rd. N19 49 B2
Chester Rd. NW1 7 C4
Chester Rd. NW1 58 A3
Chester Rd. SW19 83 J6
Chester Rd., Borwd. 22 C3
Chester Rd., Chig. 35 D2
Chester Rd., Houns. 72 B3
Chester Rd., Ilf. 52 J1
Chester Rd., Loug. 27 E2
Chester Rd., Sid. 79 H5
Chester Row SW1 19 B2
Chester Row SW1 67 A4
Chester Sq. SW1 19 C1
Chester Sq. SW1 67 A4
Chester Sq. Ms. SW1 15 D6
Chester St. E2 9 J5
Chester St. E2 59 D4
Chester St. SW1 15 C5
Chester St. SW1 67 A3
Chester Ter. NW1 7 D3
Chester Way SE11 20 F2
Chester Way SE11 67 G4
Chesterfield Dr., Esher 98 D2
Chesterfield Gdns. N4 40 H5
Chesterfield Gdns. SE10 69 D7
Crooms Hill
Chesterfield Gdns. W1 15 D1
Chesterfield Gdns. W1 67 B1
Chesterfield Gro. SE22 77 C5
Chesterfield Hill W1 15 D1
Chesterfield Hill W1 67 B1
Chesterfield Rd. E10 42 C6
Chesterfield Rd. N3 31 D6
Chesterfield Rd. W4 65 C6
Chesterfield Rd., Barn. 23 A5
Chesterfield Rd., Epsom 99 D7
Chesterfield St. W1 15 D1
Chesterfield St. W1 67 B1
Chesterfield Wk. SE10 78 D1
Chesterfield Way SE15 68 F7
Chesterfield Way, Hayes 63 A2
Chesterford Gdns. NW3 48 E4
Chesterford Ho. SE18 70 A7
Shooter's Hill Rd.
Chesterford Rd. E12 52 C5
Chesters, The, N.Mal. 92 E1
Chesterton Clo. SW18 75 D5
Ericcson Clo.
Chesterton Clo., Grnf. 54 H2
Chesterton Rd. E13 60 G3
Chesterton Rd. W10 57 A5
Chesterton Ter. E13 60 G3
Chesterton Ter., Kings.T. 92 A2
Chesthunte Rd. N17 40 J1
Chestnut All. SW6 66 C6
Lillie Rd.
Chestnut Ave. E7 51 H4
Chestnut Ave. N8 40 E5
Chestnut Ave. SW14 74 D3
Thornton Rd.
Chestnut Ave., Brent. 64 G4
Chestnut Ave., Buck.H. 35 A3
Chestnut Ave., E.Mol. 91 C3
Chestnut Ave., Edg. 29 H6
Chestnut Ave., Epsom 99 E4
Chestnut Ave., Esher 91 A7
Chestnut Ave., Hmptn. 81 G7
Chestnut Ave., Tedd. 91 C2
Chestnut Ave., Wem. 46 E5
Chestnut Ave., W.Wick. 103 E5

Chestnut Ave. N. E17 42 C4
Chestnut Ave. S. E17 42 C4
Chestnut Clo. N14 24 C5
Chestnut Clo. N16 50 A2
Lordship Gro.
Chestnut Clo. SE6 87 C5
Buckt H
Chestnut Clo., 35 A3
Buckt H
Chestnut Clo., Cars. 100 J1
North End Rd.
Chestnut Ct. SW6 66 C6
North End Rd.
Chestnut Dr. E11 42 G6
Chestnut Dr., Bexh. 80 D3
Chestnut Dr., Har. 29 C7
Chestnut Dr., Pnr. 36 D6
Chestnut Gro. SW12 76 A7
Chestnut Gro. W5 64 G3
Chestnut Gro., Barn. 23 J5
Chestnut Gro., Ilf. 35 H6
Chestnut Gro., Islw. 73 D4
Chestnut Gro., Mitch. 94 D5
Chestnut Gro., N.Mal. 92 D3
Chestnut Gro., 102 E7
S.Croy.
Chestnut Gro., Wem. 46 E5
Chestnut La. N20 31 B1
Chestnut Ri. SE18 70 H5
Chestnut Rd. SE27 85 H2
Chestnut Rd. SW20 93 A2
Chestnut Rd., 82 H7
Kings.T.
Chestnut Rd., 82 B2
Twick.
Chestnut Wk., 34 G5
Wdf.Grn.
Chestnut Way, Felt. 81 B3
Cheston Ave., Croy. 102 H2
Chettle Clo. SE1   17   B5
Chettle Ct. N8 40 G6
Chetwode Rd. SW17 84 J3
Chetwynd Ave., Barn. 31 J1
Chetwynd Rd. NW5 49 B4
Cheval Pl. SW7   14   H5
Cheval Pl. SW7 66 H3
Cheval St. E14 69 A3
Cheveney Wk., Brom. 96 G3
Marina Clo.
Chevening Rd. NW6 57 A2
Chevening Rd. SE10 69 F5
Chevening Rd. SE19 86 A6
Chevenings, The, 89 C3
Sid.
Cheverton Rd. N19 49 D1
Chevet St. E9 50 H5
Kenworthy Rd.
Cheviot Clo., Enf. 25 A2
Cheviot Gdns. NW2 48 A2
Cheviot Gate NW2 48 B2
Cheviot Rd. SE27 85 G5
Cheviot Way, Ilf. 43 H4
Chevron Clo. E16 60 G6
Butchers Rd.
Chewton Rd. E17 41 H4
Cheyne Ave. E18 42 F3
Cheyne Ave., Twick. 81 F1
Cheyne Clo. NW4 38 J6
Cheyne Wk.
Cheyne Clo., Brom. 104 B3
Cedar Cres.
Cheyne Ct. SW3   18   J5
Cheyne Gdns. SW3   18   H5
Cheyne Gdns. SW3 66 H6
Cheyne Hill, Surb. 91 J4
Cheyne Ms. SW3   18   H6
Cheyne Pl. SW3   18   J5
Cheyne Row SW3   18   G6
Cheyne Row SW3 66 H6
Cheyne Wk. N21 24 H5
Cheyne Wk. NW4 38 J6
Cheyne Wk. SW3   18   H6
Cheyne Wk. SW3 66 H6
Cheyne Wk. SW10   18   E7
Cheyne Wk. SW10 66 G7
Cheyne Wk., Croy. 102 D3
Cheyneys Ave., Edg. 29 G6
Chichele Gdns., 102 C4
Croy.
Brownlow Rd.
Chichele Rd. NW2 48 A5
Chicheley Gdns., 28 J7
Har.
Chicheley Rd., Har. 28 J7
Chicheley St. SE1   16   D3
Chicheley St. SE1 67 F2
Chichester Clo. E6 61 B6
Chichester Clo. SE3 78 J1
Chichester Clo., 81 F6
Hmptn.
Maple Clo.
Chichester Ct., Stan. 37 H3
Chichester Gdns., Ilf. 43 B7
Chichester Ms. SE27 85 G4

Chichester Rents   12   E3
WC2
Chichester Rd. E11 51 E3
Chichester Rd. N9 33 D2
Chichester Rd. NW6 57 D2
Chichester Rd. W2 10 B1
Chichester Rd., 102 B3
Crov.
Chichester St. SW1   19   G4
Chichester St. SW1 67 C5
Chichester Way E14 69 D4
Chichester Way, Felt. 72 C7
Chicksand St. E1   13   G2
Chicksand St. E1 59 C5
Chiddingfold N12 31 D3
Chiddingstone Ave., 71 F7
Bexh.
Chiddingstone St. 75 D2
SW6
Chieveley Rd., 80 H4
Bexh.
Chignell Pl. W13 64 D1
The Bdy.
Chigwell Hill E1 59 E7
Pennington St.
Chigwell Hurst Ct., 36 D2
Pnr.
Chigwell La., Loug. 25 F2
Chigwell Pk. Dr., 35 D3
Chig.
Chigwell Ri., Chig. 35 D2
Chigwell Rd. E18 42 H3
Chigwell Rd. E18 35 A7
Wdf.Grn.
Chilcot Clo. E14 60 B6
Grundy St.
Childebert Rd. SW17 85 B2
Childeric Rd. SE14 68 H7
Childerley St. SW6 75 A1
Fulham Palace Rd.
Childers, The, 35 C5
Wdf.Grn.
Childers St. SE8 68 H6
Childs La. SE19 86 B6
Westow St.
Child's Pl. SW5 66 D4
Child's St. SW5 66 D4
Child's Wk. SW5 66 D4
Child's Pl.
Childs Way NW11 39 C5
Chilham Clo., Bexh. 55 D2
Chilham Rd. SE9 88 B4
Chilham Way, Brom. 96 G7
Chillerton Rd. SW17 85 A5
Chillingworth Gdns., 82 C3
Twick.
Tower Rd.
Chillingworth Rd. N7 49 G5
Liverpool Rd.
Chilmark Gdns., 92 F7
N.Mal.
Chilmark Rd. SW16 94 D2
Chiltern Ave., 81 G1
Twick.
Chiltern Clo., Croy. 102 B3
Chiltern Clo., Wor.Pk. 99 J2
Cotswold Way
Chiltern Dene, Enf. 24 F4
Chiltern Dr., Surb. 92 A6
Chiltern Gdns. NW2 48 A3
Chiltern Gdns., Brom. 96 F4
Chiltern Rd. E3 60 A4
Knapp Rd.
Chiltern Rd., Ilf. 43 H4
Chiltern Rd., Pnr. 36 C5
Chiltern St. W1   11   B1
Chiltern St. W1 58 A5
Chiltern Way, 34 G3
Wdf.Grn.
Chilthorne Clo. SE6 77 J7
Ravensbourne Pk. Cres.
Chilton Ave. W5 64 G4
Chilton Gro. SE8 68 G4
Chilton Rd., Edg. 30 A6
Manor Pk. Cres.
Chilton Rd., Rich. 74 A3
Chilton St. E2   9   G5
Chilton St. E2 59 C4
Chiltonian Ind. Est. 78 F6
SE12
Chiltons, The E18 42 G2
Grove Hill
Chilver St. SE10 69 F5
Chilwell Gdns., Wat. 26 B1
Chilworth Ct. SW19 84 A1
Chilworth Gdns., 100 F3
Sutt.
Chilworth Ms. W2   10   E4
Chilworth Ms. W2 57 G6
Chilworth St. W2   10   D4
Chilworth St. W2 57 F6
Chimes Ave. N13 32 G5

Chinbrook Cres. 87 H3
SE12
Chinbrook Rd.
Chinbrook Est. SE9 88 A3
Chinbrook Rd. SE12 87 H3
Chinchilla Dr., 72 C2
Il...
Chine, The N10 40 C4
Chine, The N21 24 H6
Chine, The, Wem. 46 E5
Ching Ct. WC2   12   A4
Chingdale Rd. E4 34 E3
Chingford Ave. E4 34 A3
Chingford Hall Est. 33 J6
E4
Chingford Ind. Est. 33 H5
E4
Chingford La., 34 E4
Wdf.Grn.
Chingford Mt. Rd. 34 A4
E4
Chingford Rd. E4 34 A6
Chingford Rd. E17 42 B1
Chingley Clo., Brom. 87 E6
Chinnor Cres., Grnf. 54 H2
Chip St. SW4 76 D3
Chipka St. E14 69 C2
Chipley St. SE14 68 H6
Nynehead St.
Chipmunk Gro., Nthlt. 54 E3
Argus Way
Chippendale St. E5 50 G3
Chippenham Ave., 47 B5
Wem.
Chippenham Gdns. 57 D3
NW6
Chippenham Ms. W9 57 D4
Chippenham Rd. W9 57 D4
Chipping Clo., Barn. 23 B3
St. Albans Rd.
Chipstead Ave., 94 H4
Th.Hth.
Chipstead Clo. SE19 86 C7
Chipstead Gdns. NW2 47 H2
Chipstead St. SW6 75 D1
Chirk Clo., Hayes 54 E4
Braunston Clo.
Chisenhale Rd. E3 59 H2
Chisholm Rd., Croy. 102 B3
Chisholm Rd., Rich. 73 J6
Chisledon W. E9 50 J4
Trowbridge Est.
Chislehurst Ave. N12 31 F7
Chislehurst Rd., 97 A2
Brom.
Chislehurst Rd., Chis. 97 C1
Chislehurst Rd., Orp. 97 H6
Chislehurst Rd., 73 H5
Rich.
Chislehurst Rd., Sid. 89 A5
Chislet Clo., Beck. 87 A7
Abbey La.
Chisley Rd. N15 41 B6
Chiswell Sq. SE3 78 H2
Brook La.
Chiswell St. EC1   13   B1
Chiswell St. EC1 59 A5
Chiswick Bri. SW14 74 C2
Chiswick Bri. W4 74 C2
Chiswick Clo., Croy. 101 F3
Chiswick Common 65 D4
Rd. W4
Chiswick Ct., Pnr. 36 F3
Chiswick Gdns. W4 74 C1
Hartington Rd.
Chiswick High Rd. 65 A5
W4
Chiswick Ho. Grds. 65 D6
W4
Hogarth Roundabout
Chiswick La. W4 65 E5
Chiswick La. S. W4 65 F5
Chiswick Mall W4 65 F6
Chiswick Mall W6 65 G5
Chiswick Quay W4 74 C1
Chiswick Rd. N9 33 D2
Chiswick Rd. W4 65 C4
Chiswick Sq. W4 65 E6
Hogarth Roundabout
Chiswick Staithe W4 74 C1
Chiswick Vill. W4 65 B6
Chiswick Wf. W4 65 F6
Chitty St. W1   11   G1
Chitty St. W1 58 C5
Chitty's La., Dag. 53 D2
Chivalry Rd. SW11 75 H5
Chivers Rd. E4 34 B4
Choats Manor Way, 62 B4
Bark.
Renwick Rd.
Choats Rd., Dag. 62 E3
Chobham Gdns. 84 A2
SW19

Chobham Rd. E15 51 D5
Cholmeley Cres. N6 40 B7
Cholmeley Pk. N6 49 B1
Cholmley Gdns. NW6 48 D5
Fortune Grn. Rd.
Cholmley Rd., 91 E6
T.Ditt
Cholmondeley Ave. 56 G2
NW10
Cholmondeley Wk., 73 F5
Rich.
Choppins Ct. E1 68 E1
Wapping La.
Chopwell Clo. E15 51 D7
Bryant St.
Chorleywood Cres., 97 J2
Orp.
Choumert Gro. SE15 77 D2
Choumert Rd. SE15 77 C3
Choumert Sq. SE15 77 D2
Chrisp St. E14 60 B5
Christ Ch. Rd. SW14 74 B5
Christ Ch. Rd., Beck. 96 A2
Fairfield Rd.
Christchurch Ave. 31 F6
N12
Christchurch Ave. 57 A1
NW6
Christchurch Ave., 37 C4
Har.
Christchurch Ave., 82 D5
Tedd.
Christchurch Ave., 46 H6
Wem.
Christchurch Clo. 84 G7
SW19
Christchurch Gdns., 37 D4
Har.
Christchurch Grn., 46 H6
Wem.
Christchurch Hill 48 G3
NW3
Christchurch Ind. 37 C4
Cen., Har.
Christchurch La., 23 B2
Barn.
Christchurch Pk., 100 F7
Sutt.
Christchurch Pas. 48 G3
NW3
Christchurch Pas., 23 B3
Barn.
Christchurch La.
Christchurch Rd. N8 40 E6
Christchurch Rd. 85 F1
SW2
Christchurch Rd. 93 G1
SW19
Christchurch Rd., Ilf. 52 E1
Christchurch Rd., 88 J4
Sid.
Christchurch Rd., 91 J7
Surb.
Christchurch Sq. E9 59 F1
Victoria Pk. Rd.
Christchurch St. SW3 18   J5
Christchurch St. SW3 66 H6
Christchurch Ter.   18   J5
SW3
Christchurch Way 69 E5
SE10
Christian Ct. SE16 68 J1
Christian Flds. SW16 85 G7
Christian St. E1   13   J3
Christian St. E1 59 D6
Christie Gdns., Rom. 44 B6
Christie Rd. E9 50 H6
Christina Clo. N4 49 H1
Adolphus Rd.
Christina St. EC2   9   D5
Christopher Ave. W7 64 D3
Christopher Clo. 68 G2
SE16
Christopher Clo., Sid. 79 J5
Christopher Gdns., 53 D5
Dag.
Wren Rd.
Christopher Pl. NW1   7   J4
Christopher Rd., 63 B4
Sthl.
Christopher St. EC2   9   C6
Christopher St. EC2 59 A5
Christopher's Ms. 66 B1
W11
Penzance St.
Chryssell Rd. SW9 67 G7
Chubworthy St. SE14 68 H6
Chudleigh Cres., 52 H4
Ilf.
Chudleigh Gdns., 100 F3
Sutt.
Chudleigh Rd. NW6 48 A7

Chudleigh Rd. SE4	77	J5
Chudleigh Rd.,	73	B6
Twick.		
Chudleigh St. E1	59	G6
Chudleigh Way, Ruis.	45	A1
Chulsa Rd. SE26	86	E5
Chumleigh St. SE5	**21**	**D5**
Chumleigh St. SE5	68	B6
Chumleigh Wk., Surb.	91	J4
Church All., Croy.	94	H7
Handcroft Rd.		
Church App. SE21	86	A3
Church Ave. E4	34	D6
Church Ave. NW1	49	B6
Kentish Town Rd.		
Church Ave. SW14	74	D3
Church Ave., Beck.	96	A1
Church Ave., Nthlt.	45	F7
Church Ave., Pnr.	36	E6
Church Ave., Sid.	89	A5
Church Ave., Sthl.	63	E3
Church Clo. N20	31	H3
Church Clo. W8	**14**	**A3**
Church Clo., Edg.	30	C5
Church Clo., Loug.	27	C2
Church Ct., Rich.	73	G5
George St.		
Church Cres. E9	50	G7
Church Cres. N3	39	C1
Church Cres. N10	40	B4
Church Cres. N20	31	H3
Church Dr. NW9	47	D1
Church Dr., Har.	36	F6
Church Dr., W.Wick.	103	E3
Church Elm La., Dag.	53	G6
Church End E17	42	B4
Church End NW4	38	H3
Church Fm. La.,	100	B6
Sutt.		
Church Gdns. W5	64	G2
Church Gdns., Wem.	46	D4
Church Gate SW6	75	B3
Church Gro. SE13	78	B4
Church Gro.,	91	F1
Kings.T.		
Church Hill E17	42	A4
Church Hill N21	24	F7
Church Hill SE18	70	C3
Church Hill SW19	84	C5
Church Hill, Cars.	100	J5
Church Hill, Har.	46	B1
Church Hill, Loug.	27	C3
Church Hill Rd. E17	42	B4
Church Hill Rd., Barn.	23	H6
Church Hill Rd.,	91	H5
Surb.		
Church Hill Rd.,	100	A4
Sutt.		
Church Hyde SE18	70	H6
Old Mill Rd.		
Church La. E11	51	E1
Church La. E17	42	B4
Church La. N2	39	F3
Church La. N8	40	F4
Church La. N9	33	D2
Church La. N17	41	B1
Church La. NW9	38	C6
Church La. SW17	85	B5
Church La. SW19	93	C1
Church La. W5	64	F2
Church La., Brom.	104	B1
Church La., Chess.	98	J6
Church La., Chis.	97	F1
Church La., Dag.	53	H6
Church La., Enf.	25	A3
Church La., Har.	37	C1
Church La., Loug.	27	C3
Church La., Pnr.	36	E3
Church La., Tedd.	82	C5
Church La., T.Ditt.	91	C6
Church La., Twick.	82	D1
Church La., Wall.	101	D3
Church Manor Est.	67	G7
SW9		
Vassall Rd.		
Church Manorway	71	A5
SE2		
Church Meadow,	98	F2
Surb.		
Church Mt. N2	39	G5
Church Pas., Barn.	23	C4
Wood St.		
Church Pas., Surb.	91	H5
Adelaide Rd.		
Church Path E11	42	G5
Church Path N5	49	H5
Church Path N12	31	F5
Church Path N17	33	B7
White Hart La.		
Church Path NW4	31	F4
Church Path NW10	47	E7
Church Path SW14	74	D3
North Worple Way		
Church Path SW19	93	C2
Church Path W4	65	C3
Church Path W7	64	B1
Station Rd.		
Church Path, Croy.	101	J2
Keeley Rd.		
Church Path, Mitch.	93	H3
Church Path, Sthl.	63	F3
Church Pl. SW1	**11**	**G6**
Church Pl. W5	64	G2
Church Pl., Mitch.	93	H3
Church Pl., Twick.	82	E1
Church St.		
Church Ri. SE23	86	G2
Church Ri., Chess.	98	J6
Church Rd. E10	51	A1
Church Rd. E12	52	B5
Church Rd. E17	41	H2
Church Rd. N6	40	A6
Church Rd. N17	41	B1
Church Rd. NW4	38	H4
Church Rd. NW10	47	E7
Church Rd. SE19	95	B1
Church Rd. SW13	74	F2
Church Rd. (Merton)	93	G1
SW19		
Church Rd.	84	B5
(Wimbledon) SW19		
Church Rd. W3	65	C1
Church Rd. W7	55	A7
Church Rd., Bark.	52	F6
Church Rd., Bexh.	80	F3
Church Rd., Brom.	96	G2
Church Rd.	96	E3
(Shortlands), Brom.		
Church Rd., Buck.H.	34	H1
Church Rd., Croy.	101	H2
Church Rd., E.Mol.	91	A4
Church Rd., Enf.	25	F6
Church Rd.	99	D7
(West Ewell), Epsom		
Church Rd., Erith	71	J5
Church Rd., Esher	98	C6
Church Rd., Felt.	81	D5
Church Rd., Houns.	63	B5
Church Rd., Ilf.	43	H6
Church Rd., Islw.	73	A1
Church Rd., Kes.	104	A7
Church Rd.,	91	J2
Kings.T.		
Church Rd., Loug.	26	G3
Church Rd., Mitch.	93	G3
Church Rd., Nthlt.	54	D2
Church Rd.	104	F5
(Farnborough), Orp.		
Church Rd., Rich.	73	H4
Church Rd. (Ham),	82	G4
Rich.		
Church Rd., Sid.	89	A4
Church Rd., Sthl.	63	F3
Church Rd., Stan.	29	E5
Church Rd., Surb.	98	F1
Church Rd., Sutt.	100	B6
Church Rd., Tedd.	82	B4
Church Rd., Wall.	101	C3
Church Rd., Well.	80	B2
Church Rd., Wor.Pk.	99	E2
Church Row NW3	48	F4
Church Row, Chis.	97	F1
Church St. E15	60	E1
Church St. E16	70	E1
Church St. N9	33	C2
Church St. NW8	**10**	**F1**
Church St. NW8	57	G5
Church St. W2	**10**	**F1**
Church St. W4	65	F6
Church St., Croy.	101	H3
Church St., Dag.	53	H6
Church St., Enf.	24	J3
Church St., Hmptn.	90	J2
Church St., Islw.	73	E3
Church St., Kings.T.	91	G2
Church St., Sun.	90	A3
Church St., Sutt.	100	E5
High St.		
Church St., Twick.	82	D1
Church St. Est. NW8	**6**	**F6**
Church St. Est. NW8	57	G4
Church St. N. E15	60	E1
Church St. Pas. E15	60	E1
Church St.		
Church Stretton Rd.,	72	J5
Houns.		
Church Ter. NW4	38	H3
Church Ter. SE13	78	E3
Church Ter. SW8	76	E2
Church Ter., Rich.	73	G5
Church Vale N2	39	J3
Church Vale SE23	86	F2
Church Wk. N16	50	A4
Church Wk. NW2	48	C3
Church Wk. NW4	38	J3
Church Wk. NW9	47	D2
Church Wk. SW13	74	G1
Church Wk. SW15	74	H5
St. Margarets Cres.		
Church Wk. SW16	94	C2
Church Wk. SW20	92	J3
Church Wk., Brent.	64	F6
Church Wk., Rich.	73	G5
Red Lion St.		
Church Wk., T.Ditt.	91	C6
Church Way N20	31	G3
Church Way, Barn.	23	J4
Church Way, Edg.	30	A6
Station Rd.		
Church Yd. Row	**20**	**H1**
SE11		
Churchbury Clo., Enf.	25	B2
Churchbury La., Enf.	25	A3
Churchbury Rd. SE9	79	A7
Churchbury Rd., Enf.	25	A2
Churchcroft Clo.	76	A7
SW12		
Endlesham Rd.		
Churchdown, Brom.	87	E4
Churchfield Ave. N12	31	F6
Churchfield Clo.,	36	J4
Har.		
Churchfield Rd. W3	65	C1
Churchfield Rd. W7	64	B2
Churchfield Rd. W13	64	E1
Churchfield Rd.,	80	A3
Well.		
Churchfields E18	42	G1
Churchfields SE10	69	C6
Roan St.		
Churchfields, Loug.	27	B4
Churchfields, W.Mol.	90	G3
Churchfields Ave.,	81	F3
Felt.		
Churchfields Rd.,	95	G2
Beck.		
Churchill Ave., Har.	37	E6
Churchill Ct. W5	55	J4
Churchill Ct., Nthlt.	45	G5
Churchill Gdns. W3	56	A6
Churchill Gdns. Est.	**19**	**F4**
SW1		
Churchill Gdns. Est.	67	C5
SW1		
Churchill Gdns. Rd.	**19**	**E4**
SW1		
Churchill Gdns. Rd.	67	B5
SW1		
Churchill Ms.,	34	F6
Wdf.Grn.		
High Rd.		
Churchill Pl. E14	69	B1
Churchill Rd. E16	60	J6
Churchill Rd. NW2	47	H6
Churchill Rd. NW5	49	B4
Churchill Rd., Edg.	29	J6
Churchill Ter. E4	34	A4
Churchill Wk. E9	50	F5
Churchill Way, Brom.	96	G3
Ethelbort Rd.		
Churchill Way, Sun.	81	A5
Churchley Rd. SE26	86	E4
Churchmead Clo.,	23	H6
Barn.		
Churchmead Rd.	47	G6
NW10		
Churchmore Rd.	94	C1
SW16		
Churchview Rd.,	82	A1
Twick.		
Churchway NW1	**7**	**J3**
Churchway NW1	58	D3
Churchwell Path E9	50	F6
Morning La.		
Churston Ave. E13	60	H1
Churston Clo. SW2	85	H1
Tulse Hill		
Churston Dr., Mord.	93	A5
Churston Gdns. N11	32	C6
Churton Pl. SW1	**19**	**G2**
Churton St. SW1	**19**	**G2**
Churton St. SW1	67	C4
Chusan Pl. E14	59	J6
Commercial Rd.		
Chyngton Clo., Sid.	88	J3
Cibber Rd. SE23	86	G2
Cicada Rd. SW18	75	F6
Cicely Rd. SE15	77	D1
Cinderford Way,	87	E4
Brom.		
Cinema Par. W5	55	J4
Ashbourne Rd.		
Cinnamon Row SW11	175	F3
Cinnamon St. E1	68	E1
Cintra Pk. SE19	86	C7
Circle, The NW2	47	E3
Circle, The NW7	30	D5
Circle Gdns. SW19	93	D2
Circuits, The, Pnr.	36	C4
Circular Rd. N17	41	C3
Circular Way SE18	70	C6
Circus Ms. W1	**10**	**J1**
Circus Pl. EC2	**13**	**C2**
Circus Rd. NW8	**6**	**E3**
Circus Rd. NW8	57	G3
Circus St. SE10	69	C7
Cirencester St. W2	**10**	**A1**
Cirencester St. W2	57	E5
Cissbury Ring N.	31	C5
N12		
Cissbury Ring S.	31	C5
N12		
Citadel Pl. SE11	**20**	**C3**
Citizen Rd. N7	49	G3
City Gdn. Row N1	**8**	**H2**
City Gdn. Row N1	58	H2
City Rd. EC1	**8**	**G2**
City Rd. EC1	58	H2
Civic Way, Ilf.	43	F4
Clabon Ms. SW1	**14**	**J6**
Clabon Ms. SW1	66	J3
Clack St. SE16	68	F2
Clacton Rd. E6	61	A3
Clacton Rd. E17	41	H6
Clacton Rd. N17	41	C2
Sperling Rd.		
Claigmar Gdns. N3	39	E1
Claire Ct. N12	31	F3
Claire Ct., Pnr.	28	F7
Westfield Pk.		
Claire Ct., Wal.	29	A1
Claire Pl. E14	69	A3
Clairvale Rd.,	72	D1
Houns.		
Clairview Rd. SW16	85	B5
Clairville Gdns. W7	64	B1
Clairville Pt. SE23	86	G3
Clamp Hill, Stan.	29	A4
Clancarty Rd. SW6	75	D2
Clandon Clo. W3	65	B2
Avenue Rd.		
Clandon Clo., Epsom	99	F6
Clandon Gdns. N3	39	D3
Clandon Rd., Ilf.	52	H2
Clandon St. SE8	78	A2
Clanfield Way SE15	**21**	**E7**
Clanricarde Gdns.	57	D7
W2		
Clap La., Dag.	53	H3
Clapham Common	75	J4
N. Side SW4		
Clapham Common	76	B6
S. Side SW4		
Clapham Common	75	J4
W. Side SW4		
Clapham Cres. SW4	76	D4
Clapham High St.	76	D4
SW4		
Clapham Junct. Est.	75	H4
SW11		
Clapham Manor St.	76	C3
SW4		
Clapham Pk. Est.	76	D6
SW4		
Clapham Pk. Rd. SW4	76	D4
Clapham Rd. SW9	76	E3
Clapham Rd. Est.	76	D3
SW4		
Claps Gate La., Bark.	61	E4
Clapton Common E5	41	C7
Clapton Pas. E5	50	F5
Lwr. Clapton Rd.		
Clapton Sq. E5	50	F5
Clapton Ter. N16	50	D1
Oldhill St.		
Clapton Way E5	50	D4
Clara Pl. SE18	70	D2
Clare Clo. N2	39	F3
Thomas More Way		
Clare Cor. SE9	79	E7
Clare Gdns. E7	51	G4
Clare Gdns. W11	57	B6
Westbourne Pk. Rd.		
Clare Gdns., Bark.	52	J6
Clare Gdns., Stan.	29	F5
Clare La. N1	49	J7
Clare Lawn Ave.	74	D5
SW14		
Clare Ms. WC2	**12**	**C4**
Clare Ms. SW6	66	E7
Waterford Rd.		
Clare Pl. SW15	74	F6
Minstead Gdns.		
Clare Rd. E11	42	D6
Clare Rd. NW10	47	G7
Clare Rd. SE14	77	J2
Clare Rd., Grnf.	86	D3
Clare Rd., Houns.	72	F3
Clare St. E2	59	E2

Clare Way, Bexh. 80 E1
Claredale St. E2 9 J2
Claredale St. E2 59 E2
Claremont Ave., Har. 37 H5
Claremont Ave., 92 H5
N.Mal.
Claremont Ave., Sun. 90 B1
Claremont Clo. E16 70 D1
Claremont Clo. N1 8 E2
Claremont Clo. N1 58 G2
Claremont Clo. SW2 85 F1
Garden La.
Claremont Gdns., Ilf. 52 H2
Claremont Gdns., 91 H5
Surb.
Claremont Gro. W4 65 E7
Edensor Gdns.
Claremont Gro., 34 J6
Wdf.Grn.
Claremont Pk. N3 39 B1
Claremont Rd. E7 51 H5
Claremont Rd. E11 51 D3
Claremont Rd. E17 41 H2
Claremont Rd. N6 40 B7
Claremont Rd. NW2 38 J7
Claremont Rd. W9 57 C2
Claremont Rd. W13 55 D5
Claremont Rd., Brom. 97 B4
Claremont Rd., 102 D1
Croy.
Claremont Rd., 98 B7
Esher
Claremont Rd., Har. 37 B2
Claremont Rd., Surb. 91 H6
Claremont Rd., 82 C5
Tedd.
Claremont Rd., 73 E6
Twick.
Claremont Sq. N1 8 E2
Claremont Sq. N1 58 G2
Claremont St. E16 70 D1
Claremont St. N18 33 D6
Claremont St. SE10 69 B6
Claremont Way NW2 47 J1
Clarence Ave. SW4 76 D7
Clarence Ave., Brom. 97 B4
Clarence Ave., Ilf. 43 D6
Clarence Ave., 92 C2
N.Mal.
Clarence Cres. SW4 76 D6
Clarence Cres., Sid. 89 B3
Clarence Gdns. NW1 7 E4
Clarence Gdns. NW1 58 B3
Clarence La. SW15 74 E6
Clarence Ms. E5 50 E5
Clarence Pas. NW1 8 A2
Clarence Pl. E5 50 E5
Clarence Rd. E5 50 E4
Clarence Rd. E12 52 A5
Clarence Rd. E16 60 E4
Clarence Rd. E17 41 G2
Clarence Rd. N15 40 J5
Clarence Rd. N22 32 E7
Clarence Rd. NW6 48 C7
Clarence Rd. SE9 88 B2
Clarence Rd. SW19 84 E6
Clarence Rd. W4 65 A5
Clarence Rd., Bexh. 80 E4
Clarence Rd., Brom. 97 A3
Clarence Rd., Croy. 95 A7
Clarence Rd., Enf. 25 E5
Clarence Rd., Rich. 73 J1
Clarence Rd., Sid. 89 B3
Clarence Rd., Sutt. 100 E4
Clarence Rd., Tedd. 82 C6
Clarence Rd., Wall. 101 B5
Clarence St., 91 H2
Kings.T.
Clarence St., Rich. 73 H4
Clarence St., Sthl. 63 D3
Clarence Ter. NW1 7 A5
Clarence Ter., 72 H4
Houns.
Clarence Wk. SW4 76 E2
Clarence Way NW1 49 B7
Clarence Way St. 49 B7
NW1
Clarendon Clo. W2 10 G5
Clarendon Cres. W11 57 B7
Clarendon Rd.
Clarendon Cres., 57 B7
Twick.
Clarendon Cross W11 57 B7
Portland Rd.
Clarendon Dr. SW15 74 J3
Clarendon Gdns. 38 G3
NW4
Clarendon Gdns. W9 6 D6
Clarendon Gdns., Ilf. 57 F4
Clarendon Gdns., 52 C1
Ilf.
Clarendon Gdns., 46 G3
Wem.

Clarendon Gro. NW1 7 H3
Clarendon Gro., 93 J3
Mitch.
Clarendon Ms. W2 10 G5
Clarendon Ms., 22 A3
Borwd.
Clarendon Rd.
Clarendon Pl. W2 10 G5
Clarendon Pl. W2 57 H7
Clarendon Ri. SE13 78 C3
Clarendon Rd. E11 51 D1
Clarendon Rd. E17 42 B6
Clarendon Rd. E18 42 G3
Clarendon Rd. N8 40 F3
Clarendon Rd. N15 40 H4
Clarendon Rd. N18 33 D6
Clarendon Rd. N22 40 F2
Clarendon Rd. SW19 84 H7
Clarendon Rd. W5 55 H4
Clarendon Rd. W11 57 B7
Clarendon Rd., 22 A3
Borwd.
Clarendon Rd., 101 H2
Croy.
Clarendon Rd., Har. 37 B6
Clarendon Rd., 101 C6
Wall.
Clarendon St. SW1 19 E3
Clarendon St. SW1 67 B5
Clarendon Ter. W9 6 D5
Clarendon Wk. W11 57 B6
Lancaster Rd.
Clarendon Way N21 24 J6
Clarendon Way, 97 J3
Chis.
Clarens St. SE6 86 J2
Claret Gdns. SE25 95 B4
Clareville Gro. SW7 18 D2
Clareville Gro. SW7 66 F4
Clareville Rd., Orp. 104 F2
Clareville St. SW7 18 D2
Clareville St. SW7 66 F4
Clarewood Wk. SW9 76 G4
Somerleyton Rd.
Clarges Ms. W1 15 H1
Clarges Ms. W1 67 B1
Clarges St. W1 15 E1
Clarges St. W1 67 B1
Claribel Rd. SW9 76 H2
Claridge Rd., Dag. 53 D1
Clarissa Rd., Rom. 44 D7
Clarissa St. E8 57 C1
Clark St. E1 59 E5
Clark Way, Houns. 63 D7
Clarke Path N16 50 D1
Braydon St.
Clarkes Ave. 100 A1
Wor.Pk.
Clarke's Ms. W1 11 C1
Clarks Pl. EC2 13 D3
Clarks Pl. EC2 59 B6
Clarks Rd., Ilf. 52 G2
Clarkson Rd. E16 60 F6
Clarkson St. E2 59 E3
Clarksons, The, 61 F2
Bark.
Claude Rd. E10 51 C2
Claude Rd. E13 60 H1
Claude Rd. SE15 77 E2
Claude St. E14 69 A4
Claudia Jones Way 76 E6
SW2
Claudia Pl. SW19 84 B1
Claughton Rd. E13 60 J2
Clauson Ave., Nthlt. 45 H5
Clave St. E1 68 E1
Cinnamon St.
Clavell St. SE10 69 C6
Claverdale Rd. SW2 76 F7
Clavering Ave. SW13 65 H6
Clavering Clo., 82 D4
Twick.
Clavering Rd. E12 52 A1
Claverings Ind. Est. 33 G2
N9
Claverley Gro. N3 39 E1
Claverley Vill. N3 31 E7
Claverley Gro.
Claverton St. SW1 19 G4
Claverton St. SW1 67 C5
Claxton Gro. W6 66 A5
Clay Ave., Mitch. 94 B2
Clay La., Edg. 30 A2
Clay La., The, Loug. 27 A1
Clay St. W1 11 A2
Claybank Gro. SE13 78 B3
Algernon Rd.
Claybourne Ms. SW19 86 B7
Church Rd.
Claybridge Rd. SE12 87 J4
Claybrook Clo. N2 39 G3
Long La.
Claybrook Rd. W6 66 A6

Claybury Bdy., Ilf. 43 B3
Claybury Rd., 35 B7
Wdf.Grn.
Claydon Dr., Croy. 101 E4
Clayfarm Rd. SE9 88 F2
Claygate Cres., 103 C6
Croy.
Claygate La., Esher 98 D3
Claygate La., T.Ditt. 98 D1
Claygate Lo. Clo., 98 B7
Esher
Claygate Rd. W13 64 E3
Clayhall Ave., Ilf. 43 B3
Clayhill, Surb. 92 A5
Clayhill Cres. SE9 88 A4
Claylands Pl. SW8 20 E7
Claylands Pl. SW8 67 G7
Claylands Rd. SW8 20 D6
Claylands Rd. SW8 67 F6
Claymill Ho. SE18 70 F5
Claymore Clo., 93 D7
Mord.
Claypole Rd. E15 60 C2
Clayponds Ave., 64 H4
Brent.
Clayponds Gdns. W5 64 G4
Clayponds La., 64 H5
Brent.
Clays La. E15 51 B5
Clays La., Loug. 27 D1
Clays La. Clo. E15 51 B5
Clayside, Chig. 35 F5
Clayton Ave., Wem. 46 H7
Clayton Clo. E6 61 C6
Brandreth Rd.
Clayton Cres., Brent. 64 G5
Clayton Fld. NW9 30 E7
Clayton Rd. SE15 77 D1
Clayton Rd., Chess. 98 F4
Clayton Rd., Islw. 73 B3
Clayton Rd., Rom. 51 J6
Clayton St. SE11 20 E5
Clayton St. SE11 67 G5
Claywood Clo., Orp. 97 H7
Clayworth Clo., Sid. 80 B6
Cleanthus Clo. SE18 79 E1
Cleanthus Rd.
Cleanthus Rd. SE18 79 E1
Clearbrook Way E1 59 G6
West Arbour St.
Clearwell Dr. W9 6 B6
Clearwell Dr. W9 57 F4
Cleave Ave., Orp. 104 H6
Cleaveland Rd., 91 G5
Surb.
Cleaver Sq. SE11 20 F3
Cleaver St. SE11 20 F3
Cleaver St. SE11 67 G5
Cleaverholme Clo. 95 E6
SE25
Cleeve Hill SE23 86 E1
Cleeve Pk. Gdns., 89 B2
Sid.
Clegg St. E1 68 E1
Prusom St.
Clegg St. E13 60 G2
Cleland Path, Loug. 27 E1
Clem Attlee Ct. SW6 66 C6
Clematis St. W12 56 G7
Clemence St. E14 59 J5
Clement Clo. NW6 47 F7
Clement Clo. W4 65 D4
Acton La.
Clement Rd. SW19 84 B5
Clement Rd., Beck. 95 G2
Clementhorpe Rd., 53 C6
Dag.
Clementina Rd. E10 50 J1
Clementine Clo. W13 64 E2
Balfour Rd.
Clements Ave. E16 60 G7
Clements Ct., 72 D4
Houns.
Clement's Inn WC2 14 E4
Clement's Inn WC2 58 F6
Clement's Inn Pas. 14 E4
WC2
Clements La. EC4 13 C5
Clements La. EC4 59 A7
Clements La., Ilf. 52 E5
Clements Pl., 64 G5
Brent.
Clements Rd. E6 52 B7
Clements Rd. SE16 17 J6
Clements Rd. SE16 68 D3
Clements Rd., Ilf. 52 E3
Clendon Way SE18 70 G4
Polthorne Gro.
Clenham St. SE1 17 A3
Clensham La., Sutt. 100 D2
Clenston Ms. W1 10 J3
Clephane Rd. N1 49 J6

Clere St. EC2 9 C5
Clerkenwell Clo. EC1 8 F5
Clerkenwell Clo. EC1 58 G4
Clerkenwell Grn. EC1 8 F6
Clerkenwell Grn. EC1 58 G4
Clerkenwell Rd. EC1 8 E6
Clerkenwell Rd. EC1 58 C4
Clerks Piece, Loug. 27 C3
Clermont Rd. E9 59 F1
Cleve Rd. NW6 48 D7
Cleve Rd., Sid. 89 D3
Clevedon Clo. N16 50 C3
Smalley Clo.
Clevedon Gdns., 72 B1
Houns.
Clevedon Rd. SE20 95 G1
Clevedon Rd., 92 A2
Kings.T.
Clevedon Rd., 73 G6
Twick.
Cleveland Ave. SW20 93 C2
Cleveland Ave. W4 65 F4
Cleveland Ave., 81 F7
Hmptn.
Cleveland Cres., 22 C5
Borwd.
Cleveland Gdns. N4 40 J5
Cleveland Gdns. 48 A2
NW2
Cleveland Gdns. 74 F2
SW13
Cleveland Gdns. W2 10 C4
Cleveland Gdns. W2 57 F6
Cleveland Gdns., 99 E2
Wor.Pk.
Cleveland Gro. E1 59 F4
Cleveland Way
Cleveland Ms. W1 11 F1
Cleveland Pk. Ave. 42 A4
E17
Cleveland Pk. Cres. 42 A4
E17
Cleveland Pl. SW1 15 G1
Cleveland Ri., Mord. 93 A7
Cleveland Rd. E18 42 G3
Cleveland Rd. N1 50 A7
Cleveland Rd. N9 25 E7
Cleveland Rd. SW13 74 F2
Cleveland Rd. W4 65 C3
Antrobus Rd.
Cleveland Rd. W13 55 D5
Cleveland Rd., Ilf. 52 E3
Cleveland Rd., Islw. 73 D4
Cleveland Rd., 92 E4
N.Mal.
Cleveland Rd., Well. 79 J2
Cleveland Rd., 99 E2
Wor.Pk.
Cleveland Row SW1 15 F2
Cleveland Row SW1 67 C1
Cleveland Sq. W2 10 C4
Cleveland St. W1 7 E6
Cleveland St. W1 58 C4
Cleveland Ter. W2 10 C4
Cleveland Ter. W2 57 F6
Cleveland Way E1 59 F4
Cleveley Clo. SE7 70 A4
Cleveley Cres. W5 55 H2
Cleveleys Rd. E5 51 G1
Cleverley Est. W12 65 G1
Cleves Rd. E6 61 A1
Cleves Rd., Rich. 82 F3
Cleves Wk., Ilf. 35 F7
Cleves Way, Hmptn. 81 F7
Cleves Way, Ruis. 45 D1
Clewer Cres., Har. 37 A1
Clichy Est. E1 59 F5
Clifden Rd. E5 50 F5
Clifden Rd., Brent. 64 G6
Clifden Rd., Twick. 82 C1
Cliff Rd. NW1 49 D6
Cliff Ter. SE8 78 A2
Cliff Vill. NW1 49 D6
Cliff Wk. E16 60 F5
Cliffe Rd., S.Croy. 102 A5
Clifford Ave. SW14 74 B3
Clifford Ave., Chis. 88 C6
Clifford Ave., Ilf. 43 E1
Clifford Ave., Wall. 101 C4
Clifford Clo., 54 E1
Nthlt.
Clifford Dr. SW9 76 H4
Clifford Gdns. NW10 56 J2
Clifford Rd. E16 60 H4
Clifford Rd. E17 42 C2
Clifford Rd. N9 25 F6
Clifford Rd. SE25 95 D4
Clifford Rd., Barn. 23 E3
Clifford Rd., 72 D3
Houns.
Clifford Rd., Rich. 82 G2
Clifford Rd., Wem. 55 G1

Clifford St. W1 11 F6
Clifford St. W1 58 C7
Clifford Way NW10 47 F4
Clifford's Inn Pas. 12 E4
EC4
Cliffview Rd. SE13 78 A3
Clifton Ave. E17 41 G3
Clifton Ave. N3 39 C1
Clifton Ave. W12 65 F2
Clifton Ave., Felt. 81 C3
Clifton Ave., Stan. 37 E2
Clifton Ave., Wem. 46 J6
Clifton Clo., Orp. 104 F5
Clifton Ct. NW8 6 C6
Clifton Cres. SE15 68 E7
Clifton Est. SE15 77 E1
Consort Rd.
Clifton Gdns. N15 41 C6
Clifton Gdns. NW11 39 C6
Clifton Gdns. W4 65 D4
Chiswick High Rd.
Clifton Gdns. W9 6 C6
Clifton Gdns. W9 57 F4
Clifton Gdns., Enf. 24 E4
Clifton Gro. E8 50 D6
Clifton Hill NW8 6 B1
Clifton Hill NW8 57 E2
Clifton Pk. Ave. 92 J2
SW20
Clifton Pl. SE16 68 F2
Canon Beck Rd.
Clifton Pl. W2 10 F4
Clifton Pl. W2 57 G6
Clifton Rd. SE14 68 H7
Clifton Rd. E7 52 A6
Clifton Rd. E16 60 E5
Clifton Rd. N3 39 F1
Clifton Rd. N8 40 D6
Clifton Rd. N22 40 C1
Clifton Rd. SE25 95 A4
Clifton Rd. SW19 84 A6
Clifton Rd. W9 6 D5
Clifton Rd. W9 57 F4
Clifton Rd., Grnf. 54 J4
Clifton Rd., Har. 37 J5
Clifton Rd., Ilf. 43 G6
Clifton Rd., Islw. 73 A2
Clifton Rd., Kings.T. 82 J7
Clifton Rd., Loug. 27 B4
Clifton Rd., Sid. 88 H4
Clifton Rd., Sthl. 63 E4
Clifton Rd., Tedd. 82 B4
Clifton Rd., Wall. 101 B5
Clifton Rd., Well. 80 C3
Clifton St. EC2 13 D1
Clifton St. EC2 59 B5
Clifton Ter. N4 49 G2
Clifton Vill. W9 10 B1
Clifton Vill. W9 57 F5
Clifton Wk. E6 61 B5
Tollgate Rd.
Clifton Way SE15 68 F7
Clifton Way, Borwd. 22 A1
Clifton Way, Wem. 55 H1
Clinch Ct. E16 60 G5
Brent Rd.
Cline Rd. N11 32 C6
Clinger Ct. N1 59 B1
Pitfield St.
Clink St. SE1 17 B1
Clink St. SE1 67 J1
Clinton Ave., E.Mol. 90 J4
Clinton Ave., Well. 80 A4
Clinton Cres., Ilf. 35 H6
Clinton Rd. E3 59 H3
Clinton Rd. E7 51 G4
Clinton Rd. N15 41 A4
Clipper Clo. SE16 68 G2
Kinburn St.
Clipper Way SE13 78 C4
Clippesby Clo., 98 J6
Chess.
Clipstone Ms. W1 7 F6
Clipstone Ms. W1 58 C5
Clipstone Rd., 72 G3
Houns.
Clipstone St. W1 11 E1
Clipstone St. W1 58 B5
Clissold Clo. N2 39 J3
Clissold Ct. N4 49 J2
Clissold Cres. N16 50 A4
Clissold Rd. N16 50 A3
Clitheroe Ave., Har. 45 G1
Clitheroe Gdns., Wat. 28 D3
Clitheroe Rd. SW9 76 E2
Clitherow Ave. W7 64 D3
Clitherow Pas., 64 E5
Brent.
Clitherow Rd.
Clitherow Rd., Brent. 64 E5
Clitterhouse Cres. 47 J1
NW2

Clitterhouse Rd. 47 J1
NW2
Clive Ave. N18 33 D6
Claremont St.
Clive Ct. W9 6 D5
Clive Pas. SE21 86 A3
Clive Rd.
Clive Rd. SE21 86 A3
Clive Rd. SW19 84 H6
Clive Rd., Belv. 71 G4
Clive Rd., Enf. 25 D4
Clive Rd., Felt. 72 A6
Clive Rd., Twick. 82 C4
Clive Way, Enf. 25 D4
Cliveden Clo. N12 31 F4
Woodside Ave.
Cliveden Pl. SW1 19 B1
Cliveden Pl. SW1 67 A4
Cliveden Rd. SW19 93 C1
Clivedon Ct. W13 55 E5
Clivedon Rd. E4 34 E5
Clivesdale Dr., 63 A1
Hayes
Cloak La. EC4 13 B5
Cloak La. EC4 58 J7
Clock Ho. Rd., Beck. 95 H3
Clock Twr. Ms. N1 58 J1
Arlington Ave.
Clock Twr. Pl. N7 49 E6
Clock Twr. Rd., Islw. 73 C3
Clockhouse Ave., 61 F1
Bark.
Clockhouse Clo. 83 J3
SW19
Cloister Gdns. SE25 95 E6
Cloister Gdns., Edg. 30 C5
Cloister Rd. NW2 48 C3
Cloister Rd. W3 56 C5
Cloisters, The SW9 76 G1
Cloisters Ave., 97 C5
Brom.
Cloisters Mall, 91 G2
Kings.T.
Union St.
Clonard Way, Pnr. 28 G6
Clonbrock Rd. N16 50 B4
Cloncurry St. SW6 75 A2
Clonmel Clo., Har. 46 A2
Clonmel Rd., Tedd. 82 A4
Clonmel Rd. N17 41 A3
Clonmel Rd. SW6 66 C4
Clonmore St. SW18 84 C1
Cloonmore Ave., 104 J4
Orp.
Clorane Gdns. NW3 48 D3
Beech Hall Rd.
Close, The E4 34 C7
Borwd.
Close, The N14 32 D2
Close, The N20 31 C2
Close, The, Barn. 23 J6
Close, The, Beck. 95 H4
Close, The, Bex. 95 H4
Close, The, Har. 36 J2
Harrow Vw.
Close, The, Islw. 73 A2
Close, The, Mitch. 93 J4
Close, The, N.Mal. 92 C2
Close, The, Orp. 97 H6
Close, The 36 C7
(Eastcote), Pnr.
Close, The 36 F7
(Rayners La.), Pnr.
Close, The, Rich. 74 B3
Close, The, Rom. 44 A4
Close, The, Sid. 89 B4
Close, The, Sutt. 93 C7
Close, The 47 C3
(Barnhill Rd.), Wem.
Close, The 46 H6
(Lyon Pk. Ave.), Wem.
Cloth Ct. EC1 12 H2
Cloth Fair EC1 12 H2
Cloth Fair EC1 58 H5
Cloth St. EC1 12 J1
Clothworkers Rd. 70 G7
SE18
Cloudesdale Rd. 85 B2
SW17
Cloudesley Pl. N1 58 G1
Cloudesley Rd. N1 58 G1
Cloudesley Rd., 80 F1
Bexh.
Cloudesley Sq. N1 58 G1
Cloudesley St. N1 58 G1
Clouston Clo., Wall. 100 E5
Clova Rd. E7 51 F6
Clove Cres. E14 60 D7
Clove Hitch Quay 75 F3
SW11
Cotton Row
Clove St. E13 60 G4
Barking Rd.
Clovelly Ave. NW9 38 F4

Clovelly Clo., Pnr. 36 B3
Clovelly Gdns. SE19 95 C1
Clovelly Gdns., Enf. 25 B7
Clovelly Gdns., 44 H1
Rom.
Clovelly Rd. N8 40 D4
Clovelly Rd. W4 65 D2
Clovelly Rd. W5 64 F2
Clovelly Rd., Bexh. 71 E6
Clovelly Rd., 72 F2
Houns.
Clovelly Way E1 59 F6
Jamaica St.
Clovelly Way, Har. 45 F2
Clovelly Way, Orp. 97 J6
Clover Clo. E11 51 D2
Clover Ms. SW3 19 A5
Clover Way, Wall. 101 A1
Cloverdale Gdns., 79 J6
Sid.
Cloverleys (Park 27 A5
Hill), Loug.
Clowders Rd. SE6 86 J3
Clowser Clo., Sutt. 100 F5
Turnpike La.
Cloyster Wd., Edg. 29 G7
Cloysters Clo. E1 17 H1
Club Gdns. Rd., 96 G7
Brom.
Club Row E1 9 F5
Club Row E1 59 C4
Club Row E2 9 F5
Club Row E2 59 C4
Clunbury Ave., Sthl. 63 F5
Clunbury St. N1 9 C2
Clunbury St. N1 59 A2
Cluny Est. SE1 17 D5
Cluny Ms. SW5 66 D4
Cluny Pl. SE1 17 D5
Cluse Ct. N1 8 J1
Clutton St. E14 60 B5
Clydach Rd., Enf. 25 C4
Clyde Circ. N15 41 B4
Clyde Pl. E10 42 B7
Clyde Rd. N15 41 B4
Clyde Rd. N22 40 D1
Clyde Rd., Croy. 102 C2
Clyde Rd., Sutt. 100 D5
Clyde Rd., Wall. 101 C6
Clyde St. SE8 68 J6
Clyde Ter. SE23 86 F2
Clyde Vale SE23 86 F2
Clydesdale, Enf. 25 G4
Clydesdale Ave., 37 G3
Stan.
Clydesdale Clo., 22 D5
Islw.
Clydesdale Gdns., 74 B4
Rich.
Clydesdale Rd. W11 57 C6
Clymping Dene, 72 B7
Felt.
Clyston St. SW8 76 C2
Coach & Horses Yd. 11 F5
W1
Coach Ho. La. N5 49 H4
Highbury Hill
Coach Ho. La. SW19 84 A4
Coach Ho. Ms. SE20 86 E7
Coach Ho. Ms. SE23 77 H7
Coal Wf. Rd. W12 66 A2
Shepherds Bush Pl.
Coaldale Wk. SE21 76 J7
Lairdale Clo.
Coalecroft Rd. SW15 74 J4
Coate St. E2 9 J2
Coate St. E2 59 D2
Coates Hill Rd., 97 D2
Brom.
Coates Wk., Brent. 64 H5
Burford Rd.
Cobb St. E1 13 F2
Cobb St. E1 59 C5
Cobbett Rd. SE9 79 B3
Cobbett Rd., Twick. 81 G1
Cobbett St. SW8 67 F7
Cobbetts Ave., Ilf. 42 J5
Cobblers Wk., E.Mol. 91 E1
Cobblers Wk., 90 J1
Hmptn.
High St.
Cobblers Wk., 91 D1
Kings.T.
Cobblers Wk., Tedd. 82 A7
Cobblestone Pl., 101 J1
Croy.
Oakfield Rd.
Cobbold Est. NW10 47 F6
Cobbold Rd. E11 51 F3
Cobbold Rd. NW10 47 F6
Cobbold Rd. W12 65 F2
Cobb's Rd., Houns. 72 F4
Cobden Rd. E11 51 E3

Cobden Rd. SE25 95 D5
Cobden Rd., Orp. 104 G4
Cobham Ave., N.Mal. 92 G5
Cobham Clo. SW11 75 H6
Cobham Clo., Brom. 97 B7
Cobham Clo., Wall. 101 E6
Cobham Clo., Bark. 61 F1
St. Margarets
Cobham Rd. E17 80 E5
Cobham Rd. E17 42 C1
Cobham Rd. N22 40 H3
Cobham Rd., Houns. 63 C7
Cobham Rd., Ilf. 52 H2
Cobham Rd., 92 A2
Kings.T.
Cobland Rd. SE12 87 J4
Coborn Rd. E3 59 J3
Coborn St. E3 59 J3
Cobourg Rd. SE5 21 F5
Cobourg Rd. SE5 68 C6
Cobourg St. NW1 7 G4
Cobourg St. NW1 58 C3
Coburg Clo. SW1 19 G1
Coburg Cres. SW2 85 F1
Coburg Gdns., Ilf. 43 A2
Coburg Rd. N22 40 F3
Cochrane Ms. NW8 6 F2
Cochrane Rd. SW19 84 C7
Cochrane St. NW8 6 F2
Cochrane St. NW8 57 G2
Cock Hill E1 13 E2
Cock La. EC1 12 G2
Cock La. EC1 58 H5
Cockayne Way SE8 68 H4
Windlass Pl.
Cockfosters Rd., Enf. 23 J3
Cockpit Steps SW1 15 J4
Cockpit Yd. WC1 12 D1
Cocks Cres., N.Mal. 92 F4
Cocksett Ave., Orp. 104 H6
Cockspur Ct. SW1 15 J1
Cockspur St. SW1 15 J1
Cockspur St. SW1 67 D1
Cocksure La., Sid. 89 G3
Code St. E1 9 G6
Code St. E1 59 C4
Codicote Ter. N4 49 J2
Green Las.
Codling Clo. E1 17 J1
Codling Way, Wem. 46 G4
Codrington Hill SE23 77 H7
Codrington Ms. W11 57 B6
Blenheim Cres.
Cody Clo., Har. 37 G3
Cody Clo., Wall. 101 D7
Alcock Clo.
Cody Rd. E16 60 E4
Coe Ave. SE25 95 D6
Coe's All., Barn. 23 B4
Wood St.
Cofers Circ., Wem. 47 B3
Cogan Ave. E17 41 H1
Coin St. SE1 16 E1
Coin St. SE1 67 G1
Coity Rd. NW5 49 A6
Coke St. E1 13 H3
Coke St. E1 59 D6
Cokers La. SE21 86 A1
Perifield
Colas Ms. NW6 57 D1
Birchington Rd.
Colbeck Ms. SW7 18 B2
Colbeck Ms. SW7 66 E4
Colbeck Rd., Har. 36 J7
Colberg Pl. N16 41 B7
Colborne Way, 99 J3
Wor.Pk.
Colburn Ave., Pnr. 28 E6
Colburn Way, Sutt. 100 G3
Colby Rd. SE19 86 B5
Colchester Dr., Pnr. 36 D5
Colchester Rd. E10 42 C7
Colchester Rd. E17 42 A6
Colchester Rd., Edg. 30 C7
Colchester Rd., 36 A2
Nthwd.
Colchester St. E1 13 G3
Cold Blow La. SE14 68 G7
Cold Blows, Mitch. 94 A3
Cold Harbour E14 69 C2
Coldbath Sq. EC1 8 E5
Coldbath St. SE13 78 B1
Coldershaw Rd. W13 64 D1
Coldfall Ave. N10 39 J2
Coldharbour La. SE5 76 J3
Coldharbour La. SW9 76 J4
Coldharbour Pl. SE5 76 J2
Denmark Hill
Coldharbour Rd., 101 G5
Croy.
Coldharbour Way, 101 G5
Croy.

Coldstream Gdns. 75 C6
SW18
Cole Clo. SE28 71 B1
Cole Gdns., Houns. 63 A7
Cole Pk. Gdns., 73 D6
Twick
Cole Pk. Rd., Twick. 73 D7
Cole Pk. Vw., Twick. 73 D6
Cole Pk. Rd., Twick. 72 D6
Cole St. SE1 **17 A4**
Cole St. SE1 67 J2
Colebeck Rd. N1 49 H6
Colebert Ave. E1 59 F4
Colebrook Clo. SW15 75 A7
West Hill
Colebrook Gdns., 27 E2
Loug.
Colebrook Ho. E14 60 B6
Brabazon St.
Colebrook La., Loug. 27 E2
Colebrook Rd. SW16 94 E1
Colebrook Way N11 32 B5
Colebrooke Ave. W13 55 E6
Colebrooke Dr. E11 42 H7
Colebrooke Pl. N1 58 H1
St. Peters St.
Colebrooke Ri., 96 E2
Brom.
Colebrooke Row N1 8 G2
Colebrooke Row N1 58 H2
Coleby Path SE5 68 A7
Harris St.
Coledale Dr., Stan. 37 F1
Coleford Rd. SW18 75 F5
Colegrave Rd. E15 51 D5
Colegrove Rd. SE15 21 G6
Colegrove Rd. SE15 68 C6
Coleherne Ct. SW5 18 B4
Coleherne Ct. SW5 66 E5
Coleherne Ms. SW10 18 A4
Coleherne Ms. SW10 66 E5
Coleherne Rd. SW10 18 A4
Coleherne Rd. SW10 66 E5
Colehill Gdns. SW6 75 B2
Fulham Palace Rd.
Colehill La. SW6 75 B1
Coleman Clo. SE25 95 D2
Warminster Rd.
Coleman Flds. N1 58 J1
Coleman Rd. SE5 21 D7
Coleman Rd. SE5 68 B7
Coleman Rd., Belv. 71 G4
Coleman Rd., Dag. 53 E6
Coleman St. EC2 13 B3
Coleman St. EC2 59 A6
Colemans Heath SE9 88 D3
Colenso Rd. E5 50 F4
Colenso Rd., Ilf. 52 H1
Colepits Wd. Rd. SE9 79 G5
Coleraine Rd. N8 40 G3
Coleraine Rd. SE3 69 F6
Coleridge Ave. E12 52 B6
Coleridge Ave., 100 H4
Sutt.
Coleridge Clo. SW8 76 B2
Coleridge Gdns. 48 F7
NW6
Fairhazel Gdns.
Coleridge La. N8 40 E6
Coleridge Rd.
Coleridge Rd. E17 41 J4
Coleridge Rd. N4 49 G2
Coleridge Rd. N8 40 D6
Coleridge Rd. N12 31 F5
Coleridge Rd., Croy. 95 F6
Coleridge Sq. W13 55 D6
Coleridge Wk. NW11 39 D4
Coleridge Way, 54 A6
Hayes
Coles Cres., Har. 45 H2
Coles Grn., Loug. 27 D1
Coles Grn. 28 J1
(Bushey), Wat.
Coles Grn. Ct. NW2 47 G2
Coles Grn. Rd. NW2 47 G1
Colesburg Rd., Beck. 95 J3
Coleshill Rd., Tedd. 82 B6
Colestown St. SW11 75 H2
Colet Clo. N13 32 H6
Colet Gdns. W14 66 A5
Coley St. WC1 8 D6
Coley St. WC1 58 F4
Colfe Rd. SE23 86 H1
Colin Clo. NW9 38 E4
Colin Clo., Croy. 102 J3
Colin Clo., W.Wick. 103 F3
Colin Cres. NW9 38 F4
Colin Dr. NW9 38 F5
Colin Gdns. NW9 38 F5
Colin Pk. Rd. NW9 38 E3
Colin Rd. NW10 47 G6
Colina Ms. N15 40 H5
Harringay Rd.

Colina Rd. N15 40 H5
Colindale Ave. NW9 38 D3
Colindale Business 38 C3
Pk. NW9
Colindeep Gdns. 38 G5
NW4
Colindeep La. NW9 38 E3
Colinette Rd. SW15 74 J4
Colinton Rd., Ilf. 53 B1
Coliston Rd. SW18 75 D7
Collage Clo., Twick. 82 A1
Meadway
Collamore Ave. 84 H1
SW18
Collapit Clo., Har. 36 H6
Collard Ave., Loug. 27 F2
College App. SE10 69 C6
College Ave., Har. 37 B1
College Clo. E9 50 F5
Median Rd.
College Clo. N18 33 C5
College Clo., Har. 29 B7
College Clo., Twick. 82 A1
Meadway
College Cres. NW3 48 G6
College Cross N1 49 G7
College Dr., Ruis. 36 A7
College Gdns. E4 26 B7
College Gdns. N18 33 C5
College Gdns. SE21 86 B1
College Gdns. SW17 84 H2
College Gdns., Enf. 25 A1
College Gdns., Ilf. 43 B5
College Gdns., 92 F5
N.Mal.
College Grn. SE19 86 B7
College Gro. NW1 58 D1
St. Pancras Way
College Hill EC4 13 A5
College Hill Rd., Har. 29 B7
College La. NW5 49 B4
College Ms. SW1 16 A5
College Ms. SW18 75 E5
St. Ann's Hill
College Pk. Clo. 78 D4
SE13
College Pl. E17 42 E4
College Pl. NW1 58 C1
College Pl. SW10 66 F7
Hortensia Rd.
College Pt. E15 51 F6
Wolfe Gdns.
College Rd. E17 42 C5
College Rd. N17 33 C6
College Rd. N21 32 G2
College Rd. NW10 56 J2
College Rd. SE19 86 C5
College Rd. SE21 77 B7
College Rd. SW19 84 G6
College Rd. W13 55 E6
College Rd., Brom. 96 G1
College Rd., Croy. 102 A2
College Rd., Enf. 25 A1
College Rd. Har. 37 B6
(Harrow on the Hill)
College Rd., Har. 37 B1
(Harrow Weald)
College Rd., Islw. 73 C1
College Rd., Wem. 46 G1
College Row E9 50 G5
Homerton High St.
College Slip, Brom. 96 G1
College St. EC4 13 B5
College Ter. E3 59 J3
College Ter. N3 39 C2
Hendon La.
College Vw. SE9 88 A1
College Wk., Kings.T. 91 H2
Grange Rd.
College Yd. NW5 49 B4
College La.
Collent St. E9 50 F6
Colless Rd. N15 41 C5
Collett Rd. SE16 17 J6
Collett Rd. SE16 68 D3
Collett Way, Sthl. 63 H1
Collier Clo., Epsom 99 A6
Collier Dr., Edg. 38 A2
Collier Row Rd., 44 G1
Rom.
Collier St. N1 8 C2
Collier St. N1 58 F2
Colliers Shaw, Kes. 104 A5
Colliers Water La., 94 G5
Th.Hth.
Collindale Ave. 71 H6
Erith
Collindale Ave. 89 A1
Sid.
Collingbourne Rd. 65 H1
W12
Collingham Gdns. 18 B2
SW5

Collingham Gdns. 66 E4
SW5
Collingham Pl. SW5 18 A2
Collingham Pl. SW5 66 E4
Collingham Rd. SW5 18 B1
Collingham Rd. SW5 66 E4
Collings Clo. N22 32 F6
Whittington Rd.
Collington Rd. 96 E4
SE26
Collingwood Ave. 40 A3
N10
Collingwood Ave., 99 C1
Surb.
Collingwood Clo. 95 E1
SE20
Collingwood Clo., 72 G7
Twick.
Collingwood Rd. E17 42 A6
Collingwood Rd. N15 41 B3
Collingwood Rd., 93 H2
Mitch.
Collingwood Rd., 100 C3
Sutt.
Collingwood St. E1 59 E4
Collins Ave., Stan. 37 H2
Collins Dr., Ruis. 45 C2
Collins Rd. N5 49 J4
Collins Sq. SE3 78 F2
Tranquil Vale
Collins St. SE3 78 E2
Collin's Yd. N1 58 H1
Islington Grn.
Collinson St. SE1 16 J4
Collinson Wk. SE1 16 J4
Collinwood Ave., 25 F3
Enf.
Collinwood Gdns., 43 C5
Ilf.
Colls Rd. SE15 77 F1
Collyer Ave., Croy. 101 E4
Collyer Pl. SE15 77 D1
Peckham High St.
Collyer Rd., Croy. 101 E4
Colman Rd. E16 60 J5
Colmar Clo. E1 59 G4
Alderney Rd.
Colmer Pl., Har. 29 A7
Colmer Rd. SW16 94 E1
Colmore Ms. SE15 77 E1
Colmore Rd., Enf. 25 F4
Colnbrook St. SE1 16 G6
Colnbrook St. SE1 67 H3
Colne Ct., Epsom 99 C4
Colne Ho., Bark. 52 E6
Colne Rd. E5 50 H4
Colne Rd. N21 24 J7
Colne Rd., Twick. 82 B1
Colne St. E13 60 G3
Grange Rd.
Colney Hatch La. N10 32 A7
Colney Hatch La. N11 31 J6
Cologne Rd. SW11 75 G4
Colomb St. SE10 69 E5
Colombo Rd., Ilf. 52 F1
Colombo St. SE1 16 G2
Colombo St. SE1 67 H1
Colonial Ave., 72 J5
Twick.
Colonnade WC1 8 B6
Colonnade WC1 59 E4
Colonnade Wk. SW1 19 D2
Colonnades, The W2 10 B3
Colson Gdns., Loug. 27 E4
Colson Rd.
Colson Path, Loug. 27 D4
Colson Rd., Croy. 102 B2
Colson Rd., Loug. 27 D4
Colson Way SW16 85 C4
Colsterworth Rd. 41 C4
N15
Colston Ave., Cars. 100 H4
Colston Clo., Cars. 100 J4
West Hill
Colston Rd. E7 52 A6
Colston Rd. SW14 74 C4
Coltness Cres. SE2 71 B5
Colton Gdns. N17 40 J3
Colton Rd., Har. 37 B5
Columbia Ave., Edg. 38 B1
Columbia Ave., Ruis. 45 B1
Columbia Ave., 92 F7
Wor.Pk.
Columbia Ctyd. E14 69 A1
West India Ave.
Columbia Rd. E2 9 F3
Columbia Rd. E2 59 C3
Columbia Rd. E13 60 F4
Columbia Sq. SW14 74 C4
Upper Richmond Rd.
Columbine Ave. E6 61 B5
Columbine Ave., 101 H7
S.Croy.

Columbine Way 78 C2
SE13
Columbus Gdns., 36 A1
Nthwd.
Colva Wk. N19 49 B2
Chester Rd.
Colvestone Cres. E8 50 L5
Colview Ct. SE9 88 A1
Mottingham La.
Colville Est. N1 59 B1
Colville Gdns. W11 57 C6
Colville Hos. W11 57 C6
Colville Ms. W11 57 C6
Lonsdale Rd.
Colville Pl. W1 11 G2
Colville Rd. E11 51 C3
Colville Rd. E17 41 H2
Colville Rd. N9 33 E1
Colville Rd. W3 65 B3
Colville Rd. W11 57 C6
Colville Sq. W11 57 C6
Colville Ter. W11 57 C6
Colvin Clo. SE26 86 F5
Colvin Gdns. E4 34 C3
Colvin Gdns. E11 42 H4
Colvin Gdns., Ilf. 43 F1
Colvin Rd. E6 52 B7
Colvin Rd., Th.Hth. 94 G5
Colwell Rd. SE22 77 C5
Colwick Clo. N6 40 D7
Colwith Rd. W6 65 J6
Colwood Gdns. 84 G7
SW19
Colworth Gro. SE17 21 A2
Colworth Rd. E11 42 E6
Colworth Rd., Croy. 102 D1
Colwyn Ave., Grnf. 55 C2
Colwyn Cres., 72 J1
Houns.
Colwyn Grn. NW9 38 E6
Snowdon Dr.
Colwyn Rd. NW2 47 H3
Colyer Clo. SE9 88 E2
Colyer Clo. N1 80 J1
Colyers La., Erith 80 J1
Colyton Clo., Well. 80 D1
Colyton Clo., Wem. 46 F6
Bridgewater Rd.
Colyton Rd. SE22 77 E5
Combe Ave. SE3 69 F7
Combe Lea, Brom. 97 B3
Combe Lo. SE7 69 J6
Elliscombe Rd.
Combe Ms. SE3 69 F7
Combedale Rd. SE10 69 G5
Combemartin Rd. 75 B7
SW18
Comber Clo. NW2 47 H2
Comber Gro. SE5 67 J7
Combermere Rd. 76 F3
SW9
Combermere Rd., 93 E5
Mord.
Comberton Rd. E5 50 E2
Combeside SE18 70 J7
Combwell Cres. SE2 71 A3
Comely Bank Rd. E17 42 C5
Comeragh Ms. W14 66 B5
Comeragh Rd.
Comeragh Rd. W14 66 B5
Comerford Rd. SE4 77 H4
Comet Pl. SE8 69 A7
Comet St. SE8 69 A7
Commerce Rd. N22 40 F1
Commerce Rd., 64 F6
Brent.
Commerce Way, 101 F2
Croy.
Commercial Rd. E1 13 H3
Commercial Rd. E1 59 D6
Commercial Rd. E14 59 H6
Commercial Rd. N17 33 B6
Commercial Rd. N18 33 B5
Commercial St. E1 9 F6
Commercial St. E1 59 C4
Commercial Way 56 B2
NW10
Commercial Way 68 C7
SE15
Commerell St. SE10 69 E5
Commodity Quay E1 13 G6
Commodore Sq. 75 F1
SW10
Commodore St. E1 59 H4
Common, The W5 55 H7
Common, The, Rich. 82 G3
Common, The, Sthl. 63 C4
Common, The, Stan. 29 B2
Common La., Esher 98 D7
Common Rd. SW13 74 G3
Common Rd., Esher 98 D6
Common Rd., Stan. 29 A3
Commondale SW15 74 J3

Commonside, Kes.	103	J4
Commonside E.,	94	A3
Mitch.		
Commonside W.,	93	J3
Mitch.		
Commonwealth Ave.	56	H7
W12		
Commonwealth Rd.	33	D7
N17		
Commonwealth Way	71	B5
SE2		
Community Clo.,	72	B1
Houns.		
Community Rd. E15	51	D5
Community Rd.,	54	J1
Grnf.		
Como Rd. SE23	86	H2
Compass Hill, Rich.	73	G6
Compayne Gdns.	48	E7
NW6		
Compton Ave. E6	61	A2
Compton Ave. N1	49	H6
Compton Ave. N6	39	H7
Compton Clo. NW1	**7**	**E4**
Compton Clo. W13	55	D6
Compton Clo., Edg.	30	C7
Pavilion Way		
Compton Ct. SE19	86	B5
Victoria Cres.		
Compton Cres. N17	32	J7
Compton Cres. W4	65	C6
Compton Cres.,	98	H6
Chess.		
Compton Cres.,	54	D1
Nthlt.		
Compton Pas. EC1	**8**	**H5**
Compton Pl. WC1	**8**	**A5**
Compton Pl., Wat.	28	E3
Compton Ri., Pnr.	36	E5
Compton Rd. N1	49	H6
Compton Rd. N21	32	G1
Compton Rd. NW10	57	A3
Compton Rd. SW19	84	C6
Compton Rd., Croy.	102	E1
Compton St. EC1	**8**	**G5**
Compton St. EC1	58	H4
Compton Ter. N1	49	H6
Comreddy Clo., Enf.	24	H1
Comus Pl. SE17	**21**	**D2**
Comus Pl. SE17	68	B4
Comyn Rd. SW11	75	H4
Comyns, Thr.	28	J1
(Bushey), Wat.		
Comyns Clo. E16	60	F5
Comyns Rd., Dag.	53	G7
Conant Ms. E1	**13**	**H5**
Concanon Rd. SW2	76	F4
Concert Hall App.	**16**	**D2**
SE1		
Concert Hall App.	67	F1
SE1		
Concord Clo.,	54	D3
Nthlt.		
Britannia Clo.		
Concord Rd. W3	56	B4
Concord Rd., Enf.	25	E5
Concorde Clo.,	72	H2
Houns.		
Lampton Rd.		
Concorde, Dr. E6	61	C5
Concourse, The NW9	38	F1
Long Mead		
Condell Rd. SW8	76	C1
Conder St. E14	59	H6
Conderton Rd. SE5	76	J3
Condover Cres. SE18	70	E7
Condray Pl. SW11	66	H7
Conduit Ct. WC2	**12**	**A5**
Conduit La. N18	33	F5
Conduit La., Croy.	102	D5
Conduit La.,	102	D5
S.Croy.		
Conduit Ms. W2	**10**	**E4**
Conduit Ms. W2	57	G6
Conduit Pas. W2	**10**	**E4**
Conduit Pl. W2	**10**	**E4**
Conduit Pl. W2	57	G6
Conduit Rd. SE18	70	E5
Conduit St. W1	**11**	**E5**
Conduit St. W1	58	B7
Conduit Way NW10	47	C7
Conewood St. N5	49	H3
Coney Acre SE21	85	J1
Coney Burrows E4	34	E2
Wyemead Cres.		
Coney Hill Rd.,	103	E2
W.Wick.		
Coney Way SW8	**20**	**D6**
Coney Way SW8	67	F6
Conference Clo. E4	34	C2
Greenbank Clo.		
Conference Rd. SE2	71	C4
Congleton Gro. SE18	70	F5

Congo Rd. SE18	70	G5
Congress Rd. SE2	71	C4
Congreve Rd. SE9	79	C3
Congreve St. SE17	**21**	**D2**
Congreve St. SE17	68	B4
Congreve Wk. E16	61	A5
Fulmer Rd.		
Conical Cor., Enf.	24	J2
Conifer Clo., Orp.	104	G4
Conifer Gdns. SW16	85	E3
Conifer Gdns., Enf.	25	A6
Conifer Gdns.,	100	E3
Sutt.		
Conifer Way, Hayes	54	A7
Conifer Way, Wem.	46	F3
Conifers Clo., Tedd.	82	F7
Coniger Rd. SW6	75	D2
Coningham Ms. W12	65	G1
Percy Rd.		
Coningham Rd. W12	65	H1
Coningsby Cotts. W5	64	G2
Coningsby Rd.		
Coningsby Gdns. E4	34	B6
Coningsby Rd. N4	40	H7
Coningsby Rd. W5	64	G2
Conington Rd. SE13	78	B2
Conisbee Ct. N14	24	C5
Conisborough Cres.	87	C3
SE6		
Coniscliffe Rd. N13	32	J3
Coniston Ave.,	52	H7
Bark.		
Coniston Ave., Grnf.	55	E3
Coniston Ave., Well.	79	H3
Coniston Clo. N20	31	F3
Coniston Clo. SW13	65	F7
Lonsdale Ave.		
Coniston Clo. SW20	93	A6
Coniston Clo. W4	65	C7
Coniston Clo., Bark.	52	H7
Coniston Ave.		
Coniston Clo.,	80	J1
Bexh.		
Coniston Gdns. N9	33	F1
Coniston Gdns. NW9	38	D5
Coniston Gdns., Ilf.	43	B4
Coniston Gdns., Pnr.	36	A4
Coniston Gdns.,	100	G6
Sutt.		
Coniston Gdns.,	46	F1
Wem.		
Coniston Ho. SE5	**20**	**J7**
Coniston Rd. N10	40	B2
Coniston Rd. N17	33	D6
Coniston Rd., Bexh.	80	J1
Coniston Rd., Brom.	87	D6
Coniston Rd., Croy.	95	D7
Coniston Rd.,	72	H6
Twick.		
Coniston Wk. E9	50	F5
Clifden Rd.		
Coniston Way,	98	H3
Chess.		
Conistone Way N7	49	E7
Conlan St. W10	57	B4
Conley Rd. NW10	47	F6
Conley St. SE10	69	E5
Pelton Rd.		
Connaught Ave. E4	26	D7
Connaught Ave.	74	C3
SW14		
Connaught Ave.,	31	J1
Barn.		
Connaught Ave.,	25	B2
Enf.		
Connaught Ave.,	72	E5
Houns.		
Connaught Ave.,	27	A4
Loug.		
Connaught Clo. E10	50	H2
Connaught Clo. W2	**10**	**G4**
Connaught Clo.,	25	B2
Enf.		
Connaught Clo.,	100	G6
Sutt.		
Connaught Crossing	61	A7
E16		
Connaught Dr. NW11	39	D4
Connaught Gdns.	40	B5
N10		
Connaught Gdns.	32	H4
N13		
Connaught Gdns.,	93	F4
Mord.		
Connaught Hill,	27	A4
Loug.		
Connaught La., Ilf.	52	G2
Connaught Rd.		
Connaught Ms. W2	**10**	**J4**
Connaught Ms., Ilf.	52	G2
Connaught Rd.		
Connaught Pl. W2	**10**	**J4**
Connaught Pl. W2	57	J7

Connaught Rd. E4	26	E7
Connaught Rd. E11	51	D1
Connaught Rd. E16	70	A1
Connaught Crossing		
Connaught Rd. E17	42	A5
Connaught Rd. N4	40	G7
Connaught Rd.	56	E1
NW10		
Connaught Rd. SE18	70	D5
Connaught Rd. W13	55	E7
Connaught Rd.,	23	A6
Barn.		
Connaught Rd., Har.	37	C1
Connaught Rd., Ilf.	52	G2
Connaught Rd.,	92	E4
N.Mal.		
Connaught Rd., Rich.	73	J5
Albert Rd.		
Connaught Rd.,	100	G2
Sutt.		
Connaught Rd.,	82	A5
Tedd.		
Connaught Sq. W2	**10**	**J4**
Connaught Sq. W2	57	J6
Connaught St. W2	**10**	**H4**
Connaught St. W2	57	H6
Connaught Way N13	32	H4
Connell Cres. W5	55	J4
Connemara Clo.,	22	D6
Borwd.		
Percheron Rd.		
Connington Cres. E4	34	D3
Connor Rd., Dag.	53	F4
Connor St. E9	59	G1
Lauriston Rd.		
Conolly Rd. W7	64	B1
Conrad Dr., Wor.Pk.	99	J1
Conrad Ho. N16	50	B5
Cons St. SE1	**16**	**F3**
Consfield Ave.,	92	G4
N.Mal.		
Consort Ms., Islw.	73	A5
Consort Rd. SE15	77	E1
Constable Clo. NW11	39	E6
Constable Cres. N15	41	D5
Constable Gdns.,	38	A1
Edg.		
Constable Gdns.,	73	A5
Islw.		
Constable Wk. SE21	86	C3
Ferrings		
Constance Cres.,	96	F7
Brom.		
Constance Rd., Croy.	94	H7
Constance Rd., Enf.	25	B6
Constance Rd.,	100	F4
Sutt.		
Constance St. E16	70	B1
Albert Rd.		
Constantine Rd. NW3	48	H4
Constitution Hill	**15**	**D3**
SW1		
Constitution Hill	67	B2
SW1		
Constitution Ri.	79	D1
SE18		
Consul Ave., Dag.	62	J4
Content St. SE17	**21**	**A2**
Content St. SE17	68	A4
Contessa Clo., Orp.	104	H5
Convair Wk., Nthlt.	54	D3
Kittiwake Rd.		
Convent Gdns. W5	64	F4
Convent Gdns. W11	57	C6
Kensington Pk. Rd.		
Convent Hill SE19	85	J6
Convent Way, Sthl.	63	C4
Conway Clo., Stan.	29	D6
Conway Cres., Grnf.	55	B2
Conway Cres., Rom.	44	C6
Conway Dr., Sutt.	100	E6
Conway Gdns.	94	D4
Mitch.		
Conway Gdns., Wem.	37	F7
Conway Gro. W3	56	D5
Conway Ms. W1	**7**	**F6**
Conway Rd. N14	32	E3
Conway Rd. N15	40	H5
Conway Rd. NW2	47	J2
Conway Rd. SE18	70	G4
Conway Rd. SW20	92	J1
Conway Rd., Felt.	81	D5
Conway Rd., Houns.	72	F7
Conway Rd., Houns.	60	G4
Conway St. W1	**7**	**F6**
Conway St. W1	58	C4
Conway Wk., Hmptn.	81	F6
Fearnley Cres.		
Conybeare NW3	48	H7
King Henry's Rd.		
Conyer St. E3	59	H2

Conyers Clo.,	34	E6
Wdf.Grn.		
Conyers Rd. SW16	85	D5
Conyers Way, Loug.	27	E3
Cooden Clo., Brom.	87	H7
Cooderidge Clo. N17	33	C6
Brantwood Rd.		
Cookes Clo. E11	51	F2
Cookes La., Sutt.	100	B6
Cookham Cres. SE16	68	G2
Marlow Way		
Cookham Dene Clo.,	97	G1
Chis.		
Cookham Rd., Sid.	89	G7
Cookhill Rd. SE2	71	B2
Cooks Clo., Rom.	44	J1
Cook's Rd. E15	60	B2
Cooks Rd. SE17	**20**	**G5**
Cooks Rd. SE17	67	H6
Cool Oak La. NW9	47	E1
Coolfin Rd. E16	60	G6
Coolgardie Ave. E4	34	D5
Coolgardie Ave.,	35	D3
Chig.		
Coolhurst Rd. N8	40	D6
Coomassie Rd. W9	57	C4
Bravington Rd.		
Coombe Ave., Croy.	102	B4
Coombe Bank,	92	E1
Kings.T.		
Coombe Clo., Edg.	37	J2
Coombe Clo., Houns.	72	G4
Coombe Cor. N21	32	H1
Orpington Rd.		
Coombe Cres.,	81	E7
Hmptn.		
Coombe Dr.,	83	D7
Kings.T.		
Coombe Dr., Ruis.	45	B1
Coombe End,	83	D7
Kings.T.		
Coombe Gdns. SW20	92	G2
Coombe Gdns.,	92	F4
N.Mal.		
Coombe Heights,	83	E7
Kings.T.		
Coombe Hill Glade,	83	E7
Kings.T.		
Coombe Hill Rd.,	83	E7
Kings.T.		
Coombe Ho. Chase,	92	D1
N.Mal.		
Coombe La. SW20	92	F1
Coombe La., Croy.	102	E5
Coombe La. W.,	92	B1
Kings.T.		
Coombe Lea, Brom.	97	B3
Coombe Neville,	83	D7
Kings.T.		
Coombe Pk.,	83	D5
Kings.T.		
Coombe Ridings,	83	C5
Kings.T.		
Coombe Ri.,	92	C1
Kings.T.		
Coombe Rd. N22	40	G2
Coombe Rd. NW10	47	D3
Coombe Rd. SE26	86	E4
Coombe Rd. W4	65	E5
Coombe Rd. W13	64	E3
Northcroft Rd.		
Coombe Rd., Croy.	101	J4
Coombe Rd., Hmptn.	81	F6
Coombe Rd.,	92	A1
Kings.T.		
Coombe Rd., N.Mal.	92	E2
Coombe Wk., Sutt.	100	E3
Coombe Wd. Rd.,	83	C5
Kings.T.		
Coombefield Clo.,	92	E5
N.Mal.		
Coomber Way, Croy.	94	D7
Coombes Rd., Dag.	62	F1
Coombewood Dr.,	44	G6
Rom.		
Coombs St. N1	8	H2
Coombs St. N1	58	H2
Coomer Ms. SW6	66	C6
Coomer Pl.		
Coomer Pl. SW6	66	C6
Coomer Rd. SW6	66	C6
Coomer Pl.		
Coomes Wk., Edg.	38	C1
East Rd.		
Cooper Ave. E17	41	H1
Cooper Clo. SE1	**16**	**F4**
Cooper Ct. E15	51	B5
Clays La.		
Cooper Cres., Cars.	100	J3
Cooper Rd. NW10	47	G5
Cooper Rd., Croy.	101	H4

Cooper St. E16　60　F5
　Lawrence St.
Coopers Clo. E1　59　F4
Coopers Cres.,　22　C1
　Borwd.
Coopers La. E10　51　B1
Coopers La. NW1　**7**　**J2**
　Hurst Rd.
Coopers La. NW1　58　D2
Cooper's La. SE12　87　H2
Coopers Rd. SE1　**21**　**G4**
Coopers Rd. SE1　68　C5
Cooper's Row EC3　**13**　**F5**
Cooper's Yd. SE19　86　B6
　Westow Hill
Coopersale Clo.,　34　J7
　Wdf.Grn.
　Navestock Cres.
Coopersale Rd. E9　50　G5
Coote Gdns., Dag.　53　F3
　Nicholas Rd.
Coote Rd., Bexh.　80　F1
Coote Rd., Dag.　53　F3
Cope Pl. W8　66　D3
Cope St. SE16　68　G4
Copeland Dr. E14　69　A4
Copeland Rd. E17　42　B5
Copeland Rd. SE15　77　D2
Copeman Clo. SE26　86　F5
Copenhagen Gdns.　65　D2
　W4
Copenhagen Pl. E14　59　J6
Copenhagen St. N1　58　E1
Copers Cope Rd.,　86　J7
　Beck.
Copford Clo.,　35　B6
　Wdf.Grn.
Copford Wk. N1　58　J1
　Popham St.
Copinger Way., Edg.　38　B1
　North Rd.
Copland Ave., Wem.　46　G5
Copland Clo., Wem.　46　F5
Copland Rd., Wem.　46　H6
Copleston Ms. SE15　77　C2
Copleston Pas. SE15　77　C2
Copleston Rd. SE15　77　C3
Copley Clo. SE17　**20**　**H6**
Copley Clo. W7　55　C4
Copley Dene, Brom.　97　A1
Copley Pk. SW16　85　F6
Copley Rd., Stan.　29　F5
Copley St. E1　59　G5
　Stepney Grn.
Copnor Way SE15　**21**　**E7**
Copped Hall SE21　86　A2
　Glazebrook Clo.
Coppelia Rd. SE3　78　F4
Coppen Rd., Dag.　44　F7
Copper Beech Clo.,　43　D1
　Ilf.
Copper Beech Ct.,　27　D1
　Loug.
Copper Beeches,　73　A1
　Islw.
　Eversley Cres.
Copper Clo. SE19　86　C7
Copper Mead Clo.　47　J3
　NW2
Copper Mill Dr., Islw.　73　C2
Copper Mill La.　84　F4
　SW17
Copperas St. SE8　69　B6
Copperbeech Clo.　48　G5
　NW3
　Akenside Rd.
Copperdale Rd.,　63　A2
　Hayes
Copperfield, Chig.　35　G5
Copperfield App.,　35　G5
　Chig.
Copperfield Ms. N18　33　B5
Copperfield Rd. E3　59　H4
Copperfield Rd.　62　C6
　SE28
Copperfield St. SE1　**16**　**H3**
Copperfield St. SE1　67　H2
Copperfield Way,　88　F6
　Chis.
Copperfield Way,　36　F4
　Pnr.
Coppergate Clo.,　96　H1
　Brom.
Coppermill La. E17　41　F6
Coppetts Clo. N12　31　J7
　North Circular Rd.
Coppetts Rd. N10　31　J7
Coppice, The, Enf.　24　H4
Coppice Clo. SW20　92　J3
Coppice Clo., Stan.　29　C6
Coppice Dr. SW15　74　G6
Coppice Wk. N20　31　D3
Coppice Way E18　42　F4
Coppies Gro. N11　32　K4

Copping Clo., Croy.　102　B4
　Tipton Dr.
Coppins, The, Croy.　103　B6
Coppins, The, Har.　29　B6
Coppock Clo. SW11　75　H2
Coppsfield, W.Mol.　90　G3

Copse, The E4　34　F1
Copse Ave., W.Wick.　103　B3
Copse Clo. SE7　69　H6
Copse Glade, Surb.　98　G1
Copse Hill SW20　92　G1
Copse Hill, Sutt.　100　E7
Coptefield Dr., Belv.　71　D3
Copthall Ave. EC2　**13**　**C3**
Copthall Ave. EC2　59　A6
Copthall Bldgs. EC2　**13**　**C3**
Copthall Clo. EC2　**13**　**B3**
Copthall Ct. EC2　**13**　**C3**
Copthall Ct. EC2　59　A6
Copthall Dr. NW7　30　G7
Copthall Gdns. NW7　30　G7
Copthall Gdns.,　82　C1
　Twick.
Copthorne Ave.　76　D7
　SW12
Copthorne Ave., Ilf.　35　E6
Coptic St. WC1　**12**　**A2**
Coptic St. WC1　58　E5
Copwood Clo. N12　31　G4
Coral Clo., Rom.　44　C3
Coral Row SW11　75　F3
　Gartons Way
Coral St. SE1　**16**　**F4**
Coral St. SE1　67　G2
Coraline Clo.,　54　F3
　Sthl.
Coralline Wk. SE2　71　C2
Coram St. WC1　**8**　**A6**
Coram St. WC1　58　E4
Coran Clo. N9　25　G7
Corban Rd., Houns.　72　G3
Corbar Clo., Barn.　23　G1
Corbet Clo., Wall.　101　A1
Corbet Ct. EC3　**13**　**C4**
Corbet Pl. E1　**13**　**F1**
Corbett Gro. N22　32　E7
　Bounds Grn. Rd.
Corbett Ho., Wat.　28　C3
Corbett Rd. E11　42　J6
Corbett Rd. E17　42　C3
Corbetts La. SE16　68　F4
　Rotherhithe New Rd.
Corbetts Pas. SE16　68　F4
　Rotherhithe New Rd.
Corbicum E11　42　E7
Corbiere Ct. SW19　84　A6
　Thornton Rd.
Corbiere Ho. N1　59　B1
Corbins La., Har.　45　H3
Corbridge Cres. E2　59　E2
Corby Cres., Enf.　24　E4
Corby Rd. NW10　56　D2
Corby Way E3　60　A4
　Knapp Rd.
Corbylands Rd., Sid.　79　H7
Corbyn St. N4　49　J1
Cord Way E14　69　A3
　Mellish St.
Cordelia St. E14　60　B6
Cording St. E14　60　B5
　Chrisp St.
Cordova Rd. E3　59　H3
Cordwainers Wk. E13　60　G2
　Clegg St.
Cordwell Rd. SE13　78　E5
Corelli Rd. SE3　79　B1
Corfe Ave., Har.　45　G4
Corfe Twr. W3　65　C2
Corfield St. E2　59　E3
Corfton Rd. W5　56　H6
Coriander Ave. E14　60　D6
Corinium Clo.,　46　J4
　Wem.
Corinne Rd. N19　49　C4
Cork Sq. E1　68　E1
　Smeaton St.
Cork St. W1　**11**　**F6**
Cork St. W1　58　C7
Cork St. Ms. W1　**11**　**F6**
Cork Tree Way E4　33　H5
Corker Wk. N7　49　F2
Corkran Rd., Surb.　91　G7
Corkscrew Hill,　103　C2
　W.Wick.
Corlett St. NW1　**10**　**G1**
Cormont Rd. SE5　76　H1
Cornbury Rd., Edg.　29　G7
Cornelia St. N7　49　F6
Cornell Clo., Sid.　89　E6
Corner Grn. SE3　78　G2

Corner Ho. St. WC2　**16**　**A1**
Corner Mead NW9　30　F7
Corney Rd. W4　65　E6
Cornflower La.,　102　G1
　Croy.
Cornflower Ter.　77　E6
　SE22
Cornford Clo., Brom.　96　G5
Cornford Gro. SW12　85　B2
Cornhill EC3　**13**　**C4**
Cornhill EC3　59　A6
Cornish Ct. N9　25　E7
Cornish Gro. SE20　95　E1
Cornish Ho. SE17　**20**　**G6**
Cornish Ho., Brent.　64　J5
Cornmill La. SE13　78　C3
Cornmow Dr. NW10　47　G4
Cornshaw Rd., Dag.　53　D1
Cornthwaite Rd. E5　50　F3
Cornwall Ave. E2　59　F3
Cornwall Ave. N3　31　D7
Cornwall Ave. N22　40　E1
Cornwall Ave., Esher　98　C7
　The Causeway
Cornwall Ave., Sthl.　54　F5
Cornwall Ave., Well.　79　H3
Cornwall Clo., Bark.　52　J6
Cornwall Cres. W11　57　B6
Cornwall Dr., Orp.　89　C7
Cornwall Gdns.　47　H6
　NW10
Cornwall Gdns. SW7　**14**　**B6**
Cornwall Gdns. SW7　66　E3
Cornwall Gdns. Wk.　**14**　**B6**
　SW7
Cornwall Gro. W4　65　E5
Cornwall Ms. S. SW7　**14**　**C6**
Cornwall Ms. S. SW7　66　F3
Cornwall Ms. W. SW7　**14**　**B6**
Cornwall Rd. N4　40　G7
Cornwall Rd. N15　41　A5
Cornwall Rd. N18　33　D5
　Fairfield Rd.
Cornwall Rd. SE1　**16**　**E1**
Cornwall Rd. SE1　67　G1
Cornwall Rd., Croy.　101　H2
Cornwall Rd., Har.　36　J6
Cornwall Rd., Pnr.　28　F7
Cornwall Rd., Sutt.　100　C7
Cornwall Rd.,　73　D7
　Twick.
Cornwall St. E1　59　E7
　Watney St.
Cornwall Ter. NW1　**7**　**A6**
Cornwall Ter. Ms.　**7**　**A6**
　NW1
Cornwallis Ave. N9　33　E2
Cornwallis Ave. SE9　88　G2
Cornwallis Gro. N9　33　E2
Cornwallis Rd. E17　41　G4
Cornwallis Rd. N9　33　E2
Cornwallis Rd. N19　49　E2
Cornwallis Rd., Dag.　53　D4
Cornwallis Wk. SE9　79　C3
Cornwood Clo. N2　39　G5
Cornwood Dr. E1　59　F6
Cornworthy Rd., Dag.　53　C5
Corona Rd. SE12　78　G7
Coronation Ave. N16　50　C3
　Victorian Rd.
Coronation Clo., Bex.　80　D6
Coronation Clo., Ilf.　43　F4
Coronation Rd. E13　60　J3
Coronation Rd.　55　J3
　NW10
Coronation Wk.,　81　G1
　Twick.
Coronet St. N1　**9**　**D4**
Coronet St. N1　59　B3
Corporation Ave.,　72　E4
　Houns.
Corporation Row EC1　**8**　**F5**
Corporation Row EC1　58　G4
Corporation St. E15　60　E2
Corporation St. N7　49　E5
Corrance Rd. SW2　76　E4
Corri Ave. N14　32　D4
Corrib Dr., Sutt.　100　H5
Corringham Ct.　39　E7
　NW11
　Corringham Rd.
Corringham Rd.　39　D7
　NW11
Corringham Rd.,　47　A2
　Wem.
Corringway NW11　39　E7
Corringway W5　55　J5
Corscombe Clo.,　83　C5
　Kings.T.
Corsehill St. SW16　85　C6
Corsham St. N1　**9**　**C4**
Corsham St. N1　59　A3
Corsica St. N5　49　H6

Corsley Way E9　50　J6
　Trowbridge Est.
Cortayne Rd. SW6　75　C2
Cortis Rd. SW15　74　H6
Cortis Ter. SW15　74　H6
Corunna Rd. SW8　76　C1
Corunna Ter. SW8　76　C1
Corvette Sq. SE10　69　D6
　Feathers Pl.
Coryton Path W9　57　C4
　Ashmore Rd.
Cosbycote Ave. SE24　76　J5
Cosdach Ave., Wall.　101　D7
Cosedge Cres.,　101　G5
　Croy.
Cosgrove Clo. N21　32　J2
Cosgrove Clo.,　54　E4
　Hayes
　Kingsash Dr.
Cosmo Pl. WC1　**12**　**B1**
Cosmur Clo. W12　65　F3
Cossall Wk. SE15　77　E1
Cosser St. SE1　**16**　**E5**
Cosser St. SE1　67　G3
Costa St. SE15　77　D2
Coston Wk. SE4　77　D2
　Frendsbury Rd.
Costons Ave., Grnf.　55　A3
Costons La., Grnf.　55　A3
Cosway St. NW1　**10**　**H1**
Cosway St. NW1　57　H5
Cotall St. E14　60　A6
Coteford Clo., Loug.　27　E2
Coteford Clo., Pnr.　36　A5
Coteford St. SW17　84　J4
Cotelands, Croy.　102　B3
Cotesbach Rd. E5　50　F3
Cotesmore Gdns.,　53　C3
　Dag.
Cotford Rd., Th.Hth.　94　J4
Cotherstone Rd. SW2　85　F1
Cotleigh Ave., Bex.　89　D2
Cotleigh Rd. NW6　48　D7
Cotman Clo. NW11　39　F6
Cotman Clo. SW15　74　J6
　Westleigh Ave.
Cotman Gdns., Edg.　38　A2
Cotmans Clo., Hayes　63　A1
Coton Rd., Well.　80　A3
Cotsford Ave., N.Mal.　92　C5
Cotswold Clo.,　83　B6
　Kings.T.
Cotswold Gdns. E6　61　A3
Cotswold Gdns. NW2　48　B1
Cotswold Gdns.,　43　G7
　Ilf.
Cotswold Gate NW2　48　B1
　Cotswold Gdns.
Cotswold Ms. SW11　75　G1
　Battersea High St.
Cotswold Ri., Orp.　97　J6
Cotswold Rd.,　81　G6
　Hmptn.
Cotswold St. SE27　85　H4
　Norwood High St.
Cotswold Way, Enf.　24　F3
Cotswold Way,　99　J2
　Wor.Pk.
Cottage Ave., Brom.　104　B1
Cottage Fld. Clo.,　89　C1
　Sid.
Cottage Grn. SE5　**21**　**C7**
Cottage Grn. SE5　68　A7
Cottage Gro. SW9　76　E3
Cottage Gro., Surb.　91　G6
Cottage Homes NW7　30　G4
Cottage Homes　30　G4
　Chalet Est. NW7
Cottage Pl. SW3　**14**　**G6**
Cottage Pl. SW3　66　H3
Cottage Rd., Epsom　99　D7
Cottage St. E14　60　C7
Cottage Wk. SE15　68　C7
　Sumner Est.
Cottenham Dr. NW9　38　F3
Cottenham Dr. SW20　83　H7
Cottenham Pk. Rd.　92　H1
　SW20
Cottenham Pl. SW20　83　H7
Cottenham Rd. E17　41　J4
Cotterill Rd., Surb.　98　H2
Cottesbrook St.　68　H7
　SE14
　Nynehead St.
Cottesmore Ave., Ilf.　43　D2
Cottesmore Gdns.　**14**　**B5**
　W8
Cottesmore Gdns.　66　E3
　W8
Cottimore Cres.,　90　B7
　Walt.
Cottimore La., Walt.　90　B7

Cottimore Ter., Walt.	90	B7
Cottingham Chase, Ruis.	45	A3
Cottingham Rd. SE20	86	G7
Cottingham Rd. SW8	**20**	**D7**
Cottingham Rd. SW8	87	F7
Cottington Clo. SE11	**20**	**G2**
Cottington Clo. SE11	67	H4
Cottington Rd., Felt.	81	D4
Cottington St. SE11	**20**	**F3**
Cottle St. SE16	68	F2
St. Marychurch St.		
Cotton Ave. W3	56	D6
Cotton Hill, Brom.	87	D4
Cotton Row SW11	75	G3
Cotton St. E14	60	C7
Cottongrass Clo., Croy.	102	G1
Cornflower La.		
Cottons Gdns. E2	**9**	**E3**
Cottons La. SE1	**17**	**C1**
Couchmore Ave., Esher	98	B2
Couchmore Ave., Ilf.	43	C2
Coulgate St. SE4	77	H3
Coulson Clo., Dag.	44	C7
Coulson St. SW3	**18**	**J3**
Coulson St. SW3	66	J5
Coulter Rd. W6	65	H3
Coultree Clo., Hayes	54	E4
Berrydale Rd.		
Councillor St. SE5	67	J7
Counter Ct. SE1	**17**	**B2**
Counter St. SE1	**17**	**D2**
Countess Rd. NW5	49	C5
Countisbury Ave., Enf.	25	C7
Country Way, Felt.	81	B6
Country Way, Sun.	81	A7
County Gdns., Bark.	61	H2
River Rd.		
County Gate SE9	88	F3
County Gate, Barn.	23	E6
County Gro. SE5	76	J1
County Rd. E6	61	E5
County Rd., Th.Hth.	94	H2
County St. SE1	**17**	**A6**
County St. SE1	67	J3
Coupland Pl. SE18	70	F5
Courcy Rd. N8	40	G3
Courland Gro. SW8	76	D2
Courland St. SW8	76	D1
Course, The SE9	88	D3
Court, The, Ruis.	45	E4
Court Ave., Belv.	71	F5
Court Clo., Har.	37	G3
Court Clo., Twick.	81	H3
Court Clo., Wall.	101	D7
Court Clo. Ave., Twick.	81	H3
Court Cres., Chess.	90	G5
Court Downs Rd., Beck.	96	B2
Court Dr., Croy.	101	F4
Court Dr., Stan.	29	H4
Court Dr., Sutt.	100	H4
Court Frm. Ave., Epsom	99	D5
Court Frm. Rd. SE9	88	A2
Court Frm. Rd., Nthlt.	45	G7
Court Ho. Gdns. N3	31	D6
Court La. SE21	77	B6
Court La. Gdns. SE21	77	B7
Court Mead, Nthlt.	54	F3
Court Rd. SE9	79	C6
Court Rd. SE25	95	C2
Court Rd., Sthl.	63	F4
Court St. E1	59	E5
Durward St.		
Court St., Brom.	96	G2
Court Way NW9	38	E4
Court Way W3	56	C5
Court Way, Ilf.	43	F3
Court Way, Twick.	73	C7
Court Yd. SE9	79	C6
Courtauld Clo. SE28	71	A1
Pitfield Cres.		
Courtauld Rd. N19	49	H7
Courtenay Ave. N6	39	H7
Courtenay Ave., Har.	28	J7
Courtenay Dr., Beck.	96	D2
Courtenay Gdns., Har.	36	J2
Courtenay Ms. E17	41	H5
Courtenay Pl. E17	41	H5
Courtenay Ms.		
Courtenay Rd. E11	51	F3
Courtenay Rd. E17	41	G4
Courtenay Rd. SE20	86	G7
Courtenay Rd., Wor.Pk.	99	J3
Courtenay Sq. SE11	**20**	**E4**
Courtenay St. SE11	**20**	**E3**
Courtenay St. SE11	67	G5
Courtens Ms., Stan.	29	F7
Courtfield W5	55	F5
Courtfield Ave., Har.	37	C5
Courtfield Cres., Har.	37	C5
Courtfield Gdns. SW5	**18**	**B2**
Courtfield Gdns. SW5	66	E4
Courtfield Gdns. W13	55	D6
Courtfield Ms. SW5	**18**	**B2**
Courtfield Ri., W.Wick.	103	D3
Courtfield Rd. SW7	**18**	**C1**
Courtfield Rd. SW7	66	F4
Courthill Rd. SE13	78	C4
Courthope Rd. NW3	48	J4
Courthope Rd. SW19	84	B5
Courthope Rd., Grnf.	55	A2
Courthope Vill. SW19	84	B7
Courthouse Rd. N12	31	E6
Courtland Ave. E4	34	F2
Courtland Ave. NW7	30	D3
Courtland Ave. SW16	85	F7
Courtland Ave., Ilf.	52	C2
Courtland Dr., Chig.	35	E3
Courtland Gro. SE28	62	D7
Courtland Rd. E6	61	B1
Harrow Rd.		
Courtlands, Rich.	74	A5
Courtlands Ave. SE12	78	H5
Courtlands Ave., Brom.	103	E1
Courtlands Ave., Hmptn.	81	F6
Courtlands Ave., Rich.	74	B2
Courtlands Dr., Epsom	99	E6
Courtlands Rd., Surb.	92	A7
Courtleet Dr., Erith	80	H1
Courtleigh Gdns. NW11	39	B4
Courtman Rd. N17	32	J7
Courtmead Clo. SE24	76	J6
Courtnell St. W2	57	D6
Courtney Clo. SE19	86	B6
Courtney Cres., Cars.	100	J7
Courtney Pl., Croy.	101	G3
Courtney Rd.		
Courtney Rd. N7	49	G5
Bryantwood Rd.		
Courtney Rd. SW19	84	H7
Courtney Rd., Croy.	101	G3
Courtrai Rd. SE23	77	H6
Courtside N8	40	D6
Courtway, Wdf.Grn.	34	J5
Courtway, The, Wat.	28	E2
Courtyard, The E1	59	E7
Courtyard, The N1	49	F7
Barnsbury Ter.		
Cousin La. EC4	**13**	**B6**
Couthurst Rd. SE3	69	H6
Coutts Ave., Chess.	98	H5
Coutts Cres. NW5	49	A3
Coval Gdns. SW14	74	B4
Coval La. SW14	74	B4
Coval Rd. SW14	74	B4
Covelees Wall E6	61	B5
Warwall		
Covent Gdn. WC2	**12**	**B5**
Covent Gdn. WC2	58	E7
Coventry Clo. E6	61	C6
Harper Rd.		
Coventry Clo. NW6	57	D1
Kilburn High Rd.		
Coventry Cross E3	60	C4
Gillender St.		
Coventry Rd. E1	59	E4
Coventry Rd. E2	59	E4
Coventry Rd. SE25	95	D4
Coventry Rd., Ilf.	52	E2
Coventry St. W1	**11**	**H6**
Coventry St. W1	58	D7
Coverack Clo. N14	24	C6
Coverack Clo., Croy.	95	H7
Coverdale Clo., Stan.	29	E5
Coverdale Gdns., Croy.	102	C3
Park Hill Ri.		
Coverdale Rd. NW2	48	A7
Coverdale Rd. W12	65	H2
Coverdales, The, Bark.	61	G2
Coverley Clo. E1	**13**	**J1**
Coverley Clo. E1	59	D5
Covert, The, Orp.	97	H6
Covert Rd., Chig.	35	J6
Covert Way, Barn.	23	F2
Coverton Rd. SW17	84	H5
Covington Gdns. SW16	85	H7
Covington Way SW16	85	F6
Cow La., Grnf.	55	A2
Oldfield La. S.		
Cow Leaze E6	61	D6
Downings		
Cowan Clo. E6	61	B5
Oliver Gdns.		
Cowbridge La., Bark.	52	E7
Cowbridge Rd., Har.	37	J4
Cowcross St. EC1	**12**	**G1**
Cowcross St. EC1	58	H5
Cowden Rd., Orp.	97	J7
Cowden St. SE6	87	A4
Cowdenbeath Path	58	F1
Bingfield St.		
Cowdrey Clo., Enf.	25	B2
Cowdrey Rd. SW19	84	E5
Cowdry Rd. E9	50	H6
Wick Rd.		
Cowen Ave., Har.	45	J2
Cowgate Rd., Grnf.	55	A2
Cowick Rd. SW17	84	J4
Cowings Mead, Nthlt.	45	E6
Cowland Ave., Enf.	25	F4
Cowleaze Rd., Kings.T.	91	H1
Cowley La. E11	51	E3
Cathall Rd.		
Cowley Pl. NW4	38	J5
Cowley Rd. E11	42	H5
Cowley Rd. SW9	76	G1
Cowley Rd. SW14	74	E3
Cowley Rd. W3	65	F1
Cowley Rd., Ilf.	43	C7
Cowley St. SW1	**16**	**A5**
Cowling Clo. W11	66	B1
Wilsham St.		
Cowper Ave. E6	52	B7
Cowper Ave., Sutt.	100	G4
Cowper Clo., Brom.	97	A4
Cowper Clo., Well.	80	A5
Cowper Gdns. N14	24	B6
Cowper Gdns., Wall.	101	C6
Cowper Rd. N14	32	B1
Cowper Rd. N16	50	B5
Cowper Rd. N18	33	D5
Cowper Rd. SW19	84	F6
Cowper Rd. W3	65	D1
Cowper Rd. W7	55	C7
Cowper Rd., Belv.	71	G4
Cowper Rd., Brom.	97	A4
Cowper Rd., Kings.T.	82	J5
Cowper St. EC2	**9**	**C5**
Cowper St. EC2	59	A4
St. Marks Rd.		
Cowslip Rd. E18	42	H2
Cowthorpe Rd. SW8	76	D1
Cox La., Chess.	98	H4
Cox La., Epsom	99	B4
Coxmount Rd. SE7	70	A5
Cox's Wk. SE21	86	D1
Coxson Pl. SE1	**17**	**F4**
Coxwell Rd. SE18	70	G5
Coxwell Rd. SE19	86	B7
Crab Hill, Beck.	87	D7
Crabtree Ave., Rom.	44	D4
Crabtree Ave., Wem.	55	H2
Crabtree Ct. E15	51	B5
Clays La.		
Crabtree La. SW6	66	A7
Crabtree Manorway N., Belv.	71	J2
Crabtree Manorway S., Belv.	71	J3
Crabtree Wk. SE15	77	C1
Lisford St.		
Crace St. NW1	**7**	**H3**
Craddock Rd., Enf.	25	C3
Craddock St. NW5	49	A6
Prince of Wales Rd.		
Cradley Rd. SE9	88	G1
Craig Gdns. E18	42	F2
Craig Pk. Rd. N18	33	E5
Craig Rd., Rich.	82	F4
Craigen Ave., Croy.	102	E1
Craigerne Rd. SE3	69	H7
Craigholm SE18	79	D2
Craigmuir Pk., Wem.	55	J1
Craignair Rd. SW2	76	G7
Craignish Ave. SW16	94	F2
Craigs Ct. SW1	**16**	**A1**
Craigton Rd. SE9	79	C4
Craigweil Clo., Stan.	29	G5
Craigweil Dr., Stan.	29	G5
Craigwell Ave., Felt.	81	A3
Craik Ct. NW6	57	C2
Carlton Vale		
Crail Row SE17	**21**	**C2**
Cramer St. W1	**11**	**C2**
Cramond Clo. W6	66	B6
Crampton Rd. SE20	86	F6
Crampton St. SE17	**20**	**J3**
Crampton St. SE17	67	J4
Cranberry Clo., Nthlt.	54	D2
Parkfield Ave.		
Cranborne Ave., Sthl.	63	G4
Cranborne Rd., Bark.	61	G1
Cranborne Waye, Hayes	54	B6
Cranbourn All. WC2	**11**	**J5**
Cranbourn St. WC2	**11**	**J5**
Cranbourn St. WC2	58	D7
Cranbourne Ave. E11	42	H4
Cranbourne Ave., Surb.	99	A3
Cranbourne Clo. SW16	94	E3
Cranbourne Dr., Pnr.	36	D5
Cranbourne Gdns. NW11	39	B5
Cranbourne Gdns., Ilf.	43	F3
Cranbourne Rd. E12	52	B5
High St.		
Cranbourne Rd. E15	51	C4
Cranbourne Rd. N10	40	B2
Cranbrook Clo., Brom.	96	G6
Cranbrook Dr., Twick.	81	H1
Cranbrook Est. E2	59	G2
Cranbrook Ms. E17	41	J5
Cranbrook Pk. N22	40	F1
Cranbrook Pt. E16	69	G1
Cranbrook Ri., Ilf.	43	C6
Cranbrook Rd. SE8	78	A1
Cranbrook Rd. SW19	84	B7
Cranbrook Rd. W4	65	E5
Cranbrook Rd., Barn.	23	G6
Cranbrook Rd., Bexh.	80	F1
Cranbrook Rd., Houns.	72	F4
Cranbrook Rd., Ilf.	43	D5
Cranbrook Rd., Th.Hth.	94	J2
Cranbrook St. E2	59	G2
Roman Rd.		
Cranbury Rd. SW6	75	E2
Crane Ave. W3	56	C7
Crane Ave., Islw.	73	D5
Crane Clo., Dag.	53	G6
Crane Ct. EC4	**12**	**F4**
Crane Ct., Epsom	99	C4
Crane Gro. N7	49	G6
Crane Mead SE16	68	G4
Crane Pk. Rd., Twick.	81	H2
Crane Rd., Twick.	82	B1
Crane St. SE10	69	D5
Park Row		
Crane Way, Twick.	72	J7
Cranebrook, Twick.	81	J2
Manor Rd.		
Craneford Clo., Twick.	73	C7
Craneford Way, Twick.	73	B7
Cranes Dr., Surb.	91	H4
Cranes Pk.		
Cranes Pk., Surb.	91	H4
Cranes Pk. Ave., Surb.	91	H4
Cranes Pk. Cres., Surb.	91	J4
Cranes Way, Borwd.	22	C5
Craneswater Pk., Sthl.	63	F5
Cranfield Clo. SE27	85	J3
Dunelm Gro.		
Cranfield Dr. NW9	30	E7
Cranfield Rd. SE4	77	J3
Cranfield Row SE1	**16**	**F5**
Cranford Ave. N13	32	E5
Cranford Clo. SW20	83	H7
Cranford Cotts. E1	59	G7
Cranford St.		
Cranford La. (Heston), Houns.	63	B7
Cranford St. E1	59	G7
Cranford Way N8	40	F5
Cranhurst Rd. NW2	47	J3
Cranleigh Clo. SE20	95	E2
Cranleigh Clo., Bex.	80	H5
Cranleigh Gdns. N21	24	G5

Entry	Page	Ref
Cranleigh Gdns. SE25	95	B3
Cranleigh Gdns., Bark.	52	G7
Cranleigh Gdns., Har.	37	H5
Cranleigh Gdns., Kings.T.	82	J6
Cranleigh Gdns., Loug.	27	C6
Cranleigh Gdns., Sthl.	54	F6
Cranleigh Gdns., Sutt.	100	E2
Cranleigh Ms. SW11	75	H2
Cranleigh Rd. N15	40	J5
Cranleigh Rd. SW19	93	C3
Cranleigh St. NW1	**7**	**G2**
Cranleigh St. NW1	58	C2
Cranley Dene Ct. N10	40	B4
Cranley Dr., Ilf.	43	F7
Cranley Gdns. N10	40	B4
Cranley Gdns. N13	32	F3
Cranley Gdns. SW7	**18**	**D3**
Cranley Gdns. SW7	66	F5
Cranley Gdns., Wall.	101	C7
Cranley Ms. SW7	**18**	**D3**
Cranley Ms. SW7	66	F5
Cranley Pl. SW7	**18**	**E2**
Cranley Pl. SW7	66	G4
Cranley Rd. E13	60	H5
Cranley Rd., Ilf.	43	F6
Cranmer Ave. W13	64	E3
Cranmer Clo., Mord.	93	A6
Cranmer Clo., Ruis.	45	D1
Cranmer Clo., Stan.	29	F7
Cranmer Ct. SW3	**18**	**H2**
Cranmer Ct. SW4	76	D3
Cranmer Ct., Hmptn.	81	H5
Cranmer Rd.		
Cranmer Fm. Clo., Mitch.	93	J4
Cranmer Gdns., Dag.	53	J4
Cranmer Rd. E7	51	H4
Cranmer Rd. SW9	**20**	**F7**
Cranmer Rd. SW9	67	G7
Cranmer Rd., Croy.	101	H3
Cranmer Rd., Edg.	30	B3
Cranmer Rd., Hmptn.	81	H5
Cranmer Rd., Kings.T.	82	H5
Cranmer Rd., Mitch.	93	J4
Cranmer Ter. SW17	84	G5
Cranmore Ave., Islw.	63	J7
Cranmore Rd., Brom.	87	F3
Cranmore Way N10	40	C4
Cranston Clo., Houns.	72	E2
Cranston Est. N1	**9**	**C2**
Cranston Est. N1	59	A2
Cranston Gdns. E4	34	B5
Cranston Rd. SE23	86	H1
Cranswick Rd. SE16	68	E5
Crantock Rd. SE6	87	B2
Cranwell Clo. E3	60	B4
Cranwich Ave. N21	25	A7
Cranwich Rd. N16	41	A7
Cranwood St. EC1	**9**	**C4**
Cranwood St. EC1	59	A3
Cranworth Cres. E4	34	D1
Cranworth Gdns. SW9	76	G1
Craster Rd. SW2	76	F7
Crathie Rd. SE12	78	H6
Crathorn St. SE13	78	C3
Loampit Vale		
Cravan Ave., Felt.	81	A2
Craven Ave. W5	55	F7
Craven Ave., Nthlt.	54	F5
Craven Clo., Hayes	54	A6
Craven Gdns. SW19	84	D5
Craven Gdns., Bark.	61	H2
Craven Gdns., Ilf.	43	G2
Craven Hill W2	**10**	**D5**
Craven Hill W2	57	F7
Craven Hill Gdns. W2	**10**	**C5**
Craven Hill Gdns. W2	57	F7
Craven Hill Ms. W2	**10**	**D5**
Craven Hill Ms. W2	57	F7
Craven Ms. SW11	76	A3
Taybridge Rd.		
Craven Pk. NW10	56	E1
Craven Pk. Ms. NW10	56	E1
Craven Pk. Rd. N15	41	C6
Craven Pk. Rd. NW10	56	E1
Craven Pas. WC2	**16**	**A1**
Craven Rd. NW10	56	D1
Craven Rd. W2	**10**	**D5**
Craven Rd. W2	57	F6
Craven Rd. W5	55	F7
Craven Rd., Croy.	102	E1
Craven Rd., Kings.T.	91	J1
Craven St. WC2	67	E1
Craven Ter. W2	**10**	**D5**
Craven Ter. W2	57	F7
Craven Wk. N16	41	D7
Crawford Ave., Wem.	46	G5
Crawford Clo., Islw.	73	B2
Crawford Est. SE5	76	J7
Crawford Gdns. N13	32	H3
Crawford Gdns., Nthlt.	54	F3
Crawford Ms. W1	**10**	**J2**
Crawford Pas. EC1	**8**	**E6**
Crawford Pl. W1	**10**	**H3**
Crawford Pl. W1	57	H6
Crawford St. W1	**10**	**H2**
Crawford St. W1	57	J5
Crawley Rd. E10	51	B1
Crawley Rd. N22	40	J2
Crawley Rd., Enf.	25	B7
Crawshaw Ct. SW9	76	G1
Eythorne Rd.		
Crawthew Gro. SE22	77	C4
Cray Rd., Belv.	71	G6
Cray Rd., Sid.	89	C7
Craybrooke Rd., Sid.	89	B4
Craybury End SE9	88	F2
Crayford Clo. E6	61	B5
Neatscourt Rd.		
Crayford Rd. N7	49	D4
Crayke Hill, Chess.	98	H7
Crealock Gro., Wdf.Grn.	34	F5
Crealock St. SW18	75	E6
Creasy Est. SE1	**17**	**D6**
Crebor St. SE22	77	D6
Credenhall Dr., Brom.	104	C1
Lwr. Gravel Rd.		
Credenhill St. SW16	85	C6
Crediton Hill NW6	48	E5
Crediton Rd. E16	60	G6
Pacific Rd.		
Crediton Rd. NW10	57	A1
Crediton Way, Esher	94	D5
Credon Rd. E13	60	J2
Credon Rd. SE16	68	H5
Creechurch La. EC3	**13**	**E4**
Creechurch La. EC3	59	B6
Creechurch Pl. EC3	**13**	**E4**
Creed La. EC4	**12**	**H4**
Creek, The, Sun.	90	A5
Creek Rd. SE8	69	A6
Creek Rd. SE10	69	B6
Creek Rd., Bark.	61	J3
Creek Rd., E.Mol.	91	B4
Creekside SE8	69	B7
Creeland Gro. SE6	86	J1
Catford Hill		
Crefeld Clo. W6	66	A6
Creffield Rd. W3	55	J7
Creffield Rd. W5	55	J7
Creighton Ave. E6	61	A2
Creighton Ave. N2	39	H3
Creighton Ave. N10	39	J2
Creighton Rd. N17	33	B7
Creighton Rd. NW6	57	A2
Creighton Rd. W5	64	G3
Cremer St. E2	**9**	**F2**
Cremorne Est. SW10	**18**	**E7**
Cremorne Rd. SW10	**18**	**D7**
Cremorne Rd. SW10	66	F7
Crescent, The E17	41	H5
Crescent, The EC3	**13**	**F5**
Crescent, The N11	32	A4
Crescent, The NW2	47	H3
Crescent, The SW13	74	F2
Crescent, The SW19	84	D3
Crescent, The W3	56	E6
Crescent, The, Barn.	23	E3
Crescent, The, Beck.	86	A1
Crescent, The, Bex.	80	C7
Crescent, The, Croy.	95	A5
Crescent, The, Har.	45	J1
Crescent, The, Ilf.	43	D6
Crescent, The, Loug.	27	A5
Crescent, The, N.Mal.	92	C2
Crescent, The, Sid.	88	J4
Crescent, The, Sthl.	63	F2
Crescent, The, Surb.	96	H5
Crescent, The, Sutt.	100	G5
Crescent, The (Aldenham), Wat.	28	H2
Crescent, The, Wem.	46	D2
Crescent, The, W.Mol.	90	G4
Crescent, The, W.Wick.	96	E6
Crescent Dr., Orp.	97	E6
Crescent Gdns. SW19	81	D8
Crescent Gdns., Ruis.	36	B7
Crescent Gro. SW4	76	C4
Crescent Gro., Mitch.	93	H4
Crescent La. SW4	76	C4
Crescent Pl. SW3	**18**	**G1**
Crescent Pl. SW3	66	H4
Crescent Ri. N22	40	D1
Crescent Ri., Barn.	23	H5
Crescent Rd. E4	26	E7
Crescent Rd. E6	60	J1
Crescent Rd. E10	51	B2
Crescent Rd. E13	60	G1
Crescent Rd. E18	42	J2
Crescent Rd. N3	39	C1
Crescent Rd. N8	40	D6
Crescent Rd. N9	33	D1
Crescent Rd. N11	31	J4
Crescent Rd. N15	40	H3
Carlingford Rd.		
Crescent Rd. N22	40	D1
Crescent Rd. SE18	70	E5
Crescent Rd. SW20	93	A1
Crescent Rd., Barn.	23	G4
Crescent Rd., Beck.	96	B2
Crescent Rd., Brom.	87	G7
Crescent Rd., Dag.	53	H3
Crescent Rd., Enf.	24	H4
Crescent Rd., Kings.T.	83	A7
Crescent Rd., Sid.	88	J3
Crescent Row EC1	**8**	**J6**
Crescent Stables SW15	75	B4
Upper Richmond Rd.		
Crescent St. N1	49	F7
Crescent Vw., Loug.	27	A5
Crescent Way N12	31	H6
Crescent Way SE4	78	A3
Crescent Way SW16	85	F6
Crescent Way, Orp.	104	H5
Crescent W., Barn.	23	F1
Crescent Wd. Rd. SE26	86	D3
Cresford Rd. SW6	75	E1
Crespigny Rd. NW4	38	H6
Cressage Clo., Sthl.	54	G4
Cresset Rd. E9	50	F6
Cresset St. SW4	76	D3
Cressfield Clo. NW5	49	A5
Cressida Rd. N19	49	C1
Cressingham Gro., Sutt.	100	F4
Cressingham Rd. SE13	78	C3
Cressingham Rd., Edg.	30	D6
Cressington Clo. N16	50	B5
Wordsworth Rd.		
Cresswell Gdns. SW5	**18**	**C3**
Cresswell Gdns. SW5	66	F5
Cresswell Pk. SE3	78	F3
Cresswell Pl. SW10	**18**	**C3**
Cresswell Pl. SW10	66	F5
Cresswell Rd. SE25	95	D4
Cresswell Rd., Felt.	81	E4
Cresswell Rd., Twick.	73	G6
Cresswell Way N21	24	G7
Cressy Ct. E1	65	H3
Cressy Pl.		
Cressy Pl. E1	59	F5
Cressy Rd. NW3	48	J5
Crest, The N13	32	G4
Crest, The NW4	38	J5
Crest, The, Surb.	92	A5
Crest Gdns., Ruis.	45	C3
Crest Rd. NW2	47	F3
Crest Rd., Brom.	96	F7
Crest Rd., S.Croy.	102	E7
Crest Vw., Pnr.	36	D4
Crest Vw. Dr., Orp.	97	F5
Crestbrook Ave. N13	32	H3
Crestfield St. WC1	**8**	**B3**
Crestfield St. WC1	58	E3
Creston Way, Wor.Pk.	100	A1
Crestway SW15	74	G6
Crestwood Way, Houns.	72	F5
Creswick Rd. W3	56	B7
Creswick Wk. E3	60	A3
Malmesbury Rd.		
Creswick Wk. NW11	39	C4
Creton St. SE18	70	D3
Crewdson Rd. SW9	67	G7
Crewe Pl. NW10	56	F3
Crews St. E14	69	A4
Crewys Rd. NW2	48	C2
Crewys Rd. SE15	77	E2
Crichton Ave., Wall.	101	D1
Crichton Rd., Cars.	100	J7
Cricket Grn., Mitch.	93	J3
Cricket Grd. Rd., Chis.	97	E1
Cricket La., Beck.	86	H5
Cricketers Arms Rd., Enf.	24	J2
Cricketers Clo. N14	24	C7
Cricketers Clo., Chess.	98	G4
Cricketers Ct. SE11	**20**	**G2**
Cricketfield Rd. E5	50	H4
Cricklade Ave. SW2	85	E2
Cricklewood Bdy. NW2	47	J3
Cricklewood La. NW2	48	A4
Cricklewood Trd. Est. NW2	48	B3
Cridland St. E15	60	F1
Church St.		
Crieff Ct., Tedd.	82	F7
Crieff Rd. SW18	75	F6
Criffel Ave. SW2	85	D2
Crimscott St. SE1	**17**	**E6**
Crimscott St. SE1	68	B3
Crimsworth Rd. SW8	76	D1
Crinan St. N1	**8**	**B1**
Crinan St. N1	58	E2
Cringle St. SW8	**19**	**F7**
Cringle St. SW8	67	C7
Cripplegate St. EC2	**12**	**J1**
Crisp Rd. W6	65	J5
Crispe Ho., Bark.	61	G2
Dovehouse Mead		
Crispen Rd., Felt.	81	E4
Crispian Clo. NW10	47	E4
Crispin Cres., Croy.	101	D2
Crispin Rd., Edg.	30	C6
Crispin St. E1	**13**	**F2**
Crispin St. E1	59	C5
Cristowe Rd. SW6	75	C2
Criterion Ms. N19	49	D4
St. Johns Vill.		
Crockerton Rd. SW17	84	J2
Crockham Way SE9	88	D4
Crocus Clo., Croy.	102	G1
Cornflower La.		
Crocus Fld., Barn.	23	C6
Croft, The NW10	56	F2
Croft, The W5	55	H5
Croft, The, Barn.	23	B4
Croft, The, Houns.	63	E6
Croft, The, Loug.	27	D2
Croft, The, Ruis.	45	C4
Croft, The, Wem.	46	F5
Croft Ave., W.Wick.	103	C1
Croft Clo. NW7	30	E3
Croft Clo., Belv.	71	F5
Croft Clo., Chis.	88	C4
Croft Gdns. W7	64	D2
Croft Lo. Clo., Wdf.Grn.	34	H6
Croft Rd. SW16	94	G1
Croft Rd. SW19	84	F7
Croft Rd., Brom.	87	G6
Croft Rd., Enf.	25	H1
Croft Rd., Sutt.	100	H5
Croft St. SE8	68	H4
Croft Way NW3	48	D4
Ferncroft Ave.		
Croft Way, Sid.	88	H3
Croftdown Rd. NW5	49	A3
Crofters Clo., Islw.	73	A5
Ploughmans End		
Crofters Way NW1	58	D1
Crofton Ave. W4	65	C7
Crofton Ave., Bex.	80	D7
Crofton Ave., Orp.	104	F2
Crofton La., Orp.	104	G2
Crofton Pk. Rd. SE4	77	J6
Crofton Rd. E13	60	H4
Crofton Rd. SE5	77	B1
Crofton Rd., Orp.	104	D3
Crofton Ter. E5	50	H5
Studley Clo.		
Crofton Ter., Rich.	73	J4
Crofton Way, Barn.	23	E6
Wycherley Cres.		
Crofton Way, Enf.	24	G2
Croftongate Way SE4	77	H5
Crofts Rd., Har.	37	D6
Crofts St. E1	**13**	**H6**

Crofts St. E1 59 D7
Croftway NW3 48 D4
Croftway, Rich. 82 E3
Crogsland Rd. NW1 49 A7
Croham Clo., 102 B7
S.Croy.
Croham Manor Rd., 102 B7
S.Croy.
Croham Mt., S.Croy. 102 B7
Croham Pk. Ave., 102 B5
S.Croy.
Croham Rd., S.Croy. 102 A5
Croham Valley Rd., 102 C6
S.Croy.
Croindene Rd. SW16 94 E1
Cromartie Rd. N19 40 D7
Crombie Clo., Ilf. 43 C5
Crombie Clo., Sid. 88 G1
Cromer Rd. E10 42 D6
James La.
Cromer Rd. N17 41 D2
Cromer Rd. SE25 95 E6
Cromer Rd. SW17 85 A6
Cromer Rd., Barn. 23 F4
Cromer Rd., Rom. 44 J6
Cromer Rd. Rom. 44 E6
(Chadwell Heath),
Cromer Rd., Wdf.Grn. 34 G4
Cromer St. WC1 8 B4
Cromer St. WC1 58 E3
Cromer Ter. E8 50 D5
Ferncliff Rd.
Cromer Vill. Rd. 75 C6
SW18
Cromford Clo., Orp. 104 H3
Cromford Path E5 50 G4
Overbury St.
Cromford Rd. SW18 75 D5
Cromford Way, 92 D1
N.Mal.
Cromlix Clo., Chis. 97 E2
Crompton St. W2 6 E6
Crompton St. W2 57 G4
Cromwell Ave. N6 49 B1
Cromwell Ave. W6 65 H4
Cromwell Ave., 96 H3
Brom.
Cromwell Ave., 92 F5
N.Mal.
Cromwell Clo. N2 39 G4
Cromwell Clo. W3 65 C1
High St.
Cromwell Clo., 96 H4
Brom.
Cromwell Cres. SW5 66 D4
Cromwell Gdns. SW7 14 F6
Cromwell Gdns. SW7 66 G3
Cromwell Gro. W6 65 J3
Cromwell Ind. Est. 50 H1
E10
Cromwell Ms. SW7 18 F1
Cromwell Ms. SW7 66 G4
Cromwell Pl. N6 49 B1
Cromwell Ave.
Cromwell Pl. SW7 18 F1
Cromwell Pl. SW7 66 G4
Cromwell Pl. SW14 74 C3
Cromwell Pl. W3 65 C1
Grove Pl.
Cromwell Rd. E7 51 J7
Cromwell Rd. E17 42 C5
Cromwell Rd. N3 39 F2
Cromwell Rd. N10 32 A7
Cromwell Rd. SW5 66 E4
Cromwell Rd. SW7 18 E1
Cromwell Rd. SW7 66 E4
Cromwell Rd. SW9 76 H1
Cromwell Rd. SW19 84 D5
Cromwell Rd., Beck. 95 H2
Cromwell Rd., Croy. 95 A7
Cromwell Rd., Felt. 81 B1
Cromwell Rd., 72 G4
Houns.
Cromwell Rd., 91 H1
Kings.T.
Cromwell Rd., Tedd. 82 D6
Cromwell Rd., Wem. 55 H2
Cromwell Rd., 99 D3
Wor.Pk.
Cromwell St., 72 G4
Houns.
Crondace Rd. SW6 75 D1
Crondall St. N1 9 D2
Crondall St. N1 59 A2
Crook Log, Bexh. 80 D3
Crooke Rd. SE8 68 H5
Crooked Billet SW19 93 E4
Woodhayes Rd.
Crooked Billet 34 A7
Roundabout E17
Crooked Usage N3 39 B3
Crookham Rd. SW6 75 C1
Crookston Rd. SE9 79 D3

Croombs Rd. E16 60 J5
Crooms Hill SE10 69 C7
Crooms Hill Gro. 69 C7
SE10
Cropley St. N1 9 B1
Cropley St. N1 59 A2
Croppath Rd., Dag. 53 G4
Cropthorne Ct. W9 6 D4
Crosby Clo., Felt. 81 E4
Crosby Ct. SE1 17 B3
Crosby Rd. E7 51 G6
Crosby Rd., Dag. 62 H2
Crosby Row SE1 17 B3
Crosby Row SE1 68 A2
Crosby Sq. EC3 13 D4
Crosby Wk. E8 50 C6
Laurel St.
Crosby Wk. SW2 76 G7
Crosland Pl. SW11 76 A3
Taybridge Rd.
Cross Ave. SE10 69 D6
Cross Deep, Twick. 82 C3
Cross Deep Gdns., 82 C2
Twick.
Cross Keys Clo. W1 11 C2
Cross Keys Sq. EC1 12 J2
Cross Lances Rd., 72 H4
Houns.
Cross La. EC3 13 D6
Cross La. N8 40 F3
Cross La., Bex. 80 F7
Cross Rd. E4 34 E1
Cross Rd. N11 32 B5
Cross Rd. N22 32 G7
Cross Rd. SE5 77 B2
Cross Rd. SW19 84 D7
Cross Rd., Brom. 104 B2
Cross Rd., Croy. 102 A1
Cross Rd., Enf. 25 C4
Cross Rd., Felt. 81 E4
Cross Rd., Har. 37 A4
Cross Rd., Har. 45 H3
(South Harrow),
Cross Rd., Har. 37 D2
(Wealdstone),
Cross Rd., Kings.T. 82 J7
Cross Rd., Rom. 44 G4
Cross Rd., Rom. 44 C7
(Chadwell Heath),
Cross Rd., Sid. 89 B4
Sidcup Hill
Cross Rd., Sutt. 100 G5
Cross Rd., Wdf.Grn. 35 C6
Cross Rds., Loug. 26 H2
Cross St. N1 58 H1
Cross St. SW13 74 E2
Cross St., Hmptn. 81 J5
Cross Way, Pnr. 36 B2
Cross Way, The, Har. 37 B2
Crossbow Rd., Chig. 35 J5
Crossbrook Rd. SE3 79 B2
Crossfield Rd. N17 40 J3
Crossfield Rd. NW3 48 G6
Crossfield St. SE8 69 A7
Crossfields, Loug. 27 E5
Crossford St. SW9 76 E2
Crossgate, Edg. 30 A3
Crossgate, Grnf. 46 E6
Crossland Rd. 94 H5
Th.Hth.
Crosslands Ave. W5 64 J1
Crosslands Ave., 63 F5
Sthl.
Crosslands Rd., 99 D6
Epsom
Crosslet St. SE17 21 C1
Crossley St. N7 49 G6
Crossmead SE9 88 C1
Crossmead Ave., 54 G3
Grnf.
Crossmount Ho. SE5 21 A7
Crossness Rd., 61 J3
Bark.
Crossthwaite Ave. 77 A4
SE5
Crosswall EC3 13 F5
Crosswall EC3 59 C7
Crossway N12 31 G6
Crossway N16 50 B5
Crossway NW9 38 F4
Crossway SE28 62 C6
Crossway SW20 92 J4
Crossway, Dag. 53 C3
Crossway, Enf. 25 B7
Crossway, Hayes 63 A1
Crossway, Orp. 97 G4
Crossway, Ruis. 45 C4
Crossway, Wdf.Grn. 34 J4
Crossway, The N22 32 H7
Crossway, The SE9 88 A2
Crossway, The W13 55 D4
Crossways N21 24 J6
Crossways, S.Croy. 102 H7

Crossways, The, 63 F7
Houns.
Crossways, The, 47 A2
Wem.
Crossways Rd., Beck. 96 A4
Crossways Rd., 94 B3
Mitch.
Croston St. E8 59 D1
Crothall Clo. N13 32 F3
Crouch Ave., Bark. 62 B2
Crouch Clo., Beck. 87 A6
Abbey La.
Crouch Cft. SE9 88 D3
Crouch End Hill N8 40 D6
Crouch Hall Rd. N8 40 D6
Crouch Hill N4 40 E7
Crouch Hill N8 40 E6
Crouch Rd. NW10 47 D7
Crouchman Clo. 86 C3
SE26
Crow La., Rom. 44 F7
Crowborough Path, 28 D4
Wat.
Prestwick Rd.
Crowborough Rd. 85 A6
SW17
Crowden Way SE28 62 C7
Crowder St. E1 59 E7
Crowhurst Clo. SW9 76 G2
Crowland Gdns. N14 24 E7
Crowland Rd. N15 41 C5
Crowland Rd., 95 A4
Th.Hth.
Crowland Ter. N1 50 A7
Crowland Wk., Mord. 93 E6
Crowlands Ave., 44 H6
Rom.
Crowley Cres., Croy. 101 G5
Crowline Wk. N1 50 A6
Clephane Rd.
Crowmarsh Gdns. 77 F7
SE23
Tyson Rd.
Crown Arc., Kings.T. 91 G2
Union St.
Crown Clo. E3 60 A1
Crown Clo. NW6 48 E6
Lymington Rd.
Crown Clo. NW7 30 F2
Crown Clo., Walt. 90 C7
Crown Ct. EC2 13 A4
Crown Ct. SE12 78 H6
Crown Ct. WC2 12 B4
Crown Ct., Brom. 97 A5
Victoria Rd.
Crown Dale SE19 85 H6
Crown Hill, Croy. 101 J2
Crown La. N14 32 C1
Crown La. SW16 85 G5
Crown La., Brom. 97 A5
Crown La., Chis. 97 F1
Crown La., Mord. 93 D3
Crown La. Gdns. 85 G5
SW16
Crown La.
Crown La. Spur, 97 A6
Brom.
Crown Ms. W6 65 G4
Crown Office Row 12 E5
EC4
Crown Pas. SW1 15 G2
Crown Pl. NW5 49 B6
Kentish Town Rd.
Crown Pt. Par. SE19 85 H6
Beulah Hill
Crown Rd. N10 32 A7
Crown Rd. N17 33 D7
Crown Rd., Borwd. 22 A1
Crown Rd., Enf. 25 E4
Crown Rd., Ilf. 43 G4
Crown Rd., Mord. 93 D4
Crown Rd., N.Mal. 92 C1
Crown Rd., Sutt. 100 D4
Crown Rd., Twick. 73 E6
Crown St. SE5 21 A7
Crown St. SE5 67 J7
Crown St. W3 65 B1
Crown St., Dag. 53 J6
Crown St., Har. 46 A1
Crown Ter., Rich. 73 J4
Crown Wk., Wem. 46 J3
Crown Wds. La. SE9 79 F2
Crown Wds. La. 79 E2
SE18
Crown Wds. Way 79 G5
SE9
Crown Yd., Houns. 72 J3
High St.
Crowndale Rd. NW1 7 G1
Crowndale Rd. NW1 58 G2
Crownfield Ave., Ilf. 43 H6
Crownfield Rd. E15 51 D4
Crownhill Rd. NW10 56 F1

Crownhill Rd., 35 B7
Wdf.Grn.
Crownmead Way, 44 H4
Rom.
Crownstone Rd. SW2 76 G5
Crowntree Clo., Islw. 64 C6
Crows Rd. E15 60 D3
Crowshott Ave., 37 F2
Stan.
Crowther Ave., 64 H4
Brent.
Crowther Rd. SE25 95 D4
Crowthorne Clo. 84 C1
SW18
Crowthorne Rd. W10 57 A6
Croxden Clo., Edg. 37 J3
Croxden Wk., Mord. 93 F6
Croxford Gdns. N22 32 H7
Croxley Rd. W9 57 C3
Croxted Clo. SE21 76 J7
Croxted Rd. SE21 76 J7
Croxted Rd. SE24 76 J7
Croyde Ave., Grnf. 54 J3
Croyde Clo., Sid. 79 G7
Croydon Flyover, 101 H4
The, Croy.
Duppas Hill Rd.
Croydon Gro., Croy. 101 H1
Croydon Rd. E13 60 F4
Croydon Rd. SE20 95 E2
Croydon Rd., Beck. 95 H3
Croydon Rd., Brom. 103 J3
Croydon Rd., Croy. 101 B4
Croydon Rd., Kes. 104 C3
Croydon Rd., Mitch. 94 D4
Croydon Rd., Wall. 101 B4
Croydon Rd., 103 E3
W.Wick.
Croyland Rd. N9 33 D1
Croylands Dr., 91 H7
Surb.
Croysdale Ave., Sun. 90 A3
Crozier Ter. E9 50 G5
Crucible Clo., Rom. 44 B6
Crucifix La. SE1 17 D3
Crucifix La. SE1 68 B2
Cruden Ho. SE17 20 G6
Cruden St. N1 58 H1
Cruikshank Rd. E15 51 E4
Cruikshank St. WC1 8 E3
Cruikshank St. WC1 58 E3
Crummock Gdns. 38 E5
NW9
Crumpsall St. SE2 71 C4
Crundale Ave. NW9 38 A5
Crunden Rd., 102 A7
S.Croy.
Crusader Gdns., 102 B3
Croy.
Cotelands
Crusoe Rd., Mitch. 84 J7
Crutched Friars EC3 13 E5
Crutched Friars EC3 59 B7
Crutchley Rd. SE6 87 E2
Crystal Ct. SE19 86 C5
College Rd.
Crystal Palace Par. 86 C6
SE19
Crystal Palace Pk. 86 D5
Rd. SE26
Crystal Palace Rd. 77 C6
SE22
Crystal Palace Sta. 86 D7
Rd. SE19
Anerley Rd.
Crystal Ter. SE19 86 A6
Crystal Vw. Ct., 87 D4
Brom.
Winlaton Rd.
Crystal Way, Dag. 53 C1
Crystal Way, Har. 37 C5
Cuba Dr., Enf. 25 F2
Cuba St. E14 69 A2
Cubitt Steps E14 69 A1
Cabot Sq.
Cubitt St. WC1 8 D4
Cubitt St. WC1 58 F3
Cubitt St., Croy. 101 F5
Cubitt Ter. SW4 76 C3
Cubitts Yd. WC2 12 B5
Cuckoo Ave. W7 55 B4
Cuckoo Dene W7 55 A5
Cuckoo Hall La. N9 25 F7
Cuckoo Hill, Pnr. 36 C3
Cuckoo Hill Dr., Pnr. 36 C3
Cuckoo Hill Rd., Pnr. 36 C4
Cuckoo La. W7 55 B7
Cudas Clo., Epsom 99 F4
Cuddington Ave., 99 F3
Wor.Pk.
Cudham St. SE6 78 C7
Cudworth St. E1 59 E4
Cuff Cres. SE9 79 A6

Cuff Pt. E2	9	F3
Culford Gdns. SW3	19	A2
Culford Gdns. SW3	66	J4
Culford Gro. N1	50	B6
Culford Ms. N1	50	B6
Southgate Rd.		
Culford Rd. N1	50	B7
Culnaith Gdns., Enf.	24	E4
Cullen Way NW10	55	C4
Culling Rd. SE16	68	F3
Lwr. Rd.		
Cullington Clo., Har.	37	D4
Cullingworth Rd. NW10	47	G5
Culloden Rd., Enf.	24	H2
Culloden St. E14	60	C6
Cullum St. EC3	13	D5
Culmington Rd. W13	64	F1
Culmington Rd., S.Croy.	101	J7
Culmore Cross SW12	85	B1
Culmore Rd. SE15	68	E7
Culmstock Rd. SW11	76	A5
Culpeper Clo., Ilf.	35	E6
Culross Clo. N15	40	J4
Culross Clo. SW1	11	B6
Culross St. W1	58	A7
Culsac Rd., Surb.	98	H2
Culver Gro., Stan.	37	F2
Culverden Rd. SW12	85	C2
Culverden Rd., Wat.	28	B3
Culverhouse Gdns. SW16	85	F3
Culverlands Clo., Stan.	29	E4
Culverley Rd. SE6	87	B1
Culvers Ave., Cars.	100	H2
Culvers Retreat, Cars.	100	J1
Culvers Way, Cars.	100	J3
Culverstone Clo., Brom.	96	F6
Culvert Pl. SW11	76	A2
Culvert Rd. N15	41	B5
Culvert Rd. SW11	75	J1
Culworth St. NW8	6	G2
Cumberland Ave. NW10	56	B3
Cumberland Ave., Well.	79	H3
Cumberland Clo. E8	50	C6
Cumberland Clo. SW20	84	A7
Lansdowne Rd.		
Cumberland Clo., Twick.	73	E6
Westmorland Clo.		
Cumberland Cres. W14	66	B4
Cumberland Dr., Bexh.	71	E7
Cumberland Dr., Chess.	98	J3
Cumberland Dr., Esher	98	D2
Cumberland Gdns. NW4	39	A2
Cumberland Gdns. WC1	8	D3
Cumberland Gate W1	10	J5
Cumberland Gate W1	57	J7
Cumberland Mkt. NW1	7	E3
Cumberland Mkt. NW1	58	B3
Cumberland Mkt. Est. NW1	7	E3
Cumberland Mills Sq. E14	69	D5
Saunders Ness Rd.		
Cumberland Pk. W3	56	C7
Cumberland Pl. NW1	7	D3
Cumberland Pl. SE6	87	F1
Cumberland Pl., Sun.	90	A4
Cumberland Rd. E12	52	A4
Cumberland Rd. E13	60	H5
Cumberland Rd. E17	41	H2
Cumberland Rd. N9	33	F1
Cumberland Rd. N22	40	F2
Cumberland Rd. SE25	95	E6
Cumberland Rd. SW13	74	F1
Cumberland Rd. W3	56	C7
Cumberland Rd. W7	64	C2
Cumberland Rd., Brom.	96	E4
Cumberland Rd., Har.	36	H5
Cumberland Rd., Rich.	65	A7
Cumberland Rd., Stan.	37	J3
Cumberland St. SW1	19	E3
Cumberland St. SW1	67	B5
Cumberland Ter. NW1	7	D2
Cumberland Ter. Ms. NW1	7	D2
Cumberlow Ave. SE25	95	C3
Cumberton Rd. N17	41	A1
Cumbrae Gdns., Surb.	98	F1
Cumbrian Gdns. NW2	48	A2
Cumming St. N1	8	D2
Cumming St. N1	58	F2
Cumnor Gdns., Epsom	99	G6
Cumnor Rd., Sutt.	100	F6
Cunard Pl. EC3	13	E4
Cunard Rd. NW10	56	D3
Cunard Wk. SE16	68	G4
Trident St.		
Cundy Rd. E16	60	J6
Cundy St. SW1	19	C2
Cundy St. SW1	67	A4
Cundy St. Est. SW1	19	C2
Cunliffe Rd., Wor.Pk.	99	F4
Cunliffe St. SW16	85	C6
Cunningham Clo., Rom.	44	C5
Chadwell Heath La.		
Cunningham Clo., W.Wick.	103	B2
Cunningham Pk., Har.	36	J5
Cunningham Pl. NW8	6	E5
Cunningham Pl. NW8	57	G4
Cunningham Rd. N15	41	D4
Cunnington St. W4	65	C4
Cupar Rd. SW11	76	B1
Cupola Clo., Brom.	87	H5
Cureton St. SW1	19	J2
Cureton St. SW1	67	D4
Curfew Ho., Bark.	61	F1
St. Ann's		
Curlew Clo. SE28	62	D7
Curlew Ct., Surb.	98	J3
Curlew St. SE1	17	F3
Curlew St. SE1	68	C2
Curnick's La. SE27	85	J4
Chapel Rd.		
Curnock Est. NW1	58	C1
Plender St.		
Curran Ave., Sid.	79	J5
Curran Ave., Wall.	101	A3
Currey Rd., Grnf.	45	J6
Curricle St. W3	65	E1
Currie Hill Clo. SW19	84	C4
Curry Ri. NW7	31	A6
Cursitor St. EC4	12	E3
Cursitor St. EC4	58	G6
Curtain Rd. EC2	9	E4
Curtain Rd. EC2	59	B3
Curthwaite Gdns., Enf.	24	D4
Curtis Dr. W3	56	D6
Curtis Fld. Rd. SW16	85	F4
Curtis La., Wem.	46	H5
Station Gro.		
Curtis Rd., Epsom	99	C4
Curtis Rd., Houns.	72	E7
Curtis St. SE1	21	F1
Curtis St. SE1	68	C4
Curtis Way SE1	21	F1
Curtis Way SE1	68	C4
Curtis Way SE28	62	B7
Tawney Rd.		
Curve, The W12	56	G7
Curwen Ave. E7	51	H4
Woodford Rd.		
Curwen Rd. W12	65	G2
Curzon Ave., Enf.	25	G5
Curzon Ave., Stan.	37	D1
Curzon Clo., Orp.	104	G4
Curzon Cres. NW10	47	E7
Curzon Cres., Bark.	61	J2
Curzon Gate W1	15	C2
Curzon Pl. W1	15	C2
Curzon Pl., Pnr.	50	B4
Curzon Rd. N10	40	B2
Curzon Rd. W5	55	E4
Curzon Rd., Th.Hth.	94	G6
Curzon St. W1	15	C2
Curzon St. W1	67	A1
Cusack Clo., Twick.	82	G3
Waldegrave Rd.		
Cut, The SE1	16	F3
Cut, The SE1	67	G2
Cutcombe Rd. SE5	76	J2
Cuthbert Gdns. SE25	95	B3
Cuthbert Rd. E17	42	C3
Cuthbert Rd. N18	33	D5
Fairfield Rd.		
Cuthbert Rd., Croy.	101	H2
Cuthbert St. W2	10	E1
Cuthbert St. W2	57	G4
Cutler St. E1	13	E3
Cutler St. E1	59	B6
Cutlers Gdns. E1	13	E3
Cutlers Sq. E14	80	C5
Cutthroat All., Rich.	82	F2
Ham St.		
Cuxton Clo., Bexh.	90	F5
Cyclamen Clo., Hmptn.	81	G6
Gresham Rd.		
Cyclamen Way, Epsom	99	C5
Cyclops Ms. E14	69	A4
Cygnet Ave., Felt.	72	C7
Cygnet Clo. NW10	47	D5
Cygnet Clo., Borwd.	22	C1
Cygnet St. E1	9	G5
Cygnets, The, Felt.	81	E4
Cymbeline Ct., Har.	37	C6
Cynthia St. N1	8	D2
Cynthia St. N1	58	F2
Cyntra Pl. E8	50	E7
Mare St.		
Cypress Ave., Twick.	72	J7
Cypress Gro., Ilf.	35	H6
Cypress Pl. W1	7	G6
Cypress Rd. SE25	95	B2
Cypress Rd., Har.	37	A2
Cyprus Ave. N3	39	B2
Cyprus Gdns. N3	39	B2
Cyprus Pl. E2	59	F2
Cyprus Pl. E6	61	D7
Cyprus Rd. N3	39	C2
Cyprus Rd. N9	33	C2
Cyprus St. E2	59	F2
Cyrena Rd. SE22	77	C6
Cyril Mans. SW11	75	J1
Cyril Rd., Bexh.	80	E2
Cyrus St. EC1	8	H5
Cyrus St. EC1	58	H4
Czar St. SE8	69	A6

D

Dabbs Hill La., Nthlt.	45	G5
Dabin Cres. SE10	78	C1
Dacca St. SE8	68	J6
Dace Rd. E3	60	A1
Dacre Ave., Ilf.	43	D2
Dacre Clo., Chig.	35	F4
Dacre Clo., Grnf.	54	H2
Dacre Gdns. SE13	78	E4
Dacre Gdns., Borwd.	22	D5
Dacre Gdns., Chig.	35	F4
Dacre Pk. SE13	78	E3
Dacre Pl. SE13	78	E3
Dacre Rd. E11	51	F1
Dacre Rd. E13	60	H1
Dacre Rd., Croy.	94	E7
Dacre St. SW1	15	H5
Dacre St. SW1	67	D3
Dacres Rd. SE23	86	G3
Dade Way, Sthl.	63	F5
Daerwood Clo., Brom.	104	C1
Daffodil Clo., Croy.	102	G1
Primrose La.		
Daffodil Pl., Hmptn.	81	G6
Gresham Rd.		
Daffodil St. W12	56	F7
Dafforne Rd. SW17	84	J3
Dagenham Ave., Dag.	62	E1
Dagenham Rd. E10	50	J1
Dagenham Rd., Dag.	53	H4
Dagmar Ave., Wem.	46	J4
Dagmar Gdns. NW10	57	A2
Dagmar Pas. N1	58	H1
Cross St.		
Dagmar Rd. N4	40	G7
Dagmar Rd. N15	41	A4
Cornwall Rd.		
Dagmar Rd. N22	40	D1
Dagmar Rd. SE5	77	B1
Dagmar Rd. SE25	95	B5
Dagmar Rd., Dag.	53	J7
Dagmar Rd., Kings.T.	91	J1
Dagmar Ter. N1	58	H1
Dagnall Pk. SE25	95	B6
Dagnall Rd. SE25	95	B5
Dagnall St. SW11	75	J2
Dagnan Rd. SW12	76	B7
Dagonet Gdns., Brom.	87	G3
Shroffold Rd.		
Dagonet Rd., Brom.	87	G3
Dahlia Gdns., Mitch.	94	D4
Dahlia Rd. SE2	71	B4
Dahomey Rd. SW16	85	C6
Daimler Way, Wall.	101	E7
Daines Clo. E12	52	C3
Colchester Ave.		
Dainford Clo., Brom.	87	D5
Dainton Clo., Brom.	96	H1
Dairy Clo., Har.	37	D4
Daintry Way E9	50	J6
Eastway		
Dairsie Rd. SE9	79	D3
Dairy Clo., Th.Hth.	94	J2
Dairy La. SE18	70	C4
Rideout St.		
Dairy Ms. SW9	76	E3
Dairy Wk. SW19	84	B4
Daisy Clo., Croy.	102	G1
Primrose La.		
Daisy La. SW6	75	D3
Daisy Rd. E18	42	H2
Dakota Gdns., Nthlt.	54	E3
Argus Way		
Dalberg Rd. SW2	76	G5
Dalberg Way SE2	71	D3
Lanridge Rd.		
Dalby Rd. SW18	75	F4
Dalby St. NW5	49	B6
Dalcross Rd., Houns.	72	E2
Dale, The, Kes.	104	A4
Dale Ave., Edg.	37	J1
Dale Ave., Houns.	72	E3
Dale Clo. SE3	78	G3
Dale Clo., Barn.	23	E6
Dale Clo., Pnr.	26	B3
Dale Gdns., Wdf.Grn.	34	H4
Dale Grn. Rd. N11	32	B3
Dale Gro. N12	31	F5
Dale Pk. Ave., Cars.	100	J3
Dale Pk. Rd. SE19	94	J1
Dale Rd. NW5	49	A5
Grafton Rd.		
Dale Rd. SE17	20	H6
Dale Rd. SE17	67	H6
Dale Rd., Grnf.	54	H5
Dale Rd., Sutt.	100	C4
Dale Row W11	57	B6
St. Marks Rd.		
Dale St. W4	65	E5
Dale Vw. Ave. E4	34	C2
Dale Vw. Cres. E4	34	C2
Dale Vw. Gdns. E4	34	D3
Dale Wd. Rd., Orp.	97	H7
Dalebury Rd. SW17	84	H2
Daleham Gdns. NW3	48	G5
Daleham Ms. NW3	48	G6
Dalehead NW1	7	F2
Dalehead NW1	58	C2
Dales Path, Borwd.	22	D5
Farriers Way		
Dales Rd., Borwd.	22	D5
Daleside Gdns., Chig.	35	F3
Daleside Rd. SW16	85	B5
Daleside Rd., Epsom	99	D6
Daleview Rd. N15	41	B6
Dalewood Gdns., Wor.Pk.	99	H2
Daley St. E9	50	G6
Daley Thompson Way SW8	76	B3
Dalgarno Gdns. W10	56	J5
Dalgarno Gdns. Est. W10	56	J4
Dalgarno Way W10	56	J4
Dalgleish St. E14	59	H2
Daling Way E3	59	H2
Dalkeith Gro., Stan.	29	G5
Dalkeith Rd. SE21	85	J1
Dalkeith Rd., Ilf.	52	F3
Dallas Rd. NW4	38	G7
Dallas Rd. SE26	86	E4
Dallas Rd. W5	55	J5
Dallas Rd., Sutt.	100	B6
Dallin Rd. SE18	78	E7
Dallin Rd., Bexh.	80	D4
Dalling Rd. W6	65	H4
Dallinger Rd. SE12	78	F6
Dallington St. EC1	8	H5
Dallington St. EC1	58	H4
Dalmain Rd. SE23	86	G1
Dalmally Rd., Croy.	95	C7
Dalmeny Ave. N7	49	D4
Dalmeny Ave. SW16	94	G2
Dalmeny Clo., Wem.	46	F6
Dalmeny Cres., Houns.	73	D4
Dalmeny Rd. N7	49	D3
Dalmeny Rd., Barn.	23	F6
Dalmeny Rd., Cars.	101	A7

Dalmeny Rd., Erith 80 H1
Dalmeny Rd., Wor.Pk. 99 H3
Dalmeyer Rd. NW10 47 F6
Dalmore Ave., Esher 98 C6
Dalmore Rd. SE21 85 J2
Dalrymple Rd. SE4 77 H4
Dalston Gdns., Stan. 37 H1
Dalston La. E8 50 C6
Dalton Ave., Mitch. 93 H2
Dalton Clo., Orp. 104 H3
Dalton Rd., Har. 37 A2
Athelstone Rd.
Dalton St. SE27 85 H2
Dalwood St. SE5 77 B1
Daly Ct. E15 51 C5
Clays La.
Dalyell Rd. SW9 76 F3
Dame St. N1 8 J1
Dame St. N1 58 J2
Damer Ter. SW10 66 F7
Tadema Rd.
Dames Rd. E7 51 G3
Damien St. E1 59 E6
Damon Clo., Sid. 89 B3
Damsonwood Clo., Sthl. 63 G3
Dan Leno Wk. SW6 66 E7
Britannia Rd.
Danbrook Rd. SW16 94 E1
Danbury Clo., Rom. 44 D3
Danbury Ms., Wall. 101 B4
Danbury Rd., Loug. 27 B7
Danbury St. N1 8 H1
Danbury St. N1 58 H2
Danbury Way, Wdf.Grn. 34 J6
Danby St. SE15 77 C3
Dancer Rd. SW6 75 C1
Dancer Rd., Rich. 74 A3
Dando Cres. SE3 78 H3
Dandridge Clo. SE10 69 F5
Dane Clo., Bex. 80 G7
Dane Clo., Orp. 104 G5
Dane Pl. E3 59 H2
Roman Rd.
Dane Rd. N18 33 F4
Dane Rd. SW19 93 F1
Dane Rd. W13 64 F1
Dane Rd., Ilf. 52 F5
Dane Rd., Sthl. 54 E7
Dane St. WC1 12 C2
Danebury, Croy. 103 B6
Danebury Ave. SW15 74 E6
Daneby Rd. SE6 87 B3
Danecourt Gdns., Croy. 102 C3
Danecroft Rd. SE24 76 J5
Danehill Wk., Sid. 89 A3
Hatherley Rd.
Danehurst Gdns., Ilf. 43 B5
Danehurst St. SW6 75 B1
Daneland, Barn. 23 J5
Danemead Gro., Nthlt. 45 H5
Danemere St. SW15 74 J3
Danes Gate, Har. 37 B3
Danes Rd., Rom. 44 J7
Danesbury Rd., Felt. 81 B1
Danescombe SE12 87 G1
Winn Rd.
Danescourt Cres., Sutt. 100 F2
Danescroft NW4 39 A5
Danescroft Ave. NW4 39 A5
Danescroft Gdns. NW4 39 A5
Danesdale Rd. E9 50 H6
Danesfield SE5 21 D5
Daneswood Ave. SE6 87 C3
Danethorpe Rd., Wem. 46 G6
Danetree Clo., Epsom 99 C7
Danetree Rd., Epsom 99 C7
Danette Gdns., Dag. 53 F2
Daneville Rd. SE5 77 A1
Dangan Rd. E11 42 G6
Daniel Bolt Clo. E14 60 B5
Uamvar St.
Daniel Clo. N18 33 F4
Daniel Clo. SW17 84 H6
Daniel Gdns. SE15 21 F7
Daniel Gdns. SE15 68 C7
Daniel Pl. NW4 38 H6
Daniel Rd. W5 55 J7
Daniels Rd. SE15 77 F3
Dansey Pl. W1 11 H5
Dansington Rd., Well. 80 A4
Danson Cres., Well. 80 B3
Danson La., Well. 80 A4
Danson Mead, Well. 80 C3
Danson Rd., Bex. 80 D5
Danson Rd., Bexh. 80 D5
Dante Pl. SE11 20 H2
Dante Rd. SE11 20 G1
Dante Rd. SE11 67 H4
Danube St. SW3 18 H3
Danvers Rd. N8 40 D4
Danvers St. SW3 18 F6
Danvers St. SW3 66 G6
Danziger Way, Borwd. 22 C1
Daphne Gdns. E4 34 C3
Gunners Gro.
Daphne St. SW18 75 F6
Daplyn St. E1 13 H1
D'Arblay St. W1 11 G4
D'Arblay St. W1 58 C6
Darby Cres., Sun. 90 C2
Darby Gdns., Sun. 90 C2
Darcy Ave., Wall. 101 C4
Darcy Clo. N20 31 G2
D'Arcy Dr., Har. 37 G4
Darcy Gdns., Dag. 62 F1
D'Arcy Gdns., Har. 37 H4
Darcy Rd. SW16 94 E2
D'Arcy Rd., Sutt. 100 A4
Dare Gdns., Dag. 53 E3
Grafton Rd.
Darell Rd., Rich. 74 A3
Darenth Rd. N16 41 C7
Darenth Rd., Well. 80 A1
Darfield Rd. SE4 77 J5
Darfield Way W10 57 A6
Darfur St. SW15 75 A3
Dargate Clo. SE19 86 C7
Chipstead Clo.
Darien Rd. SW11 75 G3
Darlan Rd. SW6 66 C7
Darlaston Rd. SW19 84 A7
Darley Clo., Croy. 95 H6
Darley Dr., N.Mal. 92 D2
Darley Gdns., Mord. 93 F6
Darley Rd. N9 33 C1
Darley Rd. SW11 75 J6
Darling Rd. SE4 78 A3
Darling Row E1 59 E4
Darlington Rd. SE27 85 H5
Darmaine Clo., S.Croy. 101 J7
Churchill Rd.
Darnley Ho. E14 59 H6
Camdenhurst St.
Darnley Rd. E9 50 F6
Darnley Rd., Wdf.Grn. 42 G1
Darnley Ter. W11 66 B1
St. James Gdns.
Darrell Rd. SE22 77 D5
Darren Clo. N4 40 F7
Darrick Wd. Rd., Orp. 104 G2
Darris Clo., Hayes 54 E4
Darsley Dr. SW8 76 E1
Dart St. W10 57 B3
Dartford Ave. N9 25 F6
Dartford Rd., Bex. 89 J1
Dartford St. SE17 21 A5
Dartford St. SE17 67 J6
Dartmoor Wk. E14 69 A4
Charnwood Gdns.
Dartmouth Clo. W11 57 D6
Dartmouth Gro. SE10 78 C1
Dartmouth Hill SE10 78 C1
Dartmouth Pk. Ave. NW5 49 B3
Dartmouth Pk. Hill N19 49 B1
Dartmouth Pk. Hill NW5 49 C3
Dartmouth Pk. Rd. NW5 49 B4
Dartmouth Pl. SE23 86 F2
Dartmouth Rd.
Dartmouth Pl. W4 65 E6
Dartmouth Rd. E16 60 G6
Fords Pk. Rd.
Dartmouth Rd. NW2 48 A6
Dartmouth Rd. NW4 38 G6
Dartmouth Rd. SE23 86 F2
Dartmouth Rd. SE26 86 E3
Dartmouth Rd., Brom. 96 G7
Dartmouth Rd., Ruis. 45 A3
Dartmouth Row SE10 78 C1
Dartmouth St. SW1 15 J4
Dartmouth St. SW1 67 D2
Dartnell Rd., Croy. 95 C7
Dartrey Wk. SW10 18 E7
Darville Rd. N16 50 C3
Darwell Clo. E6 61 D2
Darwin Clo. N11 32 B3
Darwin Clo., Orp. 104 G5
Darwin Dr., Sthl. 54 H6
Darwin Gdns., Wat. 28 C5
Barnhurst Path
Darwin Rd. N22 40 H1
Darwin Rd. W5 64 F5
Darwin Rd., Well. 79 J3
Darwin St. SE17 21 C1
Darwin St. SE17 68 A4
Daryngton Dr., Grnf. 55 A2
Dashwood Clo., Bexh. 80 G5
Dashwood Rd. N8 40 F6
Dassett Rd. SE27 85 H5
Datchelor Pl. SE5 77 A1
Datchet Rd. SE6 86 J3
Datchworth Ct. N4 49 J3
Queens Dr.
Date St. SE17 21 A4
Date St. SE17 67 J5
Daubeney Gdns. N17 32 J7
Daubeney Rd. E5 50 H4
Daubeney Rd. N17 32 J7
Daubeney Twr. SE8 68 J4
Dault Rd. SW18 75 F6
Davema Clo., Chis. 97 D1
Davenant Rd. N19 49 D2
Davenant Rd., Croy. 101 H4
Duppas Hill Rd.
Davenant St. E1 13 J2
Davenant St. E1 59 D5
Davenport Clo., Tedd. 82 D6
Davenport Rd. SE6 78 C6
Davenport Rd., Sid. 89 D2
Daventer Dr., Stan. 29 C7
Daventry Ave. E17 42 A5
Daventry St. NW1 10 G1
Daventry St. NW1 57 H5
Davern Clo. SE10 69 F4
Davey Clo. N7 49 F6
Davey Rd. E9 51 A7
White Post La.
Davey St. SE15 21 G6
Davey St. SE15 68 C6
David Ave., Grnf. 55 B3
David Ms. W1 11 B1
David Rd., Dag. 53 E2
David St. E15 51 D6
Davidge St. SE1 16 H4
Davidge St. SE1 67 H2
Davids Rd. SE23 86 F1
Davids Way, Ilf. 35 H7
Davidson Gdns. SW8 67 E7
Davidson La., Har. 37 C7
Grove Hill
Davidson Rd., Croy. 102 B1
Davies Clo., Croy. 95 C6
Davies La. E11 51 E2
Davies Ms. W1 11 D5
Davies St. W1 11 D5
Davies St. W1 58 B7
Davington Gdns., Dag. 53 B5
Davington Rd., Dag. 53 B6
Davinia Clo., Wdf.Grn. 35 C6
Deacon Way
Davis Rd. W3 65 F1
Davis Rd., Chess. 99 A4
Davis St. E13 60 H2
Davisville Rd. W12 65 G2
Dawes Ave., Islw. 73 D5
Dawes Ho. SE17 21 B2
Dawes Rd. SW6 66 B7
Dawes St. SE17 21 C3
Dawes St. SE17 68 A5
Dawlish Ave. N13 32 E4
Dawlish Ave. SW18 84 E2
Dawlish Ave., Grnf. 55 D2
Dawlish Dr., Ilf. 52 H4
Dawlish Dr., Pnr. 36 E5
Dawlish Dr., Ruis. 45 A2
Dawlish Rd. E10 51 C1
Dawlish Rd. N17 41 D3
Dawlish Rd. NW2 48 A6
Dawn Clo., Houns. 72 E3
Dawnay Gdns. SW18 84 G2
Dawnay Rd. SW18 84 F2
Dawpool Rd. NW2 47 F2
Daws Hill E4 26 C2
Daws La. NW7 30 F5
Dawson Ave., Bark. 52 J7
Dawson Clo. SE18 70 F4
Dawson Gdns., Bark. 52 J7
Dawson Ave.
Dawson Heights Est. SE22 77 D7
Dawson Pl. W2 57 D7
Dawson Rd. NW2 47 J5
Dawson Rd., Kings.T. 91 J3
Dawson St. E2 9 G2
Dawson St. E2 59 C2
Dax Ct., Sun. 90 C3
Thames St.
Daybrook Rd. SW19 93 E2
Daylesford Ave. SW15 74 G4
Daymer Gdns., Pnr. 36 B4
Days La., Sid. 79 H7
Daysbrook Rd. SW2 85 F2
Dayton Gro. SE15 77 F1
De Beauvoir Cres. N1 59 B1
De Beauvoir Est. N1 59 A1
De Beauvoir Rd. N1 59 B1
De Beauvoir Sq. N1 50 B7
De Bohun Ave. N14 24 B6
De Crespigny Pk. SE5 77 A2
De Frene Rd. SE26 86 G4
De Havilland Rd., Edg. 38 A2
De Havilland Rd., Wall. 101 E7
De Laune St. SE17 20 G4
De Laune St. SE17 67 H5
De Luci Rd., Erith 71 J5
De Lucy St. SE2 71 B4
De Montfort Rd. SW16 85 E3
De Morgan Rd. SW6 75 E3
De Quincey Rd. N17 41 A1
De Vere Cotts. W8 14 C5
De Vere Gdns. W8 14 C4
De Vere Gdns. W8 66 F2
De Vere Gdns., Ilf. 52 C2
De Vere Ms. W8 14 C5
De Walden St. W1 11 C2
Deacon Rd. NW2 47 G5
Deacon Rd., Kings.T. 91 J1
Deacon Way SE17 20 J1
Deacon Way SE17 67 J4
Deacon Way, Wdf.Grn. 35 C7
Deacons Clo., Borwd. 22 A4
Deacons Clo., Pnr. 36 B2
Deacons Leas, Orp. 104 G4
Deacons Wk., Hmptn. 81 F4
Bishops Gro.
Deal Porters Way SE16 68 F3
Deal Rd. SW17 85 A6
Deal St. E1 13 H1
Deal St. E1 59 D5
Deal Wk. SW9 67 G7
Mandela St.
Deal's Gateway SE10 78 B1
Deptford Bri.
Dealtry Rd. SW15 74 J4
Dean Bradley St. SW1 16 A6
Dean Bradley St. SW1 67 E3
Dean Clo. E9 50 F5
Churchill Wk.
Dean Clo. SE16 68 G1
Surrey Water Rd.
Dean Ct., Wem. 46 E3
Dean Dr., Stan. 37 H2
Dean Farrar St. SW1 15 J5
Dean Farrar St. SW1 67 D3
Dean Gdns. E17 42 D4
Dean Rd. NW2 47 J6
Dean Rd., Croy. 102 A4
Dean Rd., Hmptn. 81 F5
Dean Rd., Houns. 72 H5
Dean Ryle St. SW1 20 A1
Dean Ryle St. SW1 67 E4
Dean Stanley St. SW1 16 A6
Dean Stanley St. SW1 67 E3
Dean St. E7 51 G5
Dean St. W1 11 H3
Dean St. W1 58 D6
Dean Trench St. SW1 16 A6
Dean Wk., Edg. 30 C6
Deansbrook Rd.
Dean Way, Sthl. 63 H2
Deancross St. E1 59 F6
Deane Ave., Ruis. 45 B5
Deane Cft. Rd., Pnr. 36 C6
Deane Way, Ruis. 36 B6
Deanery Clo. N2 39 H4
Deanery Ms. W1 15 C1
Deanery Rd. E15 51 E6
Deanery St. W1 15 C1
Deanery St. W1 67 A1
Deanhill Rd. SW14 74 B4
Deans Bldgs. SE17 21 C2
Deans Bldgs. SE17 68 A4

Deans Clo. W4 65 B6
Dean's Clo., Croy. 102 C3
Deans Clo., Edg. 30 C6
Dean's Ct. EC4 12 H4
Deans Dr. N10 32 H6
Deans Dr., Edg. 30 B1
Duan's Gate Clo. 86 G3
SE23
Deans La., Edg. 30 C6
Deans Ms. W1 11 E3
Dean's Pl. SW1 19 H3
Dean's Pl. SW1 67 D5
Deans Rd. W7 64 C1
Deans Rd., Sutt. 100 E3
Deans Way, Edg. 30 C5
Dean's Yd. SW1 15 J5
Deansbrook Clo., 30 C6
Edg.
Deansbrook Rd., 30 B7
Edg.
Deanscroft Ave. NW9 47 C2
Deansway N2 39 G4
Deansway N9 33 B3
Dearn Gdns., Mitch. 93 H3
Dearne Clo., Stan. 29 D5
Deason St. E15 60 C1
High St.
Debden Clo., 35 A7
Wdf.Grn.
Debden Ind. Group, 27 G4
Loug.
Debnams Rd. SE16 68 F4
Rotherhithe New Rd.
Deborah Clo., Islw. 73 B1
DeBurgh Rd. SW19 84 F7
Decima St. SE1 17 D5
Decima St. SE1 68 B3
Deck Clo. SE16 68 G2
Thame Rd.
Decoy Ave. NW11 39 B5
Dee Rd., Rich. 73 J4
Dee St. E14 60 C6
Deeley Rd. SW8 76 D1
Deena Clo. W3 55 J6
Deepdale SW19 84 A4
Deepdale Ave., 96 F4
Brom.
Deepdene W5 55 J4
Deepdene Ave., 102 C3
Croy.
Deepdene Clo. E11 42 G4
Deepdene Ct. N21 24 H6
Deepdene Gdns. 76 F7
SW2
Deepdene Path, 27 D4
Loug.
Deepdene Rd. SE5 77 A4
Deepdene Rd., Loug. 27 D4
Deepdene Rd., Well. 80 A3
Deepwell Clo., Islw. 73 D1
Deepwood La., Grnf. 55 A3
Cowgate Rd.
Deer Pk. Clo., 83 B7
Kings.T.
Deer Pk. Gdns., 93 G3
Mitch.
Deer Pk. Rd. SW19 93 E2
Deer Pk. Way, 103 G2
W.Wick.
Deerbrook Rd. SE24 85 H1
Deerdale Rd. SE24 76 J4
Deerhurst Clo., Felt. 81 A4
Deerhurst Rd. NW2 48 A6
Deerhurst Rd. SW16 85 F5
Deerings Dr., Pnr. 36 A5
Deerleap Gro. E4 26 B5
Deeside Rd. SW17 84 G3
Defiance Wk. SE18 70 C3
Antelope Rd.
Defiant Way, Wall. 101 E7
Defoe Ave., Rich. 65 A7
Defoe Clo. SW17 84 H6
Defoe Rd. N16 50 B2
Degema Rd., Chis. 88 E5
Dehar Cres. NW9 38 F7
Dekker Rd. SE21 77 B6
Delacourt Rd. SE3 69 H7
Old Dover Rd.
Delafield Rd. SE7 69 H5
Delaford Rd. SE16 68 E5
Delaford St. SW6 66 B7
Delamere Cres. 95 F6
Croy.
Delamere Gdns. NW7 30 D6
Delamere Rd. SW20 93 A1
Delamere Rd. W5 64 H1
Delamere Rd., 27 J4
Borwd.
Delamere Rd., Hayes 54 D7
Delamere Ter. W2 10 B1
Delamere Ter. W2 57 E5
Delancey Pas. NW1 58 B1
Delancey St.

Delancey St. NW1 58 B1
Delaware Rd. W9 6 A5
Delaware Rd. W9 57 E4
Delawyk Cres. SE24 76 J6
Delcombe Ave., 99 J1
Wor.Pk.
Dell Clo. SE27 77 B5
East Dulwich Gro.
Delhi Rd., Enf. 25 C7
Delhi St. N1 58 E1
Delia St. SW18 75 E7
Dell, The SE2 71 A5
Dell, The SE19 95 C1
Dell, The, Brent. 64 F6
Dell, The, Felt. 72 B7
Harlington Rd. W.
Dell, The, Pnr. 36 D2
Dell, The, Wem. 46 E5
Dell, The, Wdf.Grn. 34 H3
Dell Clo. E15 60 D1
Dell Clo., Wall. 101 C4
Dell Clo., Wdf.Grn. 34 H3
Dell La., Epsom 99 G5
Dell Rd., Epsom 99 G6
Dell Wk., N.Mal. 92 E2
Dell Way W13 55 F6
Della Path E5 50 E3
Napoleon Rd.
Dellbow Rd., Felt. 72 B5
Central Way
Dellfield Clo., Beck. 87 C7
Foxgrove Rd.
Dellors Clo., Barn. 23 A5
Dellow Clo., Ilf. 43 G7
Dellow St. E1 59 E7
Dell's Ms. SW1 19 G2
Dellwood Gdns., Ilf. 43 D3
Delmare Clo. SW9 76 F4
Brighton Ter.
Delme Cres. SE3 78 H2
Delmey Clo., Croy. 102 C3
Radcliffe Rd.
Deloraine St. SE8 78 A1
Delorme St. W6 66 A6
Delta Clo., Wor.Pk. 99 F3
Delta Ct. NW2 47 G2
Delta Gain, Wat. 28 D2
Delta Gro., Nthlt. 54 D3
Delta Rd., Wor.Pk. 99 E3
Delta St. E2 9 H3
Delvan Clo. SE18 70 D7
Ordnance Rd.
Delvers Mead, Dag. 53 J4
Delverton Rd. SE17 20 H4
Delverton Rd. SE17 67 H5
Delvino Rd. SW6 75 D1
Demesne Rd., Wall. 101 D4
Demeta Clo., Wem. 47 C3
Dempster Clo., 91 F7
Surb.
Dempster Rd. SW18 75 F5
Den Clo., Beck. 96 D3
Den Rd., Brom. 96 D3
Denberry Dr., Sid. 89 B3
Denbigh Clo. NW10 47 E7
Denbigh Clo. W11 57 C7
Denbigh Clo., Chis. 88 C6
Denbigh Clo., Sutt. 100 C5
Denbigh Gdns., 73 J5
Rich.
Denbigh Ms. SW1 19 F2
Denbigh Pl. SW1 19 F3
Denbigh Rd. SW1 67 C5
Denbigh Rd. E6 61 A3
Denbigh Rd. W11 57 C7
Denbigh Rd. W13 55 E7
Denbigh Rd., Houns. 72 H2
Denbigh Rd., Sthl. 54 F6
Denbigh St. SW1 19 F2
Denbigh St. SW1 67 C4
Denbigh Ter. W11 57 C7
Denbridge Rd., 97 C2
Brom.
Dendy St. SW12 85 A1
Dene, The W13 55 E5
Dene, The, Croy. 102 G4
Dene, The, Wem. 46 H4
Dene, The, W.Mol. 90 F5
Dene Ave., Houns. 72 F3
Dene Ave., Sid. 80 B7
Dene Clo. SE4 77 H3
Dene Clo., Brom. 103 F1
Dene Clo., Wor.Pk. 99 F2
Dene Gdns., Stan. 29 F5
Dene Gdns., T.Ditt. 98 D2
Dene Rd., Buck.H. 35 A1
Denehurst Gdns. 38 J6
NW4
Denehurst Gdns. W3 65 B1
Denehurst Gdns., 74 A4
Rich.
Denehurst Gdns., 73 A7
Twick.

Denehurst Gdns., 34 H4
Wdf.Grn.
Denewood, Barn. 23 F5
Denewood Rd. N6 39 J6
Dengie Wk. N1 58 J1
Basire St.
Denham Clo., Well. 80 C3
Park Vw. Rd.
Denholm Gdns. 93 J4
Denham Dr., Esher 98 D5
Denham Dr., Ilf. 43 F6
Denham Rd. N20 31 J3
Denham Rd., Felt. 72 B5
Denham Rd. SE10 69 G5
Denham Way, Bark. 61 H1
Denham Way, Borwd. 22 C1
Denholme Rd. W9 57 C3
Denison Clo. N2 39 F3
Denison Rd. SW19 94 B5
Denison Rd. W5 55 F4
Deniston Ave., Bex. 89 E1
Denleigh Gdns. N21 32 G1
Denleigh Gdns., 91 B6
T.Ditt.
Denman Dr. NW11 39 D5
Denman Dr. N. NW11 39 D5
Denman Dr. S. NW11 39 D5
Denman Rd. SE15 77 C1
Denman St. W1 11 H6
Denmark Ave. SW19 84 B7
Denmark Ct., Mord. 93 D5
Denmark Gdns., 100 J3
Cars.
Denmark Gro. N1 8 E1
Denmark Gro. N1 58 G2
Denmark Hill SE5 77 A1
Denmark Hill Dr. 38 F4
NW9
Denmark Hill Est. 77 A4
SE5
Denmark Pl. WC2 11 J3
Denmark Rd. N8 40 G4
Denmark Rd. NW6 57 C2
Denmark Rd. SE5 76 J1
Denmark Rd. SE25 95 D5
Denmark Rd. SW19 84 A6
Denmark Rd. W13 55 E7
Denmark Rd., Brom. 96 H1
Denmark Rd., Cars. 100 J3
Denmark Rd., 91 H3
Kings.T.
Denmark Rd., Twick. 82 A3
Denmark St. E11 51 E3
Denmark St. E13 60 H5
Denmark St. N17 41 E1
Denmark St. WC2 11 J4
Denmark St. WC2 58 D6
Denmark Wk. SE27 95 J1
Denmead Ho. SW15 74 F6
Highcliffe Dr.
Denmead Rd., Croy. 101 H1
Denmead Way SE15 68 C7
Pentridge St.
Dennan Rd., Surb. 98 J1
Denne Ter. E8 59 C1
Denner Rd. E4 34 A2
Dennett's Rd., Croy. 101 J4
Dennett's Gro. SE14 77 G2
Dennetts Rd.
Dennetts Rd. SE14 77 F1
Denning Ave., Croy. 101 G4
Denning Clo. NW8 6 D3
Denning Clo. NW8 57 F3
Denning Clo., 81 F6
Hmptn.
Denning Rd. NW3 48 G4
Dennington Clo. E5 50 E2
Detmold Rd.
Dennington Pk. Rd. 48 D6
NW6
Denningtons, The, 99 E2
Wor.Pk.
Dennis Ave., Wem. 46 J5
Dennis Gdns., Stan. 29 E5
Dennis La., Stan. 29 E3
Dennis Pk. Cres. 93 B1
SW20
Dennis Reeve Clo., 93 J1
Mitch.
Dennis Rd., E.Mol. 90 H3
Dennis Way SW4 76 D3
Gauden Rd.
Dennison Pt. E15 51 C7
Denny Clo. E6 61 B5
Linton Gdns.
Denny Cres. SE11 20 F3
Denny Gdns., Dag. 53 B7
Canonsleigh Rd.
Denny Rd. N9 33 E1
Denny St. SE11 20 F3
Denny St. SE11 67 G5
Densham Rd. E15 60 E1

Densole Clo., Beck. 95 H1
Kings Hall Rd.
Densworth Gro. N9 33 F2
Denton Clo., Barn. 22 J5
Denton Rd. N8 40 F5
Denton Rd. N18 33 B4
Denton Rd., Twick. 73 G6
Denton Rd., Well. 71 C7
Denton St. SW18 75 E6
Denton Way E5 50 G3
Denver Clo., Orp. 97 H6
Denver Rd. N16 41 B7
Denyer St. SW3 18 H2
Denyer St. SW3 66 H4
Denzil Rd. NW10 47 F5
Deodar Rd. SW15 75 B4
Deodara Clo. N20 31 H3
Depot App. N3 39 E1
Depot Rd., Houns. 73 A3
Deptford Bri. SE8 78 A1
Deptford Bdy. SE8 78 A1
Deptford Ch. St. 69 A6
SE8
Deptford Ferry Rd. 69 A4
E14
Deptford Grn. SE8 69 A6
Deptford High St. 69 A6
SE8
Deptford Strand SE8 68 J4
Deptford Wf. SE8 68 J4
Derby Ave. N12 31 F5
Derby Ave., Har. 37 A1
Derby Ave., Rom. 44 J6
Derby Ct. E5 50 G4
Overbury St.
Derby Est., Houns. 72 G4
Derby Gate SW1 16 A3
Derby Hill SE23 86 F2
Derby Hill Cres. 86 F2
SE23
Derby Rd. E7 52 A7
Derby Rd. E9 59 G1
Derby Rd. E18 42 F1
Derby Rd. N18 33 F5
Derby Rd. SW14 74 B4
Derby Rd. SW19 84 D7
Russell Rd.
Derby Rd., Croy. 101 H2
Derby Rd., Enf. 25 E5
Derby Rd., Grnf. 54 H1
Derby Rd., Houns. 72 H4
Derby Rd., Surb. 99 A1
Derby Rd., Sutt. 100 C6
Derby St. W1 15 C2
Derbyshire St. E2 9 J4
Derbyshire St. E2 59 D3
Dereham Pl. EC2 9 E4
Dereham Rd., Bark. 52 J6
Derek Ave., Epsom 99 A6
Derek Ave., Wall. 101 B3
Derek Ave., Wem. 47 B7
Derek Clo., Epsom 99 B5
Dericote St. E8 59 D1
Derifall Clo. E6 61 C5
Dering Pl., Croy. 101 J4
Dering Rd., Croy. 101 J4
Dering St. W1 11 D4
Dering St. W1 58 B6
Derinton Rd. SW17 84 J4
Derley Rd., Sthl. 63 C5
Dermody Gdns. SE13 78 D5
Dermody Rd. SE13 78 D5
Deronda Rd. SE24 85 H1
Deroy Clo., Cars. 100 J6
Derrick Gdns. SE7 69 J4
Anchor & Hope La.
Derrick Rd., Beck. 95 J3
Derry Rd., Croy. 101 E3
Derry St. W8 14 A4
Derry St. W8 66 E2
Dersingham Ave. 52 C4
E12
Dersingham Rd. 48 B3
NW2
Derwent Ave. N18 33 A5
Derwent Ave. NW7 30 D6
Derwent Ave. NW9 38 E5
Derwent Ave. SW15 83 A4
Derwent Ave., Barn. 31 J1
Derwent Ave., Pnr. 28 E6
Derwent Clo., Esher 98 B6
Derwent Cres. N20 31 F3
Derwent Cres., Bexh. 80 G2
Derwent Cres., Stan. 37 F2
Derwent Dr., Orp. 97 F3
Derwent Gdns., Ilf. 43 B4
Derwent Gdns., Wem. 37 F7
Derwent Gro. SE22 77 C4
Derwent Ri. NW9 38 E5
Derwent Rd. N13 32 F4
Derwent Rd. SE20 95 D2
Derwent Rd. SW20 93 A6

Derwent Rd. W5 64 F3
Derwent Rd., Sthl. 54 F6
Derwent Rd., Twick. 72 H6
Derwent St. SE10 69 E5
Derwent Wk., Wall. 101 B7
Derwent Yd. W5 64 F3
Northfield Ave.
Derwentwater Rd. 65 C1
W3
Desborough St. W2 10 A1
Desenfans Rd. SE21 77 B6
Desford Rd. E16 60 E4
Desmond St. SE14 68 H6
Despard Rd. N19 49 C1
Detling Rd., Brom. 87 G5
Detmold Rd. E5 50 F2
Devalls Clo. E6 61 D7
Devana End, Cars. 100 J3
Devas Rd. SW20 92 J1
Devas St. E3 60 B4
Devenay Rd. E15 51 F7
Devenish Rd. SE2 71 A2
Deventer Cres. SE22 77 B5
East Dulwich Gro.
Deverell St. SE1 17 B6
Deverell St. SE1 68 A3
Devereux Ct. WC2 12 E4
Devereux Rd. SW11 75 J6
Deverill Ct. SE20 95 F1
Devizes St. N1 59 A1
Poole St.
Devon Ave., Twick. 81 J1
Devon Clo. N17 41 C3
Devon Clo., Buck.H. 34 H2
Devon Clo., Grnf. 55 F1
Devon Gdns. N4 40 H6
Devon Ri. N2 39 G4
Devon Rd., Bark. 61 H1
Devon St. SE15 68 E6
Devon Way, Chess. 98 F5
Devon Way, Epsom 99 B5
Devon Waye, Houns. 63 F7
Devoncroft Gdns., 73 D7
Twick.
Devonia Gdns. N18 32 J6
Devonia Rd. N1 8 H1
Devonia Rd. N1 58 H2
Devonport Gdns., Ilf. 43 C6
Devonport Ms. W12 65 H1
Devonport Rd.
Devonport Rd. W12 65 H2
Devonport St. E1 59 G6
Devons Est. E3 60 B3
Devons Rd. E3 60 A5
Devonshire Ave., 100 F7
Sutt.
Devonshire Clo. E15 51 E4
Devonshire Clo. N13 32 G4
Devonshire Rd.
Devonshire Clo. W1 11 D1
Devonshire Clo. W1 58 B5
Devonshire Cres. 31 A7
NW7
Devonshire Dr. SE10 69 B7
Devonshire Dr., 98 G2
Surb.
Devonshire Gdns. 32 J6
N17
Devonshire Gdns. 24 J/
N21
Devonshire Gdns. 65 C7
W4
Devonshire Gro. 68 E6
SE15
Devonshire Hill La. 32 H6
N17
Devonshire Ms. W4 65 E5
Glebe St.
Devonshire Ms. N. 11 D1
W1
Devonshire Ms. S. 11 D1
W1
Devonshire Ms. S. 58 B5
W1
Devonshire Ms. W. 7 D6
W1
Devonshire Ms. W. 58 A4
W1
Devonshire Pas. W4 65 E5
Duke Rd.
Devonshire Pl. NW2 48 D3
Devonshire Pl. W1 7 C6
Devonshire Pl. W1 58 A4
Devonshire Pl. W4 65 E5
Devonshire Pl. Ms. 7 C6
W1
Devonshire Rd. E15 51 E4
Janson Rd.
Devonshire Rd. E16 60 H6
Devonshire Rd. E17 42 A6
Devonshire Rd. N9 33 F1
Devonshire Rd. N13 32 F4
Devonshire Rd. N17 32 J6

Devonshire Rd. NW7 31 A7
Devonshire Rd. SE9 88 B2
Devonshire Rd. SE23 86 F1
Devonshire Rd. 84 H7
SW19
Devonshire Rd. W4 65 E5
Devonshire Rd. W5 64 F3
Devonshire Rd., 80 E4
Bexh.
Devonshire Rd., 101 A4
Cars.
Devonshire Rd., 95 A7
Croy.
Devonshire Rd., Felt. 81 E3
Devonshire Rd., Har. 37 A6
Devonshire Rd., Ilf. 43 G7
Devonshire Rd. 36 C6
(Eastcote), Pnr.
Devonshire Rd. 36 F1
(Hatch End), Pnr.
Devonshire Rd., Sthl. 54 G5
Devonshire Rd., 100 F7
Sutt.
Devonshire Row EC2 13 E2
Devonshire Row Ms. 7 E6
W1
Devonshire Sq. EC2 13 E2
Devonshire Sq., 96 H4
Brom.
Devonshire St. W1 11 C1
Devonshire St. W1 58 B5
Devonshire St. W4 65 E5
Devonshire Ter. W2 10 D4
Devonshire Ter. W2 57 F6
Devonshire Way, 102 H2
Croy.
Devonshire Way, 54 B6
Hayes
Dewar St. SE15 77 D3
Dewberry Gdns. E6 61 B5
Dewberry St. E14 60 C5
Dewey Rd. N1 8 E1
Dewey Rd. N1 58 G2
Dewey Rd., Dag. 53 H6
Dewey St. SW17 84 J5
Dewhurst Rd. W14 66 A3
Dewsbury Clo., Pnr. 36 E6
Dewsbury Ct. W4 65 C4
Chiswick Rd.
Dewsbury Gdns., 99 G3
Wor.Pk.
Dewsbury Rd. NW10 47 G5
Dewsbury Ter. NW1 58 B1
Camden High St.
Dexter Rd., Barn. 23 A6
Deyncourt Rd. N17 40 J1
Deynecourt Gdns. 42 J4
E11
D'Eynsford Rd. SE5 77 A1
Diadem Ct. W1 11 H4
Dial Wk., The W8 14 B3
Diameter Rd., Orp. 97 E7
Diamond Clo., Dag. 53 C1
Diamond Rd., Ruis. 45 D4
Diamond St. SE15 68 B7
Diamond Ter. SE10 78 C1
Diana Clo. E18 42 H1
Diana Gdns., Surb. 98 J2
Diana Ho. SW13 74 F1
Diana Pl. NW1 7 F5
Diana Pl. NW1 58 B4
Diana Rd. E17 41 J3
Dianna Way, Barn. 23 H5
Dianthus Clo. SE2 71 B5
Carnation St.
Dibden St. N1 58 J1
Dibdin Clo., Sutt. 100 D3
Dibdin Rd., Sutt. 100 D3
Dicey Ave. NW2 47 J4
Dickens Ave. N3 39 F1
Dickens Clo., Rich. 82 H2
Dickens Dr., Chis. 88 F6
Dickens Est. SE1 17 H4
Dickens Est. SE1 68 C2
Dickens Est. SE16 17 H5
Dickens Est. SE16 68 C2
Dickens La. N18 33 B5
Dickens Ri., Chig. 35 E3
Dickens Rd. E6 61 A2
Dickens Sq. SE1 17 A5
Dickens Sq. SE1 67 J3
Dickens St. SW8 76 B2
Dickenson Rd. N8 40 E7
Dickenson Rd., Felt. 81 D5
Dickensons La. SE25 95 D5
Dickensons Pl. SE25 95 D6
Dickerage La., N.Mal. 92 C3
Dickerage Rd., 92 C1
Kings.T.
Dickerage Rd., 92 C1
N.Mal.
Dickson Fold, Pnr. 36 D4
Dickson Rd. SE9 79 B3

Didsbury Clo. E6 61 C1
Barking Rd.
Digby Cres. N4 49 J2
Digby Gdns., Dag. 62 G1
Digby Pl., Croy. 102 C3
Digby Rd. E5 50 G5
Digby Rd. Bark. 52 J7
Digby St. E2 59 F3
Dighton Ct. SE5 20 J6
Dighton Rd. SW18 75 F5
Digswell St. N7 49 G6
Holloway Rd.
Dilhorne Clo. SE12 87 H3
Dilke St. SW3 19 A5
Dilke St. SW3 66 J6
Dillwyn Clo. SE26 86 H4
Dilston Clo., Nthlt. 54 C3
Yeading La.
Dilston Gro. SE16 68 F4
Abbeyfield Rd.
Dilton Gdns. SW15 83 H1
Dimes Pl. W6 65 H4
King St.
Dimmock Dr., Grnf. 46 A5
Dimond Clo. E7 51 G4
Dimsdale Dr. NW9 47 C1
Dimsdale Dr., Enf. 25 D6
Dimsdale Wk. E13 60 G1
Stratford Rd.
Dingle Clo., Barn. 22 F6
Dingle Gdns. E14 60 A7
Dingley La. SW16 85 D2
Dingley Pl. EC1 9 A4
Dingley Pl. EC1 58 J3
Dingley Rd. EC1 8 J4
Dingley Rd. EC1 58 J3
Dingwall Ave., 101 J2
Croy.
Dingwall Gdns. 39 D6
NW11
Dingwall Pl., Croy. 102 A2
Dingwall Rd.
Dingwall Rd. SW18 75 F7
Dingwall Rd., Croy. 102 A1
Dinmont St. E2 59 E2
Coate St.
Dinsdale Gdns. SE25 95 B5
Dinsdale Gdns., 23 E5
Barn.
Dinsdale Rd. SE3 69 F6
Dinsmore Rd. SW12 76 B7
Dinton Rd. SW19 84 G6
Dinton Rd., Kings.T. 82 J7
Diploma Ave. N2 39 H4
Dirleton Rd. E15 60 F1
Disbrowe Rd. W6 66 B6
Discovery Wk. E1 68 E1
Waterman Way
Dishforth La. NW9 38 E1
Disney Pl. SE1 17 A3
Disney St. SF1 17 A3
Dison Clo., Enf. 25 G1
Disraeli Clo. SE28 71 C1
Disraeli Rd. E7 51 G6
Disraeli Rd. NW10 66 D2
Disraeli Rd. SW15 75 B4
Disraeli Rd. W5 64 G1
Diss St. E2 9 F3
Diss St. E2 59 C3
Distaff La. EC4 12 J5
Distaff La. EC4 58 J7
Distillery La. W6 65 J5
Fulham Palace Rd.
Distillery Rd. W6 65 J5
Distin St. SE11 20 E2
District Rd., Wem. 46 E5
Ditch All. SE10 78 B1
Ditchburn St. E14 60 C7
Ditchfield Rd., 54 E4
Hayes
Dittisham Rd. SE9 88 B4
Ditton Clo., T.Ditt. 91 D7
Ditton Gra. Clo., 98 G1
Surb.
Ditton Gra. Dr., 98 G1
Surb.
Ditton Hill, Surb. 98 F1
Ditton Hill Rd., 98 F1
Surb.
Ditton Lawn, T.Ditt. 98 D1
Ditton Reach, 91 E6
T.Ditt.
Ditton Rd., Bexh. 80 D5
Ditton Rd., Sthl. 63 F5
Ditton Rd., Surb. 98 G2
Divis Way SW15 74 H6
Dover Pk. Dr.
Dixon Clark Ct. N1 49 H6
Canonbury Rd.
Dixon Clo. E6 61 C6
Brandreth Rd.

Dixon Pl., W.Wick. 103 B1
Dixon Rd. SE14 77 H1
Dixon Rd. SE25 95 B3
Dixons All. SE16 68 E2
West La.
Dobbin Clo., Har. 37 D2
Dobell Rd. SE9 79 C5
Dobree Ave. NW10 47 H7
Dobson Clo. NW6 48 G7
Dock Hill Ave. SE16 68 G2
Dock Rd. E16 60 F7
Dock Rd., Brent. 64 G7
Dock St. E1 13 H5
Dock St. E1 59 D7
Dockers Tanner Rd. 69 A4
E14
Dockhead SE1 17 G4
Dockhead SE1 68 C2
Dockland St. E16 70 D1
Dockley Rd. SE16 17 H6
Dockley Rd. SE16 68 D3
Dockwell Clo., Felt. 72 A4
Doctor Johnson Ave. 85 B3
SW17
Doctors Clo. SE26 86 F5
Docwra's Bldgs. N1 50 B6
Dod St. E14 60 A6
Dodbrooke Rd. SE27 85 G3
Doddington Gro. 20 G5
SE17
Doddington Gro. 67 H6
SE17
Doddington Pl. SE17 20 G5
Doddington Pl. SE17 67 H6
Dodsley Pl. N9 33 F3
Dodson St. SE1 16 F4
Dodson St. SE1 67 J3
Doel Clo. SW19 84 F7
Dog Kennel Hill 77 H6
SE22
Dog Kennel Hill 77 B3
Est. SE22
Dog La. NW10 47 E4
Doggets Clo., Barn. 23 H5
Doggett Rd. SE6 78 A7
Doherty Rd. E13 60 G4
Dolben St. SE1 16 H2
Dolben St. SE1 67 H1
Dolby Ct. EC4 58 J7
Garlick Hill
Dolby Rd. SW6 75 C2
Dolland St. SE11 20 D4
Dolland St. SE11 67 F5
Dollis Ave. N3 39 C1
Dollis Brook Wk., 23 B6
Barn.
Alan Dr.
Dollis Cres., Ruis. 45 C1
Dollis Hill Ave. NW2 47 H3
Dollis Hill Est. NW2 47 G3
Dollis Hill La. NW2 47 F4
Dollis Pk. N3 39 C1
Dollis Rd. N3 39 B1
Dollis Rd. NW7 31 B7
Dollis Valley Grn.Wk. 31 F2
N20
Totteridge La.
Dollis Valley Grn.Wk., 23 B6
Barn.
Leeside
Dollis Valley Way, 23 C5
Barn.
Dolman Rd. W4 65 D4
Dolman St. SW4 76 F3
Dolphin Clo. SE16 68 G2
Kinburn St.
Dolphin Clo. SE28 62 D6
Dolphin Clo., Surb. 91 G6
Dolphin Ct. NW11 39 B6
Dolphin La. E14 60 B7
Dolphin Rd., Nthlt. 54 F2
Dolphin Sq. SW1 19 G4
Dolphin Sq. SW1 76 B6
Dolphin Sq. W4 65 E7
Dolphin St., Kings.T. 91 H1
Wood St.
Dombey St. WC1 12 C1
Dombey St. WC1 58 F5
Dome Hill Pk. SE26 86 C4
Domett Clo. SE5 77 A4
Domfe Pl. E5 50 F4
Rushmore Rd.
Domingo St. EC1 8 J5
Dominion Rd., Croy. 95 C7
Dominion Rd., Sthl. 63 C4
Dominion St. EC2 13 C1
Dominion St. EC2 58 E4
Domville Clo. N20 31 G2
Don Phelan Clo. SE5 77 A1
Donald Dr., Rom. 63 G4
Donald Rd. E13 60 H1
Donald Rd., Croy. 94 F6
Donaldson Rd. NW6 57 C1

Donaldson Rd. SE18 79 D1
Doncaster Dr., 45 F5
Nthlt.
Doncaster Gdns. N4 40 J6
Stanhope Gdns.
Doncaster Pl., 45 F5
Nthlt.
Doncaster Grn., Wat. 28 C5
Doncaster Rd. N9 26 E7
Doncel Ct. E4 26 D7
Donegal St. N1 8 D2
Donegal St. N1 58 F2
Doneraile St. SW6 75 A2
Dongola Rd. E13 60 H3
Dongola Rd. N17 41 B3
Dongola Rd. W. E13 60 H3
Balaam St.
Donington Ave., Ilf. 43 F5
Donkey All. SE22 77 D7
Donkey La., Enf. 25 D2
Donne Ct. SE24 76 J6
Burbage Rd.
Donne Pl. SW3 18 H1
Donne Pl. SW3 66 H4
Donne Pl., Mitch. 94 B4
Donne Rd., Dag. 53 C2
Donnefield Ave., 29 H7
Edg.
Donnington Rd. 47 H7
NW10
Donnington Rd., 37 F5
Har.
Donnington Rd., 99 G2
Wor.Pk.
Donnybrook Rd. 85 C7
SW16
Donovan Ave. N10 40 B3
Doon St. SE1 16 E1
Doone Clo., Tedd. 82 D6
Dora Rd. SW19 84 D5
Dora St. E14 59 J6
Doral Way, Cars. 100 J5
Doran Gro. SE18 70 H7
Doran Mans. N2 39 J5
Great N. Rd.
Doran Wk. E15 51 C7
Dorchester Ave. N13 32 J4
Dorchester Ave., 89 D1
Bex.
Dorchester Ave., Har. 36 J6
Dorchester Clo., 45 H5
Nthlt.
Dorchester Clo., Orp. 89 A7
Grovelands Rd.
Dorchester Ct. N14 24 B7
Dorchester Ct. SE24 76 J5
Dorchester Dr. SE24 76 J5
Dorchester Gdns. E4 34 A4
Dorchester Gdns. 39 D4
NW11
Dorchester Gro. W4 65 E5
Dorchester Ms., 92 D4
N.Mal.
Elm Rd.
Dorchester Rd., 93 E7
Mord.
Dorchester Rd., 45 H5
Nthlt.
Dorchester Rd., 99 J1
Wor.Pk.
Dorchester Way, Har. 37 J6
Dorchester Waye, 54 B6
Hayes
Dorcis Ave., Bexh. 80 E2
Dordrecht Rd. W3 65 E1
Dore Ave. E12 52 D5
Dore Gdns., Mord. 93 E7
Doreen Ave. NW9 47 D1
Dorell Clo., Sthl. 54 F5
Doria Rd. SW6 75 C2
Doric Way NW1 7 H3
Doric Way NW1 58 D3
Dorien Rd. SW20 93 A2
Doris Ave., Erith 80 J1
Doris Rd. E7 51 G7
Dorking Clo. SE8 68 J6
Dorking Clo., 100 A2
Wor.Pk.
Dorlcote Rd. SW18 75 H7
Dorma Trd. Est. E10 50 G1
Dorman Pl. N9 33 D2
Balham Rd.
Dorman Wk. NW10 47 D5
Garden Way
Dormay St. SW18 57 G1
Dormay St. SW18 75 E5
Dormer Clo. E15 51 F6
Dormer Clo., Barn. 23 A5
Dormers Ave., Sthl. 54 G6
Dormers Ri., Sthl. 54 H5
Dormers Wells La., 54 G6
Sthl.
Dornberg Clo. SE3 69 G7

Dornberg Rd. SE3 69 H7
Banchory Rd.
Dorncliffe Rd. SW6 75 B2
Dorney NW3 48 H7
Dorney Ri., Orp. 97 J4
Dorney Way, Houns. 72 E5
Dornton Rd. SW12 85 DL
Dornton Rd., 102 A5
S.Croy.
Dorothy Ave., Wem. 46 H7
Dorothy Evans Clo., 80 H4
Bexh.
Dorothy Gdns., Dag. 53 B4
Dorothy Rd. SW11 75 J3
Dorrell Pl. SW9 76 G4
Brixton Rd.
Dorrington Ct. SE25 95 B2
Dorrington Pt. E3 60 B3
Bromley High St.
Dorrington St. EC1 12 E1
Dorrington St. EC1 58 G5
Dorrit Ms. N18 33 B5
Dorrit Way, Chis. 88 F6
Dors Clo. NW9 47 D1
Dorset Ave., Sthl. 63 G4
Dorset Ave., Well. 79 J4
Dorset Bldgs. EC4 12 G4
Dorset Clo. NW1 10 J1
Dorset Dr., Edg. 29 J6
Dorset Est. E2 9 G3
Dorset Est. E2 59 C3
Dorset Gdns. 94 F4
Mitch.
Dorset Ms. SW1 15 D5
Dorset Pl. E15 51 D6
Dorset Ri. EC4 11 H3
Dorset Ri. EC4 12 G4
Dorset Ri. EC4 58 H6
Dorset Rd. E7 51 J7
Dorset Rd. N15 41 A4
Dorset Rd. N22 40 E1
Dorset Rd. SE9 88 B2
Dorset Rd. SW8 20 B7
Dorset Rd. SW8 67 E7
Dorset Rd. SW19 93 D1
Dorset Rd. W5 64 F3
Dorset Rd., Beck. 95 G3
Dorset Rd., Har. 36 J6
Dorset Rd., Mitch. 93 H2
Dorset Sq. NW1 8 A6
Dorset Sq. NW1 57 J4
Dorset St. W1 11 A2
Dorset St. W1 57 J5
Dorset Way, Twick. 82 A1
Dorset Waye, Houns. 63 F7
Dorville Cres. W6 65 H3
Dorville Rd. SE12 78 F5
Dothill Rd. SE18 70 G7
Douai Gro., Hmptn. 90 J1
Doubleday Rd., 27 F3
Loug.
Doughty Ms. WC1 8 C6
Doughty Ms. WC1 58 F4
Doughty St. WC1 8 C5
Doughty St. WC1 58 F4
Douglas Ave. E17 42 A1
Douglas Ave., 92 H4
N.Mal.
Douglas Ave., Wem. 46 H7
Douglas Clo., Stan. 29 D5
Douglas Clo., Wall. 101 E6
Douglas Cres., 54 C4
Hayes
Douglas Dr., Croy. 103 A3
Douglas Pl. E14 69 C5
Manchester Rd.
Douglas Rd. E4 26 E7
Douglas Rd. E16 60 G5
Douglas Rd. N1 49 J7
Douglas Rd. N22 40 G1
Douglas Rd. NW6 57 C1
Douglas Rd., Houns. 72 H3
Douglas Rd., Ilf. 44 A7
Douglas Rd., 92 B2
Kings.T.
Douglas Rd., Surb. 98 J2
Douglas Rd., Well. 80 B1
Douglas St. SW1 19 H2
Douglas St. SW1 67 D4
Douglas Way SE8 68 J7
Doulton Ms. NW6 48 E6
Lymington Rd.
Dounesforth Gdns. 84 E1
SW18
Douro Pl. W8 14 B5
Douro Pl. W8 66 E3
Douro St. E3 60 A2
Douthwaite Sq. E1 17 J1
Dove App. E6 61 B5
Dove Clo., Nthlt. 54 D4
Wayfarer Rd.
Dove Ct. EC2 13 B4

Dove Ho. Gdns. E4 34 A2
Dove Ms. SW5 18 C2
Dove Ms. SW5 66 F4
Dove Pk., Pnr. 28 G7
Dove Rd. N1 50 A6
Dove Row E2 59 D1
Dove Wk. SW1 19 B3
Dove Wk. SW1 67 A2
Dovecott Gdns. 40 G3
SW14
North Worple Way
Dovedale Ave., Har. 37 F6
Dovedale Ave., Ilf. 43 D2
Dovedale Clo., 80 A1
Well.
Dovedale Ri., 94 J7
Mitch.
Dovedale Rd. SE22 77 E5
Dovedon Clo. N14 32 E2
Dovehouse Mead, 61 G3
Bark.
Dovehouse St. SW3 18 G3
Dovehouse St. SW3 66 G5
Dover Clo., Rom. 44 J2
Dover Ct. Est. N1 50 A6
Dover Ho. Rd. SW15 74 G4
Dover Pk. Dr. SW15 74 H6
Dover Rd. E12 51 J2
Dover Rd. N9 33 F2
Dover Rd. SE19 86 A6
Dover Rd., Rom. 44 E6
Dover St. W1 11 E6
Dover St. W1 58 B7
Dover Yd. W1 15 E1
Dovercourt Ave., 94 G5
Th.Hth.
Dovercourt Gdns., 29 H5
Stan.
Dovercourt La., 100 F3
Sutt.
Dovercourt Rd. SE21 77 B6
Dovercourt Rd. SE22 77 B6
Doverfield Rd. SW2 76 E6
Doveridge Gdns. N13 32 H4
Doves Clo., Brom. 104 B2
Doveton Rd., 102 A5
S.Croy.
Doveton St. E1 59 F4
Malcolm Rd.
Dowanhill Rd. SE6 87 D1
Dowdeswell Clo. 74 E4
SW15
Dowding Pl., Stan. 29 D6
Dowgate Hill EC4 13 B5
Dowgate Hill EC4 59 J4
Dowland St. W10 57 B3
Dowlas Est. SE5 21 D7
Dowlas St. SE5 68 B7
Dowlerville Rd., 104 J6
Orp.
Dowman Clo. SW19 93 E1
Nelson Gro. Rd.
Down Clo., Nthlt. 54 B2
Down End SE18 70 E7
Moordown
Down Hall Rd., 91 G1
Kings.T.
Down Pl. W6 65 H5
Down Rd., Tedd. 82 E6
Down St. W1 15 D2
Down St., W.Mol. 90 G5
Down St. Ms. SW1 15 D2
Down Way, Nthlt. 54 B3
Downage NW4 38 J3
Downalong (Bushey), 29 A1
Wat.
Downbarns Rd., 45 D3
Ruis.
Downderry Rd., 87 D3
Brom.
Downe Clo., Well. 71 C7
Downe Rd., Mitch. 93 J2
Downers Cotts. SW4 76 C4
The Pavement
Downes Clo., Twick. 73 E6
St. Margarets Rd.
Downes Ct. N21 32 G1
Downfield, Wor.Pk. 99 F1
Downfield Clo. W9 6 A6
Downfield Clo. W9 57 E4
Downham Rd. N1 50 A7
Downham Way, 87 D5
Brom.
Downhills Ave. N17 41 A3
Downhills Pk. Rd. 40 J3
N17
Downhills Way N17 40 J2
Downhurst Ave. NW7 30 D5
Downing Dr., Grnf. 55 A1
Downing Rd., Dag. 62 F1

Downing St. SW1 16 A3
Downing St. SW1 67 E2
Downings E6 61 D6
Downland Clo. N20 31 F1
Downleys Clo. SE9 88 B2
Downman Rd. SE9 79 B3
Downs, The SW20 84 A7
Downs Ave., Chis. 88 C5
Downs Bri. Rd., 36 F6
Beck.
Downs Hill, Beck. 97 D7
Downs Pk. Rd. E5 50 D5
Downs Pk. Rd. E8 50 C5
Downs Rd. E5 50 D4
Downs Rd., Beck. 96 B2
Downs Rd., Enf. 25 B4
Downs Rd., Th.Hth. 94 J1
Downs Vw., Islw. 73 C1
Downsbury Ms. 75 D5
SW18
Merton Rd.
Downsell Rd. E15 51 C4
Downsfield Rd. E17 41 H6
Downshall Ave., Ilf. 43 H6
Downshire Hill NW3 48 G4
Downside, Sun. 90 A1
Downside, Twick. 82 C3
Downside Clo. SW19 84 F6
Downside Cres. NW3 48 H5
Downside Cres. W13 55 D4
Downside Rd., Sutt. 100 G6
Downsview Gdns. 85 J7
SE19
Downsview Rd. SE19 85 J7
Downsview, Orp. 104 H5
Southlands Ave.
Downton Ave. SW2 85 E2
Downtown Rd. SE16 68 H2
Downway N12 31 H7
Dowrey St. N1 58 G1
Richmond Ave.
Dowsett Rd. N17 41 C2
Dowson Clo. SE5 77 A4
Doyce St. SE1 16 J3
Doyle Gdns. NW10 56 G1
Doyle Rd. SE25 95 D4
D'Oyley St. SW1 19 B1
D'Oyley St. SW1 67 A4
Doynton St. N19 49 B2
Draco St. SE17 20 J5
Draco St. SE17 67 J6
Dragmire La., Mitch. 93 G4
Dragoon Rd. SE8 68 J5
Dragor Rd. NW10 56 C4
Drake Clo. SE16 68 G2
Middleton Dr.
Drake Ct. SE19 86 C5
Drake Ct., Har. 45 F1
Drake Cres. SE28 62 C6
Drake Rd. SE4 78 A3
Drake Rd., Chess. 99 A5
Drake Rd., Croy. 94 F7
Drake Rd., Har. 45 F2
Drake Rd., Mitch. 94 A6
Drake St. W1 12 C2
Drake St., Enf. 25 A1
Drakefell Rd. SE4 77 H3
Drakefell Rd. SE14 77 G2
Drakefield Rd. SW17 85 A3
Drakely Ct. N5 49 H4
Highbury Hill
Drakes Wk. E6 61 D2
Talbot Rd.
Drakewood Rd. 85 D7
SW16
Draper Clo., Belv. 71 F4
Drapers Rd. E15 51 D4
Drapers Rd. N17 41 C3
Drapers Rd., Enf. 24 H2
Drappers Way SE16 21 J1
Drawdock Rd. SE10 69 D1
Drawell Clo. SE18 70 H5
Drax Ave. SW20 83 G7
Draxmont SW19 84 B6
Dray Gdns. SW2 76 F5
Draycot Rd. E11 42 H6
Draycot Rd., Surb. 99 A1
Draycott Ave. SW3 18 H1
Draycott Ave. SW3 66 H4
Draycott Ave., Har. 37 E6
Draycott Clo., Har. 37 E6
Draycott Ms. SW6 75 C2
New Kings Rd.
Draycott Pl. SW3 18 J2
Draycott Pl. SW3 66 J4
Draycott Ter. SW3 19 A2
Draycott Ter. SW3 66 J4
Drayford Clo. W9 57 C4
Drayside Ms., Sthl. 63 F2
Kingston Rd.
Drayson Ms. W8 66 D2
Drayton Ave. W13 55 D7

Drayton Ave., Loug. 27 C6
Drayton Ave., Orp. 104 E1
Drayton Bri. Rd. W7 55 C7
Drayton Bri. Rd. 55 D6
  W13
Drayton Clo., Houns. 72 F5
  Bramley Way
Drayton Gdns. N21 24 H7
Drayton Gdns. SW10 18 D3
Drayton Gdns. SW10 66 F5
Drayton Gdns. W13 55 D7
Drayton Grn. W13 55 D7
Drayton Grn. Rd. 55 E7
  W13
Drayton Gro. W13 55 D7
Drayton Pk. N5 49 G5
Drayton Rd. E11 51 D1
Drayton Rd. N17 41 B2
Drayton Rd. NW10 56 F1
Drayton Rd. W13 55 D7
Drayton Rd., Borwd. 22 A4
Drayton Rd., Croy. 101 H2
Drayton Waye, Har. 37 E6
Dreadnought St. 69 E3
  SE10
Dresden Clo. NW6 48 E5
  Lymington Rd.
Dresden Rd. N19 49 C1
Dressington Ave. 78 A6
  SE4
Drew Ave. NW7 31 B6
Drew Gdns., Grnf. 46 C6
Drew Rd. E16 70 B1
Drewstead Rd. SW16 85 D2
Driffield Rd. E3 59 H2
Drift, The, Brom. 104 A3
Drift Way, Rich. 82 J1
Driftway, The, 94 A1
  Mitch.
Drinkwater Rd., Har. 45 H2
Drive, The E4 26 D7
Drive, The E17 42 B3
Drive, The E18 42 G4
Drive, The N3 31 D7
Drive, The N6 39 J5
  Fordington Rd.
Drive, The N11 32 C6
Drive, The NW10 56 F1
  Longstone Ave.
Drive, The NW11 39 B7
Drive, The SW16 94 F3
Drive, The SW20 83 J7
Drive, The W3 56 C6
Drive, The, Bark. 52 J7
Drive, The, Barn. 23 B3
Drive, The, Barn., 23 F6
  (New Barnet)
Drive, The, Beck. 96 A2
Drive, The, Bex. 80 C6
Drive, The, Buck.H. 26 J7
Drive, The, Chis. 97 J3
Drive, The, Edg. 30 A5
Drive, The, Enf. 25 A1
Drive, The, Epsom 99 F6
Drive, The, Erith 71 H7
Drive, The, Felt. 72 C7
Drive, The, Har. 36 G7
Drive, The, Houns. 72 J2
Drive, The, Ilf. 43 B6
Drive, The, Islw. 73 A2
Drive, The, 83 C7
  Kings.T.
Drive, The, Loug. 27 B3
Drive, The, Mord. 93 F5
Drive, The, Orp. 104 J2
Drive, The, Rom. 44 J1
Drive, The, Sid. 89 B3
Drive, The, Surb. 91 H7
Drive, The, Th.Hth. 95 A4
Drive, The, Wem. 47 C2
Drive, The, W.Wick. 96 D7
Driveway, The E17 42 B6
  Hoe St.
Droitwich Clo. SE26 86 D3
Dromey Gdns., Har. 29 C7
Dromore Rd. SW15 75 B6
Dronfield Gdns., 53 C5
  Dag.
Droop St. W10 57 B4
Drove Way, Loug. 27 C2
Drover La. SE15 68 E7
Drovers Pl. SE15 68 E7
Drovers Rd., 102 A5
  S.Croy.
Druce Rd. SE21 77 B6
Druid St. SE1 17 E3
Druid St. SE1 68 B2
Druids Way, Brom. 96 D4
Drum St. E1 13 G3
Drumaline Ridge, 99 E2
  Wor.Pk.
Drummond Cres. NW1 7 H3
Drummond Cres. NW1 58 D3

Drummond Dr., Stan. 29 C7
Drummond Gate 19 J3
  SW1
Drummond Gate 67 D5
  SW1
Drummond Pl., 73 E7
  Twick.
Drummond Rd. E11 42 J6
Drummond Rd. SE16 68 E3
Drummond Rd., 101 J2
  Croy.
Drummond St. NW1 7 F5
Drummond St. NW1 58 C4
Drummonds, The, 34 H2
  Buck.H.
Drury Cres., Croy. 101 G2
Drury Ind. Est. 47 C5
  NW10
Drury La. WC2 12 B3
Drury La. SE2 58 E6
Drury Rd., Har. 36 J7
Drury Way NW10 47 D5
Dryad St. SW15 75 A3
Dryburgh Gdns. NW9 38 A3
Dryburgh Rd. SW15 74 H3
Dryden Ave. W7 55 C6
Dryden Clo., Ilf. 35 J6
Dryden Ct. SE11 20 F2
Dryden Rd. SW19 84 F6
Dryden Rd., Enf. 25 B6
Dryden Rd., Har. 46 C4
Dryden Rd., Well. 79 H1
Dryden St. WC2 12 B4
Dryfield Clo. NW10 47 C6
Dryfield Rd., Edg. 30 C6
Dryfield Wk. SE8 69 A6
  New King St.
Dryhill Rd., Belv. 71 F6
Dryland Ave., Orp. 104 J4
Drylands Rd. N8 40 E6
Drysdale Ave. E4 26 B7
Drysdale Pl. N1 9 E3
Drysdale St. N1 9 E3
Drysdale St. N1 59 B3
Du Burstow Ter. W7 64 B2
Du Cane Ct. SW17 85 A1
Du Cane Rd. W12 56 F6
Du Cros Dr., Stan. 29 G6
Du Cros Rd. W3 65 F1
  The Vale
Dublin Cres. E8 59 D1
Ducal St. E2 9 G4
Duchess Ms. W1 11 E2
Duchess of 66 D2
  Bedford's Wk. W8
Duchess St. W1 11 E2
Duchess St. W1 58 B5
Duchy St. SE1 16 F1
Duchy St. SE1 67 G1
Ducie St. SW4 76 F4
Duck La. W1 11 H4
Duck Lees La., Enf. 25 H4
Duckett Rd. N4 40 G6
Duckett St. E1 59 G4
Ducks Wk., Twick. 73 F5
Dudden Hill La. 47 F4
  NW10
Duddington Clo. SE9 88 A4
Dudley Ave., Har. 37 F3
Dudley Ct. NW11 39 C4
Dudley Dr., Mord. 100 B1
Dudley Dr., Ruis. 45 B5
Dudley Gdns. W13 64 E2
Dudley Gdns., Har. 46 A1
Dudley Rd. E17 42 A2
Dudley Rd. N3 39 E2
Dudley Rd. NW6 57 B2
Dudley Rd. SW19 84 D6
Dudley Rd., Har. 45 J2
Dudley Rd., Ilf. 52 E4
Dudley Rd., 91 J3
  Kings.T.
Dudley Rd., Rich. 73 J2
Dudley Rd., Sthl. 63 D2
Dudley Rd., Walt. 90 A6
Dudley St. W2 10 E2
Dudlington Rd. E5 50 F2
Dudmaston Ms. SW3 18 F3
Dudsbury Rd., Sid. 89 B6
Dudset La., Houns. 72 A1
Duff St. E14 60 D6
Dufferin Ave. EC1 9 B6
Dufferin St. EC1 9 A6
Dufferin St. EC1 58 J4
Dufferin Clo., Har. 37 C5
Dufour's Pl. W1 11 G4
Duke Gdns., Ilf. 43 G4
Duke Humphrey Rd. 78 E1
  SE3
Duke of Cambridge 73 A6
  Clo., Twick.
Duke of Edinburgh 100 G2
  Rd., Sutt.

Duke of Wellington 15 C3
  Pl. SW1
Duke of Wellington 67 A2
  Pl. SW1
Duke of York St. 15 G1
  SW1
Duke of York St. 67 C1
  SW1
Duke Rd. W4 65 D5
Duke Rd., Ilf. 43 G4
Duke Shore Pl. E14 59 J7
  Narrow St.
Duke St. SW1 15 G1
Duke St. SW1 67 C1
Duke St. W1 11 C3
Duke St. W1 58 A6
Duke St., Rich. 73 G5
Duke St., Sutt. 100 G4
Duke St. Hill SE1 17 C1
Dukes Ave. N3 39 E1
Dukes Ave. N10 40 C3
Dukes Ave. W4 65 D5
Dukes Ave., Edg. 29 J6
Dukes Ave., Har. 36 F6
Dukes Ave. 37 B4
  (Wealdstone), Har.
Dukes Ave., Houns. 72 E4
Dukes Ave., 82 F4
  Kings.T.
Dukes Ave., N.Mal. 92 F3
Dukes Ave., Nthlt. 45 E7
Dukes Ave., Rich. 82 F4
Dukes Clo., Hmptn. 81 F5
Dukes Clo., Kings.T. 82 G4
Dukes Ct. E6 61 D1
Dukes Grn. Ave., 72 A5
  Felt.
Dukes La. W8 66 E2
Dukes Ms. N10 40 B3
Duke's Ms. W1 11 C3
Dukes Orchard, Bex. 89 J1
Dukes Pl. EC3 13 E4
Dukes Pl. EC3 59 B6
Dukes Rd. E6 61 D1
Dukes Rd. W3 56 A4
Duke's Rd. WC1 7 J4
Duke's Rd. WC1 58 D3
Dukes Way, W.Wick. 103 E3
Duke's Yd. W1 11 C5
Dukestreet Rd. 86 G4
  SE26
Dulas St. N4 49 F1
  Everleigh St.
Dulford St. W11 57 B7
Dulka Rd. SW11 75 J5
Dulverton Rd. SE9 88 F2
Dulverton Rd., Ruis. 45 A1
Dulwich Common 86 B1
  SE21
Dulwich Oaks, The 86 C3
  SE21
Dulwich Rd. SE24 76 G5
Dulwich Village 77 B6
  SE21
Dulwich Wd. Ave. 86 B4
  SE19
Dulwich Wd. Pk. 86 B4
  SE19
Dumbarton Rd. SW2 76 E6
Dumbleton Clo., 92 B1
  Kings.T.
  Gloucester Rd.
Dumbreck Rd. SE9 79 C4
Dumont Rd. N16 50 B3
Dumpton Pl., NW1 49 A7
  Gloucester Ave.
Dunbar Ave. SW16 94 G2
Dunbar Ave., Beck. 95 H4
Dunbar Ave., Dag. 53 G3
Dunbar Clo., Hayes 54 A6
Dunbar Ct., Sutt. 100 G5
Dunbar Gdns., Dag. 53 G5
Dunbar Rd. E7 51 G6
Dunbar Rd. N22 40 G1
Dunbar Rd., N.Mal. 92 C4
Dunbar St. SE27 85 J3
Dunblane Clo., Edg. 30 B2
  Tayside Dr.
Dunblane Rd. SE9 79 B2
Dunboyne Rd. NW3 48 J5
Dunbridge St. E2 9 H5
Dunbridge St. E2 59 D4
Duncan Clo., Barn. 23 F4
Duncan Gro. W3 56 G6
Duncan Rd. E8 59 E1
Duncan Rd., Rich. 73 H4
Duncan St. N1 11 G1
Duncan St. N1 58 H2
Duncan Ter. N1 8 G2
Duncan Ter. N1 58 H2
Duncannon St. WC2 12 A6
Duncannon St. WC2 58 E7

Dunch St. E1 59 E6
  Watney St.
Duncombe Hill SE23 77 H7
Duncombe Rd. N19 49 D1
Duncrievie Rd. SE13 78 D6
Duncroft SE18 70 H7
Dundalk Rd. SE4 77 H3
Dundas Gdns., 90 H3
  W.Mol.
Dundas Rd. SE15 77 F2
Dundee Rd. E13 60 H2
Dundee Rd. SE25 95 E5
Dundee St. E1 68 E1
Dundela Gdns., 99 H4
  Wor.Pk.
Dundonald Clo. E6 61 B6
  Northumberland Rd.
Dundonald Rd. 57 A1
  NW10
Dundonald Rd. 84 B7
  SW19
Dunedin Rd. E10 51 B3
Dunedin Rd., Ilf. 52 F1
Dunedin Way, Hayes 54 C4
Dunelm Gro. SE27 85 J4
Dunelm St. E1 59 G6
Dunfield Gdns. SE6 87 B5
Dunfield Rd. SE6 87 B5
Dunford Rd. N7 49 F4
Dungarvan Ave. 74 G4
  SW15
Dunheved Clo., 94 G6
  Th.Hth.
Dunheved Rd. N., 94 G6
  Th.Hth.
Dunheved Rd. S., 94 G6
  Th.Hth.
Dunheved Rd. W., 94 G6
  Th.Hth.
Dunholme Grn. N9 33 C3
Dunholme La. N9 33 C3
  Dunholme Rd.
Dunholme Rd. N9 33 C3
Dunkeld Rd. SE25 95 A4
Dunkeld Rd., Dag. 53 B2
Dunkery Rd. SE9 88 A4
Dunkirk St. SE27 85 J4
  Waring St.
Dunlace Rd. E5 50 F4
Dunleary Clo., 72 F7
  Houns.
Dunley Dr., Croy. 103 B7
Dunlin Ho. W13 55 C4
Dunloe Ave. N17 41 A3
Dunloe St. E2 9 G2
Dunloe St. E2 59 C2
Dunlop Pl. SE16 17 G6
Dunlop Pl. SE16 69 G1
Dunmore Pt. E2 9 F4
Dunmore Rd. NW6 57 B1
Dunmore Rd. SW20 92 J1
Dunmow Clo., Felt. 81 D4
Dunmow Clo., Loug. 27 B6
Dunmow Clo., Rom. 44 C5
Dunmow Ho., Dag. 62 B1
Dunmow Rd. E15 51 D4
Dunmow Wk. N1 58 J1
  Popham St.
Dunn Mead NW9 30 F7
  Field Mead
Dunn St. E8 50 C5
Dunnock Clo. N9 33 G1
Dunnock Clo., 22 A4
  Borwd.
  Siskin Clo.
Dunnock Rd. E6 61 B6
Dunns Pas. WC1 12 B3
Dunollie Pl. NW5 49 C5
  Dunollie Rd.
Dunollie Rd. NW5 49 C5
Dunoon Rd. SE23 77 F7
Dunraven Dr., Enf. 24 G2
Dunraven Rd. W12 65 G1
Dunraven St. W1 11 A5
Dunsany Rd. W14 66 A3
Dunsfold Way, Croy. 103 B7
Dunsford Way SW15 74 H4
  Dover Pk. Dr.
Dunsmore Clo., 54 E4
  Hayes
  Kingsash Dr.
Dunsmore Rd., Walt. 90 B6
Dunsmure Rd. N16 50 B1
Dunspring La., Ilf. 43 E2
Dunstable Ms. W1 11 C1
Dunstable Rd., Rich. 73 H4
Dunstable Rd., 90 F4
  W.Mol.
Dunstall Rd. SW20 83 H6
Dunstall Way, 90 H3
  W.Mol.
Dunstan Clo. N2 39 F3
  Thomas More Way

Dunstan Rd. NW11	48	C1
Dunstans Gro. SE22	77	E6
Dunstans Rd. SE22	77	D7
Dunster Ave., Mord.	100	A1
Dunster Clo., Barn.	23	A4
Dunster Clo., Rom.	44	J2
Dunster Ct. EC3	13	D6
Dunster Dr. NW9	47	C1
Dunster Gdns. NW6	48	C7
Dunster Way, Har.	45	E3
Dunsterville Way	17	C4
SE1		
Dunston Rd. E8	59	C1
Dunston Rd. SW11	76	A3
Dunston St. E8	59	C1
Dunton Clo., Surb.	98	H1
Dunton Rd. E10	42	B7
Dunton Rd. SE1	21	F2
Dunton Rd. SE1	68	C4
Duntshill Rd. SW18	84	E1
Dunvegan Clo.,	90	H4
W.Mol.		
Dunvegan Rd. SE9	79	C4
Dunwich Rd., Bexh.	80	F1
Dunworth Ms. W11	57	C6
Portobello Rd.		
Duplex Ride SW1	15	A4
Dupont Rd. SW20	93	A2
Dupont St. E14	59	H5
Mardon St.		
Duppas Ave., Croy.	101	H4
Violet La.		
Duppas Hill La.,	101	H4
Croy.		
Duppas Hill Rd.		
Duppas Hill Rd.,	101	G4
Croy.		
Duppas Hill Ter.,	101	H3
Croy.		
Duppas Rd., Croy.	101	G3
Dupree Rd. SE7	69	H5
Dura Den Clo., Beck.	87	B7
Durand Clo., Cars.	100	J1
Durand Gdns. SW9	76	F1
Durand Way NW10	47	C7
Durands Wk. SE16	68	H2
Salter Rd.		
Durant St. E2	9	H3
Durant St. E2	59	D3
Durants Pk. Ave., Enf.	25	G4
Durants Rd., Enf.	25	F4
Durban Gdns., Dag.	53	J7
Durban Rd. E15	60	E3
Durban Rd. E17	41	J1
Durban Rd. N17	33	B6
Durban Rd. SE27	85	J4
Durban Rd., Beck.	95	J2
Durban Rd., Ilf.	52	H1
Durbin Rd., Chess.	98	H4
Durdans Rd., Sthl.	54	F6
Durell Gdns., Dag.	53	D5
Durell Rd., Dag.	53	D5
Durford Cres. SW15	83	H1
Durham Ave., Brom.	96	F4
Durham Ave., Houns.	63	F6
Durham Ave.,	35	A5
Wdf.Grn.		
Durham Clo. SW20	92	H2
Durham Hill, Brom.	87	F4
Durham Ho. St. WC2	12	B6
Durham Pl. SW3	18	J4
Durham Pl., Ilf.	52	F4
Eton Rd.		
Durham Ri. SE18	70	F5
Durham Rd. E12	52	A4
Durham Rd. E16	60	E4
Durham Rd. N2	39	H3
Durham Rd. N7	49	F2
Durham Rd. N9	33	D2
Durham Rd. SW20	92	H1
Durham Rd. W5	64	G3
Durham Rd., Borwd.	22	C3
Durham Rd., Brom.	96	F3
Durham Rd., Dag.	53	J5
Durham Rd., Felt.	72	C7
Durham Rd., Har.	36	H5
Durham Rd., Sid.	89	B5
Durham Row E1	59	H5
Durham St. SE11	20	C4
Durham St. SE11	67	F5
Durham Ter. W2	10	A3
Durham Ter. W2	57	E6
Durham Wf., Brent.	64	F7
High St.		
Durley Ave., Pnr.	36	E7
Durley Rd. N16	41	B7
Durlston Rd. E5	50	D2
Durlston Rd.,	82	H6
Kings.T.		
Durnell Way, Loug.	27	D3
Durnford St. N15	41	B5
Durnford St. SE10	69	C6
Greenwich Ch. St.		

Durning Rd. SE19	86	A5
Durnsford Ave.	84	D2
SW19		
Durnsford Rd. N11	40	D1
Durnsford Rd. SW19	84	D2
Durrant Way, Orp.	104	G5
Durrington Ave.	75	C1
SW20		
Durrington Pk. Rd.	83	J1
SW20		
Durrington Rd. E5	50	H4
Dursley Clo. SE3	78	J2
Dursley Gdns. SE3	79	A1
Dursley Rd. SE3	78	J2
Durward St. E1	59	E5
Durweston Ms. W1	11	A1
Durweston St. W1	11	A2
Dury Rd., Barn.	23	C2
Dutch Gdns.,	83	B6
Kings.T.		
Windmill Ri.		
Dutch Yd. SW18	75	D5
Wandsworth High St.		
Duthie St. E14	60	C7
Dutton St. SE10	78	C1
Dwight Ct. SW6	75	B2
Burlington Rd.		
Dye Ho. La. E3	60	A1
Dyer's Bldgs. EC1	12	E2
Dyers Hall Rd. E11	51	E2
Dyers La. SW15	74	H4
Dykes Way, Brom.	96	F3
Dylan Rd., Belv.	71	G3
Dylan Thomas Ho.	40	F4
N8		
Dylways SE5	77	A4
Dymchurch Clo., Ilf.	43	D3
Dymchurch Clo.,	104	H4
Orp.		
Dymes Path SW19	84	A2
Queensmere Rd.		
Dymock St. SW6	75	E3
Dymond Est. SW17	84	H3
Glenburnie Rd.		
Dyne Rd. NW6	48	B7
Dyneley Rd. SE12	87	J4
Dynevor Rd. N16	50	C3
Dynevor Rd., Rich.	73	H6
Dynham Rd. NW6	48	D7
Dyott St. WC1	11	J3
Dyott St. WC1	58	D6
Dysart Ave., Kings.T.	82	F5
Dysart St. EC2	9	D6
Dyson Rd. E11	42	E6
Dyson Rd. E15	51	F6
Dysons Rd. N18	33	E5

E

Eade Rd. N4	40	J7
Eagans Clo. N2	39	H3
Market Pl.		
Eagle Ave., Rom.	44	E6
Eagle Clo., Enf.	25	F4
Eagle Ct. EC1	12	G1
Eagle Ct. EC1	58	H5
Eagle Dr. NW9	38	E2
Eagle Hill SE19	86	A6
Eagle La. E11	42	G4
Eagle Ms. N1	50	B6
Tottenham Rd.		
Eagle Pl. SW1	11	G6
Eagle Rd., Wem.	46	G7
Eagle St. WC1	12	C2
Eagle St. WC1	58	F5
Eagle Ter., Wdf.Grn.	34	H7
Eagle Wf. Rd. N1	9	A1
Eagle Wf. Rd. N1	58	C1
Eaglesfield Rd. SE18	79	E2
Ealdham Sq. SE9	78	J4
Ealing Clo., Borwd.	22	D1
Ealing Downs Ct.,	55	D3
Grnf.		
Perivale La.		
Ealing Grn. W5	64	G1
Ealing Pk. Gdns. W5	64	F4
Ealing Rd., Brent.	64	G4
Ealing Rd., Nthlt.	54	G1
Ealing Rd., Wem.	46	H6
Ealing Village W5	55	H6
Eamont St. NW8	6	G1
Eamont St. NW8	57	H2
Eardley Cres. SW5	66	D5
Eardley Pt. SE18	70	E4
Wilmount St.		
Eardley Rd. SW16	85	C5
Eardley Rd., Belv.	71	G5
Earl Ri. SE18	70	G4
Earl Rd. SE1	21	F3
Earl Rd. SE1	68	C5
Earl Rd. SW14	74	C4
Elm Rd.		

Earl St. EC2	13	C1
Earl St. EC2	59	A5
Earldom Rd. SW15	74	J4
Earle Gdns., Kings.T.	82	H7
Earlham Gro. E7	51	F5
Earlham Gro. N22	32	F7
Earlham St. WC2	11	J4
Earlham St. WC2	58	D6
Earls Ct. Gdns. SW5	18	A2
Earls Ct. Gdns. SW5	66	E4
Earls Ct. Rd. SW5	18	A2
Earls Ct. Rd. W8	66	D4
Earls Ct. Sq. SW5	18	A3
Earls Ct. Sq. SW5	66	E5
Earls Cres., Har.	37	B4
Earl's Path, Loug.	26	J2
Earls Ter. W8	66	C3
Earls Wk. W8	66	D3
Earls Wk., Dag.	53	B4
Earlsdown Ho., Bark.	61	G2
Wheelers Cross		
Earlsferry Way N1	49	F7
Earlsfield Rd. SW18	84	F1
Earlshall Rd. SE9	79	C4
Earlsmead, Har.	45	F4
Earlsmead Rd. N15	41	C5
Earlsmead Rd. NW10	56	J3
Earlsthorpe Ms.	76	A6
SW12		
Earlsthorpe Rd.	86	G4
SE26		
Earlstoke St. EC1	8	G3
Earlston Gro. E9	59	E1
Earlswood Ave.,	94	G5
Th.Hth.		
Earlswood Clo. SE10	69	E5
Earlswood St.		
Earlswood Gdns.,	43	D3
Ilf.		
Earlswood St. SE10	69	E5
Early Ms. NW1	58	B1
Arlington Rd.		
Earnshaw St. WC2	11	J3
Earnshaw St. WC2	58	D6
Earsby St. W14	66	B4
Easby Rd., Mord.	93	E6
Easebourne Rd.,	53	C5
Dag.		
Easedale Ho., Islw.	73	C5
Easley's Ms. W1	11	C3
East Acton La. W3	56	E7
East Arbour St. E1	59	G6
East Ave. E12	52	B7
East Ave. E17	42	B4
East Ave., Sthl.	54	F7
East Ave., Wall.	101	F5
East Bank N16	41	B7
East Barnet Rd.,	23	G4
Barn.		
East Churchfield Rd.	65	D1
W3		
East Clo. W5	56	A4
East Clo., Barn.	24	A4
East Clo., Grnf.	54	J2
East Ct., Wem.	46	F2
East Cres. N11	31	J4
East Cres., Enf.	25	B5
East Cross Route E3	50	J7
East Dulwich Gro.	77	B5
SE22		
East Dulwich Rd.	77	D4
SE15		
East Dulwich Rd.	77	C4
SE22		
East End Rd. N2	39	E3
East End Rd. N3	39	C2
East End Way, Pnr.	36	E3
East Entrance, Dag.	62	H2
Oval Rd. S.		
East Ferry Rd. E14	69	B4
East Gdns. SW17	84	H6
East Glade, Pnr.	36	F3
East Ham Ind. Est.	61	A4
E6		
East Ham Manor Way E6	61	D6
East Harding St. EC4	12	F3
East Heath Rd. NW3	48	F3
East Hill SW18	75	E5
East Hill, Wem.	47	A2
East Holme, Hayes	64	A5
East India Dock Rd.	60	A6
E14		
East India Dock	60	D7
Wall Rd E14		
East La. SE16	17	H4
East La. SE16	68	D2
East La., Kings.T.	91	G3
East La., Wem.	46	E3
East Mascalls SE7	69	J6
East Mead, Ruis.	45	D3
East Mt. St. E1	59	E5

East Pk. Clo., Rom.	44	D5
East Pas. EC1	12	J1
East Pier E1	68	E1
Wapping High St.		
East Pl. SE27	85	J4
Pilgrim Hill		
East Poultry Ave.	12	G2
EC1		
East Ramp, Houns.	60	G1
East Rd. N1	9	C3
East Rd. N1	59	A3
East Rd. SW19	81	F6
East Rd., Barn.	24	A7
East Rd., Edg.	38	B1
East Rd., Kings.T.	91	H1
East Rd., Rom.	44	E5
(Chadwell Heath)		
East Rd., Well.	80	B2
East Rochester Way	79	G4
SE9		
East Rochester Way,	80	D6
Bex.		
East Rochester Way,	79	H4
Sid.		
East Row E11	42	G6
East Row W10	57	B4
East Sheen Ave.	74	D5
SW14		
East Smithfield E1	13	G6
East Smithfield E1	59	C7
East St. SE17	21	A3
East St. SE17	67	J5
East St., Bark.	52	F7
East St., Bexh.	80	G4
East St., Brent.	64	F7
East St., Brom.	96	G2
East Surrey Gro.	68	C7
SE15		
East Tenter St. E1	13	G4
East Tenter St. E1	59	C6
East Twrs., Pnr.	36	D5
East Vw. E4	34	C5
East Vw., Barn.	23	C2
East Wk. NW7	30	G7
Northway		
East Wk., Barn.	24	A7
East Wk., Hayes	63	A1
East Way E11	42	H5
East Way, Brom.	96	G7
East Way, Croy.	102	H2
East Way, Hayes	63	A1
East Way, Ruis.	45	A1
East Woodside, Bex.	89	E1
Maiden Erlegh Ave.		
Eastbank Rd.,	81	J5
Hmptn.		
Eastbourne Ave. W3	56	D6
Eastbourne Gdns.	74	C3
SW14		
Eastbourne Ms. W2	10	D3
Eastbourne Ms. W2	57	F6
Eastbourne Rd. E6	61	D3
Eastbourne Rd. E15	60	E1
Eastbourne Rd. N15	41	B6
Eastbourne Rd.	85	A6
SW17		
Eastbourne Rd. W4	65	C6
Eastbourne Rd.,	64	G5
Brent.		
Eastbourne Rd., Felt.	81	D2
Eastbourne Ter. W2	10	D3
Eastbourne Ter. W2	57	F6
Eastbournia Ave. N9	33	E3
Eastbrook Ave. N9	25	F7
Eastbrook Ave., Dag.	53	J4
Eastbrook Rd. SE3	78	H1
Eastbury Ave., Bark.	61	H1
Eastbury Ave., Enf.	25	B1
Eastbury Ct., Bark.	61	H1
Eastbury Gro. W4	65	E5
Eastbury Ho., Bark.	61	J1
Eastbury Rd. E6	61	D4
Eastbury Rd.,	82	H7
Kings.T.		
Eastbury Rd., Orp.	97	G6
Eastbury Sq., Bark.	61	J1
Eastbury Ter. E1	59	G4
Eastcastle St. W1	11	F3
Eastcastle St. W1	58	C6
Eastcheap EC3	13	C5
Eastcheap EC3	59	A7
Eastcombe Ave. SE7	69	H6
Eastcote, Orp.	104	J1
Eastcote Ave., Grnf.	46	D6
Eastcote Ave., Har.	45	H2
Eastcote Ave.,	90	F5
W.Mol.		
Eastcote High Rd.,	36	A6
Pnr.		
Eastcote La., Har.	45	E4
Eastcote La., Nthlt.	45	F6
Eastcote La. N.,	45	F6
Nthlt.		

Eastcote Rd., Har.	45 J3
Eastcote Rd., Pnr.	36 D5
Eastcote Rd., Ruis.	36 A6
Eastcote Rd., Well.	79 G2
Eastcote St. SW9	76 F2
Eastcote Vw., Pnr.	36 C4
Eastcroft Rd.,	99 E7
Epsom	
Eastdown Pk. SE13	78 D4
Eastern Ave. E11	42 H6
Eastern Ave., Ilf.	43 A6
Eastern Ave., Pnr.	36 D7
Eastern Ave., Rom.	44 C4
Eastern Ave. W.,	44 E4
Rom.	
Eastern Gateway	61 E7
Access Rd. E6	
Eastern Ind. Est.,	71 F2
Belv.	
Eastern Ind. Est.,	71 F2
Erith	
Eastern Rd. E13	60 H2
Eastern Rd. E17	42 C5
Eastern Rd. N2	39 J3
Eastern Rd. N22	40 E1
Eastern Rd. SE4	78 A4
Eastern Way, Erith	71 E1
Easternville Gdns.,	43 F6
Ilf.	
Eastfield Gdns.,	53 G4
Dag.	
Eastfield Rd. E17	42 A4
Eastfield Rd. N8	40 E3
Eastfield Rd., Dag.	53 F4
Eastfields, Pnr.	36 C5
Eastfields Rd. W3	56 C5
Eastfields Rd.,	94 A2
Mitch.	
Eastgate Clo. SE28	62 D6
Eastholm NW11	39 E4
Eastlake Rd. SE5	76 J2
Eastlands Cres.	77 C6
SE21	
Eastleigh Ave.,	45 H2
Har.	
Eastleigh Clo. NW2	47 E3
Eastleigh Clo.,	100 E7
Sutt.	
Eastleigh Rd.,	80 J2
Bexh.	
Eastleigh Wk. SW15	74 G7
Alton Rd.	
Eastman Rd. W3	65 D2
Eastmead Ave.,	54 H3
Grnf.	
Eastmead Clo.,	97 B2
Brom.	
Eastmearn Rd. SE21	85 J2
Eastmont Rd., Esher	98 C2
Eastmoor Pl. SE7	70 A3
Eastmoor St.	
Eastmoor St. SE7	70 A3
Eastney Rd., Croy.	101 H1
Eastney St. SE10	69 D5
Eastnor Rd. SE9	88 F1
Easton Gdns.,	22 D4
Borwd.	
Easton St. WC1	**8 E4**
Eastry Ave., Brom.	96 F6
Eastry Rd., Erith	71 G6
Eastside Rd. NW11	39 C4
Eastview Ave. SE18	70 H7
Eastville Ave. NW11	39 C6
Eastway E9	50 J6
Eastway E10	51 A4
Eastway, Mord.	93 A5
Eastway, Wall.	101 C4
Eastwell Clo., Beck.	86 H7
Eastwood Clo. E18	42 G2
The Viaduct	
Eastwood Rd. E18	42 G2
Eastwood Rd. N10	40 A2
Eastwood Rd., Ilf.	44 A7
Eastwood St. SW16	85 C6
Eatington Rd. E10	42 D5
Eaton Clo. SW1	**19 B2**
Eaton Clo. SW1	67 A4
Eaton Clo., Stan.	29 E4
Eaton Dr. SW9	76 H4
Eaton Dr., Kings.T.	83 A7
Eaton Gdns., Dag.	53 E7
Eaton Gate SW1	**19 B1**
Eaton Gate SW1	67 A4
Eaton La. SW1	**15 E6**
Eaton La. SW1	67 B3
Eaton Ms. N. SW1	**15 B6**
Eaton Ms. N. SW1	67 A4
Eaton Ms. S. SW1	**15 D6**
Eaton Ms. S. SW1	67 A4
Eaton Ms. W. SW1	**19 C1**
Eaton Ms. W. SW1	67 A4
Eaton Pk. Rd. N13	32 G2

Eaton Pl. SW1	**15 B6**
Eaton Pl. SW1	67 A3
Eaton Ri. E11	42 J5
Eaton Ri. W5	55 F5
Eaton Rd. NW4	38 J5
Eaton Rd., Enf.	25 B3
Eaton Rd., Houns.	73 A4
Eaton Rd., Sid.	89 D2
Eaton Rd., Sutt.	100 G6
Eaton Row SW1	**15 D6**
Eaton Row SW1	67 B3
Eaton Sq. SW1	**19 C1**
Eaton Sq. SW1	67 A4
Eaton Ter. SW1	**19 B1**
Eaton Ter. SW1	67 A4
Eaton Ter. Ms. SW1	**19 B1**
Eaton Wk. SE15	68 C7
Sumner Est.	
Eatons Mead E4	34 A2
Eatonville Rd. SW17	84 J2
Eatonville Vill. SW17	84 J2
Eatonville Rd.	
Ebbisham Dr. SW8	20 C6
Ebbisham Dr. SW8	67 F6
Ebbisham Rd.,	99 J2
Wor.Pk.	
Ebbsfleet Rd. NW2	48 B5
Ebdon Way SE3	78 H3
Ebenezer St. N1	**9 B3**
Ebenezer Wk. SW16	94 C1
Meopham Rd.	
Ebley Clo. SE15	**21 F6**
Ebner St. SW18	75 E5
Ebor St. E1	**9 F5**
Ebor St. E1	59 C4
Ebrington Rd., Har.	37 F6
Ebsworth St. SE23	77 G7
Eburne Rd. N7	49 E3
Ebury Bri. SW1	**19 D3**
Ebury Bri. SW1	67 B5
Ebury Bri. Est. SW1	**19 D3**
Ebury Bri. Est. SW1	67 B5
Ebury Bri. Rd. SW1	**19 C4**
Ebury Bri. Rd. SW1	67 A5
Ebury Clo., Kes.	104 B3
Ebury Ms. SE27	85 H3
Norwood Rd.	
Ebury Ms. SW1	**19 D1**
Ebury Ms. SW1	67 B4
Ebury Ms. E. SW1	**15 D6**
Ebury Sq. SW1	19 C2
Ebury Sq. SW1	67 A4
Ebury St. SW1	**19 C2**
Ebury St. SW1	67 A4
Eccles Rd. SW11	75 J4
Ecclesbourne Clo.	32 G5
N13	
Ecclesbourne Gdns.	32 G5
N13	
Ecclesbourne Rd. N1	49 J7
Ecclesbourne Rd.,	94 J5
Th.Hth.	
Eccleston Bri. SW1	**19 E1**
Eccleston Bri. SW1	67 B4
Eccleston Clo.,	23 J4
Barn.	
Eccleston Clo., Orp.	104 G1
Eccleston Cres.,	44 A7
Rom.	
Eccleston Ms. SW1	**15 C6**
Eccleston Ms. SW1	67 A3
Eccleston Pl. SW1	**19 D1**
Eccleston Pl. SW1	67 B4
Eccleston Rd. W13	55 D7
Eccleston Sq. SW1	**19 E2**
Eccleston Sq. SW1	67 B4
Eccleston Sq. Ms.	**19 E2**
SW1	
Eccleston St. SW1	**15 C6**
Eccleston St. SW1	67 B4
Ecclestone Ms.,	46 H5
Wem.	
Ecclestone Pl.,	46 J5
Wem.	
Echo Heights E4	34 B1
Mount Echo Dr.	
Eckford St. N1	**8 E1**
Eckford St. N1	58 G2
Eckstein Rd. SW11	75 H4
Eclipse Rd. E13	60 H5
Ector Rd. SE6	87 E2
Edbrooke Rd. W9	57 D4
Eddiscombe Rd. SW6	75 C2
Eddy Clo., Rom.	44 H6
Eddystone Rd. SE4	77 H5
Ede Clo., Houns.	72 F3
Eden Clo. W8	66 D3
Adam & Eve Ms.	
Eden Clo., Wem.	55 G1
Eden Gro. E17	42 B5
Eden Gro. N7	49 F5
Eden Ms. SW17	84 F3
Huntspill St.	

Eden Pk. Ave., Beck.	95 H4
Eden Rd. E17	42 B5
Eden Rd. SE27	85 H5
Eden Rd., Beck.	95 H4
Eden Rd., Bex.	89 J4
Eden Rd., Croy.	102 A4
Eden St., Kings.T.	91 G2
Eden Wk., Kings.T.	91 H2
Eden St.	
Eden Way, Beck.	95 J5
Edenbridge Rd. E9	50 G7
Edenbridge Rd., Enf.	25 B6
Edencourt Rd. SW16	85 B6
Edenfield Gdns.,	99 F3
Wor.Pk.	
Edenham Way W10	57 C5
Elkstone Rd.	
Edenhurst Ave. SW6	75 C3
Edensor Gdns. W4	65 E7
Edensor Rd. W4	65 E7
Edenvale Rd.,	85 A7
Mitch.	
Edenvale St. SW6	75 E2
Ederline Ave. SW16	94 F3
Edgar Rd. E3	60 B3
Edgar Rd., Houns.	72 F7
Edgar Rd., Rom.	44 D7
Edgarley Ter. SW6	75 B1
Edgbaston Rd., Wat.	28 B3
Holmside Ri.	
Edge Hill SE18	70 E6
Edge Hill SW19	84 A7
Edge Hill Ave. N3	39 D4
Edge Hill Ct. SW19	84 A7
Edge St. W8	66 D1
Kensington Ch. St.	
Edgeborough Way,	88 A7
Brom.	
Edgebury, Chis.	88 E4
Edgebury Wk., Chis.	88 F4
Edgehill Rd.	
Edgecombe Clo.,	83 D7
Kings.T.	
Edgecombe Ho.	84 B1
SW19	
Edgecoombe Rd. E11	51 F1
Harvey Rd.	
Edgecoombe, S.Croy.	102 F7
Edgecot Gro. N15	41 A5
Oulton Rd.	
Edgecote Clo. W3	65 C1
Cheltenham Pl.	
Edgefield Ave.,	52 J7
Bark.	
Edgehill Gdns., Dag.	53 G4
Edgehill Rd. W13	55 F5
Edgehill Rd., Chis.	88 F3
Edgehill Rd., Mitch.	94 B1
Edgel St. SW18	75 E4
Ferrier St.	
Edgeley La. SW4	76 D3
Edgeley Rd.	
Edgeley Rd. SW4	76 D3
Edgepoint Clo. SE27	85 H5
Knights Hill	
Edgewood Dr., Orp.	104 J5
Edgewood Grn.,	102 G1
Croy.	
Edgeworth Ave. NW4	38 G5
Edgeworth Clo. NW4	38 G5
Edgeworth Cres.	38 G5
NW4	
Edgeworth Rd. SE9	78 J4
Edgeworth Rd., Barn.	23 H4
Edgington Rd. SW16	85 D6
Edgington Way, Sid.	89 C7
Edgware Rd. NW2	47 H1
Edgware Rd. W2	**6 E6**
Edgware Rd. W2	57 G4
Edgware Way, Edg.	29 J4
Edgwarebury Gdns.,	30 A5
Edg.	
Edgwarebury La.,	30 A2
Edg.	
Edinburgh Ct. SW20	93 A5
Edinburgh Gate SW1	**14 J4**
Edinburgh Gate SW1	66 J2
Edinburgh Ho. W9	**6 B3**
Edinburgh Ho. W9	57 E3
Edinburgh Rd. E13	60 H2
Edinburgh Rd. E17	42 A5
Edinburgh Rd. N18	33 D5
Edinburgh Rd. W7	64 C2
Edinburgh Rd.,	100 F2
Sutt.	
Edington Rd. SE2	71 B3
Edington Rd., Enf.	25 F2
Edis St. NW1	58 A1
Edison Dr., Sthl.	54 H6
Edison Gro. SE18	70 J7
Edison Rd. N8	40 D6
Edison Rd., Brom.	96 G2

Edison Rd., Enf.	25 J2
Edison Rd., Well.	79 J1
Edith Gdns., Surb.	92 B7
Edith Gro. SW10	**18 C6**
Edith Gro. SW10	66 F6
Edith Rd. E6	52 A7
Edith Rd. E15	51 D5
Chandos Rd.	
Edith Rd. N11	32 D7
Edith Rd. SE25	95 A5
Edith Rd. SW19	84 E6
Edith Rd. W14	66 B4
Edith Rd., Rom.	44 D6
Edith Row SW6	75 E1
Edith St. E2	**9 H1**
Edith Ter. SW10	**18 C7**
Edith Ter. SW10	66 F7
Edith Vill. W14	66 C5
Edith Yd. SW10	**18 D7**
Edithna St. SW9	76 E3
Edmansons Clo. N17	41 B1
Bruce Gro.	
Edmeston Clo. E9	50 H6
Edmonds Ct., W.Mol.	90 H4
Avern Rd.	
Edmund Rd., Mitch.	93 H3
Edmund Rd., Well.	80 A3
Edmund St. SE5	**21 B7**
Edmund St. SE5	68 A7
Edmunds Clo., Hayes	54 C5
Edmunds Wk. N2	39 H4
Edna Rd. SW20	93 A2
Edna St. SW11	75 H1
Edric Rd. SE14	68 G7
Edrich Ho. SW4	76 E1
Edrick Rd., Edg.	30 C6
Edrick Wk., Edg.	30 C6
Edridge Rd., Croy.	101 J3
Edulf Rd., Borwd.	22 B1
Edward Ave. E4	34 B6
Edward Ave., Mord.	93 G5
Edward Clo. N9	25 C7
Edward Clo., Hmptn.	81 J5
Edward Rd.	
Edward Clo., Nthlt.	54 C2
Edward Ct. E16	60 G5
Alexandra St.	
Edward Gro., Barn.	23 G5
Edward Ms. NW1	**7 E2**
Edward Pl. SE8	68 J6
Edward Rd. E17	41 G4
Edward Rd. SE20	86 G7
Edward Rd., Barn.	23 G4
Edward Rd., Brom.	87 H7
Edward Rd., Chis.	88 E5
Edward Rd., Croy.	95 B7
Edward Rd., Hmptn.	81 J5
Edward Rd., Har.	36 J3
Edward Rd., Nthlt.	54 C2
Edward Rd., Rom.	44 D6
Edward Sq. N1	58 F1
Caledonian Rd.	
Edward St. E16	60 G4
Edward St. SE8	68 J6
Edward St. SE14	68 H7
Edward Temme Ave.	51 F7
E15	
Edwardes Sq. W8	66 C3
Edward's Ave., Ruis.	45 B6
Edwards Clo.,	100 A2
Wor.Pk.	
Edwards Cotts. N1	49 H6
Compton Ave.	
Edwards Dr. N11	32 D7
Gordon Way	
Edwards La. N16	50 A2
Edwards Ms. N1	**11 B4**
Edwards Ms. W1	58 A6
Edwards Rd., Belv.	71 G4
Edwin Ave. E6	61 D2
Edwin Clo., Bexh.	71 F6
Edwin Pl., Croy.	102 A1
Cross Rd.	
Edwin Rd., Edg.	30 D6
Edwin Rd., Twick.	82 B1
Edwin St. E1	59 F4
Edwin St. E16	60 G5
Edwin Way, Ilf.	43 B5
Edwins Mead E9	50 H4
Lindisfarne Way	
Edwyn Clo., Barn.	22 J6
Eel Brook Studios	66 D7
SW6	
Moore Pk. Rd.	
Effie Pl. SW6	66 D7
Effie Rd. SW6	66 D7
Effingham Clo.,	100 E7
Sutt.	
Effingham Rd. N8	40 G5
Effingham Rd. SE12	78 E5
Effingham Rd.,	94 F7
Croy.	

Effingham Rd., Surb. 91 E7
Effort St. SW17 84 H5
Effra Par. SW2 76 G5
Effra Rd. SW2 76 G4
Effra Rd. SW19 84 D6
Egan Way SE16 68 E5
Egbert St. NW1 58 A1
Egerton Clo., Pnr. 36 A2
Egerton Cres. SW3 18 H1
Egerton Cres. SW3 66 H4
Egerton Dr. SE10 78 B1
Egerton Gdns. NW4 38 H4
Egerton Gdns. NW10 56 J1
Egerton Gdns. SW3 14 G6
Egerton Gdns. SW3 66 H4
Egerton Gdns. W13 55 E6
Egerton Gdns., Ilf. 52 J3
Egerton Gdns. Ms. 14 H6
SW3
Egerton Gdns. Ms. 66 H3
SW3
Egerton Pl. SW3 14 H6
Egerton Pl. SW3 66 H3
Egerton Rd. N16 41 C7
Egerton Rd. SE25 95 B3
Egerton Rd., N.Mal. 92 F4
Egerton Rd., Twick. 73 B7
Egerton Rd., Wem. 46 J7
Egerton Ter. SW3 14 H6
Egerton Ter. SW3 66 H3
Egham Clo. SW19 84 B2
Winterfold Clo.
Egham Clo., Sutt. 100 B2
Egham Cres., Sutt. 100 A3
Egham Rd. E13 60 H5
Eglantine Rd. SW18 75 F5
Egleston Rd., Mord. 93 E6
Eglington Ct. SE17 20 J5
Eglington Rd. E4 26 D7
Eglinton Hill SE18 70 E6
Eglinton Rd. SE18 70 E6
Egliston Ms. SW15 74 J3
Egliston Rd. SW15 74 J3
Eglon Ms. NW1 48 J7
Berkley Rd.
Egmont Ave., Surb. 98 J1
Egmont Rd., N.Mal. 92 F4
Egmont Rd., Surb. 98 J1
Egmont Rd., Sutt. 100 F7
Egmont Rd., Walt. 90 B7
Egmont St. SE14 68 G7
Egremont Rd. SE27 85 G3
Eighteenth Rd., 94 E4
Mitch.
Eighth Ave. E12 52 C4
Eighth Ave., Hayes 63 A1
Eileen Rd. SE25 95 A5
Eisenhower Dr. E6 61 B5
Elaine Gro. NW5 49 A5
Elam Clo. SE5 76 H2
Elam St. SE5 76 H2
Eland Rd. SW11 75 J3
Eland Rd., Croy. 101 H3
Elba Pl. SE17 21 A1
Elbe St. SW6 75 F2
Elberon Ave., Croy. 94 C6
Elborough Rd. SE25 95 D5
Elborough St. SW18 84 D1
Elbury Dr. E16 60 G6
Elcho St. SW11 66 H7
Elcot Ave. SE15 68 D7
Elder Ave. N8 40 E5
Elder Ct. (Bushey), 29 B2
Wat.
Elder Oak Clo. SE20 95 E1
Elder Rd. SE27 85 J5
Elder St. E1 9 F6
Elder St. E1 59 C5
Elder Wk. N1 58 H1
Essex Rd.
Elderberry Gro. SE27 85 J5
Linton Gro.
Elderberry Rd. W5 64 H2
Elderfield Rd. E5 50 G4
Elderfield Wk. E11 42 H5
Elderslie Clo., 96 A5
Beck.
Elderslie Rd. SE9 79 D5
Elderton Rd. SE26 86 H4
Eldertree Pl., Mitch. 94 C1
Eldertree Way
Eldertree Way, 94 C1
Mitch.
Elderwood Pl. SE27 85 J5
Eldred Rd.
Eldon Ave., Borwd. 22 A2
Eldon Ave., Croy. 102 F2
Eldon Ave., Houns. 63 G7
Eldon Gro. NW3 48 G5
Eldon Pk. SE25 95 E4
Lincoln Rd.
Eldon Rd. E17 41 J4
Eldon Rd. N9 33 F2

Eldon Rd. N22 40 H1
Eldon Rd. W8 14 B6
Eldon Rd. W8 66 E3
Eldon St. EC2 13 C2
Eldon St. EC2 59 A5
Eldon Way NW10 56 B2
Eldonwall Trd. Est. 47 G1
NW8
Eldred Rd., Bark. 61 H1
Eldridge Clo., Felt. 81 A1
Eleanor Clo. SE16 69 G2
Eleanor Cres. NW7 31 A4
Eleanor Gdns., Barn. 23 A5
Chesterfield Rd.
Eleanor Gdns., Dag. 53 F3
Nicholas Rd.
Eleanor Gro. SW13 74 E3
Eleanor Rd. E8 50 E6
Eleanor Rd. E15 51 F6
Eleanor Rd. N11 32 E6
Eleanor St. E3 60 A3
Eleanor Wk. SE18 70 C4
Samuel St.
Electric Ave. SW9 76 G4
Electric La. SW9 76 G4
Electric Par., Surb. 91 G6
Elephant & Castle 20 H1
SE1
Elephant & Castle 67 H3
SE1
Elephant La. SE16 68 F2
Elephant Rd. SE17 20 J1
Elephant Rd. SE17 67 J4
Elers Rd. W13 64 F2
Eleven Acre Ri., 27 C3
Loug.
Eley Est. N18 33 F4
Eley Rd. N18 33 F4
Eley's Est. N18 33 G5
Angel Rd.
Elf Row E1 59 F7
Elfin Gro., Tedd. 82 C5
Broad St.
Elfindale Rd. SE24 76 J5
Elford Clo. SE3 78 J4
Elfort Rd. N5 49 G4
Elfrida Cres. SE6 87 A4
Elfwine Rd. W7 55 B5
Elgar Ave. NW10 47 D6
Mitchellbrook Way
Elgar Ave. SW16 94 E3
Elgar Ave. W5 64 H2
Elgar Ave., Surb. 99 A1
Elgar Clo. SE8 69 A7
Comet St.
Elgar Clo., Buck.H. 35 A2
Elgar St. SE16 68 H2
Elgin Ave. W9 57 D4
Elgin Ave., Har. 37 E2
Elgin Cres. W11 57 B7
Elgin Est. W9 57 D4
Elgin Ms. W11 57 B6
Ladbroke Gro.
Elgin Ms. N. W9 6 B3
Elgin Ms. S. W9 6 B3
Elgin Rd. N22 40 C2
Elgin Rd., Croy. 102 C2
Elgin Rd., Ilf. 52 H1
Elgin Rd., Sutt. 100 F3
Elgin Rd., Wall. 101 C6
Elgood Clo. W11 57 B7
Avondale Pk. Rd.
Elham Clo., Brom. 88 A7
Elia Ms. N1 8 G2
Elia Ms. N1 58 H2
Elia St. N1 8 G2
Elia St. N1 58 H2
Elias Pl. SW8 20 E6
Elias Pl. SW8 67 G6
Elibank Rd. SE9 79 C4
Elim Est. SE1 17 D5
Elim Est. SE1 68 A3
Elim Way E13 60 F3
Eliot Bank SE23 86 E2
Eliot Cotts. SE3 78 E2
Eliot Pl.
Eliot Dr., Har. 45 H2
Eliot Gdns. SW15 74 G4
Eliot Hill SE13 78 C2
Eliot Pk. SE13 78 C2
Eliot Pl. SE3 78 E2
Eliot Rd., Dag. 53 D4
Eliot Vale SE3 78 D2
Elizabeth Ave. N1 49 J7
Elizabeth Ave., Enf. 24 H3
Elizabeth Ave., Ilf. 52 G2
Elizabeth Blackwell 40 G1
Ho. N22
Progress Way
Elizabeth Bri. SW1 19 D2
Elizabeth Bri. SW1 67 B4
Elizabeth Clo. E14 60 B6
Grundy St.

Elizabeth Clo. W9 6 D6
Elizabeth Clo., Barn. 23 A3
Elizabeth Clo., Rom. 44 H1
Elizabeth Clyde Clo. 41 B4
N15
Elizabeth Cotts., 73 J1
Rich.
Elizabeth Ct. SW1 15 J6
Elizabeth Est. SE17 81 B5
Elizabeth Est. SE17 68 A6
Flizabeth Fry Rd. 50 E7
E8
Elizabeth Gdns. W3 65 F1
Elizabeth Gdns., 29 F6
Stan.
Elizabeth Gdns., 90 C3
Sun.
Elizabeth Ms. NW3 48 J6
Elizabeth Pl. N15 41 A4
Elizabeth Ride N9 25 E7
Elizabeth Rd. E6 61 A1
Elizabeth Rd. N15 41 B5
Elizabeth St. SW1 19 C1
Elizabeth St. SW1 67 A4
Elizabeth Ter. SE9 79 C6
Elizabeth Way, SE19 86 A7
Elizabeth Way, Felt. 81 C4
Elkington Rd. E13 60 H4
Elkstone Rd. W10 57 C5
Ella Rd. N8 40 E7
Ellaline Rd. W6 66 A6
Ellanby Cres. N18 33 E4
Elland Rd. SE15 77 F4
Ellement Clo., Pnr. 36 D5
Ellen Clo., Brom. 97 A3
Ellen Ct. N9 33 F2
Densworth Gro.
Ellen St. E1 13 J4
Ellen St. E1 59 D6
Ellenborough Pl. 74 G4
SW15
Ellenborough Rd. 40 J1
N22
Ellenborough Rd., 89 D5
Sid.
Elleray Rd., Tedd. 82 C6
Ellerby St. SW6 75 A1
Ellerdale Clo. NW3 48 H4
Ellerdale Rd.
Ellerdale Rd. NW3 48 F5
Ellerdale St. SE13 78 B4
Ellerdine Rd., 73 A4
Houns.
Ellerker Gdns., Rich. 73 H5
Ellerman Ave., 81 F1
Twick.
Ellerslie Gdns. 56 G1
NW10
Ellerslie Rd. W12 65 H1
Ellerslie Sq. Ind. 76 E4
Est. SW2
Ellerton Gdns., 53 C7
Dag.
Ellerton Rd. SW13 74 G1
Ellerton Rd. SW18 84 B1
Ellerton Rd. SW20 83 G7
Ellerton Rd., Dag. 53 C7
Ellerton Rd., Surb. 98 J2
Ellery Rd. SE19 86 A7
Ellery St. SE15 77 E2
Ellesborough Clo., 28 A7
Wat.
Ellesmere Ave. NW7 30 D3
Ellesmere Ave., 96 B2
Beck.
Ellesmere Clo. E11 42 F5
Ellesmere Gdns., Ilf. 43 B5
Ellesmere Gro., 23 C5
Barn.
Ellesmere Rd. E3 59 H2
Ellesmere Rd. NW10 47 G5
Ellesmere Rd. W4 65 D6
Ellesmere Rd., 54 J4
Grnf.
Ellesmere Rd., 73 F6
Twick.
Ellesmere St. E14 60 B6
Ellingfort Rd. E8 50 F7
Ellingham Rd. E15 51 D4
Ellingham Rd. W12 65 G2
Ellingham Rd., 98 G6
Chess.
Ellington Rd. N10 40 B4
Ellington Rd., 72 H2
Houns.
Ellington St. N7 49 G6
Elliot Ave., Ruis. 45 B2
Elliot Clo. E15 51 E7
Elliot Rd. NW4 38 H6
Elliot Rd., Stan. 29 D6
Elliott Clo., Wem. 46 J3
Elliott Rd. SW9 67 H7

Elliott Rd. W4 65 E4
Elliott Rd., Brom. 97 A4
Elliott Rd., 94 H4
Th.Hth.
Elliott Sq. NW3 48 H7
Elliott's Pl. N1 58 H1
St. Peters St.
Elliotts Row SE11 20 G1
Elliotts Row SE11 67 H4
Ellis Clo. SE9 80 F1
Ellis Ct. W7 55 C5
Ellis Ms. SE7 69 J6
Ellis Rd., Mitch. 93 J6
Ellis St. SW1 19 A1
Ellis St. SW1 66 J4
Elliscombe Rd. SE7 69 J5
Ellisfield Dr. SW15 74 F7
Ellison Gdns., Sthl. 63 F4
Ellison Rd. SW13 74 F2
Ellison Rd. SW16 85 D7
Ellison Rd., Sid. 88 G1
Elliston Ho. SE18 70 D4
Wellington St.
Ellora Rd. SW16 85 D5
Ellsworth St. E2 59 E3
Ellwood Ct. W9 6 A6
Elm Ave. W5 64 H1
Elm Ave., Ruis. 45 A1
Elm Bank N14 24 E7
Elm Bank, Brom. 97 A2
Elm Bank Gdns. 74 E2
SW13
Elm Clo. E11 42 H6
Elm Clo. N19 49 C2
Hargrave Pk.
Elm Clo. NW4 39 A5
Elm Clo. SW20 92 J4
Grand Dr.
Elm Clo., Buck.H. 35 A2
Elm Clo., Cars. 100 J1
Elm Clo., Har. 36 H6
Elm Clo., Hayes 54 A6
Elm Clo., Rom. 44 H1
Elm Clo., S.Croy. 102 B6
Elm Clo., Surb. 92 C7
Elm Clo., Twick. 81 H2
Elm Ct. EC4 12 E5
Elm Cres. W5 64 H1
Elm Cres., Kings.T. 91 H1
Elm Dr., Har. 36 H6
Elm Dr., Sun. 90 C2
Elm Friars Wk. NW1 49 D7
Maiden La.
Elm Gdns. N2 39 F3
Elm Gdns., Esher 98 C6
Elm Gdns., Mitch. 94 D4
Elm Grn. W3 56 E6
Elm Gro. N8 40 E6
Elm Gro. NW2 48 A4
Elm Gro. SE15 77 C2
Elm Gro. SW19 84 B7
Elm Gro., Har. 36 G7
Elm Gro., Kings.T. 91 H1
Elm Gro., Orp. 104 J1
Elm Gro., Sutt. 100 E4
Elm Gro., Wdf.Grn. 34 F5
Elm Gro. Par., Wall. 101 A3
Butter Hill
Elm Gro. Rd. SW13 74 G2
Elm Gro. Rd. W5 64 H2
Elm Hall Gdns. E11 42 H6
Elm La. SE6 86 J2
Elm Ms., Rich. 73 J6
Grove Rd.
Elm Pk. SW2 76 F6
Elm Pk., Stan. 29 E5
Elm Pk. Ave. N15 41 C5
Elm Pk. Ct., Pnr. 36 C3
Elm Pk. Gdns. NW4 39 A5
Elm Pk. Gdns. SW10 18 E4
Elm Pk. Gdns. SW10 66 G5
Elm Pk. La. SW3 18 E4
Elm Pk. La. SW3 66 G5
Elm Pk. Mans. SW10 18 D5
Elm Pk. Rd. E10 50 H1
Elm Pk. Rd. N3 31 C7
Elm Pk. Rd. N21 24 J7
Elm Pk. Rd. SE25 95 C3
Elm Pk. Rd. SW3 18 E5
Elm Pk. Rd. SW3 66 G6
Elm Pk. Rd., Pnr. 36 C2
Elm Pl. SW7 18 E3
Elm Pl. SW7 66 G5
Elm Quay Ct. SW8 19 H6
Elm Quay Ct. SW8 67 D6
Elm Rd. E7 51 F6
Elm Rd. E11 51 D2
Elm Rd. E17 42 C5
Elm Rd. N22 40 H1
Granville Rd.
Elm Rd. SW14 74 C3
Elm Rd., Barn. 23 C4
Elm Rd., Beck. 95 J2

Elm Rd., Chess. 98 H4
Elm Rd., Epsom 99 F6
Elm Rd., Esher 98 C6
Elm Rd., Kings.T. 91 J1
Elm Rd., N.Mal. 92 D3
Elm Rd., Rom. 44 H2
Elm Rd., Sid. 89 A4
Elm Rd., Th.Hth. 95 A4
Elm Rd., Wall. 101 A1
Elm Rd., Wem. 46 H5
Elm Rd. W., Sutt. 93 C7
Elm Row NW3 48 F3
Elm St. WC1 8 D6
Elm St. WC1 58 F4
Elm Ter. NW2 48 D3
Elm Ter. SE9 79 D6
Elm Ter., Har. 37 A1
Elm Tree Ave., 91 A7
Esher
Elm Tree Clo. NW8 6 E3
Elm Tree Clo. NW8 57 G3
Elm Tree Clo., 54 F2
Nthlt.
Elm Tree Rd. NW8 6 E3
Elm Tree Rd. NW8 57 G3
Elm Wk. NW3 48 D2
Elm Wk. SW20 92 J4
Elm Wk., Orp. 104 C3
Elm Way N11 32 A6
Elm Way NW10 47 E4
Elm Way, Epsom 99 D5
Elm Way, Wor.Pk. 99 J3
Elmar Rd. N15 41 A4
Elmbank Ave., Barn. 22 J4
Elmbank Way W7 55 A5
Elmbourne Dr., 71 H4
Belv.
Elmbourne Rd. SW17 85 A3
Elmbridge Ave., 92 B5
Surb.
Elmbridge Clo., 36 A6
Ruis.
Elmbridge Wk. E8 50 D7
Wilman Gro.
Elmbrook Clo., Sun. 90 B1
Elmbrook Gdns. SE9 79 B4
Elmbrook Rd., Sutt. 100 C4
Elmcourt Rd. SE27 85 H2
Elmcroft Ave. E11 42 H4
Elmcroft Ave. N9 25 E6
Elmcroft Ave. NW11 39 C7
Elmcroft Ave., Sid. 79 J7
Elmcroft Clo. E11 42 H4
Elmcroft Clo. W5 55 G6
Elmcroft Clo., 98 H3
Chess.
Elmcroft Cres. NW11 39 A7
Elmcroft Cres., Har. 36 G3
Elmcroft Dr., 98 H3
Chess.
Elmcroft Gdns. NW9 38 A5
Elmcroft St. E5 50 F4
Elmdale Rd. N13 32 F5
Elmdene, Surb. 99 C1
Elmdene Clo., Beck. 95 J5
Elmdene Rd. SE18 70 E5
Elmdon Rd., Houns. 72 D2
Elmer Clo., Enf. 24 F1
Elmer Gdns., Edg. 30 B7
Elmer Gdns., Islw. 73 A3
Elmer Rd. SE6 78 C7
Elmers Dr., Tedd. 82 E6
St. Mark's Rd.
Elmers End Rd. SE20 95 F2
Elmers End Rd., 95 F3
Beck.
Elmers Rd. SE25 95 D7
Elmerside Rd., Beck. 95 H4
Elmfield Ave. N8 40 E5
Elmfield Ave., 94 A1
Mitch.
Elmfield Ave., 82 C5
Tedd.
Elmfield Clo., Har. 46 B2
Elmfield Pk., Brom. 96 G3
Elmfield Rd. E4 34 C2
Elmfield Rd. E17 41 G5
Elmfield Rd. N2 39 G3
Elmfield Rd. SW17 85 A2
Elmfield Rd., Brom. 96 G3
Elmfield Rd., Sthl. 63 E3
Elmgate Ave., Felt. 81 B3
Elmgate Gdns., Edg. 30 D5
Elmgreen Clo. E15 60 E1
Church St. N.
Elmgrove Cres., Har. 37 C5
Elmgrove Gdns., Har. 37 D5
Elmgrove Rd., Croy. 95 E7
Elmgrove Rd., Har. 37 C5
Elmhurst, Belv. 71 E6
Elmhurst Ave. N2 39 G3
Elmhurst Ave., 85 A7
Mitch.

Elmhurst Cres. N2 39 F4
Elmhurst Dr. E18 42 G2
Elmhurst Gdns. E18 42 H1
Elmhurst Rd. E7 51 H7
Elmhurst Rd. N17 41 B2
Elmhurst Rd. SE9 88 B2
Elmhurst St. SW4 76 D3
Elmhurst Way, Loug. 27 C7
Elmington Clo., Bex. 80 H6
Elmington Est. SE5 21 C7
Elmington Est. SE5 68 A7
Elmington Rd. SE5 77 A1
Elmira St. SE13 78 B3
Elmlee Clo., Chis. 88 C6
Elmley Clo. E6 61 B5
Northumberland Rd.
Elmley St. SE18 70 G4
Elmore Clo., Wem. 55 H2
Elmore Rd. E11 51 C3
Elmore St. N1 50 A7
Elmores, Loug. 27 D3
Elms, The SW13 74 F3
Elms Ave. N10 40 B3
Elms Ave. NW4 39 A5
Elms Ct., Wem. 46 D4
Elms Cres. SW4 76 C6
Elms Gdns., Dag. 53 F4
Elms Gdns., Wem. 46 D4
Elms La., Wem. 46 D3
Elms Ms. W2 10 E5
Elms Ms. W2 57 G7
Elms Pk. Ave., Wem. 46 D4
Elms Rd. SW4 76 C5
Elms Rd., Har. 29 B7
Elms Wk. SE3 78 F4
Elmscott Gdns. N21 24 J6
Elmscott Rd., Brom. 87 E5
Elmscroft N8 40 F5
Tottenham La.
Elmsdale Rd. E17 41 J4
Elmshaw Rd. SW15 74 G5
Elmside, Croy. 103 B6
Elmside Rd., Wem. 47 A3
Elmsleigh Ave., 37 E4
Har.
Elmsleigh Rd., 82 A2
Twick.
Elmslie Clo., 35 C6
Wdf.Grn.
Elmslie Pt. E3 59 J5
Ackroyd Dr.
Elmstead Ave., 88 C5
Chis.
Elmstead Ave., Wem. 46 H1
Elmstead Clo. N20 31 D2
Elmstead Clo., 99 E5
Epsom
Elmstead Cres., 71 C6
Well.
Elmstead Gdns., 99 G3
Wor.Pk.
Elmstead Glade, 88 C6
Chis.
Elmstead La., Chis. 88 B7
Elmstead Rd., Ilf. 52 H2
Elmstone Rd. SW6 75 D1
Elmsworth Ave., 72 H2
Houns.
Elmton Way E5 50 D3
Rendlesham Rd.
Elmtree Rd., Tedd. 82 B4
Elmwood Ave. N13 32 E5
Elmwood Ave., 22 B4
Borwd.
Elmwood Ave., Felt. 81 A2
Elmwood Ave., Har. 37 D5
Elmwood Clo., 99 G7
Epsom
Elmwood Clo., Wall. 101 A2
Elmwood Ct., Wem. 46 D3
Elmwood Cres. NW9 38 C4
Elmwood Dr., Bex. 80 E7
Elmwood Dr., Epsom 99 G6
Elmwood Gdns. W7 55 B6
Elmwood Rd. SE24 77 A5
Elmwood Rd. W4 65 C6
Elmwood Rd., Croy. 94 H7
Elmwood Rd., Mitch. 93 J3
Elmworth Gro. SE21 86 A3
Elnathan Ms. W9 6 B6
Elphinstone Rd. E17 41 J2
Elphinstone St. N5 49 H4
Avenell Rd.
Elrington Rd. E8 50 D6
Elsa Rd., Well. 80 B2
Elsa St. E1 59 H5
Elsdale St. E9 50 F6
Elsden Ms. E2 59 F2
Old Ford Rd.
Elsden Rd. N17 41 C1
Elsenham Rd. E12 52 D5
Elsenham St. SW18 84 C1
Elsham Rd. E11 51 E3

Elsham Rd. W14 66 B2
Elsham Ter. W14 66 B2
Elsie Rd. SE22 77 C4
Elsiedene Rd. N21 24 J7
Elsiemaud Rd. SE4 77 J5
Elsinore Rd. SE23 86 H1
Elsinore Way, Rich. 74 B3
Lwr. Richmond Rd.
Elsley Rd. SW11 75 J3
Elspeth Rd. SW11 75 J4
Elspeth Rd., Wem. 46 H5
Elsrick Ave., Mord. 93 D5
Chalgrove Ave.
Elstan Way, Croy. 95 H7
Elsted St. SE17 21 C2
Elsted St. SE17 68 A4
Elstow Clo. SE9 79 D5
Elstow Clo., Ruis. 36 D7
Elstow Gdns., Dag. 62 E1
Elstow Rd., Dag. 53 E7
Elstree Gdns. N9 33 E1
Elstree Gdns., 71 E4
Belv.
Elstree Gdns., Ilf. 52 F5
Elstree Hill, Brom. 87 E7
Elstree Way, Borwd. 22 B3
Elswick Rd. SE13 78 B2
Elswick St. SW6 75 F2
Elsworthy, T.Ditt. 91 B6
Elsworthy Ri. NW3 48 H7
Elsworthy Rd. NW3 57 H1
Elsworthy Ter. NW3 48 H7
Elsynge Rd. SW18 75 G5
Eltham Grn. SE9 78 J5
Eltham Grn. Rd. SE9 78 J4
Eltham High St. SE9 79 C6
Eltham Hill SE9 79 A5
Eltham Palace Rd. 78 J6
SE9
Eltham Pk. Gdns. 79 D4
SE9
Eltham Rd. SE9 78 J5
Eltham Rd. SE12 78 G5
Elthiron Rd. SW6 75 D1
Elthorne Ave. W7 64 C2
Elthorne Ct., Felt. 81 C1
Elthorne Pk. Rd. W7 64 C2
Elthorne Rd. N19 49 D2
Elthorne Rd. NW9 38 D7
Elthorne Way NW9 38 D6
Elthruda Rd. SE13 78 D6
Eltisley Rd., Ilf. 52 E4
Elton Ave., Barn. 23 C5
Elton Ave., Grnf. 46 B6
Elton Ave., Wem. 46 E5
Elton Clo., 82 F7
Kings.T.
Elton Ho. E3 59 J1
Elton Pl. N16 50 B5
Elton Rd., Kings.T. 91 J1
Eltringham St. SW18 75 F4
Elvaston Ms. SW7 14 D6
Elvaston Ms. SW7 66 F3
Elvaston Pl. SW7 14 C6
Elvaston Pl. SW7 66 F3
Elveden Pl. NW10 56 A2
Elveden Rd. NW10 56 A2
Elvendon Rd. N13 32 E6
Elver Gdns. E2 9 J2
Elverson Rd. SE8 78 B2
Elverton St. SW1 19 H1
Elverton St. SW1 67 D4
Elvington Grn., 96 F5
Brom.
Elvington La. NW9 38 E1
Elvino Rd. SE26 86 G5
Elvis Rd. NW2 47 J6
Elwill Way, Beck. 96 C4
Elwin St. E2 9 H3
Elwood St. N5 49 H3
Elwyn Gdns. SE12 78 G7
Ely Clo., N.Mal. 92 F2
Ely Ct. EC1 12 F2
Ely Gdns., Borwd. 22 D5
Ely Gdns., Dag. 53 J3
Ely Gdns., Ilf. 43 B7
Canterbury Ave.
Ely Pl. EC1 12 F2
Ely Pl., Wdf.Grn. 35 D6
Ely Rd. E10 42 C7
Ely Rd., Croy. 95 A5
Ely Rd. (TW4), 72 C3
Houns.
Elyne Rd. N4 40 G6
Elysian Ave., Orp. 97 H6
Elysium Pl. SW6 75 C2
Fulham Pk. Gdns.
Elysium St. SW6 75 C2
Fulham Pk. Gdns.
Elystan Pl. SW3 18 H3
Elystan Pl. SW3 66 H5
Elystan St. SW3 18 G2

Elystan St. SW3 66 H4
Elystan Wk. N1 58 G1
Cloudesley Rd.
Emanuel Ave. W3 56 C6
Emba St. SE16 17 J4
Emba St. SE16 68 D2
Embankment SW15 75 A2
Embankment, The, 82 D1
Twick.
Embankment Gdns. 19 A5
SW3
Embankment Gdns. 66 J6
SW3
Embankment Pl. WC2 16 B1
Embankment Pl. WC2 67 E1
Embassy Ct., Sid. 89 B3
Embassy Ct., Well. 80 B3
Ember Clo., Orp. 97 F7
Ember Fm. Ave., 91 A6
E.Mol.
Ember Fm. Way, 91 A6
E.Mol.
Ember Gdns., 91 B7
T.Ditt.
Ember La., E.Mol. 91 A6
Ember La., Esher 91 A7
Embercourt Rd., 91 B6
T.Ditt.
Emberton SE5 21 D5
Embleton Rd. SE13 78 B4
Embleton Rd., Wat. 28 A3
Embleton Wk., 81 F6
Hmptn.
Fearnley Cres.
Embley Pt. E5 50 E4
Tiger Way
Embry Clo., Stan. 29 D4
Embry Dr., Stan. 29 D6
Embry Way, Stan. 29 D4
Emden St. SW6 75 E1
Emerald Clo. E16 61 B6
Emerald Gdns., Dag. 53 G1
Emerald St. WC1 12 C1
Emerald St. WC1 58 F5
Emerson Gdns., Har. 37 J6
Emerson Rd., Ilf. 43 D7
Emerson St. SE1 16 J1
Emerson St. SE1 67 J1
Emerton Clo., Bexh. 80 E4
Emery Hill St. SW1 15 G6
Emery Hill St. SW1 67 C3
Emery St. SE1 16 F5
Emes Rd., Erith 71 J7
Emily Pl. N7 49 G4
Emlyn Gdns. W12 65 E2
Emlyn Rd. W12 65 E2
Emma Rd. E13 60 F2
Emma St. E2 59 E2
Emmanuel Rd. SW12 85 C1
Emmaus Way, Chig. 35 D5
Emmott Ave., Ilf. 43 F5
Emmott Clo. E1 59 H4
Emmott Clo. NW11 39 F6
Emms Pas., Kings.T. 91 G2
High St.
Emperor's Gate SW7 14 B6
Emperor's Gate SW7 66 E3
Empire Ave. N18 32 J5
Empire Ct., Wem. 47 B3
Empire Rd., Grnf. 55 E1
Empire Way, Wem. 46 J4
Empire Wf. Rd. E14 59 D4
Empire Yd. N7 49 E3
Holloway Rd.
Empress Ave. E4 34 B7
Empress Ave. E12 51 J2
Empress Ave., Ilf. 52 C2
Empress Ave., 34 F7
Wdf.Grn.
Empress Dr., Chis. 88 E6
Empress Pl. SW6 66 D5
Empress St. SE17 21 A5
Empress St. SE17 68 A6

Empson St. E3 60 B4
Emsworth Clo. N9 33 F1
Emsworth Rd., Ilf. 43 E2
Emsworth St. SW2 85 E2
Emu Rd. SW8 76 B2
Ena Rd. SW16 94 E3
Enbrook St. W10 57 B3
End Way, Surb. 92 A7
Endale Clo., Cars. 100 J2
Endeavour Way 84 E4
SW19
Endeavour Way, 92 A2
Bark.
Endeavour Way, 94 D7
Croy.
Endell St. WC1 12 A3
Endell St. WC2 58 E6
Enderby St. SE10 69 E5
Enderley Clo., Har. 37 B1
Enderley Rd., Har. 37 B1

Endersby Rd., Barn. 22 J5
Endersleigh Gdns. 38 G4
NW4
Endlebury Rd. E4 34 C2
Endlesham Rd. SW12 76 A7
Endsleigh Gdns. WC1 7 H5
Endsleigh Gdns. WC1 58 D4
Endsleigh Gdns., Ill. 92 C2
Endsleigh Gdns., 91 F6
Surb.
Endsleigh Pl. WC1 7 J5
Endsleigh Pl. WC1 58 D4
Endsleigh Rd. W13 55 D7
Endsleigh Rd., 63 E4
Sthl.
Endsleigh St. WC1 7 J5
Endsleigh St. WC1 58 D4
Endwell Rd. SE4 77 H2
Endymion Rd. N4 40 G7
Endymion Rd. SW2 76 F6
Enfield Rd. N1 50 B7
Enfield Rd. W3 65 B2
Enfield Rd., Brent. 64 G5
Enfield Rd., Enf. 24 E4
Enfield Wk., Brent. 64 G5
Enfield Rd.
Enford St. W1 10 J1
Enford St. W1 57 J5
Engadine Clo., 102 C3
Croy.
Engadine St. SW18 84 C1
Engate St. SE13 78 C4
Engel Pk. NW7 30 J6
Engineer Clo. SE18 70 D6
Engineers Way, 47 A4
Wem.
Englands La. NW3 48 J6
Englands La., Loug. 27 D2
Englefield Clo., Croy. 94 J6
Queens Rd.
Englefield Clo., Enf. 24 G2
Chase Ridings
Englefield Cres., Orp. 97 J4
Englefield Cres., Orp. 97 J4
Englefield Rd. N1 50 A7
Engleheart Rd. SE6 78 B7
Englewood Rd. SW12 76 B6
English Grds. SE1 17 D2
English St. E3 59 J4
Enid St. SE16 17 G5
Enid St. SE16 68 C3
Enmore Ave. SE25 95 D5
Enmore Gdns. SW14 74 D5
Enmore Rd. SE25 95 D5
Enmore Rd. SW15 74 J4
Enmore Rd., Sthl. 54 G4
Ennerdale Ave. 37 F3
Stan.
Ennerdale Clo. 100 C4
(Cheam), Sutt.
Ennerdale Dr. NW9 38 E5
Ennerdale Gdns., 46 F1
Wem.
Ennerdale Ho. E3 59 J4
Ennerdale Rd., Bexh. 80 G1
Ennerdale Rd., Rich. 73 J2
Ennersdale Rd. SE13 78 D5
Ennis Rd. N4 49 G1
Ennis Rd. SE18 70 F6
Ennismore Ave. W4 65 F4
Ennismore Ave., 46 B6
Grnf.
Ennismore Gdns. 14 G5
SW7
Ennismore Gdns. 66 H2
SW7
Ennismore Gdns., 91 B6
T.Ditt.
Ennismore Gdns. Ms. 14 G5
SW7
Ennismore Gdns. Ms. 66 H3
SW7
Ennismore Ms. SW7 14 G5
Ennismore Ms. SW7 66 H3
Ennismore St. SW7 14 G5
Ennismore St. SW7 66 H3
Ensign Dr. N13 32 J3
Ensign St. E1 13 H5
Ensign St. E1 59 D7
Enslin Rd. SE9 79 D7
Ensor Ms. SW7 18 E3
Enstone Rd., Enf. 25 H3
Enterprise Clo., 101 G1
Croy.
Enterprise Way 56 G3
NW10
Enterprise Way 75 D4
SW18
Enterprise Way, 82 C5
Tedd.
Enterprize Way SE8 68 J4
Epirus Ms. SW6 66 D7
Epirus Rd.

Epirus Rd. SW6 66 C7
Epping Clo. E14 69 A4
Epping Clo., Rom. 44 H3
Epping Glade E4 26 C6
Epping New Rd., 34 G3
Buck.H.
Epping New Rd., 26 J3
Loug.
Epping Pl. N1 49 G6
Liverpool Rd.
Epping Way E4 20 D8
Epple Rd. SW6 75 C1
Epsom Clo., Bexh. 80 H3
Epsom Clo., Nthlt. 45 F5
Epsom Rd. E10 42 C6
Epsom Rd., Croy. 101 G8
Epsom Rd., Ilf. 43 J6
Epsom Rd., Mord. 93 D6
Epsom Rd., Sutt. 93 C7
Epstein Rd. SE28 71 A1
Epworth Rd., Islw. 73 E1
Epworth St. EC2 9 C6
Epworth St. EC2 59 A4
Erasmus St. SW1 19 J2
Erasmus St. SW1 67 D4
Erconwald St. W12 56 F6
Eresby Dr., Beck. 103 A1
Eresby Pl. NW6 48 D7
Eric Clo. E7 51 G4
Eric Rd. E7 51 G4
Eric Rd. NW10 47 F6
Church Rd.
Eric Rd., Rom. 44 D7
Eric St. E3 59 J4
Erica Gdns., Croy. 103 A3
Erica St. W12 56 G7
Ericcson Clo. SW18 75 D5
Eridge Rd. W4 65 D3
Erin Clo., Brom. 87 E7
Erindale SE18 70 G6
Erindale Ter. SE18 70 G6
Erith Cres., Rom. 44 J1
Erith Rd., Belv. 71 G5
Erith Rd., Bexh. 80 H4
Erith Rd., Erith 80 J1
Erlanger Rd. SE14 77 G1
Erlesmere Gdns. W13 64 D3
Ermine Clo., Houns. 72 C2
Ermine Ho. N17 33 C7
Ermine Rd. N15 41 C6
Ermine Rd. SE13 78 B4
Ermine Side, Enf. 25 D5
Ermington Rd. SE9 88 F2
Ernald Ave. E6 61 B2
Erncroft Way, 73 C6
Twick.
Ernest Ave. SE27 85 H4
Ernest Clo., Beck. 96 A5
Ernest Gdns. W4 65 B6
Ernest Gro., Beck. 95 J3
Ernest Rd., 92 B2
Kings.T.
Ernest Sq., 92 B2
Kings.T.
Ernest St. E1 59 G4
Ernle Rd. SW20 83 H7
Ernshaw Pl. SW15 75 B5
Carlton Dr.
Erpingham Rd. SW15 74 J3
Erridge Rd. SW19 93 D2
Errington Rd. W9 57 C4
Errol Gdns., Hayes 54 D4
Errol Gdns., N.Mal. 92 G4
Errol St. EC1 9 A6
Errol St. EC1 58 J4
Erskine Clo., Sutt. 100 H3
Erskine Cres. N17 41 E4
Erskine Hill NW11 39 D5
Erskine Ms. NW3 48 J7
Erskine Rd.
Erskine Rd. E17 41 J4
Erskine Rd. NW3 48 J7
Erskine Rd., Sutt. 100 G4
Erwood Rd. SE7 70 B5
Esam Way SW16 85 G5
Escot Way, Barn. 22 J5
Escott Gdns. SE9 88 A4
Escreet Gro. SE18 70 D4
Esher Ave., Rom. 44 J6
Esher Ave., Sutt. 100 A3
Esher Ave., Walt. 90 A6
Esher Bypass, 98 F4
Chess.
Esher Clo., Bex. 89 E1
Esher Gdns. SW19 84 A2
Esher Ms., Mitch. 93 J3
Esher Rd., E.Mol. 91 A6
Esher Rd., Ilf. 67 H3
Esk Rd. E13 60 G4
Eskdale Ave., Nthlt. 54 F1
Eskdale Clo., Wem. 46 G2
Eskdale Rd., Bexh. 80 G2
Eskmont Ridge SE19 86 B7

Esmar Cres. NW9 38 G7
Esme Ho. SW16 74 F4
Ludovick Rd.
Esmeralda Rd. SE1 21 J2
Esmeralda Rd. SE1 68 D4
Esmond Rd. NW6 57 C1
Esmond Rd. W4 65 D4
Esmond St. SW15 75 B4
Esparto St. SW18 75 E7
Essenden Rd., Belv. 71 G5
Essenden Rd., 102 B7
S.Croy.
Essendine Rd. W9 57 D3
Essex Ave., Islw. 73 B3
Essex Clo. E17 41 H4
Essex Clo., Mord. 93 A7
Essex Clo., Rom. 44 H4
Essex Clo., Ruis. 45 D1
Essex Ct. EC4 12 E4
Essex Ct. SW13 74 F2
Essex Gdns. N4 40 H6
Essex Gro. SE19 86 A6
Essex Ho. E14 60 B6
Giraud St.
Essex Pk. N3 31 G6
Essex Pk. Ms. W3 65 E1
Essex Pl. W4 65 C4
Essex Rd. E4 34 E1
Essex Rd. E10 42 C6
Essex Rd. E12 52 B5
Essex Rd. E17 41 H6
Essex Rd. E18 42 H2
Essex Rd. N1 58 H1
Essex Rd. NW10 47 E7
Essex Rd. W3 56 C7
Essex Rd. W4 65 D4
Belmont Rd.
Essex Rd., Bark. 52 G7
Essex Rd., Borwd. 22 A3
Essex Rd., Dag. 53 J5
Essex Rd., Enf. 25 A4
Essex Rd., Rom. 44 G4
Essex Rd., Rom. 44 C7
(Chadwell Heath)
Essex Rd. S. E11 42 D7
Essex St. E7 51 G5
Essex St. WC2 12 E5
Essex Twr. SE20 95 F1
Essex Vill. W8 66 D2
Essex Wf. E5 50 F2
Essian St. E1 59 H5
Essoldo Way, Edg. 37 J3
Estate Way E10 50 J1
Estcourt Rd. SE25 95 E6
Estcourt Rd. SW6 66 C7
Este Rd. SW11 75 H3
Estella Ave., 92 H4
N.Mal.
Estelle Rd. NW3 48 J4
Esterbrooke St. SW1 19 H2
Esterbrooke St. SW1 67 D4
Esther Clo. N21 24 G7
Esther Rd. E11 42 E7
Estreham Rd. SW16 85 D6
Estridge Clo., 72 G4
Houns.
Eswyn Rd. SW17 84 J4
Etchingham Pk. Rd. 31 F7
N3
Etchingham Rd. E15 51 C4
Eternit Wk. SW6 74 J1
Etfield Gro., Sid. 89 B5
Ethel Rd. E16 60 H6
Ethel St. SE17 21 A2
Ethelbert Clo., 96 G3
Brom.
Ethelbert Gdns., Ilf. 43 C5
Ethelbert Rd. SW20 93 A1
Ethelbert Rd., 96 G3
Brom.
Ethelbert Rd., Erith 71 J7
Hengist Rd.
Ethelbert St. SW12 85 B1
Fernlea Rd.
Ethelburga St. SW11 75 H1
Ethelden Rd. W12 65 H1
Etheldene Ave. N10 40 C4
Etheridge Rd. NW2 38 J7
Etheridge Rd., 27 E2
Loug.
Etherley Rd. N15 40 J5
Etherow St. SE22 77 D6
Etherstone Grn. 85 G4
SW16
Etherstone Rd.
Etherstone Rd. SW16 85 G4
Ethnard Rd. SE15 68 E6
Ethronvi Rd., Bexh. 80 E3
Etloe Rd. E10 51 A2
Eton Ave. N12 31 F7
Eton Ave. NW3 48 G7
Eton Ave., Barn. 23 H6
Eton Ave., Houns. 63 F6

Eton Ave., N.Mal. 92 D5
Eton Ave., Wem. 46 E5
Eton College Rd. 48 J6
NW3
Eton Ct. NW3 48 G7
Eton Ave.
Eton Ct., Wem. 46 F4
Eton Ave.
Eton Garages NW3 48 H6
Lambolle Pl.
Eton Gro. NW9 38 A3
Eton Gro. SE13 70 E0
Eton Hall NW3 48 J6
Eton College Rd.
Eton Pl. NW3 49 A7
Eton College Rd.
Eton Ri. NW3 48 J6
Eton College Rd.
Eton Rd. NW3 48 J7
Eton Rd., Ilf. 52 F5
Eton St., Rich. 73 H5
Eton Vill. NW3 48 J6
Etta St. SE8 68 H6
Ettrick St. E14 60 C6
Etwell Pl., Surb. 91 J6
Eugenia Rd. SE16 68 F4
Eureka Rd., Kings.T. 92 A2
Washington Rd.
Europa Pl. EC1 8 J4
Europe Rd. SE18 70 C3
Eustace Rd. E6 61 B3
Eustace Rd. SW6 66 D7
Eustace Rd., Rom. 44 D7
Euston Gro. NW1 7 H4
Euston Gro. NW1 58 D3
Euston Rd. NW1 7 E6
Euston Rd. NW1 58 B4
Euston Rd., Croy. 101 G1
Euston Sq. NW1 7 H4
Euston Sq. NW1 58 D3
Euston Sta. 7 H4
Colonnade NW1
Euston St. NW1 7 G4
Euston St. NW1 58 C3
Eva Rd., Rom. 44 C7
Evandale Rd. SW9 76 G2
Evangelist Rd. NW5 49 B4
Evans Clo. E8 50 C6
Buttermere Wk.
Evans Gro., Felt. 81 G2
Evans Rd. SE6 87 E2
Evanston Ave. E4 34 C7
Evanston Gdns., Ilf. 43 B6
Eve Rd. E11 51 E4
Eve Rd. E15 60 E2
Eve Rd. N17 41 B3
Eve Rd., Islw. 73 D4
Evelina Rd. SE15 77 F3
Evelina Rd. SE20 86 G7
Eveline Lowe Est. 17 H6
SE16
Eveline Lowe Est. 68 D3
SE16
Eveline Rd., Mitch. 93 J1
Evelyn Ave. NW9 38 D3
Evelyn Clo., Twick. 72 H7
Evelyn Ct. N1 9 B2
Evelyn Dennington 61 C5
Rd. E6
Evelyn Dr., Pnr. 28 D7
Evelyn Fox Ct. W10 56 J5
Evelyn Gdns. SW7 18 E4
Evelyn Gdns. SW7 66 G5
Evelyn Gdns., Rich. 73 H4
Kew Rd.
Evelyn Gro. W5 64 J1
Evelyn Gro., Sthl. 54 F6
Evelyn Rd. E16 42 C4
Evelyn Rd. E17 42 C4
Evelyn Rd. SW19 84 E5
Evelyn Rd. W4 65 D3
Evelyn Rd., Barn. 23 J4
Evelyn Rd., Rich. 73 H3
Evelyn St. SE8 68 H5
Evelyn Ter., Rich. 73 H3
Evelyn Wk. N1 9 B2
Evelyn Wk. N1 59 A2
Evelyn Way, Wall. 101 D4
Evelyn Yd. W1 11 H3
Evening Hill, Beck. 87 C7
Evenwood Clo. 75 B5
SW15
Everard Ave., Brom. 103 G1
Everard Way, Wem. 46 H3
Everatt Clo. SW18 75 C6
Amerland Rd.
Everdon Rd. SW13 65 G6
Everest Pl. E14 60 C5
Everest Rd. SE9 79 C5
Everett Wk., Belv. 71 F5
Osborne Rd.
Everglade Strand 38 F1
NW9
Everilda St. N1 58 F1

Evering Rd. E5	50	D3	
Evering Rd. N16	50	D3	
Everington Rd. N10	39	J2	
Everington St. W6	66	A6	
Everitt Rd. NW10	56	D3	
Everleigh St. N4	49	F1	
Eversfield Gdns. NW7	30	E6	
Eversholt St. NW1	**7**	**G1**	
Eversholt St. NW1	58	C2	
Evershot Rd. N4	49	F1	
Eversleigh Rd. E6	61	A1	
Eversleigh Rd. N3	31	C7	
Eversleigh Rd. SW11	75	J3	
Eversleigh Rd., Barn.	23	F5	
Eversley Ave., Wem.	47	A2	
Eversley Clo. N21	24	F6	
Eversley Cres. N21	24	F6	
Eversley Cres., Islw.	73	A1	
Eversley Mt. N21	24	F6	
Eversley Pk. SW19	83	H5	
Eversley Pk. Rd. N21	24	F6	
Eversley Rd. SE7	69	H6	
Eversley Rd. SE19	86	A7	
Eversley Rd., Surb.	91	J4	
Eversley Way, Croy.	103	A4	
Everthorpe Rd. SE15	77	C3	
Everton Bldgs. NW1	**7**	**F4**	
Everton Dr., Stan.	37	J3	
Everton Rd., Croy.	102	D1	
Evesham Ave. E17	42	A2	
Evesham Clo., Grnf.	54	H2	
Evesham Clo., Sutt.	100	D7	
Evesham Grn., Mord.	93	E6	
Evesham Rd. E15	51	F7	
Evesham Rd. N11	32	C5	
Evesham Rd., Felt.	72	C7	
Sparrow Fm. Dr.			
Evesham Rd., Mord.	93	E6	
Evesham St. W11	57	A7	
Evesham Wk. SE5	77	A2	
Love Wk.			
Evesham Wk. SW9	76	G2	
Evesham Way SW11	76	A3	
Evesham Way, Ilf.	43	D3	
Evry Rd., Sid.	89	C6	
Ewald Rd. SW6	75	C2	
Wdf.Grn.			
Ewanrigg Ter., Wdf.Grn.	34	J5	
Ewart Gro. N22	40	G1	
Ewart Pl. E3	59	J2	
Ewart Rd. SE23	77	G7	
Ewe Clo. N7	49	E6	
Ewell Bypass, Epsom	99	G6	
Ewell Ct. Ave., Epsom	99	E5	
Ewell Pk. Way, Epsom	99	G6	
Ewell Rd., Surb.	91	H5	
Ewell Rd., Surb. (Long Ditton),	91	E7	
Ewell Rd., Sutt.	100	A7	
Ewellhurst Rd., Ilf.	43	B2	
Ewelme Rd. SE23	86	F1	
Ewen Cres. SW2	76	G7	
Ewer St. SE1	**16**	**J2**	
Ewer St. SE1	67	J1	
Jamaica St.			
Ewhurst Rd. SE4	77	J6	
Exbury Rd. SE6	87	A2	
Excel Ct. WC2	**11**	**J6**	
Excelsior Clo., Kings.T.	92	A2	
Washington Rd.			
Excelsior Gdns. SE13	78	C2	
Exchange Arc. EC2	**13**	**E1**	
Exchange Rd. EC2	59	B5	
Exchange Ct. WC2	**12**	**B6**	
Exchange Pl. EC2	**13**	**D1**	
Exchange Pl. EC2	59	B5	
Exchange Sq. EC2	**13**	**D1**	
Exchange Sq. EC2	59	B5	
Exeter Clo. E6	61	C6	
Harper Rd.			
Exeter Gdns., Ilf.	52	B1	
Exeter Ho. SW15	74	J6	
Putney Heath			
Exeter Ms. NW6	48	E6	
West Hampstead Ms.			
Exeter Rd. E16	60	G5	
Exeter Rd. E17	42	A5	
Exeter Rd. N9	33	F2	
Exeter Rd. N14	32	B1	
Exeter Rd. NW2	48	B5	
Exeter Rd. SE15	77	C1	
Exeter Rd., Croy.	95	B7	
Exeter Rd., Dag.	53	H6	
Exeter Rd., Enf.	25	G3	
Exeter Rd., Felt.	81	F3	
Exeter Rd., Har.	45	E2	
Exeter Rd., Well.	79	J2	
Exeter St. WC2	**12**	**B5**	
Exeter St. WC2	58	E7	
Exeter Way SE14	68	J7	
Exford Gdns. SE12	87	H1	
Exford Rd. SE12	87	H2	
Exhibition Clo. W12	56	J7	
Exhibition Rd. SW7	**14**	**F5**	
Exhibition Rd. SW7	66	G2	
Exmoor Clo., Ilf.	43	F1	
Exmoor St. W10	57	A5	
Exmouth Mkt. EC1	**8**	**E5**	
Exmouth Mkt. EC1	58	G4	
Exmouth Ms. NW1	**7**	**G4**	
Exmouth Pl. E8	50	E7	
Exmouth Rd. E17	41	J5	
Exmouth Rd., Brom.	96	H3	
Exmouth Rd., Ruis.	45	C3	
Exmouth Rd., Well.	80	C1	
Exmouth St. E1	59	F6	
Commercial Rd.			
Exning Rd. E16	60	F4	
Exon St. SE17	**21**	**D2**	
Exon St. SE17	68	B4	
Express Dr., Ilf.	53	B1	
Exton Cres. NW10	47	C7	
Exton Gdns., Dag.	53	C5	
Exton St. SE1	**16**	**E2**	
Exton St. SE1	67	G1	
Eyhurst Clo. NW2	47	G2	
Eylewood Rd. SE27	85	J5	
Eynella Rd. SE22	77	C7	
Eynham Rd. W12	56	J6	
Eynsford Clo., Orp.	97	F7	
Eynsford Cres., Bex.	89	C1	
Eynsford Rd., Ilf.	52	H2	
Eynsham Dr. SE2	71	A4	
Eynswood Dr., Sid.	89	B5	
Eyot Gdns. W6	65	F5	
Eyot Grn. W4	65	F6	
Chiswick Mall			
Eyre Ct. NW8	**6**	**E1**	
Eyre St. Hill EC1	**8**	**E6**	
Eythorne Rd. SW9	76	G1	
Ezra St. E2	**9**	**G3**	
Ezra St. E2	59	C3	

F

Faber Gdns. NW4	38	G5	
Fabian Rd. SW6	66	C7	
Fabian St. E6	61	C4	
Factory La. N17	41	C2	
Factory La., Croy.	101	G1	
Factory Pl. E14	69	B5	
Factory Rd. E16	70	B1	
Factory Sq. SW16	85	E6	
Factory Yd. W7	64	B1	
Uxbridge Rd.			
Faggs Rd., Felt.	72	A5	
Fair Acres, Brom.	96	G5	
Fair St. SE1	**17**	**E3**	
Fair St., Houns.	72	J3	
High St.			
Fairacre, N.Mal.	92	E3	
Fairacres SW15	74	G5	
Fairbairn Grn. SW9	76	G1	
Fairbank Ave., Orp.	104	E2	
Fairbanks Rd. N17	41	C3	
Fairbourne Rd. N17	41	B3	
Fairbridge Rd. N19	49	D2	
Fairbrook Clo. N13	32	G5	
Fairbrook Rd. N13	32	G6	
Fairburn Clo., Borwd.	22	A1	
Fairburn Ct. SW15	75	B5	
Mercier Rd.			
Fairby Rd. SE12	78	H5	
Fairchild Pl. EC2	**9**	**E6**	
Fairchild St. EC2	**9**	**E6**	
Fairclough St. E1	**13**	**J4**	
Fairclough St. E1	59	D6	
Faircross Ave., Bark.	52	F6	
Fairdale Gdns. SW15	74	H4	
Fairdale Gdns., Hayes	63	A2	
Fairfax Gdns. SE3	78	J1	
Fairfax Pl. NW6	48	F7	
Fairfax Rd. N8	40	G4	
Fairfax Rd. NW6	48	F7	
Fairfax Rd. W4	65	E3	
Fairfax Rd., Tedd.	82	D6	
Fairfield Ave. NW4	38	H6	
Fairfield Ave., Edg.	30	B6	
Fairfield Ave., Twick.	81	H1	
Fairfield Ave., Wat.	28	C3	
Fairfield Clo. N12	31	F4	
Fairfield Clo., Epsom	99	E5	
Fairfield Clo., Mitch.	84	H7	
Fairfield Clo., Sid.	79	J6	
Fairfield Ct. NW10	56	G1	
Fairfield Cres., Edg.	30	B6	
Fairfield Dr. SW18	75	E5	
Fairfield Dr., Grnf.	55	F1	
Fairfield Dr., Har.	36	J3	
Fairfield E., Kings.T.	91	H2	
Fairfield Gdns. N8	40	E5	
Elder Ave.			
Fairfield Gro. SE7	70	A6	
Fairfield Ind. Est., Kings.T.	92	A3	
Fairfield N., Kings.T.	91	H2	
Fairfield Path, Croy.	102	A3	
Fairfield Pl., Kings.T.	91	H3	
Fairfield Rd. E3	60	A2	
Fairfield Rd. E17	41	H2	
Fairfield Rd. N8	40	E5	
Fairfield Rd. N18	33	D4	
Fairfield Rd. W7	64	D3	
Southdown Ave.			
Fairfield Rd., Beck.	96	A2	
Fairfield Rd., Bexh.	80	F2	
Fairfield Rd., Brom.	87	G7	
Fairfield Rd., Croy.	102	B3	
Fairfield Rd., Ilf.	52	E6	
Fairfield Rd., Kings.T.	91	H2	
Fairfield Rd., Orp.	97	G6	
Fairfield Rd., Sthl.	54	F6	
Fairfield Rd., Wdf.Grn.	34	G6	
Fairfield S., Kings.T.	91	H3	
Fairfield St. SW18	75	E5	
Fairfield Way, Barn.	23	D5	
Fairfield Way, Epsom	99	E5	
Fairfield W., Kings.T.	91	H2	
Fairfields Clo. NW9	38	C5	
Fairfields Cres. NW9	38	C5	
Fairfields Rd., Houns.	72	J3	
Fairfoot Rd. E3	60	A4	
Fairford Ave., Croy.	95	G5	
Fairford Clo., Croy.	95	G5	
Fairford Gdns., Wor.Pk.	99	F2	
Fairgreen, Barn.	23	J3	
Fairgreen E., Barn.	23	J3	
Fairgreen Rd., Th.Hth.	94	H5	
Fairhaven Ave., Croy.	95	G6	
Fairhaven Cres., Wat.	28	A3	
Fairhazel Gdns. NW6	48	E6	
Fairholme Clo. N3	39	B4	
Fairholme Gdns. N3	39	B3	
Fairholme Rd. W14	66	B5	
Fairholme Rd., Croy.	94	G7	
Fairholme Rd., Har.	37	C5	
Fairholme Rd., Ilf.	43	C7	
Fairholme Rd., Sutt.	100	C6	
Fairholt Clo. N16	50	B1	
Fairholt Rd.			
Fairholt Rd. N16	50	A1	
Fairholt St. SW7	**14**	**H5**	
Fairland Rd. E15	51	F6	
Fairlands Ave. Buck.H.	34	G2	
Fairlands Ave., Sutt.	100	D2	
Fairlands Ave., Th.Hth.	94	F4	
Fairlands Ct. SE9	79	D6	
North Pk.			
Fairlawn SE7	70	A6	
Fairlawn Ave. N2	39	H4	
Fairlawn Ave. W4	65	C4	
Fairlawn Ave., Bexh.	80	D2	
Fairlawn Clo. N14	24	C6	
Fairlawn Clo., Esher	98	C6	
Fairlawn Clo., Felt.	81	F4	
Fairlawn Clo., Kings.T.	83	C6	
Fairlawn Dr., Wdf.Grn.	34	G7	
Fairlawn Gdns., Sthl.	54	F7	
Fairlawn Gro. W4	65	C4	
Fairlawn Pk. SE26	86	H5	
Fairlawn Rd. SW19	84	C7	
Fairlawns, Sun.	90	A3	
Fairlawns, Twick.	73	F6	
Fairlea Pl. W5	55	F5	
Fairlie Gdns. SE23	77	F7	
Fairlight Ave. E4	34	D2	
Fairlight Ave. NW10	56	E2	
Fairlight Ave., Wdf.Grn.	34	D2	
Fairlight Clo. E4	34	D2	
Fairlight Clo., Wor.Pk.	99	J4	
Fairlight Rd. SW17	84	G4	
Fairlop Gdns., Ilf.	35	F7	
Fairlop Rd. E11	42	D7	
Fairlop Rd., Ilf.	43	F2	
Fairmead, Brom.	97	C4	
Fairmead, Surb.	99	B1	
Fairmead Clo., Brom.	97	C4	
Fairmead Clo., Houns.	63	D7	
Fairmead Clo., N.Mal.	92	D3	
Fairmead Cres., Edg.	30	C3	
Fairmead Gdns., Ilf.	43	B5	
Fairmead Rd. N19	49	D3	
Fairmead Rd., Croy.	101	F1	
Fairmead Rd., Loug.	26	H5	
Fairmead Side, Loug.	26	J5	
Fairmile Ave. SW16	85	D5	
Fairmont Clo., Belv.	71	F5	
Lullingstone Rd.			
Fairmount Rd. SW2	76	F6	
Fairoak Clo., Orp.	97	E7	
Fairoak Dr. SE9	79	G5	
Fairseat Clo. (Bushey), Wat.	29	B2	
Hive Rd.			
Fairstead Wk. N1	58	J1	
Popham Rd.			
Fairthorn Rd. SE7	69	G5	
Fairview Ave., Wem.	46	G6	
Fairview Clo. E17	41	H1	
Fairview Cres., Har.	45	G1	
Fairview Dr., Chig.	35	H4	
Fairview Dr., Orp.	104	G4	
Fairview Gdns., Wdf.Grn.	42	H1	
Fairview Pl. SW2	76	F7	
Fairview Rd. N15	41	C5	
Fairview Rd. SW16	94	F1	
Fairview Rd., Chig.	35	H4	
Fairview Rd., Enf.	24	G1	
Fairview Rd., Sutt.	100	G5	
Fairview Way, Edg.	30	A4	
Fairwater Ave., Well.	80	A4	
Fairway SW20	92	J3	
Fairway, Bexh.	80	E5	
Fairway, Orp.	97	G5	
Fairway, Wdf.Grn.	34	J5	
Fairway, The N13	32	J3	
Fairway, The N14	24	B6	
Fairway, The NW7	30	D3	
Fairway, The W3	56	E6	
Fairway, The, Barn.	23	E6	
Fairway, The, Brom.	97	C5	
Fairway, The, N.Mal.	92	D1	
Fairway, The, Nthlt.	45	J6	
Fairway, The, Ruis.	45	C4	
Fairway, The, Wem.	46	E3	
Fairway, The, W.Mol.	90	H3	
Fairway Ave. NW9	38	B3	
Fairway Ave., Borwd.	22	B2	
Fairway Clo. NW11	39	F7	
Fairway Clo., Beck.	96	D6	
Fairway Clo., Croy.	95	H5	
Fairway Clo., Epsom	99	C4	
Fairway Clo., Houns.	72	C5	
Fairway Ct. NW7	30	D3	
The Fairway			

Name	Page	Grid
Fairway Dr., Grnf.	45	H7
Fairway Est., Grnf.	45	J7
Fairway Gdns., Ilf.	52	F5
Fairways, Stan.	37	H2
Fairways, Tedd.	82	G7
Fairweather Clo. N15		
Fairweather Rd. N16	41	D6
Fulmer Rd. SE26	86	H4
Fakenham Clo., Nthlt.	45	G6
Goodwood Dr.		
Fakruddin St. E1	**9**	**J6**
Fakruddin St. E1	59	D4
Falcon Ave., Brom.	97	B4
Falcon Clo. SE1	**16**	**H1**
Falcon Cres., Enf.	25	G5
Falcon Gro. SW11	75	H3
Falcon Ho. W13	55	C4
Falcon La. SW11	75	H3
Falcon Rd. SW11	75	H2
Falcon Rd., Enf.	25	G5
Falcon Rd., Hmptn.	81	F7
Falcon St. E13	60	F4
Falcon Ter. SW11	75	H3
Falcon Trd. Est. NW10	47	E4
Falcon Way E11	42	G4
Falcon Way E14	69	B4
Falcon Way NW9	38	E2
Falcon Way, Felt.	72	B5
Falcon Way, Har.	37	H5
Falconberg Ct. W1	**11**	**J3**
Falconberg Ms. W1	**11**	**H3**
Falconer Wk. N7	49	F2
Newington Barrow Way		
Falconwood Ave., Well.	79	G2
Falconwood Par., Well.	79	H4
Falcourt Clo., Sutt.	100	C5
Falkirk Gdns., Wat.	28	D5
Blackford Rd.		
Falkirk Ho. W9	**6**	**B3**
Falkirk Ho. W9	57	E3
Falkirk St. N1	**9**	**E2**
Falkirk St. N1	59	B2
Falkland Ave. N3	31	D7
Falkland Ave. N11	32	A4
Falkland Pk. Ave. SE25	95	B3
Falkland Rd. N8	40	G4
Falkland Rd. NW5	49	C5
Falkland Rd., Barn.	23	B2
Fallaize Ave., Ilf.	52	E4
Riverdene Rd.		
Falloden Way NW11	39	D4
Fallow Clo., Chig.	35	J5
Fallow Ct. Ave. N12	31	F7
Fallowfield, Stan.	29	D4
Fallowfield Ct., Stan.	29	D3
Stanmore Hill		
Fallsbrook Rd. SW16	85	B6
Falmer Rd. E17	42	B3
Falmer Rd. N15	40	J5
Falmer Rd., Enf.	25	B4
Falmouth Ave. E4	34	D5
Falmouth Clo. N22	32	F7
Truro Rd.		
Falmouth Clo. SE12	78	F5
Falmouth Gdns., Ilf.	43	A4
Falmouth Rd. SE1	**17**	**A6**
Falmouth Rd. SE1	67	J3
Falmouth St. E15	51	D5
Fambridge Clo. SE26	86	J4
Fambridge Rd., Dag.	53	G1
Fane St. W14	66	C6
North End Rd.		
Fann St. EC1	**8**	**J6**
Fann St. EC1	58	J4
Fanshaw St. N1	**9**	**D3**
Fanshaw St. N1	59	B3
Fanshawe Ave., Bark.	52	F6
Fanshawe Cres., Dag.	53	E5
Fanshawe Rd., Rich.	82	F4
Fanthorpe St. SW15	74	J3
Faraday Ave., Sid.	89	A2
Faraday Clo. N7	49	F6
Bride St.		
Faraday Rd. E15	51	F6
Faraday Rd. SW19	84	D6
Faraday Rd. W3	56	C7
Faraday Rd. W10	57	B5
Faraday Rd., Sthl.	54	H7
Faraday Rd., Well.	80	A3
Faraday Rd., W.Mol.	90	G4
Faraday Way SE18	70	A3
Faraday Way, Croy.	101	F1
Ampere Way		
Fareham Rd., Felt.	72	C7
Fareham St. W1	**11**	**H3**
Farewell Pl., Mitch.	93	H1
Faringdon Ave., Brom.	97	D7
Faringford Rd. E15	51	E7
Farjeon Rd. SE3	79	A1
Farleigh Ave., Brom.	96	F6
Farleigh Pl. N16	50	B1
Farleigh Rd.		
Farleigh Rd. N16	50	B1
Farley Dr., Ilf.	52	H1
Farley Pl. SE25	95	D4
Farley Rd. SE6	78	C7
Farley Rd., S.Croy.	102	D7
Farlington Pl. SW15	74	H7
Roehampton La.		
Farlow Rd. SW15	74	J3
Farlton Rd. SW18	75	E7
Farm Ave. NW2	48	B3
Farm Ave. SW16	85	E4
Farm Ave., Har.	36	F7
Farm Ave., Wem.	46	F6
Farm Clo., Barn.	22	H5
Farm Clo., Buck.H.	34	J3
Farm Clo., Dag.	53	J7
Farm Clo., Sthl.	54	H7
Farm Clo., Sutt.	100	H7
Farm Clo., W.Wick.	103	E3
Farm Ct. NW4	38	G3
Farm Dr., Croy.	102	J2
Farm End E4	26	E5
Farm La. N14	24	A6
Farm La. SW6	66	D6
Farm La., Croy.	102	J2
Uxbridge St.		
Farm Rd. N21	32	J1
Farm Rd., Edg.	30	B6
Farm Rd., Houns.	81	E1
Farm Rd., Mord.	93	E5
Farm Rd., Sutt.	100	G7
Farm St. W1	**11**	**D6**
Farm St. W1	58	B7
Farm Vale, Bex.	80	H6
Farm Wk. NW11	39	C5
Farm Way, Buck.H.	34	J4
Farm Way, Wor.Pk.	99	J3
Farman Gro., Nthlt.	54	D3
Wayfarer Rd.		
Farmborough Clo., Har.	37	A7
Pool Rd.		
Farmcote Rd. SE12	87	G1
Farmdale Rd. SE10	69	G5
Farmdale Rd., Cars.	100	H7
Farmer Rd. E10	51	B1
Farmer St. W8	66	D1
Uxbridge St.		
Farmers Rd. SE5	67	H7
Farmfield Rd., Brom.	87	E5
Farmhouse Rd. SW16	85	C7
Farmilo Rd. E17	41	J7
Farmington Ave., Sutt.	100	G3
Farmland Wk., Chis.	88	E5
Farmlands, Enf.	24	G1
Farmlands, Pnr.	36	A4
Farmlands, The, Nthlt.	45	G6
Moat Fm. Rd.		
Farmleigh N14	24	C7
Farmstead Rd. SE6	87	B4
Farmstead Rd., Har.	37	A1
Farmway, Dag.	53	C3
Farnaby Rd. SE9	78	J4
Farnaby Rd., Brom.	87	D7
Farnan Ave. E17	42	A2
Farnan Rd. SW16	85	E5
Farnborough Ave. E17	41	H3
Farnborough Ave., S.Croy.	102	G7
Farnborough Clo., Wem.	47	B2
Chalkhill Rd.		
Farnborough Common, Orp.	104	C3
Farnborough Cres., Brom.	103	F1
Saville Row		
Farnborough Hill, Orp.	104	G5
Farnborough Way SE15	**21**	**E7**
Farnborough Way, Orp.	104	E5
Farncombe St. SE16	**17**	**J4**
Farncombe St. SE16	68	D2
Farndale Ave. N13	32	H3
Farndale Cres., Grnf.	54	J3
Farnell Ms. SW5	18	A3
Farnell Rd., Islw.	73	A4
Farnham Clo. N20	23	F7
Farnham Gdns. SW20	92	H2
Farnham Pl. SE1	**16**	**H2**
Farnham Rd., Ilf.	43	J7
Farnham Rd., Well.	80	C2
Farnham Royal SE11	**20**	**D4**
Farnham Royal SE11	67	F5
Farningham Rd. N17	33	D7
Farnley Rd. E4	26	E7
Farnley Rd. SE25	95	A4
Faro Clo., Brom.	97	D2
Faroe Rd. W14	66	A3
Farorna Wk., Enf.	24	G1
Farquhar Rd. SE19	86	C5
Farquhar Rd. SW19	84	D3
Farquharson Rd., Croy.	101	J1
Farr Ave., Bark.	62	A2
Farr Rd., Enf.	25	A1
Farrance Rd., Rom.	44	E6
Farrance St. E14	60	A6
Farrans Ct., Har.	37	E7
Farrant Ave. N22	40	G2
Farrell Ho. E1	59	F6
Devonport St.		
Farren Rd. SE23	86	H2
Farrer Ms. N8	40	C4
Farrer Rd.		
Farrer Rd. N8	40	C4
Farrer Rd., Har.	37	H5
Farrier Clo., Sun.	90	A4
Farrier Rd., Nthlt.	54	G2
Farrier St. NW1	49	B7
Farriers Way, Borwd.	22	D5
Farringdon La. EC1	**8**	**F6**
Farringdon La. EC1	58	G4
Farringdon Rd. EC1	**8**	**E5**
Farringdon Rd. EC1	58	G4
Farringdon St. EC4	**12**	**G3**
Farringdon St. EC4	58	H5
Farrington Pl., Chis.	88	G7
Farrins Rents SE16	68	H1
Farrow La. SE14	68	F7
Farrow Pl. SE16	68	H3
Ropemaker Rd.		
Farthing All. SE1	**17**	**H4**
Farthing Flds. E1	68	E1
Raine St.		
Farthing St., Orp.	104	C7
Farthings, The, Kings.T.	92	A1
Brunswick Rd.		
Farthings Clo. E4	34	E3
Farthings Clo., Pnr.	36	B6
Farwell Rd., Sid.	89	B3
Farwig La., Brom.	96	F1
Fashion St. E1	**13**	**G2**
Fashion St. E1	59	C5
Fashoda Rd., Brom.	96	J4
Fassett Rd. E8	50	D6
Fassett Rd., Kings.T.	91	H4
Fassett Sq. E8	50	D6
Fauconberg Rd. W4	65	C6
Faulkner Clo., Dag.	44	D7
Faulkner St. SE14	77	F1
Faulkner's All. EC1	**12**	**G1**
Fauna Clo., Rom.	44	C6
Faunce St. SE17	**20**	**G4**
Favart Rd. SW6	75	D1
Faversham Ave. E4	34	E1
Faversham Ave., Enf.	25	A6
Faversham Rd. SE6	77	J7
Faversham Rd., Beck.	95	J2
Faversham Rd., Mord.	93	E6
Fawcett Clo. SW11	75	G2
Fawcett Est. E5	50	D1
Fawcett Rd. NW10	47	F7
Fawcett Rd., Croy.	101	J3
Fawcett St. SW10	**18**	**C6**
Fawcett St. SW10	66	E6
Fawcus Clo., Esher	98	C6
Dalmore Ave.		
Fawe Pk. Rd. SW15	75	C4
Fawe St. E14	60	B5
Fawley Rd. NW6	48	E5
Fawn Rd. E13	60	J2
Fawn Rd., Chig.	35	J5
Fawnbrake Ave. SE24	76	H5
Fawood Ave. NW10	47	D7
Faygate Cres., Bexh.	80	G5
Faygate Rd. SW2	85	F2
Fayland Ave. SW16	85	C5
Fearnley Cres., Hmptn.	81	E5
Fearon St. SE10	69	G5
Featherbed La., Croy.	102	J7
Feathers Pl. SE10	69	D6
Featherstone Ave. SE23	86	E2
Featherstone Gdns., Borwd.	22	C4
Featherstone Rd. NW7	30	H6
Featherstone Rd., Sthl.	63	E3
Featherstone St. EC1	**9**	**B5**
Featherstone St. EC1	59	A4
Featherstone Ter., Sthl.	63	E3
Featley Rd. SW9	76	H3
Federal Rd., Grnf.	55	F2
Federation Rd. SE2	71	B4
Fee Fm. Rd., Esher	98	C7
Felbridge Ave., Stan.	37	D1
Felbridge Clo. SW16	85	G4
Felbridge Rd., Ilf.	52	J2
Felday Rd. SE13	78	B6
Felden Clo., Pnr.	28	E7
Felden St. SW6	75	C1
Feldman Clo. N16	50	D1
Oldhill St.		
Felgate Ms. W6	65	H4
Felhampton Rd. SE9	88	E2
Felhurst Cres., Dag.	53	H4
Felix Ave. N8	40	E6
Felix Rd. W13	55	D7
Felix Rd., Walt.	90	A6
Felix St. E2	59	E2
Hackney Rd.		
Felixstowe Rd. N9	33	D3
Felixstowe Rd. N17	41	C3
Felixstowe Rd. NW10	56	H3
Felixstowe Rd. SE2	71	B3
Fell Rd., Croy.	101	J3
Fell Wk., Edg.	38	B1
East Rd.		
Fellbrigg Rd. SE22	77	C5
Fellbrigg St. E1	59	E4
Headlam St.		
Fellbrook, Rich.	82	E3
Fellowes Clo., Hayes	54	D4
Paddington Clo.		
Fellowes Rd., Cars.	100	H3
Fellows Ct. E2	**9**	**F2**
Fellows Rd. NW3	48	G7
Felltram Way SE7	69	G4
Felmersham Clo. SW4	76	D4
Haselrigge Rd.		
Felmingham Rd. SE20	95	F2
Fels Clo., Dag.	53	H3
Fels Fm. Ave., Dag.	53	J3
Felsberg Rd. SW2	76	E6
Felsham Rd. SW15	75	A3
Felspar Clo. SE18	70	J5
Felstead Ave., Ilf.	43	D1
Felstead Gdns. E14	69	C5
Ferry St.		
Felstead Rd. E11	42	G7
Felstead Rd., Loug.	22	B7
Felstead St. E9	50	J6
Felsted Rd. E16	61	A6
Feltham Ave., E.Mol.	91	B4
Feltham Rd., Mitch.	93	J2
Felthambrook Ind. Est., Felt.	81	B3
Felthambrook Way, Felt.	81	B3
Felthamhill Rd., Felt.	81	A4
Felton Clo., Orp.	97	E6
Felton Lea, Sid.	88	J5
Felton Rd. W13	64	F2
Camborne Ave.		
Felton Rd., Bark.	61	H2
Sutton Rd.		
Felton St. N1	59	A1
Fen Ct. EC3	**13**	**D5**
Fen Gro., Sid.	79	G3
Fen St. E16	60	F7
Caxton St. N.		
Fencepiece Rd., Chig.	35	F5
Fencepiece Rd., Ilf.	35	F6
Fenchurch Ave. EC3	**13**	**D4**
Fenchurch Ave. EC3	59	B6

Fenchurch Bldgs. EC3	13	E4
Fenchurch Pl. EC3	13	E5
Fenchurch St. EC3	13	D5
Fenchurch St. EC3	59	B7
Fendall Rd., Epsom	99	C5
Fendall St. SE1	17	E6
Fendall St. SE1	68	B3
Fendt Clo. E16	60	F7
Bowman Ave.		
Fendyke Rd., Belv.	71	D3
Fenelon Pl. W14	66	C4
Fenham Rd. SE15	68	D7
Fenman Ct. N17	41	E1
Shelbourne Rd.		
Fenman Gdns., Ilf.	53	B1
Fenn Clo., Brom.	87	G6
Fenn St. E9	50	F5
Fennel Clo., Croy.	102	G1
Primrose La.		
Fennel St. SE18	70	D6
Fenner Clo. SE16	68	E4
Layard Rd.		
Fenner Sq. SW11	75	G3
Thomas Baines Rd.		
Fenning St. SE1	17	D3
Fenstanton Ave. N12	31	G6
Fentiman Rd. SW8	20	C6
Fentiman Rd. SW8	67	E6
Fenton Clo. E8	50	C6
Laurel St.		
Fenton Clo. SW9	76	F2
Fenton Clo., Chis.	88	C5
Fenton Rd. N17	32	J7
Fentons Ave. E13	60	H2
Fenwick Clo. SE18	70	D6
Ritter St.		
Fenwick Gro. SE15	77	D3
Fenwick Pl. SW9	76	E3
Fenwick Rd. SE15	77	D3
Ferdinand Pl. NW1	49	A7
Ferdinand St.		
Ferdinand St. NW1	49	A7
Fergus Rd. N5	49	H5
Calabria Rd.		
Ferguson Ave., Surb.	91	J5
Ferguson Clo., Brom.	96	D3
Ferguson Dr. W3	56	D6
Ferme Pk. Rd. N4	40	F7
Ferme Pk. Rd. N8	40	E5
Fermor Rd. SE23	86	H1
Fermoy Rd. W9	57	C4
Fermoy Rd., Grnf.	54	H4
Fern Ave., Mitch.	94	D4
Fern Dene W13	55	E5
Templewood		
Fern Gro., Felt.	72	B7
Fern La., Houns.	63	F5
Fern St. E3	60	A4
Fernbank, Buck.H.	34	H1
Fernbank Ave. Walt.	90	E7
Fernbank Ave., Wem.	46	C4
Fernbrook Ave., Sid.	79	H5
Blackfen Rd.		
Fernbrook Cres. SE13	78	E6
Fernbrook Rd.		
Fernbrook Dr., Har.	36	H7
Fernbrook Rd. SE13	78	E6
Ferncliff Rd. E8	50	D5
Ferncroft Ave. N12	31	H6
Ferncroft Ave. NW3	48	D3
Ferncroft Ave., Ruis.	45	C2
Ferndale, Brom.	96	J2
Ferndale Ave. E17	42	D5
Ferndale Ave., Houns.	72	E3
Ferndale Ct. SE3	69	F7
Ferndale Rd. E7	51	H7
Ferndale Rd. E11	51	E2
Ferndale Rd. N15	41	C6
Ferndale Rd. SE25	95	E5
Ferndale Rd. SW4	76	E4
Ferndale Rd. SW9	76	E4
Ferndale Rd., Rom.	44	J2
Ferndale St. E6	61	E7
Ferndale Ter., Har.	31	J7
Ferndale Way, Orp.	104	G5
Fernden Way, Rom.	44	H6
Ferndene Rd. SE24	76	J4
Ferndown, Nthwd.	36	A2
Ferndown Ave., Orp.	104	G1
Ferndown Clo., Pnr.	28	E7
Ferndown Clo., Sutt.	100	G6
Ferndown Rd. SE9	79	A7
Ferndown Rd., Wat.	28	C3
Ferney Rd., Barn.	24	A7
Fernhall Dr., Ilf.	43	A5
Fernham Rd., Th.Hth.	94	J3
Fernhead Rd. W9	57	C3
Fernhill Ct. E17	42	D2
Fernhill Gdns., Kings.T.	82	G5
Fernhill St. E16	70	C1
Fernholme Rd. SE15	77	G5
Fernhurst Gdns., Edg.	30	A6
Fernhurst Rd. SW6	75	B1
Fernhurst Rd., Croy.	95	D7
Fernlea Rd. SW12	85	B1
Fernlea Rd., Mitch.	94	A2
Fernleigh Clo., Croy.	101	G4
Stafford Rd.		
Fernleigh Ct., Har.	36	H2
Fernleigh Ct., Wem.	46	H2
Fernleigh Rd. N21	32	G2
Ferns Rd E15	51	F6
Fernsbury St. WC1	8	E4
Fernshaw Rd. SW10	18	C6
Fernshaw Rd. SW10	66	F6
Fernside NW11	48	D2
Finchley Rd.		
Fernside, Buck.H.	34	H1
Fernside Ave. NW7	30	D3
Fernside Ave., Felt.	81	B4
Fernside Rd. SW12	84	J1
Fernthorpe Rd. SW16	85	C6
Ferntower Rd. N5	50	A5
Fernways, Ilf.	52	E4
Cecil Rd.		
Fernwood Ave. SW16	85	D4
Fernwood Ave., Wem.	46	F5
Bridgewater Rd.		
Fernwood Clo., Brom.	96	J2
Fernwood Cres. N20	31	J3
Ferranti Clo. SE18	70	A3
Ferraro Clo., Houns.	63	G6
Ferrers Ave., Wall.	101	D4
Ferrers Rd. SW16	85	D5
Ferrestone Rd. N8	40	F4
Ferriby Clo. N1	49	G7
Bewdley St.		
Ferrier Pt. E16	60	H5
Forty Acre La.		
Ferrier St. SW18	75	E4
Ferring Clo., Har.	45	J1
Ferrings SE21	86	B2
Ferris Ave., Croy.	102	J3
Ferris Rd. SE22	77	D4
Ferron Rd. E5	50	E3
Ferry App. SE18	70	D3
Ferry La. N17	41	E4
Ferry La. SW13	65	F6
Ferry La., Brent.	64	H6
Ferry La., Rich.	64	J6
Ferry Pl. SE18	70	D3
Woolwich High St.		
Ferry Rd. SW13	65	G7
Ferry Rd., Tedd.	82	E5
Ferry Rd., T.Ditt.	91	E6
Ferry Rd., Twick.	82	E1
Ferry Rd., W.Mol.	90	G3
Ferry Sq., Brent.	64	H6
Ferry St. E14	69	C5
Ferryhills Clo., Wat.	28	C3
Ferrymead Ave., Grnf.	54	G3
Ferrymead Dr., Grnf.	54	G3
Ferrymead Gdns., Grnf.	54	J2
Ferrymoor, Rich.	82	E3
Festing Rd. SW15	75	A3
Festival Clo., Bex.	89	D1
Fetter La. EC4	12	F4
Fetter La. EC4	58	G6
Ffinch St. SE8	69	A7
Field Clo. E4	34	B6
Field Clo., Brom.	96	J2
Field Clo., Buck.H.	34	J3
Field Clo., Chess.	99	F5
Field Clo., Houns.	72	B1
Field Ct. WC1	12	D2
Field End, Barn.	22	H4
Field End, Nthlt.	45	D6
Field End, Ruis.	45	D6
Field End, Twick.	82	C4
Field End Rd., Pnr.	46	B3
Field End Rd., Ruis.	45	C1
Field La., Brent.	64	F7
Field La., Tedd.	82	D5
Field Mead NW7	30	E7
Field Mead NW9	30	E7
Field Pl., N.Mal.	92	F6
Field Rd. E7	51	G4
Field Rd. N17	41	A3
Field Rd. W6	66	B5
Field Rd., Felt.	72	B6
Field St. WC1	8	C3
Field St. WC1	58	F3
Field Way NW10	47	C7
Twybridge Way		
Field Way, Croy.	103	B7
Field Way, Grnf.	54	H1
Fieldend Rd. SW16	94	C1
Fielders Clo., Enf.	25	B4
Woodfield Clo.		
Fielders Clo., Har.	45	J1
Fieldfare Rd. SE28	62	C7
Fieldgate La., Mitch.	93	H3
Fieldgate St. E1	13	J2
Fieldgate St. E1	59	D5
Fieldhouse Rd. SW12	85	C1
Fielding Ave., Twick.	81	J3
Fielding Ho. NW6	57	D3
Fielding Rd. W4	65	D3
Fielding Rd. W14	66	A3
Fielding St. SE17	21	A5
Fielding St. SE17	67	J6
Fieldings, The SE23	86	F1
Fields Est. E8	50	D7
Fields Pk. Cres., Rom.	44	C5
Fieldsend Rd., Sutt.	100	B5
Fieldside Rd., Brom.	87	D5
Fieldview SW18	84	G1
Fieldway, Dag.	53	C3
Fieldway, Orp.	97	G6
Fieldway Cres. N5	49	G5
Fiennes Clo., Dag.	53	C1
Fiesta Dr., Dag.	62	J4
Fife Rd. E16	60	G5
Fife Rd. N22	32	H7
Fife Rd. SW14	74	C5
Fife Rd., Kings.T.	91	H2
Fife Ter. N1	8	D1
Fifield Path SE23	86	G3
Bampton Rd.		
Fifth Ave. E12	52	C4
Fifth Ave. W10	57	B3
Fifth Cross Rd., Twick.	82	A2
Fifth Way, Wem.	47	B4
Fig Tree Clo. NW10	56	E1
Craven Pk.		
Figges Rd., Mitch.	85	A7
Filby Rd., Chess.	98	J6
Filey Ave. N16	50	D1
Filey Clo., Sutt.	100	F7
Filey Waye, Ruis.	45	A2
Fillebrook Ave., Enf.	25	B2
Fillebrook Rd. E11	51	D1
Filmer Rd. SW6	75	B1
Filston Rd., Erith	71	H5
Riverdale Rd.		
Finborough Rd. SW10	18	A4
Finborough Rd. SW10	66	E5
Finborough Rd. SW17	84	J6
Finch Ave. SE27	86	A4
Finch Clo. NW10	47	D5
Finch Clo., Barn.	23	D5
Finch Clo.		
Finch Dr., Felt.	72	D7
Finch La. EC3	13	C4
Finchale Rd. SE2	71	A3
Finchdale Rd. SE2	71	A3
Finchdean Way SE15	68	C7
Daniel Gdns.		
Finchingfield Ave., Wdf.Grn.	34	J7
Finchley Ct. N3	31	E6
Finchley La. NW4	38	J4
Finchley Pk. N12	31	F4
Finchley Pl. NW8	6	E1
Finchley Pl. NW8	57	G2
Finchley Rd. NW2	48	D3
Finchley Rd. NW3	48	G7
Finchley Rd. NW8	48	G7
Finchley Rd. NW11	39	C4
Finchley Way N3	31	D7
Finck St. SE1	67	F2
Finden Rd. E7	51	H5
Findhorn Ave., Hayes	48	A2
Findhorn St. E14	60	C6
Findon Clo. SW18	75	D6
Wimbledon Pk. Rd.		
Findon Clo., Har.	45	H3
Findon Rd. N9	33	E1
Findon Rd. W12	65	G2
Fingal St. SE10	69	F5
Finland Quay SE16	68	H3
Finland Rd. SE4	77	H3
Finland St. SE16	68	H3
Finlay St. SW6	75	A1
Finlays Clo., Chess.	99	A5
Finnis St. E2	59	E3
Finnymore Rd., Dag.	53	E7
Finsbury Ave. EC2	13	C2
Finsbury Circ. EC2	13	C2
Finsbury Circ. EC2	59	A5
Finsbury Cotts. N22	32	E7
Clarence Rd.		
Finsbury Est. EC1	8	F4
Finsbury Est. EC1	58	G3
Finsbury Ho. N22	40	E1
Finsbury Mkt. EC2	9	D6
Finsbury Mkt. EC2	59	B4
Finsbury Pk. Ave. N4	40	J2
Finsbury Pk. Rd. N4	49	H2
Finsbury Pavement EC2	13	C1
Finsbury Pavement EC2	59	A5
Finsbury Rd. N22	40	F1
Finsbury Sq. EC2	9	C6
Finsbury Sq. EC2	59	A5
Finsbury St. EC2	13	B1
Finsbury St. EC2	59	A5
Finsbury Way, Bex.	80	F6
Finsen Rd. SE5	76	J3
Finstock Rd. W10	57	A6
Finucane Ri. (Bushey), Wat.	28	J2
Fir Clo., Walt.	90	A7
Fir Dene, Orp.	104	C3
Fir Gro., N.Mal.	92	F6
Fir Rd., Felt.	81	D5
Fir Rd., Sutt.	100	C1
Fir Tree Clo. SW16	85	C5
Fir Tree Clo. W5	55	H6
Fir Tree Clo. Epsom	99	F4
Fir Tree Gdns., Croy.	103	A4
Fir Tree Gro., Cars.	100	J7
Fir Tree Rd., Houns.	72	E4
Fir Tree Wk., Dag.	53	J3
Wheel Fm. Dr.		
Fir Tree Wk., Enf.	25	A3
Firbank Clo. E16	68	H1
Firbank Clo., Enf.	24	J4
Gladbeck Way		
Firbank Rd. SE15	77	E2
Fircroft Ave., Chess.	98	J4
Fircroft Gdns., Har.	46	B3
Fircroft Rd. SW17	84	J2
Firdene, Surb.	99	C1
Fire Bell All., Surb.	91	HG
Fire Sta. All., Barn.	23	C2
Christchurch La.		
Firecrest Dr. NW3	48	E3
Firefly Clo., Wall.	101	E7
Defiant Way		
Firhill Rd. SE6	87	A4
Firs, The N20	31	G4
Firs, The W5	55	G5
Firs Ave. N10	40	A3
Firs Ave. N11	31	J6
Firs Ave. SW14	74	C4
Firs Clo. N10	40	A3
Firs Ave.		
Firs Clo. SE23	77	G7
Firs Clo., Esher	98	B6
Firs Clo., Mitch.	94	B2
Firs Dr., Houns.	72	B1
Firs Dr., Loug.	27	D1
Firs La. N13	32	J3
Firs La. N21	32	J2
Firs Pk. Ave. N21	33	A1
Firs Pk. Gdns. N21	32	J1
Firs Wk., Wdf.Grn.	34	G5
Firsby Ave., Croy.	102	G1
Firsby Rd. N16	50	C1
Firscroft N13	32	H3
Firside Gro., Sid.	88	J1
First Ave. E12	52	B4
First Ave. E13	60	G3
First Ave. E17	42	A5
First Ave. N18	33	F4
First Ave. NW4	38	J4
First Ave. SW14	74	E3
First Ave. W3	65	F1
First Ave. W10	57	C4
First Ave., Bexh.	71	C7

First Ave., Dag. 62 H2
First Ave., Enf. 25 C5
First Ave., Rom. 44 C5
First Ave., Walt. 90 B6
First Ave., Wem. 46 G2
First Ave., W.Mol. 90 F4
First Clo., W.Mol. 58 J0
First Cross Rd., 82 B2
Twff
First St. SW3 18 H1
First St. SW3 66 H4
First Way, Wem. 47 B4
Firstway SW20 92 J2
Firswood Ave., 99 F5
Epsom
Firth Gdns. SW6 75 B1
Firtree Ave., 94 A2
Mitch.
Firtree Clo., Orp. 104 J5
Highfield Ave.
Fish St. Hill EC3 13 C6
Fish St. Hill EC3 59 A7
Fisher Clo., Croy. 102 C1
Lwr. Addiscombe Rd.
Fisher Clo., Grnf. 54 G3
Gosling Clo.
Fisher Rd., Har. 37 C2
Fisher St. E16 60 G5
Fisher St. WC1 12 C2
Fisher St. WC1 58 F5
Fisherman Clo., 82 F4
Rich.
Locksmeade Rd.
Fishermans Dr. SE16 68 G2
Fishermans Pl. W4 65 F6
Fisherman's Wk. E14 69 A1
Cabot Sq.
Fishers Ct. SE14 77 G1
Besson St.
Fishers La. W4 65 D4
Fishers Way, Belv. 71 J1
Fishersdene, Esher 98 D6
Fisherton Est. NW8 6 F5
Fisherton St. NW8 6 E5
Fisherton St. NW8 57 G4
Fisherton St. Est. 57 G4
NW8
Fishponds Rd. SW17 84 H4
Fishponds Rd., Kes. 104 A5
Fisons Ct. E16 69 G1
Fitzalan Rd. N3 39 B3
Fitzalan Rd., Esher 98 B7
Fitzalan St. SE11 20 E1
Fitzalan St. SE11 67 F4
Fitzgeorge Ave. W14 66 B4
Fitzgeorge Ave., 92 D1
N.Mal.
Fitzgerald Ave. 74 E3
SW14
Fitzgerald Clo. E11 42 G5
Fitzgerald Rd.
Fitzgerald Ho. E14 60 B6
Kerbey St.
Fitzgerald Ho., 63 B1
Hayes
Fitzgerald Rd. E11 42 G5
Fitzgerald Rd. SW14 74 D3
Fitzgerald Rd., 91 D6
T.Ditt.
Fitzhardinge St. W1 11 B3
Fitzhardinge St. W1 58 A6
Fitzhugh Gro. SW18 75 G6
Fitzhugh Gro. Est. 75 G6
SW18
Fitzjames Ave. W14 66 B4
Fitzjames Ave., 102 D2
Croy.
Fitzjohn Ave., 23 B5
Barn.
Fitzjohn's Ave. NW3 48 G5
Fitzmaurice Pl. W1 15 E1
Fitzmaurice Pl. W1 67 B1
Fitzneal St. W12 48 J1
Fitzroy Clo. N6 48 J1
Fitzroy Ct. W1 7 G6
Fitzroy Cres. W4 65 D7
Fitzroy Gdns. SE19 86 B7
Fitzroy Ms. W1 7 F6
Fitzroy Pk. N6 48 J2
Fitzroy Rd. NW1 58 A1
Fitzroy Sq. W1 7 F6
Fitzroy Sq. W1 58 C4
Fitzroy St. W1 7 F6
Fitzroy St. W1 58 C4
Fitzroy Yd. NW1 58 A1
Fitzroy Rd.
Fitzstephen Rd., 53 B5
Dag.
Fitzwarren Gdns. 49 C1
Fitzwilliam Ave., 73 J2
Rich.
Fitzwilliam Rd. SW4 76 C3

Fitzwygram Clo., 81 J5
Hmptn.
Five Acre NW9 38 F1
Five Bell All. E14 59 J7
Three Colt St.
Five Elms Rd., Brom. 103 H3.
Five Elms Rd., Dag. 53 F3
Five Ways Rd. SW9 70 0B
Fiveacre Clo., 94 G6
Fladbury Rd. N15 41 A6
Fladgate Rd. E11 42 E6
Flag Clo., Croy. 102 G1
Primrose La.
Flag Wk., Pnr. 36 A6
Flambard Rd., Har. 37 D6
Flamborough Rd., 45 A3
Ruis.
Flamborough St. E14 59 H6
Flamingo Gdns., 54 E3
Nthlt.
Jetstar Way
Flamstead Gdns., 53 C7
Dag.
Flamstead Rd.
Flamstead Rd. SE7 70 B5
Flamstead Rd., Dag. 53 C7
Flamsted Ave., Wem. 47 A6
Flanchford Rd. W12 65 F3
Flanders Cres. SW17 84 J7
Flanders Rd. E6 61 C2
Flanders Rd. W4 65 E4
Flanders Way E9 50 G6
Flank St. E1 13 H5
Flask Wk. NW3 48 F4
Flast Cotts. NW3 48 G4
New End Sq.
Flaxen Rd. E4 34 B3
Flaxley Rd., Mord. 93 E6
Flaxman Ct. W1 11 H4
Flaxman Rd. SE5 76 H3
Flaxman Ter. WC1 7 J4
Flaxman Ter. WC1 58 D3
Flaxmore Pl., Beck. 96 D6
Flaxton Rd. SE18 70 G7
Flecker Clo., Stan. 29 C5
Fleece Rd., Surb. 98 F1
Fleece Wk. N7 49 E6
Manger Rd.
Fleeming Clo. E17 41 J2
Pennant Ter.
Fleeming Rd. E17 41 J2
Fleet Clo., W.Mol. 90 G5
Fleet La. EC4 12 G3
Fleet La., W.Mol. 90 F6
Fleet Rd. NW3 48 H5
Fleet Sq. WC1 8 D4
Fleet St. EC4 12 F4
Fleet St. EC4 58 G6
Fleet St. Hill E1 59 H6
Fleetside, W.Mol. 90 F5
Fleetway W. 55 E2
Business Pk., Grnf.
Fleetwood Clo. E16 61 A5
Fleetwood Clo., 94 H1
Chess.
Fleetwood Gro. W3 56 E7
East Acton La.
Fleetwood Rd. NW10 47 G5
Fleetwood Rd., 92 B3
Kings.T.
Fleetwood Sq., 92 B3
Kings.T.
Fleetwood St. N16 50 B2
Stoke Newington
Ch. St.
Fleetwood Way, Wat. 28 C4
Fleming Ave., Ruis. 45 B2
Fleming Ct. W2 10 E1
Fleming Ct., Croy. 101 G5
Fleming Mead 84 H7
Mitch.
Fleming Rd. SE17 20 H5
Fleming Rd. SE17 67 H6
Fleming Rd., Sthl. 54 H6
Fleming Way SE28 62 D7
Fleming Way, Islw. 73 C3
Flempton Rd. E10 50 H1
Fletcher La. E10 42 C7
Fletcher Path SE8 69 A7
New Butt La.
Fletcher Rd. W4 65 C3
Fletcher Rd., Chig. 35 J5
Fletcher St. E1 13 J5
Fletchers Clo., Brom. 96 H4
Fletching Rd. E5 50 F3
Fletching Rd. SE7 69 A6
Fletton Rd. N11 32 E7
Fleur de Lis St. E1 13 D6
Fleur de Lis St. E1 59 B4
Fleur Gates SW19 75 A7
Princes Way

Flexmere Gdns. N17 41 A1
Flexmere Rd.
Flexmere Rd. N17 41 A1
Flimwell Clo., 87 E5
Brom.
Flint St. SE17 21 C2
Flint St. SE17 68 A4
Flintmill Cres. SE3 79 B2
Flinton St. SE17 21 C3
Flinton St. SE17 68 B5
Flitcroft St. WC2 11 J4
Flockton St. SE16 17 H4
Flodden Rd. SE5 76 J1
Flood La., Twick. 82 D1
Church La.
Flood Pas. SE18 70 C4
Samuel St.
Flood St. SW3 18 H4
Flood St. SW3 66 H5
Flood Wk. SW3 18 H5
Flood Wk. SW3 66 H6
Flora Clo. E14 60 B6
Flora Gdns. W6 65 H4
Ravenscourt Rd.
Flora Gdns., Rom. 44 C6
Flora St., Belv. 71 F5
Floral St. WC2 12 A5
Floral St. WC2 58 E7
Florence Ave., 24 J3
Mord.
Florence Ave., Enf. 24 J3
Florence Ave., 93 F5
Mord.
Florence Clo., Walt. 90 B7
Florence Rd.
Florence Dr., Enf. 24 J3
Florence Gdns. W4 65 C6
Florence Nightingale 50 A6
Ho. N1
Clephane Rd.
Florence Rd. E6 60 J1
Florence Rd. E13 60 F2
Florence Rd. N4 49 G1
Florence Rd. SE2 71 C3
Florence Rd. SE14 77 J1
Florence Rd. SW19 84 E6
Florence Rd. W4 65 D3
Florence Rd. W5 55 H7
Florence Rd., Beck. 95 H2
Florence Rd., Brom. 96 G1
Florence Rd., Felt. 81 B1
Florence Rd., 82 J7
Kings.T.
Florence Rd., Sthl. 63 D4
Florence Rd., Walt. 90 B7
Florence St. E16 60 F4
Florence St. N1 49 H7
Florence St. NW4 38 J4
Florence Ter. SE14 77 J1
Florfield Rd. E8 50 E6
Reading La.
Florian Ave., Sutt. 100 G4
Florian Rd. SW15 75 B4
Florida Clo. 29 A2
(Bushey), Wat.
Florida Rd., 94 H1
Th.Hth.
Florida St. E2 9 J4
Florida St. E2 59 D3
Floriston Clo., Stan. 37 E1
Floriston Gdns., 37 E1
Stan.
Floss St. SW15 74 J2
Flower & Dean Wk. 13 G2
E1
Flower La. NW7 30 F5
Flower Wk., The 14 D4
SW7
Flower Wk., The SW7 66 F2
Flowersmead SW17 85 A2
Floyd Rd. SE7 69 J5
Fludyer St. SE13 78 E4
Folair Way SE16 68 E5
Catlin St.
Foley Rd., Esher 98 B7
Foley St. W1 11 F2
Foley St. W1 58 C5
Folgate St. E1 13 E1
Folgate St. E1 59 B5
Foliot St. W12 56 F6
Folkestone Rd. E6 61 D2
Folkestone Rd. E17 42 B4
Folkestone Rd. N18 33 D4
Folkingham La. NW9 38 D1
Folkington Cor. N12 31 C5
Follett St. E14 60 C6
Folly La. E17 41 H1
Folly Ms. W11 57 C6
Kensington Pk. Rd.
Folly Wall E14 69 C2
Font Hills N2 39 F2
Fontaine Rd. SW16 85 F1
Fontarabia Rd. SW11 76 A4
Fontayne Ave., 35 F4
Chig.

Fontenoy Rd. SW12 85 B2
Fonteyne Gdns., 43 A2
Wdf.Grn.
Lechmere Ave.
Fonthill Clo. SE20 95 D2
Selby Rd.
Fonthill Ms. N4 49 G2
Lennox Rd.
Fonthill Rd. N4 49 F1
Fontley Way SW15 74 D7
Fontwell Clo., Har. 29 B7
Fontwell Dri., 45 G6
Nthlt.
Fontwell Dr., Brom. 97 D5
Football La., Har. 46 B1
Footpath, The SW15 74 G5
Parkstead Rd.
Foots Cray High 89 C6
St., Sid.
Foots Cray La., 89 C1
Sid.
Footscray Rd. SE9 79 D6
Footway, The S9 79 F7
Forbes Ct. SE19 86 B5
Forbes St. E1 13 J4
Forburg Rd. N16 50 D1
Ford Clo., Har. 37 A7
Ford Clo., Th.Hth. 94 H5
Ford End, Wdf.Grn. 34 H6
Ford Rd. E3 59 H1
Ford Rd., Dag. 53 F7
Ford Sq. E1 59 E5
Ford St. E3 59 H1
Ford St. E16 60 F6
Forde Ave., Brom. 96 J3
Fordel Rd. SE6 87 D1
Fordham Clo., Barn. 23 H3
Fordham Rd., Barn. 23 G3
Fordham St. E1 13 J3
Fordham St. E1 59 D6
Fordhook Ave. W5 55 J7
Fordingley Rd. W9 57 C3
Fordington Rd. N6 39 J5
Fordmill Rd. SE6 87 A2
Fords Gro. N21 32 J1
Fords Pk. Rd. E16 60 G6
Fordwich Clo., Orp. 97 J7
Fordwych Rd. NW2 48 B4
Fordyce Rd. SE13 78 C6
Fordyke Rd., Dag. 53 F2
Fore St. EC2 13 A2
Fore St. EC2 58 J5
Fore St. N9 33 D4
Fore St. N18 33 C6
Fore St. Ave. EC2 13 B2
Foreland Ct. NW4 39 A1
Foreland St. SE18 70 G4
Plumstead Rd.
Foreman Ct. W6 65 J4
Hammersmith Bdy.
Foremark Clo., Ilf. 35 J6
Foreshore SE8 68 J4
Forest, The E11 42 E4
Forest App. E4 26 E7
Forest App., 34 G7
Wdf.Grn.
Forest Ave. E4 26 E7
Forest Ave., Chig. 35 D5
Forest Business Pk. 41 H7
E17
Forest Clo. E11 42 F5
Forest Clo., Chis. 97 D1
Forest Clo., 34 H4
Wdf.Grn.
Forest Ct. E4 34 F1
Forest Ct. E11 42 E4
Forest Cft. SE23 86 E2
Forest Cft. SE26 86 E2
Forest Dr. E12 52 A3
Forest Dr., Kes. 104 B4
Forest Dr., 34 D7
Wdf.Grn.
Forest Dr. E. E11 42 D7
Forest Dr. W. E11 42 C7
Forest Edge, 34 J4
Buck.H.
Forest Gdns. N17 41 C2
Forest Gate NW9 38 E5
Forest Glade E4 34 E4
Forest Glade E11 42 E4
Forest Gro. E8 50 C6
Forest Heights, 34 G7
Buck.H.
Forest Hill Rd. SE22 77 E5
Forest Hill Rd. SE23 77 F6
Forest Ind. Est., Ilf. 43 H1
Forest La. E7 51 G5
Forest La. E15 51 E6
Forest La., Chig. 35 D5
Forest Mt. Rd., 34 D7
Wdf.Grn.
Forest Ridge, Beck. 96 A3
Forest Ridge, Kes. 104 B4

Forest Ri. E17 42 D5
Forest Rd. E7 51 G4
Forest Rd. E8 50 C6
Forest Rd. E11 42 D7
Forest Rd. E17 41 F4
Forest Rd. N9 33 E1
Forest Rd., Felt. 81 C2
Forest Rd., Ilf. 43 H1
Forest Rd., Loug. 27 A3
Forest Rd., Rich. 65 A7
Forest Rd., Rom. 44 H3
Forest Rd., Sutt. 100 D1
Forest Rd., 34 G3
   Wdf.Grn.
Forest Side E4 26 F7
Forest Side E7 51 H4
   Capel Rd.
Forest Side, 34 H1
   Buck.H.
Forest Side, 91 F1
   Wor.Pk.
Forest Rd. E7 51 G5
Forest Vw. E4 26 D7
Forest Vw. E11 42 F7
Forest Vw. Ave. E10 42 D5
Forest Vw. Rd. E12 52 B4
Forest Vw. Rd. E17 42 C1
Forest Vw. Rd., 27 A4
   Loug.
Forest Way N19 49 C2
   Hargrave Pk.
Forest Way, Loug. 27 B3
Forest Way, Orp. 97 J5
Forest Way, Sid. 79 G7
Forest Way, 34 H4
   Wdf.Grn.
Forestdale N14 32 D4
Forester Rd. SE15 77 E4
Forestholme Clo. 86 F2
   SE23
Forfar Rd. N22 40 H1
Forfar Rd. SW11 76 A1
Forge Clo., Brom. 103 G1
Forge Dr., Esher 98 D7
Forge La., Felt. 81 E5
Forge La., Sun. 90 A3
Forge La., Sutt. 100 B7
Forge Pl. NW1 49 A6
   Malden Cres.
Forman Pl. N16 50 C4
   Farleigh Rd.
Formby Ave., Stan. 37 F3
Formosa St. W9 6 B6
Formosa St. W9 57 E4
Formunt Clo. E16 60 F5
   Vincent St.
Forres Gdns. NW11 39 D6
Forrest Gdns. SW16 94 F3
Forrester Path SE26 86 F4
Forset St. W1 10 H3
Forset St. W1 57 H6
Forstal Clo., Brom. 96 G3
   Ridley Rd.
Forster Rd. E17 41 H6
Forster Rd. N17 41 C3
Forster Rd. SW2 76 E7
Forster Rd., Beck. 95 H3
Forster Rd., Croy. 94 J7
   Windmill Rd.
Forsters Clo., Rom. 44 F6
Forsters Way, Hayes 54 B6
Forston St. N1 9 B1
Forsyte Clo. SE19 95 B1
Forsyth Gdns. SE17 20 H5
Forsyth Gdns. SE17 67 H6
Forsyth Pl., Enf. 25 B5
Forsythia Clo., Ilf. 52 E5
Fort Rd. SE1 21 G2
Fort Rd. SE1 68 C4
Fort Rd., Nthlt. 45 G7
Fort St. E1 13 E2
Fort St. E1 59 B5
Fort St. E16 69 H1
Forterie Gdns., Ilf. 53 A3
Fortescue Ave. E8 50 E7
   Mentmore Ter.
Fortescue Ave., 81 J3
   Twick.
Fortescue Rd. SW19 84 G7
Fortescue Rd., Edg. 38 C1
Fortess Gro. NW5 49 B5
   Fortess Rd.
Fortess Rd. NW5 49 B5
Fortess Wk. NW5 49 B5
   Fortess Rd.
Forthbridge Rd. 76 A4
   SW11

Fortis Clo. E16 60 J6
Fortis Grn. N2 39 H4
Fortis Grn. N10 40 A3
Fortis Grn. N10 39 J3
Fortis Grn. Rd. N10 40 A3
Fortismere Ave. N10 40 A3
Fortnam Rd. N19 49 D2
Fortnums Acre, 29 C6
   Stan.
Fortrose Gdns. SW2 85 D1
   New Pk. Rd.
Fortuna Clo. N7 49 F6
   Vulcan Way
Fortune Gate Rd. 56 E1
   NW10
Fortune Grn. Rd. 48 D4
   NW6
Fortune St. EC1 9 A6
Fortune St. EC1 58 J4
Fortune Wk. SE28 70 G3
   Broadwater Rd.
Fortune Way NW10 56 G3
Fortunes Mead, 45 E6
   Nthlt.
Forty Acre La. E16 60 G5
Forty Ave., Wem. 46 J3
Forty Clo., Wem. 46 J3
Forty La., Wem. 47 B2
Forum, The, W.Mol. 90 H4
Forum Way, Edg. 30 A6
   High St.
Forumside, Edg. 30 A6
   Forum Way
Forval Clo., Mitch. 93 J5
Forward Dr., Har. 37 C4
Fosbury Ms. W2 10 B6
Foscote Ms. W9 57 D5
   Amberley Rd.
Foscote Rd. NW4 38 H5
Foskett Rd. SW6 75 C2
Foss Ave., Croy. 101 G5
Foss Rd. SW17 84 G4
Fossdene Rd. SE7 69 H5
Fossdyke Clo., 54 E5
   Hayes
Fosse Way W13 55 D5
Fossil Rd. SE13 78 A3
Fossington Rd., 71 D4
   Belv.
Fossway, Dag. 53 C2
Foster La. EC2 12 J3
Foster La. EC2 58 J6
Foster Rd. E13 60 G4
Foster Rd. W3 56 F7
Foster Rd. W4 65 D5
Foster St. NW4 38 J4
Foster Wk. NW4 38 J4
   New Brent St.
Fosters Clo. E18 42 H1
Fosters Clo., Chis. 88 C5
Fothergill Clo. E13 60 G2
Fotheringham Rd., 25 C4
   Enf.
Foubert's Pl. W1 11 F4
Foubert's Pl. W1 58 C6
Foulden Rd. N16 50 C4
Foulis Ter. SW7 18 F3
Foulis Ter. SW7 66 G5
Foulser Rd. SW17 84 J3
Foulsham Rd., 94 J3
   Th.Hth.
Founders Ct. EC2 13 B3
Founders Gdns. 85 J7
   SE19
Foundry Clo. SE16 68 H1
Foundry Ms. NW1 7 G5
Fount St. SW8 67 D1
Fountain Ct. EC4 12 E5
Fountain Dr. SE19 86 E4
Fountain Pl. SW9 76 G1
Fountain Rd. SW17 84 G5
Fountain Rd., 94 J2
   Th.Hth.
Fountain Sq. SW1 19 D1
Fountains Ave., 81 F3
   Felt.
Fountains Clo., 81 F2
   Felt.
Fountains Cres. N14 24 E7
Fountayne Rd. N15 41 D4
Fountayne Rd. N16 50 D2
Four Seasons Cres., 100 C2
   Sutt.
   Kimpton Rd.
Four Seasons Ind. 63 H3
   Est., Sthl.
Four Wents, The E4 34 D2
   Kings Rd.
Fouracres, Enf. 25 H1
Fourland Wk., Edg. 30 C6
Fournier St. E1 13 G1
Fournier St. E1 59 C5
Fourth Ave. E12 52 C4

Fourth Ave. W10 57 B3
Fourth Ave., Rom. 53 J1
Fourth Cross Rd., 82 A2
   Twick.
Fourth Way, Wem. 47 C4
Fowey Ave., Ilf. 43 A5
Fowey Clo. E1 68 E1
   Kennet St.
Fowler Clo. SW11 75 G3
Fowler Rd. E7 51 G4
Fowler Rd. N1 49 H7
   Halton Rd.
Fowler Rd., Mitch. 94 A2
Fowlers Clo., Sid. 89 E5
   Thursland Rd.
Fowlers Wk. W5 55 G4
Fownes St. SW11 75 H3
Fox and Knot St. 12 H1
   EC1
Fox Clo. E1 59 F4
Fox Clo. E16 60 G5
Fox Hill SE19 86 C7
Fox Hill, Kes. 103 H5
Fox Hill Gdns. SE19 86 C7
Fox Hollow Dr., 80 D3
   Bexh.
Fox Ho. Rd., Belv. 71 H4
Fox La. N13 32 E2
Fox La. W5 55 H4
Fox La., Kes. 103 H5
Fox Rd. E16 60 F5
Foxberry Rd. SE4 77 H3
Foxborough Gdns. 78 A6
   SE4
Foxbourne Rd. SW17 85 A2
Foxbury Ave., Chis. 88 G6
Foxbury Clo., Brom. 87 H6
Foxbury Rd., Brom. 87 G6
Foxcombe, Croy. 103 B6
Foxcombe Clo. E6 61 A2
   Boleyn Rd.
Foxcombe Rd. SW15 83 G1
   Alton Rd.
Foxcote SE5 21 E4
Foxcroft Rd. SE18 79 E1
Foxes Dale SE3 78 G3
Foxes Dale, Brom. 96 D3
Foxfield Rd., Orp. 104 G2
Foxglove La., 99 A4
   Chess.
Foxglove St. W12 56 F7
Foxglove Way, Wall. 101 B1
Foxgrove N14 32 E3
Foxgrove Ave., 87 B7
   Beck.
Foxgrove Path, Wat. 28 D5
Foxgrove Rd., Beck. 87 B7
Foxham Rd. N19 49 D3
Foxhole Rd. SE9 79 B5
Foxholt Gdns. NW10 47 C7
Foxhome Clo., Chis. 88 D6
Foxlands Cres., 53 J5
   Dag.
Foxlands Rd., Dag. 53 J5
Foxlees, Wem. 46 D4
Foxley Clo. E8 50 D5
   Ferncliff Rd.
Foxley Clo., Loug. 27 E2
Foxley Rd. SW9 67 G7
Foxley Rd., Th.Hth. 94 H4
Foxley Sq. SW9 67 H7
   Cancell Rd.
Foxleys, Wat. 28 E3
Foxmead Clo., Enf. 24 F3
Foxmore St. SW11 75 J1
Fox's Path, Mitch. 93 H2
Foxwell St. SE4 77 H3
Foxwood Clo., Felt. 81 B3
Foxwood Rd. SE3 78 F4
Foyle Rd. N17 41 D1
Foyle Rd. SE3 69 F6
Framfield Clo. N12 31 D3
Framfield Ct., Enf. 25 B6
Framfield Rd. N5 49 H5
Framfield Rd. W7 55 C6
Framfield Rd., 85 A7
   Mitch.
Framlingham Clo. E5 50 F2
   Detmold Rd.
Framlingham Cres. 88 B4
   SE9
Frampton Clo., 100 D7
   Sutt.
Frampton Pk. Est. 50 F7
   E9
Frampton Pk. Rd. E9 50 F6
Frampton Rd., 72 E5
   Houns.
Frampton St. NW8 6 F6
Frampton St. NW8 57 G4
Francemary Rd. SE4 78 A5
Frances Rd. E4 34 A6

Frances St. SE18 70 C4
Franche Ct. Rd. 84 F3
   SW17
Francis Ave., Bexh. 80 G2
Francis Ave., Felt. 81 A3
Francis Ave., Ilf. 52 G2
Francis Barber Clo. 85 F4
   SW16
   Valley Rd.
Francis Chichester 76 A1
   Way SW11
Francis Clo. E14 69 D4
   Saunders Ness Rd.
Francis Clo., Epsom 99 D4
Francis Gro. SW19 84 C6
Francis Rd. E10 51 C1
Francis Rd. N2 39 J4
   Lynmouth Rd.
Francis Rd., Croy. 94 H6
Francis Rd., Grnf. 55 E2
Francis Rd., Har. 37 D5
Francis Rd., Houns. 72 D2
Francis Rd., Ilf. 52 G2
Francis Rd., Pnr. 36 C5
Francis Rd., Wall. 101 C6
Francis St. E15 51 E5
Francis St. SW1 19 F1
Francis St. SW1 67 C4
Francis St., Ilf. 52 G2
Francis Ter. N19 49 C3
   Junction Rd.
Franciscan Rd. SW17 84 J5
Francklyn Gdns., 30 A3
   Edg.
Franconia Rd. SW4 76 D5
Frank Bailey Wk. 52 D5
   E12
   Gainsborough Ave.
Frank Dixon Clo. 86 B1
   SE21
Frank Dixon Way 86 B1
   SE21
Frank St. E13 60 G4
Frank Trowell Ct., 81 A1
   Felt.
Frankfurt Rd. SE24 76 J5
Frankham St. SE8 69 A7
Frankland Clo. SE16 68 F4
Frankland Clo., 34 J5
   Wdf.Grn.
Frankland Rd. E4 34 A5
Frankland Rd. SW7 14 E6
Frankland Rd. SW7 66 G3
Franklin Clo. N20 23 F7
Franklin Clo. SE27 85 H3
Franklin Clo., 92 A3
   Kings.T.
Franklin Cres., 94 C4
   Mitch.
Franklin Ho. NW9 38 F7
Franklin Pas. SE9 79 B3
   Phineas Pett Rd.
Franklin Rd. SE20 86 F7
Franklin Rd., Bexh. 80 E1
Franklin Sq. W14 66 C5
   Marchbank Rd.
Franklin St. E3 60 B3
   Leonard St.
Franklin St. N15 41 B6
Franklin Way, Croy. 101 E1
Franklin's Row SW3 19 A3
Franklin's Row SW3 66 J5
Franklyn Gdns., 35 G6
   Ilf.
Franklyn Rd. NW10 47 F7
Franklyn Rd., Walt. 90 A6
Franks Ave., N.Mal. 92 C4
Frankswood Ave., 97 E5
   Orp.
Franlaw Cres. N13 32 J4
Fransfield Gro. 86 E3
   SE26
Frant Clo. SE20 86 F7
Frant Rd., Th.Hth. 94 H5
Franthorne Way SE6 87 B2
Fraser Clo. E6 61 B6
   Linton Gdns.
Fraser Clo., Bex. 89 J1
   Dartford Rd.
Fraser Ho., Brent. 64 J5
Fraser Rd. E17 42 B5
Fraser Rd. N9 33 E3
Fraser Rd., Erith 71 J3
Fraser Rd., Grnf. 55 E1
Fraser St. W4 65 E5
Frating Cres., 34 H6
   Wdf.Grn.
Frazer Ave., Ruis. 45 C5
Frazier St. SE1 16 E4
Frazier St. SE1 67 G2
Frean St. SE16 17 H5
Frean St. SE16 68 D3

Fred Wigg Twr. E11 51 F2
Freda Corbett Clo. 21 H7
SE15
Frederic Ms. SW1 15 A4
Frederic St. E17 41 H5
Frederica Rd. E4 26 D7
Frederica Rd. N4 43 J7
Caledonian Rd.
Frederick Clo. W2 10 H5
Frederick Clo. W2 57 H7
Frederick Clo. 100 C4
Sutt.
Frederick Cres. SW9 67 H7
Frederick Gdns. 100 C5
Sutt.
Frederick Pl. SE18 70 E5
Frederick Rd. SE17 20 H5
Frederick Rd. 100 C5
Sutt.
Frederick St. WC1 8 C4
Frederick St. WC1 58 F3
Frederick Ter. E8 59 C1
Haggerston Rd.
Frederick's Pl. EC2 13 B4
Fredericks Pl. N12 31 F4
Frederick's Row EC1 8 G3
Freedom Clo. E17 41 H4
Freedom St. SW11 75 J2
Freegrove Rd. N7 49 E5
Freeland Pk. NW4 39 B2
Freeland Rd. W5 55 J7
Freelands Gro. 96 H1
Brom.
Freelands Rd. 96 H1
Brom.
Freeling St. N1 49 F7
Caledonian Rd.
Freeman Clo. 45 E7
Nthlt.
Freeman Rd., Mord. 93 G5
Fremantle Ave. 25 G5
Enf.
Freemasons Rd. E16 60 H5
Freemasons Rd. 102 B1
Croy.
Freesia Clo., Orp. 104 J5
Briarswood Way
Freethorpe Clo. 95 B1
SE19
Freke Rd. SW11 76 A3
Fremantle Rd., Belv. 71 G4
Fremantle Rd., Ilf. 43 F2
Fremantle St. SE17 21 D3
Fremantle St. SE17 68 B5
Fremont St. E9 59 F1
French Ordinary Ct. 59 B7
EC3
Crutched Friars
French Pl. E1 9 E5
French St., Sun. 90 C2
Frendsbury Rd. SE4 77 H4
Frensham Clo., 54 F4
Sthl.
Frensham Dr. SW15 83 F3
Frensham Dr., Croy. 103 C7
Frensham Rd. SE9 88 G2
Frensham St. SE15 21 J6
Frensham St. SE15 68 D6
Frere St. SW11 75 H2
Fresh Wf. Rd., 61 E1
Bark.
Freshfield Clo. SE13 78 D4
Marischal Rd.
Freshfield Dr. N14 24 B7
Freshfields, Croy. 95 J7
Freshford St. SW18 84 F3
Freshwater Clo. 85 A6
SW17
Freshwater Rd. 85 A6
SW17
Freshwater Rd., Dag. 53 D1
Rom.
Freshwell Ave., 44 C4
Rom.
Freshwood Clo. 96 B1
Beck.
Freston Gdns., Barn. 23 J5
Freston Pk. N3 39 C2
Freston Rd. W10 57 A7
Freston Rd. W11 57 A7
Freta Rd., Bexh. 80 F5
Frewin Rd. SW18 84 G1
Friar Ms. SE27 85 H3
Prioress Rd.
Friar Rd., Hayes 54 D4
Friar St. EC4 12 H4
Friars, The, Chig. 35 H4
Friars Ave. N20 31 H3
Friars Ave. SW15 83 F3
Friars Clo. N2 39 G4
Friars Clo., Nthlt. 54 D3
Broomcroft Ave.
Friars Gdns. W3 56 D6
St. Dunstans Ave.

Friars Gate Clo., 34 G4
Wdf.Grn.
Friars La., Rich. 73 G5
Friars Mead E14 69 C3
Friars Ms. SE9 79 D5
Friars Pl. La. W3 56 D7
Friars Pl. La. W3 61 A1
Friars Stile Rd., Rich. 10 I18
Friars Wk. N14 24 B7
Friars Way W3 71 D5
Friars Way W3 56 D6
Friary Clo. N12 31 H5
Friary Ct. SW1 15 G2
Friary Est. SE15 21 J6
Friary Est. SE15 68 D6
Friary Rd. N12 31 G4
Friary Rd. SE15 21 J6
Friary Rd. SE15 68 D7
Friary Rd. W3 56 D6
Friary Way N12 31 H4
Friday Hill E4 34 E2
Friday Hill E. E4 34 E3
Friday Hill W. E4 34 E2
Friday Rd., Mitch. 84 J7
Friday St. EC4 12 J5
Friday St. EC4 58 J7
Frideswide Pl. NW5 49 C5
Islip St.
Friend St. EC1 8 G3
Friend St. EC1 58 H3
Friendly St. SE8 78 A2
Friendly St. Ms. SE8 78 A2
Friendly St.
Friends Rd., Croy. 102 A3
Friendship Wk., 54 D3
Nthlt.
Wayfarer Rd.
Friern Barnet La. 31 J4
N11
Friern Barnet La. 31 F2
N20
Friern Barnet Rd. 31 J5
N11
Friern Ct. N20 31 G3
Friern Mt. Dr. N20 23 F7
Friern Pk. N12 31 F5
Friern Rd. SE22 77 D7
Friern Watch Ave. 31 F4
N12
Frigate Ms. SE8 69 A6
Watergate St.
Frimley Clo. SW19 84 B2
Frimley Clo., Croy. 103 C7
Frimley Ct., Sid. 89 C5
Frimley Cres. 103 C7
Croy.
Frimley Gdns., 93 H3
Mitch.
Frimley Rd., Chess. 98 G5
Frimley Rd., Ilf. 52 H3
Frimley Way E1 59 G4
Frimley Way, Wall. 101 E5
Frinton Clo., Wat. 28 B2
Frinton Dr., 34 D7
Wdf.Grn.
Frinton Ms., Ilf. 43 D6
Bramley Cres.
Frinton Rd. E6 61 A3
Frinton Rd. N15 41 B6
Frinton Rd. SW17 85 A6
Frinton Rd., Sid. 89 E2
Friston Path, Chig. 35 H5
Manford Way
Friston St. SW6 75 E2
Friswell Pl., Bexh. 80 G4
Frith Ct. NW7 31 B7
Frith La. NW7 31 B7
Frith Rd. E11 51 C4
Frith Rd., Croy. 101 J2
Frith St. W1 11 H4
Frith St. W1 58 D6
Fritham Clo., 92 E6
N.Mal.
Frithville Gdns. 65 J1
W12
Frizlands La., Dag. 53 H4
Frobisher Clo., Pnr. 36 D7
Frobisher Pas. E14 69 A1
North Colonnade
Frobisher Rd. E6 61 C6
Frobisher Rd. N8 40 G4
Frobisher St. SE10 69 E6
Froghall La., Chig. 35 G4
Frogley Rd. SE22 77 C4
Frogmore SW18 75 D5
Frogmore Clo., 100 A3
Sutt.
Frogmore Gdns. 100 B4
Sutt.
Frognal NW3 48 F5
Frognal Ave., Har. 37 C4

Frognal Ave., Sid. 89 A5
Frognal Clo. NW3 48 F5
Frognal
Frognal Ct. NW3 48 F6
Frognal Gdns. NW3 48 F4
Frognal La. NW3 48 E5
Frognal Par. NW3 48 F6
Frognal Pl., Sid. 88 A5
Frognal Ri. NW3 48 F3
Frognal Way NW3 48 F4
Froissart Rd. SE9 79 A5
Frome Rd. N15 40 H3
Westbury Ave.
Frome St. N1 8 J1
Frome St. N1 58 J2
Fromondes Rd., 100 B5
Sutt.
Frostic Wk. E1 13 H2
Froude St. SW8 76 B2
Fry Rd. E6 52 A7
Fry Rd. NW10 56 F1
Fryatt Rd. N17 33 A7
Fryatt St. E14 60 E6
Fryent Clo. NW9 38 A5
Fryent Cres. NW9 38 E6
Fryent Flds. NW9 38 E6
Fryent Gro. NW9 38 E6
Fryent Way NW9 38 A5
Frye's Bldgs. N1 8 F1
Frying Pan All. E1 13 F2
Fryston Ave., Croy. 102 D2
Fuchsia St. SE2 71 B5
Fulbeck Dr. NW9 38 E1
Fulbeck Way, Har. 36 J2
Fulbourne Rd. E17 42 C1
Fulbourne St. E1 59 E5
Durward St.
Fulbrook Ms. N19 49 C4
Junction Rd.
Fulbrook Rd. N19 49 C4
Junction Rd.
Fulbrooks Ave., 99 F1
Wor.Pk.
Fulford Gro., Wat. 28 B2
Fulford Rd., Epsom 99 D7
Fulford St. SE16 68 E2
Fulham Bdy. SW6 66 D7
Fulham Ct. SW6 66 D7
Fulham Rd.
Fulham High St. SW6 75 B2
Fulham Palace Rd. 66 A6
SW6
Fulham Palace Rd. 65 J5
W6
Fulham Pk. Gdns. 75 C2
SW6
Fulham Pk. Rd. SW6 75 C2
Fulham Rd. SW3 18 E4
Fulham Rd. SW3 66 G5
Fulham Rd. SW6 75 B2
Fulham Rd. SW10 18 D5
Fulham Rd. SW10 66 G5
Fuller Clo., Orp. 104 J5
Fuller Rd., Dag. 53 B3
Fuller St. E2 9 H5
Fuller St. NW4 38 J4
Fullers Ave., Surb. 98 J2
Fullers Ave., 34 F7
Wdf.Grn.
Fullers Rd. E18 42 F1
Fullers Way N., 98 J3
Surb.
Fullers Way S. 98 H4
Chess.
Fullers Wd., Croy. 103 A5
Fullerton Rd. SW18 75 F5
Fullerton Rd., 95 C7
Croy.
Fullwell Ave., Ilf. 43 C1
Fullwoods Ms. N1 9 C3
Fulmar Ct., Surb. 91 J6
Fulmead St. SW6 75 E1
Fulmer Clo., Hmptn. 81 E5
Fulmer Rd. E16 61 A5
Fulmer Way W13 64 E3
Fulready Rd. E10 42 D5
Fulstone Clo., 72 F4
Houns.
Fulthorp Rd. SE3 78 F2
Fulton Ms. W2 10 C5
Fulton Rd., Wem. 47 A3
Fulwell Pk. Ave., 81 H2
Twick.
Fulwell Rd., Tedd. 82 A4
Fulwood Ave., Wem. 55 J2
Fulwood Gdns., 73 C6
Twick.
Fulwood Pl. WC1 12 D2
Fulwood Wk. SW19 84 B1
Furber St. W6 65 H3

Furham Feild, Pnr. 28 G7
Furley Rd. SE15 68 D7
Furlong Clo., Wall. 101 A1
Furlong Rd. N7 49 G6
Furmage St. SW18 75 E7
Furneaux Ave. SE27 85 H5
Furness Rd. NW10 56 G2
Furness Rd. SW6 75 E2
Furness Rd., Har. 36 H7
Furness Rd., Mord. 88 F1
Furnival St. EC4 12 E3
Furnival St. EC4 58 G6
Furrow La. E9 50 F0
Fursby Ave. N3 31 D6
Further Acre NW9 38 F2
Further Grn. Rd. 78 E7
SE6
Furtherfield Clo. 94 G6
Croy.
Furze Clo., Wat. 28 C5
Furze Fm. Clo., Rom. 44 E2
Furze La., Th.Hth. 94 J3
Furze St. E3 60 A5
Furzedown Dr. SW17 85 B5
Furzedown Rd. SW17 85 B5
Furzefield Clo. 88 E6
Chis.
Furzefield Rd. SE3 69 H7
Furzehill Rd., 22 A3
Borwd.
Furzewood, Sun. 90 A1
Fyfield Clo., Brom. 96 D4
Fyfield Rd. E17 42 D3
Fyfield Rd. SW9 76 G3
Fyfield Rd., Enf. 25 B3
Fyfield Rd., 34 J7
Wdf.Grn.
Fynes St. SW1 19 H1
Fynes St. SW1 67 D4

G

Gable Clo. SE26 86 E4
Lawrie Pk. Ave.
Gable Clo., Pnr. 28 G7
Gable Ct. SE26 86 E5
Lawrie Pk. Ave.
Gables Clo. SE5 77 B1
Gables Clo. SE12 87 G1
Gabriel Clo., Felt. 81 D4
Gabriel St. SE23 77 G7
Gabrielle Clo., Wem. 46 J3
Gabrielle Ct. NW3 48 G6
Gaddesden Ave., 46 J6
Wem.
Gade Clo., Hayes 63 B1
Gadesden Rd., 99 C6
Epsom
Gadsbury Clo. NW9 38 F6
Gadwall Clo. E16 60 H6
Freemasons Rd.
Gadwall Way SE28 70 G2
Goldfinch Rd.
Gage Rd. E16 60 E5
Malmesbury Rd.
Gage St. WC1 12 B1
Gainford St. N1 58 G1
Richmond Ave.
Gainsborough Ave. 52 D5
E12
Gainsborough Clo., 87 A7
Beck.
Gainsborough Clo., 98 B3
Esher
Lime Tree Ave.
Gainsborough Ct. 31 E5
N12
Gainsborough Gdns. 48 G3
NW3
Gainsborough Gdns. 39 C7
NW11
Gainsborough Gdns., 37 J2
Edg.
Gainsborough Gdns., 46 B5
Grnf.
Gainsborough Gdns., 73 A5
Islw.
Gainsborough Ms. 86 E3
SE26
Panmure Rd.
Gainsborough Rd. 42 E7
E11
Gainsborough Rd. 60 E3
E15
Gainsborough Rd. 31 E5
N12
Gainsborough Rd. W4 65 F4
Gainsborough Rd., 53 B4
Dag.
Gainsborough Rd., 92 D6
N.Mal.
Gainsborough Rd., 73 J2
Rich.

Gainsborough Rd., 35 B6
Wdf.Grn.
Gainsborough Sq., 80 D3
Bexh.
Regency Way
Gainsford Rd. E17 41 J4
Gainsford St. SE1 17 F3
Gainsford St. SE1 68 C2
Gairloch Rd. SE5 77 B2
Gaisford St. NW5 49 C6
Gaitskell Rd. SE9 88 F1
Galahad Rd., Brom. 87 G3
Galata Rd. SW13 65 G7
Galatea Sq. SE15 77 E3
Scylla Rd.
Galbraith St. E14 69 C3
Galdana Ave., Barn. 23 F3
Gale Clo., Hmptn. 81 E6
Stewart Clo.
Gale Clo., Mitch. 93 G3
Gale St. E3 60 A5
Gale St., Dag. 53 C5
Galeborough Ave., 34 D7
Wdf.Grn.
Galen Pl. WC1 12 B2
Galena Rd. W6 65 H4
Gales Gdns. E2 59 E3
Gales Way, Wdf.Grn. 35 B7
Galesbury Rd. SW18 75 F6
Galgate Clo. SW19 84 B1
Gallants Fm. Rd., 23 H7
Barn.
Galleon Clo. SE16 68 G2
Kinburn St.
Gallery Gdns., 54 D2
Nthlt.
Gallery Rd. SE21 86 A1
Galleywall Rd. SE16 68 E4
Gallia Rd. N5 49 H5
Galliard Clo. N9 25 F6
Galliard Rd. N9 33 D1
Gallions Clo., 62 A3
Bark.
Gallions Rd. SE7 69 H4
Gallon Clo. SE7 69 J4
Gallop, The, 102 E7
S.Croy.
Gallosson Rd. SE18 70 H4
Galloway Rd. W12 65 G1
Gallus Clo. N21 24 F6
Gallus Sq. SE3 78 H3
Galpins Rd., 94 E5
Th.Hth.
Galsworthy Ave. SW15 75 C5
Galway St. EC1 9 A4
Galway St. EC1 58 J3
Gambetta St. SW8 76 B2
Gambia St. SE1 16 H2
Gambole Rd. SW17 84 H4
Games Rd., Barn. 23 J3
Gamlen Rd. SW15 75 A4
Gander Grn. La., 100 B2
Sutt.
Gandhi Clo. E17 42 A6
Gane Clo., Wall. 101 E7
Kingsford Ave.
Ganton St. W1 11 F5
Ganton Wk., Wat. 28 E4
Woodhall La.
Gantshill Cres., Ilf. 43 D5
Gantshill Cross, Ilf. 43 D6
Eastern Ave.
Gap Rd. SW19 84 D5
Garage Rd. W3 56 A6
Garbutt Pl. W1 11 C1
Gard St. EC1 8 H3
Garden Ave., Bexh. 80 G3
Garden Ave., Mitch. 85 B7
Garden City, Edg. 30 A6
Garden Clo. E4 34 A5
Garden Clo. SE12 87 H3
Garden Clo. SW15 74 H7
Garden Clo., Barn. 22 H4
Garden Clo., Hmptn. 81 F5
Garden Clo., Nthlt. 54 E1
Garden Clo., Wall. 101 E5
Garden Ct. EC4 12 E5

Garden Ct. SE15 77 C1
Sumner Est.
Garden Ct., Rich. 73 J1
Lichfield Rd.
Garden Ct., W.Mol. 90 H4
Avern Rd.
Garden La. SW2 85 F1
Garden La., Brom. 87 H6
Garden Ms. W2 57 D7
Linden Gdns.
Garden Rd. NW8 6 D3
Garden Rd. NW8 68 D2
Garden Rd. SE20 95 F1
Garden Rd., Brom. 87 H7
Garden Rd., Rich. 74 A3
Garden Rd., Walt. 90 B6
Garden Row SE1 16 G6
Garden Row SE1 67 H3
Garden St. E1 59 G5
Garden Ter. SW1 19 H3
Garden Wk. EC2 9 D4
Garden Wk., Beck. 95 J1
Hayne Rd.
Garden Way NW10 47 C6
Gardeners La. EC4 12 J5
Gardeners Rd. E3 59 G2
Gardeners Rd., 101 H1
Croy.
Gardenia Rd., Enf. 28 B5
Gardenia Way, 34 H5
Wdf.Grn.
Harts Gro.
Gardens, The SE22 77 D4
Gardens, The, Beck. 96 C1
Gardens, The, Har. 36 J6
Gardens, The, Pnr. 36 F6
Gardiner Ave. NW2 47 J5
Gardiner Clo. E11 42 H6
Gardner Gro., Felt. 81 F2
Gardner Rd. E13 60 H4
Gardnor Rd. NW3 48 G4
Flask Wk.
Garendon Gdns., 93 E7
Mord.
Garendon Rd., Mord. 93 D7
Gareth Clo., 100 A2
Wor.Pk.
Burnham Dr.
Gareth Gro., Brom. 87 G4
Garfield Rd. E4 34 D1
Garfield Rd. E13 60 F4
Garfield Rd. SW11 76 A3
Garfield Rd. SW19 84 F5
Garfield Rd., Enf. 25 F4
Garfield Rd., Twick. 82 D1
York St.
Garford St. E14 60 A7
Garganey Wk. SE28 62 C7
Garibaldi St. SE18 70 H4
Garland Dr., 100 A2

Garrick Clo., Rich. 73 G5
The Grn.
Garrick Cres., 102 B2
Croy.
Garrick Dr. NW4 38 J2
Garrick Dr. SE28 70 G3
Broadwater Rd.
Garrick Gdns., 90 G3
W.Mol.
Garrick Pk. NW4 39 A2
Garrick Rd. NW9 38 F6
Garrick Rd., Grnf. 54 H4
Garrick Rd., Rich. 74 A2
Garrick St. WC2 12 A5
Garrick St. WC2 58 E7
Garrick Way NW4 39 A4
Garrison Clo. SE18 70 D7
Red Lion La.
Garrison La., 98 G7
Chess.
Garside Clo. SE28 70 G3
Goosander Way
Garside Clo., 81 H6
Hmptn.
Garsington Ms. SE4 77 J3
Garth, The, Hmptn. 81 H6
Uxbridge Rd.
Garth, The, Har. 37 J6
Garth Clo. W4 65 D5
Garth Clo., 82 J5
Kings.T.
Garth Clo., Mord. 93 A7
Garth Clo., Ruis. 45 D1
Garth Ct. W4 65 D5
Garth Rd.
Garth Ms. W5 55 H4
Greystoke Gdns.
Garth Rd. NW2 48 C2
Garth Rd. W4 65 D6
Garth Rd., Kings.T. 82 J5
Garth Rd., Mord. 92 J6
Garth Rd. Ind. Est., 93 A7
Mord.
Garthland Dr., Barn. 22 H5
Garthorne Rd. SE23 77 G7
Garthside, Rich. 82 H5
Garthway N12 31 H6
Gartmoor Gdns. 84 C1
SW19
Gartmore Rd., Ilf. 52 J2
Garton Pl. SW18 75 F6
Gartons Clo., Enf. 25 F4
Gartons Way SW11 75 F3
Garvary Rd. E16 60 H4
Garway Rd. W2 10 A4
Garway Rd. W2 57 E6
Gascoigne Gdns., 34 E7
Wdf.Grn.
Gascoigne Pl. E2 9 F3
Gascoigne Pl. E2 59 C3
Gascoigne Rd., 61 F1
Bark.
Gascony Ave. NW6 48 D7
Gascoyne Rd. E9 50 G7
Gaselee St. E14 60 C7
Gasholder Pl. SE11 20 D4
Gaskarth Rd. SW12 78 B6
Gaskarth Rd., Edg. 38 C1
Gaskell Rd. N6 39 J6
Gaskell St. SW4 76 E2
Gaskin St. N1 58 H1
Gaspar Clo. SW5 18 B1
Gaspar Ms. SW5 18 B1
Gassiot Rd. SW17 84 J4
Gassiot Way, Sutt. 100 G3
Gastein Rd. W6 66 A6
Gaston Bell Clo., 73 J3
Rich.
Gaston Rd., Mitch. 94 A3
Gataker St. SE16 68 E3
Gatcombe Rd. N19 49 D3
Gate Clo., Borwd. 22 C1
Gate End, Nthwd. 28 A7
Gate Ms. SW7 14 H4
Gate Ms. SW7 66 H2
Gate St. WC2 12 C3
Gateforth St. NW8 6 G6
Gateforth St. NW8 57 H4
Gatehouse Clo., 83 C7
Kings.T.
Gateley Rd. SW9 76 F3
Gates Grn. Rd., 103 H4
Kes.
Gates Grn. Rd., 103 F3
W.Wick.
Gatesborough St. 9 D5
EC2
Gateside Rd. SW17 84 J3
Gatestone Rd. SE19 86 B6
Gateway SE17 21 A5
Gateway Ind. Est. 56 F3
NW10

Gateway Ms. E8 50 C5
Shacklewell La.
Gateways, The SW3 18 H2
Gatfield Gro., 81 G2
Felt.
Gathorne Rd. N22 40 G2
Gathorne St. E2 59 G2
Mace St.
Gatley Ave., Epsom 99 B5
Gatliff Rd. SW1 19 D4
Gatliff Rd. SW1 67 B5
Gatling Rd. SE2 71 A5
Gatting Clo., Edg. 30 C7
Pavilion Way
Gatton Rd. SW17 84 H4
Gattons Way, Sid. 89 F4
Gatward Clo. N21 24 H6
Gatward Grn. N9 33 C2
Gatwick Rd. SW18 75 C7
Gauden Clo. SW4 76 D3
Gauden Rd. SW4 76 D2
Gaunt St. SE1 16 H5
Gaunt St. SE1 67 J3
Gauntlet Clo., 45 F7
Nthlt.
Gauntlett Ct., Wem. 46 E5
Gauntlett Rd., Sutt. 100 G5
Gautrey Rd. SE15 77 F2
Gautrey Sq. E6 61 C6
Truesdale Rd.
Gavel St. SE17 21 C1
Gaverick St. E14 69 A4
Gavestone Cres. 78 H7
SE12
Gavestone Rd. SE12 78 H7
Gaviller Pl. E5 50 E4
Clarence Rd.
Gavin St. SE18 70 H4
Gavina Clo., Mord. 93 G5
Gawber St. E2 59 F3
Gawsworth Clo. E15 51 E5
Ash Rd.
Gawthorne Ave. 31 B5
NW7
Lane App.
Gay Clo. NW2 47 H5
Gay Gdns., Dag. 53 J4
Gay Rd. E15 60 D2
Gay St. SW15 75 A3
Waterman St.
Gaydon Ho. W2 10 A1
Gaydon Ho. W2 57 E5
Gaydon La. NW9 38 E1
Gayfere Rd., Epsom 99 G5
Gayfere Rd., Ilf. 43 C3
Gayfere St. SW1 16 A6
Gayfere St. SW1 67 E3
Gayford Rd. W12 65 F2
Gayhurst SE17 21 C5
Gayhurst Rd. E8 50 D7
Gaylor Rd., Nthlt. 45 F5
Gaynes Hill Rd., 35 B6
Wdf.Grn.
Gaynesford Rd. SE23 86 G2
Gaynesford Rd., 100 J7
Cars.
Gaysham Ave., Ilf. 43 D5
Gaysham Hall, Ilf. 43 E3
Gayton Ct., Har. 37 C6
Gayton Cres. NW3 48 G4
Gayton Rd. NW3 48 G4
Gayton Rd. SE2 71 C3
Gayton Rd., Har. 37 C6
Gayville Rd. SW11 75 J6
Gaywood Clo. SW2 85 F1
Gaywood Est. SE1 16 H6
Gaywood Rd. E17 42 A3
Gaywood St. SE1 16 H6
Gaza St. SE17 20 G4
Geariesville Gdns., 43 E4
Ilf.
Geary Rd. NW10 47 G5
Geary St. N7 49 F5
GEC Est., Wem. 46 G3
Gedeney Rd. N17 40 J1
Gedling Pl. SE1 17 G5
Gedling Pl. SE1 68 C3
Gee St. EC1 8 J5
Gee St. EC1 58 J4
Geere Rd. E15 60 F7
Gees Ct. W1 11 C4
Geffrye Ct. N1 9 E2
Geffrye St. E2 9 E2
Geffrye St. E2 59 C2
Geldart Rd. SE15 68 F7
Geldeston Rd. E5 50 D2
Gellatly Rd. SE14 77 F2
Gelston Pt. E1 59 E6
Gemini Gro., Nthlt. 54 E3
Javelin Way
General Gordon Pl. 70 E4
SE18

General Wolfe Rd. 78 D1
  SE10
Genesta Rd. SE18 70 E6
Geneva Dr. SW9 76 G4
Geneva Gdns., Rom. 44 E5
Geneva Rd., 91 H4
  Kings.T.
Geneva Rd., Th.Hth. 94 J5
Genever Clo. E4 34 A5
Genista Rd. N18 33 E5
Genoa Ave. SW15 74 J5
Genoa Rd. SE20 95 F1
Genotin Rd., Enf. 25 A3
Genotin Ter., Enf. 25 A3
  Genotin Rd.
Gentian Row SE13 78 C1
  Sparta Rd.
Gentlemans Row, 24 J3
  Enf.
Gentry Gdns. E13 60 G4
  Whitwell Rd.
Geoffrey Clo. SE5 76 J2
Geoffrey Gdns. E6 61 B2
Geoffrey Rd. SE4 77 J3
George Beard Rd. 68 J4
  SE8
George Comberton 52 D5
  Wk. E12
  Gainsborough Ave.
George Ct. WC2 12 B6
George Cres. N10 32 A7
George Downing Est. 50 C2
  N16
  Cazenove Rd.
George Fifth Way, 55 E1
  Grnf.
George V Ave., Pnr. 36 F1
George V Clo., Pnr. 36 G3
  George V Ave.
George Gros. Rd. 95 D1
  SE20
George Inn Yd. SE1 17 B2
George La. E18 42 G2
George La. SE13 78 C6
George La., Brom. 103 H1
George Lansbury Ho. 40 G1
  N22
  Progress Way
George Loveless Ho. 9 G3
  E2
George Ms. NW1 7 F4
George Rd. E4 34 A6
George Rd., 83 B7
  Kings.T.
George Rd., N.Mal. 92 F4
George Row SE16 17 H4
George Row SE16 68 D2
George Sq. SW19 93 C3
  Mostyn Rd.
George St. E16 60 F6
George St. EC4 13 B4
George St. W1 10 J3
George St. W1 57 J6
George St. W7 64 B1
  The Bdy.
George St., Bark. 52 F7
George St., Croy. 101 J2
George St., Houns. 72 F2
George St., Rich. 73 G5
George St., Sthl. 63 E4
George St., Sutt. 100 E5
George Wyver Clo. 75 B7
  SW19
  Beaumont Rd.
George Yd. EC3 13 C4
George Yd. W1 11 C5
George Yd. W1 58 A7
Georges Rd. N7 49 F5
Georges Rd., Brom. 97 C3
Georges Sq. SW6 66 C6
  North End Rd.
Georgetown Clo. 86 A5
  SE19
  St. Kitts Ter.
Georgette Pl. SE10 69 C7
  King George St.
Georgeville Gdns., 43 E4
  Ilf.
Georgia Rd., N.Mal. 92 C4
Georgia Rd., Th.Hth. 94 H1
Georgian Clo., 96 H7
  Brom.
Georgian Clo., Stan. 29 D7
Georgian Ct., Wem. 44 A4
Georgian Way, Har. 46 A2
Georgiana St. NW1 58 C1
Georgina Gdns. E2 9 G3
Geraint Rd., Brom. 87 G4
Gerald Ms. SW1 19 C1
Gerald Rd. E16 60 F4
Gerald Rd. SW1 19 C1
Gerald Rd. SW1 44 A4
Gerald Rd., Dag. 53 F2

Geraldine Rd. SW18 75 F5
Geraldine Rd. W4 65 A6
Geraldine St. SE11 16 G6
Geraldine St. SE11 67 H3
Gerard Ave., Houns. 72 G7
  Redfern Ave.
Gerard Rd. SW13 74 F1
Gerard Rd., Har. 37 D6
Gerards Clo. SE16 68 F5
Gerda Rd. SE9 88 F2
Germander Way E15 60 E3
Gernon Rd. E3 59 H2
Geron Way NW2 47 H2
Gerrard Gdns., Pnr. 36 A5
Gerrard Pl. W1 11 J5
Gerrard Rd. N1 8 G1
Gerrard Rd. N1 58 H2
Gerrard St. W1 11 J5
Gerrard St. W1 58 D7
Gerrards Clo. N14 24 C5
Gerridge St. SE1 16 F5
Gerridge St. SE1 67 G3
Gerry Raffles Sq. 51 D6
  E15
  Salway Rd.
Gertrude Rd., Belv. 71 G4
Gertrude St. SW10 18 D6
Gertrude St. SW10 66 F6
Gervase Clo., Wem. 47 C3
Gervase Rd., Edg. 38 C1
Gervase St. SE15 68 E7
Ghent St. SE6 87 A2
Ghent Way E8 50 C6
Giant Tree Hill 29 A1
  (Bushey), Wat.
Gibbard Ms. SW19 84 A5
Gibbins Rd. E15 51 C7
Gibbon Rd. SE15 77 F2
Gibbon Rd. W3 56 E7
Gibbon Rd., 91 H1
  Kings.T.
Gibbon Wk. SW15 74 G4
  Swinburne Rd.
Gibbons Rd. NW10 47 E6
Gibbs Ave. SE19 86 A5
Gibbs Clo. SE19 86 A5
Gibbs Couch, Wat. 28 D3
Gibbs Grn. W14 66 C5
Gibbs Grn., Edg. 30 C5
Gibbs Rd. N18 33 F4
Gibbs Sq. SE19 86 A5
Gibraltar Wk. E2 9 G4
Gibraltar Wk. E2 59 C3
Gibson Clo. E1 59 F4
  Colebert Ave.
Gibson Clo., Chess. 98 F6
Gibson Clo., Islw. 73 A3
Gibson Gdns. N16 50 C2
  Northwold Rd.
Gibson Rd. SE11 20 D2
Gibson Rd. SE11 67 F4
Gibson Rd., Dag. 53 C1
Gibson Rd., Sutt. 100 E5
Gibson Sq. N1 58 G1
Gibson St. SE10 69 E5
Gibson's Hill SW16 85 G7
Gideon Clo., Belv. 71 H4
Gideon Rd. SW11 76 A3
Giesbach Rd. N19 49 C2
Giffard St. N18 33 B5
Giffin St. SE8 69 A7
Gifford Gdns. W7 55 A5
Gifford St. N1 49 E7
Gift La. E15 60 F1
Giggs Hill Gdns., 98 D1
  T.Ditt.
Giggs Hill Rd., 91 D7
  T.Ditt.
Gilbert Gro., Edg. 38 D1
Gilbert Ho. SE8 69 A6
  McMillan St.
Gilbert Pl. WC1 12 A2
Gilbert Rd. SE11 20 F2
Gilbert Rd. SE11 67 G4
Gilbert Rd. SW19 84 F7
Gilbert Rd., Belv. 71 G3
Gilbert Rd., Brom. 87 G7
Gilbert Rd., Pnr. 36 D4
Gilbert St. E15 51 F7
Gilbert St. W1 11 C4
Gilbert St. W1 58 A6
Gilbert St., Houns. 72 J3
  High St.
Gilbey Rd. SW17 84 H4
Gilbourne Rd. SE18 70 J6
Gilda Ave., Enf. 25 H5
Gilda Cres. N16 50 D1
Gildea St. W1 11 E2
Gilden Cres. NW5 49 A5
Gilders Rd., Chess. 98 J7
Giles Coppice SE19 86 C4
Gilkes Cres. SE21 77 B6
Gilkes Pl. SE21 77 B6

Gill Ave. E16 60 G6
Gill St. E14 59 J7
Gillan Grn. 28 J2
  (Bushey), Wat.
Gillender St. E3 60 C4
Gillender St. E14 60 C4
Gillespie Rd. N5 49 G3
Gillett Ave. E6 61 B7
Gillett Pl. N16 50 B5
Gillett Rd., Th.Hth. 95 A4
Gillett Rd. N16 50 B5
Gillett St. N16 58 C2
Gillham Ter. N17 33 D6
Gillian Pk. Rd., 100 C1
  Sutt.
Gillian St. SE13 78 B5
Gillies St. NW5 49 A5
Gilling Ct. NW3 48 H6
Gillingham Ms. SW1 19 F1
Gillingham Rd. NW2 48 B3
Gillingham Row SW1 19 F1
Gillingham St. SW1 19 E1
Gillingham St. SW1 67 C4
Gillison Wk. SE16 17 J5
Gillman Dr. E15 60 F1
Gillum Clo., Barn. 31 J1
Gilmore Rd. SE13 78 D4
Gilpin Ave. SW14 74 D4
Gilpin Clo., Mitch. 93 H2
Gilpin Cres. N18 33 C5
Gilpin Cres., Twick. 72 H7
Gilpin Rd. E5 50 H4
Gilsland Rd., 95 A4
  Th.Hth.
Gilstead Ho., Bark. 62 B2
Gilston Rd. SW10 18 D4
Gilston Rd. SW10 66 F5
Gilton Rd. SE6 87 E3
Giltspur St. EC1 12 H3
Giltspur St. EC1 58 H6
Gilwell La. E4 26 D4
Gippeswyck Clo., 36 D1
  Pnr.
  Uxbridge Rd.
Gipsy Hill SE19 86 B5
Gipsy La. SW15 74 G3
Gipsy Rd., Well. 80 D1
Gipsy Rd. SE27 85 J4
Gipsy Rd. Gdns. 85 J4
  SE27
Giralda Clo. E16 61 A5
  Fulmer Rd.
Giraud St. E14 60 B6
Girdlers Rd. W14 66 A4
Girdlestone Wk. N19 49 C2
Girdwood Rd. SW18 75 B7
Girling Way, Felt. 72 A3
Gironde Rd. SW6 66 C7
Girton Ave. NW9 38 A3
Girton Clo., Nthlt. 45 J6
Girton Gdns., Croy. 103 B3
Girton Rd. SE26 86 G5
Girton Rd., Nthlt. 45 J6
Girton Vill. N10 57 A6
  Cambridge Gdns.
Gisburn Rd. N8 40 F4
Gissing Wk. N1 49 G7
  Lofting Rd.
Given Wilson Wk. 60 F2
  E13
  Stride Rd.
Gladbeck Way, Enf. 24 H5
Gladding Rd. E12 52 A4
Glade, The N21 24 F6
Glade, The SE7 69 J7
Glade, The, Brom. 97 A2
Glade, The, Croy. 95 G5
Glade, The, Enf. 24 G2
  Chase Ridings
Glade, The, Epsom 99 G5
Glade, The, Ilf. 43 C1
Glade, The, W.Wick. 103 B3
Glade, The, 34 H3
  Wdf.Grn.
Glade Clo., Surb. 98 G2
Glade Ct., Ilf. 43 C1
  The Glade
Glade Gdns., Croy. 95 H7
Glade La., Sthl. 63 H2
Glades Shop. Cen., 96 B2
  The, Brom.
Gladeside N21 24 F7
Gladeside, Croy. 95 G7
Gladeside Clo., 98 G7
  Chess.
  Leatherhead Rd.
Gladesmore Rd. N15 41 C6
Gladeswood Rd., 71 H4
  Belv.
Gladiator St. SE23 77 H7

Glading Ter. N16 50 C3
Gladioli Clo., Hmptn. 81 G6
  Gresham Rd.
Gladsdale Dr., Pnr. 36 B4
Gladsmuir Rd. N19 49 C1
Gladsmuir Rd., 23 B2
  Barn.
Gladstone Ave. E12 52 B7
Gladstone Ave. N22 40 B1
Gladstone Ave., 72 A6
  Felt.
Gladstone Ave., 73 A7
  Twick.
Gladstone Ms. SE20 86 F7
Gladstone Pk. Gdns. 47 H4
  NW2
Gladstone Pl. E3 59 J2
  Roman Rd.
Gladstone Pl., 23 A4
  Barn.
Gladstone Rd. SW19 84 D7
Gladstone Rd. W4 65 D3
  Acton La.
Gladstone Rd., 34 H1
  Buck.H.
Gladstone Rd., 95 A7
  Croy.
Gladstone Rd., 92 A3
  Kings.T.
Gladstone Rd., Orp. 104 F5
Gladstone Rd., 63 E2
  Sthl.
Gladstone Rd., 98 G2
  Surb.
Gladstone St. SE1 16 G5
Gladstone St. SE1 67 H3
Gladstone Ter. SE27 85 J4
Gladstone Ter. SW8 76 B1
Gladstone Way, Har. 37 B3
Gladwell Rd. N8 40 F6
Gladwell Rd., Brom. 87 G6
Gladwyn Rd. SW15 75 A3
Gladys Rd. NW6 48 D7
Glaisher St. SE10 69 C7
  Straightsmouth
Glamis Pl. E1 59 F7
Glamis Rd. E1 59 F7
Glamis Way, Nthlt. 45 J6
Glamorgan Clo., 94 E3
  Mitch.
Glamorgan Rd., 82 F7
  Kings.T.
Glanfield Rd., 95 J4
  Beck.
Glanleam Rd., Stan. 29 G4
Glanville Rd. SW2 76 E5
Glanville Rd., 96 H3
  Brom.
Glasbrook Ave., 81 F1
  Twick.
Glasbrook Rd. SE9 79 A7
Glaserton Rd. N16 41 B7
Glasford St. SW17 84 J6
Glasgow Ho. W9 6 B2
Glasgow Rd. E13 60 H2
Glasgow Rd. N18 33 E5
  Aberdeen Rd.
Glasgow Ter. SW1 19 F4
Glasgow Ter. SW1 67 C5
Glass St. E2 59 E4
  Coventry Rd.
Glass Yd. SE18 70 D3
Glasse Clo. W13 55 D7
Glasshill St. SE1 16 H3
Glasshill St. SE1 67 H2
Glasshouse All. EC4 14 E3
Glasshouse St. W1 11 G6
Glasshouse St. W1 58 C7
Glasshouse Wk. 20 B3
  SE11
Glasshouse Yd. EC1 8 J6
Glasslyn Rd. N8 40 D5
Glassmill La., 96 F2
  Brom.
Glastonbury Ave., 35 A7
  Wdf.Grn.
Glastonbury Rd. N9 33 D1
Glastonbury Rd., 93 D7
  Mord.
Glastonbury St. NW6 48 C5
Glaucus St. E3 60 B5
Glazbury Rd. W14 66 B4
Glazebrook Clo. 86 A2
  SE21
Glazebrook Rd., 82 C7
  Tedd.
Glebe, The SE3 78 E3
Glebe, The SW16 85 D4
Glebe, The, Chis. 97 F1

Glebe, The, Wor.Pk.	99	F1
Glebe Ave., Enf.	24	H3
Glebe Ave., Har.	37	H3
Glebe Ave., Mitch.	93	H2
Glebe Ave., Ruis.	45	B6
Glebe Ave., Wdf.Grn.	34	G6
Glebe Clo. W4	65	E5
Glebe St.		
Glebe Ct. W7	55	A7
Glebe Ct., Mitch.	93	J3
Glebe Ct., Stan.	29	F5
Glebe Rd.		
Glebe Cres. NW4	38	J4
Glebe Cres., Har.	37	H3
Glebe Gdns., N.Mal.	92	E7
Glebe Ho. Dr.,	103	H1
Brom.		
Glebe Hyrst SE19	86	C4
Giles Coppice		
Glebe La., Barn.	22	G5
Glebe La., Har.	37	H4
Glebe Path, Mitch.	93	H3
Glebe Pl. SW3	**18**	**G5**
Glebe Pl. SW3	66	H6
Glebe Rd. E8	50	C7
Middleton Rd.		
Glebe Rd. N3	39	F1
Glebe Rd. N8	40	F4
Glebe Rd. NW10	47	F6
Glebe Rd. SW13	74	G2
Glebe Rd., Brom.	96	G1
Glebe Rd., Cars.	100	J6
Glebe Rd., Dag.	53	H6
Glebe Rd., Stan.	29	F5
Glebe Side, Twick.	73	C7
Glebe St. W4	65	E5
Glebe Ter. E3	60	A3
Bow Rd.		
Glebe Way, Felt.	81	G3
Glebe Way, W.Wick.	103	J3
Glebelands, W.Mol.	90	H5
Glebelands Ave. E18	42	G2
Glebelands Ave., Ilf.	43	G7
Glebelands Clo. SE5	77	B3
Grove Hill Rd.		
Glebelands Rd., Felt.	72	A7
Glebeway, Wdf.Grn.	34	J5
Gledhow Gdns. SW5	**18**	**C2**
Gledhow Gdns. SW5	66	F4
Gledstanes Rd. W14	66	B5
Gleed Ave.	29	A2
(Bushey), Wat.		
Gleeson Dr., Orp.	104	J5
Glegg Pl. SW15	75	A4
Glen, The, Brom.	96	E2
Glen, The, Croy.	102	G3
Glen, The, Enf.	24	H4
Glen, The, Orp.	104	C3
Glen, The, Pnr.	36	B9
Glen, The	36	E7
(Eastcote), Pnr.		
Glen, The, Sthl.	63	F6
Glen, The, Wem.	46	G4
Glen Albyn Rd.	84	A7
SW19		
Glen Cres.,	34	H6
Wdf.Grn.		
Glen Gdns., Croy.	101	H3
Glen Mill, Hmptn.	81	F5
Glen Ri., Wdf.Grn.	34	H6
Glen Rd. E13	60	J4
Glen Rd. E17	41	J5
Glen Rd., Chess.	98	H3
Glen Wk., Islw.	73	A5
Glena Mt., Sutt.	100	F4
Glenaffric Ave. E14	69	D4
Glenalmond Rd.,	37	H4
Har.		
Glenalvon Way SE18	70	B4
Glenarm Rd. E5	50	F5
Glenavon Clo.,	98	D6
Esher		
Glenavon Rd. E15	51	E7
Glenbarr Clo. SE9	79	E3
Dumbreck Rd.		
Glenbow Rd., Brom.	87	E6
Glenbrook N., Enf.	24	F4
Glenbrook Rd. NW6	48	D5
Glenbrook S., Enf.	24	F4
Glenbuck Ct., Surb.	91	G6
Glenbuck Rd.		
Glenbuck Rd., Surb.	91	G6
Glenburnie Rd.	84	H3
SW17		
Glencairn Dr. W5	55	F4
Glencairn Rd. SW16	85	E7
Glencairne Clo. E16	61	A5
Glencoe Ave., Ilf.	43	G7
Glencoe Dr., Dag.	53	G4
Glencoe Rd., Hayes	54	D4
Wat.		
Glencourse Grn.	28	D4
Caldwell Rd.		
Glendale Ave. N22	32	G7
Glendale Ave., Edg.	30	A4
Glendale Ave., Rom.	44	C7
Glendale Clo. SE9	79	D3
Dumbreck Rd.		
Glendale Dr. SW19	84	C5
Glendale Gdns.,	46	G1
Wem.		
Glendale Ms., Beck.	96	B1
Glendale Rd., Erith	71	J4
Glendale Way SE28	62	C7
Glendall St. SW9	76	F4
Glendarvon St.	75	A3
SW15		
Glendevon Clo., Edg.	30	B3
Tayside Dr.		
Glendish Rd. N17	41	D1
Glendor Gdns. NW7	30	D4
Glendower Gdns.	74	D3
SW14		
Glendower Rd.		
Glendower Pl. SW7	**18**	**E1**
Glendower Pl. SW7	66	G4
Glendower Rd. E4	34	D1
Glendower Rd. SW14	74	D3
Glendown Rd. SE2	71	A5
Glendun Rd. W3	56	E7
Gleneagle Ms. SW16	85	D5
Ambleside Ave.		
Gleneagle Rd. SW16	85	D6
Gleneagles, Stan.	29	E6
Gleneagles Clo.,	104	G1
Orp.		
Gleneagles Clo.,	29	E6
Stan.		
Gleneagles Clo.,	28	D4
Wat.		
Gleneagles Twr.,	54	J6
Sthl.		
Gleneldon Ms. SW16	85	E4
Gleneldon Rd. SW16	85	E4
Glenelg Rd. SW2	76	E5
Glenesk Rd. SE9	79	D3
Glenfarg Rd. SE6	87	D1
Glenfield Rd. SW12	85	C1
Glenfield Rd. W13	64	E2
Glenfield Ter. W13	64	E1
Glenfinlas Way SE5	**20**	**H7**
Glenfinlas Way SE5	77	J4
Glenforth St. SE10	69	F5
Glengall Causeway	69	A3
E14		
Ferry Rd.		
Glengall Gro. E14	69	C3
Glengall Rd. NW6	57	C1
Glengall Rd. SE15	**21**	**G5**
Glengall Rd. SE15	68	C5
Glengall Rd., Bexh.	80	E3
Glengall Rd., Edg.	30	B3
Glengall Rd.,	34	E6
Wdf.Grn.		
Glengall Ter. SE15	21	G5
Glengall Ter. SE15	68	C6
Glengarnock Ave.	69	C4
E14		
Glengarry Rd. SE22	77	B5
Glenham Dr., Ilf.	43	E5
Glenhaven Ave.,	22	A3
Borwd.		
Glenhead Clo. SE9	79	E3
Dumbreck Rd.		
Glenhill Clo. N3	39	D2
Glenhouse Rd. SE9	79	D5
Glenhurst Ave. NW5	49	A4
Glenhurst Ave., Bex.	89	F1
Glenhurst Ct. SE19	86	C5
Glenhurst Ri. SE19	85	J7
Glenhurst Rd. N12	31	G5
Glenhurst Rd.,	64	F6
Brent.		
Glenilla Rd. NW3	48	H6
Glenister Ho.,	63	B1
Hayes		
Glenister Pk. Rd.	85	D7
SW16		
Glenister Rd. SE10	69	F5
Glenister St. E16	70	D1
Glenlea Rd. SE9	79	D5
Glenloch Rd. NW3	48	H6
Glenloch Rd., Enf.	25	F2
Glenluce Rd. SE3	69	G6
Glenlyon Rd. SE9	79	D5
Glenmere Ave. NW7	30	G7
Glenmore Rd. NW3	48	H6
Glenmore Rd., Well.	70	J7
Glenmore Way, Bark.	62	A3
Glenmount Path	70	F5
SE18		
Raglan Rd.		
Glennie Rd. SE27	85	G3
Glenny Rd., Bark.	52	F6
Glenorchy Clo.,	54	E5
Hayes		
Glenparke Rd. E7	51	H6
Glenrosa St. SW6	75	F2
Glenrose Ct., Sid.	89	B5
Glenroy St. W12	56	J6
Glensdale Rd. SE4	77	J3
Glenshiel Rd. SE9	79	D5
Glenside, Chig.	35	E6
Glentanner Way	84	G3
SW17		
Aboyne Rd.		
Glentham Gdns.	65	H6
SW13		
Glentham Rd.		
Glentham Rd. SW13	65	G6
Glenthorne Ave.,	102	E1
Croy.		
Glenthorne Clo.,	100	D1
Sutt.		
Glenthorne Gdns.,	43	D3
Ilf.		
Glenthorne Gdns.,	100	D1
Sutt.		
Glenthorne Rd. E17	41	H5
Glenthorne Rd. N11	31	J5
Glenthorne Rd. W6	65	H4
Glenthorne Rd.,	91	J4
Kings.T.		
Glenthorpe Rd.,	93	A5
Mord.		
Glenton Rd. SE13	78	E4
Glentrammon Ave.,	104	J6
Orp.		
Glentrammon Clo.,	104	J5
Orp.		
Glentrammon Gdns.,	104	J6
Orp.		
Glentrammon Rd.,	104	J6
Orp.		
Glentworth St. NW1	**7**	**A6**
Glentworth St. NW1	57	J4
Glenure Rd. SE9	79	D5
Glenview SE2	71	D6
Glenview Rd., Brom.	97	A2
Glenville Gro. SE8	68	J7
Glenville Ms. SW18	75	E7
Glenville Rd.,	92	A1
Kings.T.		
Glenwood Ave. NW9	47	E1
Glenwood Clo., Har.	37	C5
Glenwood Gdns.,	43	D5
Ilf.		
Glenwood Gro. NW9	47	C1
Glenwood Rd. N15	40	H5
Glenwood Rd. NW7	30	E3
Glenwood Rd. SE6	86	J1
Glenwood Rd.,	99	G6
Epsom		
Glenwood Rd.,	73	A3
Houns.		
Glenwood Way,	95	G6
Croy.		
Glenworth Ave. E14	69	D4
Gliddon Rd. W14	66	B4
Glimpsing Grn.,	71	E3
Erith		
Global App. E3	60	B2
Hancock Rd.		
Globe Pond Rd. SE16	68	H1
Globe Rd. E1	59	G4
Globe Rd. E2	59	F3
Globe Rd. E15	51	F5
Globe Rd., Wdf.Grn.	34	J6
Globe Robe Wk. E14	69	C4
East Ferry Rd.		
Globe St. SE1	**17**	**B4**
Globe St. SE1	68	A2
Globe Ter. E2	59	F3
Globe Yd. W1	**11**	**D4**
Gloster Rd., N.Mal.	92	E4
Gloucester Ave. NW1	49	A7
Gloucester Ave.,	88	H2
Sid.		
Gloucester Ave.,	79	J4
Well.		
Gloucester Circ.	69	C7
SE10		
Gloucester Clo.	47	D7
NW10		
Gloucester Clo.,	98	D1
T.Ditt.		
Gloucester Ct. EC3	**13**	**E6**
Gloucester Ct.,	65	A7
Rich.		
Gloucester Cres.	58	B1
NW1		
Gloucester Dr. N4	49	H2
Gloucester Dr. NW11	39	D4
Gloucester Gdns.	39	C7
NW11		
Gloucester Gdns. W2	**10**	**B3**
Gloucester Gdns.,	24	A4
Barn.		
Gloucester Gdns.,	43	B7
Ilf.		
Gloucester Gdns.,	100	E2
Sutt.		
Gloucester Gate NW1	**7**	**D1**
Gloucester Gate NW1	58	B2
Gloucester Gate Ms.	**7**	**D1**
NW1		
Gloucester Gro.,	38	D1
Edg.		
Gloucester Gro. Est.	68	B6
SE15		
Gloucester Ho. N7	49	E3
Gloucester Ho. NW6	57	D2
Gloucester Ms. W2	**10**	**D4**
Gloucester Ms. W2	57	F6
Gloucester Ms. W.	**10**	**C4**
W2		
Gloucester Par., Sid.	80	A5
Gloucester Pl. NW1	**6**	**J5**
Gloucester Pl. NW1	57	J4
Gloucester Pl. W1	**11**	**A1**
Gloucester Pl. W1	57	J5
Gloucester Pl. Ms.	**11**	**A2**
W1		
Gloucester Rd. E10	42	A7
Gloucester Rd. E11	42	H5
Gloucester Rd. E12	52	C3
Gloucester Rd. E17	41	G2
Gloucester Rd. N17	41	A3
Gloucester Rd. N18	33	C5
Gloucester Rd. SW7	**14**	**C5**
Gloucester Rd. SW7	66	F3
Gloucester Rd. W3	65	C2
Gloucester Rd. W5	64	F2
Gloucester Rd.,	23	E5
Barn.		
Gloucester Rd.,	71	F5
Belv.		
Gloucester Rd.,	102	A1
Croy.		
Gloucester Rd.,	81	C1
Felt.		
Gloucester Rd.,	81	H7
Hmptn.		
Gloucester Rd., Har.	36	H5
Gloucester Rd.,	72	E4
Houns.		
Gloucester Rd.,	92	A2
Kings.T.		
Gloucester Rd., Rich.	65	A7
Gloucester Rd., Tedd.	81	J1
Gloucester Rd.,	81	J1
Twick.		
Gloucester Sq. E2	59	D1
Whiston Rd.		
Gloucester Sq. W2	**10**	**F4**
Gloucester Sq. W2	57	G6
Gloucester St. SW1	**19**	**F4**
Gloucester St. SW1	67	C5
Gloucester Ter. W2	**10**	**B3**
Gloucester Ter. W2	57	E6
Gloucester Wk. W8	66	D2
Gloucester Way EC1	**8**	**F4**
Gloucester Way EC1	58	G3
Glover Dr. N18	33	F6
Glover Rd., Pnr.	36	D6
Gloxinia Wk.,	81	G6
Hmptn.		
The Ave.		
Glycena Rd. SW11	75	J3
Glyn Ave., Barn.	23	G4
Glyn Clo. SE25	95	B2
Glyn Ct. SW16	85	G3
Glyn Dr., Sid.	89	B4
Glyn Rd. E5	50	G4
Glyn Rd., Enf.	25	F4
Glyn Rd., Wor.Pk.	100	A2
Glyn St. SE11	**20**	**C4**
Glynde Ms. SW3	**14**	**H6**
Glynde Rd., Bexh.	80	D3
Glynde St. SE4	77	J6
Glyndebourne Pk.,	104	E2
Orp.		
Glyndon Rd. SE18	70	F4
Glynfield Rd. NW10	47	E7
Glynne Rd. N22	40	G2
Glynwood Dr. SE23	86	F3
Goat La., Surb.	98	E2
Goat La., Mitch.	93	J7
Goat St. SE1	**17**	**F3**
Goat Wf., Brent.	64	H6
Goaters All. SW6	66	C7
Dawes Rd.		
Godalming Ave.,	101	E5
Wall.		
Godalming Rd. E14	60	B5
Godbold Rd. E15	60	E3
Goddard Rd., Beck.	95	G4
Godfrey Ave., Nthlt.	54	E1
Godfrey Ave., Twick.	73	A7
Godfrey Hill SE18	70	B4
Godfrey Rd. SE18	70	C4

Godfrey St. E15 60 C2
Abbey La.
Godfrey St. SW3 18 H3
Godfrey St. SW3 66 H5
Godfrey Way, Houns. 72 F7
Goding St. SE11 20 B4
Godley Rd. SW18 84 G1
Godliman St. EC4 12 J4
Godliman St. EC4 58 J6
Godman Rd. SE15 77 E2
Godolphin Clo. N13 32 H6
Godolphin Pl. W3 56 D7
Vyner Rd.
Godolphin Rd. W12 65 H1
Godson Rd., Croy. 101 G3
Godson St. N1 8 E1
Godstone Rd., Sutt. 100 F4
Godstone Rd., 73 D6
Twick.
Godstone Rd. SE2 71 B2
Godwin Clo. N1 9 A1
Godwin Clo., Epsom 99 C6
Godwin Ct. NW1 7 G1
Godwin Rd. E7 51 H4
Godwin Rd., Brom. 96 J3
Goffers Rd. SE3 78 E2
Goidel Clo., Wall. 101 D4
Golborne Gdns. W10 57 C4
Golborne Rd.
Golborne Ms. W10 57 B5
Portobello Rd.
Golborne Rd. W10 57 B5
Gold Hill, Edg. 30 D6
Gold La., Edg. 30 D6
Golda Clo., Barn. 23 A6
Goldbeaters Gro., 30 E6
Edg.
Goldcliff Clo., Mord. 93 D7
Goldcrest Clo. E16 61 A5
Sheerwater Rd.
Goldcrest Clo. SE28 62 C7
Goldcrest Ms. W5 55 G5
Montpelier Ave.
Goldcrest Way 28 J1
(Bushey), Wat.
Golden Ct., Rich. 73 G5
George St.
Golden La. EC1 8 J6
Golden La. EC1 58 J4
Golden La. Est. EC1 8 J6
Golden Manor W7 55 B7
Golden Plover Clo. 60 H6
E16
Maplin Rd.
Golden Sq. W1 11 G5
Golden Sq. W1 58 C7
Golden Yd. NW3 48 F4
Heath St.
Golders Clo., Edg. 30 B5
Golders Gdns. NW11 39 B7
Golders Grn. Cres. 39 C7
NW11
Golders Grn. Rd. 39 B6
NW11
Golders Manor Dr. 39 A6
NW11
Golders Pk. Clo. 48 D1
NW11
Golders Ri. NW4 39 A5
Golders Way NW11 39 C7
Goldfinch Rd. SE28 70 G3
Goldfinch Way, 22 A4
Borwd.
Siskin Clo.
Goldhawk Ms. W12 65 H2
Devonport Rd.
Goldhawk Rd. W6 65 F4
Goldhawk Rd. W12 65 G3
Goldhaze Clo., 35 A7
Wdf.Grn.
Goldhurst Ter. NW6 48 E7
Golding St. E1 13 J4
Golding St. E1 59 D6
Goldingham Ave., 27 F2
Loug.
Goldings Ri., Loug. 27 D1
Goldings Rd., Loug. 27 D1
**Goldington Cres. 7 H1
NW1**
Goldington Cres. 58 D2
NW1
Goldington Cres. 58 D2
Gdns. NW1
Goldington St. NW1 7 H1
Goldington St. NW1 58 D2
Goldman Clo. E2 9 H5
Goldman Clo. E2 59 D4
Goldney Rd. W9 57 D4
Goldsborough Cres. 34 B2
E4
Goldsborough Rd. 76 D1
SW8

Goldsdown Clo., 25 H2
Enf.
Goldsdown Rd., Enf. 25 G2
Goldsmid St. SE18 70 H5
Sladedale Rd.
Goldsmith Ave. E12 52 B6
Goldsmith Ave. NW9 38 E5
Goldsmith Ave. W3 44 G7
RoIII.
Goldsmith Clo. W3 65 E1
East Acton La.
Goldsmith Clo., 45 H1
Har.
Goldsmith La. NW9 38 B4
Goldsmith Rd. E10 51 A1
Goldsmith Rd. E17 41 G2
Goldsmith Rd. N11 31 J5
Goldsmith Rd. SE15 77 D1
Goldsmith Rd. W3 65 D1
Goldsmith St. EC2 13 A3
Goldsmith's Row E2 9 J1
Goldsmith's Row E2 59 D2
Goldsmith's Sq. E2 9 J1
Goldsmith's Sq. E2 59 D2
Goldsworthy Gdns. 68 F4
SE16
Goldwell Rd., 94 F4
Th.Hth.
Goldwin Clo. SE14 77 F1
Golf Clo., Stan. 29 F7
Golf Club Dr., 83 D7
Kings.T.
Golf Rd. W5 55 J6
Boileau Rd.
Golf Rd., Brom. 97 D3
Golf Side, Twick. 82 A3
Golfe Rd., Ilf. 52 G3
Golfside Clo. N20 31 H3
Golfside Clo., 92 E2
N.Mal.
Goliath Clo., Wall. 101 E7
Avro Way
Gollogly Ter. SE7 69 J5
Gomer Gdns., Tedd. 82 D6
Gomer Pl., Tedd. 82 D6
Gomm Rd. SE16 68 F3
Gomshall Ave., 101 E5
Wall.
Gondar Gdns. NW6 48 C5
Gonson Pl. SE8 69 A6
Gonson St. SE8 69 B6
Gonston Clo. SW19 84 B2
Bodicott Clo.
Gonville Cres. 45 H6
Nthlt.
Gonville Rd., 94 F5
Th.Hth.
Gonville St. SW6 75 B3
Putney Bri. App.
Goodall Rd. E11 51 C3
Gooden Ct., Har. 46 B3
Goodenough Rd. 84 C7
SW19
Goodge Pl. W1 11 G2
Goodge St. W1 11 G2
Goodge St. W1 58 C5
Goodhall St. NW10 56 E3
Goodhart Pl. E14 59 H7
Goodhart Way, 96 E7
W.Wick.
Goodhew Rd., Croy. 95 D6
Gooding Clo., 92 C4
N.Mal.
Goodinge Clo. N7 49 E6
Goodman Cres. SW2 85 D2
Goodman Rd. E10 42 C7
Goodmans Ct., Wem. 46 G4
Goodman's Flds. E1 13 H4
Goodman's Stile E1 13 H3
Goodman's Stile E1 59 D6
Goodmans Yd. E1 13 F5
Goodmayes Ave., 53 A1
Ilf.
Goodmayes La., Ilf. 53 A2
Goodmayes Rd., Ilf. 53 A1
Goodrich Rd. SE22 77 C6
Goods Way NW1 8 A1
Goods Way NW1 58 E2
Goodson Rd. NW10 47 E7
Goodway Gdns. E14 60 D6
Goodwin Clo., 93 G3
Mitch.
Goodwin Dr., Sid. 89 D3
Goodwin Gdns., 101 H6
Croy.
Goodwin Rd. N9 33 F1
Goodwin Rd. W12 65 G2
Goodwin Rd., Croy. 101 H5
Goodwin St. N4 49 G2
Fonthill Rd.
Goodwins Ct. WC2 12 A5

Goodwood Clo., 93 D4
Mord.
Goodwood Clo., 29 F5
Stan.
Marsh La.
Goodwood Dr., 45 G6
Nthlt.
Goodwood...
Borwd.
Stratfield Rd.
Goodwood Rd. SE14 88 HJ
Goodwyn Ave. NW7 30 E5
Goodwyns Vale N10 40 A1
Goodyers Gdns. NW4 39 A5
Goosander Way 70 G3
SE28
Goose Sq. E6 61 C6
Harper Rd.
Gooseacre La., Har. 37 G5
Gooseley La. E6 61 D3
Goossens Clo., 100 F5
Sutt.
Turnpike La.
Gophir La. EC4 13 B5
Gopsall St. N1 59 A1
Gordon Ave. E4 34 E6
Gordon Ave. SW14 74 E4
Gordon Ave., Stan. 29 C7
Gordon Ave., Twick. 73 D5
Gordon Clo. E17 42 A6
Gordon Clo. N19 49 C1
Highgate Hill
Gordon Ct. W12 56 H6
Gordon Cres., Croy. 102 B1
Gordon Cres., Hayes 63 A3
Gordon Gdns., Edg. 38 B2
Gordon Gro. SE5 76 H2
Gordon Hill, Enf. 24 J1
Gordon Ho. Rd. NW5 49 A4
Gordon Pl. W8 66 D2
Gordon Rd. E4 26 E7
Gordon Rd. E11 42 G6
Gordon Rd. E15 51 C4
Gordon Rd. E18 42 H1
Gordon Rd. N3 31 C7
Gordon Rd. N9 33 E2
Gordon Rd. N11 32 D7
Gordon Rd. SE15 77 E2
Gordon Rd. W4 65 B6
Gordon Rd. W5 55 F7
Gordon Rd. W13 55 F7
Gordon Rd., Bark. 61 H1
Gordon Rd., Beck. 95 J3
Gordon Rd., Belv. 71 J4
Gordon Rd., Cars. 100 J6
Gordon Rd., Enf. 25 A1
Gordon Rd., Esher 98 B7
Gordon Rd., Har. 37 B3
Gordon Rd., Houns. 72 J4
Gordon Rd., Ilf. 52 G3
Gordon Rd., 91 J1
Kings.T.
Gordon Rd., Rich. 73 J2
Gordon Rd., Rom. 44 F6
Gordon Rd., Sid. 79 H5
Gordon Rd., Sthl. 63 E4
Gordon Rd., Surb. 91 J7
Gordon Sq. WC1 7 H5
Gordon Sq. WC1 58 D4
Gordon St. E13 60 G3
Grange Rd.
Gordon St. WC1 7 H5
Gordon St. WC1 58 D4
Gordon Way, Barn. 23 C4
Gordonbrock Rd. SE4 78 A5
Gordondale Rd. 84 D2
SW19
Gore Ct. NW9 38 A5
Gore Rd. E9 59 F1
Gore Rd. SW20 92 J2
Gore St. SW7 14 D5
Gore St. SW7 66 F3
Gorefield Pl. NW6 57 D2
Goresbrook Rd., 62 B1
Dag.
Gorham Pl. W11 57 B7
Mary Pl.
Goring Clo., Rom. 44 J1
Goring Rd. N11 32 E6
Goring St. EC3 13 E3
Goring St. EC3 59 B6
Goring Way, Grnf. 54 J2
Gorleston Rd. N15 41 A5
Gorleston St. W14 66 B4
Gorman Rd. SE18 70 C4
Gorringe Pk. Ave., 84 J7
Mitch.
Gorse Ri. SW17 85 A5
Gorse Rd., Croy. 103 A3
Gorst Rd. NW10 56 C4
Gorst Rd. SW11 75 J6
Gorsuch Pl. E2 9 F3
Gorsuch St. E2 9 F3

Gorsuch St. E2 59 C3
Gosberton Rd. SW12 84 J1
Gosbury Hill, 98 H4
Chess.
Gosfield Rd., Dag. 53 G2
Gosfield St. W1 11 F1
Gosfield St. W1 58 C5
Gosford Gdns., Ilf. 43 C5
Gosforth La., Wat. 28 A3
Gosforth Path, Wat. 28 A3
Goslett Yd. WC2 11 J4
Gosling Clo., Grnf. 54 G3
Gosling Way SW9 76 G1
Gospatric Rd. N17 32 J7
Gospel Oak Est. NW5 48 J5
Gosport Rd. E17 41 J5
Gosport Way SE15 21 F7
Gossage Rd. SE18 70 G5
Ancona Rd.
Gosset St. E2 9 G4
Gosset St. E2 59 C3
Gosshill Rd., Chis. 97 D2
Gossington Clo., 88 E4
Chis.
Beechwood Ri.
Gosterwood St. SE8 68 H6
Gostling Rd., 81 G1
Twick.
Goston Gdns., 94 G3
Th.Hth.
Goswell Rd. EC1 8 G2
Goswell Rd. EC1 58 H2
Gothic Rd., Twick. 82 A2
Goudhurst Rd., 87 E5
Brom.
Gough Rd. E15 51 F4
Gough Rd., Enf. 25 E2
Gough Sq. EC4 12 F3
Gough St. WC1 8 D5
Gough St. WC1 58 F4
Gough Wk. E14 60 A6
Saracen St.
Gould Ct. SE19 86 B5
Gould Rd., Twick. 82 B1
Gould Ter. E8 50 E5
Kenmure Rd.
Goulston St. E1 13 F3
Goulston St. E1 59 C6
Goulton Rd. E5 50 E4
Gourley St. N15 41 B5
Gourley St.
Gourley St. N15 41 B5
Gourock Rd. SE9 79 D5
Govan St. E2 59 D1
Whiston Rd.
Govier Clo. E15 51 E7
Gowan Ave. SW6 75 B1
Gowan Rd. NW10 47 H6
Gower Ct. WC1 7 H5
Gower Ms. WC1 11 J2
Gower Ms. WC1 58 D5
Gower Pl. WC1 7 G5
Gower Pl. WC1 58 C4
Gower Rd. E7 51 G6
Gower Rd., Islw. 64 C6
Gower St. WC1 7 H6
Gower St. WC1 58 C4
Gower's Wk. E1 13 H3
Gower's Wk. E1 59 D6
Gowland Pl., Beck. 95 J2
Gowlett Rd. SE15 77 D3
Gowrie Rd. SW11 76 A3
Graburn Way, E.Mol. 91 A3
Grace Ave., Bexh. 80 F2
Grace Clo. SE9 88 A3
Grace Clo., Borwd. 22 D1
Grace Clo., Edg. 30 C7
Pavilion Way
Grace Clo., Ilf. 35 J6
Grace Jones Clo. E8 50 D6
Parkholme Rd.
Grace Rd., Croy. 94 J6
Grace St. E3 60 B3
Gracechurch St. EC3 13 C5
Gracechurch St. EC3 59 A7
Gracedale Rd. SW16 85 B5
Gracefield Gdns. 85 E3
SW16
Grace's All. E1 13 H5
Graces Ms. SE5 77 A2
Graces Rd. SE5 77 B2
Gradient, The SE26 86 D4
Graeme Rd., Enf. 25 A2
Graemesdyke Ave. 74 B3
SW14
Grafton Clo. W13 55 D6
Grafton Clo., 81 E1
Houns.
Grafton Clo., 99 E3
Wor.Pk.
Grafton Cres. NW1 49 B6
Grafton Gdns. N4 40 J6

Grafton Gdns., Dag. 53 E2
Grafton Ho. E3 60 A3
Wellington Way
Grafton Ms. W1 7 F6
Grafton Pk. Rd., 99 E2
Wor.Pk.
Grafton Pl. NW1 7 H4
Grafton Pl. NW1 58 D3
Grafton Rd. NW5 49 A5
Grafton Rd. W3 56 C7
Grafton Rd., Croy. 101 G1
Grafton Rd., Dag. 53 E1
Grafton Rd., Enf. 24 F3
Grafton Rd., Har. 36 J5
Grafton Rd., N.Mal. 92 E3
Grafton Rd., 99 D4
Wor.Pk.
Grafton Sq. SW4 76 C3
Grafton St. W1 11 E6
Grafton St. W1 58 B7
Grafton Ter. NW5 48 J5
Grafton Way W1 7 F6
Grafton Way W1 58 C4
Grafton Way WC1 7 G6
Grafton Way WC1 58 C4
Grafton Way, W.Mol. 90 F4
Grafton Yd. NW5 49 B6
Prince of Wales Rd.
Graftons, The NW2 48 D3
Hermitage La.
Graham Ave. W13 64 E2
Graham Ave., Mitch. 94 A1
Graham Clo., Croy. 103 A2
Graham Gdns., Surb. 98 H1
Graham Rd. E8 50 D6
Graham Rd. E13 60 G3
Graham Rd. N15 40 H3
Graham Rd. NW4 38 H6
Graham Rd. SW19 84 C7
Graham Rd. W4 65 D3
Graham Rd., Bexh. 80 G4
Graham Rd., Hmptn. 81 G4
Graham Rd., Har. 37 B3
Graham Rd., Mitch. 94 A1
Graham St. N1 8 H2
Graham St. N1 58 H2
Graham Ter. SW1 19 B2
Graham Ter. SW1 67 A4
Grahame Pk. Est. 30 F7
NW9
Grahame Pk. Way 30 F7
NW7
Grahame Pk. Way 38 F2
NW9
Grainger Clo., Nthlt. 45 J5
Lancaster Rd.
Grainger Rd. N22 40 J1
Grainger Rd., Islw. 73 C2
Gramer Clo. E11 51 D2
Grampian Clo., Orp. 97 J6
Cotswold Ri.
Grampian Gdns. NW2 48 B1
Granard Ave. SW15 74 H5
Granard Rd. SW12 75 J7
Granary Clo. N9 25 F7
Turin Rd.
Granary St. NW1 58 D1
Granby Bldgs. SE11 20 C2
Granby Rd. SE9 79 C2
Granby St. E2 9 H5
Granby St. E2 59 C4
Granby Ter. NW1 7 F2
Granby Ter. NW1 58 C2
Grand Ave. EC1 12 H1
Grand Ave. N10 40 A4
Grand Ave., Surb. 92 B5
Grand Ave., Wem. 47 A5
Grand Ave. E., Wem. 47 A6
Victoria Ave.
Grand Depot Rd. 70 D5
SE18
Grand Dr. SW20 92 J2
Grand Par. Ms. SW15 75 B5
Upper Richmond Rd.
Grand Union Cres. 59 D1
E8
Grand Union Ind. 56 B2
Est. NW10
Grand Wk. E1 59 H4
Solebay St.
Granden Rd. SW16 94 E2
Grandison Rd. SW11 75 J5
Grandison Rd., 99 J2
Wor.Pk.
Granfield St. SW11 75 G1
Grange, The N2 39 G2
Grange, The N20 31 F1
Grange, The SE1 17 F5
Grange, The SE1 68 C3
Grange, The SW19 84 A6
Grange, The, Croy. 102 J2
Grange, The, Wem. 47 A7

Grange, The, 99 D3
Wor.Pk.
Grange Ave. N12 31 F5
Grange Ave. N20 23 B7
Grange Ave. SE25 95 B2
Grange Ave., Barn. 31 H1
Grange Ave., 37 E2
Stan.
Grange Ave., Twick. 82 B2
Grange Ave., 34 G6
Wdf.Grn.
Grange Clo., Edg. 30 C5
Grange Clo., Houns. 63 F6
Grange Clo., Sid. 89 A3
Grange Clo., W.Mol. 90 H4
Grange Clo., 34 G7
Wdf.Grn.
Grange Ct. E8 50 C7
Grange Ct. WC2 12 D4
Grange Ct., Chig. 35 F2
Grange Ct., Loug. 27 A5
Grange Ct., Nthlt. 54 C2
Grange Cres. SE28 62 C6
Grange Cres., Chig. 35 G5
Grange Dr., Chis. 88 B6
Grange Fm. Clo., 45 J2
Har.
Grange Gdns. N14 32 D1
Grange Gdns. NW3 48 E3
Grange Gdns. SE25 95 B2
Grange Gdns., Pnr. 36 E3
Grange Gro. N1 49 J6
Grange Hill SE25 95 B2
Grange Hill, Edg. 30 C5
Grange Ho., Bark. 61 G1
St. Margarets
Grange La. SE21 86 C2
Grange Mans., 99 F7
Epsom
Grange Ms. SE10 69 D7
Crooms Hill
Grange Pk. W5 64 H1
Grange Pk. Ave. N21 24 J6
Grange Pk. Pl. SW20 83 H7
Grange Pk. Rd. E10 51 B1
Grange Pk. Rd., 37 J3
Th.Hth.
Grange Pl. NW6 48 D7
Grange Pl. SE16 17 H6
Grange Pl. SE16 68 D3
Grange Rd. E10 51 A1
Grange Rd. E13 60 F3
Grange Rd. E17 41 H5
Grange Rd. N6 40 A6
Grange Rd. N17 33 D6
Grange Rd. N18 33 D6
Grange Rd. NW10 47 H6
Grange Rd. SE1 17 E6
Grange Rd. SE1 68 B5
Grange Rd. SE19 95 A2
Grange Rd. SE25 95 A3
Grange Rd. SW13 74 G1
Grange Rd. W4 65 B5
Grange Rd. W5 64 G1
Grange Rd., Chess. 97 H3
Grange Rd., Edg. 30 D6
Grange Rd. 37 D6
(Greenhill), Har.
Grange Rd. 46 A2
(Roxeth), Har.
Grange Rd., Ilf. 52 E4
Grange Rd., 91 H3
Kings.T.
Grange Rd., Orp. 104 F2
Grange Rd., Sthl. 63 E2
Grange Rd., Sutt. 100 D7
Grange Rd., Th.Hth. 95 A4
Grange Rd., W.Mol. 90 H4
Grange Vale, Sutt. 100 E7
Grange Vw. Rd. N20 31 F1
Chandos Ave.
Grange Wk. SE1 17 E5
Grange Wk. SE1 68 B3
Grange Way N12 31 E4
Grange Yd. SE1 17 F6
Grange Yd. SE1 68 C3
Grangecliffe Gdns. 95 B2
SE25
Grangecourt Rd. N16 50 B1
Grangehill Pl. SE9 79 C3
Westmount Rd.
Grangehill Rd. SE9 79 C3
Grangemill Rd. SE6 87 A3
Grangemill Way SE6 87 A2
Grangeway NW6 48 D7
Messina Ave.
Grangeway, Wdf.Grn. 34 J4
Grangeway, The N21 24 H6
Grangeway Gdns., 43 B5
Ilf.
Grangewood, Bex. 89 F1
Hurst Rd.
Grangewood Clo., 36 A5
Pnr.

Grangewood La., 86 J6
Beck.
Grangewood St. E6 61 A1
Granham Gdns. N9 33 C2
Granite St. SE18 70 J5
Granleigh Rd. E11 51 E2
Gransden Ave. E8 50 E7
Gransden Rd. W12 65 F2
Wendell Rd.
Grant Clo. N14 24 C7
Grant Pl., Croy. 102 C1
Grant Rd. SW11 75 G4
Grant Rd., Croy. 102 C1
Grant Rd., Har. 37 B3
Grant St. E13 60 G3
Grant St. N1 8 E1
Grant Way, Islw. 64 D7
Grantbridge St. N1 8 H1
Grantbridge St. N1 58 H2
Grantchester Clo., 46 C3
Har.
Grantham Clo., Edg. 29 H3
Grantham Gdns., 44 F6
Rom.
Grantham Grn., 22 C5
Borwd.
Grantham Pl. W1 15 D2
Grantham Rd. E12 52 D4
Grantham Rd. SW9 76 E3
Grantham Rd. W4 65 E7
Grantley Rd., 72 C2
Houns.
Grantley St. E1 59 G3
Grantock Rd. E17 42 D1
Granton Rd. SW16 94 C1
Granton Rd., Ilf. 53 A1
Granton Rd., Sid. 89 C6
Grants Clo. NW7 30 J7
Grantully Rd. W9 6 A4
Grantully Rd. W9 57 E3
Granville Ave. N9 33 F3
Granville Ave., Felt. 81 A2
Granville Ave., 72 G5
Houns.
Granville Clo., 102 B2
Croy.
Granville Ct. N1 59 A1
Granville Gdns. 94 F1
SW16
Granville Gdns. W5 64 J1
Granville Gro. SE13 78 C3
Granville Ms., Sid. 89 A4
Granville Pk. SE13 78 C3
Granville Pl. 31 F7
(North Finchley) N12
High Rd.
Granville Pl. W1 11 B4
Granville Pl. W1 58 A6
Granville Rd. E17 42 B6
Granville Rd. E18 42 H2
Granville Rd. N4 40 F6
Granville Rd. N12 31 E6
Granville Rd. N13 32 F6
Russell Rd.
Granville Rd. N22 40 H1
Granville Rd. NW2 48 C2
Granville Rd. NW6 57 D2
Granville Rd. SW18 75 C7
Granville Rd. SW19 84 D7
Russell Rd.
Granville Rd., Barn. 22 J4
Granville Rd., Ilf. 52 E7
Granville Rd., Sid. 89 A4
Granville Rd., Well. 80 C3
Granville Sq. SE15 21 E7
Granville Sq. WC1 8 D4
Granville Sq. WC1 58 F3
Granville St. WC1 8 D4
Granville St. WC1 58 F3
Grape St. WC2 12 A3
Graphite Sq. SE11 20 C6
Grasdene Rd. SE18 71 A7
Grasmere Ave. 83 D4
SW15
Grasmere Ave. 93 D3
SW19
Grasmere Ave. W3 56 D7
Grasmere Ave., 72 H6
Houns.
Grasmere Ave., Orp. 104 E3
Grasmere Ave., 37 F7
Wem.
Grasmere Clo., 27 C2
Loug.
Grasmere Ct. N22 32 F6
Palmerston Rd.
Grasmere Gdns., 37 D2
Har.
Grasmere Gdns., Ilf. 43 C5
Grasmere Gdns., 104 E3
Orp.
Grasmere Rd. E13 60 G2
Grasmere Rd. N10 40 B1

Grasmere Rd. N17 33 D6
Grasmere Rd. SE25 95 E6
Grasmere Rd. SW16 85 F5
Grasmere Rd., Bexh. 80 J1
Grasmere Rd., Brom. 96 F1
Grasmere Rd., Orp. 104 E3
Grass Pk. N3 39 C1
Grassington Rd., 89 A4
Sid.
Grassmount SE23 86 E2
Grassway, Wall. 101 C4
Grasvenor Ave., 23 E6
Barn.
Grately Way SE15 21 F7
Gratton Rd. W14 66 B3
Gratton Ter. NW2 48 A3
Gravel Hill N3 39 C2
Gravel Hill, Bexh. 80 H5
Gravel Hill, Croy. 102 G6
Gravel Hill Clo., 80 H5
Bexh.
Gravel La. E1 13 F3
Gravel La., Chig. 27 J4
Gravel Pit La. SE9 79 F5
Gravel Rd., Brom. 104 B3
Gravel Rd., Twick. 82 B1
Graveley Rd., 22 C4
Borwd.
Gravelly Ride SW19 83 F4
Gravelwood Clo., 88 F3
Chis.
Graveney Gro. SE20 86 F7
Graveney Rd. SW17 84 H4
Gravesend Rd. W12 56 G7
Gray Ave., Dag. 53 F1
Gray St. SE1 16 F4
Grayham Cres., 92 D4
N.Mal.
Grayham Rd., N.Mal. 92 D4
Grayland Clo., 97 A1
Brom.
Grayling Rd. N16 50 A2
Gray's Inn Pl. WC1 12 D2
Gray's Inn Rd. WC1 8 B3
Gray's Inn Rd. WC1 58 E3
Gray's Inn Sq. WC1 12 E1
Gray's Yd. W1 11 C3
Grayscroft Rd. SW16 85 D7
Grayshott Rd. SW11 76 A2
Grayswood Gdns. 92 H2
SW20
Farnham Gdns.
Graywood Ct. N12 31 F7
Grazebrook Rd. N16 50 A2
Grazeley Clo., Bexh. 80 J5
Grazeley Ct. SE19 86 B4
Gipsy Hill
Great Bell All. EC2 13 B3
Great Brownings 86 C4
SE21
Great Bushey Dr. 31 E1
N20
Great Cambridge Rd. 33 A3
N9
Great Cambridge Rd. 33 A7
N17
Great Cambridge Rd. 33 A4
N18
Great Cambridge 25 D3
Rd., Enf.
Great Castle St. W1 11 E3
Great Castle St. W1 58 B6
Great Cen. Ave., 45 C5
Ruis.
Great Cen. St. NW1 10 J1
Great Cen. St. NW1 57 J5
Great Cen. Way 47 C4
NW10
Great Chapel St. W1 11 H3
Great Chapel St. W1 58 D6
Great Chertsey Rd. 74 C2
W4
Great Chertsey Rd., 81 G3
Felt.
Great Chertsey Rd., 81 J1
Twick.
Great Ch. La. W6 66 A5
Great College St. 16 A5
SW1
Great College St. 67 E3
SW1
Great Cross Ave. 69 E7
SE10
Great Cumberland 10 J4
Ms. W1
Great Cumberland 11 A3
Pl. W1
Great Cumberland 57 J6
Pl. W1
Great Dover St. W1 17 B4
Great Dover St. SE1 68 A2
Great Eastern Rd. 51 D7
E15

Great Eastern St. EC2	9	D4
Great Eastern St. EC2	59	B3
Great Eastern Wk. EC2	13	D2
Great Ellis Rd., Brom.	66	J1
Great Fld. NW9	38	E1
Great George St. SW1	15	J4
Great George St. SW1	67	D2
Great Guildford St. SE1	16	J2
Great Guildford St. SE1	67	J1
Great Harry Dr. SE9	88	D3
Great James St. WC1	12	C1
Great James St. WC1	58	F5
Great Marlborough St. W1	11	F4
Great Marlborough St. W1	58	C6
Great Maze Pond SE1	17	C3
Great Maze Pond SE1	68	A1
Great New St. EC4	12	F3
Great Newport St. WC2	11	J5
Great N. Rd. N2	39	H4
Great N. Rd. N6	39	J5
Great N. Rd., Barn.	23	C2
Great N. Way NW4	38	H1
Great Oaks, Chig.	35	F4
Great Ormond St. WC1	12	B1
Great Ormond St. WC1	58	E5
Great Owl Rd., Chig.	35	D3
Great Percy St. WC1	8	D3
Great Percy St. WC1	58	F3
Great Peter St. SW1	15	H6
Great Peter St. SW1	67	D3
Great Portland St. W1	11	E1
Great Portland St. W1	58	B4
Great Pulteney St. W1	11	G5
Great Pulteney St. W1	58	C7
Great Queen St. WC2	12	B4
Great Queen St. WC2	58	E6
Great Russell St. WC1	11	J3
Great Russell St. WC1	58	D6
Great St. Helens EC3	13	D3
Great St. Thomas Apostle EC4	13	A5
Great Scotland Yd. SW1	16	A1
Great Scotland Yd. SW1	67	E1
Great Smith St. SW1	15	J5
Great Smith St. SW1	67	D3
Great Spilmans SE22	77	E3
Great Strand NW9	38	F1
Great Suffolk St. SE1	16	H2
Great Suffolk St. SE1	67	H1
Great Sutton St. EC1	8	H6
Great Sutton St. EC1	58	H4
Great Swan All. EC2	13	B3
Great Thrift, Orp.	97	F4
Great Titchfield St. W1	11	F1
Great Titchfield St. W1	58	C5
Great Twr. St. EC3	13	D5
Great Twr. St. EC3	59	B7
Great Trinity La. EC4	13	A5
Great Turnstile WC1	12	D2
Great W. Rd. W4	65	G5
Great W. Rd. W6	65	G5
Great W. Rd., Brent.	65	B5
Great W. Rd., Houns.	72	E2
Great W. Rd., Islw.	64	A7
Great Western Ind. Pk., Sthl.	63	H2
Great Western Rd. W9	57	C5
Great Western Rd. W11	57	C5
Great Winchester St. EC2	13	C3
Great Winchester St. EC2	59	A6
Great Windmill St. W1	11	H5
Great Windmill St. W1	58	D7
Greatdown Rd. W7	55	C4
Greatfield Ave. E6	61	C4
Greatfield Clo. N13	19	C1
Warrender Rd.		
Greatfield Clo. SE4	78	A4
Greatfields Rd., Bark.	61	G1
Greatham Wk. SW15	83	G1
Bessborough Rd.		
Greatorex St. E1	13	H1
Greatorex St. E1	59	D5
Greatwood, Chis.	88	D7
Greaves Pl. SW17	84	H4
Grebe Clo. E17	33	H7
Banbury Rd.		
Grecian Cres. SE19	85	H6
Gredo Ho., Bark.	62	B3
Greek St. W1	11	J4
Greek St. W1	58	D6
Greek Yd. WC2	12	A5
Green, The E4	34	C1
Green, The E11	42	H6
Green, The E15	51	E6
Green, The N9	33	D2
Green, The N14	32	D3
Green, The N21	24	G7
Green, The SW19	84	A5
Green, The W3	56	E6
Green, The, Bexh.	80	G1
Green, The, Brom.	96	G7
Green, The, Cars.	101	A4
Green, The, Esher	98	C6
Green, The, Felt.	81	B2
Green, The, Houns.	63	G6
Heston Rd.		
Green, The, Mord.	93	B4
Green, The, N.Mal.	92	C3
Green, The, Orp.	89	B7
The Ave.		
Green, The, Rich.	73	G5
Green, The, Sid.	89	A4
Green, The, Sthl.	63	E3
Green, The, Sutt.	100	E3
Green, The, Twick.	82	B6
Green, The, Well.	79	H4
Green, The, Wem.	46	D2
Green, The, Wdf.Grn.	34	G5
Green Acres, Croy.	102	C3
Green Arbour Ct. EC1	12	G3
Green Ave. NW7	30	D4
Green Ave. W13	64	E3
Green Bank E1	68	E1
Green Bank N12	31	E4
Green Clo. NW9	38	C6
Green Clo. NW11	39	F7
Green Clo., Brom.	96	E3
Green Clo., Cars.	100	J2
Green Clo., Felt.	81	E5
Green Dale SE22	77	B5
Green Dale Clo. SE22	77	B5
Green Dale		
Green Dragon Ct. SE1	17	B1
Green Dragon La. N21	24	G5
Green Dragon La., Brent.	64	H5
Green Dragon Yd. E1	13	H2
Green Dr., Sthl.	63	G1
Green End N21	32	H2
Green End, Chess.	98	H4
Green Gdns., Orp.	106	F5
Green Hill, Buck.H.	34	J1
Green Hundred Rd. SE15	21	J6
Green Hundred Rd. SE15	68	E6
Green La. E4	26	D3
Green La. NW4	39	A4
Green La. SE9	88	E1
Green La. SE20	85	H7
Green La. SW16	85	F7
Green La. W7	64	B2
Green La., Chig.	35	F1
Green La., Chis.	88	E3
Green La., Dag.	53	D2
Green La., Edg.	29	J4
Green La., Felt.	81	E5
Green La., Har.	46	B4
South Vale		
Green La., Houns.	72	B3
Green La., Ilf.	52	F2
Green La., Mord.	93	D6
Green La., N.Mal.	92	C5
Green La., Stan.	29	E4
Green La., Th.Hth.	94	H1
Green La., Wat.	28	C1
Green La., W.Mol.	90	H5
Green La., Wor.Pk.	99	G1
Green La. Gdns., Th.Hth.	87	H8
Green Las. N4	40	H7
Green Las. N8	40	H3
Green Las. N13	32	F6
Green Las. N16	49	J3
Green Las. N21	32	H2
Green Lawns, Ruis.	45	C1
Green Man Gdns. W13	55	D7
Green Man La. W13	55	D7
Green Man La., Felt.	72	A4
Green Moor Link N21	24	H7
Green Pt. E15	51	E6
Green Pond Clo. E17	41	H3
Green Pond Rd. E17	41	H3
Green Ride, Loug.	26	G5
Green Rd. N14	24	B6
Green Rd. N20	31	F3
Green Shield Ind. Est. E16	69	G1
Green St. E7	51	H6
Green St. E13	51	J7
Green St. W1	11	A5
Green St. W1	57	J7
Green St., Enf.	25	F2
Green St., Sun.	90	A1
Green Vale W5	55	J6
Green Vale, Bexh.	80	D5
Green Verges, Stan.	29	G7
Green Vw., Chess.	98	J7
Green Wk. NW4	39	A5
Green Wk. SE1	17	D6
Green Wk., Hmptn.	81	F6
Orpwood Clo.		
Green Wk., Sthl.	63	G5
Green Wk., Wdf.Grn.	35	B6
Green Wk., The E4	34	C1
Green Way SE9	79	A5
Green Way, Brom.	97	B6
Green Way, Sun.	90	A4
Green Wrythe Cres., Cars.	100	H1
Green Wrythe La., Cars.	93	G6
Greenacre Gdns. E17	42	C4
Greenacre Sq. SE16	68	G2
Fishermans Dr.		
Greenacre Wk. N14	32	E3
Greenacres SE9	79	D6
Greenacres (Bushey), Wat.	29	A2
Greenacres Dr., Stan.	29	E6
Greenaway Gdns. NW3	48	E4
Greenbank Ave., Wem.	46	D5
Greenbank Clo. E4	34	C2
Greenbank Cres. NW4	39	B4
Greenbay Rd. SE7	70	A7
Greenberry St. NW8	6	G2
Greenbrook Ave., Barn.	23	F1
Greencoat Pl. SW1	19	G1
Greencoat Pl. SW1	67	C4
Greencoat Row SW1	15	G6
Greencourt Ave., Croy.	102	E2
Greencourt Ave., Edg.	38	B1
Greencourt Gdns. Croy.	102	E1
Greencourt Rd., Orp.	93	G6
Greencrest Pl. NW2	47	H3
Dollis Hill La.		
Greencroft Ave. Ruis.	45	C2
Greencroft Clo. E6	61	B5
Neatscourt Rd.		
Greencroft Gdns. NW6	90	E7
Greencroft Gdns., Enf.	25	B3
Greencroft Rd., Houns.	72	F1
Greenend Rd. W4	65	E2
Greenfarm Clo., Orp.	104	J5
Greenfell St. SE10	69	E3
Greenfield Ave., Surb.	92	B7
Greenfield Ave., Wat.	28	D2
Greenfield Gdns. NW2	48	B2
Greenfield Gdns., Dag.	62	D1
Greenfield Gdns., Orp.	97	G7
Greenfield Rd. E1	13	J2
Greenfield Rd. E1	59	D5
Greenfield Rd. N15	41	D5
Greenfield Rd., Dag.	53	C7
Greenfield Way, Har.	36	H3
Greenfields, Loug.	27	D4
Greenfields Clo., Loug.	27	D4
Greenford Ave. W7	55	B4
Greenford Ave., Sthl.	54	F7
Greenford Gdns., Grnf.	54	H3
Greenford Rd., Grnf.	54	J6
Greenford Rd., Har.	46	C4
Greenford Rd. Sthl.	54	J6
Greenford Rd., Sutt.	100	E4
Greengate, Grnf.	46	E6
Greengate St. E13	60	H2
Greenhalgh Wk. N2	39	F4
Greenham Clo. SE1	16	E4
Greenham Clo. SE1	67	G2
Greenham Rd. N10	40	A2
Greenheys Dr. E18	42	F3
Greenhill NW3	48	G4
Hampstead High St.		
Greenhill SE18	70	C5
Greenhill, Sutt.	100	F2
Greenhill, Wem.	47	B2
Greenhill Gdns., Nthlt.	54	F2
Greenhill Gro. E12	52	B4
Greenhill Pk. NW10	56	E1
Greenhill Pk., Barn.	23	E5
Greenhill Rd. NW10	56	E1
Greenhill Rd., Har.	37	B6
Greenhill Ter. SE18	70	C5
Greenhill Ter., Nthlt.	54	F2
Greenhill Way, Har.	37	B6
Greenhill Way, Wem.	47	B2
Greenhill's Rents EC1	12	G1
Baxter Rd.		
Greenhills Ter. N1	50	A6
Greenhithe Clo., Sid.	79	H7
Greenholm Rd. SE9	79	H5
Greenhurst Rd. SE27	85	G5
Greening St. SE2	71	C4
Greenland Cres., Sthl.	63	C3
Greenland Pl. NW1	58	B1
Greenland Rd.		
Greenland Quay SE16	68	G4
Greenland Rd. NW1	58	B1
Greenland Rd., Barn.	22	J5
Greenland St. NW1	58	B1
Camden High St.		
Greenlaw Gdns., N.Mal.	92	F7
Greenlaw St. SE18	70	D3
Greenlea Trd. Pk. SW19	93	G1
Greenleaf Clo. SW2	76	G7
Tulse Hill		
Greenleaf Rd. E6	60	J1
Redclyffe Rd.		
Greenleaf Rd. E17	41	J3
Greenleafe Dr., Ilf.	43	E3
Greenman St. N1	49	J7
Greenmoor Rd., Enf.	25	F2
Greenoak Way SW19	84	A4
Greenock Rd. SW16	90	D1
Greenock Rd. W3	65	B3
Greens Clo., The, Loug.	27	D4
Green's Ct. W1	11	H5
Green's End SE18	70	E4
Greenside, Bex.	89	S3
Greenside, Dag.	53	C1
Greenside Clo. N20	31	G2
Greenside Clo. W12	65	G3
Greenside Rd., Croy.	93	G7
Greenstead Ave., Wdf.Grn.	34	J7
Greenstead Clo., Wdf.Grn.	34	J6
Greenstead Gdns.		

Name	Page	Grid
Greenstead Gdns. SW15	74	G5
Greenstead Gdns., Wdf.Grn.	34	J6
Greensted Rd., Loug.	27	B7
Greenstone Ms. E11	42	G6
Greenvale Rd. SE9	79	C4
Greenview Ave., Beck.	95	H6
Greenview Ave., Croy.	95	H6
Greenway N14	32	E2
Greenway N20	31	D2
Greenway SW20	92	J4
Greenway, Chis.	88	D5
Greenway, Dag.	53	C2
Greenway, Har.	37	H5
Greenway, Hayes	54	A3
Greenway, Pnr.	36	B2
Greenway, Wall.	101	C4
Greenway, Wdf.Grn.	34	J5
Greenway, The NW9	38	D2
Greenway, The, Har.	37	B1
Greenway, The, Houns.	72	F4
Greenway, The, Pnr.	36	F6
Greenway Ave. E17	42	D4
Greenway Clo. N4	49	J2
Greenway Clo. N11	32	A6
Greenway Clo. N20	31	D2
Greenway Clo. NW9	38	D2
Greenway Gdns. NW9	38	D2
Greenway Gdns., Croy.	102	J3
Greenway Gdns., Grnf.	54	G3
Greenway Gdns., Har.	37	B2
Greenways, Beck.	96	A2
Greenways, Esher	98	B4
Greenways, The, Twick.	73	D6
Greenwell St. W1	**7**	**E6**
Greenwell St. W1	58	B4
Greenwich Ch. St. SE10	69	C6
Greenwich Cres. E6 Swan App.	61	B5
Greenwich High Rd. SE10	78	B1
Greenwich Ind. Est. SE7	69	H4
Greenwich Mkt. SE10	69	C6
Greenwich Pk. SE10	69	D7
Greenwich Pk. St. SE10	69	D5
Greenwich S. St. SE10	78	B1
Greenwich Vw. Pl. E14	69	B3
Greenwood Ave., Dag.	53	H4
Greenwood Ave., Enf.	25	H2
Greenwood Clo., Mord.	93	B4
Greenwood Clo., Orp.	97	H6
Greenwood Clo., Sid. Hurst Rd.	89	A2
Greenwood Clo., T.Ditt.	98	D1
Greenwood Ct. SW1 Avril Way	**19**	**G4**
Greenwood Dr. E4	34	C5
Greenwood Gdns. N13	32	H3
Greenwood Gdns., Ilf.	35	F7
Greenwood La., Hmptn.	81	H5
Greenwood Pk., Kings.T.	83	E7
Greenwood Pl. NW5 Highgate Rd.	49	B5
Greenwood Rd. E8	50	D6
Greenwood Rd. E13 Maud Rd.	60	F2
Greenwood Rd., Croy.	94	H7
Greenwood Rd., Islw.	73	C3
Greenwood Rd., Mitch.	94	D3
Greenwood Rd., T.Ditt.	98	D1
Greenwood Ter. NW10	56	D1
Greer Rd., Har.	36	J1
Greet St. SE1	**16**	**F2**
Greet St. SE1	67	G1
Gregor Ms. SE3	69	G7
Gregory Cres. SE9	79	A7
Gregory Pl. W8	**14**	**A3**
Gregory Pl. W8	66	E2
Gregory Rd., Rom.	44	D4
Gregory Rd., Sthl.	63	G3
Gregson Clo., Borwd.	22	C1
Greig Clo. N8	40	E5
Greig Ter. SE17	**20**	**H5**
Grena Gdns., Rich.	73	J4
Grena Rd., Rich.	73	J4
Grenaby Ave., Croy.	95	A7
Grenaby Rd., Croy.	95	A7
Grenada Rd. SE7	69	J7
Grenade St. E14	59	J7
Grenadier St. E16	70	D1
Grendon Gdns., Wem.	47	A2
Grendon St. NW8	**6**	**G5**
Grendon St. NW8	57	H4
Grenfell Gdns., Har.	37	H7
Grenfell Rd. W11	57	A7
Grenfell Rd., Mitch.	84	J6
Grenfell Twr. W11	57	A7
Grennell Clo., Sutt.	100	G2
Grennell Rd., Sutt.	100	F3
Grenoble Gdns. N13	32	G6
Grenville Clo. N3	39	C1
Grenville Clo., Surb.	99	C1
Grenville Gdns., Wdf.Grn.	42	J1
Grenville Ms. SW7	**18**	**D1**
Grenville Ms. SW7	66	F4
Grenville Ms., Hmptn.	81	H5
Grenville Pl. NW7	30	D5
Grenville Pl. SW7	**14**	**C6**
Grenville Pl. SW7	66	F3
Grenville Rd. N19	49	E1
Grenville St. WC1	**8**	**B6**
Grenville St. WC1	58	E4
Gresham Ave. N20	31	J4
Gresham Clo., Bex.	80	E6
Gresham Dr., Rom.	44	B5
Gresham Gdns. NW11	48	B1
Gresham Rd. E6	61	C2
Gresham Rd. E16	60	H6
Gresham Rd. NW10	47	D5
Gresham Rd. SE25	95	D4
Gresham Rd. SW9	76	G3
Gresham Rd., Beck.	95	H2
Gresham Rd., Edg.	29	J6
Gresham Rd., Hmptn.	81	G6
Gresham Rd., Houns.	72	J1
Gresham St. EC2	**13**	**A3**
Gresham St. EC2	58	J6
Gresham Way SW19	84	D3
Gresley Clo. N15 Clinton Rd.	41	A4
Gresley Rd. N19	49	C1
Gresse St. W1	**11**	**H3**
Gresse St. W1	58	D5
Gressenhall Rd. SW18	75	C6
Greswell Clo., Sid.	89	A
Greswell St. SW6	75	A1
Gretton Rd. N17	33	B7
Greville Clo., Twick.	73	E7
Greville Hall NW6	**6**	**B1**
Greville Hall NW6	57	E2
Greville Pl. NW6	**6**	**B1**
Greville Pl. NW6	57	E2
Greville Rd. E17	42	C4
Greville Rd. NW6	**6**	**A1**
Greville Rd. NW6	57	E2
Greville Rd., Rich.	73	J6
Greville St. EC1	**12**	**F2**
Greville St. EC1	58	G5
Grey Clo. NW11	39	F6
Grey Eagle St. E1	**9**	**G6**
Grey Eagle St. E1	59	C5
Greycoat Pl. SW1	**15**	**H6**
Greycoat Pl. SW1	67	D3
Greycoat St. SW1	**15**	**H6**
Greycoat St. SW1	67	D3
Greycot Rd., Beck.	87	A5
Greyfell Clo., Stan. Coverdale Clo.	29	E5
Greyfriars Pas. EC1	**12**	**H3**
Greyhound Hill NW4	38	G3
Greyhound La. SW16	85	D6
Greyhound Rd. N17	41	B3
Greyhound Rd. NW10	56	H3
Greyhound Rd. W6	66	A6
Greyhound Rd. W14	66	B6
Greyhound Rd., Sutt.	100	F5
Greyhound Ter. SW16	94	C1
Greys Pk. Clo., Kes.	104	A5
Greystead Rd. SE23	77	F7
Greystoke Ave. Pnr.	36	G3
Greystoke Gdns. W5	55	H4
Greystoke Gdns., Enf.	24	D4
Greystoke Pk. Ter. W5	55	G3
Greystoke Pl. EC4	**12**	**E3**
Greystone Gdns., Har.	37	F6
Greystone Gdns., Ilf.	43	F2
Greyswood St. SW16	85	B6
Grierson Rd. SE23	77	G7
Griffin Clo. NW10	47	H5
Griffin Manor Way SE28	70	G3
Griffin Rd. N17	41	B2
Griffin Rd. SE18	70	G5
Griffin Way, Sun.	90	A2
Griffith Clo., Dag. Gibson Rd.	53	C1
Griffiths Clo., Wor.Pk.	99	H2
Griffiths Rd. SW19	84	D7
Griggs App., Ilf.	52	F2
Griggs Pl. SE1	**17**	**E5**
Griggs Rd. E10	42	C6
Grilse Clo. N9 Parr Clo.	33	E4
Grimsby St. E2	**9**	**G6**
Grimsdyke Cres., Barn.	22	J3
Grimsdyke Rd., Pnr.	28	E7
Grimsel Path SE5	**20**	**H7**
Grimshaw Clo. N6	40	A7
Grimston Rd. SW6	75	C2
Grimwade Ave., Croy.	102	D3
Grimwood Rd., Twick.	73	C7
Grindal St. SE1	**16**	**E4**
Grindall Clo., Croy. Hillside Rd.	101	H4
Grinling Pl. SE8	69	A6
Grinstead Rd. SE8	68	H5
Grittleton Ave., Wem.	47	B6
Grittleton Rd. W9	57	D4
Grizedale Ter. SE23	86	E2
Grocer's Hall Ct. EC2	**13**	**B4**
Grogan Clo., Hmptn.	81	F6
Groom Cres. SW18	75	G7
Groom Pl. SW1	**15**	**C5**
Groom Pl. SW1	67	A3
Groombridge Clo., Well.	80	A5
Groombridge Rd. E9	50	G7
Groomfield Clo. SW17	85	A4
Gronms Dr., Pnr.	36	A5
Grosmont Rd. SE18	70	J6
Grosse Way SW15	74	H6
Grosvenor Ave. N5	49	J5
Grosvenor Ave. SW14	74	E3
Grosvenor Ave., Cars.	100	J6
Grosvenor Ave., Har.	36	H6
Grosvenor Ave., Rich. Grosvenor Rd.	73	H5
Grosvenor Clo., Loug.	27	E1
Grosvenor Cotts. SW1	**19**	**B1**
Grosvenor Ct. N14	24	C7
Grosvenor Cres. NW9	38	A4
Grosvenor Cres. SW1	**15**	**C4**
Grosvenor Cres. SW1	67	A2
Grosvenor Cres. Ms. SW1	**15**	**B4**
Grosvenor Cres. Ms. SW1	67	A2
Grosvenor Dr., Loug.	27	E2
Grosvenor Est. SW1	**19**	**J1**
Grosvenor Est. SW1	67	D4
Grosvenor Gdns. E6	61	A3
Grosvenor Gdns. N10	40	D3
Grosvenor Gdns. N14	24	D4
Grosvenor Gdns. NW2	47	J5
Grosvenor Gdns. NW11	39	C6
Grosvenor Gdns. SW1	**15**	**E6**
Grosvenor Gdns. SW1	67	B3
Grosvenor Gdns. SW14	74	E3
Grosvenor Gdns., Kings.T.	82	G6
Grosvenor Gdns., Wall.	101	C7
Grosvenor Gdns., Wdf.Grn.	34	G6
Grosvenor Gdns. Ms. E. SW1	**15**	**E5**
Grosvenor Gdns. Ms. N. SW1	**15**	**D6**
Grosvenor Gdns. Ms. S. SW1	**15**	**E6**
Grosvenor Gate W1	**11**	**A6**
Grosvenor Hill SW19	84	B6
Grosvenor Hill W1	**11**	**D5**
Grosvenor Hill W1	58	B7
Grosvenor Pk. SE5	**20**	**J6**
Grosvenor Pk. SE5	67	J7
Grosvenor Pk. Rd. E17	42	A5
Grosvenor Path, Loug.	27	E1
Grosvenor Pl. SW1	**15**	**C4**
Grosvenor Pl. SW1	67	A2
Grosvenor Ri. E. E17	42	B5
Grosvenor Rd. E6	61	A1
Grosvenor Rd. E7	51	H6
Grosvenor Rd. E10	51	C1
Grosvenor Rd. E11	42	G5
Grosvenor Rd. N3	31	C7
Grosvenor Rd. N9	33	E1
Grosvenor Rd. N10	40	B1
Grosvenor Rd. SE25	95	D4
Grosvenor Rd. SW1	**19**	**F5**
Grosvenor Rd. SW1	67	B6
Grosvenor Rd. W4	65	B5
Grosvenor Rd. W7	64	D1
Grosvenor Rd., Belv.	71	G6
Grosvenor Rd., Bexh.	80	D5
Grosvenor Rd., Borwd.	22	A3
Grosvenor Rd., Brent.	64	G6
Grosvenor Rd., Dag.	53	F1
Grosvenor Rd., Houns.	72	F3
Grosvenor Rd., Ilf.	52	F3
Grosvenor Rd., Orp.	97	H6
Grosvenor Rd., Rich.	73	H5
Grosvenor Rd., Sthl.	63	F3
Grosvenor Rd., Twick.	73	D7
Grosvenor Rd., Wall.	101	B6
Grosvenor Rd., W.Wick.	103	B1
Grosvenor Sq. W1	**11**	**C5**
Grosvenor Sq. W1	58	A7
Grosvenor St. W1	**11**	**D5**
Grosvenor St. W1	58	B7
Grosvenor Ter. SE5	**20**	**J6**
Grosvenor Ter. SE5	67	J6
Grosvenor Wf. Rd. E14	69	D4
Grote's Bldgs. SE3	78	E2
Grote's Pl. SE3	78	E2
Groton Rd. SW18	84	E2
Grotto Pas. W1	**11**	**C1**
Grotto Rd., Twick.	82	C2
Grove, The E15	51	E6
Grove, The N3	39	D1
Grove, The N4	40	F7
Grove, The N6	49	A1
Grove, The N8	40	D5
Grove, The N13	32	G5
Grove, The N14	24	C5
Grove, The NW9	38	D5
Grove, The NW11	39	B7
Grove, The W5	64	C1
Grove, The, Bexh.	80	D4
Grove, The, Edg.	30	B4
Grove, The, Enf.	24	G2
Grove, The, Grnf.	54	J8
Grove, The, Islw.	73	B1
Grove, The, Sid.	89	E5
Grove, The, Tedd.	82	D4
Grove, The, Twick. Bridge Rd.	73	E6
Grove, The, Walt.	90	B7
Grove, The, W.Wick.	103	B3
Grove Ave. N3	31	D7
Grove Ave. N10	40	C2
Grove Ave. W7	55	B6
Grove Ave., Pnr.	36	E5
Grove Ave., Sutt. Grove Rd.	100	D6

Grove Ave., Twick.	82	C1
Grove Clo. SE23	86	H1
Grove Clo., Brom.	103	G2
Grove Clo., Felt.	81	E4
Grove Clo.,	91	J4
Kings.T.		
Grove Cotts. SW3	18	IIC
Grove Ct. SE3	78	G1
Grove Ct., E.Mol	91	A5
Walton Rd.		
Grove Cres. E18	42	F2
Grove Cres. NW9	38	C4
Grove Cres. SE5	77	B2
Grove Cres., Felt.	81	E4
Grove Cres.,	91	H3
Kings.T.		
Grove Cres., Walt.	90	B7
Grove Cres. Rd. E15	51	D6
Grove End E18	42	F2
Grove Hill		
Grove End La.,	98	A1
Esher		
Grove End Rd. NW8	6	E3
Grove End Rd. NW8	57	G2
Grove Footpath,	91	H4
Surb.		
Grove Gdns. E15	51	E6
Grove Gdns. NW4	38	G5
Grove Gdns. NW8	6	H4
Grove Gdns., Dag.	53	J3
Grove Gdns., Tedd.	82	D4
Grove Grn. Rd. E11	51	C3
Grove Hall Ct. NW8	6	D3
Grove Hill E18	42	F2
Grove Hill, Har.	37	B7
Grove Hill Rd. SE5	77	B3
Grove Hill Rd., Har.	37	B7
Grove Ho. Rd. N8	40	E4
Grove La. SE5	77	B2
Grove La., Chig.	35	J3
Grove La., Kings.T.	91	H4
Grove Mkt. Pl. SE9	79	C6
Grove Ms. W6	65	J3
Grove Ms. W11	57	C6
Portobello Rd.		
Grove Pk. E11	42	H6
Grove Pk. NW9	38	C4
Grove Pk. SE5	77	B2
Grove Pk. Ave. E4	34	B7
Grove Pk. Bri. W4	65	C7
Grove Pk. Gdns. W4	65	C7
Grove Pk. Ms. W4	65	C7
Grove Pk. Rd. N15	41	B4
Grove Pk. Rd. SE9	87	J3
Grove Pk. Rd. W4	65	B7
Grove Pk. Ter. W4	65	B7
Grove Pas. E2	59	E2
The Oval		
Grove Pas., Tedd.	82	D5
Grove Pl. NW3	48	G4
Christchurch Hill		
Grove Pl. W3	65	C1
Grove Pl., Bark.	61	F1
Clockhouse Ave.		
Grove Rd. E3	59	G1
Grove Rd. E4	34	C4
Grove Rd. E11	42	F7
Grove Rd. E17	42	B6
Grove Rd. E18	42	F2
Grove Rd. N11	32	B5
Grove Rd. N12	31	G5
Grove Rd. N15	41	B5
Grove Rd. NW2	47	J6
Grove Rd. SW13	74	F2
Grove Rd. SW19	84	F7
Grove Rd. W3	65	C1
Grove Rd. W5	55	G7
Grove Rd., Barn.	23	H3
Grove Rd., Belv.	71	F6
Grove Rd., Bexh.	80	J4
Grove Rd., Borwd.	22	A1
Grove Rd., Brent.	64	F5
Grove Rd., E.Mol.	91	A4
Grove Rd., Edg.	30	A6
Grove Rd., Houns.	72	G4
Grove Rd., Islw.	73	B1
Grove Rd., Mitch.	94	A3
Grove Rd., Pnr.	36	F5
Grove Rd., Rich.	73	J6
Grove Rd., Rom.	44	B7
Grove Rd., Surb.	91	G5
Grove Rd., Sutt.	100	D6
Grove Rd., Th.Hth.	94	G4
Grove Rd., Twick.	82	A3
Grove St. N18	33	C5
Grove St. SE8	68	J4
Grove Ter. NW5	49	B3
Grove Ter., Tedd.	82	D4
Grove Vale SE22	77	B4
Grove Vale, Chis.	88	D6
Grove Vill. E14	60	B7
Grove Way, Esher	90	J7
Grovebury Ct. N14	24	D7

Grovebury Rd. SE2	71	B2
Grovedale Rd. N19	49	D2
Groveland Ave.	85	F7
SW16		
Groveland Ct. EC4	13	A4
Groveland Rd.,	95	J3
Beck.		
Groveland Way,	92	L5
N.Mal.		
Grovelands, W.Mol.	88	G1
Grovelands Clo. SE5	77	B2
Grovelands Clo.,	45	H3
Har.		
Grovelands Ct. N14	24	D7
Grovelands Rd. N13	32	F4
Grovelands Rd. N15	41	D6
Grovelands Rd.,	89	A7
Orp.		
Groveside Clo. W3	56	B6
Groveside Clo.,	100	H2
Cars.		
Groveside Rd. E4	34	E2
Groveway SW9	76	F1
Groveway, Dag.	53	D4
Groveway, Wem.	47	C5
Grovewood, Rich.	73	J1
Sandycombe Rd.		
Grummant Rd. SE15	77	C1
Grundy St. E14	60	B6
Gruneisen Rd. N3	31	E7
Gubyon Ave. SE24	76	H5
Guerin Sq. E3	59	J3
Malmesbury Rd.		
Guernsey Clo.,	72	G1
Houns.		
Guernsey Gro. SE24	76	J7
Guernsey Rd. E11	51	D1
Guibal Rd. SE12	78	H7
Guild Rd. SE7	70	A5
Guildersfield Rd.	85	E7
SW16		
Guildford Gro. SE10	78	B1
Guildford Rd. E6	61	C6
Guildford Rd. E17	42	C1
Guildford Rd. SW8	76	E1
Guildford Rd.,	95	A6
Croy.		
Guildford Rd., Ilf.	52	H2
Guildford Way,	101	E5
Wall.		
Guildhall Bldgs. EC2	13	B3
Guildhouse St. SW1	19	F1
Guildhouse St. SW1	67	C4
Guildown Ave. N12	31	E4
Guildsway E17	41	J1
Guilford Ave., Surb.	91	J5
Guilford Pl. WC1	8	C6
Guilford Pl. WC1	58	F4
Guilford St. WC1	8	B6
Guilford St. WC1	58	F4
Guilsborough Clo.	47	E7
NW10		
Guinness Bldgs. SE1	17	D6
Guinness Bldgs. SE1	68	B4
Guinness Clo. E9	50	H7
Guinness Sq. SE1	21	D1
Guinness Trust	20	G3
Bldgs. SE11		
Guinness Trust	67	H5
Bldgs. SE11		
Guinness Trust	18	J2
Bldgs. SW3		
Guinness Trust Est.	50	B1
N16		
Guinness Trust Est.	76	H4
SW9		
Guion Rd. SW6	75	C2
Gull Clo., Wall.	101	E7
Gulland Wk. N1	49	J6
Marquess Est.		
Gulliver Clo., Nthlt.	54	F1
Gulliver Rd., Sid.	88	H2
Gulliver St. SE16	68	J3
Gumleigh Rd. W5	64	F4
Gumley Gdns., Islw.	73	D3
Gumping Rd., Orp.	104	F1
Gun St. E1	13	F2
Gun St. E1	59	C5
Gundulph Rd., Brom.	96	J3
Gunmakers La. E3	59	H1
Gunner La. SE18	70	D5
Gunners Gro. E4	34	C3
Gunners Rd. SW18	84	G2
Gunnersbury Ave.	65	A3
W3		
Gunnersbury Ave.	64	J1
W5		
Gunnersbury Clo. W4	65	B5
Grange Rd.		
Gunnersbury Ct. W3	65	B2
Bollo La.		
Gunnersbury Cres.	65	A2
W3		

Gunnersbury Dr. W5	64	J2
Gunnersbury Gdns.	65	A2
W3		
Gunnersbury La. W3	65	A3
Gunnersbury Ms. W4	65	B5
Chiswick High Rd.		
Gunnersbury Pk. W3	64	J4
Gunnersbury Pk. W5	64	J4
Gunning St. SE18	70	H4
Gunpowder Sq. EC4	12	F3
Gunpowder Sq. EC4	58	G6
Gunstor Rd. N16	50	B4
Gunter Gro. SW10	66	F6
Gunter Gro., Edg.	38	D1
Gunterstone Rd. W14	66	B4
Gunthorpe St. E1	13	G2
Gunthorpe St. E1	59	C5
Gunton Rd. E5	50	E2
Gunton Rd. SW17	85	A6
Gunwhale Clo. SE16	68	K1
Gurdon Rd. SE7	69	G5
Gurnell Gro. W13	55	C4
Gurney Clo. E15	51	E5
Gurney Rd.		
Gurney Clo. E17	41	G1
Gurney Clo., Bark.	52	E6
Gurney Cres., Croy.	101	F1
Gurney Dr. N2	39	F4
Gurney Rd. E15	51	E5
Gurney Rd., Cars.	101	A3
Gurney Rd., Nthlt.	54	B3
Guthrie St. SW3	18	G3
Gutter La. EC2	13	A3
Gutter La. EC2	58	J6
Guy Rd., Wall.	101	D3
Guy St. SE1	17	C3
Guy St. SE1	68	A2
Guyatt Gdns., Mitch.	94	A2
Ormerod Gdns.		
Guyscliff Rd. SE13	78	C5
Gwalior Rd. SW15	75	A3
Felsham Rd.		
Gwendoline Ave.	75	A4
SW15		
Gwendolen Clo.	75	A5
SW15		
Gwendoline Ave. E13	60	H1
Gwendwr Rd. W14	66	B5
Gwillim Clo., Sid.	80	A5
Gwydor Rd., Beck.	95	G4
Gwydyr Rd., Brom.	96	F3
Gwyn Clo. SW6	66	F7
Gwynne Ave., Croy.	95	G7
Gwynne Pk. Ave.	35	C6
Wdf.Grn.		
Gwynne Pl. WC1	8	D4
Gwynne Rd. SW11	75	G2
Gylcote Clo. SE5	77	A4
Gyles Pk., Stan.	29	F7
Gyllyngdune Gdns.,	52	J3
Ilf.		

H

Ha-Ha Rd. SE18	70	C6
Haarlem Rd. W14	66	A3
Haberdasher Pl. N1	9	C3
Haberdasher St. N1	9	C3
Haberdasher St. N1	59	A3
Habgood Rd., Loug.	28	B3
Haccombe Rd. SW19	84	F6
Hackbridge Grn.	101	A2
Wall.		
Hackbridge Pk.	101	A2
Gdns., Cars.		
Hackbridge Rd.,	101	A2
Wall.		
Hackforth Clo.,	22	H5
Barn.		
Hackington Cres.,	87	A6
Beck.		
Hackney Clo.,	22	D5
Borwd.		
Hackney Gro. E8	50	E6
Reading La.		
Hackney Rd. E2	9	F3
Hackney Rd. E2	59	C3
Hadden Rd. SE28	70	H3
Hadden Way, Grnf.	46	A6
Haddington Rd.,	87	D4
Brom.		
Haddo St. SE10	69	G1
Haddon Clo., Borwd.	22	A2
Haddon Clo., N.Mal.	92	F5
Haddon Gro., Sid.	79	J7
Haddon Rd., Sutt.	100	E4
Haddonfield SE8	68	G4
Hadleigh Clo. E1	59	F4
Mantus Rd.		
Hadleigh Rd. N9	25	E7

Hadleigh St. E2	59	F3
Hadleigh Wk. E6	61	B6
Dunnock Rd.		
Hadley Clo. N21	24	G6
Hadley Common,	23	D2
Barn.		
Hadley Gdns. W4	65	D5
Hadley Gdns., Sthl.	63	F5
Hadley Grn., Barn.	23	C2
Hadley Grn. Rd.,	23	C2
Barn.		
Hadley Grn. W.,	23	B2
Barn.		
Hadley Gro., Barn.	23	B2
Hadley Highstone,	23	C1
Barn.		
Hadley Ridge, Barn.	23	C3
Hadley Rd., Barn.	23	E3
Hadley Rd., Belv.	71	F4
Hadley Rd., Mitch.	94	D4
Hadley St. NW1	49	B6
Hadley Way N21	24	G6
Hadlow Pl. SE19	86	D7
Hadlow Rd., Sid.	89	A4
Hadlow Rd., Well.	71	C7
Hadrian Clo., Wall.	101	E7
De Havilland Rd.		
Hadrian Est. E2	9	J2
Hadrian St. SE10	69	E5
Hadrians Ride, Enf.	25	C5
Hadyn Pk. Rd. W12	65	G2
Hafer Rd. SW11	75	J4
Hafton Rd. SE6	87	E1
Haggard Rd., Twick.	73	D7
Haggerston Rd. E8	50	C7
Hague St. E2	9	J4
Haig Rd., Stan.	29	F5
Haig Rd. E. E13	60	J3
Haig Rd. W. E13	60	J3
Haigville Gdns., Ilf.	43	E4
Hailes Clo. SW19	84	F6
North Rd.		
Hailey Rd., Erith	71	G2
Haileybury Ave.,	25	C6
Enf.		
Hailsham Ave. SW2	85	F2
Hailsham Clo.,	91	G7
Surb.		
Hailsham Dr., Har.	37	A3
Hailsham Rd. SW17	85	A6
Hailsham Ter. N18	32	J5
Haimo Rd. SE9	79	A5
Hainault Ct. E17	42	D4
Hainault Gore, Rom.	44	E5
Hainault Gro.,	35	F4
Chig.		
Hainault Rd. E11	51	C1
Hainault Rd., Chig.	35	E3
Hainault Rd., Rom.	44	B1
Hainault Rd., Rom.	44	F6
Hainault Rd., Rom.	44	J2
Hainault St. SE9	88	E1
Hainault St., Ilf.	52	F2
Hainford Clo. SE4	77	G4
Haining Clo. W4	65	A5
Wellesley Rd.		
Hainthorpe Rd. SE27	85	H3
Hainton Path E1	59	E6
Commercial Rd.		
Halberd Ms. E5	50	E2
Knightland Rd.		
Halbutt Gdns., Dag.	53	F3
Halbutt St., Dag.	53	F4
Halcomb St. N1	59	B1
Halcot Ave., Bexh.	80	H5
Halcrow St. E1	59	E5
Haldan Rd. E4	34	C6
Haldane Clo. N10	32	B7
Haldane Pl. SW18	84	E1
Haldane Rd. E6	61	A3
Haldane Rd. SE28	62	D7
Haldane Rd. SW6	66	C7
Haldane Rd., Sthl.	54	J7
Haldon Clo., Chig.	35	H5
Haldon Rd. SW18	75	C5
Hale, The E4	34	D7
Hale, The N17	41	D3
Hale Clo. E4	34	C3
Hale Clo., Edg.	30	C5
Hale Clo., Orp.	104	F4
Hale Dr. NW7	30	C6
Hale End Clo., Ruis.	36	A6
Hale End Rd. E4	34	D6
Hale End Rd. E17	42	D1
Hale End Rd.,	34	D7
Wdf.Grn.		
Hale Gdns. N17	41	D3
Hale Gdns. W3	65	A1
Hale Gro. Gdns. NW7	30	D5
Hale La. NW7	30	D5
Hale La., Edg.	30	B5
Hale Path SE27	85	H4
Hale Rd. E6	61	B4

Hale Rd. N17	41	D3
Hale St. E14	60	B7
Hale Wk. W7	55	B5
Benham Rd.		
Halefield Rd. N17	41	D1
Hales St. SE8	69	A7
Halesowen Rd.,	93	E7
Mord.		
Halesworth Clo. E5	50	F2
Theydon Rd.		
Halesworth Rd. SE13	78	B3
Haley Rd. NW4	38	J6
Half Acre, Brent.	64	G6
Half Acre Rd. W7	64	B1
Half Moon Ct. EC1	12	J2
Half Moon Cres. N1	8	D1
Half Moon Cres. N1	58	F2
Half Moon La. SE24	76	J6
Half Moon Pas. E1	13	G4
Half Moon St. W1	15	E1
Half Moon St. W1	67	B1
Halford Rd. E10	42	D5
Halford Rd. SW6	66	D6
Halford Rd., Rich.	73	H5
Halfway St., Sid.	79	G7
Haliburton Rd.,	73	D5
Twick.		
Haliday Wk. N1	50	A6
Mildmay St.		
Halidon Clo. E9	50	F5
Urswick Rd.		
Halifax Rd., Enf.	24	J2
Halifax Rd., Grnf.	54	H1
Halifax St. SE26	86	E4
Halifield Dr., Belv.	71	E3
Haling Gro.,	101	J7
S.Croy.		
Haling Pk. Gdns.,	101	H6
S.Croy.		
Haling Pk. Rd.,	101	H6
S.Croy.		
Haling Rd., S.Croy.	102	A6
Halkin Arc. SW1	15	B5
Halkin Ms. SW1	15	B5
Halkin Pl. SW1	15	B5
Halkin Pl. SW1	67	A3
Halkin St. SW1	15	C4
Halkin St. SW1	67	A2
Hall, The SE3	78	G3
Hall Ave. N18	33	A6
Weir Hall Ave.		
Hall Clo. W5	55	H5
Hall Ct., Tedd.	82	C5
Teddington Pk.		
Hall Dr. SE26	86	F5
Hall Dr. W7	55	B6
Hall Fm. Clo., Stan.	29	E4
Hall Fm. Dr., Twick.	73	A7
Hall Gdns. E4	33	J4
Hall Gate NW8	6	D3
Hall La. E4	33	H5
Hall La. NW4	38	G1
Hall Oak Wk. NW6	48	C6
Maygrove Rd.		
Hall Pl. W2	6	E6
Hall Pl. W2	57	G4
Hall Pl. Cres., Bex.	80	J5
Hall Rd. E6	61	C1
Hall Rd. E15	51	D4
Hall Rd. NW8	6	D4
Hall Rd. NW8	57	F3
Hall Rd., Islw.	73	A5
Hall Rd., Rom.	44	C6
Hall St. EC1	8	H3
Hall St. EC1	58	H3
Hall St. N12	31	F5
Hall Vw. SE9	88	A2
Hallam Clo., Chis.	88	C5
Hallam Gdns., Pnr.	28	E7
Hallam Ms. W1	11	E1
Hallam Rd. N15	40	H4
Hallam St. W1	7	E6
Hallam St. W1	58	B5
Halley Gdns. SE13	78	D4
Halley Rd. E7	51	J6
Halley Rd. E12	52	A6
Halley St. E14	59	H5
Hallfield Est. W2	10	C4
Halliards, The, Walt.	90	A6
Felix Rd.		
Halliford St. N1	49	J7
Hallingbury Ct. E17	42	B3
Halliwell Rd. SW2	76	F6
Halliwick Rd. N10	40	A1
Hallmead Rd., Sutt.	100	E3
Hallowell Ave.,	101	E4
Croy.		
Hallowell Clo.,	94	A3
Mitch.		
Hallowes Cres., Wat.	28	A3
Hayling Rd.		
Hallsville Rd. E16	60	F6
Hallswelle Rd. NW11	39	C5

Hallywell Cres. E6	61	C5
Halons Rd. SE9	79	D7
Halpin Pl. SE17	21	C2
Halsbrook Rd. SE3	78	J3
Halsbury Clo.,	29	E4
Stan.		
Halsbury Rd. W12	65	G1
Halsbury Rd. E.,	45	J4
Nthlt.		
Halsbury Rd. W.,	45	H5
Nthlt.		
Halsend, Hayes	63	B1
Halsey Ms. SW3	18	J1
Halsey St. SW3	18	J1
Halsey St. SW3	66	J4
Halsham Cres., Bark.	52	J6
Halsmere Rd. SE5	76	H1
Halstead Ct. N1	9	C2
Halstead Gdns. N21	33	A1
Halstead Rd. E11	42	G5
Halstead Rd. N21	33	A1
Halstead Rd., Enf.	25	B4
Halston Clo. SW11	75	J6
Halstow Rd. NW10	57	A3
Halstow Rd. SE10	69	G5
Halsway, Hayes	63	A1
Halt Robin La., Belv.	71	H4
Halt Robin Rd.		
Halt Robin Rd.,	71	G4
Belv.		
Halter Clo., Borwd.	22	D5
Clydesdale Rd.		
Halton Cross St. N1	58	H1
Halton Rd.		
Halton Rd. N1	49	H7
Ham, The, Brent.	64	F7
Ham Clo., Rich.	82	F3
Ham Fm. Rd., Rich.	82	G4
Ham Gate Ave.,	82	H4
Rich.		
Ham Pk. Rd. E7	51	G7
Ham Pk. Rd. E15	51	F7
Ham Ridings, Rich.	82	J5
Ham St., Rich.	82	E1
Ham Vw., Croy.	95	H6
Ham Yd. W1	11	H5
Hambalt Rd. SW4	76	C5
Hamble Ct.,	82	G7
Kings.T.		
Hamble St. SW6	75	E3
Hambleden Pl. SE21	86	B1
Hambledon Gdns.	95	C3
SE25		
Hambledon Rd.	75	C7
SW18		
Hambledown Rd.,	79	G7
Sid.		
Hambleton Clo.,	99	J2
Wor.Pk.		
Cotswold Way		
Hambridge Way	76	G7
SW2		
Hambro Ave., Brom.	103	G1
Hambro Rd. SW16	85	D6
Hambrook Rd. SE25	95	E3
Hambrough Rd.,	63	E1
Sthl.		
Hamden Cres., Dag.	53	H3
Hamelin St. E14	60	C6
St. Leonards Rd.		
Hameway E6	61	D4
Hamfrith Rd. E15	51	F6
Hamilton Ave. N9	25	D7
Hamilton Ave., Ilf.	43	E4
Hamilton Ave.,	99	A2
Surb.		
Hamilton Ave.,	100	B1
Sutt.		
Hamilton Clo. N17	41	C3
Hamilton Clo. NW8	6	E4
Hamilton Clo. NW8	57	F3
Hamilton Clo. SE16	68	H2
Somerford Way		
Hamilton Clo., Barn.	23	H4
Hamilton Clo., Stan.	29	C2
Hamilton Ct. W5	55	J7
Hamilton Ct. W9	6	C3
Hamilton Cres. N13	32	G4
Hamilton Cres., Har.	45	F3
Hamilton Cres.,	72	H5
Houns.		
Hamilton Gdns. NW8	6	D3
Hamilton Gdns. NW8	57	F3
Hamilton La. N5	49	H4
Hamilton Pk.		
Hamilton Ms. W1	15	D3
Hamilton Pk. N5	49	H4
Hamilton Pk. W. N5	49	H4
Hamilton Pl. W1	15	C2
Hamilton Pl. W1	67	A1
Hamilton Pl., Sun.	81	B7
Hamilton Rd. E15	60	E3
Hamilton Rd. E17	41	H2

Hamilton Rd. N2	39	F3
Hamilton Rd. N9	25	D7
Hamilton Rd. NW10	47	G5
Hamilton Rd. NW11	39	A7
Hamilton Rd. SE27	86	A4
Hamilton Rd. SW19	84	E7
Hamilton Rd. W4	65	E2
Hamilton Rd. W5	56	H7
Hamilton Rd., Barn.	23	H4
Hamilton Rd., Bexh.	80	E2
Hamilton Rd., Brent.	64	G6
Hamilton Rd., Har.	37	B5
Hamilton Rd., Hayes	54	B7
Hamilton Rd., Ilf.	52	E4
Hamilton Rd., Sid.	89	A4
Hamilton Rd., Sthl.	63	F1
Hamilton Rd.,	95	A3
Th.Hth.		
Hamilton Rd., Wat.	28	B3
Hamilton Sq. SE1	17	C3
Hamilton St. SE8	69	A6
Deptford High St.		
Hamilton Ter. NW8	6	B2
Hamilton Ter. NW8	57	E2
Hamilton Way N3	31	D6
Hamilton Way N13	32	H4
Hamlea Clo. SE12	78	G5
Hamlet, The SE5	77	A3
Hamlet Clo. SE13	78	E4
Old Rd.		
Hamlet Gdns. W6	65	G4
Hamlet Rd. SE19	86	C7
Hamlet Sq. NW2	48	B3
Cricklewood Trd. Est.		
Hamlet Sq. NW11	48	B3
The Vale		
Hamlet Way SE1	17	C3
Hamlets Way E3	59	J4
Hamlin Cres., Pnr.	36	C5
Hamlyn Clo., Edg.	29	H3
Hamlyn Gdns. SE19	86	B7
Hammelton Grn.	76	H1
SW9		
Cromwell Rd.		
Hammelton Rd.,	96	F1
Brom.		
Hammers La. NW7	30	G5
Hammersmith Bri.	65	H5
SW13		
Hammersmith Bri.	65	J5
Rd. W6		
Hammersmith Bdy.	65	J4
W6		
Hammersmith	65	J5
Flyover W6		
Hammersmith Gro.	65	J2
W6		
Hammersmith Rd.	66	A4
W6		
Hammersmith Rd.	66	B4
W14		
Hammersmith Ter.	65	G5
W6		
Hammet Clo., Hayes	54	D5
Willow Tree La.		
Hammett St. EC3	13	F5
Hammond Ave.,	94	B2
Mitch.		
Hammond Clo., Barn.	23	B5
Hammond Clo., Grnf.	46	A5
Lilian Board Way		
Hammond Clo.,	90	G1
Hmptn.		
Hammond Rd., Enf.	25	E2
Hammond Rd., Sthl.	63	E3
Hammond St. NW5	49	C6
Hammond Way SE28	62	B7
Oriole Way		
Hamonde Clo., Edg.	30	B2
Hampden Ave., Beck.	95	H2
Hampden Clo. NW1	7	J2
Hampden Gurney St.	10	J4
W1		
Hampden La. N17	41	C1
Hampden Rd. N8	40	G4
Hampden Rd. N10	32	A7
Hampden Rd. N17	41	D1
Hampden Rd. N19	49	D2
Holloway Rd.		
Hampden Rd., Beck.	95	H2
Hampden Rd., Har.	36	J1
Hampden Rd.,	92	A3
Kings.T.		
Hampden Way N14	32	B2
Hampshire Clo. N18	33	E5
Hampshire Hog La.	65	H4
W6		
King St.		
Hampshire Rd. N22	32	F7
Hampshire St. NW5	49	D6
Torriano Ave.		

Hampson Way SW8	76	F1
Hampstead Clo. SE28	71	B1
Hampstead Gdns.	39	D6
NW11		
Hampstead Grn. NW3	48	H5
Hampstead Gro. NW3	48	F3
Hampstead High St.	48	F4
NW3		
Hampstead Hill	48	G4
Gdns. NW3		
Hampstead La. N6	39	G7
Hampstead La. NW3	39	G7
Hampstead Rd. NW1	7	F2
Hampstead Rd. NW1	58	C2
Hampstead Sq. NW3	48	F3
Hampstead Way	39	C5
NW11		
Hampton Clo. NW6	57	D3
Hampton Clo. SW20	83	J7
Hampton Ct. N1	49	H6
Upper St.		
Hampton Ct. Ave.,	91	A5
E.Mol.		
Hampton Ct. Palace,	91	B3
E.Mol.		
Hampton Ct. Par.,	91	B4
E.Mol.		
Creek Rd.		
Hampton Ct. Rd.,	91	C3
E.Mol.		
Hampton Ct. Rd.,	90	J2
Hmptn.		
Hampton Ct. Rd.,	91	F2
Kings.T.		
Hampton Ct. Way,	91	B6
E.Mol.		
Hampton Ct. Way,	98	B2
T.Ditt.		
Hampton Fm. Ind.	81	E3
Est., Felt.		
Hampton La., Felt.	81	E4
Hampton Mead,	27	E3
Loug.		
Hampton Ri., Har.	37	H6
Hampton Rd. E4	33	J5
Hampton Rd. E7	51	H5
Hampton Rd. E11	51	D1
Hampton Rd., Croy.	94	J6
Hampton Rd., Ilf.	52	E4
Hampton Rd., Tedd.	82	A5
Hampton Rd., Twick.	82	A3
Hampton Rd.,	99	G2
Wor.Pk.		
Hampton Rd. E., Felt.	81	F3
Hampton Rd. W.,	81	E2
Felt.		
Hampton St. SE1	20	H2
Hampton St. SE1	67	J4
Hampton St. SE17	20	H2
Hampton St. SE17	67	H4
Hamshades Clo.,	88	J3
Sid.		
Hanah Ct. SW19	84	A7
Hanameel St. E16	69	H1
Hanbury Ms. N1	58	J1
Mary St.		
Hanbury Rd. N17	41	E2
Hanbury Rd. W3	65	B2
Hanbury St. E1	13	G1
Hanbury St. E1	59	C5
Hancock Ct., Borwd.	22	C2
Banks Rd.		
Hancock Rd. E3	60	C3
Hancock Rd. SE19	86	A6
Hand Ct. WC1	12	D2
Handa Wk. N1	50	A6
Clephane Rd.		
Handcroft Rd., Croy.	94	H7
Handel Clo., Edg.	29	J6
Handel Pl. NW10	47	D6
Mitchellbrook Way		
Handel St. WC1	8	A5
Handel St. WC1	58	E4
Handel Way, Edg.	30	A7
Handen Rd. SE12	78	E5
Handforth Rd. SW9	20	E7
Handforth Rd. SW9	67	G7
Handforth Rd., Ilf.	52	E3
Winston Way		
Handley Rd. E9	59	F1
Handowe Clo. NW4	38	G4
Hands Wk. E16	60	G6
Butchers Rd.		
Handside Clo.,	100	A1
Wor.Pk.		
Carters Clo.		
Handsworth Ave. E4	34	D6
Handsworth Rd. N17	41	A3
Handsworth Way,	28	A3
Wat.		
Handtrough Way,		
Bark.		
Fresh Wf. Rd.		

Hanford Clo. SW18 84 D1
Hanford Row SW19 83 J6
Hangar Ruding, Wat. 28 F3
Hanger Grn. W5 56 A4
Hanger La. W5 55 H2
Hanger Vale La. W3 55 J6
Hanger Vale La. W5
Hanger Vw. Way W3 56 A6
Hankey Pl. SE1 17 C4
Hankey Pl. SE1 68 A2
Hankins La. NW7 30 E2
Hanley Rd. N4 49 E1
Hanmer Wk. N7 49 F2
Newington Barrow
Way
Hannah Clo. NW10 47 C4
Hannah Mary Way 21 J2
SE1
Hannah Ms., Wall. 101 C7
Hannay Wk. SW16 85 D2
Dingley La.
Hannell Rd. SW6 66 B7
Hannen Rd. SE27 85 H3
Norwood High St.
Hannibal Rd. E1 59 F5
Hannibal Way, Croy. 101 F5
Hannington Rd. SW4 76 B3
Hanover Ave., Felt. 81 A1
Hanover Clo., Rich. 65 A7
Hanover Clo., Sutt. 100 B4
Hanover Ct. W12 55 H2
Uxbridge Rd.
Hanover Dr., Chis. 88 F4
Hanover Gdns. SE11 20 E6
Hanover Gdns. SE11 67 G6
Hanover Gdns., Ilf. 35 F7
Hanover Gate NW1 6 H4
Hanover Gate NW1 57 H3
Hanover Pk. SE15 77 D1
Hanover Pl. WC2 12 B4
Hanover Rd. N15 41 C4
Hanover Rd. NW10 47 J7
Hanover Rd. SW19 84 F7
Hanover Sq. W1 11 E4
Hanover Sq. W1 58 B6
Hanover St. W1 11 E4
Hanover St. W1 58 B6
Hanover St., Croy. 101 H3
Abbey Rd.
Hanover Ter. NW1 6 H4
Hanover Ter. NW1 57 H3
Hanover Ter., Islw. 73 D1
Hanover Ter. Ms. 6 H4
NW1
Hanover Way, Bexh. 80 D3
Hanover W. Ind. 56 D3
Est. NW10
Acton La.
Hanover Yd. N1 8 H1
Hans Cres. SW1 14 J5
Hans Cres. SW1 66 J3
Hans Pl. SW1 15 A5
Hans Pl. SW1 66 J3
Hans Rd. SW3 14 J5
Hans Rd. SW3 66 J3
Hans St. SW1 15 A6
Hansard Ms. W14 66 A2
Holland Rd.
Hansart Way, Enf. 24 G1
The Ridgeway
Hanselin Clo., Stan. 29 C5
Chenduit Way
Hasha Dr., Edg. 38 D1
Hansler Gro., E.Mol. 91 A5
Hansler Rd. SE22 77 C5
Hansol Rd., Bexh. 80 E5
Hanson Clo. SW12 76 B7
Hanson Clo., Loug. 27 F2
Hanson Dr.
Hanson Dr., Loug. 27 F2
Hanson Gdns., Sthl. 63 E2
Hanson Grn., Loug. 27 F2
Hanson Dr.
Hanson St. W1 11 F1
Hanson St. W1 58 C5
Hanway Pl. W1 11 H3
Hanway Rd. W7 55 A6
Hanway St. W1 11 H3
Hanway St. W1 58 D6
Hanworth Rd., Felt. 81 B1
Hanworth Rd., 81 F4
Hmptn.
Hanworth Rd. (TW3), 72 H4
Houns.
Hanworth Rd. (TW4), 81 E1
Houns.
Hanworth Rd., Sun. 81 A7
Hanworth Ter., 72 H4
Houns.
Hanworth Trd. Est., 81 E3
Felt.
Hapgood Clo., Grnf. 46 A5
Harben Rd. NW6 48 F7

Harberson Rd. E15 60 F1
Harberson Rd. SW12 85 B1
Harberton Rd. N19 49 C1
Harbet Rd. N18 33 G5
Harbet Rd. W2 10 F2
Harbet Rd. W2 57 G5
Harbinger Rd. E14 89 B4
Harbledown Rd. SW6 75 D1
Harbord Clo. SE5 77 A9
De Crespigny Pk.
Harbord St. SW6 75 A1
Harborne Clo., Wat. 28 C5
Anglesey Rd.
Harborough Ave., 79 H7
Sid.
Harborough Rd. 85 F4
SW16
Harbour Ave. SW10 75 F1
Harbour Ex. Sg. E14 69 B2
Harbour Rd. SE5 76 J3
Harbridge Ave. SW15 74 F7
Harbut Rd. SW11 75 G4
Harcombe Rd. N16 50 B3
Harcourt Ave. E12 52 C4
Harcourt Ave., Edg. 30 C3
Harcourt Ave., Sid. 80 C6
Harcourt Ave., Wall. 101 B4
Harcourt Clo., Islw. 73 D3
Harcourt Fld., Wall. 101 B4
Harcourt Rd. E15 60 F7
Harcourt Rd. N22 40 D1
Harcourt Rd. SE4 77 H4
Harcourt Rd. SW19 84 D7
Russell Rd.
Harcourt Rd., Bexh. 80 E4
Harcourt Rd., Th.Hth. 94 F6
Harcourt Rd., Wall. 101 B4
Harcourt St. W1 10 H2
Harcourt Ter. SW10 18 B4
Harcourt Ter. SW10 66 E5
Hardcastle Clo., 95 C6
Croy.
Hardcourts Clo., 103 B3
W.Wick.
Hardel Ri. SW2 85 H1
Hardel Wk. SW2 76 G7
Papworth Way
Hardens Manorway 70 A3
SE7
Harders Rd. SE15 77 E2
Hardess St. SE24 77 J3
Herne Hill Rd.
Hardie Clo. NW10 47 D5
Hardie Rd., Dag. 53 J3
Harding Clo. SE17 20 J6
Harding Ho., Hayes 54 A6
Harding Rd., Bexh. 80 F2
Hardinge Rd. N18 33 B5
Hardinge Rd. NW10 56 H1
Hardinge St. E1 59 F6
Hardings La. SE20 86 G6
Hardman Rd. SE7 69 H5
Hardman Rd., 91 H2
Kings.T.
Hardwick Clo., 29 F5
Stan.
Hardwick Grn. W13 55 E5
Hardwick St. EC1 8 F4
Hardwick St. EC1 58 G3
Hardwicke Ave., 72 G1
Houns.
Hardwicke Rd. N13 32 E6
Hardwicke Rd. W4 65 C4
Hardwicke Rd., Rich. 82 F4
Hardwicke St., Bark. 61 F1
Hardwicks Way 75 D5
SW18
Buckhold Rd.
Hardwidge St. SE1 17 D3
Hardy Ave., Ruis. 45 B5
Hardy Clo. SE16 68 G2
Middleton Rd.
Hardy Clo., Pnr. 36 D7
Hardy Rd. SE3 69 F6
Hardy Rd. SW19 84 E7
Hardy Way, Enf. 24 G1
Hare & Billet Rd. 78 D1
SE3
Hare Ct. EC4 12 E4
Hare La., Esher 98 A5
Hare Marsh E2 9 H5
Hare Pl. EC4 12 F4
Hare Row E2 59 E2
Hare St. SE18 70 D3
Hare Wk. N1 9 E2
Hare Wk. N1 59 B2
Harecastle Clo., 54 E4
Hayes
Braunston Dr.
Harecourt Rd. N1 49 J6
Haredale Rd. SE24 76 J4

Haredon Clo. SE23 77 F7
Harefield, Esher 98 B3
Harefield Clo., Enf. 24 G1
Harefield Ms. SE4 77 J3
Harefield Rd. N8 40 D5
Harefield Rd. SE4 77 J3
Harefield Rd. SW16 85 F7
Harefield Rd., Sid. 80 D2
Haresfield Rd., Dag. 53 G6
Harewood Ave. NW1 6 H6
Harewood Ave. NW1 57 H4
Harewood Ave., 45 E7
Nthlt.
Harewood Clo., 45 F7
Nthlt.
Harewood Dr., Ilf. 43 C2
Harewood Pl. W1 11 E4
Harewood Rd. SW19 84 H6
Harewood Rd., Islw. 64 C7
Harewood Rd., 102 B6
S.Croy.
Harewood Rd., Wat. 28 B2
Harewood Row NW1 10 H1
Harewood Ter., Sthl. 63 F4
Harfield Gdns. SE5 77 B3
Harfield Rd., Sun. 90 D2
Harford Clo. E4 26 B7
Harford Rd. E4 26 B7
Harford St. E1 59 H4
Harford Wk. N2 39 G4
Hargood Clo., Har. 37 H6
Hargood Rd. SE3 78 J1
Hargrave Pk. N19 49 C2
Hargrave Pl. N7 49 D5
Brecknock Rd.
Hargrave Rd. N19 49 C2
Hargwyne St. SW9 76 F3
Haringey Pk. N8 40 E6
Haringey Pas. N4 40 H5
Warham Rd.
Haringey Pas. N8 40 H4
Haringey Rd. N8 40 E4
Harington Ter. N9 33 A3
Harington Ter. N18 33 A3
Harkett Clo., Har. 37 C2
Byron Rd.
Harland Ave., Croy. 102 C3
Harland Ave., Sid. 88 G3
Harland Rd. SE12 87 G1
Harlech Gdns., 63 C6
Houns.
Harlech Rd. N14 32 E3
Harlech Twr. W3 65 C2
Harlequin Ave., 64 D6
Brent.
Harlequin Clo., Islw. 73 B5
Harlequin Rd., 82 E7
Tedd.
Harlescott Rd. SE15 77 G4
Harlesden Gdns. 56 F1
NW10
Harlesden La. NW10 56 G1
Harlesden Rd. NW10 56 G1
Harleston Clo. E5 50 F2
Theydon Rd.
Harley Clo., Wem. 46 G6
Harley Ct. E11 42 G7
Harley Cres., Har. 37 A4
Harley Gdns. SW10 18 D4
Harley Gdns. SW10 66 F5
Harley Gdns., Orp. 104 H4
Harley Gro. E3 69 J3
Harley Pl. W1 11 D2
Harley Pl. W1 58 B5
Harley Rd. NW3 48 G7
Harley Rd. NW10 56 E2
Harley Rd., Har. 37 A4
Harley St. W1 7 D6
Harley St. W1 58 B5
Harley St., Brom. 96 H1
Harleyford Rd. SE11 20 C5
Harleyford Rd. SE11 67 H3
Harleyford St. SE11 20 E6
Harleyford St. SE11 67 G6
Harlington Rd., 80 E3
Bexh.
Harlington Rd. E. 72 B7
Felt.
Harlington Rd. W., 72 B6
Felt.
Harlow Rd. N13 33 A3
Harlow Rd., Pnr. 36 B3
Harman Ave., 34 F6
Wdf.Grn.
Harman Clo. E4 34 D4
Harman Clo. NW2 48 B3
Harman Dr. NW2 48 B3
Harman Dr., Sid. 79 J6
Harman Rd., Enf. 25 C5
Harmony Clo. NW11 39 B5
Harmood Gro. NW1 49 B7
Clarence Way

Harmood Pl. NW1 49 B7
Harmood St.
Harmood St. NW1 49 B6
Harmsworth St. 20 G4
SE17
Harmsworth St. 67 H5
SE17
Harmsworth Way 31 C1
N20
Harnage Rd., Brent. 64 E7
Harness Rd. SE28 71 A0
Harold Ave., Belv. 71 F5
Harold Ave., 80 E3
Nthlt.
Harold Clo., 45 F7
Nthlt.
Harold Est. SE1 17 E6
Harold Est. SE1 68 B3
Harold Gibbons Ct. 69 J6
SE7
Victoria Way
Harold Pl. SE11 20 E4
Harold Rd. E4 34 C4
Harold Rd. E11 51 E1
Harold Rd. E13 60 H1
Harold Rd. N8 40 F5
Harold Rd. N15 41 C5
Harold Rd. NW10 56 D3
Harold Rd. SE19 86 A7
Harold Rd., Sutt. 100 G4
Harold Rd., 42 G1
Wdf.Grn.
Haroldstone Rd. E17 41 G5
Harp All. EC4 12 G3
Harp Island Clo. 47 D2
NW10
Harp La. EC3 13 D6
Harp Rd. W7 55 B4
Harpenden Rd. E12 51 J2
Harpenden Rd. SE27 85 H2
Harper Rd. E6 61 C6
Harper Rd. SE1 17 A5
Harper Rd. SE1 67 J3
Harpley Sq. E1 59 F3
Harpour Rd., Bark. 52 F6
Harpsden St. SW11 76 A1
Harpur Ms. WC1 12 C1
Harpur St. WC1 12 C1
Harpur St. WC1 58 F5
Harraden Rd. SE3 78 J1
Harrier Ms. SE28 70 G3
Harrier Rd. NW9 38 E2
Harrier Way E6 61 C5
Harriers Clo. W5 55 H7
Harries Rd., Hayes 54 C4
Harriet Clo. E8 59 D1
Harriet Gdns. 102 D2
Croy.
Harriet St. SW1 15 A4
Harriet Wk. SW1 15 A4
Harriet Wk. SW1 66 J2
Harringay Gdns. N8 40 H4
Harringay Rd. N15 40 H5
Harrington Clo., 101 E2
Croy.
Harrington Gdns. 18 B2
SW7
Harrington Gdns. 66 F4
SW7
Harrington Hill E5 50 E1
Harrington Rd. E11 51 E1
Harrington Rd. SE25 95 D4
Harrington Rd. SW7 18 F1
Harrington Rd. SW7 66 G4
Harrington Sq. NW1 7 F2
Harrington Sq. NW1 58 C2
Harrington St. NW1 7 F2
Harrington St. NW1 58 C3
Harrington Way SE18 70 A3
Harriott Clo. SE10 69 F4
Harris Clo., Enf. 24 H1
Harris Clo., Houns. 72 G1
Harris Rd., Bexh. 80 E1
Harris Rd., Dag. 53 F5
Harris St. E17 41 J7
Harris St. SE5 68 A7
Harrison Rd., Dag. 53 H6
Harrison St. WC1 8 B4
Harrison St. WC1 58 E3
Harrisons Ri., 101 H3
Croy.
Harrogate Rd., Wat. 28 C3
Harrold Rd., Dag. 53 B5
Harrow Ave., Enf. 25 C6
Harrow Clo., Chess. 98 G7
Harrow Dr. N9 33 C1
Harrow Flds. Gdns., 46 B3
Har.
Harrow La. E14 60 C7
Harrow Manorway 71 C3
SE2
Harrow Pas., 91 G2
Kings.T.
Market Pl.
Harrow Pl. E1 13 F3
Harrow Pl. E1 59 B6

Harrow Rd. E6	61	B1
Harrow Rd. E11	51	E3
Harrow Rd. NW10	56	H3
Harrow Rd. W2	57	D5
Harrow Rd. W9	57	C4
Harrow Rd. W10	57	B4
Harrow Rd., Bark.	61	H1
Harrow Rd., Cars.	100	H5
Harrow Rd., Ilf.	52	F4
Harrow Rd., Wem.	46	C4
Harrow Vw., Har.	36	J1
Harrow Vw., Hayes	54	A6
Harrow Vw. Rd. W5	55	E4
Harrow Way, Wat.	28	E3
Harrow Weald Pk., Har.	29	A6
Harroway Rd. SW11	75	G2
Harrowby St. W1	**10**	**H3**
Harrowby St. W1	57	H6
Harrowdene Clo., Wem.	46	G4
Harrowdene Gdns., Tedd.	82	D6
Harrowdene Rd., Wem.	46	G5
Harrowes Meade, Edg.	30	A3
Harrowgate Rd. E9	50	H6
Hart Cres., Chig.	35	J5
Hart Gro. W5	65	A1
Hart Gro., Sthl.	54	G5
Hart St. EC3	**13**	**E5**
Harte Rd., Houns.	72	F2
Hartfield Ave., Borwd.	22	A5
Hartfield Ave., Nthlt.	54	B2
Hartfield Clo., Borwd.	22	A5
Hartfield Cres. SW19	84	C7
Hartfield Cres., W.Wick.	103	G3
Hartfield Gro. SE20	95	F1
Hartfield Rd. SW19	84	C6
Hartfield Rd., Chess.	98	G5
Hartfield Rd., W.Wick.	103	G4
Hartfield Ter. E3	60	A2
Hartford Ave., Har.	37	D3
Hartford Rd., Bex.	80	G6
Hartford Rd., Epsom	99	A6
Hartforde Rd., Borwd.	22	A2
Hartham Clo. N7	49	E5
Hartham Clo., Islw.	73	D1
Hartham Rd. N7	49	E5
Hartham Rd. N17	41	C2
Hartham Rd., Islw.	73	C1
Harting Rd. SE9	88	B4
Hartington Clo., Har.	46	B4
Hartington Ct. W4	65	B7
Hartington Rd. E16	60	H6
Hartington Rd. E17	41	H6
Hartington Rd. SW8	76	E1
Hartington Rd. W4	65	B7
Hartington Rd. W13	55	E7
Hartington Rd., Sthl.	63	E3
Hartington Rd., Twick.	73	E7
Hartismere Rd. SW6	66	C7
Hartlake Rd. E9	50	G6
Hartland Clo., Edg.	30	A2
Hartland Dr., Edg.	30	A2
Hartland Dr., Ruis.	45	B3
Hartland Rd. E15	51	F7
Hartland Rd. N11	31	J5
Hartland Rd. NW1	49	B7
Hartland Rd. NW6	57	C2
Hartland Rd., Hmptn.	81	H4
Hartland Rd., Islw.	73	D3
Hartland Rd., Mord.	93	D7
Hartland Way, Croy.	102	H2
Hartland Way, Mord.	93	C7
Hartlands Clo., Bex.	80	F6
Hartley Ave. E6	61	B1
Hartley Ave. NW7	30	F5
Hartley Clo. NW7	30	F5
Hartley Clo., Brom.	97	C2
Hartley Rd. E11	51	F1
Hartley Rd., Croy.	94	H7
Hartley Rd., Well.	71	C7
Hartley St. E2	59	F3
Hartnoll St. N7	49	F5
Eden Gro.		
Harton Clo., Brom.	97	A1
Harton Rd. N9	33	E2
Harton St. SE8	78	A1

Harts Gro., Wdf.Grn.	34	G5
Harts La. SE14	68	H7
Harts La., Bark.	52	E6
Hartsbourne Ave. (Bushey), Wat.	28	J2
Hartsbourne Clo. (Bushey), Wat.	29	A2
Hartsbourne Rd. (Bushey), Wat.	29	A2
Hartshorn All. EC3	**13**	**E4**
Hartshorn Gdns. E6	61	D4
Hartslock Dr. SE2	71	D2
Hartsmead Rd. SE9	88	C2
Hartsway, Enf.	25	F4
Hartswood Grn. (Bushey), Wat.	29	A2
Hartswood Rd. W12	65	F2
Hartsworth Clo. E13	60	F2
Hartville Rd. SE18	70	H4
Hartwell Dr. E4	34	C6
Hartwell St. E8	50	C6
Dalston La.		
Harvard Hill W4	65	B5
Wolseley Gdns.		
Harvard La. W4	65	B5
Harvard Rd.		
Harvard Rd. SE13	78	C5
Harvard Rd. W4	65	B5
Harvard Rd., Islw.	73	B1
Harvel Cres. SE2	71	D5
Harvest Bank Rd., W.Wick.	103	F3
Harvest La., T.Ditt.	91	D6
Harvest Rd., Felt.	81	A4
Harvesters Clo., Islw.	73	A5
Harvey Gdns. E11	51	F1
Harvey Rd.		
Harvey Gdns. SE7	69	J5
Harvey Gdns., Loug.	27	E3
Harvey Ho., Brent.	64	H5
Harvey Pl. E16	60	H5
Fife Rd.		
Harvey Rd. E11	51	E1
Harvey Rd. N8	40	F5
Harvey Rd. SE5	77	A1
Harvey Rd., Houns.	72	F7
Harvey Rd., Ilf.	52	E5
Harvey Rd., Nthlt.	45	C7
Harvey Rd., Walt.	90	A7
Harvey St. N1	59	A1
Harvill Rd., Sid.	89	D5
Harvington Wk. E8	50	D7
Wilman Gro.		
Harvist Est. N7	49	G4
Harvist Rd. NW6	57	A2
Harwater Dr., Loug.	27	C2
Harwell Pas. N2	39	J4
Harwich La. EC2	**13**	**E1**
Harwich La. EC2	59	B5
Harwood Ave., Brom.	96	H2
Harwood Ave., Mitch.	93	H3
Harwood Clo., Wem.	46	G4
Harrowdene Rd.		
Harwood Rd. SW6	66	D7
Harwood Ter. SW6	75	E1
Harwoods Yd. N21	24	G7
Wades Hill		
Hascombe Ter. SE5	77	A2
Haselbury Rd. N9	33	B3
Haselbury Rd. N18	33	B4
Haseley End SE23	77	F7
Tyson Rd.		
Haselrigge Rd. SW4	76	D4
Haseltine Rd. SE26	86	A4
Haselwood Dr., Enf.	24	H4
Haskard Rd., Dag.	53	D4
Haskell Ho. NW10	56	D1
Hasker St. SW3	**18**	**H1**
Hasker St. SW3	66	H4
Haslam Ave., Sutt.	100	B1
Haslam Clo. N1	49	G7
Haslemere Ave. NW4	39	A6
Haslemere Ave. SW18	84	E2
Haslemere Ave. W7	64	D3
Haslemere Ave. W13	64	D3
Haslemere Ave., Barn.	31	J1
Haslemere Ave., Houns.	72	C2
Haslemere Ave., Mitch.	93	G2
Haslemere Clo., Hmptn.	81	F5
Haslemere Clo., Wall.	101	E5
Stafford Rd.		
Haslemere Gdns. N3	39	C3
Haslemere Heathrow Est., Houns.	72	B2

Haslemere Rd. N8	40	D7
Haslemere Rd. N21	32	H2
Haslemere Rd., Bexh.	80	F2
Haslemere Rd., Ilf.	52	J2
Haslemere Rd., Th.Hth.	94	H5
Hasler Clo. SE28	62	B7
Hasluck Gdns., Barn.	23	E6
Hassard St. E2	**9**	**G2**
Hassendean Rd. SE3	69	H6
Hassett Rd. E9	50	G6
Hassock Wd., Kes.	104	A4
Hassocks Clo. SE26	86	E3
Hassocks Rd. SW16	94	C1
Hassop Rd. NW2	48	A4
Hassop Wk. SE9	88	B4
Hasted Rd. SE7	70	A5
Hastings Ave., Ilf.	43	F4
Hastings Clo. SE15	68	D7
Hastings Clo., Barn.	23	F4
Leicester Rd.		
Hastings Ho. SE18	70	C4
Cardwell Rd.		
Hastings Rd. N11	32	C5
Hastings Rd. N17	41	A3
Hastings Rd. W13	55	E7
Hastings Rd., Brom.	104	B1
Hastings Rd., Croy.	102	C1
Hastings St. WC1	**8**	**A4**
Hastings St. WC1	58	E3
Hastoe Clo., Hayes	54	E4
Kingsash Dr.		
Hat and Mitre Ct. EC1	**8**	**H6**
Hatch, The, Enf.	25	G1
Hatch Gro., Rom.	44	E4
Hatch La. E4	34	D4
Hatch Pl., Kings.T.	82	J5
Hatch Rd. SW16	94	E2
Hatch Side, Chig.	35	D5
Hatcham Pk. Ms. SE14	77	G1
Hatcham Pk. Rd. SE14	77	G1
Hatcham Rd. SE15	68	F6
Hatchard Rd. N19	49	D2
Hatchcroft NW4	38	H3
Hatchwood Clo., Wdf.Grn.	34	F4
Sunset Ave.		
Hatcliffe Clo. SE3	78	F3
Hatcliffe St. SE10	69	F5
Woolwich Rd.		
Hatfield Clo. SE14	68	G7
Hatfield Clo., Ilf.	43	E3
Hatfield Clo., Mitch.	93	G4
Hatfield Mead, Mord.	93	D5
Central Rd.		
Hatfield Rd. E15	51	E5
Hatfield Rd. W4	65	D2
Hatfield Rd. W13	64	D1
Hatfield Rd., Dag.	53	E6
Hatfields SE1	**16**	**F1**
Hatfields SE1	67	G1
Hatfields, Loug.	27	E3
Hathaway Clo., Brom.	104	C1
Hathaway Clo., Stan.	29	D5
Hathaway Cres. E12	52	G6
Hathaway Gdns. W13	55	C5
Hathaway Gdns., Rom.	44	D5
Hathaway Rd., Croy.	94	H7
Hatherleigh Clo., Chess.	98	G5
Hatherleigh Clo., Mord.	93	D4
Hatherleigh Rd., Ruis.	45	A2
Hatherley Cres., Sid.	89	A2
Hatherley Gdns. E6	61	A2
Hatherley Gdns. N8	58	E6
Hatherley Gro. W2	**10**	**A3**
Hatherley Gro. W2	57	E6
Hatherley Ms. E17	41	J4
Hatherley Rd. E17	41	J4
Hatherley Rd., Rich.	73	J1
Hatherley Rd., Sid.	89	A2
Hatherley St. SW1	**19**	**G2**
Hathern Gdns. SE9	88	D4
Hatherop Rd., Hmptn.	81	F7
Hathorne Clo. SE15	77	E2
Hathway St. SE15	77	F2
Gibbon Rd.		

Hathway Ter. SE14	77	F2
Gibbon Rd.		
Hatley Ave., Ilf.	43	F4
Hatley Clo. N11	31	J5
Hatley Rd. N4	49	F2
Hatteraick St. SE16	68	F2
Church St.		
Hattersfield Clo., Belv.	71	F4
Hatton Clo. SE18	70	G7
Hatton Ct. E5	50	H4
Gilpin Rd.		
Hatton Gdn. EC1	**12**	**F1**
Hatton Gdn. EC1	58	G5
Hatton Gdns., Mitch.	93	J5
Hatton Grn., Felt.	72	A4
Hatton Ho. E1	**13**	**J5**
Hatton Pl. EC1	58	G5
Hatton Rd., Croy.	101	G1
Hatton Row NW8	**6**	**F6**
Hatton St. NW8	**6**	**F6**
Hatton Wall EC1	**12**	**E1**
Hatton Wall EC1	58	G5
Haunch of Venison Yd. W1	**11**	**D4**
Havana Rd. SW19	84	D2
Havannah St. E14	69	A2
Havant Rd. E17	42	C3
Havant Way SE15	**21**	**F7**
Havelock Pl., Har.	37	B6
Havelock Rd. N17	41	D2
Havelock Rd. SW19	84	F5
Havelock Rd., Belv.	71	F4
Havelock Rd., Brom.	96	J4
Havelock Rd., Croy.	102	C2
Havelock Rd., Har.	37	B3
Havelock Rd., Sthl.	63	E3
Havelock St. N1	58	E1
Havelock St., Ilf.	52	E2
Havelock Ter. SW8	67	B7
Havelock Wk. SE23	86	F1
Haven, The, Rich.	74	A3
Haven Clo. SE9	88	C3
Haven Clo. SW19	84	A3
Haven Clo., Sid.	89	C6
Haven Grn. W5	55	G6
Haven Grn. Ct. W5	55	G6
Haven La. W5	55	H6
Haven Pl. W5	55	G7
The Bdy.		
Haven St. NW1	49	B7
Castlehaven Rd.		
Havenhurst Ri., Enf.	24	G2
Havenwood, Wem.	47	B3
Haverfield Gdns., Rich.	65	A7
Haverfield Rd. E3	59	H3
Haverford Way, Edg.	37	J1
Haverhill Rd. E4	34	C1
Haverhill Rd. SW12	85	C1
Havering Gdns., Rom.	44	C5
Havering St. E1	59	G6
Devonport St.		
Havering Way, Bark.	62	B3
Haversfield Est., Brent.	64	H5
Haversham Clo., Twick.	73	G6
Haversham Pl. SE19	85	H7
Biggin Hill		
Haverstock Hill NW3	48	J6
Haverstock Rd. NW5	49	A5
Haverstock St. N1	**8**	**H2**
Haverstock St. N1	58	H2
Haverthwaite Rd., Orp.	104	G3
Havil St. SE5	68	B7
Hawarden Gro. SE24	76	J7
Hawarden Hill NW2	47	G3
Hawarden Rd. E17	41	G4
Hawbridge Rd. E11	51	D1
Hawes La., W.Wick.	103	C1
Hawes Rd. N18	33	E6
Hawes Rd., Brom.	96	H1
Hawes St. N1	49	H7
Haweswater Ho., Islw.	73	C5
Hawgood St. E3	60	A5
Hawkdene E4	26	B6
Hawke Pk. Rd. N22	40	H3
Hawke Pl. SE16	68	G2
Middleton Dr.		
Hawke Rd. SE19	86	A6
Hawker Clo., Wall.	101	E7
Kingsford Ave.		
Hawkes Rd., Mitch.	93	H1
Hawkesbury Rd. SW15	74	H5
Hawkesfield Rd. SE23	86	H2
Hawkesley Clo., Twick.	82	D4

Hawkewood Rd., 90 A3
Sun.
Hawkhurst Gdns., 98 H4
Chess.
Hawkhurst Rd. SW16 94 D1
Hawkhurst Way, 92 D5
N. Mal.
Hawkhurst Way, 103 B2
W.Wick.
Hawkins Clo., Borwd. 22 C2
Banks Rd.
Hawkins Clo., Har. 37 A7
Hawkins Rd., Tedd. 82 E6
Hawkley Gdns. SE27 85 H2
Hawkridge Clo., Rom. 44 C6
Hawks Ms. SE10 69 C7
Luton Pl.
Hawks Rd., Kings.T. 91 J2
Hawksbrook La., 96 B6
Beck.
Hawkshaw Clo. SW2 76 E7
Tierney Rd.
Hawkshead Clo., 87 E7
Brom.
Hawkshead Rd. 47 F7
NW10
Hawkshead Rd. W4 65 E2
Hawkslade Rd. SE15 77 G5
Hawksley Rd. N16 50 A3
Hawksmoor Clo. E6 61 B6
Allhallows Rd.
Hawksmoor Ms. E1 59 E7
Cable St.
Hawksmoor St. W6 66 A6
Hawksmouth E4 26 B7
Hawkstone Rd. SE16 68 F4
Hawkwell Wk. N1 58 J1
Basire St.
Hawkwood Cres. E4 26 B6
Hawkwood La., Chis. 97 F1
Hawkwood Mt. E5 50 E1
Hawlands Dr., Pnr. 36 E7
Hawley Clo., Hmptn. 81 F6
Hawley Cres. NW1 49 B7
Hawley Ms. NW1 49 B7
Hawley St.
Hawley Rd. NW1 49 B7
Hawley St. NW1 49 B7
Hawstead Rd. SE6 78 B6
Hawsted, Buck.H. 26 H7
Hawthorn Ave. N13 32 E5
Hawthorn Ave., 101 A7
Cars.
Hawthorn Ave., Rich. 73 H2
Kew Rd.
Hawthorn Ave., 94 H1
Th.Hth.
Hawthorn Clo., 81 G5
Hmptn.
Hawthorn Clo., 63 B7
Houns.
Hawthorn Clo., Orp. 97 G6
Hawthorn Ct., Rich. 74 B1
Hawthorn Cres. 85 A5
SW17
Hawthorn Dr., Har. 36 G6
Hawthorn Dr., 103 E4
W.Wick.
Hawthorn Gdns. W5 64 G3
Hawthorn Gro. SE20 86 E7
Hawthorn Gro., 22 F6
Barn.
Hawthorn Hatch, 64 E7
Brent.
Hawthorn Ms. NW7 39 B1
Holders Hill Rd.
Hawthorn Pl., Erith 71 J5
Hawthorn Rd. N8 40 D3
Hawthorn Rd. N18 33 C6
Hawthorn Rd. NW10 47 G7
Hawthorn Rd., Bexh. 80 F4
Hawthorn Rd., 64 E7
Brent.
Hawthorn Rd., 35 A4
Buck.H.
Hawthorn Rd., Sutt. 100 H5
Hawthorn Rd., Wall. 101 B7
Hawthorn Wk. W10 57 B4
Droop St.
Hawthorn Way N9 33 B2
Hawthorndene Clo., 103 F2
Brom.
Hawthorndene Rd., 103 F2
Brom.
Hawthorne Ave., 37 D6
Har.
Hawthorne Ave., 93 G2
Mitch.
Hawthorne Ave., 36 B7
Ruis.
Hawthorne Clo. N1 50 B6
Hawthorne Clo., 97 C3
Brom.

Hawthorne Clo., 100 E2
Sutt.
Aultone Way
Hawthorne Fm. Ave., 54 E1
Nthlt.
Hawthorne Gro. NW9 38 C7
Hawthorne Rd. E17 42 A3
Hawthorne Rd., 97 C3
Brom.
Hawthornes Gro., 27 C4
Har.
Hawthorns, Wdf.Grn. 34 G3
Hawthorns, The, 99 F6
Epsom
Ewell Bypass
Hawthorns, The, 27 D4
Loug.
Hawtrey Ave., Nthlt. 54 D2
Hawtrey Dr., Ruis. 36 A7
Hawtrey Rd. NW3 48 H7
Haxted Rd., Brom. 96 H1
North Rd.
Hay Clo. E15 51 E7
Hay Clo., Borwd. 22 C2
Banks Rd.
Hay Currie St. E14 60 B6
Hay Hill W1 11 E6
Hay Hill W1 58 B7
Hay La. NW9 38 C4
Hay St. E2 59 D1
Haycroft Gdns. 56 G1
NW10
Haycroft Rd. SW2 76 E5
Haycroft Rd., Surb. 98 G3
Hayday Rd. E16 60 G5
Hayden Way, Rom. 44 J2
Haydens Pl. W11 57 C6
Portobello Rd.
Haydns Ms. W3 56 C6
Emanuel Ave.
Haydock Ave., Nthlt. 45 G6
Haydock Grn., Nthlt. 45 G6
Haydock Ave.
Haydon Clo. NW9 38 C4
Haydon Clo., Enf. 25 B6
Mortimer Dr.
Haydon Dr., Pnr. 36 B4
Haydon Pk. Rd. 84 D5
SW19
Haydon Rd., Dag. 53 C2
Haydon St. EC3 13 F5
Haydon Wk. E1 13 G5
Haydons Rd. SW19 84 E5
Hayes Chase, 96 D6
W.Wick.
Hayes Clo., Brom. 103 G2
Hayes Ct. SW2 85 E1
Hayes Cres. NW11 39 C5
Hayes Cres., Sutt. 100 A4
Hayes Gdns., Brom. 103 G2
Hayes Hill, Brom. 103 E1
Hayes Hill Rd., 103 F1
Brom.
Hayes La., Beck. 96 C3
Hayes La., Brom. 96 G5
Hayes Mead Rd., 103 E1
Brom.
Hayes Pl. NW1 6 H6
Hayes Rd., Brom. 96 G4
Hayes Rd., Sthl. 63 B4
Hayes St., Brom. 103 H1
Hayes Way, Beck. 96 C4
Hayes Wd. Ave., 103 H1
Brom.
Hayesford Pk. Dr., 96 F5
Brom.
Hayfield Pas. E1 59 F4
Stepney Grn.
Hayfield Yd. E1 59 F4
Mile End Rd.
Haygarth Pl. SW19 84 A5
Haygreen Clo., 83 B6
Kings.T.
Kingsnympton Pk.
Hayland Clo. NW9 38 D4
Hayles St. SE11 20 G1
Hayles St. SE11 67 H4
Haylett Gdns., 91 G4
Kings.T.
Anglesea Rd.
Hayling Ave., Felt. 81 A3
Hayman St. N1 49 H7
Cross St.
Haymarket SW1 11 H6
Haymarket SW1 58 D7
Haymarket Arc. SW1 11 H6
Haymer Gdns., 99 G3
Wor.Pk.
Haymerle Rd. SE15 21 H6
Haymerle Rd. SE15 68 D6
Haymill Clo., Grnf. 55 C3
Hayne Rd., Beck. 95 J2
Hayne St. EC1 12 H1

Haynes Clo. N17 33 E7
Haynes Clo. SE3 78 E3
Haynes La. SE19 86 B6
Haynes Rd., Wem. 46 H7
Haynt Wk. SW20 93 B3
Hay's La. SE1 17 D2
Hay's Ms. W1 15 D1
Hay's Ms. W1 67 B1
Haysleigh Gdns. 95 D2
SE20
Hayter Rd. SW2 76 E5
Hayton Clo. E8 50 C6
Buttermere Wk.
Hayward Clo. SW19 84 E7
Hayward Gdns. 74 J6
SW15
Hayward Rd. N20 31 F2
Hayward's Pl. EC1 8 G6
Haywood Clo., Pnr. 36 D2
Haywood Ri., Orp. 104 H4
Haywood Rd., Brom. 97 A4
Hayworth Clo., Enf. 25 H2
Green St.
Hazel Bank, Surb. 99 C1
Hazel Clo. N13 33 A3
Hazel Clo. N19 49 C2
Hargrave Pk.
Hazel Clo. SE15 77 D2
Copeland Rd.
Hazel Clo., Brent. 64 E7
Hazel Clo., Croy. 102 G1
Primrose La.
Hazel Clo., Mitch. 94 D4
Hazel Clo., Twick. 72 J7
Hazel Gdns., Edg. 30 B4
Hazel Gro. SE26 86 G4
Hazel Gro., Enf. 25 D6
Dimsdale Dr.
Hazel Gro., Orp. 104 E2
Hazel Gro., Rom. 44 E3
Hazel Gro., Wem. 55 H1
Carlyon Rd.
Hazel Gro. Est. 86 G4
SE26
Hazel La., Rich. 82 H2
Hazel Mead, Barn. 22 H5
Hazel Rd. E15 51 E5
Wingfield Rd.
Hazel Rd. NW10 56 H3
Hazel Wk., Brom. 97 D6
Hazel Way E4 33 J6
Hazel Way SE1 21 F1
Hazelbank Rd. SE6 87 D2
Hazelbourne Rd. 76 B6
SW12
Hazelbrouck Gdns., 35 G7
Ilf.
Hazelbury Clo. SW19 93 D2
Hazelbury Grn. N9 33 B3
Hazelbury La. N9 33 B3
Hazelcroft, Pnr. 28 H6
Hazeldean Rd. NW10 47 D7
Hazeldene Dr., Pnr. 36 C3
Hazeldene Rd., Ilf. 53 B2
Hazeldene Rd., 80 C2
Well.
Hazeldon Rd. SE4 77 H5
Hazeleigh Gdns., 35 B5
Wdf.Grn.
Hazelgreen Clo. N21 32 H1
Hazelhurst, Beck. 96 D1
Hazelhurst Rd. SW17 84 F4
Hazell Cres., Rom. 44 H1
Hazellville Rd. N19 40 D7
Hazelmere Clo., 54 F2
Nthlt.
Hazelmere Dr., 54 F2
Nthlt.
Hazelmere Rd. NW6 57 C1
Hazelmere Rd., 54 F2
Nthlt.
Hazelmere Rd., Orp. 97 F4
Hazelmere Wk., 54 F2
Nthlt.
Hazelmere Way, 96 G6
Brom.
Hazeltree La., Nthlt. 54 E3
Hazelwood, Loug. 27 A5
Hazelwood Ave., 93 E4
Mord.
Hazelwood Clo. W5 64 H2
Hazelwood Clo., 36 H4
Har.
Hazelwood Ct. NW10 47 E3
Neasden La. N.
Hazelwood Cres. N13 32 G4
Hazelwood Cres. W10 57 B4
Hazelwood Cft., 111 H6
Surb.
Hazelwood Dr., Pnr. 36 B2
Hazelwood La. N13 32 G4
Hazelwood Pk. Clo., 35 H5
Chig.

Hazelwood Rd. E17 41 H5
Hazelwood Rd., Enf. 25 C6
Hazlebury Rd. SW6 75 E2
Hazledean Rd., 102 A2
Croy.
Hazledene Rd. W4 65 C6
Hazlemere Gdns., 99 G1
Wor.Pk.
Hazlewell Rd. SW15 74 H5
Hazlitt Ms. W14 66 B3
Hazlitt Rd.
Hazlitt Rd. W14 66 B3
Head St. E1 59 G6
Headcorn Pl., 94 F4
Th.Hth.
Headcorn Rd.
Headcorn Rd. N17 33 C7
Headcorn Rd., Brom. 87 G5
Headcorn Rd., 94 F4
Th.Hth.
Headfort Pl. SW1 15 C4
Headfort Pl. SW1 67 A2
Headingley Clo., Ilf. 35 J6
Headington Rd. 84 F2
SW18
Headlam Rd. SW4 76 D6
Headlam St. E1 59 E4
Headley App., Ilf. 43 E5
Headley Ave., Wall. 101 F5
Headley Clo., Epsom 99 A6
Headley Ct. SE26 86 F5
Headley Dr., Croy. 103 D7
Headley Dr., Ilf. 43 E6
Head's Ms. W11 57 D6
Artesian Rd.
Headstone Dr., Har. 37 B3
Headstone Gdns., 36 J4
Har.
Headstone La., Har. 28 H7
Headstone Rd., Har. 37 B5
Headway Clo., Rich. 82 F4
Locksmeade Rd.
Heald St. SE14 77 J1
Healey Dr., Orp. 104 J4
Healey St. NW1 49 B6
Heanor Ct. E5 50 G3
Pedro St.
Hearn Ri., Nthlt. 54 D1
Hearn St. EC2 9 E6
Hearn St. EC2 59 B4
Hearne Rd. W4 65 A6
Hearn's Bldgs. SE17 21 C2
Hearnville Rd. SW12 85 A1
Heath, The W7 64 B1
Lwr. Boston Rd.
Heath Ave., Bexh. 71 D6
Heath Brow NW3 48 F3
North End Way
Heath Clo. NW11 39 E7
Heath Clo. W5 55 J4
Heath Ct., Houns. 72 F4
Heath Dr. NW3 48 E4
Heath Dr. SW20 92 J4
Heath Gdns., Twick. 82 C1
Heath Gro. SE20 86 F7
Maple Rd.
Heath Hurst Rd. NW3 48 H4
Heath La. SE3 78 D2
Heath Mead SW19 84 A3
Heath Pk. Dr., 97 B3
Brom.
Heath Ri. SW15 75 A6
Heath Ri., Brom. 96 F6
Heath Rd. SW8 76 B2
Heath Rd., Bex. 89 J1
Heath Rd., Har. 36 J7
Heath Rd., Houns. 72 H4
Heath Rd., Rom. 44 D7
Heath Rd., Th.Hth. 82 C1
Heath Rd., Twick. 82 C1
Heath Side NW3 48 G4
Heath Side, Orp. 104 F1
Heath St. NW3 48 F3
Heath Vw. N2 39 F4
Heath Vw. Clo. N2 39 F4
Heath Vill. SE18 70 J5
Heath Way, Erith 80 J1
Heatham Pk., Twick. 73 C7
Heathbourne Rd. 38 E3
(Bushey), Wat.
Heathcock Ct. WC2 58 E7
Strand
Heathcote Ave., 43 C2
Ilf.
Heathcote Gro. E4 34 C3
Heathcote Rd., 73 E6
Twick.
Heathcote St. WC1 8 C5
Heathcote St. WC1 58 F4
Heathcroft NW11 48 E1
Heathcroft W5 55 J4
Heathdale Ave., 72 E3
Houns.

Heathdene Dr., Belv.	71	H4
Heathdene Rd. SW16	85	F7
Heathdene Rd., Wall.	101	A7
Heathedge SE26	86	E2
Heather Clo. E6	61	E6
Heather Clo. SW8	76	B3
Heather Clo., Hmptn.	90	F1
Heather Dr., Enf.	24	H2
Chasewood Ave.		
Heather Gdns. NW11	39	B6
Heather Gdns., Sutt.	100	D6
Heather Pk. Dr., Wem.	47	A7
Heather Rd. NW2	47	F2
Heather Rd. SE12	87	G2
Heather Wk. W10	57	B4
Droop St.		
Heather Wk., Edg.	30	B5
Heather Way, Stan.	29	C6
Heatherbank SE9	79	C2
Heatherbank, Chis.	97	D2
Heatherdale Clo., Kings.T.	83	B7
Heatherdene Clo. N12	39	F1
Bow La.		
Heatherdene Clo., Mitch.	93	H4
Heatherlands, Sun.	81	A6
Heatherley Dr., Ilf.	43	B3
Heatherset Gdns. SW16	85	F7
Heatherside Rd., Epsom	99	D7
Heatherside Rd., Sid.	89	D3
Wren Rd.		
Heatherwood Clo. E12	51	J2
Heathfield E4	34	C3
Heathfield, Chis.	88	F6
Heathfield Ave. SW18	75	G7
Heathfield Rd.		
Heathfield Clo. E16	61	A5
Heathfield Clo., Kes.	103	J5
Heathfield Dr., Mitch.	93	H1
Heathfield Gdns. NW11	39	A6
Heathfield Gdns. SW18	75	G6
Heathfield Rd.		
Heathfield Gdns. W4	65	C5
Heathfield La., Chis.	88	E6
Heathfield N., Twick.	73	C7
Heathfield Pk. NW2	47	J6
Heathfield Rd. SW18	75	F6
Heathfield Rd. W3	65	B2
Heathfield Rd., Bexh.	80	F4
Heathfield Rd., Brom.	87	F7
Heathfield Rd., Croy.	102	A4
Heathfield Rd., Kes.	103	J5
Heathfield S., Twick.	73	C7
Heathfield Sq. SW18	75	G7
Heathfield St. W11	57	B7
Portland Rd.		
Heathfield Ter. SW18	70	H6
Heathfield Ter. W4	65	C5
Heathfields Ct., Houns.	72	E5
Frampton Rd.		
Heathgate NW11	39	E6
Heathland Rd. N16	50	B1
Heathlands Clo., Twick.	82	C1
Heathlands Way, Houns.	72	E5
Frampton Rd.		
Heathlee Rd. SE3	78	F4
Heathley End, Chis.	88	F6
Heathmans Rd. SW6	75	C1
Heathrow International Trd. Est., Houns.	72	B3
Heaths Clo., Enf.	25	B2
Heathside, Esher	98	B3
Heathside, Houns.	72	F7
Heathside Ave., Bexh.	80	E2
Heathside Clo., Esher	98	B3
Heathstan Rd. W12	56	G6
Heathview Clo. SW19	84	A2
Heathview Dr. SE2	71	D6
Heathview Gdns. SW15	74	J7
Heathview Rd., Th.Hth.	94	G4
Heathville Rd. N19	40	E7
Heathwall St. SW11	75	J3
Heathway SE3	69	G7
Heathway, Croy.	102	J3
Heathway, Dag.	53	F3
Heathway, Wdf.Grn.	34	J4
Heathwood Gdns. SE7	70	B4
Heaton Rd. SE15	77	D3
Heaton Rd., Mitch.	85	A7
Heaver Rd. SW11	75	G3
Wye St.		
Heavitree Rd. SE18	70	G5
Hebden Ct. E2	59	C1
Laburnum St.		
Hebdon Rd. SW17	84	H3
Heber Rd. NW2	48	A5
Heber Rd. SE22	77	C6
Hebron Rd. W6	65	H3
Hecham Clo. E17	41	H2
Heckfield Pl. SW6	66	D7
Fulham Rd.		
Heckford St. E1	59	G7
The Highway		
Hector St. SE18	70	H4
Heddington Gro. N7	49	F5
Heddon Clo., Islw.	73	D4
Heddon Ct. Ave., Barn.	23	J5
Heddon Rd., Barn.	23	J5
Heddon St. W1	**11**	**F5**
Heddon St. W1	58	C7
Hedge Hill, Enf.	24	H1
Hedge La. N13	32	H3
Hedge Wk. SE6	87	B5
Lushington Rd.		
Hedgeley, Ilf.	43	C4
Hedgeley St. SE12	78	F5
Hedgemans Rd., Dag.	53	D7
Hedgemans Way, Dag.	53	E6
Hedgerley Gdns., Grnf.	54	J2
Hedgers Gro. E9	50	H6
Hedgewood Gdns., Ilf.	43	D4
Hedingham Clo. N1	49	J7
Popham Rd.		
Hedingham Rd., Dag.	53	B5
Hedley Rd., Twick.	72	E2
Hedley Row N5	50	A5
Poets Rd.		
Heenan Clo., Bark.	52	F6
Glenny Rd.		
Heene Rd., Enf.	25	A1
Heigham Rd. E6	52	B7
Heighton Gdns., Croy.	101	H5
Heights, The SE7	69	J5
Heights, The, Beck.	81	J2
Heights, The, Loug.	27	C2
Heights, The, Nthlt.	45	F5
Heights Clo. SW20	83	H7
Heiron St. SE17	**20**	**H6**
Heiron St. SE17	67	H6
Helby Rd. SW4	76	D6
Helder Gro. SE12	78	F7
Helder St., S.Croy.	102	A6
Heldmann Clo., Houns.	73	A4
Helen Ave., Felt.	72	B7
Helen Clo. N2	39	F3
Thomas More Way		
Helen Clo., W.Mol.	90	H4
Helen St. SE18	70	E4
Wilmount St.		
Helena Clo., Wall.	101	E7
Kingsford Ave.		
Helena Pl. E9	59	F1
Fremont St.		
Helena Rd. E13	60	F2
Helena Rd. E17	42	A5
Helena Rd. NW10	47	H5
Helena Rd. W5	55	G5
Helens Pl. E2	59	F3
Roman Rd.		
Helenslea Ave. NW11	48	C1
Helix Gdns. SW2	76	F6
Helix Rd.		
Helix Rd. SW2	76	F6
Hellings St. E1	**17**	**J2**
Helme Clo. SW19	84	C5
Helmet Row EC1	**9**	**A5**
Helmet Row EC1	58	J4
Helmsdale Clo., Hayes	54	E4
Berrydale Rd.		
Helmsdale Rd. SW16	94	D1
Helmsley Pl. E8	50	E7
Helston Clo., Pnr.	28	F7
Helvetia St. SE6	86	J2
Hemans St. SW8	67	D7
Hemberton Rd. SW9	76	E3
Hemery Rd., Grnf.	46	A5
Lilian Board Way		
Heming Rd., Edg.	30	B7
Hemingford Rd. N1	58	F1
Hemingford Rd., Sutt.	99	J4
Hemington Ave. N11	31	J5
Hemlock Rd. W12	56	F7
Hemming Clo., Hmptn.	90	G1
Chandler Clo.		
Hemming St. E1	**9**	**J6**
Hemming St. E1	59	D4
Hemp Wk. SE17	**21**	**C5**
Hempstead Clo., Buck.H.	34	G2
Hempstead Rd. E17	42	D2
Hemsby Rd., Chess.	98	J6
Hemstal Rd. NW6	48	D7
Hemswell Dr. NW9	38	E1
Hemsworth Ct. N1	**9**	**D1**
Hemsworth St. N1	**9**	**D1**
Hemsworth St. N1	59	B2
Hemus Pl. SW3	**18**	**H4**
Hen & Chicken Ct. EC4	58	G6
Fleet St.		
Henbury Way, Wat.	28	D3
Henchman St. W12	56	F6
Hendale Ave. NW4	38	G3
Henderson Clo. NW10	47	C6
Henderson Dr. NW8	**6**	**E5**
Henderson Rd. E7	51	J6
Henderson Rd. N9	33	E1
Henderson Rd. SW18	75	H7
Henderson Rd., Croy.	95	A6
Henderson Rd., Hayes	54	A3
Hendham Rd. SW17	84	H2
Hendon Ave. N3	39	B1
Hendon La. N3	39	B3
Hendon Pk. Row NW11	39	C6
Hendon Rd. N9	33	D2
Hendon Way NW2	39	A7
Hendon Way NW4	38	H6
Hendon Wk. La. NW7	22	F7
Hendre Rd. SE1	**21**	**E2**
Hendren Clo., Grnf.	46	A5
Dimmock Dr.		
Hendrick Ave. SW12	75	J7
Heneage La. EC3	**13**	**E4**
Heneage St. E1	**13**	**G1**
Heneage St. E1	59	C5
Henfield Clo. N19	49	C1
Henfield Clo., Bex.	80	G6
Henfield Rd. SW19	93	C1
Hengelo Gdns., Mitch.	93	G4
Hengist Rd. SE12	78	H7
Hengist Rd., Erith	71	H7
Hengist Way, Brom.	96	D4
Hengrave Rd. SE23	77	F7
Hengrove Ct., Bex.	89	E1
Hurst Rd.		
Henley Ave., Sutt.	100	B3
Henley Clo., Grnf.	54	J2
Henley Clo., Islw.	73	C1
Henley Ct. N14	24	C7
Henley Dr. SE1	**21**	**G1**
Henley Dr., Kings.T.	83	F7
Henley Gdns., Pnr.	36	B3
Henley Gdns., Rom.	44	E5
Henley Rd. E16	70	C2
Henley Rd. N18	33	B4
Henley Rd. NW10	56	J1
Henley Rd., Ilf.	52	F4
Henley St. SW11	76	A2
Henley Way, Felt.	81	D5
Conway Rd.		
Hennel Clo. SE23	86	F3
Henniker Gdns. E6	61	A3
Henniker Ms. SW3	**18**	**E5**
Henniker Rd. E15	51	E5
Henniker Rd. E15	51	D5
Henning St. SW11	75	H1
Henningham Rd. N17	41	A1
Henrietta Ms. WC1	**8**	**B5**
Henrietta Pl. W1	**11**	**D3**
Henrietta Pl. W1	58	B6
Henrietta St. E15	51	C5
Henrietta St. WC2	**12**	**B5**
Henrietta St. WC2	58	E7
Henriques St. E1	**13**	**J3**
Henriques St. E1	59	D6
Henry Cooper Way SE9	88	A3
Henry Darlot Dr. NW7	31	A5
Henry Dickens Ct. W11	57	A7
Henry Jackson Rd. SW15	75	A3
Henry Rd. E6	61	B2
Henry Rd. N4	49	J1
Henry Rd., Barn.	23	G5
Henry St., Brom.	96	H1
Henry's Ave., Wdf.Grn.	34	F5
Henry's Wk., Ilf.	35	G7
Henryson Rd. SE4	78	A5
Hensford Gdns. SE26	86	E4
Wells Pk. Rd.		
Henshall St. N1	50	A6
Henshaw St. SE17	**21**	**B1**
Henshaw St. SE17	68	A4
Henshawe Rd., Dag.	53	D3
Henshill Pt. E3	60	B3
Bromley High St.		
Henslowe Rd. SE22	77	D5
Henson Ave. NW2	47	J5
Henson Clo., Orp.	104	E2
Henson Path, Har.	37	G3
Brancker Rd.		
Henson Pl., Nthlt.	54	C1
Henstridge Pl. NW8	57	H2
Henty Clo. SW11	66	H7
Henty Wk. SW15	74	H5
Henville Rd., Brom.	96	J1
Henwick Rd. SE9	79	A3
Henwood Rd. SE16	68	F3
Gomm Rd.		
Henwood Side, Wdf.Grn.	35	C6
Love La.		
Hepburn Gdns., Brom.	103	E1
Hepburn Ms. SW11	75	J5
Webbs Rd.		
Hepple Clo., Islw.	73	E2
Hepplestone Clo. SW15	74	H6
Dover Pk. Dr.		
Hepscott Rd. E9	51	A6
Hepworth Ct., Bark.	53	A5
Hepworth Gdns., Bark.	53	A5
Hepworth Rd. SW16	85	E7
Hepworth Wk. NW3	48	H5
Haverstock Hill		
Heracles Clo., Wall.	101	E7
Gull Clo.		
Herald Gdns., Wall.	101	B3
Herald St. E2	59	E4
Three Colts La.		
Herald's Ct. SE11	**20**	**G2**
Herald's Pl. SE11	**20**	**F1**
Herbal Hill EC1	**8**	**F6**
Herbal Hill EC1	58	G4
Herbert Cres. SW1	**15**	**A5**
Herbert Gdns. NW10	56	H1
Herbert Gdns., Rom.	44	D7
Magnolia Rd.		
Herbert Pl. SE18	70	E6
Plumstead Common Rd.		
Herbert Rd. E12	52	B4
Herbert Rd. E17	41	J7
Herbert Rd. N11	32	E7
Herbert Rd. N15	41	C5
Herbert Rd. NW9	38	G6
Herbert Rd. SE18	70	D7
Herbert Rd. SW19	84	C7
Herbert Rd., Bexh.	80	E2
Herbert Rd., Brom.	97	A5
Herbert Rd., Ilf.	52	H2
Herbert Rd., Kings.T.	91	J3
Herbert Rd., Sthl.	63	F1
Herbert St. E13	60	G2
Herbert St. NW5	46	A6
Herbert Ter. SE18	70	E6
Herbert Rd.		
Herbrand St. WC1	**8**	**A5**
Herbrand St. WC1	58	E4
Hercules Pl. N7	49	E3
Hercules St.		
Hercules Rd. SE1	**16**	**D6**
Hercules Rd. SE1	67	F3
Hercules St. N7	49	E3
Hercules Twr. SE13	68	H6
Milton Ct. Rd.		
Hereford Ave., Barn.	31	J1
Hereford Gdns., Ilf.	43	B7
Hereford Gdns., Pnr.	36	E5

Hereford Gdns.,	81	J1
Twick.		
Hereford Ho. NW6	57	D2
Hereford Ms. W2	57	D6
Hereford Pl. SE14	68	A7
Hereford Retreat		
SE15		
Hereford Rd. E11	42	H5
Hereford Rd. W2	57	D6
Hereford Rd. W3	56	B7
Hereford Rd. W5	64	F3
Hereford Rd., Felt.	81	C1
Hereford Sq. SW7	**18**	**D2**
Hereford Sq. SW7	66	F4
Hereford St. E2	59	D4
Hereford Way,	98	F5
Chess.		
Herent Dr., Ilf.	43	B4
Hereward Gdns. N13	32	G5
Hereward Grn.,	27	F1
Loug.		
Hereward Rd. SW17	84	H4
Herga Ct., Har.	46	B3
Herga Rd., Har.	37	C4
Heriot Ave. E4	34	A2
Heriot Rd. NW4	38	J5
Heriots Clo., Stan.	29	D4
Heritage Hill, Kes.	103	J5
Heritage Vw., Har.	46	C3
Herlwyn Gdns.	84	J4
SW17		
Hermes Pt. W9	57	D4
Harrow Rd.		
Hermes St. N1	**8**	**E2**
Hermes Wk., Nthlt.	54	G2
Hotspur Rd.		
Hermes Way, Wall.	101	D7
Hermiston Ave. N4	40	E5
Hermit Pl. NW6	57	E1
Belsize Rd.		
Hermit Rd. E16	60	F4
Hermit St. EC1	**8**	**G3**
Hermit St. EC1	58	H3
Hermitage, The SE23	86	F1
Hermitage, The	74	F1
SW13		
Hermitage, The,	73	H5
Rich.		
Hermitage Clo. E18	42	F4
Hermitage Clo., Enf.	24	H2
Hermitage Clo.,	98	D6
Esher		
Hermitage Ct. E18	42	G4
Hermitage Ct. NW2	48	D3
Hermitage La.		
Hermitage Gdns.	48	D3
NW2		
Hermitage Gdns.	85	J7
SE19		
Hermitage La. N18	33	A5
Great Cambridge Rd.		
Hermitage La. NW2	48	D3
Hermitage La. SE25	95	D6
Hermitage La. SW16	85	F7
Hermitage La., Croy.	95	D6
Hermitage Path	94	E1
SW16		
Hermitage Rd. N4	40	H7
Hermitage Rd. N15	40	H7
Hermitage Rd. SE19	85	J7
Hermitage St. W2	**10**	**E2**
Hermitage Wk. E18	42	F4
Hermitage Wall E1	**17**	**J2**
Hermitage Wall E1	68	D1
Hermitage Way,	37	D1
Stan.		
Hermon Gro., Hayes	63	A1
Hermon Hill E11	42	G5
Hermon Hill E18	42	H3
Herndon Rd. SW18	75	F5
Herne Clo. NW10	47	D5
North Circular Rd.		
Herne Hill SE24	76	J5
Herne Hill Rd. SE24	76	J3
Herne Ms. N18	33	D4
Lyndhurst Rd.		
Herne Pl. SE24	76	H5
Herne Rd., Surb.	98	G2
Heron Clo. E17	41	J2
Heron Clo. NW10	47	D5
Heron Clo., Buck.H.	34	G1
Heron Ct., Brom.	96	J4
Heron Cres., Sid.	88	H3
Heron Hill, Belv.	71	F5
Heron Ms., Ilf.	52	E2
Balfour Rd.		
Heron Pl. SE16	68	H1
Heron Quay E14	69	A1
Heron Rd. SE24	76	J4
Heron Rd., Croy.	102	B2
Tunstall Rd.		
Heron Rd., Twick.	73	D4

Herondale Ave.	84	G1
SW18		
Herongate Rd. E12	51	J2
Herons, The E11	42	F6
Heron's Pl., Islw.	73	E3
Herons Ri., Barn.	23	H4
Heronsforde W13	55	F6
Heronsgate, Edg.	30	A5
Heronslea Dr., Stan.	29	H5
Heronway, Wdf.Grn.	34	J4
Herrick Rd. N5	49	J3
Herrick St. SW1	**19**	**J2**
Herrick St. SW1	67	D4
Herries St. W10	57	B2
Herringham Rd. SE7	69	J3
Herrongate Clo.,	25	C2
Enf.		
Hersant Clo. NW10	56	G1
Herschell Rd. SE23	77	H7
Hersham Clo. SW15	74	D2
Hertford Ave. SW14	74	D5
Hertford Clo., Barn.	23	G3
Hertford Pl. W1	**7**	**F6**
Hertford Rd. N1	59	B1
Hertford Rd. N2	39	H3
Hertford Rd. N9	33	D2
Hertford Rd., Bark.	52	E7
Hertford Rd., Barn.	23	F3
Hertford Rd., Enf.	25	F2
Hertford Rd., Ilf.	43	H6
Hertford St. W1	**15**	**C2**
Hertford St. W1	67	A1
Hertford Wk., Belv.	71	G5
Hertford Way, Mitch.	94	E4
Hertslet Rd. N7	49	F3
Hertsmere Rd. E14	60	A7
Hervey Clo. N3	39	D1
Hervey Pk. Rd. E17	41	H4
Hervey Rd. SE3	78	H1
Hesa Rd., Hayes	54	A6
Hesketh Pl. W11	57	B7
Hesketh Rd. E7	51	G3
Heslop Rd. SW12	84	J1
Hesper Ms. SW5	**18**	**A3**
Hesper Ms. SW5	66	E5
Hesperus Cres. E14	69	B4
Hessel Rd. W13	64	D2
Hessel St. E1	59	E6
Hester Rd. N18	33	D5
Hester Rd. SW11	66	H7
Hestercombe Ave.	75	B2
SW6		
Heston Ave., Houns.	63	E6
Heston Gra. La.,	63	F6
Houns.		
Heston Ind. Cen.,	63	C6
Houns.		
Heston Ind. Mall,	63	F7
Houns.		
Heston Rd., Houns.	63	G6
Heston St. SE14	78	A1
Heswell Grn., Wat.	28	A3
Fairhaven Cres.		
Hetherington Rd.	84	E4
SW4		
Hetley Gdns. SE19	86	C7
Fox Hill		
Hetley Rd. W12	65	H1
Heton Gdns. NW4	38	G4
Hevelius Clo. SE10	69	F5
Hever Cft. SE9	88	D4
Hever Gdns., Brom.	97	D2
Heverham Rd. SE18	70	H4
Heversham Rd.,	80	G2
Bexh.		
Hewer St. W10	57	A5
Hewett Clo., Stan.	29	E4
Hewett Rd., Dag.	53	C5
Hewett St. EC2	**9**	**E6**
Hewish Rd. N18	33	B4
Hewitt Ave. N22	40	H2
Hewitt Rd. N8	40	G5
Hewlett Rd. E3	59	H2
Hexagon, The N6	48	J1
Hexal Rd. SE6	87	E3
Hexham Gdns., Islw.	64	D7
Hexham Rd. SE27	85	J2
Hexham Rd., Barn.	23	E4
Hexham Rd., Mord.	100	E1
Heybourne Rd. N17	33	E7
Heybridge Ave.	85	E1
SW16		
Heybridge Dr., Ilf.	43	G2
Heybridge Way E10	41	H7
Heyford Ave. SW8	**20**	**B7**
Heyford Ave. SW8	67	E7
Heyford Ave. SW20	93	C3
Heyford Rd., Mitch.	93	H2
Heygate St. SE17	**20**	**J2**
Heygate St. SE17	67	J4
Heylyn Sq. E3	59	J3
Malmesbury Rd.		
Heynes Rd., Dag.	53	C4

Heysham Dr., Wat.	28	C5
Heysham La. NW3	48	E3
Heysham Rd. N15	41	A6
Heythorp St. SW18	84	C1
Heywood Ave. NW9	38	E1
Heyworth Rd. E5	50	E4
Heyworth Rd. E15	51	F1
Hibbert Rd. E17	41	J7
Hibbert Rd. N14	32	D2
Hibbert St. SW11	76	F0
Hibernia Gdns.,	72	G4
Houns.		
Hibernia Rd., Houns.	72	G4
Hichisson Rd. SE15	77	F5
Hickin Clo. SE7	70	A4
Hickin St. E14	69	C3
Plevna St.		
Hickling Rd., Ilf.	52	E5
Hickman Ave. E4	34	C6
Hickman Clo. E16	61	A5
Hickman Rd., Rom.	44	C7
Hickmore Wk. SW4	76	C3
Hickory Clo. N9	25	D7
Hicks Ave., Grnf.	55	A2
Hicks Clo. SW11	75	H3
Hicks St. SE8	68	H5
Hidcote Gdns. SW20	93	H3
Hide Pl. SW1	**19**	**H2**
Hide Pl. SW1	67	D4
Hide Rd., Har.	36	J4
Hides St. N7	49	F6
Sheringham Rd.		
Higgins Wk., Hmptn.	81	E6
Abbott Clo.		
High Beech, S.Croy.	102	B7
High Beech,	27	B4
Loug.		
High Beeches, Sid.	89	E5
High Bri. SE10	69	D5
Eastney St.		
High Broom Cres.,	96	B7
W.Wick.		
High Cedar Dr. SW20	83	H7
High Coombe Pl.,	83	D7
Kings.T.		
High Cross Cen. N15	41	D4
High Cross Rd. N17	41	D3
High Dr., N.Mal.	92	C1
High Elms, Wdf.Grn.	34	G5
High Foleys, Esher	98	E7
High Gables, Loug.	27	A5
High Gro. SE18	70	G7
High Gro., Brom.	96	J1
High Hill Est. E5	50	E1
Mount Pleasant La.		
High Holborn WC1	**12**	**A3**
High Holborn WC1	58	E6
High Lawns, Har.	46	B3
High Level Dr. SE26	86	D4
High Mead, Chig.	35	F2
High Mead, Har.	37	B5
High Mead, W.Wick.	103	D2
High Meadow Clo.,	36	B4
Pnr.		
Daymer Gdns.		
High Meadow Cres.	38	D5
NW9		
High Meadows, Chig.	35	G5
High Meads Rd. E16	61	A6
Aleston Beck Rd.		
High Mt. NW4	38	G6
High Pk. Ave., Rich.	74	A1
High Pk. Rd., Rich.	74	A1
High Path SW19	93	E1
High Pt. N6	40	A7
High Pt. SE9	88	E3
High Rd. E18	42	G1
High Rd. N2	39	G1
High Rd. N11	32	B5
High Rd. N12	31	F4
High Rd. N15	41	C6
High Rd. N17	41	C3
High Rd. N20	31	F2
High Rd. N22	32	F6
High Rd.	47	F6
(Willesden) NW10		
High Rd., Buck.H.	34	H3
High Rd., Chig.	35	D5
High Rd. (Harrow	29	B7
Weald), Har.		
High Rd., Ilf.	52	F2
High Rd., Loug.	26	J6
High Rd., Rom.	53	A1
High Rd. (Bushey),	29	A1
Wat.		
High Rd., Wem.	46	H5
High Rd., Wdf.Grn.	34	F6
High Rd. Leyton E10	51	C4
High Rd. Leyton E15	51	C4
High Rd.	51	E4
Leytonstone E11		

High Rd.	51	E4
Leytonstone E15		
High Silver, Loug.	27	A4
High St. E11	42	G5
High St. E13	60	G2
High St. E15	60	C2
High St. E17	41	H5
High St. N8	40	E4
High St. N14	32	D2
High St.	32	D1
(Southgate) N14		
High St. NW7	30	H4
Wills Gro.		
High St.	56	F7
(Harlesden) NW10		
High St. SE20	86	F7
High St. (South	95	C4
Norwood) SE25		
High St. SW6	75	B3
High St. SW19	84	G7
(Colliers Wd.)		
High St. SW19	84	A5
(Wimbledon)		
High St. W3	65	B1
High St. W5	55	G7
High St., Beck.	96	A2
High St., Brent.	64	H6
High St., Brom.	96	G2
High St., Cars.	100	J4
High St., Chis.	88	E6
High St., Croy.	101	J3
High St., Edg.	30	A6
High St., Enf.	25	F4
(Ponders End),		
High St.	98	C3
(Claygate), Esher		
High St., Hmptn.	90	H7
High St., Har.	37	B2
High St.	46	B1
(Wealdstone), Har.		
High St., Houns.	72	H3
High St.	63	A7
(Cranford), Houns.		
High St., Ilf.	43	F3
High St., Kings.T.	91	G3
High St., Kings.T.	91	F1
(Hampton Wick)		
High St., N.Mal.	92	E4
High St., Orp.	104	E5
(Farnborough)		
High St., Orp.	104	J7
(Green St.Grn.)		
High St., Pnr.	36	E3
High St., Sthl.	63	F1
High St., Sutt.	100	E4
High St. (Cheam)	100	B6
Sutt.		
High St., Tedd.	82	C5
High St., T.Ditt.	91	D7
High St., Th.Hth.	94	J4
High St. (Whitton),	72	J7
Twick.		
High St., Wem.	46	J4
High St., W.Mol.	90	G4
High St., W.Wick.	103	B1
High St. Ms. SW19	84	B5
High St. N. E6	52	B7
High St. N. E12	52	B7
High St. S. E6	52	C7
High Timber St. EC4	**12**	**J5**
High Timber St. EC4	58	J7
High Tor Clo., Brom.	87	H7
Babbacombe Rd.		
High Trees Ct. W7	55	B7
High Trees SW2	85	G1
High Trees, Barn.	23	H5
High Trees, Croy.	102	H1
High Vw., Pnr.	36	C3
High Vw. Clo. SE19	95	C2
High Vw. Clo., Loug.	26	J5
High Vw. Rd. E18	42	F3
High Vw. Rd., Sid.	89	B4
High Worple, Har.	36	E7
Higham Hill Rd. E17	41	H1
Higham Pl. E17	41	H3
Higham Rd. N17	41	A3
Higham Rd.,	34	G6
Wdf.Grn.		
Higham Sta. Ave. E4	34	A6
Higham St. E17	41	H3
Highams Lo.	41	G3
Business Cen. E17		
Highams Pk. Ind.	34	C6
Est. E4		
Highbanks Clo., Well.	71	B7
Highbanks Rd., Pnr.	28	G6
Highbarrow Rd.,	95	D7
Croy.		
Highbridge Rd., Bark.	61	L1
Highbrook Rd. SE3	79	A3
Highbury Ave.	94	G2
Th.Hth.		

Highbury Clo., 92 C4
N.Mal.
Highbury Clo., 103 B2
W.Wick.
Highbury Cor. N5 49 H6
Highbury Cres. N5 49 H5
Highbury Est. N5 49 J5
Highbury Gdns., Ilf. 52 H2
Highbury Gra. N5 49 J4
Highbury Gro. N5 49 H6
Highbury Hill N5 49 G3
Highbury Ms. N7 49 G6
Holloway Rd.
Highbury New Pk. N5 49 J5
Highbury Pk. N5 49 H4
Highbury Pk. Ms. N5 49 J4
Highbury Gra.
Highbury Pl. N5 49 H6
Highbury Quad. N5 49 J3
Highbury Rd. SW19 84 B5
Highbury Sta. Rd. 49 G6
N1
Highbury Ter. N5 49 H5
Highbury Ter. Ms. 49 H5
N5
Highclere Rd., 92 D3
N.Mal.
Highclere St. SE26 86 H4
Highcliffe Dr. SW15 74 F6
Highcliffe Gdns., 43 B5
Ilf.
Highcombe SE7 69 H6
Highcombe Clo. SE9 88 A1
Highcroft NW9 38 E5
Highcroft Ave., 56 A1
Wem.
Highcroft Gdns. 39 C6
NW11
Highcroft Rd. N19 40 E7
Highcross Way SW15 83 G1
Highdaun Dr. SW16 94 F4
Highdown, Wor.Pk. 99 E2
Highdown Rd. SW15 74 H6
Highfield, Felt. 81 A1
Highfield Ave. NW9 38 C5
Highfield Ave. NW11 39 A7
Highfield Ave., 71 H6
Erith
Highfield Ave., 46 B5
Grnf.
Highfield Ave., 104 J5
Orp.
Highfield Ave., 36 F5
Pnr.
Highfield Ave., 46 H3
Wem.
Highfield Clo. NW9 38 C5
Highfield Clo., 98 F1
Surb.
Highfield Ct. N14 24 C6
Highfield Dr., 96 E4
Brom.
Highfield Dr., 99 F7
Epsom
Highfield Dr., 103 B2
W.Wick.
Highfield Gdns. 39 B6
NW11
Highfield Hill SE19 86 A7
Highfield Rd. N21 32 H2
Highfield Rd. NW11 39 B6
Highfield Rd. W3 56 B5
Highfield Rd., 80 F5
Bexh.
Highfield Rd., 97 C4
Brom.
Highfield Rd., 97 J3
Chis.
Highfield Rd., 81 A1
Felt.
Highfield Rd., 73 C1
Islw.
Highfield Rd., 92 C7
Surb.
Highfield Rd., 100 H5
Sutt.
Highfield Rd., 35 B7
Wdf.Grn.
Highfields Gro. N6 48 J1
Highgate Ave. N6 40 B7
Highgate Clo. N6 40 A7
Highgate High St. 49 A1
N6
Highgate Hill N19 49 B1
Highgate Rd. NW5 49 B4
Highgate Wk. SE23 86 F2
Highgate W. Hill N6 49 A1
Highgrove Clo., 97 B1
Chis.
Highgrove Rd., Dag. 53 C5
Highgrove Way, 36 A6
Ruis.
Highland Ave. W7 55 B6

Highland Ave., Dag. 53 J3
Highland Ave., 27 B6
Loug.
Highland Cotts., 101 B4
Wall.
Highland Ct. E18 42 H1
Highland Cft., 87 B5
Beck.
Highland Rd. SE19 86 B6
Highland Rd., Bexh. 80 G5
Highland Rd., Brom. 96 F1
Highlands, Wat. 28 C1
Highlands, The, 38 B2
Edg.
Highlands Ave. W3 56 C7
Highlands Clo. N4 40 E7
Highlands Clo., 72 H1
Mount Vw. Rd.
Highlands Clo., 72 H1
Houns.
Highlands Gdns., 52 C1
Ilf.
Highlands Heath 74 J7
SW15
Highlands Rd., 23 D5
Barn.
Highlea Clo. NW9 38 E1
Highlever Rd. W10 56 J5
Highmead SE18 70 J7
Highmead Cres., 46 J7
Wem.
Highmore Rd. SE3 69 E7
Highshore Rd. SE15 77 C2
Highstone Ave. E11 42 G6
Highview Ave., Edg. 30 C4
Highview Ave., 101 F5
Wall.
Highview Gdns. N3 39 B4
Highview Gdns. N11 32 C5
Highview Gdns., 30 C5
Edg.
Highview Ho., Rom. 44 E4
Highview Rd. SE19 86 A6
Highview Rd. W13 55 D5
Highwood Clo. NW7 30 D5
Highwood Hill NW7 30 F2
Highwood La., Loug. 27 D5
Highwood Rd. N19 49 E3
Highworth Rd. N11 32 D6
Hilary Ave., Mitch. 94 A3
Hilary Clo. SW6 18 A7
Hilary Clo. SW6 66 E7
Hilary Clo., Erith 80 H1
Hilary Rd. W12 56 F6
Hilbert Rd., Sutt. 100 A3
Hilborough Way, 104 G5
Orp.
Hilda Rd. E6 52 A7
Hilda Rd. E16 60 E4
Hilda Ter. SW9 76 G2
Hilda Vale Clo., 104 E4
Orp.
Hilda Vale Rd., 104 D4
Orp.
Hildenborough 87 E6
Gdns., Brom.
Hildenlea Pl., 96 E2
Brom.
Hildreth St. SW12 85 B1
Hildyard Rd. SW6 66 D6
Hiley Rd. NW10 56 J3
Hilgrove Rd. NW6 48 F7
Hiliary Gdns., 37 F2
Stan.
Hill Brow, Brom. 97 A1
Hill Clo. NW2 47 H3
Hill Clo. NW11 39 D6
Hill Clo., Barn. 22 J5
Hill Clo., Chis. 88 E5
Hill Clo., Har. 46 B3
Hill Clo., Stan. 29 E4
Hill Ct., Nthlt. 45 G5
Hill Cres. N20 31 E2
Hill Cres., Bex. 89 J1
Hill Cres., Har. 37 D5
Hill Cres., Surb. 91 J5
Hill Cres., Wor.Pk. 99 J2
Hill Crest, Sid. 89 B4
Hill Crest Gdns. N3 39 B4
Hill Dr. NW9 47 C1
Hill Dr. SW16 94 F3
Hill End, Orp. 104 J2
The App.
Hill Fm. Rd. W10 56 J5

Hill Ho. Ave., Stan. 29 C7
Hill Ho. Clo. N21 24 G7
Hill Ho. Rd. SW16 85 F5
Hill Path SW16 85 F5
Valley Rd.
Hill Ri. N9 25 E6
Hill Ri. NW11 39 E4
Hill Ri. SE23 86 E1
London Rd.
Hill Ri., Esher 98 E2
Hill Ri., Grnf. 45 J7
Hill Ri., Rich. 73 G5
Hill Rd. N10 39 J1
Hill Rd. NW8 6 D3
Hill Rd. NW8 57 F2
Hill Rd., Cars. 100 H6
Hill Rd., Har. 37 D5
Hill Rd., Mitch. 94 B1
Hill Rd., Pnr. 36 E6
Hill Rd., Sutt. 100 C5
Hill Rd., Wem. 46 E3
Hill St. W1 15 C1
Hill St. W1 58 A7
Hill St., Rich. 73 G5
Hill Top NW11 39 E4
Hill Top, Loug. 27 D2
Hill Top Clo., 27 D3
Loug.
Hill Top Vw., 35 C6
Wdf.Grn.
Hill Vw. Cres., 104 J1
Orp.
Hill Vw. Dr., Well. 79 H2
Hill Vw. Gdns. NW9 38 D5
Hill Vw. Rd., Esher 98 D7
Hill Vw. Rd., Orp. 104 J1
Hill Vw. Rd., 82 D1
Twick.
Hillary Ri., Barn. 23 D4
Hillary Rd., Sthl. 63 G3
Hillbeck Clo. SE15 68 F7
Hillbeck Way, Grnf. 55 A1
Hillborne Clo., 63 A5
Hayes
Hillborough Clo. 84 F7
SW19
Hillbrook Rd. SW17 84 J3
Hillbrow, N.Mal. 92 F3
Hillbrow Rd., Brom. 87 F1
Hillbury Ave., Har. 37 E5
Hillbury Rd. SW17 85 B3
Hillcote Ave. SW16 85 G7
Hillcourt Ave. N12 31 E6
Hillcourt Est. N16 50 A1
Hillcourt Rd. SE22 77 E6
Hillcrest N6 40 A7
Hillcrest N21 24 G7
Hillcrest Ave. NW11 39 B5
Hillcrest Ave., 30 B4
Edg.
Hillcrest Ave., 36 D4
Pnr.
Hillcrest Clo. SE26 86 D4
Hillcrest Clo., 95 J5
Beck.
Hillcrest Gdns. NW2 47 G3
Hillcrest Gdns., 98 C3
Esher
Hillcrest Rd. E17 42 D2
Hillcrest Rd. E18 42 F2
Hillcrest Rd. W3 65 A1
Hillcrest Rd. W5 55 H5
Hillcrest Rd., 87 G4
Brom.
Hillcrest Rd., 27 A6
Loug.
Hillcrest Vw., 95 J6
Beck.
Hillcroft, Loug. 27 D2
Hillcroft Ave., Pnr. 36 F6
Hillcroft Cres. W5 55 G6
Hillcroft Cres. 45 D3
Ruis.
Hillcroft Cres., 28 A1
Wat.
Hillcroft Cres., 46 J4
Wem.
Hillcroft Rd. E6 61 E5
Hillcroome Rd., 100 G6
Sutt.
Hillcross Ave., 93 A6
Mord.
Hilldale Rd., Sutt. 100 C4
Hilldown Rd. SW16 85 E7
Hilldown Rd., Brom. 103 E1
Hilldrop Cres. N7 49 D5
Hilldrop Est. N7 49 D5
Hilldrop La. N7 49 D5
Hilldrop Rd. N7 49 D5
Hilldrop Rd., Brom. 87 G6
Hillend SE18 79 E1
Hillersdon Ave. 74 G2
SW13

Hillersdon Ave., 29 J5
Edg.
Hillery Clo. SE17 21 C2
Hillfield Ave. N8 40 E5
Hillfield Ave. NW9 38 E5
Hillfield Ave., 93 H6
Mord.
Hillfield Ave., 46 H7
Wem.
Hillfield Clo., 36 J4
Har.
Hillfield Ct. NW3 48 H5
Hillfield Pk. N10 40 B3
Hillfield Pk. N21 32 G2
Hillfield Pk. Ms. 40 B4
N10
Hillfield Rd. NW6 48 C5
Hillfield Rd., 81 F7
Hmptn.
Hillfoot Ave., Rom. 44 J1
Hillfoot Rd., Rom. 44 J1
Hillgate Pl. SW12 76 B7
Hillgate Pl. W8 66 D1
Hillgate St. W8 66 D1
Hilliards Ct. E1 68 E1
Hilliards St. E1 68 F1
Wapping High St.
Hillier Clo., Barn. 23 E6
Hillier Gdns., 101 G5
Croy.
Crowley Cres.
Hillier Rd. SW11 75 J6
Hilliers La., Croy. 101 E3
Hillingdon Rd., 80 J2
Bexh.
Hillingdon St. SE5 20 G7
Hillingdon St. SE5 67 H6
Hillingdon St. SE17 20 J6
Hillingdon St. SE17 67 H6
Hillington Gdns., 43 A2
Wdf.Grn.
Hillman St. E8 50 E6
Hillmarton Rd. N7 49 E5
Hillmead Dr. SW9 76 H4
Hillmont Rd., Esher 98 B3
Hillmore Gro. SE26 86 G5
Hillreach SE18 70 C5
Hillrise Rd. N19 40 E7
Hills Ms. W5 55 H1
Hills Pl. W1 11 F4
Hills Pl. W1 17 F5
Hills Rd., Buck.H. 34 H1
Hillsborough Grn., 28 A3
Wat.
Ashburnham Dr.
Hillsborough Rd. 77 B5
SE22
Hillside NW9 38 D4
Hillside NW10 47 C7
Hillside SW19 84 A6
Hillside, Barn. 23 F5
Hillside Ave. N11 31 J6
Hillside Ave., 22 B4
Borwd.
Hillside Ave., Wem. 46 J4
Hillside Ave., 34 J5
Wdf.Grn.
Hillside Clo. NW8 6 B2
Hillside Clo. NW8 57 E2
Hillside Clo., 93 B4
Mord.
Hillside Clo., 34 J5
Wdf.Grn.
Hillside Cres., 45 J1
Har.
Hillside Cres., 36 A1
Nthwd.
Hillside Dr., Edg. 30 A6
Hillside Est. N15 41 C6
Hillside Gdns. E17 42 D3
Hillside Gdns. N6 40 A6
Hillside Gdns. SW2 85 G2
Hillside Gdns., 23 B4
Barn.
Hillside Gdns., 29 J4
Edg.
Hillside Gdns., 37 H7
Har.
Hillside Gdns., 28 A7
Nthwd.
Hillside Gdns., 101 C7
Wall.
Hillside Gro. N14 24 D7
Hillside Gro. NW7 30 G7
Hillside Pas. SW2 85 F2
Hillside Ri., 28 A7
Nthwd.
Hillside Rd. N15 41 B6
Hillside Rd. SW2 85 F2
Hillside Rd. W5 55 H5
Hillside Rd., Brom. 96 F3
Hillside Rd., Croy. 101 H5

Hillside Rd., Nthwd.   28 A7
Hillside Rd., Sthl.   54 G4
Hillside Rd., Surb.   91 J4
Hillside Rd., Sutt.   100 C7
Hillsleigh Rd. W8   66 C1
Hillstowe St. E5   50 F3
Hilltop, Bans.   **11**   **B7**
Hilltop Gdns. NW4   38 H1
Great N. Way
Hilltop Gdns., Orp.   104 H2
Hilltop Rd. NW6   48 D7
Hilltop Way, Stan.   29 D3
Hillview SW20   83 H7
Hillview, Mitch.   94 E4
Hillview Ave., Har.   37 H5
Hillview Clo., Pnr.   28 F6
Hillview Cres., Ilf.   43 C6
Hillview Gdns. NW4   39 A4
Hillview Gdns., Har.   36 G3
Hillview Rd. NW7   31 A4
Hillview Rd., Chis.   88 D5
Hillview Rd., Pnr.   28 F7
Hillview Rd., Sutt.   100 F3
Hillway N6   49 A1
Hillway NW9   38 E7
Hillworth Rd. SW2   76 G7
Hilly Flds. Cres. SE4   78 A3
Hillyard Rd. W7   55 B5
Hillyard St. SW9   76 G1
Hillyfield E17   41 H3
Hillyfields, Loug.   27 D2
Hilsea St. E5   50 F4
Hilton Ave. N12   31 G5
Hilversum Cres.   77 B5
SE22
East Dulwich Gro.
Himley Rd. SW17   84 H5
Hinchcliffe Clo.,   101 F7
Wall.
Roe Way
Hinchley Clo.,   98 C3
Esher
Hinchley Dr., Esher   98 C3
Hinchley Way, Esher   98 D3
Hinckler Clo., Wall.   101 E7
Kingsford Ave.
Hinckley Rd. SE15   77 D4
Hind Clo., Chig.   35 J5
Hind Ct. EC4   **12**   **F4**
Hind Gro. E14   60 A6
Hinde Ms. W1   58 A6
Marylebone La.
Hinde St. W1   **11**   **C3**
Hinde St. W1   58 A6
Hindes Rd., Har.   37 A5
Hindhead Clo. N16   50 B1
East Bank
Hindhead Gdns.,   54 E1
Nthlt.
Hindhead Grn., Wat.   28 C5
Hindhead Way, Wall. 101 E5
Hindmans Rd. SE22   77 D5
Hindmans Way, Dag.   62 F4
Hindmarsh Clo. E1   **13**   **J5**
Hindrey Rd. E5   50 E5
Hindsley Pl. SE23   86 F2
Hinkler Rd., Har.   37 G3
Hinksey Path SE2   71 D2
Hinstock Rd. SE18   70 F6
Hinton Ave., Houns.   72 D4
Hinton Clo. SE9   88 B1
Hinton Rd. N18   33 B4
Hinton Rd. SE24   76 H3
Hinton Rd., Wall.   101 C6
Hippodrome Ms.   57 B7
W11
Portland Rd.
Hippodrome Pl. W11   57 B7
Hiroshima Wk. SE7   69 H3
Hiscocks Ho. NW10   47 C7
Hitcham Rd. E17   41 J7
Hitchin Sq. E3   59 H2
Hither Grn. La. SE13   78 C5
Hitherbroom Rd.,   63 A1
Hayes
Hitherfield Rd.   85 F2
SW16
Hitherfield Rd., Dag.   53 E2
Hitherlands SW12   85 B2
Hitherwell Dr.,   37 A1
Har.
Hitherwood Dr. SE19   86 C4
Hive Clo. (Bushey),   29 A2
Wat.
Hive Rd. (Bushey),   29 A2
Wat.
Hoadly Rd. SW16   85 D3
Hobart Clo. N20   31 H2
Hobart Clo., Hayes   54 D4
Hobart Dr., Hayes   54 D4
Hobart Gdns.,   95 A3
Th.Hth.
Hobart La., Hayes   54 D4

Hobart Pl. SW1   **15**   **D5**
Hobart Pl. SW1   67 B3
Hobart Pl., Rich.   73 J6
Chisholm Rd.
Hobart Rd., Dag.   53 D4
Hobart Rd., Hayes   54 D4
Hobart Rd., IIf.   37 E2
Hobart Rd., Wor.Pk.   99 H3
Hobbayne Rd. W7   55 A6
Hobbes Wk. SW15   74 H5
Hobbs Grn. N2   39 F3
Hobbs Rd. SE27   85 J4
Hobday St. E14   60 B5
Hobill Wk., Surb.   91 J6
Hoblands End, Chis.   88 H6
Hobury St. SW10   **18**   **D6**
Hobury St. SW10   66 F6
Hocker St. E2   **9**   **F4**
Hockett Clo. SE8   68 J4
Carteret Way
Hockley Ave. E6   61 B2
Hocroft Ave. NW2   48 C3
Hocroft Rd. NW2   48 C4
Hocroft Wk. NW2   48 C3
Hodder Dr., Grnf.   55 C2
Hoddesdon Rd.,   71 G5
Belv.
Hodford Rd. NW11   48 C1
Hodgkin Clo. SE28   62 D7
Fleming Way
Hodnet Gro. SE16   68 G4
Hawkstone Rd.
Hodson Clo., Har.   45 F3
Hoe, The, Wat.   28 D2
Hoe St. E17   42 A5
Hofland Rd. W14   66 A3
Hogan Way E5   50 D2
Geldeston Rd.
Hogans Ms. W2   **10**   **E1**
Hogarth Clo. E16   61 A5
Hogarth Clo. W5   55 H5
Hogarth Ct. EC3   **13**   **E5**
Hogarth Ct. SE19   86 C4
Fountain Dr.
Hogarth Cres. SW19   93 G1
Hogarth Cres.,   94 J7
Croy.
Hogarth Gdns.,   63 G7
Houns.
Hogarth Hill NW11   39 C4
Hogarth La. W4   65 E6
Hogarth Pl. SW5   **18**   **A2**
Hogarth Reach,   27 C5
Loug.
Hogarth Rd. SW5   18 A2
Hogarth Rd. SW5   66 D4
Hogarth Rd., Edg.   38 A2
Hogarth Roundabout 65 E6
W4
Hogarth Way,   90 J1
Hmptn.
Hogshead Pas. E1   59 E7
Pennington St.
Hogsmill Way,   99 C5
Epsom
Holbeach Gdns.,   79 H6
Sid.
Holbeach Ms. SW12   85 B1
Harberson Rd.
Holbeach Rd. SE6   78 A7
Holbeck Row SE15   68 D7
Holbein Ms. SW1   **19**   **B3**
Holbein Ms. SW1   67 A5
Holbein Pl. SW1   **19**   **B2**
Holbein Pl. SW1   67 A4
Holberton Gdns.   56 H3
NW10
Holborn EC1   **12**   **E2**
Holborn EC1   58 G5
Holborn Circ. EC1   **12**   **F2**
Holborn Pl. WC1   **12**   **F2**
Holborn Pl. E13   60 H4
Holborn Viaduct EC1   **12**   **G2**
Holborn Viaduct EC1   58 G5
Holbrook Clo. N19   49 B1
Dartmouth Pk. Hill
Holbrook Clo., Enf.   25 C1
Holbrook La., Chis.   88 G7
Holbrook Rd. E15   60 F2
Holbrook Way, Brom. 97 C6
Holbrooke Ct. N7   49 E4
Holbrooke Pl., Rich.   73 G5
Hill Ri.
Holburne Clo. SE3   78 J1
Holburne Gdns. SE3   79 A1
Holburne Rd. SE3   78 J1
Holcombe Hill NW7   30 G3
Highwood Hill
Holcombe Rd. N17   41 C3
Holcombe Rd., Ilf.   43 D7
Holcombe St. W6   65 H5
Holcote Clo., Belv.   71 E3
Blakemore Way

Holcroft Rd. E9   50 F7
Holden Ave. N12   31 E5
Holden Ave. NW9   47 C1
Holden Clo., Dag.   53 B3
Holden Pt. E15   51 D6
Waddington Rd.
Holden St. SW11   76 A2
Holdenby Rd. SE4   77 H5
Holdenhurst Ave.   31 E7
N12
Holderness Way   85 H5
SE27
Holdernesse Rd.   84 J3
SW17
Holders Hill Ave.   39 A2
NW4
Holders Hill Circ.   31 B7
NW7
Dollis Rd.
Holders Hill Cres.   39 A2
NW4
Holders Hill Dr.   39 A3
NW4
Holders Hill Gdns.   39 B2
NW4
Holders Hill Rd.   39 A2
NW4
Holders Hill Rd.   39 B1
NW7
Holdgate St. SE7   70 A3
Westmoor St.
Holford Pl. WC1   **8**   **D3**
Holford Rd. NW3   48 F3
Holford St. WC1   **8**   **E3**
Holford St. WC1   58 G3
Holgate Ave. SW11   75 G3
Holgate Gdns., Dag.   53 G6
Holgate Rd., Dag.   53 G5
Holland Ave. SW20   92 F1
Holland Ave., Sutt.   100 D7
Holland Clo., Barn.   23 G7
Holland Clo., Brom.   103 F2
Holland Clo., Stan.   29 E5
Holland Dr. SE23   86 H3
Holland Gdns. W14   66 B3
Holland Gro. SW9   67 G7
Holland Pk. W11   66 B1
Holland Pk. Ave.   66 B1
W11
Holland Pk. Ave.,   43 H6
IIf.
Holland Pk. Gdns.   66 B2
W14
Holland Pk. Ms. W11   66 C1
Holland Pk. Rd. W14   66 C3
Holland Pl. W8   **14**   **A3**
Holland Rd. E6   61 C1
Holland Rd. E15   60 E3
Holland Rd. NW10   56 G1
Holland Rd. SE25   95 D5
Holland Rd. W14   66 A2
Holland Rd., Wem.   46 G6
Holland St. SE1   **16**   **H1**
Holland St. SE1   67 H1
Holland St. W8   66 D2
Holland Vill. Rd.   66 B2
W14
Holland Wk. N19   49 D1
Duncombe Rd.
Holland Wk. W8   66 C2
Holland Wk., Stan.   29 D5
Holland Way, Brom.   103 F2
Hollands, The,   81 D4
Felt.
Hollands, The,   99 F1
Wor.Pk.
Hollar Rd. N16   50 C3
Stoke Newington
High St.
Hollen St. W1   **11**   **G3**
Hollen St. W1   58 D6
Holles Clo., Hmptn.   81 G6
Holles St. W1   **11**   **E3**
Holles St. W1   58 B6
Holley Rd. W3   65 E2
Hollickwood Ave.   31 J6
N12
Holliday Sq. SW11   75 G3
Fowler Clo.
Hollidge Way, Dag.   53 H6
Hollies, The E11   42 G5
Hollies, The N20   31 G1
Hollies Ave., Sid.   88 J2
Hollies Clo. SW16   85 G6
Hollies Clo.,   82 C2
Twick.
Hollies End NW7   30 H5
Hollies Rd. W5   64 F4
Hollies Way SW12   76 A7
Bracken Ave.
Holligrave Rd.,   96 G1
Brom.

Hollingbourne Ave.,   71 F7
Bexh.
Hollingbourne Gdns.   55 E5
W13
Hollingbourne Rd.   76 J5
SE24
Hollingsworth Rd.   102 F6
Croy.
Hollington Cres.,   92 F6
N.Mal.
Hollington Rd. E6   61 C3
Hollington Rd. N17   41 D2
Hollingworth Rd.,   97 E7
Orp.
Hollman Gdns. SW16 85 H6
Hollow, The,   34 F4
Wdf.Grn.
Hollow Wk., Rich.   64 H7
Kew Rd.
Holloway Rd. E6   61 C3
Holloway Rd. E11   51 E3
Holloway Rd. N7   49 F3
Holloway Rd. N19   49 C2
Holloway St.,   72 H3
Houns.
Hollowfield Wk.,   45 E6
Nthlt.
Hollows, The, Brent.   64 J6
Kew Bri. Rd.
Holly Ave., Stan.   37 H2
Holly Bush Hill NW3   48 F4
Holly Bush La.,   81 F7
Hmptn.
Holly Bush Steps   48 F4
NW3
Heath St.
Holly Bush Vale NW3 48 F4
Heath St.
Holly Clo. NW10   47 E7
Holly Clo., Buck.H.   35 A3
Holly Clo., Felt.   81 E5
Holly Clo., Wall.   101 B7
Holly Cres., Beck.   95 J5
Holly Cres.,   34 D7
Wdf.Grn.
Holly Dr. E4   26 B7
Holly Fm. Rd., Sthl.   63 E5
Holly Gro. NW9   38 C7
Holly Gro. SE15   77 C2
Holly Gro., Pnr.   36 E1
Holly Hedge Ter.   78 D5
SE13
Holly Hill N21   24 F6
Holly Hill NW3   48 F4
Holly Hill Rd., Belv.   71 H5
Holly Hill Rd.,   71 J5
Erith
Holly Lo. Gdns. N6   49 A1
Holly Ms. SW10   **18**   **D4**
Holly Mt. NW3   48 F4
Holly Bush Hill
Holly Pk. N3   39 C5
Holly Pk. N4   40 E7
Holly Pk. Est. N4   40 F7
Blythwood Rd.
Holly Pk. Gdns. N3   39 D3
Holly Pk. Rd. N11   32 A5
Holly Pk. Rd. W7   64 C1
Holly Rd. E11   42 F7
Holly Rd. W4   65 D4
Dolman Rd.
Holly Rd., Hmptn.   81 J6
Holly Rd., Houns.   72 H4
Holly Rd., Twick.   82 D1
Holly St. E8   50 C7
Holly St. Est. E8   50 C7
Holly St.
Holly Ter. N20   31 F2
Swan La.
Holly Vw. Clo. NW4   38 G6
Holly Wk. NW3   48 F4
Holly Wk., Enf.   24 J3
Gentlemans Row
Holly Wk., Rich.   73 H2
Holly Way, Mitch.   94 D4
Hollybank Clo.,   81 G5
Hmptn.
Hollyberry La. NW3   48 F4
Holly Wk.
Hollybrake Clo.,   88 G7
Chis.
Hollybush Clo. E11   42 G5
Hollybush Clo.,   37 B1
Har.
Hollybush Gdns. E2   59 E3
Hollybush Hill E11   42 F7
Hollybush Pl. E2   59 E3
Bethnal Grn. Rd.
Hollybush Rd.,   82 H5
Kings.T.
Hollybush St. E13   60 H3
Hollybush Wk. SW9   76 H4
Hollycroft Ave. NW3   48 D3
Hollycroft Ave.,   46 J2
Wem.

Hollydale Dr., Brom. 104 C3
Hollydale Rd. SE15 77 F1
Hollydene SE15 77 E1
Hollydown Way E11 51 D3
Hollyfield Ave. N11 31 J5
Hollyfield Rd., 91 J7
Surb.
Hollymead, Cars. 100 J3
Hollymount Clo. 78 C1
SE10
Hollytree Clo. SW19 84 A1
Hollywood Gdns., 54 B6
Hayes
Hollywood Ms. SW10 18 C5
Hollywood Rd. E4 33 H5
Hollywood Rd. SW10 18 C5
Hollywood Rd. SW10 66 F6
Hollywood Way, 34 D7
Wdf.Grn.
Holm Oak Clo. SW15 75 C6
West Hill
Holm Oak Ms. SW4 76 E5
King's Ave.
Holm Wk. SE3 78 G2
Blackheath Pk.
Holman Rd. SW11 75 G2
Holman Rd., Epsom 99 C5
Holmbridge Gdns., 25 G4
Enf.
Holmbrook Dr. NW4 39 A5
Holmbury Ct. SW17 84 J3
Holmbury Ct. SW19 84 H7
Cavendish Rd.
Holmbury Gro., 102 J7
Croy.
Holmbury Pk., Brom. 88 B7
Holmbury Vw. E5 50 E1
Holmbush Rd. SW15 75 B6
Holmcote Gdns. N5 49 J5
Holmcroft Way, 97 C5
Brom.
Holmdale Gdns. NW4 39 A5
Holmdale Rd. NW6 48 D5
Holmdale Rd., Chis. 88 F5
Holmdale Ter. N15 41 B7
Holmdene Ave. NW7 30 G6
Holmdene Ave. SE24 76 J5
Holmdene Ave., Har. 36 H3
Holmdene Clo., 96 C2
Beck.
Holme Lacey Rd. 78 F6
SE12
Holme Rd. E6 61 B1
Holme Way, Stan. 29 C6
Holmead Rd. SW6 66 E7
Holmebury Clo. 29 B2
(Bushey), Wat.
Holmefield Ct. NW3 48 H6
Holmes Ave. E17 41 J3
Holmes Ave. NW7 31 B5
Holmes Pl. SW10 18 D5
Holmes Rd. NW5 49 B6
Holmes Rd. SW19 84 F7
Holmes Rd., Twick. 82 C2
Holmes Ter. SE1 16 E3
Holmes Ter. SE1 67 G2
Holmesdale Ave. 74 B3
SW14
Holmesdale Clo. 95 C3
SE25
Holmesdale Rd. N6 40 B7
Holmesdale Rd. SE25 95 A5
Holmesdale Rd., 80 D2
Bexh.
Holmesdale Rd., 95 A5
Croy.
Holmesdale Rd., 73 J1
Rich.
Holmesdale Rd., 82 F7
Tedd.
Holmesley Rd. SE23 77 H6
Holmewood Gdns. 76 F7
SW2
Holmewood Rd. 95 B3
SE25
Holmewood Rd. SW2 76 E7
Holmfield Ave. NW4 39 A5
Holmhurst Rd., 71 H5
Belv.
Holmleigh Rd. N16 50 B3
Holms St. E2 9 H1
Holmshaw Clo. SE26 86 H4
Holmside Ri., Wat. 28 B3
Holmside Rd. SW12 76 A6
Holmsley Clo., 92 F6
N.Mal.
Holmstall Ave., Edg. 38 C3
Holmwood Clo., Har. 36 J3
Holmwood Clo., 45 H6
Nthlt.
Holmwood Gdns. N3 39 D2
Holmwood Gdns., 101 B6
Wall.

Holmwood Gro. NW7 30 D5
Holmwood Rd., 98 G5
Chess.
Holmwood Rd., Ilf. 52 H2
Holmwood Vill. SE7 69 G5
Holne Chase N2 39 F6
Holne Chase, Mord. 93 C6
Holness Rd. E15 51 F6
Holroyd Rd. SW15 74 J4
Holstein Way, Erith 71 D3
Holstock Rd., Ilf. 52 F2
Holsworth Clo., Har. 36 J5
Holsworthy Sq. WC1 8 D6
Holsworthy Way, 98 F5
Chess.
Holt, The, Ilf. 35 F6
Holt, The, Wall. 101 C4
Holt Clo. N10 40 A4
Holt Clo. SE28 62 B7
Holt Clo., Chig. 35 J5
Holt Ct. E15 51 C5
Clays La.
Holt Rd. E16 70 B1
Holt Rd., Wem. 46 E3
Holt Way, Chig. 35 J5
Holton St. E1 59 G4
Holtwhite Ave., Enf. 24 J2
Holtwhites Hill, Enf. 24 H1
Holwell Pl., Pnr. 36 E4
Holwood Pk. Ave., 104 C4
Orp.
Holwood Pl. SW4 76 D4
Holybourne Ave. 74 G7
SW15
Holyhead Clo. E3 60 A3
Holyoak Rd. SE11 20 G1
Holyoak Rd. SE11 67 H4
Holyoake Ct. SE16 68 J2
Bryan Rd.
Holyoake Wk. N2 39 F3
Holyoake Wk. W5 55 F4
Holyport Rd. SW6 65 J7
Holyrood Ave., Har. 45 E4
Holyrood Gdns., 38 B3
Edg.
Holyrood Rd., Barn. 23 F6
Holyrood St. SE1 17 D2
Holywell Clo. SE3 69 G6
Holywell La. EC2 9 E5
Holywell Row EC2 59 B4
Holywell Row EC2 9 D6
Holywell Row EC2 59 B4
Home Clo., Cars. 100 J2
Home Clo., Nthlt. 54 F3
Home Ct., Felt. 81 A1
Home Fm. Clo., 91 C7
T.Ditt.
Home Gdns., Dag. 53 J3
Home Lea, Orp. 104 J5
Home Mead, Stan. 37 F1
Home Pk. Rd. SW19 84 C4
Home Pk. Wk., 91 G5
Kings.T.
Home Rd. SW11 75 H2
Homecroft Gdns., 27 E4
Loug.
Homecroft Rd. N22 40 H1
Homecroft Rd. SE26 86 F5
Homefarm Rd. W7 55 B6
Homefield Ave., Ilf. 43 H5
Homefield Clo. NW10 47 C6
Homefield Gdns. N2 39 G3
Homefield Gdns., 93 F2
Mitch.
Homefield Pk., Sutt. 100 E6
Homefield Rd. SW19 84 A6
Homefield Rd. W4 65 F5
Homefield Rd., 96 J1
Brom.
Homefield Rd., Edg. 30 D6
Homefield Rd., Walt. 90 E7
Homefield Rd., Wem. 46 D4
Homefield St. N1 9 D2
Homelands Dr. SE19 86 B7
Homeleigh Rd. SE15 77 G5
Homemead SW12 85 B2
Homemead Rd., 97 F6
Brom.
Homemead Rd., 95 F6
Croy.
Homer Clo., Bexh. 80 J1
Homer Dr. E14 69 A4
Homer Rd. E9 50 H6
Homer Rd., Croy. 95 G6
Homer Row W1 10 H2
Homer Row W1 57 H5
Homer St. W1 10 H2
Homer St. W1 57 H5
Homersham Rd., 92 A2
Kings.T.
Homerton Gro. E9 50 G5
Homerton High St. 50 F5
E9

Homerton Rd. E9 50 H5
Homerton Row E9 50 F5
Homerton Ter. E9 50 F6
Morning La.
Homesdale Clo. E11 42 G5
Homesdale Rd., 96 J4
Brom.
Homesdale Rd., Orp. 97 H7
Homesfield NW11 39 D5
Homestall Rd. SE22 77 F5
Homestead, The N11 32 B4
Homestead Gdns., 98 B5
Esher
Homestead Paddock 24 B5
N14
Homestead Rd. NW2 47 F3
Homestead Rd. SW6 66 C7
Homestead Rd., Dag. 53 F2
Homewillow Clo. N21 24 H6
Homewood Clo., 81 F6
Hmptn.
Fearnley Cres.
Homewood Cres., 88 H6
Chis.
Honduras St. EC1 8 J5
Honey La. EC2 13 A4
Honeybourne Rd. 48 E5
NW6
Honeybourne Way, 104 G1
Orp.
Honeybrook Rd. 76 C7
SW12
Honeycroft, Loug. 27 D4
Honeyden Rd., Sid. 89 E6
Honeyman Clo. NW6 48 A7
Honeypot Clo. NW9 37 J4
Honeypot La. NW9 38 A5
Honeypot La., Stan. 37 G3
Honeysett Rd. N17 41 C2
Reform Row
Honeysuckle Gdns., 102 G1
Croy.
Primrose La.
Honeywell Rd. SW11 75 H6
Honeywood Rd. 56 F2
NW10
Honeywood Rd., 73 D4
Islw.
Honeywood Wk., 100 J4
Cars.
Honister Clo., Stan. 37 E1
Honister Gdns., 37 E1
Stan.
Honister Pl., Stan. 37 E1
Honiton Rd. NW6 57 C2
Honiton Rd., Well. 79 J2
Honley Rd. SE6 78 B7
Honor Oak Pk. SE23 77 F6
Honor Oak Ri. SE23 77 F6
Honor Oak Rd. SE23 86 F1
Hood Ave. N14 24 B6
Hood Ave. SW14 74 C5
Hood Clo., Croy. 101 H1
Parsons Mead
Hood Ct. EC4 12 F4
Hood Rd. SW20 83 F7
Hood Wk., Rom. 44 H1
Hoodcote Gdns. N21 24 H7
Hook, The, Barn. 23 G6
Hook Fm. Rd., Brom. 97 A5
Hook La., Well. 79 J4
Hook Ri. N., Surb. 99 A3
Hook Ri. S., Surb. 99 A3
Hook Rd., Chess. 98 G5
Hook Rd., Epsom 99 C7
Hook Rd., Surb. 98 H3
Hook Wk., Edg. 30 C6
Hookers Rd. E17 41 G3
Hooking Grn., Har. 36 H5
Hooks Clo. SE15 77 E1
Woods Rd.
Hooks Hall Dr., Dag. 53 J3
Hooks Way SE22 86 D1
Dulwich Common
Hookstone Way, 35 A7
Wdf.Grn.
Hoop La. NW11 39 C7
Hooper St. E16 60 G6
Hooper St. E1 13 H4
Hooper St. E1 59 D7
Hooper's Clo. SW3 14 J4
Hop Gdns. WC2 12 A6
Hope Clo. SE12 87 H3
Hope Clo., Sutt. 100 F5
Hope Clo., Wdf.Grn. 34 J6
West Gro.
Hope Pk., Brom. 87 F7
Hope St. SW11 75 G3
Hopedale Rd. SE7 69 H6
Hopefield Ave. NW6 57 B2
Hopetown St. E1 13 G2
Hopewell St. SE5 68 A7
Hopewell Yd. SE5 68 A7

Hopgood St. W12 65 J1
Macfarlane Rd.
Hopkins St. W1 11 G4
Hopkinsons Pl. NW1 58 A1
Fitzroy Rd.
Hoppers Rd. N13 32 G2
Hoppers Rd. N21 32 G2
Hoppett Rd. E4 34 E2
Hopping La. N1 49 H6
St. Mary's Gro.
Hoppingwood Ave., 92 E3
N.Mal.
Hopton Gdns. SE1 16 H1
Hopton Gdns., 92 G6
N.Mal.
Hopton Rd. SW16 85 E5
Hopton St. SE1 16 H1
Hopton St. SE1 67 H1
Hopwood Rd. SE17 21 C5
Hopwood Rd. SE17 68 A6
Hopwood Wk. E8 50 D7
Wilman Gro.
Horace Ave., Rom. 53 J1
Horace Rd. E7 51 H4
Horace Rd., Ilf. 43 F3
Horace Rd., 91 J3
Kings.T.
Horatio Pl. SW19 84 D7
Kingston Rd.
Horatio St. E2 9 G2
Horatio St. E2 59 G2
Horatius Way, Croy. 101 F5
Horbury Cres. W11 57 D7
Horbury Ms. W11 57 C7
Ladbroke Rd.
Horder Rd. SW6 75 B1
Hordle Prom. E. 21 G7
SE15
Hordle Prom. N. 21 F7
SE15
Hordle Prom. S. 68 C7
SE15
Pentridge St.
Hordle Prom. W. 21 E7
SE15
Horizon Way SE7 69 H4
Horley Clo., Bexh. 80 G5
Horley Rd. SE9 88 B4
Hormead Rd. W9 57 C4
Horn La. SE10 69 G4
Horn La. W3 65 C1
Horn La., Bexh. 80 J2
Horn La., Wdf.Grn. 34 G6
Horn Pk. Clo. SE12 78 H5
Horn Pk. La. SE12 78 H5
Hornbeam Clo. SE11 20 E1
Hornbeam Clo., 22 A1
Borwd.
Hornbeam Clo., 35 A3
Buck.H.
Hornbeam Rd.
Hornbeam Clo., 45 F5
Nthlt.
Hornbeam Cres., 64 E7
Brent.
Hornbeam Gro. E4 34 C3
Hornbeam La. E4 26 E5
Hornbeam La., Bexh. 80 J2
Hornbeam Rd., 35 A3
Buck.H.
Hornbeam Rd., 54 C5
Hayes
Hornbeam Ter. 100 H1
Cars.
Hornbeam Twr. E11 51 D3
Hornbeam Wk., Rich. 82 J2
Hornbeam Way, 97 D6
Brom.
Hornbeams Ri. N11 32 A6
Hornblower Clo. 68 H4
SE16
Greenland Quay
Hornbuckle Clo., 46 A2
Har.
Hornby Clo. NW3 48 G7
Horncastle Clo. 78 G7
SE12
Horncastle Rd. SE12 78 G7
Horndean Clo. SW15 83 G1
Bessborough Rd.
Horndon Clo., Rom. 44 J1
Horndon Grn., Rom. 44 J1
Horndon Rd., Rom. 44 J1
Horne Way SW15 74 J2
Horner La., Mitch. 93 G2
Hornfair Rd. SE7 69 A7
Horniman Dr. SE23 86 E1
Horning Clo. SE9 88 B4
Horns End, Pnr. 36 C4
Horns Rd., Ilf. 53 F6
Hornsey La. N6 49 B1
Hornsey La. Est. 40 D7
N19

Hornsey La. Gdns. N6	40	C7
Hornsey Pk. Rd. N8	40	F3
Hornsey Ri. N19	40	D7
Hornsey Ri. Gdns. N19	40	D7
Hornsey Rd. N7	49	J6
Hornsey Rd. N19	49	E1
Hornsey Gro. N7	49	F5
Hornshay St. SE15	68	F6
Hornton St. W8	66	D2
Horsa Clo., Wall. Kingsford Ave.	101	E7
Horsa Rd. SE12	78	J7
Horsa Rd., Erith	71	H7
Horse and Dolphin Yd. W1	11	J5
Horse Fair, Kings.T. Wood St.	91	G2
Horse Guards Ave. SW1	16	A2
Horse Guards Ave. SW1	67	E1
Horse Guards Rd. SW1	15	J2
Horse Guards Rd. SW1	67	D1
Horse Leaze E6	61	D6
Horse Ride SW1	15	H2
Horse Rd. E7 Centre Rd.	51	H3
Horse Shoe Cres., Nthlt.	54	G2
Horse Shoe Yd. W1	11	E5
Horsebridges Clo., Dag.	62	E1
Horsecroft Rd., Edg.	30	D7
Horseferry Pl. SE10	69	C6
Horseferry Rd. E14	59	G7
Horseferry Rd. SW1	15	H6
Horseferry Rd. SW1	67	D4
Horsell Rd. N5	49	G5
Horselydown La. SE1	17	F3
Horselydown La. SE1	68	C2
Horsenden Ave., Grnf.	46	B5
Horsenden Cres., Grnf.	46	C5
Horsenden La. N., Grnf.	46	C6
Horsenden La. S., Grnf.	55	D1
Horseshoe Clo. E14 Ferry St.	69	C5
Horseshoe Clo. NW2	47	H2
Horseshoe Grn., Sutt. Aultone Way	100	E2
Horseshoe La. N20	31	A1
Horsfeld Gdns. SE9	79	B5
Horsfeld Rd. SE9	79	A5
Horsford Rd. SW2	76	F5
Horsham Ave. N12	31	H5
Horsham Rd., Bexh.	80	G6
Horsley Dr., Croy.	103	C7
Horsley Rd. E4	34	C2
Horsley Rd., Brom. Palace Rd.	96	H1
Horsley St. SE17	21	B5
Horsley St. SE17	68	A6
Horsmonden Clo., Orp.	97	J7
Horsmonden Rd. SE4	77	J5
Hortensia Rd. SW10	18	C7
Hortensia Rd. SW10	66	F7
Horticultural Pl. W4 Heathfield Ter.	65	D5
Horton Ave. NW2	48	B4
Horton Rd. E8	50	E6
Horton St. SE13	78	B3
Hortus Rd. E4	34	C2
Hortus Rd., Sthl.	63	F2
Hosack Rd. SW17	84	J1
Hoser Ave. SE12	87	G2
Hosier La. EC1	12	G2
Hosier La. EC1	58	H5
Hoskins Clo. E16	60	J6
Hoskins St. SE10	69	D5
Hospital Bri. Rd., Twick.	72	H7
Hospital La., Islw.	73	C5
Hospital Rd. E9 Homerton Row	50	G5
Hospital Rd., Houns.	72	G3
Hotham Clo., W.Mol. Garrick Gdns.	90	G3
Hotham Rd. SW15	74	J3
Hotham Rd. SW19	84	F7
Hotham Rd. Ms. SW19 Haydons Rd.	84	F7

Hotham St. E15	60	E1
Hothfield Pl. SE16 Lwr. Rd.	68	F3
Hotspur Rd., Nthlt.	54	G2
Hotspur St. SE11	20	E3
Hotspur St. SE11	67	H5
Houghton Clo. E8	60	C0
Buttermere Wk.		
Houghton Clo., Hmptn.	81	F6
Houghton Rd. N15 West Grn. Rd.	41	C5
Houghton St. WC2	12	D4
Houlder Cres., Croy.	101	H6
Houndsden Rd. N21	24	F6
Houndsditch EC3	13	E3
Houndsditch EC3	59	B6
Houndsfield Rd. N9	25	E7
Hounslow Ave., Houns.	72	H5
Hounslow Gdns., Houns.	72	H5
Hounslow Rd. (Feltham), Felt.	81	B1
Hounslow Rd. (Hanworth), Felt.	81	D4
Hounslow Rd., Twick.	72	H6
Houseman Way SE5 Benhill Rd.	68	A7
Houston Pl., Esher Lime Tree Ave.	98	B1
Houston Rd. SE23	86	H2
Hove Ave. E17	41	J5
Hove Gdns., Sutt.	100	E1
Hoveden Rd. NW2	48	B5
Hoveton Rd. SE28	62	C6
Howard Ave., Bex.	89	C1
Howard Clo. N11	32	A2
Howard Clo. NW2	48	B4
Howard Clo. W3	56	B6
Howard Clo., Hmptn.	81	J6
Howard Dr., Borwd.	22	D4
Howard Ms. N5 Hamilton Pk.	49	H4
Howard Pl. SW1	15	F6
Howard Rd. E6	61	C2
Howard Rd. E11	51	E3
Howard Rd. E17	42	A3
Howard Rd. N15	41	B6
Howard Rd. N16	50	A4
Howard Rd. NW2	48	A4
Howard Rd. SE20	95	F1
Howard Rd. SE25	95	D5
Howard Rd., Bark.	61	G1
Howard Rd., Brom.	87	J6
Howard Rd., Ilf.	52	E4
Howard Rd., Islw.	73	C3
Howard Rd., N.Mal.	92	E3
Howard Rd., Sthl.	54	H6
Howard Rd., Surb.	91	J6
Howard St., T.Ditt.	91	E7
Howard Wk. N2	39	F4
Howards Clo., Pnr.	36	B2
Howards Crest Clo., Beck.	96	C2
Howards La. SW15	74	H5
Howards Rd. E13	60	G3
Howarth Ct. E15 Taylor Ct.	51	C5
Howarth Rd. SE2	71	A5
Howberry Rd., Edg.	29	G6
Howberry Rd., Edg.	29	G6
Howberry Rd., Stan.	29	G6
Howberry Rd., Th.Hth.	95	A1
Howbury Rd. SE15	77	F3
Howcroft Cres. N3	31	D7
Howcroft La., Grnf. Cowgate Rd.	55	A3
Howden Clo. SE28	62	D7
Howden Rd. SE25	95	C2
Howden St. SE15	77	D3
Howe Clo., Rom.	44	G1
Howell Clo., Rom.	44	D5
Howell Wk. SE1	20	H2
Howes Clo. N3	39	D3
Howgate Rd. SW14	74	D3
Howick Pl. SW1	15	G6
Howick Pl. SW1	67	C3
Howie St. SW11	66	H7
Howitt Rd. NW3	48	H6
Howland Ms. E. W1	11	G1
Howland St. W1	11	F1
Howland St. W1	58	C5
Howland Way SE16	68	H2
Howletts Rd. SE24	76	J6
Howley Pl. W2	10	D1
Howley Pl. W2	57	F5
Howley Rd., Croy.	101	H3
Hows St. E2	9	F1

Hows St. E2	59	C2
Howsman Rd. SW13	65	G6
Howson Rd. SE4	77	H4
Howson Ter., Rich.	73	H6
Howton Pl. (Bushey), Wat.	29	A1
Hoxton Mkt. N1	9	D4
Hoxton Mkt. N1	9	D4
Hoxton Sq. N1	59	B3
Hoxton Sq. N1	9	D4
Hoxton St. N1	59	B1
Hoy St. E16	00	F0
Hoylake Gdns., Mitch.	94	C3
Hoylake Gdns., Ruis.	45	B1
Hoylake Gdns., Wat.	28	D4
Hoylake Rd. W3	56	E6
Hoyland Clo. SE15 Commercial Way	68	E7
Hoyle Rd. SW17	84	H5
Hubbard Rd. SE27	85	J4
Hubbard St. E15	60	E1
Hubert Gro. SW9	76	E3
Hubert Rd. E6	61	A3
Huddart St. E3	59	J5
Huddleston Rd. N7	49	C3
Huddlestone Rd. E7	51	H4
Huddlestone Rd. NW2	47	H6
Hudson Ct. SW19	84	E7
Hudson Pl. SE18	70	F5
Hudson Rd., Bexh.	80	F2
Hudson's Pl. SW1	19	F1
Huggin Ct. EC4	13	A5
Huggin Hill EC4	13	A5
Hugh Ms. SW1	19	E2
Hugh Pl. SW1	19	H1
Hugh St. SW1	19	E2
Hugh St. SW1	67	B4
Hughan Rd. E15	51	D5
Hughenden Ave., Har.	37	E5
Hughenden Gdns., Nthlt.	54	C3
Hughenden Rd., Wor.Pk.	92	G7
Hughenden Ter. E15 Westdown Rd.	51	C4
Hughes Rd., Hayes	54	A7
Hughes Wk., Croy. St. Saviours Rd.	94	J7
Hugo Rd. N19	49	C4
Hugon Rd. SW6	75	E3
Huguenot Pl. SW18	75	F5
Huguenot Pl. SE15 Scylla Rd.	77	E3
Hull Clo. SE16	68	G2
Hull St. EC1	8	J4
Hullbridge Ms. N1 Sherborne St.	59	A1
Hulse Ave., Bark.	52	G6
Hulse Ave., Rom.	44	H1
Humber Rd. NW2	47	H2
Humber Rd. SE3	69	F6
Humberstone Rd. E13	60	J3
Humberton Clo. E9 Marsh Hill	50	H5
Humbolt Rd. W6	66	B6
Hume Pt. E16	60	H5
Hume Way, Ruis.	36	A6
Humes Ave. W7	64	B3
Humphrey Clo., Ilf.	43	C1
Humphrey St. SE1	21	F3
Humphrey St. SE1	68	C5
Humphries Clo., Dag.	53	F4
Hundred Acre NW9	38	F2
Hungerdown E4	34	C1
Hungerford Bri. SE1	16	C2
Hungerford Bri. SE1	67	F1
Hungerford Bri. WC2	16	C2
Hungerford Bri. WC2	67	F1
Hungerford La. WC2	16	B1
Hungerford Rd. N7	49	D6
Hungerford St. E1 Commercial Rd.	59	E6
Hunsdon Clo., Dag.	53	E6
Hunsdon Rd. SE14	68	G7
Hunslett St. E2	59	F2
Hunston Rd., Mord.	100	E1
Hunt Rd., Sthl.	63	G3
Hunt St. W11	66	A1
Hunt Way SE22 Dulwich Common	86	D1
Hunter Clo. SE1	17	C6
Hunter Clo., Borwd.	22	C5
Hunter Ho., Felt.	81	A1
Hunter Rd. SW20	92	D1
Hunter Rd., Ilf.	52	E5
Hunter Rd., Th.Hth.	95	A3
Hunter St. WC1	8	B5

Hunter St. WC1	58	E4
Hunter Wk. E13	60	G1
Stratford Rd.		
Hunter Wk., Borwd. Ashley Dr.	22	C5
Huntercrombe Gdns., Wat.	28	C5
Hunters, The, Beck.	96	C1
Hunters Gro. NW10 Balham Pk. Rd.	95	A1
Hunters Ct., Rich. Friars La.	73	G5
Hunters Gro., Har.	37	F4
Hunters Gro., Hayes	63	A1
Hunters Gro., Orp. State Fm. Ave.	104	F4
Hunters Hall Rd., Dag.	53	G4
Hunters Hill, Ruis.	45	C3
Hunters Meadow SE19 Dulwich Wd. Ave.	86	B4
Hunters Rd., Chess.	98	H3
Hunters Sq., Dag.	53	G4
Hunters Way, Croy. Brownlow Rd.	102	B4
Hunters Way, Enf.	24	G1
Hunting Clo., Esher	24	G3
Hunting Gate Dr., Chess.	98	H7
Hunting Gate Ms., Sutt.	100	E3
Hunting Gate Ms., Twick. Colne Rd.	82	B1
Huntingdon Clo., Mitch.	94	E4
Huntingdon Gdns. W4	65	C7
Huntingdon Gdns., Wor.Pk.	99	J3
Huntingdon Rd. N2	39	H3
Huntingdon Rd. N9	33	F1
Huntingdon St. E16	60	F6
Huntingdon St. N1	49	F7
Huntingfield, Croy.	102	J7
Huntingfield Rd. SW15	74	G4
Huntings Rd., Dag.	53	G6
Huntley Dr. N3	31	D6
Huntley St. WC1	7	G6
Huntley St. WC1	58	C4
Huntley Way SW20	92	G2
Huntly Rd. SE25	95	B4
Hunton St. E1	9	H6
Hunton St. E1	59	D5
Hunt's Clo. SE3	78	G2
Hunt's Ct. WC2	11	J6
Hunts La. E15	60	C2
Hunts Mead, Enf.	25	G3
Hunts Slip Rd. SE21	86	B3
Huntsman St. SE17	21	C2
Huntsman St. SE17	68	B4
Huntsmans Clo., Felt.	81	B4
Huntsmead Clo., Chis.	88	C7
Huntsmoor Rd., Epsom	99	D5
Huntspill St. SW17	84	F1
Huntsworth Ms. NW1	6	J6
Hurley Cres. SE16 Marlow Way	68	G2
Hurley Rd., Grnf.	54	H6
Hurlingham Ct. SW6	75	C3
Hurlingham Gdns. SW6	75	C3
Hurlingham Rd. SW6	75	C2
Hurlingham Rd., Bexh.	71	F7
Hurlingham Sq. SW6 Peterborough Rd.	75	E3
Hurlock St. N5	49	H3
Hurlstone Rd. SE25	95	A5
Hurn Ct. Rd., Houns. Renfrew Rd.	72	D2
Huron Rd. SW17	85	A2
Hurren Clo. SE3	78	E3
Hurry Clo. E15	51	E7
Hurst Ave. E4	34	A4
Hurst Ave. N6	40	C4
Hurst Clo. E4	34	A3
Hurst Clo. NW11	39	E6
Hurst Clo., Brom.	103	F1
Hurst Clo., Chess.	99	A5
Hurst Clo., Nthlt.	45	F6
Hurst Est. SE2	71	D5
Hurst La. SE2	71	D5
Hurst La., E.Mol.	90	J4
Hurst Ri., Barn.	23	D3
Hurst Rd. E17	42	B3

Hurst Rd. N21 32 G1
Hurst Rd., Bex. 89 C1
Hurst Rd., Buck.H. 35 A1
Hurst Rd., Croy. 102 A5
Hurst Rd., E.Mol. 90 G3
Hurst Rd., Erith 80 J1
Hurst Rd., Sid. 89 A2
Hurst Rd., Walt. 90 C5
Hurst Rd., W.Mol. 90 G3
Hurst Springs, Bex. 89 E1
Hurst St. SE24 76 H6
Hurst Vw. Rd., 102 B7
  S.Croy.
Hurst Way, S.Croy. 102 B6
Hurstbourne, Esher 98 C6
Hurstbourne Gdns., 52 H6
  Bark.
Hurstbourne Rd. 86 H1
  SE23
Hurstcourt Rd., Sutt. 100 E1
Hurstdene Ave., 103 F1
  Brom.
Hurstdene Gdns. N15 41 B7
Hurstfield, Brom. 96 G5
Hurstfield Rd., 90 G3
  W.Mol.
Hurstleigh Gdns., 43 C1
  Ilf.
Hurstmead Ct., Edg. 30 B4
Hurstway Wk. W11 57 A7
  Whitchurch Rd.
Hurstwood Ave. E18 42 H4
Hurstwood Ave., 89 E1
  Bex.
Hurstwood Dr., 97 C3
  Brom.
Hurstwood Rd. NW11 39 B4
Hurtwood Rd., Walt. 90 F7
Huson Clo. NW3 48 H7
Husseywell Cres., 103 G1
  Brom.
Hutchings St. E14 69 A2
Hutchings Wk. NW11 39 E4
Hutchins Clo. E15 51 C7
  Gibbins Rd.
Hutchinson Ter., 46 G3
  Wem.
Hutton Clo., Grnf. 46 A5
  Mary Peters Dr.
Hutton Clo., 34 H6
  Wdf.Grn.
Hutton Gdns., Har. 28 J7
  Hutton Wk.
Hutton Gro. N12 31 E5
Hutton La., Har. 28 J7
Hutton Row, Edg. 30 C7
  Pavilion Way
Hutton St. EC4 12 F4
Hutton Wk., Har. 28 J7
Huxbear St. SE4 77 J5
Huxley Dr., Rom. 44 B7
Huxley Gdns. NW10 55 J3
Huxley Par. N18 32 J5
Huxley Pl. N13 32 H3
Huxley Rd. E10 51 C2
Huxley Rd. N18 33 A4
Huxley Rd., Well. 79 J3
Huxley Sayze N18 32 J5
Huxley St. W10 57 B3
Hyacinth Clo., 81 G6
  Hmptn.
  Gresham Rd.
Hyacinth Ct., Pnr. 36 C3
  Tulip Ct.
Hyacinth Rd. SW15 83 G1
Hycliffe Gdns., 35 F4
  Chig.
Hyde, The NW9 38 E4
Hyde Clo. E13 60 G1
  Pelly Rd.
Hyde Clo., Barn. 23 C3
Hyde Ct. N20 31 G3
Hyde Cres. NW9 38 E5
Hyde La. SW11 75 H1
  Battersea Bri. Rd.
Hyde Pk. W2 14 G1
Hyde Pk. W2 66 H1
Hyde Pk. Ave. N21 32 J2
Hyde Pk. Cor. W1 15 C3
Hyde Pk. Cor. W1 67 A2
Hyde Pk. Cres. W2 10 G4
Hyde Pk. Cres. W2 57 H6
Hyde Pk. Gdns. N21 32 J1
  Hyde Pk. Ave.
Hyde Pk. Gdns. W2 10 F5
Hyde Pk. Gdns. W2 57 G7
Hyde Pk. Gdns. Ms. 10 F5
  W2
Hyde Pk. Gate SW7 14 D4
Hyde Pk. Gate SW7 66 F2
Hyde Pk. Gate Ms. 14 D4
  SW7

Hyde Pk. Pl. W2 10 H5
Hyde Pk. Sq. W2 10 G4
Hyde Pk. Sq. Ms. W2 10 G4
Hyde Pk. St. W2 10 G4
Hyde Pk. St. W2 57 H6
Hyde Rd. N1 59 B1
Hyde Rd., Bexh. 80 F2
Hyde Rd., Rich. 73 J5
  Albert Rd.
Hyde St. SE8 69 A6
  Deptford High St.
Hyde Vale SE10 78 D1
Hyde Way N9 33 C2
Hydefield Clo. N21 33 A1
Hydefield Ct. N9 33 B2
Hydes Pl. N1 49 H7
  Compton Ave.
Hydeside Gdns. N9 33 C2
Hydethorpe Ave. N9 33 C2
Hydethorpe Rd. 85 C1
  SW12
Hylands Rd. E17 42 D2
Hylton St. SE18 70 J4
Hyndewood SE23 86 G3
Hyndman St. SE15 68 E6
Hynton Rd., Dag. 53 C2
Hyrst Dene, S.Croy. 101 H4
Hyson Rd. SE16 68 E4
Hythe Ave., Bexh. 71 E7
Hythe Clo. N18 33 D4
Hythe Rd. NW10 56 G4
Hythe Rd., Th.Hth. 95 A2
Hyver Hill NW7 22 D6

I

Ibbetson Path, 27 E3
  Loug.
Ibbotson Ave. E16 60 F6
Ibbott St. E1 59 F4
  Mantus Rd.
Iberian Ave., Wall. 101 D4
Ibis La. W4 74 C1
Ibscott Clo., Dag. 53 J6
Ibsley Gdns. SW15 83 G1
Ibsley Way, Barn. 23 H5
Iceland Rd. E3 60 A1
Ickburgh Est. E5 50 E3
Ickburgh Rd. E5 50 E3
Ickleton Rd. SE9 88 B4
Icklefield Dr., Ilf. 43 E5
Ickworth Pk. Rd. E17 41 H4
Ida Rd. N15 41 A5
Ida St. E14 60 C6
Iden Clo., Brom. 96 E3
Idlecombe Rd. SW17 85 A6
Idmiston Rd. E15 51 F5
Idmiston Rd. SE27 85 J3
Idmiston Rd., 92 F7
  Wor.Pk.
Idmiston Sq., 99 F1
  Wor.Pk.
Idol La. EC3 13 D6
Idonia St. SE8 69 A7
Iffley Rd. W6 05 H3
Ifield Rd. SW10 18 B5
Ifield Rd. SW10 66 H6
Ightham Rd., Erith 71 G7
Ikea Twr. NW10 47 D5
Ilbert St. W10 57 A3
Ilchester Gdns. W2 10 A5
Ilchester Gdns., W2 57 E7
Ilchester Pl. W14 66 C3
Ilchester Rd., Dag. 53 B5
Ildersley Gro. SE21 86 A2
Ilderton Rd. SE15 68 F7
Ilderton Rd. SE16 68 E5
Ilex Clo., Sun. 90 C2
  Oakington Dr.
Ilex Ho. N4 40 F7
Ilex Rd. NW10 47 F6
Ilex Way SW16 85 G5
Ilford Hill, Ilf. 52 D3
Ilford La., Ilf. 52 E3
Ilfracombe Gdns., 44 B7
  Rom.
Ilfracombe Rd., 87 F3
  Brom.
Iliffe St. SE17 20 H3
Iliffe St. SE17 67 H5
Iliffe Yd. SE17 20 H3
Ilkeston Ct. E5 50 G4
  Overbury St.
Ilkley Clo. SE19 86 A6
Ilkley Rd. E16 60 J5
Ilkley Rd., Wat. 28 D5
Illingworth Clo., 93 G3
  Mitch.
Illingworth Way, 25 B4
  Enf.

Ilmington Rd., Har. 37 G6
Ilminster Gdns. 75 H4
  SW11
Imber Clo. N14 24 C7
Imber Clo., Esher 98 A1
  Ember La.
Imber Ct. Ind. Est., 91 A6
  E.Mol.
Imber Gro., Esher 91 A7
Imber Pk. Rd., 98 A1
  Esher
Imber St. N1 59 A1
Imperial Ave. N16 50 C3
  Victorian Rd.
Imperial Clo., Har. 36 G6
Imperial College 14 E5
  Rd. SW7
Imperial College 66 G3
  Rd. SW7
Imperial Dr., Har. 36 G7
Imperial Gdns., 94 B3
  Mitch.
Imperial Ms. E6 60 J2
  Central Pk. Rd.
Imperial Rd. N22 40 E1
Imperial Rd. SW6 75 E1
Imperial Rd. SW6 75 E1
Imperial St. E3 60 C3
Imperial Way, Chis. 88 F3
Imperial Way, Croy. 101 G6
Imperial Way, Har. 37 H6
Inca Dr. SE9 79 E7
Inchmery Rd. SE6 87 B2
Inchwood, Croy. 103 B4
Independent Pl. E8 50 C5
  Downs Pk. Rd.
Independents Rd. 78 F3
  SE3
  Blackheath Village
Inderwick Rd. N8 40 F5
Indescon Ct. E14 69 A2
India St. EC3 13 F4
India Way W12 56 H7
Indus Rd. SE7 69 J7
Industry Ter. SW9 76 G3
  Canterbury Cres.
Ingal Rd. E13 60 G4
Ingate Pl. SW8 76 B1
Ingatestone Rd. E12 51 J1
Ingatestone Rd. 95 E5
  SE25
Ingelow Rd. SW8 76 B2
Ingersoll Rd. W12 65 H1
Ingestre Pl. W1 11 G4
Ingestre Rd. E7 51 G4
Ingestre Rd. NW5 49 B4
Ingham Rd. NW6 48 D4
Ingle Clo., Pnr. 36 F3
Inglebert St. EC1 8 E3
Ingleborough St. 76 G2
  SW9
Ingleby Clo., Dag. 53 H6
Ingleby Dr., Har. 46 A3
Ingleby Rd. N7 49 E3
Ingleby Rd., Dag. 53 H6
Ingleby Rd., Ilf. 52 E1
Ingleby Way, Chis. 88 D5
Ingledew Rd. SE18 70 G5
Inglehurst Gdns., 43 C5
  Ilf.
Inglemere Rd. SE23 86 G3
Inglemere Rd., 84 J7
  Mitch.
Inglesham Wk. E9 50 J6
  Trowbridge Est.
Ingleside Clo., 87 A7
  Beck.
Ingleside Gro. SE3 69 F6
Inglethorpe St. SW6 75 A1
Ingleton Ave., 80 A5
  Well.
Ingleton Rd. N18 33 D6
Ingleton St. SW9 76 G2
Ingleway N12 31 G6
Inglewood Clo. E14 69 A4
Inglewood Clo., Ilf. 35 J6
Inglewood Copse, 97 B2
  Brom.
Inglewood Rd. NW6 48 D5
Inglis Barracks NW7 31 B5
Inglis Rd. W5 55 J7
Inglis Rd., Croy. 102 C1
Inglis St. SE5 76 H1
Ingram Ave. NW11 54 H1
Ingram Clo. SE11 20 D1
Ingram Clo., Stan. 29 F5
Ingram Rd. N2 39 H4
Ingram Rd., Th.Hth. 94 J1
Ingram Way, Grnf. 55 A1
Ingrave Ho., Dag. 62 B1
Ingrave St. SW11 75 G3

Ingress St. W4 65 E5
  Devonshire Rd.
Inigo Jones Rd. SE7 70 B7
Inigo Pl. WC2 12 A5
Inkerman Rd. NW5 49 B6
Inks Grn. E4 34 B5
Inman Rd. NW10 56 E1
Inman Rd. SW18 75 F7
Inmans Row, 34 G4
  Wdf.Grn.
Inner Circle NW1 7 B4
Inner Circle NW1 58 A3
Inner Pk. Rd. SW19 84 A1
Inner Temple La. 12 E4
  EC4
Innes Clo. SW20 93 B2
Innes Gdns. SW15 74 H6
Innes Yd., Croy. 101 J3
  High St.
Inniskilling Rd. E13 60 J2
Inskip Clo. E10 51 B2
Inskip Rd., Dag. 53 D1
Institute Pl. E8 50 E5
  Amhurst Rd.
Instone Clo., Wall. 101 E7
  De Havilland Rd.
Insurance St. WC1 8 E4
Integer Gdns. E11 42 D7
  Forest Rd.
International Ave., 63 C5
  Houns.
International Trd. 63 B3
  Est., Sthl.
Inver Clo. E5 50 F2
  Theydon Rd.
Inver Ct. W2 10 B4
Inveraray Pl. SE18 70 G6
  Old Mill Rd.
Inverclyde Gdns., 44 D4
  Rom.
Inveresk Gdns., 99 F3
  Wor.Pk.
Inverforth Clo. NW3 48 F2
  North End Way
Inverforth Rd. N11 32 B5
Inverine Rd. SE7 69 H5
Invermore Pl. SE18 70 F4
Inverness Ave., Enf. 25 B1
Inverness Dr., Ilf. 35 H6
Inverness Gdns. W8 14 A2
Inverness Ms. W2 10 B5
Inverness Pl. W2 10 B5
Inverness Pl. W2 57 E7
Inverness Rd. N18 33 E5
Inverness Rd., 72 F4
  Houns.
Inverness Rd., Sthl. 63 E4
Inverness Rd., 100 A1
  Wor.Pk.
Inverness St. NW1 58 B1
Inverness Ter. W2 10 B5
Inverness Ter. W2 57 E6
Inverton Rd. SE15 77 G4
Invicta Clo., Chis. 88 D5
Invicta Gro., 54 F3
  Nthlt.
Invicta Rd. SE3 69 G7
Invicta Rd., Bexh. 71 F6
Inville Rd. SE17 21 C4
Inville Rd. SE17 68 A5
Inwood Ave., Houns. 72 J3
Inwood Clo., Croy. 102 H2
Inwood Rd., Houns. 72 H4
Inworth St. SW11 75 H2
Inworth Wk. N1 58 J1
  Popham St.
Ion Sq. E2 9 H2
Iona Clo. SE6 78 A7
Ipswich Rd. SW17 85 A6
Ireland Pl. N22 32 E7
  Whittington Rd.
Ireland Row E14 59 J6
  Commercial Rd.
Ireland Yd. EC4 12 H1
Irene Rd. SW6 75 D1
Irene Rd., Orp. 97 J3
Iris Ave., Bex. 80 E6
Iris Clo., Croy. 102 G1
  Primrose La.
Iris Clo., Surb. 91 J7
Iris Ct., Pnr. 36 C3
Iris Cres., Bexh. 71 F6
Iris Rd., Epsom 99 B5
Iris Way E4 33 J6
Irkdale Ave., Enf. 25 C1
Iron Mill Pl. SW18 75 E6
  Garratt La.
Iron Mill Rd. SW18 75 H4
Ironmonger La. EC2 13 A4
Ironmonger Pas. EC1 9 A4
Ironmonger Row EC1 9 A4
Ironmonger Row EC1 58 J3
Ironmongers Pl. E14 69 A4
  Spindrift Ave.

Ironside Clo. SE16	68	G2
Kinburn St.		
Irvine Ave., Har.	37	D3
Irvine Clo. N20	31	H2
Irving Way, Orp.	97	J7
Irving Ave., Hdn.	54	D1
Irving Gro. SW9	76	F2
Irving Rd. W14	66	A3
Irving St. WC2	11	**J6**
Irving St. WC2	58	D7
Irving Way NW9	38	F5
Irwin Ave. SE18	70	H7
Irwin Gdns. NW10	56	H1
Isabel St. SW9	76	F1
Isabella Clo. N14	24	C7
Old Fm. Ave.		
Isabella Dr., Orp.	104	F4
Isabella Rd. E9	50	F5
Isabella St. SE1	16	**G2**
Isabella St. SE1	67	H1
Isambard Ms. E14	69	C3
Isambard Pl. SE16	68	F1
Rotherhithe St.		
Isel Way SE22	77	B5
East Dulwich Gro.		
Isham Rd. SW16	94	E2
Isis Clo. SW15	74	J4
Isis St. SW18	84	F2
Isla Rd. SE18	70	F6
Island Fm. Ave.,	90	F5
W.Mol.		
Island Fm. Rd.,	90	F5
W.Mol.		
Island Rd., Mitch.	84	J7
Island Row E14	59	H6
Commercial Rd.		
Islay Gdns., Houns.	72	D5
Islay Wk. N1	49	J6
Douglas Rd.		
Isledon Rd. N7	49	G3
Islehurst Clo.,	97	D1
Chis.		
Islington Grn. N1	58	H1
Islington High St.	8	**G1**
N1		
Islington High St.	58	H2
N1		
Islington Pk. Ms.	49	G7
N1		
Islington Pk. St.		
Islington Pk. St.	49	G7
N1		
Islip Gdns., Edg.	30	D7
Islip Gdns., Nthlt.	45	E7
Islip Manor Rd.,	45	E7
Nthlt.		
Islip St. NW5	49	C5
Ismailia Rd. E7	51	H7
Isom Clo. E13	60	J4
Belgrave Rd.		
Ivanhoe Dr., Har.	37	D3
Ivanhoe Rd. SE5	77	C3
Ivanhoe Rd., Houns.	72	D3
Ivatt Pl. W14	66	C5
Ivatt Way N17	40	H3
Ive Fm. Clo. E10	51	A2
Ive Fm. La. E10	51	A2
Iveagh Ave. NW10	56	A2
Iveagh Clo. E9	59	G1
Iveagh Clo. NW10	56	A2
Ivedon Rd., Well.	80	C2
Iveley Rd. SW4	76	C2
Ivere Dr., Barn.	23	E6
Iverhurst Clo., Bexh.	80	D5
Iverna Ct. W8	66	D3
Iverna Gdns. W8	66	D3
Ivers Way, Croy.	103	B3
Iverson Rd. NW6	48	C6
Ives Rd. E16	60	E5
Ives St. SW3	18	**H1**
Ives St. SW3	66	H4
Ivestor Ter. SE23	77	F7
Ivimey St. E2	9	**J3**
Ivimey St. E2	59	D3
Ivinghoe Clo., Enf.	25	B1
Ivinghoe Rd., Dag.	53	B5
Ivor Gro. SE9	88	E1
Ivor Pl. NW1	6	**J6**
Ivor Pl. NW1	57	J4
Ivor St. NW1	49	C7
Ivory Sq. SW11	75	F3
Gartons Way		
Ivorydown, Brom.	87	G4
Ivy Clo., Har.	45	F4
Ivy Clo., Pnr.	36	C7
Ivy Clo., Sun.	90	C2
Ivy Cotts. E14	60	B7
Grove Vill.		
Ivy Cres. W4	65	C4
Bollo La.		
Ivy Gdns. N8	40	E6
Ivy Gdns., Mitch.	94	D3
Ivy La., Houns.	72	F4

Ivy Rd. E16	60	G6
Pacific Rd.		
Ivy Rd. E17	42	A6
Ivy Rd. N14	24	C7
Ivy Rd. NW2	47	J4
Ivy Rd. SE4	77	J4
Ivy Rd. SW17	73	H4
Ivy Rd., Surb.	96	A2
Ivy St. N1	9	**D1**
Ivy St. N1	59	B2
Ivy Wk., Dag.	53	E6
Ivybridge Clo.,	73	D7
Twick.		
Ivybridge Est.,	73	C5
Islw.		
Ivybridge La. WC2	12	**B6**
Ivychurch Clo. SE20	86	F7
Laurel Gro.		
Ivychurch La. SE17	21	**E3**
Ivydale Rd. SE15	77	G3
Ivydale Rd., Cars.	100	J2
Ivyday Gro. SW16	85	F3
Ivydene, W.Mol.	90	F5
Ivydene Clo., Sutt.	100	F4
Ivyhouse Rd., Dag.	53	D6
Ivymount Rd. SE27	85	G3
Ixworth Pl. SW3	18	**G3**
Ixworth Pl. SW3	66	H4
Izane Rd., Bexh.	80	F4

J

Jack Cornwell St.	52	D4
E12		
Jack Walker Ct. N5	49	H4
Jackass La., Kes.	103	H5
Jacklin Grn.,	34	G4
Wdf.Grn.		
Jackman Ms. NW10	47	E3
Jackman St. E8	59	E1
Jackson Rd. N7	49	F4
Jackson Rd., Bark.	61	G1
Jackson Rd., Barn.	23	G6
Jackson St. SE18	70	D6
Jackson Way, Sthl.	63	H2
Jacksons La. N6	40	A7
Jacksons Pl., Croy.	102	A1
Cross Rd.		
Jacob St. SE1	17	**H3**
Jacob St. SE1	68	C2
Jacobs Clo., Dag.	53	H4
Jacobs Ho. E14	60	J3
Jacob's Well Ms. W1	11	**C3**
Jacqueline Clo.,	54	F1
Nthlt.		
Canford Ave.		
Jade Clo. E16	61	A6
Jade Clo., Dag.	53	C1
Jaffray Pl. SE27	85	H4
Chapel Rd.		
Jaffray Rd., Brom.	92	A4
Jaggard Way SW12	75	J7
Jago Clo. SE18	70	F6
Jago Wk. SE5	68	A7
Lomond Gro.		
Jamaica Rd. SE1	17	**G4**
Jamaica Rd. SE1	68	C2
Jamaica Rd. SE16	17	**H5**
Jamaica Rd. SE16	68	D3
Jamaica Rd.,	94	H6
Th.Hth.		
Jamaica St. E1	59	F5
James Ave. NW2	47	J5
James Ave., Dag.	53	F1
James Bedford Clo.,	36	C2
Pnr.		
James Boswell Clo.	85	G4
SW16		
Curtis Fld. Rd.		
James Clo. NW11	39	B6
Woodlands		
James Collins Clo.	57	C4
W9		
Fermoy Rd.		
James Ct. N1	49	J7
Morton Rd.		
James Dudson Ct.	47	C7
NW10		
James Gdns. N22	32	H7
James Hammett Ho.	9	**G3**
E2		
James La. E10	42	D6
James La. E11	42	D6
James Newman Ct.	88	D3
SE9		
Great Harry Dr.		
James Sinclair Pt.	60	J1
E13		
James St. W1	11	**C3**
James St. W1	58	A6
James St. WC2	12	**B5**
James St., Bark.	52	F7

James St., Enf.	25	C5
James St., Houns.	73	A3
James Yd. E4	34	D6
Larkshall Rd.		
Jameson St. W8	66	D1
James's Cotts.,	65	A7
Rich.		
Kew Rd.		
Jamestown Rd. NW1	60	B1
Jamieson Ho.,	72	F6
Houns.		
Jane St. E1	59	E6
Commercial Rd.		
Janet St. E14	69	A3
Janeway Pl. SE16	68	E2
Janeway St.		
Janeway St. SE16	17	**J4**
Janeway St. SE16	68	D2
Janice Ms., Ilf.	52	E3
Oakfield Rd.		
Jansen Wk. SW11	75	G4
Hope St.		
Janson Clo. E15	51	E5
Janson Rd.		
Janson Clo. NW10	47	E3
Janson Rd. E15	51	E5
Jansons Rd. N15	41	B3
Japan Cres. N4	40	F7
Japan Rd., Rom.	44	D6
Jarrett Clo. SW2	85	H1
Jarrow Clo., Mord.	93	E5
Jarrow Rd. N17	41	E4
Jarrow Rd. SE16	68	F4
Jarrow Rd., Rom.	44	C6
Jarrow Way E9	50	J5
Jarvis Clo., Barn.	23	A5
Jarvis Rd. SE22	77	B4
Melbourne Gro.		
Jarvis Rd., S.Croy.	102	A6
Jasmin Rd., Epsom	99	B6
Jasmine Clo., Ilf.	52	E5
Jasmine Clo., Orp.	104	E2
Jasmine Gdns.,	103	A3
Croy.		
Jasmine Gdns., Har.	45	G2
Jasmine Gro. SE20	95	E1
Jasmine Way, E.Mol.	91	B4
Hampton Ct. way		
Jason Ct. W1	58	A6
Marylebone La.		
Jason Wk. SE9	88	D4
Jasper Pas. SE19	86	C6
Jasper Rd. E16	61	A6
Jasper Rd. SE19	86	C6
Jasper Wk. N1	9	**B3**
Javelin Way, Nthlt.	54	D3
Jay Ms. SW7	14	**D4**
Jay Ms. SW7	66	F2
Jaycroft, Enf.	24	G1
The Ridgeway		
Jebb Ave. SW2	76	E6
Jebb St. E3	60	A2
Jedburgh Rd. E13	60	J3
Jedburgh St. SW11	76	A4
Jeddo Rd. W12	65	F2
Jefferies Ho. NW10	47	D7
Jefferson Clo. W13	64	E3
Jefferson Clo., Ilf.	43	E5
Jeffreys Pl. NW1	49	C7
Jeffreys St.		
Jeffreys Rd. SW4	76	E2
Jeffreys Rd., Enf.	25	J3
Jeffreys St. NW1	49	C7
Jeffreys Wk. SW4	76	E2
Jeffs Clo., Hmptn.	81	H6
Uxbridge Rd.		
Jeffs Rd., Sutt.	100	C4
Jeken Rd. SE9	78	J4
Jelf Rd. SW2	76	G5
Jellicoe Gdns.,	29	C6
Stan.		
Jellicoe Rd. E13	60	G4
Jutland Rd.		
Jellicoe Rd. N17	33	A7
Jengar Clo., Sutt.	100	E4
Jenkins La. E6	61	D2
Jenkins La., Bark.	61	E2
Jenkins Rd. E13	60	H4
Jenner Ave. W3	56	D5
Jenner Ho. SE3	69	E6
Jenner Pl. SW13	65	H6
Jenner Rd. N16	50	C2
Jennett Rd., Croy.	101	G3
Jennifer Rd., Brom.	87	F3
Jennings Rd. SE22	77	C6
Jennings Way, Barn.	22	J3
Jenningtree Way,	71	J2
Belv.		
Jenny Hammond	51	F3
Clo. E11		
Newcomen Rd.		
Jenson Way SE19	86	C7

Jenton Ave., Bexh.	80	E1
Jephson Rd. E7	51	J7
Jephson St. SE5	77	A1
Grove La.		
Jephtha Rd. SW18	75	D6
Jeppos La., Mitch.	93	J4
Jerdan Pl. SW6	66	D7
Fulham Bdy.		
Jeremiah St. E14	60	B6
Jeremys Grn. N18	39	F1
Jermyn St. SW1	15	**G1**
Jermyn St. SW1	67	C1
Jerningham Ave.,	43	E2
Ilf.		
Jerningham Rd. SE14	77	H2
Jerome Cres. NW8	6	**G5**
Jerome Cres. NW8	57	H4
Jerome St. E1	9	**F6**
Jerome St. E1	58	D2
Jerrard St. N1	9	**E2**
Jerrard St. SE13	78	B3
Jersey Ave., Stan.	37	E2
Jersey Dr., Orp.	97	G6
Jersey Par., Houns.	72	H1
Jersey Rd. E11	51	D1
Jersey Rd. E16	60	J6
Jersey Rd. SW17	85	B6
Jersey Rd. W7	64	D2
Jersey Rd., Houns.	72	H1
Jersey Rd., Ilf.	52	E4
Jersey Rd., Islw.	64	A7
Jersey St. E2	59	E3
Bethnal Grn. Rd.		
Jerusalem Pas. EC1	8	**G6**
Jervis Ct. W1	11	**E4**
Jerviston Gdns.	85	G5
SW16		
Jesmond Ave., Wem.	46	J6
Jesmond Rd., Croy.	95	C7
Jesmond Way, Stan.	29	H5
Jessam Ave. E5	50	E1
Jessamine Rd. W7	64	B1
Jesse Rd. E10	51	C1
Jessel Dr., Loug.	27	F1
Jessica Rd. SW18	75	F6
Jessop Ave., Sthl.	63	F4
Jessops Way, Croy.	94	C6
Jessup Clo. SE18	70	F4
Jetstar Way, Nthlt.	54	E3
Jevington Way SE12	87	H1
Jewel Rd. E17	42	A3
Jewry St. EC3	13	**F4**
Jewry St. EC3	59	C6
Jew's Row SW18	75	E4
Jews Wk. SE26	86	E4
Jeymer Ave. NW2	47	H5
Jeymer Dr., Grnf.	54	J1
Jeypore Rd. SW18	75	F7
Jillian Clo., Hmptn.	81	G7
Jim Bradley Clo.	70	D4
SE18		
John Wilson St.		
Joan Cres. SE9	79	A7
Joan Gdns., Dag.	53	E2
Joan Rd., Dag.	53	E1
Joan St. SE1	16	**G2**
Joan St. SE1	67	H1
Jocelyn Rd., Rich.	73	H3
Jockey's Flds. WC1	12	**D1**
Jockey's Flds. WC1	58	F5
Jodrell Rd. E3	59	J1
Joel St., Nthwd.	36	A3
Joel St., Pnr.	36	A3
Johanna St. SE1	16	**E4**
John Adam St. WC2	12	**B6**
John Adam St. WC2	58	E7
John Aird Ct. W2	10	**D1**
John Ashby Clo.	76	E6
SW2		
John Barnes Wk. E15	51	F6
John Bradshaw Rd.	32	D1
N14		
Bark.		
John Burns Dr.,	52	H7
Bark.		
John Campbell Rd.	50	B5
N16		
John Carpenter St.	12	**F5**
EC4		
John Carpenter St.	58	H7
EC4		
John Cornwall VC	52	D4
Ho. E12		
John Felton Rd.	17	**H4**
SE16		
John Felton Rd.	68	D2
John Fisher St. E1	13	**H5**
John Fisher St. E1	59	D7
John Gooch Dr.,	24	H1
Enf.		
John Groom's Est.,	30	C4
Edg.		
John Islip St. SW1	19	**J3**

John Islip St. SW1 67 D5
John Keats Ho. N22 32 F7
John McKenna Wk. 17 J5
SE16
John Newton Ct., 80 B3
Well.
Danson La.
John Parker Clo., 53 H7
Dag.
John Parker Sq. 75 G3
SW11
Thomas Baines Rd.
John Penn St. SE13 78 B1
John Perrin Pl., 31 H7
Har.
John Princes St. W1 11 E3
John Princes St. W1 58 B6
John Rennie Wk. E1 68 E1
Wine Clo.
John Roll Way SE16 17 J5
John Roll Way SE16 68 D3
John Ruskin St. SE5 20 H7
John Ruskin St. SE5 67 H7
John Spencer Sq. N1 49 H6
John St. E15 60 F1
John St. SE25 95 D4
John St. WC1 8 D6
John St. W1 58 F4
John St., Enf. 25 C5
John St., Houns. 72 E2
John Walsh Twr. E11 51 F2
John Wilson St. 70 D3
SE18
John Woolley Clo. 78 D4
SE13
Johns Ave. NW4 38 J4
Johns La., Mord. 93 F5
John's Ms. WC1 8 D6
John's Ms. WC1 58 F4
John's Pl. E1 59 E6
Damien St.
Johns Ter., Croy. 102 B1
Johnson Clo. E8 59 D1
Johnson Rd., Brom. 97 A5
Johnson Rd., Croy. 95 A7
Johnson Rd., Houns. 63 C7
Johnson St. E1 59 F7
Cable St.
Johnson St., Sthl. 63 C3
Cars.
Johnsons Clo., 100 H3
Johnson's Ct. EC4 58 G6
Fleet St.
Johnsons Dr., 90 J1
Hmptn.
Johnson's Pl. SW1 19 F4
Johnson's Pl. SW1 67 C5
Johnsons Way NW10 56 B4
Johnston Rd., 34 G5
Wdf.Grn.
Johnston Ter. NW2 48 A3
Campion Ter.
Johnstone Rd. E6 61 C3
Joiner St. SE1 17 C2
Joiner's Arms Yd. 77 A1
SE5
Denmark Hill
Jollys La., Har. 46 A1
Lwr. Rd.
Jolly's La., Hayes 54 D5
Jonathan St. SE11 20 C3
Jonathan St. SE11 67 F5
Jones Rd. E13 60 H4
Holborn Rd.
Jones St. W1 11 D6
Jonquil Gdns., 81 F6
Hmptn.
Partridge Rd.
Jonson Clo., Hayes 54 A5
Jonson Clo., Mitch. 94 B4
Joram Way SE16 68 E5
Egan Way
Jordan Clo., Dag. 53 H4
Muggeridge Rd.
Jordan Clo., Har. 45 F3
Hamilton Cres.
Jordan Rd., Grnf. 55 E1
Jordans Clo., Islw. 73 B1
Joseph Ave. W3 56 D6
Joseph Powell Clo. 76 B6
SW12
Hazelbourne Rd.
Joseph St. E3 59 J4
Josephine Ave. SW2 76 F5
Joshua St. E14 60 C6
St. Leonards Rd.
Joubert St. SW11 75 J2
Jowett St. SE15 68 C7
Joyce Ave. N18 33 C5
Joyce Dawson Way 62 A7
SE28
Thamesmere Dr.
Joyce Page Clo. SE7 70 A6

Lansdowne La.
Joydon Dr., Rom. 44 B6
Joyners Clo., Dag. 53 F4
Jubb Powell Ho. N15 41 B6
Jubilee Ave. E4 34 C6
Jubilee Ave., Rom. 44 H5
Jubilee Ave., 2 J7
Twick.
Jubilee Clo. NW9 38 D6
Jubilee Clo., Pnr. 36 C2
Jubilee Clo., Rom. 44 H5
Jubilee Cres. E14 69 C3
Jubilee Cres. N9 33 D1
Jubilee Dr., Ruis. 45 D4
Jubilee Gdns., 54 G6
Sthl.
Jubilee Pl. SW3 18 H3
Jubilee Pl. SW3 66 H5
Jubilee Rd., Grnf. 55 E1
Jubilee Rd., Sutt. 100 A7
Jubilee St. E1 59 F6
Jubilee Way SW19 93 E1
Jubilee Way, Chess. 99 A4
Jubilee Way, 89 A2
Sidc.
Judd St. WC1 8 A4
Judd St. WC1 58 E3
Jude St. E16 60 F6
Judge Wk., Esher 98 B6
Juer St. SW11 66 H7
Julia Gdns., Bark. 62 D2
Julia St. NW5 49 A4
Oak Village
Julian Ave. W3 56 B7
Julian Clo., Barn. 23 E3
Julian Hill, Har. 46 B2
Julian Pl. E14 69 B5
Julien Rd. W5 64 H4
Junction App. SE13 78 C3
Loampit Vale
Junction App. SW11 75 H3
Junction Ave. W10 56 J3
Harrow Rd.
Junction Ms. W2 10 G3
Junction Pl. W2 10 F3
Junction Rd. E13 60 H4
Junction Rd. N9 33 D1
Junction Rd. N17 41 D3
Junction Rd. N19 49 C4
Junction Rd. W5 64 G4
Junction Rd., Har. 37 B6
Junction Rd., 102 A5
S.Croy.
Junction Rd. E., 44 E7
Rom.
Kenneth Rd.
Junction Rd. W., 44 E7
Rom.
Junction Wf. N1 8 J2
Junction Wf. N1 58 J2
Juniper Clo., Wem. 47 A5
Juniper Gdns. SW16 94 C1
Leonard Rd.
Juniper La. E6 61 B5
Juniper Pl., Ilf. 52 E4
Juniper St. E1 59 F7
Juno Way SE14 68 G6
Jupiter Way N7 49 F6
Jupp Rd. E15 51 D7
Jupp Rd. W. E15 60 C1
Justice Wk. SW3 18 G6
Justin Clo., Brent. 64 G7
Justin Rd. E4 33 J6
Jute La., Enf. 25 H2
Jutland Clo. N19 49 E1
Sussex Way
Jutland Rd. E13 60 G4
Jutland Rd. SE6 78 C7
Jutsums Ave., Rom. 44 H6
Jutsums La., Rom. 44 H6
Juxon Clo., Har. 36 H1
Augustine Rd.
Juxon St. SE11 20 D1
Juxon St. SE11 67 F4

K

Kaduna Clo., Pnr. 36 B5
Kale Rd., Erith 71 E2
Kambala Rd. SW11 75 G3
Kangley Bri. Rd. 86 J4
SE26
Karen Ct. SE4 77 J2
Wickham Rd.
Karen Ct., Brom. 96 F1
Blyth Rd.
Karoline Gdns., 55 A2
Grnf.
Oldfield La. N.
Kashgar Rd. SE18 70 J4
Kashmir Rd. SE7 70 J4
Kassala Rd. SW11 75 J1
Katella Trd. Est., 61 H3
Bark.

Kates Clo., Barn. 22 G5
Katharine St., 101 J3
Croy.
Katherine Gdns. SE9 79 A4
Katherine Gdns., Ilf. 35 F7
Katherine Rd. E6 52 A7
Katherine Rd. E7 51 J6
Katherine Rd., 82 D1
Twick.
London Rd.
Katherine Sq. W11 66 B1
Wilsham St.
Kathleen Ave. W3 56 C5
Kathleen Ave., Wem. 46 H7
Kathleen Rd. SW11 75 J3
Kay Rd. SW9 76 E2
Kay St. E2 9 J1
Kay St. E2 59 D2
Kay St. E15 51 D7
Kay St., Well. 80 D2
Kayemoor Rd., Sutt. 100 H7
Kean St. WC2 12 C4
Kean St. WC2 58 F6
Keats Clo. E11 42 H5
Nightingale La.
Keats Clo. NW3 48 H4
Keats Gro.
Keats Clo. SE1 21 F2
Keats Clo. SW19 84 G6
North Rd.
Keats Clo., Chig. 35 F6
Keats Clo., Hayes 54 A5
Keats Ho., Beck. 87 A6
Keats Pl. EC2 13 B2
Keats Rd., Belv. 71 J3
Keats Rd., Well. 79 H1
Keats Way, Croy. 95 F6
Keats Way, Grnf. 54 H5
Keble Clo., Nthlt. 45 J5
Keble Clo., Wor.Pk. 99 F1
Keble St. SW17 84 F4
Kechill Gdns., 96 G7
Brom.
Kedelston Ct. E5 50 G4
Redwald Rd.
Kedleston Dr., Orp. 97 J6
Kedleston Wk. E2 59 E3
Middleton St.
Keedonwood Rd., 87 E5
Brom.
Keel Clo. SE16 68 G1
Keeley Rd., Croy. 101 J2
Keeley St. WC2 12 C4
Keeley St. WC2 58 F6
Keeling Rd. SE9 79 A5
Keely Clo., Barn. 23 H5
Keemor Clo. SE18 70 D7
Llanover Rd.
Keens Rd., Croy. 101 J4
Keens Yd. N1 49 H6
St. Pauls Rd.
Keep, The SE3 78 G2
Keep, The, Kings.T. 82 J6
Keetons Rd. SE16 68 E3
Keevil Dr. SW19 75 A7
Keighley Clo. N7 49 E5
Penn Rd.
Keightley Dr. SE9 88 F1
Keildon Rd. SW11 75 J4
Keir Hardie Est. E5 50 E1
Springfield
Keir Hardie Ho. W6 65 J6
Lochaline St.
Keir Hardie Way, 53 A7
Bark.
Keir Hardie Way, 54 A3
Hayes
Keith Connor Clo. 76 B3
SW8
Daley Thompson
Way
Keith Gro. W12 65 G2
Keith Rd. E17 41 J1
Keith Rd., Bark. 61 G2
Kelbrook Rd. SE3 79 B2
Kelby Path SE9 88 E3
Kelceda Clo. NW2 47 G2
Kelfield Gdns. W10 56 J6
Kell St. SE1 16 H5
Kelland Clo. N8 40 D5
Palace Rd.
Kelland Rd. E13 60 G4
Kellaway Rd. SE3 78 J2
Kellerton Rd. SE13 78 E5
Kellett Rd. SW2 76 G4
Kelling Gdns., 94 H7
Croy.
Kellino St. SW17 84 J4
Kellner Rd. SE28 70 J3
Kelly Ct., Borwd. 22 C2
Banks Rd.
Kelly Rd. NW7 31 B6

Kelly St. NW1 49 B6
Kelly Way, Rom. 44 E5
Kelman Clo. SW4 76 D2
Kelmore Gro. SE22 77 D4
Kelmscott Clo. E17 41 J3
Kelmscott Gdns. W12 65 G3
Kelmscott Rd. SW11 75 H5
Kelross Pas. N5 49 J4
Kelross Rd.
Kelross Rd. N5 49 J4
Kelsall Clo. SE3 78 H2
Kelsey La., Beck. 96 A3
Kelsey Pk. Ave., 96 B2
Beck.
Kelsey Pk. Rd., Beck. 96 A2
Kelsey St. E2 9 J5
Kelsey St. E2 59 D4
Kelsey Way, Beck. 96 A3
Kelshall Ct. N4 49 J2
Brownswood Rd.
Kelsie Way, Ilf. 35 H6
Kelso Pl. W8 14 B5
Kelso Pl. W8 66 E3
Kelso Rd., Cars. 93 F7
Kelson Ho. E14 69 C3
Kelston Rd., Ilf. 43 E2
Kelvedon Clo., 83 A6
Kings.T.
Kelvedon Rd. SW6 66 C7
Kelvedon Way, 35 C6
Wdf.Grn.
Kelvin Ave. N13 32 F6
Kelvin Ave., Tedd. 82 B6
Kelvin Clo., Epsom 99 A6
Kelvin Cres., Har. 29 B7
Kelvin Dr., Twick. 73 E6
Kelvin Gdns., Sthl. 54 G6
Kelvin Gro. SE26 86 E3
Kelvin Gro., Chess. 98 H3
Kelvin Ind. Est., Grnf. 45 H7
Kelvin Par., Orp. 104 H1
Kelvin Rd. N5 49 H4
Kelvin Rd., Well. 80 A3
Kelvinbrook, W.Mol. 90 H3
Kelvington Clo., 95 H7
Croy.
Kelvington Rd. SE15 77 G3
Kember St. N1 49 F7
Carnoustie Dr.
Kemble Dr., Brom. 104 B3
Kemble Rd. N17 41 D1
Kemble Rd. SE23 86 G1
Kemble Rd., Croy. 101 G3
Kemble St. WC2 12 C4
Kemble St. WC2 58 F6
Kemerton Rd. SE5 76 J3
Kemerton Rd., Beck. 96 B2
Kemerton Rd., Croy. 95 C7
Kemeys St. E9 50 H5
Kemnal Rd., Chis. 88 F7
Kemp Gdns., Croy. 94 J6
St. Saviours Rd.
Kemp Rd., Dag. 53 D1
Kempe Rd. NW6 57 A2
Kempis Way SE22 77 B5
East Dulwich Gro.
Kemplay Rd. NW3 48 G4
Kemp's St. W1 11 G4
Kemps Dr. E14 60 A7
Morant St.
Kemps Gdns. SE13 78 C5
Thornford Rd.
Kempsford Gdns. 66 D5
SW5
Kempsford Rd. SE11 20 G2
Kempsford Rd. SE11 67 G4
Kempshott Rd. SW16 85 D7
Kempson Rd. SW6 75 D1
Kempt St. SE18 70 D6
Kempthorne Rd. SE8 68 H4
Kempton Ave., 45 G6
Nthlt.
Kempton Ave., Sun. 90 B1
Kempton Clo., Erith 71 J4
Kempton Ct., Sun. 90 B1
Kempton Rd. E6 61 C1
Kempton Rd., Hmptn. 90 F2
Kempton Wk., Croy. 95 H6
Kemsing Clo., Bex. 80 E7
Kemsing Clo., Brom. 103 F2
Bourne Way
Kemsing Clo., 94 J4
Th.Hth.
Kemsing Rd. SE10 69 G5
Ken Way, Wem. 47 C2
Kenbury St. SE5 76 J2
Kenchester Clo. SW8 67 E7
Kencot Way, Erith 71 F2
Kendal Ave. N18 33 A4
Kendal Ave. W3 56 H4
Kendal Ave., Bark. 52 H7
Kendal Clo. SW9 20 G7
Kendal Clo. SW9 67 H7

Kendal Clo., 34 F2
  Wdf.Grn.
Kendal Gdns. N18 33 A4
Kendal Gdns., Sutt. 100 F2
Kendal Par. N18 33 A4
  Green Canning Rd.,
Kendal Pl. SW15 75 L5
  Upper Richmond Rd.
Kendal Rd. NW10 47 C4
Kendal St. W2 10 H4
Kendal St. W2 57 H6
Kendale Rd., Brom. 87 G5
Kendall Ave., Beck. 95 H2
Kendall Pl. W1 11 B2
Kendall Rd., Beck. 95 H2
Kendall Rd., Islw. 73 D2
Kender St. SE14 77 F1
Kendoa Rd. SW4 76 D4
Kendon Clo. E11 42 H5
  The Ave.
Kendra Hall Rd., 101 H7
  S.Croy.
Kendrey Gdns., 73 B6
  Twick.
Kendrick Ms. SW7 18 E1
Kendrick Pl. SW7 18 E2
Kendrick Rd. SW7 66 G4
Kenelm Clo., Har. 46 D3
Kenerne Dr., Barn. 23 B5
Kenilford Rd. SW12 76 B7
Kenilworth Ave. E17 42 A2
Kenilworth Ave. 84 D5
  SW19
Kenilworth Ave., 45 F4
  Har.
Kenilworth Clo., 22 C3
  Borwd.
Kenilworth Ct. SW15 75 A3
Kenilworth Cres., 25 B1
  Enf.
Kenilworth Dr., 22 C3
  Borwd.
Kenilworth Gdns. 79 E2
  SE18
Kenilworth Gdns., 52 J2
  Ilf.
Kenilworth Gdns., 27 C6
  Loug.
Kenilworth Gdns., 54 F3
  Sthl.
Kenilworth Gdns., 28 C5
  Wat.
Kenilworth Rd. E3 59 H2
Kenilworth Rd. NW6 57 C1
Kenilworth Rd. SE20 95 G1
Kenilworth Rd. W5 64 H1
Kenilworth Rd., 30 C3
  Edg.
Kenilworth Rd., 99 G5
  Epsom
Kenilworth Rd., Orp. 97 F6
Kenley Ave. NW9 38 E1
Kenley Clo., Bex. 80 G7
Kenley Clo., Chis. 97 H3
Kenley Gdns., 94 H4
  Th.Hth.
Kenley Rd. SW19 93 C2
Kenley Rd., Kings.T. 92 B2
Kenley Rd., Twick. 73 D6
Kenley Wk., W11 57 B7
  Princedale Rd.
Kenley Wk., Sutt. 100 A4
Kenlor Rd. SW17 84 G5
Kenmare Dr., Mitch. 84 J7
Kenmare Gdns. N13 32 J4
Kenmare Rd., 94 G6
  Th.Hth.
Kenmere Gdns., 56 A1
  Wem.
Kenmere Rd., Well. 80 C2
Kenmont Gdns. 56 H3
  NW10
Kenmore Ave., Har. 37 H4
Kenmore Clo., Rich. 65 A7
  Kent Rd.
Kenmore Gdns., Edg. 38 B2
Kenmore Rd., Har. 37 G3
Kenmure Rd. E8 50 E5
Kennard Rd. E15 51 D7
Kennard Rd. N11 31 J5
Kennard St. E16 70 C1
Kennard St. SW11 76 A1
Kennedy Ave., Enf. 25 F6
Kennedy Clo. E13 60 G2
Kennedy Clo., Orp. 104 G1
Kennedy Path W7 55 C4
  Harp Rd.
Kennedy Rd. W7 55 B5
Kennedy Rd., Bark. 61 H1
Kennet Clo. SW11 75 G4
  Maysoule Rd.
Kennet Rd. W9 57 C4
Kennet Rd., Islw. 73 C3

Kennet Sq., Mitch. 93 H1
Kennet St. E1 17 J1
Kennet St. E1 68 D1
Kennet Wf. La. EC4 13 A5
Kenneth Ave., Ilf. 52 E4
Kenneth Cres. NW2 47 H5
  Ronald Gdns. 29 D6
  Stan.
Kenneth More Rd., 52 E3
  Ilf.
  Oakfield Rd.
Kenneth Rd., Rom. 44 D7
Kenneth Robbins Ho. 33 E7
  N17
Kennett Dr., Hayes 54 E5
Kenning St. SE16 68 F2
  Railway Ave.
Kenning Ter. N1 57 J1
Kenninghall Rd. E5 50 D3
Kenninghall Rd. N18 33 F5
Kennings Way SE11 20 G3
Kennings Way SE11 67 G5
Kennington Grn. 20 E4
  SE11
Kennington Gro. 20 D5
  SE11
Kennington La. SE11 20 C4
Kennington La. SE11 67 E5
Kennington Oval 20 D5
  SE11
Kennington Oval 67 F6
  SE11
Kennington Pk. Est. 20 E6
  SE11
Kennington Pk. 20 G5
  Gdns. SE11
Kennington Pk. Pl. 20 F5
  SE11
Kennington Pk. Pl. 67 G6
  SE11
Kennington Pk. Rd. 20 F5
  SE11
Kennington Pk. Rd. 67 G6
  SE11
Kennington Rd. SE1 16 E5
Kennington Rd. SE1 67 G3
Kennington Rd. SE11 20 E1
Kennington Rd. SE11 67 G3
Kenny Rd. NW7 31 B5
Kenrick Pl. W1 11 B2
Kensal Rd. W10 57 A4
Kensington Ave. E12 52 B6
Kensington Ave., 94 G1
  Th.Hth.
Kensington Ch. Ct. 14 A4
  W8
Kensington Ch. Ct. 66 E2
  W8
Kensington Ch. St. 66 D1
  W8
Kensington Ch. Wk. 14 A3
  W8
Kensington Ch. Wk. 66 E2
  W8
Kensington Ct. W8 14 B4
Kensington Ct. W8 66 E2
Kensington Ct. Ms. 14 B4
  W8
Kensington Ct. Pl. 14 B5
  W8
Kensington Ct. Pl. 66 E3
  W8
Kensington Dr., 43 A2
  Wdf.Grn.
Kensington Gdns., 52 C1
  Ilf.
Kensington Gdns. 10 A4
  Sq. W2
Kensington Gdns. 57 E6
  Sq. W2
Kensington Gate W8 14 C5
Kensington Gate W8 66 F3
Kensington Gore 14 E4
  SW7
Kensington Gore 66 F2
  SW7
Kensington Hall 66 C5
  Gdns. W14
  Beaumont Ave.
Kensington High St. 66 D3
  W8
Kensington High St. 66 C3
  W14
Kensington Mall W8 66 D1
Kensington Palace 14 A1
  Gdns. W8
Kensington Palace 66 E1
  Gdns. W8
Kensington Pk. 57 C7
  Gdns. W11
Kensington Pk. Ms. 57 C6
  W11
  Kensington Pk. Rd.

Kensington Pk. Rd. 57 C6
  W11
Kensington Pl. W8 66 D1
Kensington Rd. SW7 14 C4
Kensington Rd. SW7 66 F2
Kensington Rd. W8 14 B4
Kensington Rd. W8 66 E2
Kensington Rd., 54 G3
  Nthlt.
Kensington Rd., 44 J6
  Rom.
Kensington Sq. W8 14 A4
Kensington Sq. W8 66 E2
Kensington Ter., 102 A7
  S.Croy.
  Sanderstead Rd.
Kent Ave. W13 55 E5
Kent Ave., Dag. 62 G4
Kent Ave., Well. 79 J5
Kent Clo., Mitch. 94 E4
Kent Clo., Orp. 104 H6
Kent Dr., Barn. 24 A4
Kent Dr., Tedd. 82 B5
Kent Gdns. W13 55 E5
Kent Gdns., Ruis. 36 B6
Kent Gate Way, 102 J6
  Croy.
Kent Ho. La., Beck. 86 H5
Kent Ho. Rd. SE26 86 H5
Kent Ho. Rd., Beck. 86 G7
Kent Pas. NW1 6 J5
Kent Rd. N21 33 A1
Kent Rd. W4 65 C3
Kent Rd., Dag. 53 H5
Kent Rd., E.Mol. 90 J4
Kent Rd., Kings.T. 91 G3
Kent Rd., Rich. 65 A7
Kent Rd., W.Wick. 103 B1
Kent St. E2 9 G1
Kent St. E2 59 C2
Kent St. E13 60 H3
Kent Ter. NW1 6 H4
Kent Ter. NW1 57 H3
Kent Twrs. SE20 86 E7
Kent Vw. Gdns., 52 H2
  Ilf.
Kent Wk. SW9 76 H4
  Moorland Rd.
Kent Way SE15 77 C1
  Sumner Est.
Kent Way, Surb. 98 H3
Kent Yd. SW7 14 H4
  Nthlt.
Kentford Way, 54 E1
  Nthlt.
Kentish Bldgs. SE1 17 B3
Kentish Rd., Belv. 71 G4
Kentish Town Rd. 49 B7
  NW1
Kentish Town Rd. 49 B6
  NW5
Kentish Way, Brom. 96 G2
Kentmere Rd. SE18 70 H4
Kenton Ave., Har. 37 C7
Kenton Ave., Sthl. 54 G7
Kenton Ave., Sun. 90 D2
Kenton Gdns., Har. 37 F5
Kenton La., Har. 29 C6
Kenton Pk. Ave., 37 F4
  Har.
Kenton Pk. Clo., Har. 37 F4
Kenton Pk. Cres., 37 G4
  Har.
Kenton Pk. Rd., Har. 37 F4
Kenton Rd. E9 50 G6
Kenton Rd., Har. 37 F5
Kenton St. WC1 8 A5
Kenton St. WC1 58 E4
Kents Pas., Hmptn. 90 F1
Kentwode Grn. SW13 65 G7
Kenver Ave. N12 31 G6
Kenward Rd. SE9 78 J5
Kenway, Rom. 44 J2
Kenway Rd. SW5 18 A2
Kenway Rd. SW5 66 E4
Kenwood Ave. N14 24 D5
Kenwood Ave. SE14 77 G1
  Besson St.
Kenwood Clo. NW3 48 G1
Kenwood Dr., Beck. 96 G3
Kenwood Gdns. E18 42 H3
Kenwood Gdns., Ilf. 43 D4
Kenwood Rd. N6 39 J6
Kenwood Rd. N9 33 D1
Kenworthy Rd. E9 50 H5
Kenwyn Dr. NW2 47 E3
Kenwyn Rd. SW4 76 H3
Kenwyn Rd. SW20 92 J1
Kenya Rd. SE7 70 H7
Kenyngton Dr., Sun. 81 A5
Kenyngton Pl., Har. 37 F6
Kenyon St. SW6 75 A1
Keogh Rd. E15 51 E6
Kepler Rd. SW4 76 E4

Keppel Rd. E6 52 C7
Keppel Rd., Dag. 53 E4
Keppel Row SE1 16 J2
Keppel St. WC1 11 J1
Keppel St. WC1 58 D5
Kerbela St. E2 9 H5
Kerbey St. E14 60 B6
Kerfield Cres. SE5 77 A1
  Grove La.
Kerfield Pl. SE5 77 A1
Kerri Clo., Barn. 22 J4
Kerridge Ct. N1 50 B6
  Kingsbury Rd.
Kerrison Pl. W5 64 G1
Kerrison Rd. E15 60 D1
Kerrison Rd. SW11 75 H3
Kerrison Rd. W5 64 G1
Kerry Ave., Stan. 29 G4
Kerry Clo. E16 60 H6
Kerry Ct., Stan. 29 G4
Kerry Path SE14 68 J6
  Edward St.
Kersey Gdns. SE9 88 B4
Kersfield Rd. SW15 75 A6
Kershaw Clo. SW18 75 G6
  Westover Rd.
Kershaw Rd., Dag. 53 G3
Kersley Ms. SW11 75 J2
Kersley Rd. N16 50 B2
Kersley St. SW11 75 J2
Kerswell Clo. N15 41 B5
Kerwick Clo. N7 49 F7
  Sutterton St.
Keslake Rd. NW6 57 A2
Kessock Clo. N17 41 E5
Kesteven Clo., Ilf. 35 J6
Keston Ave., Kes. 103 J5
Keston Clo. N18 33 A3
Keston Clo., Well. 71 C7
Keston Gdns., Kes. 103 J4
Keston Pk. Clo., 104 C3
  Kes.
Keston Rd. N17 41 A3
Keston Rd. SE15 77 D3
Keston Rd., Th.Hth. 94 F6
Kestrel Ave. E6 61 B5
  Swan App.
Kestrel Ave. SE24 76 H5
Kestrel Clo. NW9 38 E2
Kestrel Clo. NW10 47 D5
Kestrel Ho. EC1 8 J3
Kestrel Ho. W13 55 C4
Keswick Ave. SW15 83 E5
Keswick Ave. SW19 93 D2
Keswick Clo., Sutt. 100 F4
Keswick Gdns., Ilf. 43 B5
Keswick Gdns., Wem. 46 H4
Keswick Ms. W5 64 H1
Keswick Rd. SW15 75 B5
Keswick Rd., Bexh. 80 G2
Keswick Rd., Orp. 104 J1
Keswick Rd., Twick. 72 J6
Keswick Rd., 103 E2
  W.Wick.
Kett Gdns. SW2 76 F5
Kettering St. SW16 85 C6
Kettlebaston Rd. 50 J1
  E10
Kevan Ho. SE5 67 J7
  Wyndham Rd.
Kevelioc Rd. N17 40 J1
Kevin Clo., Houns. 72 C2
Kevington Clo., 97 J4
  Orp.
Kevington Dr., Chis. 97 H4
Kew Bri., Brent. 64 J6
Kew Bri., Rich. 64 J6
Kew Bri. Ct. W4 65 A5
Kew Bri. Rd., Brent. 64 J6
Kew Cres., Sutt. 100 B3
Kew Foot Rd., Rich. 73 H4
Kew Gdns. Rd., Rich. 64 J7
Kew Grn., Rich. 64 J6
Kew Meadows Path, 74 B1
  Rich.
Kew Palace, Rich. 64 H7
Kew Rd., Rich. 73 H4
Key Clo. E1 59 E4
Keybridge Ho. SW8 20 B6
Keybridge Ho. SW8 67 E6
Keyes Rd. NW2 48 A5
Keymer Rd. SW2 85 F2
Keynes Clo. N2 39 J4
Keynsham Ave., 34 E4
  Wdf.Grn.
Keynsham Gdns. SE9 79 B5
Keynsham Rd. SE9 79 A5
Keynsham Rd., 100 E1
  Mord.
Keynsham Wk., 100 E1
  Mord.
  Hunston Rd.
Keyse Rd. SE1 17 F6

Keysham Ave., 72 A1
Houns.
The Ave.
Keystone Cres. N1 8 B2
Keywood Dr., Sun. 81 A6
Keyworth Pl. SE1 16 H5
Keyworth St. SE1 16 H5
Keyworth St. SE1 67 H3
Kezia St. SE8 68 H5
Trundleys Rd.
Khama Rd. SW17 84 H4
Khartoum Rd. E13 60 H3
Khartoum Rd. SW17 84 G4
Khartoum Rd., Ilf. 52 E5
Khyber Rd. SW11 75 H2
Kibworth St. SW8 67 F7
Kidbrooke Gdns. SE3 78 G2
Kidbrooke Gro. SE3 78 G1
Kidbrooke La. SE9 79 B4
Kidbrooke Pk. Clo. 78 H1
SE3
Kidbrooke Pk. Rd. 78 H1
SE3
Kidbrooke Way SE3 78 H2
Kidd Pl. SE7 70 B5
Kidderminster Pl., 101 H1
Croy.
Kidderminster Rd.
Kidderminster Rd., 101 H1
Croy.
Kidderpore Ave. 48 D4
NW3
Kidderpore Gdns. 48 D4
NW3
Kidlington Way NW9 38 E2
Kidron Way E9 59 F1
Clermont Rd.
Kielder Clo., Ilf. 35 J6
Kiffen St. EC2 9 C5
Kilberry Clo., 73 A1
Islw.
Kilburn Bldgs. NW6 57 E1
Kilburn High Rd.
Kilburn Gate NW6 6 A1
Kilburn High Rd. 48 C7
NW6
Kilburn La. W9 57 B3
Kilburn La. W10 57 A3
Kilburn Pk. Rd. NW6 57 D3
Kilburn Pl. NW6 57 D1
Kilburn Priory NW6 57 E1
Kilburn Sq. NW6 57 D1
Kilburn High Rd.
Kilburn Vale NW6 57 E1
Belsize Rd.
Kildare Clo., Ruis. 45 C1
Kildare Gdns. W2 57 D6
Kildare Rd. E16 60 G5
Kildare Ter. W2 57 D6
Kildare Wk. E14 60 A6
Farrance St.
Kildoran Rd. SW2 76 E5
Kildowan Rd., Ilf. 53 A1
Kilgour Rd. SE23 77 H6
Kilkie St. SW6 75 F2
Killarney Rd. SW18 75 F6
Killearn Rd. SE6 87 D1
Killester Gdns., 99 H4
Wor.Pk
Killick St. N1 8 C1
Killick St. N1 58 F2
Killieser Ave. SW2 85 E1
Killip Clo. E16 60 F6
Killowen Ave., Nthlt. 45 J5
Killowen Rd. E9 50 G6
Killyon Rd. SW8 76 C2
Killyon Ter. SW8 76 C2
Killyon Rd.
Kilmaine Rd. SW6 66 B7
Kilmarnock Gdns., 53 C3
Dag.
Lindsey Rd.
Kilmarnock Rd., 28 D4
Wat.
Kilmarsh Rd. W6 65 J4
Kilmartin Ave. SW16 94 F3
Kilmartin Rd., Ilf. 53 A2
Kilmeston Way SE15 21 G7
Kilmington Rd. SW13 65 G6
Kilmorey Gdns., 73 E4
Twick.
Kilmorey Rd., 73 E4
Twick.
Kilmorie Rd. SE23 86 H1
Kiln Pl. NW5 49 A4
Kilner St. E14 60 A5
Kilnside, Esher 98 D7
Kilpatrick Way, 54 E5
Hayes
Kilravock St. W10 57 B3
Kilsby Wk., Dag. 53 B6
Rugby Rd.
Kilsha Rd., Walt. 90 B6

Kimbell Gdns. SW6 75 B1
Kimber Rd. SW18 75 D7
Kimberley Ave. E6 61 B2
Kimberley Ave. SE15 77 E2
Kimberley Ave., 43 G7
Ilf.
Kimberley Ave., 44 J6
Rom.
Kimberley Dr., Sid. 89 D2
Kimberley Gdns. N4 40 H5
Kimberley Gdns., 25 C3
Enf.
Kimberley Rd. E4 34 E1
Kimberley Rd. E11 51 D2
Kimberley Rd. E16 60 F4
Kimberley Rd. E17 41 J1
Kimberley Rd. N17 41 D2
Kimberley Rd. N18 33 E6
Kimberley Rd. NW6 57 B1
Kimberley Rd. SW9 76 E2
Kimberley Rd., 95 G2
Beck.
Kimberley Rd., 94 H6
Croy.
Kimberley Way E4 34 E1
Kimble Rd. SW19 84 G6
Kimbolton Clo. SE12 78 F6
Kimbolton Grn., 22 C4
Borwd.
Kimbolton Row SW3 18 G2
Kimmeridge Gdns. 88 B4
SE9
Kimmeridge Rd. SE9 88 B4
Kimpton Ind. Est., 100 C2
Sutt.
Kimpton Rd. SE5 77 A1
Kimpton Rd., Sutt. 100 C3
Kinburn St. SE16 68 G2
Kincaid Rd. SE15 68 F2
Kincardine Gdns. W9 57 C4
Harrow Rd.
Kinch Gro., Har. 37 J7
Kinder Clo. SE28 62 D7
Kinder St. E1 59 E6
Cannon St. Rd.
Kinfauns Rd. SW2 85 G2
Kinfauns Rd., Ilf. 53 A1
King Alfred Ave. 87 A4
SE6
King & Queen St. 21 A3
SE17
King & Queen St. 67 J5
SE17
King Arthur Clo. 68 F7
SE15
King Charles Cres., 91 J7
Surb.
King Charles Rd., 91 J5
Surb.
King Charles St. 16 A3
SW1
King Charles St. 67 D2
SW1
King Charles Wk. 84 B1
SW19
Princes Way
King David La. E1 59 F7
King Edward Dr., 98 H3
Chess.
Kelvin Gro.
King Edward Ms. 74 G1
SW13
King Edward Rd. E10 51 C1
King Edward Rd. E17 41 H3
King Edward Rd., 23 D4
Barn.
King Edward St. EC1 12 J3
King Edward St. EC1 58 J6
King Edward Wk. 16 F5
SE1
King Edward Wk. 67 A2
SE1
King Edwards Gdns. 65 A1
W3
King Edwards Gro., 82 E6
Tedd.
King Edwards Rd. E9 59 E1
King Edwards Rd. N9 25 E7
King Edwards Rd., 53 D7
Bark.
King Edward's Rd., 25 G4
Enf.
King Gdns., Croy. 101 H5
King George Ave. 61 A6
E16
King George Ave., 43 G5
Ilf.
King George Clo., 44 J3
Rom.
King George VI 93 J4
Ave., Mitch.
King George Sq., 73 J6
Rich.

King George St. 69 C7
SE10
King Georges Dr., 54 F5
Sthl.
King Harolds Way, 71 D7
Bexh.
King Henry Ms., 104 J5
Orp.
Osgood Ave.
King Henry St. N16 50 B5
King Henry's Rd. 48 H7
NW3
King Henrys Rd., 92 B3
Kings.T.
King Henry's Wk. N1 50 B6
King James St. SE1 16 H4
King James St. SE1 67 H2
King John Ct. EC2 9 E5
King John St. E1 59 G5
King John's Wk. SE9 88 A1
King Sq. EC1 8 J4
King Stairs Clo. 68 E2
SE16
Elephant La.
King St. E13 60 G4
King St. EC2 13 A4
King St. EC2 58 J6
King St. N2 39 G3
King St. SW1 15 G2
King St. SW1 67 C1
King St. W3 65 B1
King St. W6 65 G4
King St. WC2 12 A5
King St. WC2 58 E7
King St., Rich. 73 G5
King St., Sthl. 63 E3
King St., Twick. 82 D1
King William IV 86 F6
Gdns. SE20
St. Johns Rd.
King William La. 69 E5
SE10
Orlop St.
King William St. EC4 13 C6
King William St. EC4 59 A7
King William Wk. 69 C6
SE10
Kingcup Clo., Croy. 102 G1
Primrose La.
Kingdon Rd. NW6 48 D6
Kingfield Rd. W5 55 G4
Kingfield St. E14 69 C4
Kingfisher Clo. 62 C7
SE28
Kingfisher Ct. SW19 84 B2
Queensmere Rd.
Kingfisher Dr., 82 E4
Rich.
Kingfisher St. E6 61 B5
Kingfisher Way 47 D6
NW10
Kingham Clo. SW18 75 F7
Kingham Clo. W11 66 B2
Kinghorn St. EC1 12 J2
Kinglake Est. SE17 21 E3
Kinglake St. SE17 21 D4
Kinglake St. SE17 68 B5
Kingly Ct. W1 11 G5
Kingly St. W1 11 F5
Kingly St. W1 58 C7
Kings Arbour, Sthl. 63 E5
Ringway
Kings Arms St. E1 13 H2
Kings Arms Yd. EC2 13 B3
Kings Ave. N10 40 A3
Kings Ave. N21 32 H1
King's Ave. SW4 76 E5
King's Ave. SW12 85 D1
Kings Ave. W5 55 G6
Kings Ave., Brom. 87 F6
Kings Ave., Buck.H. 35 A2
Kings Ave., Cars. 100 H7
Kings Ave., Grnf. 54 H6
Kings Ave., Houns. 72 H1
Kings Ave., N.Mal. 92 E4
Kings Ave., Rom. 44 F6
Kings Ave., 34 H6
Wdf.Grn.
Kings Bench St. SE1 16 H3
Kings Bench Wk. EC4 12 F4
Kings Chase, E.Mol. 90 J3
Kings Clo. E10 42 B7
Kings Clo. NW4 39 A4
Kings College Rd. 48 H7
NW3
Kings Ct. E13 60 H1
Kings Ct. W6 65 G4
King St.
Kings Ct., Wem. 47 B2
Kings Cres. N4 49 J3
Kings Cres. Est. N4 49 J2
King's Cross Rd. 8 C3
WC1

King's Cross Rd. 58 F3
WC1
Kings Dr., Edg. 29 J4
Kings Dr., Surb. 92 A7
Kings Dr., Tedd. 82 A5
Kings Dr., T.Ditt. 91 E6
Kings Dr., Wem. 47 B2
Kings Fm. Ave., 74 A4
Rich.
Kings Gdns. NW6 48 D7
West End La.
Kings Gdns., Ilf. 52 G1
King's Garth Ms. 86 F2
SE23
London Rd.
Kings Grn., Loug. 27 B3
Kings Gro. SE15 77 E1
Kings Hall Rd., 86 H7
Beck.
Kings Head Hill E4 26 B7
Kings Head Yd. SE1 17 B2
Kings Highway SE18 70 H6
Kings Hill, Loug. 27 B2
Kings Keep, 91 H4
Kings.T.
Beaufort Rd.
Kings La., Sutt. 100 G6
Kings Mead Pk., 98 B7
Esher
Kings Ms. SW4 76 E5
King's Ms. WC1 8 D6
King's Ms. WC1 58 F4
Kings Ms., Chig. 35 F2
King's Orchard SE9 79 B6
Kings Paddock, 90 J1
Hmptn.
Kings Pas. E11 42 E7
Kings Pas. 91 G2
Kings.T.
Kings Pl. SE1 16 J4
Kings Pl. W4 65 C4
Chiswick High Rd.
Kings Pl., Buck.H. 35 A2
King's Reach Twr. 16 F1
SE1
Kings Ride Gate, 74 A4
Rich.
Kings Rd. E4 34 D1
Kings Rd. E6 60 J1
Kings Rd. E11 42 E7
King's Rd. N17 41 C1
Kings Rd. N18 33 D5
Kings Rd. N22 40 F1
Kings Rd. NW10 41 H7
Kings Rd. SE25 95 D3
King's Rd. SW1 19 C1
King's Rd. SW1 67 A4
King's Rd. SW3 18 F5
King's Rd. SW3 66 G6
King's Rd. SW6 66 E7
King's Rd. SW10 66 F7
King's Rd. SW14 74 D3
King's Rd. SW19 84 D6
Kings Rd. W5 55 G5
Kings Rd., Bark. 52 F7
North St.
Kings Rd., Barn. 22 J3
Kings Rd., Felt. 81 C1
Kings Rd., Har. 45 F2
Kings Rd., Kings.T. 82 H7
Kings Rd., Mitch. 94 A3
Kings Rd., Orp. 104 J4
Kings Rd., Rich. 73 J6
Kings Rd., Surb. 98 F1
Kings Rd., Tedd. 82 A5
Kings Rd., Twick. 73 E6
King's Scholars' Pas. 15 F6
SW1
King's Ter. NW1 58 C1
Plender St.
Kings Wk., Kings.T. 91 G1
Kings Way, Har. 37 B4
Kingsand Rd. SE12 87 G2
Kingsash Dr., Hayes 54 E4
Kingsbridge Ave. W3 64 J2
Kingsbridge Cres., 54 F5
Sthl.
Kingsbridge Rd. W10 56 H9
Kingsbridge Rd., 61 G2
Bark.
Kingsbridge Rd., 93 A7
Mord.
Kingsbridge Rd., 63 F4
Sthl.
Kingsbridge Rd., 90 B7
Walt.
Kingsbury Circ. NW9 38 A5
Kingsbury Rd. N1 50 B6
Kingsbury Rd. NW9 38 A5
Kingsbury Ter. N1 50 B6
Kingsbury Trd. Est. 38 D6
NW9

Kingsclere Clo. 74 G7
SW15
Kingscliffe Gdns. 84 C1
SW19
Kingscote Rd. W4 65 D3
Kingscote Rd., 95 E7
Croy.
Kingscote Rd., 92 D3
N.Mal.
Kingscote St. EC4 12 G5
Kingscourt Rd. SW16 85 D3
Kingscroft Rd. NW2 48 C6
Kingsdale Gdns. W11 66 A1
Kingsdale Rd. SE18 70 J6
Kingsdale Rd. SE20 86 G7
Kingsdown Ave. W3 56 E7
Kingsdown Ave. W13 64 E2
Kingsdown Clo. W10 57 A6
Kingsdown Rd. E11 51 E3
Kingsdown Rd. N19 49 E3
Kingsdown Rd., 100 B5
Sutt.
Kingsdown Way, 96 G7
Brom.
Kingsdowne Rd., 91 H7
Surb.
Kingsfield Ave., Har. 36 H4
Kingsfield Ho. SE9 88 A3
Kingsfield Rd., 37 A7
Har.
Kingsford Ave., 101 E7
Wall.
Kingsford St. NW5 48 J5
Kingsgate, Wem. 47 C3
Kingsgate Ave. N3 39 D3
Kingsgate Clo., 80 E1
Bexh.
Kingsgate Pl. NW6 48 D7
Kingsgate Rd. NW6 48 D7
Kingsgate Rd., 91 H1
Kings.T.
Kingsground SE9 79 B7
Kingshill Ave., Har. 37 E4
Kingshill Ave., 54 A3
Nthlt.
Kingshill Ave., 92 G7
Wor.Pk.
Kingshill Dr., Har. 37 E2
Kingshold Rd. E9 50 F7
Kingsholm Gdns. 79 A4
SE9
Kingshurst Rd. SE12 78 G7
Kingsland NW8 57 H1
Broxwood Way
Kingsland Grn. E8 50 B6
Kingsland High St. 50 C6
E8
Kingsland Pas. E8 50 B6
Kingsland Grn.
Kingsland Rd. E2 9 E3
Kingsland Rd. E2 59 B3
Kingsland Rd. E8 59 B1
Kingsland Rd. E13 60 J3
Kingslaven Clo. 74 H5
SW15
Howards La.
Kingsleigh Pl., 93 J3
Mitch.
Whitford Gdns.
Kingsleigh Wk., 96 F4
Brom.
Stamford Dr.
Kingsley Ave. W13 55 D6
Kingsley Ave., 72 J2
Houns.
Kingsley Ave., 54 G7
Sthl.
Kingsley Ave., 100 G4
Sutt.
Kingsley Clo. N2 39 F5
Kingsley Clo., Dag. 53 H4
Kingsley Ct., Edg. 30 B2
Kingsley Dr., 99 F2
Wor.Pk.
Badgers Copse
Kingsley Gdns. E4 34 A5
Kingsley Ms. W8 14 B6
Kingsley Pl. N6 40 A7
Kingsley Rd. E7 51 G7
Kingsley Rd. E17 42 C2
Kingsley Rd. N13 32 G4
Kingsley Rd. NW6 57 C1
Kingsley Rd. SW19 84 E5
Kingsley Rd., Croy. 101 G1
Kingsley Rd., Har. 45 J4
Kingsley Rd., 72 H1
Houns.
Kingsley Rd., Ilf. 43 F1
Kingsley Rd., Loug. 27 G3
Kingsley Rd., Orp. 104 J6
Kingsley Rd., Pnr. 36 F4
Kingsley St. SW11 75 J3
Kingsley Way N2 39 F5

Kingsley Wd. Dr. 88 C3
SE9
Kingslyn Cres. SE19 95 B1
Kingsman Par. SE18 70 C3
Woolwich Ch. St.
Kingsman St. SE18 70 C3
Kingsmead Barn, 23 D4
Kingsmead, Rich. 73 J0
Kingsmead Ave. N9 33 E1
Kingsmead Ave., 38 D7
NW9
Kingsmead Ave., 94 C3
Mitch.
Kingsmead Ave., 90 C2
Sun.
Kingsmead Ave., 99 A2
Surb.
Kingsmead Ave., 99 H2
Wor.Pk.
Kingsmead Clo., 99 D7
Epsom
Kingsmead Clo., 89 A2
Sid.
Kingsmead Clo., 82 E6
Tedd.
Kingsmead Dr., 45 F7
Nthlt.
Kingsmead Rd. SW2 85 G2
Kingsmead Way E9 50 H4
Kingsmere Clo. 75 B3
SW15
Weimar St.
Kingsmere Pk. NW9 47 B1
Kingsmere Rd. SW19 84 A2
Kingsmill Gdns., 53 F5
Dag.
Kingsmill Rd., Dag. 53 F5
Kingsmill Ter. NW8 6 F1
Kingsmill Ter. NW8 57 G2
Kingsnympton Pk., 83 B7
Kings.T.
Kingspark Ct. E18 42 G3
Kingsridge SW19 84 B2
Kingsthorpe Rd. 86 G4
SE26
Kingston Ave., Sutt. 100 B3
Kingston Bri., 91 G2
Kings.T.
Kingston Bypass 83 E4
SW15
Kingston Bypass 83 E6
SW20
Kingston Bypass, 98 B2
Esher
Kingston Bypass, 92 G4
N.Mal.
Kingston Bypass, 98 E3
Surb.
Kingston Clo., Nthlt. 45 F7
Kingston Clo., Rom. 44 E3
Kingston Clo., Tedd. 82 E6
Kingston Ct. N4 40 J6
Wiltshire Gdns.
Kingston Cres., 95 J1
Beck.
Kingston Gdns., 101 E3
Croy.
Wandle Rd.
Kingston Hall Rd., 91 G3
Kings.T.
Kingston Hill, 92 A1
Kings.T.
Kingston Hill Ave., 44 E3
Rom.
Kingston La., Tedd. 82 D5
Kingston Pk. Est., 83 B6
Kings.T.
Kingston Pl., Har. 29 C7
Richmond Gdns.
Kingston Rd. N9 33 D2
Kingston Rd. SW15 83 D4
Kingston Rd. SW19 93 B2
Kingston Rd. SW20 92 J2
Kingston Rd., Barn. 23 G5
Kingston Rd., Epsom 99 E4
Kingston Rd., Ilf. 52 E4
Kingston Rd., 92 B3
Kings.T.
Kingston Rd., 92 D4
N.Mal.
Kingston Rd., Sthl. 63 F2
Kingston Rd., Surb. 99 B2
Kingston Rd., Tedd. 82 E5
Kingston Rd., 99 C3
Wor.Pk.
Kingston Sq. SE19 86 A5
Kingston Vale SW15 83 D4
Kingstown St. NW1 58 A1
Kingswater Pl. SW11 66 H7
Battersea Ch. Rd.
Kingsway N12 31 F6
Kingsway SW14 74 B3
Kingsway WC2 12 C3

Kingsway WC2 58 F6
Kingsway, Croy. 101 F5
Kingsway, Enf. 25 C5
Kingsway, N.Mal. 92 J4
Kingsway, Wem. 46 H4
Kingsway, W.Wick. 103 E3
Kingsway, Wdf.Grn. 34 J5
Kingsway Business 90 F1
Pk., Hmptn.
Kingsway Cres., 36 J4
Har.
Kingsway Ind. Est. 33 G6
Kingsway Rd., Sutt. 100 B6
Kingswear Rd. NW5 49 B3
Kingswear Rd., 45 A2
Ruis.
Kingswood Ave. 57 B1
NW6
Kingswood Ave., 71 F4
Belv.
Kingswood Ave., 96 E3
Brom.
Kingswood Ave., 81 H6
Hmptn.
Kingswood Ave., 72 F1
Houns.
Kingswood Ave., 94 G5
Th.Hth.
Kingswood Clo. N20 23 F7
Kingswood Clo. SW8 67 E7
Kenchester Clo.
Kingswood Clo., 25 B5
Enf.
Kingswood Clo., 92 F6
N.Mal.
Motspur Pk.
Kingswood Clo., 97 G7
Orp.
Kingswood Clo., 91 H7
Surb.
Kingswood Clo., 98 A7
Wey.
Kingswood Dr. SE19 86 B4
Kingswood Dr., 100 J1
Cars.
Kingswood Est. SE21 86 B4
Bowen Dr.
Kingswood Pk. N3 39 C2
Kingswood Pl. SE13 78 E4
Kingswood Rd. SE20 86 F6
Kingswood Rd. SW2 76 E6
Kingswood Rd., 84 C7
SW19
Kingswood Rd. W4 65 C3
Kingswood Rd., 96 D4
Brom.
Kingswood Rd., Ilf. 53 A1
Kingswood Way, 101 E5
Wall.
Kingsworth Clo., 95 H5
Beck.
Shirley Cres.
Kingsworthy Clo., 91 J3
Kings.T.
Kingthorpe Rd. 47 D7
NW10
Kingthorpe Ter. 47 D6
NW10
Kingwood Rd. SW6 66 B7
Kinlet Rd. SE18 79 F1
Kinloch Dr. NW9 38 D7
Kinloch St. N7 49 F3
Hornsey Rd.
Kinloss Gdns. N3 39 C3
Kinloss Rd., Cars. 93 F7
Kinnaird Ave. W4 65 C7
Kinnaird Ave., 87 F6
Brom.
Kinnaird Clo., 87 F6
Brom.
Kinnaird Way, 35 C6
Wdf.Grn.
Kinnear Rd. W12 65 F2
Kinnerton Pl. N. 15 A4
SW1
Kinnerton Pl. S. 15 A4
SW1
Kinnerton St. SW1 15 B4
Kinnerton St. SW1 67 A2
Kinnerton Yd. SW1 15 A4
Kinnoul Rd. W6 66 B6
Kinross Ave., 99 G2
Wor.Pk.
Kinross Clo., Edg. 30 B2
Tayside Dr.
Kinross Clo., Har. 37 H5
Kinsale Rd. SE15 77 D3
Kintore Way SE1 21 F1
Kintyre Clo. SW16 94 F1
Kinveachy Gdns. SE7 70 B5
Kinver Rd. SE26 86 F4
Kipling Dr. SW19 84 G6

Kipling Est. SE1 17 C4
Kipling Est. SE1 68 A2
Kipling Pl., Stan. 29 C6
Uxbridge Rd.
Kipling Rd., Bexh. 80 E1
Kipling St. SE1 17 C4
Kipling St. SE1 68 A2
Kipling Ter. N9 33 A3
Kippington Dr. SE9 88 A1
Kirby Clo., Epsom 99 J3
Kirby Clo., Ilf. 35 H6
Kirby Clo., Loug. 27 B7
Kirby Est. SE16 68 E3
Kirby Gro. SE1 17 D3
Kirby Gro. SE1 68 B2
Kirby St. EC1 12 F1
Kirby Way, Walt. 90 C6
Kirchen Rd. W13 55 E7
Kirk La. SE18 70 F6
Kirk Ri., Sutt. 100 E3
Kirk Rd. E17 41 J6
Kirkcaldy Grn., Wat. 28 C3
Trevose Way
Kirkdale SE26 86 F4
Kirkdale Rd. E11 51 E1
Kirkham Rd. E6 61 B6
Kirkham St. SE18 70 H6
Kirkland Ave., Ilf. 43 D2
Kirkland Clo., Sid. 79 H6
Kirkland Wk. E8 50 C6
Laurel St.
Kirkleas Rd., Surb. 98 H1
Kirklees Rd., Dag. 53 C5
Kirklees Rd., 94 G5
Th.Hth.
Kirkley Rd. SW19 93 D1
Kirkman Pl. W1 11 H2
Kirkmichael Rd. E14 60 C6
Dee St.
Kirks Pl. E14 59 J5
Rhodeswell Rd.
Kirkside Rd. SE3 69 G6
Kirkstall Ave. N17 41 A4
Kirkstall Gdns. SW2 85 D1
Kirkstall Rd. SW2 85 D1
Kirkstead Ct. E5 50 H3
Mandeville St.
Kirksted Rd., Mord. 100 E1
Kirkstone Way, 87 E6
Brom.
Kirkton Rd. N15 41 B4
Kirkwall Pl. E2 59 F3
Kirkwood Rd. SE15 77 E2
Kirn Rd. W13 55 E7
Kirchen Rd.
Kirtley Rd. SE26 86 H4
Kirtling St. SW8 19 F7
Kirtling St. SW8 67 C7
Kirton Clo. W4 65 D4
Dolman Rd.
Kirton Gdns. E2 9 G4
Kirton Rd. E13 60 J2
Kirton Wk., Edg. 30 C7
Kirwyn Way SE5 20 H7
Kirwyn Way SE5 67 H7
Kitcat Ter. E3 60 A3
Kitchener Rd. E7 51 H6
Kitchener Rd. E17 42 B1
Kitchener Rd. N2 39 H3
Kitchener Rd. N17 41 A3
Kitchener Rd., Dag. 53 H6
Kitchener Rd., 95 A3
Th.Hth.
Kitley Gdns. SE19 95 C1
Kitson Rd. SE5 21 A7
Kitson Rd. SE5 68 A7
Kitson Rd. SW13 74 G1
Kittiwake Rd., 54 D3
Nthlt.
Kitto Rd. SE14 77 G2
Kiver Rd. N19 49 D2
Klea Ave. SW4 76 C6
Knapdale Clo. SE23 86 E2
Knapmill Rd. SE6 87 A2
Knapmill Way SE6 87 B2
Knapp Clo. NW10 47 E6
Knapp Rd. E3 60 A4
Knapton Ms. SW17 85 A6
Seely Rd.
Knaresborough Pl. 18 A1
SW5
Knaresborough Pl. 66 E4
SW5
Knatchbull Rd. NW10 56 D1
Knatchbull Rd. SE5 76 H2
Knebworth Ave. E17 42 A1
Knebworth Path, 22 D4
Borwd.
Knebworth Rd. N16 50 B4
Nevill Rd.
Knee Hill SE2 71 C4
Knee Hill Cres. SE2 71 C4
Kneller Gdns., Islw. 73 A6

Kneller Rd. SE4 77 H4
Kneller Rd., N.Mal. 92 E7
Kneller Rd., Twick. 72 J6
Knighten St. E1 17 J2
Knightland Rd. E5 50 E2
Knighton Clo., 101 H7
S.Croy.
Knighton Clo., 34 H4
Wdf.Grn.
Knighton Dr., 34 H4
Wdf.Grn.
Knighton La., 34 H2
Buck.H.
Knighton Pk. Rd. 86 G5
SE26
Knighton Rd. E7 51 G3
Knighton Rd., Rom. 44 J6
Knightrider Ct. EC4 58 J7
Knightrider St.
Knightrider St. EC4 12 H5
Knights Arc. SW1 14 J4
Knights Ave. W5 64 H2
Knights Clo. E9 50 F5
Churchill Wk.
Knights Ct., 91 H3
Kings.T.
Knights Ct., Rom. 44 E6
Knights Hill SE27 85 H5
Knights Hill Sq. SE27 85 H4
Knights Hill
Knights La. N9 33 D3
Knights Pk., 91 H3
Kings.T.
Knights Rd. E16 69 G2
Knights Rd., Stan. 29 F4
Knights Wk. SE11 20 G2
Knights Way, Ilf. 35 F6
Knightsbridge SW1 15 A3
Knightsbridge SW1 66 J2
Knightsbridge SW7 14 H4
Knightsbridge SW7 66 H2
Knightsbridge Grn. 14 J4
SW1
Knightsbridge Grn. 66 J2
SW1
Knightswood Clo., 30 C2
Edg.
Knightwood Cres., 92 E6
N.Mal.
Knivet Rd. SW6 66 D6
Knobs Hill Rd. E15 60 B1
Knockholt Rd. SE9 79 A5
Knole, The SE9 88 D4
Knole Clo., Croy. 95 F6
Stockbury Rd.
Knole Gate, Sid. 88 H3
Woodside Cres.
Knoll, The W13 55 F5
Knoll, The, Beck. 96 B1
Knoll, The, Brom. 103 G1
Knoll Ct. SE19 86 C5
Knoll Dr. N14 24 A7
Knoll Ri., Orp. 104 J1
Knoll Rd. SW18 75 F5
Knoll Rd., Bex. 80 G7
Knoll Rd., Sid. 89 B5
Knollmead, Surb. 99 C1
Knolls Clo., 99 H3
Wor.Pk.
Knollys Clo. SW16 85 G3
Knollys Rd. SW16 85 F3
Knottisford St. E2 59 F3
Knotts Grn. Rd. E10 42 B6
Knowle Ave., Bexh. 71 E7
Knowle Clo. SW9 76 G3
Knowle Rd., Brom. 104 B2
Knowle Rd., Twick. 82 B1
Knowles Hill Cres. 78 D5
SE13
Knowles Wk. SW4 76 C3
Knowlton Grn., 96 F5
Brom.
Knowsley Ave., Sthl. 63 H1
Knowsley Rd. SW11 75 J2
Knox Rd. E7 51 F6
Knox St. W1 10 J1
Knox St. W1 57 J5
Knoyle St. SE14 68 H6
Chubworthy St.
Kohat Rd. SW19 84 E5
Kossuth St. SE10 69 E5
Kotree Way SE1 21 J2
Kramer Ms. SW5 66 D5
Kempsford Gdns.
Kreisel Wk., Rich. 64 J6
Kuala Gdns. SW16 94 F1
Kuhn Way E7 51 G5
Brooking Rd.
Kydbrook Clo., Orp. 97 F7
Kylemore Clo. E6 61 A2
Parr Rd.
Kylemore Rd. NW6 48 D7
Kymberley Rd., Har. 37 B6

Kynance Gdns., 37 F1
Stan.
Kynance Ms. SW7 14 B6
Kynance Pl. SW7 14 C6
Kynance Pl. SW7 66 F3
Kynaston Ave. N16 50 C3
Dynevor Rd.
Kynaston Ave., 94 J5
Th.Hth.
Kynaston Clo., Har. 29 A7
Kynaston Cres., 94 J5
Th.Hth.
Kynaston Rd. N16 50 B3
Kynaston Rd., Brom. 87 G5
Kynaston Rd., Enf. 25 A1
Kynaston Rd., 94 J5
Th.Hth.
Kynaston Wd., Har. 29 A7
Kynnersley Clo., 100 J3
Cars.
William St.
Kynock Rd. N18 33 F4
Kyrle Rd. SW11 75 J6
Kyverdale Rd. N16 41 C7

L

La Tourne Gdns., 104 F3
Orp.
Laburnham Ct., Stan. 29 F4
Laburnum Ave. N9 33 B2
Laburnum Ave. N17 33 A7
Laburnum Ave., 100 H3
Sutt.
Laburnum Clo. E4 33 J6
Laburnum Clo. N11 32 A6
Laburnum Clo. SE15 68 F7
Clifton Way
Laburnum Ct. E2 59 C1
Laburnum St.
Laburnum Cres., 90 B1
Sun.
Batavia Rd.
Laburnum Gdns. N21 32 J2
Laburnum Gro.
Laburnum Gdns., 102 G1
Croy.
Primrose La.
Laburnum Gro. N21 32 J2
Laburnum Gro. NW9 38 C7
Laburnum Gro., 72 F4
Houns.
Laburnum Gro., 92 D2
N.Mal.
Laburnum Gro., 54 F4
Sthl.
Laburnum Ho., Dag. 53 G2
Laburnum Rd. SW19 84 F7
Laburnum Rd., 94 A2
Mitch.
Laburnum St. E2 59 C1
Laburnum Way, 97 D7
Brom.
Lacebark Clo., Sid. 79 J7
Lacey Clo. N9 33 D2
Lacey Dr., Edg. 29 H4
Lacey Dr., Hmptn. 90 F1
Lacey Wk. E3 60 A2
Lackington St. EC2 13 C1
Lackington St. EC2 59 A5
Lacock Clo. SW19 84 F6
Lacon Rd. SE22 77 D4
Lacy Rd. SW15 75 A4
Ladas Rd. SE27 85 J4
Ladbroke Cres. W11 57 B6
Ladbroke Gro.
Ladbroke Gdns. W11 57 C7
Ladbroke Gro. W10 57 A4
Ladbroke Gro. W11 57 B6
Ladbroke Ms. W11 66 B1
Ladbroke Rd.
Ladbroke Rd. W11 66 C1
Ladbroke Rd., Enf. 25 C6
Ladbroke Sq. W11 57 C7
Ladbroke Ter. W11 57 C7
Ladbroke Wk. W11 66 C1
Ladbrook Clo., Pnr. 36 F5
Ladbrook Rd. SE25 95 A3
Ladbrooke Cres., 89 D3
Sid.
Ladderstile Ride, 92 C5
Kings.T.
Ladderswood Way 32 C5
N11
Lady Booth Rd., 91 H2
Kings.T.
Lady Hay, Wor.Pk. 99 F2
Lady Margaret Rd. 49 C4
N19
Lady Margaret Rd. 49 C5
NW5
Lady Margaret Rd., 54 F5
Sthl.

Lady Somerset Rd. 49 B4
NW5
Ladybower Ct. E5 50 H4
Gilpin Rd.
Ladycroft Gdns., 104 F5
Orp.
Ladycroft Rd. SE13 78 B3
Ladycroft Wk., 37 G1
Stan.
Ladycroft Way, Orp. 104 F5
Ladyfield Clo., 27 E4
Loug.
Ladyfields, Loug. 27 E4
Ladysmith Ave. E6 61 B2
Ladysmith Ave., Ilf. 43 G7
Ladysmith Rd. E16 60 F3
Ladysmith Rd. N17 41 D2
Ladysmith Rd. N18 33 E5
Ladysmith Rd. SE9 79 D6
Ladysmith Rd., Enf. 25 B3
Ladysmith Rd., Har. 37 B2
Ladywell Rd. SE13 78 B5
Ladywell St. E15 60 F1
Plaistow Gro.
Ladywood Ave., Orp. 97 H5
Ladywood Rd., Surb. 99 A2
Lafone Ave., Felt. 81 C1
Alfred Rd.
Lafone St. SE1 17 F3
Lafone St. SE1 68 C2
Lagado Ms. SE16 68 G1
Lagonda Ave., Ilf. 35 J6
Laing Clo., Ilf. 35 G6
Laing Dean, Nthlt. 54 C1
Laings Ave., Mitch. 93 J2
Lainlock Pl., Houns. 72 H1
Spring Gro. Rd.
Lainson St. SW18 75 D7
Laird Ho. SE5 67 J7
Redcar St.
Lairdale Clo. SE21 85 J1
Lairs Clo. N7 49 E6
Manger Rd.
Laitwood Rd. SW12 85 B1
Lake, The (Bushey), 28 J1
Wat.
Lake Ave., Brom. 87 G6
Lake Dr. (Bushey), 28 J2
Wat.
Lake Gdns., Dag. 53 G5
Lake Gdns., Rich. 82 E2
Lake Gdns., Wall. 101 B3
Lake Ho. Rd. E11 51 G3
Lake Rd. SW19 84 C5
Lake Rd., Croy. 102 J2
Lake Rd., Rom. 44 D4
Lake Vw., Edg. 29 J5
Lakedale Rd. SE18 70 H5
Lakefield Rd. N22 40 H2
Lakehall Gdns. 94 H5
Th.Hth.
Lakehall Rd., 94 H5
Th.Hth.
Lakehurst Rd., 99 E5
Epsom
Lakeland Clo., Har. 29 A6
Lakenheath N14 24 C5
Laker Pl. SW15 75 B6
Lakes Clo., Kes. 103 J5
Lakeside N3 39 E2
Lakeside W13 55 F6
Edgehill Rd.
Lakeside, Beck. 96 B3
Lakeside, Enf. 24 D4
Lakeside, Wall. 101 B3
Derek Ave.
Lakeside Ave., Ilf. 43 A4
Lakeside Clo. SE25 95 D2
Lakeside Clo., Sid. 80 C5
Lakeside Clo. N4 49 H2
Lakeside Cres., 23 J5
Barn.
Lakeside Dr., Brom. 104 B3
Lakeside Rd. N13 32 F4
Lakeside Rd. W14 66 A3
Lakeside Way, Wem. 47 A4
Lakeswood Rd., Orp. 97 E5
Lakeview Ct. SW19 84 B2
Victoria Dr.
Lakeview Rd. SE27 85 G5
Lakeview Rd., Well. 80 B4
Lakis Clo. NW3 48 F4
Flask Wk.
Laleham Ave. NW7 30 D3
Laleham Rd. SE6 78 C7
Lalor St. SW6 75 B2
Lamb La. E8 50 E7
Lamb St. E1 13 F1
Lamb St. E1 59 C5
Lamb Wk. SE1 20 D4
Lambarde Ave. SE9 88 D4
Lamberhurst Rd. 85 G4
SE27

Lamberhurst Rd., 53 E1
Dag.
Lambert Ave., Rich. 74 A3
Lambert Rd. E16 60 H6
Lambert Rd. N12 31 F5
Lambert Rd. N22 31 F5
Lambert Rd. SW2 76 E5
Lambert St. N1 49 G7
Lambert Way N12 31 F5
Woodhouse Rd.
Lamberts Pl., Croy. 102 A1
Lamberts Rd., Surb. 91 H5
Lambeth Bri. SE1 20 B1
Lambeth Bri. SE1 67 E4
Lambeth Bri. SW1 20 B1
Lambeth Bri. SW1 67 E4
Lambeth High St. 20 C1
SE1
Lambeth High St. 67 F4
SE1
Lambeth Hill EC4 12 J5
Lambeth Hill EC4 58 J7
Lambeth Palace Rd. 16 C6
SE1
Lambeth Palace Rd. 67 F3
SE1
Lambeth Rd. SE1 16 E6
Lambeth Rd. SE1 67 F3
Lambeth Rd., Croy. 94 G7
Lambeth Wk. SE11 20 D1
Lambeth Wk. SE11 67 F4
Lamble St. NW5 49 A5
Lambley Rd., Dag. 53 B6
Lambolle Pl. NW3 48 H6
Lambolle Rd. NW3 48 H6
Lambourn Clo. W7 64 C2
Lambourn Rd. SW4 76 B3
Lambourne Ave. 84 C4
SW19
Lambourne Gdns. E4 34 A2
Lambourne Gdns., 52 J7
Bark.
Lambourne Rd.
Lambourne Gdns., 25 C2
Enf.
Lambourne Gro. 92 B2
Kings.T.
Kenley Rd.
Lambourne Pl. SE3 78 H1
Shooter's Hill Rd.
Lambourne Rd. E11 42 D7
Lambourne Rd., 52 H7
Bark.
Lambourne Rd., 35 J4
Chig.
Lambourne Rd., Ilf. 52 H2
Lambrook Ter. SW6 75 B1
Lamb's Bldgs. EC1 9 B6
Lambs Conduit Pas. 12 C1
WC1
Lamb's Conduit St. 8 C6
WC1
Lamb's Conduit St. 58 F4
WC1
Lambs Meadow, 43 A2
Wdf.Grn.
Lambs Ms. N1 50 H1
Colebrooke Row
Lamb's Pas. EC1 13 B1
Lamb's Pas. EC1 59 A5
Lambs Ter. N9 33 A2
Lambs Wk., Enf. 24 J2
Lambscroft Ave. SE9 87 J3
Lambton Pl. W11 57 C6
Westbourne Gro.
Lambton Rd. N19 49 E1
Lambton Rd. SW20 92 J1
Lamerock Rd., Brom. 87 F4
Lamerton Rd., Ilf. 43 E2
Lamerton St. SE8 69 A6
Lamford Clo. N17 33 A7
Lamington St. W6 65 H4
Lamlash St. SE11 20 B1
Lammas Ave., Mitch. 94 A2
Lammas Grn. SE26 86 E3
Lammas Pk. Gdns. 65 F1
W5
Lammas Pk. Rd. W5 64 F1
Lammas Rd. E9 51 G1
Lammas Rd. E10 50 H2
Lea Bri. Rd.
Lammas Rd., Rich. 82 F4
Lammermoor Rd. 76 B7
SW12
Lamont Rd. SW10 18 D6
Lamont Rd. Pas. 18 E6
SW10
Lamorbey Clo., Sid. 88 J1
Lamorna Gro., Stan. 37 G1
Lampard Gro. N16 50 C1
Lampern Sq. E2 9 J3
Lampeter Sq. W6 66 B6
Humbolt Rd.

Lamplighter Clo. E1 59 F4
Cleveland Way
Lampmead Rd. SE12 78 F5
Lamport Clo. SE18 70 C4
Lampton Ave., 72 H1
Houns.
Lampton Ho. Clo. 84 A4
SW19
Lampton Pk. Rd 72 H2
Houns.
Lampton Rd., Houns. 72 H2
Lanacre Ave. NW9 38 D1
Lanark Clo. W5 55 F5
Lanark Clo. W5 6 D5
Lanark Pl. W9 57 F4
Lanark Rd. W9 6 B2
Lanark Rd. W9 57 E2
Lanark Sq. E14 69 B3
Lanbury Rd. SE15 77 G4
Lancashire Ct. W1 11 E5
Lancaster Ave. E18 42 H4
Lancaster Ave. SE27 85 H2
Lancaster Ave. SW19 84 A5
Lancaster Ave., 52 H7
Bark.
Lancaster Ave., 94 E5
Mitch.
Lancaster Clo. N1 50 B7
Hertford Rd.
Lancaster Clo. N17 33 D7
Park La.
Lancaster Clo. SE27 85 H2
Lancaster Clo., 96 F4
Brom.
Lancaster Clo., 82 G5
Kings.T.
Lancaster Cotts.,Rich. 73 H6
Lancaster Pk.
Lancaster Ct. SW6 66 C7
Lancaster Ct. W2 10 D6
Lancaster Ct., 90 A7
Walt.
Lancaster Dr. E14 69 C1
Prestons Rd.
Lancaster Dr. NW3 48 H6
Lancaster Gdns. 84 B5
SW19
Lancaster Gdns. W13 64 E2
Lancaster Gdns., 82 G5
Kings.T.
Lancaster Gate W2 10 D6
Lancaster Gate W2 57 F7
Lancaster Gro. NW3 48 G6
Lancaster Ms. W2 10 D5
Lancaster Ms. W2 57 F7
Lancaster Ms., Rich. 73 H6
Richmond Hill
Lancaster Pk., Rich. 73 H5
Lancaster Pl. SW19 84 A5
Lancaster Rd.
Lancaster Pl. WC2 12 C5
Lancaster Pl. WC2 58 F7
Lancaster Pl., 72 C2
Houns.
Lancaster Pl., Ilf. 52 F5
Staines Rd.
Lancaster Pl., 73 D6
Twick.
Lancaster Rd. E7 51 G7
Lancaster Rd. E11 51 E2
Lancaster Rd. E17 41 G2
Lancaster Rd. N4 40 F7
Lancaster Rd. N11 32 D6
Lancaster Rd. N18 33 C5
Lancaster Rd. NW10 47 G5
Lancaster Rd. SE25 95 C2
Lancaster Rd. SW19 84 A5
Lancaster Rd. W11 57 B6
Lancaster Rd., 23 G5
Barn.
Lancaster Rd., Enf. 25 A1
Lancaster Rd., Har. 36 G5
Lancaster Rd., Nthlt. 45 J6
Lancaster Rd., Sthl. 54 E7
Lancaster St. SE1 16 H4
Lancaster St. SE1 67 H2
Lancaster Ter. W2 10 E5
Lancaster Ter. W2 57 G7
Lancaster Wk. W2 14 D1
Lancaster Wk. W2 66 G1
Lance Rd., Har. 36 J7
Lancefield St. W10 57 C3
Lancell St. N16 50 B2
Stoke Newington
Ch. St.
Lancelot Ave., Wem. 46 G4
Lancelot Cres., Wem. 46 G4
Lancelot Gdns., 24 A7
Barn.
Lancelot Pl. SW7 14 J4
Lancelot Pl. SW7 66 J2
Lancelot Rd., Ilf. 35 H6
Lancelot Rd., Well. 80 A4

Lancelot Rd., Wem. 46 G4
Lancer Sq. W8 14 A3
Cleveley Clo.
Lanchester Rd. N6 39 J5
Lancing Gdns. N9 33 C1
Lancing Rd. W13 55 E7
Drayton Grn. Rd.
Lancing Rd., Croy. 94 F6
Lancing Rd., Ilf. 53 G6
Lancing St. NW1 7 H4
Lancresse Ct. N1 59 B1
Landcroft Rd. SE22 77 C5
Landells Rd. SE22 77 C6
Landford Rd. SW15 74 J3
Landgrove Rd. SW19 84 D5
Landmann Way SE14 68 G6
Landon Pl. SW1 14 J5
Landon Pl. SW1 66 J3
Landon Wk. E14 60 B7
Cottage St.
Landons Clo. E14 69 C1
Landor Rd. SW9 76 E3
Landor Wk. W12 65 G2
Landport Way SE15 21 G7
Landra Gdns. N21 24 H6
Landridge Rd. SW6 75 C2
Landrock Rd. N8 40 E6
Landscape Rd., 34 H7
Wdf.Grn.
Landseer Ave. E12 52 D5
Landseer Clo. SW19 93 F1
Brangwyn Cres.
Landseer Clo., Edg. 38 A2
Landseer Rd. N19 49 E3
Landseer Rd., Enf. 25 D5
Landseer Rd., 92 D7
N.Mal.
Landseer Rd., Sutt. 100 D6
Landstead Rd. SE18 70 G7
Lane, The NW8 6 C2
Lane, The SE3 78 G3
Lane App. NW7 31 B5
Lane Clo. NW2 47 H3
Lane End, Bexh. 80 H3
Lanercost Clo. SW2 85 G2
Lanercost Gdns. N14 24 E7
Lanercost Rd. SW2 85 G2
Lanesborough Pl. 15 C3
SW1
Laneside, Chis. 88 E5
Laneside, Edg. 30 C5
Laneside Ave., Dag. 44 F7
Laneway SW15 74 H5
Sunnymead Rd.
Lanfranc Rd. E3 59 H2
Lanfrey Pl. W14 66 C5
North End Rd.
Lang St. E1 59 F4
Langbourne Ave. N6 49 A2
Langbourne Way, 98 D6
Esher
Langbrook Rd. SE3 79 A3
Langcroft Clo., 100 J3
Cars.
Langdale Ave., 93 J3
Mitc.
Langdale Clo. SE17 20 J5
Langdale Clo. SE17 67 J6
Langdale Clo. SW14 74 B4
Clifford Ave.
Langdale Cres., 71 G7
Bexh.
Langdale Gdns., 55 E3
Grnf.
Langdale Rd. SE10 69 C7
Langdale Rd., 94 G4
Th.Hth.
Langdale St. E1 59 E6
Burslem St.
Langdon Ct. NW10 56 E1
Langdon Cres. E6 61 D2
Langdon Dr. NW9 47 C7
Langdon Pk. Rd. N6 40 C7
Langdon Pl. SW14 74 C3
Rosemary La.
Langdon Rd. E6 61 D1
Langdon Rd., Brom. 96 H3
Langdon Rd., Mord. 93 F5
Langdon Shaw, Sid. 88 J5
Langdon Wk., Mord. 93 F5
Langdon Rd.
Langdon Way SE1 21 J2
Langford Clo. E8 50 D5
Langford Clo. N15 41 B6
Langford Clo. NW8 6 D1
Langford Clo. NW8 6 D2
Langford Cres., 23 J4
Barn.
Langford Grn. SE5 77 B3
Langford Pl. NW8 6 D1
Langford Pl. NW8 57 F2
Langford Pl., Sid. 89 A3

Langford Rd. SW6 75 E2
Gilstead Rd.
Langford Rd., Barn. 23 H4
Langford Rd., 34 J6
Wdf.Grn.
Langfords, Buck.H. 35 A2
Langham Dr., Rom. 44 B6
Langham Gdns. N21 13 C6
Langham Gdns. W13 55 E7
Langham Gdns., Edg. 30 C7
Langham Gdns., 82 F4
Rich.
Langham Gdns., 46 F2
Wem.
Langham Ho. Clo., 82 G4
Rich.
Langham Pl. N15 40 H3
Langham Pl. W1 11 E2
Langham Pl. W1 58 B5
Langham Pl. W4 65 E6
Hogarth Roundabout
Langham Rd. N15 40 H3
Langham Rd. SW20 92 J1
Langham Rd., Edg. 30 C6
Langham Rd., Tedd. 82 D5
Langham St. W1 11 E2
Langham St. W1 58 B5
Langhedge Clo. N18 33 C6
Langhedge La.
Langhedge La. N18 33 C5
Langhedge La. Ind. 33 C6
Est. N18
Langholm Clo. SW12 76 D7
King's Ave.
Langholme (Bushey), 28 J1
Wat.
Langhorne Rd., Dag. 53 G7
Langland Cres., 37 G2
Stan.
Langland Dr., Pnr. 28 E7
Langland Gdns. NW3 48 E5
Langland Gdns., 102 J2
Croy.
Langler Rd. NW10 56 J2
Langley Ave., Ruis. 45 B2
Langley Ave., Surb. 98 G1
Langley Ave., 100 A1
Wor.Pk.
Langley Ct. SE9 79 D6
Langley Ct. WC2 12 A5
Langley Cres. E11 42 H7
Langley Cres., Dag. 53 C7
Langley Cres., Edg. 30 C3
Langley Dr. E11 42 H7
Langley Dr. W3 65 B2
Langley Gdns., 96 J4
Brom.
Langley Gdns., Dag. 53 D7
Langley Gdns., Orp. 97 E6
Langley Gro., N.Mal. 92 E2
Langley La. SW8 20 B5
Langley La. SW8 67 E6
Langley Meadow, 27 G2
Loug.
Langley Pk. NW7 30 E6
Langley Pk. Rd., 100 F5
Sutt.
Langley Rd. SW19 93 C1
Langley Rd., Beck. 95 H4
Langley Rd., Islw. 73 C2
Langley Rd., Surb. 91 H7
Langley Rd., Well. 71 C6
Langley St. WC2 12 A4
Langley St. WC2 58 E6
Langley Way, 103 D1
W.Wick.
Langmead St. SE27 85 H4
Beadman St.
Langmore Ct., Bexh. 80 D3
Regency Way
Langroyd Rd. SW17 84 J2
Langside Ave. SW15 74 G4
Langside Cres. N14 32 D3
Langston Rd., Loug. 27 F5
Langthorn Ct. EC2 13 C3
Langthorne Rd. E11 51 C3
Langthorne St. SW6 75 A1
Langton Ave. E6 61 D3
Langton Ave. N20 23 F7
Langton Clo. WC1 8 D5
Langton Ri. SE23 77 E7
Langton Rd. NW2 47 J3
Langton Rd. SW9 67 H7
Langton Rd., Har. 28 J7
Langton Rd., W.Mol. 90 J5
Langton St. SW10 18 D6
Langton St. SW10 66 F6
Langton Way SE3 78 F1
Langton Way, Croy. 102 B3
Langtry Rd. NW8 57 D1
Langtry Rd., Nthlt. 54 D2
Langtry Wk. NW8 48 F7
Alexandra Pl.

Langwood Chase, 82 F6
Tedd.
Langworth Dr., 54 A6
Hayes
Lanhill Rd. W9 57 D4
Lanier Rd. SE13 78 C6
Lankaster Gdns. N2 39 G1
Lankers Dr. Har. 36 F6
Lankton Clo., Beck. 96 C1
Lannoy Rd. SE9 88 F1
Lanrick Rd. E14 60 D6
Lanridge Rd. SE2 71 D3
Lansbury Ave. N18 33 A5
Lansbury Ave., Bark. 53 A7
Lansbury Ave., Felt. 72 B6
Lansbury Ave., Rom. 44 E5
Lansbury Clo. NW10 47 C5
Lansbury Est. E14 60 B6
Lansbury Gdns. E14 60 C6
Lansbury Rd., Enf. 25 G1
Lansbury Way N18 33 B5
Lansbury Ave.
Lansdell Rd., Mitch. 94 A2
Lansdown Rd. E7 51 J7
Lansdown Rd., Sid. 89 B3
Lansdowne Ave., 71 C7
Bexh.
Lansdowne Ave., 104 E1
Orp.
Lansdowne Clo. 84 A7
SW20
Lansdowne Clo., 82 C1
Twick.
Lion Rd.
Lansdowne Ct., 99 G2
Wor.Pk.
Lansdowne Cres. 57 C7
W11
Lansdowne Dr. E8 50 D6
Lansdowne Gdns. 76 E1
SW8
Lansdowne Gro. 47 E4
NW10
Lansdowne Hill SE27 85 H3
Lansdowne La. SE7 70 A5
Lansdowne Ms. SE7 70 A5
Lansdowne Ms. W11 66 C1
Lansdowne Rd.
Lansdowne Pl. SE1 17 C5
Lansdowne Pl. SE19 86 C7
Lansdowne Ri. W11 57 B7
Lansdowne Rd. E4 34 A2
Lansdowne Rd. E11 51 F2
Lansdowne Rd. E17 42 A6
Lansdowne Rd. E18 42 G3
Lansdowne Rd. N3 31 C7
Lansdowne Rd. N10 40 C2
Lansdowne Rd. N17 41 D1
Lansdowne Rd. 83 J7
SW20
Lansdowne Rd. W11 57 B7
Lansdowne Rd., 87 G7
Brom.
Lansdowne Rd., 101 J2
Croy.
Lansdowne Rd., 99 C7
Epsom
Lansdowne Rd., Har. 37 B7
Lansdowne Rd., 72 H3
Houns.
Lansdowne Rd., Ilf. 52 J1
Lansdowne Rd., 29 F6
Stan.
Lansdowne Row W1 15 E1
Lansdowne Ter. WC1 8 B6
Lansdowne Ter. WC1 58 E4
Lansdowne Wk. W11 66 C1
Lansdowne Way 76 D1
SW8
Lansdowne Wd. Clo. 85 H3
SE27
Lansfield Ave. N18 33 D4
Lant St. SE1 16 J3
Lant St. SE1 67 J2
Lantern Clo. SW15 74 G4
Lantern Clo., Wem. 46 G5
Lanterns Ct. E14 69 A2
Lanvanor Rd. SE15 77 F2
Lapford Clo. W9 57 C4
Lapse Wd. Wk. SE23 86 E2
Lapstone Gdns., 37 F6
Har.
Lapwing Ct., Surb. 99 A3
Chaffinch Clo.
Lara Clo. SE13 78 G3
Lara Clo., Chess. 98 H7
Larbert Rd. SW16 95 C7
Larch Ave. W3 65 E1
Larch Clo. N11 32 A4
Larch Clo. N19 49 C2
Bredgar Rd.
Larch Clo. SE8 68 J6
Clyde St.

Larch Clo. SW12 85 B1
Larch Cres., Epsom 99 B6
Larch Cres., Hayes 54 C4
Larch Dr. W4 65 A5
Gunnersbury Ave.
Larch Gro., Sid. 88 J1
Larch Ms. N19 49 C2
Bredgar Rd.
Larch Rd. NW2 47 J4
Larch Tree Way, 103 A3
Croy.
Larch Way, Brom. 97 D7
Larchdene, Orp. 104 D2
Larches, The N13 32 J3
Larches Ave. SW14 74 D4
Larchwood Rd. SE9 88 E2
Larcom St. SE17 21 A2
Larcom St. SE17 67 J4
Larcombe Clo., 102 C4
Croy.
Larden Rd. W3 65 E1
Largewood Av., 98 J2
Surb.
Larissa St. SE17 21 C3
Lark Row E2 59 F1
Larkbere Rd. SE26 86 H4
Larken Dr. 28 J1
(Bushey), Wat.
Larkfield Ave., Har. 37 E3
Larkfield Clo., 103 F2
Brom.
Larkfield Rd., Rich. 73 H4
Larkfield Rd., Sid. 88 J3
Larkhall Ct., Rom. 44 J2
Larkhall La. SW4 76 D2
Larkhall Ri. SW4 76 C3
Larkhill Ter. SE18 70 D7
Larks Gro., Bark. 52 H7
Larksfield Gro., 25 E1
Enf.
Larkshall Cres. E4 34 C4
Larkshall Rd. E4 34 C5
Larkspur Clo. E6 61 B5
Larkspur Clo. N17 33 A7
Fryatt Rd.
Larkspur Way, 99 B5
Epsom
Larkswood Ct. E4 34 D5
Larkswood Ri., Pnr. 36 C4
Larkswood Rd. E4 34 A4
Larkway Clo. NW9 38 D4
Larnach Rd. W6 66 A6
Larpent Ave. SW15 74 J5
Larwood Clo., Grnf. 46 A5
Lascelles Ave., 37 A7
Har.
Lascelles Clo. E11 51 D2
Lascotts Rd. N22 32 F6
Lassa Rd. SE9 79 B5
Lassell St. SE10 69 D5
Lasterton St. E8 50 E6
Wilton Way
Latchett Rd. E18 42 H1
Latchingdon Ct. E17 41 G4
Latchingdon Gdns., 35 B6
Wdf.Grn.
Latchmere Clo., Rich. 82 H5
Latchmere La., 32 J8
Kings.T.
Latchmere Pas. SW11 75 H2
Cabul Rd.
Latchmere Rd. SW11 75 J2
Latchmere Rd., 82 H7
Kings.T.
Latchmere St. SW11 75 J2
Lateward Rd., 64 G6
Brent.
Latham Clo. E6 61 B6
Oliver Gdns.
Latham Clo., Twick. 73 D7
Latham Ho. E1 59 G6
Latham Rd., Bexh. 80 G5
Latham Rd., Twick. 73 C7
Lathams Way, Croy. 101 F1
Lathkill Clo., Enf. 25 C7
Lathom Rd. E6 52 B7
Latimer SE17 21 D4
Latimer Ave. E6 61 C1
Latimer Clo., Pnr. 36 C1
Latimer Clo., 99 H4
Wor.Pk.
Latimer Gdns., Pnr. 36 C1
Latimer Pl. W10 56 J6
Latimer Rd. E7 51 H4
Latimer Rd. N15 41 B6
Latimer Rd. SW19 84 E6
Latimer Rd. W10 56 J5
Latimer Rd., Barn. 23 E3
Latimer Rd., Croy. 101 H3
Abbey Rd.
Latimer Rd., Tedd. 82 C5
Latimer St. E1 59 G5
Stepney Way

Latona Rd. SE15 21 H6
Latona Rd. SE15 68 D6
Latton Clo., Walt. 90 E7
Latymer Ct. W6 66 A4
Latymer Rd. N9 33 C2
Latymer Way N9 33 A2
Laud St. SE11 20 C3
Laud St., Croy. 101 J3
Lauder Clo., Nthlt. 54 D2
Lauderdale Dr., 82 G3
Rich.
Lauderdale Rd. W9 6 A4
Lauderdale Rd. W9 57 E3
Laughton Ct., 22 D2
Borwd.
Banks Rd.
Laughton Rd., Nthlt. 54 D1
Launcelot St. SE1 16 E4
Launceston Gdns., 55 F1
Grnf.
Launceston Pl. W8 14 C5
Launceston Pl. W8 66 F3
Launceston Rd., 55 F1
Grnf.
Launch St. E14 69 C3
Laundry La. N1 58 J1
Greenman St.
Laundry Rd. W6 66 B6
Laura Clo. E11 42 J5
Laura Clo., Enf. 25 B5
Laura Pl. E5 50 F4
Lauradale Rd. N2 39 J4
Laurel Ave., Twick. 82 C1
Laurel Bank Gdns. 75 C2
SW6
New Kings Rd.
Laurel Bank Rd., 24 J1
Enf.
Laurel Clo. N19 49 C2
Hargrave Pk.
Laurel Clo., Ilf. 35 F6
Laurel Clo., Sid. 89 A3
Laurel Cres., Croy. 103 A3
Laurel Dr. N21 24 G7
Laurel Gdns. E4 26 B7
Laurel Gdns. NW7 30 D3
Laurel Gdns. W7 64 B1
Laurel Gdns., 72 E4
Houns.
Laurel Gro. SE20 86 E7
Laurel Gro. SE26 86 G4
Laurel Pk., Har. 29 C7
Laurel Rd. SW13 74 G2
Laurel Rd. SW20 92 H1
Laurel St. E8 50 C6
Laurel Vw. N12 31 E3
Laurel Way E18 42 F4
Laurel Way N20 31 D3
Laurence Ms. W12 65 G2
Askew Rd.
Laurence Pountney 13 B5
Hill EC4
Laurence Pountney 13 B5
La. EC4
Laurie Gro. SE14 77 H1
Laurie Rd. W7 55 B5
Laurier Rd. NW5 49 B3
Laurier Rd., Croy. 95 C7
Laurimel Clo., 29 E6
Stan.
September Way
Laurino Pl. 28 J2
(Bushey), Wat.
Lauriston Rd. E9 59 G1
Lauriston Rd. SW19 84 A6
Lausanne Rd. N8 40 G4
Lausanne Rd. SE15 77 F1
Lavell St. N16 50 A4
Lavender Ave. NW9 47 C1
Lavender Ave., 93 H1
Mitch.
Lavender Ave., 99 J3
Wor.Pk.
Lavender Clo. SW3 18 F6
Lavender Clo., 101 B4
Cars.
Lavender Ct., 90 H3
W.Mol.
Molesham Way
Lavender Gdns. 75 J4
SW11
Lavender Gdns., 24 H1
Enf.
Lavender Gro. E8 50 D7
Lavender Gro., 93 H1
Mitch.
Lavender Hill SW11 75 J4
Lavender Hill, Enf. 24 G1
Lavender Pl., Ilf. 52 E5
Lavender Rd. SE16 68 H1

Lavender Rd. SW11 75 G3
Lavender Rd., Cars. 101 A4
Lavender Rd., Croy. 94 F6
Lavender Rd., Enf. 25 A1
Lavender Rd., 99 B5
Epsom
Lavender Rd., Sutt. 100 G4
Lavender St. E15 51 E6
Manbey Gro.
Lavender Sweep 75 J4
SW11
Lavender Ter. SW11 75 H3
Falcon Rd.
Lavender Vale, 101 D6
Wall.
Lavender Wk. SW11 75 J4
Lavender Wk., 94 A3
Mitch.
Lavender Way, Croy. 95 G6
Lavengro Rd. SE27 85 J2
Lavenham Rd. SW18 84 C2
Lavernock Rd., 80 G2
Bexh.
Lavers Rd. N16 50 B3
Laverstoke Gdns. 74 F7
SW15
Laverton Ms. SW5 18 B2
Laverton Pl. SW5 18 B2
Laverton Pl. SW5 66 E4
Lavidge Rd. SE9 88 B2
Lavina Gro. N1 8 C1
Lavington Rd. W13 64 E1
Lavington Rd., 101 F3
Croy.
Lavington St. SE1 16 H2
Lavington St. SE1 67 H1
Law Ho., Bark. 62 A2
Law St. SE1 17 C5
Law St. SE1 68 A3
Lawdons Gdns., 101 H4
Croy.
Lawford Rd. N1 50 B7
Lawford Rd. NW5 49 C6
Lawford Rd. W4 65 C7
Lawless St. E14 60 B7
Lawley Rd. N14 24 B7
Lawley St. E5 50 F4
Lawn, The, Sthl. 63 G5
Lawn Clo. N9 25 C7
Lawn Clo., Brom. 87 H6
Lawn Clo., N.Mal. 92 E2
Lawn Cres., Rich. 74 A2
Lawn Fm. Gro., Rom. 44 E4
Lawn Gdns. W7 64 B1
Lawn Ho. Clo. E14 69 C2
Lawn La. SW8 20 B6
Lawn La. SW8 67 E6
Lawn Pl. SE15 77 C1
Sumner Est.
Lawn Rd. NW3 48 J5
Lawn Rd., Beck. 86 J7
Lawn Ter. SE3 78 B3
Lee Ter.
Lawns, The E4 34 A5
Lawns, The SE3 78 E3
Lee Ter.
Lawns, The SE19 95 A1
Lawns, The, Pnr. 28 H7
Lawns, The, Sid. 89 B4
Lawns, The, Sutt. 100 B7
Lawnside SE3 78 F4
Lawrence Ave. E12 52 D4
Lawrence Ave. E17 41 G1
Lawrence Ave. N13 32 H4
Lawrence Ave. NW7 30 E4
Lawrence Ave., 92 D6
N.Mal.
Lawrence Bldgs. N16 50 C3
Lawrence Campe 31 G3
Clo. N20
Friern Barnet La.
Lawrence Clo. E3 60 A3
Lawrence Clo. N15 41 B3
Lawrence Rd.
Lawrence Ct. NW7 30 E5
Lawrence Cres. 53 H3
Dag.
Lawrence Cres., 38 A2
Edg.
Lawrence Est., 72 C4
Houns.
Lawrence Gdns. NW7 30 F3
Lawrence Hill E4 34 A2
Lawrence La. EC2 13 A4
Lawrence Pl. N1 58 E1
Outram Pl.
Lawrence Rd. E6 61 H1
Lawrence Rd. E13 60 H1
Lawrence Rd. N15 41 B4
Lawrence Rd. N18 33 E4
Lawrence Rd. SE25 95 C4
Lawrence Rd. W5 64 G4

Lawrence Rd., 81 F7
Hmptn.
Lawrence Rd., 72 C3
Houns.
Lawrence Rd., Pnr. 36 D6
Lawrence Rd., Rich. 82 F4
Lawrence Rd., 103 G4
W.Wick.
Lawrence St. E16 60 F5
Lawrence St. NW7 30 F5
Lawrence St. SW3 18 G6
Lawrence St. SW3 66 H6
Lawrence Weaver 93 E6
Clo., Mord.
Green La.
Lawrie Pk. Ave. 86 E5
SE26
Lawrie Pk. Cres. 86 E5
SE26
Lawrie Pk. Gdns. 86 E5
SE26
Lawrie Pk. Rd. SE26 86 E6
Lawson Clo. E16 60 J5
Lawson Clo. SW19 84 A3
Lawson Est. SE1 17 B6
Lawson Gdns., Pnr. 36 B3
Lawson Rd., Enf. 25 F1
Lawson Rd., Sthl. 54 F4
Lawton Rd. E3 59 H3
Lawton Rd. E10 51 D1
Lawton Rd., Barn. 23 G3
Lawton Rd., Loug. 27 E2
Laxcon Clo. NW10 47 C5
Laxey Rd., Orp. 104 J6
Laxley Clo. SE5 20 H7
Laxley Clo. SE5 67 H7
Laxton Pl. NW1 7 E5
Layard Rd. SE16 68 E4
Layard Rd., Enf. 25 C1
Layard Rd., Th.Hth. 95 A2
Layard Sq. SE16 68 E4
Laycock St. N1 49 G6
Layer Gdns. W3 56 A7
Layfield Clo. NW4 38 H7
Layfield Cres. NW4 38 H7
Layfield Rd. NW4 38 H7
Layhams Rd., Kes. 103 F5
Layhams Rd., 103 D3
W.Wick.
Laymarsh Clo., Belv. 71 F3
Laymead Clo., Nthlt. 45 E7
Laystall St. EC1 8 E6
Laystall St. EC1 58 E4
Layton Cres., Croy. 101 G5
Layton Pl. N1 8 F1
Layton Rd. N1 58 G2
Layton Rd., Brent. 64 G5
Layton Rd., Houns. 72 H4
Laytons Bldgs. SE1 17 B3
Layzell Wk. SE9 88 A1
Mottingham La.
Lazar Wk. N7 49 F2
Briset Way
Le May Ave. SE12 87 H3
Lea Bri. Rd. E5 50 E3
Lea Bri. Rd. E10 42 A7
Lea Bri. Rd. E17 42 D5
Lea Gdns., Wem. 46 J4
Lea Hall Rd. E10 51 A1
Lea Pk. Way N9 33 G5
Lea Rd., Beck. 96 A2
Fairfield Rd.
Lea Rd., Enf. 25 A1
Lea Rd., Sthl. 63 E4
Lea Side Ind. Est., 25 J3
Enf.
Lea Valley Rd. E4 26 A6
Lea Valley Rd. 25 G5
Enf.
Lea Valley Viaduct 33 G5
E4
Lea Valley Viaduct 33 G5
N18
Lea Vw. Hos. E5 50 E1
Springfield
Leabank Clo., Har. 46 B3
Leabank Sq. E9 51 A6
Leabank Vw. N15 41 D6
Leabourne Rd. N16 41 D6
Leacroft Ave. SW12 75 J7
Leadale Ave. E4 33 J2
Leadale Rd. N15 41 D6
Leadale Rd. N16 41 D6
Leadenhall Mkt. EC3 13 D4
Leadenhall Pl. EC3 13 D4
Leadenhall St. EC3 13 D4
Leadenhall St. EC3 59 B6
Leader Ave. E12 52 D5
Leadings, The, Wem. 47 C3
Leaf Clo., T.Ditt. 91 B5
Leaf Gro. SE27 85 G5
Leafield Clo. SW16 85 H6
Leafield La., Sid. 89 G4

Leafield Rd. SW20 93 C3
Leafield Rd., Sutt. 100 D2
Leafy Gro., Kes. 103 J5
Leafy Oak Rd. SE12 87 J4
Leafy Way, Croy. 102 C2
Leahurst Rd. E5 50 F3
Leahurst Rd. SE13 78 D3
Leake Ct. SE1 16 D3
Leake St. SE1 16 D3
Leake St. SE1 67 F2
Lealand Rd. N15 41 C6
Leamington Ave. E17 42 A5
Leamington Ave., 87 J5
Brom.
Leamington Ave., 93 B4
Mord.
Leamington Ave., 104 H4
Orp.
Leamington Clo. E12 52 C5
Leamington Clo., 87 J5
Brom.
Leamington Clo., 72 J5
Houns.
Leamington Cres., 45 E3
Har.
Leamington Gdns., 52 J2
Ilf.
Leamington Pk. W3 56 D5
Leamington Rd., 63 D4
Sthl.
Leamington Rd. 57 C5
Vill. W11
Leamore St. W6 65 H4
Leamouth Rd. E6 61 B6
Leamouth Rd. E14 60 D6
Leander Ct. SE8 78 A1
Leander Rd. SW2 76 F7
Leander Rd., Nthlt. 54 G2
Leander Rd., Th.Hth. 94 F4
Learoyd Gdns. E6 61 D7
Leas Clo., Chess. 98 J7
Leas Dale SE9 88 D3
Leas Grn., Chis. 88 J6
Leaside Ave. N10 40 A3
Leaside Rd. E5 50 F1
Leasowes Rd. E10 51 A1
Leather Bottle La., 71 F4
Belv.
St. Augustine's Rd.
Leather Clo., 94 A2
Mitch.
Leather Gdns. E15 60 E1
Abbey Rd.
Leather La. EC1 12 E1
Leather La. EC1 58 G5
Leatherbottle Grn., 71 F3
Erith
Leatherdale St. E1 59 F4
Portelet Rd.
Leatherhead Clo. 50 B1
N16
Leathermarket St. 17 D4
SE1
Leathermarket St. 68 B2
SE1
Leathersellers Clo., 23 B4
Barn.
The Ave.
Leathsail Rd., Har. 45 H3
Leathwaite Rd. SW11 75 J4
Leathwell Rd. SE8 78 B2
Leaveland Clo., 96 A4
Beck.
Leaver Gdns., Grnf. 55 A2
Leavesden Rd., Stan. 29 D6
Leaway E10 50 G1
Lebanon Ave., Felt. 81 D5
Lebanon Ct., Twick. 73 E7
Lebanon Gdns. SW18 75 D5
Lebanon Pk., Twick. 73 E7
Lebanon Rd. SW18 75 D5
Lebanon Rd., Croy. 102 B1
Lebrun Sq. SE3 78 H3
Lechmere App., 42 J2
Wdf.Grn.
Lechmere Ave., Chig. 35 F4
Lechmere Ave., 43 A2
Wdf.Grn.
Lechmere Rd. NW2 47 H6
Leckford Rd. SW18 84 F2
Leckwith Ave., 71 E6
Bexh.
Lecky St. SW7 18 E3
Lecky St. SW7 66 G5
Leconfield Ave. 74 F3
SW13
Leconfield Rd. N5 50 A4
Leda Rd. SE18 70 C3
Ledbury Est. SE15 68 E7
Ledbury Rd.
Ledbury Ms. N. W11 57 D7
Ledbury Rd.
Ledbury Ms. W. W11 57 D7
Ledbury Rd.

Ledbury Pl., Croy. 101 J4
Ledbury Rd.
Ledbury Rd. W11 57 C6
Ledbury Rd., Croy. 101 J4
Ledbury St. SE15 21 J7
Ledbury St. SE15 68 D7
Ledrington Rd. SE19 86 D6
Anerley Rd.
Ledway Dr., Wem. 37 J7
Lee Ave., Rom. 11 E6
Lee Bri. SE13 78 C3
Lee Ch. St. SE13 78 E4
Lee Clo. E17 41 G1
Lee Conservancy Rd. 50 J5
E9
Lee Grn. SE12 78 F5
Lee Gro., Chig. 35 D2
Lee High Rd. SE12 78 F4
Lee High Rd. SE13 78 D4
Lee Pk. SE3 78 F4
Lee Pk. Way N9 33 H3
Lee Pk. Way N18 33 G5
Lee Rd. NW7 31 A7
Lee Rd. SE3 78 F3
Lee Rd. SW19 93 E1
Lee Rd., Enf. 25 D6
Lee Rd., Grnf. 55 F1
Lee St. E8 59 C1
Lee Ter. SE3 78 E3
Lee Valley Trd. Est. 33 G5
N18
Lee Vw., Enf. 24 H1
Leechcroft Ave., Sid. 79 J5
Leechcroft Rd., 101 A3
Wall.
Leecroft Rd., Barn. 23 B5
Leeds Pl. N4 49 F2
Tollington Pk.
Leeds Rd., Ilf. 52 G1
Leeds St. N18 33 D5
Leefern Rd. W12 65 G2
Leegate SE12 78 F5
Leeke St. WC1 8 C3
Leeke St. WC1 58 F3
Leeland Rd. W13 64 D1
Leeland Ter. W13 64 D1
Leeland Way NW10 47 F4
Leerdam Dr. E14 69 C3
Lees, The, Croy. 102 J2
Lees Pl. W1 11 B5
Lees Pl. W1 58 A7
Leeside, Barn. 23 B5
Leeside Cres. NW11 39 B6
Leeside Rd. N17 33 H4
Leeson Rd. SE24 76 G4
Leesons Hill, Chis. 97 H3
Leesons Way, Orp. 97 J2
Leeward Gdns. 84 C5
SW19
Leeway SE8 68 J5
Leeway Clo., Pnr. 28 F7
Woodridings Clo.
Lefevre Wk. E3 59 J1
Old Ford Rd.
Lefroy Rd. W12 65 F2
Legard Rd. N5 49 H3
Legatt Rd. SE9 79 A5
Leggatt Rd. E15 60 C2
Legge St. SE13 78 C5
Leghorn Rd. NW10 56 F2
Leghorn Rd. SE18 70 G5
Legion Clo. N1 49 G7
Legion Ct., Mord. 93 D6
Legion Rd., Grnf. 54 J1
Legion Way N12 31 H7
Downay
Legon Ave., Rom. 53 J1
Legrace Ave., 72 D2
Houns.
Leicester Ave., 94 E4
Mitch.
Leicester Clo., 99 J4
Wor.Pk.
Leicester Ct. WC2 11 J5
Leicester Gdns., 53 H7
Ilf.
Leicester Pl. WC2 11 J5
Leicester Rd. E11 42 H5
Leicester Rd. N2 39 H3
Leicester Rd. NW10 47 D7
Leicester Rd., Barn. 23 E5
Leicester Rd., 95 B7
Croy.
Leicester Sq. WC2 11 J5
Leicester Sq. WC2 58 D7
Leicester St. WC2 11 J5
Leigh Ave., Ilf. 43 A4
Leigh Clo., N.Mal. 92 D3
Leigh Ct., Borwd. 22 D2
Banks Rd.
Leigh Ct., Har. 46 B1
Leigh Cres., Croy. 103 B7
Leigh Gdns. NW10 56 J2

Leigh Hunt St. SE1 16 J3
Leigh Orchard Clo. 85 F3
SW16
Leigh Pl., Well. 80 A2
Leigh Pl. E6 52 D6
Leigh Rd. E10 42 C7
Leigh Rd. N5 49 H4
Leigh Rd., Houns. 72 H1
Leigh Rodd, Wat. 28 F3
Leigh St. WC1 8 A5
Leigh St. WC1 58 E4
Leigham Ave. SW16 85 E3
Leigham Ct. Rd. 85 E2
SW16
Leigham Dr., Islw. 64 B7
Leigham Vale SW2 85 G2
Leigham Vale SW16 85 F3
Leighton Ave. E12 52 D5
Leighton Ave., Pnr. 36 E3
Leighton Clo., Edg. 38 A2
Leighton Cres. NW5 49 C5
Leighton Gro.
Leighton Gdns. 56 H2
NW10
Leighton Gro. NW5 49 C5
Leighton Pl. NW5 49 C5
Leighton Rd. NW5 49 C5
Leighton Rd. W13 64 D2
Leighton Rd., Enf. 25 C5
Leighton Rd., Har. 37 A2
Leighton St. E., 101 H1
Croy.
Leighton St. W., 101 H1
Croy.
Leinster Ave. SW14 74 C3
Leinster Gdns. W2 10 C4
Leinster Gdns. W2 57 F6
Leinster Ms. W2 10 C6
Leinster Ms. W2 57 F7
Leinster Pl. W2 10 B4
Leinster Pl. W2 57 F6
Leinster Rd. N10 40 B4
Leinster Rd. NW6 57 D3
Stafford Rd.
Leinster Sq. W2 57 D6
Leinster Ter. W2 10 C5
Leinster Ter. W2 57 F7
Leith Clo. NW9 47 D1
Leith Rd. N22 40 H1
Leith Yd. NW6 57 D1
Quex Rd.
Leithcote Gdns. 85 F4
SW16
Leithcote Path SW16 85 F3
Lela Ave., Houns. 72 C2
Lelitia Clo. E8 59 D1
Pownall Rd.
Leman St. E1 13 G4
Leman St. E1 59 C6
Lemark Clo., Stan. 29 F5
Lemmon Rd. SE10 69 E6
Lemna Rd. E11 42 E7
Lemonwell Ct. SE9 79 F5
Lemsford Clo. N15 41 D5
Lemsford Ct. N4 49 J2
Brownswood Rd.
Lemsford Ct., 22 C4
Borwd.
Lemuel St. SW18 75 E6
St. Ann's Hill
Lena Gdns. W6 65 J3
Lena Kennedy Clo. 38 D6
E4
Lenanton Steps E14 69 A2
Manilla St.
Lendal Ter. SW4 76 D3
Lenelby Rd., Surb. 99 A1
Lenham Rd. SE12 78 F4
Lenham Rd., Bexh. 71 F6
Lenham Rd., Sutt. 100 E4
Lenham Rd., Th.Hth. 95 A2
Lennard Ave., 103 E2
W.Wick.
Lennard Clo., 103 E2
W.Wick.
Lennard Rd. SE20 86 G6
Lennard Rd., Beck. 86 H7
Lennard Rd., Brom. 104 C1
Lennard Rd., Croy. 101 J1
Lennon Rd. NW2 47 J6
Lennox Gdns. NW10 47 J4
Lennox Gdns. SW1 14 J6
Lennox Gdns. SW1 66 J3
Lennox Gdns., Croy. 101 H4
Lennox Gdns., Ilf. 52 C1
Lennox Gdns. Ms. 14 J6
SW1
Lennox Gdns. Ms. 66 J3
SW1
Lennox Rd. E17 41 J6
Lennox Rd. N4 49 F2
Lenor Clo., Bexh. 80 E4
Lens Rd. E7 51 J7

Lensbury Way SE2 71 C3
Lenthall Pl. SW7 18 C1
Lenthall Rd. E8 50 C7
Lenthall Rd., Loug. 27 G4
Lenthorp Rd. SE10 69 F4
Lentmead Rd., Brom. 87 F3
Lenton Ri., Rich. 73 H3
Evelyn Ter.
Lenton St. SE18 70 G4
Lenville Way SE16 21 J4
Leo St. SE15 68 F7
Leo Yd. EC1 8 H6
Leof Cres. SE6 87 B5
Leominster Rd., 93 F6
Mord.
Leominster Wk., 93 F6
Mord.
Leonard Ave., Mord. 93 F5
Leonard Rd. E4 34 A6
Leonard Rd. E7 51 G4
Leonard Rd. N9 33 C3
Leonard Rd. SW16 94 C1
Leonard Rd., Sthl. 63 D3
Leonard Robbins 62 B7
Path SE28
Tawney Rd.
Leonard St. E16 70 B1
Leonard St. EC2 9 C5
Leonard St. EC2 59 A4
Leontine Clo. SE15 68 D7
Leopards Ct. EC1 12 E1
Leopold Ave. SW19 84 C5
Leopold Ms. E9 59 F1
Fremont St.
Leopold Rd. E17 42 A5
Leopold Rd. N2 39 G3
Leopold Rd. N18 33 E5
Leopold Rd. NW10 47 E7
Leopold Rd. SW19 84 C4
Leopold Rd. W5 64 J1
Leopold St. E3 59 J5
Lepe Clo., Brom. 87 E4
Winlaton Rd.
Leppoc Rd. SW4 76 D3
Leroy St. SE1 17 D6
Leroy St. SE1 68 B4
Lescombe Clo. SE23 86 H3
Lescombe Rd. SE23 86 H3
Lesley Clo., Bex. 80 H7
Leslie Gdns., Sutt. 100 D6
Leslie Gro., Croy. 102 A1
Leslie Pk. Rd., Croy. 102 B1
Leslie Rd. E11 51 C4
Leslie Rd. E16 60 H6
Leslie Rd. N2 39 G3
Leslie Smith Sq. 70 D6
SE18
Nightingale Vale
Lessar Ave. SW4 76 B5
Lessing St. SE23 77 H7
Lessingham Ave. 84 J4
SW17
Lessingham Ave., 43 D3
Ilf.
Lessington Ave., 44 J6
Rom.
Lessness Ave., 71 D7
Bexh.
Lessness Pk., Belv. 71 F5
Lessness Rd., Belv. 71 G5
Stapley Rd.
Lessness Rd., Mord. 93 F6
Lester Ave. E15 60 E4
Leswin Pl. N16 50 C3
Leswin Rd.
Leswin Rd. N16 50 C3
Letchford Gdns. 56 G3
NW10
Letchford Ms. NW10 56 G3
Letchford Gdns.
Letchford Ter., 36 H1
Har.
Letchworth Clo., 96 G5
Brom.
Letchworth Clo., 28 D5
Wat.
Letchworth Dr., 96 G5
Brom.
Letchworth St. SW17 84 J4
Lethbridge Clo. 78 C1
SE13
Lett Rd. E15 51 D7
Letterstone Rd. SW6 66 C7
Varna Rd.
Lettice St. SW6 75 C1
Lettsom St. SE5 77 B2
Lettsom Wk. E13 60 G2
Hunter Wk.
Leucha Rd. E17 41 H5
Levana Clo. SW19 84 B1
Levehurst Way SW4 76 E2
Leven Clo., Wat. 28 D5
Benton Rd.

Leven Rd. E14	60	C5
Levendale Rd. SE23	86	H2
Lever St. EC1	**8**	**H4**
Lever St. EC1	8	H4
Leverett St. SW3	58	H3
Leverett St. SW3	**18**	**H1**
Leverholme Gdns.	88	D3
SE9		
Leverson St. SW16	85	C6
Leverton Pl. NW5	49	C5
Leverton St.		
Leverton St. NW5	49	C5
Levett Gdns., Ilf.	52	J4
Levett Rd., Bark.	52	H6
Levine Gdns., Bark.	62	D2
Lewes Clo., Nthlt.	45	G6
Lewes Rd. N12	31	H5
Lewes Rd., Brom.	97	A2
Lewesdon Clo. SW19	84	A1
Leweston Pl. N16	41	C7
Lewey Ho. E3	59	J4
Lewgars Ave. NW9	38	C6
Lewin Rd. SW14	74	D3
Lewin Rd. SW16	85	D6
Lewin Rd., Bexh.	80	E5
Lewis Ave. E17	42	A1
Lewis Cres. NW10	47	C5
Lewis Gdns. N2	39	G2
Lewis Gro. SE13	78	C3
Lewis Rd., Mitch.	93	G2
Lewis Rd., Rich.	73	G5
Red Lion St.		
Lewis Rd., Sid.	89	C3
Lewis Rd., Sthl.	63	E2
Lewis Rd., Sutt.	100	E4
Lewis Rd., Well.	80	C3
Lewis St. NW1	49	B6
Lewisham High St.	78	B6
SE13		
Lewisham Hill SE13	78	C2
Lewisham Pk. SE13	78	C5
Lewisham Rd. SE13	78	B1
Lewisham St. SW1	**15**	**J4**
Lewisham Way SE4	78	A2
Lewisham Way SE14	77	J1
Lexden Dr., Rom.	44	B6
Lexden Rd. W3	65	B1
Lexden Rd., Mitch.	94	D4
Lexham Gdns. W8	**14**	**A6**
Lexham Gdns. W8	66	D4
Lexham Gdns. Ms.	**14**	**B6**
W8		
Lexham Ho., Bark.	61	G1
St. Margarets		
Lexham Ms. W8	66	D4
Lexham Wk. W8	**14**	**B6**
Lexington St. W1	**11**	**G5**
Lexington St. W1	58	C7
Lexington Way,	23	A4
Barn.		
Lexton Gdns. SW12	85	D1
Ley St., Ilf.	52	E2
Leyborne Ave. W13	64	E2
Leyborne Pk., Rich.	74	A1
Leybourne Clo.,	96	G6
Brom.		
Leybourne Rd. E11	51	F1
Leybourne Rd. NW1	49	B7
Leybourne Rd. NW9	38	A5
Leybourne St. NW1	49	B7
Hawley St.		
Leybridge Ct. SE13	78	G5
Leyburn Clo. E17	42	C4
Leyburn Gdns.,	102	C2
Croy.		
Leyburn Gro. N18	33	D6
Leyburn Rd. N18	33	D6
Leycroft Clo.,	27	D5
Loug.		
Leyden St. E1	**13**	**F2**
Leydon Clo. SE16	68	G1
Lagado Ms.		
Leyes Rd. E16	60	J6
Leyfield, Wor.Pk.	99	E1
Leyland Ave., Enf.	25	H2
Leyland Gdns.,	34	J5
Wdf.Grn.		
Leyland Rd. SE12	78	F5
Leylang Rd. SE14	68	G7
Leys, The N2	39	F4
Leys, The, Har.	37	H6
Leys Ave., Dag.	62	J1
Leys Clo., Dag.	53	J7
Leys Clo., Har.	37	A5
Leys Gdns., Barn.	24	A5
Leys Rd. E., Enf.	25	H1
Leys Rd. W., Enf.	25	H1
Leysdown Ave.,	80	J4
Bexh.		
Leysdown Rd. SE9	88	B2
Leysfield Rd. W12	65	G3
Leyspring Rd. E11	51	F1
Leyswood Dr., Ilf.	43	H5
Leythe Rd. W3	65	C2
Leyton Business	51	A2
Cen. E10		
Leyton Gra. E10	51	B1
Leyton Gra. Est. E10	51	A1
Leyton Grn. Rd. E10	42	C6
Leyton Ind. Village	41	G7
E10		
Leyton Pk. Rd. E10	51	C3
Leyton Rd. E15	51	D5
Leyton Rd. SW19	84	F7
Leytonstone Rd. E15	51	E6
Leywick St. E15	60	E2
Lezayre Rd., Orp.	104	J6
Liardet St. SE14	68	H6
Liberia Rd. N5	49	H6
Liberty Ave. SW19	93	F1
Liberty Ms. SW12	76	B6
Liberty St. SW9	76	F1
Libra Rd. E3	59	J1
Libra Rd. E13	60	G2
Library Pl. E1	59	E7
Cable St.		
Library St. SE1	**16**	**G4**
Library St. SE1	67	H2
Lichfield Gdns., Rich.	73	H4
Lichfield Gro. N3	39	D1
Lichfield Rd. E3	59	H3
Lichfield Rd. E6	61	A3
Lichfield Rd. N9	33	D2
Winchester Rd.		
Lichfield Rd. NW2	48	B4
Lichfield Rd., Dag.	53	B4
Lichfield Rd.,	72	C3
Houns.		
Lichfield Rd.,	36	A3
Nthwd.		
Lichfield Rd., Rich.	73	J1
Lichfield Rd.,	34	E4
Wdf.Grn.		
Lichlade Clo., Orp.	104	J4
Lidbury Rd. NW7	31	B6
Lidcote Gdns. SW9	76	G2
Liddall Clo., Har.	37	G3
Liddell Gdns. NW10	56	J2
Liddell Rd. NW6	48	D6
Lidding Rd., Har.	37	G5
Liddington Rd. E15	60	F1
Liddon Rd. E13	60	H3
Liddon Rd., Brom.	96	J3
Liden Clo. E17	50	J1
Hitcham Rd.		
Lidfield Rd. N16	50	A4
Lidiard Rd. SW18	84	F2
Lidlington Pl. NW1	7	G2
Lidlington Pl. NW1	50	C3
Lidyard Rd. N19	49	C1
Liffler Rd. SE18	70	H5
Lifford St. SW15	75	A4
Liffords Pl. SW13	74	F2
Lightcliffe Rd. N13	32	G4
Lightermans Rd. E14	69	A2
Lightfoot Rd. N8	40	E5
Lightley Clo., Wem.	46	B2
Stanley Ave.		
Ligonier St. E2	**9**	**F5**
Lilac Clo. E4	33	J6
Lilac Gdns. W5	64	G3
Lilac Gdns., Croy.	103	A3
Lilac Pl. SE11	**20**	**C2**
Lilac Pl. SE11	67	F4
Lilac St. W12	56	G7
Lilburne Gdns. SE9	79	B5
Lilburne Rd. SE9	79	B5
Lilburne Wk. NW10	47	C6
Pitfield Way		
Lile Cres. W7	55	B5
Lilestone Est. NW8	6	E6
Lilestone St. NW8	**6**	**G5**
Lilestone St. NW8	57	H4
Lilford Rd. SE5	76	H2
Lilian Barker Clo.	78	G3
SE12		
Lilian Board Way,	46	A5
Grnf.		
Lilian Clo. N16	50	B3
Barbauld Rd.		
Lilian Gdns.,	42	H1
Wdf.Grn.		
Lilian Rd. SW16	94	C1
Lillechurch Rd.,	53	B6
Dag.		
Lilleshall Rd.,	93	G5
Mord.		
Lilley La. NW7	30	D5
Lillian Ave. W3	65	A2
Lillian Rd. SW13	65	G6
Lillie Rd. SW6	66	A6
Lillie Yd. SW6	66	D6
Lillieshall Rd. SW4	76	B3
Lillington Gdns.	**19**	**G2**
Est. SW1		
Lilliput Ave., Nthlt.	54	E1
Lily Clo. W14	66	A4
Gliddon Rd.		
Lily Gdns., Wem.	55	F2
Lily Pl. EC1	**12**	**F1**
Lily Pl. EC1	58	G5
Lily Rd. E17	42	A6
Lilyville Rd. SW6	75	C1
Limbourne Ave.,	44	F7
Dag.		
Limburg Rd. SW11	75	J4
Lime Clo. E1	**17**	**J1**
Lime Clo. E1	68	D1
Lime Clo., Brom.	97	B4
Lime Clo., Buck.H.	35	A3
Lime Clo., Cars.	100	J2
Lime Clo., Har.	37	D2
Lime Clo., Rom.	44	J4
Lime Ct., Mitch.	93	G2
Lime Cres., Sun.	90	C2
Lime Gro. N20	31	C1
Lime Gro. W12	65	J2
Lime Gro., Ilf.	35	J6
Lime Gro., N.Mal.	92	D3
Lime Gro., Orp.	104	E2
Lime Gro., Ruis.	36	B6
Lime Gro., Sid.	79	J6
Lime Gro., Twick.	73	C6
Lime Rd., Rich.	73	J4
St. Mary's Gro.		
Lime Row, Erith	71	F3
Northwood Pl.		
Lime St. E17	41	H4
Lime St. EC3	**13**	**D5**
Lime St. EC3	59	B7
Lime St. Pas. EC3	**13**	**D5**
Lime Tree Ave.,	98	A1
Esher		
Lime Tree Ave.,	98	B1
T.Ditt.		
Lime Tree Gro.,	102	J3
Croy.		
Lime Tree Pl., Mitch.	94	B1
Lime Tree Rd.,	72	H1
Houns.		
Lime Tree Wk.	29	B1
(Bushey), Wat.		
Lime Tree Wk.,	103	F4
W.Wick.		
Lime Wk. E15	60	E1
Church St. N.		
Limecroft Clo.,	99	D7
Epsom		
Limedene Clo., Pnr.	36	D1
Limeharbour E14	69	B3
Limehouse	59	J7
Causeway E14		
Limehouse Flds. Est.	59	H5
E14		
Limerick Clo. SW12	76	C7
Limerston St. SW10	**18**	**D5**
Limerston St. SW10	66	F6
Limes, The W2	57	D7
Linden Gdns.		
Limes, The, Brom.	104	B2
Oakley Rd.		
Limes Ave. E11	42	H4
Limes Ave. N12	31	F4
Limes Ave. NW7	30	E6
Limes Ave. NW11	39	B7
Limes Ave. SE20	86	E7
Limes Ave. SW13	74	F2
Limes Ave., Cars.	100	J1
Limes Ave., Chig.	35	F5
Limes Ave., Croy.	101	G3
Limes Ave., The N11	32	B5
Limes Gdns. SW18	75	D6
Limes Gro. SE13	78	C4
Limes Pl., Croy.	95	A7
Limes Rd., Beck.	96	B2
Limes Rd., Croy.	95	A6
Limes Wk. SE15	77	E4
Limes Wk. W5	64	G2
Chestnut Gro.		
Limesdale Gdns.,	38	C2
Edg.		
Limesford Rd. SW14	74	E3
White Hart La.		
Limesford Rd. SE15	77	G4
Limestone Wk., Erith	71	D3
Alsike Rd.		
Limetree Clo. SW2	85	F1
Limetree Wk. SW17	85	A5
Limewood Clo. W13	55	E6
St. Stephens Rd.		
Limewood Ct., Ilf.	43	C5
Beehive La.		
Limewood Rd., Erith	71	J7
Limpsfield Ave.	84	A2
SW19		
Limpsfield Ave.,	94	F5
Th.Hth.		
Linacre Ct. W6	66	A5
Linacre Rd. NW2	47	H6
Linberry Wk. SE8	68	H4
Carteret Way		
Linchmere Rd. SE12	78	F7
Lincoln Ave. N14	32	C3
Lincoln Ave. SW19	84	A3
Lincoln Ave.,	81	H2
Twick.		
Lincoln Clo. SE25	95	D6
Woodside Grn.		
Lincoln Clo., Grnf.	54	J1
Lincoln Clo., Har.	36	F5
Lincoln Ct. N16	41	A7
Lincoln Ct., Borwd.	22	D5
Lincoln Cres., Enf.	25	B5
Lincoln Dr., Wat.	28	C3
Lincoln Gdns., Ilf.	43	B7
Lincoln Grn. Rd.,	97	J5
Orp.		
Lincoln Ms. NW6	57	C1
Willesden La.		
Lincoln Ms. SE21	86	A1
Lincoln Rd. E7	52	A6
Lincoln Rd. E13	60	H4
Lincoln Rd. E18	42	G1
Grove Rd.		
Lincoln Rd. N2	39	H3
Lincoln Rd. SE25	95	E3
Lincoln Rd., Enf.	25	B4
Lincoln Rd., Felt.	81	F3
Lincoln Rd., Har.	36	F5
Lincoln Rd., Mitch.	94	E5
Lincoln Rd., N.Mal.	92	C3
Lincoln Rd., Sid.	89	B5
Lincoln Rd., Wem.	46	G6
Lincoln Rd.,	99	H1
Wor.Pk.		
Lincoln Rd. E11	51	E2
Lincoln St. SW3	**18**	**J2**
Lincoln St. SW3	66	J4
Lincoln Way, Enf.	25	E5
Lincolns, The NW7	30	F3
Lincoln's Inn Flds.	**12**	**C3**
WC2		
Lincoln's Inn Flds.	58	F6
WC2		
Lincombe Rd., Brom.	87	F3
Lind Rd., Sutt.	100	F5
Lind St. SE8	78	A2
Lindal Cres., Enf.	24	E5
Lindal Rd. SE4	77	J3
Lindales, The N17	33	C6
Brantwood Rd.		
Lindbergh Rd.,	101	E7
Wall.		
Linden Ave. NW10	57	A2
Linden Ave., Enf.	25	D1
Linden Ave., Houns.	72	H5
Linden Ave., Ruis.	45	A1
Linden Ave.,	94	H4
Th.Hth.		
Linden Ave., Wem.	46	J5
Linden Clo. N14	24	C6
Linden Clo., Ruis.	45	A1
Linden Clo., Stan.	29	E5
Linden Clo.,	95	C7
T.Ditt.		
Linden Ct. W12	65	J1
Linden Cres., Grnf.	46	C6
Linden Cres.,	91	J2
Kings.T.		
Linden Cres.,	34	H6
Wdf.Grn.		
Linden Gdns. W2	57	D7
Linden Gdns. W4	65	E5
Linden Gdns., Enf.	25	D1
Linden Gro. SE15	77	E3
Linden Gro. SE26	86	F6
Linden Gro., N.Mal.	92	E3
Linden Gro., Tedd.	82	C5
Waldegrave Rd.		
Linden Lawns, Wem.	46	J4
Linden Lea N2	39	F5
Linden Leas,	103	D2
W.Wick.		
Linden Ms. W2	57	D7
Linden Rd. N10	40	B4
Linden Rd. N11	31	J2
Linden Rd. N15	40	J4
Linden Rd., Hmptn.	81	G7
Linden Way N14	24	C6
Lindenfield, Chis.	97	E2
Lindens, The N12	31	G5
Lindens, The W4	74	C1
Hartington Rd.		
Lindens, The, Croy.	103	C6
Lindens, The, Loug.	27	C5
Lindeth Clo., Stan.	29	F6
Old Ch. La.		
Lindfield Gdns. NW3	48	F5
Lindfield Rd. W5	55	F4
Lindfield Rd., Croy.	95	C6
Lindfield St. E14	60	A6

Lindisfarne Rd. SW20 83 G7
Lindisfarne Rd., Dag. 53 C3
Lindisfarne Way E9 50 H4
Lindley Est. SE15 21 H7
Lindley Rd. E10 61 B1
Lindley St. E1 59 F5
Lindo St. SE15 77 F2
Selden Rd.
Lindore Rd. SW11 75 J4
Lindores Rd., Cars. 93 F7
Lindrop St. SW6 75 F2
Lindsay Clo., Chess. 98 H7
Lindsay Dr., Har. 37 H6
Lindsay Rd., Hmptn. 81 H4
Lindsay Rd., Wor.Pk. 99 H2
Lindsay Sq. SW1 19 J4
Lindsay Sq. SW1 67 D5
Lindsell St. SE10 78 C1
Lindsey Clo., Brom. 97 A3
Lindsey Clo., Mitch. 94 E4
Lindsey Ms. N1 49 J7
Lindsey Rd., Dag. 53 C4
Lindsey St. EC1 12 H1
Lindsey St. EC1 58 H5
Lindum Rd., Tedd. 82 F7
Lindway SE27 85 H5
Lindwood Clo. E6 61 B5
Northumberland Rd.
Linford Rd. E17 42 C3
Linford St. SW8 76 C1
Ling Rd. E16 60 G5
Ling Rd., Erith 71 J6
Lingards Rd. SE13 78 C4
Lingey Clo., Sid. 88 J2
Lingfield Ave., Kings.T. 91 H4
Lingfield Clo., Enf. 25 B6
Lingfield Cres. SE9 79 G4
Lingfield Gdns. N9 25 E7
Lingfield Rd. SW19 84 A6
Lingfield Rd., Wor.Pk. 99 J3
Lingham St. SW9 76 E2
Lingholm Way, Barn. 23 A4
Lingmere Clo., Chig. 35 F2
Lingrove Gdns., Buck.H. 34 H2
Beech La.
Lings Coppice SE21 86 A2
Lingwell Rd. SW17 84 H3
Lingwood Gdns., Islw. 64 B7
Lingwood Rd. E5 41 D7
Linhope St. NW1 6 J5
Linhope St. NW1 57 J4
Link, The W3 56 B6
Link, The, Enf. 25 H1
Link, The, Nthlt. 45 F5
Eastcote La.
Link, The, Pnr. 36 C7
Link, The, Wem. 46 F1
Nathans Rd.
Link La., Wall. 101 D6
Link Rd. N11 32 A4
Link Rd., Dag. 62 H2
Link Rd., Wall. 101 A1
Link St. E9 50 F5
Link Way, Brom. 97 B7
Link Way, Dag. 53 C4
Link Way, Pnr. 36 D1
Linkfield, Brom. 96 G6
Linkfield, W.Mol. 90 H3
Linkfield Rd., Islw. 73 C2
Linklea Clo. NW9 30 E7
Links, The E17 41 H4
Links Ave., Mord. 93 D4
Links Dr. N20 31 D1
Links Gdns. SW16 85 G7
Links Rd. NW2 47 F2
Links Rd. SW17 85 A6
Links Rd. W3 56 A6
Links Rd., W.Wick. 103 C1
Links Rd., Wdf.Grn. 34 G5
Links Side, Enf. 24 F3
Links Vw. N3 31 C7
Links Vw. Clo., Stan. 29 D6
Links Vw. Rd., Croy. 103 A3
Links Vw. Rd., Hmptn. 81 J5
Links Way, Beck. 96 A6
Linkside N12 31 C6
Linkside, Chig. 35 F5
Linkside, N.Mal. 92 E2
Linkside Clo., Enf. 24 F3

Linkside Gdns., Enf. 24 F3
Linksway NW4 39 A2
Linkway N4 40 J7
Linkway SW20 92 H3
Linkway, Rich. 82 E3
Linkway, The, Barn. 23 E6
Maiden La.
Linley Cres., Rom. 44 H3
Linley Rd. N17 41 B2
Linnell Clo. NW11 39 E6
Linnell Dr. NW11 39 E6
Linnell Rd. N18 33 D5
Fairfield Rd.
Linnell Rd. SE5 77 B2
Linnet Clo. N9 33 G1
Linnet Clo. SE28 62 C7
Linnet Ms. SW12 76 A7
Linnett Clo. E4 34 C4
Linom Rd. SW4 76 E4
Linscott Rd. E5 50 F4
Linsdell Rd., Bark. 61 F1
Linsey St. SE16 21 H1
Linsey St. SE16 68 D4
Linslade Clo., Houns. 72 E5
Frampton Rd.
Linslade Clo., Pnr. 36 B3
Linstead Ct. SE9 79 H6
Linstead St. NW6 48 D7
Linstead Way SW18 75 J7
Linster Gro., Borwd. 22 C5
Lintaine Clo. W6 66 B6
Moylan Rd.
Linthorpe Ave., Wem. 46 F6
Linthorpe Rd. N16 41 B7
Linthorpe Rd., Barn. 23 H3
Linton Clo., Well. 80 B1
Anthony Rd.
Linton Gdns. E6 61 B6
Linton Gro. SE27 85 H5
Linton Rd., Bark. 52 F7
Linton St. N1 58 J1
Lintons, The, Bark. 75 C2
Linver Rd. SW6 75 C2
Linwood Clo. E6 61 B5
Northumberland Rd.
Linwood Clo. SE5 77 C2
Linwood Way SE15 21 F7
Linzee Rd. N8 40 E4
Lion Ave., Twick. 82 C1
Lion Rd.
Lion Clo. SE4 78 A6
Lion Ct., Borwd. 22 C1
Lion Gate Gdns., Rich. 73 J3
Lion Pk. Ave., Chess. 99 A4
Lion Rd. E6 61 C5
Lion Rd. N9 33 D2
Lion Rd., Bexh. 80 F4
Lion Rd., Croy. 94 J5
Lion Rd., Twick. 82 C1
Lion Way, Brent. 64 G7
Lionel Gdns. SE9 79 A5
Lionel Ms. W10 57 B5
Telford Rd.
Lionel Rd. SE9 79 A5
Lionel Rd., Brent. 64 H3
Lions Clo. SE9 87 J3
Liphook Cres. SE23 77 F7
Liphook Rd., Wat. 28 D4
Lippitts Hill, Loug. 26 E1
Lipton Clo. SE28 62 C7
Aisher Rd.
Lipton Rd. E1 59 G6
Bower Rd.
Lisbon Ave., Twick. 81 J2
Lisburne Rd. NW3 48 J4
Lisford St. SE15 77 C1
Lisgar Ter. W14 66 C4
Liskeard Clo., Chis. 93 J6
Liskeard Gdns. SE3 78 G1
Lisle St. WC2 11 J5
Lisle St. WC2 57 D7
Lismore Circ. NW5 49 A5
Wellesley Rd.
Lismore Clo., Islw. 73 G1
Lismore Rd. N17 41 A3
Lismore Rd., S.Croy. 102 B6
Lismore Wk. N1 49 J6
Clephane Rd.
Liss Way SE15 21 G7
Lissenden Gdns. NW5 49 A4
Lisson Grn. Est. NW8 6 G4

Lisson Grn. Est. NW8 57 H3
Lisson Gro. NW1 6 H6
Lisson Gro. NW1 57 H4
Lisson Gro. NW8 6 F5
Lisson Gro. NW8 57 G4
Lisson St. NW1 10 G1
Lisson St. NW1 57 H5
Lister Clo. W3 56 D5
Lister Clo., Mitch. 93 H1
Lister Gdns. N18 32 J5
Lister Ho. SE3 69 E6
Lister Ms. N7 49 F4
Lister Rd. E11 51 E1
Lister St. E13 60 G3
Sewell St.
Lister Wk. SE28 62 D7
Haldane Rd.
Liston Rd. N17 41 D1
Liston Rd. SW4 76 C3
Liston Way, Wdf.Grn. 34 J7
Listowel Clo. SW9 67 G7
Mandela St.
Listowel Rd., Dag. 53 G3
Listria Pk. N16 50 B2
Litchfield Ave. E15 51 E6
Litchfield Ave., Mord. 93 C7
Litchfield Gdns. NW10 47 G6
Litchfield Rd., Sutt. 100 F4
Litchfield St. WC2 11 J5
Litchfield St. WC2 58 D7
Litchfield Way NW11 39 E5
Lithos Rd. NW3 48 F6
Little Acre, Beck. 96 A3
Little Albany St. NW1 7 E4
Little Argyll St. W1 11 F4
Little Birches, Sid. 88 H2
Little Boltons, The SW10 18 B3
Little Boltons, The SW10 66 E5
Little Bornes SE21 86 B4
Little Britain EC1 12 H2
Little Britain EC1 58 H5
Little Brownings SE23 86 E2
Little Bury St. N9 33 A1
Little Cedars N12 31 F4
Woodside Ave.
Little Chester St. SW1 15 D5
Little Chester St. SW1 67 B3
Little College St. SW1 16 A5
Little Ct., W.Wick. 103 E2
Little Dean's Yd. SW1 16 A5
Little Dimocks SW12 85 B2
Little Dorrit Ct. SE1 17 A3
Little Dorrit Ct. SE1 67 J2
Little Dragons, Loug. 27 A4
Little Ealing La. W5 64 F4
Little Edward St. NW1 7 E3
Little Essex St. WC2 12 E5
Little Ferry Rd., Twick. 82 E1
Ferry Rd.
Little Friday Rd. E4 34 E2
Little Gearies, Ilf. 43 E4
Little George St. SW1 16 A4
Little Gra., Grnf. 55 D3
Perivale La.
Little Grn., Rich. 73 G4
Little Grn. St. NW5 49 B4
College La.
Little Halliards, Walt. 90 A6
Felix Rd.
Little Heath SE7 70 B5
Little Heath, Rom. 44 B4
Little Heath Rd., Bexh. 80 E1
Little Ilford La. E12 52 C4
Little Marlborough St. W1 11 F4
Little Moss La., Pnr. 36 E2
Little New St. EC4 12 F3
Little Newport St. WC2 11 J5
Little Newport St. WC2 58 D7
Little Orchard Clo., Pnr. 36 E2
Barrow Pt. La.
Little Oxhey La., Wat. 28 D5

Little Pk. Dr., Felt. 81 D2
Little Pk. Gdns., Enf. 24 J3
Little Plucketts Way, Buck.H. 34 J1
Little Portland St. W1 11 E3
Little Portland St. W1 58 C6
Little Queens Rd., Tedd. 82 C6
Little Redlands, Brom. 97 B2
Little Rd., Croy. 102 B1
Lwr. Addiscombe Rd.
Little Russell St. WC1 12 A2
Little Russell St. WC1 58 E5
Little St. James's St. SW1 15 F2
Little St. James's St. SW1 67 C1
Little St. Leonards SW14 74 C3
Little Sanctuary SW1 15 J4
Little Smith St. SW1 15 J5
Little Somerset St. E1 13 F4
Little Strand NW9 38 F2
Little Thrift, Orp. 97 F4
Little Titchfield St. W1 11 F2
Little Trinity La. EC4 13 A5
Little Turnstile WC1 12 C2
Littlebrook Clo., Croy. 95 G6
Littlebury Rd. SW4 76 D3
Littlecombe SE7 69 H6
Littlecombe Clo. SW15 75 A6
Littlecote Clo. SW19 75 A7
Littlecroft SE9 79 D3
Littledale SE2 71 A6
Littlefield Clo. N19 49 C4
Junction Rd.
Littlefield Clo., Kings.T. 91 H2
Fairfield W.
Littlefield Rd., Edg. 30 C7
Littlegrove, Barn. 23 H6
Littleheath Rd., S.Croy. 102 E7
Littlejohn Rd. W7 55 C6
Littlemead, Esher 98 A4
Littlemede SE9 88 C3
Littlemoor Rd., Ilf. 52 G3
Littlemore Rd. SE2 71 A2
Littlers Clo. SW19 93 G1
Runnymede
Littlestone Clo., Beck. 87 A6
Abbey La.
Littleton Ave. E4 34 F1
Littleton Cres., Har. 46 C2
Littleton Rd., Har. 46 C2
Littleton St. SW18 84 F2
Littlewood SE13 78 C5
Littlewood Clo. W13 64 E3
Littleworth Ave., Esher 98 A5
Littleworth Common Rd., Esher 98 A3
Littleworth La., Esher 98 A4
Littleworth Pl., Esher 98 A4
Littleworth Rd., Esher 98 A5
Livermere Rd. E8 59 C1
Liverpool Gro. SE17 21 B4
Liverpool Gro. SE17 68 A5
Liverpool Rd. E10 42 C6
Liverpool Rd. E16 60 E5
Liverpool Rd. N1 49 G7
Liverpool Rd. N7 49 G5
Liverpool Rd. W5 64 G2
Liverpool Rd., Kings.T. 83 A7
Liverpool Rd., Th.Hth. 94 J3
Liverpool St. EC2 13 D2
Liverpool St. EC2 59 B5
Livesey Pl. SE15 21 J5
Livingston College Twrs. E10 42 C6
Livingstone Pl. E14 69 C5
Ferry St.

Livingstone Rd. E15	60	C1
Livingstone Rd. E17	42	B6
Livingstone Rd. N13	32	E6
Livingstone Rd. SW11	75	G3
Winstanley Rd.		
Livingstone Rd., Houns.	72	J4
Livingstone Rd., Sthl.	54	D7
Livingstone Rd., Th.Hth.	94	J2
Livingstone Wk. SW11	75	G3
Livonia St. W1	**11**	**G4**
Lizard St. EC1	**9**	**A4**
Lizard St. EC1	58	J3
Lizban St. SE3	69	H7
Llanelly Rd. NW2	48	C2
Llanover Rd. SE18	70	D6
Llanover Rd., Wem.	46	G3
Llanthony Rd., Mord.	93	G6
Llanvanor Rd. NW2	48	C2
Llewellyn St. SE16	**17**	**J4**
Lloyd Ave. SW16	94	E1
Lloyd Baker St. WC1	8	D4
Lloyd Baker St. WC1	58	F3
Lloyd Ct., Pnr.	36	D5
Lloyd Pk. Ave.	102	C4
Croy.		
Lloyd Rd. E6	61	C1
Lloyd Rd. E17	41	G4
Lloyd Rd., Dag.	53	F6
Lloyd Rd., Wor.Pk.	99	J3
Lloyd Sq. WC1	**8**	**E3**
Lloyd Sq. WC1	58	G3
Lloyd St. WC1	**8**	**E3**
Lloyd St. WC1	58	G3
Lloyd's Ave. EC3	**13**	**E4**
Lloyd's Ave. EC3	59	B6
Lloyds Pl. SE3	78	E2
Lloyd's Row EC1	**8**	**G4**
Lloyds Way, Beck.	95	H5
Loampit Hill SE13	78	A2
Loampit Vale SE13	78	B3
Loanda Clo. E8	59	C1
Clarissa St.		
Loats Rd. SW2	76	E6
Lobelia Clo. E6	61	B5
Sorrell Gdns.		
Locarno Rd. W3	65	C1
High St.		
Locarno Rd., Grnf.	54	J4
Lochaber Rd. SE13	78	E4
Lochaline St. W6	65	J6
Lochan Clo., Hayes	54	E4
Lochinvar St. SW12	76	B7
Lochmere Clo., Erith	71	H6
Lochnagar St. E14	60	C5
Lock Chase SE3	78	E3
Lock Rd., Rich.	82	F4
Lockesfield Pl. E14	69	B5
Lockesley Dr., Orp.	97	J6
Lockesley Sq., Surb.	91	G6
Locket Rd., Har.	37	B3
Lockfield Ave., Enf.	25	H2
Lockhart Clo. N7	49	F6
Lockhart St. E3	59	J4
Lockhurst St. E5	50	G4
Lockie Pl. SE25	95	D3
Lockington Rd. SW8	76	B1
Lockmead Rd. N15	41	D6
Lockmead Rd. SE13	78	C3
Locks La., Mitch.	93	J1
Lockside E14	59	H7
Northey St.		
Locksley Est. E14	59	J6
Locksley St. E14	59	J5
Locksmeade Rd., Rich.	82	F4
Lockwood Clo. SE26	86	G4
Lockwood Ind. Pk. N17	41	E3
Lockwood Sq. SE16	68	E3
Lockwood Way E17	41	G2
Lockwood Way, Chess.	99	A5
Lockyer Est. SE1	**17**	**C3**
Lockyer St. SE1	**17**	**C4**
Loddiges Rd. E9	50	F7
Loder St. SE15	68	F7
Lodge Ave. SW14	74	E3
Lodge Ave., Croy.	101	G3
Lodge Ave., Dag.	62	A1
Lodge Ave., Har.	37	H4
Lodge Clo. N18	32	J5
Lodge Clo., Edg.	29	J6
Lodge Clo., Islw.	73	E1
Lodge Clo., Wall.	101	A1

Lodge Ct., Wem.	46	H5
Lodge Dr. N13	32	G4
Lodge Gdns., Beck.	95	J5
Lodge Hill, Ilf.	43	B4
Lodge Hill, Well.	71	B7
Lodge La. N12	31	F5
Lodge La., Bex.	80	D6
Lodge La., Croy.	103	A6
Lodge Pl., Sutt.	100	E5
Lodge Rd. NW4	38	J4
Lodge Rd. NW8	**6**	**F4**
Lodge Rd. NW8	57	G3
Lodge Rd., Brom.	87	H7
Lodge Rd., Croy.	94	H6
Lodge Rd., Wall.	101	B5
Lodge Vill., Wdf.Grn.	34	F7
Lodgehill Pk. Clo., Har.	45	H2
Lodore Gdns. NW9	38	E5
Lodore St. E14	60	C6
Loftie St. SE16	**17**	**J4**
Loftie St. SE16	68	D2
Lofting Rd. N1	49	F7
Loftus Rd. W12	65	H1
Logan Clo., Enf.	25	G1
Logan Clo., Houns.	72	F3
Logan Ms. W8	66	D4
Logan Pl. W8	66	D4
Logan Rd. N9	33	E2
Logan Rd., Wem.	46	H2
Loggetts, The SE21	86	A3
Logs Hill, Chis.	88	B7
Logs Hill Clo., Chis.	97	B1
Lolesworth Clo. E1	13	G2
Lollard St. SE11	**20**	**D1**
Lollard St. SE11	67	G4
Loman St. SE1	**16**	**H3**
Loman St. SE1	67	H2
Lomas Clo., Croy.	103	C7
Lomas Ct. E8	50	C7
Lomas St. E1	**13**	**J1**
Lomas St. E1	59	D5
Lombard Ave., Enf.	25	F1
Lombard Ave., Ilf.	52	H1
Lombard Business Pk. SW19	93	E2
Lombard Ct. EC3	**13**	**C5**
Lombard La. EC4	**12**	**F4**
Lombard Rd. N11	32	B5
Lombard Rd. SW11	75	G2
Lombard Rd. SW19	93	E2
Lombard St. EC3	**13**	**C4**
Lombard St. EC3	59	A6
Lombard Wall SE7	69	H3
Lombardy Pl. W2	**10**	**A6**
Lomond Clo. N15	41	B5
Lomond Clo., Wem.	46	J7
Lomond Gdns., S.Croy.	102	H7
Lomond Gro. SE5	**21**	**B7**
Lomond Gro. SE5	68	A7
Lomond Ho. SE5	77	A1
Camberwell Grn.		
Loncroft Rd. SE5	**21**	**E5**
Loncroft Rd. SE5	68	B6
Londesborough Rd. N16	50	B4
London Bri. EC4	**17**	**C1**
London Bri. EC4	59	A7
London Bri. SE1	**17**	**C1**
London Bri. SE1	68	A1
London Bri. St. SE1	**17**	**C2**
London Bri. St. SE1	68	A1
London Flds. E8	50	E7
London Flds. E. E8	50	E7
Side E8		
London Flds. W. E8	50	D7
Side E8		
London Ind. Pk. E6	61	E5
London La. E8	50	E7
London La., Brom.	87	F7
London Ms. W2	**10**	**F4**
London Rd. E13	60	G2
London Rd. SE1	**16**	**G5**
London Rd. SE1	67	H3
London Rd. SE23	86	E1
London Rd. SW16	94	F1
London Rd. SW17	84	J7
London Rd., Bark.	52	G7
London Rd., Brom.	87	F7
London Rd., Croy.	95	A6
London Rd., Enf.	25	A4
London Rd., Epsom	99	G7
London Rd., Har.	46	B2
London Rd., Houns.	72	J3
London Rd., Islw.	73	C2
London Rd., Kings.T.	91	J2
London Rd., Mitch.	93	H4
London Rd. Mitch. (Mitcham Junct.)	94	A7

London Rd., Mord.	93	D5
London Rd., Rom.	44	G6
London Rd., Stan.	29	F5
London Rd., Sutt.	99	J4
London Rd., Th.Hth.	94	G5
London Rd., Twick.	73	D7
London Rd., Wall.	101	B4
London Rd., Wem.	46	H5
London Stile W4	65	A5
Wellesley Rd.		
London St. EC3	**13**	**E5**
London St. W2	**10**	**E3**
London St. W2	57	G6
London Wall EC2	**13**	**A2**
London Wall EC2	58	J5
Long Acre WC2	**12**	**A5**
Long Acre WC2	58	E7
Long Ct. WC2	**11**	**J6**
Long Deacon Rd. E4	34	E1
Long Dr. W3	56	E6
Long Dr., Grnf.	54	H1
Long Dr., Ruis.	45	D4
Long Elmes, Har.	36	H1
Long Fld. NW9	30	E7
Long Grn., Chig.	35	H4
Long Hedges, Houns.	72	G1
Great W. Rd.		
Long La. EC1	**12**	**H1**
Long La. EC1	58	H5
Long La. N2	39	F2
Long La. N3	31	E7
Long La. SE1	**17**	**B4**
Long La. SE1	68	A2
Long La., Bexh.	71	D7
Long La., Croy.	95	E6
Long Leys E4	34	B6
Long Mark Rd. E16	61	A5
Fulmer Rd.		
Long Mead NW9	38	F1
Long Meadow NW5	49	D5
Torriano Ave.		
Long Meadow Clo., W.Wick.	96	C7
Long Pond Rd. SE3	78	E1
Long Reach Ct., Bark.	61	G2
Long Reach Rd., Bark.	61	J4
Long Rd. SW4	76	B4
Long St. E2	**9**	**F3**
Long St. E2	59	C3
Long Wk. SE1	**17**	**E5**
Long Wk. SE18	70	E6
Long Wk. SW13	74	E2
The Ter.		
Long Wk., N.Mal.	92	C3
Long Yd. WC1	**8**	**C6**
Long Yd. WC1	58	F4
Longacre Pl., Cars.	101	A6
Beddington Gdns.		
Longacre Rd. E17	42	D1
Longbeach Rd. SW11	75	J3
Longberrys NW2	48	C3
Longboat Row, Sthl.	54	F6
Longbridge Rd., Bark.	52	G6
Longbridge Rd., Dag.	53	A4
Longbridge Way SE13	78	C5
Longcliffe Path, Wat.	28	A3
Gosforth La.		
Longcroft SE9	88	C3
Longcroft Ri., Loug.	27	D5
Longcroft Rd., Edg.	29	G7
Longdon Wd. Ave. Kes.	104	B3
Longdown Rd. SE6	87	A4
Longfellow Rd. E17	41	J6
Longfellow Rd., Wor.Pk.	99	G1
Longfellow Way SE1	21	G2
Longfield, Brom.	96	F1
Longfield, Loug.	26	J5
Longfield Ave. E17	41	H4
Longfield Ave. NW7	30	G7
Longfield Ave. W5	55	F7
Longfield Ave., Wall.	101	A1
Longfield Ave., Wem.	46	H1
Longfield Cres. SE26	86	F3
Longfield Dr. SW14	74	B5
Longfield Dr., Mitch.	84	H7
Longfield Est. SE1	**21**	**G2**
Longfield Est. SE1	68	C4
Longfield Rd. W5	55	F6
Longfield St. SW18	75	D7
Longfield Wk. W5	55	F6

Longford Ave., Sthl.	54	G7
Longford Clo., Hmptn.	81	G4
Longford Ct. E5	50	G4
Pedro St.		
Longford Ct. NW4	39	A4
Longford Ct., Epsom	99	C4
Longford Gdns., Hayes	54	D7
Longford Gdns., Sutt.	100	F3
Longford Rd., Twick.	81	G1
Longford St. NW1	**7**	**E5**
Longford St. NW1	58	B4
Longford Wk. SW2	76	G7
Papworth Way		
Longhayes Ave., Rom.	44	D4
Longheath Gdns., Croy.	95	F5
Longhedge Ho. SE26	86	C4
Longhedge St. SW11	76	A2
Longhill Rd. SE6	87	D2
Longhook Gdns., Nthlt.	54	A2
Longhope Clo. SE15	**21**	**F6**
Longhope Clo. SE15	68	B6
Longhurst Rd. SE13	78	D5
Longhurst Rd., Croy.	95	E6
Longland Ct. SE1	**21**	**H3**
Longland Dr. N20	31	E3
Longlands Ct. W11	57	C7
Portobello Rd.		
Longlands Ct., Mitch.	94	A1
Summerhill Way		
Longlands Pk. Cres., Sid.	88	H3
Longlands Rd., Sid.	88	H3
Longleat Rd., Enf.	25	B5
Longleigh La. SE2	71	C6
Longleigh La., Bexh.	71	C6
Longlents Ho. NW10	56	D1
Shrewsbury Cres.		
Longley Ave., Wem.	55	J1
Longley Rd. SW17	84	H6
Longley Rd., Croy.	94	H7
Longley Rd., Har.	36	J5
Longley St. SE1	**21**	**H1**
Longley St. SE1	68	D4
Longley Way NW2	47	J3
Longmead, Chis.	97	D2
Longmead Dr., Sid.	89	D2
Longmead Rd. SW17	84	J5
Longmead Rd., T.Ditt.	91	B7
Longmeadow Rd., Sid.	88	H1
Longmoor Pt. SW15	83	H1
Norley Vale		
Longmoore St. SW1	**19**	**F2**
Longmoore St. SW1	67	C4
Longmore Ave., Barn.	23	F6
Longnor Rd. E1	59	G3
Longridge La., Sthl.	54	H6
Longridge Rd. SW5	66	D4
Longs Ct., Rich.	73	J4
Crown Ter.		
Longshaw Rd. E4	34	D3
Longshore SE8	68	J4
Longstaff Cres. SW18	75	D6
Longstaff Rd. SW18	75	D6
Longstone Ave. NW10	47	F7
Longstone Rd. SW17	85	B5
Longthornton Rd. SW16	94	C2
Longton Ave. SE26	86	D4
Longton Gro. SE26	86	E4
Longville Rd. SE11	**20**	**H1**
Longwood Dr. SW15	74	G6
Longwood Gdns., Ilf.	43	C4
Longworth Clo. SE28	62	D6
Loning, The NW9	38	E4
Lonsdale Ave. E6	61	A3
Lonsdale Ave., Rom.	44	H5
Lonsdale Ave., Wem.	46	H5
Lonsdale Clo. E6	61	B4
Lonsdale Ave.		
Lonsdale Clo. SE9	88	A3
Lonsdale Clo., Pnr.	36	E1
Uxbridge Rd.		
Lonsdale Cres., Ilf.	43	E6
Lonsdale Dr., Enf.	24	D4
Lonsdale Gdns., Th.Hth.	94	F4

Lonsdale Ms., Rich. 74 A1
Lonsdale Pl. N1 49 G7
Barnsbury St.
Lonsdale Rd. E11 42 F7
Lonsdale Rd. NW6 57 C1
Lonsdale Rd. SE25 95 E4
Lonsdale Rd. SW13 91 F1
Lonsdale Rd. W4 65 F4
Lonsdale Rd. W11 57 C6
Lonsdale Rd., Bexh. 80 F2
Lonsdale Rd., Sthl. 63 D3
Lonsdale Sq. N1 58 G1
Loobert Rd. N15 41 B3
Looe Gdns., Ilf. 43 E3
Loop Rd., Chis. 88 F6
Lopen Rd. N18 33 B4
Loraine Clo., Enf. 25 F5
Loraine Rd. N7 49 F4
Loraine Rd. W4 65 B6
Lord Ave., Ilf. 43 C4
Lord Chancellor 92 C1
Wk., Kings.T.
Lord Gdns., Ilf. 43 B4
Lord Hills Bri. W2 10 B2
Lord Hills Rd. W2 10 B1
Lord Hills Rd. W2 57 E5
Lord Holland La. 76 G1
SW9
Myatts Flds. S.
Lord Napier Pl. W6 65 G5
Upper Mall
Lord N. St. SW1 16 A6
Lord N. St. SW1 67 E3
Lord Roberts Ms. 66 E7
SW6
Moore Pk. Rd.
Lord Roberts Ter. 70 D5
SE18
Lord St. E16 70 B1
Lord Warwick St. 70 C3
SE18
Lorden Wk. E2 9 H4
Lord's Clo. SE21 85 J2
Lords Clo., Felt. 81 E2
Lord's Vw. NW8 6 F4
Lordship Gro. N16 50 A2
Lordship La. N17 40 J1
Lordship La. N22 40 G2
Lordship La. SE22 77 C6
Lordship La. Est. 86 D1
SE22
Lordship Pk. N16 49 J2
Lordship Pk. Ms. 49 J2
N16
Allerton Rd.
Lordship Pl. SW3 18 G6
Lordship Rd. N16 50 A1
Lordship Rd., 45 E7
Nthlt.
Lordship Ter. N16 50 A2
Lordsmead Rd. N17 41 B1
Lorenzo St. WC1 8 C2
Lorenzo St. WC1 58 F3
Loretto Gdns., Har. 37 H4
Lorian Clo. N12 31 E4
Loring Rd. N20 31 H2
Loring Rd., Islw. 73 C2
Loris Rd. W6 65 J3
Lorn Rd. SW9 76 F2
Lorne Ave., Croy. 95 G7
Lorne Clo. NW8 6 H4
Lorne Gdns. E11 42 J4
Lorne Gdns. W11 66 A2
Lorne Gdns., Croy. 95 G7
Lorne Rd. E7 51 H4
Lorne Rd. E17 42 A5
Lorne Rd. N4 49 F1
Lorne Rd., Har. 37 C2
Lorne Rd., Rich. 73 J5
Albert Rd.
Lorraine Rd., Har. 29 B7
Lorrimore Rd. SE17 20 H5
Lorrimore Rd. SE17 67 H6
Lorrimore Sq. SE17 20 H5
Lorrimore Sq. SE17 67 H6
Losberne Way SE16 21 J4
Loseberry Rd., 98 A5
Esher
Lothair Rd. W5 64 G2
Lothair Rd. N. N4 40 H6
Lothair Rd. S. N4 40 H6
Lothbury EC2 13 B3
Lothbury EC2 59 A6
Lothian Ave., Hayes 54 B5
Lothian Clo., Wem. 46 D4
Lothian Rd. SW9 76 H1
Lothrop St. W10 57 B3
Lots Rd. SW10 66 F7
Loubet St. SW17 84 J6
Loudoun Ave., Ilf. 54 D3
Loudoun Rd. NW8 57 F1
Loudwater Clo., 90 A4
Sun.

Loudwater Rd., Sun. 90 A4
Lough Rd. N7 49 F5
Loughborough Est. 76 H2
SW9
Loughborough Rd.
Loughborough Pk. 76 H4
SW9
Loughborough Rd. 76 G2
SW9
Loughborough St. 20 D4
SE11
Loughborough St. 67 F5
SE11
Loughton Way, 35 A1
Buck.H.
Louisa Gdns. E1 59 G4
Louisa St.
Louisa Ho. SW15 74 F4
Arabella Dr.
Louisa St. E1 59 G4
Louise Rd. E15 51 E6
Louisville Rd. SW17 85 A3
Louvaine Rd. SW11 75 G4
Lovage App. E6 61 B5
Lovat Clo. NW2 47 F3
Lovat La. EC3 13 D6
Lovat Wk., Houns. 63 E7
Cranford La.
Lovatt Clo., Edg. 30 B6
Love La. EC2 13 A3
Love La. EC2 58 J6
Love La. N17 33 C7
Love La. SE18 70 E4
Love La. SE25 95 E3
Love La., Bex. 80 F6
Love La., Mitch. 93 H3
Love La., Mord. 93 D7
Love La., Pnr. 36 E3
Love La., Surb. 98 F2
Love La., Sutt. 100 B6
Love La., Wdf.Grn. 35 C6
Love Wk. SE5 77 A2
Loveday Rd. W13 64 E1
Lovegrove St. SE1 21 J5
Lovegrove St. SE1 68 D5
Lovegrove Wk. E14 69 C1
Lovekyn Clo., 91 J2
Kings.T.
Queen Elizabeth Rd.
Lovel Ave., Well. 80 A2
Lovelace Ave., 97 D6
Brom.
Lovelace Gdns., 53 A4
Bark.
Lovelace Gdns., 91 G7
Surb.
Lovelace Grn. SE9 79 C3
Lovelace Rd. SE21 85 J2
Lovelace Rd., Barn. 23 H7
Lovelace Rd., Surb. 91 F7
Lovelinch Clo. SE15 68 F6
Lovell Ho. E8 59 D1
Lovell Pl. SE16 68 H3
Ropemaker Rd.
Lovell Rd., Rich. 82 F3
Lovell Rd., Sthl. 54 H6
Loveridge Ms. NW6 48 C6
Loveridge Rd.
Loveridge Rd. NW6 48 C6
Lovers Wk. N3 31 D7
Lovers Wk. NW7 31 D7
Lovers Wk. SE10 69 E7
Lover's Wk. W1 15 B1
Lover's Wk. W1 67 A1
Lovett Dr., Cars. 93 F7
Lovett Way NW10 47 C5
Lovibonds Ave., 104 E3
Orp.
Low Cross Wd. La. 86 C3
SE21
Low Hall Clo. E4 26 A7
Low Hall La. E17 41 H6
Lowbrook Rd., Ilf. 54 E6
Lowden Rd. N9 33 E1
Lowden Rd. SE24 91 H5
Lowden Rd., Sthl. 54 E7
Lowe Ave. E16 60 G5
Charford Rd.
Lowell St. E14 59 H6
Lwr. Addiscombe 102 B1
Rd., Croy.
Lwr. Addison Gdns. 66 B2
W14
Lwr. Alderton Hall 27 D5
La., Loug.
Lwr. Belgrave St. 15 D6
SW1
Lwr. Belgrave St. 67 B3
SW1
Lwr. Boston Rd. W7 64 B1
Lwr. Broad St., 62 G1
Dag.
Lwr. Camden, Chis. 88 C7

Lwr. Clapton Rd. E5 50 F5
Lwr. Clarendon Wk. 57 B6
W11
Lancaster Rd.
Lwr. Common S. 74 H3
SW15
Lwr. Coombe St. 101 J4
Croy.
Lwr. Downs Rd. 93 A1
SW20
Lwr. Drayton Pl., 101 H2
Croy.
Drayton Rd.
Lwr. George St., 73 G5
Rich.
George St.
Lwr. Gravel Rd., 104 B1
Brom.
Lwr. Grn. W., Mitch. 93 H3
Lwr. Grosvenor Pl. 15 D5
SW1
Lwr. Grosvenor Pl. 67 B3
SW1
Lwr. Gro. Rd., 73 J6
Rich.
Lwr. Hall La. E4 33 H5
Lwr. Ham Rd., 82 G6
Kings.T.
Lwr. Hampton Rd., 90 C3
Sun.
Lwr. James St. W1 11 G5
Lwr. John St. W1 11 G5
Lwr. Kenwood Ave., 24 D5
Enf.
Lwr. Lea Crossing 60 E7
E14
Lwr. Maidstone Rd. 32 C6
N11
Telford Rd.
Lwr. Mall W6 65 H5
Lwr. Mardyke Ave., 62 J2
Rain.
Lwr. Marsh SE1 16 E4
Lwr. Marsh SE1 67 F2
Lwr. Marsh La., 91 J4
Kings.T.
Lwr. Merton Ri. NW3 48 H7
Lwr. Morden La., 93 A6
Mord.
Lwr. Mortlake Rd., 73 H4
Rich.
Lwr. Pk. Rd. N11 32 C5
Lwr. Pk. Rd., Belv. 71 G3
Lwr. Pk. Rd., Loug. 27 A5
Lwr. Queens Rd., 35 A2
Buck.H.
Lwr. Richmond Rd. 74 B3
SW14
Lwr. Richmond Rd. 74 H3
SW15
Lwr. Richmond Rd., 74 A3
Rich.
Lwr. Rd. SE8 68 G4
Lwr. Rd. SE16 68 F3
Lwr. Rd., Belv. 71 H3
Lwr. Rd., Har. 46 A1
Lwr. Rd., Loug. 27 D1
Lwr. Rd., Sutt. 100 F4
Lwr. Robert St. WC2 12 B6
Lwr. Sloane St. SW1 19 B2
Lwr. Sloane St. SW1 67 A4
Lwr. Sq., Islw. 73 E3
Lwr. Strand NW9 38 F2
Lwr. Sunbury Rd., 90 F2
Hmptn.
Lwr. Sydenham Ind. 86 J5
Est. SE26
Rollesby Way
Lwr. Tail, Wat. 28 E3
Lwr. Talbot Wk. W11 57 B6
Lancaster Rd.
Lwr. Teddington 82 G7
Rd., Kings.T.
Lwr. Ter. NW3 48 F3
Lwr. Thames St. EC3 13 C6
Lwr. Thames St. EC3 59 A7
Lwr. Wd. Rd., Esher 98 D6
Lowestoft Clo. E5 50 F2
Theydon Rd.
Loweswater Clo., 46 G2
Wem.
Lowfield Rd. NW6 48 D7
Lowfield Rd. W3 56 C6
Lowick Rd., Har. 37 B4
Lowlands Gdns., 44 H6
Rom.
Lowlands Rd., Har. 36 B6
Lowlands Rd., Pnr. 36 C6
Lowman Rd. N7 49 F4
Lowndes Clo. SW1 15 C6
Lowndes Clo. SW1 67 A3
Lowndes Pl. SW1 15 B6
Lowndes Pl. SW1 67 A3
Lowndes Sq. SW1 15 A4

Lowndes Sq. SW1 66 J2
Lowndes St. SW1 15 A5
Lowndes St. SW1 66 J3
Lowood Ct. SE19 86 C5
Lowood St. E1 59 E7
Dellow St.
Lowry Cres. Mitch. 93 H2
Lowshoe La., Rom. 44 B1
Lowth Rd. SE5 76 J2
Lowther Dr. Enf. 24 E4
Lowther Gdns. SW7 14 E4
Lowther Hill SE23 77 H7
Lowther Rd. E17 41 H2
Lowther Rd. N7 49 G5
Mackenzie Rd.
Lowther Rd. SW13 74 F1
Lowther Rd., 91 J1
Kings.T.
Lowther Rd., Stan. 37 J3
Loxford Ave. E6 61 A2
Loxford Gdns., Ilf. 52 F5
Loxford Rd., Bark. 52 E6
Loxham Rd. E4 34 A7
Loxham St. WC1 8 B4
Loxley Clo. SE26 86 G5
Loxley Rd. SW18 84 G1
Loxley Rd., Hmptn. 81 F4
Loxton Rd. SE23 86 G1
Loxwood Rd. N17 41 B3
Lubbock Rd., Chis. 88 C7
Lubbock St. SE14 68 F7
Lucan Pl. SW3 18 G2
Lucan Pl. SW3 66 H4
Lucan Rd., Barn. 23 B3
Lucas Ave. E13 60 H1
Lucas Ave., Har. 45 G2
Lucas Ct., Har. 45 G1
Lucas Rd. SE20 86 F6
Lucas Sq. NW11 39 D6
Hampstead Way
Lucas St. SE8 78 A1
Lucerne Clo. N13 32 E3
Lucerne Ct., Erith 71 E3
Middle Way
Lucerne Gro. E17 42 D4
Lucerne Ms. W8 66 D1
Kensington Mall
Lucerne Rd. N5 49 H4
Lucerne Rd., Orp. 104 J1
Lucerne Rd., 94 H5
Th.Hth.
Lucey Rd. SE16 17 H6
Lucey Rd. SE16 68 D3
Lucey Way SE16 17 J6
Lucien Rd. SW17 85 A4
Lucien Rd. SW19 84 E2
Lucknow St. SE18 70 H7
Lucorn Clo. SE12 78 F6
Luctons Ave., 34 J1
Buck.H.
Lucy Cres. W3 56 C5
Lucy Gdns., Dag. 53 E3
Grafton Rd.
Luddesdon Rd., 71 G6
Erith
Ludford Clo. NW9 38 E2
Ludford Clo., Croy. 101 H4
Warrington Rd.
Ludgate Bdy. EC4 12 G4
Ludgate Bdy. EC4 58 H6
Ludgate Circ. EC4 12 G4
Ludgate Ct. EC4 12 G4
Ludgate Hill EC4 12 G4
Ludgate Hill EC4 58 H6
Ludgate Sq. EC4 12 H4
Ludham Clo. SE28 62 C6
Rollesby Way
Ludlow Clo., Brom. 96 G3
Ludlow Clo., Har. 45 F4
Ludlow Mead, Wat. 28 B3
Ludlow Rd. W5 55 F4
Ludlow Rd., Felt. 81 A4
Ludlow St. EC1 8 J5
Ludlow Way N2 39 F4
Ludovick Ms. SW15 74 E4
Ludwick Ms. SE14 68 H7
Luffield Rd. SE2 71 B3
Luffman Rd. SE12 87 H3
Lugard Rd. SE15 77 E2
Lugg App. E12 52 D3
Romford Rd.
Luke Ho. E1 59 E6
Luke St. EC2 9 D5
Luke St. EC2 59 B4
Lukin Cres. E4 34 D3
Lukin St. E1 59 F6
Lullingstone Clo., 89 B7
Orp.
Lullingstone Cres.
Lullingstone Cres., 89 A7
Orp.
Lullingstone Rd., 71 F6
Belv.

Name	Pg	Ref
Lullington Garth N12	31	C5
Lullington Garth, Borwd.	22	B5
Lullington Garth, Brom.	87	E7
Lullington Rd. SE20	86	D7
Lullington Rd., Dag.	53	E7
Lulot Gdns. N19	49	B2
Dartmouth Pk. Hill		
Lulworth SE17	21	B3
Lulworth Ave., Houns.	63	H7
Lulworth Ave., Wem.	37	F7
Lulworth Clo., Har.	45	F3
Lulworth Cres., Mitch.	93	H2
Lulworth Dr., Pnr.	36	D7
Lulworth Gdns., Har.	45	E2
Lulworth Rd. SE9	88	B2
Lulworth Rd. SE15	77	E2
Lulworth Rd., Well.	79	J2
Lulworth Waye, Hayes	54	B6
Lumley Clo., Belv.	71	G6
Lumley Ct. WC2	12	B6
Lumley Gdns., Sutt.	100	B5
Lumley Rd., Sutt.	100	B6
Lumley St. W1	11	C4
Lumley St. W1	58	A6
Luna Rd., Th.Hth.	94	J3
Lunar Ho., Croy.	101	J1
Lundin Wk., Wat.	28	D4
Woodhall La.		
Lundy Wk. N1	49	J6
Marquess Est.		
Lunham Rd. SE19	86	B6
Lupin Clo. SW2	85	H2
Palace Rd.		
Lupin Clo., Croy.	102	G1
Primrose La.		
Lupton Clo. SE12	87	H4
Lupton St. NW5	49	C4
Lupus St. SW1	19	E4
Lupus St. SW1	67	B5
Luralda Gdns. E14	69	C5
Saunders Ness Rd.		
Lurgan Ave. W6	66	A6
Lurline Gdns. SW11	76	A1
Luscombe Ct., Brom.	96	E2
Luscombe Way SW8	20	A7
Luscombe Way SW8	67	E7
Lushes Rd., Loug.	27	E5
Lushington Rd. NW10	56	H2
Wayland Ave.		
Lushington Rd. SE6	87	B5
Lushington Ter. E8	50	D5
Luther Rd., Tedd.	82	C5
Luton Pl. SE10	69	C7
Luton Rd. E17	41	J3
Luton Rd., Sid.	89	C3
Luton St. NW8	6	F6
Luton St. NW8	57	G4
Lutton Ter. NW3	48	G3
Flask Wk.		
Luttrell Ave. SW15	74	H5
Lutwyche Rd. SE6	86	J2
Luxborough La., Chig.	35	B3
Luxborough St. W1	7	B6
Luxborough St. W1	58	A5
Luxemburg Gdns. W6	66	A4
Luxfield Rd. SE9	88	B1
Luxford St. SE16	68	G4
Luxmore Gdns. SE4	77	J1
Luxmore St.		
Luxmore St. SE4	77	J1
Luxor St. SE5	76	J3
Lyal Rd. E3	59	H2
Lyall Ave. SE21	86	B3
Lyall Ms. SW1	15	B6
Lyall Ms. W. SW1	15	B6
Lyall St. SW1	15	B6
Lyall St. SW1	67	A3
Lycett Pl. W12	65	G2
Becklow Rd.		
Lyconby Gdns., Croy.	95	H7
Lydd Clo., Sid.	88	H3
Lydd Rd., Bexh.	71	F7
Lydden Ct. SE9	79	H6
Lydden Gro. SW18	75	E7
Lydden Rd. SW18	75	E7
Lydeard Rd. E6	52	C7
Lydford Rd. N15	41	A5
Lydford Rd. NW2	47	J6
Lydford Rd. W9	57	C4
Lydhurst Ave. SW2	85	F2
Lydney Clo. SE15	21	E7
Lydney Clo. SW19	84	B2
Princes Way		
Lydon Rd. SW4	76	C3
Lydstep Rd., Chis.	88	D4
Lyford Rd. SW18	75	G7
Lygon Pl. SW1	15	D6
Lyham Clo. SW2	76	E6
Lyham Rd. SW2	76	E5
Lyme Fm. Rd. SE12	78	G4
Lyme Rd., Well.	80	B1
Lyme St. NW1	49	C7
Lyme Ter. NW1	49	C7
Royal College St.		
Lymer Ave. SE19	86	C5
Lymescote Gdns., Sutt.	100	D2
Lyminge Clo., Sid.	88	J4
Lyminge Gdns. SW18	84	H1
Lymington Ave. N22	40	G2
Lymington Clo. SW16	94	D2
Lymington Gdns., Epsom	99	F5
Lymington Rd. NW6	48	E6
Lymington Rd., Dag.	53	D1
Lympstone Gdns. SE15	21	J7
Lympstone Gdns. SE15	68	D7
Lynbridge Gdns. N13	32	H4
Lynbrook Clo. SE15	21	E7
Lynch Wk. SE8	68	J6
Prince St.		
Lynchen Clo., Houns.	72	A1
The Ave.		
Lyncott Cres. SW4	76	B4
Lyncroft Ave., Pnr.	36	E5
Lyncroft Gdns. NW6	48	D5
Lyncroft Gdns. W13	64	F2
Lyncroft Gdns., Houns.	72	J5
Lyndale NW2	48	C4
Lyndale Ave. NW2	48	C3
Lyndale Clo. SE3	69	F6
Lyndhurst Ave. N12	31	J6
Lyndhurst Ave. NW7	30	E6
Lyndhurst Ave. SW16	94	D2
Lyndhurst Ave., Pnr.	36	B1
Lyndhurst Ave., Sthl.	90	A3
Lyndhurst Ave., Sun.	99	B1
Lyndhurst Ave., Surb.	81	F1
Lyndhurst Ave., Twick.	63	H1
Lyndhurst Clo. NW10	47	D3
Lyndhurst Clo., Bexh.	80	H3
Lyndhurst Clo., Croy.	102	C3
Lyndhurst Clo., Orp.	104	E4
Lyndhurst Dr. E10	42	C7
Lyndhurst Dr., N.Mal.	92	E6
Lyndhurst Gdns. N3	39	B1
Lyndhurst Gdns. NW3	48	G5
Lyndhurst Gdns., Bark.	52	H6
Lyndhurst Gdns., Enf.	25	B4
Lyndhurst Gdns., Ilf.	43	G6
Lyndhurst Gdns., Pnr.	36	B1
Lyndhurst Gro. SE15	77	B2
Lyndhurst Ri., Chig.	35	D4
Lyndhurst Rd. E4	34	C7
Lyndhurst Rd. N18	33	D4
Lyndhurst Rd. N22	32	F6
Lyndhurst Rd. NW3	48	G5
Lyndhurst Rd., Bexh.	80	H3
Lyndhurst Rd., Grnf.	54	H4
Lyndhurst Rd., Th.Hth.	94	G4
Lyndhurst Sq. SE15	77	C1
Lyndhurst Ter. NW3	48	G5
Lyndhurst Way SE15	77	C1
Lyndhurst Way, Sutt.	100	D7
Lyndon Ave., Pnr.	28	E6
Lyndon Ave., Sid.	79	J5
Lyndon Ave., Wall.	101	A3
Lyndon Rd., Belv.	71	G4
Lyne Cres. E17	41	J1
Lyneham Wk. E5	50	H5
Ashenden Rd.		
Lynett Rd., Dag.	53	D2
Lynette Ave. SW4	76	B6
Lynford Clo., Edg.	38	C1
Lynford Gdns., Edg.	30	B3
Lynford Gdns., Ilf.	52	J2
Lynmere Rd., Well.	80	B2
Lynmouth Ave., Enf.	25	C6
Lynmouth Ave., Mord.	93	A7
Lynmouth Dr., Ruis.	45	B2
Lynmouth Gdns., Grnf.	55	E1
Lynmouth Gdns., Houns.	72	D1
Lynmouth Rd. E17	41	H6
Lynmouth Rd. N2	39	J4
Lynmouth Rd. N16	50	C1
Lynmouth Rd., Grnf.	55	E1
Lynn Clo., Har.	37	A2
Lynn Ms. E11	51	E2
Lynn Rd.		
Lynn Rd. E11	51	E2
Lynn Rd. SW12	76	B7
Lynn Rd., Ilf.	43	G7
Lynn St., Enf.	25	A1
Lynne Clo., Orp.	104	J6
Lynne Way NW10	47	E6
Lynne Way, Nthlt.	54	D2
Lynsted Clo., Bexh.	80	H5
Lynsted Clo., Brom.	96	J2
Lynsted Ct., Beck.	95	H2
Churchfields Rd.		
Lynsted Gdns. SE9	79	A3
Lynton Ave. N12	31	G4
Lynton Ave. NW9	38	F4
Lynton Ave. W13	55	D6
Lynton Ave., Rom.	44	G1
Lynton Clo., Chess.	98	H4
Lynton Clo., Islw.	73	C4
Lynton Cres., Ilf.	43	E6
Lynton Est. SE1	21	H2
Lynton Gdns. N11	32	D6
Lynton Gdns., Enf.	25	B7
Lynton Mead N20	31	D3
Lynton Rd. E4	34	B5
Lynton Rd. N8	40	D5
Lynton Rd. NW6	57	C1
Lynton Rd. SE1	21	G2
Lynton Rd. SE1	68	C4
Lynton Rd. W3	56	A7
Lynton Rd., Croy.	94	G6
Lynton Rd., Har.	45	E2
Lynton Rd., N.Mal.	92	D5
Lynwood Clo. E18	42	J1
Lynwood Clo., Har.	45	E3
Lynwood Dr., Wor.Pk.	99	G2
Lynwood Gdns., Croy.	101	F4
Lynwood Gdns., Sthl.	54	F5
Lynwood Gro. N21	32	G1
Lynwood Gro., Orp.	97	H7
Lynwood Rd. SW17	84	J3
Lynwood Rd. W5	55	H4
Lynwood Rd., T.Ditt.	98	C2
Lyon Ind. Est., Bark.	61	H2
Lyon Meade, Stan.	37	F1
Lyon Pk. Ave., Wem.	46	H6
Lyon Rd. SW19	93	F1
Lyon Rd., Har.	37	C6
Lyon St. N1	49	F7
Caledonian Rd.		
Lyon Way, Grnf.	55	B1
Lyons Pl. NW8	6	E6
Lyons Pl. NW8	57	G4
Lyons Wk. W14	66	B4
Lyonsdown Ave., Barn.	23	F6
Lyonsdown Rd., Barn.	23	E6
Lyoth Rd., Orp.	104	F2
Lyric Dr., Grnf.	54	H4
Lyric Rd. SW13	74	F1
Lysander Gro. N19	49	D1
Lysander Rd., Croy.	101	F6
Lysander Way, Orp.	104	F3
Lysia St. SW6	66	A7
Lysias Rd. SW12	76	B6
Lysons Wk. SW15	74	G5
Swinburne Rd.		
Lytchet Rd., Brom.	87	H7
Lytchet Way, Enf.	25	F1
Lytchgate Clo., S.Croy.	102	B7
Lyte St. E2	59	F2
Bishops Way		
Lytham Ave., Wat.	28	D5
Lytham Gro. W5	55	J3
Lytham St. SE17	21	B4
Lytham St. SE17	68	A5
Lyttelton Clo. NW3	48	H7
Hawtrey Rd.		
Lyttelton Rd. E10	51	B3
Lyttelton Rd. N8	40	G3
Lytton Ave. N13	32	G2
Lytton Clo. N2	39	F6
Lytton Clo., Loug.	27	G3
Lytton Clo., Nthlt.	45	F7
Lytton Gdns., Wall.	101	D4
Lytton Gro. SW15	75	A3
Lytton Rd. E11	42	E7
Lytton Rd., Barn.	23	F4
Lytton Rd., Pnr.	28	E7
Lytton Strachey Path SE28	62	B7
Titmuss Ave.		
Lyveden Rd. SE3	69	H7
Lyveden Rd. SW17	84	H6

M

Name	Pg	Ref
Maberley Cres. SE19	86	D7
Maberley Rd. SE19	95	C1
Maberley Rd., Beck.	95	G3
Mabledon Pl. WC1	7	J4
Mabledon Pl. WC1	58	D3
Mablethorpe Rd. SW6	66	B7
Mabley St. E9	50	H5
Macaret Clo. N20	23	F7
Macarthur Ter. SE7	70	A6
Macaulay Ave., Esher	98	B2
Macaulay Ct. SW4	76	B3
Macaulay Rd. E6	61	A2
Macaulay Rd. SW4	76	B3
Macaulay Sq. SW4	76	B4
Macaulay Way SE28	62	B7
Booth Clo.		
Macauley Ms. SE13	78	C1
Macbean St. SE18	70	E3
Macbeth St. W6	65	H5
Macclesfield Bri. NW1	6	H1
Macclesfield Bri. NW1	57	H2
Macclesfield Rd. EC1	8	J3
Macclesfield Rd. EC1	58	J3
Macclesfield Rd. SE25	95	E5
Macclesfield St. W1	11	J5
Macdonald Ave., Dag.	53	H3
Macdonald Rd. E7	51	G4
Macdonald Rd. E17	42	C2
Macdonald Rd. N11	31	J5
Macdonald Rd. N19	49	C2
Macduff Rd. SW11	76	A1
Mace Clo. E1	68	E1
Kennet St		
Mace St. E2	59	G2
MacFarlane La., Islw.	64	C6
Macfarlane Rd. W12	65	J1
Macgregor Rd. E16	60	J5
Machell Rd. SE15	77	F3
Mackay Rd. SW4	76	B3
Mackennal St. NW8	6	H1
Mackennal St. NW8	57	H2
Mackenzie Rd. N7	49	F6
Mackenzie Rd., Beck.	95	F2
Mackenzie Wk. E14	69	A1
Cabot Sq.		
Mackeson Rd. NW3	48	J4
Mackie Rd. SW2	76	G7
Mackintosh La. E9	50	G6
High St.		
Macklin St. WC2	12	B3
Macklin St. WC2	58	E6
Mackrow Wk. E14	60	C7
Poplar High St.		
Macks Rd. SE16	21	J1
Macks Rd. SE16	68	D4
Mackworth St. NW1	7	F3
Mackworth St. NW1	58	C3
Maclaren Ms. SW15	74	J4
Clarendon Dr.		
Maclean Rd. SE23	77	H6
Macleod St. SE17	21	A4
Macleod St. SE17	68	A6
Maclise Rd. W14	66	B3
Macoma Rd. SE18	70	G6
Macoma Ter. SE18	70	G6
Maconochies Rd. E14	69	B5
Macquarie Way E14	69	B4

Macready Pl. N7 49 E4
Warlters Rd.
Macroom Rd. W9 57 C3
Mada Rd., Orp. 104 E2
Maddams St. E3 60 B4
Maddison Clo., Tedd. 82 C6
Maddock Way SE17 20 H6
Maddocks Clo., Sid. 89 D5
Maddox St. W1 11 F5
Maddox St. W1 58 B7
Madeira Ave., Brom. 87 E7
Madeira Gro., 34 J6
Wdf.Grn.
Madeira Rd. E11 51 D1
Madeira Rd. N13 32 H4
Madeira Rd. SW16 85 E5
Madeira Rd., Mitch. 93 J4
Madeley Rd. W5 55 H6
Madeline Rd. SE20 86 D7
Madison Cres., 71 C7
Bexh.
Madison Gdns., 71 C7
Bexh.
Madison Gdns., 96 F3
Brom.
Madras Pl. N7 49 G6
Madras Rd., Ilf. 52 E4
Madrid Rd. SW13 74 G1
Madrigal La. SE5 67 H7
Madron St. SE17 21 E3
Madron St. SE17 68 B5
Mafeking Ave. E6 61 B2
Mafeking Ave., 64 H6
Brent.
Mafeking Ave., Ilf. 43 G7
Mafeking Rd. E16 60 F4
Mafeking Rd. N17 41 D2
Mafeking Rd., Enf. 25 C3
Magdala Ave. N19 49 B2
Magdala Rd., Islw. 73 D3
Magdala Rd., 102 A7
S.Croy.
Napier Rd.
Magdalen Pas. E1 13 G5
Magdalen Rd. SW18 84 F1
Magdalen St. SE1 17 D2
Magdalen St. SE1 68 B1
Magdalene Clo. SE15 77 E2
Heaton Rd.
Magdalene Gdns. E6 61 D4
Magee St. SE11 20 E5
Magee St. SE11 67 G6
Maggie Blake's 17 F2
Cause SE1
Magnin Clo. E8 59 D1
Wilde Clo.
Magnolia Clo., 83 B6
Kings.T.
Magnolia Ct., Har. 37 J7
Magnolia Ct., Rich. 74 B1
West Hall Rd.
Magnolia Pl. SW4 76 E5
Magnolia Pl. W5 55 H5
Montpelier Rd.
Magnolia Rd. W4 65 B6
Magnolia Way, 99 C5
Epsom
Magnolia St. EC4 12 F4
Magpie All. EC4 12 F4
Magpie Clo. NW9 38 E2
Eagle Dr.
Magpie Clo., Enf. 25 D1
Magpie Hall Clo., 97 B6
Brom.
Magpie Hall La., 97 B7
Brom.
Magpie Hall Rd. 29 B2
(Bushey), Wat.
Magri Wk. E1 59 F5
Ashfield St.
Maguire Dr., Rich. 82 F4
Maguire St. SE1 17 G3
Maguire St. SE1 68 C2
Mahatma Gandhi 46 J5
Ho., Wem.
Mahlon Ave., Ruis. 45 B5
Mahogany Clo. SE16 68 H1
Mahon Clo., Enf. 25 C1
Maida Ave. E4 26 B7
Maida Ave. W2 10 D1
Maida Ave. W2 57 F5
Maida Rd., Belv. 71 G3
Maida Vale W9 6 A1
Maida Vale W9 57 E2
Maida Way E4 26 B7
Maiden Erlegh Ave., 89 E1
Bex.
Maiden La. NW1 49 D7
Maiden La. E1 17 A1
Maiden La. WC2 12 B5
Maiden La. WC2 58 E7
Maiden Rd. E15 51 E7
Maidenstone Hill 78 C1
SE10

Maidstone Ave., 44 J2
Rom.
Maidstone Bldgs. 17 B2
SE1
Maidstone Ho. E14 60 B6
Carmen St.
Maidstone Rd. N11 32 C0
Maidstone Rd., Sid. 89 D6
Mail Coach Yd. N1 9 F3
Main Ave., Enf. 25 C5
Main Rd., Sid. 88 H3
Main St., Felt. 81 D5
Mainridge Rd., 88 D4
Chis.
Maisemore St. SE15 21 H7
Maitland Clo. SE10 69 B7
Maitland Clo., 72 F3
Houns.
Maitland Pk. Est. 48 J6
NW3
Maitland Pk. Rd. 48 J6
NW3
Maitland Pk. Vill. 48 J6
NW3
Maitland Rd. E15 51 F6
Maitland Rd. SE26 86 G6
Maize Row E14 59 J6
Oak La.
Majendie Rd. SE18 70 G5
Majestic Way, Mitch. 93 J2
Major Rd. E15 51 D5
Major Rd. SE16 17 J5
Makepeace Ave. N6 49 A2
Makepeace Rd., 54 E1
Nthlt.
Makins St. SW3 18 H2
Makins St. SW3 66 H4
Malabar St. E14 69 A2
Malam Gdns. E14 60 B7
Wades Pl.
Malbrook Rd. SW15 74 H4
Malcolm Ct., Stan. 29 F5
Malcolm Cres. NW4 38 G6
Malcolm Dr., Surb. 98 G1
Malcolm Pl. E2 59 F4
Malcolm Rd. E1 59 F4
Malcolm Rd. SE20 86 F7
Malcolm Rd. SE25 95 D6
Malcolm Rd. SW19 84 B6
Malcolm Way E11 42 G5
Malden Ave. SE25 95 E3
Malden Ave., Grnf. 46 B5
Malden Cres. NW1 49 A6
Malden Grn. Ave., 99 F1
Wor.Pk.
Malden Hill, N.Mal. 92 F3
Malden Hill Gdns., 92 F3
N.Mal.
Malden Pk., N.Mal. 92 F6
Malden Pl. NW5 49 A5
Grafton Ter.
Malden Rd. NW5 48 J5
Malden Rd., Borwd. 22 A3
Malden Rd., N.Mal. 92 E5
Malden Rd., Sutt. 99 J4
Malden Rd., Wor.Pk. 92 F7
Malden Way, N.Mal. 92 D6
Maldon Clo. E15 51 D5
Maryland St.
Maldon Clo. N1 58 J1
Maldon Clo. SE5 77 B3
Maldon Rd. N9 33 C3
Maldon Rd. W3 56 C7
Maldon Rd., Rom. 44 J7
Maldon Rd., Wall. 101 B5
Maldon Wk., 34 J6
Wdf.Grn.
Malet Pl. WC1 7 H6
Malet Pl. WC1 58 D4
Malet St. WC1 7 H6
Malet St. WC1 58 D4
Maley Ave. SE27 85 H2
Malford Ct. E18 42 G2
Malford Gro. E18 42 F4
Malfort Rd. SE5 77 B3
Malham Rd. SE23 86 G1
Malins Clo., Barn. 22 H5
Mall, The E15 51 D7
Broadway
Mall, The N14 32 E3
Mall, The SW1 15 G3
Mall, The SW1 67 C1
Mall, The SW14 74 C5
Mall, The W5 55 H7
Mall, The, Brom. 96 G3
High St.
Mall, The, Croy. 101 J1
Poplar Wk.
Mall, The, Har. 37 J6
Mall, The, Surb. 91 G5
Mall Rd. W6 65 H5
Mallams Ms. SW9 76 H3
St. James's Cres.

Mallard Clo. E9 50 J6
Mallard Clo., Barn. 23 G6
The Hook
Mallard Clo., 72 G7
Twick.
Stephenson Rd.
Mallard Pl. E3 60 B3
Rainhill Way
Mallard Wk. SE18 70 G3
Goosander Way
Mallard Wk., Sid. 89 C6
Cray Rd.
Mallard Way NW9 38 C7
Mallards Rd., 34 H7
Wdf.Grn.
Malling Clo., Croy. 95 F6
Malling Gdns., 93 F6
Mord.
Malling Way, Brom. 96 F7
Mallinson Rd. SW11 75 H5
Mallinson Rd., 101 D3
Croy.
Mallord St. SW3 18 F5
Mallord St. SW3 66 G6
Mallory Clo. SE4 77 H4
Mallory Gdns., 24 A7
Barn.
Mallory St. NW8 6 G6
Mallory St. NW8 57 H4
Mallow Clo., Croy. 102 G1
Marigold Way
Mallow Mead NW7 31 B7
Mallow St. EC1 9 B5
Mallow St. EC1 96 D4
Malmains Clo., 96 D4
Beck.
Malmains Way, 96 C4
Beck.
Malmesbury Rd. E3 59 J3
Malmesbury Rd. E16 60 E5
Malmesbury Rd. E18 42 F1
Malmesbury Rd., 93 F7
Mord.
Malmesbury Ter. E16 60 F5
Malpas Dr., Pnr. 36 D5
Malpas Rd. E8 50 E6
Malpas Rd. SE4 77 J2
Malpas Rd., Dag. 53 D6
Malt St. SE1 21 H5
Malt St. SE1 68 D6
Malta Rd. E10 51 A1
Malta St. EC1 8 H5
Maltby Rd., Chess. 99 A6
Maltby St. SE1 17 F4
Maltby St. SE1 68 C3
Malthouse Dr., 81 D5
Felt.
Malting Ho. E14 59 J7
Oak La.
Maltings, The, Orp. 104 J1
Maltings Clo. SW13 74 E2
Cleveland Gdns.
Maltings Ms., Sid. 89 A3
Station Rd.
Maltings Pl. SW6 75 E1
Malton Ms. W10 57 B6
Cambridge Gdns.
Malton Rd. W10 57 B6
St. Marks Rd.
Malton St. SE18 70 H6
Maltravers St. WC2 12 D5
Malva Clo. SW18 75 E5
St. Ann's Hill
Malvern Ave. E4 34 D7
Malvern Ave., Bexh. 71 E7
Malvern Ave., Har. 45 E3
Malvern Clo. SE20 95 D2
Derwent Rd.
Malvern Clo. W10 57 C5
Malvern Clo., 94 C3
Mitch.
Malvern Clo., Surb. 98 H1
Malvern Ct. SE14 66 F7
Avonley Rd.
Malvern Ct. SW7 18 F1
Malvern Ct. SW7 66 G4
Malvern Dr., Felt. 81 D5
Malvern Dr., Ilf. 52 J4
Malvern Dr., 34 J5
Wdf.Grn.
Malvern Gdns. NW2 48 B2
Malvern Gdns. NW6 57 C2
Malvern Gdns., Har. 37 H4
Malvern Gdns., 27 C6
Loug.
Malvern Ms. NW6 57 D3
Malvern Rd.
Malvern Pl. NW6 57 C2
Malvern Rd. E6 61 B1
Malvern Rd. E8 50 D7
Malvern Rd. E11 51 E2

Malvern Rd. N8 40 F3
Malvern Rd. N17 41 D3
Malvern Rd. NW6 57 D3
Malvern Rd., Hmptn. 81 G7
Malvern Rd., Surb. 98 H2
Malvern Rd., 94 G4
Th.Hth.
Malvern Ter. N1 58 G1
Malvern Ter. N9 33 C1
Malvern Way W13 55 E5
Templewood
Malwood Rd. SW12 76 B6
Malyons St. SE13 78 B6
Malyons Ter. SE13 78 B5
Managers St. E14 69 C1
Prestons Rd.
Manaton Clo. SE15 77 E3
Manaton Cres., 54 G6
Sthl.
Manbey Gro. E15 51 E6
Manbey Pk. Rd. E15 51 E6
Manbey Rd. E15 51 E6
Manbey St. E15 51 E6
Manborough Ave. E6 61 C3
Manbre Rd. W6 65 J6
Manchester Dr. W10 57 B4
Manchester Gro. E14 69 C5
Manchester Ms. W1 11 B2
Manchester Rd. E14 69 C5
Manchester Rd. N15 41 A6
Manchester Rd., 94 J3
Th.Hth.
Manchester Sq. W1 11 B3
Manchester Sq. W1 58 A6
Manchester St. W1 11 B2
Manchester St. W1 58 A5
Manchester Way, 53 H4
Dag.
Manchuria Rd. SW11 76 A6
Manciple St. SE1 17 C4
Manciple St. SE1 68 A2
Mandalay Rd. SW4 76 C5
Mandarin St. E14 60 A7
Salter St.
Mandela Clo. NW10 47 C7
Mandela Rd. E16 60 G6
Mandela St. NW1 58 C1
Mandela St. SW9 67 G1
Mandela Way SE1 21 E1
Mandela Way SE1 68 B4
Mandeville Clo. SE3 69 F7
Vanbrugh Pk.
Mandeville Clo. 93 B1
SW20
Mandeville Ct. E4 33 H4
Mandeville Dr., 98 G1
Surb.
Mandeville Pl. W1 11 C3
Mandeville Pl. W1 58 A6
Mandeville Rd. N14 32 B2
Mandeville Rd., 73 D2
Islw.
Mandeville Rd., 45 F7
Nthlt.
Mandeville St. E5 50 H3
Mandrake Rd. SW17 84 J2
Mandrell Rd. SW2 76 E5
Manette St. W1 11 J4
Manette St. W1 58 D6
Manford Way, Chig. 35 H4
Manfred Rd. SW15 75 C5
Manger Rd. N7 49 E6
Mangold Way, Erith 71 E3
Manhattan Ct., 54 D3
Nthlt.
Manilla St. E14 69 A2
Manister Rd. SE2 71 A3
Manley Ct. N16 50 C3
Stoke Newington
High St.
Manley St. NW1 58 A1
Mannin Rd., Rom. 44 B7
Manning Gdns., Har. 37 G7
Manning Rd. E17 41 H5
Southcote Rd.
Manning Rd., Dag. 53 G6
Manningford Clo. EC1 8 G3
Manningtree Clo. 84 B1
SW19
Manningtree Rd., 45 B4
Ruis.
Manningtree St. E1 13 H3
Mannock Dr., Loug. 27 F2
Mannock Rd. N22 40 H3
Manns Clo., Islw. 73 C5
Manns Rd., Edg. 30 A6
Manoel St. Twick. 81 J2
Manor Ave. SE4 77 J2
Manor Ave., Houns. 72 D3
Manor Ave., Nthlt. 45 F7
Manor Clo. NW7 30 D5
Manor Dr.
Manor Clo. NW9 38 B5

Manor Clo. SE28 62 C7
Manor Clo., Barn. 23 B4
Manor Clo., Wor.Pk. 99 E1
Manor Cotts. App. N2 39 F2
Manor Ct. N2 39 J5
Manor Ct. SW6 75 E1
Bagley's La.
Manor Ct., Twick. 81 J2
Manor Ct., Wem. 46 H5
Manor Ct. Rd. W7 55 B7
Manor Cres., Surb. 92 A6
Manor Dr. N14 24 B7
Manor Dr. N20 31 H3
Manor Dr. NW7 30 D5
Manor Dr., Epsom 99 E6
Manor Dr., Esher 98 C3
Manor Dr., Felt. 81 D5
Manor Dr., Sun. 90 A2
Manor Dr., Surb. 91 J6
Manor Dr., Wem. 46 J4
Manor Dr., The, Wor.Pk. 99 E1
Manor Dr. N., N.Mal. 92 D6
Manor Dr. N., Wor.Pk. 99 E1
Manor Est. SE16 68 E4
Manor Fm. Dr. E4 34 E3
Manor Fm. Rd., Th.Hth. 94 G2
Manor Fm. Rd., Wem. 55 G1
Manor Flds. SW15 75 A6
Manor Gdns. N7 49 E3
Manor Gdns. SW20 93 C2
Manor Gdns. W3 65 A4
Manor Gdns., Hmptn. 81 H7
Manor Gdns., Rich. 73 J4
Manor Gdns., Ruis. 45 C5
Manor Gdns., S.Croy. 102 C6
Manor Gdns., Sun. 90 A1
Manor Gate, Nthlt. 45 E7
Manor Gro. SE15 68 F6
Manor Gro., Beck. 96 B2
Manor Gro., Rich. 74 A4
Manor Hall Ave. NW4 38 J2
Manor Hall Dr. NW4 39 A2
Manor Ho. Dr. NW6 48 A7
Manor Ho. Way, Islw. 73 E3
Manor La. SE12 78 E6
Manor La. SE13 78 E5
Manor La., Felt. 81 A2
Manor La., Sun. 90 A2
Manor La., Sutt. 100 F5
Manor La. Ter. SE13 78 E4
Manor Ms. NW6 57 D2
Cambridge Ave.
Manor Ms. SE4 77 J2
Manor Mt. SE23 86 F1
Manor Pk. SE13 78 D5
Manor Pk., Chis. 97 G2
Manor Pk., Rich. 73 J4
Manor Pk. Clo., W.Wick. 103 B1
Manor Pk. Cres., Edg. 30 A6
Manor Pk. Dr., Har. 36 H3
Manor Pk. Gdns., Edg. 30 A5
Manor Pk. Rd. E12 52 A4
Manor Pk. Rd. N2 39 F3
Manor Pk. Rd. NW10 56 F1
Manor Pk. Rd., Chis. 97 F1
Manor Pk. Rd., Sutt. 100 F5
Manor Pk. Rd., W.Wick. 103 B1
Manor Pl. SE17 20 J3
Manor Pl. SE17 67 H5
Manor Pl., Chis. 97 G2
Manor Pl., Felt. 81 A1
Manor Pl., Mitch. 94 C3
Manor Pl., Sutt. 100 E5
Manor Rd. E10 42 A7
Manor Rd. E15 60 E2
Manor Rd. E16 60 E4
Manor Rd. E17 41 H2
Manor Rd. N16 50 A2
Manor Rd. N17 41 D1
Manor Rd. N22 32 E6
Manor Rd. SE25 95 D4
Manor Rd. SW20 93 C2
Manor Rd. W13 55 D7
Manor Rd., Bark. 52 J6
Manor Rd., Barn. 23 B5
Manor Rd., Beck. 96 A2
Manor Rd., Bex. 89 H1
Manor Rd., Chig. 35 D6
Manor Rd., Dag. 53 J6
Manor Rd., E.Mol. 91 A4
Manor Rd., Enf. 24 J2
Manor Rd., Har. 37 D6
Manor Rd., Hayes 54 A6
Manor Rd., Loug. 26 H6
Manor Rd. (High Beach), Loug. 26 H1
Manor Rd., Mitch. 94 C4
Manor Rd., Rich. 73 J3
Manor Rd., Rom. (Chadwell Heath) 44 D6
Manor Rd., Sid. 89 A3
Manor Rd., Sutt. 100 C7
Manor Rd., Tedd. 82 D5
Manor Rd., Twick. 81 J2
Manor Rd., Wall. 101 B4
Manor Rd., W.Wick. 103 B2
Manor Rd., Wdf.Grn. 35 C6
Manor Rd. N., Esher 98 C3
Manor Rd. N., T.Ditt. 98 D2
Manor Rd. N., Wall. 101 B4
Manor Rd. S., Esher 98 B4
Manor Sq., Dag. 53 C2
Manor Vale, Brent. 64 F5
Manor Vw. N3 39 E2
Manor Way E4 34 D4
Manor Way NW9 38 E4
Manor Way SE3 78 F4
Manor Way, Beck. 96 A2
Manor Way, Bex. 89 G1
Manor Way, Borwd. 22 C2
Manor Way, Brom. 97 B6
Manor Way, Har. 36 H4
Manor Way, Mitch. 94 C3
Manor Way, S.Croy. 102 B6
Manor Way, Sthl. 63 D4
Manor Way, Wor.Pk. 99 E1
Manor Way, The, Wall. 101 B4
Manorbrook SE3 78 G4
Manordene Clo., T.Ditt. 98 D1
Manordene Rd. SE28 62 C6
Manorgate Rd., Kings.T. 92 A1
Manorhall Gdns. E10 51 A1
Manorside, Barn. 23 B4
Manorside Clo. SE2 71 C4
Manorway, Enf. 25 B7
Manorway, Wdf.Grn. 34 J5
Manresa Rd. SW3 18 G4
Manresa Rd. SW3 66 H5
Mansard Beeches SW17 85 A5
Mansard Clo., Pnr. 36 D3
Manse Rd. N16 50 C3
Mansel Gro. E17 42 A1
Mansel Rd. SW19 84 B6
Mansell Rd. W3 65 D2
Mansell Rd., Grnf. 54 H5
Mansell St. E1 13 G4
Mansell St. E1 59 C6
Mansergh Clo. SE18 70 B7
Mansfield Ave. N15 41 A4
Mansfield Ave., Barn. 23 J6
Mansfield Ave., Ruis. 45 B1
Mansfield Clo. N9 25 D6
Mansfield Hill E4 34 B1
Mansfield Ms. W1 11 D2
Mansfield Pl. NW3 48 F4
New End
Mansfield Rd. E11 42 H6
Mansfield Rd. E17 41 J4
Mansfield Rd. NW3 48 J5
Mansfield Rd. W3 56 B4
Mansfield Rd., Chess. 98 F5
Mansfield Rd., Ilf. 52 D2
Mansfield Rd., S.Croy. 102 A6
Mansfield St. W1 11 D2
Mansfield St. W1 58 B5
Mansford St. E2 9 J2
Mansford St. E2 59 D2
Manship Rd., Mitch. 85 A7
Mansion Gdns. NW3 48 E3
Mansion Ho. Pl. EC4 13 B4
Manson Ms. SW7 18 E2
Manson Ms. SW7 66 F4
Manson Pl. SW7 18 E2
Manson Pl. SW7 66 G4
Mansted Gdns., Rom. 44 C7
Manston Ave., Sthl. 63 G4
Manston Clo. SE20 95 F1
Garden Rd.
Manstone Rd. NW2 48 B5
Manthorp Rd. SE18 70 F5
Mantilla Rd. SW17 85 A4
Mantle Rd. SE4 77 H3
Mantlet Clo. SW16 85 C7
Manton Ave. W7 64 C2
Manton Rd. SE2 71 A4
Mantua St. SW11 75 G3
Mantus Clo. E1 59 F4
Mantus Rd.
Mantus Rd. E1 59 F4
Manus Way N20 31 F2
Blakeney Clo.
Manville Gdns. SW17 85 B2
Manville Rd. SW17 85 A2
Manwood Rd. SE4 77 J5
Manwood St. E16 70 C1
Manygates SW12 85 B2
Mape St. E2 59 E4
Mapesbury Rd. NW2 48 B7
Maple Ave. E4 33 J5
Maple Ave. W3 65 E1
Maple Ave., Har. 45 H2
Maple Clo. N16 41 D6
Maple Clo. SW4 76 D6
Maple Clo., Buck.H. 35 A3
Maple Clo., Hmptn. 81 F6
Maple Clo., Hayes 54 D3
Maple Clo., Ilf. 35 H5
Maple Clo., Mitch. 94 B1
Maple Clo., Orp. 97 G5
Maple Clo., Ruis. 36 B6
Maple Ct., N.Mal. 92 D3
Maple Cres., Sid. 80 A6
Maple Gate, Loug. 27 D2
Maple Gro. NW9 38 C7
Maple Gro. W5 64 F3
Maple Gro., Brent. 64 E7
Maple Gro., Sthl. 54 F5
Maple Ind. Est., Felt. 81 A3
Maple Leaf Dr., Sid. 88 J1
Maple Leaf Sq. SE16 68 G2
St. Elmos Rd.
Maple Ms. NW6 6 A1
Maple Ms. SW16 85 F5
Maple Pl. W1 7 G6
Maple Rd. E11 42 E6
Maple Rd. SE20 95 E1
Maple Rd., Hayes 54 C3
Maple Rd., Surb. 91 G6
Maple St. W1 11 F1
Maple St. W1 58 C5
Maple St., Rom. 44 J4
Maple Wk. W10 57 A4
Droop St.
Maple Way, Felt. 81 A3
Maplecroft Clo. E6 61 B6
Allhallows Rd.
Mapledale Ave., Croy. 102 D2
Mapledene, Chis. 88 F5
Kemnal Rd.
Mapledene Rd. E8 50 D7
Maplehurst Clo., Kings.T. 91 H4
Mapleleafe Gdns., Ilf. 43 E3
Maples Pl. E1 59 E5
Raven Row
Maplestead Rd. SW2 76 F7
Maplestead Rd., Dag. 62 B1
Maplethorpe Rd., Th.Hth. 94 G4
Mapleton Clo., Brom. 96 G6
Mapleton Cres. SW18 75 E6
Mapleton Rd. E4 34 C3
Mapleton Rd. SW18 75 D6
Mapleton Rd., Enf. 25 E2
Maplin Clo. N21 24 F6
Maplin Rd. E16 60 G6
Maplin St. E3 59 J3
Maran Way, Erith 71 D2
Marban Rd. W9 57 C3
Marble Arch W1 10 J5
Marble Arch W1 57 J7
Marble Clo. W3 65 B1
Marble Hill Clo., Twick. 73 E7
Marble Hill Gdns., Twick. 73 E7
Marble Quay E1 17 H1
Marble Quay E1 68 D1
Marbrook Ct. SE12 87 J3
Marcellina Way, Orp. 104 H3
March Rd., Twick. 73 D7
Marchant Rd. E11 51 D2
Marchbank Rd. W14 66 C6
Marchmont Rd., Rich. 73 J5
Marchmont Rd., Wall. 101 C7
Marchmont St. WC1 8 A5
Marchmont St. WC1 58 E4
Marchside Clo., Houns. 72 D1
Springwell Rd.
Marchwood Clo. SE5 68 B7
Marchwood Cres. W5 55 F6
Marcia Rd. SE1 21 E2
Marcia Rd. SE1 68 B4
Marcilly Rd. SW18 75 G5
Marco Rd. W6 65 H3
Marcon Pl. E8 50 E5
Marconi Way, Sthl. 54 H6
Marcourt Lawns W5 55 H4
Marcus Ct. E15 60 E1
Marcus Garvey Way SE24 76 G4
Marcus St. E15 60 E1
Marcus St. SW18 75 E6
Marcus Ter. SW18 75 E6
Mardale Dr. NW9 38 D5
Mardell Rd., Croy. 95 G5
Marden Ave., Brom. 96 F6
Marden Cres., Bex. 80 J5
Marden Cres., Croy. 94 F6
Marden Rd. N17 41 B3
Marden Rd., Croy. 94 F6
Marden Sq. SE16 68 E3
Marder Rd. W13 64 D2
Mardon St. E14 59 H5
Mare St. E8 59 E1
Marechal Niel Ave., Sid. 88 G3
Mares Fld., Croy. 102 B3
Maresfield Gdns. NW3 48 F5
Marfleet Clo., Cars. 100 H2
Margaret Ave. E4 26 B6
Margaret Bondfield Ave., Bark. 53 A7
Margaret Bldgs. N16 50 C1
Margaret Rd.
Margaret Ct. W1 11 F3
Margaret Rd. N16 50 C1
Margaret Rd., Barn. 23 G4
Margaret Rd., Bex. 80 D6
Margaret St. W1 11 E3
Margaret St. W1 58 B6
Margaret Way, Ilf. 43 B6
Margaretta Ter. SW3 18 G5
Margaretta Ter. SW3 66 H6
Margaretting Rd. E12 51 J1
Margate Rd. SW2 76 E5
Margeholes, Wat. 28 E2
Margery Pk. Rd. E7 51 G6
Margery Rd., Dag. 53 D3
Margery St. WC1 8 E4
Margery St. WC1 58 G3
Margin Dr. SW19 84 A5
Margravine Gdns. W6 66 A5
Margravine Rd. W6 66 A5
Marham Gdns. SW18 84 H1
Marham Gdns., Mord. 93 F6
Maria Ter. E1 59 G4
Maria Theresa Clo., N.Mal. 92 D5
Marian Clo., Hayes 54 D4
Marian Ct., Sutt. 100 E5
Marian Pl. E2 59 E2
Marian Rd. SW16 94 C1
Marian Sq. E2 9 J1
Marian St. E2 59 E2
Hackney Rd.
Marian Way NW10 47 F7
Maricas Ave., Har. 29 A7
Marie Lloyd Gdns. N19 40 E7
Hornsey Ri. Gdns.
Marie Lloyd Wk. E8 50 D6
Forest Rd.
Marigold All. SE1 12 G6
Marigold Rd. N17 33 F7
Marigold St. SE16 68 E2
Marigold Way, Croy. 102 G1
Marina App., Hayes 54 E5
Marina Ave., N.Mal. 92 H5
Marina Clo., Brom. 96 G3
Marina Dr., Well. 79 H2
Marina Gdns., Rom. 44 H5
Marina Way, Tedd. 82 G7
Fairways
Marine Dr. SE18 70 C4
Marine St. SE16 17 H5
Marinefield Rd. SW6 75 E2
Mariner Gdns., Rich. 82 F3
Mariner Rd. E12 52 C4
Dersingham Ave.
Mariners Ms. E14 69 D4

202 Mar-Mar

Marion Clo., Ilf. 35 G7
Marion Gro., Wdf.Grn. 34 E5
Marion Rd. NW7 30 G5
Marion Rd., Th.Hth. 94 J5
Marischal Rd. SE13 78 D3
Maritime St. E3 59 J4
Marius Pas. SW17 85 A2
Marius Rd.
Marius Rd. SW17 85 A2
Marjorams Ave., Loug. 27 C2
Marjorie Gro. SW11 75 J4
Mark Ave. E4 26 B6
Mark Clo., Bexh. 80 E1
Mark Clo., Sthl. 63 H1
Longford Ave.
Mark La. EC3 13 E5
Mark La. EC3 59 B7
Mark Rd. N22 40 H2
Mark St. E15 51 E7
West Ham La.
Mark St. EC2 9 D5
Markab Rd., Nthwd. 28 A5
Atria Rd.
Marke Clo., Kes. 104 B4
Markeston Grn., Wat. 28 D4
Market Ct. W1 11 F3
Market Est. N7 49 E6
Clock Twr. Pl.
Market Hill SE18 70 D3
Market La., Edg. 38 C1
Market Ms. W1 15 D2
Market Par. SE15 77 D2
Rye La.
Market Pl. N2 39 H3
Market Pl. NW11 39 F4
Market Pl. SE16 21 J1
Market Pl. W1 11 F3
Market Pl. W3 65 C1
Market Pl., Bexh. 80 G4
Market Pl., Brent. 64 G7
Lion Way
Market Pl., Enf. 25 A3
The Town
Market Pl., Kings.T. 91 G2
Market Rd. N7 49 E6
Market Rd., Rich. 74 A3
Market Sq. E14 60 B6
Chrisp St.
Market Sq. N9 33 D2
New Rd.
Market Sq., Brom. 96 G2
Market St. E6 61 C2
Market St. SE18 70 D4
Market Way E14 60 B6
Kerbey St.
Markfield Gdns. E4 26 B7
Markfield Rd. N15 41 D4
Markham Pl. SW3 18 J3
Markham Sq. SW3 18 J3
Markham Sq. SW3 66 J5
Markham St. SW3 18 H3
Markham St. SW3 66 H5
Markhole Clo., Hmptn. 81 F7
Priory Rd.
Markhouse Ave. E17 41 H6
Markhouse Rd. E17 41 J5
Markmanor Ave. E17 41 H7
Marks Rd., Rom. 44 J5
Marksbury Ave., Rich. 74 A3
Markway, The, Sun. 90 C2
Markwell Clo. SE26 86 E4
Taylors La.
Markyate Rd., Dag. 53 B5
Marl Rd. SW18 75 E4
Marlands Rd., Ilf. 43 B3
Marlborough Ave. E8 59 D1
Marlborough Ave. N14 32 C3
Marlborough Ave., Edg. 30 B3
Marlborough Bldgs. SW3 18 H1
Marlborough Bldgs. SW3 66 H4
Marlborough Clo. SE17 20 J2
Marlborough Clo. SW19 84 H7
Marlborough Clo., Orp. 97 J7
Aylesham Rd.
Marlborough Ct. W8 66 D4
Marlborough Cres. W4 65 D3
Marlborough Dr., Ilf. 43 B3
Marlborough Gdns. N20 31 J3
Marlborough Gate Ho. W2 10 E5
Marlborough Gro. SE1 21 H4
Marlborough Gro. SE1 68 D5
Marlborough Hill NW8 57 F1
Marlborough Hill, Har. 37 A4
Marlborough La. SE7 69 J6
Marlborough Pk. Ave., Sid. 89 A1
Marlborough Pl. NW8 6 C2
Marlborough Pl. NW8 57 F2
Marlborough Rd. E4 34 A6
Marlborough Rd. E7 51 J7
Marlborough Rd. E15 51 E4
Borthwick Rd.
Marlborough Rd. E18 42 G3
Marlborough Rd. N9 33 C1
Marlborough Rd. N19 49 D2
Marlborough Rd. N22 32 E7
Marlborough Rd. SW1 15 G2
Marlborough Rd. SW1 67 C1
Marlborough Rd. SW19 84 H6
Marlborough Rd. W4 65 C5
Marlborough Rd. W5 64 G2
Marlborough Rd., Bexh. 80 D3
Marlborough Rd., Brom. 96 J4
Marlborough Rd., Dag. 53 B4
Marlborough Rd., Felt. 81 D2
Marlborough Rd., Hmptn. 81 G6
Marlborough Rd., Islw. 73 E1
Marlborough Rd., Rich. 73 H6
Marlborough Rd., Rom. 44 G4
Marlborough Rd., S.Croy. 101 J7
Marlborough Rd., Sthl. 63 C3
Marlborough Rd., Sutt. 100 D3
Marlborough St. SW3 18 G2
Marlborough St. SW3 66 H4
Marlborough Yd. N19 49 D2
Marlborough Rd.
Marler Rd. SE23 86 H1
Marlescroft Way, Loug. 27 E5
Marley Ave., Bexh. 71 D6
Marley Clo., Grnf. 54 G3
Marley Wk. NW2 47 J5
Lennon Rd.
Marlingdene Clo., Hmptn. 81 G6
Marlings Clo., Chis. 97 H4
Marlings Pk. Ave., Chis. 97 H4
Marloes Clo., Wem. 46 G4
Marloes Rd. W8 14 A6
Marloes Rd. W8 66 E3
Marlow Clo. SE20 95 E3
Marlow Ct. NW6 48 A7
Marlow Ct. NW9 38 E3
Marlow Cres., Twick. 73 C6
Marlow Dr., Sutt. 100 A2
Marlow Rd. E6 61 C3
Marlow Rd. SE20 95 E3
Marlow Rd., Sthl. 63 F3
Marlow Way SE16 68 G2
Marlowe Clo., Chis. 88 G6
Marlowe Clo., Ilf. 43 F1
Marlowe Gdns. SE9 79 D6
Marlowe Rd. E17 42 C4
Marlowe Sq., Mitch. 94 C3
Tamworth La.
Marlowe Way, Croy. 101 E2
Marlowes, The NW8 57 G1
Marlton St. SE10 69 F5
Woolwich Rd.
Marmadon Rd. SE18 70 J4
Marmion App. E4 34 A4
Marmion Ave. E4 33 J4
Marmion Clo. E4 33 J4
Marmion Ms. SW11 76 A3
Taybridge Rd.
Marmion Rd. SW11 76 A4
Marmont Rd. SE15 77 D1
Marmora Rd. SE22 77 F6
Marmot Rd., Houns. 72 D3
Marne Ave. N11 32 B4
Marne Ave., Well. 80 A3
Marne St. W10 57 B3
Marnell Way, Houns. 72 D3
Marney Rd. SW11 76 A4
Marnham Ave. NW2 48 B4
Marnham Cres., Grnf. 54 H3
Marnock Rd. SE4 77 J5
Maroon St. E14 59 H5
Maroons Way SE6 87 A5
Marquess Est. N1 49 J6
Marquess Rd. N1 50 A6
Marquis Clo., Wem. 46 J7
Marquis Rd. N4 49 F1
Marquis Rd. N22 32 F6
Marquis Rd. NW1 49 D6
Marrick Clo. SW15 74 G4
Marriot Rd., Barn. 23 A3
Marriots Clo. NW9 38 F6
Marriott Rd. E15 60 E1
Marriott Rd. N4 49 F1
Marriott Rd. N10 39 J1
Marryat Pl. SW19 84 B4
Marryat Rd. SW19 84 A5
Marsala Rd. SE13 78 B4
Marsden Rd. N9 33 E2
Marsden Rd. SE15 77 C3
Marsden St. NW5 49 A6
Marsden Way, Orp. 104 H3
Marsh Ave., Mitch. 93 J2
Marsh Clo. NW7 30 F3
Marsh Ct. SW19 93 F1
Marsh Dr. NW9 38 F6
Marsh Fm. Rd., Twick. 82 C1
Marsh Grn. Rd., Dag. 62 G1
Marsh Hill E9 50 H5
Marsh La. E10 51 A2
Marsh La. N17 41 E1
Marsh La. NW7 30 D4
Marsh La., Stan. 29 F5
Marsh Rd., Pnr. 36 E4
Marsh Rd., Wem. 55 G3
Marsh St. E14 69 B4
Harbinger Rd.
Marsh Wall E14 69 A1
Marshall Clo. SW18 75 F6
Allfarthing La.
Marshall Clo., Har. 37 A7
Bowen Rd.
Marshall Clo., Houns. 72 F5
Marshall Path SE28 62 B7
Attlee Rd.
Marshall Rd. N17 41 A1
Marshall St. W1 11 G4
Marshall St. W1 58 C6
Marshalls Clo. N11 32 B4
Marshall's Gro. SE18 70 B4
Marshalls Pl. SE16 17 G6
Marshall's Rd., Sutt. 100 E4
Marshalsea Rd. SE1 17 A3
Marshalsea Rd. SE1 67 J2
Marsham Clo., Chis. 88 E5
Marsham St. SW1 15 J6
Marsham St. SW1 67 D3
Marshbrook Clo. SE3 79 A3
Marshfield St. E14 69 C3
Marshgate La. E15 51 B7
Marshgate Path SE18 70 F4
Tom Cribb Rd.
Marsland Clo. SE17 20 H4
Marsland Clo. SE17 67 H5
Marston Ave., Chess. 98 H6
Marston Ave., Dag. 53 G2
Marston Clo. NW6 48 F7
Fairfax Rd.
Marston Clo., Dag. 53 G3
Marston Ave.
Marston Rd., Ilf. 43 B1
Marston Rd., Tedd. 82 E5
Kingston Rd.
Marston Way SE19 85 H7
Marsworth Ave., Pnr. 36 D1
Marsworth Clo., Hayes 54 E5
Mart St. WC2 12 B5
Martaban Rd. N16 50 C2
Martel Pl. E8 50 C6
Dalston La.
Martell Rd. SE21 86 A3
Martello St. E8 50 E7
Martello Ter. E8 50 E7
Marten Rd. E17 42 A2
Martens Ave., Bexh. 80 H4
Martens Clo., Bexh. 80 J4
Martha Ct. E2 59 E2
Cambridge Heath Rd.
Martha Rd. E15 51 E6
Martha St. E1 59 F6
Martham Clo. SE28 62 D7
Marthorne Cres., Har. 37 A2
Martin Bowes Rd. SE9 79 C3
Martin Clo. N9 33 G1
Martin Cres., Croy. 101 G1
Martin Dale Ind. Est., Enf. 25 E3
Martin Dene, Bexh. 80 F5
Martin Dr., Nthlt. 45 F5
Martin Gdns., Dag. 53 C4
Martin Gro., Mord. 93 D3
Martin La. EC4 13 C5
Martin Ri., Bexh. 80 F5
Martin Rd., Dag. 53 C4
Martin Way SW20 93 A2
Martin Way, Mord. 93 D3
Martinbridge Trd. Est., Enf. 25 D4
Martindale SW14 74 C5
Martindale Rd. SW12 76 B7
Martindale Rd., Houns. 72 E4
Martineau Clo., Esher 98 A4
Martineau Est. E1 59 F7
Martineau Rd. N5 49 H4
Martineau St. E1 59 F7
Lukin St.
Martingale Clo., Sun. 90 A4
Martingales Clo., Rich. 82 G3
Martins Mt., Barn. 23 D4
Martins Rd., Brom. 96 E2
Martins Wk. N10 39 J1
Coppetts Rd.
Martinsfield Clo., Chig. 35 H4
Martlet Gro., Nthlt. 54 D3
Javelin Way
Martlett Ct. WC2 12 B4
Martley Dr., Ilf. 43 E5
Martock Clo., Har. 37 D4
Marton Clo. SE6 87 A3
Marton Rd. N16 50 B2
Martys Yd. NW3 48 G4
Hampstead High St.
Marvell Ave., Hayes 54 A5
Marvels Clo. SE12 87 H2
Marvels La. SE12 87 H2
Marville Rd. SW6 66 C7
Marvin St. E8 50 E6
Sylvester Rd.
Marwell Clo., W.Wick. 103 F2
Deer Pk. Way
Marwood Clo., Well. 80 B3
Marwood Way SE16 68 E5
Catlin St.
Mary Adelaide Clo. SW15 83 E4
Mary Ann Gdns. SE8 69 A6
Mary Clo., Stan. 37 J4
Mary Datchelor Clo. SE5 77 A1
Mary Datchelor Pl. SE5 77 A1
Mary Gardener Dr. SE9 88 C2
Mary Grn. NW8 57 E1
Mary Macarthur Ho. W6 66 B6
Field Rd.
Mary Peters Dr., Grnf. 46 A5
Mary Pl. W11 57 B7
Mary Rose Clo., Hmptn. 90 G1
Ashley Rd.
Mary Rose Mall E6 61 D5
Frobisher Rd.
Mary Rose Way N20 31 G1
Mary Seacole Clo. E8 59 C1
Clarissa St.
Mary St. E16 60 F5
Barking Rd.
Mary St. N1 58 J1
Mary Ter. NW1 58 B1
Arlington Rd.
Maryatt Ave., Har. 45 H2
Marybank SE18 70 C4
Maryland Pk. E15 51 E5
Maryland Rd. E15 51 D5

Maryland Rd. N22	32	F6	
Maryland Rd.,	94	H1	
Th.Hth.			
Maryland Sq. E15	51	E5	
Maryland St. E15	51	D5	
Maryland Wk. N1	58	J1	
Popham St.			
Maryland Way, Sun.	90	A2	
Marylands Rd. W9	57	D4	
Marylebone Flyover	**10**	**G2**	
NW1			
Marylebone Flyover	**10**	**F2**	
W2			
Marylebone High St.	**11**	**C1**	
W1			
Marylebone High St.	58	A5	
W1			
Marylebone La. W1	**11**	**C3**	
Marylebone La. W1	58	A6	
Marylebone Ms. W1	**11**	**D2**	
Marylebone Ms. W1	58	B5	
Marylebone Pas. W1	**11**	**G3**	
Marylebone Rd. NW1	**11**	**A1**	
Marylebone Rd. NW1	57	H5	
Marylebone St. W1	**11**	**C2**	
Marylebone St. W1	58	A5	
Marylee Way SE11	**20**	**D3**	
Marylee Way SE11	67	F4	
Maryon Gro. SE7	70	B4	
Maryon Ms. NW3	48	H4	
South End Rd.			
Maryon Rd. SE7	70	B4	
Maryon Rd. SE18	70	B4	
Mary's Clo. N17	41	C1	
Kemble Rd.			
Mary's Ter., Twick.	73	D7	
Masbro Rd. W14	66	A3	
Mascalls Ct. SE7	69	J6	
Victoria Way			
Mascalls Rd. SE7	69	J6	
Mascotte Rd. SW15	75	A4	
Mascotts Clo. NW2	47	H3	
Masefield Ave.,	22	B5	
Borwd.			
Masefield Ave.,	54	G7	
Sthl.			
Masefield Ave.,	29	C5	
Stan.			
Masefield Cres. N14	24	C5	
Masefield Gdns. E6	61	D4	
Masefield La.,	54	B4	
Hayes			
Masefield Rd.,	81	F4	
Hmptn.			
Wordsworth Rd.			
Masefield Vw., Orp.	104	F3	
Mashie Rd. W3	56	E6	
Maskall Clo. SW2	85	G1	
Maskani Wk. SW16	85	C7	
Bates Cres.			
Maskell Rd. SW17	84	F3	
Maskelyn Clo. SW11	75	H1	
Mason Bradbear Ct.	50	A6	
N1			
St. Pauls Rd.			
Mason Clo. E16	60	G7	
Mason Clo., Bexh.	80	H3	
Mason Clo., Borwd.	22	D2	
Banks Rd.			
Mason Clo., Hmptn.	90	F1	
Mason Rd., Wdf.Grn.	34	E4	
Mason St. SE17	**21**	**C1**	
Mason St. SE17	68	A4	
Masons Arms Ms. W11	**11**	**E5**	
Masons Ave. EC2	**13**	**B3**	
Masons Ave., Croy.	101	J3	
Masons Ave., Har.	37	C4	
Masons Ct., Wem.	47	A2	
Masons Grn. La. W3	56	A4	
Dukes Rd.			
Masons Hill SE18	70	E4	
Masons Hill, Brom.	96	G3	
Mason's Pl. EC1	**8**	**J3**	
Mason's Pl. EC1	58	J3	
Masons Pl., Mitch.	93	J1	
Mason's Yd. SW1	**15**	**G1**	
Mason's Yd. SW19	84	A5	
High St.			
Massey Clo. N11	32	B5	
Grove Rd.			
Massie Rd. E8	50	D6	
Graham Rd.			
Massinger St. SE17	**21**	**D2**	
Massingham St. E1	59	G4	
Masson Ave., Ruis.	45	C6	
Mast Ho. Ter. E14	69	A4	
Master Gunner Pl.	70	B7	
SE18			
Masterman Ho. SE5	**21**	**B7**	
Masterman Rd. E6	61	B3	
Masters St. E1	59	G5	
Mastmaker Rd. E14	69	A2	
Maswell Pk. Cres.,	72	J5	
Houns.			
Maswell Pk. Rd.,	72	H5	
Houns.			
Matcham Rd. E11	51	E3	
Matchless Dr. SE18	70	D7	
Red Lion La.			
Matfield Clo.,	96	G5	
Brom.			
Matfield Rd., Belv.	71	G6	
Matham Gro. SE22	77	C4	
Matham Rd., E.Mol.	91	A5	
Matheson Rd. W14	66	C4	
Mathews Pk. Ave.	51	F6	
E15			
Matilda St. N1	58	F1	
Matlock Clo. SE24	76	J4	
Matlock Ct. SE5	77	A4	
Denmark Hill Est.			
Matlock Cres.,	100	B4	
Sutt.			
Matlock Cres., Wat.	28	C3	
Matlock Gdns.,	100	B4	
Sutt.			
Matlock Pl., Sutt.	100	B4	
Matlock Rd. E10	42	C6	
Matlock St. E14	59	H6	
Matlock Way, N.Mal.	92	D1	
Matrimony Pl. SW8	76	C2	
Wandsworth Rd.			
Matthew Clo. W10	57	A4	
Matthew Ct., Mitch.	94	D5	
Matthew Parker St.	**15**	**J4**	
SW1			
Matthew Parker St.	67	D2	
SW1			
Matthews Ave. E6	61	D2	
Matthews Rd., Grnf.	46	A5	
Matthews St. SW11	75	J2	
Matthews Yd. WC2	**12**	**A4**	
Matthias Rd. N16	50	A5	
Mattingley Way SE15	68	C7	
Daniel Gdns.			
Mattison Rd. N4	40	G6	
Mattock La. W5	64	F1	
Mattock La. W13	64	E1	
Maud Gdns. E13	60	F1	
Maud Gdns., Bark.	61	J2	
Maud Rd. E10	51	C3	
Maud Rd. E13	60	F2	
Maud St. E16	60	F5	
Maude Rd. E17	41	H5	
Maude Rd. SE5	77	B1	
Maude Ter. E17	41	H4	
Maudlins Grn. E1	**17**	**H1**	
Maudslay Rd. SE9	79	C3	
Maudsley Ho.,	64	H5	
Brent.			
Mauleverer Rd. SW2	76	E5	
Maundeby Wk.	47	E6	
NW10			
Neasden La.			
Maunder Rd. W7	64	B1	
Maunsel St. SW1	**19**	**H1**	
Maunsel St. SW1	67	D4	
Maurice Ave. N22	40	H2	
Maurice Brown Clo.	31	A5	
NW7			
Maurice St. W12	56	H6	
Maurice Wk. NW11	39	F4	
Maurier Clo.,	54	C1	
Nthlt.			
Mauritius Rd. SE10	69	E4	
Maury Rd. N16	50	D2	
Mavelstone Clo.,	97	B1	
Brom.			
Mavelstone Rd.,	97	A1	
Brom.			
Maverton Rd. E3	60	A1	
Mavis Ave., Epsom	99	E5	
Mavis Clo., Epsom	99	E5	
Mavis Wk. E6	61	B5	
Tollgate Rd.			
Mawbey Est. SE1	**21**	**H4**	
Mawbey Est. SE1	68	C5	
Mawbey Pl. SE1	**21**	**G4**	
Mawbey Pl. SE1	68	C5	
Mawbey Rd. SE1	**21**	**G4**	
Mawbey St. SW8	67	E7	
Mawney Clo., Rom.	44	H2	
Mawney Rd., Rom.	44	H2	
Mawson Clo. SW20	93	B2	
Mawson La. W4	65	B6	
Great W. Rd.			
Maxey Gdns., Dag.	53	E4	
Maxey Rd. SE18	70	F4	
Maxey Rd., Dag.	53	E5	
Maxfield Clo. N20	23	F7	
Maxilla Gdns. W10	57	A6	
Cambridge Gdns.			
Maxilla Wk. W10	57	A6	
Bartle Rd.			
Maxim Rd. N21	24	G6	
Maxted Pk., Har.	37	B7	
Maxted Rd. SE15	77	C3	
Maxwell Gdns., Orp.	104	J3	
Maxwell Rd. SW6	66	E7	
Maxwell Rd., Borwd.	22	B3	
Maxwell Rd., Well.	80	A3	
Maxwelton Ave. NW7	30	D5	
Maxwelton Clo. NW7	30	D5	
May Ct. SW19	93	E1	
May Gdns., Wem.	55	F3	
May Rd. E4	34	A6	
May Rd. E13	60	G2	
May Rd., Twick.	82	B1	
May St. W14	66	C5	
North End Rd.			
May Tree La., Stan.	29	C7	
May Wk. E13	60	H2	
Queens Rd. W.			
Maya Rd. N2	39	F4	
Mayall Rd. SE24	76	H5	
Maybank Ave. E18	42	H2	
Maybank Ave., Wem.	46	C5	
Maybank Gdns., Pnr.	36	A5	
Maybank Rd. E18	42	H1	
Maybells	62	D2	
Commercial Est.,			
Bark.			
Mayberry Pl., Surb.	91	J7	
Maybourne Clo.	86	E5	
SE26			
Maybrook Meadow	53	A5	
Est., Bark.			
Maybury Clo., Orp.	97	E5	
Maybury Gdns.	47	H6	
NW10			
Maybury Ms. N6	40	C7	
Maybury Rd. E13	60	J4	
Maybury Rd., Bark.	61	J2	
Maybury St. SW17	84	H5	
Maychurch Clo.,	29	G7	
Stan.			
Maycroft, Pnr.	36	B2	
Maycross Ave.,	93	C3	
Mord.			
Mayday Gdns. SE3	79	B2	
Mayday Rd., Th.Hth.	94	H6	
Mayerne Rd. SE9	79	A5	
Mayes Rd. N22	40	F2	
Mayesbrook Rd.	61	J1	
Bark.			
Mayesbrook Rd.,	53	B3	
Dag.			
Mayesbrook Rd., Ilf.	53	A3	
Mayesford Rd., Rom.	44	C7	
Mayeswood Rd.	87	J3	
SE12			
Mayfair Ave., Bexh.	80	D1	
Mayfair Ave., Ilf.	52	C2	
Mayfair Ave., Rom.	44	D6	
Mayfair Ave.,	72	J7	
Twick.			
Mayfair Ave.,	99	F1	
Wor.Pk.			
Mayfair Clo., Beck.	96	B1	
Mayfair Clo., Surb.	98	H1	
Mayfair Gdns. N17	32	J6	
Mayfair Gdns.,	34	G7	
Wdf.Grn.			
Mayfair Ms. NW1	48	J7	
Regents Pk. Rd.			
Mayfair Pl. W1	**15**	**E1**	
Mayfair Pl. W1	67	B1	
Mayfair Ter. N14	24	D7	
Mayfield, Bexh.	80	F3	
Mayfield Ave. N12	31	F4	
Mayfield Ave. N14	32	C2	
Mayfield Ave. W4	65	E4	
Mayfield Ave. W13	64	E3	
Mayfield Ave., Har.	37	E5	
Mayfield Ave., Orp.	97	J7	
Mayfield Ave.,	34	G6	
Wdf.Grn.			
Mayfield Clo. E8	50	C6	
Forest Rd.			
Mayfield Clo. SW4	76	D5	
Mayfield Clo.,	98	E1	
T.Ditt.			
Mayfield Cres. N9	25	E6	
Mayfield Cres.,	94	F3	
Th.Hth.			
Mayfield Dr., Pnr.	36	F4	
Mayfield Gdns. NW4	39	A6	
Mayfield Gdns. W7	55	A6	
Mayfield Rd. E4	34	C2	
Mayfield Rd. E8	50	C7	
Mayfield Rd. E13	60	F4	
Mayfield Rd. E17	41	H2	
Mayfield Rd. N8	40	F5	
Mayfield Rd. SW19	93	C1	
Mayfield Rd. W3	56	B7	
Mayfield Rd. W12	65	E2	
Mayfield Rd., Belv.	71	J4	
Mayfield Rd., Brom.	97	B5	
Mayfield Rd., Dag.	53	C1	
Mayfield Rd., Enf.	25	G2	
Mayfield Rd., Sutt.	100	G6	
Mayfield Rd.,	94	F4	
Th.Hth.			
Mayfields, Wem.	47	A2	
Mayfields Clo.,	47	A2	
Wem.			
Mayflower Clo. SE16	68	G4	
Greenland Quay			
Mayflower Ct. SE16	68	F2	
St. Marychurch St.			
Mayflower Rd. SW9	76	E3	
Mayflower St. SE16	68	F2	
St. Marychurch St.			
Mayfly Gdns., Nthlt.	54	D3	
Ruislip Rd.			
Mayford Clo. SW12	75	J7	
Mayford Clo., Beck.	95	G3	
Mayford Rd. SW12	75	J7	
Maygood St. N1	**8**	**E1**	
Maygood St. N1	58	F2	
Maygrove Rd. NW6	48	C6	
Mayhew Clo. E4	34	A3	
Mayhill Rd. SE7	69	H6	
Mayhill Rd., Barn.	23	B5	
Maylands Dr., Sid.	89	D3	
Maylands Rd., Wat.	28	C4	
Maynard Clo. SW6	66	E7	
Cambria St.			
Maynard Rd. E17	42	C5	
Maynards Quay E1	59	F7	
Garnet St.			
Mayo Rd. NW10	47	E6	
Mayo Rd., Croy.	95	A5	
Mayola Rd. E5	50	F4	
Mayow Rd. SE23	86	G3	
Mayow Rd. SE26	86	G4	
Mayplace Clo.,	80	H3	
Bexh.			
Mayplace La. SE18	70	E7	
Mayplace Rd. E.,	80	H3	
Bexh.			
Mayplace Rd. W.,	80	G4	
Bexh.			
Maypole Cres., Ilf.	35	G7	
Mayroyd Ave., Surb.	99	A2	
Mays Ct. WC2	**12**	**A6**	
Mays Hill Rd.,	96	E2	
Brom.			
Mays La. E4	34	D2	
Mays La., Barn.	22	G7	
Mays Rd., Tedd.	82	A5	
Maysoule Rd. SW11	75	G4	
Mayswood Gdns.,	53	J6	
Dag.			
Mayton St. N7	49	F3	
Maytree Clo., Edg.	30	C3	
Maytree Wk. SW2	85	G2	
Mayville Est. N16	50	B5	
Woodville Rd.			
Mayville Rd. E11	51	E2	
Mayville Rd., Ilf.	52	E5	
Maywood Clo., Beck.	87	B7	
Maze Hill SE3	69	E7	
Maze Hill SE10	69	E6	
Maze Rd., Rich.	65	A7	
Mazenod Ave. NW6	48	D7	
McAdam Dr., Enf.	24	H2	
Rowantree Rd.			
McAuley Clo. SE1	**16**	**E5**	
McAuley Clo. SE1	67	G3	
McAuley Clo. SE9	79	E5	
McCall Clo. SW4	76	E2	
Jeffreys Rd.			
McCall Cres. SE7	70	B5	
McCarthy Rd., Felt.	81	D5	
McCoid Way SE1	**16**	**J4**	
McCrone Ms. NW3	48	G6	
Belsize La.			
McCullum Rd. E3	59	J2	
Wrights Rd.			
McDermott Clo.	75	H3	
SW11			
McDermott Rd. SE15	77	D3	
McDonough Clo.,	98	H4	
Chess.			
McDowall Rd. SE5	76	J1	
McDowell Clo. E16	60	F5	
McEntee Ave. E17	41	J1	
McEwan Way E15	60	D1	
McGrath Rd. E15	51	F5	
McGregor Rd. W11	57	C5	
McIntosh Clo.,	101	E7	
Wall.			
McKay Rd. SW20	83	H7	
McKellar Clo.	28	J2	
(Bushey), Wat.			
McKerrell Rd. SE15	77	D1	
McLeod Rd. SE2	71	A4	
McLeod's Ms. SW7	**18**	**B1**	
McLeod's Ms. SW7	66	E4	

McMillan St. SE8 69 A6
McNeil Rd. SE5 77 B2
Mead, The N2 39 F2
Mead, The W13 55 E5
Mead, The, Beck. 96 C1
Mead, The, Stan. 37 F1
Mead, The, Wall. 101 B6
Mead, The, Wat. 28 E2
Mead, The, W.Wick. 103 D1
Mead Clo., Har. 37 A1
Mead Ct. NW9 38 C5
Mead Cres. E4 34 C4
Mead Cres., Sutt. 100 H4
Mead Gro., Rom. 44 D3
Mead Path SW17 84 F4
Mead Pl. E9 50 F6
Mead Pl., Croy. 101 H1
Mead Plat NW10 47 C6
Mead Rd., Chis. 88 F6
Mead Rd., Edg. 30 A6
Mead Rd., Rich. 82 F3
Mead Row SE1 16 E5
Mead Way, Brom. 96 E6
Mead Way, Croy. 102 H2
Meadcroft Rd. SE11 20 G6
Meadcroft Rd. SE11 67 H6
Meade Clo. W4 65 A6
Meadfield, Edg. 30 B2
Meadfield Grn., Edg. 30 B2
Meadfoot Rd. SW16 85 C7
Meadgate Ave., Wdf.Grn. 35 B5
Meadlands Dr., Rich. 82 G2
Meadow, The, Chis. 88 F6
Meadow Ave., Croy. 95 G6
Meadow Bank N21 24 F6
Meadow Clo. E4 34 B1
Mount Echo Ave.
Meadow Clo. SE6 87 A5
Meadow Clo. SW20 92 J4
Meadow Clo., Barn. 23 C6
Meadow Clo., Chis. 88 E5
Meadow Clo., Esher 98 C3
Meadow Clo., Houns. 72 G6
Meadow Clo., Nthlt. 54 G2
Meadow Clo., Rich. 82 H1
Meadow Clo., Sutt. 100 E2
Aultone Way
Meadow Dr. N10 40 A3
Meadow Dr. NW4 38 J2
Meadow Gdns., Edg. 30 B6
Meadow Garth NW10 47 C6
Meadow Hill, N.Mal. 92 E6
Meadow Ms. SW8 20 C6
Meadow Ms. SW8 67 F6
Meadow Pl. SW8 20 B7
Meadow Pl. SW8 67 E7
Meadow Pl. W4 65 E7
Edensor Rd.
Meadow Rd. SW8 20 C6
Meadow Rd. SW8 67 F7
Meadow Rd. SW19 84 F7
Meadow Rd., Bark. 52 J7
Meadow Rd., Borwd. 22 B2
Meadow Rd., Brom. 96 E1
Meadow Rd., Dag. 53 F6
Meadow Rd., Esher 98 B5
Meadow Rd., Felt. 81 E2
Meadow Rd., Loug. 27 B5
Meadow Rd., Pnr. 36 D4
Meadow Rd., Rom. 53 J1
Meadow Rd., Sthl. 54 F7
Meadow Rd., Sutt. 100 H5
Meadow Row SE1 16 J6
Meadow Row SE1 67 J3
Meadow Stile, Croy. 101 J3
High St.
Meadow Vw., Sid. 80 B7
Meadow Vw. Rd., Th.Hth. 94 H5
Meadow Wk. E18 42 G4
Meadow Wk., Dag. 53 F6
Meadow Wk., Epsom 99 E6
Meadow Wk., Wall. 101 B3
Meadow Way NW9 38 D5
Meadow Way, Chess. 98 H5
Meadow Way, Chig. 35 F3
Meadow Way, Orp. 104 D3
Meadow Way, Ruis. 36 B6
Meadow Way, Wem. 66 A6
Meadow Way, The, Har. 37 B1
Meadow Waye, Houns. 63 E6
Meadowbank NW3 48 J7
Meadowbank SE3 78 F3
Meadowbank, Surb. 91 J6
Meadowbank Clo. SW6 65 J7
Meadowbank Gdns., Houns. 72 A1

Meadowbank Rd. NW9 38 D7
Meadowcourt Rd. SE3 78 F4
Meadowcroft, Brom. 97 C3
Meadowcroft Rd. N13 32 G2
Meadows Clo. E10 51 A2
Meadows End, Sun. 90 A1
Meadowside SE9 78 J4
Meadowsweet Clo. E16 61 A5
Monarch Dr.
Meadowview Rd. SE6 87 A4
Meadowview Rd., Bex. 80 E6
Meads, The, Edg. 30 D6
Meads, The, Sutt. 100 B3
Meads La., Ilf. 43 H7
Meads Rd. N22 40 H2
Meads Rd., Enf. 25 H1
Meadvale Rd. W5 55 E4
Meadvale Rd., Croy. 95 C7
Meadway N14 32 D2
Meadway NW11 39 E6
Meadway SW20 92 J4
Meadway, Barn. 23 C4
Meadway, Beck. 96 C1
Meadway, Ilf. 52 H4
Meadway, Surb. 99 C1
Meadway, Twick. 82 A1
Meadway, Wdf.Grn. 34 J5
Meadway, The SE3 78 D2
Heath La.
Meadway, The, Buck.H. 35 A1
Meadway, The, Loug. 27 C6
Meadway Clo. NW11 39 E6
Meadway Clo., Barn. 23 D4
Meadway Clo., Pnr. 28 H6
Highbanks Rd.
Meadway Ct. NW11 39 E6
Meadway Gate NW11 39 D6
Meaford Way SE20 86 E7
Meakin Est. SE1 17 D5
Meakin Est. SE1 68 B3
Meanley Rd. E12 52 B4
Meard St. W1 11 H4
Meard St. W1 58 D6
Meath Rd. E15 60 F2
Meath Rd., Ilf. 52 F3
Meath St. SW11 76 B1
Mechanics Path SE8 69 A7
Deptford High St.
Mecklenburgh Pl. WC1 8 C5
Mecklenburgh Pl. WC1 58 F4
Mecklenburgh Sq. WC1 8 C5
Mecklenburgh Sq. WC1 58 F4
Mecklenburgh St. WC1 8 C5
Medburn St. NW1 7 H1
Medburn St. NW1 58 D6
Medcroft Gdns. SW14 74 C4
Medebourne Clo. SE3 78 G3
Medesenge Way N13 32 H6
Medfield St. SW15 74 G7
Medhurst Clo. E3 59 H2
Arbery Rd.
Medhurst Rd. E3 59 H2
Arbery Rd.
Median Rd. E5 50 F5
Medina Ave., Esher 98 B3
Medina Gro. N7 49 G3
Medina Rd.
Medina Rd. N7 49 G3
Medland Clo., Wall. 101 A1
Medlar Clo., Nthlt. 54 E2
Parkfield Ave.
Medlar St. SE5 76 J1
Medley Rd. NW6 48 D6
Medora Rd. SW2 76 F7
Medusa Rd. SE6 78 B6
Medway Bldgs. E3 59 H2
Medway Rd.
Medway Clo., Croy. 95 F6
Medway Clo., Ilf. 52 F5
Loxford La.
Medway Dr., Grnf. 55 C2
Medway Gdns., Wem. 46 D4
Medway Ms. E3 59 H2
Medway Rd.
Medway Par., Grnf. 55 C2
Medway Rd. E3 59 H2
Medway St. SW1 15 J6

Medway St. SW1 67 D3
Medwin St. SW4 76 B4
Meerbrook Rd. SE3 78 J3
Meeson Rd. E15 60 F1
Meeson St. E5 50 H4
Meeting Flds. Path E9 50 F6
Homerton Ter.
Meeting Ho. La. SE15 77 E1
Meetinghouse All. E1 68 E1
Chandler St.
Mehetabel Rd. E9 50 F6
Melancholy Wk. SE1 55 F3
Melanda Clo., Chis. 88 C5
Melanie Clo., Bexh. 80 E1
Melba Way SE13 78 B1
Melbourne Ave. N13 32 F6
Melbourne Ave. W13 64 D1
Melbourne Ave., Pnr. 36 H3
Melbourne Clo., Orp. 97 H7
Melbourne Clo., Wall. 101 C5
Melbourne Ct. E5 50 H4
Daubeney Rd.
Melbourne Ct. SE20 86 D7
Melbourne Gdns., Rom. 44 E5
Melbourne Gro. SE22 77 B4
Melbourne Ho., Hayes 54 C4
Melbourne Ms. SE6 78 C7
Melbourne Ms. SW9 76 G1
Melbourne Pl. WC2 12 D4
Melbourne Pl. WC2 58 F7
Melbourne Rd. E6 61 C1
Melbourne Rd. E10 42 B7
Melbourne Rd. E17 41 H4
Melbourne Rd. SW19 93 D1
Melbourne Rd., Ilf. 52 F6
Melbourne Rd., Tedd. 82 F6
Melbourne Rd., Wall. 101 B5
Melbourne Sq. SW9 76 G1
Melbourne Ms.
Melbourne Ter. SW6 66 E7
Waterford Rd.
Melbourne Way, Enf. 25 H6
Melbury Ave., Sthl. 63 H3
Melbury Clo., Chis. 88 B6
Melbury Clo., Esher 98 E6
Melbury Ct. W8 66 C3
Melbury Dr. SE5 68 B7
Sedgmoor Pl.
Melbury Gdns. SW20 92 H1
Melbury Rd. W14 66 C3
Melbury Rd., Har. 37 J5
Melbury Ter. NW1 6 H6
Melbury Ter. NW1 57 H4
Melcombe Gdns., Har. 37 J6
Melcombe Pl. NW1 10 J1
Melcombe Pl. NW1 57 J5
Melcombe St. NW1 7 A6
Melcombe St. NW1 57 J4
Meldon Clo. SW6 75 E1
Bagley's La.
Meldrum Rd., Ilf. 53 A2
Melfield Gdns. SE6 87 B4
Melford Ave., Bark. 52 H6
Melford Rd. E6 61 C4
Melford Rd. E11 51 E2
Melford Rd. E17 41 H4
Melford Rd. SE22 77 D7
Melford Rd., Ilf. 52 G2
Melfort Ave., Th.Hth. 94 H3
Melfort Rd., Th.Hth. 94 H3
Melgund Rd. N5 49 G5
Melina Pl. NW8 6 E4
Melina Pl. NW8 57 G3
Melina Rd. W12 65 H2
Melior Pl. SE1 17 D3
Melior St. SE1 17 D3
Melior St. SE1 68 B2
Mell St. SE10 69 E5
Trafalgar Rd.
Meller Clo., Croy. 101 E3
Melling St. SE18 70 H6
Mellish Clo., Bark. 61 J1
Mellish Gdns., Wdf.Grn. 34 G5
Harts Gro.
Mellish St. E14 69 A3
Mellison Rd. SW17 84 H5
Mellitus St. W12 56 F6
Mellor Clo., Walt. 90 F7

Mellows Rd., Ilf. 43 C3
Mellows Rd., Wall. 101 D5
Mells Cres. SE9 88 C4
Melody Rd. SW18 75 F5
Melon Rd. SE15 77 D1
Melrose Ave. N22 40 H1
Melrose Ave. NW2 47 H5
Melrose Ave. SW16 94 F3
Melrose Ave. SW19 84 C2
Melrose Ave., Borwd. 22 D5
Melrose Ave., Grnf. 54 H2
Melrose Ave., Mitch. 85 B7
Melrose Ave., Twick. 72 H7
Melrose Clo. SE12 87 G1
Melrose Clo., Grnf. 54 H2
Melrose Clo., Hayes 54 A5
Melrose Cres., Orp. 104 G4
Melrose Dr., Sthl. 63 G1
Melrose Gdns. W6 65 J3
Melrose Gdns., Edg. 38 B2
Melrose Gdns., N.Mal. 92 D3
Melrose Rd. SW13 74 F2
Melrose Rd. SW18 75 C6
Melrose Rd. SW19 93 D2
Melrose Rd. W3 65 C3
Stanley Rd.
Melrose Rd., Pnr. 36 F4
Melrose Ter. W6 65 J2
Melsa Rd., Mord. 93 F6
Meltham Way SE16 68 E5
Egan Way
Melthorne Dr., Ruis. 45 C3
Melthorpe Gdns. SE3 79 A1
Melton Clo., Ruis. 45 C1
Melton Ct. SW7 18 F2
Melton Ct. SW7 66 G4
Melton St. NW1 7 G4
Melton St. NW1 58 C3
Melville Ave. SW20 83 G7
Melville Ave., Grnf. 46 C5
Melville Ave., S.Croy. 102 C5
Melville Gdns. N13 32 G5
Melville Rd. E17 41 J3
Melville Rd. NW10 47 D7
Melville Rd. SW13 74 G1
Melville Rd., Sid. 89 C2
Melville Vill. Rd. W3 65 D1
High St.
Melvin Rd. SE20 95 F1
Melyn Clo. N7 49 C4
Anson Rd.
Memel Ct. EC1 8 J6
Memel St. EC1 8 J6
Memorial Ave. E15 60 E3
Memorial Clo., Houns. 63 F6
Queensmere Rd.
Mendip Clo. SE26 86 F4
Mendip Clo. SW19 84 B2
Queensmere Rd.
Mendip Clo., Wor.Pk. 99 J2
Cotswold Way
Mendip Dr. NW2 48 B2
Mendip Rd. SW11 75 F3
Mendip Rd., Ilf. 43 H5
Mendora Rd. SW6 66 B7
Menelik Rd. NW2 48 B4
Menlo Gdns. SE19 86 A7
Menotti St. E2 9 J5
Mentmore Clo., Har. 37 F6
Mentmore Ter. E8 50 E7
Meon Ct., Islw. 73 B2
Meon Rd. W3 65 C2
Meopham Rd., Mitch. 94 C1
Mepham Cres., Har. 28 J7
Mepham Gdns., Har. 28 J7
Mepham St. SE1 16 E2
Mepham St. SE1 67 F1
Mera Dr., Bexh. 80 G4
Merantun Way SW19 93 F1
Merbury Clo. SE13 78 D5
Merbury Rd. SE28 70 H2
Mercator Rd. SE13 78 D4
Mercer Clo., T.Ditt. 91 C7
Mercer St. WC2 12 A4
Mercer St. WC2 58 E6
Merceron St. E1 59 E4
Mercers Clo. SE10 69 F4
Mercers Pl. W6 65 J4
Mercers Rd. N19 49 D3
Merchant St. E3 59 J3
Merchiston Rd. SE6 87 D2
Merchland Rd. SE9 88 F1
Mercia Gro. SE13 78 C4
Mercier Rd. SW15 75 B5

Mercury Cen. Ind. Est., Felt.	72	A5	Merton Ind. Pk. SW19	93	F1	**Middle Temple La. EC4**	**12**	**E4**	Mildred Ave., Borwd.	22	A4
Mercury Way SE14	68	G6	Merton La. N6	48	J2	Middle Temple La. EC4	58	G6	Mildred Ave., Nthlt.	45	H5
Mercy Ter. SE13	78	B4	Merton Mans. SW20	93	A2				Mile End, The E17	41	G1
Mere Clo. SW15	75	A7	Merton Ri. NW3	48	H7	Middle Way SW16	94	D2	Mile End Pl. E1	59	G4
Mere Clo., Orp.	104	D2	Merton Rd. E17	42	C5	Middle Way, Erith	71	E3	Mile End Rd. E1	59	F5
Mere End, Croy.	95	G7	Merton Rd. SE25	95	D5	Middle Way, Hayes	54	D4	Mile End Rd. E3	59	H4
Mere Side, Orp.	104	D2	Merton Rd. SW18	75	D5	Douglas Cres.			Mile Rd., Wall.	101	B1
Merebank La., Croy.	101	F5	Merton Rd. SW19	84	E7	Middle Way, The,	37	C2	**Miles Pl. NW1**	**10**	**G1**
Meredith Ave. NW2	47	J5	Merton Rd., Bark.	52	J7	Har.			Miles Pl., Surb.	91	G4
Meredith Clo., Pnr.	28	D7	Merton Rd., Har.	45	J1	**Middle Yd. SE1**	**17**	**D1**	Villiers Ave.		
Meredith St. E13	60	G3	Merton Rd., Ilf.	43	J7	Middlefield Gdns.,	43	E6	Miles Rd. N8	40	E3
Meredith St. EC1	**8**	**G4**	Merton Way, W.Mol.	90	H4	Ilf.			Miles Rd., Mitch.	93	G3
Meredyth Rd. SW13	74	G2	Merttins Rd. SE15	77	G5	Middlefielde W13	55	E5	**Miles St. SW8**	**20**	**A6**
Meretone Clo. SE4	77	H4	Mervan Rd. SW2	76	G4	Middleham Gdns.	33	D6	Miles St. SW8	67	E6
Merevale Cres.,	93	F6	Mervyn Ave. SE9	88	F3	N18			Miles Way N20	31	H2
Mord.			Mervyn Rd. W13	64	D3	Middleham Rd. N18	33	D6	Milespit Hill NW7	30	H5
Mereway Rd., Twick.	82	A1	Messaline Ave. W3	56	C6	Middlesborough Rd.	33	D6	Milestone Clo.,	100	G6
Merewood Clo.,	97	D2	Messent Rd. SE9	78	J5	N18			Sutt.		
Brom.			Messeter Pl. SE9	79	D6	Middlesex Business	63	F2	Milestone Rd. SE19	86	C6
Merewood Rd., Bexh.	80	J2	Messina Ave. NW6	48	D7	Cen., The, Sthl.			Milfoil St. W12	56	G7
Mereworth Clo.,	96	F5	Metcalfe Wk., Felt.	81	E4	Middlesex Ct. W4	65	F4	Milford Clo. SE2	71	E6
Brom.			Gabriel Clo.			British Gro.			Milford Gdns., Edg.	30	A7
Mereworth Dr. SE18	70	E7	Meteor St. SW11	76	A4	**Middlesex Pas. EC1**	**12**	**H2**	Milford Gdns., Wem.	46	G4
Meriden Clo., Brom.	88	A7	Meteor Way, Wall.	101	E7	Middlesex Rd.,	94	E4	Milford Gro., Sutt.	100	F4
Meriden Clo., Ilf.	43	F1	Metheringham Way	38	E1	Mitch.			**Milford La. WC2**	**12**	**E5**
Meridian Gate E14	69	C2	NW9			**Middlesex St. E1**	**13**	**E2**	Milford La. WC2	58	F7
Meridian Rd. SE7	70	A7	**Methley St. SE11**	**20**	**F4**	Middlesex St. E1	59	B5	Milford Ms. SW16	85	F3
Meridian Trd. Est.	69	H4	Methley St. SE11	67	G5	Middlesex Wf. E5	50	F2	Milford Rd. W13	64	E1
SE7			Methuen Clo., Edg.	30	A7	Middleton Ave. E4	33	J4	Milford Rd., Sthl.	54	G7
Meridian Way N9	33	G2	Methuen Pk. N10	40	B2	Middleton Ave.,	55	A2	Milford Way SE15	77	C1
Meridian Way N18	33	F6	Methuen Rd., Belv.	71	H4	Grnf.			Sumner Est.		
Meridian Way, Enf.	25	G6	Methuen Rd., Bexh.	80	F5	Middleton Ave.,	89	C6	Milk St. E16	70	E1
Merifield Rd. SE9	78	J4	Methuen Rd., Edg.	30	A7	Sid.			**Milk St. EC2**	**13**	**A3**
Merino Pl., Sid.	80	A6	Methwold Rd. W10	57	A5	**Middleton Bldgs. W1**	**11**	**F2**	Milk St., Brom.	87	H6
Blackfen Rd.			Metro Ind. Cen.,	73	B2	Middleton Clo. E4	33	J3	Milk Yd. E1	57	F7
Merivale Rd. SW15	75	B4	Islw.			Middleton Dr. SE16	68	G2	Milkwell Gdns.,	34	H7
Merivale Rd., Har.	36	J7	Metropolitan Cen.,	54	H1	Middleton Dr., Pnr.	36	A3	Wdf.Grn.		
Merlewood Dr., Chis.	97	C1	The, Grnf.			Middleton Gdns.,	43	E6	Milkwell Yd. SE5	76	J1
Merley Ct. NW9	47	C1	Mews, The N1	58	J1	Ilf.			Milkwood Rd. SE24	76	H5
Merlin Clo., Croy.	102	B4	St. Paul St.			Middleton Gro. N7	49	E5	Mill Clo., Cars.	101	A2
Minster Dr.			Mews, The, Ilf.	43	A5	Middleton Ms. N7	49	E5	Mill Cor., Barn.	23	C1
Merlin Clo., Nthlt.	54	C3	Mews, The, Twick.	73	E6	Middleton Gro.			Mill Ct. E10	51	C3
Merlin Cres., Edg.	37	J1	Bridge Rd.			Middleton Rd. E8	50	D7	Mill Fm. Clo., Pnr.	36	C2
Merlin Gdns., Brom.	87	G3	**Mews St. E1**	**17**	**H1**	Middleton Rd. NW11	39	D7	Mill Fm. Cres.,	81	E1
Merlin Gro., Beck.	95	J4	Mews St. E1	68	D1	Middleton Rd.,	93	G7	Houns.		
Merlin Gro., Ilf.	35	E6	Mexfield Rd. SW15	75	C5	Cars.			Mill Gdns. SE26	86	E4
Merlin Rd. E12	52	A2	Meyer Rd., Erith	71	J6	Middleton Rd.,	93	E6	Mill Grn. Rd., Mitch.	93	J7
Merlin Rd., Well.	80	A4	**Meymott St. SE1**	**16**	**G2**	Mord.			Mill Hill SW13	74	G2
Merlin Rd. N., Well.	80	A4	Meymott St. SE1	67	H1	Middleton St. E2	59	E3	Mill Hill Rd.		
Merlin St. WC1	**8**	**E4**	Meynell Cres. E9	50	G7	Middleton Way SE13	78	D4	Mill Hill Circ. NW7	30	F5
Merlins Ave., Har.	45	F3	Meynell Gdns. E9	50	G7	Middleway NW11	39	E5	Watford Way		
Mermaid Ct. SE1	**17**	**B3**	Meynell Rd. E9	50	G7	Midfield Ave.,	80	J3	Mill Hill Gro. W3	65	B1
Mermaid Ct. SE1	68	A2	Meyrick Rd. NW10	47	G6	Bexh.			Mill Hill Rd.		
Mermaid Ct. SE16	68	J1	Meyrick Rd. SW11	75	G3	**Midford Pl. W1**	**7**	**G6**	Mill Hill Rd. SW13	74	G2
Merredene St. SW2	76	F6	Miall Wk. SE26	86	H4	Midholm NW11	39	E4	Mill Hill Rd. W3	65	B2
Merrick Rd., Sthl.	63	F2	**Micawber St. N1**	**9**	**A3**	Midholm, Wem.	47	A1	Mill La. E4	26	B3
Merrick Sq. SE1	**17**	**B5**	Micawber St. N1	58	J3	Midholm Clo. NW11	39	E4	Mill La. NW6	48	B5
Merrick Sq. SE1	67	J3	**Michael Faraday Ho.**	**21**	**C4**	Midholm Rd., Croy.	102	H2	Mill La. SE18	70	D5
Merridene N21	24	H6	**SE17**			**Midhope St. WC1**	**8**	**B4**	Mill La., Cars.	100	A4
Merrielands Cres.,	62	F1	Michael Gaynor Clo.	64	C1	Midhope St. WC1	58	B4	Mill La., Croy.	101	F3
Dag.			W7			Midhurst Ave. N10	40	A3	Mill La., Rom.	44	E6
Merrilands Rd.,	99	J1	Michael Rd. E11	51	E1	Midhurst Ave.,	94	G7	(Chadwell Heath),		
Wor.Pk.			Michael Rd. SE25	95	B3	Croy.			Mill La., Wdf.Grn.	34	F5
Merrilees Rd., Sid.	88	H1	Michael Rd. SW6	75	E1	Midhurst Hill,	80	G6	Mill Mead Ind. Cen.	41	E2
Merrilyn Clo.,	98	D6	Michaels Clo. SE13	78	E4	Bexh.			N17		
Esher			Micheldever Rd.	78	E6	Midhurst Rd. W13	64	D2	Mill Mead Rd. N17	41	E3
Merriman Rd. SE3	78	J1	SE12			Midland Pl. E14	69	C5	Mill Pl. E14	59	J6
Merrington Rd. SW6	66	D6	Michelham Gdns.,	82	D3	Ferry St.			East India Dock Rd.		
Merrion Ave., Stan.	29	G5	Twick.			Midland Rd. E10	42	C7	Mill Pl., Chis.	97	E1
Merritt Rd. SE4	77	J5	Michels Row, Rich.	73	H4	**Midland Rd. NW1**	**7**	**J2**	Mill Pl., Kings.T.	91	J3
Merrivale N14	24	D6	Kew Foot Rd.			Midland Rd. NW1	58	D2	Mill Plat, Islw.	73	D2
Merrivale Ave., Ilf.	43	A4	Michigan Ave. E12	52	C4	Midland Ter. NW2	48	A3	Mill Plat Ave., Islw.	73	D2
Merrow St. SE17	**21**	**B4**	Michleham Down	31	C4	Midland Ter. NW10	56	E4	Mill Ridge, Edg.	29	J5
Merrow St. SE17	67	J6	N12			Midleton Rd.,	92	C2	Mill Rd. E16	69	H1
Merrow Wk. SE17	**21**	**C3**	Mickleham Clo., Orp.	97	J2	N.Mal.			Mill Rd. SE13	78	C3
Merrow Way, Croy.	103	C6	Mickleham Gdns.,	100	B6	Midlothian Rd. E3	59	H5	Loampit Vale		
Merry Hill Mt.	28	H1	Sutt.			Midmoor Rd. SW12	85	C1	Mill Rd. SW19	84	F7
(Bushey), Wat.			Mickleham Rd., Orp.	97	J1	Midmoor Rd. SW19	93	A1	Mill Rd., Erith	71	J7
Merrydown Way,	97	B1	Mickleham Way,	103	D7	Midship Clo. SE16	68	G1	Mill Rd., Ilf.	52	D3
Chis.			Croy.			Surrey Water Rd.			Mill Rd., Twick.	81	J2
Merryfield SE3	78	F2	Micklethwaite Rd.	66	D6	Midstrath Rd. NW10	47	E4	Mill Row N1	59	B1
Merryfield Gdns.,	29	F5	SW6			Midsummer Ave.,	72	F4	Mill Shot Clo. SW6	74	J1
Stan.			Middle Dene NW7	30	D3	Houns.			**Mill St. SE1**	**17**	**G4**
Merryhill Clo. E4	26	B7	Middle Fld. NW8	57	G1	Midway, Sutt.	93	C7	Mill St. SE1	68	C2
Merryhills Ct. N14	24	C5	Middle Grn. Clo.,	91	J6	Midwood Clo. NW2	47	H3	**Mill St. W1**	**11**	**F5**
Merryhills Dr., Enf.	24	D4	Surb.			Miers Clo. E6	61	D1	Mill St. W1	58	C7
Mersea Ho., Bark.	52	E6	Alpha Rd.			Mighell Ave., Ilf.	43	A5	Mill St., Kings.T.	91	H3
Mersey Rd. E17	41	J3	Middle La. N8	40	E5	**Milborne Gro. SW10**	**18**	**D4**	Mill Trd. Est., The	56	C3
Mersham Dr. NW9	38	A5	Middle La., Tedd.	82	C6	Milborne Gro. SW10	66	F5	NW10		
Mersham Pl. SE20	95	E1	Middle La. Ms. N8	40	E5	Milborne St. E9	50	F6	Mill Vale, Brom.	96	F2
Mersham Rd.,	95	A3	Middle La.			Milborough Cres.	78	E6	Mill Vw. Gdns.,	102	G3
Th.Hth.			Middle Pk. Ave. SE9	79	A6	SE12			Croy.		
Merten Rd., Rom.	44	E7	Middle Path, Har.	46	A1	**Milcote St. SE1**	**16**	**G4**	Mill Way, Felt.	72	B5
Merthyr Ter. SW13	65	H6	Middle Rd.			Milcote St. SE1	67	H2	**Mill Yd. E1**	**13**	**H5**
Merton Ave. W4	65	F4	Middle Rd. E13	60	G2	Mildenhall Rd. E5	50	F4	Millais Ave. E12	52	D5
Merton Ave., Nthlt.	45	J5	London Rd.			Mildmay Ave. N1	50	A6	Millais Gdns., Edg.	38	A2
Merton Hall Gdns.	93	B1	Middle Rd. SW16	94	C2	Mildmay Gro. N1	50	A5	Millais Rd. E11	51	C4
SW20			Middle Rd., Barn.	23	H6	Mildmay Pk. N1	50	A5	Millais Rd., Enf.	25	C5
Merton Hall Rd.	84	B7	Middle Rd., Har.	46	A2	Mildmay Rd. N1	50	A5	Millais Rd., N.Mal.	92	E7
SW19			Middle Row W10	57	B4	Mildmay Rd., Ilf.	52	E3	Millais Way, Epsom	99	C4
Merton High St.	84	F7	**Middle St. EC1**	**12**	**J1**	Winston Way			Millard Clo. N16	50	B5
SW19						Mildmay St. N1	50	A6	Boleyn Rd.		

Millard Ter., Dag. 53 G6
Church Elm La.
Millbank SW1 16 A5
Millbank SW1 67 E4
Millbank Twr. SW1 20 A2
Millbank Twr. SW1 67 E4
Millbank Way SE12 70 G5
Millbourne Rd., 81 E4
Erith
Millbrook Ave., Well. 79 G4
Millbrook Gdns. 44 F6
(Chadwell Heath)
Rom.
Millbrook Rd. N9 33 E1
Millbrook Rd. SW9 76 H3
Millender Wk. SE16 68 F4
Miller Clo., Pnr. 36 C2
Miller Rd. SW19 84 G6
Miller Rd., Croy. 101 F1
Miller St. NW1 7 F1
Miller St. NW1 58 C2
Millers Ave. E8 50 C5
Millers Clo. NW7 30 G4
Millers Ct. W4 65 F5
Chiswick Mall
Millers Grn. Clo., Enf. 24 H3
Millers Ter. E8 50 C5
Millers Way W6 65 J2
Millet Rd., Croy. 54 H3
Millfield Ave. E17 41 H1
Millfield La. N6 48 J2
Millfield Pl. N6 49 A2
Millfield Rd., Edg. 38 C2
Millfield Rd., 81 E1
Houns.
Millfields Rd. E5 50 F4
Millgrove St. SW11 76 A1
Millharbour E14 69 B3
Millhaven Clo., 44 B6
Rom.
Millhouse Pl. SE27 85 H4
Millicent Rd. E10 50 J1
Milligan St. E14 59 J7
Three Colt St.
Milling Rd., Edg. 30 D7
Millman Ms. WC1 8 C6
Millman Ms. WC1 58 F4
Millman St. WC1 8 C6
Millman St. WC1 58 F4
Millmark Gro. SE14 77 H2
Millmarsh La., Enf. 25 H2
Millpond Est. SE16 68 E2
West La.
Mills Ct. EC2 9 D5
Mills Gro. E14 60 C5
Dewberry St.
Mills Gro. NW4 39 A3
Mills Row W4 65 D4
Bridge St.
Millside, Cars. 100 J2
Millside Pl., Islw. 73 E2
Millsmead Way, 27 C2
Loug.
Millson Clo. N20 31 G2
Millstream Rd. SE1 17 F4
Millstream Rd. SE1 68 E2
Millwall Dock Rd. 69 A3
E14
Millway NW7 30 E5
Millway Gdns., Nthlt. 45 F6
Millwell Cres., Chig. 35 G5
Millwood Rd., 72 J5
Houns.
Millwood St. W10 57 B5
St. Charles Sq.
Milman Clo., Pnr. 36 D3
Milman Rd. NW6 57 A2
Milmans St. SW10 18 E6
Milmans St. SW10 66 G6
Milne Feild, Pnr. 28 G7
Milne Gdns. SE9 79 B5
Milne Dr., Twick. 73 A7
Milner Pl. N1 58 G1
Milner Pl., Cars. 101 A4
High St.
Milner Rd. E15 60 E3
Milner Rd. SW19 93 E1
Milner Rd., Dag. 53 C2
Milner Rd., 91 G3
Kings.T.
Milner Rd., Mord. 93 G5
Milner Rd., Th.Hth. 95 A3
Milner Sq. N1 49 H7
Milner St. SW3 18 J1
Milner St. SW3 66 J4
Milnthorpe Rd. W4 65 D6
Milo Rd. SE22 77 C6
Milroy Wk. SE1 16 G1
Milson Rd. W14 66 A3
Milton Ave. E6 52 A7
Milton Ave. N6 40 C7
Milton Ave. NW9 38 C3
Milton Ave. NW10 56 C1

Milton Ave., Barn. 23 C5
Milton Ave., Croy. 95 A7
Milton Ave., Sutt. 100 G3
Milton Clo. N2 39 F5
Milton Clo. SE1 21 F2
Milton Clo. SE1 68 C4
Milton Clo., Hayes 51 A8
Milton Clo., Sutt. 100 G3
Milton Ct. EC2 13 B1
Milton Ct. Rd. SE14 68 H6
Milton Cres., Ilf. 43 F7
Milton Dr., Borwd. 22 B5
Milton Gro. N11 32 C5
Milton Gro. N16 50 A4
Milton Pk. N6 40 C7
Milton Pl. N7 49 G5
Georges Rd.
Milton Rd. E17 42 A4
Milton Rd. N6 40 C7
Milton Rd. N15 40 H4
Milton Rd. NW7 30 G5
Milton Rd. NW9 38 G7
West Hendon Bdy.
Milton Rd. SE24 76 H6
Milton Rd. SW14 74 D3
Milton Rd. SW19 84 F6
Milton Rd. W3 65 D1
Milton Rd. W7 55 C7
Milton Rd., Belv. 71 G4
Milton Rd., Croy. 102 A1
Milton Rd., Hmptn. 81 G7
Milton Rd., Har. 37 B4
Milton Rd., Mitch. 85 A7
Milton Rd., Sutt. 100 D3
Milton Rd., Wall. 101 C6
Milton Rd., Well. 79 J1
Milton St. EC2 13 B1
Milton St. EC2 59 A5
Milverton Gdns., Ilf. 52 J2
Milverton Rd. NW6 47 J7
Milverton St. SE11 20 F4
Milverton St. SE11 67 G5
Milverton Way SE9 88 D4
Milward St. E1 59 E5
Stepney Way
Milward Wk. SE18 70 D6
Spearman St.
Mimosa Rd., Hayes 54 C5
Mimosa St. SW6 75 C1
Mina Rd. SE17 21 E4
Mina Rd. SE17 68 B5
Mina Rd. SW19 93 D1
Minard Rd. SE6 78 E7
Minchenden Cres. 32 C3
N14
Mincing La. EC3 13 D5
Mincing La. EC3 59 B7
Minden Rd. SE20 95 E1
Minden Rd., Sutt. 100 C2
Minehead Rd. SW16 85 F5
Minehead Rd., Har. 45 G3
Minera Ms. SW1 19 C1
Minera Ms. SW1 67 A4
Mineral St. SE18 70 H4
Minerva Clo. SW9 67 G7
Minerva Clo., Sid. 88 H3
Minerva Rd. E4 34 B7
Minerva Rd. NW10 56 C3
Minerva Rd., 91 J2
Kings.T.
Minerva St. E2 59 E2
Minet Ave. NW10 56 E2
Minet Dr., Hayes 63 A1
Minet Gdns. NW10 56 E2
Minet Gdns., Hayes 63 A1
Minet Rd. SW9 76 H2
Minford Gdns. W14 66 A2
Ming St. E14 60 A7
Mingard Wk. N7 49 F2
Hornsey Rd.
Ministry Way SE9 88 C2
Miniver Pl. EC4 58 J7
Garlick Hill
Mink Ct., Houns. 72 C2
Minniedale, Surb. 91 J5
Minnow Wk. SE17 21 E2
Minories EC3 13 F4
Minories EC3 59 C6
Minshull Pl., Beck. 87 A7
Minshull St. SW8 76 D1
Wandsworth Rd.
Minson Rd. E9 59 G1
Minstead Gdns. 74 F7
SW15
Minstead Way, 92 E6
N.Mal.
Minster Ave., Sutt. 100 D2
Burford Rd.
Minster Dr., Croy. 102 B4
Minster Gdns., 90 F5
W.Mol.
Molesey Ave.
Minster Rd. NW2 48 B5

Minster Rd., Brom. 87 H7
Minster Wk. N8 40 E4
Lightfoot Rd.
Minstrel Gdns., Surb. 91 J5
Mint Rd., Wall. 101 B4
Mint St. SE1 16 J3
Mint Wk., Croy. 101 J3
High St.
Mintern Clo. N13 32 H3
Mintern St. N1 8 D1
Mintern St. N1 59 A2
Minterne Ave., 63 G4
Sthl.
Minterne Rd., Har. 37 J5
Minterne Way, Hayes 54 C6
Minton Ms. NW6 48 E6
Lymington Rd.
Mirabel Rd. SW6 66 C7
Miranda Ct. W3 55 J6
Miranda Rd. N19 49 C1
Mirfield St. SE7 70 A3
Miriam Rd. SE18 70 H5
Missenden Gdns., 93 F6
Mord.
Mission Gro. E17 41 H5
Mission Pl. SE15 77 D1
Mistletoe Clo., 102 G1
Croy.
Marigold Way
Mitcham Gdn. Vill., 94 A5
Mitch.
Mitcham Ind. Est., 94 A1
Mitch.
Mitcham La. SW16 85 B6
Mitcham Pk., Mitch. 93 H4
Mitcham Rd. E6 61 B3
Mitcham Rd. SW17 84 J5
Mitcham Rd., Croy. 94 G5
Mitcham Rd., Ilf. 43 J7
Mitchell Clo. SE2 71 C4
Mitchell Clo., Belv. 71 J3
Lwr. Rd.
Mitchell Rd. N13 32 H5
Mitchell Rd., Orp. 104 J4
Mitchell St. EC1 11 J5
Mitchell St. EC1 58 J4
Mitchell Wk. E6 61 B5
Oliver Gdns.
Mitchell Way NW10 47 C4
Mitchell Way, Brom. 96 G1
Mitchellbrook Way 47 D6
NW10
Mitchison Rd. N1 50 A6
Mitchley Rd. N17 41 D3
Mitford Rd. N19 49 E2
Mitre, The E14 59 J7
Three Colt St.
Mitre Clo., Brom. 96 F2
Beckenham La.
Mitre Clo., Sutt. 100 F7
Mitre Ct. EC2 13 A3
Mitre Ct. EC4 12 F4
Mitre Rd. E15 60 E2
Mitre Rd. SE1 16 F3
Mitre Rd. SE1 67 G2
Mitre Sq. EC3 13 E4
Mitre St. EC3 13 E4
Mitre St. EC3 59 B6
Mitre Way NW10 56 H4
Moat, The, N.Mal. 92 E1
Moat Cres. N3 39 E3
Moat Cft., Well. 80 C3
Moat Dr. E13 60 J2
Boundary Rd.
Moat Dr., Har. 36 J4
Moat Fm. Rd., Nthlt. 45 F6
Moat Pl. SW9 76 F3
Moat Pl. W3 56 B6
Moatside, Enf. 25 F4
Moatside, Felt. 81 C4
Moberley Rd. SW4 76 D7
Modbury Gdns. NW5 49 A6
Queens Cres.
Modder Pl. SW15 75 A4
Cardinal Pl.
Model Fm. Clo. SE9 88 B3
Modling Ho. E2 59 G3
Mace St.
Moelwyn Hughes Ct. 49 D5
N7
Hilldrop Cres.
Moelyn Ms., Har. 37 D5
Moffat Gdns., 93 G3
Mitch.
Moffat Rd. N13 32 E6
Moffat Rd. SW17 84 H4
Moffat Rd., Th.Hth. 94 J2
Mogden La., Islw. 73 H5
Moiety Rd. E14 69 A2
Moira Clo. N17 41 B2
Moira Rd. SE9 79 C4

Moland Mead SE16 68 G5
Crane Mead
Molasses Row SW11 75 F3
Cinnamon Row
Mole Ct., Epsom 99 C4
Molember Ct., 91 B5
E.Mol.
Molember Rd., 91 A5
E.Mol.
Molescroft SE9 89 F2
Molesey Ave., 90 F5
W.Mol.
Molesey Dr., Sutt. 100 B2
Molesey Pk. Ave., 90 H5
W.Mol.
Molesey Pk. Clo., 90 J5
E.Mol.
Molesey Pk. Rd., 90 H5
E.Mol.
Molesey Pk. Rd., 90 H5
W.Mol.
Molesey Rd., W.Mol. 90 E5
Molesford Rd. SW6 75 D1
Molesham Clo., 90 H3
W.Mol.
Molesham Way, 90 H3
W.Mol.
Molesworth St. SE13 78 C4
Molineaux Pl., Tedd. 82 D5
Mollison Dr., Wall. 101 D7
Mollison Way, Edg. 37 J2
Molly Huggins Clo. 76 C7
SW12
Molyneux St. W1 10 H2
Molyneux St. W1 57 H5
Mona Rd. SE15 77 F2
Mona St. E16 60 F5
Monarch Clo., 103 F4
W.Wick.
Monarch Dr. E16 61 A5
Monarch Ms. SW16 85 G5
Monarch Rd., Belv. 71 G3
Monastery Gdns., 25 A2
Enf.
Monaveen Gdns., 90 G3
W.Mol.
Monck St. SW1 15 J6
Monck St. SW1 67 D3
Monclar Rd. SE5 77 A4
Moncorvo Clo. SW7 14 G4
Linton Gdns.
Moncrieff Clo. E6 61 B6
Moncrieff St. SE15 77 D2
Monega Rd. E7 51 J6
Monega Rd. E12 52 A6
Monfitchet Rd. E6 61 E6
Warwall
Monier Rd. E3 51 A7
Monivea Rd., Beck. 86 J7
Monk Dr. E16 60 G6
Monk Pas. E16 60 G7
Monk Dr.
Monk St. SE18 70 D4
Monkchester Clo., 27 D1
Loug.
Monkfrith Ave. N14 24 B6
Monkfrith Clo. N14 24 B7
Monkfrith Way N14 24 A7
Monkhams Ave., 34 G5
Wdf.Grn.
Monkhams Dr., 34 H5
Wdf.Grn.
Monkhams La., 34 H3
Buck.H.
Monkhams La., 34 G5
Wdf.Grn.
Monkleigh Rd., 93 B3
Mord.
Monks Ave., Barn. 23 F6
Monks Ave., W.Mol. 90 F5
Monks Clo. SE2 71 D4
Monks Clo., Enf. 24 J2
Monks Clo., Har. 45 H2
Monks Clo., Ruis. 45 D4
Monks Dr. W3 56 A5
Monks Orchard Rd., 103 A1
Beck.
Monks Pk., Wem. 47 B6
Monks Pk. Gdns., 47 B7
Wem.
Monks Rd., Enf. 24 J2
Monks Way NW11 39 C4
Hurstwood Rd.
Monks Way, Beck. 96 A6
Monks Way, Orp. 104 F1
Monksdene Gdns., 100 E3
Sutt.
Monksgrove, Loug. 27 D5
Monksmead, Borwd. 22 C4
Monkswell Ct. N10 40 A1
Pembroke Rd.
Monkswood Gdns., 22 D5
Borwd.

Monkswood Gdns., Ilf.	43	D3
Monkton Rd., Well.	79	J2
Monkton St. SE11	**20**	**F1**
Monkton St. SE11	67	G4
Monkville Ave. NW11	39	C4
Monkwell Sq. EC2	**13**	**A2**
Monmouth Ave. E18	42	H3
Monmouth Ave., Kings.T.	82	F7
Monmouth Clo., Mitch.	94	E4
Recreation Way		
Monmouth Clo., Well.	80	A4
Monmouth Gro. W5	64	H4
Sterling Pl.		
Monmouth Pl. W2	**10**	**A4**
Monmouth Pl. W2	57	D6
Monmouth Rd.		
Monmouth Rd. E6	61	C3
Monmouth Rd. N9	33	E2
Monmouth Rd. W2	57	D6
Monmouth Rd., Dag.	53	F5
Monmouth St. WC2	**12**	**A5**
Monmouth St. WC2	58	E6
Monnery Rd. N19	49	C3
Monnow Rd. SE1	**21**	**H2**
Monnow Rd. SE1	68	D5
Mono La., Felt.	81	B2
Monoux Gro. E17	42	A1
Monro Gdns., Har.	29	B7
Monroe Cres., Enf.	25	E1
Monroe Dr. SW14	74	B5
Mons Way, Brom.	97	B6
Monsal Ct. E5	50	G4
Redwald Rd.		
Monsell Rd. N4	49	H3
Monson Rd. NW10	56	G2
Monson Rd. SE14	68	G7
Montacute Rd. SE6	77	J7
Montacute Rd., Mord.	93	F6
Montagu Cres. N18	33	E4
Montagu Gdns. N18	33	E4
Montagu Gdns., Wall.	101	C4
Montagu Mans. W1	**11**	**A1**
Montagu Ms. N. W1	**11**	**A2**
Montagu Ms. N. W1	57	J5
Montagu Ms. S. W1	**11**	**A3**
Montagu Ms. W. W1	**11**	**A3**
Montagu Pl. W1	**10**	**J2**
Montagu Pl. W1	57	J5
Montagu Rd. N9	33	F3
Montagu Rd. N18	33	E5
Montagu Rd. NW4	38	G6
Montagu Row W1	**11**	**A2**
Montagu Sq. W1	**11**	**A2**
Montagu Sq. W1	57	J5
Montagu St. W1	**11**	**A3**
Montagu St. W1	57	J6
Montague Ave. SE4	77	J4
Montague Ave. W7	64	C1
Montague Clo. SE1	**17**	**B1**
Montague Clo. SE1	68	A1
Montague Clo., Walt.	90	A7
Montague Gdns. W3	56	A7
Montague Pl. WC1	**11**	**J1**
Montague Pl. WC1	58	D5
Montague Rd. E8	50	D5
Montague Rd. E11	51	F3
Montague Rd. N8	40	F5
Montague Rd. N15	41	D4
Montague Rd. SW19	84	E7
Montague Rd. W7	64	C2
Montague Rd. W13	55	E6
Montague Rd., Croy.	101	H1
Montague Rd., Houns.	72	H3
Montague Rd., Rich.	73	H6
Montague Rd., Sthl.	63	E4
Montague Rd. Ind. Est. N18	33	F4
Montague Sq. SE15	68	F7
Clifton Way		
Montague St. EC1	**12**	**J2**
Montague St. EC1	58	J5
Montague St. WC1	**12**	**A1**
Montague St. WC1	58	E5
Montague Waye, Sthl.	63	E3
Montalt Rd., Wdf.Grn.	34	F5
Montana Rd. SW17	85	A4
Montana Rd. SW20	92	J1
Montbelle Rd. SE9	88	E3
Montcalm Clo., Brom.	96	G6
Montcalm Clo., Hayes	54	B3
Ayles Rd.		
Montcalm Rd. SE7	70	A7
Montclare St. E2	**9**	**F5**
Monteagle Ave., Bark.	52	F6
Monteagle Way E5	50	D3
Rendlesham Rd.		
Monteagle Way SE15	77	E3
Montefiore St. SW8	76	B2
Monteith Rd. E3	59	J1
Montem Rd. SE23	77	J7
Montem Rd., N.Mal.	92	E4
Montem St. N4	49	F1
Thorpedale Rd.		
Montenotte Rd. N8	40	C5
Monterey Clo., Bex.	89	J2
Montford Pl. SE11	**20**	**E4**
Montford Pl. SE11	67	G5
Montford Rd., Sun.	90	A4
Montfort Gdns., Ilf.	35	F6
Montfort Pl. SW19	84	A1
Montgolfier Wk., Nthlt.	54	E3
Jetstar Way		
Montgomery Ave., Esher	98	B3
Montgomery Clo., Mitch.	94	E4
Montgomery Clo., Sid.	79	J6
Montgomery Rd. W4	65	C4
Montgomery Rd., Edg.	29	J6
Montholme Rd. SW11	75	J6
Monthope Rd. E1	**13**	**H2**
Montolieu Gdns. SW15	74	H5
Montpelier Ave. W5	55	F5
Montpelier Ave., Bex.	80	D7
Montpelier Gdns. E6	61	A3
Montpelier Gdns., Rom.	44	C7
Montpelier Gro. NW5	49	C5
Montpelier Ms. SW7	**14**	**H5**
Montpelier Pl. SW7	**14**	**H5**
Montpelier Pl. SW7	66	H3
Montpelier Ri. NW11	39	B7
Montpelier Ri., Wem.	46	G1
Montpelier Rd. N3	39	F1
Montpelier Rd. SE15	77	E1
Montpelier Rd. W5	55	G5
Montpelier Rd., Sutt.	100	F4
Montpelier Row SE3	78	F2
Montpelier Row, Twick.	73	E7
Montpelier Sq. SW7	**14**	**H5**
Montpelier Sq. SW7	66	H2
Montpelier St. SW7	**14**	**H4**
Montpelier St. SW7	66	H3
Montpelier Ter. SW7	**14**	**H4**
Montpelier Vale SE3	78	F2
Montpelier Wk. SW7	**14**	**G5**
Montpelier Wk. SW7	66	H3
Montpelier Way NW11	39	B7
Montrave Rd. SE20	86	F7
Montreal Pl. WC2	**12**	**C5**
Montreal Rd., Ilf.	35	F7
Montrell Rd. SW2	85	E1
Montrose Ave. NW6	57	B2
Montrose Ave., Sid.	80	A7
Montrose Ave., Twick.	72	H7
Montrose Ave., Well.	79	G3
Montrose Clo., Well.	79	J3
Montrose Clo., Wdf.Grn.	34	G4
Montrose Ct. SW7	**14**	**F4**
Montrose Ct. SW7	66	G2
Montrose Cres. N12	31	F6
Montrose Cres., Wem.	46	H6
Montrose Gdns., Mitch.	93	J3
Montrose Gdns., Sutt.	100	D2
Montrose Pl. SW1	**15**	**C4**
Montrose Pl. SW1	67	A2
Montrose Rd., Har.	37	B2
Montrose Way SE23	86	G1
Montserrat Ave., Wdf.Grn.	34	D7
Montserrat Clo. SE19	86	A5
Montserrat Rd. SW15	75	B4
Monument Gdns. SE13	78	C5
Monument St. EC3	**13**	**C5**
Monument St. EC3	59	A7
Monument Way N17	41	C3
Monza St. E1	59	F7
Moodkee St. SE16	68	F3
Moody St. E1	59	G3
Moon La., Barn.	23	C3
Moon St. N1	58	H1
Moor La. EC2	**13**	**B2**
Moor La. EC2	59	A5
Moor La., Chess.	98	H4
Moor Mead Rd., Twick.	73	D6
Moor Pl. EC2	**13**	**B2**
Moor St. W1	**11**	**J4**
Moorcroft Rd. SW16	85	E3
Moorcroft Way, Pnr.	36	E5
Moordown SE18	79	D1
Moore Clo. SW14	74	C3
Little St. Leonards		
Moore Clo., Mitch.	94	B2
Moore Cres., Dag.	62	B1
Moore Pk. Rd. SW6	66	E7
Moore Rd. SE19	85	J6
Moore St. SW3	**18**	**J1**
Moore St. SW3	66	J4
Moore Wk. E7	51	G4
Stracey Rd.		
Moore Way SE22	86	D1
Lordship La.		
Moorefield Rd. N17	41	C3
Moorehead Way SE3	78	H3
Mooreland Rd., Brom.	87	F7
Moorey Clo. E15	60	F1
Stephen's Rd.		
Moorfield Ave. W5	55	G4
Moorfield Rd., Chess.	98	H5
Moorfield Rd., Enf.	25	F1
Moorfields EC2	**13**	**B2**
Moorfields EC2	59	A5
Moorgate EC2	**13**	**B2**
Moorgate EC2	59	A5
Moorgate Pl. EC2	**13**	**B3**
Moorhouse Rd. W2	57	D6
Moorhouse Rd., Har.	37	G3
Moorland Clo., Rom.	44	H1
Moorland Clo., Twick.	72	G7
Telford Rd.		
Moorland Rd. SW9	76	H4
Moorlands Ave. NW7	30	H6
Moorlands Est. SW9	76	G4
Moormead Dr., Epsom	99	E5
Moorside Rd., Brom.	87	E3
Moortown Rd., Wat.	28	C4
Moot Ct. NW9	38	A5
Mora Rd. NW2	47	J4
Mora St. EC1	**9**	**A4**
Mora St. EC1	58	J3
Morant Pl. N22	40	F1
Commerce Rd.		
Morant St. E14	60	A7
Morat St. SW9	76	F1
Moravian Pl. SW10	**18**	**F6**
Moravian St. E2	59	F3
Moray Ms. N7	49	F2
Durham Rd.		
Moray Rd. N4	49	F2
Mordaunt Gdns., Dag.	53	E7
Mordaunt Ho. NW10	56	D1
Mordaunt Rd. NW10	56	D1
Mordaunt St. SW9	76	F3
Morden Clo. SE13	78	C2
Morden Ct., Mord.	93	E4
Morden Gdns., Grnf.	46	C5
Morden Gdns., Mitch.	93	G4
Morden Hall Rd. Mord.	93	E3
Morden Hill SE13	78	C2
Morden La. SE13	78	C1
Morden Rd. SE3	78	G2
Morden Rd. SW19	93	E1
Morden Rd., Mitch.	93	F4
Morden Rd., Rom.	44	E7
Morden Rd. Ms. SE3	78	G2
Morden St. SE13	78	B1
Morden Way, Sutt.	93	D7
Morden Wf. Rd. SE10	69	E3
Mordon Rd., Ilf.	54	A6
Mordred Rd. SE6	87	E2
More Clo. E16	60	F6
More Clo. W14	66	A4
Morecambe Clo. E1	59	G5
Morecambe Gdns., Stan.	29	G4
Morecambe St. SE17	**21**	**A2**
Morecambe St. SE17	67	J4
Morecambe Ter. N18	33	A4
Morecombe Clo., Kings.T.	83	B7
Moree Way N18	33	D4
Moreland Clo. NW11	48	E1
Moreland St. EC1	**8**	**H3**
Moreland St. EC1	58	H3
Moreland Way E4	34	B3
Morella Rd. SW12	75	J7
Moremead Rd. SE6	86	J4
Morena St. SE6	78	B7
Moresby Ave., Surb.	92	B7
Moresby Rd. E5	50	E1
Moresby Wk. SW8	76	B2
Moreton Ave., Islw.	73	B1
Moreton Clo. E5	50	F2
Moreton Clo. N15	41	A6
Moreton Clo. NW7	30	J6
Moreton Gdns., Wdf.Grn.	35	B5
Moreton Pl. SW1	**19**	**G3**
Moreton Pl. SW1	67	C5
Moreton Rd. N15	41	A6
Moreton Rd., S.Croy.	102	A5
Moreton Rd., Wor.Pk.	99	G2
Moreton St. SW1	**19**	**G3**
Moreton St. SW1	67	C5
Moreton Ter. SW1	**19**	**G3**
Moreton Ter. SW1	67	C5
Moreton Ter. Ms. N. SW1	**19**	**G3**
Moreton Ter. Ms. S. SW1	**19**	**G3**
Moreton Twr. W3	65	B1
Morford Clo., Ruis.	36	B7
Morford Way, Ruis.	36	B7
Morgan Ave. E17	42	D4
Morgan Clo., Dag.	63	G7
Morgan Rd. N7	49	G5
Morgan Rd. W10	57	C5
Morgan Rd., Brom.	87	G7
Morgan St. E3	59	H3
Morgan St. E16	60	F5
Morgan Way, Wdf.Grn.	35	B6
Morgans La. SE1	**17**	**D2**
Morgans La. SE1	68	B1
Moriatry Clo. N7	49	E4
Morie St. SW18	75	E4
Morieux Rd. E10	50	J1
Moring Rd. SW17	85	A4
Morkyns Wk. SE21	86	B3
Morland Ave., Croy.	102	B1
Morland Clo., Hmptn.	81	F5
Morland Clo., Mitch.	93	H3
Morland Gdns., NW10	47	D7
Morland Gdns., Sthl.	63	H1
Morland Ms. N1	49	G7
Lofting Rd.		
Morland Rd. E17	41	G5
Morland Rd. SE20	86	G6
Morland Rd., Croy.	102	B1
Morland Rd., Dag.	53	G7
Morland Rd., Har.	37	H5
Morland Rd., Ilf.	52	E2
Morland Rd., Sutt.	100	F5
Morley Ave. E4	34	D7
Morley Ave. N18	33	D4
Morley Ave. N22	40	G2
Morley Clo., Orp.	104	E2
Morley Clo., Ruis.	45	C2
Morley Cres., Edg.	30	C2
Morley Cres. E., Stan.	37	F2
Morley Cres. W., Stan.	37	F3
Morley Rd. E10	51	C1
Morley Rd. E15	60	F2
Morley Rd. SE13	78	C4
Morley Rd., Bark.	61	G1
Morley Rd., Chis.	97	F1
Morley Rd., Rom.	44	E5
Morley Rd., Sutt.	100	C1
Morley Rd., Twick.	73	G6
Morley St. SE1	**16**	**F5**
Morley St. SE1	67	G2
Morna Rd. SE5	76	J2
Morning La. E9	50	F6
Morningside Rd., Wor.Pk.	99	H2
Mornington Ave. W14	66	C4
Mornington Ave., Brom.	96	J3
Mornington Ave., Ilf.	43	D7
Mornington Clo., Wdf.Grn.	34	G4

Mornington Ct., Bex. 89 J1
Mornington Cres. NW1 7 F1
Mornington Cres. NW1 58 C2
Mornington Cres., NW1 72 B1
Hourls.
Mornington Gro. E3 60 A3
Mornington Ms. SE5 76 J1
Mornington Pl. NW1 7 E1
Mornington Rd. E4 26 D7
Mornington Rd. E11 51 F1
Mornington Rd. SE8 68 J7
Mornington Rd., 54 H5
Grnf.
Mornington Rd., 27 F3
Loug.
Mornington Rd., 34 F4
Wdf.Grn.
Mornington St. NW1 7 E1
Mornington St. NW1 58 B2
Mornington Ter. NW1 58 B2
Mornington Wk., 82 F4
Rich.
Morocco St. SE1 17 D4
Morocco St. SE1 68 B2
Morpeth Gro. E9 59 G1
Morpeth Rd. E9 59 F1
Morpeth St. E2 59 G3
Morpeth Ter. SW1 15 F6
Morpeth Ter. SW1 67 C3
Morpeth Wk. N17 33 E7
West Rd.
Morrab Gdns., Ilf. 52 J3
Morrell Clo., Barn. 23 F3
Galdana Ave.
Morris Ave. E12 52 C5
Morris Clo., Orp. 104 H3
Morris Gdns. SW18 75 D7
Morris Pl. N4 49 G2
Morris Rd. E14 60 B5
Morris Rd. E15 51 D4
Morris Rd., Dag. 53 F2
Morris Rd., Islw. 73 C3
Morris St. E1 59 E6
Morrish Rd. SW2 76 E7
Morrison Ave. N17 41 B3
Morrison Rd., Bark. 62 E2
Morrison Rd., Hayes 54 B3
Morrison St. SW11 76 A3
Morriston Clo. 28 C5
Wat.
Morse Clo. E13 60 G3
Morshead Rd. W9 57 D3
Morson Rd., Enf. 25 H6
Morston Gdns. SE9 88 C4
Morten Clo. SW4 76 D6
Morteyne Rd. N17 41 A1
Mortham St. E15 60 E1
Mortimer Clo. NW2 48 C3
Mortimer Clo. SW16 85 D2
Mortimer Cres. NW6 57 E1
Mortimer Cres., 99 D3
Wor.Pk.
Mortimer Dr., Enf. 25 B5
Mortimer Est. NW6 57 E1
Mortimer Mkt. WC1 7 G6
Mortimer Pl. NW6 57 E1
Mortimer Rd. E6 61 C3
Mortimer Rd. N1 50 B7
Mortimer Rd. NW10 56 J3
Mortimer Rd. W13 55 F6
Mortimer Rd., 93 J1
Mitch.
Mortimer Sq. W11 57 A7
St. Anns Rd.
Mortimer St. W1 11 F3
Mortimer St. W1 58 C6
Mortimer Ter. NW5 49 B4
Gordon Ho. Rd.
Mortlake Clo., 101 E3
Croy.
Richmond Rd.
Mortlake Dr., 93 H1
Mitch.
Mortlake High St. 74 D3
SW14
Mortlake Rd. E16 60 H6
Mortlake Rd., Ilf. 52 F4
Mortlake Rd., Rich. 65 A7
Mortlock Clo. SE15 77 E2
Kirkwood Rd.
Morton Cres. N14 32 D4
Morton Gdns., Wall. 101 C5
Morton Ms. SW5 18 A2
Morton Pl. SE1 16 E6
Morton Rd. E15 51 F7
Morton Rd. N1 49 J7
Morton Rd., Mord. 93 G5
Morton Way N14 32 C3
Morval Rd. SW2 76 G5
Morvale Clo., Belv. 71 F4
Morven Rd. SW17 84 J3

Morville St. E3 60 A2
Morwell St. WC1 11 J2
Moscow Pl. W2 10 A5
Moscow Rd. W2 10 A5
Moscow Rd. W2 57 E7
Moselle Ave. N22 40 G2
Moselle Clo. N8 40 F3
Miles Rd.
Moselle Ho. N17 33 C7
Moselle Pl. N17 33 C7
High Rd.
Moselle St. N17 33 C7
Moss Clo. E1 13 J2
Moss Clo., Pnr. 36 F2
Moss Gdns., S.Croy. 102 G7
Warren Ave.
Moss Hall Cres. N12 31 E6
Moss Hall Gro. N12 31 E6
Moss La., Pnr. 36 E1
Moss Rd., Dag. 53 G7
Mossborough Clo. 31 E6
N12
Mossbury Rd. SW11 75 H3
Mossdown Clo., 71 G4
Belv.
Mossford Ct., Ilf. 43 E3
Mossford Grn., Ilf. 43 E3
Mossford La., Ilf. 43 E2
Mossford St. E3 59 J4
Mossington Gdns. 68 F4
SE16
Abbeyfield Rd.
Mosslea Rd. SE20 86 F6
Mosslea Rd., Brom. 97 A5
Mosslea Rd., Orp. 104 F3
Mossop St. SW3 18 H1
Mossop St. SW3 66 H4
Mossville Gdns., 93 C3
Mord.
Mostyn Ave., Wem. 46 J5
Mostyn Gdns. NW10 57 A3
Mostyn Gro. E3 60 A2
Mostyn Rd. SW9 76 G1
Mostyn Rd. SW19 93 C1
Mostyn Rd., Edg. 30 D7
Mosul Way, Brom. 97 B6
Motcomb St. SW1 15 A5
Motcomb St. SW1 67 A3
Motley St. SW8 76 C2
St. Rule St.
Motspur Pk., N.Mal. 92 F6
Mott St., Loug. 26 E1
Mottingham Gdns. 88 A1
SE9
Mottingham La. SE9 87 J1
Mottingham La. SE12 87 J1
Mottingham Rd. N9 25 G6
Mottingham Rd. SE9 88 B2
Mottisfont Rd. SE2 71 A3
Moulins Rd. E9 50 F7
Moulton Ave., 72 E2
Houns.
Mound, The SE9 88 D3
Moundfield Rd. N16 41 D6
Mount, The N20 31 F2
Mount, The NW3 48 F4
Heath St.
Mount, The W3 65 B1
High St.
Mount, The N.Mal. 92 F3
Mount, The, Wem. 47 B2
Mount, The, Wor.Pk. 99 H4
Mount Adon Pk. 77 D7
SE22
Mount Angelus Rd. 74 F7
SW15
Laverstoke Gdns.
Mount Ararat Rd., 73 H5
Rich.
Mount Ash Rd. SE26 86 E3
Mount Ave. E4 34 A3
Mount Ave. W5 55 F5
Mount Ave., Sthl. 54 G6
Mount Clo. W5 55 F5
Mount Clo., Barn. 24 A4
Mount Clo., Brom. 97 B1
Mount Cor., Felt. 81 D2
Mount Ct. SW15 75 B3
Weimar St.
Mount Ct., W.Wick. 103 E2
Mount Culver Ave., 89 D6
Sid.
Mount Dr., Bexh. 80 E5
Mount Dr., Har. 36 F5
Mount Dr., Wem. 47 C2
Mount Echo Ave. E4 34 B2
Mount Echo Dr. E4 34 B1
Mount Ephraim La. 85 D3
SW16
Mount Ephraim Rd. 85 D3
SW16
Mount Est., The E5 50 E2
Mount Pleasant

Mount Gdns. SE26 86 E3
Mount Gro., Edg. 30 C3
Mount Ms., Hmptn. 90 H1
Mount Mills EC1 8 H4
Mount Nod Rd. SW16 85 F3
Mount Pk. Ave., Har. 46 A2
Mount Pk. Rd. W5 55 G5
Mount Pk. Rd., Har. 46 A3
Mount Pk. Rd., Pnr. 36 A5
Mount Pleasant SE27 85 J4
Mount Pleasant WC1 8 E6
Mount Pleasant WC1 58 G4
Mount Pleasant, 23 H4
Barn.
Mount Pleasant, 45 C2
Ruis.
Mount Pleasant, 55 H1
Wem.
Mount Pleasant 40 F7
Cres. N4
Mount Pleasant Hill 50 E2
E5
Mount Pleasant La. 50 E2
E5
Mount Pleasant Rd. 41 H2
E17
Mount Pleasant Rd. 41 B1
N17
Mount Pleasant Rd. 47 J7
NW10
Mount Pleasant Rd. 78 C6
SE13
Mount Pleasant Rd. 55 F4
W5
Mount Pleasant Rd., 35 G4
Chig.
Mount Pleasant Rd., 92 C3
N.Mal.
Mount Pleasant 40 F7
Vill. N4
Mount Pleasant Wk., 80 J5
Bex.
Mount Rd. NW2 47 H3
Mount Rd. NW4 38 G6
Mount Rd. SE19 86 A6
Mount Rd. SW19 84 D2
Mount Rd., Barn. 23 H5
Mount Rd., Bexh. 80 D5
Mount Rd., Chess. 98 J5
Mount Rd., Dag. 53 F1
Mount Rd., Felt. 81 E3
Mount Rd., Ilf. 52 E5
Mount Rd., Mitch. 93 G2
Mount Rd., N.Mal. 92 D3
Mount Row W1 11 D6
Mount Row W1 58 B7
Mount Sq., The NW3 48 F3
Mount Stewart Ave., 37 G6
Har.
Mount St. W1 11 B6
Mount St. W1 58 A7
Mount Ter. E1 59 E5
New Rd.
Mount Vernon NW3 48 F4
Mount Vw. NW7 30 D3
Mount Vw. W5 55 G4
Mount Vw. Rd. E4 26 C7
Mount Vw. Rd. N4 40 E7
Mount Vw. Rd. NW9 38 D5
Mount Vill. SE27 85 H3
Mountacre Clo. SE26 86 C4
Montague Pl. E14 60 C7
SE18
Mountbatten Clo. 70 H6
SE18
Mountbatten Clo. 86 B5
SE19
Mountbatten Ct., 35 A2
Buck.H.
Mountbatten Ms. 84 F1
SW18
Inman Rd.
Mountbel Rd., Stan. 37 D1
Mountcombe Clo., 91 H7
Surb.
Mountearl Gdns. 85 F5
SW16
Mountfield Rd. E6 61 D2
Mountfield Rd. N3 39 C3
Mountfield Rd. W5 55 G6
Mountford St. E1 13 H3
Mountfort Cres. N1 49 G7
Barnsbury Sq.
Mountfort Ter. N1 49 G7
Barnsbury Sq.
Mountgrove Rd. N5 49 H3
Mounthurst Rd., 96 F7
Brom.
Mountington Pk. 37 G6
Clo., Har.
Mountjoy Clo. SE2 71 B2
Mounts Pond Rd. SE3 78 D2

Mountsfield Ct. 78 D6
SE13
Mountside, Felt. 81 E3
Mountside, Stan. 37 C1
Mountview Ct. N8 40 H4
Green Las.
Mountview Rd., 00 E7
Esher
Mountwood, W.Mol. 90 G3
Movers La., Bark. 61 G1
Mowatt Clo. N19 49 D1
Mowbray Rd. NW6 48 B7
Mowbray Rd. SE19 95 C1
Mowbray Rd., Barn. 23 F4
Mowbray Rd., Edg. 30 A4
Mowbray Rd., Rich. 82 F3
Mowbrays Clo., Rom. 44 J1
Mowbrays Rd., Rom. 44 J2
Mowbray Gdns., 27 F1
Loug.
Mowlem St. E2 59 E2
Mowlem Trd. Est. 33 F7
N17
Mowll St. SW9 67 G7
Moxon Clo. E13 60 F2
Whitelegg Rd.
Moxon St. W1 11 B2
Moxon St. W1 58 A5
Moxon St., Barn. 23 C3
Moye Clo. E2 9 J1
Moye Clo. E2 59 D1
Dove Row
Moyers Rd. E10 42 C7
Moylan Rd. W6 66 B6
Moyne Pl. NW10 56 A2
Moyser Rd. SW16 85 B5
Mozart St. W10 57 C3
Mozart Ter. SW1 19 C2
Muchelney Rd., 93 F6
Mord.
Mud La. W5 55 G5
Mudlarks Way SE7 69 H3
Mudlarks Way SE10 69 F3
Muggeridge Rd., 53 H4
Dag.
Muir Rd. E5 50 D4
Muir St. E16 70 C1
Tate Rd.
Muirdown Ave. 74 D4
SW14
Muirfield W3 56 E6
Muirfield Clo., 28 C5
Wat.
Muirfield Cres. E14 69 B3
Millharbour
Muirfield Grn., 28 C4
Wat.
Muirfield Rd., Wat. 28 B4
Muirkirk Rd. SE6 87 C1
Mulberry Clo. E4 34 A2
Mulberry Clo. NW3 48 G4
Hampstead High St.
Mulberry Clo. NW4 38 J3
Mulberry Clo. SE7 70 A6
Mulberry Clo. SE22 77 D6
Mulberry Clo. SW16 85 C4
Mulberry Clo., Barn. 23 G4
Mulberry Clo., 54 E2
Nthlt.
Parkfield Ave.
Mulberry Clo., Bark. 52 J7
Westrow Dr.
Mulberry Cres., 64 E7
Brent.
Mulberry La., Croy. 102 C1
Mulberry Ms., Wall. 101 C6
Ross Rd.
Mulberry Pl. W6 65 G5
Chiswick Mall
Mulberry St. E1 13 H3
Mulberry Wk. SW3 18 F5
Mulberry Wk. SW3 66 G6
Mulberry Way E18 42 H2
Mulberry Way, Belv. 71 J2
Mulberry Way, Ilf. 43 F4
Mulgrave Rd. NW10 47 F4
Mulgrave Rd. SW6 66 C6
Mulgrave Rd. W5 55 G4
Mulgrave Rd., Croy. 102 A3
Mulgrave Rd., Har. 46 D2
Mulgrave Rd., Sutt. 100 C7
Mulholland Clo., 94 B2
Mitch.
Mulkern Rd. N19 49 D1
Mull Wk. N1 49 J6
Clephane Rd.
Muller Rd. SW4 76 D6
Mullet Gdns. E2 9 J3
Mullins Path SW14 74 D3
Mullion Clo., Har. 36 H1
Mullion Wk., Wat. 28 D4
Ormskirk Rd.
Mulready St. NW8 6 G6

Multon Rd. SW18	75	G7
Mulvaney Way SE1	**17**	**C4**
Mulvaney Way SE1	68	A2
Mumford Ct. EC2	**13**	**A3**
Mumford Rd. SE24	76	H5
Railton Rd.		
Muncaster Rd. SW11	75	J5
Muncies Ms. SE6	87	C2
Mund St. W14	66	C5
Mundania Rd. SE22	77	E6
Munday Rd. E16	60	G6
Munden St. W14	66	B4
Mundesley Clo.,	28	C4
Wat.		
Mundford Rd. E5	50	F2
Mundon Gdns., Ilf.	52	G1
Mundy St. N1	**9**	**E3**
Mundy St. N1	59	B3
Mungo Pk. Clo.	28	J2
(Bushey), Wat.		
Munnery Way, Orp.	104	D2
Munnings Gdns.,	73	A5
Islw.		
Munro Dr. N11	32	C6
Munro Ms. W10	57	B5
Munro Ter. SW10	**18**	**E7**
Munro Ter. SW10	66	G6
Munster Ave.,	72	E4
Houns.		
Munster Ct., Tedd.	82	F6
Munster Gdns. N13	32	H4
Munster Rd. SW6	66	B7
Munster Rd., Tedd.	82	E6
Munster Sq. NW1	**7**	**E4**
Munster Sq. NW1	58	B3
Munton Rd. SE17	**21**	**A1**
Munton Rd. SE17	67	J4
Murchison Ave.,	89	D1
Bex.		
Murchison Rd. E10	51	C2
Murdock Clo. E16	60	F6
Rogers Rd.		
Murdock St. SE15	68	E6
Murfett Clo. SW19	84	B2
Muriel St. N1	58	F1
Murphy St. SE1	**16**	**E4**
Murphy St. SE1	67	G2
Murray Ave., Brom.	96	H3
Murray Ave., Houns.	72	H5
Murray Cres., Pnr.	36	D1
Murray Gro. N1	**9**	**A2**
Murray Gro. N1	58	J2
Murray Ms. NW1	49	D7
Murray Rd. SW19	84	A6
Murray Rd. W5	64	G4
Murray Rd., Rich.	82	E2
Murray Sq. E16	60	G6
Murray St. NW1	49	D7
Murray Ter. NW3	48	G4
Flask Wk.		
Mursell Est. SW8	76	F1
Murtwell Dr., Chig.	35	F6
Musard Rd. W6	66	B6
Musbury St. E1	59	F6
Muscal W6	66	B6
Muscatel Pl. SE5	77	B1
Dalwood St.		
Muschamp Rd. SE15	77	C3
Muschamp Rd.,	100	H2
Cars.		
Muscovy St. EC3	**13**	**E6**
Museum Pas. E2	59	E3
Victoria Pk. Sq.		
Museum St. WC1	**12**	**A2**
Museum St. WC1	58	E5
Musgrave Clo.,	23	F1
Barn.		
Musgrave Cres. SW6	66	D7
Musgrave Rd., Islw.	73	C1
Musgrove Rd. SE14	77	G1
Musjid Rd. SW11	75	G2
Kambala Rd.		
Musquash Way,	72	C2
Houns.		
Muston Rd. E5	50	E2
Mustow Pl. SW6	75	C2
Munster Rd.		
Muswell Ave. N10	40	B1
Muswell Hill N10	40	B3
Muswell Hill Bdy.	40	B3
N10		
Muswell Hill Pl. N10	40	B4
Muswell Hill Rd. N6	40	A6
Muswell Hill Rd. N10	40	A5
Muswell Ms. N10	40	B3
Muswell Rd.		
Muswell Rd. N10	40	B3
Mutrix Rd. NW6	57	D1
Mutton Pl. NW1	49	B6
Harmood St.		
Muybridge Rd.,	92	C2
N.Mal.		

Myatt Rd. SW9	76	H1
Myatt's Flds. N.	76	G1
SW9		
Eythorne Rd.		
Myatt's Flds. S.	76	G2
SW9		
Mycenae Rd. SE3	69	G7
Myddelton Clo., Enf.	25	C1
Myddelton Ave.		
Myddelton Gdns.	24	H7
N21		
Myddelton Pk. N20	31	G3
Myddelton Pas. EC1	**8**	**F3**
Myddelton Rd. N8	40	E4
Myddelton Sq. EC1	**8**	**F3**
Myddelton Sq. EC1	58	G3
Myddelton St. EC1	**8**	**F4**
Myddelton St. EC1	58	G3
Myddleton Rd. N22	32	E7
Myers La. SE14	68	G6
Mylis Clo. SE26	86	E4
Mylne St. EC1	**8**	**E3**
Mylne St. EC1	58	G2
Myra St. SE2	71	A4
Myrdle St. E1	**13**	**J3**
Myrdle St. E1	59	D5
Myrna Clo., Mitch.	84	H7
Myron Pl. SE13	78	C3
Myrtle Ave., Ruis.	36	A7
Myrtle Clo., Barn.	31	J1
Myrtle Gdns. W7	64	B1
Myrtle Gro., N.Mal.	92	C2
Myrtle Rd. E6	61	B1
Myrtle Rd. E17	41	H6
Myrtle Rd. N13	32	J2
Myrtle Rd. W3	65	C1
Myrtle Rd., Croy.	103	A3
Myrtle Rd., Hmptn.	81	J6
Myrtle Rd., Houns.	72	J2
Myrtle Rd., Ilf.	52	E2
Myrtle Rd., Sutt.	100	F5
Myrtle Wk. N1	**9**	**D2**
Myrtle Wk. N1	59	B2
Myrtleberry Clo. E8	50	C6
Beechwood Rd.		
Myrtledene Rd. SE2	71	A5
Mysore Rd. SW11	75	J3
Myton Rd. SE21	86	A3

N

Nadine St. SE7	69	J5
Nagasaki Wk. SE7	69	J3
Nagle Clo. E17	42	D2
Nag's Head Ct. EC1	**9**	**A6**
Nags Head La., Well.	80	B3
Nags Head Rd., Enf.	25	F4
Nairn Grn., Wat.	28	A3
Nairn Rd., Ruis.	45	C6
Nairn St. E14	60	C5
Nairne Gro. SE24	77	A5
Naish Ct. N1	58	E1
Nallhead Rd., Felt.	81	C5
Namton Dr., Th.Hth.	94	F4
Nan Clark's La. NW7	30	F2
Nankin St. E14	60	A6
Nansen Rd. SW11	76	A4
Nant Rd. NW2	48	C2
Nant St. E2	59	E3
Cambridge Heath Rd.		
Nantes Clo. SW18	75	F4
Nantes Pas. E1	**13**	**F1**
Napier Ave. E14	69	A5
Napier Ave. SW6	75	C3
Napier Clo. SE8	68	J7
Amersham Vale		
Napier Clo. W14	66	C3
Napier Rd.		
Napier Ct. SW6	75	C3
Ranelagh Gdns.		
Napier Gro. N1	58	J2
Napier Pl. W14	66	C3
Napier Rd. E6	61	D1
Napier Rd. E11	51	E4
Napier Rd. E15	60	E2
Napier Rd. N17	41	B3
Napier Rd. NW10	56	H3
Napier Rd. W14	66	B3
Napier Rd. SE25	95	E4
Napier Rd., Belv.	71	F4
Napier Rd., Brom.	96	H4
Napier Rd., Enf.	25	G5
Napier Rd., Islw.	73	F4
Napier Rd., S.Croy.	102	A7
Napier Rd., Wem.	49	H6
Napier Ter. N1	58	H7
Napoleon Rd. E5	50	E3
Napoleon Rd.,	73	E7
Twick.		
Napton Clo., Hayes	54	E4
Kingsash Dr.		
Narbonne Ave. SW4	76	C5
Narborough St. SW6	75	E2

Narcissus Rd. NW6	48	D5
Naresby Fold, Stan.	29	F6
Narford Rd. E5	50	D3
Narrow St. E14	59	H7
Narrow Way, Brom.	97	B6
Nascot St. W12	56	J6
Naseby Clo. NW6	48	F7
Fairfax Rd.		
Naseby Clo., Islw.	73	B1
Naseby Rd. SE19	86	A6
Naseby Rd., Dag.	53	G3
Naseby Rd., Ilf.	43	C1
Nash Grn., Brom.	87	G6
Nash La., Kes.	103	G7
Nash Pl. E14	69	B1
South Colonnade		
Nash Rd. N9	33	F2
Nash Rd. SE4	77	H4
Nash Rd., Rom.	44	D4
Nash St. NW1	**7**	**E3**
Nasmyth St. W6	65	H3
Nassau Path SE28	71	C1
Disraeli Clo.		
Nassau Rd. SW13	74	F1
Nassau St. W1	**11**	**F2**
Nassau St. W1	58	C5
Nassington Rd. NW3	48	H4
Natal Rd. N11	32	E6
Natal Rd. SW16	85	D6
Natal Rd., Ilf.	52	E4
Natal Rd., Th.Hth.	95	A3
Nathan Way SE28	70	H3
Nathaniel Clo. E1	**13**	**G2**
Nathans Rd., Wem.	46	F1
Naval Row E14	60	C7
Naval Wk., Brom.	96	G3
High St.		
Navarino Gro. E8	50	D6
Navarino Rd. E8	50	D6
Navarre Rd. E6	61	B2
Navarre St. E2	**9**	**F5**
Navarre St. E2	59	C4
Navenby Wk. E3	60	A4
Rounton Rd.		
Navestock Clo. E4	34	C3
Mapleton Rd.		
Navestock Cres.,	42	J1
Wdf.Grn.		
Navestock Ho.,	62	B2
Bark.		
Navy St. SW4	76	D3
Naylor Gro., Enf.	25	G5
South St.		
Naylor Rd. N20	31	F2
Naylor Rd. SE15	68	E7
Nazrul St. E2	**9**	**F3**
Nazrul St. E2	59	C3
Neagle Clo., Boreh.B.	22	C1
Neal Ave., Sthl.	54	F3
Neal Clo., Nthwd.	36	A1
Neal St. WC2	**12**	**A4**
Neal St. WC2	58	E6
Nealden St. SW9	76	F3
Neale Clo. N2	39	F3
Neal's Yd. WC2	**12**	**A4**
Near Acre NW9	38	F1
Neasden Clo. NW10	47	E5
Neasden La. NW10	47	E4
Neasden La. N.	47	D3
NW10		
Neasham Rd., Dag.	53	B5
Neate St. SE5	**21**	**D6**
Neate St. SE5	68	B6
Neath Gdns., Mord.	93	F6
Neathouse Pl. SW1	**19**	**F1**
Neatscourt Rd. E6	61	A5
Nebraska St. SE1	**17**	**B4**
Neckinger SE16	17	G5
Neckinger SE16	68	C3
Neckinger Est. SE16	**17**	**G5**
Neckinger Est. SE16	68	C3
Neckinger St. SE1	**17**	**G5**
Neckinger St. SE1	68	C2
Nectarine Way SE13	78	B2
Needham Rd. W11	57	D6
Westbourne Gro.		
Needham Ter. NW2	48	A3
Needleman St. SE16	68	G2
Neeld Cres. NW4	38	H5
Neeld Cres., Wem.	47	A5
Nelgarde Rd. SE6	78	A7
Nella Rd. W6	66	A6
Nelldale Rd. SE16	68	F4
Nello James Gdns.	86	A4
SE27		
Nelson Clo., Croy.	101	H1
Nelson Clo., Rom.	44	H1
Nelson Gdns. E2	**9**	**J3**
Nelson Gdns. E2	59	D3
Nelson Gdns.,	72	G6
Houns.		
Nelson Gro. Rd.	93	E1
SW19		

Nelson Mandela Clo.	40	A2
N10		
Nelson Mandela Rd.	78	J3
SE3		
Nelson Pas. EC1	**9**	**A4**
Nelson Pas. EC1	58	J3
Nelson Pl. N1	**8**	**H2**
Nelson Pl. N1	58	H2
Nelson Pl. W3	65	B1
Steyne Rd.		
Nelson Pl., Sid.	89	A4
Nelson Rd. E4	34	A6
Nelson Rd. E11	42	G4
Nelson Rd. N8	40	F5
Nelson Rd. N9	33	E2
Nelson Rd. N15	41	B4
Nelson Rd. SE10	69	C6
Nelson Rd. SW19	84	E7
Nelson Rd., Belv.	71	F5
Nelson Rd., Brom.	96	J4
Nelson Rd., Enf.	25	G6
Nelson Rd., Har.	46	A1
Nelson Rd., Houns.	72	G6
Nelson Rd., N.Mal.	92	D5
Nelson Rd., Sid.	89	A4
Nelson Rd., Stan.	29	F6
Nelson Rd., Twick.	72	H7
Nelson Sq. SE1	**16**	**G3**
Nelson Sq. SE1	67	H2
Nelson St. E1	59	E6
Nelson St. E6	61	C2
Nelson St. E16	60	F7
Huntingdon St.		
Nelson Ter. N1	**8**	**H2**
Nelson Ter. N1	58	H2
Nelson Trd. Est.	93	E1
SW19		
Nelson Wk. SE16	68	H1
Rotherhithe St.		
Nelson's Row SW4	76	D4
Nemoure Rd. W3	56	C7
Nene Gdns., Felt.	81	F2
Nepaul Rd. SW11	75	H2
Afghan Rd.		
Nepean St. SW15	74	G6
Neptune Rd., Har.	37	A6
Neptune St. SE16	68	F3
Nesbit Clo. SE3	78	E3
Hurren Clo.		
Nesbit Rd. SE9	79	A4
Nesbitt Sq. SE19	86	B7
Coxwell Rd.		
Nesbitts All., Barn.	23	C3
Bath Pl.		
Nesham St. E1	**17**	**H1**
Nesham St. E1	68	D1
Ness St. SE16	**17**	**H5**
Nesta Rd., Wdf.Grn.	34	E6
Nestor Ave. N21	24	H6
Nether Clo. N3	31	D7
Nether Clo. N3	39	D1
Nether St. N12	31	E6
Netheravon Rd. W7	64	C1
Netheravon Rd. N.	65	F4
W4		
Netheravon Rd. S.	65	F5
W4		
Netherbury Rd. W5	64	G3
Netherby Gdns.,	24	E4
Enf.		
Netherby Rd. SE23	77	F7
Nethercourt Ave. N3	31	D6
Netherfield Gdns.,	52	G6
Bark.		
Netherfield Rd. N12	31	E5
Netherfield Rd. SW17	85	A3
Netherford Rd. SW4	76	C2
Netherhall Gdns.	48	F6
NW3		
Netherhall Way NW3	48	F5
Netherhall Gdns.		
Netherlands Rd.,	23	G6
Barn.		
Netherleigh Clo. N6	49	C1
Netherton Gro.	**18**	**D6**
SW10		
Netherton Gro.	66	F6
SW10		
Netherton Rd.,	73	D5
Twick.		
Netherwood N2	39	G2
Netherwood Pl. W14	66	A3
Netherwood Rd.		
Netherwood Rd. W14	66	A3
Netherwood St. NW6	48	C7
Netley Clo., Croy.	103	C7
Netley Clo., Sutt.	100	A5
Netley Dr., Walt.	90	F7
Netley Gdns., Mord.	93	F7
Netley Rd. E17	41	J5
Netley Rd., Brent.	64	H6
Netley Rd., Ilf.	43	G5

Netley Rd., Mord.	93	F7
Netley St. NW1	7	F4
Nettleden Ave., Wem.	47	A6
New Goulston St. E1	13	F3
Nettlefold Pl. SE27	85	H3
Nettleton Rd. SE14	77	G1
Nettlewood Rd. SW16	85	D7
Neuchatel Rd. SE6	86	J2
Nevada Clo., N.Mal.	92	C4
Georgia Rd.		
Nevada St. SE10	69	C6
Nevern Pl. SW5	66	D4
Nevern Rd. SW5	66	D4
Nevern Sq. SW5	66	D4
Nevill Rd. N16	50	B3
Neville Ave., N.Mal.	92	D1
Neville Clo. E11	51	F3
Neville Clo. NW1	7	J2
Neville Clo. NW6	57	C2
Neville Clo. SE15	68	D7
Neville Clo. W3	65	C2
Acton La.		
Neville Clo., Houns.	72	H2
Neville Clo., Sid.	88	J4
Neville Dr. N2	39	F6
Neville Gdns., Dag.	53	D3
Neville Gill Clo. SW18	75	E6
Neville Pl. N22	40	F1
Neville Rd. E7	51	G7
Neville Rd. NW6	57	C2
Neville Rd. W5	55	G4
Neville Rd., Croy.	95	A7
Neville Rd., Dag.	53	D2
Neville Rd., Ilf.	43	F1
Neville Rd., Kings.T.	92	A2
Neville Rd., Rich.	82	F2
Neville St. SW7	18	E3
Neville St. SW7	66	G5
Neville Ter. SW7	18	E3
Neville Ter. SW7	66	G5
Neville Wk., Cars.	93	H7
Green Wrythe La.		
Nevilles Ct. NW2	47	G3
Nevin Dr. E4	34	B1
Nevis Rd. SW17	85	A2
New Ash Clo. N2	39	G3
Oakridge Dr.		
New Barn St. E13	60	G4
New Barns Ave., Mitch.	94	D4
New Barns Way, Chig.	35	E3
New Bond St. W1	11	D4
New Bond St. W1	58	B6
New Brent St. NW4	38	J5
New Bri., Erith	71	J4
New Bri. St. EC4	12	G4
New Bri. St. EC4	58	H6
New Broad St. EC2	13	D2
New Bdy. W5	55	F7
New Burlington Ms. W1	11	F5
New Burlington Pl. W1	11	F5
New Burlington St. W1	11	F5
New Burlington St. W1	58	C7
New Butt La. SE8	69	A7
New Cavendish St. W1	11	C2
New Cavendish St. W1	58	A5
New Change EC4	12	J4
New Change EC4	58	J6
New Chapel Sq., Felt.	81	B1
New Charles St. EC1	8	H3
New Ch. Rd. SE5	21	B7
New Ch. Rd. SE5	68	A7
New City Rd. E13	60	J3
New Clo. SW19	93	F3
New Clo., Felt.	81	E5
New College Ms. N1	49	G7
Islington Pk. St.		
New Compton St. WC2	11	J4
New Compton St. WC2	58	D6
New Ct. EC4	12	E5
New Covent Gdn. Mkt. SW8	67	D7
New Coventry St. W1	11	J6
New Crane Pl. E1	68	F1
Garnet St.		
New Cross Rd. SE14	68	F7
New End NW3	48	G4
New End Sq. NW3	48	G4
New Fm. Ave., Brom.	96	G4
New Fetter La. EC4	12	F3
New Fetter La. EC4	58	G6
New Forest La., Chig.	35	D6
New Goulston St. E1	13	F3
New Heston Rd., Houns.	63	F7
New Horizon St., Brent.	84	D8
New Inn Bdy. EC2	9	E5
New Inn Pas. WC2	12	D4
New Inn St. EC2	9	E5
New Inn Yd. EC2	9	E5
New Inn Yd. EC2	59	B4
New James Ct. SE15	77	E3
Nunhead La.		
New Kent Rd. SE1	16	J6
New Kent Rd. SE1	67	J3
New King St. SE8	69	A6
New Kings Rd. SW6	75	C2
New London St. EC3	13	E5
New Lydenburgh St. SE7	69	J3
New Mt. St. E15	51	D7
New N. Pl. EC2	9	D6
New N. Rd. N1	9	B1
New N. Rd. N1	49	J7
New N. Rd., Ilf.	35	F2
New N. St. WC1	12	C1
New N. St. WC1	58	F5
New Oak Rd. N2	39	F2
New Orleans Wk. N19	40	D7
New Oxford St. WC1	11	J3
New Oxford St. WC1	58	D6
New Pk. Ave. N13	32	J3
New Pk. Clo., Nthlt.	45	E6
New Pk. Ct. SW2	76	E7
New Pk. Rd. SW2	85	D1
New Pl. Sq. SE16	68	E3
New Plaistow Rd. E15	60	E1
New Priory Ct. NW6	48	D7
Mazenod Ave.		
New Quebec St. W1	11	A4
New Quebec St. W1	57	J6
New Ride SW7	14	G3
New River Cres. N13	32	H4
New River Wk. N1	49	A6
Arran Wk.		
New Rd. E1	59	E5
New Rd. E4	34	B4
New Rd. N8	40	E5
New Rd. N9	33	D3
New Rd. N17	41	C1
New Rd. N22	40	J1
New Rd. NW7	31	B7
New Rd. NW7 (Barnet Gate)	22	F7
New Rd. SE2	71	D4
New Rd., Brent.	64	G5
New Rd., Dag.	62	G3
New Rd. (East Bedfont), Felt.	81	B1
New Rd. (Hanworth), Felt.	81	E5
New Rd., Har.	46	C4
New Rd., Houns.	72	H4
Station Rd.		
New Rd., Ilf.	52	H2
New Rd., Kings.T.	83	A7
New Rd., Mitch.	101	A1
New Rd., Rain.	62	J2
New Rd., Rich.	82	F4
New Rd., Well.	80	G2
New Rd., W.Mol.	90	G3
New Row WC2	12	A5
New Row WC2	58	E7
New Spring Gdns. Wk. SE11	20	B4
New Sq. WC2	12	D3
New Sq. WC2	58	F6
New St. EC2	13	E2
New St. EC2	59	B5
New St. Hill, Brom.	87	H5
New St. Sq. EC4	12	F3
New Trinity Rd. N2	39	G3
New Turnstile WC1	12	C2
New Union Clo. E14	69	C3
New Union St. EC2	13	B2
New Union St. EC2	59	A5
New Wanstead E11	52	A4
New Way Rd. NW9	38	E4
New Wf. Rd. N1	8	B1
New Wf. Rd. N1	58	E2
New Zealand Way W12	56	H7
India Way		
Newark Cres. NW10	56	D3
Newark Grn., Borwd.	22	D3
Newark Knok E6	61	D5
Newark Rd., S.Croy.	102	A6
Newark St. E1	59	E5
Newark Way NW4	38	G4
Newbiggin Path, Wat.	28	C4
Newbolt Ave., Sutt.	99	A3
Newbolt Rd., Stan.	29	C5
Newborough Grn., N.Mal.	92	D4
Newburgh Rd. W3	65	C1
Newburgh St. W1	11	F4
Newburgh St. W1	58	C6
Newburn St. SE11	20	D4
Newburn St. SE11	67	F5
Newbury Clo., Nthlt.	45	F6
Newbury Gdns., Epsom	99	F4
Newbury Ho. N22	40	E1
Newbury Ms. NW5	49	A6
Malden Rd.		
Newbury Rd. E4	34	C6
Newbury Rd., Brom.	96	G3
Newbury Rd., Ilf.	43	H6
Newbury St. EC1	12	J1
Newbury Way, Nthlt.	45	F6
Newby Clo., Enf.	25	B2
Newby Pl. E14	60	C7
Newby St. SW8	76	B3
Newcastle Clo. EC4	12	G3
Newcastle Pl. W2	10	F2
Newcastle Pl. W2	57	G5
Newcastle Row EC1	8	F6
Newcombe Gdns. SW16	85	E4
Newcombe Pk. NW7	30	E5
Newcombe Pk., Wem.	55	J1
Newcombe St. W8	66	D1
Kensington Pl.		
Newcomen Rd. E11	51	F3
Newcomen Rd. SW11	75	G3
Newcomen St. SE1	17	B3
Newcomen St. SE1	68	A2
Newcourt St. NW8	6	G2
Newcourt St. NW8	57	H2
Newdales Clo. N9	33	D2
Balham Rd.		
Newdene Ave., Nthlt.	54	D2
Newell St. E14	59	G5
Newent Clo. SE15	21	D7
Newent Clo. SE15	68	B7
Newent Clo., Cars.	100	J1
Newfield Clo., Hmptn.	90	G1
Percy Rd.		
Newgale Gdns., Edg.	37	J1
Newgate, Croy.	101	J1
Newgate Clo., Felt.	81	E2
Newgate St. E4	34	F3
Newgate St. EC1	12	H3
Newgate St. EC1	58	H6
Newham Way E6	61	D4
Newham Way E16	60	F5
Newhams Clo., Brom.	97	C3
Newhams Row SE1	17	E4
Newhaven Gdns. SE9	79	A4
Newhaven Rd. SE25	95	A5
Newhouse Ave., Rom.	44	D3
Newhouse Clo., N.Mal.	92	E7
Newhouse Wk., Mord.	93	F7
Newick Clo., Bex.	80	H6
Newick Rd. E5	50	E3
Newing Grn., Brom.	88	A7
Newington Barrow Way N7	49	F3
Newington Butts SE1	20	H2
Newington Butts SE11	20	H2
Newington Butts SE11	67	H4
Newington Causeway SE1	16	H6
Newington Causeway SE1	67	H3
Newington Grn. N1	50	A5
Newington Grn. N16	50	A5
Newington Grn. Rd. N1	50	A6
Newington Way N7	49	F2
Hornsey Rd.		
Newland Clo., Pnr.	28	E6
Newland Ct., Wem.	47	A2
Forty Ave.		
Newland Dr., Enf.	25	B1
Newland Gdns. W13	64	D2
Newland Rd. N8	40	E3
Newland St. E16	70	B1
Newlands, The, Wall.	101	C7
Newlands Ave., T.Ditt.	98	B1
Newlands Clo., Edg.	29	H3
Newlands Clo., Sthl.	63	E5
Newlands Clo., Wem.	46	F6
Newlands Ct. SE9	79	D6
Newlands Pk. SE26	86	G5
Newlands Pl., Barn.	23	A5
Newlands Quay E1	69	F7
Newlands Rd. SW16	94	E2
Newlands Rd., Wdf.Grn.	34	F2
Newlands Way, Chess.	98	F5
Newling Clo. E6	61	C6
Porter Rd.		
Newlyn Gdns., Har.	36	F7
Newlyn Rd. N17	41	C1
Newlyn Rd., Barn.	23	C4
Newlyn Rd., Well.	79	J2
Newman Pas. W1	11	G2
Newman Rd. E13	60	H3
Newman Rd. E17	41	G5
Southcote Rd.		
Newman Rd., Brom.	96	G1
Newman Rd., Croy.	101	F1
Newman Rd., Hayes	54	B7
Newman St. W1	11	G2
Newman St. W1	58	C5
Newman Yd. W1	11	G3
Newmans Clo., Loug.	27	E3
Newman's Ct. EC3	13	C4
Newmans La., Loug.	27	D3
Newmans La., Surb.	91	G6
Newman's Row WC2	12	D2
Newmans Way, Barn.	23	F1
Newmarket Ave., Nthlt.	45	H5
Newmarket Grn. SE9	79	A7
Newminster Rd., Mord.	93	F6
Newnes Path SW15	74	H4
Putney Pk. La.		
Newnham Ave., Ruis.	45	C1
Newnham Clo., Loug.	27	A6
Newnham Clo., Nthlt.	45	J5
Newnham Clo., Th.Hth.	94	J2
Newnham Gdns., Nthlt.	45	J6
Newnham Ms. N22	40	F1
Newnham Rd.		
Newnham Rd. N22	40	F1
Newnham Ter. SE1	16	E5
Newnham Way, Har.	37	H5
Newnhams Clo., Brom.	97	C3
Newton Clo. N4	41	A7
Newpiece, Loug.	27	E3
Newport Ave. E13	60	H4
Palmer Rd.		
Newport Ct. WC2	11	J5
Newport Mead, Wat.	28	D4
Kilmarnock Rd.		
Newport Pl. WC2	11	J5
Newport Pl. WC2	58	D7
Newport Rd. E10	51	C2
Newport Rd. E17	41	H4
Newport Rd. SW13	74	G1
Newport St. SE11	20	C2
Newport St. SE11	67	F4
Newquay Cres., Har.	45	E2
Newquay Gdns., Wat.	28	B2
Fulford Gro.		
Newquay Rd. SE6	87	B2
Newry Rd., Twick.	73	D5
Newsam Ave. N15	41	A5
Newstead Ave., Orp.	104	G3
Newstead Rd. SE12	78	F7
Newstead Wk., Cars.	93	F7
Newstead Way SW19	84	A4
Newton Ave. N10	40	A1
Newton Ave. W3	65	C2
Newton Cres., Borwd.	22	C4
Newton Gro. W4	65	E4
Newton Rd. E15	51	D5
Newton Rd. N15	41	C5
Newton Rd. NW2	47	J3
Newton Rd. SW19	84	B7
Newton Rd. W2	57	E6
Newton Rd., Har.	37	B2
Newton Rd., Islw.	73	C2
Newton Rd., Well.	80	A3
Newton Rd., Wem.	46	J7
Newton St. WC2	12	B3
Newton St. WC2	58	E6
Newton Wk., Edg.	38	B1
North Rd.		
Newton Way N18	32	J5

Newtons Yd. SW18	75	E5
Wandsworth High St.		
Newtown St. SW11	76	B1
Strasburg Rd.		
Niagara Ave. W5	64	F4
Nibthwaite Rd.,	37	B5
Har.		
Nichol Clo. N14	32	D1
Nichol La., Brom.	87	G7
Nicholas Clo., Grnf.	54	H2
Nicholas Gdns. W5	64	G2
Nicholas St. EC4	**13**	**C5**
Nicholas Rd. E1	59	F4
Nicholas Rd., Croy.	101	E4
Nicholas Rd., Dag.	53	F2
Nicholay Rd. N19	49	D1
Calverley Gro.		
Nicholes Rd.,	72	G4
Houns.		
Nicholl St. E2	59	D1
Nichollsfield Wk.	49	F5
N7		
Hillmarton Rd.		
Nichols Grn. W5	55	H5
Montpelier Rd.		
Nicholson Dr.	28	J1
(Bushey), Wat.		
Nicholson Rd.,	102	C1
Croy.		
Nicholson St. SE1	**16**	**G2**
Nicholson St. SE1	67	H1
Nickelby Clo. SE28	62	C6
Nicol Clo., Twick.	73	E6
Cassilis Rd.		
Nicola Clo., Har.	37	A2
Nicola Clo., S.Croy.	101	J6
Nicola Ms., Ilf.	35	E7
Nicoll Pl. NW4	38	H6
Nicoll Rd. NW10	56	E1
Nicoll Way, Borwd.	22	D5
Nicosia Rd. SW18	75	H7
Niederwald Rd. SE26	86	H4
Nigel Clo., Nthlt.	54	E1
Church Rd.		
Nigel Ms., Ilf.	52	E4
Nigel Playfair Ave.	65	H4
W6		
King St.		
Nigel Rd. E7	51	J5
Nigel Rd. SE15	77	D3
Nigeria Rd. SE7	69	J7
Nightingale Ave. E4	34	E5
Nightingale Clo. E4	34	E4
Nightingale Clo. W4	65	C6
Grove Pk. Ter.		
Nightingale Clo.,	101	A2
Cars.		
Nightingale Clo.,	36	C5
Pnr.		
Nightingale Dr.,	99	B6
Epsom		
Nightingale Est. E5	50	D3
Nightingale Gro.	78	D5
SE13		
Nightingale La. E11	42	H5
Nightingale La. N6	39	H7
Nightingale La. N8	40	E4
Nightingale La. SW4	76	B6
Nightingale La.	75	J7
SW12		
Nightingale La.,	96	J2
Brom.		
Nightingale La.,	73	H7
Rich.		
Nightingale Pl.	70	D6
SE18		
Nightingale Rd. E5	50	E3
Nightingale Rd. N9	25	F6
Nightingale Rd. N22	40	E1
Nightingale Rd.	56	F2
NW10		
Nightingale Rd. W7	64	C1
Nightingale Rd.,	100	J3
Cars.		
Nightingale Rd.,	81	G5
Hmptn.		
Nightingale Rd.,	97	F6
Orp.		
Nightingale Rd.,	90	B7
Walt.		
Nightingale Rd.,	90	H5
W.Mol.		
Nightingale Sq.	76	A7
SW12		
Nightingale Vale	70	D6
SE18		
Nightingale Wk. SW4	76	B6
Nightingale Way E6	61	B5
Nile Path SE18	70	D6
Jackson St.		
Nile Rd. E13	60	J2
Nile St. N1	**9**	**A3**
Nile St. N1	59	A3
Nile Ter. SE15	**21**	**G4**
Nile Ter. SE15	68	C5
Nimegate Way SE22	77	B5
East Dulwich Gro.		
Nimrod Clo., Nthlt.	54	D3
Britannia Clo.		
Nimrod Rd. SW16	85	B6
Nine Acres Clo. E12	52	B5
Nine Elms La. SW8	19	G7
Nine Elms La. SW8	67	C7
Nineteenth Rd.,	94	E4
Mitch.		
Ninhams Wd., Orp.	104	D4
Ninth Ave., Hayes	71	H1
Nisbet Ho. E9	50	G5
Homerton High St.		
Nithdale Rd. SE18	70	E7
Niton Clo., Barn.	23	A6
Niton Rd., Rich.	74	A3
Niton St. SW6	66	A7
Niven Clo., Borwd.	22	C1
Nobel Rd. N18	33	F4
Noble St. EC2	**12**	**J3**
Noble St. EC2	58	J6
Noel Pk. Rd. N22	40	G2
Noel Rd. E6	61	B4
Noel Rd. N1	**8**	**H1**
Noel Rd. N1	58	H2
Noel Rd. W3	56	A6
Noel Sq., Dag.	53	C4
Noel St. W1	**11**	**G4**
Noel St. W1	58	C6
Nolan Way E5	50	D4
Nolton Pl., Edg.	37	J1
Nonsuch Clo., Ilf.	35	E6
Nora Gdns. NW4	39	A4
Nora Ter., Har.	46	B1
Norbiton Ave.,	92	A1
Kings.T.		
Norbiton Common	92	B3
Rd., Kings.T.		
Norbiton Rd. E14	59	J6
Norbreck Gdns.	55	J3
NW10		
North Circular Rd.		
Norbreck Par. NW10	55	J3
North Circular Rd.		
Norbroke St. W12	56	F7
Norburn St. W10	57	B5
Chesterton Rd.		
Norbury Ave. SW16	94	F1
Norbury Ave.,	73	A4
Th.Hth.		
Norbury Ave.,	94	G2
Th.Hth.		
Norbury Clo. SW16	94	G1
Norbury Ct. E5	50	H4
Norbury Ct. Rd.	94	E3
SW16		
Norbury Cres. SW16	94	F1
Norbury Cross SW16	94	E3
Norbury Gdns., Rom.	44	D5
Norbury Gro. NW7	30	E3
Norbury Hill SW16	85	G7
Norbury Ri. SW16	94	E3
Norbury Rd. E4	34	A5
Norbury Rd.,	94	J2
Th.Hth.		
Norcombe Gdns.,	37	F6
Har.		
Norcott Clo., Hayes	54	C4
Willow Tree La.		
Norcott Rd. N16	50	D2
Norcroft Gdns. SE22	77	D7
Norcutt Rd., Twick.	82	B1
Norfield Rd. Dart.	89	J4
Norfolk Ave. N13	32	H6
Norfolk Ave. N15	41	C6
Norfolk Clo. N2	39	H3
Park Rd.		
Norfolk Clo. N13	32	H6
Norfolk Clo., Barn.	24	A4
Norfolk Clo., Twick.	73	E6
Cassilis Rd.		
Norfolk Cres. W2	**10**	**G3**
Norfolk Cres. W2	57	H6
Norfolk Cres., Sid.	79	H7
Norfolk Gdns., Bexh.	80	F1
Norfolk Gdns.,	21	D4
Borwd.		
Norfolk Ho. SE3	69	E6
Norfolk Ho. Rd.	85	D3
SW16		
Norfolk Pl. W2	**10**	**F3**
Norfolk Pl. W2	57	G6
Norfolk Pl., Well.	80	A2
Norfolk Rd. E6	61	C1
Norfolk Rd. E17	41	G2
Norfolk Rd. NW8	57	G1
Norfolk Rd. NW10	47	E7
Norfolk Rd. SW19	84	H7
Norfolk Rd., Bark.	52	H7
Norfolk Rd., Barn.	23	D3
Norfolk Rd., Dag.	53	H5
Norfolk Rd., Enf.	25	E6
Norfolk Rd., Esher	98	B5
Norfolk Rd., Felt.	81	C1
Norfolk Rd., Har.	36	H5
Norfolk Rd., Ilf.	52	H1
Norfolk Rd., Rom.	44	J6
Norfolk Rd., Th.Hth.	94	J3
Norfolk Row SE1	**20**	**C1**
Norfolk Row SE1	67	F3
Norfolk Sq. W2	**10**	**F4**
Norfolk Sq. W2	57	G6
Norfolk Sq. Ms. W2	**10**	**F4**
Norfolk St. E7	51	G5
Norfolk Ter. W6	66	B5
Field Rd.		
Norgrove St. SW12	85	A1
Norhyrst Ave. SE25	95	C3
Norland Pl. W11	66	B1
Norland Rd. W11	66	A1
Norland Sq. W11	66	B1
Norlands Cres., Chis.	97	E1
Norley Vale SW15	83	G1
Norlington Rd. E10	51	C1
Norlington Rd. E11	51	D1
Norman Ave. N22	40	H1
Norman Ave., Felt.	81	G2
Norman Ave., Sthl.	54	E7
Norman Ave., Twick.	78	E7
Norman Clo., Orp.	104	F3
Norman Clo., Rom.	44	H2
Norman Ct., Ilf.	43	G7
Norman Cres.,	63	D7
Houns.		
Norman Cres., Pnr.	36	C1
Norman Gro. E3	59	H2
Norman Rd. E6	61	C4
Norman Rd. E11	51	D2
Norman Rd. N15	41	C5
Norman Rd. SE10	69	B7
Norman Rd. SW19	84	F7
Norman Rd., Belv.	71	H3
Norman Rd., Ilf.	52	E5
Norman Rd., Sutt.	100	D5
Norman Rd., Th.Hth.	94	H5
Norman St. EC1	**8**	**J4**
Norman Way N14	32	E2
Norman Way W3	56	B5
Normanby Clo. SW15	75	C5
Manfred Rd.		
Normanby Rd. NW10	47	F4
Normand Gdns. W14	66	B6
Greyhound Rd.		
Normand Ms. W14	66	B6
Normand Rd.		
Normand Rd. W14	66	C6
Normandy Ave.,	23	C5
Barn.		
Normandy Rd. SW9	76	G1
Normandy Ter. E16	60	H6
Normanhurst Ave.,	80	D1
Bexh.		
Normanhurst Dr.,	73	E5
Twick.		
St. Margarets Rd.		
Normanhurst Rd.	85	F2
SW2		
Normans Clo. NW10	47	D6
Normans Mead	47	D6
NW10		
Normansfield Ave.,	82	F7
Tedd.		
Normanshire Ave. E4	34	C4
Normanshire Dr.		
Normanshire Dr. E4	34	A4
Normanton Ave.	84	D2
SW19		
Normanton Pk. E4	34	E3
Normanton Rd.,	102	B5
S.Croy.		
Normanton St. SE23	86	G2
Normington Clo.	85	G5
SW16		
Norrice Lea N2	39	G5
Norris St. SW1	**11**	**H6**
Norroy Rd. SW15	75	A4
Norrys Clo., Barn.	23	J4
Norrys Rd., Barn.	23	J4
Norseman Clo., Ilf.	53	B1
Norseman Way, Grnf.	54	H1
Olympic Way		
Norstead Pl. SW15	83	G2
North Access Rd.	41	G6
E17		
North Acre NW9	38	E1
North Acton Rd.	56	D2
NW10		
North Audley St. W1	**11**	**B4**
North Audley St. W1	58	A7
North Ave. N18	33	D4
North Ave. W13	55	E5
North Ave., Cars.	101	A7
North Ave., Har.	36	H6
North Ave., Hayes	54	A7
North Ave., Rich.	73	G1
Sandycombe Rd.		
North Ave., Sthl.	54	F7
North Bank NW8	6	G4
North Bank NW8	57	H3
North Birkbeck Rd.	51	D3
E11		
North Branch Ave.	56	J3
W10		
Harrow Rd.		
North Carriage Dr.	**10**	**G5**
W2		
North Carriage Dr.	57	H7
W2		
North Circular Rd.	33	J7
E4		
North Circular Rd.	42	H1
E18		
North Circular Rd.	39	C4
N3		
North Circular Rd.	39	G1
N12		
North Circular Rd.	32	G5
N13		
North Circular Rd.	47	E3
NW2		
North Circular Rd.	47	E4
NW10		
North Circular Rd.	39	A6
NW11		
North Clo., Barn.	22	J5
North Clo., Bexh.	80	D4
North Clo., Dag.	62	G1
North Clo., Mord.	93	B4
North Colonnade E14	69	A1
North Common Rd.	55	H7
W5		
North Countess Rd.	41	J2
E17		
North Ct. W1	**11**	**G1**
North Cray Rd.,	89	G2
Bex.		
North Cray Rd.,	89	E6
Sid.		
North Cres. N3	39	C2
North Cres. WC1	**11**	**H1**
North Cross Rd.	77	C5
SE22		
North Cross Rd., Ilf.	43	F4
North Dene NW7	30	D3
North Dene, Houns.	72	H1
North Dr. SW16	85	C4
North Dr., Houns.	72	J2
North Dr., Orp.	104	H4
North End NW3	48	F2
North End, Buck.H.	26	J7
North End, Croy.	101	J2
North End Ave. NW3	48	F2
North End Cres. W14	66	C4
North End Ho. W14	66	B4
North End Rd. NW11	48	D1
North End Rd. SW6	66	C6
North End Rd. W14	66	C4
North End Rd., Wem.	47	A3
North End Way NW3	48	F2
North Eyot Gdns. W6	65	F5
St. Peters Sq.		
North Feltham Trd.	72	B5
Est., Felt.		
North Flockton St.	**17**	**H3**
SE16		
North Gdns. SW19	84	G7
North Glade, The,	80	F7
Bex.		
Camden Rd.		
North Gower St. NW1	**7**	**G4**
North Gower St. NW1	58	C3
North Grn. NW9	30	E7
Clayton Fld.		
North Gro. N6	40	A7
North Gro. N15	41	A5
North Hill N6	39	J6
North Hill Ave. N6	39	J6
North Hyde Gdns.,	63	A4
Hayes		
North Hyde La.,	63	E6
Houns.		
North Hyde La., Sthl.	63	D5
North La., Tedd.	82	C6
North Lo. Clo. SW15	75	A5
Westleigh Ave.		
North Mall N9	33	E2
St. Martins Rd.		
North Ms. WC1	**8**	**D6**
North Ms. WC1	58	F4
North Par., Chess.	98	H5
North Pk. SE9	79	D6
North Pas. SW18	75	D5
North Peckham Est.	**21**	**F7**
SE15		
North Peckham Est.	68	B7
SE15		

North Pl., Mitch.	84	J7
North Pl., Tedd.	82	C6
North Pole La., Kes.	103	F6
North Pole Rd. W10	56	J5
North Ride W2	**10**	**G6**
North Ride W2	66	H1
Harall. Rd. 118	*18*	*J7*
North Rd. N7	49	E6
North Rd. N9	33	E1
North Rd. SE18	70	H4
North Rd. SW19	84	F6
North Rd. N6	64	G3
North Rd., Belv.	71	H3
North Rd., Brent.	64	H6
North Rd., Brom.	96	H1
North Rd., Edg.	38	B1
North Rd., Ilf.	52	H2
North Rd., Rich.	74	A3
North Rd., Rom.	44	E5
North Rd., Sthl.	54	G6
North Rd., Surb.	91	G6
North Rd., W.Wick.	103	B1
North Row W1	**11**	**A5**
North Row W1	57	J7
North Several SE3	78	D2
Orchard Dr.		
North Sq. N9	33	E2
St. Martins Rd.		
North Sq. NW11	39	D5
North St. E13	60	H2
North St. NW4	38	J5
North St. SW4	76	C3
North St., Bark.	52	E6
North St., Bexh.	80	G4
North St., Brom.	96	G1
North St., Cars.	100	J3
North St., Islw.	73	D3
North St. Pas. E13	60	H2
North St.		
North Tenter St. E1	**13**	**G4**
North Tenter St. E1	59	C6
North Ter. SW3	**14**	**G6**
North Verbena Gdns.	65	G5
W6		
St. Peters Sq.		
North Vw. SW19	83	J5
North Vw. W5	55	F4
North Vw., Pnr.	36	C7
North Vw. Cres.	47	F4
NW10		
North Vw. Dr.,	43	A2
Wdf.Grn.		
North Vw. Rd. N8	40	D3
North Vill. NW1	49	D6
North Wk. W2	**10**	**C6**
North Wk., Croy.	103	B6
North Way N9	33	G2
North Way N11	32	C6
North Way NW9	38	B3
North Way, Mord.	93	B3
North Way, Pnr.	36	C3
North Wf. Rd. W2	**10**	**E2**
North Wf. Rd. W2	57	G5
North Woolwich Rd.	69	G1
E16		
North Worple Way	74	D3
SW14		
Northall Rd., Bexh.	80	J2
Northampton Gro. N1	50	A6
St. Paul's Pl.		
Northampton Pk. N1	49	J6
Northampton Rd. EC1	**8**	**F5**
Northampton Rd.	58	G4
EC1		
Northampton Rd.,	102	D3
Croy.		
Northampton Rd.,	25	H4
Enf.		
Northampton Sq. EC1	**8**	**G4**
Northampton Sq. EC1	58	H3
Northampton St. N1	49	J7
Northanger Rd.	85	E6
SW16		
Northbank Rd. E17	42	C2
Northborough Rd.	94	D3
SW16		
Northbourne, Brom.	96	G7
Northbourne Rd.	76	D4
SW4		
Northbrook Rd. N22	32	E7
Northbrook Rd. SE13	78	D5
Northbrook Rd.,	23	B6
Barn.		
Northbrook Rd.,	95	A5
Croy.		
Northbrook Rd.,	52	D2
Ilf.		
Northburgh St. EC1	**8**	**H6**
Northburgh St. EC1	58	H4
Northchurch SE17	**21**	**C3**
Northchurch Rd. N1	50	A7
Northchurch Rd.,	47	A6
Wem.		

Northchurch Ter. N1	50	B7
Northcliffe Clo.,	99	E3
Wor.Pk.		
Northcliffe Dr. N20	31	C1
Northcote Ave. W5	55	H7
Northcote Ave.,	73	D5
Islw.		
Northcote Ave.,	54	E7
Sthl.		
Northcote Ave.,	92	A7
Surb.		
Northcote Ms. SW11	75	H4
Northcote Rd.		
Northcote Rd. E17	41	H4
Northcote Rd. NW10	47	E7
Northcote Rd. SW11	75	H5
Northcote Rd., Croy.	95	A6
Northcote Rd.,	92	D3
N.Mal.		
Northcote Rd., Sid.	88	H4
Northcote Rd.,	73	D5
Twick.		
Northcott Ave. N22	40	E1
Northcroft Rd. W13	64	E2
Northcroft Rd.,	99	D7
Epsom		
Northdene, Chig.	35	G5
Northdene Gdns. N15	41	C6
Northdown Gdns.,	43	H5
Ilf.		
Northdown Rd.,	80	B2
Well.		
Northdown St. N1	**8**	**B1**
Northdown St. N1	58	E2
Northern Ave. N9	33	B2
Northern Relief Rd.	52	E7
Bark.		
Northern Rd. E13	60	H2
Northern Service	23	B3
Rd., Barn.		
Northernhay Wk.,	93	B4
Mord.		
Northey St. E14	59	H7
Northfield, Loug.	27	A4
Northfield Ave. W5	64	E1
Northfield Ave. W13	64	E1
Northfield Ave.,	36	D4
Pnr.		
Northfield Clo.,	97	B1
Brom.		
Northfield Cres.,	100	B4
Sutt.		
Northfield Gdns.,	53	F4
Dag.		
Northfield Rd.		
Northfield Path,	53	F4
Dag.		
Connor Rd.		
Northfield Rd. E6	52	C7
Northfield Rd. N16	41	B7
Northfield Rd. W13	64	E2
Northfield Rd.,	23	H3
Barn.		
Northfield Rd.,	22	B1
Borwd.		
Northfield Rd., Dag.	53	F4
Northfield Rd.,	25	E5
Enf.		
Northfield Rd.,	63	D7
Houns.		
Northfields SW18	75	D4
Northfields Ind. Est.,	56	A1
Wem.		
Northfields Rd. W3	56	B5
Northgate Dr. NW9	38	E6
Northiam N12	31	D4
Northiam St. E9	59	E1
Northington St. WC1	**8**	**D6**
Northington St. WC1	58	F4
Northlands Ave.,	104	H4
Orp.		
Northlands St. SE5	76	J2
Northolm, Edg.	30	D4
Northolme Gdns.,	38	A1
Edg.		
Northolme Ri., Orp.	104	H2
Northolme Rd. N5	49	J4
Northolt Ave., Ruis.	45	B5
Northolt Gdns.,	46	C5
Grnf.		
Northolt Ind. Est.,	45	H7
Nthlt.		
Northolt Rd., Har.	45	H4
Northover, Brom.	87	F3
Northport St. N1	59	A1
Northside Rd.,	96	G1
Brom.		
Mitchell Way		
Northspur Rd.,	100	D3
Sutt.		
Northstead Rd. SW2	85	G2
Northumberland All.	**13**	**E4**
EC3		

Northumberland All.	59	B6
EC3		
Northumberland Ave.	51	J1
E12		
Northumberland Ave. 16		**A1**
WC2		
Northumberland Ave. 117	*81*	
WC2		
Northumberland	25	E1
Ave., Enf.		
Northumberland	73	C1
Ave., Islw.		
Northumberland	79	G4
Ave., Well.		
Northumberland	71	J7
Clo., Erith		
Northumberland	33	C3
Gdns. N9		
Northumberland	64	D7
Gdns., Islw.		
Northumberland Ave.		
Northumberland	94	D5
Gdns., Mitch.		
Northumberland Gro. 33		E7
N17		
Northumberland Pk.	33	C7
N17		
Northumberland Pk.,	71	J7
Erith		
Northumberland Pl.	57	D6
W2		
Northumberland Pl.,	73	G6
Rich.		
Northumberland Rd.	61	B6
E6		
Northumberland Rd.	42	A7
E17		
Northumberland Rd.,	23	F6
Barn.		
Northumberland Rd.,	36	F5
Har.		
Northumberland Row,82		B1
Twick.		
Colne Rd.		
Northumberland St.	**16**	**A1**
WC2		
Northumberland St.	67	E1
WC2		
Northumberland	80	J1
Way, Erith		
Northumbria St. E14	60	A6
Northway NW7	30	G7
Northway NW11	39	E5
Northway, Wall.	101	C4
Northway Circ. NW7	30	D4
Northway Cres. NW7	30	D4
Northway Rd. SE5	76	J3
Northway Rd., Croy.	95	C6
Northwest Pl. N1	**8**	**F1**
Northwick Ave.,	37	D6
Har.		
Northwick Circle,	37	F6
Har.		
Northwick Clo. NW8	**6**	**E5**
Northwick Pk. Rd.,	37	C6
Har.		
Northwick Rd., Wat.	28	C4
Northwick Rd., Wem.	55	G1
Northwick Ter. NW8	**6**	**E5**
Northwick Ter. NW8	57	G4
Northwick Wk., Har.	37	C7
Peterborough Rd.		
Northwold Est. E5	50	D2
Northwold Rd. E5	50	D2
Northwold Rd. N16	50	C2
Northwood Gdns.	31	G5
N12		
Northwood Gdns.,	46	C5
Grnf.		
Northwood Gdns.,	43	D4
Ilf.		
Northwood Hall N6	40	C7
Northwood Ho. SE27	86	A4
Northwood Pl.,	71	F3
Erith		
Northwood Rd. N6	40	B7
Northwood Rd. SE23	86	J1
Northwood Rd.,	101	A6
Cars.		
Northwood Rd.,	94	H2
Th.Hth.		
Northwood Way	86	A6
SE19		
Roman Rd.		
Norton Ave., Surb.	92	B7
Norton Clo. E4	34	A5
Norton Clo., Borwd.	22	A1
Norton Clo., Enf.	25	E2
Brick La.		
Norton Folgate E1	**13**	**E1**
Norton Folgate E1	59	B5
Norton Gdns. SW16	94	E2
Norton Rd. E10	50	J1

Norton Rd., Wem.	46	G6
Norval Rd., Wem.	46	E2
Norway Gate SE16	68	H3
Norway Pl. E14	59	J6
East India Dock Rd.		
Norway St. SE10	69	B6
Haunton Hau 1111	*11*	*11*
Cordelia St.		
Norwich Ms., Ilf.	53	A1
Ashgrove Rd.		
Norwich Rd., Bexh.	80	G4
Norwich Rd. E7	51	G5
Norwich Rd., Dag.	62	G2
Norwich Rd., Grnf.	54	H1
Norwich Rd., Th.Hth.	94	J3
Norwich St. EC4	**12**	**E3**
Norwich St. EC4	58	G6
Norwich Wk., Edg.	30	C7
Norwood Ave., Wem.	55	J1
Norwood Clo., Sthl.	63	G4
Norwood Dr., Har.	36	F6
Norwood Gdns.,	54	C4
Hayes		
Norwood Gdns.,	63	F4
Sthl.		
Norwood Grn. Rd.,	63	G4
Sthl.		
Norwood High St.	85	H3
SE27		
Norwood Pk. Rd.,	85	J5
SE27		
Norwood Rd. SE24	85	H1
Norwood Rd. SE27	85	H2
Norwood Rd., Sthl.	63	F4
Notley St. SE5	**21**	**B7**
Notley St. SE5	68	A7
Notre Dame Est. SW4	76	C4
Notson Rd. SE25	95	E4
Belfast Rd.		
Notting Barn Rd.	57	A4
W10		
Notting Hill Gate	66	D1
W11		
Nottingham Ave. E16	60	J5
Nottingham Ct. WC2 12		**A4**
Nottingham Pl. W1	**7**	**B6**
Nottingham Pl. W1	58	A5
Nottingham Rd. E10	42	C6
Nottingham Rd.	84	J1
SW17		
Nottingham Rd.,	73	C2
Islw.		
Nottingham Rd.,	101	J4
S.Croy.		
Nottingham St. W1	**11**	**B1**
Nottingham St. W1	58	A5
Nottingham Ter. NW1	**7**	**B6**
Nova Ms., Sutt.	93	B7
Nova Rd., Croy.	101	H1
Novar Clo., Orp.	97	J7
Novar Rd. SE9	88	F1
Novello St. SW6	75	D1
Nowell Rd. SW13	65	G6
Nower Hill, Pnr.	36	F4
Noyna Rd. SW17	84	J8
Nuding Clo. SE13	78	A3
Nugent Rd. N19	49	E1
Nugent Rd. SE25	95	C3
Nugent Ter. NW8	**6**	**D2**
Nugent Ter. NW8	57	F2
Nugents Ct., Pnr.	36	E1
St. Thomas' Dr.		
Nugents Pk., Pnr.	36	E1
Nun Ct. EC2	**13**	**B3**
Nuneaton Rd., Dag.	53	D7
Nunhead Cres. SE15	77	E3
Nunhead Grn. SE15	77	E3
Nunhead Gro. SE15	77	E3
Nunhead La. SE15	77	E3
Nunhead Pas. SE15	77	D3
Peckham Rye		
Nunnington Clo. SE9	88	B3
Nunns Rd., Enf.	24	J2
Nupton Dr., Barn.	22	J5
Nursery Ave. N3	39	F2
Nursery Ave., Bexh.	80	F3
Nursery Ave., Croy.	102	G2
Nursery Clo. SW15	75	A4
Nursery Clo., Croy.	102	G2
Nursery Clo., Enf.	25	G1
Nursery Clo., Felt.	72	B7
Nursery Clo., Orp.	97	J7
Nursery Clo., Rom.	44	D6
Nursery Clo.,	34	H5
Wdf.Grn.		
Nursery Ct. N17	33	C7
Nursery St.		
Nursery Gdns., Enf.	25	G1
Nursery La. E7	51	G6
Nursery La. W10	56	J5
Nursery La. E9	50	F6
Morning La.		
Nursery Rd. N2	39	G1

Nursery Rd. N14 24 C7
Nursery Rd. SW9 76 F4
Nursery Rd. (Merton) SW19 93 E2
Nursery Rd. (Wimbledon) SW19 84 B7
Worple Rd.
Nursery Rd., Loug. 26 J5
Nursery Rd. (High Beach), Loug. 26 H1
Nursery Rd., Pnr. 36 C3
Nursery Rd., Sutt. 100 F4
Nursery Rd., Th.Hth. 95 A4
Nursery Row, Barn. 23 B3
St. Albans Rd.
Nursery St. N17 33 C7
Nursery Wk. NW4 38 H3
Nurstead Rd., Erith 71 G7
Nutbourne St. W10 57 B3
Nutbrook St. SE15 77 D3
Nutbrowne Rd., Dag. 62 F1
Nutcroft Rd. SE15 68 E7
Nutfield Clo. N18 33 D6
Nutfield Clo., Cars. 100 H3
Nutfield Gdns., Ilf. 52 J2
Nutfield Gdns., Nthlt. 54 C2
Nutfield Rd. E15 51 C4
Nutfield Rd. NW2 47 G2
Nutfield Rd. SE22 77 C5
Nutfield Rd., Th.Hth. 94 H4
Nutfield Way, Orp. 104 D2
Nutford Pl. W1 10 H3
Nutford Pl. W1 57 H6
Nuthatch Gdns. SE28 70 G2
Nuthurst Ave. SW2 85 F2
Nutley Ter. NW3 48 F6
Nutmead Clo., Bex. 89 J1
Nutmeg La. E14 60 D6
Nutt Gro., Edg. 29 G2
Nutt St. SE15 21 G7
Nutt St. SE15 68 C7
Nuttall St. N1 9 E1
Nuttall St. N1 59 B2
Nutter La. E11 42 J6
Nutwell St. SW17 84 H5
Nuxley Rd., Belv. 71 F6
Nyanza St. SE18 70 G6
Nye Bevan Est. E5 50 G3
Nylands Ave., Rich. 74 A1
Nymans Gdns. SW20 92 H3
Hidcote Gdns.
Nynehead St. SE14 68 H7
Nyon Gro. SE6 86 J2
Nyssa Clo., Wdf.Grn. 35 C6
Gwynne Pk. Ave.
Nyton Clo. N19 49 E1
Courtauld Rd.

O

Oak Ave. N8 40 E4
Oak Ave. N10 32 B7
Oak Ave. N17 33 A7
Oak Ave., Croy. 103 A1
Oak Ave., Enf. 24 F1
Oak Ave., Hmptn. 81 E5
Oak Ave., Houns. 63 E7
Oak Bank, Croy. 103 C6
Oak Clo. N14 24 B7
Oak Clo., Sutt. 100 F2
Oak Cottage Clo. SE6 87 F1
Oak Cres. E16 60 E5
Oak Dene W13 55 E5
The Dene
Oak Gdns., Croy. 103 A2
Oak Gdns., Edg. 38 C2
Oak Gro. NW2 48 A4
Oak Gro., Ruis. 36 B7
Oak Gro., Sun. 81 B7
Oak Gro., W.Wick. 103 C2
Oak Gro. Rd. SE20 95 F2
Oak Hall Rd. E11 42 H6
Oak Hill, Wdf.Grn. 34 D7
Oak Hill Ave. NW3 48 E4
Oak Hill Clo., Wdf.Grn. 34 D7
Oak Hill Ct. SW19 84 A7
Oak Hill Cres., Wdf.Grn. 34 D7
Oak Hill Gdns., Wdf.Grn. 42 E1
Oak Hill Pk. NW3 48 E4
Oak Hill Pk. Ms. NW3 48 F4
Oak Hill Way NW3 48 F4
Oak La. E14 59 J7
Oak La. N2 39 G2
Oak La. N11 32 D6
Oak La., Islw. 73 B4
Oak La., Twick. 73 D7
Oak La., Wdf.Grn. 34 F4
Oak Lo. Ave., Chig. 35 G5
Oak Lo. Clo., Stan. 29 F5
Dennis La.
Oak Lo. Dr., W.Wick. 96 B7
Oak Manor Dr., Wem. 46 J5
Oakington Manor Dr.
Oak Pk. Gdns. SW19 75 A7
Oak Pl. SW18 75 E5
East Hill
Oak Ri., Buck.H. 35 A3
Oak Rd. W5 55 G7
The Bdy.
Oak Rd. Erith (Northumberland Heath), 71 J7
Oak Rd., N.Mal. 92 D2
Oak Row SW16 94 C2
Oak St., Rom. 44 J5
Oak Tree Clo. W5 55 F6
Pinewood Gro.
Oak Tree Clo., Stan. 29 E7
Oak Tree Dell NW9 38 C5
Oak Tree Dr. N20 31 E1
Oak Tree Gdns., Brom. 87 H5
Oak Tree Rd. NW8 6 F4
Oak Tree Rd. NW8 57 H3
Oak Village NW5 49 A4
Oak Way N14 24 B7
Oak Way W3 65 E1
Oak Way, Croy. 95 G6
Oakapple Ct. SE12 87 G2
Oakbank Ave., Walt. 90 F7
Oakbank Gro. SE24 76 J4
Oakbrook Clo., Brom. 87 H4
Oakbury Rd. SW6 75 E2
Oakcombe Clo., N.Mal. 92 E1
Traps La.
Oakcroft Clo., Pnr. 36 B2
Oakcroft Rd. SE13 78 D2
Oakcroft Rd., Chess. 98 J4
Oakcroft Vill., Chess. 98 J4
Oakdale N14 32 B1
Oakdale Ave., Har. 37 H5
Oakdale Ave., Nthwd. 36 A2
Oakdale Clo., Wat. 28 C4
Oakdale Ct. E4 34 C5
Oakdale Rd. E7 51 H7
Oakdale Rd. E11 51 D2
Oakdale Rd. E18 42 H2
Oakdale Rd. N4 40 J6
Oakdale Rd. SE15 77 F3
Oakdale Rd. SW16 85 E5
Oakdale Rd., Wat. 28 C3
Oakden St. SE11 20 F1
Oakden St. SE11 67 G4
Oakdene SE15 77 E1
Carlton Gro.
Oakdene Ave., Chis. 88 D5
Oakdene Ave., Erith 71 J6
Oakdene Ave., T.Ditt. 98 D1
Oakdene Clo., Pnr. 28 F7
Oakdene Dr., Surb. 92 C7
Oakdene Ms., Sutt. 100 C1
Oakdene Pk. N3 31 C7
Oakdene Rd., Orp. 97 J5
Oake Ct. SW15 75 B5
Oaken Dr., Esher 98 C6
Oaken La., Esher 98 B4
Oakenshaw Clo., Surb. 91 H7
Oakes Clo. E6 61 C6
Savage Gdns.
Oakeshott Ave. N6 49 A2
Oakey La. SE1 16 E5
Oakfield E4 34 B5
Oakfield Ave., Har. 37 E3
Oakfield Clo., N.Mal. 92 F5
Blakes La.
Oakfield Ct. N8 40 E7
Oakfield Ct. NW2 39 A7
Hendon Way
Oakfield Gdns. N18 33 B4
Oakfield Gdns. SE19 86 C5
Oakfield Gdns., Beck. 96 A5
Oakfield Gdns., Cars. 100 H1
Oakfield Gdns., Grnf. 55 A4
Oakfield La., Kes. 103 J4
Oakfield Rd. E6 61 B1
Oakfield Rd. E17 41 H2
Oakfield Rd. N3 39 E1
Oakfield Rd. N4 40 G6
Oakfield Rd. N14 32 E3
Oakfield Rd. SE20 95 E1
Oakfield Rd. SW19 84 A3
Oakfield Rd., Croy. 101 J1
Oakfield Rd., Ilf. 52 E2
Oakfield St. SW10 18 C5
Oakfield St. SW10 66 F6
Oakfields Rd. NW11 39 B6
Oakford Rd. NW5 49 C4
Oakham Clo. SE6 86 J2
Rutland Wk.
Oakham Dr., Brom. 96 F4
Oakhampton Rd. NW7 31 A7
Oakhill, Esher 98 D6
Oakhill, Surb. 91 H7
Oakhill Ave., Pnr. 36 E2
Oakhill Ct. E11 42 H6
Eastern Ave.
Oakhill Ct. SW19 84 A7
Edge Hill
Oakhill Cres., Surb. 91 H7
Oakhill Dr., Surb. 91 H7
Oakhill Gro., Surb. 91 H6
Oakhill Path, Surb. 91 H6
Glenbuck Rd.
Oakhill Pl. SW15 75 D5
Oakhill Rd.
Oakhill Rd. SW15 75 C5
Oakhill Rd. SW16 94 E1
Oakhill Rd., Beck. 96 C2
Oakhill Rd., Orp. 104 J1
Oakhill Rd., Surb. 91 H6
Oakhill Rd., Sutt. 100 E3
Oakhouse Rd., Bexh. 80 G5
Oakhurst Ave., Barn. 23 H7
Oakhurst Ave., Bexh. 71 E7
Oakhurst Clo. E17 42 E4
Oakhurst Clo., Ilf. 43 F1
Oakhurst Clo., Tedd. 82 B5
Oakhurst Gdns. E4 34 F1
Oakhurst Gdns. E17 42 E4
Oakhurst Gdns., Bexh. 71 E7
Oakhurst Gro. SE22 77 D4
Oakhurst Rd., Epsom 99 C6
Oakington Ave., Har. 36 G7
Oakington Ave., Wem. 46 J3
Oakington Dr., Sun. 90 C2
Oakington Manor Dr., Wem. 47 A5
Oakington Rd. W9 57 D4
Oakington Way N8 40 E6
Oakland Way, Epsom 99 D6
Oaklands N21 32 F2
Oaklands, Twick. 72 J7
Oaklands Ave. N9 25 E6
Oaklands Ave., Esher 98 A1
Oaklands Ave., Islw. 64 C6
Oaklands Ave., Sid. 79 J7
Oaklands Ave., Th.Hth. 94 G4
Oaklands Ave., Wat. 28 B1
Oaklands Ave., W.Wick. 103 B3
Oaklands Clo., Bexh. 80 F5
Oaklands Clo., Chess. 98 F4
Oaklands Clo., Orp. 97 H6
Oaklands Ct., Wem. 46 G5
Oaklands Est. SW4 76 C6
Oaklands Gro. W12 65 G1
Oaklands La., Barn. 22 H4
Oaklands Pk. Ave., Ilf. 52 G2
High Rd.
Oaklands Pl. SW4 76 C4
St. Alphonsus Rd.
Oaklands Rd. N20 23 C7
Oaklands Rd. NW2 48 A4
Oaklands Rd. SW14 74 D3
Oaklands Rd. W7 64 C2
Oaklands Rd., Bexh. 80 F4
Oaklands Rd., Brom. 87 E7
Oaklands Way, Wall. 101 D7
Oaklea Pas., Kings.T. 91 G3
Oakleafe Gdns., Ilf. 43 E3
Oakleigh Ave. N20 31 G2
Oakleigh Ave., Edg. 38 B2
Oakleigh Ave., Surb. 99 A1
Oakleigh Clo. N20 31 J3
Oakleigh Ct., Barn. 23 H6
Church Hill Rd.
Oakleigh Ct., Edg. 38 C2
Oakleigh Cres. N20 31 H2
Oakleigh Gdns. N20 31 F1
Oakleigh Gdns., Edg. 29 J5
Oakleigh Gdns., Orp. 104 H4
Oakleigh Ms. N20 31 F2
Oakleigh Rd. N.
Oakleigh Pk. Ave., Chis. 97 D2
Oakleigh Pk. N. N20 31 G1
Oakleigh Pk. S. N20 23 H7
Oakleigh Rd., Pnr. 28 F6
Oakleigh Rd. N. N20 31 H2
Oakleigh Rd. S. N11 32 A3
Oakleigh Way, Mitch. 94 B1
Oakleigh Way, Surb. 99 A1
Oakley Ave. W5 56 A7
Oakley Ave., Bark. 52 J7
Oakley Ave., Croy. 101 F4
Oakley Clo. E4 34 C3
Mapleton Rd.
Oakley Clo. E6 61 B6
Northumberland Rd.
Oakley Clo. W7 55 B7
Oakley Clo., Islw. 73 A1
Oakley Cres. EC1 8 H2
Oakley Dr. SE9 88 G1
Oakley Dr., Brom. 104 B3
Oakley Gdns. N8 40 F5
Oakley Gdns. SW3 18 H5
Oakley Gdns. SW3 66 H6
Oakley Pk., Bex. 80 C7
Oakley Pl. SE1 21 F4
Oakley Pl. SE1 68 C5
Oakley Rd. N1 50 A7
Oakley Rd. SE25 95 E5
Oakley Rd., Brom. 104 B3
Oakley Rd., Har. 37 B6
Oakley Sq. NW1 7 G1
Oakley Sq. NW1 58 C2
Oakley St. SW3 18 G5
Oakley St. SW3 66 H6
Oakley Wk. W6 66 A6
Greyhound Rd.
Oakmead Ave., Brom. 96 G6
Oakmead Gdns., Edg. 30 D4
Oakmead Pl., Mitch. 93 H1
Oakmead Rd. SW12 85 A1
Oakmead Rd., Croy. 95 F6
Oakmeade, Pnr. 28 G6
Oakmere Rd. SE2 71 A6
Oakmoor Way, Chig. 35 H5
Oakmount Pl., Orp. 104 G1
Oakridge Dr. N2 39 G3
Oakridge Rd., Brom. 87 D4
Oaks, The N12 31 E4
Oaks, The SE18 70 F5
Oaks, The, Wdf.Grn. 34 E7
Oaks Ave. SE19 86 B5
Oaks Ave., Felt. 81 E2
Oaks Ave., Rom. 44 J2
Oaks Ave., Wor.Pk. 99 H3
Oaks Gro. E4 34 E2
Oaks La., Croy. 102 F3
Oaks La., Ilf. 43 H5
Oaks Rd., Croy. 102 E5
Oaks Way, Cars. 100 J7
Oaks Way, Surb. 98 G2
Oaksford Ave. SE26 86 E3
Oakshade Rd., Brom. 87 D4
Oakshaw Rd. SW18 75 E7
Oakthorpe Rd. N13 32 G5
Oaktree Ave. N13 32 H3
Oakview Gdns. N2 39 G4
Oakview Gro., Croy. 102 H1
Oakview Rd. SE6 87 B5
Oakway SW20 92 J4
Oakway, Brom. 96 D2
Oakway Clo., Bex. 80 E6
Oakways SE9 79 E6
Oakwood Ave. N14 24 D7
Oakwood Ave., Beck. 96 C2
Oakwood Ave., Borwd. 22 B4
Oakwood Ave., Brom. 96 H3
Oakwood Ave., Mitch. 93 G2
Oakwood Ave., Sthl. 54 G7
Oakwood Clo. N14 24 C6
Oakwood Clo., Chis. 88 C6
Oakwood Clo., Wdf.Grn. 35 B6
Green Wk.
Oakwood Ct. W14 66 C3
Oakwood Cres. N21 24 E6
Oakwood Cres., Grnf. 46 D6
Oakwood Dr. SE19 86 A6
Oakwood Dr., Edg. 30 C6

Oakwood Gdns., Ilf.	52	J2
Oakwood Gdns., Orp.	104	F2
Oakwood Gdns., Sutt.	100	D2
Oakwood Hill, Loug.	27	C6
Oakwood Hill Ind. Est. (Oakwood Hill), Loug.	27	E5
Oakwood La. W14	66	C3
Oakwood Pk. Rd. N14	24	D7
Oakwood Pl., Croy.	94	G6
Oakwood Rd. NW11	39	D4
Oakwood Rd. SW20	92	G1
Oakwood Rd., Croy.	94	G6
Oakwood Rd., Orp.	104	F2
Oakwood Rd., Pnr.	36	B2
Oakwood Vw. N14	24	D5
Oakworth Rd. W10	56	J5
Oat La. EC2	13	A3
Oat La. EC2	58	J6
Oates Clo., Brom.	96	D3
Oatfield Rd., Orp.	104	J1
Oatland Ri. E17	41	H2
Oatlands Rd., Enf.	25	F1
Oban Ho., Bark.	61	G2
Wheelers Cross		
Oban Rd. E13	60	J3
Oban Rd. SE25	95	A4
Oban St. E14	60	D6
Oberstein Rd. SW11	75	G4
Oborne Clo. SE24	76	H5
Observatory Gdns. W8	66	D2
Observatory Rd. SW14	74	C4
Occupation La. SE18	79	E1
Occupation La. W5	64	G4
Occupation Rd. SE17	20	J3
Occupation Rd. SE17	67	J5
Occupation Rd. W13	64	E2
Ocean Est. E1	59	G4
Ocean St. E1	59	G5
Ockenden Rd. N1	50	A6
Ockham Dr., Orp.	89	A7
Ockley Rd. SW16	85	E4
Ockley Rd., Croy.	94	F7
Octagon Arc. EC2	13	D2
Octavia Clo., Mitch.	93	H5
Octavia Rd., Islw.	73	C3
Octavia St. SW11	75	H1
Octavia Way SE28	62	B7
Booth Clo.		
Octavius St. SE8	69	A7
Odard Rd., W.Mol.	90	G4
Down St.		
Oddesey Rd., Borwd.	22	B1
Odessa Rd. E7	51	F4
Odessa Rd. NW10	56	G2
Odessa St. SE16	68	J2
Odger St. SW11	75	J2
Odhams Wk. WC2	12	A4
Odyssey Business Pk., Ruis.	45	B5
Offas Mead E9	50	H4
Lindisfarne Way		
Offenbach Ho. E2	59	G2
Mace St.		
Offenham Rd. SE9	88	C4
Offerton Rd. SW4	76	C3
Offham Slope N12	31	C5
Offley Rd. SW9	20	E7
Offley Rd. SW9	67	G7
Offord Clo. N17	33	D7
Offord Rd. N1	49	F7
Offord St. N1	49	F7
Ogilby St. SE18	70	C4
Oglander Rd. SE15	77	C4
Ogle St. W1	11	F1
Ogle St. W1	58	C5
Oglethorpe Rd., Dag.	53	F3
Ohio Rd. E13	60	F4
Okeburn Rd. SW17	85	A5
Okehampton Clo. N12	31	G5
Okehampton Cres., Well.	80	B1
Okehampton Rd. NW10	56	J1
Olaf St. W11	57	A7
Old Bailey EC4	12	H4
Old Bailey EC4	58	H6
Old Barge Ho. All. SE1	16	F1
Old Barn Clo., Sutt.	100	B7
Old Barrack Yd. SW1	15	B4
Old Barrowfield E15	60	E1
New Plaistow Rd.		
Old Bethnal Grn. Rd. E2	9	J3
Old Bethnal Grn. Rd. E2	59	D3
Old Bond St. W1	11	F6
Old Bond St. W1	58	C7
Old Brewers Yd. WC2	12	A4
Old Brewery Ms. NW3	48	G4
Hampstead High St.		
Old Brk. Ms., N.Mal.	51	C2
Old Bri. St., Kings.T.	91	G2
Old Broad St. EC2	13	C4
Old Broad St. EC2	59	A6
Old Bromley Rd., Brom.	87	D5
Old Brompton Rd. SW5	66	E5
Old Brompton Rd. SW7	18	D3
Old Brompton Rd. SW7	66	E5
Old Bldgs. WC2	12	E3
Old Burlington St. W1	11	F5
Old Burlington St. W1	58	C7
Hindes Rd.		
Old Castle St. E1	13	F3
Old Castle St. E1	59	C6
Old Cavendish St. W1	11	D3
Old Cavendish St. W1	58	B6
Old Chelsea Ms. SW3	18	F6
Old Ch. La. NW9	47	D2
Old Ch. La., Grnf.	55	D3
Perivale La.		
Old Ch. La., Stan.	29	E5
Old Ch. Rd. E1	59	G6
Old Ch. Rd. E4	34	A4
Old Ch. St. SW3	18	F4
Old Ch. St. SW3	66	G5
Old Claygate La., Esher	98	D6
Old Compton St. W1	11	H5
Old Compton St. W1	58	D7
Old Cote Dr., Houns.	63	G6
Old Ct. Pl. W8	14	A3
Old Ct. Pl. W8	66	E2
Old Deer Pk. Gdns., Rich.	73	H3
Old Devonshire Rd. SW12	76	B7
Old Dock Clo., Rich.	65	A6
Watcombe Cotts.		
Old Dover Rd. SE3	69	G7
Old Fm. Ave. N14	24	C7
Old Fm. Ave., Sid.	88	G1
Old Fm. Clo., Houns.	72	F4
Old Fm. Pas., Hmptn.	90	J1
Old Fm. Rd. N2	39	G1
Old Fm. Rd., Hmptn.	81	F6
Old Fm. Rd. E., Sid.	89	A2
Old Fm. Rd. W., Sid.	88	J2
Old Fish St. Hill EC4	12	J5
Old Fold Clo., Barn.	23	C1
Old Fold La.		
Old Fold La., Barn.	23	C1
Old Fold Vw., Barn.	22	J3
Old Ford Rd. E2	59	F2
Old Ford Rd. E3	59	G2
Old Forge Clo., Stan.	29	D4
Old Forge Ms. W12	65	H2
Goodwin Rd.		
Old Forge Way, Sid.	89	B4
Old Fox Footpath, S.Croy.	102	B7
Essenden Rd.		
Old Gloucester St. WC1	12	B1
Old Gloucester St. WC1	58	E5
Old Hall Clo., Pnr.	36	E1
Old Hall Dr., Pnr.	36	E1
Old Hill, Chis.	97	D1
Old Hill, Orp.	104	G6
Old Homesdale Rd., Brom.	96	J4
Old Ho. Clo. SW19	84	B5
Old Ho. Gdns., Twick.	59	J3
Old Jamaica Rd. SE16	17	H5
Old Jamaica Rd. SE16	68	D3
Old James St. SE15	77	E3
Old Jewry EC2	12	J3
Old Jewry EC2	59	A6
Old Kent Rd. SE1	21	D1
Old Kent Rd. SE1	68	B4
Old Kent Rd. SE15	21	J5
Old Kent Rd. SE15	68	E6
Old Kenton La. NW9	38	B5
Old Kingston Rd., Wor.Pk.	99	C3
Old Lo. Pl., Twick.	73	E6
St. Margarets Rd.		
Old Lo. Way, Stan.	29	D5
Old Maidstone Rd., Sid.	89	F7
Old Malden La., Wor.Pk.	99	D3
Old Manor Dr., Islw.	72	J6
Old Manor Way, Chis.	88	C5
Old Manor Yd. SW5	18	A2
Old Marylebone Rd. NW1	10	H2
Old Marylebone Rd. NW1	57	H5
Old Ms., Har.	37	B5
Old Mill Ct. E18	42	J3
Old Mill La. W6	65	G5
Old Mill Rd. SE18	70	G6
Old Montague St. E1	13	H2
Old Montague St. E1	59	D5
Old Nichol St. E2	9	F5
Old Nichol St. E2	59	C4
Old N. St. WC1	12	C1
Old Oak Common La. NW10	56	E4
Old Oak Common La. W3	56	E5
Old Oak La. NW10	56	F7
Old Oak Rd. W3	56	F7
Old Orchard, Sun.	90	C2
Old Orchard, The NW3	48	J4
Nassington Rd.		
Old Palace La., Rich.	73	F5
Old Palace Rd., Croy.	101	H3
Old Palace Ter., Rich.	73	G5
King St.		
Old Palace Yd. SW1	16	A5
Old Palace Yd. SW1	67	E3
Old Palace Yd., Rich.	73	G5
Old Paradise St. SE11	20	C1
Old Paradise St. SE11	67	F4
Old Pk. Ave. SW12	76	A6
Old Pk. Ave., Enf.	24	J4
Old Pk. Gro., Enf.	24	J4
Old Pk. La. W1	15	C2
Old Pk. La. W1	67	A1
Old Pk. Ms., Houns.	63	F7
Old Pk. Ridings N21	24	H6
Old Pk. Rd. N13	32	F4
Old Pk. Rd. SE2	71	A5
Old Pk. Rd., Enf.	24	H3
Old Pk. Rd. S., Enf.	24	H4
Old Pk. Vw., Enf.	24	G3
Old Perry St., Chis.	88	H6
Old Pl. N1	58	G1
Liverpool Rd.		
Old Pye St. SW1	15	H5
Old Pye St. SW1	67	D3
Old Quebec St. W1	11	A4
Old Quebec St. W1	57	J6
Old Queen St. SW1	15	J4
Old Queen St. SW1	67	D2
Old Rectory Gdns., Edg.	30	A6
Old Redding, Har.	28	H5
Old Rd. SE13	78	E4
Old Rd., Enf.	25	F1
Old Rope Wk., Sun.	90	B3
The Ave.		
Old Ruislip Rd., Nthlt.	54	C2
Old Savill's Cotts., Chig.	35	F4
The Chase		
Old Sch. Clo. SW19	93	D2
Old Sch. Clo., Beck.	95	G2
Old Seacoal La. EC4	12	G4
Old S. Clo., Pnr.	36	D1
Old S. Lambeth Rd. SW8	20	B7
Old S. Lambeth Rd. SW8	67	E7
Old Sq. N1	58	G1
Liverpool Rd.		
Old Sq. WC2	12	D3
Old Sq. WC2	58	F6
Old Sta. Rd., Loug.	27	B5
Old St. E13	60	H2
Old St. EC1	8	J6
Old St. EC1	58	J4
Old Swan Yd., Cars.	100	J4
Old Town SW4	76	C3
Old Town, Croy.	101	H3
Old Tram Yd. SE18	70	H4
Lakedale Rd.		
Old Woolwich Rd. SE10	63	D6
Old York Rd. SW18	75	E5
Oldberry Rd., Edg.	30	D6
Oldborough Rd., Wem.	46	F2
Oldbury Pl. W1	11	C1
Oldbury Pl. W1	58	A5
Oldbury Rd., Enf.	25	D2
Oldfield Circ., Nthlt.	45	J6
Currey Rd.		
Oldfield Clo., Brom.	97	C4
Oldfield Clo., Grnf.	46	B5
Oldfield Clo., Stan.	29	D5
Oldfield Fm. Gdns., Grnf.	55	A1
Oldfield Gro. SE16	68	G4
Oldfield La. N., Grnf.	55	A2
Oldfield La. S., Grnf.	54	J3
Oldfield Ms. N6	40	C7
Oldfield Pk., Brom.	97	D4
Oldfield Rd. N16	50	B3
Oldfield Rd. NW10	47	F7
Oldfield Rd. SW19	84	B6
Oldfield Rd. W3	65	F2
Valetta Rd.		
Oldfield Rd., Bexh.	80	E2
Oldfield Rd., Brom.	97	B4
Oldfield Rd., Hmptn.	90	F1
Oldfields Rd., Sutt.	100	C3
Oldham Ter. W3	65	C1
Oldhill St. N16	50	D1
Oldridge Rd. SW12	76	A7
Oldstead Rd., Brom.	87	D4
Oleander Clo., Orp.	104	G5
O'Leary Sq. E1	59	F5
Oley Pl. E1	59	G5
Redman's Rd.		
Olga St. E3	59	H2
Conyer St.		
Olinda Rd. N16	41	C6
Oliphant St. W10	57	A3
Olive Rd. E13	60	J3
Olive Rd. NW2	47	J4
Olive Rd. SW19	84	F7
Norman Rd.		
Olive Rd. W5	64	G3
Oliver Ave. SE25	95	C3
Oliver Clo. E10	51	A2
Oliver Clo. W4	65	B6
Oliver Gdns. E6	61	B6
Oliver Goldsmith Est. SE15	77	D1
Goldsmith Rd.		
Oliver Gro. SE25	95	C4
Oliver Rd. E10	51	B2
Oliver Rd. E17	42	C5
Oliver Rd., N.Mal.	92	C2
Oliver Rd., Sutt.	100	G4
Olivers Yd. EC1	9	C5
Olivette St. SW15	75	A3
Felsham Rd.		
Ollards Gro., Loug.	27	A4
Ollerton Grn. E3	59	J1
Ollerton Rd. N11	32	D5
Olley Clo., Wall.	101	E6
Ollgar Clo. W12	65	F1
Olliffe St. E14	69	C3
Olmar St. SE1	21	H5
Olmar St. SE1	68	D6
Olney Rd. SE17	20	J5
Olney Rd. SE17	67	H6
Olron Cres., Bexh.	80	D5
Olven Rd. SE18	70	F6
Olveston Wk., Cars.	93	G6
Olwen Ms., Pnr.	36	D2
Olyffe Ave., Well.	80	A1
Olyffe Dr., Beck.	96	C1
Olympia Ms. W2	10	B6
Olympia Way W14	66	B3
Olympic Ind. Est., Wem.	47	B4
Olympic Way, Grnf.	54	H1
Olympic Way, Wem.	47	A3
Olympus Sq. E5	50	D4
Nolan Way		
Oman Ave. NW2	47	H4
O'Meara St. SE1	17	A2
O'Meara St. SE1	67	J1
Omega Pl. N1	8	B2

Omega St. SE14 78 A1
Ommaney Rd. SE14 77 G1
On The Hill, Wat. 28 E2
Ondine Rd. SE15 77 C4
One Tree Clo. SE23 77 F6
Onega Gate SE16 68 H3
Ongar Clo., Rom. 44 C5
Ongar Rd. SW6 66 D6
Onra Rd. E17 42 A7
Onslow Ave., Rich. 73 H5
Onslow Clo. E4 34 D2
Onslow Clo., T.Ditt. 98 B1
Onslow Cres., Chis. 97 E1
Onslow Dr., Sid. 89 D3
Onslow Gdns. E18 42 H3
Onslow Gdns. N10 40 B5
Onslow Gdns. N21 24 G5
Onslow Gdns. SW7 18 E3
Onslow Gdns. SW7 66 G5
Onslow Gdns., 98 B1
T.Ditt.
Onslow Gdns., Wall. 101 C6
Onslow Ms. E. SW7 18 E2
Onslow Ms. W. SW7 18 E2
Onslow Rd., Croy. 101 G1
Onslow Rd., N.Mal. 92 G4
Onslow Rd., Rich. 73 H5
Onslow Sq. SW7 18 F2
Onslow Sq. SW7 66 G4
Onslow St. EC1 8 F6
Onslow Way, T.Ditt. 98 B1
Ontario St. SE1 16 H6
Opal Clo. E16 61 A6
Opal Ms., Ilf. 52 E2
Ley St.
Opal St. SE11 20 G3
Opal St. SE11 67 H4
Openshaw Rd. SE2 71 B4
Openview SW18 84 F1
Ophelia Gdns. NW2 48 B3
The Vale
Ophir Ter. SE15 77 D1
Opossum Way, 72 C2
Houns.
Oppenheim Rd. SE13 78 C2
Oppidans Ms. NW3 48 J7
Meadowbank
Oppidans Rd. NW3 48 J7
Orange Ct. E1 17 J2
Orange Hill Rd., Edg. 30 C7
Orange Pl. SE16 68 F3
Lwr. Rd.
Orange St. WC2 11 J6
Orange St. WC2 58 D7
Orange Yd. W1 11 J4
Orangery, The, 82 F2
Rich.
Orangery La. SE9 79 C5
Oratory La. SW3 18 F3
Orb St. SE17 21 B2
Orb St. SE17 68 A4
Orbain Rd. SW6 66 B7
Orbel St. SW11 75 H1
Orchard, The N14 24 B5
Orchard, The N21 25 A6
Orchard, The NW11 39 D5
Orchard, The SE3 78 D2
Orchard, The W4 65 D4
Orchard, The W5 55 G5
Orchard, The, Epsom 99 F7
Orchard, The, 72 J2
Houns.
Orchard Ave. N3 39 D3
Orchard Ave. N14 24 C6
Orchard Ave. N20 31 G2
Orchard Ave., Belv. 71 E6
Orchard Ave., Croy. 102 H2
Orchard Ave., 63 E7
Houns.
Orchard Ave., Mitch. 101 A1
Orchard Ave., 92 E2
N.Mal.
Orchard Ave., Sthl. 63 E1
Orchard Ave., 98 D1
T.Ditt.
Orchard Clo. E4 34 A4
Chingford Mt. Rd.
Orchard Clo. E11 42 H4
Orchard Clo. NW2 47 G3
Orchard Clo. SE23 77 F6
Brenchley Gdns.
Orchard Clo. SW20 92 J4
Grand Dr.
Orchard Clo. W10 57 B5
Orchard Clo., Bexh. 80 E1
Orchard Clo., Edg. 29 H6
Orchard Clo., Epsom 99 B6
Orchard Clo., 45 J5
Nthlt.
Orchard Clo., Surb. 91 E7
Orchard Clo. 29 A1
(Bushey), Wat.
Orchard Clo., Wem. 55 H1
Orchard Ct., Islw. 73 A1
Orchard Ct., Twick. 82 A2
Orchard Ct., 99 G1
Wor.Pk.
Orchard Cres., Edg. 30 C5
Orchard Cres., Enf. 25 C1
Orchard Dr. SE3 78 E2
Orchard Dr., Edg. 29 J5
Orchard Gdns., 98 H4
Chess.
Orchard Gdns., 100 D5
Sutt.
Orchard Gate NW9 38 E4
Orchard Gate, Esher 98 A1
Orchard Gate, Grnf. 46 E5
Orchard Grn., Orp. 104 H2
Orchard Gro. SE20 86 D7
Orchard Gro., Croy. 95 H7
Orchard Gro., Edg. 38 A1
Orchard Gro., Har. 37 J5
Orchard Gro., Orp. 104 J2
Orchard Hill SE13 78 B2
Coldbath St.
Orchard Hill, Cars. 100 J5
Orchard La., E.Mol. 91 A6
Orchard La., 34 J4
Wdf.Grn.
Orchard Ms. N1 50 A7
Southgate Gro.
Orchard Pl. E14 60 E7
Orchard Pl. N17 33 C7
Orchard Ri., Croy. 102 H1
Orchard Ri., 92 C1
Kings.T.
Orchard Ri., Rich. 74 B4
Orchard Ri. E., Sid. 79 H5
Orchard Ri. W., Sid. 79 H5
Orchard Rd. N6 40 B7
Orchard Rd. SE3 78 E2
Eliot Pl.
Orchard Rd. SE18 70 G4
Orchard Rd., Barn. 23 B4
Orchard Rd., Belv. 71 G4
Orchard Rd., Brent. 64 F6
Orchard Rd., Brom. 96 J1
Orchard Rd., Chess. 98 H4
Orchard Rd., Dag. 62 G1
Orchard Rd., Enf. 25 F5
Orchard Rd., Hmptn. 81 F7
Orchard Rd., Houns. 72 F5
Orchard Rd., 91 H2
Kings.T.
Orchard Rd., Mitch. 101 A1
Orchard Rd. Orp. 104 E6
(Farnborough)
Orchard Rd., Rich. 74 A3
Orchard Rd., Rom. 44 H2
Orchard Rd., Sid. 88 H4
Orchard Rd., Sun. 81 B7
Hanworth Rd.
Orchard Rd., Sutt. 100 D4
Orchard Rd., Twick. 73 D5
Orchard Rd., Well. 80 B3
Orchard Sq. W14 66 C5
Sun Rd.
Orchard St. E17 41 H4
Orchard St. W1 11 B4
Orchard St. W1 58 A6
Orchard Ter., Enf. 25 D6
Great Cambridge Rd.
Orchard Way, Beck. 95 H5
Orchard Way, Croy. 102 H1
Orchard Way, Enf. 25 B3
Orchard Way, Sutt. 100 G4
Orchardleigh Ave., 25 F2
Enf.
Orchardmede N21 25 A6
Orchardson St. NW8 6 E6
Orchardson St. NW8 57 G4
Orchid Clo. E6 61 B5
Orchid Rd. N14 24 C7
Orchid St. W12 56 G7
Orde Hall St. WC1 12 C1
Orde Hall St. WC1 58 F5
Ordell Rd. E3 59 J2
Ordnance Clo., 81 A3
Felt.
Ordnance Cres. SE10 69 E2
Ordnance Hill NW8 57 G1
Ordnance Ms. NW8 6 F1
Ordnance Rd. E16 60 F5
Ordnance Rd. SE18 70 D6
Oregano Dr. E14 60 D6
Oregon Ave. E12 52 C4
Oregon Clo., N.Mal. 92 C4
Georgia Rd.
Oregon Sq., Orp. 104 G1
Orestes Ms. NW6 48 D5
Aldred Rd.
Orford Ct. SE27 85 H2
Orford Gdns., 82 C2
Twick.
Orford Rd. E17 42 A5
Orford Rd. E18 42 H3
Organ La. E4 34 C2
Oriel Clo., Mitch. 94 D4
Oriel Ct. NW3 48 F4
Heath St.
Oriel Gdns., Ilf. 43 C3
Oriel Pl. NW3 48 F4
Heath St.
Oriel Rd. E9 50 G6
Oriel Way, Nthlt. 45 H7
Orient Ind. Pk. E10 51 A2
Orient St. SE11 20 G1
Orient Way E5 50 G3
Oriental Rd. E16 70 A1
Oriental St. E14 60 A7
Morant St.
Oriole Way SE28 62 B7
Orissa Rd. SE18 70 H5
Orkney St. SW11 76 A2
Orlando Rd. SW4 76 C3
Orleans Rd. SE19 86 A6
Orleans Rd., Twick. 73 E7
Orleston Ms. N7 49 G6
Orleston Rd. N7 49 G6
Orley Fm. Rd., Har. 46 B3
Orlop St. SE10 69 E5
Ormanton Rd. SE26 86 D4
Orme Ct. W2 10 A6
Orme Ct. W2 57 E7
Orme Ct. Ms. W2 10 B6
Orme La. W2 10 A6
Orme La. W2 57 E7
Orme Rd., Kings.T. 92 B2
Orme Sq. W2 10 A6
Ormeley Rd. SW12 76 B7
Ormerod Gdns., 94 A2
Mitch.
Ormesby Clo. SE28 62 D7
Wroxham Rd.
Ormesby Way, Har. 37 J6
Ormiston Gro. W12 65 H1
Ormiston Rd. SE10 69 G5
Ormond Ave., Hmptn. 90 H1
Ormond Clo. WC1 12 B1
Ormond Cres., 90 H1
Hmptn.
Ormond Dr., Hmptn. 81 H7
Ormond Ms. WC1 8 B6
Ormond Rd. N19 49 E1
Ormond Rd., Rich. 73 G5
Ormond Yd. SW1 15 G1
Ormonde Ave., Orp. 104 F2
Ormonde Gate SW3 19 A4
Ormonde Gate SW3 66 J5
Ormonde Pl. SW1 19 B2
Ormonde Ri., 34 J1
Buck.H.
Ormonde Rd. SW14 74 C3
Ormonde Ter. NW8 57 J1
Ormsby Gdns., Grnf. 54 J2
Ormsby Pl. N16 50 C3
Victorian Gro.
Ormsby Pt. SE18 70 E4
Troy Ct.
Ormsby St. E2 9 F2
Ormsby St. E2 59 C2
Ormside St. SE15 68 F6
Ormskirk Rd., Wat. 28 D4
Ornan Rd. NW3 48 H5
Oronsay Wk. N1 49 J6
Marquess Est.
Orpen Wk. N16 50 B3
Orpheus St. SE5 77 A1
Orpington Gdns. N18 33 B3
Orpington Rd. N21 32 G1
Orpington Rd., 97 H3
Chis.
Orpwood Clo., 81 F6
Hmptn.
Orsett St. SE11 20 D3
Orsett St. SE11 67 F5
Orsett Ter. W2 10 B3
Orsett Ter. W2 57 E6
Orsett Ter., 34 J7
Wdf.Grn.
Orsman Rd. N1 59 B1
Orton St. E1 17 H2
Orville Rd. SW11 75 G2
Orwell Ct. N5 49 J4
Orwell Rd. E13 60 J1
Osbaldeston Rd. N16 50 D2
Osbert St. SW1 19 H2
Osberton Rd. SE12 78 G5
Osborn Clo. E8 59 D1
Osborn Gdns. NW7 31 A7
Osborn La. SE23 77 H7
Osborn St. E1 13 G2
Osborn St. E1 59 C5
Osborn Ter. SE3 78 F4
Lee Rd.
Osborne Clo., Beck. 95 H4
Osborne Clo., Felt. 81 D5
Osborne Gdns., 94 J2
Th.Hth.
Osborne Gro. E17 41 J4
Osborne Gro. N4 49 G1
Osborne Ms. E17 41 J4
Osborne Gro.
Osborne Pl., Sutt. 100 G5
Osborne Rd. E7 51 H5
Osborne Rd. E9 50 J6
Osborne Rd. E10 51 B3
Osborne Rd. N4 49 G1
Osborne Rd. N13 32 G3
Osborne Rd. NW2 47 H6
Osborne Rd. W3 65 B2
Osborne Rd., Belv. 71 F5
Osborne Rd., 34 H1
Buck.H.
Osborne Rd., Dag. 53 F5
Osborne Rd., Enf. 25 H2
Osborne Rd., Houns. 72 F3
Osborne Rd., 82 H7
Kings.T.
Osborne Rd., Sthl. 54 J6
Osborne Rd., 94 J2
Th.Hth.
Osborne Sq., Dag. 53 F4
Oscar St. SE8 78 A1
Oseney Cres. NW5 49 C6
Osgood Ave., Orp. 104 J5
Osgood Gdns., Orp. 104 J5
O'Shea Gro. E3 59 J1
Osidge La. N14 32 A1
Osier St. E1 59 F4
Osier Way E10 51 B3
Osier Way, Mitch. 93 H5
Osiers Rd. SW18 75 D4
Oslac Rd. SE6 87 B5
Oslo Sq. SE16 68 H3
Norway Gate
Osman Clo. N15 41 A6
Tewkesbury Rd.
Osman Rd. N9 33 D3
Osman Rd. W6 65 J3
Batoum Gdns.
Osmond Clo., Har. 45 J2
Osmond Gdns., 101 C5
Wall.
Osmund St. W12 56 F6
Braybrook St.
Osnaburgh St. NW1 7 E5
Osnaburgh St. NW1 58 B4
Osnaburgh Ter. NW1 7 E5
Osney Wk., Cars. 93 G6
Osprey Clo. E6 61 B5
Dove App.
Osprey Clo. E11 42 G4
Osprey Ms., Enf. 25 E5
Ospringe Clo. SE20 86 F7
Ospringe Ct. SE9 79 G6
Ospringe Rd. NW5 49 C4
Osric Path N1 9 D2
Ossian Rd. N4 40 F7
Ossington Bldgs. W1 11 B1
Ossington St. W2 10 A6
Ossington St. W2 57 E7
Ossory Rd. SE1 21 H6
Ossory Rd. SE1 68 D6
Ossulston St. NW1 7 H2
Ossulston St. NW1 58 D2
Ossulton Pl. N2 39 F3
East End Rd.
Ossulton Way N2 39 F4
Ostade Rd. SW2 76 F7
Osten Ms. SW7 14 B6
Osterley Ave., 64 A7
Islw.
Osterley Ct., Islw. 73 A1
Osterley Cres., 73 B1
Islw.
Osterley Gdns., 94 J2
Th.Hth.
Osterley Ho. E14 60 B6
Giraud St.
Osterley La., Islw. 63 J5
Osterley La., Sthl. 63 G5
Osterley Pk. Rd., 63 F3
Sthl.
Osterley Pk. Vw. 64 B2
Rd. W7
Osterley Rd. N16 50 B4
Osterley Rd., Islw. 64 B7
Ostliffe Rd. N13 32 H5
Oswald Rd., Sthl. 63 E1
Oswald St. E5 50 G3
Oswalds Mead E9 50 H4
Lindisfarne Way
Osward Pl. N9 33 E2
Osward Rd. SW17 84 J2
Oswell Ho. E1 68 E1
Penang St.
Oswin St. SE11 20 H1
Oswin St. SE11 67 H4
Oswyth Rd. SE5 77 B2

Otford Clo., Bex. 80 H6
 Southwold Rd.
Otford Clo., Brom. 97 D3
Otford Cres. SE4 77 J6
Othello Clo. SE11 20 G3
Otis St. E3 60 C3
Otley App., Ilf. 43 E6
Otley Dr., Ilf. 43 E6
Otley Rd. E16 60 J6
Otley Ter. E5 50 G3
Otley Way, Wat. 28 C3
Ottaway St. E5 50 D3
 Stellman Clo.
Otter Rd., Grnf. 54 J4
Otterbourne Rd. E4 34 D3
Otterbourne Rd., 101 H2
 Croy.
Otterburn Gdns., 64 D7
 Islw.
Otterburn Ho. SE5 20 J7
Otterburn St. SW17 84 J6
Otterden Clo., Orp. 104 H4
 Southfleet Rd.
Otterden St. SE6 87 A4
Otto Clo. SE26 86 E3
Otto St. SE17 20 G6
Otto St. SE17 67 H6
Oulton Clo. E5 50 F2
 Mundford Rd.
Oulton Clo. SE28 62 C6
 Rollesby Way
Oulton Cres., Bark. 52 J6
Oulton Rd. N15 41 A5
Oulton Way, Wat. 28 E4
Ouseley Rd. SW12 84 J1
Outer Circle NW1 6 J1
Outer Circle NW1 57 H3
Outgate Rd. NW10 47 F7
Outram Pl. N1 58 E1
Outram Rd. E6 61 B1
Outram Rd. N22 40 D1
Outram Rd., 102 C2
 Croy.
Outwich St. EC3 13 E3
Outwich St. EC3 59 B6
Oval, The E2 59 E2
Oval, The, Sid. 80 A7
Oval Pl. SW8 20 C7
Oval Pl. SW8 67 F7
Oval Rd. NW1 58 B1
Oval Rd., Croy. 102 A2
Oval Rd. N., Dag. 62 H1
Oval Rd. S., Dag. 62 H2
Oval Way SE11 20 D4
Oval Way SE11 67 F5
Overbrae, Beck. 87 A6
Overbrook Wk., Edg. 30 A7
 Edg.
Overbury Ave., 96 B3
 Beck.
Overbury Rd. N15 41 A6
Overbury St. E5 50 G4
Overcliff Rd. SE13 78 A3
Overcourt Clo., Sid. 80 B6
Overdale Ave., 92 C2
 N.Mal.
Overdale Rd. W5 64 F3
Overdown Rd. SE6 87 A4
Overhill Rd. SE22 77 D7
Overhill Way, Beck. 96 C5
Overlea Rd. E5 41 D7
Overmead, Sid. 79 G7
Oversley Ho. W2 57 D5
Overstand Clo., 96 A5
 Beck.
Overstone Gdns., 95 J7
 Croy.
Overstone Rd. W6 65 J3
Overton Clo. NW10 47 C6
Overton Clo., Islw. 73 C1
 Avenue Rd.
Overton Ct. E11 42 G7
Overton Dr. E11 42 G7
Overton Dr., Rom. 44 C7
Overton Rd. E10 50 H1
Overton Rd. N14 24 E5
Overton Rd. SE2 71 C3
Overton Rd. SW9 76 G2
Overton Rd., Sutt. 100 D6
Overton Rd. E. SE2 71 D4
Overtons Yd., Croy. 101 J3
Ovesdon Ave., Har. 45 F1
Ovett Clo. SE19 86 B6
Ovex Clo. E14 69 C2
Ovington Gdns. 14 H6
 SW3
Ovington Gdns. SW3 66 H3
Ovington Ms. SW3 14 H6
Ovington Ms. SW3 66 H3
Ovington Sq. SW3 14 H6
Ovington Sq. SW3 66 H3
Ovington St. SW3 14 H6
Ovington St. SW3 66 H4

Owen Clo. SE28 71 C1
Owen Clo., Hayes 54 B3
Owen Gdns., 35 B6
 Wdf.Grn.
Owen Rd. N13 32 J4
Owen Rd., Hayes 54 B3
Owen St. EC1 8 F2
Owen Wk. SE20 95 D1
 Sycamore Gro.
Owen Waters Ho., 43 D1
 Ilf.
Owen Way NW10 47 C5
Owenite St. SE2 71 B4
Owen's Ct. EC1 8 G3
Owen's Row EC1 8 G3
Owens Way SE23 77 H7
Owgan Clo. SE5 68 A7
 Benhill Rd.
Oxberry Ave. SW6 75 B2
Oxendon St. SW1 11 H6
Oxendon St. SW1 58 D7
Oxenford St. SE15 77 C3
Oxenholme NW1 7 G2
Oxenholme NW1 58 C2
Oxenpark Ave., 46 H1
 Wem.
Oxestalls Rd. SE8 68 H5
Oxford Ave. SW20 93 B2
Oxford Ave., Houns. 63 G5
Oxford Circ. Ave. 11 F4
 W1
Oxford Ct. EC4 13 B5
Oxford Ct. W3 56 A6
 Queens Dr.
Oxford Ct., Felt. 81 D4
 Oxford Way
Oxford Cres., 92 D6
 N.Mal.
Oxford Dr., Ruis. 45 C2
Oxford Gdns. N20 31 G1
Oxford Gdns. N21 24 J7
Oxford Gdns. W4 65 A5
Oxford Gdns. W10 57 A6
Oxford Gate W6 66 A4
Oxford Ms., Bex. 80 G7
 Bexley High St.
Oxford Rd. E15 51 D6
Oxford Rd. N4 49 G1
Oxford Rd. N9 57 D2
Oxford Rd. NW6 57 D2
Oxford Rd. SE19 86 A6
Oxford Rd. SW15 75 B4
Oxford Rd. W5 55 G7
Oxford Rd., Cars. 100 H6
Oxford Rd., Enf. 25 E5
Oxford Rd., Har. 36 J6
Oxford Rd., Har. 37 C3
 (Wealdstone)
Oxford Rd., Ilf. 52 F5
Oxford Rd., Sid. 89 B5
Oxford Rd., Tedd. 82 A5
Oxford Rd., Wall. 100 C5
Oxford Rd., 35 A5
 Wdf.Grn.
Oxford Rd. N. W4 65 B5
Oxford Rd. S. W4 65 A5
Oxford Sq. W2 10 H4
Oxford Sq. W2 57 H6
Oxford St. W1 11 B4
Oxford St. W1 57 H6
Oxford Wk., Sthl. 63 F1
Oxford Way, Felt. 81 D4
Oxgate Gdns. NW2 47 H3
Oxgate La. NW2 47 H2
Oxhawth Cres., 97 D5
 Brom.
Oxhey Dr., Nthwd. 28 A4
Oxhey Dr., Wat. 28 C3
Oxhey La., Wat. 28 E1
Oxhey Ridge Clo., 28 A5
 Nthwd.
Oxleas E6 61 E6
Oxleas Clo., Well. 79 G2
Oxleay Ct., Har. 45 G1
Oxleay Rd., Har. 45 G1
Oxleigh Clo., 92 E5
 N.Mal.
Oxley Clo. SE1 21 G3
Oxley Clo. SE1 54 A4
Oxleys Rd. NW2 47 H3
Oxlip Clo., Croy. 103 G1
 Marigold Way
Oxlow La., Dag. 53 F4
Oxonian St. SE22 77 C4
Oxted Clo., Mitch. 93 G3
Oxtoby Way SW16 94 D1
Oyster Catchers 60 H6
 Clo. E16
 Freemasons Rd.
Oyster Row E1 59 F6
 Lukin St.

Ozalins Way E16 60 G6

P

Pace Pl. E1 59 E6
 Bigland St.
Pacific Rd. E16 80 G0
Packington Rd. W3 65 C3
Packington Sq. N1 58 J1
Packington St. N1 58 H1
Packmores Rd. SE9 79 G5
Padbury SE17 21 D4
Padbury Ct. E2 9 G4
Paddenswick Rd. W6 65 G3
Paddington Clo., 54 D4
 Hayes
Paddington Grn. W2 10 F1
Paddington Grn. W2 57 G5
Paddington St. W1 11 B1
Paddington St. W1 58 A5
Paddock Clo. SE3 78 G3
Paddock Clo. SE26 86 G4
Paddock Clo., Nthlt. 54 G2
Paddock Clo., 99 E1
 Wor.Pk.
Paddock Gdns. SE19 86 B6
 Westow St.
Paddock Rd. NW2 47 G3
Paddock Rd., Bexh. 80 E4
Paddock Rd., Ruis. 45 D3
Paddock Way, Chis. 88 G7
Paddocks, The, 23 J3
 Barn.
Paddocks, The, Wem. 47 B2
Paddocks Clo., Har. 45 H4
Padfield Rd. SE5 76 J3
Padnall Rd., Rom. 44 D3
Padstow Rd., Enf. 24 H2
Padua Rd. SE20 95 F1
Pagden St. SW8 76 B1
Page Clo., Dag. 53 E5
Page Clo., Hmptn. 81 E6
Page Clo., Har. 37 J6
Page Cres., Croy. 101 G5
Page Grn. Rd. N15 41 D5
Page Grn. Ter. N15 41 C5
Page Heath La., 97 A3
 Brom.
Page Heath Vill., 97 A3
 Brom.
Page Meadow NW7 30 G7
Page St. NW7 30 G6
Page St. SW1 19 J1
Page St. SW1 67 D4
Pageant Ave. NW9 38 E1
Pageant Wk., Croy. 102 B3
Pagehurst Rd., 95 E7
 Croy.
Pages Hill N10 40 A2
Pages La. N10 40 A2
Pages Wk. SE1 21 D1
Pages Wk. SE1 68 B4
Pages Yd. W4 65 E6
 Church St.
Paget Ave., Sutt. 100 G3
Paget Clo., Hmptn. 82 A4
Paget Gdns., Chis. 97 E1
Paget La., Islw. 73 A3
Paget Pl., Kings.T. 83 C6
Paget Ri. SE18 70 D6
Paget Rd. N16 50 A1
Paget Rd., Ilf. 52 E4
Paget St. EC1 8 G3
Paget Ter. SE18 70 D6
Pagitts Gro., Barn. 23 J7
Pagnell St. SE14 68 J7
Pagoda Ave., Rich. 73 J3
Pagoda Gdns. SE3 78 D2
Paignton Rd. N15 41 B6
Paignton Rd., Ruis. 45 A3
Paines Clo., Pnr. 36 E2
Paines La., Pnr. 36 E1
Pains Clo., Mitch. 94 B2
Painters Rd., Ilf. 43 J3
Paisley Rd. N22 40 H1
Paisley Rd., Cars. 100 G1
Pakeman St. N7 49 F3
Pakenham Clo. SW12 85 A1
 Balham Pk. Rd.
Pakenham St. WC1 8 D4
Pakenham St. WC1 58 F3
Palace Ave. W8 14 B2
Palace Ave. W8 66 E1
Palace Ct. NW3 48 E5
Palace Ct. W2 10 A5
Palace Ct. W2 57 E7
 Palace Gro.
Palace Ct., Brom. 96 H1
 Palace Gro.
Palace Gdn. Ms. W8 66 D1
Palace Gdns., 35 A1
 Buck.H.

Palace Gdns. Ter. 66 D1
 W8
Palace Gate W8 14 C4
Palace Gate W8 66 F2
Palace Gates Rd. 40 D2
 N22
Palace Grn. W8 14 A2
Palace Grn. W8 66 E2
Palace Grn., Croy. 102 B7
Palace Gro. SE19 86 C7
Palace Gro., Brom. 96 H1
Palace Ms. E17 41 J4
Palace Ms. SW1 19 C2
Palace Ms. SW6 66 C7
 Hartismere Rd.
Palace Pl. SW1 15 F5
Palace Rd. N8 40 D5
Palace Rd. N11 32 D7
Palace Rd. SE19 86 C7
Palace Rd. SW2 85 F1
Palace Rd., Brom. 96 H1
Palace Rd., E.Mol. 91 A3
Palace Rd., 91 G4
 Kings.T.
Palace Rd., Ruis. 45 E4
Palace Rd. Est. SW2 85 F1
Palace Sq. SE19 86 C7
Palace St. SW1 15 F5
Palace St. SW1 67 C3
Palace Vw. SE12 87 G2
Palace Vw., Brom. 96 H3
Palace Vw. Rd. E4 34 B5
Palamos Rd. E10 51 A1
Palatine Ave. N16 50 C4
 Stoke Newington Rd.
Palatine Rd. N16 50 B4
Palermo Rd. NW10 56 G2
Palestine Gro. SW19 93 G1
Palewell Common Dr. 74 D5
 SW14
Palewell Pk. SW14 74 D5
Paley Gdns., Loug. 27 E3
Palfrey Pl. SW8 67 F7
Palgrave Ave., Sthl. 54 G2
Palgrave Rd. W12 65 F3
Palissy St. E2 9 F4
Pall Mall SW1 15 G2
Pall Mall SW1 67 C1
Pall Mall E. SW1 15 J1
Pall Mall E. SW1 67 D1
Pall Mall Pl. SW1 15 G2
Pallant Way, Orp. 104 D3
Pallet Way SE18 79 B1
Palliser Rd. W14 66 B5
Palm Ave., Sid. 89 D6
Palm Gro. W5 64 H3
Palm Rd., Rom. 44 J5
Palmar Cres., Bexh. 80 G2
Palmar Rd., Bexh. 80 G2
Palmeira Rd., Bexh. 80 D3
Palmer Ave., Sutt. 99 J4
Palmer Clo., Houns. 72 G1
Palmer Clo., W.Wick. 103 D4
Palmer Cres., 91 H3
 Kings.T.
Palmer Gdns., Barn. 23 A5
Palmer Pl. N7 49 G5
Palmer Rd. E13 60 H4
Palmer Rd., Dag. 53 D1
Palmer St. SW1 15 H5
Palmer St. SW1 67 D3
Palmers Gro., 90 G4
 W.Mol.
Palmers La., Enf. 25 F1
Palmers Pas. SW14 74 C3
 Palmers Rd.
Palmers Rd. E2 59 G2
Palmers Rd. N11 32 C5
Palmers Rd. SW14 74 C3
Palmers Rd. SW16 94 F2
Palmers Rd., Borwd. 22 B1
Palmerston Cres. 32 F5
 N13
Palmerston Cres. 70 F6
 SE18
Palmerston Gro. 84 D7
 SW19
Palmerston Rd. E7 51 H5
Palmerston Rd. E17 41 J3
Palmerston Rd. N22 32 F7
Palmerston Rd. NW6 48 C7
Palmerston Rd. 74 C4
 SW14
Palmerston Rd. 84 D7
 SW19
Palmerston Rd. W3 65 C3
Palmerston Rd., 34 H2
 Buck.H.
Palmerston Rd., 100 J4
 Cars.
Palmerston Rd., 37 B3
 Har.

Name	Page	Grid
Palmerston Rd., Orp.	104	F4
Palmerston Rd., Sutt.	100	F4
Vernon Rd.		
Palmerston Rd., Th.Hth.	95	A5
Palmerston Rd. Twick.	73	B6
Palmerston Way SW8	67	B7
Bradmead		
Pamber St. W10	57	A6
Pamela Gdns., Pnr.	36	B5
Pamela Wk. E8	59	D1
Marlborough Ave.		
Pams Way, Epsom	99	D5
Pancras La. EC4	13	A4
Pancras Rd. NW1	7	H1
Pancras Rd. NW1	58	D2
Pandora Rd. NW6	48	D6
Panfield Ms., Ilf.	43	D6
Cranbrook Rd.		
Panfield Rd. SE2	71	A3
Pangbourne Ave. W10	56	J5
Pangbourne Dr., Stan.	29	G5
Pankhurst Clo. SE14	68	G7
Briant St.		
Pankhurst Rd., Walt.	90	C7
Panmuir Rd. SW20	92	H1
Panmure Clo. N5	49	H4
Panmure Rd. SE26	86	E3
Pannard Pl., Sthl.	54	H7
Pansy Gdns. W12	56	G7
Pantiles, The NW11	39	C5
Willifield Way		
Pantiles, The, Bexh.	71	F7
Pantiles, The, Brom.	97	B3
Panton St. SW1	11	H6
Panyer All. EC4	12	J3
Papillons Wk. SE3	78	G3
Papworth Gdns. N7	49	F5
Chillingworth Rd.		
Papworth Way SW2	76	G7
Parade, The SW11	19	A7
Parade, The SW11	66	J7
Parade, The, Esher	98	B6
Parade, The, Wat.	28	E3
Parade Ms. SE27	85	H2
Norwood Rd.		
Paradise Pas. N7	49	G5
Sheringham Rd.		
Paradise Rd. SW4	76	E2
Paradise Rd., Rich.	73	H5
Paradise Row E2	59	E3
Bethnal Grn. Rd.		
Paradise St. SE16	68	E2
Paradise Wk. SW3	19	A5
Paradise Wk. SW3	66	J6
Paragon, The SE3	78	F2
Paragon Gro., Surb.	91	J6
Paragon Ms. SE1	21	C1
Paragon Pl. SE3	78	F2
Paragon Pl., Surb.	91	J6
Berrylands Rd.		
Paragon Rd. E9	50	F6
Parbury Ri., Chess.	98	H6
Parbury Rd. SE23	77	H6
Parchmore Rd., Th.Hth.	94	H2
Parchmore Way, Th.Hth.	94	H2
Pardon St. EC1	8	H5
Pardoner St. SE1	17	C5
Pardoner St. SE1	68	A3
Parfett St. E1	13	J2
Parfett St. E1	59	D5
Parfitt Clo. NW3	48	F2
North End		
Parfrey St. W6	65	J6
Parham Dr., Ilf.	43	E6
Paris Gdn. SE1	16	G1
Paris Gdn. SE1	67	H1
Parish Gate Dr., Sid.	79	H6
Parish La. SE20	86	G6
Parish Ms. SE20	86	G7
Park, The N6	40	A6
Park, The NW11	48	E1
Park, The SE19	86	B7
Park, The SE23	86	E1
Park Hill		
Park, The W5	64	G1
Park, The, Cars.	100	J5
Park, The, Sid.	89	A4
Park App., Well.	80	B4
Park Ave. E6	61	D1
Park Ave. E15	51	E6
Park Ave. N3	39	E1
Park Ave. N13	32	G3
Park Ave. N18	33	D4
Park Ave. N22	40	E2
Park Ave. NW2	47	H6
Park Ave. NW10	55	J2
Park Ave. NW11	48	E1
Park Ave. SW14	74	D4
Park Ave., Bark.	52	F6
Park Ave., Barn.	23	F5
Park Ave., Brom.	87	F7
Park Ave., Cars.	101	A6
Park Ave., Chis.	97	H3
Park Ave., Enf.	25	A5
Park Ave., Houns.	72	H6
Park Ave., Ilf.	52	D1
Park Ave., Mitch.	85	B7
Park Ave., Orp. (Farnborough)	104	C3
Park Ave., Sthl.	63	F2
Park Ave., W.Wick.	103	C2
Park Ave., Wdf.Grn.	34	H5
Park Ave. E., Epsom	99	G6
Park Ave. Ms., Mitch.	85	B7
Park Ave.		
Park Ave. N. N8	40	D3
Park Ave. N. NW10	47	H5
Park Ave. Rd. N17	33	E7
Park Ave. S. N8	40	D4
Park Ave. W., Epsom	99	G6
Park Chase, Wem.	46	J4
Park Clo. E9	59	F1
Skipworth Rd.		
Park Clo. NW2	47	H4
Park Clo. NW10	55	J3
Park Clo. SW1	14	J4
Park Clo. W4	65	D5
Park Clo. W14	66	C3
Park Clo., Cars.	100	J6
Park Clo., Hmptn.	90	J1
Park Clo., Har.	37	B1
Park Clo., Houns.	72	J5
Park Ct. SE26	86	E6
Park Ct., Kings.T.	91	F1
Park Ct., Wem.	46	H5
Park Cres. N3	31	E7
Park Cres. W1	7	D6
Park Cres. W1	58	B4
Park Cres., Enf.	25	A4
Park Cres., Erith	71	J6
Park Cres., Har.	37	B1
Park Cres., Twick.	82	A1
Park Cres. Ms. E. W1	7	E6
Park Cres. Ms. W. W1	7	D6
Park Cft., Edg.	38	C1
Park Dale N11	32	D6
Bounds Grn. Rd.		
Park Dr. N21	24	J6
Park Dr. NW11	48	E1
Park Dr. SE7	70	B6
Park Dr. SW14	74	D4
Park Dr. W3	65	A3
Park Dr., Dag.	53	J3
Park Dr., Har.	36	G7
Park Dr., Har. (Harrow Weald)	29	B6
Uxbridge Rd.		
Park Dr. Clo. SE7	70	B5
Park End NW3	48	H4
South Hill Pk.		
Park End, Brom.	96	F1
Park Fm. Clo. N2	39	F3
Park Fm. Clo., Pnr.	36	B5
Field End Rd.		
Park Fm. Rd., Brom.	97	A1
Park Fm. Rd., Kings.T.	82	H7
Park Gdn. Pl. W2	10	F4
Park Gdns. NW9	38	B3
Park Gdns., Kings.T.	82	J5
Park Gate N2	39	G3
Park Gate N21	24	F7
Park Gate W5	55	G5
Mount Ave.		
Park Gate Clo., Kings.T.	83	B6
Warboys App.		
Park Gate Clo., Kings.T.	83	B6
Warboys App.		
Park Gro. E15	60	G1
Park Gro. N11	32	D7
Park Gro., Bexh.	80	J4
Park Gro., Brom.	86	J5
Park Gro., Edg.	29	J5
Park Gro. Rd. E11	51	E2
Park Hall Rd. N2	39	H4
Park Hall Rd. SE21	86	A3
Park Hill SE23	86	E2
Park Hill SW4	76	D5
Park Hill W5	55	G5
Park Hill, Brom.	97	B4
Park Hill, Cars.	100	H6
Park Hill, Loug.	27	A5
Park Hill, Rich.	73	J6
Park Hill Clo., Cars.	100	H5
Park Hill Ct. SW17	84	J3
Beeches Rd.		
Park Hill Ri., Croy.	102	B2
Park Hill Rd., Brom.	96	E2
Park Hill Rd., Croy.	102	B2
Park Hill Rd., Sid.	88	H3
Park Hill Rd., Wall.	101	B6
Park Ho. N21	24	F7
Park Ho. Gdns., Twick.	73	F6
Park La. E15	60	D1
High St.		
Park La. N9	33	B3
Park La. N17	33	C7
Park La. N18	33	B4
Sheldon Rd.		
Park La. W1	11	A5
Park La. W1	57	J7
Park La., Cars.	101	A4
Park La., Croy.	102	A3
Park La., Har.	45	H3
Park La. (Cranford), Houns.	63	A7
Park La., Rich.	73	G4
Park La., Rom. (Chadwell Heath)	44	D6
Park La., Stan.	29	D3
Park La., Sutt.	100	B6
Park La., Tedd.	82	C6
Park La., Wem.	46	H5
Park La. Clo. N17	33	D7
Park Lawns, Wem.	46	J4
Park Mead, Har.	45	H3
Park Mead, Sid.	80	B5
Park Ms. SE24	76	J6
Croxted Rd.		
Park Ms., E.Mol.	90	J4
Park Ms., Hmptn.	81	J5
Park Rd.		
Park Par. NW10	56	F2
Park Pl. E14	69	A1
Park Pl. SW1	15	F2
Park Pl. SW1	67	C1
Park Pl. W3	65	A4
Park Pl. W5	64	G1
Park Pl., Hmptn.	81	J6
Park Pl., Wem.	46	J4
Park Pl. Vill. W2	10	D1
Park Pl. Vill. W2	57	F5
Park Ridings N8	40	G3
Park Ri. SE23	86	H1
Park Ri., Har.	37	B1
Park Ri. Rd. SE23	86	H1
Park Rd. E6	60	J1
Park Rd. E10	51	A1
Park Rd. E12	51	H1
Park Rd. E15	60	G1
Park Rd. E17	41	J5
Park Rd. N2	39	G3
Park Rd. N8	40	C4
Park Rd. N11	32	D7
Park Rd. N14	24	D7
Park Rd. N15	40	H4
Park Rd. N18	33	C4
Park Rd. NW1	6	J5
Park Rd. NW1	57	J4
Park Rd. NW4	38	G7
Park Rd. NW8	6	G3
Park Rd. NW8	57	H3
Park Rd. NW9	38	D7
Park Rd. NW10	56	E1
Park Rd. SE25	95	B4
Park Rd. SW19	84	G7
Park Rd. W4	65	C7
Park Rd. W7	55	C7
Park Rd., Barn.	23	C4
Park Rd. (New Barnet), Barn.	23	G4
Park Rd., Beck.	86	J7
Park Rd., Brom.	96	H1
Park Rd., Chis.	88	E6
Park Rd., E.Mol.	90	J4
Park Rd., Felt.	81	D4
Park Rd., Hmptn.	81	H4
Park Rd., Houns.	72	H5
Park Rd., Ilf.	52	G3
Park Rd., Islw.	73	E1
Park Rd., Kings.T.	82	J5
Park Rd., Kings.T. (Hampton Wick)	91	F1
Park Rd., N.Mal.	92	D4
Park Rd., Rich.	73	J6
Park Rd., Sun.	81	B7
Park Rd., Surb.	91	J6
Park Rd., Sutt.	100	B6
Park Rd., Tedd.	82	C7
Park Rd., Twick.	73	F6
Park Rd., Wall.	101	B5
Park Rd. (Hackbridge), Wall.	101	B2
Park Rd., Wem.	46	H6
Park Rd. E. W3	65	B2
Park Rd. N. W3	65	B2
Park Rd. N. W4	65	D5
Park Rd. W., Kings.T.	91	F1
Park Row SE10	69	D6
Park Royal Rd. NW10	56	C4
Park Royal Rd. W3	56	C4
Park Side, Sutt.	100	B6
Park Sq. E. NW1	7	D5
Park Sq. E. NW1	58	B4
Park Sq. Ms. NW1	7	D6
Park Sq. Ms. NW1	58	B4
Park Sq. W. NW1	7	D5
Park Sq. W. NW1	58	B4
Park St. SE1	16	J1
Park St. SE1	67	J1
Park St. W1	11	B5
Park St. W1	58	A7
Park St., Croy.	101	J2
Park St., Tedd.	82	B6
Park Ter., Wor.Pk.	99	G1
Park Vw. N21	24	F7
Park Vw. W3	56	G2
Park Vw., N.Mal.	92	F3
Park Vw., Pnr.	36	F1
Park Vw., Wem.	47	B5
Park Vw. Ct., Ilf.	43	H6
Brancaster Rd.		
Park Vw. Cres. N11	32	B4
Park Vw. Est. E2	59	G2
Park Vw. Gdns. NW4	39	A6
Park Vw. Gdns., Bark.	61	H2
River Rd.		
Park Vw. Gdns., Ilf.	43	C4
Woodford Ave.		
Park Vw. Rd. N3	39	E1
Park Vw. Rd. N17	41	D3
Park Vw. Rd. NW10	47	F4
Park Vw. Rd. W5	55	H5
Park Vw. Rd., Pnr.	28	B7
Park Vw. Rd., Sthl.	63	G1
Park Vw. Rd., Well.	80	B3
Park Village E. NW1	7	D1
Park Village E. NW1	58	B2
Park Village W. NW1	7	D1
Park Village W. NW1	58	B2
Park Vill., Rom.	44	D6
Park Vista SE10	69	D6
Park Wk. N6	40	A7
North Rd.		
Park Wk. SW10	18	D5
Park Wk. SW10	66	F6
Park Way N20	31	J4
Park Way NW11	39	B5
Park Way, Edg.	38	B1
Park Way, Enf.	24	G2
Park Way, Felt.	72	B7
Park Way, Ilf.	52	J3
Park Way, Ruis.	45	A1
Park Way, W.Mol.	90	H3
Park W. W2	10	F4
Park W. Pl. W2	10	H3
Parkcroft Rd. SE12	78	F7
Parkdale Cres., Wor.Pk.	99	D3
Parkdale Rd. SE18	70	H5
Parke Rd. SW13	74	G1
Parke Rd., Sun.	90	A4
Parker Clo. E16	70	B1
Parker Ms. WC2	12	B3
Parker Rd., Croy.	101	J4
Parker St. E16	70	B1
Parker St. WC2	12	B3
Parker St. WC2	58	E6
Parkers Row SE1	17	G4
Chambers St.		
Parkes Rd., Chig.	35	H5
Parkfield Ave. SW14	74	E4
Parkfield Ave., Felt.	81	A3
Parkfield Ave., Har.	36	J2
Parkfield Ave., Nthlt.	54	D2
Parkfield Clo., Edg.	30	B6
Parkfield Clo., Nthlt.	54	E2
Parkfield Cres., Felt.	81	A3
Parkfield Cres., Har.	36	J2
Parkfield Cres., Ruis.	45	E3
Parkfield Dr., Nthlt.	54	D2
Parkfield Gdns., Har.	36	H3

Name	Pg	Grid
Parkfield Rd. NW10	47	G7
Parkfield Rd. SE14	77	J1
Parkfield Rd., Felt.	81	A3
Parkfield Rd., Har.	45	J3
Parkfield Rd., Nthlt.	54	E2
Parkfield St. N1	8	F1
Parkfield St. N1	58	G2
Parkfield Way, Brom.	97	C6
Parkfields SW15	74	J4
Parkfields, Croy.	102	J1
Parkfields Ave. NW9	47	D1
Parkfields Ave. SW20	92	H2
Parkfields Rd., Kings.T.	82	J5
Parkgate SE3	78	F3
Parkgate Ave., Barn.	23	F1
Parkgate Cres., Barn.	23	F1
Parkgate Gdns. SW14	74	D5
Parkgate Rd. SW11	66	H7
Parkgate Rd., Wall.	101	A5
Parkham Ct., Brom.	96	E2
Parkham St. SW11	75	G1
Parkhill Rd. E4	34	C1
Parkhill Rd. NW3	48	J5
Parkhill Rd., Bex.	80	F7
Parkhill Wk. NW3	48	J5
Parkholme Rd. E8	50	D6
Parkhouse St. SE5	21	C7
Parkhouse St. SE5	68	A7
Parkhurst Gdns., Bex.	80	G7
Parkhurst Rd. E12	52	D4
Parkhurst Rd. E17	41	H4
Parkhurst Rd. N7	49	E4
Parkhurst Rd. N11	32	A4
Parkhurst Rd. N17	41	D2
Parkhurst Rd. N22	32	F6
Parkhurst Rd., Bex.	80	G7
Parkhurst Rd., Sutt.	100	G4
Parkland Clo., Chig.	35	F3
Parkland Gdns. SW19	84	A1
Parkland Rd. N22	40	F2
Parkland Rd., Wdf.Grn.	34	G7
Parkland Wk. N4	40	G7
Parkland Wk. N6	40	C7
Parkland Wk. N10	40	A4
Cranley Gdns.		
Parklands, Chig.	35	F3
Parklands, Surb.	91	J5
Parklands Clo. SW14	74	C5
Parklands Ct., Houns.	72	D2
Parklands Dr. N3	39	B3
Parklands Rd. SW16	85	B5
Parklands Way, Wor.Pk.	99	E2
Parklea Clo. NW9	38	E1
Parkleigh Rd. SW19	93	E2
Parkleys, Rich.	82	G4
Parkmead SW15	74	H6
Parkmead, Loug.	27	D5
Parkmead Gdns. NW7	30	F6
Parkmore Clo., Wdf.Grn.	34	G4
Parkshot, Rich.	73	H4
Parkside N3	39	E1
Parkside NW2	47	G3
Parkside NW7	30	G6
Parkside SE3	69	F7
Parkside SW19	84	A4
Parkside, Buck.H.	34	H2
Parkside, Hmptn.	82	A5
Parkside, Sid.	89	B2
Parkside Ave. SW19	84	A4
Parkside Ave., Brom.	97	B4
Parkside Cres., Surb.	92	C6
Parkside Dr., Edg.	30	A3
Parkside Est. E9	59	F1
Rutland Rd.		
Parkside Gdns. SW19	84	A4
Parkside Gdns., Barn.	31	J1
Parkside Ho., Dag.	53	J3
Parkside Rd. SW11	76	A1
Parkside Rd., Belv.	71	H4
Parkside Rd., Houns.	72	H5
Parkside Ter. N18	33	H4
Great Cambridge Rd.		
Parkside Way, Har.	36	H4
Parkstead Rd. SW15	74	G5
Parkstone Ave. N18	33	C5
Parkstone Rd. E17	42	C3
Parkstone Rd. SE15	77	D2
Rye La.		
Parkthorne Clo., Har.	36	H6
Parkthorne Dr., Har.	36	G6
Parkthorne Rd. SW12	76	D7
Parkview Rd. SE9	88	E1
Parkville Rd., Orp.	100	D1
Parkville Rd. SW6	66	C7
Parkway N14	32	E2
Parkway NW1	98	B1
Calvedon Way		
Parkway SW20	93	A4
Parkway, Erith	71	E3
Parkway, Wdf.Grn.	34	J5
Parkway, The, Hayes	54	C6
Parkway, The (Cranford), Houns.	63	A6
Parkway Trd. Est., Houns.	63	C6
Parkwood N20	31	J3
Parkwood, Beck.	96	A1
Parkwood Gro., Sun.	90	A3
Parkwood Ms. N6	40	B6
Parkwood Rd. SW19	84	C5
Parkwood Rd., Bex.	80	F7
Parkwood Rd., Islw.	73	C1
Parliament Hill NW3	48	H4
Parliament Ms. SW14	74	C2
Thames Bank		
Parliament Sq. SW1	16	A4
Parliament Sq. SW1	67	E2
Parliament St. SW1	16	A4
Parliament St. SW1	67	E2
Parma Cres. SW11	75	J4
Parmiter St. E2	59	E2
Parnell Clo., Edg.	30	B4
Parnell Rd. E3	59	J1
Parnham St. E14	59	H6
Blount St.		
Parolles Rd. N19	49	C1
Paroma Rd., Belv.	71	G3
Parr Clo. N9	33	E4
Parr Ct., Felt.	81	C4
Parr Rd. E6	61	A1
Parr Rd., Stan.	37	G1
Parr St. N1	9	B1
Parr St. N1	59	A2
Parrs Pl., Hmptn.	81	G7
Parry Ave. E6	61	C6
Parry Clo., Epsom	99	G6
Parry Pl. SE18	70	E4
Parry Rd. SE25	95	B3
Parry Rd. W10	57	B3
Dart St.		
Parry St. SW8	20	A5
Parry St. SW8	67	E6
Parsifal Rd. NW6	48	D5
Parsloes Ave., Dag.	53	D4
Parson St. NW4	38	J4
Parsonage Gdns., Enf.	24	J2
Parsonage La., Enf.	25	A2
Parsonage La., Sid.	89	F4
Parsonage Manorway, Belv.	71	G6
Parsonage St. E14	69	C4
Parsons Cres., Edg.	30	A3
Parsons Gro. SW6	75	D2
Parsons Grn. La. SW6	75	D1
Parsons Gro., Edg.	30	A3
Parson's Ho. W2	6	E6
Parson's Mead, Croy.	101	H1
Parsons Mead, E.Mol.	90	J3
Parsons Rd. E13	60	J2
Old St.		
Parthenia Rd. SW6	75	D1
Partingdale La. NW7	31	A5
Partington Clo. N19	49	D1
Partridge Clo. E16	61	A5
Fulmer Rd.		
Partridge Clo. (Bushey), Wat.	28	H1
Partridge Dr., Orp.	104	F3
Partridge Grn. SE9	88	D3
Partridge Rd., Hmptn.	81	F6
Partridge Rd., Sid.	88	H3
Partridge Sq. E6	61	B5
Nightingale Way		
Partridge Way N22	40	E1
Parvin St. SW8	76	D1
Pasadena Clo., Hayes	63	A2
Pascal St. SW8	19	J7
Pascal St. SW8	67	D7
Pascoe Rd. SE13	78	D5
Pasley Clo. SE17	20	J4
Pasquier Rd. E17	41	H3
Passey Pl. SE9	79	C6
Passfield Dr. E14	60	B5
St. Leonards Rd.		
Passfield Path SE28	62	B7
Booth Clo.		
Passing All. EC1	8	G6
Passmore Gdns. N11	32	D6
Passmore St. SW1	19	B2
Passmore St. SW1	67	A5
Rector Clo. NW9	38	F2
Pasteur Gdns. N18	32	H5
Paston Clo. E5	50	G3
Caldecott Way		
Paston Cres. SE12	78	H7
Pastor St. SE11	20	H1
Pastor St. SE11	67	H4
Pasture Clo., Wem.	46	B3
Pasture Rd. SE6	87	E1
Pasture Rd., Dag.	53	F4
Pasture Rd., Wem.	46	E2
Pastures, The N20	31	C1
Patcham Ter. SW8	76	B1
Pater St. W8	66	D3
Paternoster Row EC4	12	J4
Paternoster Sq. EC4	12	H3
Path, The SW19	93	E1
Pathfield Rd. SW16	85	D6
Pathway, The, Wat.	28	D1
Anthony Clo.		
Patience Rd. SW11	75	H2
Patio Clo. SW4	76	D6
Patmore Est. SW8	76	C1
Patmore St. SW8	76	C1
Patmos Rd. SW9	67	H7
Paton Clo. E3	60	A3
Paton St. EC1	8	J4
Patricia Clo., Chis.	97	G1
Manor Pk. Rd.		
Patricia Ct., Well.	71	B7
Patrick Connolly Gdns. E3	60	B3
Talwin St.		
Patrick Pas. SW11	75	H2
Patrick Rd. E13	60	J3
Patriot Sq. E2	59	E2
Patrol Pl. SE6	78	B6
Patshull Pl. NW5	49	C6
Patshull Rd.		
Patshull Rd. NW5	49	C6
Patten All., Rich.	73	G5
The Hermitage		
Patten Rd. SW18	75	H7
Pattenden Rd. SE6	86	J1
Patterdale Clo., Brom.	87	F6
Patterdale Rd. SE15	68	F7
Patterson Ct. SE19	86	G6
Patterson Rd. SE19	86	C6
Pattinson Pt. E16	60	H5
Fife Rd.		
Pattison Rd. NW2	48	D3
Pattison Wk. SE18	70	F5
Sandbach Pl.		
Paul Clo. E15	51	E7
Paul St.		
Paul Gdns., Croy.	102	C2
Paul St. E15	60	E1
Paul St. EC2	9	C6
Paul St. EC2	59	A4
Paulet Rd. SE5	76	H2
Paulhan Rd., Har.	37	F4
Paulin Dr. N21	24	G7
Pauline Cres., Twick.	81	J1
Paultons Sq. SW3	18	F5
Paultons Sq. SW3	66	G6
Paultons St. SW3	18	F6
Paultons St. SW3	66	G6
Pauntley St. N19	49	C1
Paved Ct., Rich.	73	G5
King St.		
Paveley Dr. SW11	75	H7
Paveley St. NW8	6	H4
Paveley St. NW8	57	H4
Pavement, The SW4	76	C4
Pavement, The W5	64	H3
Popes La.		
Pavement Ms., Rom.	44	D7
Clarissa Rd.		
Pavement Sq., Croy.	102	D1
Pavet Clo., Dag.	53	H6
Pavilion Rd. SW1	15	A4
Pavilion Rd. SW1	66	J3
Pavilion Rd., Ilf.	43	C7
Pavilion St. SW1	15	A6
Pavilion Ter., E.Mol.	91	C4
Pavilion Ter., Ilf.	43	H5
Southdown Cres.		
Pavilion Way, Edg.	30	B7
Pavilion Way, Ruis.	45	C2
Pawleyne Clo. SE20	86	F7
Pawsey Clo. E13	60	G1
Plashet Rd.		
Pawson's Rd., Croy.	94	J6
Paxford Rd., Wem.	46	E2
Paxton Clo., Rich.	73	J2
Paxton Clo., Walt.	90	C7
Shaw Dr.		
Paxton Pl. SE27	86	B4
Paxton Rd. N17	33	C7
Paxton Rd. SE23	86	H3
Paxton Rd. W4	65	F6
Paxton Rd., Brom.	87	G7
Paxton Ter. SW1	19	E5
Paxton Ter. SW1	67	B6
Payne Rd. E3	60	B2
Payne St. SE8	68	B6
Paynell Ct. SE3	78	E3
Lawn Ter.		
Paynes Wk. W6	66	B6
Ancill Clo.		
Paynesfield Ave. SW14	74	D3
Peabody Ave. SW1	19	D4
Peabody Clo. SE10	78	B1
Devonshire Dr.		
Peabody Dws. WC1	8	A5
Peabody Est. EC1	9	A6
Peabody Est. N17	41	B1
Peabody Est. SE1	16	F2
Peabody Est. SE24	76	J7
Peabody Est. SW3	18	H5
Peabody Est. W6	65	J5
Peabody Est. W10	56	J4
Dalgarno Gdns.		
Peabody Hill SE21	85	H1
Peabody Hill Est. SE21	85	H1
Peabody Sq. SE1	16	G4
Peabody Sq. SE1	67	H2
Peabody Yd. N1	58	J1
Greenman St.		
Peace Clo. N14	24	B5
Peace Gro., Wem.	47	B2
Peach Rd. W10	57	A3
Peaches Clo., Sutt.	100	B7
Peachum Rd. SE3	69	F6
Peacock St. SE17	20	H2
Peacock Wk. E16	60	H6
Sophia Rd.		
Peacock Yd. SE17	20	H2
Peak, The SE26	86	F3
Peak Hill SE26	86	F4
Peak Hill Ave. SE26	86	F4
Peak Hill Gdns. SE26	86	F4
Peaketon Ave., Ilf.	43	A4
Peal Gdns. W13	55	D4
Ruislip Rd. E.		
Peall Rd., Croy.	94	F6
Pear Clo. NW9	38	D4
Pear Clo. SE14	68	H7
Southergate Way		
Pear Pl. SE1	16	E3
Pear Tree Ct. EC1	8	F6
Pear Tree Ct. EC1	58	G4
Pear Tree St. EC1	8	H5
Pear Tree St. EC1	58	H4
Pearce Rd., W.Mol.	90	H3
Pearcefield Ave. SE23	86	F1
Pearcroft Rd. E11	51	D2
Peardon St. SW8	76	B2
Peareswood Gdns., Stan.	37	G1
Pearfield Rd. SE23	86	H3
Pearl Clo. E6	61	D6
Pearl Rd. E17	42	A3
Pearl St. E1	68	E1
Penang St.		
Pearman St. SE1	16	F5
Pearman St. SE1	67	G3
Pears Rd., Houns.	72	J3
Pearscroft Ct. SW6	75	E1
Pearscroft Rd. SW6	75	E1
Pearson St. E2	9	F1
Pearson St. E2	59	C2
Pearsons Ave. SE14	78	A1
Tanners Hill		
Peartree Clo., Mitch.	93	H2
Peartree Gdns., Dag.	53	B4
Peartree Gdns., Rom.	44	H2
Peartree La. E1	59	F7
Glamis Rd.		
Peartree Rd., Enf.	25	B3
Peary Pl. E2	59	F3
Kirkwall Pl.		
Peatfield Clo., Sid.	88	H3
Woodside Rd.		
Pebworth Rd., Har.	46	D2
Peckarmans Wd. SE26	86	F3
Peckett Sq. N5	49	J4
Highbury Gra.		
Peckford Pl. SW9	76	G2

Peckham Gro. SE15 21 E7
Peckham Gro. SE15 68 B7
Peckham High St. SE15 77 D1
Peckham Hill St. SE15 21 H7
Peckham Hill St. SE15 68 D7
Peckham Pk. Rd. SE15 68 D7
Peckham Rd. SE5 77 B1
Peckham Rd. SE15 77 C1
Peckham Rye SE15 77 D3
Peckham Rye SE22 77 D4
Peckwater St. NW5 49 C5
Pedlars Wk. N7 49 E6
Pedley Rd., Dag. 53 C1
Pedley St. E1 9 G6
Pedley St. E1 59 D4
Pedro St. E5 50 G3
Pedworth Gdns. SE16 68 F4
Rotherhithe New Rd.
Peek Cres. SW19 84 A5
Peel Clo. E4 34 B2
Peel Clo. N9 33 D3
Plevna Rd.
Peel Dr. NW9 38 F3
Peel Dr., Ilf. 43 B3
Peel Gro. E2 59 F2
Peel Pas. W8 66 D1
Peel St.
Peel Pl., Ilf. 43 B2
Peel Prec. NW6 57 D2
Peel Rd. E18 42 F1
Peel Rd. NW6 57 C3
Peel Rd., Har. 37 C3
Peel Rd., Orp. 104 F5
Peel Rd., Wem. 46 G3
Peel St. W8 66 D1
Peerless St. EC1 9 B4
Peerless St. EC1 59 A3
Pegamoid Rd. N18 33 F3
Pegasus Ct., Kings.T. 91 G3
Pegasus Pl. SE11 20 E5
Pegg Rd., Houns. 63 D7
Pegley Gdns. SE12 87 G2
Pegwell St. SE18 70 H7
Pekin Clo. E14 60 A6
Pekin St.
Pekin St. E14 60 A6
Peldon Ct., Rich. 73 J4
Peldon Wk. N1 58 H1
Britannia Row
Pelham Ave., Bark. 61 J1
Pelham Clo. SE5 77 B3
Pelham Cres. SW7 18 G2
Pelham Cres. SW7 66 H4
Pelham Pl. SW7 18 G1
Pelham Pl. SW7 66 H4
Pelham Rd. E18 42 H3
Pelham Rd. N15 41 C4
Pelham Rd. N22 40 G2
Pelham Rd. SW19 84 D7
Pelham Rd., Beck. 95 F2
Pelham Rd., Bexh. 80 G3
Pelham Rd., Ilf. 52 G2
Pelham St. SW7 18 F1
Pelham St. SW7 66 G4
Pelican Est. SE15 77 C1
Pelican Pas. E1 59 F4
Cambridge Heath Rd.
Pelican Wk. SW9 76 H4
Loughborough Pk.
Pelier St. SE17 21 A5
Pelinore Rd. SE6 87 E2
Pellant Rd. SW6 66 B7
Pellatt Gro. N22 40 G1
Pellatt Rd. SE22 77 C5
Pellerin Rd. N16 50 B5
Pelling St. E14 60 A6
Pellipar Clo. N13 32 G3
Pellipar Gdns. SE18 70 C5
Pelly Rd. E13 60 G1
Pelter St. E2 9 F3
Pelter St. E2 59 C3
Pelton Rd. SE10 69 E5
Pembar Ave. E17 41 H3
Pember Rd. NW10 57 A3
Pemberton Gdns. N19 49 C3
Pemberton Gdns., Rom. 44 E5
Pemberton Ho. SE26 86 D4
High Level Dr.
Pemberton Pl. E8 50 E7
Mare St.
Pemberton Rd. N4 40 G5
Pemberton Rd., E.Mol. 90 J4
Pemberton Row EC4 12 F3
Pemberton Ter. N19 49 C3
Pembridge Ave., Twick. 81 F1
Pembridge Cres. W11 57 D7
Pembridge Gdns. W2 57 D7
Pembridge Ms. W11 57 D7
Pembridge Pl. W2 57 D7
Pembridge Rd. W11 57 D7
Pembridge Sq. W2 57 D7
Pembridge Vill. W11 57 D7
Pembroke Ave., Har. 37 D3
Pembroke Ave., Surb. 92 B5
Pembroke Clo. SW1 15 C4
Pembroke Clo. SW1 67 A2
Pembroke Gdns. W8 66 C4
Pembroke Gdns., Dag. 53 H3
Pembroke Gdns. Clo. W8 66 C3
Pembroke Ms. E3 59 H3
Morgan St.
Pembroke Ms. N10 40 A1
Pembroke Rd.
Pembroke Ms. W8 66 D3
Earls Wk.
Pembroke Pl. W8 66 D3
Pembroke Pl., Edg. 30 A7
Pembroke Pl., Islw. 73 B2
Clifton Rd.
Pembroke Rd. E6 61 C5
Pembroke Rd. E17 42 B5
Pembroke Rd. N8 40 E4
Pembroke Rd. N10 40 A1
Pembroke Rd. N13 32 J3
Pembroke Rd. N15 41 C5
Pembroke Rd. SE25 95 B4
Pembroke Rd. W8 66 D4
Pembroke Rd., Brom. 96 J2
Pembroke Rd., Erith 71 J5
Pembroke Rd., Grnf. 54 H3
Pembroke Rd., Ilf. 52 J1
Pembroke Rd., Mitch. 94 A2
Pembroke Rd., Wem. 46 G3
Pembroke Sq. W8 66 D3
Pembroke St. N1 49 E7
Pembroke Studios W8 66 C3
Pembroke Vill. W8 66 D4
Pembroke Vill., Rich. 73 G4
Pembroke Wk. W8 66 D4
Pembury Ave., Wor.Pk. 99 G1
Pembury Clo., Brom. 96 F7
Pembury Cres., Sid. 89 E3
Pembury Pl. E5 50 E5
Pembury Rd. E5 50 E5
Pembury Rd. N17 41 C1
Pembury Rd. SE25 95 D4
Pembury Rd., Bexh. 71 E7
Pemdevon Rd., Croy. 94 G7
Pemell Clo. E1 59 F4
Colebert Ave.
Pempath Pl., Wem. 46 G2
Penally Pl. N1 59 A1
Shepperton Rd.
Penang St. E1 68 E1
Penarth St. SE15 68 F6
Penates, Esher 98 A4
Penberth Rd. SE6 87 C1
Penbury Rd., Sthl. 63 F4
Pencombe Ms. W11 57 C7
Denbigh Rd.
Pencraig Way SE15 68 E6
Penda Rd., Erith 71 H7
Pendarves Rd. SW20 92 J1
Penda's Mead E9 50 H4
Lindisfarne Way
Pendennis Rd. N17 41 A3
Pendennis Rd. SW16 85 E4
Penderel Rd., Houns. 72 G5
Penderry Ri. SE6 87 D2
Penderyn Way N7 49 D4
Pendle Rd. SW16 85 B6
Pendlestone Rd. E17 42 B5
Pendragon Rd., Brom. 87 F3
Pendragon Wk. NW9 38 E6
Pendrell Rd. SE4 77 H2
Pendrell St. SE18 70 G6
Pendula Dr., Hayes 54 D4
Penerley Rd. SE6 87 B1
Penfold Clo., Croy. 101 G3
Epsom Rd.
Penfold La., Bex. 89 D1
Carisbrooke Ave.
Penfold Pl. NW1 10 G1
Penfold Pl. NW1 57 H5
Penfold Rd. N9 33 G1
Penfold St. NW1 10 G1
Penfold St. NW1 57 H5
Penfold St. NW8 6 F6
Penfold St. NW8 57 J4
Penford Gdns. SE9 79 A3
Penford St. SE5 76 H2
Pengarth Rd., Bex. 80 D5
Penge Ho. SW11 75 G3
Wye St.
Penge La. SE20 86 F7
Penge Rd. E13 60 J1
Penge Rd. SE20 95 D3
Penge Rd. SE25 95 D3
Penhall Rd. SE7 70 A4
Penhill Rd., Bex. 80 C6
Penhurst Rd., Ilf. 35 E7
Penifather La., Grnf. 55 A3
Penistone Rd. SW16 85 E7
Penketh Dr., Har. 46 A3
Penmon Rd. SE2 71 A3
Penn Clo., Grnf. 54 H2
Penn Clo., Har. 37 F4
Penn Gdns., Chis. 97 E2
Penn La., Bex. 80 D6
Penn Rd. N7 49 E5
Penn St. N1 59 A1
Pennack Rd. SE15 21 G6
Pennack Rd. SE15 68 C6
Pennant Ms. W8 18 A1
Pennant Ms. W8 66 E4
Pennant Ter. E17 41 J2
Pennard Rd. W12 65 J2
Pennards, The, Sun. 90 C2
Penner Clo. SW19 84 B2
Victoria Dr.
Pennethorne Clo. E9 59 F1
Victoria Pk. Rd.
Pennethorne Rd. SE15 68 E7
Pennine Dr. NW2 48 A2
Pennine La. NW2 48 B2
Pennine Dr.
Pennington Clo. SE27 86 A4
Hamilton Rd.
Pennington St. E1 13 J6
Pennington St. E1 59 D7
Penny Rd. NW10 56 B3
Pennyfields E14 60 A7
Pennymoor Wk. W9 57 C3
Ashmore Rd.
Pennyroyal Ave. E6 61 D6
Penpoll Rd. E8 50 E6
Penpool La., Well. 80 B3
Penrhyn Ave. E17 41 J1
Penrhyn Cres. E17 42 A1
Penrhyn Ave.
Penrhyn Cres. SW14 74 C4
Penrhyn Gro. E17 42 A1
Penrhyn Rd., Kings.T. 91 H4
Penrith Clo. SW15 75 B5
Penrith Clo., Beck. 96 B1
Albemarle Rd.
Penrith Pl. SE27 85 H2
Harpenden Rd.
Penrith Rd. N15 41 A5
Penrith Rd., Ilf. 35 J6
Penrith Rd., N.Mal. 92 D4
Penrith Rd., Th.Hth. 94 J2
Penrith St. SW16 85 C6
Penrose Ave., Wat. 28 D2
Penrose Gro. SE17 20 J4
Penrose Gro. SE17 67 J5
Penrose Ho. SE17 20 J4
Penrose St. SE17 20 J4
Penrose St. SE17 67 J5
Penry St. SE1 21 E2
Penryn St. NW1 7 H1
Penryn St. NW1 58 D2
Pensbury Pl. SW8 76 C2
Pensbury St. SW8 76 C2
Penscroft Gdns., Borwd. 22 D4
Pensford Ave., Rich. 74 A2
Penshurst Ave., Sid. 80 A6
Penshurst Gdns., Edg. 30 B5
Penshurst Grn., Brom. 96 F5
Penshurst Rd. E9 50 G7
Penshurst Rd. N17 33 C7
Penshurst Rd., Bexh. 80 F1
Penshurst Rd., Th.Hth. 94 H5
Penshurst Wk., Brom. 96 F5
Hayesford Pk. Dr.
Penshurst Way, Sutt. 100 D7
Penstock Footpath N22 40 E3
Pentelowe Gdns., Felt. 72 A6
Pentire Rd. E17 42 D1
Pentland Clo. NW11 48 B2
Pentland Gdns. SW18 75 F6
St. Ann's Hill
Pentland Pl., Nthlt. 54 E1
Pentland St. SW18 75 F6
Pentlands Clo., Mitch. 94 B3
Pentlow St. SW15 74 J3
Pentlow Way, Buck.H. 27 B7
Pentney Rd. E4 34 D1
Pentney Rd. SW12 85 C1
Pentney Rd. SW19 93 B1
Midmoor Rd.
Penton Gro. N1 8 E2
Penton Pl. SE17 20 H3
Penton Pl. SE17 67 H5
Penton Ri. WC1 8 D3
Penton Ri. WC1 58 F3
Penton St. N1 8 E2
Penton St. N1 58 G2
Pentonville Rd. N1 8 C2
Pentonville Rd. N1 58 F2
Pentridge St. SE15 68 C7
Pentyre Ave. N18 33 A5
Penwerris Ave., Islw. 63 J7
Penwith Rd. SW18 84 D2
Penwortham Rd. SW16 85 B6
Penylan Pl., Edg. 30 A7
Penywern Rd. SW5 66 D5
Penzance Pl. W11 66 B1
Penzance St. W11 66 B1
Peony Gdns. W12 56 G7
Peploe Rd. NW6 57 A2
Pepper All., Loug. 26 F2
Pepper Clo. E6 61 C5
Pepper St. E14 69 B3
Pepper St. SE1 16 J3
Peppermint Clo., Croy. 94 E7
Pepys Cres., Barn. 22 J5
Pepys Ri., Orp. 104 J1
Pepys Rd. SE14 77 G1
Pepys Rd. SW20 92 J2
Pepys St. EC3 13 E5
Pepys St. EC3 59 B7
Perceval Ave. NW3 48 H5
Perch St. E8 50 C4
Percheron Rd., Borwd. 22 D6
Percival Ct. N17 33 C7
High Rd.
Percival Ct., Nthlt. 45 G5
Percival Gdns., Rom. 44 C6
Percival Rd. SW14 74 C4
Percival Rd., Enf. 25 C4
Percival Rd., Orp. 104 E2
Percival St. EC1 8 G5
Percival St. EC1 58 H4
Percival Way, Epsom 99 C4
Percy Circ. WC1 8 D3
Percy Circ. WC1 58 F3
Percy Gdns., Enf. 25 G5
Percy Gdns., Islw. 73 D3
Percy Gdns., Wor.Pk. 99 E1
Percy Ms. W1 11 H2
Percy Pas. W1 11 G2
Percy Rd. E11 42 E7
Percy Rd. E16 60 E5
Percy Rd. N12 31 F5
Percy Rd. N21 24 J7
Percy Rd. NW6 57 D3
Stafford Rd.
Percy Rd. SE20 95 G1
Percy Rd. SE25 95 D5
Percy Rd. W12 65 G2
Percy Rd., Bexh. 80 E2
Percy Rd., Dag. 62 F4
Percy Rd., Hmptn. 81 G7
Percy Rd., Ilf. 44 A7
Percy Rd., Islw. 73 D4
Percy Rd., Mitch. 94 A7
Percy Rd., Rom. 44 H3
Percy Rd., Twick. 81 H1
Percy St. W1 11 H2
Percy St. W1 58 D5
Percy Way, Twick. 81 J1
Percy Yd. WC1 8 D3
Peregrine Clo. NW10 47 D5
Peregrine Ct. SW16 85 F4
Leithcote Gdns.
Peregrine Gdns., Croy. 102 H2
Peregrine Ho. EC1 8 H3
Peregrine Ho. EC1 58 H3

Peregrine Way SW19 83 J7
Perham Rd. W14 66 B5
Peridot St. E6 61 B5
Perifield SE21 85 J1
Perimeade Rd., Grnf. 55 F2
Periton Rd. SE9 79 A4
Perivale Gdns. W13 55 E1
Bellevue Rd.
Perivale Gra., 55 D3
Grnf.
Perivale Ind. Pk., 55 D1
Grnf.
Perivale La., Grnf. 55 D3
Perivale New 55 E2
Business Cen., Grnf.
Perkins Clo., Wem. 46 E5
Perkin's Rents SW1 15 H5
Perkin's Rents SW1 67 D3
Perkins Rd., Ilf. 43 G5
Perks Clo. SE3 78 E3
Hurren Clo.
Perpins Rd. SE9 79 G6
Perran Rd. SW2 85 H2
Christchurch Rd.
Perran Wk., Brent. 64 H5
Burford Rd.
Perren St. NW5 49 B6
Ryland Rd.
Perrers Rd. W6 65 H4
Perrin Rd., Wem. 46 D4
Perrins Ct. NW3 48 F4
Hampstead High St.
Perrins La. NW3 48 F4
Perrin's Wk. NW3 48 F4
Perry Ave. W3 56 D6
Perry Ct. N15 41 B6
Albert Rd.
Perry Gdns. N9 33 B3
Deansway
Perry Garth, Nthlt. 54 C1
Perry Hall Rd., 97 J6
Orp.
Perry Hill SE6 86 J3
Perry How, Wor.Pk. 99 F1
Perry Mead, Enf. 24 H2
Perry Ri. SE23 86 H3
Perry St., Chis. 88 G6
Perry St. Gdns., Chis. 88 H6
Perry St.
Perry Vale SE23 86 F3
Perryfield Way NW9 38 F6
Perryfield Way, 73 H3
Rich.
Perryman Ho., Bark. 61 F1
Perrymans Fm. Rd., 43 G6
Ilf.
Perrymead St. SW6 75 D1
Perryn Rd. SE16 68 E3
Drummond Rd.
Perryn Rd. W3 65 D1
Perrys Pl. W1 11 H3
Persant Rd. SE6 87 E3
Perseverance Pl. 67 G7
SW9
Mandela St.
Perseverance Pl., 73 H3
Rich.
Shaftesbury Rd.
Pershore Clo., Ilf. 43 E5
Pershore Gro., Cars. 93 G6
Pert Clo. N10 32 B6
Perth Ave. NW9 38 D7
Perth Ave., Hayes 54 C4
Perth Clo. SW20 92 G2
Perth Rd. E10 50 H1
Perth Rd. E13 60 H2
Perth Rd. N4 49 G1
Perth Rd. N22 40 H1
Perth Rd., Bark. 61 G1
Perth Rd., Beck. 96 C2
Perth Rd., Ilf. 43 D6
Perth Ter., Ilf. 43 F7
Perwell Ave., Har. 45 F1
Perwell Ct., Har. 45 F1
Peter Ave. NW10 47 H7
Peter St. W1 11 H5
Peter St. W1 58 D7
Peterboat Clo. SE10 69 E4
Tunnel Ave.
Peterborough Gdns., 43 B7
Ilf.
Peterborough Ms. 75 D2
SW6
Peterborough Rd. 42 C5
E10
Peterborough Rd. 75 D2
SW6
Peterborough Rd., 93 H6
Cars.
Peterborough Rd., 46 B1
Har.
Peterborough Vill. 75 E1
SW6

Peterchurch Ho. 68 E6
SE15
Commercial Way
Petergate SW11 75 F4
Peters Clo., Dag. 53 D1
Peters Clo., Stan. 29 G6
Peters Clo., Well. 70 H2
Peters Hill EC4 12 J5
Peters La. EC1 12 G1
Peters Path SE26 86 E4
Petersfield Clo. 32 J5
N18
Petersfield Ri. 83 H1
SW15
Petersfield Rd. W3 65 C2
Petersham Clo., 82 G2
Rich.
Petersham Clo., 100 C5
Sutt.
Petersham Dr., Orp. 97 J2
Petersham Gdns., 97 J2
Orp.
Petersham La. SW7 14 C5
Petersham Ms. SW7 66 F3
Petersham Ms. SW7 14 C6
Petersham Ms. SW7 66 F3
Petersham Pl. SW7 14 C5
Petersham Pl. SW7 66 F3
Petersham Rd., 73 G6
Rich.
Peterstone Rd. SE2 71 B3
Peterstow Clo. SW19 84 B2
Peterwood Way, 101 F2
Croy.
Petherton Rd. N5 49 J5
Petley Rd. W6 65 J6
Peto Pl. NW1 7 E5
Peto Pl. NW1 58 B4
Peto St. N. E16 60 F7
Victoria Dock Rd.
Petrie Clo. NW2 48 B6
Pett St. SE18 70 C3
Petticoat Sq. E1 13 F3
Pettits Pl., Dag. 53 G5
Pettits Rd., Dag. 53 G5
Pettiward Clo. SW15 74 J4
Pettman Cres. SE28 70 G3
Petts Hill, Nthlt. 45 H5
Pettsgrove Ave., 46 F5
Wem.
Petty France SW1 15 G5
Petty France SW1 67 C3
Petworth Clo., 45 F7
Nthlt.
Petworth Gdns. 92 H3
SW20
Hidcote Gdns.
Petworth Rd. N12 31 H5
Petworth Rd., Bexh. 80 G5
Petworth St. SW11 75 H1
Petyt Pl. SW3 18 G6
Petyward SW3 18 H2
Petyward SW3 66 H4
Pevel Ho., Dag. 53 G2
Pevensey Ave. N11 32 D5
Pevensey Ave., Enf. 25 A2
Pevensey Clo., 63 J7
Islw.
Pevensey Rd. E7 51 F4
Pevensey Rd. SW17 84 G4
Pevensey Rd., Felt. 81 K1
Peveret Clo. N11 32 B5
Woodland Rd.
Peveril Dr., Tedd. 82 A5
Pewsey Clo. E4 34 A5
Peyton Pl. SE10 69 C7
Pheasant Clo. E16 60 H6
Maplin Rd.
Phelp St. SE17 21 B5
Phelp St. SE17 68 A6
Phene St. SW3 18 H5
Phene St. SW3 66 H6
Philbeach Gdns. SW5 66 D5
Philchurch Pl. E1 13 J4
Philip Gdns., Croy. 102 J2
Philip La. N15 41 A4
Philip St. E13 60 G4
Philip Wk. SE15 77 E3
Philpot Path SE9 79 E2
Court Yd.
Philippa Gdns. SE9 79 A5
Phillimore Gdns. 56 J1
NW10
Phillimore Gdns. W8 66 D2
Phillimore Gdns. 66 D3
Clo. W8
Phillimore Gdns.
Phillimore Pl. W8 66 D2
Phillimore Wk. W8 66 D3
Phillipp St. N1 58 D1
Philpot La. EC3 13 D5
Philpot Path, Ilf. 52 F3
Sunnyside Rd.

Philpot Sq. SW6 75 E3
Peterborough Rd.
Philpot St. E1 59 E6
Phineas Pett Rd. 79 B3
SE9
Phipp St. EC2 9 D5
Phipp St. EC2 59 B4
Phipps Bri. Rd. 93 F2
SW19
Phipps Bri. Rd., 93 F2
Mitch.
Phipp's Ms. SW1 15 D6
Phoebeth Rd. SE4 78 A5
Phoenix Clo. E8 59 C1
Stean St.
Phoenix Clo., 103 D2
W.Wick.
Phoenix Dr., Kes. 104 A3
Phoenix Pk., Brent. 64 G5
Phoenix Pl. WC1 8 D5
Phoenix Pl. WC1 58 F4
Phoenix Pl. NW1 7 H3
Phoenix Rd. NW1 58 D3
Phoenix Rd. SE20 86 F6
Phoenix St. WC2 11 J4
Phoenix Way, Houns. 63 C6
Phyllis Ave., 92 H5
N.Mal.
Physic Pl. SW3 18 J4
Picardy Manorway, 71 H3
Belv.
Pinchin St. E1 13 J5 (?)
Picardy Rd., Belv. 71 G5
Picardy St., Belv. 71 G3
Piccadilly W1 15 E2
Piccadilly W1 67 B1
Piccadilly Arc. SW1 15 F1
Piccadilly Circ. W1 11 H6
Piccadilly Circ. W1 58 C7
Piccadilly Pl. W1 11 G6
Pickard St. EC1 8 H3
Pickering Ave. E6 61 D3
Vicarage La.
Pickering Ms. W2 10 B3
Pickering Pl. SW1 15 G2
Pickering St. N1 58 H1
Essex Rd.
Pickets Clo. 29 A1
(Bushey), Wat.
Pickets St. SW12 76 B7
Pickett Cft., Stan. 37 G1
Picketts Lock La. N9 33 F2
Pickford Clo., 80 E2
Bexh.
Pickford La., Bexh. 80 E2
Pickford Rd., Bexh. 80 E4
Pickford Wf. N1 8 J2
Pickford Wf. N1 58 J2
Pickhurst Grn. 96 F7
Brom.
Pickhurst La., 96 F7
W.Wick.
Pickhurst Mead, 96 F7
Brom.
Pickhurst Pk., 96 E5
Brom.
Pickhurst Ri. 96 C7
W.Wick.
Pickwick Clo., 72 E5
Houns.
Dorney Way
Pickwick Ms. N18 33 B5
Pickwick Pl., Har. 37 B7
Pickwick Rd. SE21 77 A7
Pickwick St. SE1 16 J4
Pickwick Way, Chis. 88 F6
Pickworth Clo. SW8 67 E7
Kenchester Clo.
Picton Pl. W1 11 C4
Picton St. SE5 68 A7
Piedmont Rd. SE18 70 G5
Pier Head E1 68 E1
Wapping High St.
Pier Rd. E16 70 D2
Pier Rd., Felt. 72 B5
Pier St. E14 69 C4
Pier Ter. SW18 75 F4
Jew's Row
Pier Way SE28 70 G3
Piermont Pl., Brom. 97 B2
Piermont Rd. SE22 77 E3
Pierrepoint Rd. W3 56 B7
Pierrepoint Row N1 8 G1
Pigeon La., Hmptn. 81 G3
Piggott St. E14 60 A6
Pike Clo., Brom. 87 H5
Pike Rd. NW7 30 D4
Ellesmere Ave.
Pikes End, Pnr. 36 B4
Pikestone Clo., 54 E4
Hayes
Berrydale Rd.

Pilgrim Hill SE27 85 J4
Pilgrim St. EC4 12 G4
Pilgrim St. EC4 58 H6
Pilgrimage St. SE1 17 B4
Pilgrimage St. SE1 68 A2
Pilgrims Clo. N13 32 F4
Pilgrims Clo., 45 J5
Nthlt.
Pilgrims Ct. SE3 78 G1
Pilgrim's La. NW3 48 G4
Pilgrims Pl. NW3 48 G4
Hampstead High St.
Pilgrims Ri., Barn. 23 H5
Pilgrims Way N19 49 D1
Pilgrims Way, 102 C6
Bench Fld.
Pilgrim's Way, Wem. 47 B1
Pilkington Rd. SE15 77 E2
Pilkington Rd., 104 F2
Orp.
Pilot Ind. Est. 56 D7
NW10
Pilsdon Clo. SW19 84 A1
Inner Pk. Rd.
Piltdown Rd., Wat. 28 D4
Pimlico Rd. SW1 19 B3
Pimlico Rd. SW1 67 A5
Pimlico Wk. N1 9 D3
Pinchbeck Rd., Orp. 104 J6
Pinchin St. E1 13 J5
Pinchin St. E1 59 D7
Pincott Rd. SW19 84 F7
Pincott Rd., Bexh. 80 G5
Pindar St. EC2 13 D1
Pindar St. EC2 59 B5
Pindock Ms. W9 6 B6
Pine Ave. E15 51 D5
Pine Ave., W.Wick. 103 B1
Pine Clo. N14 24 C7
Pine Clo. N19 49 C2
Hargrave Pk.
Pine Clo., Stan. 29 E4
Pine Coombe, Croy. 102 G4
Pine Gdns., Ruis. 45 B1
Pine Gdns., Surb. 92 A6
Pine Glade, Orp. 104 C4
Pine Gro. N4 49 E2
Pine Gro. N20 31 C1
Pine Gro. SW19 84 C5
Pine Rd. N11 32 A2
Pine Rd. NW2 47 J4
Pine St. EC1 8 E5
Pine St. EC1 58 G4
Pine Tree Clo., 72 B1
Houns.
Pine Wk., Surb. 92 A6
Pine Wal., Sun. 90 A1
Pineapple Ct. SW1 15 F5
Pinecrest Gdns., 104 E4
Orp.
Pinedene SE15 77 E1
Meeting Ho. La.
Pinefield Clo. E14 60 A7
Pinelands Clo. SE3 69 F7
St. John's Pk.
Pines, The N14 24 C5
Pines, The, Sun. 90 A3
Pines, The, 34 G3
Wdf.Grn.
Pines Rd., Brom. 97 B2
Pinewood Ave., Pnr. 28 H6
Pinewood Ave., Sid. 88 H1
Pinewood Clo., 22 D1
Borwd.
Pinewood Clo., 102 H3
Croy.
Pinewood Clo., Orp. 104 G1
Pinewood Clo., Pnr. 28 H6
Pinewood Dr., Orp. 104 H5
Pinewood Gro. W5 55 F6
Pinewood Rd. SE2 71 D6
Pinewood Rd., Brom. 96 G4
Pinewood Rd., Felt. 81 B3
Pinfold Rd. SW16 85 E4
Pinkcoat Clo., 81 B3
Felt.
Tanglewood Way
Pinkerton Pl. SW16 85 D4
Riggindale Rd.
Pinkham Way N11 32 A7
Pinley Gdns., Dag. 62 B1
Stamford Rd.
Pinnacle Hill, 80 H4
Bexh.
Pinnacle Hill N., 80 H3
Bexh.
Pinnell Pl. SE9 79 A4
Pinnell Rd. SE9 79 A4
Pinner Ct., Pnr. 36 G4
Pinner Grn., Pnr. 36 C2
Pinner Gro., Pnr. 36 E4
Pinner Hill, Pnr. 28 B7

Pinner Hill Rd., Pnr. 36 C1
Pinner Pk. Ave., 36 H3
Har.
Pinner Pk. Gdns., 36 J2
Har.
Pinner Rd., Har. 36 H5
Pinner Rd., Pnr. 36 F4
Pinner Vw., Har. 36 J4
Pintail Clo. E6 61 B5
Swan App.
Pintail Rd., 34 H7
Wdf.Grn.
Pinto Clo., Borwd. 22 D6
Percheron Rd.
Pinto Way SE3 78 H4
Pioneer Way W12 56 H6
Du Cane Rd.
Piper Clo. N7 49 F5
Piper Rd., Kings.T. 92 A3
Pipers Gdns., Croy. 95 H7
Pipers Grn. NW9 38 C5
Pipers Grn. La., 29 H3
Edg.
Pipewell Rd., Cars. 93 H6
Pippin Clo., Croy. 102 J1
Piquet Rd. SE20 95 F2
Pirbright Cres., 103 C6
Croy.
Pirbright Rd. SW18 84 C1
Pirie Clo. SE5 77 H3
Denmark Hill
Pirie St. E16 69 H1
Pitcairn Clo., Rom. 44 G4
Pitcairn Rd., 84 J7
Mitch.
Pitchford St. E15 51 D7
Pitfield Cres. SE28 71 A1
Pitfield Est. N1 9 D3
Pitfield St. N1 9 D4
Pitfield St. N1 59 B3
Pitfield Way NW10 47 C6
Pitfield Way, Enf. 25 F1
Pitfold Clo. SE12 78 G6
Pitfold Rd. SE12 78 G6
Pitlake, Croy. 101 H2
Pitman St. SE5 20 J7
Pitman St. SE5 67 J7
Pitsea Pl. E1 59 G6
Pitsea St.
Pitsea St. E1 59 G6
Pitshanger La. W5 55 E4
Pitshanger Pk. W13 55 D4
Pitt Cres. SW19 84 E4
Pitt Rd., Har. 45 J2
Pitt Rd., Orp. 104 F4
Pitt Rd., Th.Hth. 94 J5
Pitt St. SE15 68 C7
Pitt St. W8 66 D2
Pittman Gdns., Ilf. 52 F5
Pitt's Head Ms. W1 15 C2
Pitt's Head Ms. W1 67 A1
Pittsmead Ave., 96 G7
Brom.
Pittville Gdns. SE25 95 D3
Pixfield Ct., Brom. 96 F2
Beckenham La.
Pixley St. E14 59 J6
Place Fm. Ave., 104 G1
Orp.
Plaistow Gro. E15 60 F1
Plaistow Gro., 87 H7
Brom.
Plaistow La., Brom. 87 G7
Plaistow Pk. Rd. 60 H2
E13
Plaistow Rd. E15 60 F1
Plane St. SE26 86 E3
Plane Tree Cres., 81 B3
Felt.
Plane Tree Wk. SE19 86 B6
Central Ave.
Plantagenet Clo., 99 D4
Wor.Pk.
Plantagenet Gdns., 44 D7
Rom.
Broomfield Rd.
Plantagenet Pl., 44 D7
Rom.
Broomfield Rd.
Plantagenet Rd., 23 F4
Barn.
Plantain Pl. SE1 17 B3
Plantation, The SE3 78 G2
Plasel Ct. E13 60 G1
Plashet Rd.
Plashet Gro. E6 60 J1
Plashet Rd. E13 60 G1
Plassy Rd. SE6 86 E3
Platina St. EC2 9 C5
Plato Rd. SW2 76 D4
Platt, The SW15 75 A3
Platt St. NW1 7 H1
Platt St. NW1 58 D2

Platt's La. NW3 48 D4
Platts Rd., Enf. 25 F1
Plawsfield Rd., 95 G1
Beck.
Plaxtol Clo., Brom. 96 J1
Plaxtol Rd., Erith 71 G6
Playfield Ave. 44 J1
Rom.
Playfield Cres. 77 C5
SE22
Playfield Rd., Edg. 38 C2
Playford Rd. N4 49 F2
Playgreen Way SE6 87 A3
Playground Clo., 95 G2
Beck.
Churchfields Rd.
Playhouse Yd. EC4 12 G4
Plaza W., Houns. 72 H1
Pleasance, The SW15 74 H4
Pleasance Rd. SW15 74 H5
Pleasant Gro., 102 J3
Croy.
Pleasant Pl. N1 49 H7
Pleasant Rd., 92 C3
Kings.T.
Pleasant Row NW1 58 B1
Camden High St.
Pleasant Way, Wem. 55 F2
Plender St. NW1 58 C1
Plender St. Est. NW1 58 C1
Plender St.
Pleshey Rd. N7 49 D4
Plevna Cres. N15 41 B6
Plevna Rd. N9 33 D3
Plevna Rd., Hmptn. 90 H1
Plevna St. E14 69 C3
Pleydell Ave. SE19 86 C7
Pleydell Ave. W6 65 F4
Pleydell Ct. EC4 58 G6
Fleet St.
Pleydell St. EC4 12 F4
Plimsoll Clo. E14 60 B6
Grundy St.
Plimsoll Rd. N4 49 G3
Plough Ct. EC3 13 C5
Plough La. SE22 77 C6
Plough La. SW17 84 F4
Plough La. SW19 84 E5
Plough La., Wall. 101 E4
Plough La. Clo., 101 E5
Wall.
Plough Pl. EC4 12 F3
Plough Rd. SW11 75 G3
Plough Ter. SW11 75 G4
Plough Way SE16 68 G4
Plough Yd. EC2 9 E6
Plough Yd. EC2 59 B4
Ploughmans Clo. 58 D1
NW1
Crofters Way
Ploughmans End, 73 A5
Islw.
Plover Way SE16 68 H3
Plowman Clo. N18 33 A5
Plowman Way, Dag. 53 C1
Plum Garth, Brent. 64 G4
Plum La. SE18 70 E7
Plumbers Row E1 13 J2
Plumbers Row E1 59 D5
Plumbridge St. SE10 78 C1
Blackheath Hill
Plummer La., Mitch. 93 J2
Plummer Rd. SW4 76 D7
Plumpton Clo., 45 G6
Nthlt.
Plumpton Way, 100 H3
Cars.
Plumstead Common 70 E6
Rd. SE18
Plumstead High St. 70 G4
SE18
Plumstead Rd. SE18 70 E4
Plumtree Clo., 101 D7
Wall.
Plumtree Ct. EC4 12 G3
Plumtree Mead, 27 D3
Loug.
Plymouth Rd. E16 60 G5
Plymouth Rd., Brom. 96 H1
Plymouth Wf. E14 69 D4
Plympton Ave. NW6 46 C7
Plympton Clo., 71 E3
Belv.
Halifield Dr.
Plympton Pl. NW8 6 G6
Plympton Rd. NW6 46 C7
Plympton St. NW8 6 G6
Plympton St. NW8 57 H4
Plymstock Rd., 71 C7
Well.
Pocklington Clo. 38 E2
NW9
Pocock St. SE1 16 G3

Pocock St. SE1 67 H2
Podmore Rd. SW18 75 F4
Poets Rd. N5 50 A5
Poets Way, Har. 37 B4
Blawith Rd.
Point Clo. SE10 78 C1
Point Hill
Point Hill SE10 69 C7
Point Pleasant SW18 75 D4
Pointalls Clo. N3 39 F2
Pointer Clo. SE28 62 D6
Pointers Clo. E14 69 B5
Pointers Cotts., 82 F2
Rich.
Poland St. W1 11 G3
Poland St. W1 58 C6
Pole Cat All., 103 F2
Brom.
Pole Hill Rd. E4 26 C7
Polebrook Rd. SE3 78 J3
Polecroft La. SE6 86 J2
Polesden Gdns. 92 H2
SW20
Polesworth Ho. W2 57 D5
Polesworth Rd., 53 D7
Dag.
Pollard Clo. E16 60 G7
Pollard Clo. N7 49 F4
Pollard Rd. N20 31 H2
Pollard Rd., Mord. 93 G5
Pollard Row E2 9 J3
Pollard Row E2 59 D3
Pollard St. E2 9 J3
Pollard St. E2 59 D3
Pollard Wk., Sid. 89 C6
Evry Rd.
Pollards Clo., Loug. 26 J5
Pollards Cres. SW16 94 E3
Pollards Hill E. 94 F3
SW16
Pollards Hill N. 94 E3
SW16
Pollards Hill S. 94 E3
SW16
Pollards Hill W. 94 E3
SW16
Pollards Wd. Rd. 94 E2
SW16
Pollen St. W1 11 F4
Pollitt Dr. NW8 6 F5
Polperro Clo., Orp. 97 J6
Cotswold Ri.
Polsted Rd. SE6 77 J7
Polthorne Gro. SE18 70 F4
Polworth Rd. SW16 85 E5
Polygon, The SW4 76 C4
Old Town
Polygon Rd. NW1 7 H2
Polygon Rd. NW1 58 D2
Polytechnic St. 70 D4
SE18
Pomell Way E1 13 G3
Pomeroy St. SE14 77 F1
Pomfret Rd. SE5 76 H3
Flaxman Rd.
Pond Clo. SE3 78 F2
Pond Cottage La., 103 A1
W.Wick.
Pond Cotts. SE21 86 B1
Pond Hill Gdns., 100 B6
Sutt.
Pond Mead SE21 77 A6
Pond Pl. SW3 18 G2
Pond Pl. SW3 66 H4
Pond Rd. E15 60 E2
Pond Rd. SE3 78 F2
Pond Sq. N6 49 A1
South Gro.
Pond St. NW3 48 H5
Pond Way, Tedd. 82 F6
Holmesdale Rd.
Ponder St. N7 49 F7
Ponders End Ind. 25 J4
Est., Enf.
Pondfield Rd., 103 E1
Brom.
Pondfield Rd., Dag. 53 H5
Pondfield Rd., Orp. 104 E3
Pondwood Ri., Orp. 97 H7
Ponler St. E1 59 E6
Ponsard Rd. NW10 56 H3
Ponsford St. E9 50 F5
Ponsonby Pl. SW1 19 J3
Ponsonby Pl. SW1 67 D5
Ponsonby Rd. SW15 74 H7
Ponsonby Ter. SW1 19 J3
Ponsonby Ter. SW1 67 D5
Pont St. SW1 14 J6
Pont St. SW1 66 J3
Pont St. Ms. SW1 14 J6
Pont St. Ms. SW1 66 J3
Pontefract Rd., 87 F5
Brom.

Ponton Rd. SW8 19 J6
Ponton Rd. SW8 67 D6
Pontypool Pl. SE1 16 G3
Pool Clo., Beck. 87 A5
Pool Clo., W.Mol. 90 F5
Pool Rd., Har. 37 A7
Pool Rd., W.Mol. 90 F5
Poole Ct. Rd., 72 E2
Houns.
Vicarage Fm. Rd.
Poole Rd. E9 50 G6
Poole Rd., Epsom 99 D6
Poole St. N1 59 A1
Pooles Bldgs. EC1 8 E6
Pooles La. SW10 66 F7
Lots Rd.
Pooles La., Dag. 62 E2
Pooles Pk. N4 49 G2
Seven Sisters Rd.
Poolmans St. SE16 68 G2
Poolsford Rd. NW9 38 E4
Poonah St. E1 59 F6
Hardinge St.
Pope Clo. SW19 84 G6
Shelley Way
Pope Rd., Brom. 97 A5
Pope St. SE1 17 E4
Pope St. SE1 68 B2
Popes Ave., Twick. 82 B2
Popes Dr. N3 39 D1
Popes Gro., Croy. 102 J3
Popes Gro., Twick. 82 B2
Pope's Head All. 59 A6
EC3
Cornhill
Popes La. W5 64 G3
Popes Rd. SW9 76 G3
Popham Clo., Felt. 81 F3
Popham Rd. N1 58 J1
Popham St. N1 58 J1
Poplar Ave., Mitch. 93 J1
Poplar Ave., Orp. 104 E2
Poplar Ave., Sthl. 63 H3
Poplar Bath St. E14 60 B7
Lawless St.
Poplar Clo., Pnr. 36 D1
Poplar Ct. SW19 84 D5
Poplar Cres., Epsom 99 C6
Poplar Fm. Clo., 99 C6
Epsom
Poplar Gdns., 92 D2
N.Mal.
Poplar Gro. N11 32 A6
Poplar Gro. W6 65 J2
Poplar Gro., N.Mal. 92 D3
Poplar Gro., Wem. 47 C3
Poplar High St. E14 60 B7
Poplar Mt., Belv. 71 H4
Poplar Pl. SE28 62 C7
Poplar Pl. W2 10 A5
Poplar Pl. W2 58 E7
Poplar Pl., Hayes 54 A7
Central Ave.
Poplar Rd. SE24 76 J4
Poplar Rd. SW19 93 D2
Poplar Rd., Sutt. 100 C1
Poplar Rd. S. SW19 93 D3
Poplar St., Rom. 44 J4
Poplar Wk. SE24 76 J4
Poplar Wk., Croy. 101 J2
Poplar Way, Felt. 81 A3
Poplar Way, Ilf. 43 F4
Poplars, The N14 24 B5
Poplars Ave. NW2 47 J6
Poplars Rd. E17 42 B6
Poppins Ct. EC4 12 G4
Poppleton Rd. E11 42 E6
Poppy Clo., Wall. 101 A1
Poppy La., Croy. 95 F7
Porch Way N20 31 J3
Porchester Gdns. W2 10 B5
Porchester Gdns., 57 E7
Beck.
**Porchester Gdns. 10 B4
Ms. W2**
Porchester Mead, 87 A6
Beck.
Porchester Ms. W2 10 H4
Porchester Pl. W2 57 H6
Porchester Pl. W2 15 H3
Porchester Rd. W2 10 B3
Porchester Rd., 92 B2
Kings.T.
Porchester Sq. W2 10 B3
Porchester Sq. W2 57 E6
Porchester Ter. W2 10 C5
Porchester Ter. W2 57 F7
**Porchester Ter. N. 10 B3
W2**
Porchester Ter. N. 57 E6
W2
Porcupine Clo. SE9 88 B2
Porden Rd. SW2 76 F4

Name	Page	Grid
Porlock Ave., Har.	45	J1
Porlock Rd. W10	57	A4
Ladbroke Gro.		
Porlock Rd., Enf.	25	C7
Porlock St. SE1	17	C3
Porlock St. SE1	68	A2
Porrington Clo.,	97	D1
Chis.		
Port Cres. E13	60	H4
Jenkins Rd.		
Portal Clo. SE27	85	G3
Portal Clo., Ruis.	45	A4
Portbury Clo. SE15	77	D1
Clayton Rd.		
Portchester Clo. SE5	77	A4
Portcullis Lo. Rd.,	25	A3
Enf.		
Portelet Rd. E1	59	G3
Porten Rd. W14	66	B3
Porter Rd. E6	61	C6
Porter St. SE1	17	A1
Porter St. W1	11	A1
Porters Ave., Dag.	53	B6
Porters Wk. E1	59	E7
Pennington St.		
Portersfield Rd.,	25	B4
Enf.		
Porteus Rd. W2	10	D1
Porteus Rd. W2	57	F5
Portgate Clo. W9	57	C4
Porthcawe Rd. SE26	86	H4
Porthkerry Ave.,	80	A4
Well.		
Portia Way E3	59	J4
Portinscale Rd.	75	B5
SW15		
Portland Ave. N16	41	C7
Portland Ave.,	92	F7
N.Mal.		
Portland Ave., Sid.	80	A6
Portland Clo., Rom.	44	E5
Portland Cres. SE9	88	B2
Portland Cres.,	54	H4
Grnf.		
Portland Cres., Stan.	37	G2
Portland Gdns. N4	40	H6
Portland Gro. SW8	76	F1
Portland Ms. W1	11	G4
Portland Pl. W1	7	D6
Portland Pl. W1	58	B5
Portland Ri. N4	49	H1
Portland Ri. Est.	49	J1
N4		
Portland Rd. N15	41	C4
Portland Rd. SE9	88	B2
Portland Rd. SE25	95	D4
Portland Rd. W11	57	B7
Portland Rd., Brom.	87	J4
Portland Rd.,	91	H3
Kings.T.		
Portland Rd.,	93	H2
Mitch.		
Portland Rd., Sthl.	63	F3
Portland Sq. E1	68	E1
Vinegar St.		
Portland St. SE17	21	B3
Portland St. SE17	68	A5
Portland Ter.,	73	G4
Rich.		
Portland Wk. SE15	21	C5
Portland Wk. SE17	21	C5
Portman Ave. SW14	74	D3
Portman Clo. W1	11	A3
Portman Clo. W1	57	J6
Portman Clo., Bexh.	80	D3
Queen Anne's Gate		
Portman Dr.,	43	A2
Wdf.Grn.		
Portman Gdns. NW9	38	D2
Portman Ms. S. W1	11	B4
Portman Ms. S. W1	58	A6
Portman Pl. E2	59	F3
Portman Rd.,	91	J2
Kings.T.		
Portman Sq. W1	11	B3
Portman Sq. W1	58	A6
Portman St. W1	11	B4
Portman St. W1	58	A6
Portmeadow Wk. SE2	71	D2
Lennox Rd.		
Portmeers Clo. E17	41	J6
Lennox Rd.		
Portnall Rd. W9	57	C2
Portobello Ct. W11	57	C7
Westbourne Gro.		
Portobello Ms. W11	57	D7
Portobello Rd.		
Portobello Rd. W10	57	B5
Portobello Rd. W11	57	C6
Porton Ct., Surb.	91	F6
Portpool La. EC1	12	E1
Portpool La. EC1	58	G5
Portree Clo. N22	32	F7
Nightingale Rd.		
Portree St. E14	60	D6
Portsdown Ave.	39	C6
NW11		
Portsdown Ms.	39	C6
NW11		
Portsea Ms. W2	10	H4
Portsea Pl. W2	10	H4
Portslade Rd. SW8	76	C2
Portsmouth Ave.,	91	D7
T.Ditt.		
Portsmouth Rd.	74	H7
SW15		
Portsmouth Rd.,	91	G4
Kings.T.		
Portsmouth Rd.,	91	F6
Surb.		
Portsmouth Rd.,	98	B2
T.Ditt.		
Portsmouth St. WC2	12	C4
Portsoken St. E1	13	F5
Portsoken St. E1	59	C7
Portswood Pl. SW15	74	F7
Danebury Ave.		
Portugal Gdns.,	81	J2
Twick.		
Fulwell Pk. Ave.		
Portugal St. WC2	12	C4
Portugal St. WC2	58	F6
Portway E15	60	F1
Portway Gdns. SE18	70	A7
Shooter's Hill Rd.		
Post La., Twick.	82	A1
Post Office App. E7	61	H6
Post Office Ct. EC3	13	C4
Post Office Way SW8	19	H7
Post Office Way SW8	67	D7
Postern Grn., Enf.	24	G2
Postway Ms., Ilf.	52	E3
Clements Rd.		
Potier St. SE1	17	C6
Potier St. SE1	68	A3
Pott St. E2	59	E3
Potter Clo., Mitch.	94	B2
Potter St., Nthwd.	36	A1
Potter St., Pnr.	36	B1
Potter St. Hill, Pnr.	28	B6
Potterne Clo. SW19	75	A7
Castlecombe Dr.		
Potters Clo., Croy.	102	H1
Potters Clo., Loug.	27	B2
Potters Gro.,	92	C4
N.Mal.		
Potters Heights	28	B7
Clo., Pnr.		
Potters La. SW16	85	D6
Potters La., Barn.	23	D4
Potters La., Borwd.	22	C1
Potters Rd., Barn.	23	E4
Pottery La. W11	57	B7
Portland Rd.		
Pottery Rd., Bex.	89	J2
Pottery Rd., Brent.	64	H6
Pottery St. SE16	68	E2
Poulett Gdns.	82	C1
Twick.		
Poulett Rd. E6	61	C2
Poulner Way SE15	68	C7
Daniel Gdns.		
Poulters Wd., Kes.	104	A5
Poulton Ave., Sutt.	100	G3
Poulton Clo. E8	50	E5
Spurstowe Ter.		
Poultry EC2	13	B4
Poultry EC2	59	A6
Pound Clo., Orp.	104	G2
Pound Clo., Surb.	98	F1
Pound Ct. Dr., Orp.	104	G2
Pound La. NW10	47	G6
Pound Pk. Rd. SE7	70	A4
Pound Pl. SE9	79	D6
Pound St., Cars.	100	J5
Poundfield Rd.,	27	D5
Loug.		
Pountney Rd. SW11	76	A3
Poverest Rd., Orp.	97	J5
Powder Mill La.,	72	F7
Twick.		
Powell Clo., Edg.	29	J6
Powell Clo., Wall.	101	D7
Hermes Way		
Powell Gdns., Dag.	53	G4
Powell Rd. E5	50	E3
Powell Rd., Buck.H.	26	J7
Powell's Wk. W4	65	E6
Power Rd. W4	65	A4
Powers Ct., Twick.	73	G7
Powerscroft Rd. E5	50	F4
Powerscroft Rd.,	89	C6
Sid.		
Powis Gdns. NW11	39	C7
Powis Gdns. W11	57	C6
Powis Ms. W11	57	C6
Westbourne Pk. Rd.		
Powis Pl. WC1	8	B6
Powis Pl. WC1	58	E4
Powis Rd. E3	60	B3
Powis Sq. W11	57	C6
Powis St. SE18	70	D3
Powis Ter. W11	57	C6
Powlett Pl. NW1	49	B6
Harmood St.		
Pownall Gdns.,	72	H4
Hounsl.		
Pownall Rd. E8	59	D1
Pownall Rd., Houns.	72	H4
Powster Rd., Brom.	87	H5
Powys Clo., Bexh.	71	D6
Powys La. N13	32	E4
Powys La. N14	32	E4
Poynders Ct. SW4	76	C6
Poynders Rd.		
Poynders Gdns. SW4	76	C7
Poynders Rd. SW4	76	C6
Poynings N19	49	C3
Poynings Way N12	31	D5
Poyntell Cres., Chis.	97	G1
Poynter Rd., Enf.	25	D5
Poynton Rd. N17	41	D2
Poyntz Rd. SW11	75	J2
Poyser St. E2	59	E2
Praed Ms. W2	10	F3
Praed St. W2	10	F3
Praed St. W2	57	G6
Pragel St. E13	60	H2
Pragnell Rd. SE12	87	H2
Prague Pl. SW2	76	E5
Prah Rd. N4	49	G2
Prairie St. SW8	76	A2
Pratt Ms. NW1	58	C1
Pratt St.		
Pratt St. NW1	58	C1
Pratt Wk. SE11	20	D1
Pratt Wk. SE11	67	F4
Pratts Pas., Kings.T.	91	H2
Eden St.		
Prayle Gro. NW2	48	A1
Prebend Gdns. W4	65	F4
Prebend Gdns. W6	65	F4
Prebend St. N1	58	J1
Precinct Rd., Hayes	54	A7
Precinct, The,	93	E6
Mord.		
Green La.		
Precincts, The,	93	F5
Mord.		
Premier Cor. W9	57	C2
Kilburn La.		
Prendergast Rd. SE3	78	E3
Prentis Rd. SW16	85	D4
Prentiss Ct. SE7	70	A4
Presburg Rd.,	92	E5
N.Mal.		
Prescelly Pl., Edg.	37	J1
Prescot St. E1	13	G5
Prescot St. E1	59	C7
Prescott Ave., Orp.	104	A7
Prescott Clo. SW16	85	E7
Prescott Grn.,	27	E2
Loug.		
Prescott Ho. SE17	20	H6
Prescott Pl. SW4	76	D3
President Dr. E1	68	E1
Waterman Way		
President St. EC1	8	J3
Press Rd. NW10	47	D3
Prestbury Rd. E7	51	J7
Prestbury Sq. SE9	88	C4
Prested Rd. SW11	75	H4
St. Johns Hill		
Preston Ave. E4	34	D6
Preston Clo. SE1	21	D1
Preston Clo.,	82	B3
Twick.		
Preston Dr. E11	42	J5
Preston Dr., Bexh.	80	D1
Preston Dr., Epsom	99	E6
Preston Gdns. NW10	47	G6
Church Rd.		
Preston Gdns., Ilf.	43	B6
Preston Hill, Har.	37	H7
Preston Pl. NW2	47	G6
Preston Pl., Rich.	73	H5
Preston Rd. E11	42	G6
Preston Rd. SE19	85	H6
Preston Rd. SW20	83	F7
Preston Rd., Har.	37	H7
Preston Rd., Wem.	46	H2
Preston Waye, Har.	46	H1
Prestons Rd. E14	69	C2
Prestons Rd., Brom.	103	G3
Prestwick Clo.,	63	E5
Sthl.		
Ringway		
Prestwick Rd., Wat.	28	C1
Prestwood Ave.,	37	E4
Har.		
Prestwood Clo. SE18	71	A7
Prestwood Clo.,	37	E4
Har.		
Prestwood Gdns.,	94	J7
Croy.		
Prestwood St. N1	9	A2
Pretoria Ave. E17	41	H4
Pretoria Clo. N17	33	C7
Pretoria Rd.		
Pretoria Cres. E4	34	C1
Pretoria Rd. E4	34	C1
Pretoria Rd. E11	51	D1
Pretoria Rd. E16	60	F4
Pretoria Rd. N17	33	C7
Pretoria Rd. SW16	85	B6
Pretoria Rd., Ilf.	52	E5
Pretoria Rd. N. N18	33	C6
Prevost Rd. N11	32	A2
Price Clo. NW7	31	B6
Price Clo. SW17	84	J3
Price Rd., Croy.	101	H4
Price Way, Hmptn.	81	E6
Victors Dr.		
Price's St. SE1	16	H2
Price's St. SE1	67	H1
Pricklers Hill,	23	E6
Barn.		
Prickley Wd., Brom.	103	F1
Priddy's Yd., Croy.	101	J2
Crown Hill		
Prideaux Pl. W3	56	D7
Friars Pl. La.		
Prideaux Pl. WC1	8	D3
Prideaux Pl. WC1	58	F3
Prideaux Rd. SW9	76	E3
Pridham Rd.,	95	A4
Th.Hth.		
Priest Ct. EC2	12	J3
Priest Pk. Ave., Har.	45	G2
Priestfield Rd.	86	H3
SE23		
Priestlands Pk.	88	J3
Rd., Sid.		
Priestley Clo. N16	41	C7
Ravensdale Rd.		
Priestley Gdns.,	44	B6
Rom.		
Priestley Rd.,	94	A2
Mitch.		
Priestley Way E17	41	G3
Priestley Way NW2	47	G1
Priests Bri. SW14	74	E3
Prima Rd. SW9	20	E7
Prima Rd. SW9	67	G2
Primrose Ave., Enf.	25	A1
Primrose Ave., Rom.	44	A7
Primrose Clo. SE6	87	C5
Primrose Clo., Har.	45	F3
Primrose Clo.,	94	B7
Wall.		
Primrose Gdns. NW3	48	H6
Primrose Gdns.,	45	C5
Ruis.		
Primrose Hill EC4	12	F4
Primrose Hill Ct.	48	J7
NW3		
Primrose Hill Rd.	48	J7
NW3		
Primrose Hill	58	A1
Studios NW1		
Fitzroy Rd.		
Primrose La., Croy.	102	F1
Primrose Ms. NW1	48	J7
Sharpleshall St.		
Primrose Rd. E10	51	B1
Primrose Rd. E18	42	H2
Primrose St. EC2	13	D1
Primrose St. EC2	59	B5
Primrose Way, Wem.	55	G2
Primula St. W12	56	G6
Prince Albert Rd.	6	H2
NW1		
Prince Albert Rd.	58	A1
NW1		
Prince Albert Rd.	6	H2
NW8		
Prince Albert Rd.	57	H3
NW8		
Prince Arthur Ms.	48	F4
NW3		
Perrins La.		
Prince Arthur Rd.	48	F5
NW3		
Prince Charles Dr.	38	J7
NW4		
Prince Charles Rd.	78	F2
SE3		
Prince Charles Way,	101	B3
Wall.		

Prince Consort Dr., 97 G1
Chis.
Prince Consort Rd. 14 E5
SW7
Prince Consort Rd. 66 F3
SW7
Prince Edward Rd. 50 J6
E9
Prince George Ave. 24 C4
N14
Prince George Duke 88 G7
of Kent Ct., Chis.
Holbrook La.
Prince George Rd. 50 B4
N16
Prince George's Ave. 92 J2
SW20
Prince George's Rd. 93 G1
SW19
Prince Henry Rd. 70 A7
SE7
Prince Imperial Rd. 79 C1
SE18
Prince Imperial Rd. 88 E7
Chis.
Prince John Rd. SE9 79 B5
Prince of Orange 69 C7
La. SE10
Greenwich High Rd.
Prince of Wales 38 H4
Clo. NW4
Church Ter.
Prince of Wales Dr. 67 B7
SW8
Prince of Wales Dr. 75 H1
SW11
Prince of Wales 14 G4
Gate SW7
Prince of Wales 66 H2
Gate SW7
Prince of Wales 7 F4
Pas. NW1
Prince of Wales Rd. 60 J6
E16
Prince of Wales Rd. 49 A6
NW5
Prince of Wales Rd. 78 F1
SE3
Prince of Wales 100 G2
Rd., Sutt.
Prince of Wales 65 E5
Ter. W4
Prince of Wales 14 B4
Ter. W8
Prince Regent La. 60 H3
E13
Prince Regent La. 60 J5
E16
Prince Regent Rd., 72 J3
Houns.
Prince Rd. SE25 95 B5
Prince Rupert Rd. 79 C4
SE9
Prince St. SE8 68 J6
Princedale Rd. W11 66 B1
Princelet St. E1 13 G1
Princelet St. E1 59 C5
Prince's Arc. SW1 15 G1
Princes Ave. N3 39 D1
Princes Ave. N10 40 B3
Princes Ave. N13 32 G5
Princes Ave. N22 40 D1
Princes Ave. W3 65 A3
Princes Ave., Cars. 100 J7
Princes Ave., Grnf. 54 H6
Princes Ave., Orp. 97 H5
Princes Ave., Surb. 99 A1
Princes Ave., 34 H4
Wdf.Grn.
Princes Clo. NW9 38 A4
Princes Clo. SW4 76 C3
Old Town
Princes Clo., Edg. 30 A5
Princes Clo., Sid. 89 D3
Princes Clo., Tedd. 82 A4
Princes Ct. E1 59 E7
Princes Ct., Wem. 46 H5
Princes Dr., Har. 37 B3
Princes Gdns. SW7 14 F5
Princes Gdns. SW7 66 G3
Princes Gdns. W3 56 A5
Princes Gdns. W5 55 F4
Princes Gate SW7 14 F4
Princes Gate SW7 66 H2
Princes Gate Ct. 14 F4
SW7
Princes Gate Ms. 14 F5
SW7
Princes Gate Ms. 66 G3
SW7
Princes La. N10 40 B3
Princes Ms. W2 10 A5

Princes Ms. W2 57 D7
Hereford Rd.
Princes Pk. Ave. 39 B6
NW11
Princes Pl. SW1 15 G1
Princes Pl. W11 66 B1
Brom.
Princes Ri. SE13 78 C2
Princes Rd. N18 33 F4
Princes Rd. SE20 86 G6
Princes Rd. SW14 74 D3
Princes Rd. SW19 84 D6
Princes Rd. W13 64 E1
Broomfield Rd.
Princes Rd., Buck.H. 34 J2
Princes Rd., Ilf. 43 G4
Princes Rd., 92 A1
Kings.T.
Princes Rd., Rich. 73 J5
Princes Rd. (Kew), 73 J1
Rich.
Princes Rd., Tedd. 82 A4
Princes Sq. W2 10 A5
Princes Sq. W2 57 E7
Princes St. EC2 13 B4
Princes St. EC2 59 A6
Princes St. N17 33 B6
Queen St.
Princes St. W1 11 E4
Princes St. W1 58 B6
Princes St., Bexh. 80 F4
Princes St., Rich. 73 H5
Sheen Rd.
Princes St., Sutt. 100 G4
Princes Ter. E13 60 H1
Princes Way SW19 75 A7
Princes Way, 34 J2
Buck.H.
Princes Way, Croy. 101 F5
Princes Way, Ruis. 45 E4
Princes Way, 103 F4
W.Wick.
Princes Yd. W11 66 B1
Princedale Rd.
Princess Ave., Wem. 46 H2
Princess Ct. SE16 68 J3
Princess Cres. N4 49 H2
Princess May Rd. 50 B4
N16
Princess Ms. NW3 48 G6
Belsize Cres.
Princess Rd. NW1 58 A1
Princess Rd. NW6 57 D2
Princess Rd., Croy. 94 J6
Princess St. SE1 16 H6
Princess St. SE1 67 H3
Princesses Wk., 64 H7
Rich.
Kew Rd.
Princethorpe Ho. W2 10 A1
Princethorpe Rd. W2 57 E5
Princethorpe Rd. 86 G4
SE26
Princeton St. WC1 12 C2
Princeton St. WC1 58 F5
Pringle Gdns. SW16 85 C4
Printer St. EC4 12 F3
Printing Ho. Yd. E2 9 E4
Priolo Rd. SE7 69 J5
Prior Ave., Sutt. 100 H7
Prior Bolton St. N1 49 H6
Prior Rd., Ilf. 52 D3
Prior St. SE10 69 C7
Prioress Rd. SE27 85 H3
Prioress St. SE1 17 C6
Prioress St. SE1 68 A3
Priors Cft. E17 41 H2
Priors Fld., Nthlt. 45 E6
Arnold Rd.
Priors Gdns., Ruis. 45 C5
Priors Mead, Enf. 25 B1
Priory, The SE3 78 F4
Priory Ave. E4 33 J3
Priory Ave. E17 42 A5
Priory Ave. N8 40 D4
Priory Ave. W4 65 E4
Priory Ave., Orp. 97 G6
Priory Ave., Sutt. 100 A4
Priory Ave., Wem. 46 C4
Priory Clo. E4 33 J3
Priory Clo. E18 42 G1
Priory Clo. N3 39 C1
Church Cres.
Priory Clo. N14 24 B5
Priory Clo. N20 23 C7
Priory Clo. SW19 93 E1
High Path
Priory Clo., Beck. 95 H3
Priory Clo., Chis. 90 F1
Priory Clo., Hmptn. 90 F1
Priory Gdns.
Priory Clo., Hayes 54 B7

Priory Clo., Stan. 29 C3
Priory Clo., Sun. 81 A7
Priory Clo. 46 C4
(Sudbury), Wem.
Priory Ct. E17 41 J2
Priory Ct. SW8 76 D1
Priory Ct. 28 J1
(Bushey), Wat.
Sparrows Herne
Priory Ct. Est. E17 41 J2
Priory Cres. SE19 85 J7
Priory Cres., Sutt. 100 A4
Priory Cres., Wem. 46 D3
Priory Dr. SE2 71 D5
Priory Dr., Stan. 29 C3
Priory Fld. Dr., 30 B4
Edg.
Priory Gdns. N6 40 B6
Priory Gdns. SW13 74 F3
Priory Gdns. W4 65 E4
Priory Gdns. W5 55 H3
Hanger La.
Priory Gdns., 81 F7
Hmptn.
Priory Gdns., Wem. 46 D4
Priory Grn. Est. N1 8 D1
Priory Grn. Est. N1 58 F2
Priory Gro. SW8 76 E1
Priory Hill, Wem. 46 D4
Priory La. SW15 74 E6
Priory La., Rich. 65 A7
Forest Rd.
Priory La., W.Mol. 90 E1
Priory Ms. SW8 76 E1
Priory Pk. SE3 78 F3
Priory Pk. Rd. NW6 57 C1
Priory Pk. Rd., 46 D4
Wem.
Priory Rd. E6 61 A1
Priory Rd. N8 40 C4
Priory Rd. NW6 57 E1
Priory Rd. SW19 84 G7
Priory Rd. W4 65 D3
Priory Rd., Bark. 52 G2
Priory Rd., Chess. 98 H3
Priory Rd., Croy. 94 G7
Priory Rd., Hmptn. 81 F7
Priory Rd., Houns. 72 J5
Priory Rd., Loug. 27 B4
Priory Rd., Rich. 65 A7
Priory Rd., Sutt. 100 A4
Priory St. E3 60 B3
Leonard St.
Priory Ter. NW6 57 E1
Priory Ter., Sun. 81 A7
Priory Clo.
Priory Wk. SW10 18 D4
Priory Wk. SW10 66 F5
Priory Way, Har. 36 H4
Pritchard's Rd. E2 59 D2
Priter Rd. SE16 17 J6
Priter Rd. SE16 68 D3
Private Rd., Enf. 25 A5
Probert Rd. SW2 76 G5
Probyn Rd. SW2 85 H2
Procter St. WC1 12 C2
Procter St. WC1 58 F5
Proctors Clo., 81 A1
Felt.
Progress Business 101 F2
Pk., The, Croy.
Progress Way N22 40 G1
Progress Way, Croy. 101 F2
Progress Way, Enf. 25 D5
Promenade, The W4 74 E1
Promenade App. Rd. 65 E7
W4
Prospect Clo. SE26 86 E4
Prospect Clo., 71 G4
Belv.
Prospect Clo., 72 F1
Houns.
Prospect Clo., 36 D7
Ruis.
Prospect Cotts. 75 D4
SW18
Point Pleasant
Prospect Cres., 72 J6
Twick.
Prospect Hill E17 42 B4
Prospect Pl. E1 68 F1
Prospect Pl. N2 39 G4
Prospect Pl. N17 41 B1
Church Rd.
Prospect Pl. NW2 48 C3
Ridge Rd.
Prospect Pl. NW3 48 F4
Holly Wk.
Prospect Pl., Brom. 96 H3
Prospect Pl., Rom. 44 J2
Prospect Ring N22 39 G3
Prospect Rd. NW2 48 C3
Prospect Rd., Barn. 23 D5

Priory Clo., Surb. 91 F6
Prospect Rd., 34 J6
Wdf.Grn.
Prospect St. SE16 68 E2
Jamaica Rd.
Prospect Vale SE18 70 B4
Prospero Rd. N19 49 C1
Prothero Gdns. NW4 38 H5
Prothero Ho. NW10 47 D7
Prothero Rd. SW6 66 B7
Prout Gro. NW10 47 E4
Prout Rd. E5 50 E3
Providence Ct. W1 11 C5
Providence Ct. W1 58 A7
Providence Pl. N1 58 H1
Upper St.
Providence Pl., 44 F2
Rom.
Providence Row N1 8 C2
Providence Yd. E2 9 H3
Provident Ind. Est. 63 A2
Hayes
Provost Est. N1 9 B3
Provost Est. N1 59 A2
Provost Rd. NW3 48 J7
Provost St. N1 9 B2
Provost St. N1 59 A2
Prowse Ave. 28 J2
(Bushey), Wat.
Prowse Pl. NW1 49 B7
Bonny St.
Pruden Clo. N14 32 C2
Prudent Pas. EC2 13 B3
Prusom St. E1 68 E1
Pryors, The NW3 48 G3
Pudding La. EC3 13 C6
Pudding La. EC3 59 A7
Pudding La., Chig. 27 J6
Pudding Mill La. 60 B1
E15
Puddle Dock EC4 12 H5
Pulborough Rd. 75 C7
SW18
Pulborough Way, 72 C4
Houns.
Pulford Rd. N15 41 A6
Pulham Ave. N2 39 F4
Puller Rd., Barn. 23 B2
Pulleyns Ave. E6 61 B3
Pullman Ct. SW2 85 E1
Pullman Gdns. SW15 74 J6
Pulross Rd. SW9 76 F3
Pulteney Clo. E3 59 J1
Pulteney Rd. E18 42 H3
Pulteney Ter. N1 58 F1
Pulton Pl. SW6 66 D7
Puma Ct. E1 13 F1
Pump All., Brent. 64 G7
Pump Clo., Nthlt. 54 G2
Union Rd.
Pump Ct. EC4 12 E4
Pump Hill, Loug. 27 C2
Old Town
Pump La. SE14 68 F7
Farrow La.
Pump Pail N., Croy. 101 J3
Old Town
Pump Pail S., Croy. 101 J3
Southbridge Rd.
Pumping Sta. Rd. W4 65 E7
Pundersons Gdns. E2 59 E3
Purbeck Ave., 92 F6
N.Mal.
Purbeck Dr. NW2 48 A2
Purbrook Est. SE1 17 E4
Purbrook St. SE1 17 E5
Purcell Cres. SW6 66 A7
Purcell Rd., Grnf. 54 H5
Purcell St. N1 9 D1
Purcell St. N1 59 B2
Purcells Ave., Edg. 30 A5
Purchese St. NW1 7 J1
Purchese St. NW1 58 D2
Purdy St. E3 60 B4
Purex Rd., Grnf. 55 A1
Purland Clo., Dag. 53 F1
Purland Rd. SE28 70 J2
Purleigh Ave., 35 B6
Wdf.Grn.
Purley Ave. NW2 48 B2
Purley Clo., Ilf. 43 D2
Purley Pl. N1 49 H7
Islington Pk. St.
Purley Rd. N9 33 A3
Purley Rd., S.Croy. 102 A3
Purley Way, Croy. 94 F7
Purneys Rd. SE9 79 A4
Purrett Rd. SE18 70 J5
Purser's Cross Rd. 75 C1
SW6
Pursewardens Clo. 64 F1
W13
Pursley Rd. NW7 30 H7
Purves Rd. NW10 56 H2

Puteaux Ho. E2 59 G2
  Mace St.
Putney Bri. SW6 75 B3
Putney Bri. SW15 75 B3
Putney Bri. App. 75 B3
  CME
Putney Bri. Rd. 75 B4
  SW15
Putney Dri. Rd 75 D5
  SW18
Putney Common 74 J3
  SW15
Putney Heath SW15 74 H7
Putney Heath La. 75 A6
  SW15
Putney High St. 75 A4
  SW15
Putney Hill SW15 75 A6
Putney Pk. Ave. 74 G4
  SW15
Putney Pk. La. SW15 74 H4
Puttenham Clo., 28 D2
  Wat.
Pycroft Way N9 33 D3
Pyecombe Cor. N12 31 C4
Pylbrook Rd., Sutt. 100 D3
Pylon Way, Croy. 101 E1
Pym Clo., Barn. 23 G5
Pymers Mead SE21 85 J1
Pymmes Clo. N13 32 F5
Pymmes Clo. N17 41 E1
Pymmes Gdns. N. N9 33 C3
Pymmes Gdns. S. N9 33 C3
Pymmes Grn. Rd. N11 32 B4
Pymmes Rd. N13 32 E6
Pymms Brook Dr., 23 H4
  Barn.
Pyne Rd., Surb. 99 A1
Pynham Clo. SE2 71 B3
Pynnacles Clo., 29 E5
  Stan.
Pyrland Rd. N5 50 A5
Pyrland Rd., Rich. 73 J6
Pyrles Grn., Loug. 27 E1
Pyrles La., Loug. 27 E2
Pyrmont Gro. SE27 85 H3
Pyrmont Rd. W4 65 A6
Pytchley Cres. SE19 85 J6
Pytchley Rd. SE22 77 B3

Q

Quadrant, The SE24 76 J5
  Herne Hill
Quadrant, The SW20 93 B1
Quadrant, The, Bexh. 71 D7
Quadrant, The, 73 H4
  Rich.
Quadrant, The, 100 F6
  Sutt.
Quadrant Arc. W1 11 G6
Quadrant Gro. NW5 48 J5
Quadrant Rd., Rich. 73 G4
Quadrant Rd., 94 H4
  Th.Hth.
Quaggy Wk. SE3 78 G4
Quainton St. NW10 47 D3
Quaker La., Sthl. 63 G3
Quaker St. E1 9 F6
Quaker St. E1 59 C4
Quakers Course NW9 38 F1
Quakers La., Islw. 73 D1
Quakers Wk. N21 25 A6
Quality Ct. WC2 12 E3
Quantock Dr., 99 J2
  Wor.Pk.
  Cotswold Way
Quantock Gdns. NW2 48 A2
Quarley Way SE15 21 F7
Quarr Rd., Cars. 93 G6
Quarrendon St. SW6 75 D2
Quarry Pk. Rd., 100 C6
  Sutt.
Quarry Ri., Sutt. 100 C6
Quarry Rd. SW18 75 F6
Quarter Mile La. 51 B4
  E10
Quarterdeck, The 69 A2
  E14
Quay W., Tedd. 82 E5
Quebec Ms. W1 11 A4
Quebec Rd., Hayes 54 C7
Quebec Rd., Ilf. 43 E7
Quebec Way SE16 68 G2
Queen Adelaide Rd. 86 F6
  SE20
Queen Alexandra's 84 C5
  Ct. SW19
Queen Anne Ave. 41 C5
  N15
  Suffield Rd.
Queen Anne Ave., 96 F3
  Brom.

Puteaux Ho. E2 98 B7
Queen Anne Clo.,
  Esher
Queen Anne Ms. W1 11 E2
Queen Anne Rd. E9 50 G6
Queen Anne St. W1 11 D3
Queen Anne St, W1 58 B5
  Twick.
Queen Anne's Gdns. 65 E3
  W4
Queen Annes Gdns. 64 H2
  W5
Queen Annes Gdns., 25 B6
  Enf.
Queen Anne's Gdns., 93 J3
  Mitch.
Queen Anne's Gate 15 H4
  SW1
Queen Anne's Gate 67 D2
  SW1
Queen Anne's Gate, 80 D3
  Bexh.
Queen Annes Gro. 65 E3
  W4
Queen Annes Gro. 64 H2
  W5
Queen Annes Gro., 25 A7
  Enf.
Queen Annes Pl., 25 B6
  Enf.
Queen Anne's Wk. 8 B6
  WC1
Queen Caroline Est. 65 J5
  W6
Queen Caroline St. 65 J5
  W6
Queen Elizabeth 93 D4
  Gdns., Mord.
Queen Elizabeth Rd. 41 H3
  E17
Queen Elizabeth 91 J2
  Rd., Kings.T.
Queen Elizabeth St. 17 F3
  SE1
Queen Elizabeth St. 68 C2
  SE1
Queen Elizabeth Wk. 74 G1
  SW13
Queen Elizabeth 101 D4
  Wk., Wall.
Queen Elizabeths 50 A2
  Clo. N16
Queen Elizabeths 32 D1
  Dr. N14
Queen Elizabeths 50 A2
  Wk. N16
Queen Margarets 50 B5
  Gro. N1
Queen Mary Ave., 93 A5
  Mord.
Queen Mary Rd. 85 H6
  SE19
Queen Mary's Ave., 100 J7
  Cars.
Queen of Denmark 68 J3
  Ct. SE16
Queen Sq. WC1 12 B1
Queen Sq. WC1 58 E4
Queen Sq. Pl. WC1 8 B6
Queen St. EC4 13 A5
Queen St. EC4 58 J7
Queen St. N17 50 C2
Queen St. W1 15 D1
Queen St. W1 67 B1
Queen St., Bexh. 80 F3
Queen St., Croy. 101 J3
  Church Rd.
Queen St. Pl. EC4 13 A6
Queen Victoria 46 G7
  Ave., Wem.
Queen Victoria St. 12 H5
  EC4
Queen Victoria St. 58 H7
  EC4
Queenborough 88 G6
  Gdns., Chis.
Queenborough 43 D4
  Gdns., Ilf.
Queenhithe EC4 13 A5
Queenhithe EC4 58 J7
Queens Acre, Sutt. 100 A7
Queens Ave. N3 31 F7
Queens Ave. N10 40 A3
Queens Ave. N20 31 G2
Queen's Ave. N21 32 H1
Queens Ave., Felt. 81 C4
Queens Ave., Grnf. 54 H6
Queens Ave., Stan. 37 E3
Queens Ave., 34 H5
  Wdf.Grn.
Queen's Circ. SW8 67 B7
  Queenstown Rd.
Queens Clo., Edg. 30 A5

Queens Clo., Wall. 101 B5
  Queens Rd.
Queens Club Gdns. 66 B6
  W14
Queens Ct. SE23 86 F2
Queens Ct., Rich. 73 J6
Queens Cres. NW5 48 B6
Queens Cres., Rich. 73 J5
Queens Dr. E10 42 A7
Queens Dr. N4 48 H2
Queens Dr. W3 55 J6
Queens Dr., Surb. 92 A7
Queens Dr., T.Ditt. 91 D7
Queen's Elm Sq. 18 F4
  SW3
Queens Gdns. NW4 38 J5
Queens Gdns. W2 10 C5
Queens Gdns. W2 57 F6
Queens Gdns. W5 55 F5
Queen's Gdns., 72 E1
  Houns.
Queen's Gate SW7 14 D4
Queen's Gate SW7 66 F3
Queen's Gate Gdns. 14 D6
  SW7
Queens Gate Gdns. 66 F3
  SW7
Queens Gate Gdns. 74 H4
  SW15
  Upper Richmond Rd.
Queen's Gate Ms. 14 D4
  SW7
Queen's Gate Ms. 66 F3
  SW7
Queen's Gate Pl. 14 D6
  SW7
Queen's Gate Pl. 66 F3
  SW7
Queen's Gate Pl. 14 D6
  Ms. SW7
Queen's Gate Pl. 66 F3
  Ms. SW7
Queen's Gate Ter. 14 C5
  SW7
Queen's Gate Ter. 66 F3
  SW7
Queen's Gro. NW8 57 G1
Queen's Gro. Ms. 57 G1
  NW8
  Queen's Gro.
Queens Gro. Rd. E4 34 D1
Queens Head Yd. SE1 17 B2
Queens Ho., Tedd. 82 C6
Queens La. N10 40 B3
Queens Mkt. E13 60 J1
  Green St.
Queens Ms. W2 10 A5
Queens Par. N11 31 J5
  Colney Hatch La.
Queen's Par. W5 55 J6
Queen's Pk. Ct. W10 57 A3
Queens Pk. Gdns., 81 A3
  Felt.
  Vernon Rd.
Queens Pas., Chis. 88 E6
  High St.
Queens Pl., Mord. 93 D4
Queen's Prom., 91 G3
  Kings.T.
  Portsmouth Rd.
Queens Reach, 91 B4
  E.Mol.
Queen's Ride SW13 74 G3
Queen's Ride, Rich. 83 B1
Queens Ri., Rich. 73 J6
Queens Rd. E11 42 D7
Queens Rd. E13 60 H1
Queen's Rd. E17 41 J6
Queens Rd. N3 39 F1
Queens Rd. N9 33 E3
Queen's Rd. N11 32 E7
Queens Rd. NW4 38 J5
Queens Rd. SE14 77 E1
Queens Rd. SE15 77 E1
Queens Rd. SW14 74 D3
Queens Rd. SW19 84 C6
Queens Rd. W5 55 H6
Queens Rd., Bark. 52 F6
Queens Rd., Barn. 23 A3
Queens Rd., Beck. 95 H2
Queens Rd., Brom. 96 G2
Queens Rd., Buck.H. 34 J2
Queens Rd., Chis. 88 E6
Queens Rd., Croy. 94 H6
Queens Rd., Enf. 25 B4
Queens Rd., Felt. 81 B1
Queens Rd., Hmptn. 81 H6
Queens Rd., Houns. 72 H3
Queens Rd., Ilf. 52 F6
Queens Rd., 83 A7
  Kings.T.
Queens Rd., Loug. 27 B3

Queens Rd., Mitch. 93 G2
Queens Rd., Mord. 93 D4
Queens Rd., N.Mal. 92 F4
Queens Rd., Rich. 73 J6
Queens Rd., Sthl. 63 D2
Queens Rd., Tedd. 82 B6
Queens Rd., Twick. 73 G1
Queens Rd., Wall. 101 B5
Queen's Rd., Well. 98 B3
Queen's Row SE17 21 B5
Queen's Row SE17 68 A6
Queens Ter. E13 60 H1
Queens Ter. NW8 57 G1
Queens Ter., Islw. 73 D4
Queens Ter. Cotts. 64 B2
  W7
  Boston Rd.
Queens Wk. E4 34 D1
  The Grn. Wk.
Queens Wk. NW9 47 C2
Queen's Wk. SW1 15 F2
Queen's Wk. SW1 67 C1
Queens Wk. W5 55 F4
Queens Wk., Har. 37 B4
Queens Wk., Ruis. 45 D3
Queens Way NW4 38 J5
Queens Way, Felt. 81 C4
Queens Well Ave. 31 H4
  N20
Queen's Wd. Rd. N10 40 B6
Queens Yd. WC1 7 G6
Queensberry Ms. W. 18 E1
  SW7
Queensberry Pl. SW7 18 E1
Queensberry Pl. SW7 66 G4
Queensberry Way 18 E1
  SW7
Queensborough Ms. 10 C5
  W2
Queensborough Pas. 10 C5
  W2
Queensborough 10 C5
  Studios W2
Queensborough Ter. 10 B5
  W2
Queensborough Ter. 57 E7
  W2
Queensbridge Pk., 73 B5
  Islw.
Queensbridge Rd. E2 9 G2
Queensbridge Rd. E2 50 C7
Queensbridge Rd. E8 50 C7
Queensbury Rd. NW9 38 D7
Queensbury Rd., 55 J2
  Wem.
Queensbury Sta. 37 J3
  Par., Edg.
Queensbury St. N1 49 J7
Queenscourt, Wem. 46 H4
Queenscroft Rd. SE9 79 A6
Queensdale Cres. 66 A1
  W11
Queensdale Pl. W11 66 B1
Queensdale Rd. W11 66 A1
Queensdale Wk. W11 66 B1
Queensdown Rd. E5 50 E4
Queensgate Gdns., 97 G1
  Chis.
Queensgate Pl. NW6 48 D7
Queensland Ave. N18 32 J4
Queensland Ave. 93 E1
  SW19
Queensland Pl. N7 49 G4
  Queensland Rd.
Queensland Rd. N7 49 G4
Queensmead NW8 57 G1
Queensmead Rd., 96 F2
  Brom.
Queensmere Clo. 84 A2
  SW19
Queensmere Rd. 84 A2
  SW19
Queensmill Rd. SW6 66 A7
Queensthorpe Rd. 86 G4
  SE26
Queenstown Rd. 19 D6
  SW8
Queenstown Rd. 67 B6
  SW8
Queensville Rd. 76 D7
  SW12
Queensway W2 10 B4
Queensway W2 57 E6
Queensway, Croy. 101 F6
Queensway, Enf. 25 E4
Queensway, Orp. 97 F5
Queensway, Sun. 90 B2
Queensway, 103 E3
  W.Wick.
Queenswood Ave. 42 C1
  E17

Queenswood Ave., 81 H6
Hmptn.
Queenswood Ave., 72 F2
Houns.
Queenswood Ave., 94 G5
Th.Hth.
Queenswood Ave., 101 D4
Wall.
Queenswood Gdns. 51 H1
E11
Queenswood Pk. N3 39 B2
Queenswood Rd. 86 G3
SE23
Queenswood Rd., 79 J5
Sid.
Quemerford Rd. N7 49 F5
Quentin Pl. SE13 78 E3
Quentin Rd. SE13 78 E3
Quernmore Clo., 87 G6
Brom.
Quernmore Rd. N4 40 G6
Quernmore Rd., 87 G6
Brom.
Querrin St. SW6 75 F2
Quex Ms. NW6 57 D1
Quex Rd.
Quex Rd. NW6 57 D1
Quick Rd. W4 65 E5
Quick St. N1 8 H2
Quick St. N1 58 H2
Quicks Rd. SW19 84 E7
Quickswood NW3 48 H7
King Henry's Rd.
Quiet Nook, Kes. 104 A3
Croydon Rd.
Quill La. SW15 75 A4
Quilp St. SE1 16 J3
Quilter St. E2 9 H3
Quilter St. E2 59 D3
Quinta Dr., Barn. 22 H5
Quintin Ave. SW20 93 C1
Quinton Clo., Beck. 96 C3
Quinton Clo., Wall. 101 B4
Quinton Rd., 98 D1
T.Ditt.
Quinton St. SW18 84 F2
Quixley St. E14 60 D7
Quorn Rd. SE22 77 B4

R

Rabbit Row W8 66 D1
Kensington Mall
Rabbits Rd. E12 52 B4
Rabournmead Dr., 45 E5
Nthlt.
Raby Rd., N.Mal. 92 D4
Raby St. E14 59 H6
Salmon La.
Raccoon Way, Houns. 72 C2
Rachel Pt. E5 50 D4
Muir Rd.
Rackham Ms. SW16 85 C6
Westcote Rd.
Racton Rd. SW6 66 D6
Radbourne Ave. W5 64 F4
Radbourne Clo. E5 50 G4
Overbury St.
Radbourne Cres. E17 42 D2
Radbourne Rd. SW12 76 C7
Radcliffe Ave. NW10 56 G2
Radcliffe Ave., Enf. 24 J1
Radcliffe Gdns., 100 H7
Cars.
Radcliffe Rd. N21 32 H1
Radcliffe Rd., 102 C2
Croy.
Radcliffe Rd., Har. 37 D2
Radcliffe Sq. SW15 75 A6
Radcliffe Way, 54 D3
Nthlt.
Radcot Pt. SE23 86 G3
Radcot St. SE11 20 F4
Raddington Rd. W10 57 B5
Radfield Way, Sid. 79 G7
Radford Rd. SE13 78 C5
Radford Way, Bark. 61 J3
Radipole Rd. SW6 75 C1
Radland Rd. E16 60 F6
Radlet Ave. SE26 86 E3
Radlett Clo. E7 51 F6
Radlett Pl. NW8 57 H1
Radley Ave., Ilf. 52 J4
Radley Ct. SE16 68 G2
Thame Rd.
Radley Gdns., Har. 37 H4
Radley Ms. W8 66 D3
Radley Rd. N17 41 B2
Radleys La. E18 42 G2
Radleys Mead, Dag. 53 H6
Radlix Rd. E10 51 A1
Radnor Ave., Har. 37 B5
Radnor Ave., Well. 80 B5

Radnor Clo., Chis. 88 H6
Homewood Cres.
Radnor Clo., Mitch. 94 E4
Radnor Cres. SE18 71 A7
Radnor Cres., Ilf. 43 C5
Radnor Gdns., Enf. 25 B1
Radnor Gdns., 82 C2
Twick.
Radnor Ms. W2 10 F4
Radnor Pl. W2 10 G4
Radnor Pl. W2 57 H6
Radnor Rd. NW6 57 B1
Radnor Rd. SE15 21 H7
Radnor Rd. SE15 68 D7
Radnor Rd., Har. 37 A5
Radnor Rd., Twick. 82 C1
Radnor St. EC1 9 A4
Radnor St. EC1 58 J3
Radnor Ter. W14 66 C4
Radnor Wk. E14 69 A4
Barnsdale Ave.
Radnor Wk. SW3 18 H4
Radnor Wk. SW3 66 H5
Radnor Wk., Croy. 95 H6
Radnor Way NW10 56 B4
Radstock Ave., Har. 37 D3
Radstock St. SW11 66 H7
Raeburn Gdns., 22 H5
Barn.
Raeburn Ave., Surb. 99 B1
Raeburn Clo. NW11 59 J5
Raeburn Clo., 82 G7
Kings.T.
Raeburn Rd., Edg. 38 A2
Raeburn Rd., Sid. 79 H6
Raeburn Rd. SW2 76 E4
Rafford Way, Brom. 96 H2
Raft Rd. SW18 75 D4
North Pas.
Raggleswood, Chis. 97 D1
Raglan Clo., Houns. 72 E5
Vickers Way
Raglan Ct. SE12 78 G5
Raglan Ct., S.Croy. 101 H5
Raglan Ct., Wem. 46 J4
Raglan Gdns., Wat. 28 B1
Raglan Rd. E17 42 C5
Raglan Rd. SE18 70 F5
Raglan Rd., Belv. 71 F5
Raglan Rd., Brom. 96 J4
Raglan Rd., Enf. 25 B7
Raglan St. NW5 49 B6
Raglan Ter., Har. 45 H4
Raglan Way, Nthlt. 45 J4
Ragley Clo. W3 65 C2
Avenue Rd.
Raider Clo., Rom. 44 G1
Railey Ms. NW5 49 C5
Railshead Rd., 73 E4
Twick.
Railton Rd. SE24 76 G4
Railway App. SE1 17 C2
Railway App. SE1 68 A1
Railway App., Har. 37 C4
Railway App., 73 D7
Twick.
Railway App., Wall. 101 B6
Railway Ave. SE16 68 F2
Railway Ms. E3 60 A3
Wellington Way
Railway Ms. W10 57 B6
Ladbroke Gro.
Railway Pas., Tedd. 82 D6
Victoria Rd.
Railway Pl., Belv. 71 G3
Railway Ri. SE22 77 B4
Grove Vale
Railway Rd., Tedd. 82 C4
Railway Side SW13 74 E3
Railway St. N1 8 B2
Railway St. N1 58 E2
Railway St., Rom. 53 C1
Railway Ter. SE13 78 B5
Ladywell Rd.
Railway Ter., Felt. 81 A1
Rainborough Clo. 47 C6
NW10
Rainbow Ave. E14 69 B5
Rainbow St. SE5 20 D1
Rainbow St. SE5 68 B7
Raine St. E1 68 E7
Rainham Clo. SE9 79 G6
Rainham Clo. SW11 75 H6
Rainham Rd. NW10 56 J3
Rainham Rd. N., 53 H3
Dag.
Rainham Rd. S., 53 H4
Dag.
Rainhill Way E3 60 A3
Rainsborough Ave. 68 H4
SE8
Rainsford Clo., 29 F5
Stan.

Rainsford Rd. NW10 56 B2
Rainsford St. W2 10 G3
Rainton Rd. SE7 69 G5
Rainville Rd. W6 65 J6
Raisins Hill, Pnr. 36 C3
Raith Ave. N14 32 D3
Raleana Rd. E14 69 C1
Raleigh Ave., Hayes 54 B5
Raleigh Ave., Wall. 101 D4
Raleigh Clo. NW4 38 J5
Raleigh Clo., Pnr. 36 D7
Raleigh Ct., Wall. 101 B6
Raleigh Dr. N20 31 H3
Raleigh Dr., Esher 98 A5
Raleigh Dr., Surb. 99 C1
Raleigh Gdns. SW2 76 F6
Brixton Hill
Raleigh Gdns., 93 J3
Mitch.
Raleigh Ms., Orp. 104 J5
Osgood Ave.
Raleigh Rd. N8 40 G4
Raleigh Rd. SE20 86 G7
Raleigh Rd., Enf. 25 A4
Raleigh Rd., Rich. 73 J3
Raleigh Rd., Sthl. 63 E5
Raleigh St. N1 58 H1
Raleigh Way N14 32 D1
Raleigh Way, Felt. 81 C4
Ralph Ct. W2 10 B3
Ralph Perring Ct., 96 A4
Beck.
Ralston St. SW3 18 J4
Ralston Way, Wat. 28 D2
Ram Pas., Kings.T. 91 G2
High St.
Ram Pl. E9 50 F6
Chatham Pl.
Ram St. SW18 75 E5
Rama Ct., Har. 46 B2
Ramac Ind. Est. SE7 69 G5
Ramac Way SE7 69 H5
Rambler Clo. SW16 85 C4
Ramillies Clo. SW2 76 E6
Ramillies Pl. W1 11 F4
Ramillies Rd. NW7 30 E2
Ramillies Rd. W4 65 D4
Ramillies Rd., Sid. 80 B6
Ramillies St. W1 11 F4
Rampart St. E1 59 E6
Commercial Rd.
Rampayne St. SW1 19 H3
Rampayne St. SW1 67 D5
Rampton Clo. E4 34 A3
Rams Gro., Rom. 44 E4
Ramsay Pl., Har. 46 B1
West St.
Ramsay Rd. E7 51 E4
Ramsay Rd. W3 65 C3
Ramscroft Clo. N9 25 B7
Ramsdale Rd. SW17 85 A5
Ramsden Rd. N11 31 J5
Ramsden Rd. SW12 76 A6
Ramsey Clo. NW9 38 F6
West Hendon Bdy.
Ramsey Clo., Grnf. 46 A5
Ramsey Ho., Wem. 46 H6
Ramsey Rd., Th.Hth. 94 F6
Ramsey St. E2 9 J5
Ramsey St. E2 59 D4
Ramsey Wk. N1 50 A6
Marquess Est.
Ramsey Way N14 24 C7
Ramsgate St. E8 50 C6
Dalston La.
Ramsgill App., Ilf. 43 J4
Ramsgill Dr., Ilf. 43 J5
Ramulis Dr., Hayes 54 D4
Ramus Wd. Ave., 104 H5
Orp.
Rancliffe Gdns. SE9 79 B4
Rancliffe Rd. E6 61 B2
Randall Ave. NW2 47 E2
Randall Clo. SW11 75 H1
Randall Clo., Erith 71 J6
Randall Pl. SE10 69 C7
Randall Rd. SE11 20 C2
Randall Rd. SE11 67 F5
Randall Row SE11 20 C2
Randell's Rd. N1 58 E1
Randle Rd., Rich. 82 F4
Randlesdown Rd. 86 A4
SE6
Randolph App. E16 60 J6
Baxter Rd.
Randolph Ave. W9 6 A2
Randolph Ave. W9 57 E2
Randolph Clo., 80 J3
Bexh.
Randolph Clo., 83 C5
Kings.T.
Randolph Cres. W9 6 C6

Randolph Cres. W9 57 F4
Randolph Gdns. NW6 6 A2
Randolph Gdns. NW6 57 F2
Randolph Gro., Rom. 44 C5
Donald Dr.
Randolph Ho., Croy. 101 J1
Randolph Ms. W9 6 D6
Randolph Ms. W9 57 F4
Randolph Rd. E17 42 B5
Randolph Rd. W9 6 C6
Randolph Rd. W9 57 F4
Randolph Rd., Sthl. 63 F2
Randolph St. NW1 49 C7
Randon Clo., Har. 36 H2
Ranelagh Ave. SW6 75 C3
Ranelagh Ave. SW13 74 G2
Ranelagh Clo., Edg. 30 A4
Ranelagh Dr., Edg. 30 A4
Ranelagh Dr., 73 E2
Twick.
Ranelagh Gdns. E11 42 J5
Ranelagh Gdns. SW6 75 C3
Ranelagh Gdns. W4 65 C3
Grove Pk. Gdns.
Ranelagh Gdns. W6 65 F3
Ranelagh Gdns., 52 C1
Ilf.
Ranelagh Gro. SW1 19 C3
Ranelagh Gro. SW1 67 A5
Ranelagh Ms. W5 64 G2
Ranelagh Rd.
Ranelagh Pl., 92 E5
N.Mal.
Rodney Rd.
Ranelagh Rd. E6 61 D1
Ranelagh Rd. E11 51 E4
Ranelagh Rd. E15 60 E1
Ranelagh Rd. N17 41 B3
Ranelagh Rd. N22 40 F1
Ranelagh Rd. NW10 56 F2
Ranelagh Rd. SW1 19 G4
Ranelagh Rd. W5 64 G2
Ranelagh Rd., Sthl. 63 D1
Ranelagh Rd., Wem. 46 G6
Ranfurly Rd., Sutt. 100 D2
Rangefield Rd., 87 E5
Brom.
Rangemoor Rd. N15 41 C5
Rangers Rd. E4 26 E7
Rangers Rd., Loug. 26 G7
Rangers Sq. SE10 78 D1
Rangeworth Pl., 88 J3
Sid.
Priestlands Pk. Rd.
Rankin Clo. NW9 38 E3
Ranleigh Gdns., 71 F7
Bexh.
Ranmere St. SW12 85 B1
Ormeley Rd.
Ranmoor Clo., Har. 37 A4
Ranmoor Gdns., Har. 37 A4
Ranmore Ave., Croy. 102 C3
Rannoch Rd. W6 65 J6
Rannock Ave. NW9 38 D7
Ranskill Rd., 22 A1
Borwd.
Ransom Rd. SE7 69 J5
Harvey Gdns.
Ransom Wk. SE7 69 J5
Woolwich Rd.
Ranston St. NW1 10 G1
Ranulf Rd. NW2 48 C4
Ranwell Clo. E3 59 J1
Beale Rd.
Ranwell St. E3 59 J1
Ranworth Rd. N9 33 F2
Ranyard Clo., 98 J3
Chess.
Raphael St. SW7 11 J4
Raphael St. SW7 66 J2
Rashleigh St. SW8 76 B2
Peardon St.
Rasper Rd. N20 31 F2
Rastell Ave. SW2 85 D2
Ratcliff Rd. E7 51 J5
Ratcliffe Cross St. 59 G6
E1
Ratcliffe La. E14 59 H6
Ratcliffe Orchard E1 59 G7
Rathbone Mkt. E16 60 F5
Barking Rd.
Rathbone Pl. W1 11 H2
Rathbone Pl. W1 58 D5
Rathbone Pt. E5 50 D4
Nolan Way
Rathbone St. E16 60 F5
Rathbone St. W1 11 G2
Rathbone St. W1 58 C5
Rathcoole Ave. N8 40 F5
Rathcoole Gdns. N8 40 F5
Rathfern Rd. SE6 86 F1
Rathgar Ave. W13 64 E1
Rathgar Clo. N3 39 C2

Rathgar Rd. SW9 76 H3
Coldharbour La.
Rathlin Wk. N1 49 J6
Marquess Est.
Rathmell Dr. SW4 76 D6
Rathmore Rd. SE7 69 H5
Halliway Rd. SW1 71 B1
Raul Rd. SE15 77 D1
Raunley St. NW5 49 C4
Raven Clo. NW9 38 E2
Eagle Dr.
Raven Ct. E5 50 D3
Stellman Clo.
Raven Rd. E18 42 J2
Raven Row E1 59 E5
Ravenet St. SW11 76 B1
Strasburg Rd.
Ravenfield Rd. SW17 84 J3
Ravenhill Rd. E13 60 J2
Ravenna Rd. SW5 75 A5
Ravenor Pk. Rd., 54 H3
Grnf.
Ravens Clo., Brom. 96 F2
Ravens Clo., Enf. 25 B2
Ravens Ms. SE12 78 G5
Ravens Way
Ravens Way SE12 78 G5
Ravensbourne Ave., 87 D7
Brom.
Ravensbourne Gdns. 55 E5
W13
Ravensbourne Gdns., 43 D1
Ilf.
Ravensbourne Pk. 78 A7
SE6
Ravensbourne Pk. 77 J7
Cres. SE6
Ravensbourne Pl. 78 B2
SE13
Ravensbourne Rd. 86 J1
SE6
Ravensbourne Rd., 96 G3
Brom.
Ravensbourne Rd., 73 F6
Twick.
Ravensbury Ave., 93 F5
Mord.
Ravensbury Gro., 93 G4
Mitch.
Ravensbury La., 93 G4
Mitch.
Ravensbury Path, 93 G4
Mitch.
Ravensbury Rd. 84 D2
SW18
Ravensbury Rd. 97 J3
Orp.
Ravensbury Ter. 84 E1
SW18
Ravenscar Rd., 87 E4
Brom.
Ravenscar Rd., 98 J2
Surb.
Ravenscourt Ave. W6 65 G4
Ravenscourt Gdns. 65 G4
W6
Ravenscourt Pk. W6 65 G3
Ravenscourt Pl. W6 65 H4
Ravenscourt Rd. W6 65 H4
Ravenscourt Sq. W6 65 G3
Ravenscraig Rd. N11 32 B4
Ravenscroft Ave. 39 C7
NW11
Ravenscroft Ave., 46 H1
Wem.
Ravenscroft Clo. 60 G5
E16
Ravenscroft Cres. 88 C3
SE9
Ravenscroft Pk. 23 A4
Barn.
Ravenscroft Rd. E16 60 G5
Ravenscroft Rd. W4 65 C4
Ravenscroft Rd., 95 F2
Beck.
Ravenscroft St. E2 9 G2
Ravenscroft St. E2 59 C2
Ravensdale Ave. N12 31 F4
Ravensdale Gdns. 86 A7
SE19
Ravensdale Rd. N16 41 C7
Ravensdale Rd., 72 E3
Houns.
Ravensdon St. SE11 20 F4
Ravensdon St. SE11 67 G5
Ravensfield Clo., 53 D4
Dag.
Ravensfield Gdns., 99 E5
Epsom
Ravenshaw St. NW6 48 C5
Ravenshill, Chis. 97 E1
Ravenshurst Ave. 38 J4
NW4

Ravenside Clo. N18 33 G5
Ravenslea Rd. SW12 75 J7
Ravensmead Rd., 87 D7
Brom.
Ravensmede Way 65 F4
W4
Ravenstone SE17 21 F4
Ravenstone Rd. N8 40 G3
Ravenstone Rd. NW9 38 F6
West Hendon Bdy.
Ravenstone St. 85 A1
SW12
Ravenswood, Bex. 89 E1
Ravenswood Ave., 98 J2
Surb.
Ravenswood Ave., 103 C1
W.Wick.
Ravenswood Ct., 83 B6
Kings.T.
Ravenswood Cres., 45 F2
Har.
Ravenswood Cres., 103 C1
W.Wick.
Ravenswood Gdns., 73 B1
Islw.
Ravenswood Pk., 28 A6
Nthwd.
Ravenswood Rd. E17 42 C4
Ravenswood Rd. 76 B7
SW12
Ravenswood Rd., 101 H3
Croy.
Ravensworth Rd. 56 H3
NW10
Ravensworth Rd. 88 C3
SE9
Ravent Rd. SE11 20 D1
Ravent Rd. SE11 67 F4
Ravey St. EC2 9 D5
Ravine Gro. SE18 70 H6
Rawlings Clo., Orp. 104 J5
Rawlings St. SW3 18 J1
Rawlings St. SW3 66 J4
Rawlins Clo. N3 39 B3
Rawlins Clo., 102 H7
S.Croy.
Rawnsley Ave., 93 G5
Mitch.
Rawreth Wk. N1 58 J1
Basire St.
Rawson St. SW11 76 A1
Strasburg Rd.
Rawsthorne Clo. E16 70 C1
Kennard St.
Rawstone Wk. E13 60 G2
Grasmere Rd.
Rawstorne Pl. EC1 8 G3
Rawstorne St. EC1 8 G3
Rawstorne St. EC1 58 H3
Ray Gdns., Bark. 62 A2
Ray Gdns., Stan. 29 E5
Ray Lo. Rd., 34 J6
Wdf.Grn.
Ray Rd., W.Mol. 90 H5
Ray St. EC1 8 F6
Ray St. Bri. EC1 8 F6
Ray Wk. N7 49 F2
Andover Rd.
Raydean Rd., Barn. 23 E5
Raydon St. N19 49 B2
Raydons Gdns., Dag. 53 E5
Raydons Rd., Dag. 53 E5
Rayfield Clo., 97 B6
Brom.
Rayford Ave. SE12 78 F7
Rayleas Clo. SE18 79 E1
Rayleigh Ave., 82 B6
Tedd.
Rayleigh Clo. N13 33 A3
Rayleigh Rd.
Rayleigh Ct., 91 J2
Kings.T.
Rayleigh Ri., 102 B6
S.Croy.
Rayleigh Rd. N13 32 J3
Rayleigh Rd. SW19 93 J1
Rayleigh Rd., 34 J6
Wdf.Grn.
Raymead NW4 38 J4
Raymead Ave., 94 G5
Th.Hth.
Raymere Gdns. SE18 70 G7
Raymond Ave. E18 42 F3
Raymond Ave. W13 64 D3
Raymond Bldgs. 12 D1
WC1
Raymond Clo. SE26 86 F5
Raymond Rd. E13 51 J7
Raymond Rd. SW19 34 B6
Raymond Rd., Beck. 95 H4
Raymond Rd., Ilf. 43 G7
Raymond Way, Esher 98 D6

Raymouth Rd. SE16 68 E4
Rayne Ct. E18 42 F4
Rayner Twr. E10 42 A7
Rayners Clo., Wem. 46 G5
Rayner Ct., Har. 45 G1
Rayners Cres., 54 B3
Nthlt.
Rayners Gdns., 54 DE
Nthlt.
Rayners La., Har. 45 G1
Rayners La., Pnr. 36 F5
Rayners Rd. SW15 75 B5
Raynes Ave. E11 42 J7
Raynham Ave. N18 33 D6
Raynham Rd. N18 33 D5
Raynham Rd. W6 65 H4
Raynham Ter. N18 33 D5
Raynor Clo., Sthl. 63 F1
Raynor Pl. N1 58 J1
Elizabeth Ave.
Raynton Clo., Har. 45 E1
Rays Ave. N18 33 F4
Rays Rd. N18 33 F4
Rays Rd., W.Wick. 96 C7
Raywood St. SW8 76 B1
Gladstone Ter.
Reachview Clo. NW1 49 C7
Baynes St.
Reade Wk. NW10 47 E7
Denbigh Clo.
Reading La. E8 50 E6
Reading Rd., Nthlt. 45 H5
Reading Rd., Sutt. 100 F5
Reading Way NW7 31 A5
Reads Clo., Ilf. 52 E3
Chapel La.
Reapers Clo. NW1 58 D1
Crofters Way
Reardon Path E1 68 E1
Reardon St. E1 68 E1
Reaston St. SE14 68 F7
Rebecca Ter. SE16 68 F3
Gomm Rd.
Reckitt Rd. W4 65 E5
Record St. SE15 68 F6
Recovery St. SW17 84 H5
Recreation Ave., 44 J5
Rom.
Recreation Rd. SE26 86 G4
Recreation Rd., 96 F2
Brom.
Recreation Rd., Sid. 88 J3
Recreation Rd., 63 E4
Sthl.
Recreation Way, 94 E3
Mitch.
Rector St. N1 58 J1
Rectory Clo. E4 34 A3
Rectory Clo. N3 39 C2
Rectory Clo. SW20 92 J3
Rectory Clo., Sid. 89 B4
Rectory Clo., Stan. 29 E5
Rectory Clo., Surb. 98 F1
Rectory Cres. E11 42 J6
Rectory Fld. Cres. 69 J7
SE7
Rectory Gdns. N8 40 E4
Rectory Gdns. SW4 76 C3
Rectory Gdns., 54 F1
Nthlt.
Rectory Grn., Beck. 95 J1
Rectory Gro. SW4 76 C3
Rectory Gro., Croy. 101 H2
Rectory Gro., 81 F4
Hmptn.
Rectory La. SW17 85 A6
Rectory La., Edg. 30 A6
Rectory La., Loug. 27 D2
Rectory La., Sid. 89 B4
Rectory La., Stan. 29 E5
Rectory La., Surb. 98 E1
Rectory La., Wall. 101 C3
Rectory Orchard 84 B4
SW19
Rectory Pk. Ave., 54 E3
Nthlt.
Rectory Pl. SE18 70 D4
Rectory Rd. E12 52 C5
Rectory Rd. E17 42 B3
Rectory Rd. N16 50 C2
Rectory Rd. SW13 74 G2
Rectory Rd. W3 65 B1
Rectory Rd., Beck. 96 A1
Rectory Rd., Dag. 53 G6
Rectory Rd., Hayes 54 A6
Rectory Rd., Houns. 72 B1
Rectory Rd., Kes. 104 A7
Rectory Rd., Sthl. 63 F3
Rectory Rd., Sutt. 100 D3
Rectory Sq. E1 59 G5
Reculver Ms. N18 33 D4
Lyndhurst Rd.
Reculver Rd. SE16 68 G5

Red Anchor Clo. SW3 18 G6
Red Barracks Rd. 70 C4
SE18
Red Cedars Rd., 97 H7
Orp.
Red Hill, Chis. 88 E5
Red Ho. La., Bexh. 80 D4
Red La., D.l., Croy 91 D6
Red La., Esher 98 D6
Red Lion Clo. SE17 21 B5
Red Lion Ct. EC4 12 F4
Red Lion Ct. EC4 58 G6
Red Lion Hill N2 39 G2
Red Lion La. SE18 79 D1
Red Lion Pl. SE18 79 D1
Shooter's Hill Rd.
Red Lion Rd., Surb. 98 J2
Red Lion Row SE17 21 A5
Red Lion Row SE17 67 J6
Red Lion Sq. WC1 12 C2
Red Lion Sq. WC1 58 F5
Red Lion St. WC1 12 C1
Red Lion St. WC1 58 F5
Red Lion St., Rich. 73 G5
Red Lion Yd. W1 15 C1
Red Lo. Rd., 103 C1
W.Wick.
Red Oak Clo., Orp. 104 E3
Red Path E9 50 J6
Eastway
Red Pl. W1 11 B5
Red Post Hill SE21 77 A5
Red Post Hill SE24 77 A4
Redan Pl. W2 10 A4
Redan Pl. W2 57 E6
Redan St. W14 66 A3
Redan Ter. SE5 76 J2
Flaxman Rd.
Redberry Gro. SE26 86 F3
Redbourne Ave. N3 39 D1
Redbridge Gdns. SE5 68 B7
Redbridge La. E., 43 A6
Ilf.
Redbridge La. W. 42 H6
E11
Redburn St. SW3 18 J5
Redburn St. SW3 66 J6
Redcar Clo., Nthlt. 45 H6
Redcar St. SE5 67 J7
Redcastle Clo. E1 59 F7
Redchurch St. E2 9 F5
Redchurch St. E2 59 C4
Redcliffe Gdns. 18 B4
SW10
Redcliffe Gdns. 66 E5
SW10
Redcliffe Gdns., 52 D1
Ilf.
Redcliffe Ms. SW10 18 B4
Redcliffe Ms. SW10 66 E5
Redcliffe Pl. SW10 18 C6
Redcliffe Pl. SW10 66 F6
Redcliffe Rd. SW10 18 C4
Redcliffe Rd. SW10 66 F5
Redcliffe Sq. SW10 18 B5
Redcliffe Sq. SW10 66 E5
Redcliffe St. SW10 18 B5
Redcliffe St. SW10 66 E6
Redclose Ave., 93 D5
Mord.
Chalgrove Ave.
Redclyffe Rd. E6 60 J1
Redcroft Rd., Sthl. 54 J7
Redcross Way SE1 17 A3
Redcross Way SE1 67 J2
Reddings, The NW7 30 F3
Reddings Clo. NW7 30 F4
Reddins Rd. SE15 21 G7
Reddins Rd. SE15 68 D6
Reddons Rd., Beck. 86 H7
Rede Pl. W2 57 D6
Chepstow Pl.
Redesdale Gdns., 64 D7
Islw.
Redesdale St. SW3 18 H5
Redesdale St. SW3 66 H6
Redfern Ave., 72 G7
Houns.
Redfern Rd. NW10 47 E3
Redfern Rd. SE6 78 C7
Redfield La. SW5 66 D2
Redford Ave. 94 F4
Th.Hth.
Redford Ave., Wall. 101 E6
Redford Wk. N1 58 H1
Britannia Row
Redgate Dr., Brom. 103 H2
Redgate Ter. SW15 75 A6
Lytton Gro.
Redgrave Clo., 95 C6
Croy.
Redgrave Rd. SW15 75 A3
Redhill Dr., Edg. 38 C2

Redhill St. NW1 7 E3
Redhill St. NW1 58 B2
Redington Gdns. 48 E4
NW3
Redington Rd. NW3 48 E4
Redlands Ct., Brom. 87 F7
Redlands Gdns., 90 F4
W.Mol.
Dunstable Rd.
Redlands Rd., Enf. 25 H1
Redlands Way SW2 76 F7
Redlaw Way SE16 21 J4
Redleaf Clo., Belv. 71 G6
Redlees Clo., Islw. 73 D4
Redman Clo., Nthlt. 54 C2
Redman's Rd. E1 59 F5
Redmead La. E1 17 H2
Redmore Rd. W6 65 H4
Redpoll Way, Erith 71 D2
Redriff Est. SE16 68 H3
Redriff Rd. SE16 68 G3
Redriff Rd., Rom. 44 H2
Redriffe Rd. E13 60 F1
Redroofs Clo., 96 B1
Beck.
Redruth Clo. N22 32 F7
Palmerston Rd.
Redruth Rd. E9 59 F1
Redstart Clo. E6 61 B5
Columbine Ave.
Redstart Clo. SE14 68 H7
Southerngate Way
Redston Rd. N8 40 C4
Redvers Rd. N22 40 G2
Redvers St. N1 9 E3
Redwald Rd. E5 50 G4
Redway Dr., Twick. 72 J7
Redwing Path SE28 70 G2
Whinchat Rd.
Redwood Clo. N14 24 D7
The Vale
Redwood Clo. SE16 68 H1
Redwood Clo., Wat. 28 C4
Redwood Est., 63 B6
Houns.
Redwood Twr. E11 51 D3
Redwood Wk., Surb. 98 G1
Redwood Way, Barn. 23 A5
Redwoods SW15 83 G1
Redwoods Clo., 34 H2
Buck.H.
Beech La.
Reece Ms. SW7 18 E1
Reece Ms. SW7 66 G4
Reed Ave., Orp. 104 H3
Reed Clo. E16 60 G5
Reed Clo. SE12 78 G5
Reed Rd. N17 41 C2
Reede Rd., Dag. 53 G6
Reede Way, Dag. 53 H6
Reedham Clo. N17 41 H4
Reedham St. SE15 77 D2
Reedholm Vill. N16 50 A4
Winston Rd.
Reeds Pl. NW1 49 C7
Royal College St.
Reedworth St. SE11 20 F2
Reedworth St. SE11 67 G4
Reenglass Rd., 29 G4
Stan.
Rees Gdns., Croy. 95 C6
Rees St. N1 58 J1
Reesland Clo. E12 52 D6
Reets Fm. Clo. NW9 38 E6
Reeves Ave. NW9 38 D7
Reeves Cor., Croy. 101 H2
Roman Way
Reeves Ms. W1 11 B6
Reeves Ms. W1 58 A7
Reeves Rd. E3 60 B4
Reeves Rd. SE18 70 E6
Reform Row N17 41 C2
Reform St. SW11 75 J2
Regal Clo. E1 13 J1
Regal Clo. W5 55 G5
Regal Ct. N18 33 C5
College Clo.
Regal Cres., Wall. 101 B3
Regal La. NW1 58 A1
Regents Pk. Rd.
Regal Way, Har. 37 H6
Regan Way N1 9 D2
Regan Way N1 59 B2
Regency Clo. W5 55 H6
Regency Clo., Chig. 35 F5
Regency Clo., 81 F5
Hmptn.
Regency Ct., Enf. 25 A5
Regency Cres. NW4 39 A2
Regency Lo., 35 A2
Buck.H.
Regency Ms. NW10 47 G6
High Rd.

Regency Ms., Beck. 96 C1
Regency Ms., Islw. 73 B5
Queensbridge Pk.
Regency Pl. SW1 19 J1
Regency St. SW1 19 J1
Regency St. SW1 67 D4
Regency Wk., Croy. 95 H6
Regency Way, Bexh. 80 D3
Regent Clo. N12 31 F5
Nether St.
Regent Clo., Har. 37 H6
Regent Clo., Houns. 72 B1
Regent Gdns., Ilf. 44 A6
Regent Pl. W1 11 G5
Regent Pl., Croy. 102 C1
Grant Rd.
Regent Rd. SE24 76 H6
Regent Rd., Surb. 91 J5
Regent Sq. E3 60 B3
Regent Sq. WC1 8 B4
Regent Sq. WC1 58 E3
Regent Sq., Belv. 71 H4
Regent St. NW10 57 A3
Kilburn La.
Regent St. W1 11 H6
Regent St. W1 58 D7
Regent St. W1 11 E3
Regent St. W1 58 B6
Regent St. W4 65 A5
Regents Ave. N13 32 G5
Regents Bri. Gdns. 20 B7
SW8
Regents Bri. Gdns. 67 E7
SW8
Regents Clo., 102 B6
S.Croy.
Regents Dr., Kes. 104 A5
Regents Ms. NW8 6 D1
Regents Pk. NW1 6 J2
Regents Pk. NW1 57 J2
Regents Pk. Est. 7 F4
NW1
Regents Pk. Rd. N3 39 C4
Regents Pk. Rd. NW1 48 J7
Regents Pk. Ter. 58 B1
NW1
Oval Rd.
Regent's Pl. SE3 78 G2
Regent Row E8 59 D1
Regina Clo., Barn. 23 A3
Regina Rd. N4 49 F1
Regina Rd. SE25 95 D3
Regina Rd. W13 64 D1
Regina Rd., Sthl. 63 H3
Regina Ter. W13 64 E1
Reginald Rd. E7 51 G6
Reginald Rd. SE8 69 A7
Reginald Sq. SE8 69 A7
Regis Rd. NW5 49 B5
Regnart Bldgs. NW1 7 G5
Reid Clo., Pnr. 36 A4
Reidhaven Rd. SE18 70 H4
Reigate Ave., Sutt. 100 D2
Reigate Rd., Brom. 87 F3
Reigate Rd., Ilf. 52 J2
Reigate Way, Wall. 101 E5
Heighton Rd. E5 50 D3
Relay Rd. W12 65 H1
Relf Rd. SE15 77 D3
Relko Gdns., Sutt. 100 G5
Relton Ms. SW7 14 H5
Rembrandt Clo. E14 69 D3
Rembrandt Clo. SW1 19 B2
Rembrandt Rd. SE13 78 E4
Rembrandt Rd., Edg. 38 A2
Remington Rd. E6 61 B6
Remington Rd. N15 41 A6
Remington St. N1 8 H2
Remington St. N1 58 H2
Remnant St. WC2 12 C3
Rempstone Ms. N1 9 C1
Remus Rd. E3 51 A7
Monier Rd.
Rendlesham Clo., 96 J1
Brom.
Rendlesham Rd. E5 50 D4
Rendlesham Rd., 24 H1
Enf.
Renforth St. SE16 68 F2
Renfrew Clo. E6 61 D7
Renfrew Rd. SE11 20 G1
Renfrew Rd. SE11 67 H4
Renfrew Rd., Houns. 72 D2
Renfrew Rd., 83 B7
Kings.T.
Renmuir St. SW17 84 J6
Rennell St. SE13 78 C3
Renness Rd. E17 41 H3
Rennets Clo. SE9 79 H5
Rennets Wd. Rd. SE9 79 G5
Rennie Est. SE16 68 E4
Rennie St. SE1 16 G1
Rennie St. SE1 67 H1

Renown Clo., Croy. 101 H1
Renown Clo., Rom. 44 G1
Rensburg Rd. E17 41 G5
Renshaw Clo., Belv. 71 F6
Grove Rd.
Renters Ave. NW4 38 J6
Renwick Rd., Bark. 62 B4
Repens Way, Hayes 54 D4
Stipularis Dr.
Rephidim St. SE1 17 C6
Replingham Rd. 84 C1
SW18
Reporton Rd. SW6 75 B1
Repository Rd. SE18 70 C6
Repton Ave., Wem. 46 F4
Repton Clo., Cars. 100 H5
Repton Ct. E5 50 H3
Repton Ct., Beck. 96 B1
Repton Gro., Ilf. 43 C1
Repton Rd., Har. 37 J4
Repton Rd., Orp. 104 A5
Repulse Clo., Rom. 44 H1
Reservoir Rd. N14 24 C5
Reservoir Rd. SE4 77 H2
Resolution Wk. SE18 70 C3
Venus Rd.
Restell Clo. SE3 69 E6
Reston Pl. SW7 14 C4
Restons Cres. SE9 79 G6
Restormel Clo., 72 G5
Houns.
Retcar Clo. N19 49 B2
Dartmouth Pk. Hill
Retford St. N1 9 E2
Retingham Way E4 34 B2
Retreat, The NW9 38 D5
Retreat, The SW14 74 E3
South Worple Way
Retreat, The, Har. 36 G7
Retreat, The, Surb. 91 J6
Retreat, The, 95 A4
Th.Hth.
Retreat, The, 99 H2
Wor.Pk.
Retreat Clo., Har. 37 F5
Retreat Pl. E9 50 F6
Retreat Rd., Rich. 73 G5
Reunion Row E1 59 E7
Pennington St.
Reveley Sq. SE16 68 H2
Howland Way
Revell Ri. SE18 70 J6
Revell Rd., 92 B2
Kings.T.
Revell Rd., Sutt. 100 C6
Revelon Rd. SE4 77 H3
Revelstoke Rd. SW18 84 C2
Reventlow Rd. SE9 88 F1
Reverdy Rd. SE1 21 H2
Reverdy Rd. SE1 68 D4
Reverend Clo., Har. 45 H3
Revesby Rd., Cars. 93 G6
Review Rd. NW2 47 F2
Review Rd., Dag. 62 H1
Rewell St. SW6 66 F7
Rewley Rd., Cars. 93 G6
Rex Pl. W1 11 C6
Reydon Ave. E11 42 J6
Reynard Clo., Brom. 97 C3
Reynard Dr. SE19 86 C7
Reynardson Rd. N17 32 J7
Reynolds Ave. E12 52 D5
Reynolds Ave., 98 H7
Chess.
Reynolds Ave., Rom. 44 C7
Reynolds Clo. NW11 39 E7
Reynolds Clo. SW19 93 G1
Reynolds Clo., 100 J1
Cars.
Reynolds Ct. E11 51 F3
Cobbold Rd.
Reynolds Dr., Edg. 37 J3
Reynolds Pl. SE3 69 H7
Reynolds Pl., Rich. 73 J6
Cambrian Rd.
Reynolds Rd. SE15 77 F5
Reynolds Rd. W4 65 C3
Reynolds Rd., Hayes 54 C4
Reynolds Rd., 92 D7
N.Mal.
Reynolds Way, 102 B4
Croy.
Rheidol Ms. N1 8 J1
Rheidol Ter. N1 8 H1
Rheidol Ter. N1 58 J1
Rheola Clo. N17 41 C1
Rhoda St. E2 9 G5
Rhodes Ave. N22 40 C1
Rhodes Moorhouse 93 D6
Ct., Mord.
Rhodes St. N7 49 F5
Mackenzie Rd.
Rhodesia Rd. E11 51 D2

Rhodesia Rd. SW9 76 E2
Rhodeswell Rd. E14 59 H5
Rhodrons Ave., 98 H5
Chess.
Rhondda Gro. E3 59 H3
Rhyl Rd., Grnf. 55 C2
Rhyl St. NW5 49 A6
Rhys Ave. N11 32 D7
Rialto Rd., Mitch. 94 A2
Ribble Clo., 34 J6
Wdf.Grn.
Prospect Rd.
Ribblesdale Ave., 45 H6
Nthlt.
Ribblesdale Rd. N8 40 F4
Ribblesdale Rd. 85 B6
SW16
Ribchester Ave., 55 F5
Grnf.
Ribston Clo., Brom. 104 A1
Ricardo St. E14 60 B6
Ricards Rd. SW19 84 C5
Rich La. SW5 18 A4
Rich St. E14 59 J7
Richard Clo. SE18 70 B4
Richard Foster Clo. 41 J7
E17
Richard St. E1 59 E6
Commercial Rd.
Richards Ave., Rom. 44 J5
Richards Clo., Har. 37 D5
Richards Pl. E17 42 A3
Richards Pl. SW3 18 H1
Richardson Clo. E8 59 C1
Clarissa St.
Richardson Rd. E15 60 E2
Richardson's Ms. W1 7 F6
Richbell Pl. WC1 12 C1
Richborne Ter. SW8 20 D7
Richborne Ter. SW8 67 F7
Richborough Rd. 48 B4
NW2
Riches Rd., Ilf. 52 F2
Richford Rd. E15 60 F1
Richford St. W6 65 J2
Richlands Ave., 99 G4
Epsom
Richmond Ave. E4 34 D5
Richmond Ave. N1 58 F1
Richmond Ave. 47 J6
NW10
Richmond Ave. 93 B1
SW20
Richmond Bri., 73 G5
Rich.
Richmond Bri., 73 G6
Twick.
Richmond Bldgs. W1 11 H4
Richmond Clo. E17 41 J6
Richmond Cres. E4 34 D5
Richmond Cres. N1 58 F1
Richmond Cres. N9 33 D1
Richmond Gdns. 38 G5
NW4
Richmond Gdns., 29 C7
Har.
Richmond Grn., 101 E3
Croy.
Richmond Gro. N1 49 H7
Richmond Gro., 91 J6
Surb.
Alpha Rd.
Richmond Hill, Rich. 73 H6
Richmond Hill Ct., 73 H6
Rich.
Richmond Ms. W1 11 H4
Richmond Pk. 83 C4
Heights, Kings.T.
Richmond Pk. Rd. 74 C5
SW14
Richmond Pk. Rd., 91 H1
Kings.T.
Richmond Pl. SE18 70 F5
Richmond Rd. E4 34 D1
Richmond Rd. E7 51 H5
Richmond Rd. E8 50 C7
Richmond Rd. E11 51 D2
Richmond Rd. N2 39 F2
Richmond Rd. N11 32 E6
Richmond Rd. N15 41 B6
Richmond Rd. SW20 92 H1
Richmond Rd. W5 64 H2
Richmond Rd., Barn. 23 E5
Richmond Rd., Croy. 101 E3
Richmond Rd., Ilf. 52 F3
Richmond Rd., Islw. 73 D3
Richmond Rd., 82 G5
Kings.T.
Richmond Rd., 94 H3
Th.Hth.
Richmond Rd., 82 D1
Twick.
Richmond St. E13 60 G2

Richmond Ter. SW1 16 A3
Richmond Ter. SW1 67 E2
Richmond Way E11 51 G2
Richmond Way W12 66 A2
Richmond Way W14 66 A2
Richmount Gdns. SE3 78 G3
Rickard Clo. NW4 30 G4
Rickard Clo. SW2 85 G1
Rickards Clo., Surb. 98 H1
Rickett St. SW6 66 D6
Rickman St. E1 59 F3
Mantus Rd.
Rickmansworth Rd., 36 B2
Pnr.
Rickthorne Rd. N19 49 E2
Landseer Rd.
Rickyard Path SE9 79 B4
Ridding La., Grnf. 46 C5
Riddons Rd. SE12 87 J3
Ride, The, Brent. 64 E5
Ride, The, Enf. 25 F3
Rideout St. SE18 70 C4
Rider Clo., Sid. 79 H6
Ridgdale St. E3 60 A2
Ridge, The, Bex. 80 F7
Ridge, The, Orp. 104 G2
Ridge, The, Surb. 92 A5
Ridge, The, Twick. 73 A7
Ridge Ave. N21 24 J7
Ridge Clo. NW4 39 A2
Ridge Clo. NW9 38 D4
Ridge Crest, Enf. 24 F1
Ridge Hill NW11 48 B1
Ridge Rd. N8 40 F6
Ridge Rd. N21 32 J1
Ridge Rd. NW2 48 C3
Ridge Rd., Mitch. 85 B7
Ridge Rd., Sutt. 100 B1
Ridge Way SE19 86 B6
Central Hill
Ridge Way, Felt. 81 E3
Ridgebrook Rd. SE3 78 J3
Ridgecroft Clo., 89 J1
Bex.
Ridgemont Gdns., 30 C4
Edg.
Ridgemount Ave., 102 G2
Croy.
Ridgemount Clo. 86 E7
SE20
Anerley Pk.
Ridgemount Gdns., 24 H3
Enf.
Ridgeview Clo., 23 A6
Barn.
Ridgeview Rd. N20 31 E3
Ridgeway, Brom. 103 G2
Ridgeway, Wdf.Grn. 34 J4
Ridgeway, The E4 34 B2
Ridgeway, The N3 31 E7
Ridgeway, The N11 31 J4
Ridgeway, The N14 32 E2
Ridgeway, The NW7 30 G3
Ridgeway, The NW9 38 E4
Ridgeway, The NW11 48 C1
Ridgeway, The W3 65 A3
Ridgeway, The, 101 F3
Croy.
Ridgeway, The, Enf. 24 G1
Ridgeway, The, Har. 36 F5
Ridgeway, The 37 F6
(Kenton), Har.
Ridgeway, The, 36 A7
Ruis.
Ridgeway, The, 29 F6
Stan.
Ridgeway, The, 100 G6
Sutt.
Ridgeway Ave., 23 J6
Barn.
Ridgeway Cres. 104 H3
Orp.
Ridgeway Cres. 104 H2
Gdns., Orp.
Ridgeway Dr., Brom. 87 H5
Ridgeway E., Sid. 79 J5
Ridgeway Gdns. N6 40 C7
Ridgeway Gdns., 43 B5
Ilf.
Ridgeway Rd. SW9 76 H3
Ridgeway Rd., Islw. 64 B7
Ridgeway Rd. N., 64 B6
Islw.
Ridgeway W., Sid. 79 H5
Ridgewell Clo. N1 58 J1
Basire St.
Ridgewell Clo., 62 H1
Dag.
Ridgewell Rd. E16 60 J5
Ridgmount Gdns. 11 H1
WC1
Ridgmount Pl. WC1 11 H1

Ridgmount Rd. 75 E5
SW18
Ridgmount St. WC1 11 H1
Ridgway SW19 83 J7
Ridgway Gdns. 84 A7
SW19
Ridgway Pl. SW19 84 B6
Riding, The NW11 39 C7
Golders Grn. Rd.
Riding Ho. St. W1 11 F2
Riding Ho. St. W1 58 C5
Ridings, The W5 55 J4
Ridings, The, Sun. 90 A1
Ridings, The, Surb. 92 A5
Ridings Ave. N21 24 H4
Ridings Clo. N6 40 C7
Hornsey La. Gdns.
Ridley Ave. W13 64 E3
Ridley Rd. E7 51 J4
Ridley Rd. E8 50 C5
Ridley Rd. NW10 56 G2
Ridley Rd. SW19 84 E7
Ridley Rd., Brom. 96 F3
Ridley Rd., Well. 80 B1
Ridley Several SE3 78 H2
Blackheath Pk.
Ridsdale Rd. SE20 95 E1
Riefield Rd. SE9 79 F4
Riesco Dr., Croy. 102 F6
Riffel Rd. NW2 47 J5
Rifle Pl. SE11 20 F5
Rifle Pl. W11 66 A1
Rifle St. E14 60 B5
Rigault Rd. SW6 75 B2
Rigby Clo., Croy. 101 G3
Rigby Ms., Ilf. 52 E2
Cranbrook Rd.
Rigden St. E14 60 B6
Rigeley Rd. NW10 56 G3
Rigg App. E10 50 G1
Rigge Pl. SW4 76 D4
Riggindale Rd. SW16 85 D4
Riley Rd. SE1 17 F5
Riley Rd. SE1 68 C3
Riley St. SW10 18 E7
Riley St. SW10 66 G7
Rinaldo Rd. SW12 76 B7
Ring, The W2 10 G5
Ring, The W2 57 G7
Ring Clo., Brom. 87 H7
Garden Rd.
Ringcroft St. N7 49 G5
Ringers Rd., Brom. 96 G3
Ringford Rd. SW18 75 C5
Ringlewell Clo., 25 E2
Enf.
Central Ave.
Ringmer Ave. SW6 75 B1
Ringmer Gdns. N19 49 E2
Sussex Way
Ringmer Pl. N21 25 A5
Ringmer Way, Brom. 88 A5
Ringmore Ri. SE23 77 E7
Ringslade Rd. N22 40 F2
Ringstead Rd. SE6 78 B7
Ringstead Rd., 100 G4
Sutt.
Ringway N11 32 C6
Ringway, Sthl. 63 D5
Ringwold Clo., 86 H7
Beck.
Ringwood Ave. N2 39 J2
Ringwood Ave., 94 E7
Croy.
Ringwood Clo., Pnr. 36 C3
Ringwood Gdns. 83 G2
SW15
Ringwood Rd. E17 41 J6
Ringwood Way N21 32 H1
Ringwood Way, 81 G4
Hmptn.
Ripley Clo., Brom. 97 C5
Ringmer Way
Ripley Clo., Croy. 103 C6
Ripley Gdns. SW14 74 D3
Ripley Gdns., Sutt. 100 F4
Ripley Ms. E11 42 E7
Wadley Rd.
Ripley Rd. E16 60 J6
Ripley Rd., Belv. 71 G4
Ripley Rd., Enf. 24 J1
Ripley Rd., Hmptn. 81 G7
Ripley Rd., Ilf. 53 G7
Ripley Vill. W5 55 F6
Castlebar Rd.
Riplington Ct. SW15 74 G7
Longwood Dr.
Ripon Clo., Nthlt. 45 G5
Ripon Gdns., Chess. 98 G5
Ripon Gdns., Ilf. 43 B7
Ripon Rd. N9 25 E7
Ripon Rd. N17 41 A3
Ripon Rd. SE18 70 E6

Ripon Way, Borwd. 22 C5
Rippersley Rd., 80 A1
Well.
Ripple Rd., Bark. 61 G1
Ripple Rd., Dag. 62 D1
Rippleside Ind. 62 B2
Est., Bark.
Ripplevale Gro. N1 49 F7
Rippolson Rd. SE18 70 J5
Risborough Dr., 92 G7
Wor.Pk.
Risborough St. SE1 16 H3
Risdon St. SE16 68 F2
Renforth St.
Rise, The E11 42 G5
Rise, The N13 32 G4
Rise, The NW7 30 F6
Rise, The NW10 47 D4
Rise, The, Bex. 80 C7
Rise, The, Buck.H. 27 A7
Rise, The, Edg. 30 B5
Rise, The, Grnf. 46 D5
Rise, The, Sid. 80 C7
Risedale Rd., Bexh. 80 H3
Riseldine Rd. SE23 77 H6
Rising Sun Ct. EC1 12 H2
Risinghill St. N1 8 E1
Risinghill St. N1 58 F2
Risingholme Clo., 37 B1
Har.
Risingholme Rd., 37 B2
Har.
Risings, The E17 42 D4
Risley Ave. N17 40 J1
Rita Rd. SW8 20 B6
Rita Rd. SW8 67 E6
Ritches Rd. N15 40 J5
Ritchie Rd., Croy. 95 E6
Ritchie St. N1 8 F1
Ritchie St. N1 58 G2
Ritchings Ave. E17 41 H4
Ritherdon Rd. SW17 85 A2
Ritson Rd. E8 50 D6
Ritter St. SE18 70 D6
Rivaz Pl. E9 50 F6
Rivenhall Gdns. E18 42 F4
River Ave. N13 32 H3
River Ave., T.Ditt. 91 D7
River Bank N21 24 J7
River Bank, E.Mol. 91 B3
River Bank, T.Ditt. 91 C5
River Bank, W.Mol. 90 F3
River Barge Clo. E14 69 C2
Stewart St.
River Clo. E11 42 J6
River Clo., Surb. 91 G5
Catherine Rd.
River Front, Enf. 25 A3
River Gdns., Cars. 101 A3
River Gdns., Felt. 72 B4
River Gro. Pk. 95 J1
Beck.
River La., Rich. 82 G1
River Meads Ave., 81 G3
Twick.
River Pk. Gdns., 87 D7
Brom.
River Pk. Rd. N22 40 F2
River Pl. N1 49 J7
River Reach, Tedd. 82 E5
River Rd., Bark. 61 H2
River Rd., Buck.H. 35 B1
River Rd. Business 61 J3
Pk., Bark.
River St. EC1 8 E3
River St. EC1 58 G3
River Ter. W6 65 J5
Crisp Rd.
River Vw., Enf. 24 J3
Chase Side
River Vw. Gdns., 82 C2
Twick.
River Wk., Walt. 90 A6
River Way SE10 69 F3
River Way, Epsom 99 D6
River Way, Loug. 27 C6
River Way, Twick. 81 H2
Riverbank Way, 64 F6
Brent.
Rivercourt Rd. W6 65 H4
Riverdale SE13 91 D6
Lewisham High St.
Riverdale Gdns., 73 F6
Twick.
Riverdale Rd. SE18 70 J5
Riverdale Rd., Bex. 80 E7
Riverdale Rd., 71 H5
Erith
Riverdale Rd., 81 F4
Felt.
Riverdale Rd., 73 F6
Twick.
Riverdene, Edg. 30 C3

Riverdene Rd., Ilf. 52 D3
Riverhead Clo. E17 41 G2
Rivermead Clo., 82 E5
Tedd.
Rivermead Ct. SW6 75 C3
Rivernook Clo., 90 C5
Walt.
Riversdale Rd. N5 49 H3
Riversdale Rd., 91 D6
T.Ditt.
Riversfield Rd., 25 B3
Enf.
Riverside NW4 38 H7
Riverside SE7 69 H3
Anchor & Hope La.
Riverside, Twick. 82 E1
Riverside Ave., 91 A5
E.Mol.
Riverside Clo. E5 50 F1
Riverside Clo. W7 55 B4
Riverside Clo., 91 G4
Kings.T.
Riverside Clo., 101 B3
Wall.
Riverside Ct. E4 26 B6
Chelwood Clo.
Riverside Ct. SW8 19 J5
Riverside Ct. SW8 67 D6
Riverside Dr. NW11 39 B6
Riverside Dr. W4 65 D7
Riverside Dr., 93 H5
Mitch.
Riverside Dr., 82 E2
Rich.
Riverside Gdns. W6 65 H5
Riverside Gdns., 24 J2
Enf.
Riverside Gdns., 55 H2
Wem.
Riverside Ind. 62 A3
Est., Bark.
Riverside Rd. E15 60 C2
Riverside Rd. N15 41 D6
Riverside Rd. SW17 84 E4
Riverside Rd., Sid. 89 E3
Riverside Wk. SE1 16 D1
Riverside Wk., Bex. 80 D7
Riverside Wk., 73 B3
Islw.
Riverside Wk., 91 G2
Kings.T.
High St.
Riverton Clo. W9 57 C3
Riverview Gdns. 65 H6
SW13
Riverview Gro. W4 65 B6
Riverview Pk. SE6 87 A1
Riverview Rd. W4 65 B6
Riverview Rd., 99 D5
Epsom
Riverway N13 32 G4
Riverwood La., 97 G1
Chis.
Rivington Ave., 43 A2
Wdf.Grn.
Rivington Ct. NW10 56 G1
Rivington Cres. NW7 30 F7
Rivington Pl. EC2 9 E4
Rivington St. EC2 9 D4
Rivington St. EC2 59 B3
Rivington Wk. E8 59 D1
Wilde Clo.
Rivulet Rd. N17 32 J7
Rixon Ho. SE18 70 E6
Barnfield Rd.
Rixsen Rd. E12 52 B5
Roach Rd. E3 51 A7
Roads Pl. N19 49 E2
Hornsey Rd.
Roan St. SE10 69 B7
Robb Rd., Stan. 29 D6
Robert Adam St. W1 11 B3
Robert Adam St. W1 58 A6
Robert Clo. W9 6 D6
Robert Clo., Chig. 35 J5
Robert Dashwood 20 J2
Way SE17
Robert Dashwood 67 J4
Way SE17
Robert Gentry Ho. 66 B5
W14
Comeragh Rd.
Robert Keen Clo. 77 D1
SE15
Cicely Rd.
Robert Lowe Clo. 68 G7
SE14
Robert Owen Ho. 75 A1
SW6
Robert St. E16 70 E1
Robert St. NW1 7 E4
Robert St. NW1 58 B3
Robert St. SE18 70 G5

Robert St. WC2 12 B6
Roberta St. E2 9 J4
Roberta St. E2 59 D3
Roberton Dr., Brom. 96 J1
Roberts Clo. SE9 88 G1
Roberts Clo., Pnr. 36 B5
Field End Rd.
Roberts Clo., Sutt. 100 A7
Roberts Ms. SW1 15 B6
Robert's Pl. EC1 8 F5
Roberts Rd. E17 42 B1
Roberts Rd. NW7 31 B6
Roberts Rd., Belv. 71 G5
Roberts St., Croy. 101 J3
High St.
Robertsbridge Rd., Cars. 100 F1
Robertson Rd. E15 60 C1
Robertson St. SW8 76 B3
Robeson St. E3 59 J5
Ackroyd Dr.
Robin Clo. NW7 30 E3
Robin Clo., Hmptn. 81 E5
Robin Ct. SE16 21 H1
Robin Ct. SE16 68 D4
Robin Cres. E6 61 B5
Robin Gro. N6 49 A2
Robin Gro., Brent. 64 F6
Robin Gro., Har. 37 J6
Robin Hill Dr., Chis. 88 B6
Robin Hood Dr., Har. 29 C7
Robin Hood La. E14 60 C6
Robin Hood La. SW15 83 E4
Robin Hood La., Bexh. 80 E5
Robin Hood La., Sutt. 100 D5
Robin Hood Rd. SW19 83 H5
SW19
Robin Hood Way SW15 83 E4
Robin Hood Way SW20 83 E4
Robin Hood Way, Grnf. 46 C6
Robina Clo., Bexh. 80 D4
Robinhood Clo., Mitch. 94 C4
Robinhood La., Mitch. 94 C3
Robinia Clo., Chig. 35 H5
Robins Ct. SE12 87 J3
Robins Gro., W.Wick. 103 G3
Robinscroft Ms. SE10 78 B1
Sparta St.
Robinson Cres. (Bushey), Wat. 28 J1
Robinson Rd. E2 59 F2
Robinson Rd. SW17 84 H6
Robinson Rd., Dag. 53 G4
Robinson St. SW3 18 J5
Robinson's Clo. W13 55 D5
Robinwood Pl. SW15 83 D4
Robsart St. SW9 76 F2
Robson Ave. NW10 56 G1
Robson Clo. E6 61 B6
Linton Gdns.
Robson Clo., Enf. 24 H2
Robson Rd. SE27 85 H3
Roch Ave., Edg. 37 J2
Rochdale Rd. E17 42 A7
Rochdale Rd. SE2 71 B5
Rochdale Way SE8 69 A7
Idonia St.
Roche Rd. SW16 94 E1
Roche Wk., Cars. 93 G6
Rochelle Clo. SW11 75 G4
Rochelle St. E2 9 F4
Rochemont Wk. E8 59 C1
Pownall Rd.
Rochester Ave. E13 60 J1
Rochester Ave., Brom. 96 H2
Rochester Clo. SW16 85 E7
Rochester Clo., Enf. 25 B1
Rochester Clo., Sid. 80 B6
Rochester Dr., Bex. 80 F6
Rochester Dr., Pnr. 36 D5
Rochester Gdns., Croy. 102 B3
Rochester Gdns., Ilf. 43 C7
Rochester Ms. NW1 49 C7
Rochester Pl. NW1 49 C6
Rochester Rd. NW1 49 C6
Rochester Rd., Cars. 100 J4
Rochester Row SW1 19 G1
Rochester Row SW1 67 C4
Rochester Sq. NW1 49 C7
Rochester St. SW1 15 H6
Rochester St. SW1 67 D3
Rochester Ter. NW1 49 C6
Rochester Wk. SE1 17 B1
Rochester Way SE3 78 J2
Rochester Way SE9 79 C3
Rochester Way Relief Rd. SE3 78 H1
Rochester Way Relief Rd. SE9 78 J4
Rochford Ave., Loug. 27 F3
Rochford Ave., Rom. 44 C5
Rochford Clo. E6 61 A2
Boleyn Rd.
Rochford Grn., Loug. 27 F3
Rochford St. NW5 48 J5
Rochford Wk. E8 50 D7
Wilman Gro.
Rochford Way, Croy. 94 E6
Rock Ave. SW14 74 D3
South Worple Way
Rock Gdns., Dag. 53 H5
Rockwell Rd.
Rock Gro. Way SE16 21 J1
Rock Gro. Way SE16 68 E4
Blue Anchor La.
Rock Hill SE26 86 C4
Rock St. N4 49 G2
Rockbourne Rd. SE23 86 G1
Rockells Pl. SE22 77 E6
Rockford Ave., Grnf. 55 D2
Rockhall Rd. NW2 48 A4
Rockhampton Clo. SE27 85 G4
Rockhampton Rd.
Rockhampton Rd. SE27 85 G4
Rockhampton Rd., S.Croy. 102 B6
Rockingham Clo. SW15 74 F4
Rockingham Est. SE1 16 J6
Rockingham Est. SE1 67 J3
Rockingham St. SE1 16 J6
Rockingham St. SE1 67 J3
Rockland Rd. SW15 75 B4
Rocklands Dr., Stan. 37 E2
Rockley Rd. W14 66 A2
Rockmount Rd. SE18 70 J5
Rockmount Rd. SE19 86 A6
Rocks La. SW13 74 G3
Rockware Ave., Grnf. 55 B1
Rockways, Barn. 22 F6
Rockwell Rd., Dag. 53 H5
Rockwells Gdns. SE19 86 B4
Rockwood Pl. W12 65 J2
Shepherds Bush Grn.
Rocliffe St. N1 8 H2
Rocmoale Way SE8 69 A7
Octavius St.
Rocombe Cres. SE23 77 F7
Rocque La. SE3 78 F3
Rodborough Rd. NW11 48 D1
Roden Ct. N6 40 D7
Hornsey La.
Roden Gdns., Croy. 95 B6
Roden St. N7 49 F3
Roden St., Ilf. 52 D3
Rodenhurst Rd. SW4 76 C6
Roderick Rd. NW3 48 J4
Roding Ave., Wdf.Grn. 35 B6
Roding La., Buck.H. 35 A1
Roding La., Chig. 35 E2
Roding La. N., Wdf.Grn. 35 B6
Roding La. S., Ilf. 43 A4
Roding La. S., Wdf.Grn. 43 A3
Roding Ms. E1 17 J1
Roding Rd. E5 50 H4
Roding Rd. E6 61 E5
Roding Rd., Loug. 27 B5
Roding Trd. Est., Bark. 52 E7
Roding Vw., Buck.H. 35 A1
Rodings, The, Wdf.Grn. 34 J6
Rodmarton St. W1 11 A2
Rodmarton St. W1 57 J5
Rodmell Clo., Hayes 54 E4
Rodmell Slope N12 31 C5
Rodmere St. SE10 69 E5
Trafalgar Rd.
Rodmill La. SW2 76 E7
Rodney Clo., Croy. 101 H1
Rodney Clo., N.Mal. 92 E5
Rodney Clo., Pnr. 36 E7
Rodney Ct. W9 6 D5
Rodney Gdns., Pnr. 36 B5
Rodney Gdns., W.Wick. 103 G4
Rodney Pl. E17 41 H2
Rodney Pl. SE17 21 A1
Rodney Pl. SE17 67 J4
Rodney Pl. SW19 93 F1
Rodney Rd. E11 42 H4
Rodney Rd. SE17 21 A1
Rodney Rd. SE17 67 J4
Rodney Rd., Mitch. 93 H2
Rodney Rd., N.Mal. 92 E5
Rodney Rd., Twick. 72 G7
Rodney St. N1 8 D1
Rodney St. N1 58 F2
Rodney Way, Rom. 44 G1
Rodway Rd. SW15 74 G7
Rodway Rd., Brom. 96 H1
Rodwell Clo., Ruis. 45 C1
Rodwell Pl., Edg. 30 A6
Whitchurch La.
Rodwell Rd. SE22 77 C6
Roe End NW9 38 C4
Roe Grn. NW9 38 C5
Roe La. NW9 38 B4
Roe Way, Wall. 101 E7
Roebourne Way E16 70 D2
Roebuck Clo., Felt. 81 B4
Roebuck La. N17 33 C6
High Rd.
Roebuck La., Buck.H. 26 J7
Roebuck Rd., Chess. 99 A5
Roedean Ave., Enf. 25 F1
Roedean Clo., Enf. 25 F1
Roedean Cres. SW15 74 E6
Roehampton Clo. SW15 74 G4
Roehampton Dr., Chis. 88 F6
Roehampton Gate SW15 74 E6
Roehampton High St. SW15 74 G7
Roehampton La. SW15 74 G4
Roehampton Vale SW15 83 F3
Roffey St. E14 69 C2
Rogate Ho. E5 50 D3
Muir Rd.
Roger St. WC1 8 D6
Roger St. WC1 58 F4
Rogers Gdns., Dag. 53 G5
Rogers Rd. E16 60 F6
Rogers Rd. SW17 84 G4
Rogers Rd., Dag. 53 G5
Rogers Wk. N12 31 E3
Brook Meadow
Rojack Rd. SE23 86 G1
Rokeby Gdns., Wdf.Grn. 42 G1
Rokeby Pl. SW20 83 H7
Rokeby Rd. SE4 77 J2
Rokeby St. E15 60 D1
Rokesby Clo., Well. 79 G2
Rokesby Pl., Wem. 46 G5
Rokesly Ave. N8 40 E5
Roland Gdns. SW7 18 D3
Roland Gdns. SW7 66 F5
Roland Gdns., Felt. 81 F3
Roland Ms. E1 59 G5
Stepney Grn.
Roland Rd. E17 42 D4
Roland Way SE17 21 C4
Roland Way SE17 68 A5
Roland Way SW7 18 D3
Roland Way, Wor.Pk. 99 F2
Roles Gro., Rom. 44 D4
Rolfe Clo., Barn. 23 H4
Rolinsden Way, Kes. 104 A4
Roll Gdns., Ilf. 43 D5
Rollesby Rd., Chess. 99 A6
Rollesby Way SE28 62 C7
Rolleston Ave., Orp. 97 E6
Rolleston Clo., Orp. 97 E7
Rolleston Rd., S.Croy. 102 A7
Rollins St. SE15 68 F6
Rollit Cres., Houns. 72 G5
Rollit St. N7 49 F5
Hornsey Rd.
Rolls Bldgs. EC4 12 E3
Rolls Pk. Ave. E4 34 A6
Rolls Pk. Rd. E4 34 B5
Rolls Pas. EC4 12 E3
Rolls Rd. SE1 21 G3
Rolls Rd. SE1 68 C5
Rollscourt Ave. SE24 76 J5
Rolt St. SE8 68 H6
Rolvenden Gdns., Brom. 88 A7
Rolvenden Pl. N17 41 D1
Manor Rd.
Roma Read Clo. SW15 74 H7
Bessborough Rd.
Roma Rd. E17 41 H3
Roman Clo., Felt. 72 C5
Roman Ri. SE19 86 A6
Roman Rd. E2 59 F3
Roman Rd. E3 59 H2
Roman Rd. E6 61 A4
Roman Rd. N10 32 B7
Roman Rd. W4 65 F4
Roman Rd., Ilf. 52 E6
Roman Sq. SE28 71 A1
Roman Way N7 49 F6
Roman Way SE15 68 F7
Clifton Way
Roman Way, Croy. 101 H2
Roman Way, Enf. 25 C5
Roman Way Ind. Est. N1 49 F7
Offord St.
Romanhurst Ave., Brom. 96 E4
Romanhurst Gdns., Brom. 96 E4
Romany Gdns. E17 41 H1
McEntee Ave.
Romany Gdns., Sutt. 93 D7
Romany Ri., Orp. 104 F1
Romberg Rd. SW17 85 A3
Romborough Gdns. SE13 78 C5
Romborough Way SE13 78 C5
Romero Clo. SW9 76 F3
Stockwell Rd.
Romero Sq. SE3 78 J4
Romeyn Rd. SW16 85 F3
Romford Rd. E7 51 F5
Romford Rd. E12 52 B4
Romford Rd. E15 51 E6
Romford St. E1 13 J2
Romford St. E1 59 D5
Romilly Dr., Wat. 28 E4
Romilly Rd. N4 49 H2
Romilly St. W1 11 H5
Romilly St. W1 58 D7
Rommany Rd. SE27 86 A4
Romney Clo. N17 41 E1
Romney Clo. NW11 48 F1
Romney Clo. SE14 68 F7
Kender St.
Romney Clo., Chess. 98 H4
Romney Clo., Har. 36 G7
Romney Dr., Brom. 88 A7
Romney Dr., Har. 36 G7
Romney Gdns., Bexh. 80 F1
Romney Rd. SE10 69 C6
Romney Rd., N.Mal. 92 D6
Romney St. SW1 16 A6
Romney St. SW1 67 E3
Romola Rd. SE24 85 H1
Romsey Clo., Orp. 104 E4
Romsey Gdns., Dag. 62 D1
Romsey Rd. W13 55 D7
Romsey Rd., Dag. 62 D1
Rona Rd. NW3 49 A4
Rona Wk. N1 50 A6
Marquess Est.
Ronald Ave. E15 60 E3
Ronald Clo., Beck. 95 J4
Ronald St. E1 59 F6
Devonport St.
Ronalds Rd. N5 49 G5
Ronalds Rd., Brom. 96 G1
Ronaldstone Rd., Sid. 79 H6
Ronart St., Har. 37 C3
Stuart Rd.
Rondu Rd. NW2 48 B5
Ronelean Rd., Surb. 98 J3
Ronver Rd. SE12 87 G1
Baring Rd.
Rood La. EC3 13 D5
Rood La. EC3 59 B7
Rook Wk. E6 61 B6
Allhallows Rd.
Rooke Way SE10 69 F5
Rookeries Clo., Felt. 81 B3
Rookery Clo. NW9 38 F5
Rookery Cres., Dag. 53 H7

Rookery Dr., Chis. 97 D1
Rookery La., Brom. 97 A6
Rookery Rd. SW4 76 C4
Rookery Way NW9 38 F5
Rookfield Ave. N10 40 C4
Rookfield Clo. N10 40 C4
  Drummond Way
Rookstone Rd. SW17 84 J5
Rookwood Ave., 27 F3
  Loug.
Rookwood Ave., 92 G4
  N.Mal.
Rookwood Ave., 101 D4
  Wall.
Rookwood Gdns. E4 34 F1
  Whitehall Rd.
Rookwood Gdns., 27 F3
  Loug.
Rookwood Ho., Bark. 61 G2
  St. Marys
Rookwood Rd. N16 41 C7
Rope St. SE16 68 H3
Rope Wk., Sun. 90 C3
Rope Wk. Gdns. E1 13 J3
Rope Yd. Rails SE18 70 E3
Ropemaker Rd. SE16 68 H2
Ropemaker St. EC2 13 B1
Ropemaker St. EC2 59 A5
Ropemakers Flds. 59 J7
  E14
  Narrow St.
Roper La. SE1 17 E4
Roper St. SE9 79 C6
Roper Way, Mitch. 94 A2
Ropers Ave. E4 34 B5
Ropers Wk. SW2 76 G7
  Brockwell Pk. Gdns.
Ropery St. E3 59 J4
Ropley St. E2 9 H2
Ropley St. E2 59 D2
Rosa Alba Ms. N5 49 J4
  Kelross Rd.
Rosaline Rd. SW6 66 B7
Rosamond St. SE26 86 E3
Rosary Clo., Houns. 72 E2
Rosary Gdns. SW7 18 C2
Rosary Gdns. SW7 66 F4
Rosaville Rd. SW6 66 C7
Roscoe St. EC1 9 A6
Roscoff Clo., Edg. 38 C1
Rose All. SE1 17 A1
Rose All. SE1 67 J1
Rose & Crown Ct. 12 J3
  EC2
Rose & Crown Yd. 15 G1
  SW1
Rose Ave. E18 42 H2
Rose Ave., Mitch. 93 J1
Rose Ave., Mord. 93 F5
Rose Bates Dr. NW9 38 A4
Rose Ct. E1 59 B5
  Sandys Row
Rose Ct. SE26 86 E2
Rose Ct., Pnr. 36 C3
  Nursery Rd.
Rose Dale, Ash. 104 E2
Rose Dale, Orp. 104 E2
Rose End, Wor.Pk. 100 A1
Rose Gdn. Clo., 29 H6
  Edg.
Rose Gdns. W5 64 G3
Rose Gdns., Felt. 81 A2
Rose Gdns., Sthl. 54 G4
Rose Glen NW9 38 D4
Rose Hill, Sutt. 100 E3
Rose La., Rom. 44 D3
Rose Lawn (Bushey), 28 J1
  Wat.
Rose St. WC2 12 A5
Rose Wk., Surb. 92 B5
Rose Wk., W.Wick. 103 C2
Rose Way SE12 78 G5
Roseacre Clo. W13 55 E5
  Middlefielde
Roseacre Rd., Well. 80 B3
Rosebank SE20 86 E7
Rosebank Ave., 46 C4
  Wem.
Rosebank Clo. N12 31 H5
Rosebank Gdns. E3 59 J2
Rosebank Gro. E17 41 J3
Rosebank Rd. E17 42 B6
Rosebank Rd. W7 64 B2
Rosebank Vill. E17 42 A4
Rosebank Wk. NW1 49 D7
  Maiden La.
Rosebank Way W3 56 D6
Roseberry Gdns. N4 40 H6
Roseberry Gdns. 104 H3
  Orp.
Roseberry Pl. E8 50 C6
Roseberry St. SE16 68 E4
Rosebery Ave. E12 52 B6

Rosebery Ave. EC1 8 E5
Rosebery Ave. EC1 58 G4
Rosebery Ave. N17 41 D2
Rosebery Ave., Har. 45 E4
Rosebery Ave., 92 F2
  N.Mal.
Rosebery Ave., Sid. 79 H7
Rosebery Ave., 94 J2
  Th.Hth.
Rosebery Clo., Mord. 93 A8
Rosebery Gdns. N8 40 E5
Rosebery Gdns. W13 55 D6
Rosebery Gdns., 100 E4
  Sutt.
Rosebery Ms. N10 40 C2
Rosebery Ms. SW2 76 E6
  Rosebery Rd.
Rosebery Rd. N9 33 D3
Rosebery Rd. N10 40 C2
Rosebery Rd. SW2 76 E6
Rosebery Rd., 72 J5
  Houns.
Rosebery Rd., 92 B2
  Kings.T.
Rosebery Rd., Sutt. 100 C6
Rosebery Sq. EC1 8 E6
Rosebery Sq., 92 B2
  Kings.T.
Rosebine Ave., 73 A7
  Twick.
Rosebury Rd. SW6 75 E2
Rosebury Vale, 45 A2
  Ruis.
Rosecourt Rd., 94 F6
  Croy.
Rosecroft Ave. NW3 48 D3
Rosecroft Gdns. NW2 47 G3
Rosecroft Gdns., 82 A1
  Twick.
Rosecroft Rd., 54 G4
  Sthl.
Rosecroft Wk., Pnr. 36 D5
Rosecroft Wk., Wem. 46 G5
Rosedale Clo. W7 64 C2
  Boston Rd.
Rosedale Clo., 29 E6
  Stan.
Rosedale Ct. N5 49 H4
  Panmure Clo.
Rosedale Gdns., 53 B7
  Dag.
Rosedale Rd. E7 51 J5
Rosedale Rd., Dag. 53 B7
Rosedale Rd., Epsom 99 G5
Rosedale Rd., Rich. 73 H4
Rosedale Rd., Rom. 44 J2
Rosedene NW6 57 A1
Rosedene Ave. SW16 85 F3
Rosedene Ave., 94 E7
  Croy.
Rosedene Ave., 54 G3
  Grnf.
Rosedene Ave., 93 D5
  Mord.
Rosedene Gdns., 43 D4
  Ilf.
Rosedene Ter. E10 51 B2
Rosedew Rd. W6 66 A6
Rosefield Clo., 100 H5
  Cars.
  Alma Rd.
Rosefield Gdns. E14 60 A7
Roseford Ct. W12 66 A2
  Shepherds Bush Grn.
Rosehart Ms. W11 57 D6
  Westbourne Gro.
Rosehatch Ave., 44 D3
  Rom.
Roseheath Rd., 72 F5
  Houns.
Rosehill, Esher 98 D6
Rosehill, Hmptn. 90 G1
Rosehill Ave., 100 F1
  Sutt.
Rosehill Gdns., 46 C5
  Grnf.
Rosehill Gdns., 100 E2
  Sutt.
Rosehill Pk. W., 100 E1
  Sutt.
Rosehill Rd. SW18 75 F6
Roseland Clo. N17 33 A7
  Cavell Rd.
Roseleigh Ave. N5 49 H4
Roseleigh Clo., 73 G6
  Twick.
Rosemary Ave. N3 39 E2
Rosemary Ave. N9 33 E1
Rosemary Ave., Enf. 25 A1
Rosemary Ave., 72 D2
  Houns.
Rosemary Ave., 90 G3
  W.Mol.

Rosemary Dr. E14 60 D6
Rosemary Dr., Ilf. 43 A5
Rosemary Gdns., 98 H4
  Chess.
Rosemary Gdns. 53 F1
  Dag.
Rosemary La. SW14 74 C3
Rosemary Pl. N1 59 A1
  Shepperton Rd.
Rosemary Rd. 81 G7
Rosemary Rd. SE15 68 C7
Rosemary Rd. SW17 84 F3
Rosemary Rd., Well. 79 J1
Rosemary St. N1 59 A1
  Shepperton Rd.
Rosemead NW9 38 F7
Rosemead Ave., 94 C2
  Mitch.
Rosemead Ave., 46 H5
  Wem.
Rosemont Ave. N12 31 F6
Rosemont Rd. NW3 48 F6
Rosemont Rd. W3 56 B7
Rosemont Rd., 92 C3
  N.Mal.
Rosemont Rd., Rich. 73 H6
Rosemont Rd., Wem. 55 H1
Rosemoor St. SW3 18 J2
Rosemoor St. SW3 66 E5
Rosemount Clo., 35 C6
  Wdf.Grn.
  Chapelmount Rd.
Rosemount Dr., 97 C4
  Brom.
Rosemount Rd. W13 55 D6
Rosemount Rd., 92 C3
  Kings.T.
Rosenau Cres. SW11 75 H1
Rosenau Rd. SW11 75 H1
Rosendale Rd. SE21 76 J7
Rosendale Rd. SE24 76 J7
Roseneath Ave. N21 32 H1
Roseneath Rd. SW11 76 A6
Roseneath Wk., Enf. 25 A4
Rosens Wk., Edg. 30 B3
Rosenthal Rd. SE6 78 B6
Rosenthorpe Rd. 77 G5
  SE15
Roserton St. E14 69 C2
Rosery, The, Croy. 95 G6
Roses, The, 34 F7
  Wdf.Grn.
Rosethorn Clo. SW12 76 D7
Rosetta Clo. SW8 67 E7
  Kenchester Clo.
Roseveare Rd. SE12 87 J4
Roseville Ave., 72 G5
  Houns.
Roseville Rd., 63 A5
  Hayes
Rosevine Rd. SW20 92 J1
Roseway SE21 77 A6
Rosewood Ave., 46 D5
  Grnf.
Rosewood Clo., Sid. 89 C3
Rosewood Ct., Brom. 96 J1
Rosewood Gdns. 78 C2
  SE13
  Lewisham Rd.
Rosewood Gro., 100 F2
  Sutt.
Rosewood Sq. W12 56 G6
  Primula St.
Rosher Clo. E15 51 D7
Rosina St. E9 50 G5
Roskell Rd. SW15 75 A3
Roslin Rd. W3 65 B3
Roslin Way, Brom. 87 G5
Roslyn Clo., Mitch. 93 G2
Roslyn Rd. N15 41 A5
Rosmead Rd. W11 57 B7
Rosoman Pl. EC1 8 F5
Rosoman St. EC1 8 F4
Rosoman St. EC1 58 G3
Ross Ave. NW7 31 B5
Ross Ave., Dag. 53 F2
Ross Clo., Har. 28 J7
Ross Ct. SW15 75 A7
Ross Par., Wall. 101 B6
Ross Rd. SE25 95 A3
Ross Rd., Twick. 81 H1
Ross Rd., Wall. 101 C5
Ross Way SE9 79 B3
Rossall Cres. NW10 55 J3
Rossdale, Sutt. 100 H5
Rossdale Dr. N9 25 F6
Rossdale Dr. NW9 47 C1
Rossdale Rd. SW15 74 J4
Rosse Ms. SE3 78 H1
Rossendale St. E5 50 E2
Rossendale Way 58 C1
  NW1
Rossetti Rd. SE16 68 E5

Rossignol Gdns., 101 A2
  Cars.
Rossindel Rd., 72 G5
  Houns.
Rossington St. E5 50 D2
Rossiter Flds., 23 B6
  Barn.
Rossiter Rd. SW12 85 B1
Rossland Clo., Bexh. 80 H5
Rosslyn Ave. E4 34 F2
Rosslyn Ave. SW13 74 E3
Rosslyn Ave., Barn. 23 H6
Rosslyn Ave., Dag. 44 F7
Rosslyn Ave., Felt. 72 A6
Rosslyn Clo., 103 F3
  W.Wick.
Rosslyn Cres., Har. 37 C4
Rosslyn Cres., Wem. 46 H4
Rosslyn Hill NW3 48 G4
Rosslyn Ms. NW3 48 G4
  Rosslyn Hill
Rosslyn Pk. Ms. NW3 48 G5
  Lyndhurst Rd.
Rosslyn Rd. E17 42 C4
Rosslyn Rd., Bark. 52 G7
Rosslyn Rd., Twick. 73 F6
Rossmore Rd. NW1 6 H6
Rossmore Rd. NW1 57 H4
Rosswood Gdns., 101 B6
  Wall.
Rostella Rd. SW17 84 G4
Rostrevor Ave. N15 41 C6
Rostrevor Gdns., 63 E5
  Sthl.
Rostrevor Rd. SW6 75 C1
  Rostrevor Rd.
Rostrevor Rd. SW6 75 C1
Rostrevor Rd. SW19 84 D5
Rotary St. SE1 16 G5
Roth Wk. N7 49 F3
  Durham Rd.
Rothbury Gdns., 64 D7
  Islw.
Rothbury Rd. E9 50 J7
Rothbury Wk. N17 33 D7
  Northumberland Gro.
Rotherfield Rd., 101 A4
  Cars.
Rotherfield St. N1 49 J7
Rotherham Wk. SE1 16 G2
Rotherhill Ave. 85 D6
  SW16
Rotherhithe New Rd. 21 J4
  SE16
Rotherhithe New Rd. 68 E5
  SE16
Rotherhithe Old Rd. 68 G4
  SE16
Rotherhithe St. 68 F2
  SE16
Rotherhithe Tunnel 68 G1
  E1
Rotherhithe Tunnel 59 H7
  App. E14
Rotherhithe Tunnel 68 F2
  App. SE16
Rothermere Rd., 101 F5
  Croy.
Rotherwick Hill W5 55 J4
Rotherwick Rd. NW11 39 D7
Rotherwood Clo. 93 B1
  SW20
Rotherwood Rd. 75 A3
  SW15
Rothery St. N1 58 H1
  Gaskin St.
Rothery Ter. SW9 67 H7
  Foxley Rd.
Rothesay Ave. SW20 93 B2
Rothesay Ave., 46 A6
  Grnf.
Rothesay Ave., 74 B4
  Rich.
Rothesay Rd. SE25 95 A4
Rothsay Rd. E7 51 J7
Rothsay St. SE1 17 D5
Rothsay St. SE1 68 B3
Rothsay Wk. E14 69 A4
  Charnwood Gdns.
Rothschild Rd. W4 65 C3
Rothschild St. SE27 85 H4
Rothwell Gdns., 53 C7
  Dag.
Rothwell Rd., Dag. 62 C1
Rothwell St. NW1 57 J1
Rotten Row SW1 14 J3
Rotten Row SW7 14 H3
Rotten Row SW7 66 H2
Rotterdam Dr. E14 69 C3
Rouel Rd. SE16 17 H6
Rouel Rd. SE16 68 D3
Rougemont Ave., 93 D6
  Mord.

Name	Page	Grid
Round Gro., Croy.	95	G7
Round Hill SE26	86	F3
Roundaway Rd., Ilf.	43	C1
Roundhay Clo. SE23	86	G2
Roundhill Dr., Enf.	24	F4
Roundmead Ave., Loug.	27	D2
Roundmead Clo., Loug.	27	D3
Roundtable Rd., Brom.	87	F3
Roundtree Rd., Wem.	46	E5
Roundway, The N17	40	J1
Roundway, The, Esher	98	C6
Roundwood, Chis.	97	E2
Roundwood Rd. NW10	47	F6
Rounton Rd. E3	60	A4
Roupell Rd. SW2	85	F1
Roupell St. SE1	16	F2
Roupell St. SE1	67	G1
Rous Rd., Buck.H.	35	B1
Rousden St. NW1	49	C7
Rouse Gdns. SE21	86	B4
Routh Rd. SW18	75	H7
Routh St. E6	61	C5
Routledge Clo. N19	49	D1
Rover Ave., Ilf.	35	J6
Rowallan Rd. SW6	66	B7
Rowan Ave. E4	33	J3
Rowan Clo. SW16	94	C1
Rowan Clo. W5	64	H2
Rowan Clo., N.Mal.	92	E2
Rowan Clo., Stan.	29	C6
Woodlands Dr.		
Rowan Clo., Wem.	46	D3
Rowan Ct. E8	50	C7
Rowan Cres. SW16	94	C1
Rowan Dr. NW9	38	G3
Rowan Gdns., Croy.	102	C3
Radcliffe Rd.		
Rowan Ind. Est., Croy.	95	B7
Rowan Rd. SW16	94	C2
Rowan Rd. W6	66	A4
Rowan Rd., Bexh.	80	E3
Rowan Rd., Brent.	64	E7
Rowan Ter. W6	66	A4
Bute Gdns.		
Rowan Wk. N2	39	F5
Rowan Wk. N19	49	C2
Bredgar Rd.		
Rowan Wk. W10	57	B4
Droop St.		
Rowan Wk., Brom.	104	C3
Rowan Way, Rom.	44	C3
Rowans, The N13	32	H3
Rowans Way, Loug.	27	C4
Rowantree Clo. N21	33	A1
Rowantree Rd. N21	33	A1
Rowantree Rd., Enf.	24	H2
Rowanwood Ave., Sid.	89	A1
Rowben Clo. N20	31	E1
Rowberry Clo. SW6	65	J7
Rowcross St. SE1	21	G3
Rowcross St. SE1	68	C5
Rowdell Rd., Nthlt.	54	G1
Rowden Rd. E4	34	A6
Rowden Rd., Beck.	95	H1
Rowden Rd., Epsom	99	B4
Rowditch La. SW11	76	A2
Rowdon Ave. NW10	47	H7
Rowdowns Rd., Dag.	62	F1
Rowe Gdns., Bark.	61	J2
Rowe La. E9	50	F5
Rowe Wk., Har.	45	G3
Rowena Cres. SW11	75	H2
Rowfant Rd. SW17	85	A1
Rowhill Rd. E5	60	E5
Rowington Clo. W2	10	A1
Rowington Clo. W2	57	C7
Rowland Ave., Har.	37	F3
Rowland Ct. E16	60	C7
Rowland Cres., Chig.	35	H4
Rowland Hill Ave. N17	32	J7
Rowland Hill St. NW3	48	H5
Rowland Way SW19	93	E1
Hayward Clo.		
Rowlands Ave., Pnr.	28	G5
Rowlands Clo. N6	40	A6
North Hill		
Rowlands Clo. NW7	30	G7
Rowlands Rd., Dag.	53	F2
Rowley Ave., Sid.	80	B7
Rowley Clo., Wem.	46	J7
Rowley Gdns. N4	40	J1
Rowley Grn. Rd., Barn.	22	F5
Rowley Ind. Est. W3	65	B3
Rowley La., Barn.	22	E4
Rowley La., Borwd.	22	D1
Rowley Rd. N15	40	J5
Rowley Way NW8	57	E1
Rowlls Rd., Kings.T.	91	J3
Rowney Gdns., Dag.	53	C6
Rowney Rd., Dag.	53	B6
Rowntree Path SE28	62	B7
Booth Clo.		
Rowntree Rd., Twick.	82	B1
Rowse Clo. E15	60	C1
Rowsley Ave. NW4	38	J3
Rowstock Gdns. N7	49	D5
Rowton Rd. SE18	70	F7
Roxborough Ave., Har.	37	B7
Roxborough Ave., Islw.	64	C7
Roxborough Pk., Har.	37	B7
Roxborough Rd., Har.	37	A5
Roxbourne Clo., Nthlt.	45	D6
Roxburgh Rd. SE27	85	H5
Roxby Pl. SW6	66	D6
Roxeth Grn. Ave., Har.	45	H3
Roxeth Gro., Har.	45	H4
Roxeth Hill, Har.	46	A2
Roxley Rd. SE13	78	B6
Roxton Gdns., Croy.	103	A5
Roxwell Rd. W12	65	G2
Roxwell Rd., Bark.	62	A2
Roxwell Trd. Pk. E10	41	H7
Roxwell Way, Wdf.Grn.	34	J7
Roxy Ave., Rom.	44	C7
Roy Gdns., Ilf.	43	H4
Roy Gro., Hmptn.	81	H6
Roy Sq. E14	59	H7
Narrow St.		
Royal Albert Dock E16	61	B7
Royal Albert Dock Spine Rd. E16	61	A7
Royal Arc. W1	11	F6
Royal Ave. SW3	18	J3
Royal Ave. SW3	66	J5
Royal Ave., Wor.Pk.	99	E2
Royal Circ. SE27	85	G3
Royal Clo., Ilf.	44	A7
Royal Clo., Wor.Pk.	99	E2
Royal College St. NW1	49	C7
Royal Ct. SE16	68	J3
Finland St.		
Royal Cres. W11	66	A1
Royal Cres., Ruis.	45	E4
Royal Cres. Ms. W11	66	A1
Queensdale Rd.		
Royal Ex. EC3	13	C4
Royal Ex. EC3	59	A6
Royal Ex. Ave. EC3	13	C4
Royal Ex. Bldgs. EC3	13	C4
Royal Hill SE10	69	C7
Royal Hospital Rd. SW3	18	J5
Royal Hospital Rd. SW3	66	J6
Royal London Est., The N17	33	D6
Royal London Ind. Est. NW10	56	D2
North Acton Rd.		
Royal Mint Ct. EC3	13	G6
Royal Mint Ct. EC3	59	C7
Royal Mint Pl. E1	13	G5
Royal Mint St. E1	13	G5
Royal Mint St. E1	59	C7
Royal Mt. Ct., Twick.	82	B3
Royal Naval Pl. SE14	68	J7
Royal Oak Pl. SE22	77	E6
Royal Oak Rd. E8	50	E6
Royal Oak Rd., Bexh.	80	F5
Royal Opera Arc. SW1	15	H1
Royal Orchard Clo. SW18	75	B7
Royal Par. SE3	78	F2
Royal Par. W5	55	H3
Western Ave.		
Royal Par., Chis.	88	F7
Royal Par. Ms. SE3	78	F2
Royal Par.		
Royal Par. Ms., Chis.	88	F7
Royal Pl. SE10	69	C7
Royal Rd. E16	60	J6
Royal Rd. SE17	20	G5
Royal Rd. SE17	67	H6
Royal Rd., Sid.	89	D3
Royal Rd., Tedd.	82	A5
Royal Route, Wem.	47	A4
Royal St. SE1	16	D5
Royal St. SE1	67	F3
Royal Victor Pl. E3	59	G2
Royal Victoria Dock E16	60	G7
Royal Wk., Wall.	101	B3
Prince Charles Way		
Royalty Ms. W1	11	H4
Roycraft Ave., Bark.	61	J2
Roycroft Clo., Bark.	61	J2
Roycroft Clo. E18	42	H1
Roycroft Clo. SW2	85	G1
Roydene Rd. SE18	70	H6
Roydon Clo. SW11	76	B1
Reform St.		
Roydon Clo., Loug.	27	B7
Roydon St. SW11	76	B1
Southolm St.		
Royle Cres. W13	55	D4
Royston Ave. E4	34	A5
Royston Ave., Sutt.	100	G3
Royston Ave., Wall.	101	D4
Royston Clo., Houns.	72	B1
Royston Ct. SE24	76	J6
Burbage Rd.		
Royston Ct., Rich.	73	J1
Lichfield Rd.		
Royston Ct., Surb.	99	A3
Hook Ri. N.		
Royston Gdns., Ilf.	43	A6
Royston Gro., Pnr.	28	G6
Royston Par., Ilf.	43	A6
Royston Pk. Rd., Pnr.	28	F6
Royston Rd. SE20	95	G1
Royston Rd., Rich.	73	H5
Royston St. E2	59	F2
Roystons, The, Surb.	92	B5
Rozel Ct. N1	59	B1
Rozel Rd. SW4	76	C3
Rubastic Rd., Sthl.	63	C3
Rubens Rd., Nthlt.	54	C2
Rubens St. SE6	86	J2
Ruberoid Rd., Enf.	25	J3
Ruby Ms. E17	42	A3
Ruby Rd.		
Ruby Rd. E17	42	A3
Ruby St. SE15	68	E6
Ruby Triangle SE15	68	E6
Sandgate St.		
Ruckholt Clo. E10	51	B3
Ruckholt Rd. E10	51	B4
Rucklidge Ave. NW10	56	F2
Rudall Cres. NW3	48	G4
Willoughby Rd.		
Ruddstreet Clo. SE18	70	E4
Rudland Rd., Bexh.	80	H3
Rudloe Rd. SW12	76	C7
Rudolph Rd. E13	60	F2
Rudolph Rd. NW6	57	D2
Rudyard Gro. NW7	30	C6
Ruffetts, The, S.Croy.	102	E7
Ruffetts Clo., S.Croy.	102	E7
Rufford Clo., Har.	37	D6
Rufford St. N1	58	E1
Rufford Twr. W3	65	B1
Rufus Clo., Ruis.	45	E3
Rufus St. N1	9	D4
Rugby Ave. N9	33	C1
Rugby Ave., Grnf.	46	A6
Rugby Ave., Wem.	46	E5
Rugby Clo., Har.	37	B4
Rugby Gdns., Dag.	53	C6
Rugby Rd. NW9	38	A4
Rugby Rd. W4	65	E2
Rugby Rd., Dag.	53	B6
Rugby Rd., Islw.	73	B5
Rugby Rd., Twick.	73	B5
Rugby St. WC1	8	C6
Rugby St. WC1	58	F4
Rugg St. E14	60	A7
Ruislip Clo., Grnf.	54	H4
Ruislip Rd., Grnf.	54	G3
Ruislip Rd., Nthlt.	54	C1
Ruislip Rd. E. W7	55	A4
Ruislip Rd. E. W13	55	A4
Ruislip Rd. E., Grnf.	55	A4
Ruislip St. SW17	84	J4
Rum Clo. E1	59	F7
Rumbold Rd. SW6	66	E7
Rumsey Clo., Hmptn.	81	F5
Rumsey Rd. SW9	76	F3
Runbury Circ. NW9	47	D2
Runcorn Clo. N17	41	E4
Runcorn Pl. W11	57	B7
Rundell Cres. NW4	38	H5
Runnel Fld., Har.	46	B3
Runnymede SW19	93	F1
Runnymede Clo., Twick.	72	H7
Runnymede Ct., Croy.	102	C2
Runnymede Cres. SW16	94	D1
Runnymede Gdns., Grnf.	55	A2
Runnymede Gdns., Twick.	72	H7
Runnymede Rd., Twick.	72	H6
Runway, The, Ruis.	45	B5
Rupack St. SE16	68	F2
St. Marychurch St.		
Rupert Ave., Wem.	46	H5
Rupert Ct. W1	11	H5
Rupert Gdns. SW9	76	H2
Rupert Rd. N19	49	D3
Holloway Rd.		
Rupert Rd. NW6	57	C2
Rupert Rd. W4	65	E3
Rupert St. W1	11	H5
Rupert St. W1	58	D7
Rural Way SW16	85	B7
Ruscoe Rd. E16	60	F6
Rush Grn. Gdns., Rom.	53	J1
Rush Grn. Rd., Rom.	53	J1
Rush Gro. St. SE18	70	C4
Rush Hill Ms. SW11	76	A3
Rush Hill Rd.		
Rush Hill Rd. SW11	76	A3
Rusham Rd. SW12	75	J6
Rushbrook Cres. E17	41	J1
Rushbrook Rd. SE9	88	F2
Rushcroft Rd. E4	34	A7
Rushcroft Rd. SW2	76	G4
Rushden Clo. SE19	86	A7
Rushden Gdns. NW7	30	J6
Rushden Gdns., Ilf.	43	D2
Rushdene SE2	71	C3
Rushdene Ave., Barn.	23	H7
Rushdene Clo., Nthlt.	54	C2
Rushdene Cres., Nthlt.	54	C2
Rushdene Rd., Pnr.	36	D6
Rushden Wk., Cars.	100	G1
Paisley Rd.		
Rushett Clo., T.Ditt.	98	E1
Rushett Rd., T.Ditt.	91	E7
Rushey Clo., N.Mal.	92	D4
Rushey Grn. SE6	78	B7
Rushey Hill, Enf.	24	F4
Rushey Mead SE4	78	A5
Rushford Rd. SE4	77	J4
Rushgrove Ave. NW9	38	E5
Rushley Clo., Kes.	104	A4
Rushmead E2	59	E3
Florida St.		
Rushmead, Rich.	82	E3
Croftway		
Rushmead Clo., Croy.	102	C4
Rushmere Ct., Wor.Pk.	99	G2
Rushmoor Clo., Pnr.	36	B4
Rushmore Clo., Brom.	99	F4
Rushmore Rd. E5	50	F4
Rusholme Ave., Dag.	53	G3
Rusholme Gro. SE19	86	B5
Rusholme Rd. SW15	75	A6
Rushout Ave., Har.	37	E6
Rushton St. N1	9	C1
Rushton St. N1	59	A2
Rushworth Ave. NW4	38	G3
Rushworth Gdns.		
Rushworth Gdns. NW4	38	G3
Rushworth St. SE1	16	H3
Rushworth St. SE1	67	H2
Ruskin Ave. E12	52	B6
Ruskin Ave., Rich.	65	A7
Ruskin Ave., Well.	80	A3
Ruskin Clo. NW11	39	E6
Ruskin Dr., Orp.	104	H3
Ruskin Dr., Well.	80	A3

Ruskin Dr., Wor.Pk. 99 H2
Ruskin Gdns. W5 55 G4
Ruskin Gdns., Har. 37 J4
Ruskin Gro., Well. 80 A2
Ruskin Pk. Ho. SE5 77 A3
Ruskin Rd. N17 41 C1
Ruskin Rd., Bely. 71 G4
Ruskin Rd., Cars. 100 J5
Ruskin Rd., Croy. 101 H2
Ruskin Rd., Islw. 73 C5
Ruskin Rd., Sthl. 94 E7
Ruskin Wk. N9 33 D2
  Durham Rd.
Ruskin Wk. SE24 76 J5
Ruskin Way SW19 93 G1
Rusland Ave., Orp. 104 G3
Rusland Pk. Rd., 37 B4
  Har.
Rusper Clo. NW2 47 J3
Rusper Clo., Stan. 29 F4
Rusper Rd. N22 40 H2
Rusper Rd., Dag. 53 C6
Russell Ave. N22 40 G2
Russell Clo. NW10 44 C7
Russell Clo. SE7 69 J7
Russell Clo., Beck. 96 B3
Russell Clo., Bexh. 80 G4
Russell Clo., Ruis. 45 C2
Russell Ct. SW1 **15 G2**
Russell Gdns. N20 31 H2
Russell Gdns. NW11 39 B6
Russell Gdns. W14 66 B3
Russell Gdns., 82 F2
  Rich.
Russell Gdns. Ms. 66 B2
  W14
Russell Gro. NW7 30 E5
Russell Gro. SW9 76 G1
Russell Kerr Clo. W4 65 C7
  Burlington La.
Russell La. N20 31 H2
Russell Mead, Har. 29 C7
Russell Pl. NW3 48 H5
  Aspern Rd.
Russell Pl. SE16 68 H3
  Onega Gate
Russell Rd. E4 33 J4
Russell Rd. E10 42 B6
Russell Rd. E16 60 G6
Russell Rd. E17 41 J3
Russell Rd. N8 40 D6
Russell Rd. N13 32 F6
Russell Rd. N15 41 B5
Russell Rd. N20 31 H2
Russell Rd. NW9 38 F6
Russell Rd. SW19 84 D7
Russell Rd. W14 66 B3
Russell Rd., Buck.H. 34 H1
Russell Rd., Mitch. 93 H3
Russell Rd., Nthlt. 45 J5
Russell Rd., Twick. 73 C6
Russell Rd., Walt. 90 A6
Russell Sq. WC1 **8 A6**
Russell Sq. WC1 58 E4
Russell St. WC2 **12 B5**
Russell St. WC2 58 E7
Russell Wk., Rich. 73 J6
  Park Hill
Russell Way, Sutt. 100 D5
Russell's Footpath 85 E5
  SW16
Russet Dr., Croy. 102 H1
Russett Way SE13 78 B2
  Conington Rd.
Russetts Clo. E4 34 D4
  Larkshall Rd.
Russia Ct. EC2 **13 A4**
Russia Dock Rd. 68 H1
  SE16
Russia La. E2 59 F2
Russia Row EC2 **13 A4**
Russia Wk. SE16 68 G2
  Archangel St.
Rust Sq. SE5 **21 B7**
Rust Sq. SE5 68 A7
Rusthall Ave. W4 65 D4
Rusthall Clo., 95 F6
  Croy.
Rustic Ave. SW16 85 B7
Rustic Pl., Wem. 46 G4
Rustington Wk., 93 C7
  Mord.
Ruston Ave., Surb. 96 B7
Ruston Gdns. N14 24 A6
  Farm La.
Ruston Ms. W11 57 B6
  St. Marks Rd.
Ruston St. E3 59 J1
Rutford Rd. SW16 85 E5
Ruth Clo., Stan. 37 J4
Rutherford Clo., 100 H2
  Sutt.

Rutherford St. SW1 **19 H1**
Rutherford St. SW1 67 D4
Rutherford Twr., 54 H6
  Sthl.
Rutherford Way 29 A1
  (Bushey), Wat.
Rutherford Way, 47 A3
  Wem.
Rutherglen Rd. SE2 71 A6
Rutherwyke Clo., 88 D8
  Epsom
Ruthin Rd. SE3 69 G6
Ruthven St. E9 59 G1
  Lauriston Rd.
Rutin Clo. NW9 38 E6
Rutland Ave., Sid. 80 A7
Rutland Clo. SW14 74 B3
Rutland Clo. SW19 84 H7
  Rutland Rd.
Rutland Clo., Bex. 89 D1
Rutland Clo., 98 J6
  Chess.
Rutland Ct., Enf. 25 E5
Rutland Ct., Mord. 93 C6
Rutland Dr., Rich. 82 G1
Rutland Gdns. N4 40 H6
Rutland Gdns. SW7 **14 H4**
Rutland Gdns. W13 55 D5
Rutland Gdns., 102 B4
  Croy.
Rutland Gdns., Dag. 53 C5
Rutland Gdns. Ms. **14 H4**
  SW7
Rutland Gate SW7 **14 H4**
Rutland Gate SW7 66 H2
Rutland Gate, Belv. 71 H5
Rutland Gate, Brom. 96 F4
Rutland Gate Ms. **14 G4**
  SW7
Rutland Gro. W6 65 H5
Rutland Ms. NW8 57 E1
  Boundary Rd.
Rutland Ms. E. SW7 **14 G5**
Rutland Ms. S. SW7 **14 G5**
Rutland Pk. NW2 47 J6
Rutland Pk. SE6 86 J2
Rutland Pl. EC1 **12 H1**
Rutland Pl. 29 A1
  (Bushey), Wat.
  The Rutts
Rutland Rd. E7 52 A7
Rutland Rd. E9 59 F1
Rutland Rd. E11 42 H5
Rutland Rd. E17 42 A6
Rutland Rd. SW19 84 H7
Rutland Rd., Har. 36 J6
Rutland Rd., Ilf. 52 E4
Rutland Rd., Sthl. 54 G4
Rutland Rd., Twick. 82 A2
Rutland St. SW7 **14 H5**
Rutland St. SW7 66 H3
Rutland Wk. SE6 86 J2
Rutley Clo. SE17 **20 G5**
Rutlish Rd. SW19 93 D1
Rutter Gdns., 93 G4
  Mitch.
Rutts, The 29 A1
  (Bushey), Wat.
Rutts Ter. SE14 77 G1
Ruvigny Gdns. SW15 75 A3
Ruxley Clo., Epsom 99 B5
Ruxley Clo., Sid. 89 E6
Ruxley Cor. Ind. 89 D6
  Est., Sid.
Ruxley Cres., Esher 98 E6
Ruxley La., Epsom 99 B6
Ruxley Ms., Epsom 99 B5
Ruxley Ridge, Esher 98 D7
Ryalls Ct. N20 31 J3
Ryan Clo. SE3 78 J4
Ryan Clo., Ruis. 45 B1
Ryan Dr., Brent. 64 D6
Ryarsh Cres., Orp. 104 H4
Rycott Path SE22 77 D7
  Lordship La.
Rycroft Way N17 41 C3
Ryculff Sq. SE3 78 F2
Rydal Clo. NW4 39 A1
Rydal Cres., Grnf. 55 E3
Rydal Dr., Bexh. 80 F2
Rydal Dr., W.Wick. 103 E2
Rydal Gdns. NW9 38 E5
Rydal Gdns. SW15 83 E5
Rydal Gdns., Houns. 72 H6
Rydal Gdns., Wem. 46 F1
Rydal Rd. SW16 85 D4
Rydal Way, Enf. 25 F6
Rydal Way, Ruis. 45 C4
Ryde Pl., Twick. 73 F6
Ryde Vale Rd. SW12 85 B2
Ryder Clo., Brom. 87 H5
Ryder Ct. SW1 **15 G1**

Ryder St. SW1 **15 G1**
Ryder St. SW1 67 C1
Ryder Yd. SW1 **15 G1**
Ryders Ter. NW8 **6 C1**
  Gore Rd.
Rydon St. N1 58 J1
  St. Paul St.
Rydons Clo. SE9 79 B3
Rydston Clo. N7 49 F7
  Sutterton St.
Rye Hill Est. SE15 77 G4
Rye Hill Pk. SE15 77 F4
Rye La. SE15 77 D2
Rye Rd. SE15 77 G4
Rye Wk. SW15 75 A5
  Chartfield Ave.
Rye Way, Edg. 29 J6
  Canons Dr.
Ryecotes Mead SE21 86 B1
Ryecroft Ave., Ilf. 43 E2
Ryecroft Ave., 72 H7
  Twick.
Ryecroft Cres., Barn. 22 H5
Ryecroft Rd. SE13 78 C5
Ryecroft Rd. SW16 85 G6
Ryecroft Rd., Orp. 97 G6
Ryecroft St. SW6 75 E1
Ryedale SE22 77 E6
Ryefield Path SW15 83 G1
Ryefield Rd. SE19 85 J6
Ryelands Cres. SE12 78 J6
Ryfold Rd. SW19 84 D3
Ryhope Rd. N11 32 B4
Ryland Ho., Croy. 101 J3
Ryland Rd. NW5 47 G3
Rylandes Rd. NW2 47 G3
Rylett Cres. W12 65 F2
Rylett Rd. W12 65 F3
Rylston Rd. N13 33 A3
Rylston Rd. SW6 66 C6
Rymer Rd., Croy. 95 B7
Rymer St. SE24 76 H6
Rymill St. E16 70 D1
Rysbrack St. SW3 **14 J5**
Rysbrack St. SW3 66 J3
Rythe Ct., T.Ditt. 91 D7
Rythe Rd., Esher 98 A5

S

Sabbarton St. E16 60 F6
  Victoria Dock Rd.
Sabella Ct. E3 59 J2
  Mostyn Gro.
Sabine Rd. SW11 75 J3
Sable Clo., Houns. 72 C3
Sable St. N1 49 H7
  Canonbury Rd.
Sach Rd. E5 50 E2
Sackville Ave., 103 G1
  Brom.
Sackville Clo., 46 A3
  Har.
Sackville Est. SW16 85 E3
Sackville Gdns., 52 C1
  Ilf.
Sackville Rd., 100 D7
  Sutt.
Sackville St. W1 **11 G6**
Sackville St. W1 58 C7
Sackville Way SE22 86 D1
  Dulwich Common
Saddlers Clo., 22 D6
  Borwd.
  Farriers Way
Saddlers Clo., Pnr. 28 G6
Saddlers Ms., Wem. 46 C4
  The Boltons
Saddlescombe Way 31 D5
  N12
Sadler Clo., Mitch. 93 J2
Sadlers Ride, 90 H3
  W.Mol.
Saffron Ave. E14 60 D7
Saffron Clo. NW11 39 C5
Saffron Hill EC1 **12 F1**
Saffron Hill EC1 58 G5
Saffron Rd., Rom. 44 J2
Saffron St. EC1 **12 F1**
Saffron Way, Surb. 98 G1
Sage St. E1 59 F7
  Cable St.
Sage Way WC1 **8 C4**
Saigasso Clo. E16 61 A6
  Royal Rd.
Sail St. SE11 **20 D1**
Sail St. SE11 67 F4
Sainfoin Rd. SW17 85 A2
Sainsbury Rd. SE19 86 B5
St. Agathas Dr., 82 J6
  Kings.T.

St. Agathas Gro., 100 J1
  Cars.
St. Agnes Clo. E9 59 F1
  Gore Rd.
St. Agnes Pl. SE11 **20 F6**
St. Agnes Pl. SE11 67 H6
St. Aidans Rd. SE22 77 E6
St. Aidans Rd. W13 64 E2
St. Albans Ave. E6 61 C3
St. Albans Ave. W4 64 D3
St. Albans Cres. N22 40 G1
St. Albans Cres., 34 G7
  Wdf.Grn.
St. Alban's Gdns., 82 D5
  Tedd.
St. Albans Gro. W8 **14 B5**
St. Albans Gro. W8 66 E3
St. Albans Clo., 93 H7
  Cars.
St. Albans La. NW11 48 D1
  West Heath Dr.
St. Albans Ms. W2 **10 F1**
St. Alban's Pl. N1 58 H1
St. Albans Rd. NW5 49 A3
St. Albans Rd. NW10 56 E1
St. Albans Rd., 23 A1
  Barn.
St. Albans Rd., 52 J1
  Ilf.
St. Albans Rd., 82 H6
  Kings.T.
St. Alban's Rd., 100 C4
  Sutt.
St. Albans Rd., 34 G7
  Wdf.Grn.
St. Albans St. SW1 **11 H6**
St. Albans Ter. W6 66 B6
  Margravine Rd.
St. Albans Twr. E4 33 J6
St. Alfege Pas. 69 C6
  SE10
St. Alfege Rd. SE7 70 A4
St. Alphage Gdns. **13 A2**
  EC2
St. Alphage Wk., 38 C2
  Edg.
St. Alphege Rd. N9 25 F7
St. Alphonsus Rd. 76 D4
  SW4
St. Amunds Clo. SE6 87 A4
St. Andrew St. EC4 **12 F2**
St. Andrew St. EC4 58 G5
St. Andrews Ave., 46 D4
  Wem.
St. Andrew's Clo. 31 F4
  N12
  Woodside Ave.
St. Andrews Clo. 47 H3
  NW2
St. Andrew's Clo., 73 A1
  Islw.
St. Andrews Clo., 45 D2
  Ruis.
St. Andrew's Clo., 37 F2
  Stan.
St. Andrew's Ct. 84 F2
  SW18
  Waynflete St.
St. Andrews Dr., 37 F1
  Stan.
St. Andrews Gro. 50 A1
  N16
St. Andrew's Hill **12 H5**
  EC4
St. Andrew's Hill 58 H7
  EC4
St. Andrews Ms. N16 50 B1
  Dunsmure Rd.
St. Andrews Ms. SE3 69 G7
  Mycenae Rd.
St. Andrews Pl. NW1 **7 E5**
St. Andrews Rd. E11 42 E6
St. Andrews Rd. E13 60 H3
St. Andrews Rd. E17 41 G2
St. Andrews Rd. N9 25 F7
St. Andrews Rd. NW9 47 D1
St. Andrews Rd. 47 H6
  NW10
St. Andrews Rd. 39 C6
  NW11
St. Andrews Rd. W3 56 E6
St. Andrews Rd. W7 64 B2
  Church Rd.
St. Andrews Rd. W14 66 B6
St. Andrews Rd. 100 H3
  Cars.
St. Andrews Rd., 101 J4
  Croy.
  Lwr. Coombe St.

St. Andrews Rd., 25 A3
Enf.
St. Andrews Rd., 43 C7
Ilf.
St. Andrews Rd., 89 D3
Sid.
St. Andrews Rd., 91 G6
Surb.
St. Andrews Rd., 28 D3
Wat.
Bird Rd.
St. Andrews Sq. W11 57 B6
St. Marks Rd.
St. Andrews Sq., 91 G6
Surb.
St. Andrews Twr., 54 J7
Sthl.
St. Andrews Way E3 60 B4
St. Annes Clo. N6 49 A3
Highgate W. Hill
St. Anne's Clo., 28 C4
Wat.
St. Anne's Ct. W1 11 H4
St. Annes Gdns. 55 J3
NW10
St. Anne's Ho. N16 50 B1
St. Annes Pas. E14 59 J6
Newell St.
St. Annes Rd. E11 51 D2
St. Anne's Rd., 46 G5
Wem.
St. Anne's Row E14 59 J6
St. Anne's St. E14 59 J6
Commercial Rd.
St. Ann's, Bark. 61 F1
St. Ann's Cres. 75 E6
SW18
St. Ann's Gdns. NW5 49 A6
Queens Cres.
St. Ann's Hill SW18 75 E5
St. Ann's La. SW1 15 J5
St. Ann's Pk. Rd. 75 F6
SW18
St. Ann's Pas. SW13 74 E3
Cross St.
St. Anns Rd. N9 33 C2
St. Ann's Rd. N15 40 H5
St. Ann's Rd. SW13 74 F2
St. Anns Rd. W11 57 A7
St. Ann's Rd., Bark. 61 F1
Axe St.
St. Ann's Rd., Har. 37 B6
St. Ann's St. SW1 15 J5
St. Ann's St. SW1 67 D3
St. Ann's Ter. NW8 6 F1
St. Ann's Ter. NW8 57 G2
St. Anns Vill. W11 66 A1
St. Anns Way, 101 H6
S.Croy.
St. Anselm's Pl. W1 11 D4
St. Anthonys Ave., 34 J6
Wdf.Grn.
St. Anthonys Clo. E1 17 H1
St. Anthonys Clo. 84 H2
SW17
College Gdns.
St. Antony's Rd. E7 51 I17
St. Arvans Clo., 102 B3
Croy.
St. Asaph Rd. SE4 77 G3
St. Aubyn's Ave. 84 C5
SW19
St. Aubyns Ave., 72 G5
Houns.
St. Aubyns Clo., 104 J3
Orp.
St. Aubyns Gdns., 104 J2
Orp.
St. Aubyn's Rd. 86 C6
SE19
St. Audrey Ave., 80 G2
Bexh.
St. Augustine's 55 H2
Ave. W5
St. Augustines 97 B5
Ave., Brom.
St. Augustines 101 J6
Ave., S.Croy.
St. Augustines 46 H3
Ave., Wem.
St. Augustines Rd. 49 D7
NW1
St. Augustine's 71 F4
Rd., Belv.
St. Austell Clo., 37 J2
Edg.
St. Austell Rd. 78 C2
SE13
St. Awdry's Rd., 52 G7
Bark.
St. Barnabas Clo., 96 C2
Beck.
St. Barnabas Ct., Har. 36 J1

St. Barnabas Rd. 42 A6
E17
St. Barnabas Rd., 85 A7
Mitch.
St. Barnabas Rd., 100 G5
Sutt.
St. Barnabas Rd., 42 H1
Wdf.Grn.
**St. Barnabas St. 19 C3
SW1**
St. Barnabas St. 67 A5
SW1
St. Barnabas Ter. 50 G5
E9
St. Barnabas Vill. 76 E1
SW8
St. Bartholomews 86 E4
Clo. SE26
St. Bartholomew's 61 C2
Rd. E6
St. Benedict's Clo. 85 A5
SW17
Church La.
St. Benet Gro., 93 F7
Cars.
St. Benet's Clo. 84 H2
SW17
College Gdns.
St. Benet's Pl. EC3 13 C5
St. Bernards, Croy. 102 B3
St. Bernard's Clo. 86 A4
SE27
St. Gothard Rd.
St. Bernard's Rd. 61 A1
E6
St. Blaise Ave., 96 H2
Brom.
St. Botolph Row EC3 13 F4
St. Botolph St. EC3 13 F3
St. Botolph St. EC3 59 C6
St. Bride St. EC4 12 G3
St. Bride St. EC4 58 H6
St. Brides Ave., 37 J1
Edg.
St. Brides Clo., Erith 71 D2
St. Katherines Rd.
St. Bride's Pas. EC4 12 G4
St. Catherines Clo. 84 H2
SW17
College Gdns.
St. Catherines Dr. 77 G2
SE14
Kitto Rd.
**St. Catherine's Ms. 18 J1
SW3**
St. Catherines Rd. 34 A2
E4
St. Chads Gdns., 44 E7
Rom.
St. Chad's Pl. WC1 8 B3
St. Chad's Pl. WC1 58 E3
St. Chads Rd., Rom. 44 E6
St. Chad's St. WC1 8 B3
St. Chad's St. WC1 58 E3
St. Charles Pl. W10 57 B5
Chesterton Rd.
St. Charles Sq. W10 57 B5
St. Christopher's 73 B1
Clo., Islw.
St. Christophers 94 G3
Gdns., Th.Hth.
St. Christophers 101 C5
Ms., Wall.
**St. Christopher's 11 C3
Pl. W1**
St. Clair Dr., 99 H3
Wor.Pk.
St. Clair Rd. E13 60 H2
St. Claire Clo., 43 C2
Ilf.
St. Clair's Rd., 102 C2
Croy.
St. Clare St. EC3 13 F4
St. Clements Ct. N7 49 G6
Arundel Sq.
St. Clements 86 D3
Heights SE26
**St. Clement's La. 12 D4
WC2**
St. Clements St. N1 49 G6
St. Clements St. N1 49 G6
St. Cloud Rd. SE27 85 J4
St. Crispins Clo. 48 H4
NW3
St. Crispin's Clo., 54 F6
Sthl.
St. Cross St. EC1 12 F1
St. Cross St. EC1 58 G5
St. Cuthberts Gdns., 28 F7
Pnr.
Westfield Pk.
St. Cuthberts Rd. 48 C6
NW2

St. Cyprian's St. 84 J4
SW17
St. Davids Clo., 47 C3
Wem.
St. Davids Clo., 96 B7
W.Wick.
St. David's Ct. E17 42 C3
St. Davids Dr., 37 J1
Edg.
St. Davids Pl. NW4 38 H7
St. Denis Rd. SE27 86 A4
St. Dionis Rd. SW6 75 C2
St. Donatts Rd. 77 J1
SE14
**St. Dunstan's All. 13 D6
EC3**
St. Dunstans Ave. 56 D7
W3
St. Dunstan's Ct. 58 G6
EC4
Fleet St.
St. Dunstans Gdns. 56 D7
W3
St. Dunstans Ave.
**St. Dunstan's Hill 13 D6
EC3**
St. Dunstan's Hill 59 B7
EC3
St. Dunstan's Hill, 100 B5
Sutt.
**St. Dunstan's La. 13 D6
EC3**
St. Dunstans La., 96 C6
Beck.
St. Dunstan's La. 51 J6
E7
St. Dunstans Rd. 95 C4
SE25
St. Dunstans Rd. W6 66 A5
St. Dunstans Rd. W7 64 B2
St. Dunstans Rd., 72 B2
Houns.
St. Edmunds Clo. 57 J1
NW8
St. Edmunds Ter.
St. Edmunds Clo. 84 H2
SW17
College Gdns.
St. Edmunds Clo., 71 D2
Erith
St. Katherines Rd.
St. Edmunds Dr., 37 D1
Stan.
St. Edmund's La., 72 H7
Twick.
St. Edmunds Rd. N9 25 D7
St. Edmunds Rd., 43 C6
Ilf.
**St. Edmunds Ter. 6 H1
NW8**
St. Edmunds Ter. 57 H1
NW8
St. Edwards Clo. 39 D6
NW11
St. Egberts Way E4 34 C1
St. Elmo Rd. W12 65 F1
St. Elmos Rd. SE16 68 G2
St. Erkenwald Rd., 61 G1
Bark.
**St. Ermin's Hill 15 H5
SW1**
St. Ervans Rd. W10 57 C5
St. Fabian Twr. E4 33 J6
St. Faiths Clo., 24 J1
Enf.
St. Faith's Rd. 85 H1
SE21
St. Fillans Rd. SE6 87 C1
St. Francis Clo., 97 H6
Orp.
St. Francis Clo., 28 B1
Wat.
St. Francis Rd. 77 B4
SE22
St. Francis Twr. E4 33 J6
St. Gabriel's Clo. 51 H1
E11
St. Gabriels Rd. 48 A5
NW2
St. George St. W1 11 E5
St. George St. W1 58 B7
St. Georges Ave. E7 51 H7
St. Georges Ave. N7 49 D4
St. Georges Ave. 38 C4
NW9
St. Georges Ave. 64 G2
W5
St. Georges Ave., 54 F7
Sthl.
**St. Georges Circ. 16 G5
SE1**
St. Georges Circ. 67 H3
SE1

St. Georges Clo. 39 C6
NW11
St. Georges Clo., 46 D3
Wem.
St. Georges Ct. E6 61 C4
St. Georges Ct. SW7 14 C5
**St. George's Dr. 19 E2
SW1**
St. George's Dr. 67 B4
SW1
St. Georges Dr., 28 E3
Wat.
**St. Georges Flds. 10 H4
W2**
St. Georges Flds. 57 H6
W2
St. George's Gdns., 99 B2
Surb.
Hamilton Ave.
St. Georges Gro. 84 G3
SW17
St. Georges Gro. 84 G3
Est. SW17
St. Georges Ind. 32 H7
Est. N17
St. Georges La. EC3 13 C5
St. Georges Ms. NW1 48 J7
Regents Pk. Rd.
St. Georges Pl., 82 D1
Twick.
Church St.
St. Georges Rd. E7 51 H6
St. Georges Rd. E10 51 C3
St. Georges Rd. N9 33 D3
St. Georges Rd. N13 32 F3
St. Georges Rd. 39 C6
NW11
St. Georges Rd. SE1 16 F5
St. Georges Rd. SE1 67 G3
St. George's Rd. 84 C7
SW19
St. Georges Rd. W4 65 D2
St. Georges Rd. W7 64 C1
St. George's Rd., 96 B1
Beck.
St. Georges Rd., 97 C2
Brom.
St. Georges Rd., 53 E5
Dag.
St. George's Rd., 81 D4
Felt.
St. George's Rd., 43 C7
Ilf.
St. George's Rd., 83 A7
Kings.T.
St. George's Rd., 94 B3
Mitch.
St. Georges Rd., 97 G6
Orp.
St. Georges Rd., 73 J3
Rich.
St. George's Rd., 89 D6
Sid.
St. Georges Rd., 73 E5
Twick.
St. Georges Rd., 101 B5
Wall.
St. George's Rd. W., 97 B1
Brom.
St. Georges Sq. E7 51 H7
St. Georges Sq. E14 59 H7
St. Georges Sq. SE8 68 J4
**St. George's Sq. 19 H4
SW1**
St. George's Sq. 67 D5
SW1
St. George's Sq., 92 E3
N.Mal.
**St. George's Sq. 19 H4
Ms. SW1**
St. George's Sq. 67 D5
Ms. SW1
St. Georges Ter. 48 J7
NW1
Regents Pk. Rd.
St. Georges Wk., 101 J3
Croy.
**St. Georges Way 21 D6
SE15**
St. Georges Way 68 B6
SE15
St. Gerards Clo. 76 C5
SW4
St. Germans Pl. SE3 78 G1
St. Germans Rd. 86 H1
SE23
St. Giles Clo., Dag. 53 H7
St. Giles Ave.
St. Giles Clo., Orp. 104 G5
**St. Giles High St. 11 J3
WC2**

St. Giles High St. WC2	58	D6
St. Giles Pas. WC2	**11**	**J4**
St. Giles Rd. SE5	68	B7
St. Gilles Ho. E2	59	G2
Mace St.		
St. Gothard Rd. SE27	86	A4
St. Gregory Clo.,	45	C4
Ruis.		
St. Helena Rd. SE16	69	G4
St. Helena St. WC1	**6**	**E1**
St. Helens Cres.	94	F1
SW16		
St. Helens Gdns.	57	A5
W10		
St. Helens Pl. EC3	**13**	**D3**
St. Helens Rd. SW16	94	F1
St. Helen's Rd. W13	64	E1
Dane Rd.		
St. Helens Rd., Erith	71	D2
St. Helens Rd., Ilf.	43	C6
St. Helier Ave.,	93	F7
Mord.		
St. Heliers Ave.,	72	G5
Houns.		
St. Heliers Rd. E10	42	C6
St. Hildas Clo. NW6	57	A1
St. Hildas Clo. SW17	84	H2
St. Hilda's Rd. SW13	65	H6
St. Hughe's Clo.	84	H2
SW17		
College Gdns.		
St. Hughs Rd. SE20	95	E1
Ridsdale Rd.		
St. James Ave. E2	59	F2
St. James Ave. N20	31	H3
St. James Ave. W13	64	D1
St. James Ave.,	95	H3
Beck.		
St. James Ave.,	100	D5
Sutt.		
St. James Clo. N20	31	H3
St. James Clo. SE18	70	F5
Congleton Gro.		
St. James Clo.,	92	F5
N.Mal.		
St. James Clo.,	45	C2
Ruis.		
St. James Gdns. W11	66	B1
St. James Gdns.,	46	G7
Wem.		
St. James Gate NW1	49	D7
St. Pauls Cres.		
St. James Ms. E14	69	C3
St. James Rd. E15	51	F5
St. James Rd. N9	33	E2
Queens Rd.		
St. James Rd.,	100	H3
Cars.		
St. James Rd.,	85	A7
Mitch.		
St. James Rd.,	91	G6
Surb.		
St. James Rd.,	100	D5
Sutt.		
St. James St. W6	65	J5
St. James Wk. SE15	68	C7
Sumner Est.		
St. James Way, Sid.	89	B5
St. James'S E14	77	H1
St. James's Ave.,	95	H3
Beck.		
St. James's Ave.,	81	J5
Hmptn.		
St. James's Clo.	84	J2
SW17		
St. James's Dr.		
St. James's Cotts.,	73	G5
Rich.		
Paradise Rd.		
St. James's Ct. SW1	**15**	**G5**
St. James's Ct. SW1	67	C3
St. James's Cres.	76	G3
SW9		
St. James's Dr.	84	J1
SW17		
St. James's Gro.	75	J2
SW11		
Reform St.		
St. James's La. N10	40	B4
St. James's Mkt.	**11**	**H6**
SW1		
St. James's Pk. SW1	**15**	**H5**
St. James's Pk. SW1	67	C2
St. James's Pk.,	94	J7
Croy.		
St. James's Pas. EC3	**13**	**E4**
St. James's Pl. SW1	**15**	**F2**
St. James's Pl. SW1	67	C1
St. James's Rd. SE1	**21**	**J5**
St. James's Rd. SE1	68	D5
St. James's Rd.	**17**	**J5**
SE16		

St. James's Rd.	68	D3
SE16		
St. James's Rd.,	94	H7
Croy.		
St. James's Rd.,	81	H5
Hmptn.		
St. James's Rd.	91	G2
Kings.l.		
St. James's Row EC1	**8**	**G5**
St. James's Sq. SW1	**15**	**G1**
St. James's Sq. SW1	67	D1
St. James's St. E17	41	H5
St. James's St. SW1	**15**	**F1**
St. James's St. SW1	67	C1
St. James's Ter.	**6**	**J1**
NW8		
St. James's Ter.	57	J1
Ms. NW8		
St. James's Wk. EC1	**8**	**G5**
St. James's Wk. EC1	58	H4
St. Joans Rd. N9	33	C1
St. John Fisher	71	D3
Rd., Erith		
St. John St. EC1	**8**	**G3**
St. John St. EC1	58	G2
St. Johns Ave. N11	31	J5
St. John's Ave.	56	F1
NW10		
St. John's Ave.	75	A5
SW15		
St. John's Ch. Rd.	50	F5
E9		
St. John's Clo. SW6	66	D7
Dawes Rd.		
St. John's Clo.,	46	H5
Wem.		
St. John's Cotts.	86	F7
SE20		
Maple Rd.		
St. Johns Cotts.,	73	H4
Rich.		
Kew Foot Rd.		
St. Johns Ct.,	34	H1
Buck.H.		
St. John's Ct.,	73	C2
Islw.		
St. John's Cres. SW9	76	G3
St. Johns Dr. SW18	84	E1
St. Johns Est. N1	**9**	**C2**
St. Johns Est. N1	59	A2
St. Johns Gdns. W11	57	B7
St. Johns Gro. N19	49	C2
St. Johns Gro. SW13	74	F2
Terrace Gdns.		
St. Johns Gro.,	73	H4
Rich.		
Kew Foot Rd.		
St. John's Hill	75	G4
SW11		
St. John's Hill	75	G4
Gro. SW11		
St. John's La. EC1	**8**	**G6**
St. John's La. EC1	58	H4
St. John's Ms. W11	57	D6
Ledbury Rd.		
St. Johns Par., Sid.	89	A4
Church Rd.		
St. John's Pk. SE3	69	F7
St. Johns Pas. SE23	86	F1
Davids Rd.		
St. John's Pas. SW19	84	B6
Ridgway Pl.		
St. John's Path EC1	**8**	**G6**
St. John's Pathway	86	F1
SE23		
Devonshire Rd.		
St. John's Pl. EC1	**8**	**G6**
St. John's Rd. E4	34	B3
St. Johns Rd. E6	61	B1
St. Johns Rd. E16	60	G6
St. John's Rd. E17	42	B2
St. John's Rd. N15	41	B6
St. Johns Rd. NW11	39	C6
St. John's Rd. SE20	86	F7
St. John's Rd. SW11	74	H4
St. John's Rd. SW19	84	B6
St. John's Rd.,	61	H1
Bark.		
St. Johns Rd.,	100	H3
Cars.		
St. Johns Rd.,	101	H3
Croy.		
Sylverdale Rd.		
St. Johns Rd.,	91	A4
E.Mol.		
St. John's Rd.,	81	E4
Felt.		
St. Johns Rd., Har.	37	C6
St. John's Rd., Ilf.	43	G7
St. Johns Rd., Islw.	73	B2
St. Johns Rd.,	91	F2
Kings.T.		

St. Johns Rd., Loug.	27	C2
St. John's Rd.,	92	C3
N.Mal.		
St. Johns Rd., Orp.	97	G6
St. John's Rd.,	73	H4
Rich.		
St. Johns Rd., Sid.	89	B4
St. Johns Rd.,	63	E3
Sthl.		
St. Johns Rd.,	100	D3
Sutt.		
St. John's Rd.,	80	B3
Well.		
St. John's Rd.,	46	H5
Wem.		
St. Johns Sq. EC1	**8**	**G6**
St. Johns Ter. E7	51	H6
St. Johns Ter. SE18	70	F6
St. Johns Ter. W10	57	A4
Harrow Rd.		
St. Johns Vale SE8	78	A2
St. Johns Vill. N19	49	D2
St. Johns Way N19	49	C2
St. John's Wd. Ct.	**6**	**F4**
NW8		
St. John's Wd. High	**6**	**F2**
St. NW8		
St. John's Wd. High	57	G2
St. NW8		
St. John's Wd. Pk.	57	G1
NW8		
St. John's Wd. Rd.	**6**	**E5**
NW8		
St. John's Wd. Rd.	57	G4
NW8		
St. John's Wd. Ter.	**6**	**F1**
NW8		
St. John's Wd. Ter.	57	G2
NW8		
St. Josephs Clo.	57	B5
W10		
Bevington Rd.		
St. Josephs Clo.,	104	J4
Orp.		
St. Joseph's Ct.	69	H6
SE7		
St. Josephs Dr.,	63	E1
Sthl.		
St. Joseph's Gro.	38	H4
NW4		
St. Josephs Rd. N9	25	E7
St. Joseph's Vale	78	D3
SE3		
St. Jude St. N16	50	B5
St. Jude's Rd. E2	59	E2
St. Julian's Clo.	85	G4
SW16		
St. Julian's Fm.	85	G4
Rd. SE27		
St. Julian's Rd.	57	D1
NW6		
St. Katharines Prec.	**7**	**D1**
NW1		
St. Katharine's Way	**17**	**G1**
E1		
St. Katharine's Way	68	D1
E1		
St. Katherines Rd.,	71	D2
Erith		
St. Katherine's Row	**13**	**E5**
EC3		
St. Keverne Rd. SE9	88	B4
St. Kilda Rd. W13	64	D1
St. Kilda Rd., Orp.	104	J1
St. Kilda's Rd. N16	50	A1
St. Kildas Rd.,	37	B6
Har.		
St. Kitts Ter. SE19	86	B5
St. Laurence Clo.	57	A1
NW6		
St. Lawrence Clo.,	29	J7
Edg.		
St. Lawrence Dr.,	36	B5
Pnr.		
St. Lawrence St.	69	C1
E14		
St. Lawrence Ter.	57	B5
W10		
St. Lawrence Way	76	G2
SW9		
St. Leonards Ave. E4	34	D6
St. Leonards Ave.,	37	F5
Har.		
St. Leonard's Clo.,	80	A3
Well.		
Hook La.		
St. Leonards Ct. N1	**9**	**C3**
St. Leonard's Gdns.	72	E1
Houns.		
St. Leonards Gdns.,	52	F5
Ilf.		
St. Leonards Ri.,	104	H4
Orp.		

St. Leonards Rd.	60	B5
E14		
St. Leonards Rd.	56	D4
NW10		
St. Leonard's Rd.	74	B3
SW14		
St. Leonards Rd.	55	F6
W13		
St. Leonards Rd.,	101	H3
Croy.		
St. Leonards Rd.,	99	G6
Esher		
St. Leonards Rd.,	91	G5
Surb.		
St. Leonards Rd.,	91	D6
T.Ditt.		
St. Leonards Sq.	49	A6
NW5		
St. Leonards Sq.,	91	G5
Surb.		
St. Leonards Rd.		
St. Leonard's St. E3	60	B3
St. Leonard's Ter.	**18**	**J4**
SW3		
St. Leonard's Ter.	66	J5
SW3		
St. Leonards Wk.	85	F7
SW16		
St. Loo Ave. SW3	**18**	**H5**
St. Loo Ave. SW3	66	H6
St. Louis Rd. SE27	85	J4
St. Loys Rd. N17	41	B2
St. Luke's Ave. SW4	76	D4
St. Lukes Ave., Ilf.	52	E5
St. Lukes Clo. SE25	95	E6
St. Luke's Est. EC1	**9**	**B4**
St. Luke's Est. EC1	59	A3
St. Lukes Ms. W11	57	C6
Basing St.		
St. Lukes Pas.,	91	J1
Kings.T.		
St. Lukes Rd. W11	57	C5
St. Lukes Sq. E16	60	F6
St. Luke's St. SW3	**18**	**H3**
St. Luke's St. SW3	66	H5
St. Luke's Yd. W9	57	C3
St. Malo Ave. N9	33	F3
St. Margarets,	61	F1
Bark.		
St. Margarets Ave.	40	H4
N15		
St. Margarets Ave.	31	F1
N20		
St. Margarets Ave.,	45	J3
Har.		
St. Margarets Ave.,	88	G3
Sid.		
St. Margaret's Ave.,	100	B3
Sutt.		
St. Margaret's Ct.	**17**	**B2**
SE1		
St. Margarets Cres.	74	H5
SW15		
St. Margarets Dr.,	73	E5
Twick.		
St. Margaret's Gro.	51	F3
E11		
St. Margaret's Gro.	70	F6
SE18		
St. Margarets Gro.,	73	D6
Twick.		
St. Margarets Pas.	78	E3
SE13		
Church Ter.		
St. Margaret's Rd.	51	J2
E12		
St. Margarets Rd.	41	B3
N17		
St. Margaret's Rd.	56	J3
NW10		
St. Margaret's Rd.	77	J4
SE4		
St. Margarets Rd.	64	B2
W7		
St. Margaret's Rd.,	95	G4
Beck.		
St. Margaret's Rd.,	30	B5
Edg.		
St. Margarets Rd.,	73	E6
Twick.		
St. Margarets Sq.	77	J4
SE4		
Adelaide Ave.		
St. Margaret's St.	**16**	**A4**
SW1		
St. Margaret's St.	67	E2
SW1		
St. Margaret's Ter.	70	F5
SE18		
St. Mark St. E1	**13**	**G4**
St. Mark St. E1	59	C6
St. Marks Clo. SE10	69	C7
Ashburnham Pl.		

St. Marks Clo. W11 57 B6
Lancaster Rd.
St. Mark's Clo., 23 E3
Barn.
St. Marks Cres. NW1 58 A1
St. Marks Gate E9 50 J7
Cadogan Ter.
St. Mark's Gro. 18 B7
SW10
St. Mark's Gro. 66 E6
SW10
St. Marks Hill, 91 H6
Surb.
St. Mark's Pl. SW19 84 C6
Wimbledon Hill Rd.
St. Marks Pl. W11 57 B6
St. Marks Ri. E8 50 C5
St. Marks Rd. SE25 95 G4
Coventry Rd.
St. Mark's Rd. W5 64 H1
The Common
St. Marks Rd. W7 64 B2
St. Marks Rd. W10 57 A5
St. Marks Rd. W11 57 B6
St. Marks Rd., 96 H3
Brom.
St. Marks Rd., Enf. 25 C5
St. Marks Rd., 93 J2
Mitch.
St. Marks Rd., 82 E7
Tedd.
St. Marks Sq. NW1 58 A1
Regents Pk. Rd.
St. Martins Ave. E6 61 A2
St. Martin's Clo. 58 C1
NW1
St. Martins Clo., 25 E1
Enf.
St. Martins Clo., 71 D2
Erith
St. Helens Rd.
St. Martin's Clo., 28 C4
Wat.
Muirfield Rd.
St. Martin's Ct. WC2 12 A5
St. Martins Est. SW2 85 G1
St. Martin's La. WC2 12 A5
St. Martin's La. WC2 58 E7
St. Martin's Pl. WC2 12 A6
St. Martin's Pl. WC2 58 E7
St. Martins Rd. N9 33 E2
St. Martin's Rd. SW9 76 F2
St. Martin's St. WC2 11 J6
St. Martins Way 84 F3
SW17
St. Martin's-le-Grand 12 J3
EC1
St. Martin's-le-Grand 58 J6
EC1
St. Mary Abbots Pl. 66 C3
W8
St. Mary Abbots 66 C3
Ter. W14
St. Mary at Hill EC3 13 D6
St. Mary at Hill EC3 59 B7
St. Mary Ave. 101 A3
Wall.
St. Mary Axe EC3 13 D4
St. Mary Axe EC3 59 B6
St. Mary Rd. E17 42 A4
St. Mary St. SE18 70 D4
St. Marychurch St. 68 F2
SE16
St. Marys, Bark. 61 G1
St. Marys App. E12 52 C5
St. Mary's Ave. E11 42 H6
St. Mary's Ave. N3 39 B2
St. Mary's Ave., 96 E3
Brom.
St. Mary's Ave., 63 G4
Sthl.
St. Marys Ave., 82 C6
Tedd.
St. Marys Clo., 98 J7
Chess.
St. Marys Clo., 99 G7
Epsom
St. Mary's Clo., Sun. 90 A4
Green Way
St. Marys Ct. E6 61 C4
St. Mary's Ct. SE7 70 A7
St. Mary's Ct. W5 64 G2
St. Mary's Rd.
St. Marys Cres. NW4 38 H3
St. Marys Cres., 64 A7
Islw.
St. Mary's Gdns. 20 F1
SE11
St. Mary's Gdns. 67 G4
SE11
St. Mary's Gro. N1 49 H6
St. Mary's Gro. 74 H3
SW13

St. Mary's Gro. W4 65 B6
St. Mary's Gro., 73 J4
Rich.
St. Marys Mans. W2 10 E1
St. Mary's Mans. W2 57 G5
St. Mary's Ms. NW6 48 E7
Priory Rd.
St. Mary's Path N1 58 H1
St. Mary's Pl. SE9 79 D6
Eltham High St.
St. Mary's Pl. W5 64 G2
St. Marys Rd.
St. Marys Rd. E10 51 C3
St. Marys Rd. E13 00 HJ
St. Marys Rd. N8 40 E4
High St.
St. Marys Rd. N9 33 E1
St. Marys Rd. NW10 56 E1
St. Marys Rd. NW11 39 B7
St. Mary's Rd. SE15 77 F1
St. Mary's Rd. SE25 95 B3
St. Mary's Rd. 84 B5
(Wimbledon) SW19
St. Mary's Rd. W5 64 G2
St. Mary's Rd., 23 J7
Barn.
St. Marys Rd., Bex. 89 J1
St. Mary's Rd., 91 A5
E.Mol.
St. Marys Rd., Ilf. 52 F2
St. Marys Rd., 91 G6
Surb.
St. Marys Rd. (Long 91 F7
Ditton), Surb.
St. Mary's Rd., 99 E2
Wor.Pk.
St. Marys Sq. W2 10 E1
St. Marys Sq. W2 57 G5
St. Mary's Sq. W5 64 G2
St. Mary's Rd.
St. Marys Ter. W2 10 E1
St. Mary's Ter. W2 57 G5
St. Marys Vw., Har. 37 F5
St. Matthew St. SW1 15 H6
St. Matthews Ave., 98 H1
Surb.
St. Matthew's Dr., 97 C3
Brom.
St. Matthew's Rd. 76 F4
SW2
St. Matthews Rd. W5 64 H1
The Common
St. Matthew's Row 9 H5
E2
St. Matthew's Row 59 D3
E2
St. Matthias Clo. 38 F5
NW9
St. Maur Rd. SW6 75 C1
St. Merryn Clo. 70 G7
SE18
St. Michael's All. EC3 13 C4
St Michaels Ave. 25 F7
N9
St. Michael's Ave., 47 A6
Wem.
St. Michaels Clo. 61 A5
E16
Long Mark Rd.
St. Michael's Clo. 39 C2
N3
St. Michaels Clo. 31 H5
N12
St. Michaels Clo., 97 B3
Brom.
St. Michaels Clo., 71 D2
Erith
St. Helens Rd.
St. Michaels Clo., 99 F2
Wor.Pk.
St. Michaels Cres. 36 E6
Pnr.
St. Michaels Gdns. 57 B5
W10
St. Lawrence Ter.
St. Michaels Rd. 47 J4
NW2
St. Michael's Rd. 76 F2
SW9
St. Michaels Rd., 101 J1
Croy.
St. Michaels Rd., 101 C6
Wall.
St. Michaels Rd., 80 B3
Well.
St. Michaels St. W2 10 F3
St. Michaels St. W2 57 G6
St. Michaels Ter. 40 E2
N22

St. Mildred's Ct. 13 B4
EC2
St. Mildreds Rd. 78 F7
SE12
St. Nicholas Glebe 85 A5
SW17
St. Nicholas La., 97 B1
Chis.
St. Nicholas Rd. 70 J5
SE18
St. Nicholas Rd., 100 E5
Sutt.
St. Nicholas Rd., 91 C6
T.Ditt.
St. Nicholas St. 77 J1
SE8
Lucas St.
St. Nicholas Way, 100 E4
Sutt.
St. Ninian's Ct. 31 J3
N20
St. Norbert Grn. 77 H4
SE4
St. Norbert Rd. SE4 77 G5
St. Olaf's Rd. SW6 66 B7
St. Olaves Ct. EC2 13 B4
St. Olave's Est. SE1 17 E3
St. Olaves Gdns. 20 E1
SE11
St. Olaves Rd. E6 61 D1
St. Olave's Wk. 94 C2
SW16
St. Olav's Sq. SE16 68 F2
Albion St.
St. Oswald's Pl. 20 C4
SE11
St. Oswald's Pl. 67 F5
SE11
St. Oswald's Rd. 94 H1
SW16
St. Oswulf St. SW1 19 J2
St. Pancras Way 49 C7
NW1
St. Patrick's Ct., 34 E7
Wdf.Grn.
St. Paul St. N1 58 J1
St. Paul's All. EC4 58 H6
St. Paul's Chyd.
St. Paul's Ave. NW2 47 J6
St. Paul's Ave. 68 G1
SE16
St. Pauls Ave., 37 J5
Har.
St. Paul's Chyd. EC4 12 H4
St. Paul's Chyd. EC4 58 H6
St. Paul's Clo. SE7 70 A5
St. Paul's Clo. W5 64 J2
St. Pauls Clo., 100 H1
Cars.
St. Pauls Clo., 98 G4
Chess.
St. Pauls Clo., 72 E2
Houns.
St. Paul's Ct. W14 66 A4
Colet Gdns.
St. Pauls Ctyd. SE8 69 A7
Deptford High St.
St. Pauls Cray Rd., 97 G1
Chis.
St. Pauls Cres. NW1 49 D7
St. Pauls Dr. E15 51 D5
St. Paul's Ms. NW1 49 D7
St. Pauls Cres.
St. Paul's Pl. N1 50 A6
St. Pauls Ri. N13 32 H6
St. Paul's Rd. N1 49 H6
St. Paul's Rd. N17 33 D7
St. Paul's Rd., 61 F1
Bark.
St. Paul's Rd., 64 G6
Brent.
St. Paul's Rd., 71 J7
Erith
St. Paul's Rd., 73 J3
Rich.
St. Paul's Rd., 94 J3
Th.Hth.
St. Paul's 50 A6
Shrubbery N1
St. Pauls Sq., 96 G2
Brom.
St. Pauls St. E3 59 B3
St. Paul's Ter. SE17 20 H5
St. Pauls Twr. E10 42 C7
St. Pauls Wk., 91 H2
Kings.T.
Alexandra Rd.
St. Pauls Way E3 59 J5
St. Pauls Way N3 31 E7
St. Pauls Wd. Hill, 97 H2
Orp.
St. Peter's All. EC3 13 C4
St. Peter's Ave. E2 9 J2

St. Peter's Ave. 42 E4
E17
St. Peters Ave. N18 33 D4
St. Peter's Clo. E2 9 J2
St. Peter's Clo. E2 59 D2
St. Peters Clo. 84 H2
SW17
College Gdns.
St. Peters Clo., 22 H5
Barn.
St. Peters Clo., 88 G7
Chis.
St. Peters Clo., 43 H4
Ilf.
St. Peters Clo., 45 D2
Ruis.
St. Peters Clo. 29 A1
(Bushey), Wat.
St. Peter's Ct. NW4 38 J5
St. Peters Ct. SE3 78 F4
Eltham Rd.
St. Peters Ct. SE4 77 J2
Wickham Rd.
St. Peter's Gdns. 85 G3
SE27
St. Peters Gro. W6 65 G4
St. Peters Rd. N9 33 E1
St. Peters Rd. N9 33 F1
St. Peters Rd. W6 65 G5
St. Peters Rd., 102 A4
Croy.
St. Peters Rd., 92 A2
Kings.T.
St. Peters Rd., 54 G5
Sthl.
St. Peters Rd., 73 E5
Twick.
St. Peters Rd., 90 G4
W.Mol.
St. Peter's Sq. E2 9 J2
St. Peters Sq. W6 65 G5
St. Peters Vill. N1 58 H1
St. Peter's St. N1 102 A5
S.Croy.
St. Peters Ter. SW6 66 C7
St. Peters Vill. W6 65 G4
St. Peter's Way N1 50 B7
St. Peters Way W5 55 G5
St. Petersburgh Ms. 10 A5
W2
St. Petersburgh Ms. 57 E7
W2
St. Petersburgh Pl. 10 A5
W2
St. Petersburgh Pl. 57 E7
W2
St. Philip Sq. SW8 76 B2
St. Philip St. SW8 76 B2
St. Philip's Ave., 99 H2
Wor.Pk.
St. Philip's Rd. E8 50 D6
St. Philips Rd., 91 G6
Surb.
St. Philip's Way N1 58 J1
Linton St.
St. Quentin Rd., 79 J3
Well.
St. Quintin Ave. 56 J5
W10
St. Quintin Gdns. 56 J5
W10
St. Quintin Rd. E13 60 H2
St. Raphael's Way 47 C5
NW10
St. Regis Clo. N10 40 B2
St. Ronans Cres. 34 G7
Wdf.Grn.
St. Rule St. SW8 76 C2
St. Saviour's Est. 17 F5
SE1
St. Saviour's Est. 68 C3
SE1
St. Saviour's Rd. 76 F5
SW2
St. Saviours Rd., 94 H6
Croy.
St. Silas Pl. NW5 49 A6
St. Silas St. Est. 49 A6
NW5
St. Simons Ave. 74 J5
SW15
St. Stephens Ave. 42 C5
E17
St. Stephens Ave. 65 H2
W12
St. Stephens Ave. 55 E6
W13
St. Stephens Clo. 42 B5
E17
St. Stephens Clo. 57 H1
NW8
St. Stephens Clo., 54 G5
Sthl.

St. Stephens Cres. W2 57 D6
Talbot Rd.
St. Stephens Cres., Th.Hth. 94 G3
St. Stephens Gdn. 57 D6
W2
Shrewsbury Rd.
St. Stephens Gdns. 75 C5
SW1F
Manfred Rd.
St. Stephens Gdns. W2 57 D6
St. Stephen's Gdns., Twick. 73 F6
St. Stephens Gro. SE13 78 C3
St. Stephens Ms. W2 57 D5
Chepstow Rd.
St. Stephen's Pas., Twick. 73 F6
Richmond Rd.
St. Stephens Rd. E3 59 H1
St. Stephens Rd. E6 51 J7
St. Stephen's Rd. E17 42 B5
Grove Rd.
St. Stephens Rd. W13 55 E6
St. Stephen's Rd., Barn. 23 A5
St. Stephens Rd., Houns. 72 G6
St. Stephens Row EC4 13 B5
St. Stephens Ter. SW8 67 F7
St. Stephen's Wk. SW7 18 C1
St. Swithin's La. EC4 13 B5
St. Swithin's La. EC4 59 A7
St. Swithun's Rd. SE13 78 D5
St. Thomas Ct., Bex. 80 G7
St. Thomas Dr., Orp. 104 F1
St. Thomas Dr., Pnr. 36 E1
St. Thomas Gdns., Ilf. 52 F6
St. Thomas Pl. NW1 49 D7
Maiden La.
St. Thomas Rd. E16 60 G6
St. Thomas Rd. N14 24 D7
St. Thomas Rd., Belv. 71 J2
St. Thomas St. SE1 17 C2
St. Thomas St. SE1 68 A1
St. Thomas's Gdns. NW5 49 A6
Queens Cres.
St. Thomas's Pl. E9 50 F7
St. Thomas's Rd. N4 49 G2
St. Thomas's Rd. NW10 56 E1
St. Thomas's Rd. W4 65 C6
St. Thomas's Sq. E9 50 F7
St. Thomas's Way SW6 66 C7
St. Ursula Gro., Pnr. 36 D5
St. Ursula Rd., Sthl. 54 G6
St. Vincent Clo. SE27 85 H5
St. Vincent Rd., Twick. 72 J6
St. Vincent St. W1 11 C2
St. Wilfrids Clo., Barn. 23 G5
East Barnet Rd.
St. Wilfrid's Rd., Barn. 23 G5
East Barnet Rd.
St. Winifreds Clo., Chig. 35 F5
St. Winifreds Rd., Tedd. 82 E6
St. Winifride's Ave. E12 52 C5
Saints Dr. E7 52 A5
Salamanca Pl. SE11 20 C2
Salamanca St. SE11 20 C2
Salamanca St. SE11 67 F4
Salcombe Dr., Mord. 100 A1
Salcombe Dr., Rom. 44 F6
Salcombe Gdns. NW7 30 J6
Salcombe Rd. E17 41 J7
Salcombe Rd. N16 50 B5
Salcombe Way, Ruis. 45 A2

Salcott Rd. SW11 75 H5
Salcott Rd., Croy. 101 E3
Sale Pl. W2 10 G2
Sale Pl. W2 57 H6
Sale St. E2 9 J5
Sale St. E2 59 D4
Salehurst Clo. 37 H5
Salehurst Rd. SE4 77 J6
Salem Pl., Croy. 101 J3
Salem Rd. W2 10 B5
Salem Rd. W2 57 E7
Salford Rd. SW2 85 D1
Salhouse Clo. SE28 62 C6
Rollesby Way
Salisbury Ave. N3 39 C3
Salisbury Ave., Bark. 52 G7
Salisbury Ave., Sutt. 100 C6
Salisbury Clo. SE17 21 B1
Salisbury Clo., Wor.Pk. 99 F3
Salisbury Ct. EC4 12 F4
Salisbury Ct. EC4 58 H6
Salisbury Gdns. SW19 84 B7
Salisbury Gdns., Buck.H. 35 A2
Salisbury Hall Gdns. E4 34 A6
Salisbury Ho. E14 60 B6
Hobday St.
Salisbury Ms. SW6 66 C7
Dawes Rd.
Salisbury Pl. SW9 67 H7
Salisbury Pl. W1 10 J1
Salisbury Pl. W1 57 J5
Salisbury Rd. E4 34 A3
Salisbury Rd. E7 51 G6
Salisbury Rd. E10 51 C2
Salisbury Rd. E12 52 A5
Salisbury Rd. E17 42 C5
Salisbury Rd. N4 40 H5
Salisbury Rd. N9 33 D3
Salisbury Rd. N22 40 H1
Salisbury Rd. SE25 95 D6
Salisbury Rd. SW19 84 B7
Salisbury Rd. W13 64 D2
Salisbury Rd., Barn. 23 B3
Salisbury Rd., Bex. 89 G1
Salisbury Rd., Brom. 97 B5
Salisbury Rd., Cars. 100 J6
Salisbury Rd., Dag. 53 H6
Salisbury Rd., Felt. 81 C1
Salisbury Rd., Har. 37 A5
Salisbury Rd., Houns. 72 C3
Salisbury Rd., Ilf. 52 H2
Salisbury Rd., N.Mal. 92 D3
Salisbury Rd., Pnr. 36 A4
Salisbury Rd., Rich. 73 H4
Salisbury Rd., Sthl. 63 E4
Salisbury Rd., Wor.Pk. 99 D4
Salisbury Sq. EC4 12 F4
Salisbury St. NW8 6 G6
Salisbury St. NW8 57 H4
Salisbury St. W3 65 C2
Salisbury Ter. SE15 77 F3
Salisbury Wk. N19 49 C2
Salix Clo., Sun. 81 B7
Oak Gro.
Salliesfield, Twick. 73 A6
Salmen Rd. E13 60 F2
Salmon La. E14 59 H6
Salmon La., Belv. 71 G5
Salmon St. E14 59 J6
Salmon La.
Salmon St. NW9 47 B1
Salmond Clo., Stan. 29 D6
Robb Rd.
Salmons Rd. N9 33 D1
Salmons Rd., Chess. 98 G6
Salomons Rd. E13 60 J5
Chalk Rd.
Salop Rd. E17 41 G6
Saltash Clo., Sutt. 100 C4
Saltash Rd., Ilf. 35 G7
Saltash Rd., Well. 80 C1
Saltcoats Rd. W4 65 E2
Saltcroft Clo., Wem. 47 B1
Salter Rd. SE16 68 G1
Salter St. E14 60 A7

Salter St. NW10 56 G3
Salterford Rd. SW17 85 A6
Salters Hall Ct. EC4 13 B5
Salters Hill SE19 86 A5
Salters Rd. E17 42 D4
Salters Rd. W10 57 A4
Salterton Rd. N7 49 E3
Saltram Clo. N15 41 C4
Saltram Cres. W9 57 C3
Saltwell St. E14 60 A7
Saltwood Gro. SE17 21 B4
Saltwood Rd. NW6 57 B1
Salvia Gdns., Grnf. 55 D2
Selborne Gdns.
Salvin Rd. SW15 75 A3
Salway Clo., Wdf.Grn. 34 F7
Salway Pl. E15 51 E6
Broadway
Salway Rd. E15 51 D6
Sam Bartram Clo. SE7 69 J5
Samantha Clo. E17 41 J7
Sambruck Ms. SE6 87 B2
Inchmery Rd.
Samels Ct. W6 65 G5
South Black Lion La.
Samford St. NW8 6 G6
Samford St. NW8 57 H4
Samos Rd. SE20 95 E2
Sampson Ave., Barn. 23 A5
Sampson Clo., Belv. 71 D3
Carrill Way
Sampson St. E1 17 J2
Sampson St. E1 68 D1
Samson St. E13 60 J2
Samuel Clo. E8 59 C1
Pownall Rd.
Samuel Clo. SE14 68 G6
Samuel Clo. SE18 70 B4
Samuel Johnson Clo. SW16 85 G4
Curtis Fld. Rd.
Samuel Lewis Trust Dws. E8 50 D4
Amhurst Rd.
Samuel Lewis Trust Dws. N1 49 G7
Liverpool Rd.
Samuel Lewis Trust Dws. SW3 18 G2
Samuel Lewis Trust Dws. SW6 66 D7
Samuel St. SE18 70 C4
Sancroft Clo. NW2 47 H3
Sancroft Rd., Har. 37 C2
Sancroft St. SE11 20 D3
Sancroft St. SE11 67 F5
Sanctuary, The SW1 15 J5
Sanctuary, The, Bex. 80 D6
Sanctuary, The, Mord. 93 E6
Green La.
Sanctuary, The, Mord. 93 E6
Sanctuary St. SE1 17 A4
Sandal Rd. N18 33 D5
Sandal Rd., N.Mal. 92 D5
Sandal St. E15 60 E1
Sandale Clo. N16 50 A3
Stoke Newington Ch. St.
Sandall Clo. W5 55 H4
Sandall Rd. NW5 49 C6
Sandall Rd. W5 55 H4
Sandalwood Clo. E1 59 H4
Solebay St.
Sandalwood Rd., Felt. 81 B3
Sandbach Pl. SE18 70 F5
Sandbourne Ave. SW19 93 E2
Sandbourne Rd. SE4 77 H2
Sandbrook Clo. NW7 30 D6
Sandbrook Rd. N16 50 B3
Sandby Grn. SE9 79 B3
Sandell St. SE1 16 E3
Sanders Clo., Hmptn. 81 J5
Sanders La. NW7 30 J2
Sanders Way N19 49 D1
Sussex Way
Sanderson Clo. NW5 49 B4
Sanderstead Ave. NW2 48 B2
Sanderstead Clo. SW12 76 C7
Atkins Rd.
Sanderstead Rd. E10 50 H1
Sanderstead Rd., S.Croy. 102 A7

Sandfield Gdns., Th.Hth. 94 H3
Sandfield Ind. Est., Hmptn. 90 F1
Sandfield Pas., Th.Hth. 94 J3
Sandfield Rd., Th.Hth. 94 H3
Sandford Ave. N22 40 J1
Sandford Ave., Loug. 27 E3
Sandford Clo. E6 61 C4
Sandford Ct. N16 50 B1
Bethune Rd.
Sandford Rd. E6 61 B3
Sandford Rd. N22 40 J1
Sandford Rd., Bexh. 80 E4
Sandford Rd., Brom. 96 G3
Sandford Rd. SW6 66 E7
Kings Rd.
Sandgate La. SW18 84 H1
Sandgate Rd., Well. 71 C7
Sandgate St. SE15 68 E6
Sandham Pt. SE18 70 E4
Troy Ct.
Sandhills, Wall. 101 D4
Sandhurst Ave., Har. 36 H6
Sandhurst Ave., Surb. 92 B7
Sandhurst Clo. NW9 38 A3
Sandhurst Dr., Ilf. 52 J4
Sandhurst Rd. N9 25 F6
Sandhurst Rd. NW9 38 A3
Sandhurst Rd. SE6 87 D1
Sandhurst Rd., Bex. 80 D5
Sandhurst Rd., Sid. 88 J3
Sandhurst Way, S.Croy. 102 B7
Sandiford Rd., Sutt. 100 C2
Sandiland Cres., Brom. 103 F2
Sandilands, Croy. 102 D2
Sandilands Rd. SW6 75 E1
Sandison St. SE15 77 C3
Sandland St. WC1 12 D2
Sandland St. WC1 58 F5
Sandling Ri. SE9 88 D3
Sandlings, The N22 40 G2
Sandmere Rd. SW4 76 E4
Sandon Clo., Esher 91 A7
Sandown Ave., Dag. 53 J3
Sandown Clo., Houns. 72 A1
Sandown Rd. SE25 95 E5
Sandown Way, Nthlt. 45 G6
Sandpit Pl. SE7 70 B5
Sandpit Rd., Brom. 87 E5
Sandpits Rd., Croy. 102 G4
Sandpits Rd., Rich. 82 G2
Sandra Clo. N22 40 J1
New Rd.
Sandra Clo., Houns. 72 H5
Sandridge Clo., Har. 37 B4
Sandridge Ct. N4 49 J3
Queens Dr.
Sandridge St. N19 49 C2
Sandringham Ave. SW20 93 B1
Sandringham Clo., Enf. 25 B2
Sandringham Clo., Ilf. 43 F3
Sandringham Ct. W9 6 D4
Sandringham Cres., Har. 45 G2
Sandringham Dr., Well. 79 H2
Sandringham Gdns. N8 40 E6
Sandringham Gdns. N12 31 F6
Sandringham Gdns., Houns. 72 A1
Sandringham Gdns., Ilf. 43 F3
Sandringham Rd. E7 51 J5
Sandringham Rd. E8 50 C5
Sandringham Rd. E10 42 D6
Sandringham Rd. N22 40 J3
Sandringham Rd. NW2 47 H6
Sandringham Rd. NW11 39 B7
Sandringham Rd., Bark. 52 J6
Sandringham Rd., Brom. 87 G5
Sandringham Rd., Nthlt. 45 G7

Sandringham Rd., Th.Hth.	94	J5
Sandringham Rd., Wor.Pk.	99	G3
Sandrock Pl., Croy.	102	G4
Sandrock Rd. SE13	78	A3
Sand's End La. SW6	75	E1
Sands Way, Wdf.Grn.	35	C6
Sandstone Pl. N19	49	B2
Dartmouth Pk. Hill		
Sandstone Rd. SE12	87	H2
Sandtoft Rd. SE7	69	H6
Sandwell Cres. NW6	48	D6
Sandwich St. WC1	**8**	**A4**
Sandwich St. WC1	58	E3
Sandy Bury, Orp.	104	G3
Sandy Hill Ave. SE18	70	E5
Sandy Hill Rd. SE18	70	E5
Sandy La., Har.	37	J6
Sandy La., Kings.T.	91	E1
Sandy La., Mitch.	94	A1
Sandy La., Rich.	82	F2
Sandy La., Sid.	89	D7
Sandy La., Sutt.	100	B7
Sandy La., Tedd.	82	D7
Sandy La., Walt.	90	B6
Sandy La. Est., Rich.	82	G2
Sandy La. N., Wall.	101	D6
Sandy Ridge, Chis.	88	D6
Sandy Rd. NW3	48	E2
Sandy Way, Croy.	102	J3
Sandycombe Rd., Felt.	81	A1
Sandycombe Rd., Rich.	74	A3
Sandycombe Rd., Twick.	73	F6
Sandycroft SE2	71	A6
Sandyhill Rd., Ilf.	52	E4
Sandymount Ave., Stan.	29	F5
Sandys Row E1	**13**	**E2**
Sandys Row E1	59	B5
Sanford La. N16	50	C3
Stoke Newington High St.		
Sanford St. SE14	68	H6
Sanford Ter. N16	50	C2
Sanford Wk. N16	50	C2
Smalley Clo.		
Sanford Wk. SE14	68	H6
Cold Blow La.		
Sanger Ave., Chess.	98	H5
Sangley Rd. SE6	78	B7
Sangley Rd. SE25	95	B4
Sangora Rd. SW11	75	G4
Sans Wk. EC1	**8**	**F5**
Sans Wk. EC1	58	G4
Sansom Rd. E11	51	F2
Sansom St. SE5	68	A7
Santley St. SW4	76	E4
Santos Rd. SW18	75	D5
Santway, The, Stan.	29	B5
Sapphire Clo. E6	61	D6
Sapphire Clo., Dag.	53	C1
Sapphire Rd. SE8	68	H5
Sara Ct., Beck.	96	B1
Albemarle Rd.		
Saracen Clo., Croy.	95	A6
Saracen St. E14	60	A6
Saracen's Head Yd. EC3	**13**	**F4**
Sarah Ho. SW15	74	F4
Arabella Dr.		
Saratoga Rd. E5	50	F4
Sardinia St. WC2	**12**	**C4**
Sarita Clo., Har.	37	A2
Sarjant Path SW19	84	A2
Queensmere Rd.		
Sark Clo., Houns.	63	G7
Sark Wk. E16	60	H6
Pencraig Way		
Sarnesfield Rd., Enf.	25	A3
Church St.		
Sarre Rd. NW2	48	C5
Sarsen Ave., Houns.	72	F2
Sarsfeld Rd. SW12	84	J2
Sarsfield Rd., Grnf.	55	E2
Sartor Rd. SE15	77	G4
Satanita Clo. E16	61	A6
Aleston Beck Rd.		
Satchell Mead NW9	38	F1
Satchwell Rd. E2	**9**	**G4**
Satchwell St. E2	**9**	**G4**
Napier Rd.		
Sauls Grn. E11	51	E3
Saunders Ness Rd. E14	69	C5
Saunders Rd. SE18	70	J5
Saunders Way SE28	62	B7
Oriole Way		
Saunderton Rd., Wem.	46	E5
Savage Gdns. E6	61	C6
Savage Gdns. EC3	**13**	**E5**
Savernake Rd. N9	25	D6
Savernake Rd. NW3	48	J4
Savile Clo., N.Mal.	92	E5
Savile Gdns., Croy.	102	C2
Savile Row W1	**11**	**F5**
Savile Row W1	58	C7
Savill Gdns. SW20	93	G2
Bodnant Gdns.		
Savill Row, Wdf.Grn.	34	F6
Saville Rd. E16	70	B1
Saville Rd. W4	65	D3
Saville Row, Kings.T.	44	F6
Saville Rd., Twick.	82	C1
Saville Row, Brom.	103	F1
Saville Row, Enf.	25	G2
Green St.		
Savona Clo. SW19	84	B7
Savona Est. SW8	67	C7
Savona St. SW8	67	C7
Savoy Bldgs. WC2	**12**	**C6**
Savoy Clo. E15	60	E1
Arthingworth St.		
Savoy Clo., Edg.	30	A5
Savoy Ct. WC2	**12**	**B6**
Savoy Hill WC2	**12**	**C6**
Savoy Pl. WC2	**12**	**B6**
Savoy Pl. WC2	58	E7
Savoy Row WC2	**12**	**C6**
Savoy Steps WC2	**12**	**C6**
Savoy St. WC2	**12**	**C6**
Savoy St. WC2	58	F7
Savoy Way WC2	**12**	**C6**
Sawkins Clo. SW19	84	B2
Sawley Rd. W12	65	F1
Sawtry Clo., Cars.	93	G7
Sawyer Clo. N9	33	D2
Lion Rd.		
Sawyer St. SE1	**16**	**J3**
Sawyer St. SE1	67	J2
Sawyers Clo., Dag.	53	H6
Sawyer's Hill, Rich.	73	J7
Sawyers Lawn W13	55	C6
Saxby Rd. SW2	76	E7
Saxham Rd., Bark.	61	J2
Saxlingham Rd. E4	34	D3
Saxon Ave., Felt.	81	E2
Saxon Clo., Surb.	91	G6
Saxon Dr. W3	56	B6
Saxon Rd. E3	59	J2
Saxon Rd. E6	61	C4
Saxon Rd. N22	40	H1
Saxon Rd. SE25	95	A5
Saxon Rd., Brom.	87	F7
Saxon Rd., Ilf.	52	E6
Saxon Rd., Sthl.	63	E1
Saxon Rd., Wem.	47	C3
Saxon Wk., Sid.	89	C6
Cray Rd.		
Saxon Way N14	24	D6
Saxonbury Ave., Sun.	90	B3
Saxonbury Clo., Mitch.	93	G3
Saxonbury Gdns., Surb.	98	F1
Saxton Clo. SE13	78	D3
Sayers Wk., Rich.	73	J7
Stafford Pl.		
Sayes Ct. SE8	68	J5
Sayes Ct. St.		
Sayes Ct. St. SE8	68	J6
Scads Hill Clo., Orp.	97	J3
Scala St. W1	**11**	**G1**
Scala St. W1	58	C5
Scales Rd. N17	41	C3
Scampston Ms. W10	57	A6
Scandrett St. E1	68	E1
Scarba Wk. N1	50	A6
Marquess Rd.		
Scarborough Rd. E11	51	D1
Scarborough Rd. N4	40	G1
Scarborough Rd. N9	25	F7
Scarborough St. E1	**13**	**G4**
Scarbrook Rd., Croy.	101	J3
Scarle Rd., Wem.	46	G6
Scarlet Rd. SE6	87	E3
Scarlette Manor Way SW2	76	G7
Papworth Way		
Scarsbrook Rd. SE3	79	A3
Scarsdale Pl. W8	**14**	**A5**
Scarsdale Rd., Har.	45	J3
Scarsdale Vill. W8	66	D3
Scarth Rd. SW13	74	F3
Scawen Rd. SE8	68	H5
Scawfell St. E2	**9**	**G2**
Scawfell St. E2	59	C2
Scaynes Link N12	31	D5
Sceaux Est. SE5	77	B1
Sceaux Gdns. SE5	77	C1
Sceptre Rd. E2	59	F3
Schofield Wk. SE3	69	H7
Dornberg Clo.		
Scholars Rd. E4	34	C1
Scholars Rd. SW12	85	C1
Scholefield Rd. N19	49	D2
Scholes Cres. SW2	85	G1
School Ho. La., Tedd.	82	E7
School La. SE23	86	E2
School La., Kings.T.	91	F1
School La., Pnr.	36	E4
School La., Surb.	98	J1
School La., Well.	80	B3
School Pas., Kings.T.	91	J2
School Pas., Sthl.	63	F1
School Rd. E12	52	C4
School Rd. NW10	56	D4
School Rd., Chis.	97	F1
School Rd., Dag.	62	G1
School Rd., E.Mol.	91	A4
School Rd., Hmptn.	81	J6
School Rd., Houns.	72	J3
School Rd., Kings.T.	91	F1
School Rd. Ave., Hmptn.	81	J6
School Way N12	31	F4
High Rd.		
Schoolbell Ms. E3	59	H2
Arbery Rd.		
Schoolhouse La. E1	59	G7
Schoolway N12	31	G6
Schoolway, Dag.	53	C3
Schooner Clo. SE16	68	G2
Kinburn St.		
Schubert Rd. SW15	75	C5
Sclater St. E1	**9**	**F5**
Sclater St. E1	59	C4
Scoble Pl. N16	50	C4
Amhurst Rd.		
Scoresby St. SE1	**16**	**G2**
Scoresby St. SE1	67	H1
Scorton Ave., Grnf.	55	D2
Scot Gro., Pnr.	28	D7
Scotch Common W13	55	D5
Scoter Clo., Wdf.Grn.	34	H7
Mallards Rd.		
Scotland Grn. N17	41	C2
Scotland Grn. Rd., Enf.	25	G5
Scotland Grn. Rd. N. Enf.	25	G4
Scotland Pl. SW1	**16**	**A2**
Scotland Rd., Buck.H.	34	J1
Scotsdale Clo., Orp.	97	H4
Scotsdale Clo. Sutt.	100	B7
Scotsdale Rd. SE12	78	H5
Scotswood St. EC1	**8**	**F5**
Scotswood Wk. N17	33	D7
Scott Clo. SW16	94	F1
Scott Clo., Epsom	99	C5
Scott Cres., Har.	45	H1
Scott Ellis Gdns. NW8	**6**	**E4**
Scott Ellis Gdns. NW8	57	G3
Scott Fm. Clo., T.Ditt.	98	E1
Scott Gdns., Houns.	63	D7
Scott Ho. N18	33	D5
Scott Lidgett Cres. SE16	**17**	**H4**
Scott Lidgett Cres. SE16	68	D2
Scott Russell Pl. E14	69	B5
Westferry Rd.		
Scott St. E1	59	E4
Scottes La., Dag.	53	D1
Valence Ave.		
Scotts Ave., Brom.	96	D2
Scotts Dr., Hmptn.	81	H7
Scotts Fm. Rd., Epsom	99	C6
Scotts La., Brom.	96	D3
Scotts Rd. E10	51	C1
Scotts Rd. W12	65	H2
Scotts Rd., Brom.	87	G7
Scotts Rd., Sthl.	63	C3
Scott's Yd. EC4	**13**	**B5**
Scoulding Rd. E16	60	G6
Scout App. NW10	47	E4
Scout La. SW4	76	C3
Old Town		
Scout Way NW7	30	D4
Scovell Cres. SE1	**16**	**J4**
Scovell Rd. SE1	**16**	**J4**
Scrattons Ter., Bark.	62	D1
Scriven St. E8	59	C1
Scrooby St. SE6	78	B6
Scrubs La. NW10	56	G3
Scrubs La., W10	56	H5
Scrutton Clo. SW12	76	D7
Scrutton St. EC2	**9**	**D6**
Scrutton St. EC2	59	B4
Scudamore La. NW9	38	C4
Scutari Rd. SE22	77	F5
Scylla Rd. SE15	77	E3
Seabright St. E2	59	E3
Bethnal Grn. Rd.		
Seabrook Dr., W.Wick.	103	E2
Seabrook Gdns., Rom.	44	G7
Seabrook Rd., Dag.	53	D3
Seacoal La. EC4	**12**	**G4**
Seacoal La. EC4	58	H6
Seacole Clo. W3	56	D5
Seacourt Rd. SE2	71	D2
Seacroft Gdns., Wat.	28	D3
Seafield Rd. N11	32	C4
Seaford Rd. E17	42	B3
Seaford Rd. N15	41	A4
Seaford Rd. W13	64	E1
Seaford Rd., Enf.	25	B4
Seaford St. WC1	**8**	**B4**
Seaford St. WC1	58	F3
Seaforth Ave., N.Mal.	92	H5
Seaforth Cres. N5	49	J5
Seaforth Gdns. N21	24	F7
Seaforth Gdns., Epsom	99	F4
Seaforth Gdns., Wdf.Grn.	34	J5
Seaforth Pl. SW1	**15**	**G5**
Seager Pl. E3	59	J5
Burdett Rd.		
Seagrave Rd. SW6	66	D6
Seagry Rd. E11	42	G6
Seal St. E8	50	C4
Searle Pl. N4	49	F1
Evershot Rd.		
Searles Clo. SW11	66	H7
Searles Rd. SE1	**21**	**C1**
Searles Rd. SE1	68	A4
Sears St. SE5	**21**	**B7**
Sears St. SE5	68	A7
Seasprite Clo., Nthlt.	54	D3
Ruislip Rd.		
Seaton Ave., Ilf.	52	H5
Seaton Clo. E13	60	H4
New Barn St.		
Seaton Clo. SE11	**20**	**G3**
Seaton Clo. SW15	83	H1
Seaton Clo., Twick.	73	A6
Seaton Gdns., Ruis.	45	A3
Seaton Pl. NW1	**7**	**F5**
Seaton Pt. E5	50	D4
Nolan Way		
Seaton Rd., Mitch.	93	J2
Seaton Rd., Twick.	72	J6
Seaton Rd., Well.	71	C7
Seaton Rd., Wem.	55	H2
Seaton St. N18	33	D5
Sebastian St. EC1	**8**	**H4**
Sebastian St. EC1	58	H3
Sebastopol Rd. N9	33	D4
Sebbon St. N1	49	H7
Sebert Rd. E7	51	H5
Sebright Pas. E2	**9**	**J2**
Sebright Rd., Barn.	23	A2
Secker Cres., Har.	35	J6
Secker St. SE1	**16**	**E2**
Second Ave. E12	52	B4
Second Ave. E13	60	G3
First Ave.		
Second Ave. E17	42	A5
Second Ave. N18	33	F4
Second Ave. NW4	39	J4
Second Ave. SW14	74	E3
Second Ave. W3	65	F1
Second Ave. W10	57	B4
Second Ave., Dag.	62	H1
Second Ave., Enf.	25	C5
Second Ave., Rom.	44	C5
Second Ave., Walt.	90	B6
Second Ave., Wem.	46	G2
Second Clo., W.Mol.	90	J4
Second Cross Rd., Twick.	82	A2

Second Way, Wem. 47 B4
Sedan Way SE17 21 D3
Sedcombe Clo., Sid. 89 B4
Knoll Rd.
Sedcote Rd., Enf. 25 F5
Sedding St. SW1 19 B1
Sedding St. SW1 67 A4
Seddon Rd., Mord. 93 G5
Seddon St. WC1 8 D4
Sedge Rd. N17 33 E7
Sedgebrook Rd. SE3 79 A2
Sedgecombe Ave., Har. 37 F5
Sedgeford Rd. W12 65 F1
Sedgehill Rd. SE6 87 A4
Sedgemere Ave. N2 39 F3
Sedgemere Rd. SE2 71 C3
Sedgemoor Dr., Dag. 53 G4
Sedgeway SE6 87 F1
Sedgewood Clo., Brom. 96 F7
Sedgmoor Pl. SE5 68 B7
Sedgwick Rd. E10 51 C2
Sedgwick St. E9 50 G5
Sedleigh Rd. SW18 75 C6
Sedlescombe Rd. SW6 66 C6
Sedley Pl. W1 11 D4
Sedley Ri., Loug. 27 C2
Seeley Dr. SE21 86 B4
Seelig Ave. NW9 38 G7
Seely Rd. SW17 85 A6
Seething La. EC3 13 E5
Seething La. EC3 59 B7
Seething Wells La., Surb. 91 F6
Sefton Ave. NW7 30 D5
Sefton Ave., Har. 37 A1
Sefton Clo., Orp. 97 J4
Sefton Rd., Croy. 102 D1
Sefton Rd., Orp. 97 J4
Sefton St. SW15 74 J3
Segal Clo. SE23 77 H7
Sekforde St. EC1 8 G6
Sekforde St. EC1 58 H4
Selan Gdns., Hayes 54 B5
Selbie Ave. NW10 47 F5
Selborne Ave. E12 52 D4
Walton Rd.
Selborne Ave. E17 41 J4
Selborne Ave., Bex. 89 E1
Selborne Gdns. NW4 38 G4
Selborne Gdns., Grnf. 55 D2
Selborne Rd. E17 41 J5
Selborne Rd. N14 32 E3
Selborne Rd. N22 40 F1
Selborne Rd. SE5 77 A2
Denmark Hill
Selborne Rd., Croy. 102 B3
Selborne Rd., Ilf. 52 D2
Selborne Rd., N.Mal. 92 E2
Selborne Rd., Sid. 89 B4
Selbourne Ave., Surb. 98 J2
Selby Chase, Ruis. 45 B2
Selby Clo. E6 61 B5
Linton Gdns.
Selby Clo., Chess. 98 H7
Selby Clo., Chis. 88 D6
Selby Gdns., Sthl. 54 G4
Selby Grn., Cars. 93 H7
Selby Rd. E11 51 E3
Selby Rd. E13 60 H5
Selby Rd. N17 33 B6
Selby Rd. SE20 95 D2
Selby Rd. W5 55 E4
Selby Rd., Cars. 93 H7
Selby St. E1 9 J6
Selby St. E1 59 D4
Selden Rd. SE15 77 F2
Selden Wk. N7 49 F2
Durham Rd.
Selhurst New Rd. SE25 95 B6
Selhurst Pl. SE25 95 B6
Selhurst Rd. N9 33 A3
Selhurst Rd. SE25 95 B5
Selinas La., Dag. 44 E7
Selkirk Rd. SW17 84 H4
Selkirk Rd., Twick. 81 J2
Sellers Clo., Borwd. 22 C1
Sellers Hall Clo. N3 31 D7
Sellincourt Rd. SW17 84 H5
Sellindge Clo., Beck. 86 J7
Sellon Ms. SE11 20 D2
Sellons Ave. NW10 56 F1
Sellwood Dr., Barn. 23 A5
Selsdon Ave., S.Croy. 102 A6
Selsdon Rd.
Selsdon Clo., Rom. 44 J1
Selsdon Clo., Surb. 91 H5
Selsdon Rd. E11 42 G7
Selsdon Rd. E13 60 J1
Selsdon Rd. NW2 47 F2
Selsdon Rd. SE27 85 H3
Selsdon Rd., S.Croy. 102 A5
Selsdon Rd. Ind. Est., Croy. 102 A6
Selsdon Rd.
Selsdon Way E14 69 B3
Selsea Pl. N16 50 B5
Crossway
Selsey Cres., Well. 80 D1
Selsey St. E14 60 A5
Selvage La. NW7 30 D5
Selway Clo., Pnr. 36 B3
Selwood Pl. SW7 18 E3
Selwood Pl. SW7 66 G5
Selwood Rd., Chess. 98 G4
Selwood Rd., Croy. 102 E2
Selwood Rd., Sutt. 100 C1
Selwood Ter. SW7 18 E3
Selworthy Clo. E11 42 G5
Selworthy Rd. SE6 86 J3
Selwyn Ave. E4 34 C6
Selwyn Ave., Ilf. 43 J6
Selwyn Ave., Rich. 73 H3
Selwyn Clo., Houns. 72 E4
Selwyn Ct. SE3 78 F3
Selwyn Cres., Well. 80 B3
Selwyn Rd. E3 59 J2
Selwyn Rd. E13 60 H1
Selwyn Rd. NW10 47 D7
Selwyn Rd., N.Mal. 92 D5
Semley Gate E9 50 J6
Eastway
Semley Pl. SW1 19 C2
Semley Pl. SW1 67 A4
Semley Rd. SW16 94 E2
Senate St. SE15 77 F2
Senator Wk. SE28 70 G3
Broadwater Rd.
Seneca Rd., Th.Hth. 94 J4
Senga Rd., Wall. 101 A1
Senhouse Rd., Sutt. 100 A3
Senior St. W2 10 A1
Senior St. W2 57 E5
Senlac Rd. SE12 87 H1
Sennen Rd., Enf. 25 C7
Sennen Wk. SE9 88 B3
Nunnington Clo.
Senrab St. E1 59 G6
Sentinel Clo., Nthlt. 54 E4
Sentinel Sq. NW4 38 J4
Brent St.
September Way, Stan. 29 E6
Sequoia Clo. (Bushey), Wat. 29 A1
Giant Tree Hill
Sequoia Gdns., Orp. 97 J7
Sequoia Pk., Pnr. 28 H6
Serbin Clo. E10 42 C7
Serjeants Inn EC4 12 F4
Serle St. WC2 12 D3
Serle St. WC2 58 F6
Sermon La. EC4 58 J6
Carter La.
Serpentine Rd. W2 14 J2
Serpentine Rd. W2 66 J1
Serviden Dr., Brom. 97 A1
Setchell Rd. SE1 21 F1
Setchell Way SE1 21 F1
Seth St. SE16 68 F2
Swan Rd.
Seton Gdns., Dag. 53 C7
Settle Pt. E13 60 G2
London Rd.
Settle Rd. E13 60 G2
London Rd.
Settles St. E1 13 J2
Settles St. E1 59 D5
Settrington Rd. SW6 75 E2
Seven Acres, Cars. 100 H2
Seven Acres, Nthwd. 28 A6
Seven Clo., Cars. 100 H2
Seven Kings Rd., Ilf. 52 J1
Seven Sisters Rd. N4 40 J7
Seven Sisters Rd. N7 49 F3
Seven Sisters Rd. N15 41 A6
Sevenoaks Clo., Bexh. 80 H4
Sevenoaks Ho. SE25 95 D3
Sevenoaks Rd. SE4 77 H6
Sevenoaks Rd., Orp. 104 J4
Sevenoaks Rd. (Green St. Grn.), Orp. 104 J7
Sevenoaks Way, Sid. 89 C7
Seventh Ave. E12 52 C4
Severn Dr., Esher 98 D2
Severn Way NW10 47 F5
Severnake Clo. E14 69 A4
Severus Rd. SW11 75 H4
Seville St. SW1 15 A4
Seville St. SW1 66 J2
Sevington Rd. NW4 38 H6
Sevington St. W9 6 A6
Sevington St. W9 57 E4
Seward Rd. W7 64 D2
Seward Rd., Beck. 95 G2
Seward St. EC1 8 H4
Seward St. EC1 58 H4
Sewardstone Gdns. E4 26 B5
Sewardstone Rd. E2 59 F2
Sewardstone Rd. E4 26 B7
Sewdley St. E5 50 G4
Sewell Rd. SE2 71 A2
Sewell St. E13 60 G3
Sextant Ave. E14 69 D4
Seymour Ave. N17 41 D2
Seymour Ave., Mord. 93 A7
Seymour Clo., E.Mol. 90 J5
Seymour Clo., Pnr. 36 F1
Seymour Ct. E4 34 F2
Seymour Dr., Brom. 104 C1
Seymour Gdns. SE4 77 H3
Seymour Gdns., Felt. 81 C4
Seymour Gdns., Ilf. 52 C1
Seymour Gdns., Ruis. 45 D1
Seymour Gdns., Surb. 91 J5
Seymour Gdns., Twick. 73 E7
Seymour Ms. W1 11 B3
Seymour Ms. W1 58 A6
Seymour Pl. SE25 95 E4
Seymour Pl. W1 10 H1
Seymour Pl. W1 57 H5
Seymour Rd. E4 34 B1
Seymour Rd. E6 61 A2
Seymour Rd. E10 50 J1
Seymour Rd. N3 31 E7
Seymour Rd. N8 40 H5
Seymour Rd. N9 33 E2
Seymour Rd. SW18 75 C7
Seymour Rd. SW19 84 A3
Seymour Rd. W4 65 C4
Seymour Rd., Cars. 101 A5
Seymour Rd., E.Mol. 90 J5
Seymour Rd., Hmptn. 81 J5
Seymour Rd., Kings.T. 91 G1
Seymour Rd., Mitch. 94 A7
Seymour Rd., W.Mol. 90 J5
Seymour St. W1 10 J4
Seymour St. W1 57 J6
Seymour St. W2 10 J4
Seymour St. W2 57 J6
Seymour Ter. SE20 95 E1
Seymour Vill. SE20 95 E1
Seymour Wk. SW10 18 C5
Seymour Wk. SW10 66 F6
Seymours, The, Loug. 27 D1
Seyssel St. E14 69 C4
Shaa Rd. W3 56 D7
Shacklegate La., Tedd. 82 B4
Shackleton Clo. SE23 86 E2
Shackleton Rd., Sthl. 54 F7
Shacklewell Grn. E8 50 C4
Shacklewell La.
Shacklewell La. E8 50 C5
Shacklewell Rd. N16 50 C4
Shacklewell Row E8 50 C4
Shacklewell St. E2 9 G5
Shacklewell St. E2 59 C3
Shad Thames SE1 17 F2
Shad Thames SE1 68 C2
Shadbolt Clo., Wor.Pk. 99 F2
Shadwell Dr., Nthlt. 54 F3
Shadwell Pierhead E1 59 F7
Glamis Rd.
Shadwell Pl. E1 59 F6
Martha St.
Shaef Way, Tedd. 82 D7
Shafter Rd., Dag. 53 J6
Shaftesbury, Loug. 27 A3
Shaftesbury Ave. W1 11 H5
Shaftesbury Ave. W1 58 D7
Shaftesbury Ave. WC2 11 H6
Shaftesbury Ave. WC2 58 D7
Shaftesbury Ave., Barn. 23 F3
Shaftesbury Ave., Enf. 25 G2
Shaftesbury Ave., Felt. 72 A6
Shaftesbury Ave., Har. 37 G5
Shaftesbury Ave. (Kenton), Har. 45 H1
Shaftesbury Ave., Sthl. 63 G4
Shaftesbury Circle, Har. 45 J1
Shaftesbury Ave.
Shaftesbury Ms. W8 66 D3
Stratford Rd.
Shaftesbury Pt. E13 60 H2
High St.
Shaftesbury Rd. E4 34 D1
Shaftesbury Rd. E7 51 J7
Shaftesbury Rd. E10 51 A1
Shaftesbury Rd. E17 42 B6
Shaftesbury Rd. N18 33 B6
Shaftesbury Rd. N19 49 E1
Shaftesbury Rd., Beck. 95 J2
Shaftesbury Rd., Cars. 93 G7
Shaftesbury Rd., Rich. 73 H3
Shaftesbury St. N1 9 A2
Shaftesbury St. N1 58 J2
Shaftesbury Way, Twick. 82 A3
Shaftesbury Waye, Hayes 54 C5
Shaftesburys, The, Bark. 61 F2
Shafto Ms. SW1 14 J6
Shafton Rd. E9 59 G1
Shaftsbury Rd., Beck. 95 J2
Shakespeare Ave. N11 32 C5
Shakespeare Ave. NW10 56 D1
Shakespeare Ave., Felt. 72 A6
Shakespeare Ave., Hayes 54 A6
Shakespeare Cres. E12 52 C6
Shakespeare Cres. NW10 56 D1
Shakespeare Dr., Har. 37 J6
Shakespeare Gdns. N2 39 J4
Shakespeare Ho. N14 32 D2
High St.
Shakespeare Rd. E17 41 G2
Shakespeare Rd. N3 39 D1
Popes Dr.
Shakespeare Rd. NW7 30 F4
Shakespeare Rd. SE24 76 H5
Shakespeare Rd. W3 65 C1
Shakespeare Rd. W7 55 C7
Shakespeare Rd., Bexh. 80 E1
Shakespeare Sq., Ilf. 35 F6
Shakespeare Wk. N16 50 B4
Shakespeare Way, Felt. 81 C4
Shalcomb St. SW10 18 D6
Shalcomb St. SW10 66 F6
Shaldon Dr., Mord. 93 B5
Shaldon Dr., Ruis. 45 C3
Shaldon Rd., Edg. 37 J2
Shalfleet Dr. W10 57 A7
Shalford Clo., Orp. 104 F4
Isabella Dr.
Shalimar Gdns. W3 56 C7
Shalimar Rd. W3 56 C7
Hereford Rd.
Shallons Rd. SE9 88 E4
Shalston Rd. SW14 74 B3
Shalston Vill., Surb. 91 J6
Shamrock Rd., Croy. 94 F6
Shamrock St. SW4 76 D3
Shamrock Way N14 32 B1
Shand St. SE1 17 E2
Shand St. SE1 68 B2
Shandon Rd. SW4 76 C6
Shandy St. E1 59 G5
Shanklin Gdns., Wat. 28 C4

Name	Page	Grid
Shanklin Rd. N8	40	D5
Shanklin Rd. N15	41	D4
Shanklin Way SE15	68	C7
Pentridge St.		
Shannon Clo. NW2	48	A3
Shannon Clo., Sthl.	63	D5
Shannon Gro. SW9	76	F4
Shannon Pl. NW8	**6**	**H1**
Shannon Way, Beck.	87	B6
Shap Cres., Cars.	100	J1
Shap St. E2	59	C1
Laburnum St.		
Shapland Way N13	32	F5
Shardcroft Ave.	76	H5
SE24		
Shardeloes Rd. SE14	77	J2
Sharman Ct., Sid.	89	A4
Sharnbrooke Clo.,	80	C3
Well.		
Sharon Clo., Surb.	98	F1
Sharon Gdns. E9	59	F1
Sharon Rd. W4	65	D5
Sharon Rd., Enf.	25	H2
Sharpe Clo. W7	55	C5
Templeman Rd.		
Sharpleshall St.	48	J7
NW1		
Sharpness Clo.,	54	E5
Hayes		
Sharratt St. SE15	68	F6
Sharsted St. SE17	**20**	**G4**
Sharsted St. SE17	67	H5
Shavers Pl. SW1	**11**	**H6**
Shaw Ave., Bark.	62	E2
Shaw Clo. SE28	71	B1
Shaw Clo. (Bushey),	29	B2
Wat.		
Shaw Dr., Walt.	90	C7
Shaw Gdns., Bark.	62	E2
Shaw Rd., Brom.	87	F3
Shaw Rd., Enf.	25	G1
Shaw Sq. E17	41	H1
Shaw Way, Wall.	101	E7
Shawbrooke Rd. SE9	78	J5
Shawbury Rd. SE22	77	C5
Shawfield Pk.,	97	A2
Brom.		
Shawfield St. SW3	**18**	**H4**
Shawfield St. SW3	66	H5
Shawford Ct. SW15	74	G7
Shawford Rd., Epsom	99	D6
Shaws Cotts. SE23	86	H3
Shearing Dr., Cars.	93	F7
Stavordale Rd.		
Shearling Way N7	49	E6
Shearman Rd. SE3	78	F4
Shearsmith Ho. E1	**13**	**J5**
Sheavesmill Ave.	38	E4
NW9		
Sheen Common Dr.,	74	A4
Rich.		
Sheen Clo., Rich.	74	A4
Sheen Rd.		
Sheen Ct. Rd.,	74	A4
Rich.		
Sheen Gate Gdns.	74	C4
SW14		
Sheen Gro. N1	58	G1
Richmond Ave.		
Sheen La. SW14	74	C5
Sheen Pk., Rich.	73	H4
Sheen Rd., Orp.	97	J4
Sheen Rd., Rich.	73	H5
Sheen Way, Wall.	101	F5
Sheen Wd. SW14	74	C5
Sheendale Rd.,	73	J4
Rich.		
Sheenewood SE26	86	E5
Sheep La. E8	59	E1
Sheep Wk. Ms. SW19	84	B6
Sheepcote Clo.,	63	A7
Houns.		
Sheepcote La. SW11	75	J2
Sheepcote Rd., Har.	37	C6
Sheepcotes Rd.,	44	D4
Rom.		
Sheephouse Way,	99	D1
N.Mal.		
Sheerwater Rd. E16	61	A5
Sheffield Sq. E3	59	J3
Malmesbury Rd.		
Sheffield St. WC2	**12**	**C4**
Sheffield Ter. W8	66	D1
Shefton Ri., Nthwd.	28	A7
Shelbourne Clo.,	36	F3
Pnr.		
Shelburne Rd. N17	41	E2
Shelburne Rd. N7	49	F4
Shelbury Clo., Sid.	89	A3
Shelbury Rd. SE22	77	E5
Sheldon Ave. N6	39	H7
Sheldon Ave., Ilf.	43	E2
Sheldon Clo. SE12	78	H5
Sheldon Clo. SE20	95	E1
Sheldon Rd. N18	33	B4
Sheldon Rd. NW2	48	A4
Sheldon Rd., Bexh.	80	F1
Sheldon Rd., Dag.	53	E7
Sheldon St., Croy.	101	J3
Wandle Rd.		
Sheldrake Pl. W8	66	D2
Sheldrick Clo. SW19	93	G2
Shelduck Clo. NW9	38	E2
Swan Dr.		
Sheldwich Ter.,	97	B6
Brom.		
Turpington La.		
Shelford Pl. N16	50	A3
Stoke Newington		
Ch. St.		
Shelford Ri. SE19	86	C7
Shelford Rd., Barn.	22	J5
Shelgate Rd. SW11	75	H5
Shell Clo., Brom.	97	B6
Shell Rd. SE13	78	B3
Shelley Ave. E12	52	B6
Shelley Ave., Grnf.	55	A3
Shelley Clo., Edg.	30	A4
Shelley Clo., Grnf.	55	A3
Shelley Clo., Hayes	54	A5
Shelley Clo., Orp.	104	H3
Shelley Cres.,	72	D1
Houns.		
Shelley Cres.,	54	F6
Sthl.		
Shelley Dr., Well.	79	H1
Shelley Gdns., Wem.	46	F2
Shelley Gro., Loug.	27	C4
Shelley Way SW19	84	G6
Shellgrove Est. N16	50	B5
Shellness Rd. E5	50	E5
Shellwood Rd. SW11	75	J2
Shelmerdine Clo. E3	60	A5
Shelton Rd. SW19	93	D1
Shelton St. WC2	**12**	**A4**
Shelton St. WC2	58	E6
Shenfield Ho. SE18	70	A7
Shooter's Hill Rd.		
Shenfield Rd.,	34	H7
Wdf.Grn.		
Shenfield St. N1	**9**	**E2**
Shenfield St. N1	59	B2
Shenley Rd. SE5	77	B1
Shenley Rd., Borwd.	22	A4
Shenley Rd., Houns.	72	E1
Shepcot Ho. N14	24	C6
Shepherd Mkt. W1	**15**	**D2**
Shepherd St. W1	**15**	**D2**
Shepherdess Pl. N1	**9**	**A3**
Shepherdess Wk. N1	**9**	**A2**
Shepherdess Wk. N1	58	J2
Shepherds Bush Grn.	65	J2
W12		
Shepherds Bush Mkt.	65	J2
W12		
Uxbridge Rd.		
Shepherds Bush Pl.	66	A2
W12		
Shepherds Bush Rd.	65	J3
W6		
Shepherds Clo. N6	40	B6
Shepherds Clo.,	44	D5
Rom.		
Shepherds Ct. W12	66	A2
Shepherds Bush Grn.		
Shepherds Grn.,	88	G7
Chis.		
Shepherds Hill N6	40	B6
Shepherds La. E9	50	G6
Shepherds Pl. W1	**11**	**B5**
Shepherds Wk. NW2	47	G2
Shepherds Wk. NW3	48	G4
Shepherds Wk.	29	A2
(Bushey), Wat.		
Shepherds Way,	102	G7
S.Croy.		
Shepley Clo., Cars.	101	A3
Sheppard Clo.,	91	H4
Kings.T.		
Beaufort Rd.		
Sheppard Dr. SE16	68	E5
Sheppard St. E16	60	F4
Shepperton Clo.,	22	D1
Borwd.		
Shepperton Rd. N1	58	J1
Shepperton Rd.,	97	G6
Orp.		
Sheppey Gdns., Dag.	52	C7
Sheppey Rd.		
Sheppey Rd., Dag.	53	B7
Sheppey Wk. N1	49	J7
Marquess Rd.		
Sherard Rd. SE9	79	B5
Sheraton Business	55	E2
Cen., Grnf.		
Sheraton St. W1	**11**	**H4**
Sherborne Ave.,	25	F2
Enf.		
Sherborne Ave.,	63	G4
Sthl.		
Sherborne Gdns.	38	A3
NW9		
Sherborne Gdns.	55	E5
W13		
Sherborne La. EC4	**13**	**B5**
Sherborne Rd.,	98	H5
Chess.		
Sherborne Rd., Orp.	97	J4
Sherborne Rd.,	100	D2
Sutt.		
Sherborne St. N1	59	A1
Sherboro Rd. N15	41	C6
Ermine Rd.		
Sherbourne Cres.	93	H7
Cars.		
Sherbrook Gdns.	24	H7
N21		
Green Las.		
Sherbrooke Clo.,	80	G4
Bexh.		
Sherbrooke Rd. SW6	66	B7
Shere Clo., Chess.	98	G5
Shere Rd., Ilf.	43	D5
Sheredan Rd. E4	34	D5
Sherfield Gdns.	74	F6
SW15		
Sheridan Ct.,	72	F5
Houns.		
Vickers Way		
Sheridan Cres.,	97	E2
Chis.		
Sheridan Gdns.,	37	G6
Har.		
Sheridan Pl. SW13	74	F2
Brookwood Ave.		
Sheridan Pl.,	90	H1
Hmptn.		
Sheridan Rd. E7	51	F3
Sheridan Rd. E12	52	B5
Sheridan Rd. SW19	93	C1
Sheridan Rd., Belv.	71	G4
Sheridan Rd., Bexh.	80	E3
Sheridan Rd., Rich.	82	F3
Sheridan St. E1	59	E6
Watney St.		
Sheridan Ter.,	45	H5
Nthlt.		
Whitton Ave. W.		
Sheridan Wk. NW11	39	D6
Sheridan Wk., Cars.	100	J5
Sheridan Way, Beck.	95	J1
Turners Meadow		
Way		
Sheringham Ave.	52	C4
E12		
Sheringham Ave.	24	D5
N14		
Sheringham Ave.	81	A3
Felt.		
Sheringham Ave.	44	J6
Rom.		
Sheringham Ave.,	81	F1
Twick.		
Sheringham Dr.,	52	J5
Bark.		
Sheringham Rd. N7	49	F6
Sheringham Rd.	95	F3
SE20		
Sheringham Twr.	54	H7
Sthl.		
Sherington Ave.,	28	G7
Pnr.		
Sherington Rd. SE7	69	H6
Sherland Rd.,	73	C7
Twick.		
Sherlies Ave., Orp.	104	H2
Sherlock Ms. W1	**11**	**B1**
Sherman Rd., Brom.	96	B1
Shernhall St. E17	42	C3
Sherrard Rd. E7	51	J6
Sherrard Rd. E12	52	A6
Sherrards Way,	23	D5
Barn.		
Sherrick Grn. Rd.	47	H5
NW10		
Sherriff Rd. NW6	48	D6
Sherrin Rd. E10	51	A4
Sherringham Ave.	45	A6
N17		
Sherrock Gdns. NW4	38	G4
Sherwin Rd. SE14	77	G1
Sherwood Ave. E18	42	H3
Sherwood Ave.,	85	C7
SW16		
Sherwood Ave.,	46	B6
Grnf.		
Sherwood Ave.,	54	B4
Hayes		
Sherwood Clo. SW13	74	H3
Lwr. Common S.		
Sherwood Clo. W13	64	E1
Sherwood Clo., Bex.	80	C6
Sherwood Gdns. E14	69	A4
Sherwood Gdns.,	52	G7
Bark.		
Sherwood Pk. Ave.,	80	A7
Sid.		
Sherwood Pk. Rd.,	94	C4
Mitch.		
Sherwood Pk. Rd.,	100	D5
Sutt.		
Sherwood Rd. NW4	38	J3
Sherwood Rd. SW19	84	C7
Sherwood Rd., Croy.	95	E7
Sherwood Rd.,	81	J5
Hmptn.		
Sherwood Rd., Har.	45	J2
Sherwood Rd., Ilf.	43	G4
Sherwood Rd., Well.	79	H2
Sherwood St. N20	31	G3
Sherwood St. W1	**11**	**G5**
Sherwood Ter. N20	31	G3
Green Rd.		
Sherwood Way,	103	B2
W.Wick.		
Shetland Clo.,	22	D6
Borwd.		
Percheron Rd.		
Shetland Rd. E3	59	J2
Shield Dr., Brent.	64	D6
Shieldhall St. SE2	71	C4
Shifford Path SE23	86	G3
Shillibeer Pl. W1	**10**	**H2**
Shillibeer Wk.,	35	J3
Chig.		
Shillingford St. N1	49	H7
Cross St.		
Shillitoe Rd. N13	32	H5
Shinfield St. W12	56	H2
Shinglewell Rd.,	71	G6
Erith		
Shinners Clo. SE25	95	D5
Stanger Rd.		
Ship and Mermaid	**17**	**C3**
Row SE1		
Ship La. SW14	74	C3
Ship St. SE8	78	A1
Ship Tavern Pas. EC3	**13**	**D5**
Shipka Rd. SW12	85	B1
Shipman Rd. E16	60	H6
Shipman Rd. SE23	86	G2
Shipton Clo., Dag.	53	D3
Shipton St. E2	**9**	**G3**
Shipton St. E2	59	C2
Shipwright Rd. SE16	68	H2
Shirburn Clo. SE23	77	F7
Tyson Rd.		
Shirbutt St. E14	60	B7
Shire Ct., Erith	71	D3
St. John Fisher Rd.		
Shirebrook Rd. SE3	79	A3
Shirehall Clo. NW4	39	A6
Shirehall Gdns. NW4	39	A6
Shirehall La. NW4	39	A6
Shirehall Pk. NW4	39	A6
Shires, The, Rich.	82	H4
Shirland Ms. W9	57	C3
Shirland Rd. W9	57	C3
Shirley Ave., Bex.	80	D7
Shirley Ave., Croy.	102	F1
Shirley Ave., Sutt.	100	G4
Shirley Ch. Rd.,	102	F3
Croy.		
Shirley Clo. E17	42	B5
Addison Rd.		
Shirley Clo.,	72	J5
Houns.		
Shirley Ct., Croy.	102	G3
Shirley Cres.,	95	H4
Beck.		
Shirley Dr., Houns.	72	J5
Shirley Gdns. W7	64	C3
Shirley Gdns.,	52	H6
Bark.		
Shirley Gro. N9	25	F7
Shirley Gro. SW11	76	A3
Shirley Hills Rd.,	102	G5
Croy.		
Shirley Ho. Dr. SE7	69	J7
Shirley Oaks Rd.,	102	G1
Croy.		
Shirley Pk. Rd.,	102	E1
Croy.		
Shirley Rd. E15	51	E7
Shirley Rd. W4	57	E2
Shirley Rd., Croy.	95	E7
Shirley Rd., Enf.	24	J3
Shirley Rd., Sid.	88	H3
Shirley St. E16	60	F6
Shirley Way, Croy.	102	H3
Shirlock Rd. NW3	48	J4

Shobden Rd. N17   41 A1
Shoe La. EC4   **12 F3**
Shoe La. EC4   58 G6
Shoebury Rd. E6   52 C7
Shoot Up Hill NW2   48 B5
Shooters Ave., Har.   37 F4
Shooter's Hill SE18   79 D1
Shooter's Hill,   79 F2
  Well.
Shooter's Hill Rd.   78 F1
  SE3
Shooter's Hill Rd.   79 A1
  SE18
Shooters Rd., Enf.   24 H1
Shore Clo., Felt.   72 A7
Shore Clo., Hmptn.   81 E5
  Stewart Clo.
Shore Gdns., Felt.   81 G2
Shore Pl. E9   50 F7
Shore Rd. E9   50 F7
Shoreditch High St.   **9 E6**
  E1
Shoreditch High St.   59 B4
  E1
Shoreham Clo. SW18   75 E5
  Ram St.
Shoreham Clo., Bex.   89 D1
  Stansted Cres.
Shoreham Clo.,   95 F5
  Croy.
Shoreham Way,   96 G6
  Brom.
Shorncliffe Rd. SE1   **21 F3**
Shorncliffe Rd. SE1   68 C5
Shorndean St. SE6   87 C1
Shorne Clo., Sid.   80 B6
Shornefield Clo.,   97 D3
  Brom.
Shornells Way SE2   71 C5
  Willrose Cres.
Shorrolds Rd. SW6   66 C7
Short Gate N12   31 C4
Short Hedges,   72 G1
  Houns.
  Lampton Ave.
Short Path SE18   70 E6
  Westdale Rd.
Short Rd. E11   51 E2
Short Rd. E15   60 D1
Short Rd. W4   65 E6
Short St. NW4   38 J4
  New Brent St.
Short St. SE1   **16 F3**
Short Wall E15   60 D3
  Bisson Rd.
Short Way N12   31 H6
Short Way SE9   79 B3
Short Way, Twick.   72 J7
Shortcroft Rd.,   99 F7
  Epsom
Shortcrofts Rd.,   53 F6
  Dag.
Shorter St. E1   **13 G5**
Shorter St. E1   59 C7
Shortland Rd. E10   42 B7
Shortlands W6   66 A4
Shortlands Clo. N18   33 A3
Shortlands Gdns.,   96 E2
  Brom.
Shortlands Gro.,   96 D3
  Brom.
Shortlands Rd.,   96 D3
  Brom.
Shortlands Rd.,   82 J7
  Kings.T.
Shorts Cft. NW9   38 B4
Shorts Gdns. WC2   **12 A4**
Shorts Gdns. WC2   58 E6
Shorts Rd., Cars.   100 H4
Shotfield, Wall.   101 B6
Shott Clo., Sutt.   100 F5
  Turnpike La.
Shottendane Rd.   75 D1
  SW6
Shottery Clo. SE9   88 B3
Shottfield Ave.   74 E4
  SW14
Shoulder of Mutton   59 H7
  All. E14
  Narrow St.
Shouldham St. W1   **10 H2**
Shouldham St. W1   57 H5
Showers Way, Hayes   63 A1
Shrapnel Clo. SE18   70 B7
Shrapnel Rd. SE9   79 C3
Shrewsbury Ave.   74 C4
  SW14
Shrewsbury Ave.,   37 H4
  Har.
Shrewsbury Clo.,   98 H2
  Surb.
Shrewsbury Cres.   56 D1
  NW10

Shrewsbury La. SE18   79 E1
Shrewsbury Ms. W2   57 D5
  Chepstow Rd.
Shrewsbury Rd. E7   52 A5
Shrewsbury Rd. N11   32 C6
Shrewsbury Rd. W2   57 D6
  Beck.
Shrewsbury Rd.,   93 H6
Shrewsbury Rd.,   70 D0
  Islw.
  South St.
Shrewton Rd. SW17   84 J7
Shroffold Rd.,   87 E4
  Brom.
Shropshire Clo.,   94 E4
  Mitch.
Shropshire Pl. WC1   **7 G6**
Shropshire Rd. N22   32 F7
Shroton St. NW1   10 G1
Shroton St. NW1   57 H5
Shrubberies, The   42 G2
  E18
Shrubberies, The,   35 F5
  Chig.
Shrubbery Clo. N1   58 J1
  St. Paul St.
Shrubbery Gdns.   24 H7
  N21
Shrubbery Rd. N9   33 D3
Shrubbery Rd. SW16   85 E4
Shrubbery Rd.,   63 F1
  Sthl.
Shrubland Gro.,   99 J3
  Wor.Pk.
Shrubland Rd. E8   59 C1
Shrubland Rd. E10   42 A7
Shrubland Rd. E17   42 A5
Shrublands Ave.,   103 A4
  Croy.
Shrublands Clo. N20   31 G1
Shrublands Clo.   86 F3
  SE26
Shrublands Clo.,   35 F6
  Chig.
Shuna Wk. N1   50 A6
  St. Pauls Rd.
Shurland Ave.,   23 G6
  Barn.
Shurland Gdns. SE15 21 G7
Shurlock Dr., Orp.   104 F4
Shuters Sq. W14   66 C5
  Sun Rd.
Shuttle Clo., Sid.   79 J7
Shuttle St. E1   **9 H6**
Shuttlemead, Bex.   80 F7
Shuttleworth Rd.   75 G2
  SW11
Sibella Rd. SW4   76 D2
Sibley Clo., Bexh.   80 E5
Sibley Gro. E12   52 B7
Sibthorp Rd.,   93 J2
  Mitch.
Sibthorpe Rd. SE12   78 H6
Sibton Rd., Cars.   93 H7
Sicilian Ave. WC1   **12 B2**
Sidbury St. SW6   75 B1
Sidcup Bypass, Orp.   89 B6
Sidcup Bypass, Sid.   88 H4
Sidcup High St.,   89 A4
  Sid.
Sidcup Hill, Sid.   89 B4
Sidcup Hill Gdns.,   89 C5
  Sid.
  Sidcup Hill
Sidcup Pl., Sid.   89 A5
Sidcup Rd. SE9   78 J7
Sidcup Rd. SE12   78 H5
Sidcup Technology   89 D5
  Cen., Sid.
Siddons La. NW1   7 A6
Siddons Rd. N17   41 D1
Siddons Rd. SE23   86 H2
Siddons Rd., Croy.   101 G3
Side Rd. E17   41 J5
Sidewood Rd. SE9   88 G1
Sidford Pl. SE1   **16 D6**
Sidings, The E11   51 C1
Sidmouth Ave.,   73 B2
  Islw.
Sidmouth Clo., Wat.   28 B2
Sidmouth Dr., Ruis.   45 A3
Sidmouth Rd. E10   51 C3
Sidmouth Rd. NW2   47 J7
Sidmouth Rd. SE15   77 C1
Sidmouth Rd., Well.   71 C7
Sidmouth St. WC1   **8 B4**
Sidmouth St. WC1   58 F3
Sidney Ave. N13   32 F5
Sidney Elson Way E6   61 D2
  Edwin Ave.
Sidney Est. E1   59 F6

Sidney Gdns.,   64 F6
  Brent.
Sidney Gro. EC1   **8 G2**
Sidney Rd. E7   51 G3
Sidney Rd. N22   32 F7
Sidney Rd. SE25   95 D5
  Sidney Rd., Beck.
Sidney Rd., SW9   76 F2
Sidney Rd., Har.   36 J3
Sidney Rd., Twick.   73 D6
Sidney Sq. E1   59 F5
Sidney St. E1   59 F5
Sidworth St. E8   50 E7
Siebert Rd. SE3   69 G6
Siemens Rd. SE18   70 A3
Sigdon Rd. E8   50 D5
Sigers, The, Pnr.   36 B6
Signmakers Yd. NW1   58 B1
  Delancey St.
Silbury Ave.,   93 H1
  Mitch.
Silbury St. N1   **9 B3**
Silchester Rd. W10   57 A6
Silecroft Rd.,   80 G1
  Bexh.
Silesia Bldgs. E8   50 E7
  London La.
Silex St. SE1   **16 H4**
Silex St. SE1   67 H2
Silk Clo. SE12   78 G5
Silk Mills Path SE13   78 C2
Silk St. EC2   **13 A1**
Silk St. EC2   58 J5
Silkfield Rd. NW9   38 E5
Silkin Ho., Wat.   28 C3
Silkstream Rd.,   38 C1
  Edg.
Silsoe Rd. N22   40 F2
Silver Birch Ave. E4   33 J6
Silver Birch Clo.   32 A6
  N11
Silver Clo. SE14   68 H7
  Southerngate Way
Silver Clo., Har.   29 A7
Silver Cres. W4   65 B4
Silver Jubilee Way,   72 B2
  Houns.
Silver La., W.Wick.   103 D2
Silver Pl. W1   **11 G5**
Silver Rd. W12   57 A7
Silver Spring Clo.,   71 H6
  Erith
Silver St. N18   33 A4
Silver St., Enf.   25 A3
Silver Wk. SE16   68 J1
Silver Way, Rom.   44 H3
Silverbirch Wk. NW3   49 A6
  Queens Cres.
Silvercliffe Gdns.,   23 H4
  Barn.
Silverdale SE26   86 F4
Silverdale, Enf.   24 E4
Silverdale Ave.,   43 H5
  Ilf.
Silverdale Clo. W7   64 B1
  Cherington Rd.
Silverdale Clo.,   45 F5
  Nthlt.
Silverdale Clo.,   100 C4
  Sutt.
Silverdale Dr. SE9   88 B2
Silverdale Dr.,   90 B2
  Sun.
Silverdale Gdns.,   63 A2
  Hayes
Silverdale Rd. E4   34 D6
Silverdale Rd.,   80 H2
  Bexh.
Silverdale Rd.   97 F4
  (Petts Wd.), Orp.
Silverhall St.,   73 D3
  Islw.
Silverholme Clo.,   37 H7
  Har.
Silverland St. E16   70 C1
Silverleigh Rd.,   94 F4
  Th.Hth.
Silvermere Rd. SE6   78 B6
Silverst Clo.,   45 H6
  Nthlt.
Silverston Way,   29 F6
  Stan.
Silverthorn Gdns. E4   34 A2
Silverthorne Rd.   76 B2
  SW8
Silverton Rd. W6   66 A6
Silvertown Way E16   60 H6
Silvertree La.,   55 A3
  Grnf.
  Cowgate Rd.
Silverwood Clo.,   87 A7
  Beck.

Silvester Rd. SE22   77 C5
Silvester St. SE1   **17 B4**
Silwood Est. SE16   68 F4
  Millender Wk.
Silwood St. SE16   68 F4
Simla Clo. SE16   68 H6
  Chulworthy St.
Simla Ho. SE1   **17 C4**
Simmil Rd., Esher   98 B5
  Simmons Clo. N20   31 H1
Simmons La. E4   **34 D2**
Simmons Rd. SE18   70 E5
Simmons Way N20   31 H2
Simms Clo., Cars.   100 H2
Simms Rd. SE1   **21 J2**
Simms Rd. SE1   68 D4
Simnel Rd. SE12   78 H7
Simon Clo. W11   57 C7
  Portobello Rd.
Simonds Rd. E10   51 A2
Simone Clo., Brom.   97 A1
Simons Wk. E15   51 D5
  Alma St.
Simpson Dr. W3   56 D6
Simpson Rd., Houns.   72 F6
Simpson Rd., Rich.   82 F4
Simpson St. SW11   75 H2
Simpsons Rd. E14   60 B7
Simpsons Rd., Brom.   96 G3
Sims Wk. SE3   78 F4
  Lee Rd.
Sinclair Ct., Beck.   87 A7
Sinclair Gdns. W14   66 A2
Sinclair Gro. NW11   39 A6
Sinclair Rd. E4   33 H5
Sinclair Rd. W14   66 A2
Sinclare Clo., Enf.   25 C1
Singapore Rd. W13   64 D1
Singer St. EC2   **9 C4**
Singleton Clo. SW17   84 J7
Singleton Clo.,   94 J7
  Croy.
  St. Saviours Rd.
Singleton Rd., Dag.   53 F5
Singleton Scarp N12   31 D5
Sinnott Rd. E17   41 G1
Sion Rd., Twick.   73 E7
Sir Alexander Clo.   65 F1
  W3
Sir Alexander Rd.   65 F1
  W3
Sir Thomas More   **18 F6**
  Est. SW3
Sirdar Rd. N22   40 H3
Sirdar Rd. W11   57 A7
Sirdar Rd., Mitch.   85 A6
  Grenfell Rd.
Sirinham Pt. SW8   **20 C6**
Sirinham Pt. SW8   67 F6
Sirus Rd., Nthwd.   28 A5
Sise La. EC4   **13 B4**
Siskin Clo., Borwd.   22 A4
Sisley Rd., Bark.   61 H1
Sispara Gdns. SW18   75 C6
Sissinghurst Rd.,   95 D7
  Croy.
Sister Mabel's Way   **21 H7**
  SE15
Sisters Ave. SW11   75 J3
Sistova Rd. SW12   85 B1
Sisulu Pl. SW9   76 G3
Sittingbourne Ave.,   25 A6
  Enf.
Sitwell Gro., Stan.   29 C5
Sivill Ho. E2   **9 G3**
Sivill Ho. E2   59 C3
Siviter Rd., Dag.   53 H7
Siviter Way, Dag.   53 H7
Siward Rd. N17   41 A1
Siward Rd. SW17   84 F3
Siward Rd., Brom.   96 H3
Six Acres Est. N4   49 G2
Sixth Ave. E12   52 C4
Sixth Ave. W10   57 B3
Sixth Cross Rd.,   81 J3
  Twick.
Skardu Rd. NW2   48 B5
Skeena Hill SW18   75 J7
Skeffington Rd. E6   61 C1
Skelbrook St. SW18   84 E2
Skelgill Rd. SW15   75 C4
Skelley Rd. E15   51 F7
Skelton Clo. E8   50 C6
  Buttermere Wk.
Skelton Rd. E7   51 G6
Skeltons La. E10   42 B7
Skelwith Rd. W6   65 J6
Skenfrith Ho. SE15   68 E6
  Commercial Way
Skerne Rd.,   82 G7
  Kings.T.
Sketchley Gdns.   68 G5
  SE16

Name	Page	Grid
Sketty Rd., Enf.	25	B3
Skiers St. E15	60	E1
Skiffington Clo. SW2	85	G1
Skinner Ct. E2	59	E2
Parmiter St.		
Skinner Pl. SW1	19	B2
Skinner St. EC1	8	F4
Skinner St. EC1	58	G3
Skinners La. EC4	13	A5
Skinners La.,	72	H1
Houns.		
Skinner's Row SE10	78	B1
Blackheath Rd.		
Skipsey Ave. E6	61	C3
Skipton St. SE1	16	H8
Skipworth Rd. E9	59	F1
Skomer Wk. N1	49	J6
Clephane Rd.		
Sky Peals Rd.,	34	D7
Wdf.Grn.		
Slade, The SE18	70	H6
Slade Ho., Houns.	72	F6
Slade Twr. E10	51	A2
Slade Wk. SE17	20	J5
Sladebrook Rd. SE3	79	A3
Sladedale Rd. SE18	70	H5
Sladen Pl. E5	50	E4
Clarence Rd.		
Slades Clo., Enf.	24	G3
Slades Dr., Chis.	88	F3
Slades Gdns., Enf.	24	G2
Slades Hill, Enf.	24	G3
Slades Ri., Enf.	24	G3
Slagrove Pl. SE13	78	B5
Ladywell Rd.		
Slaidburn St. SW10	18	D6
Slaidburn St. SW10	66	F6
Slaithwaite Rd.	78	C4
SE13		
Slaney Pl. N7	49	G5
Hornsey Rd.		
Sleaford Grn., Wat.	28	D3
Sleaford St. SW8	19	F7
Sleaford St. SW8	67	C7
Slievemore Clo. SW4	76	D3
Voltaire Rd.		
Slingsby Pl. WC2	12	A5
Slippers Pl. SE16	68	E3
Sloane Ave. SW3	18	H2
Sloane Ave. SW3	66	H4
Sloane Ct. E. SW3	19	B3
Sloane Ct. E. SW3	67	A5
Sloane Ct. W. SW3	19	B3
Sloane Ct. W. SW3	67	A5
Sloane Gdns. SW1	19	B2
Sloane Gdns. SW1	67	A4
Sloane Gdns., Orp.	104	F3
Partridge Dr.		
Sloane Sq. SW1	19	A2
Sloane Sq. SW1	66	J4
Sloane St. SW1	15	A5
Sloane St. SW1	66	J2
Sloane Ter. SW1	19	A1
Sloane Ter. SW1	66	J4
Sloane Wk., Croy.	95	J6
Slocum Clo. SE28	62	C7
Woodpecker Rd.		
Slough La. NW9	38	C5
Sly St. E1	59	E6
Cannon St. Rd.		
Smallberry Ave.,	73	C2
Islw.		
Smallbrook Ms. W2	10	E4
Smalley Clo. N16	50	C3
Smalley Rd. Est.	50	C3
N16		
Smalley Clo.		
Smallwood Rd. SW17	84	G4
Smardale Rd. SW18	75	F5
Alma Rd.		
Smarden Clo., Belv.	71	G5
Essenden Rd.		
Smarden Gro. SE9	88	C4
Smart St. E2	59	G3
Smarts La., Loug.	27	A4
Smarts Pl. N18	33	D5
Fore St.		
Smart's Pl. WC2	12	B3
Smeaton Rd. SW18	75	D7
Smeaton Rd.,	35	C5
Wdf.Grn.		
Smedley St. E1	68	E1
Smedley St. SW4	76	D2
Smedley St. SW8	76	D2
Smeed Rd. E3	51	A7
Smiles Pl. SE13	78	C2
Smith Clo. SE16	68	G1
Smith Sq. SW1	16	A6
Smith Sq. SW1	67	E3
Smith St. SW3	18	J3
Smith St. SW3	66	J5
Smith St., Surb.	91	J6
Smith Ter. SW3	18	J4
Smith Ter. SW3	66	J5
Smithfield St. EC1	12	G2
Smithies Ct. E15	51	C5
Clays La.		
Smithies Rd. SE2	71	B4
Smith's Ct. W1	11	G5
Smiths Fm. Est.,	54	G2
Nthlt.		
Smiths Way NW2	47	G2
Smiths Yd. SW18	84	F2
Summerley St.		
Smith's Yd., Croy.	101	J3
St. Georges Wk.		
Smithwood Clo. N17	41	A1
Smithwood Clo.	84	B1
SW19		
Smithy St. E1	59	F5
Smock Wk., Croy.	94	J6
Smugglers Way	75	E4
SW18		
Smyrks Rd. SE17	21	E4
Smyrks Rd. SE17	68	B5
Smyrna Rd. NW6	48	D7
Smythe St. E14	60	B7
Snag La., Sev.	104	G1
Snakes La., Barn.	24	C3
Snakes La. E.,	34	J6
Wdf.Grn.		
Snakes La. W.,	34	G6
Wdf.Grn.		
Snaresbrook Dr.,	29	G4
Stan.		
Snaresbrook Rd. E11	42	E4
Snarsgate St. W10	56	J5
Sneath Ave. NW11	39	C7
Snells Pk. N18	33	C6
Sneyd Rd. NW2	47	J4
Snow Hill EC1	12	G2
Snow Hill EC1	58	H5
Snow Hill Ct. EC1	12	H3
Snowbury Rd. SW6	75	E2
Snowden St. EC2	9	D6
Snowden St. EC2	59	B4
Snowdon Dr. NW9	38	E6
Snowdown Clo.	95	G1
SE20		
Snowdrop Clo.,	81	G6
Hmptn.		
Gresham Rd.		
Snowman Ho. NW6	48	E7
Snowsfields SE1	17	C3
Snowsfields SE1	68	A2
Snowshill Rd. E12	52	B5
Snowy Fielder Waye,	73	E2
Islw.		
Soames St. SE15	77	C3
Soames Wk., N.Mal.	92	E1
Socket La., Brom.	96	H6
Soho Sq. W1	11	H3
Soho Sq. W1	58	D6
Soho St. W1	11	H3
Solebay St. E1	59	H4
Solent Rd. NW6	48	D5
Soley Ms. WC1	8	E3
Solna Ave. SW15	74	J5
Solna Rd. N21	33	A1
Solomon's Pas. SE15	77	E4
Solon New Rd. SW4	76	E4
Solon New Rd. Est.	76	E4
SW4		
Solon New Rd.		
Solon Rd. SW2	76	E4
Solway Clo. E8	50	C6
Buttermere Wk.		
Solway Clo., Houns.	72	E3
Solway Rd. N22	40	H1
Solway Rd. SE22	77	E4
Somaford Gro.,	23	G6
Barn.		
Somali Rd. NW2	48	C5
Somerby Rd., Bark.	52	G7
Somercoates Clo.,	23	H3
Barn.		
Somerfield Rd. N4	49	H2
Somerford Clo.,	36	A4
Pnr.		
Somerford Gro. N16	50	C4
Somerford Gro. N17	33	D7
Somerford Gro. Est.	50	C4
N16		
Somerford Gro.		
Somerford St. E1	59	E4
Somerford Way	68	H2
SE16		
Somerhill Ave.,	80	B7
Sid.		
Somerhill Rd.,	80	B2
Well.		
Somerleyton Pas.	76	H4
SW9		
Somerleyton Rd.	76	G4
SW9		
Somers Clo. NW1	7	H1
Somers Cres. W2	10	G4
Somers Cres. W2	57	H6
Somers Ms. W2	10	G4
Somers Pl. SW2	76	F7
Somers Rd. E17	41	J4
Somers Rd. SW2	76	F6
Somersby Gdns.,	43	C5
Ilf.		
Somerset Ave.	92	H2
SW20		
Somerset Ave.,	98	G4
Chess.		
Somerset Ave.,	79	J5
Well.		
Somerset Clo.,	92	E6
N.Mal.		
Somerset Clo.,	42	G1
Wdf.Grn.		
Somerset Est. SW11	75	G1
Somerset Gdns. N	40	A7
Somerset Gdns.	78	B2
SE13		
Somerset Gdns.	94	F3
SW16		
Somerset Gdns.,	82	B5
Tedd.		
Somerset Rd. E17	42	A5
Somerset Rd. N17	41	C3
Somerset Rd. N18	33	C5
Somerset Rd. NW4	38	J4
Somerset Rd. SW19	84	A3
Somerset Rd. W4	65	D3
Somerset Rd. W13	64	E1
Somerset Rd., Barn.	23	E5
Somerset Rd.,	64	G6
Brent.		
Somerset Rd., Har.	36	J6
Somerset Rd.,	91	J2
Kings.T.		
Somerset Rd., Sthl.	54	F6
Somerset Rd., Tedd.	82	B5
Somerset Sq. W14	66	B2
Somerset Waye,	63	E7
Houns.		
Somersham Rd.,	80	E2
Bexh.		
Somerton Ave.,	74	B3
Rich.		
Somerton Rd. NW2	48	A3
Somerton Rd. SE15	77	E4
Somertrees Ave.	87	H2
SE12		
Somervell Rd., Har.	45	F5
Somerville Rd. SE20	86	G7
Somerville Rd.,	44	C6
Rom.		
Sondes St. SE17	21	B5
Sondes St. SE17	68	A6
Sonia Ct., Har.	37	C6
Sonia Gdns. N12	31	F4
Woodside Ave.		
Sonia Gdns. NW10	47	F4
Sonia Gdns., Houns.	63	G7
Sonning Gdns.,	81	E6
Hmptn.		
Sonning Rd. SE25	96	D6
Soper Clo. E4	33	J5
Sophia Clo. N7	49	F6
Mackenzie Rd.		
Sophia Rd. E10	51	B1
Sophia Rd. E16	60	H6
Sopwith Ave.,	98	H5
Chess.		
Sopwith Rd., Houns.	63	C7
Sopwith Way,	91	H1
Kings.T.		
Sorrel Clo. SE28	71	A1
Sorrell Clo. SE14	68	H7
Southerngate Way		
Sorrell Gdns. E6	61	B5
Sorrento Rd., Sutt.	100	D3
Sotheby Rd. N5	49	J3
Sotheran Clo. E8	59	D1
Sotheron Rd. SW6	66	E1
Soudan Rd. SW11	75	J1
Souldern Rd. W14	66	A3
South Access Rd.	41	H7
E17		
South Africa Rd.	65	H1
W12		
South Audley St. W1	11	C6
South Audley St. W1	58	B7
South Ave. E4	26	B7
South Ave., Cars.	101	A7
South Ave., Rich.	73	G1
Sandycombe Rd.		
South Ave. Gdns.,	54	F7
Sthl.		
South Ave. Gdns.,	54	F7
Sthl.		
South Bank, Chis.	88	F3
South Bank, Surb.	91	H6
South Bank Ter.,	91	H6
Surb.		
South Birkbeck Rd.	51	D3
E11		
South Black Lion	65	G5
La. W6		
South Bolton Gdns.	18	B3
SW5		
South Bolton Gdns.	66	E5
SW5		
South Carriage Dr.	66	H2
SW1		
South Carriage Dr.	14	G3
SW7		
South Carriage Dr.	66	H2
SW7		
South Clo. N6	40	B6
South Clo., Barn.	23	C3
South Clo., Bexh.	80	D4
South Clo., Dag.	62	G1
South Clo., Mord.	93	D6
Green La.		
South Clo., Pnr.	36	F7
South Clo., Twick.	81	G3
South Colonnade	69	C4
E14		
South Countess Rd.	41	J3
E17		
South Cres. WC1	11	H2
South Cres. WC1	58	D5
South Cross Rd.,	43	F5
Ilf.		
South Croxted Rd.	86	A3
Dag.		
South Dagenham Rd.,	53	J7
Dag.		
South Dene NW7	30	D3
South Dr., Orp.	104	H5
South Ealing Rd. W5	64	G2
South Eastern Ave.	33	C3
N9		
South Eaton Pl. SW1	19	C1
South Eaton Pl. SW1	67	A4
South Eden Pk. Rd.,	96	B6
Beck.		
South Edwardes Sq.	66	C3
W8		
South End W8	14	B5
South End, Croy.	101	J4
South End Clo. NW3	48	H4
South End Rd. NW3	48	H4
South End Row W8	14	B5
South End Row W8	66	E3
South Esk Rd. E7	51	J6
South Gdns. SW19	84	G7
Well.		
South Gipsy Rd.,	80	D3
Well.		
South Glade, The,	89	F1
Bex.		
Camden Rd.		
South Grn. NW9	38	E1
Clayton Fld.		
South Gro. E17	41	J5
South Gro. N6	49	A1
South Gro. N15	41	A5
South Gro. Ho. N6	49	A1
Highgate W. Hill		
South Hill, Chis.	88	C6
South Hill Ave.,	45	J3
Har.		
South Hill Gro.,	46	B4
Har.		
South Hill Pk. NW3	48	H4
South Hill Pk.	48	H4
Gdns. NW3		
South Hill Rd.,	96	H3
Brom.		
South Huxley N18	33	A5
South Island Pl.	67	F7
SW9		
South Lambeth Pl.	20	B5
SW8		
South Lambeth Pl.	67	E6
SW8		
South Lambeth Rd.	20	B7
SW8		
South Lambeth Rd.	67	E6
SW8		
South La., Kings.T.	91	G3
South La., N.Mal.	92	D4
South La. W.,	92	D4
N.Mal.		
South Lo. Ave.,	94	E4
Mitch.		
South Lo. Cres.,	24	D4
Enf.		
South Lo. Dr. N14	24	D4
South Mall N9	33	D3
Plevna Rd.		
South Mead NW9	38	F1
South Mead, Epsom	99	E3
South Meadows,	46	H5
Wem.		

South Molton La. W1 11 D4
South Molton La. W1 58 B6
South Molton Rd. 60 G6
E16
South Molton St. W1 11 D4
South Molton St. W1 58 B6
South Norwood Hill 95 B1
SE25
South Oak Rd. SW16 85 F4
South Par. SW3 18 F3
South Par. SW3 66 G5
South Par. W4 50 D4
South Pk. Cres. SE6 87 F1
South Pk. Cres., 52 G3
Ilf.
South Pk. Dr., Ilf. 52 H3
South Pk. Gro., 92 C4
N.Mal.
South Pk. Hill Rd., 102 A5
S.Croy.
South Pk. Ms. SW6 75 E3
South Pk. Rd. SW19 84 D6
South Pk. Rd., Ilf. 52 G3
South Pk. Ter., Ilf. 52 H3
South Pk. Way, 45 C6
Ruis.
South Penge Pk. 95 E2
Est. SE20
South Pl. EC2 13 C2
South Pl. EC2 59 A5
South Pl., Enf. 25 F5
South Pl., Surb. 91 J7
South Pl. Ms. EC2 13 C2
South Rd. N9 33 D1
South Rd. SE23 86 G2
South Rd. SW19 84 F6
South Rd. W5 64 G4
South Rd., Edg. 38 B1
South Rd., Felt. 81 D5
South Rd., Hmptn. 81 E6
South Rd., Rom. 44 E6
(Chadwell Heath)
South Rd., Rom. 44 B5
(Little Heath)
South Rd., Sthl. 63 F2
South Rd., Twick. 82 A3
South Row SE3 78 F2
South Sea St. SE16 68 J3
South Side W6 65 F3
South Side Common 83 J6
SW19
South Sq. NW11 39 E6
South Sq. WC1 12 E2
South St. W1 15 C1
South St. W1 67 A1
South St., Brom. 96 G2
South St., Enf. 25 F5
South St., Islw. 73 D3
South St., Rain. 62 J2
South Tenter St. E1 13 G4
South Tenter St. E1 59 C7
South Ter. SW7 18 G1
South Ter. SW7 66 H4
South Ter., Surb. 91 H6
South Vale SE19 86 B6
South Vale, Har. 46 B4
South Vw., Brom. 96 H2
South Vw. Dr. E18 42 H3
South Vw. Rd. N8 40 D3
South Vw. Rd., 27 C6
Loug.
South Vw. Rd., Pnr. 28 B6
South Vill. NW1 49 D6
South Wk., W.Wick. 103 E3
South Way N9 33 F2
South Way N11 32 C6
Ringway
South Way, Brom. 96 G7
South Way, Croy. 102 H3
South Way, Har. 36 G4
South Way, Wem. 47 A5
South W. India Dock 69 C2
Entrance E14
South Western Rd., 73 D6
Twick.
South Wf. Rd. W2 10 E3
South Wf. Rd. W2 57 G6
South Woodford to 52 D4
Barking Relief Rd.,
Bark.
South Worple Ave. 74 E3
SW14
South Worple Way
South Worple Way 74 D3
SW14
Southacre Way, Pnr. 36 C1
Southall La., 63 B6
Houns.
Southall Pl. SE1 17 B4
Southall Pl. SE1 68 A2
Southam St. W10 57 B4
Southampton Bldgs. 12 E2
WC2

Southampton Gdns., 94 E5
Mitch.
Southampton Pl. 12 B2
WC1
Southampton Pl. 58 E5
WC1
Southampton Rd. 48 J5
NW5
Southampton Row 12 B1
WC1
Southampton Row 58 E5
WC1
Southampton St. 12 B5
WC2
Southampton St. 58 E7
WC2
Southampton Way 21 C7
SE5
Southampton Way 68 A7
SE5
Southbank, T.Ditt. 91 E7
Southborough Clo., 98 G1
Surb.
Southborough La., 97 B5
Brom.
Southborough Rd. 50 G7
E9
Southborough Rd., 97 B3
Brom.
Southborough Rd., 98 H1
Surb.
Southbourne, Brom. 96 G7
Southbourne Ave. 38 C2
NW9
Southbourne Clo., 38 E7
Pnr.
Southbourne Cres. 39 B4
NW4
Southbourne Gdns. 78 H5
SE12
Southbourne Gdns., 52 F5
Ilf.
Southbourne Gdns., 45 B1
Ruis.
Southbridge Pl., 101 J4
Croy.
Southbridge Rd., 101 J4
Croy.
Southbridge Way, 63 E2
Sthl.
Southbrook Ms. 78 F6
SE12
Southbrook Rd. 78 F6
SE12
Southbrook Rd. 94 E1
SW16
Southbury Ave., 25 D5
Enf.
Southbury Rd., Enf. 25 A3
Southchurch Rd. E6 61 C2
Southcombe St. W14 66 B4
Southcote Ave., 92 B7
Surb.
Southcote Rd. E17 41 G5
Southcote Rd. N19 49 C4
Southcote Rd. SE25 95 E5
Southcroft Ave., 79 H3
Well.
Southcroft Ave., 103 C2
W.Wick.
Southcroft Rd. SW16 85 B6
Southcroft Rd. SW17 85 A6
Southcroft Rd., 104 H3
Orp.
Southdale, Chig. 35 G6
Southdean Gdns. 84 C2
SW19
Southdown Ave. W7 64 D3
Southdown Cres., 45 J1
Har.
Southdown Cres., 43 H5
Ilf.
Southdown Dr. 84 A7
SW20
Crescent Rd.
Southdown Rd. 93 A1
SW20
Southend Clo. SE9 79 E6
Southend Cres. SE9 79 E6
Southend La. SE6 87 A4
Southend La. SE26 86 J4
Southend Rd. E6 52 C7
Southend Rd. E17 42 D1
Southend Rd. E18 42 A7
Southend Rd., Beck. 87 A7
Southend Rd., 42 J2
Wdf.Grn.
Southern Ave. SE25 95 C3
Southern Ave., 81 A1
Felt.
Southern Dr., Loug. 27 C6
Southern Gro. E3 59 J3
Southern Rd. E13 60 H2

Southern Rd. N2 39 J4
Southern Row W10 57 B4
Southern St. N1 8 C1
Southern St. N1 58 F2
Southern Way, Rom. 44 G6
Southerngate Way 68 H7
SE14
Southernhay, Loug. 27 A4
Southerton Rd. W6 65 J3
Southey Rd. N15 41 B5
Southey Rd. SW9 76 G1
Southey Rd. SW19 84 D7
Southey St. SE20 86 G7
Southfield, Barn. 23 A6
Southfield Cotts. W7 64 C2
Southfield Gdns., 82 C4
Twick.
Southfield Pk., 36 H4
Har.
Southfield Rd. N17 41 B2
Southfield Rd. W4 65 D2
Southfield Rd., 97 J3
Chis.
Southfield Rd., 25 E6
Enf.
Southfields NW4 38 H3
Southfields, E.Mol. 91 B6
Southfields Ct. 84 B1
SW19
Southfields Pas. 75 D6
SW18
Southfields Rd.
Southfields Rd. 75 D6
SW18
Southfleet Rd., 104 H3
Orp.
Southgate Circ. N14 32 D1
The Bourne
Southgate Gro. N1 50 A7
Southgate Rd. N1 59 A1
Southholme Clo. 95 C1
SE19
Southill La., Pnr. 36 B4
Southill Rd., Chis. 88 B6
Southill St. E14 60 B6
Chrisp St.
Southland Rd. SE18 70 J7
Southland Way, 73 A5
Houns.
Southlands Ave., 104 G4
Orp.
Southlands Gro. 97 B3
Brom.
Southlands Rd., 96 J5
Brom.
Southly Clo., Sutt. 100 D3
Southmead Rd. 84 B1
SW19
Southmont Rd., 98 B2
Esher
Southmoor Way E9 50 J6
Southold Ri. SE9 88 C3
Southolm St. SW11 76 B1
Southover N12 31 D3
Southover, Brom. 87 G5
Southport Rd. SE18 70 G4
Southridge Pl. SW20 84 A7
Southsea Rd., 91 H4
Kings.T.
Southspring, Sid. 79 G7
Southvale Rd. SE3 78 E2
Southview Ave. 47 F5
NW10
Southview Clo. 80 F6
Bex.
Southview Cres., 43 E6
Ilf.
Southview Gdns., 101 C7
Wall.
Southview Rd., 87 D4
Brom.
Southville SW8 76 D1
Southville Rd., 91 D7
T.Ditt.
Southwark Bri. EC4 13 A6
Southwark Bri. EC4 67 J1
Southwark Bri. SE1 13 A6
Southwark Bri. SE1 67 H3
Southwark Bri. Rd. 16 J4
SE1
Southwark Bri. Rd. 67 H3
SE1
Southwark Gro. SE1 16 J2
Southwark Pk. Est. 68 E4
SE16
Southwark Pk. Rd. 21 G1
SE16
Southwark Pk. Rd. 68 C4
SE16
Southwark Pl., 97 C3
Brom.
St. Georges Rd.

Southwark St. SE1 16 H1
Southwark St. SE1 67 H1
Southwater Clo. E14 59 J6
Southwater Clo., 87 B7
Beck.
Southway N20 31 D2
Southway NW7 30 G7
Southway NW11 29 E6
Southway SW20 92 J4
Southway, Wall. 101 C4
Southwell Ave., 45 G6
Nthlt.
Southwell Gdns. 14 C6
SW7
Southwell Gdns. 66 F4
SW7
Southwell Gro. Rd. 51 E2
E11
Southwell Rd. SE5 76 J3
Southwell Rd., 94 G6
Croy.
Southwell Rd., Har. 37 G6
Southwest Rd. E11 51 D1
Southwick Ms. W2 10 F3
Southwick Pl. W2 10 G4
Southwick Pl. W2 57 H6
Southwick St. W2 10 G3
Southwick St. W2 57 H6
Southwold Dr., 53 A5
Bark.
Southwold Rd. E5 50 E2
Southwold Rd., Bex. 80 H6
Southwood Ave. N6 40 B7
Southwood Ave., 92 C1
Kings.T.
Southwood Clo., 97 C4
Brom.
Southwood Clo., 100 A1
Wor.Pk.
Carters Clo.
Southwood Dr., 92 C7
Surb.
Southwood Gdns., 98 D3
Esher
Southwood Gdns., 43 E4
Ilf.
Southwood La. N6 40 A7
Southwood Lawn Rd. 40 A7
N6
Southwood Rd. SE9 88 E2
Southwood Rd. SE28 71 B1
Sovereign Clo. E1 59 E7
Sovereign Clo. W5 55 F5
Sovereign Ms. E2 9 F1
Sovereign Pk. NW10 56 B4
Sowerby Clo. SE9 79 B5
Spa Clo. SE25 95 B1
Spa Grn. Est. EC1 8 F3
Spa Hill SE19 95 A1
Spa Rd. SE16 17 F6
Spa Rd. SE16 68 C3
Space Way, Felt. 72 A5
Spafield St. EC1 8 E5
Spalding Rd. NW4 38 J6
Spalding Rd. SW17 85 B5
Spanby Rd. E3 60 A4
Spaniards Clo. NW11 48 G1
Spaniards End NW3 48 F1
Spaniards Rd. NW3 48 F3
Spanish Pl. W1 11 C3
Spanish Pl. W1 58 A6
Spanish Rd. SW18 75 F5
Spareleaze Hill, 27 B5
Loug.
Sparkbridge Rd., 37 B4
Har.
Sparks Clo. W3 56 D6
Joseph Ave.
Sparks Clo., Hmptn. 81 E6
Victors Dr.
Sparrow Clo., 81 E6
Hmptn.
Sparrow Dr., Orp. 104 F1
Sparrow Fm. Dr., 72 C6
Felt.
Sparrow Fm. Rd., 99 G4
Epsom
Sparrow Grn., Dag. 53 H3
Sparrows La. SE9 79 F7
Sparrows Way 28 J1
(Bushey), Wat.
Sparrows Herne
Sparsholt Rd. N19 49 F1
Sparsholt Rd., 61 H1
Bark.
Sparta St. SE10 78 C1
Spear Ms. SW5 66 D4
Spearman St. SE18 70 D6
Spearpoint Gdns., 43 J4
Ilf.
Spears Rd. N19 49 E1
Speart La., Houns. 63 E7
Spedan Clo. NW3 48 E3

Speedwell St. SE8 69 A7
 Comet St.
Speedy Pl. WC1 8 A4
Speer Rd., T.Ditt. 91 C7
Speke Ho. SE5 67 J7
Speke Rd., Th.Hth. 95 A2
Spekehill SE9 88 C3
Speldhurst Clo., 96 G5
 Brom.
Speldhurst Rd. E9 50 G7
Speldhurst Rd. W4 65 D3
Spellbrook Wk. N1 58 J1
 Basire St.
Spelman St. E1 13 H1
Spelman St. E1 59 D5
Spencer Ave. N13 32 F6
Spencer Ave., Hayes 54 A5
Spencer Clo. N3 39 D2
Spencer Clo. NW10 55 J3
Spencer Clo., Orp. 104 H2
Spencer Clo., 34 J5
 Wdf.Grn.
Spencer Ct. NW8 6 C1
Spencer Dr. N2 39 F6
Spencer Gdns. SE9 79 C5
Spencer Gdns. SW14 74 C5
Spencer Hill SW19 84 B6
Spencer Hill Rd. 84 B7
 SW19
Spencer Ms. W6 66 B6
 Greyhound Rd.
Spencer Pk. SW18 75 G5
Spencer Pas. E2 59 E2
 Pritchard's Rd.
Spencer Pl., Croy. 95 A7
 Gloucester Rd.
Spencer Ri. NW5 49 B4
Spencer Rd. E6 61 A1
Spencer Rd. E17 42 C2
Spencer Rd. N8 40 F5
Spencer Rd. N11 32 B4
Spencer Rd. N17 41 D1
Spencer Rd. SW18 75 G4
Spencer Rd. SW20 92 H1
Spencer Rd. W3 65 C1
Spencer Rd. W4 65 C7
Spencer Rd., Brom. 87 F7
Spencer Rd., E.Mol. 91 A4
Spencer Rd., Har. 37 B2
Spencer Rd., Ilf. 52 J1
Spencer Rd., Islw. 72 J1
Spencer Rd., Mitch. 94 A3
Spencer Rd. Mitch. 94 A7
 (Beddington),
Spencer Rd., 102 B5
 S.Croy.
Spencer Rd., Twick. 82 B3
Spencer Rd., Wem. 46 F2
Spencer St. EC1 8 G4
Spencer St. EC1 58 H3
Spencer St., Sthl. 63 D2
Spencer Wk. SW15 75 A4
Spenser Gro. N16 50 B4
Spenser Rd. SE24 76 G5
Spenser St. SW1 15 G5
Spenser St. SW1 67 C3
Spensley Wk. N16 50 A3
 C/issold Rd.
Speranza St. SE18 70 J5
Sperling Rd. N17 41 B2
Spert St. E14 59 H7
Spey St. E14 60 C5
Speyside N14 24 C6
Spezia Rd. NW10 56 G2
Spicer Clo. SW9 76 H2
Spicer Clo., Walt. 90 C6
Spices Yd., Croy. 101 J4
Spiers Clo., N.Mal. 92 F6
Spigurnell Rd. N17 41 A1
Spikes Bri. Rd., 54 E6
 Sthl.
Spilsby Clo. NW9 38 E2
 Kenley Ave.
Spindlewood Gdns., 102 B4
 Croy.
Spindrift Ave. E14 69 A4
Spinel Clo. SE18 70 J5
Spinnells Rd., Har. 45 F1
Spinney, The N21 24 G7
Spinney, The SW16 85 C3
Spinney, The, Barn. 23 E2
Spinney, The, Sid. 89 E4
Spinney, The, Stan. 29 H4
Spinney, The, Sun. 90 A1
Spinney, The, Sutt. 99 J4
Spinney, The, Wem. 46 D3
Spinney Clo., 92 E5
 N.Mal.
Spinney Gdns. SE19 86 C5
Spinney Gdns., Dag. 53 E5
Spinney Oak, Brom. 97 B2
Spinneys, The, 97 C2
 Brom.

Spirit Quay E1 17 J1
Spital Sq. E1 13 E1
Spital Sq. E1 59 B5
Spital St. E1 9 H6
Spital St. E1 59 D5
Spital Yd. E1 13 E1
Spitalfields Mkt. E1 13 F1
Spitalfields Mkt. E1 59 C5
Spitfire Est., 63 C5
 Houns.
Spitfire Way, 63 C5
 Houns.
Spode Wk. NW6 48 E6
 Lymington Rd.
Spondon Rd. N15 41 D4
Spooner Wk., Wall. 101 D5
Sportsbank St. SE6 78 C7
Spottons Gro. N17 40 J1
 Gospatrick Rd.
Spout Hill, Croy. 103 A5
Spratt Hall Rd. E11 42 G6
Spray La., Twick. 73 B6
Spray St. SE18 70 E4
Spreighton Rd., 90 H4
 W.Mol.
Sprimont Pl. SW3 18 J3
Sprimont Pl. SW3 66 J4
Spring Bri. Rd. W5 55 G7
Spring Clo., Barn. 23 A5
Spring Clo., Borwd. 22 A1
Spring Clo., Dag. 53 D1
Spring Clo. La., 100 B6
 Sutt.
Spring Cotts., 91 G5
 Surb.
 St. Leonards Rd.
Spring Ct., Sid. 89 A3
 Station Rd.
Spring Dr., Pnr. 36 A6
 Eastcote Rd.
Spring Gdns. SW1 15 J1
Spring Gdns., Rom. 44 J5
Spring Gdns., Wall. 101 C5
Spring Gdns., 90 J5
 W.Mol.
Spring Gdns., 34 J7
 Wdf.Grn.
Spring Gdns. Ind. 44 J5
 Est., Rom.
Spring Gro. W4 65 A5
Spring Gro., Hmptn. 90 H1
 Plevna Rd.
Spring Gro., Loug. 27 A6
Spring Gro., Mitch. 94 A1
Spring Gro. Cres., 72 J1
 Houns.
Spring Gro. Rd., 72 H1
 Houns.
Spring Gro. Rd., 73 A1
 Islw.
Spring Gro. Rd., 73 J5
 Rich.
Spring Hill E5 41 D7
Spring Hill SE26 86 F4
Spring Lake, Stan. 29 E4
Spring La. E5 41 D7
Spring La. SE25 95 E6
Spring Ms. W1 15 J1
Spring Pk. Ave., 102 G2
 Croy.
Spring Pk. Dr. N4 49 J1
Spring Pk. Rd., 102 G2
 Croy.
Spring Pas. SW15 75 A3
 The Embk.
Spring Path NW3 48 G5
Spring Pl. NW5 49 B5
Spring St. W2 10 E4
Spring St. W2 57 G6
Spring Ter., Rich. 73 H5
Spring Vale, Bexh. 80 H4
Spring Vill. Rd., 30 A7
 Edg.
Spring Wk. E1 13 J1
Springall St. SE15 68 E7
Springbank N21 24 F6
Springbank Rd. SE13 78 D6
Springbank Wk. NW1 49 D7
 Agar Gro.
Springbourne Ct., 96 C1
 Beck.
Springclose La., 100 B6
 Sutt.
Springcroft Ave. N2 39 J4
Springdale Rd. N16 50 A4
Springfield E5 50 E1
Springfield 29 A1
 (Bushey), Wat.
Springfield Ave. 40 C3
 N10
Springfield Ave. 93 C3
 SW20

Springfield Ave., 81 H6
 Hmptn.
Springfield Clo. 31 E5
 N12
Springfield Clo., 29 D3
 Stan.
Springfield Dr., 43 F6
 Ilf.
Springfield Gdns. 50 E1
 E5
Springfield Gdns. 38 D5
 NW9
Springfield Gdns., 97 C4
 Brom.
Springfield Gdns., 45 B1
 Ruis.
Springfield Gdns., 103 B2
 W.Wick.
Springfield Gdns., 34 J7
 Wdf.Grn.
Springfield Gro. 69 J6
 SE7
Springfield La. NW6 57 E1
Springfield Mt. NW9 38 D5
Springfield Ri. 86 E3
 SE26
Springfield Rd. E4 34 E1
Springfield Rd. E6 52 C7
Springfield Rd. E15 60 E3
Springfield Rd. E17 41 J6
Springfield Rd. N11 32 B5
Springfield Rd. N15 41 D4
Springfield Rd. NW8 57 F1
Springfield Rd. 86 E5
 SE26
Springfield Rd. 84 C5
 SW19
Springfield Rd. W7 64 B1
Springfield Rd., 80 H3
 Bexh.
Springfield Rd., 97 C4
 Brom.
Springfield Rd., 37 B6
 Har.
Springfield Rd., 63 C1
 Hayes
Springfield Rd., 91 H3
 Kings.T.
Springfield Rd., 82 D5
 Tedd.
Springfield Rd., 94 J1
 Th.Hth.
Springfield Rd., 81 G1
 Twick.
Springfield Rd., 101 A5
 Wall.
Springfield Rd., 80 B3
 Well.
Springfield Wk. NW6 57 E1
Springhill Clo. SE5 77 A3
Springhurst Clo., 102 J4
 Croy.
Springpark Dr. N4 96 C3
Springpond Rd., 53 E5
 Dag.
Springrice Rd. SE13 78 D6
Springvale Ave., 64 H5
 Brent.
Springvale Est. W14 66 B3
 Blythe Rd.
Springvale Ter. W14 66 A3
Springwater Clo. 79 D1
 SE18
Springwell Ave. 56 F1
 NW10
Springwell Clo. 85 G4
 SW16
 Etherstone Rd.
Springwell Ct., 72 D2
 Houns.
Springwell Rd. SW16 85 G4
Springwell Rd., 72 D2
 Houns.
Springwood Cres. 30 B2
 Edg.
Sprowston Ms. E7 51 G6
Sprowston Rd. E7 51 G5
Spruce Ct. W4 65 D2
Spruce Ct. W5 64 H3
 Elderberry Rd.
Spruce Hills Rd. 42 C2
 E17
Spruce Pk., Brom. 96 F4
 Cumberland Rd.
Sprucedale Gdns., 102 G4
 Croy.
Sprules Rd. SE4 77 H2
Spur Rd. N15 41 A4
 Philip La.
Spur Rd. SW1 15 F4
Spur Rd. SW1 67 C2
Spur Rd., Bark. 61 F3

Spur Rd., Edg. 29 H4
Spur Rd., Felt. 72 B5
Spur Rd., Islw. 64 E7
Spur Rd. Est., Edg. 29 J4
Spurfield, W.Mol. 90 H3
Spurgeon Ave. SE19 95 A1
Spurgeon Rd. SE19 95 A1
Spurgeon St. SE1 17 B6
Spurgeon St. SE1 68 A3
Spurling Rd. SE22 77 C4
Spurling Rd., Dag. 53 F6
Spurstowe Rd. E8 50 E6
 Marcon Pl.
Spurstowe Ter. E8 50 E5
Square, The W6 65 J5
Square, The, Cars. 101 A5
Square, The, Ilf. 43 D7
Square, The, Rich. 73 G5
Square, The, 34 G5
 Wdf.Grn.
Square Rigger Row 75 F3
 SW11
 York Pl.
Squarey St. SW17 84 F3
Squires Ct. SW19 84 D4
Squires La. N3 39 E2
Squires Mt. NW3 48 G3
 East Heath Rd.
Squires Wd. Dr., 88 C7
 Chis.
 Bullers Wd. Dr.
Squirrel Clo., 72 C3
 Houns.
Squirrels, The SE13 78 D3
 Belmont Hill
Squirrels, The, 36 F3
 Pnr.
Squirrels Clo. N12 31 F4
 Woodside Ave.
Squirrels Grn., 99 G2
 Wor.Pk.
 The Ave.
Squirrels La., 35 A3
 Buck.H.
Squirrels Ms. W13 55 D7
Squirries St. E2 9 J3
Squirries St. E2 59 D3
Stable Clo., Nthlt. 54 G2
 Hotspur Rd.
Stable Wk. N2 39 G1
 Old Fm. Rd.
Stable Way W10 56 J6
 Latimer Rd.
Stable Yd. SW1 15 F3
Stable Yd. SW9 76 F2
 Broomgrove Rd.
Stable Yd. Rd. SW1 15 G3
Stable Yd. Rd. SW1 67 C2
Stables, The, 26 J7
 Buck.H.
Stables End, Orp. 104 F3
Stables Ms. SE27 85 J5
Stables Way SE11 20 E3
Stables Way SE11 67 G6
Stacey Ave. N18 33 F4
Stacey Clo. E10 42 D5
 Halford Rd.
Stacey St. WC2 11 J4
Stacey St. WC2 58 D6
Stackhouse St. SW3 14 J5
Stacy Path SE5 68 B7
 Harris St.
Stadium Rd. NW2 38 J7
Stadium Rd. SE18 70 C7
Stadium St. SW10 66 F7
Stadium Way, Wem. 46 J4
Staff St. EC1 9 C4
Staffa Rd. E10 50 G1
Stafford Clo. N14 24 C5
Stafford Clo. NW6 57 D3
Stafford Clo., 100 B6
 Sutt.
Stafford Ct. W8 66 D3
 Kensington High St.
Stafford Cross Ind. 101 F5
 Est., Croy.
Stafford Gdns., 101 F5
 Croy.
Stafford Pl. SW1 15 F5
Stafford Pl. SW1 67 C3
Stafford Pl., Rich. 73 J7
Stafford Rd. E3 59 J2
Stafford Rd. E7 51 J7
Stafford Rd. NW6 57 D3
Stafford Rd., Croy. 101 G3
Stafford Rd., Har. 28 J7
Stafford Rd., 92 C3
 N.Mal.
Stafford Rd., Sid. 88 H4
Stafford Rd., Wall. 101 B6
Stafford St. W1 15 F1
Stafford St. W1 67 C1
Stafford Ter. W8 66 D2

Staffordshire St. 77 D1
SE15
Stag Clo., Edg. 38 B2
Stag La. NW9 38 C3
Stag La. SW15 83 F2
Stag La., Buck.H. 34 H2
Stan La., Edg. 38 B2
Stag Pl. SW1 15 F5
Stag Ridg OW10 88 F2
Stag Pl. SW1 67 C3
Stags Way, Islw. 64 C6
Stainbank Rd., 94 B3
Mitch.
Stainby Rd. N15 41 C4
Stainer St. SE1 17 C2
Stainer St. SE1 68 A1
Staines Ave., Sutt. 100 A2
Staines Rd., Felt. 72 C5
Staines Rd. (TW3), 72 G3
Houns.
Staines Rd. (TW4), 72 C5
Houns.
Staines Rd., Ilf. 52 G4
Staines Rd., Twick. 81 G3
Staines Rd. E., 81 A7
Sun.
Staines Wk., Sid. 89 C6
Evry Rd.
Stainforth Rd. E17 42 A4
Stainforth Rd., 43 G7
Ilf.
Staining La. EC2 13 A3
Staining La. EC2 58 J6
Stainmore Clo., 97 G1
Chis.
Stainsbury St. E2 59 F2
Royston St.
Stainsby Pl. E14 60 A6
Stainsby Rd. E14 60 A6
Stainton Rd. SE6 78 D6
Stainton Rd., Enf. 25 F1
Stalbridge St. NW1 10 H1
Statham St. SE16 68 E3
Stambourne Way 86 B7
SE19
Stambourne Way, 103 C3
W.Wick.
Stamford Brook Ave. 65 F3
W6
Stamford Brook Rd. 65 F3
W6
Stamford Clo. N15 41 D4
Stamford Clo., Har. 29 B7
Stamford Clo., 54 G7
Sthl.
Stamford Ct. W6 65 F4
Goldhawk Rd.
Stamford Dr., Brom. 96 F4
Stamford Gdns., 53 C7
Dag.
Stamford Gro. E. 50 D1
N16
Oldhill St.
Stamford Gro. W. 50 D1
N16
Oldhill St.
Stamford Hill N16 50 C2
Stamford Hill Est. 50 C1
N16
Stamford Rd. E6 61 B1
Stamford Rd. N1 50 B7
Stamford Rd. N15 41 D4
Stamford Rd., Dag. 62 B1
Stamford St. SE1 16 E2
Stamford St. SE1 67 G1
Stamp Pl. E2 9 F3
Stamp Pl. E2 59 C3
Stanard Clo. N16 41 B7
Stanborough Clo., 81 F6
Hmptn.
Stanborough Pas. E8 50 C6
Abbot St.
Stanborough Rd., 73 A3
Houns.
Stanbridge Pl. N21 32 H2
Stanbridge Rd. SW15 74 J3
Stanbrook Rd. SE2 71 B2
Stanbury Rd. SE15 77 E1
Stancroft NW9 38 E5
Standard Ind. Est. 70 C2
E16
Standard Pl. EC2 9 E4
Standard Rd. NW10 56 C4
Standard Rd., Belv. 71 G5
Standard Rd., Bexh. 80 E4
Standard Rd., 72 E3
Houns.
Standen Rd. SW18 75 C7
Standfield Gdns., 53 G6
Dag.
Standfield Rd.
Standfield Rd., 53 G6
Dag.

Standish Rd. W6 65 G4
Standlake Pt. SE23 86 G3
Stane Clo. SW19 93 E1
Hayward Clo.
Stane Way SE18 70 B7
Stanfield Rd. E3 59 H2
Stanford Clo. 81 F6
Hmptn.
Stanford Clo., Rom. 44 H6
Stanford Rd. 26 B6
Wdf.Grn.
Stanford Ho., Bark. 62 B2
Stanford Rd. N11 31 J5
Stanford Rd. SW16 94 D2
Stanford Rd. W8 14 B5
Stanford Rd. W8 66 E3
Stanford St. SW1 19 H2
Stanford Way SW16 94 D2
Stangate Cres. 22 D5
Borwd.
Stangate Gdns., 29 E4
Stan.
Stanger Rd. SE25 95 D4
Stanhope Ave. N3 39 C3
Stanhope Ave., 103 F1
Brom.
Stanhope Ave., Har. 37 A1
Stanhope Clo. SE16 68 G2
Middleton Dr.
Stanhope Gdns. N4 40 H6
Stanhope Gdns. N6 40 B6
Stanhope Gdns. 30 F5
NW7
**Stanhope Gdns. 18 D1
SW7**
Stanhope Gdns. 66 F4
SW7
Stanhope Gdns. 53 F3
Dag.
Stanhope Rd.
Stanhope Gdns. 52 C1
Ilf.
Stanhope Gate W1 15 C1
Stanhope Gate W1 67 A1
Stanhope Gro., 95 J5
Beck.
**Stanhope Ms. E. 18 D1
SW7**
Stanhope Ms. E. 66 F4
SW7
**Stanhope Ms. S. 18 D2
SW7**
**Stanhope Ms. W. 18 D1
SW7**
Stanhope Ms. W. 66 F4
SW7
Stanhope Par. NW1 7 F3
Stanhope Pk. Rd., 54 J4
Grnf.
Stanhope Pl. W2 10 J4
Stanhope Pl. W2 57 J7
Stanhope Rd. E17 42 B5
Stanhope Rd. N6 40 C6
Stanhope Rd. N12 31 F5
Stanhope Rd., Barn. 22 J5
Stanhope Rd., Bexh. 80 E2
Stanhope Rd., Cars. 101 A7
Stanhope Rd., Croy. 102 B3
Stanhope Rd., Dag. 53 F2
Stanhope Rd., Grnf. 54 J5
Stanhope Rd., Sid. 89 A4
Stanhope Row W1 15 D2
Stanhope St. NW1 7 F3
Stanhope St. NW1 58 C3
Stanhope Ter. W2 10 F5
Stanhope Ter. W2 57 J7
Stanier Clo. W14 66 C5
Aisgill Ave.
Stanlake Ms. W12 65 J1
Stanlake Rd. W12 65 J1
Stanlake Vill. W12 65 J1
Stanley Ave., Bark. 61 J2
Stanley Ave., Beck. 96 C2
Stanley Ave., Dag. 53 F1
Stanley Ave., Grnf. 54 J1
Stanley Ave., 92 G5
N.Mal.
Stanley Ave., Wem. 46 H7
Stanley Clo. SW8 20 C6
Stanley Clo. SW8 67 F6
Stanley Clo., Wem. 46 H7
Stanley Cres. W11 57 C7
Stanley Gdns. NW2 47 J5
Stanley Gdns. SW17 85 A6
Ashbourne Rd.
Stanley Gdns. W3 65 E2
Stanley Gdns. W11 57 C7
Stanley Gdns., 101 C6
Wall.
Stanley Gdns. Ms. 57 C7
W11
Stanley Cres.

Stanley Gdns. Rd., 82 B5
Tedd.
Stanley Gro. SW8 76 A2
Stanley Gro., Croy. 94 G6
Stanley Pk. Dr., 55 J1
Wem.
Stanley Pk. Rd., 100 H7
Cars.
Stanley Pk. Rd., 101 B6
Wall.
Stanley Rd. E4 34 D1
Stanley Rd. E10 42 B6
Stanley Rd. E12 52 B5
Stanley Rd. E15 60 D1
Stanley Rd. E18 42 F1
Stanley Rd. N2 39 G3
Stanley Rd. N9 33 C1
Stanley Rd. N10 32 B7
Stanley Rd. N11 32 D6
Stanley Rd. N15 40 H4
Stanley Rd. NW9 38 G7
West Hendon Bdy.
Stanley Rd. SW14 74 B4
Stanley Rd. SW19 84 D7
Stanley Rd. W3 65 C3
Stanley Rd., Brom. 96 H4
Stanley Rd., Cars. 101 A7
Stanley Rd., Croy. 94 G7
Stanley Rd., Enf. 25 B3
Stanley Rd., Har. 45 J2
Stanley Rd., Houns. 72 J4
Stanley Rd., Ilf. 52 G2
Stanley Rd., Mitch. 85 A7
Stanley Rd., Mord. 93 D4
Stanley Rd., Nthwd. 36 A1
Stanley Rd., Sid. 89 A3
Stanley Rd., Sthl. 54 E7
Stanley Rd., Sutt. 100 E6
Stanley Rd., Tedd. 82 B4
Stanley Rd., Twick. 82 A5
Stanley Rd., Wem. 46 J6
Stanley St. SE8 68 J7
Stanley Ter. N19 49 E2
Stanleycroft Clo., 73 B1
Islw.
Stanmer St. SW11 75 H1
Stanmore Gdns., 73 J3
Rich.
Stanmore Gdns., 100 F3
Sutt.
Stanmore Hill, 29 D3
Stan.
Stanmore Pl. NW1 58 B1
Arlington Rd.
Stanmore Rd. E11 51 F1
Stanmore Rd. N15 40 H4
Stanmore Rd., Belv. 71 J4
Stanmore Rd., Rich. 73 J3
Stanmore St. N1 58 F1
Caledonian Rd.
Stanmore Ter., 96 A2
Beck.
Stanmore Way, 27 D1
Loug.
Stannard Rd. E8 50 D6
Stannary Pl. SE11 20 F5
Stannary St. SE11 20 F5
Stannary St. SE11 67 G6
Stannington Path, 22 A1
Borwd.
Warenford Way
Stansfeld Rd. E6 61 A5
Stansfield Rd. SW9 76 F3
Stansfield Rd., 72 B2
Houns.
Stansgate Rd., Dag. 53 G2
Stanstead Clo., 96 F5
Brom.
Stanstead Gro. SE6 86 J1
Catford Hill
Stanstead Manor, 100 D6
Sutt.
Stanstead Rd. E11 42 H5
Stanstead Rd. SE6 86 J1
Catford Hill
Stanstead Rd. SE23 86 G1
Stansted Cres., 89 D1
Bex.
Stanswood Gdns. 68 B7
SE5
Sedgmoor Pl.
Stanthorpe Clo. 85 E5
SW16
Stanthorpe Rd. 85 E5
SW16
Stanton Ave., Tedd. 82 B5
Stanton Clo., Epsom 99 B5
Stanton Clo., 100 A1
Wor.Pk.
Stanton Rd. SE26 86 J4
Stanton Way
Stanton Rd. SW13 74 F2

Stanton Rd. SW20 93 A1
Stanton Rd., Croy. 94 J7
Stanton Sq. SE26 86 J4
Stanton Way
Stanton St. SE15 77 D1
Stanton Way SE26 86 J4
Stanway Clo., Chig. 35 H5
Stanway Gdns., Edg. 30 C6
Stanway St. N1 9 F1
Stanway St. N1 59 B2
Stanwick Rd. W14 66 C4
Stanworth St. SE1 17 F4
Stanworth St. SE1 68 C2
Stanwyck Dr., Chig. 35 F5
Stapenhill Rd., Wem. 46 E3
**Staple Inn Bldgs. 12 E2
WC1**
Staple St. SE1 17 C4
Staple St. SE1 68 A2
Staplefield Clo. 85 E1
SW2
Staplefield Clo., 28 E7
Pnr.
Stapleford Ave., Ilf. 43 H5
Stapleford Clo. E4 34 C3
Stapleford Clo. 75 B7
SW19
Beaumont Rd.
Stapleford Clo., 92 A3
Kings.T.
Stapleford Rd., 46 G7
Wem.
Stapleford Way, 62 B3
Bark.
Staplehurst Rd. 78 E5
SE13
Staplehurst Rd., 100 H7
Cars.
Staples Clo. SE16 68 H1
Staples Cor. NW2 47 H1
Staples Cor. 47 G1
Business Pk. NW2
Staples Rd., Loug. 27 A3
Stapleton Gdns., 101 G5
Croy.
Stapleton Hall Rd. 49 F1
N4
Stapleton Rd. SW17 85 A3
Stapleton Rd., 71 F7
Bexh.
Stapleton Rd., Orp. 104 J3
Stapley Rd., Belv. 71 G5
Stapylton Rd., 23 B3
Barn.
Star & Garter Hill, 82 H1
Rich.
Star La. E16 60 E4
Star Rd. W14 66 C6
Star Rd., Islw. 73 A2
Star St. E16 60 F5
Star St. W2 10 F3
Star St. W2 57 H6
Star Yd. WC2 12 E3
Starboard Way E14 69 A3
Starch Ho. La., Ilf. 43 G2
Starcross St. NW1 7 G4
Starcross St. NW1 58 C3
Starfield Rd. W12 65 G2
Starkleigh Way SE16 68 E5
Egan Way
Starling Clo., 34 G1
Buck.H.
Starling Clo., Pnr. 36 C3
Starling Ms. SE28 70 G2
Whinchat Rd.
Starling Wk., 81 E6
Hmptn.
Oak Ave.
Starts Clo., Orp. 104 D3
Starts Hill Ave., 104 E4
Orp.
Starts Hill Rd., 104 D3
Orp.
State Fm. Ave., 104 E4
Orp.
Staten Gdns., Twick. 82 C1
Green Las.
Statham Gro. N16 49 J4
Statham Gro. N18 33 B5
Tanners End La.
Station App. E7 51 H4
Woodford Rd.
Station App. 42 G5
(Snaresbrook) E11
High St.
Station App. N11 32 B5
Station App. 31 E4
(Woodside Pk.) N12
Holden Rd.
Station App. N16 50 C2
(Stoke Newington)
Stamford Hill

Station App. NW10	56	F3
Station Rd.		
Station App. SE3	78	H3
Kidbrooke Pk. Rd.		
Station App.	88	C1
(Mottingham) SE9		
Station App. SE26	86	F4
Sydenham Rd.		
Station App. SW6	75	B3
Station App. SW16	85	D5
Station App. W7	64	B1
Station App., Bex.	80	G7
Bexley High St.		
Station App., Bexh.	80	E2
Avenue Rd.		
Station App., Bexh.	80	J2
(Barnehurst)		
Station App., Brom.	103	G1
Station App.,	35	A4
Buck.H.		
Cherry Tree Ri.		
Station App., Chis.	97	D1
Station App., Chis.	88	B6
(Elmstead Wds.)		
Station App., Epsom	99	F5
(Stoneleigh)		
Station App., Esher	98	C3
(Hinchley Wd.)		
Station App., Grnf.	46	A7
Station App.,	90	G1
Hmptn.		
Milton Rd.		
Station App., Har.	37	B7
Station App., Ilf.	43	G3
Station App.,	92	A2
Kings.T.		
Station App., Loug.	27	B5
Station App., Loug.	27	F4
(Debden)		
Station App., Orp.	104	J2
Station App., Pnr.	36	E4
Station App., Pnr.	28	G7
(Hatch End)		
Uxbridge Rd.		
Station App., Rich.	74	A1
Station App., Ruis.	45	B5
Station App., Sid.	89	A2
Station App., Sun.	90	A1
Station App., Sutt.	100	B7
(Cheam)		
Station App., Wat.	28	D3
Prestwick Rd.		
Station App., Well.	80	A2
Station App., Wem.	46	E6
Station App. Rd. W4	65	C7
Station Ave. SW9	76	H3
Coldharbour La.		
Station Ave.,	92	E3
N.Mal.		
Station Ave., Rich.	74	A1
Station Clo. N3	39	D1
Station Rd.		
Station Clo.,	90	H1
Hmptn.		
Station Cres. N15	41	A4
Station Cres. SE3	69	G5
Station Cres., Wem.	46	E6
Station Est., Beck.	95	G4
Elmers End Rd.		
Station Est. Rd.,	81	B1
Felt.		
Station Gdns. W4	65	C7
Station Hill, Brom.	103	G2
Station Ho., Wem.	47	B7
Station Par. E11	42	G5
Station Par. N14	32	D1
High St.		
Station Par. NW2	47	J6
Station Par. W3	56	A6
Station Par., Bark.	52	F7
Station Pas. E18	42	H2
Maybank Rd.		
Station Path E8	50	E6
Amhurst Rd.		
Station Pl. N4	49	G2
Seven Sisters Rd.		
Station Ri. SE27	85	H2
Norwood Rd.		
Station Rd.	34	D1
(Chingford) E4		
Station Rd. E7	51	G4
Station Rd. E10	51	C3
Station Rd. E12	52	A4
Station Rd. E17	41	H6
Station Rd. N3	39	D1
Station Rd. N11	32	B5
Station Rd. N17	41	D3
Hale Rd.		
Station Rd. N19	49	C3
Station Rd. N21	32	H1
Station Rd. N21	32	H1
(Winchmore Hill)		

Station Rd. N22	40	E2
Station Rd. NW4	38	G6
Station Rd. NW7	30	E5
Station Rd. NW10	56	F2
Station Rd. SE20	86	F6
Station Rd. SE25	95	C4
(Norwood Junct.)		
Station Rd. SW13	74	F2
Station Rd. SW19	93	F1
Station Rd. W5	55	J6
Station Rd.	64	B1
(Hanwell) W7		
Station Rd., Barn.	23	E5
Station Rd., Belv.	71	G3
Station Rd., Bexh.	80	E3
Station Rd., Borwd.	22	A4
Station Rd., Brom.	96	G1
Station Rd., Brom.	96	E2
(Shortlands)		
Station Rd., Cars.	100	J4
Station Rd., Chess.	98	H5
Station Rd., Chig.	35	E3
Station Rd., Croy.	102	A2
(East Croydon)		
Station Rd., Croy.	101	J1
(West Croydon)		
Station Rd., Edg.	30	A6
Station Rd., Enf.	24	J3
Station Rd., Esher	98	A2
Station Rd.	98	A5
(Claygate), Esher		
Station Rd., Hmptn.	90	G1
Station Rd., Har.	37	C4
Station Rd. (North	36	H5
Harrow), Har.		
Station Rd., Houns.	72	H4
Station Rd., Ilf.	52	E3
Station Rd.	43	G3
(Barkingside), Ilf.		
Station Rd.,	92	A1
Kings.T.		
Station Rd., Kings.T.	91	G1
(Hampton Wick)		
Station Rd., Loug.	27	B4
Station Rd., N.Mal.	92	H5
(Motspur Pk.)		
Station Rd., Orp.	104	J2
Station Rd., Rom.	53	D1
(Chadwell Heath)		
Station Rd., Sid.	89	A4
Station Rd., Sun.	81	A7
Station Rd., Tedd.	82	C5
Station Rd.,	91	C7
T.Ditt.		
Station Rd., Twick.	82	C1
Station Rd.,	103	C2
W.Wick.		
Station Rd. N.,	71	H3
Belv.		
Station Sq.	97	F5
(Petts Wood), Orp.		
Station St. E15	51	D7
Station St. E16	70	E1
Station Ter. NW10	57	A2
Station Ter. SE5	76	J1
Station Vw., Grnf.	55	A1
Station Way, Buck.H.	34	J4
(Roding Valley)		
Station Way	98	B6
(Claygate), Esher		
Station Way, Sutt.	100	B6
(Cheam), Sutt.		
Station Yd., Twick.	73	D7
Staunton Rd.,	82	H6
Kings.T.		
Staunton St. SE8	68	J6
Stave Yd. Rd. SE16	68	H1
Staveley Clo. E9	50	F5
Churchill Wk.		
Staveley Clo. N7	49	E4
Penn Rd.		
Staveley Clo. SE15	77	E1
Asylum Rd.		
Staveley Gdns. W4	74	D1
Staveley Rd. W4	65	C6
Staverton Rd. NW2	47	J7
Stavordale Rd. N5	49	H4
Stavordale Rd.,	100	F1
Cars.		
Stayners Rd. E1	59	G4
Stayton Rd., Sutt.	100	D3
Stead St. SE17	**21**	**B2**
Stead St. SE17	68	A4
Steadfast Rd.,	91	G1
Kings.T.		
Stean St. E8	59	C1
Stebbing Way, Bark.	62	A2
Stebondale St. E14	69	C5
Stedham Pl. WC1	**12**	**A3**
Steedman St. SE17	**20**	**J2**
Steeds Rd. N10	39	J1
Steeds Way, Loug.	27	B3
Steele Rd. E11	51	E4

Steele Rd. N17	41	B3
Steele Rd. NW10	56	C2
Steele Rd. W4	65	C3
Steele Rd., Islw.	73	D4
Steeles Ms. N. NW3	48	J6
Steeles Rd.		
Steeles Ms. S. NW3	48	J6
Steeles Rd.		
Steeles Rd. NW3	48	J6
Steel's La. E1	59	F6
Devonport St.		
Steen Way SE22	77	B5
East Dulwich Gro.		
Steep Clo., Orp.	104	J6
Steep Hill SW16	85	D3
Steep Hill, Croy.	102	B4
Steeple Clo. SW6	75	B2
Steeple Clo. SW19	84	B5
Steeple Ct. E1	59	E4
Coventry Rd.		
Steeple Wk. N1	58	J1
Basire St.		
Steeplestone Clo.	32	J5
N18		
Steerforth St. SW18	84	F2
Steers Mead, Mitch.	93	J1
Steers Way SE16	68	H2
Stella Rd. SW17	84	J6
Stellar Ho. N17	33	D6
Stellman Clo. E5	50	D3
Stembridge Rd. SE20	95	E2
Stephan Clo. E8	59	D1
Stephen Clo., Orp.	104	H3
Stephen Ms. W1	**11**	**H2**
Stephen Rd., Bexh.	80	J3
Stephen St. W1	**11**	**H2**
Stephen St. W1	58	D5
Stephendale Rd.	75	E3
SW6		
Stephen's Rd. E15	60	E1
Stephenson Rd. W7	55	C6
Stephenson Rd.,	72	G7
Twick.		
Stephenson St. E16	60	E4
Stephenson St.	56	E3
NW10		
Stephenson Way	**7**	**G5**
NW1		
Stephenson Way	58	C4
NW1		
Stepney Causeway	59	G6
E1		
Stepney Grn. E1	59	F5
Stepney High St. E1	59	G5
Stepney Way E1	59	E5
Sterling Ave., Edg.	29	J4
Sterling Ind. Est.,	53	H4
Dag.		
Sterling Pl. W5	64	H4
Sterling Rd., Enf.	25	A1
Sterling St. SW7	**14**	**H4**
Sterling Way N18	33	A4
Sterndale Rd. W14	66	A3
Sterne St. W12	66	A2
Sternhall La. SE15	77	D3
Sternhold Ave. SW2	85	D2
Storry Dr., Dag.	53	G5
Alibon Rd.		
Sterry Dr., Epsom	99	E4
Sterry Dr., T.Ditt.	91	B6
Sterry Gdns., Dag.	53	G6
Sterry Rd., Bark.	61	J1
Sterry Rd., Dag.	53	G4
Sterry St. SE1	**17**	**B4**
Sterry St. SE1	68	A2
Steucers La. SE23	86	H1
Steve Biko La. SE6	87	A4
Steve Biko Way,	72	G3
Houns.		
Stevedale Rd.,	80	C2
Well.		
Stevenage Rd. E6	52	D6
Stevenage Rd. SW6	66	A7
Stevens Ave. E9	50	F6
Stevens Clo., Beck.	87	A6
Stevens Clo.,	81	E6
Hmptn.		
Stevens Clo., Pnr.	36	C5
Bridle Rd.		
Stevens Grn.	28	J1
(Bushey), Wat.		
Stevens La., Esher	98	D7
Stevens Rd., Dag.	53	B3
Stevens St. SE1	**17**	**E5**
Stevens Way, Chig.	35	H4
Stevenson Cres.	**21**	**J3**
SE16		
Stevenson Cres.	68	D5
SE16		
Steventon Rd. W12	56	F7
Steward St. E1	**13**	**E1**
Steward St. E1	59	B5
Stewart Clo. NW9	38	C6

Stewart Clo., Chis.	88	E5
Stewart Clo.,	81	E6
Hmptn.		
Stewart Rainbird	52	D5
Ho. E12		
Stewart Rd. E15	51	C4
Stewart St. E14	69	C2
Stewart's Gro. SW3	**18**	**G3**
Stewart's Gro. SW3	66	H5
Stewart's Rd. SW8	67	C7
Stewartsby Clo. N18	32	J5
Steyne Rd. W3	65	B1
Steyning Gro. SE9	88	C4
Steyning Way,	72	C4
Houns.		
Steynings Way N12	31	D5
Steynton Ave., Bex.	89	D2
Stickland Rd.,	71	G4
Belv.		
Picardy Rd.		
Stickleton Clo.,	54	H3
Grnf.		
Stile Hall Gdns. W4	65	A5
Stile Path, Sun.	90	A3
Stilecroft Gdns.,	46	E3
Wem.		
Stiles Clo., Brom.	97	C6
Stillingfleet Rd.	65	G6
SW13		
Stillington St. SW1	**19**	**G1**
Stillington St. SW1	67	C4
Stillness Rd. SE23	77	H6
Stilton Cres. NW10	47	C7
Stipularis Dr.,	54	D4
Hayes		
Stirling Clo. SW16	94	C1
Stirling Rd. E13	60	H2
Stirling Rd. E17	41	H3
Stirling Rd. N17	41	D1
Stirling Rd. N22	40	H1
Stirling Rd. SW9	76	E2
Stirling Rd. W3	65	B3
Stirling Rd., Har.	37	C3
Stirling Rd., Hayes	54	B7
Stirling Rd.,	72	G7
Twick.		
Stirling Rd. Path	41	H3
E17		
Stirling Wk.,	92	C5
N.Mal.		
Green La.		
Stirling Wk., Surb.	92	B6
Stirling Way,	22	D6
Borwd.		
Stirling Way, Croy.	94	E7
Stiven Cres., Har.	45	F3
Stock Orchard Cres.	49	F5
N7		
Stock Orchard St.	49	F5
N7		
Stock St. E13	60	G2
Stockbury Rd.,	95	F6
Croy.		
Stockdale Rd., Dag.	53	F2
Stockdove Way,	55	C3
Grnf.		
Stockfield Rd. SW16	85	F3
Stockfield Rd.,	98	B5
Esher		
Stockholm Rd. SE16	68	F5
Stockhurst Clo.	74	J2
SW15		
Stockingswater La.,	25	H3
Enf.		
Stockport Rd. SW16	94	D1
Stocks Pl. E14	59	J7
Grenade St.		
Stocksfield Rd. E17	42	C3
Stockton Gdns. N17	32	J7
Stockton Rd.		
Stockton Gdns. NW7	30	G3
Stockton Rd. N17	32	J7
Stockton Rd. N18	33	D6
Stockwell Ave. SW9	76	H2
Stockwell Clo.,	96	H2
Brom.		
Stockwell Gdns. SW9	76	F1
Stockwell Gdns.	76	F2
Est. SW9		
Stockwell Grn. SW9	76	F2
Stockwell La. SW9	76	F2
Stockwell Ms. SW9	76	F2
Stockwell Rd.		
Stockwell Pk. Cres.	76	F2
SW9		
Stockwell Pk. Est.	76	F2
SW9		
Stockwell Pk. Rd.	76	F1
SW9		
Stockwell Pk. Wk.	76	F3
SW9		
Stockwell Rd. SW9	76	F2
Stockwell St. SE10	69	C6

Stockwell Ter. SW9   76 F1
Stodart Rd. SE20   95 F1
Stofield Gdns. SE9   88 A3
  Aldersgrove Ave.
Stoford Clo. SW19   75 B7
Stoke Newington Ch.   50 A3
  St. N16
Stoke Newington   50 C3
  Common N16
Stoke Newington   50 C3
  High St. N16
Stoke Newington Rd.   50 C5
  N16
Stokes Rd. E6   61 B4
Stokes Rd., Croy.   95 G6
Stokesby Rd.,   98 J6
  Chess.
Stokesley St. W12   56 F6
Stoll Clo. NW2   47 J3
Stoms Path SE6   87 A5
  Sedgehill Rd.
Stonard Rd. N13   32 G3
Stonard Rd., Dag.   53 B5
Stonards Hill,   27 C6
  Loug.
Stondon Pk. SE23   77 H6
Stondon Wk. E6   61 A2
  Abbots Rd.
Stone Bldgs. WC2   12 D2
Stone Bldgs. WC2   58 F6
Stone Clo. SW4   76 C2
  Larkhall Ri.
Stone Clo., Dag.   53 F2
Stone Hall Rd. N21   24 F7
Stone Ho. Ct. EC3   13 E3
Stone Pk. Ave.,   96 A4
  Beck.
Stone Pl., Wor.Pk.   99 G2
Stone Rd., Brom.   96 F5
Stone St., Croy.   101 G5
Stone Yd. La. E14   60 B7
  Poplar High St.
Stonebanks, Walt.   90 A7
Stonebridge   50 C7
  Common E8
  Mayfield Rd.
Stonebridge Pk.   47 D7
  NW10
Stonebridge Rd. N15   41 C5
Stonebridge Way,   47 B6
  Wem.
Stonechat Sq. E6   61 B5
  Peridot St.
Stonecot Clo.,   100 B1
  Sutt.
Stonecot Hill,   100 B1
  Sutt.
Stonecroft Rd.,   71 J7
  Erith
Stonecroft Way,   94 E7
  Croy.
Stonecutter St. EC4   12 G3
Stonecutter St. EC4   58 H6
Stonefield Clo.,   80 G3
  Bexh.
Stonefield Clo.,   45 E5
  Ruis.
Stonefield St. N1   58 G1
Stonefield Way SE7   70 A7
  Greenbay Rd.
Stonefield Way,   45 E4
  Ruis.
Stonegrove, Edg.   29 H4
Stonegrove Est.,   29 H4
  Edg.
Stonegrove Gdns.,   29 H5
  Edg.
Stonehall Ave.,   43 B6
  Ilf.
Stoneham Rd. N11   32 C5
Stonehill Clo. SW14   74 D5
Stonehill Grn. Rd.,   89 J7
  Dart.
  Birchwood Rd.
Stonehill Rd. SW14   74 C5
Stonehill Rd. W4   65 A5
  Wellesley Rd.
Stonehill Wds.   89 H6
  Caravan Pk., Sid.
Stonehills Ct. SE21   86 B3
Stonehorse Rd.,   25 F5
  Enf.
Stonehouse St. SW4   76 D4
Stoneleigh Ave.,   99 G3
  Wor.Pk.
Stoneleigh Cres.,   99 F5
  Epsom
Stoneleigh Pk. Ave.,   95 G6
  Croy.

Stoneleigh Pk. Rd.,   99 F6
  Epsom
Stoneleigh Pl. W11   57 A7
Stoneleigh Rd. N17   41 C3
Stoneleigh Rd.,   93 H7
  Cars.
Stoneleigh Rd., Ilf.   43 B3
Stoneleigh St. W11   57 A7
Stoneleigh Ter. N19   49 B2
  Dartmouth Pk. Hill
Stonells Rd. SW11   75 J5
  Chatham Rd.
Stonenest St. N4   49 F1
Stones End St. SE1   16 J4
Stones End St. SE1   67 J2
Stoney All. SE18   79 D2
Stoney La. E1   13 F3
Stoney La. SE19   86 C6
  Church Rd.
Stoney St. SE1   17 B1
Stoney St. SE1   68 A1
Stoneyard La. E14   60 B7
  Poplar High St.
Stoneycroft Clo.   78 F7
  SE12
Stoneycroft Rd.,   35 B6
  Wdf.Grn.
Stoneydeep, Tedd.   82 D4
  Twickenham Rd.
Stoneydown E17   41 H4
Stoneydown Ave.   41 H4
  E17
Stoneyfields Gdns.,   30 C4
  Edg.
Stoneyfields La.,   30 C5
  Edg.
Stonhouse St. SW4   76 D3
Stonor Rd. W14   66 C4
Stony Path, Loug.   27 C1
Stopford Rd. E13   60 G1
Stopford Rd. SE17   20 H4
Stopford Rd. SE17   67 H5
Store Rd. E16   70 D2
Store St. E15   51 D5
Store St. WC1   11 H2
Store St. WC1   58 H5
Storers Quay E14   69 D4
Storey Rd. E17   41 J4
Storey Rd. N6   39 J6
Storey St. E16   70 D1
Storey's Gate SW1   15 J4
Storey's Gate SW1   67 D2
Stories Ms. SE5   77 B2
Stories Rd. SE5   77 B3
Stork Rd. E7   51 F6
Storks Rd. SE16   17 J6
Storks Rd. SE16   68 D3
Storksmead Rd.,   30 E7
  Edg.
Stormont Rd. N6   39 J7
Stormont Rd. SW11   76 A3
Stormont Way,   98 F5
  Chess.
Storrington Rd.,   102 C1
  Croy.
Story St. N1   49 F7
  Carnoustie Dr.
Stothard Pl. EC2   13 E1
Stothard St. E1   59 F4
  Colebert Ave.
Stoughton Ave.,   100 A5
  Sutt.
Stoughton Clo. SE11   20 D2
Stoughton Clo.   83 G1
  SW15
  Bessborough Rd.
Stour Ave., Sthl.   63 G3
Stour Clo., Kes.   103 J4
Stour Rd. E3   51 A7
Stour Rd., Dag.   53 G2
Stourcliffe St. W1   10 J4
Stourcliffe St. W1   57 J6
Stourhead Clo.   75 A7
  SW19
  Castlecombe Dr.
Stourhead Gdns.   92 G3
  SW20
Stourton Ave.,   81 F4
  Felt.
Stow Cres. E17   33 H7
Stowage SE8   69 A6
Stowe Gdns. N9   33 C1
  Latymer Rd.
Stowe Pl. N15   41 B3
Stowe Rd. W12   65 H2
Stowting Rd., Orp.   104 H4
Stox Mead, Har.   37 A1
Stracey Rd. E7   51 G4
Stracey Rd. NW10   56 D1
Strachan Pl. SW19   83 J6
  Woodhayes Rd.
Stradbroke Dr.,   35 D6
  Chig.

Stradbroke Gro.,   35 A1
  Buck.H.
Stradbroke Gro.,   43 B3
  Ilf.
Stradbroke Pk.,   35 E6
  Chig.
Stradbroke Rd. N5   49 J4
Stradbrook Rd. SE24   76 J6
Strafford Ave.,   43 D2
  Ilf.
Strafford Rd.,   23 B3
  Barn.
Strafford Rd.,   72 F3
  Houns.
Strafford Rd.,   73 D7
  Twick.
Strafford St. E14   69 A2
Strahan Rd. E3   59 H3
Straight, The,   63 D2
  Sthl.
Straightsmouth SE10   69 C7
Strait Rd. E6   61 B7
Straker's Rd. SE15   77 E4
Strand WC2   12 A6
Strand WC2   58 E7
Strand La. WC2   12 D5
Strand on the Grn.   65 A6
  W4
Strand Pl. N18   33 B4
Strand Sch. App. W4   65 A6
Strandfield Clo.   70 H5
  SE18
Strangways Ter. W14   66 C3
  Melbury Rd.
Stranraer Way N1   49 E7
Strasburg Rd. SW11   76 B1
Stratfield Pk. Clo.   24 H7
  N21
Stratford Ave. W8   66 D3
  Stratford Rd.
Stratford Cen., The   51 D7
  E15
  Broadway
Stratford Clo.,   53 A7
  Bark.
Stratford Clo.,   53 J7
  Dag.
Stratford Ct., N.Mal.   92 D4
  Kingston Rd.
Stratford Gro. SW15   75 A4
Stratford Pl. W1   11 D4
Stratford Pl. W1   58 B6
Stratford Rd. E13   60 F1
Stratford Rd. W3   65 C2
  Bollo Bri. Rd.
Stratford Rd. W8   66 D3
Stratford Rd.,   54 B4
  Hayes
Stratford Rd.,   63 E4
  Sthl.
Stratford Rd.,   94 G4
  Th.Hth.
Strath Ter. SW11   49 C7
Strath Ter. SW11   75 H4
Strathan Clo. SW18   75 B6
Strathaven Rd. SE12   78 H6
Strathblaine Rd.   75 G5
  SW11
Strathbrook Rd.   85 F7
  SW16
Strathcona Rd.,   46 G2
  Wem.
Strathdale SW16   85 F5
Strathdon Dr. SW17   84 G3
Strathearn Ave.,   81 H1
  Twick.
Strathearn Pl. W2   10 G5
Strathearn Pl. W2   57 H7
Strathearn Rd. SW19   84 D5
Strathearn Rd.,   100 D5
  Sutt.
Stratheden SE3   78 G1
Strathfield Gdns.,   52 G6
  Bark.
Strathleven Rd. SW2   76 E4
Strathmore Gdns. N3   39 E1
Strathmore Gdns.   66 D1
  W8
  Palace Gdns. Ter.
Strathmore Gdns.,   38 B2
  Edg.
Strathmore Rd.   84 D3
  SW19
Strathmore Rd.   94 J7
  Croy.
Strathmore Rd.,   82 B4
  Tedd.
Strathnairn St. SE1   21 J2
Strathnairn St. SE1   68 D4
Strathray Gdns. NW3   48 H6
Strathville Rd.   84 D2
  SW18

Strathyre Ave. SW16   94 G3
Stratton Clo. SW19   93 D2
Stratton Clo.,   80 E3
  Bexh.
Stratton Clo., Edg.   29 J6
Stratton Clo.,   72 F1
  Houns.
Stratton Dri., Bark.   52 J5
Stratton Gdns.,   54 F6
  Sthl.
Stratton Rd. SW19   84 D3
Stratton Rd., Bexh.   80 E3
Stratton St. W1   15 E1
Stratton St. W1   67 B1
Strattondale St.   69 C3
  E14
Strauss Rd. W4   65 D2
Strawberry Hill,   82 C3
  Twick.
Strawberry Hill   82 C4
  Clo., Twick.
Strawberry Hill   82 C3
  Rd., Twick.
Strawberry La.,   100 J3
  Cars.
Strawberry Vale N2   39 G1
Strawberry Vale,   82 C3
  Twick.
Streakes Fld. Rd.   47 G2
  NW2
Stream La., Edg.   30 B5
Streamdale SE2   71 F6
Streamline Clo. N9   33 C1
Streamside Clo.,   96 G4
  Brom.
Streatfield Ave. E6   61 C1
Streatfield Rd.,   37 F3
  Har.
Streatham Clo. SW16   85 E3
Streatham Common   85 E5
  N. SW16
Streatham Common   85 E6
  S. SW16
Streatham Ct. SW16   85 E3
Streatham High Rd.   85 E5
  SW16
Streatham Hill SW2   85 E2
Streatham Pl. SW2   76 E7
Streatham Rd.,   94 A1
  Mitch.
Streatham St. WC1   12 A3
Streatham Vale   94 C1
  SW16
Streathbourne Rd.   85 A2
  SW17
Streatley Pl. NW3   48 F4
  New End Sq.
Streatley Rd. NW6   48 C7
Streeters La.,   101 D3
  Wall.
Streetfield Ms. SE3   78 G3
Streimer Rd. E15   60 C2
Strelley Way W3   56 E7
Stretton Rd., Croy.   95 B7
Stretton Rd., Rich.   82 F2
Strickland Rd.,   71 G4
  Belv.
Strickland Row SW18   75 G7
Strickland St. SE8   78 A1
Strickland Way,   104 J4
  Orp.
Stride Rd. E13   60 F2
Strode Clo. N10   32 A7
  Pembroke Rd.
Strode Rd. E7   51 G4
Strode Rd. N17   41 B2
Strode Rd. NW10   47 G6
Strode Rd. SW6   66 B7
Strone Rd. E7   51 J6
Strone Rd. E12   52 A6
Strone Way, Hayes   54 E4
Strongbow Cres. SE9   79 C5
Strongbow Rd. SE9   79 C5
Strongbridge Clo.,   45 G1
  Har.
Stronsa Rd. W12   65 F2
Stroud Cres. SW15   83 G3
Stroud Fld., Nthlt.   45 E6
Stroud Gate, Har.   45 H4
Stroud Grn. Gdns.,   95 F7
  Croy.
Stroud Grn. Rd. N4   47 F1
Stroud Grn. Way,   95 E7
  Croy.
Stroud Rd. SE25   95 D6
Stroud Rd. SW19   84 D3
Stroudes Clo.,   92 E7
  Wor.Pk.
Stroudley Wk. E3   60 B3
Strouts Pl. E2   9 F3
Strutton Grd. SW1   15 H5
Strutton Grd. SW1   67 D3

Strype St. E1 13 F2
Stuart Ave. NW9 38 G7
Stuart Ave. W5 64 J1
Stuart Ave., Brom. 103 G1
Stuart Ave., Har. 45 F3
Stuart Cres., Croy. 102 J4
Stuart Evans Clo., 80 C3
Well.
Stuart Pl., Mitch. 93 J1
Stuart Rd. NW6 57 D3
Stuart Rd. SE15 77 F4
Stuart Rd. SW19 84 D3
Stuart Rd. W3 65 C1
Stuart Rd., Bark. 52 J7
Stuart Rd., Barn. 23 H7
Stuart Rd., Har. 37 C3
Stuart Rd., Rich. 82 E2
Stuart Rd., Th.Hth. 94 J4
Stuart Rd., Well. 80 B1
Stuart Twr. W9 6 C4
Stuart Twr. W9 57 F3
Stubbs Dr. SE16 68 E5
Stubbs Pt. E13 60 G4
Stubbs Way SW19 93 G1
Brangwyn Cres.
Stucley Pl. NW1 49 B7
Hawley Cres.
Stucley Rd., Houns. 63 J7
Studd St. N1 58 H1
Studdridge St. SW6 75 D2
Studholme Ct. NW3 48 D4
Studholme St. SE15 68 E7
Studio Pl. SW1 15 A4
Studio Way, Borwd. 22 C2
Studland SE17 21 B3
Studland Clo., Sid. 88 J3
Studland Rd. SE26 86 G5
Studland Rd. W7 55 A6
Studland Rd., 82 H6
Kings.T.
Studland St. W6 65 H4
Studley Ave. E4 34 D7
Studley Clo. E5 50 H5
Studley Ct., Sid. 89 B5
Studley Dr., Ilf. 43 A6
Studley Est. SW4 76 E1
Studley Gra. Rd. W7 64 B2
Studley Rd. E7 51 H6
Studley Rd. SW4 76 E1
Studley Rd., Dag. 53 D7
Stukeley Rd. E7 51 H7
Stukeley St. WC2 12 B3
Stukeley St. WC2 58 E6
Stumps Hill La., 87 A6
Beck.
Sturdy Rd. SE15 77 E2
Sturge Ave. E17 42 B1
Sturge St. SE1 16 J3
Sturgeon Rd. SE17 20 J4
Sturgeon Rd. SE17 67 H5
Sturges Fld., Chis. 88 G6
Sturgess Ave. NW4 38 G7
Sturmer Way N7 49 F5
Stock Orchard Cres.
Sturrock Clo. N15 41 A4
Sturry St. E14 60 B6
Sturt St. N1 9 A2
Sturt St. N1 58 J2
Stutfield St. E1 13 J4
Stutfield St. E1 59 D6
Styles Gdns. SW9 76 H3
Styles Way, Beck. 96 C4
Sudbourne Rd. SW2 76 E5
Sudbrook Gdns., 82 H3
Rich.
Sudbrook La., Rich. 82 H1
Sudbrooke Rd. SW12 75 J6
Sudbury Ave., Wem. 46 F5
Sudbury Ct. E5 50 H4
Sudbury Ct. Dr., Har. 46 C3
Sudbury Ct. Rd., 46 C3
Har.
Sudbury Cres., 87 G6
Brom.
Sudbury Cres., Wem. 46 E5
Sudbury Cft., Wem. 46 C4
Sudbury Gdns., 102 B4
Croy.
Langton Way
Sudbury Heights 46 C5
Ave., Grnf.
Sudbury Hill, Har. 46 B2
Sudbury Hill Clo., 46 C4
Wem.
Sudbury Meadows, 46 F3
Wem.
Sudbury Rd., Bark. 52 J5
Sudeley St. N1 8 H2
Sudeley St. N1 58 H2
Sudlow Rd. SW18 75 D5
Sudrey St. SE1 16 J4
Suez Ave., Grnf. 55 C2

Suez Rd., Enf. 25 H4
Suffield Rd. E4 34 B3
Suffield Rd. N15 41 C5
Suffield Rd. SE20 95 F2
Suffolk Clo., Borwd. 22 D5
Clydesdale Clo.
Suffolk Ct. E10 42 A7
Suffolk Ct., Ilf. 43 H6
Suffolk La. EC4 13 B5
Suffolk Pk. Rd. E17 41 H4
Suffolk Pl. SW1 15 J1
Suffolk Rd. E13 60 G3
Suffolk Rd. N15 41 A6
Suffolk Rd. NW10 47 E7
Suffolk Rd. SE25 95 C4
Suffolk Rd. SW13 65 F7
Suffolk Rd., Bark. 52 G7
Suffolk Rd., Dag. 53 J5
Suffolk Rd., Enf. 25 E5
Suffolk Rd., Har. 36 F6
Suffolk Rd., Ilf. 43 H6
Suffolk Rd., Sid. 89 C6
Suffolk Rd., 99 F2
Wor.Pk.
Suffolk St. E7 51 G5
Suffolk St. SW1 11 J6
Sugar Bakers Ct. 13 E4
EC3
Sugar Ho. La. E15 60 C2
Sugar Loaf Wk. E2 59 F3
Victoria Pk. Sq.
Sugden Rd. SW11 76 A3
Sugden Rd., T.Ditt. 98 E1
Sugden Way, Bark. 61 J2
Sulgrave Gdns. W6 65 J2
Sulgrave Rd.
Sulgrave Rd. W6 65 J3
Sulina Rd. SW2 76 E7
Sulivan Ct. SW6 75 D2
Sulivan Rd. SW6 75 D3
Sullivan Ave. E16 61 A5
Sullivan Clo. SW11 75 H3
Sullivan Clo., 90 G3
W.Mol.
Victoria Ave.
Sullivan Rd. SE11 20 F1
Sullivan Rd. SE11 67 G4
Sultan Rd. E11 42 H4
Sultan St. SE5 20 J7
Sultan St. SE5 67 J7
Sultan St., Beck. 95 G2
Sumatra Rd. NW6 48 D5
Sumburgh Rd. SW12 76 A6
Summer Ave., E.Mol. 91 B5
Summer Gdns., 91 B5
E.Mol.
Summer Hill, Borwd. 22 A5
Summer Hill, Chis. 97 D2
Summer Hill Vill., 97 D1
Chis.
Summer Ho. Rd. N16 50 B2
Stoke Newington
Ch. St.
Summer Rd., E.Mol. 91 B5
Summer Rd., T.Ditt. 91 C5
Summer Trees, Sun. 90 B1
The Ave.
Summercourt Rd. E1 59 F6
Summerdene Clo. 85 C7
SW16
Bates Cres.
Summerfield Ave. 57 B2
NW6
Summerfield La., 98 G2
Surb.
Summerfield Rd. W5 55 E4
Summerfield Rd., 27 A6
Loug.
Summerfield St. 78 F7
SE12
Summerhill Clo. 104 H3
Orp.
Summerhill Rd. 73 C5
Enf.
Summerhill Rd. N15 41 A4
Summerhill Way, 94 A1
Mitch.
Summerhouse Ave. 72 E1
Houns.
Summerland Gdns. 40 B3
N10
Summerlands Ave. 56 C7
W3
Summerlee Ave. N2 39 J4
Summerlee Gdns. N2 39 J4
Summerley St. 84 E2
SW18
Summers Clo., Sutt. 100 D7
Overton Rd.
Summers Clo., Wem. 47 B3
Summers La. N12 31 G7
Summers Row N12 31 H6
Summers St. EC1 8 E6

Summersby Rd. N6 40 B6
Summerstown 84 F3
SW17
Summerton Way 62 D7
SE28
Summerville Gdns., 100 C6
Sutt.
Summerwood Rd., 73 C5
Islw.
Summit, The, Loug. 27 C1
Summit Ave. NW9 38 D5
Summit Clo. N14 32 C2
Summit Clo. NW9 38 D4
Summit Clo., Edg. 30 A7
Summit Ct. NW2 48 B5
Summit Dr., 43 A2
Wdf.Grn.
Summit Est. N16 41 D7
Summit Rd. E17 42 B4
Summit Rd., Nthlt. 45 G7
Summit Way N14 32 B2
Summit Way SE19 86 B7
Sumner Ave. SE15 77 C1
Sumner Rd.
Sumner Clo., Orp. 104 F4
Sumner Pl. SW7 18 F2
Sumner Pl. SW7 66 G4
Sumner Pl. Ms. SW7 18 F2
Sumner Rd. SE15 21 G6
Sumner Rd. SE15 68 C7
Sumner Rd., Croy. 101 G1
Sumner Rd., Har. 36 J7
Sumner Rd. S., 101 G1
Croy.
Sumner St. SE1 16 H1
Sumner St. SE1 67 H1
Sumpter Clo. NW3 48 F6
Sun Ct. EC3 13 C4
Sun La. SE3 69 H7
Sun Pas. SE16 17 H5
Sun Rd. W14 66 C5
Sun St. EC2 13 C1
Sun St. EC2 59 A5
Sun St. Pas. EC2 13 D2
Sunbeam Rd. NW10 56 D4
Sunbury Ave. NW7 30 D5
Sunbury Ave. SW14 74 D4
Sunbury Ct., Sun. 90 D2
Sunbury Ct. Rd., 90 C2
Sun.
Sunbury Gdns. NW7 30 D5
Sunbury La. SW11 75 G1
Sunbury La., Walt. 90 A6
Sunbury Rd., Sutt. 100 A3
Sunbury St. SE18 70 C3
Sunbury Way, Felt. 81 C5
Suncroft Pl. SE26 86 F3
Sunderland Ct. SE22 77 D7
Sunderland Rd. SE23 86 G1
Sunderland Rd. W5 64 G3
Sunderland Ter. W2 10 A3
Sunderland Ter. W2 57 E6
Sunderland Way E12 52 A2
Sundew Ave. W12 66 G7
Sundial Ave. SE25 95 C3
Sundorne Rd. SE7 69 H5
Sundra Wk. E1 59 G4
Beaumont Gro.
Sundridge Ave., 97 A2
Brom.
Sundridge Ave., 88 B7
Chis.
Sundridge Ave., 79 G2
Well.
Sundridge Ho., 87 H5
Brom.
Burnt Ash La.
Sundridge Rd., Croy. 95 C7
Sunfields Pl. SE3 69 H7
Sunland Ave., Bexh. 80 E4
Sunleigh Rd., Wem. 55 H1
Sunley Gdns., Grnf. 55 D1
Sunmead Rd., Sun. 90 A3
Sunna Gdns., Sun. 90 B2
Sunningdale N14 32 D5
Wilmer Way
Sunningdale Ave. 56 E7
W3
Sunningdale Ave., 61 G1
Bark.
Sunningdale Ave., 81 E2
Felt.
Sunningdale Ave., 45 C1
Ruis.
Sunningdale Clo. E6 61 C3
Ascot Rd.
Sunningdale Clo., 29 D7
Stan.
Sunningdale Gdns. 38 C5
NW9

Sunningdale Gdns. 66 D3
W8
Lexham Ms.
Sunningdale Rd., 97 B4
Brom.
Sunningdale Rd., 100 C4
Sutt.
Sunningfields Cres. 38 H2
NW4
Sunningfields Rd. 38 H3
NW4
Sunninghill Rd. 78 B2
SE13
Sunny Bank SE25 95 D3
Sunny Cres. NW10 47 C7
Sunny Gdns. Rd. 38 J3
NW4
Sunny Hill NW4 38 H3
Sunny Nook Gdns., 102 A6
S.Croy.
Selsdon Rd.
Sunny Rd., The, 25 G1
Enf.
Sunny Side, Walt. 90 C5
Sunny Vw. NW9 38 D5
Sunny Way N12 31 H7
Sunnycroft Rd. SE25 95 D3
Sunnycroft Rd., 72 H2
Houns.
Sunnycroft Rd., 54 G5
Sthl.
Sunnydale, Orp. 104 D2
Sunnydale Gdns. 30 D6
NW7
Sunnydale Rd. SE12 78 H5
Sunnydene Ave. E4 34 D5
Sunnydene Ave., 45 A1
Ruis.
Sunnydene Gdns., 46 F6
Wem.
Sunnydene St. SE26 86 H4
Sunnyfield NW7 30 F4
Sunnyhill Rd. SW16 85 E4
Sunnyhurst Clo., 100 D3
Sutt.
Sunnymead Ave., 94 C3
Mitch.
Sunnymead Rd. NW9 38 D7
Sunnymead Rd. 74 H5
SW15
Sunnymede Dr., Ilf. 43 E5
Sunnyside NW2 33 C3
Sunnyside SW19 84 B6
Sunnyside Dr. E4 26 C7
Sunnyside Pas. 84 B6
SW19
Sunnyside Rd. E10 51 A1
Sunnyside Rd. N19 40 D7
Sunnyside Rd. W5 64 G1
Sunnyside Rd., Ilf. 52 F3
Sunnyside Rd., 82 A4
Tedd.
Sunnyside Rd. E. N9 33 D3
Sunnyside Rd. N. N9 33 C3
Sunnyside Rd. S. N9 33 C3
Sunray Ave. SE24 77 A4
Sunray Ave., Brom. 97 D6
Sunray Ave., Surb. 99 B2
Sunrise Clo., Felt. 81 F3
Exeter Rd.
Sunset Ave. E4 34 B1
Sunset Ave., 34 F4
Wdf.Grn.
Sunset Gdns. SE25 95 C2
Sunset Rd. SE5 76 J4
Sunset Vw., Barn. 23 B2
Sunshine Way, 93 J2
Mitch.
Sunwell Clo. SE15 77 E2
Gordon Rd.
Surbiton Ct., Surb. 91 F6
Surbiton Cres., 91 H5
Kings.T.
Surbiton Hall Clo., 91 H4
Kings.T.
Surbiton Hill Pk., 91 J5
Surb.
Surbiton Hill Rd., 91 H4
Surb.
Surbiton Rd., 91 G4
Kings.T.
Surlingham Clo. 62 D7
SE28
Surr St. N7 49 E5
Surrendale Pl. W9 57 B2
Surrey Canal Rd. 68 G6
SE14
Surrey Canal Rd. 68 F6
SE15
Surrey Cres. W4 65 A5
Surrey Gdns. N4 40 G3
Surrey Gro. SE17 21 D4
Surrey Gro., Sutt. 100 C3

Surrey La. SW11	75	H1
Surrey La. Est.	75	H1
SW11		
Surrey Lo. SE1	16	E6
Surrey Ms. SE27	86	B4
Hamilton Rd.		
Surrey Ms. SE27	86	F1
Surrey Quays Rd.	68	F3
SE16		
Surrey Rd. SE15	77	D5
Surrey Rd., Bark.	82	H7
Surrey Rd., Dag.	53	H5
Surrey Rd., Har.	36	J5
Surrey Rd., W.Wick.	103	B1
Surrey Row SE1	16	G3
Surrey Row SE1	67	H2
Surrey Sq. SE17	21	D3
Surrey Sq. SE17	68	B5
Surrey St. E13	60	H3
Surrey St. WC2	12	D5
Surrey St. WC2	58	F7
Surrey St., Croy.	101	J2
Surrey Ter. SE17	21	E3
Surrey Ter. SE17	68	B4
Surrey Water Rd.	68	G1
SE16		
Surridge Gdns. SE19	86	A6
Hancock Rd.		
Susan Clo., Rom.	44	J3
Susan Rd. SE3	78	H2
Susan Wd., Chis.	97	D1
Susannah St. E14	60	B6
Sussex Ave., Islw.	73	B3
Sussex Clo. N19	49	E2
Cornwallis Rd.		
Sussex Clo., Ilf.	43	C6
Sussex Clo., N.Mal.	92	E4
Sussex Clo., Twick.	73	E6
Westmorland Clo.		
Sussex Cres.,	45	G6
Nthlt.		
Sussex Gdns. N4	40	J5
Sussex Gdns. N6	39	J5
Great N. Rd.		
Sussex Gdns. W2	10	E5
Sussex Gdns. W2	57	G6
Sussex Gdns.,	98	G6
Chess.		
Sussex Ms. E. W2	10	F4
Sussex Ms. W. W2	10	F5
Sussex Pl. NW1	6	J4
Sussex Pl. NW1	57	J4
Sussex Pl. W2	10	F4
Sussex Pl. W2	57	G6
Sussex Pl. W6	65	J5
Sussex Pl., Erith	71	H7
Sussex Pl., N.Mal.	92	E4
Sussex Ring N12	31	D5
Sussex Rd. E6	61	D1
Sussex Rd., Cars.	100	J4
Sussex Rd., Erith	71	H7
Sussex Rd., Har.	36	J5
Sussex Rd., Mitch.	94	E5
Lincoln Rd.		
Sussex Rd., N.Mal.	92	E4
Sussex Rd., Sid.	89	B5
Sussex Rd., S.Croy.	102	A6
Sussex Rd., Sthl.	63	D3
Sussex Rd., W.Wick.	103	B1
Sussex Sq. W2	10	F5
Sussex Sq. W2	57	G7
Sussex St. E13	60	H3
Sussex St. SW1	19	E4
Sussex St. SW1	67	B5
Sussex Wk. SW9	76	H4
Sussex Way N7	49	E2
Sussex Way N19	49	E1
Sussex Way, Barn.	24	B5
Sutcliffe Clo. NW11	39	E5
Sutcliffe Ho.	54	A6
Hayes		
Sutcliffe Rd. SE18	70	H6
Sutcliffe Rd.,	80	C2
Well.		
Sutherland Ave. W9	57	D4
Sutherland Ave. W13	55	E6
Sutherland Ave.,	63	A4
Hayes		
Sutherland Ave.	97	J6
Orp.		
Sutherland Ave.,	79	H4
Well.		
Sutherland Clo.,	23	B4
Barn.		
Sutherland Ct. NW9	38	B4
Sutherland Dr. SW19	93	G1
Brangwyn Cres.		
Sutherland Gdns.	74	E3
SW14		
Sutherland Gdns.,	92	H7
Wor.Pk.		
Sutherland Gro.	75	B6
SW18		
Sutherland Gro.,	82	B5
Tedd.		
Sutherland Pl. W2	57	D6
Sutherland Pt. E5	50	E4
Tiger Way		
Sutherland Rd. E17	41	G2
Sutherland Rd. N17	33	D7
Sutherland Rd. W4	65	B6
Sutherland Rd. W13	55	D6
Sutherland Rd.,	71	C2
Belv.		
Sutherland Rd.,	94	G7
Croy.		
Sutherland Rd.,	25	G5
Enf.		
Sutherland Rd.,	54	F6
Sthl.		
Sutherland Rd. Path		
E17		
Sutherland Row	19	E3
SW1		
Sutherland Row	67	B5
SW1		
Sutherland Sq. SE17	20	J4
Sutherland Sq. SE17	67	J5
Sutherland St. SW1	19	D3
Sutherland St. SW1	67	B5
Sutherland Wk. SE17	21	A4
Sutherland Wk. SE17	67	J5
Sutlej Rd. SE7	69	J7
Sutterton St. N7	49	F6
Sutton Arc., Sutt.	100	E5
Throwley Way		
Sutton Clo., Beck.	96	B1
Albemarle Rd.		
Sutton Clo., Loug.	27	B7
Sutton Clo., Pnr.	36	A5
Sutton Common Rd.,	93	C7
Sutt.		
Sutton Ct. W4	65	C6
Sutton Ct. Rd. E13	60	J3
Sutton Ct. Rd. W4	65	C7
Sutton Ct. Rd.,	100	F6
Sutt.		
Sutton Cres., Barn.	23	A5
Sutton Dene, Houns.	72	H1
Sutton Est. N1	49	H7
Upper St.		
Sutton Est. SW3	18	H3
Sutton Est. SW3	66	H5
Sutton Est. W10	56	J5
Sutton Gdns., Bark.	61	H1
Sutton Rd.		
Sutton Gdns., Croy.	95	C5
Sutton Gro., Sutt.	100	G4
Sutton Hall Rd.,	63	G7
Houns.		
Sutton La. W4	65	C5
Sutton La., Houns.	72	F3
Sutton La. S. W4	65	C6
Sutton Pk. Rd.,	100	E6
Sutt.		
Sutton Path, Borwd.	22	A2
Stratfield Rd.		
Sutton Pl. E9	50	F5
Sutton Rd. E13	60	F4
Sutton Rd. E17	41	G1
Sutton Rd. N10	40	A1
Sutton Rd., Bark.	61	H2
Sutton Rd., Houns.	72	G1
Sutton Row W1	11	J3
Sutton Row W1	58	D6
Sutton Sq. E9	50	F5
Urswick Rd.		
Sutton Sq., Houns.	72	F1
Sutton St. E1	59	F7
Sutton Way W10	56	J5
Sutton Way, Houns.	72	F1
Sutton's Way EC1	9	A6
Swaby Rd. SW18	84	F1
Swaffham Way N22	32	H7
White Hart La.		
Swaffield Rd. SW18	75	E7
Swain Rd., Th.Hth.	94	J5
Swains La. N6	49	A1
Swains Rd. SW17	84	J7
Swainson Rd. W3	65	F2
Swallands Rd. SE6	87	A3
Swallow Clo. SE14	77	G1
Swallow Clo.	28	J1
(Bushey), Wat.		
Swallow Dr. NW10	47	D6
Kingfisher Way		
Swallow Dr., Nthlt.	54	G2
Swallow Pas. W1	11	E4
Swallow Pl. W1	11	E4
Swallow St. E6	61	B5
Swallow St. W1	11	G6
Swallowfield Rd.	69	H5
SE7		
Swan App. E6	61	B5
Swan Clo. E17	41	H1
Banbury Rd.		
Swan Clo., Croy.	95	B7
Swan Clo., Felt.	81	E4
Swan St. SW3	18	H4
Swan Dr. NW9	38	E2
Swan La. EC4	13	B6
Swan La. N20	31	F3
Swan Mead SE1	17	D6
Swan Mead SE1	68	B3
Swan Ms. SW9	76	F1
Swan Rd. SE16	69	F2
Swan Rd. SE18	70	A3
Swan Rd., Felt.	81	E5
Swan Rd., Sthl.	54	H6
Swan St. SE1	17	A5
Swan St. SE1	67	J3
Swan St., Islw.	73	E3
Swan Wk. SW3	18	J5
Swan Wk. SW3	66	J6
Swan Way, Enf.	25	G2
Swan Yd. N1	49	H6
Highbury Sta. Rd.		
Swanage Rd. E4	34	C7
Swanage Rd. SW18	75	F6
Swanage Waye,	54	C6
Hayes		
Swanbridge Rd.,	80	G1
Bexh.		
Swandon Way SW18	75	E4
Swanfield St. E2	9	F4
Swanfield St. E2	59	C3
Swanley Rd., Well.	80	C1
Swanscombe Rd. W4	65	E5
Swanscombe Rd.	66	A1
W11		
Swansea Rd., Enf.	25	F4
Swanshope, Loug.	27	E2
Swansland Gdns. E17	41	H1
McEntee Ave.		
Swanston Path, Wat.	28	C3
Swanton Gdns.	84	A1
SW19		
Swanton Rd., Erith	71	H7
Swanwick Clo. SW15	74	F7
Swaton Rd. E3	60	A4
Swaylands Rd.,	71	G6
Belv.		
Swaythling Clo. N18	33	E4
Sweden Gate SE16	68	H3
Swedenborg Gdns.	59	D7
E1		
Sweeney Cres. SE1	17	G4
Sweeney Cres. SE1	68	C2
Sweet Briar Grn. N9	33	C3
Sweet Briar Rd. N9	33	C3
Sweet Briar Wk. N18	33	C4
Sweetmans Ave.,	36	D3
Pnr.		
Sweets Way N20	31	G2
Swete St. E13	60	G2
Swetenham Wk.	70	F5
SE18		
Sandbach Pl.		
Sweyn Pl. SE3	78	G2
Swift Clo. E17	33	H7
Banbury Rd.		
Swift Clo., Har.	45	H2
Swift Rd., Felt.	81	D4
Swift Rd., Sthl.	63	F3
Swift St. SW6	75	C1
Swiftsden Way,	87	E6
Brom.		
Swinbrook Rd. W10	57	B5
Swinburne Ct. SE5	77	A4
Basingdon Way		
Swinburne Cres.,	95	F6
Croy.		
Swinburne Rd. SW15	74	G4
Swinderby Rd., Wem.	46	H6
Swindon Clo., Ilf.	52	H2
Salisbury Rd.		
Swindon St. W12	65	H1
Swinfield Clo.,	81	E4
Felt.		
Swinford Gdns. SW9	76	H3
Swingate La. SE18	70	H7
Swinnerton St. E9	50	H5
Swinton Clo., Wem.	47	B1
Swinton Pl. WC1	8	C3
Swinton Pl. WC1	58	F3
Swinton St. WC1	8	C3
Swinton St. WC1	58	F3
Swires Shaw, Kes.	104	A4
Swiss Ter. NW6	48	G7
Swyncombe Ave. W5	64	E4
Swynford Gdns. NW4	38	G4
Handowe Clo.		
Sybil Ms. N4	40	H6
Lothair Rd. N.		
Sybil Thorndike Ho.	49	J6
N1		
Clephane Rd.		
Sybourn St. E17	41	J7
Sycamore Ave. W5	64	G3
Sycamore Ave., Sid.	79	J6
Sycamore Clo. E16	60	E4
Clarence Rd.		
Sycamore Clo. N9	33	D4
Pycroft Way		
Sycamore Clo., SE9	80	D2
Sycamore Clo.,	23	G6
Barn.		
Sycamore Clo.	100	J4
Cars.		
Sycamore Clo.,	81	A3
Felt.		
Sycamore Clo.,	54	E1
Nthlt.		
Sycamore Gdns. W6	65	H2
Sycamore Gdns.,	93	G2
Mitch.		
Sycamore Gro. NW9	38	C7
Sycamore Gro. SE6	78	C6
Sycamore Gro. SE20	86	D7
Sycamore Gro.,	92	D3
N.Mal.		
Sycamore Hill N11	32	A6
Sycamore Rd. SW19	83	J6
Sycamore Rd., Tedd.	82	F6
Sycamore St. EC1	8	J6
Sycamore Wk. W10	57	B4
Fifth Ave.		
Sycamore Way, Ilf.	43	F4
Civic Way		
Sycamore Way,	94	G5
Th.Hth.		
Grove Rd.		
Sydenham Ave. SE26	86	E5
Sydenham Cotts.	87	J2
SE12		
Sydenham Hill SE23	86	E1
Sydenham Hill SE26	86	C4
Sydenham Hill Est.	86	D3
SE26		
Sydenham Pk. SE26	86	F3
Sydenham Pk. Rd.	86	F3
SE26		
Sydenham Ri. SE23	86	E2
Sydenham Rd. SE26	86	G5
Sydenham Rd.,	101	J1
Croy.		
Sydmons Ct. SE23	77	F7
Sydner Ms. N16	50	C4
Sydner Rd.		
Sydner Rd. N16	50	C4
Sydney Clo. SW3	18	F2
Sydney Clo. SW3	66	G4
Sydney Gro. NW4	38	J5
Sydney Ms. SW3	18	F2
Sydney Pl. SW7	18	F2
Sydney Pl. SW7	66	G4
Sydney Rd. E11	42	H6
Mansfield Rd.		
Sydney Rd. N8	40	G4
Sydney Rd. N10	40	A1
Sydney Rd. SE2	71	C3
Sydney Rd. SW20	93	A2
Sydney Rd. W13	64	D1
Sydney Rd., Bexh.	80	D4
Sydney Rd., Enf.	25	A3
Sydney Rd., Felt.	81	A1
Sydney Rd., Ilf.	43	F2
Sydney Rd., Rich.	73	H4
Sydney Rd., Sid.	88	H4
Sydney Rd., Sutt.	100	D4
Sydney Rd., Tedd.	82	C5
Sydney Rd.,	34	G4
Wdf.Grn.		
Sydney St. SW3	18	G3
Sydney St. SW3	66	H5
Sylvan Ave. N3	39	D2
Sylvan Ave. N22	32	F7
Sylvan Ave. NW7	30	F6
Sylvan Ave., Rom.	44	F6
Sylvan Est. SE19	95	C1
Sylvan Gdns., Surb.	91	G7
Sylvan Gro. SE15	68	E6
Sylvan Hill SE19	95	B1
Sylvan Rd. E7	51	G6
Sylvan Rd. E11	42	G5
Sylvan Rd. E17	42	A5
Sylvan Rd. SE19	95	C1
Sylvan Wk., Brom.	97	C3
Sylvan Way, Dag.	53	B3
Sylvan Way,	103	E4
W.Wick.		
Sylverdale Rd.,	101	H3
Croy.		
Sylvester Ave.,	88	C6
Chis.		
Sylvester Path E8	50	E6
Sylvester Rd.		
Sylvester Rd. E8	50	E6
Sylvester Rd. E17	41	J7
Sylvester Rd. N2	39	F2

Name	Pg	Grid
Sylvester Rd., Wem.	46	F5
Sylvestrus Clo., Kings.T.	92	A1
Sylvia Ave., Pnr.	28	E6
Sylvia Gdns., Wem.	47	B7
Symes Ms. NW1	7	F1
Symons St. SW3	19	A2
Symons St. SW3	66	J4
Syon Gate Way, Brent.	64	D7
Syon La., Islw.	64	C6
Syon Pk. Gdns., Islw.	64	C7
Syon Vista, Rich.	73	G1
Kew Rd.		
T		
Tabard Gdn. Est. SE1	17	C4
Tabard Est. SE1	68	A2
Tabard St. SE1	17	B4
Tabard St. SE1	68	A2
Tabernacle Ave. E13	60	G4
Barking Rd.		
Tabernacle St. EC2	9	C6
Tabernacle St. EC2	59	A4
Tableer Ave. SW4	76	C5
Tabley Rd. N7	49	E4
Tabor Gdns., Sutt.	100	C6
Tabor Gro. SW19	84	B7
Tabor Rd. W6	65	H3
Tachbrook Est. SW1	19	J4
Tachbrook Est. SW1	67	D5
Tachbrook Ms. SW1	19	F1
Tachbrook Rd., Sthl.	63	D4
Tachbrook St. SW1	19	G2
Tachbrook St. SW1	67	C4
Tack Ms. SE4	78	A3
Tadema Rd. SW10	66	F7
Tadmor St. W12	66	A1
Tadworth Ave., N.Mal.	92	F5
Tadworth Rd. NW2	47	G2
Taeping St. E14	69	B4
Taffy's How, Mitch.	93	H3
Taft Way E3	60	B3
St. Leonards St.		
Tait Rd., Croy.	95	B7
Talacre Rd. NW5	49	A6
Talbot Ave. N2	39	G3
Talbot Clo. N15	41	C4
Talbot Ct. EC3	13	C5
Talbot Cres. NW4	38	G5
Talbot Gdns., Ilf.	53	A2
Talbot Ho. E14	60	B6
Giraud St.		
Talbot Pl. SE3	78	E2
Talbot Rd. E6	61	D2
Talbot Rd. E7	51	G4
Talbot Rd. N6	40	A6
Talbot Rd. N15	41	C4
Talbot Rd. N22	40	C2
Talbot Rd. W2	57	D6
Talbot Rd. W11	5/	C6
Talbot Rd. W13	55	D7
Talbot Rd., Brom.	96	H4
Masons Hill		
Talbot Rd., Cars.	101	A5
Talbot Rd., Dag.	53	F6
Talbot Rd., Har.	37	C2
Talbot Rd., Islw.	73	D4
Talbot Rd., Sthl.	63	E4
Talbot Rd., Th.Hth.	95	A4
Talbot Rd., Twick.	82	B1
Talbot Rd., Wem.	46	G5
Talbot Sq. W2	10	F4
Talbot Sq. W2	57	G6
Talbot Wk. NW10	47	E6
Garnet Rd.		
Talbot Wk. W11	57	B6
Lancaster Rd.		
Talbot Yd. SE1	17	B2
Talfourd Pl. SE15	77	C1
Talfourd Rd. SE15	77	C1
Talgarth Rd. W6	66	A5
Talgarth Rd. W14	66	A5
Talgarth Wk. NW9	38	E5
Talisman Clo., Ilf.	53	B1
Talisman Sq. SE26	86	D4
Talisman Way, Wem.	46	J3
Tall Elms Clo., Brom.	96	F5
Tall Trees SW16	94	F3
Tallack Clo., Har.	29	B7
College Hill Rd.		
Tallack Rd. E10	50	J1
Tallis Gro. SE7	69	H6
Tallis St. EC4	12	F5
Tallis St. EC4	58	G7
Tallis Vw. NW10	47	D6
Mitchellbrook Way		
Tally Ho Cor. N12	31	F5
Talma Gdns., Twick.	73	B6
Talma Rd. SW2	76	G4
Talmage Clo. SE23	77	F7
Tyson Rd.		
Talman Gro., Stan.	29	G6
Talwin St. E3	60	B3
Tamar Sq., Wdf.Grn.	34	H6
Tamar St. SE7	70	B3
Tamar Way N17	41	C3
Tamarind Yd. E1	17	J1
Tamarisk Sq. W12	56	F7
Tamesis Gdns., Wor.Pk.	99	E2
Tamian Est., Houns.	72	C4
Tamlan Way, Houns.	72	C4
Tamworth Ave., Wdf.Grn.	34	E6
Tamworth Gdns., Pnr.	36	B2
Tamworth La., Mitch.	94	A2
Tamworth Pk., Mitch.	94	B4
Tamworth Pl., Croy.	101	J2
Tamworth Rd., Croy.	101	H2
Tamworth St. SW6	66	D6
Tancred Rd. N4	40	H6
Tandridge Dr., Orp.	104	G1
Tanfield Ave. NW2	47	F4
Tanfield Rd., Croy.	101	J2
Tangier Rd., Rich.	74	B4
Tanglebury Clo., Brom.	97	B4
Tanglewood Clo., Croy.	102	F3
Tanglewood Clo., Stan.	29	B2
Tanglewood Way, Felt.	81	B3
Tangley Gro. SW15	74	F7
Tangley Pk. Rd., Hmptn.	81	F5
Tangmere Gdns., Nthlt.	54	C2
Tangmere Way NW9	38	E2
Tanhurst Wk. SE2	71	D3
Alsike Rd.		
Tankerton Rd., Surb.	98	J2
Tankerton St. WC1	8	B4
Tankerville Rd. SW16	85	D7
Tankridge Rd. NW2	47	H2
Tanner St. SE1	17	E4
Tanner St. SE1	68	B2
Tanner St., Bark.	52	F6
Tanners Clo., Walt.	90	B6
Tanners End La. N18	33	B4
Tanners Hill SE8	77	J1
Tanners La., Ilf.	43	F3
Tannery Clo., Beck.	95	G5
Tannery Clo., Dag.	53	H3
Tannsfeld Rd. SE26	86	G5
Tansley Clo. N7	49	D5
Hilldrop Rd.		
Tanswell Est. SE1	16	F4
Tanswell St. SE1	16	E4
Tansy Clo. E6	61	D6
Tant Ave. E16	60	F6
Tantallon Rd. SW12	85	A1
Tantony Gro., Rom.	44	D3
Tanyard La., Bex.	80	G7
Bexley High St.		
Tanza Rd. NW3	48	J4
Tapestry Clo., Sutt.	100	E7
Taplow NW3	48	G7
Taplow SE17	21	C3
Taplow SE17	68	A5
Taplow Rd. N13	32	J4
North Circular Rd.		
Taplow St. N1	9	A2
Taplow St. N1	58	J2
Tapp St. E1	59	E4
Tappesfield Rd. SE15	77	F3
Tapster St., Barn.	23	C3
Tarbert Rd. SE22	77	B5
Tarbert Wk. E1	59	F7
Juniper St.		
Tariff Rd. N17	33	D6
Tarleton Gdns. SE23	86	E1
Tarling Clo., Sid.	89	B3
Tarling Rd. E16	60	F6
Tarling Rd. N2	39	F2
Tarling St. E1	59	E6
Tarling St. Est. E1	59	F6
Tarn St. SE1	16	J6
Tarnbank, Enf.	24	E5
Tarnwood Pk. SE9	79	C7
Tarquin Ho. SE26	86	D4
Tarragon Gro. SE26	86	G6
Tarrant Pl. W1	10	J2
Tarrington Clo. SW16	85	D3
Tarry La. SE8	68	H4
Tarver Rd. SE17	20	H4
Tarver Rd. SE17	67	H5
Tarves Way SE10	69	B7
Tash Pl. N11	32	B5
Woodland Rd.		
Tasker Ho., Bark.	61	G2
Dovehouse Mead		
Tasker Rd. NW3	48	J5
Tasman Rd. SW9	76	E3
Tasman Wk. E16	61	A6
Royal Rd.		
Tasmania Ter. N18	32	J6
Tasso Rd. W6	66	B6
Tatam Rd. NW10	47	D7
Tate Rd. E16	70	C1
Newland St.		
Tate Rd., Sutt.	100	D5
Tatnell Rd. SE23	77	H6
Tattersall Clo. SE9	79	B5
Tatton Cres. N16	41	C7
Clapton Common		
Tatum St. SE17	21	C2
Tatum St. SE17	68	A4
Taunton Ave. SW20	92	H2
Taunton Ave., Houns.	72	J2
Taunton Clo., Ilf.	35	J6
Taunton Clo., Sutt.	100	D1
Taunton Ct. N17	33	B7
Taunton Dr., Enf.	24	G3
Taunton Ms. NW1	6	J6
Taunton Pl. NW1	6	J5
Taunton Pl. NW1	57	J4
Taunton Rd. SE12	78	E5
Taunton Rd., Grnf.	54	H1
Taunton Rd., Stan.	37	H2
Taunton Way, Stan.	37	H2
Tavern La. SW9	76	G2
Taverner Sq. N5	49	J4
Highbury Gra.		
Taverners Clo. W11	66	B1
Addison Ave.		
Taverners Way E4	34	E1
Douglas Rd.		
Tavistock Ave. E17	41	G3
Tavistock Ave., Grnf.	55	D2
Tavistock Clo. N16	50	B5
Crossway		
Tavistock Cres. W11	57	C5
Tavistock Cres., Mitch.	94	E4
Tavistock Gdns., Ilf.	52	H4
Tavistock Gate, Croy.	102	A1
Tavistock Gro., Croy.	95	A7
Tavistock Ms. E18	42	G4
Avon Way		
Tavistock Ms. W11	57	C6
Lancaster Rd.		
Tavistock Pl. E18	42	G3
Avon Way		
Tavistock Pl. N14	24	B7
Chase Side		
Tavistock Pl. WC1	8	A5
Tavistock Pl. WC1	58	E4
Tavistock Rd. E7	51	F4
Tavistock Rd. E15	51	F6
Tavistock Rd. E18	42	G3
Tavistock Rd. N4	41	A6
Tavistock Rd. NW10	56	F2
Tavistock Rd. W11	57	C6
Tavistock Rd., Brom.	96	F4
Tavistock Rd., Cars.	100	G1
Tavistock Rd., Croy.	102	A1
Tavistock Rd., Edg.	38	A1
Tavistock Rd., Well.	80	C1
Tavistock Sq. WC1	7	J5
Tavistock Sq. WC1	58	D4
Tavistock St. WC2	12	B5
Tavistock St. WC2	58	E7
Tavistock Ter. N19	49	D3
Tavistock Wk., Cars.	100	G1
Tavistock Rd.		
Taviton St. WC1	7	H5
Taviton St. WC1	58	D4
Tavy Clo. SE11	20	F3
Tawney Rd. SE28	62	B7
Tawny Clo., Felt.	81	A3
Chervil Clo.		
Tawny Way SE16	68	G4
Tayben Ave., Twick.	73	B6
Taybridge Rd. SW11	76	A3
Tayburn Clo. E14	60	C6
Taylor Ave., Rich.	74	B2
Taylor Clo. N17	33	D7
Taylor Clo., Hmptn.	81	J5
Taylor Clo., Orp.	104	J4
Taylor Ct. E15	51	C5
Taylor Rd., Mitch.	84	H7
Taylor Rd., Wall.	101	B5
Taylors Bldgs. SE18	70	E4
Spray St.		
Taylors Clo., Sid.	88	J4
Taylors Grn. W3	56	E6
Long Dr.		
Taylors La. NW10	47	E7
Taylors La. SE26	86	E4
Taylors La., Barn.	23	C1
Taymount Ri. SE23	86	F2
Tayport Clo. N1	49	E7
Tayside Dr., Edg.	30	B3
Taywood Rd., Nthlt.	54	F3
Invicta Gro.		
Teak Clo. SE16	68	H1
Teal Clo. E16	61	A5
Fulmer Rd.		
Teale St. E2	9	J1
Teale St. E2	59	D2
Tealing Dr., Epsom		
Teasel Clo., Croy.	102	G1
Teasel Way E15	60	E3
Tebworth Rd. N17	33	C7
Tedder Clo., Chess.	98	F6
Tedder Rd., S.Croy.	102	F7
Teddington Pk., Tedd.	82	C5
Teddington Pk. Rd., Tedd.	82	C4
Tedworth Gdns. SW3	18	J4
Tedworth Sq. SW3	18	J4
Tedworth Sq. SW3	66	J5
Tee, The W3	56	E6
Tees Ave., Grnf.	55	B2
Teesdale Ave., Islw.	73	D1
Teesdale Clo. E2	9	J2
Teesdale Clo. E2	59	D2
Teesdale Gdns. SE25		
Grange Hill		
Teesdale Gdns., Islw.	73	D1
Teesdale Rd. E11	42	F6
Teesdale St. E2	59	E2
Teeswater Ct., Erith	71	D3
Middle Way		
Teevan Clo., Croy.	95	D7
Teevan Rd., Croy.	102	D1
Teignmouth Clo. SW4	76	D4
Teignmouth Clo., Edg.	37	J2
Teignmouth Gdns., Grnf.	55	C2
Teignmouth Rd. NW2	48	A5
Teignmouth Rd., Well.	80	C2
Telegraph Hill NW3	48	E3
Telegraph La., Esher	98	C6
Telegraph Ms., Ilf.	53	A1
Telegraph Rd. SW15	74	H7
Telegraph St. EC2	13	B3
Telemann Sq. SE3	78	H3
Telephone Pl. SW6	66	C6
Lillie Rd.		
Telfer Clo. W3	65	C2
Church Rd.		
Telferscot Rd. SW12	85	D1
Telford Ave. SW2	85	D1
Telford Clo. SE19	86	C6
St. Aubyn's Rd.		
Telford Clo. W3	65	C2
Church Rd.		
Telford Dr., Walt.	90	C7
Telford Rd. N11	32	C6
Telford Rd. NW9	38	G6
West Hendon Bdy.		
Telford Rd. SE9	88	G2
Telford Rd. W10	57	B5
Telford Rd., Sthl.	54	H7
Telford Rd., Twick.	72	G7
Telford Ter. SW1	19	F5
Telford Ter. SW1	67	C6
Telford Way W3	56	E5
Telford Way, Hayes	54	E5
Telham Rd. E6	61	D2
Tell Gro. SE22	77	C4
Tellson Ave. SE18	79	A1
Telscombe Clo., Orp.	104	H2
Temeraire St. SE16	68	F2
Swan Rd.		

Name	Page	Grid
Temperley Rd. SW12	76	A7
Templar Dr. SE28	62	D6
Templar Ho. NW2	48	C6
Shoot Up Hill		
Templar Pl., Hmptn.	81	G7
Templar St. SE5	76	H2
Templars Ave. NW11	00	C6
Templars Cres. N3	39	D2
Templars Way, Har.	29	A6
Temple EC4	12	E9
Temple EC4	58	G7
Temple Ave. EC4	12	F5
Temple Ave. EC4	58	G7
Temple Ave. N20	23	G1
Temple Ave., Croy.	102	J2
Temple Ave., Dag.	53	G1
Temple Clo. E11	42	E7
Wadley Rd.		
Temple Clo. N3	39	C2
Cyprus Rd.		
Temple Clo. SE28	70	F3
Temple Fortune Hill NW11	39	D5
Temple Fortune La. NW11	39	C5
Temple Gdns. NW11	39	C6
Temple Gdns., Dag.	53	D3
Temple Gro. NW11	39	D6
Temple Gro., Enf.	24	H3
Temple La. EC4	12	F4
Temple Mead Clo., Stan.	29	E6
Temple Mill La. E15	51	A4
Temple Pl. WC2	12	D5
Temple Pl. WC2	58	F7
Temple Rd. E6	61	B1
Temple Rd. N8	40	F4
Temple Rd. NW2	47	J4
Temple Rd. W4	65	C3
Temple Rd. W5	64	G3
Temple Rd., Croy.	102	A4
Temple Rd., Houns.	72	H4
Temple Rd., Rich.	73	J2
Temple Sheen SW14	74	B4
Temple Sheen Rd. SW14	74	B4
Temple St. E2	59	E2
Temple Way, Sutt.	100	G3
Temple W. Ms. SE11	16	G6
Temple W. Ms. SE11	67	H3
Templecombe Rd. E9	59	F1
Templecombe Way, Mord.	93	B5
Templehof Ave. NW2	38	J7
Templeman Rd. W7	55	C5
Templemead Clo. W3	56	E6
Templeton Ave. E4	34	A4
Templeton Clo. SE19	95	A1
Templeton Pl. SW5	66	D4
Templeton Rd. N15	41	A6
Templewood W13	55	E5
Templewood Ave. NW3	48	E3
Templewood Gdns. NW3	48	E3
Tempsford Ave., Borwd.	22	D4
Tempsford Clo., Enf.	24	J3
Gladbeck Way		
Temsford Clo., Har.	36	J2
Tenbury Clo. E7	52	A5
Romford Rd.		
Tenbury Ct. SW2	85	D1
Tenby Ave., Har.	37	E2
Tenby Clo. N15	41	C4
Hanover Rd.		
Tenby Clo., Rom.	44	E6
Tenby Gdns., Nthlt.	45	G6
Tenby Rd. E17	41	H5
Tenby Rd., Edg.	37	J1
Tenby Rd., Enf.	25	F3
Tenby Rd., Rom.	44	E6
Tenby Rd., Well.	80	D1
Tench St. E1	68	E1
Tenda Rd. SE16	68	E4
Roseberry St.		
Tendring Way, Rom.	44	C5
Tenham Ave. SW2	85	D2
Tenison Ct. W1	11	F5
Tenison Way SE1	16	D2
Tenison Way SE1	67	F1
Tenniel Clo. W2	10	C5
Tennis Ct. La., E.Mol.	91	C3
Hampton Ct. Way		
Tennis St. SE1	17	B3
Tennis St. SE1	68	A2
Tennison Ave., Borwd.	22	B5
Tennison Rd. SE25	95	C4
Tenniswood Rd., Enf.	25	B1
Tennyson Ave. E11	42	G7
Tennyson Ave. E12	52	B7
Tennyson Ave. NW9	38	C3
Tennyson Ave., N.Mal.	92	H5
Tennyson Ave., Twick	82	C1
Tennyson Clo., Well.	79	J1
Tennyson Rd. E10	51	B1
Tennyson Rd. E15	51	E7
Tennyson Rd. E17	41	J6
Tennyson Rd. NW6	57	C1
Tennyson Rd. NW7	30	G5
Tennyson Rd. SE20	86	G7
Tennyson Rd. SW19	84	F6
Tennyson Rd. W7	55	C7
Tennyson Rd., Houns.	72	J2
Tennyson Rd., Well.	79	J1
Tennyson St. SW8	76	B2
Tensing Rd., Sthl.	63	G3
Tent St. E1	59	E4
Tentelow La., Sthl.	63	G5
Tenter Grd. E1	13	F2
Tenterden Clo. NW4	39	A3
Tenterden Clo. SE9	88	C4
Tenterden Dr. NW4	39	A3
Tenterden Gdns. NW4	39	A3
Tenterden Gdns., Croy.	95	D7
Tenterden Gro. NW4	39	A3
Tenterden Rd. N17	33	C7
Tenterden Rd., Croy.	95	D7
Tenterden Rd., Dag.	53	F2
Tenterden St. W1	11	E4
Tenterden St. W1	58	B6
Terborch Way SE22	77	B5
East Dulwich Gro.		
Teresa Ms. E17	42	A4
Teresa Wk. N10	40	B5
Connaught Gdns.		
Terling Clo. E11	51	F3
Terling Rd., Dag.	53	G2
Terling Wk. N1	58	J1
Britannia Row		
Terminus Pl. SW1	15	E6
Terminus Pl. SW1	67	B3
Terrace, The E4	34	E3
Chingdale Rd.		
Terrace, The N3	39	C2
Hendon La.		
Terrace, The NW6	57	D1
Terrace, The SW13	74	E2
Terrace, The, Wdf.Grn.	34	G6
Terrace Gdns. SW13	74	F2
Terrace La., Rich.	73	H6
Terrace Rd. E9	50	F7
Terrace Rd. E13	60	G1
Terrace Rd., Walt.	90	A7
Terrace Wk., Dag.	53	E5
Terrapin Rd. SW17	85	B3
Terretts Pl. N1	49	H7
Upper St.		
Terrick Rd. N22	40	E1
Terrick St. W12	56	H6
Terrilands, Pnr.	36	F3
Terront Rd. N15	40	J5
Tessa Sanderson Pl. SW8	76	B3
Heath Rd.		
Tessa Sanderson Way, Grnf.	46	A5
Lilian Board Way		
Testerton Wk. W11	57	A7
Whitchurch Rd.		
Tetbury Pl. N1	58	H1
Upper St.		
Tetcott Rd. SW10	18	C7
Tetcott Rd. SW10	76	F7
Tetherdown N10	40	A3
Tetterby Way SE16	21	J4
Tetty Way, Brom.	96	G2
Teversham La. SW8	76	E1
Teviot Clo., Well.	80	B1
Teviot St. E14	60	C5
Tewkesbury Ave. SE23	77	E7
Tewkesbury Ave., Pnr.	36	E5
Tewkesbury Clo. N15	41	A6
Tewkesbury Rd.		
Tewkesbury Gdns. NW9	38	B3
Tewkesbury Rd. N15	41	A6
Tewkesbury Rd. W13	55	D7
Tewkesbury Rd., Cars.	100	G1
Tewkesbury Ter. N11	32	C6
Tewson Rd. SE18	70	H4
Teynham Ave., Enf.	25	A6
Teynham Grn., Brom.	96	G5
Teynton Ter. N17	40	J1
Thackeray Ave. N17	41	D2
Thackeray Clo. SW19	84	A7
Thackeray Dr., Ilf.	44	A7
Thackeray Dr., Rom.	44	A7
Thackeray Rd. E6	61	A2
Thackeray Rd. SW8	76	B4
Thackeray St. W8	14	B4
Thackeray St. W8	66	E2
Thackery Clo., Har.	45	G1
Thakeham Clo. SE26	86	E5
Thakrah Clo. N2	39	F2
Thalia Clo. SE10	69	D6
Feathers Pl.		
Thame Rd. SE16	68	G2
Thames Ave. SW10	75	C1
Thames Ave., Dag.	62	G4
Thames Ave., Grnf.	55	C2
Thames Bank SW14	74	C2
Thames Clo., Hmptn.	90	H2
Thames Ct., W.Mol.	90	H2
Thames Mead, Walt.	90	A7
Thames Meadow, W.Mol.	90	G2
Thames Rd. E16	70	A1
Thames Rd. W4	65	A6
Thames Rd., Bark.	61	H3
Thames Rd. Ind. Est. E16	70	A1
Thames Side, Kings.T.	91	G1
Thames Side, Tedd.	82	G7
Thames St. SE10	69	B6
Thames St., Hmptn.	90	H1
Thames St., Kings.T.	91	G2
Thames St., Sun.	90	A4
Thames Vill. W4	74	C1
Thamesbank Pl. SE28	62	C6
Thamesgate Clo., Rich.	82	E4
Locksmeade Rd.		
Thameshill Ave., Rom.	44	J2
Thameside, Tedd.	82	F7
Thameside Ind. Est. E16	70	B2
Thamesmead Wk. SE28	62	B6
Thamesmead, Walt.	90	A7
Thamesmere Dr. SE29	62	A7
Thamesvale Clo., Houns.	72	G2
Thane Vill. N7	49	F3
Thanescroft Gdns., Croy.	102	B3
Thanet Dr., Kes.	104	A3
Phoenix Dr.		
Thanet Pl., Croy.	101	J4
Thanet Rd., Bex.	80	G7
Thanet St. WC1	8	A4
Thanet St. WC1	58	E3
Thanington Ct. SE9	79	H6
Thant Clo. E10	51	B3
Tharp Rd., Wall.	101	D5
Thatcham Gdns. N20	23	F7
Thatchers Clo., Loug.	27	F2
Thatchers Way, Islw.	73	A5
Thatches Gro., Rom.	44	E4
Thavies Inn EC1	12	F3
Thaxted Pl. SW20	84	A7
Thaxted Rd. SE9	88	F2
Thaxted Rd., Buck.H.	27	A7
Thaxton Rd. W14	66	C6
Thayer St. W1	11	C2
Thayer St. W1	58	A5
Thayers Fm. Rd., Beck.	95	H1
Theatre St. SW11	75	J3
Theberton St. N1	58	H1
Theed St. SE1	16	F2
Theed St. SE1	67	G1
Thelma Gdns. SE3	79	A1
Thelma Gdns., Felt.	81	E3
Thelma Gro., Tedd.	82	D6
Theobald Cres., Har.	36	H1
Theobald Rd. E17	41	J7
Theobald Rd., Croy.	101	H2
Theobald St. SE1	17	B6
Theobalds Ave. N12	31	F4
Theobalds Clo. N4	49	J2
Queens Dr.		
Theobald's Rd. WC1	12	B2
Theobald's Rd. WC1	58	F5
Theodore Rd. SE13	78	D6
Therapia La., Croy.	94	D7
Therapia Rd. SE22	77	F6
Theresa Rd. W6	65	G4
Therfield Ct. N4	49	J2
Brownswood Rd.		
Thermopylae Gate E14	69	B4
Theseus Wk. N1	8	H2
Thesiger Rd. SE20	86	G7
Thessaly Rd. SW8	67	C7
Thetford Clo. N13	32	H6
Thetford Gdns., Dag.	53	D7
Thetford Rd., Dag.	53	D7
Thetford Rd., N.Mal.	92	D6
Thetis Ter., Rich.	65	A6
Theydon Gro., Wdf.Grn.	34	J6
Theydon Pk. Rd., Epp.	27	H1
Theydon Rd. E5	50	F2
Theydon St. E17	41	J7
Thicket Cres., Sutt.	100	F4
Thicket Gro., Dag.	53	C6
Thicket Rd. SE20	86	D7
Thicket Rd., Sutt.	100	F4
Third Ave. E12	52	B4
Third Ave. E13	60	G3
Third Ave. E17	42	A5
Third Ave. W3	65	F1
Third Ave. W10	57	B3
Third Ave., Dag.	62	H1
Third Ave., Enf.	25	C5
Third Ave., Rom.	44	C6
Third Ave., Wem.	46	G2
Third Clo., W.Mol.	90	H4
Third Cross Rd., Twick.	82	A2
Third Way, Wem.	47	B4
Thirleby Rd. SW1	15	G6
Thirleby Rd. SW1	67	C3
Thirleby Rd., Edg.	38	D1
Thirlmere Ave., Grnf.	55	F3
Thirlmere Gdns., Wem.	46	F1
Thirlmere Ho., Islw.	73	C5
Thirlmere Ri., Brom.	87	F6
Thirlmere Rd. N10	40	B1
Thirlmere Rd. SW16	85	D4
Thirlmere Rd., Bexh.	80	J2
Thirsk Clo., Nthlt.	45	G6
Thirsk Rd. SE25	95	A4
Thirsk Rd. SW11	76	A3
Thirsk Rd., Mitch.	85	A7
Thistle Gro. SW10	18	D3
Thistle Gro. SW10	66	F5
Thistle Mead, Loug.	27	D3
Thistlebrook SE2	71	C3
Thistlecroft Gdns., Stan.	37	G1
Thistledene, T.Ditt.	91	B6
Thistledene Ave., Har.	45	E3
Thistlemead, Chis.	97	E2
Thistlewaite Rd. E5	50	E3
Thistlewood Clo. N7	49	F2
Thistleworth Clo., Islw.	64	A7
Thomas à Beckett Clo., Wem.	46	C4
Thomas Baines Rd. SW11	75	G3
Thomas Darby Ct. W11	57	B6
Thomas Doyle St. SE1	16	H5
Thomas Doyle St. SE1	67	H3
Thomas Hardy Ho. N22	32	F7
Thomas La. SE6	78	A7
Thomas More St. E1	13	H6
Thomas More St. E1	59	D7
Thomas More Way N2	39	F3
Thomas Rd. E14	59	J6
Thomas St. SE18	70	E4
Thompson Ave., Rich.	74	A3
Thompson Clo., Ilf.	52	F2
High Rd.		
Thompson Rd. SE22	77	C6
Thompson Rd., Dag.	53	F3
Thompson's Ave. SE5	20	J7

Thompson's Ave. 67 J7
SE5
Thomson Cres., 101 G1
Croy.
Thomson Rd., Har. 37 B3
Thorburn Sq. SE1 21 H2
Thorburn Sq. SE1 68 D4
Thorburn Way SW19 93 G1
Phipps Bri. Rd.
Thoresby St. N1 9 A3
Thoresby St. N1 58 J3
Thorkhill Gdns., 98 D1
T.Ditt.
Thorkhill Rd., 98 D1
T.Ditt.
Thorn Ave. 28 J1
(Bushey), Wat.
Thorn Clo., Brom. 97 D6
Thorn Clo., Nthlt. 54 F3
Thorn Ho., Beck. 95 H1
Thornaby Gdns. N18 33 D6
Thornbury Ave., 64 A7
Islw.
Thornbury Gdns., 22 C3
Borwd.
Thornbury Rd. SW2 76 E6
Thornbury Rd., 64 A7
Islw.
Thornby Rd. E5 50 F3
Thorncliffe Rd. SW2 76 E6
Thorncliffe Rd., 63 F5
Sthl.
Thorncombe Rd. 77 B5
SE22
Thorncroft Rd., 100 E4
Sutt.
Thorncroft St. SW8 67 E7
Thorndean St. SW18 84 F2
Thorndene Ave. N11 32 A1
Thorndike Ave., 54 D1
Nthlt.
Thorndike Clo. SW10 18 C7
Thorndike Clo. SW10 66 F7
Thorndike St. SW1 19 H2
Thorndike St. SW1 67 D4
Thorndon Clo., Orp. 97 J2
Thorndon Gdns., 99 E5
Epsom
Thorndon Rd., Orp. 97 J2
Westfield Pk.
Thorndyke Ct., Pnr. 28 F7
Thorne Clo. E11 51 E4
Thorne Clo. E16 60 F6
Thorne Clo., Erith 71 J6
Thorne Pas. SW13 74 E2
Thorne Rd. SW8 67 E7
Thorne St. SW13 74 E3
Thorneloe Gdns., 101 G5
Croy.
Thornes Clo., Beck. 96 C3
Thornet Wd. Rd., 97 D3
Brom.
Thorney Cres. SW11 66 G7
Thorney Hedge Rd. 65 B4
W4
Thorney St. SW1 20 A1
Thorney St. SW1 67 E4
Thorneycroft Clo., 90 C6
Walt.
Thornfield Ave. NW7 39 B1
Thornfield Rd. W12 65 H2
Thornford Rd. SE13 78 C5
Thorngate Rd. W9 57 D4
Thorngrove Rd. E13 60 H1
Thornham Gro. E15 51 D5
Thornham St. SE10 69 B6
Thornhaugh Ms. WC1 7 J6
Thornhaugh St. WC1 11 J1
Thornhaugh St. WC1 58 D5
Thornhill Ave. SE18 70 H7
Thornhill Ave., 98 H2
Surb.
Thornhill Bri. Wf. 58 F1
N1
Caledonian Rd.
Thornhill Cres. N1 49 F7
Thornhill Gdns. E10 51 B2
Thornhill Gdns., 52 H7
Bark.
Thornhill Gro. N1 49 F7
Lofting Rd.
Thornhill Ho. N1 49 G7
Thornhill Rd.
Thornhill Rd. E10 51 B2
Thornhill Rd. N1 49 G7
Thornhill Rd., 94 J7
Croy.
Thornhill Rd., 98 H2
Surb.
Thornhill Sq. N1 49 F7
Thornlaw Rd. SE27 85 G4
Thornley Clo. N17 33 D7
Thornley Dr., Har. 45 H2

Thornley Pl. SE10 69 E5
Caradoc St.
Thornsbeach Rd. SE6 87 C1
Thornsett Pl. SE20 95 E2
Thornsett Rd. SE20 95 E2
Thornsett Rd. SW18 84 E1
Thornside, Edg. 30 A6
High St.
Thornton Ave. SW2 85 D1
Thornton Ave. W4 65 E4
Thornton Ave., 94 F6
Croy.
Thornton Ct. SW20 93 A5
Thornton Dene, 96 A2
Beck.
Thornton Gdns. 85 D1
SW12
Thornton Gro., Pnr. 28 G6
Thornton Hill SW19 84 B7
Thornton Pl. W1 10 J1
Thornton Pl. W1 57 J5
Thornton Rd. E11 51 D2
Thornton Rd. N18 33 F3
Thornton Rd. SW12 76 D7
Thornton Rd. SW14 74 D3
Thornton Rd. SW19 84 A6
Thornton Rd., Barn. 23 B3
Thornton Rd., Belv. 71 H4
Thornton Rd., Brom. 87 G5
Thornton Rd., Cars. 100 G1
Thornton Rd., Croy. 94 F7
Thornton Rd., Ilf. 52 E4
Thornton Rd. 94 G5
Th.Hth.
Thornton Rd. E. 84 A6
SW19
Thornton Rd.
Thornton Row, 94 G5
Th.Hth.
London Rd.
Thornton St. SW9 76 G2
Thornton Way NW11 39 E5
Thorntons Fm. Ave., 53 J1
Rom.
Thorntree Rd. SE7 70 A5
Thornville St. SE8 78 A1
Thornwood Clo. E18 42 H2
Thornwood Rd. SE13 78 E5
Thorogood Gdns. 51 E5
E15
Thorold Rd. N22 32 E7
Thorold Rd., Ilf. 52 E2
Thorparch Rd. SW8 76 D1
Thorpe Clo. W10 57 B6
Cambridge Gdns.
Thorpe Clo., Orp. 104 H2
Thorpe Cres. E17 41 J2
Thorpe Hall Rd. E17 42 C1
Thorpe Rd. E6 61 C1
Thorpe Rd. E7 51 F4
Thorpe Rd. E17 42 C2
Thorpe Rd. N15 41 B6
Thorpe Rd., Bark. 52 G7
Thorpe Rd., 82 H7
Kings.T.
Thorpebank Rd. W12 65 G1
Thorpedale Gdns., 43 D4
Ilf.
Thorpedale Rd. N4 49 E2
Thorpewood Ave. 86 E2
SE26
Thorsden Way SE19 86 B4
Oaks Ave.
Thorverton Rd. NW2 48 B3
Thoydon Rd. E3 59 H2
Thrale Rd. SW16 85 C4
Thrale St. SE1 17 A2
Thrale St. SE1 67 J1
Thrasher Clo. E8 59 C1
Stean St.
Thrawl St. E1 13 G2
Thrawl St. E1 59 C5
Threadneedle St. 13 C4
EC2
Threadneedle St. 59 A6
EC2
Three Colt St. E14 59 J6
Three Colts La. E2 59 E4
Three Cors., Bexh. 80 H2
Three Cups Yd. WC1 12 D2
Three Kings Yd. 94 A3
Mitch.
Three Kings Rd. W1 11 D5
Three Kings Yd. W1 58 B7
Three Mill La. E3 61 A3
Three Oak La. SE1 17 F3
Threshers Pl. W11 57 B7
Thriffwood SE26 86 F3
Thrift Fm. La., 22 C2
Borwd.
Thrigby Rd., Chess. 98 J6
Throckmorten Rd. 60 H6
E16

Throgmorton Ave. 13 C3
EC2
Throgmorton Ave. 59 A6
EC2
Throgmorton St. EC2 13 C3
Throgmorton St. EC2 59 A6
Throwley Clo. SE2 71 C3
Throwley Rd., Sutt. 100 E5
Throwley Way, Sutt. 100 E4
Thrupp Clo., Mitch. 94 B2
Thrush Grn., Har. 36 G4
Thrush St. SE17 20 J3
Thruxton Way SE15 21 G7
Thurbarn Rd. SE6 87 B5
Thurland Rd. SE16 17 H5
Thurland Rd. SE16 68 D3
Thurlby Clo., Har. 37 D6
Gayton Rd.
Thurlby Clo. 35 C5
Wdf.Grn.
Thurlby Rd. SE27 85 G4
Thurlby Rd., Wem. 46 G6
Thurleigh Ave. SW12 76 A6
Thurleigh Rd. SW12 75 J7
Thurleston Ave. 93 B5
Mord.
Thurlestone Ave. 31 J6
N12
Thurlestone Ave., 52 J4
Ilf.
Thurlestone Rd. 85 G3
SE27
Thurloe Clo. SW7 18 G1
Thurloe Clo. SW7 66 H4
Thurloe Pl. SW7 18 F1
Thurloe Pl. SW7 66 G4
Thurloe Pl. Ms. SW7 18 F1
Thurloe Sq. SW7 18 G1
Thurloe Sq. SW7 66 H4
Thurloe St. SW7 66 G4
Thurlow Clo. E4 34 B6
Higham Sta. Ave.
Thurlow Gdns., Ilf. 35 G6
Thurlow Gdns., 46 G5
Wem.
Thurlow Hill SE21 85 J1
Thurlow Pk. Rd. 85 H1
SE21
Thurlow Rd. NW3 48 G5
Thurlow Rd. W7 64 D2
Thurlow St. SE17 21 C3
Thurlow St. SE17 68 A5
Thurlow Ter. NW5 49 A5
Thurlston Rd., 45 A3
Ruis.
Thurnby Ct., Twick. 82 B3
Thursland Rd., Sid. 89 E5
Thursley Cres., 103 C7
Croy.
Thursley Gdns. 84 A2
SW19
Thursley Rd. SE9 88 C3
Thurso St. SW17 84 G4
Thurstan Rd. SW20 83 H7
Thurston Rd. SE13 78 B2
Thurston Rd., Sthl. 54 F6
Thurtle Rd. E2 59 C1
Thwaite Clo., Erith 71 J6
Thyra Gro. N12 31 E6
Tibbatts Rd. E3 60 B4
Tibbenham Wk. E13 60 F2
Stride Rd.
Tibberton Sq. N1 49 J7
Popham Rd.
Tibbets Clo. SW19 84 A1
Tibbets Cor. SW19 75 A7
Tibbet's Ride SW15 75 A7
Tiber Gdns. N1 58 F1
Treaty St.
Ticehurst Clo., 89 A7
Orp.
Grovelands Rd.
Ticehurst Rd. SE23 86 H2
Tickford Clo. SE2 71 C2
Ampleforth Rd.
Tidal Basin Rd. E16 60 F7
Tidenham Gdns., 102 B3
Croy.
Tideswell Rd. SW15 74 J4
Tideswell Rd., 103 A3
Croy.
Tideway Clo., Rich. 82 E4
Locksmeade Rd.
Tidey St. E3 60 A5
Tidford Rd., Well. 79 J2
Tidworth Rd. E3 60 A4
Tiepigs La., Brom. 103 F1
Tiepigs La., 103 E2
W.Wick.
Tierney Rd. SW2 76 E7
Tiger La., Brom. 96 H4
Tiger Way E5 50 E4

Tilbrook Rd. SE3 78 J3
Tilbury Clo. SE15 21 G7
Tilbury Rd. E6 61 C2
Tilbury Rd. E10 42 C7
Tildesley Rd. SW15 74 J6
Tile Fm. Rd., Orp. 104 G3
Tile Kiln La. N6 49 C1
Winchester Rd.
Tile Kiln La. N13 32 J5
Tile Kiln La., Bex. 89 J2
Tile Yd. E14 59 J6
St. Anne's St.
Tile Yd. E14 59 J6
Commercial Rd.
Tilehurst Rd. SW18 84 G1
Tilehurst Rd., 100 B5
Sutt.
Tileyard Rd. N7 49 E7
Tilford Ave., Croy. 103 C7
Tilford Gdns. SW19 84 A1
Tilia Rd. E5 50 E4
Clarence Rd.
Tiller Rd. E14 69 A3
Tillett Clo. NW10 47 C6
Tillett Way E2 9 H3
Tilling Rd. NW2 47 J1
Tillingbourne Gdns. 39 C3
N3
Tillingbourne Grn., 97 J4
Orp.
Tillingbourne Way 39 C3
N3
Tillingbourne Gdns.
Tillingham Way N12 31 D4
Tillman St. E1 59 E6
Bigland St.
Tilloch St. N1 49 F7
Carnoustie Dr.
Tillotson Rd. N9 33 C2
Tillotson Rd., Har. 28 H7
Tillotson Rd., Ilf. 43 D7
Tilney Ct. EC1 9 A5
Tilney Dr., Buck.H. 34 G2
Tilney Gdns. N1 50 A6
Baxter Rd.
Tilney Rd., Dag. 53 F6
Tilney Rd., Sthl. 63 C4
Tilney St. W1 15 C1
Tilney St. W1 67 A1
Tilson Gdns. SW2 76 E7
Tilson Ho. SW2 76 E7
Tilson Gdns.
Tilson Rd. N17 41 D1
Tilt Yd. App. SE9 79 C6
Tilton St. SW6 66 B6
Tiltwood, The W3 56 C7
Acacia Rd.
Timber Clo., Chis. 97 D2
Timber Mill Way 76 D3
SW4
Timber Pond Rd. 68 G1
SE16
Timber St. EC1 8 J5
Timbercroft, Epsom 99 E4
Timbercroft La. 70 H6
SE18
Timberdene NW4 39 A2
Timberdene Ave., 43 F1
Ilf.
Timberland Rd. E1 59 E6
Timberwharf Rd. N16 41 D6
Times Sq., Sutt. 100 E5
High St.
Timothy Rd. E3 59 J5
Timsbury Wk. SW15 83 G1
Tindal St. SW9 76 H1
Tinderbox All. SW14 74 D3
Tine Rd., Chig. 35 H5
Tinsley Rd. E1 59 F5
Tintagel Cres. SE22 77 C4
Tintagel Dr., Stan. 29 G4
Tintern Ave. NW9 38 B3
Tintern Clo. SW15 75 B5
Tintern Clo. SW19 84 F7
Tintern Gdns. N14 24 E7
Tintern Path NW9 38 E6
Ruthin Clo.
Tintern Rd. N22 40 J1
Tintern Rd., Cars. 100 G1
Tintern St. SW4 76 E4
Tintern Way, Har. 45 H1
Tinto Rd. E16 60 G4
Tinwell Ms., Borwd. 22 C5
Cranes Way
Tinworth St. SE11 20 B3
Tinworth St. SE11 67 E5
Tippetts Clo., Enf. 24 J1
Tipthorpe Rd. SW11 76 A3
Tipton Dr., Croy. 102 B4
Tiptree Clo. E4 34 C3
Tiptree Cres., Ilf. 43 D3
Tiptree Dr., Enf. 25 A4
Tiptree Est., Ilf. 43 D3

Name	Page	Grid
Tiptree Rd., Ruis.	45	B4
Tirlemont Rd., S.Croy.	101	J7
Tirrell Rd., Croy.	94	J6
Tisbury Ct. W1	11	H5
Tisbury Rd. SW16	94	E2
Tisdall Pl. SE17	21	C2
Titchborne Row W2	10	H4
Titchfield Rd. NW8	57	J1
Titchfield Rd., Cars.	100	G1
Titchfield Wk., Cars.	93	G7
Titchfield Rd.		
Titchwell Rd. SW18	75	G7
Tite St. SW3	18	J4
Tite St. SW3	66	J6
Tithe Barn Clo., Kings.T.	91	J1
Tithe Barn Way, Nthlt.	54	B2
Tithe Clo. NW7	38	G1
Tithe Fm. Ave., Har.	45	G3
Tithe Fm. Clo., Har.	45	G3
Tithe Wk. NW7	38	G1
Titley Clo. E4	34	A5
Titmuss Ave. SE28	62	B7
Titmuss St. W12	65	H2
Tiverton Ave., Ilf.	43	D3
Tiverton Dr. SE9	88	F1
Tiverton Rd. N15	41	A6
Tiverton Rd. N18	33	B5
Tiverton Rd. NW10	57	A1
Tiverton Rd., Edg.	37	J2
Tiverton Rd., Houns.	72	J2
Tiverton Rd., Ruis.	45	A3
Tiverton Rd., Th.Hth.	94	G5
Willett Rd.		
Tiverton Rd., Wem.	55	H2
Tiverton St. SE1	16	J6
Tiverton St. SE1	67	J3
Tiverton Way, Chess.	98	F5
Tivoli Ct. SE16	68	J2
Tivoli Gdns. SE18	70	B4
Tivoli Rd. N8	40	D5
Tivoli Rd. SE27	85	J5
Tivoli Rd., Houns.	72	E4
Tobacco Quay E1	59	E7
Wapping La.		
Tobago St. E14	69	A2
Manilla St.		
Tobin Clo. NW3	48	H7
Toby La. E1	59	H4
Todds Wk. N7	49	F2
Tokenhouse Yd. EC2	13	B3
Tokyngton Ave., Wem.	47	A6
Toland Sq. SW15	74	G5
Tolcarne Dr., Pnr.	36	A2
Toley Ave., Wem.	37	H7
Tollbridge Clo. W10	57	H4
Kensal Rd.		
Tollesbury Gdns., Ilf.	43	G3
Tollet St. E1	59	G4
Tollgate Dr. SE21	86	B2
Tollgate Gdns. NW6	6	A1
Tollgate Gdns. NW6	57	J2
Tollgate Rd. E6	61	A5
Tollgate Rd. E16	60	J5
Tollhouse Way N19	49	C2
Tollington Pk. N4	49	F2
Tollington Pl. N4	49	F2
Tollington Rd. N7	49	F4
Tollington Way N7	49	E3
Tolmers Sq. NW1	7	G5
Tolpuddle St. N1	8	E1
Tolpuddle St. N1	58	G2
Tolsford Rd. E5	50	E5
Tolson Rd., Islw.	73	D3
Tolverne Rd. SW20	92	J1
Tolworth Clo., Surb.	99	B1
Tolworth Gdns., Rom.	44	D5
Tolworth Pk. Rd., Surb.	98	J2
Tolworth Ri. N., Surb.	92	D6
South La.		
Tolworth Ri. S., Surb.	92	D6
South La.		
Tolworth Rd., Surb.	98	H2
Tom Coombs Clo. SE9	79	B4
Well Hall Rd.		
Tom Cribb Rd. SE28	70	F3
Tom Hood Clo. E15	51	D5
Maryland St.		
Tom Mann Clo., Bark.	61	H1
Tom Smith Clo. SE10	69	E6
Maze Hill		
Tomahawk Gdns., Nthlt.	54	D3
Javelin Way		
Tomlins Gro. E3	60	A3
Tomlins Orchard, Bark.	61	F1
Tomlins Ter. E14	59	J5
Rhodeswell Rd.		
Tomlins Wk. N7	49	F2
Briset Way		
Tomlinson Clo. E2	9	G4
Tomlinson Clo. E2	59	C3
Tomlinson Clo. W4	65	B5
Oxford Rd. N.		
Tompion St. EC1	8	G4
Tomswood Hill, Ilf.	35	E7
Tomswood Rd., Chig.	35	D6
Tonbridge Cres., Har.	37	H4
Tonbridge Ho. SE25	95	D3
Tonbridge Rd., W.Mol.	90	E4
Tonbridge St. WC1	8	A3
Tonbridge St. WC1	58	E3
Tonbridge Wk. WC1	8	A3
Tonfield Rd., Sutt.	100	C1
Tonge Clo., Beck.	96	A5
Tonsley Hill SW18	75	E5
Tonsley Pl. SW18	75	E5
Tonsley Rd. SW18	75	E5
Tonsley St. SW18	75	E5
Tonstall Rd., Mitch.	94	A2
Tooke Clo., Pnr.	36	E1
Took's Ct. EC4	12	E3
Tooley St. SE1	17	C1
Tooley St. SE1	68	B1
Toorack Rd., Har.	37	A2
Tooting Bec Gdns. SW16	85	D4
Tooting Bec Rd. SW16	85	B4
Tooting Gro. SW17	84	H5
Tooting High St. SW17	84	H6
Tootswood Rd., Brom.	96	E5
Top Ho. Ri. E4	26	C7
Parkhill Rd.		
Top Pk., Beck.	96	E5
Topcliffe Dr., Orp.	104	G5
Topham Sq. N17	40	J1
Topham St. EC1	8	E5
Topiary Sq., Rich.	73	J3
Topley St. SE9	79	A4
Topp Wk. NW2	47	J2
Topsfield Rd. N8	40	E5
Topsham Rd. SW17	84	J3
Tor Gdns. W8	66	D2
Tor Rd., Well.	80	C1
Torbay Rd. NW6	48	C7
Torbay Rd., Har.	45	E2
Torbay St. NW1	49	B7
Hawley Rd.		
Torbridge Clo., Edg.	29	H7
Torbrook Clo., Bex.	80	E6
Torcross Dr. SE23	86	F2
Torcross Rd., Ruis.	45	B3
Tormead Clo., Sutt.	100	D6
Tormount Rd. SE18	70	H6
Toronto Ave. E12	52	C4
Toronto Rd. E11	51	D4
Toronto Rd., Ilf.	52	E1
Torquay Gdns., Ilf.	43	A4
Torquay St. W2	10	A2
Torr Rd. SE20	86	G7
Torre Wk., Cars.	100	H1
Torrens Rd. E15	51	F6
Torrens Rd. SW2	76	F5
Torrens Sq. E15	51	F6
Torrens St. EC1	8	F2
Torrens St. EC1	58	G2
Torriano Ave. NW5	49	D5
Torriano Cotts. NW5	49	C5
Torriano Ave.		
Torridge Gdns. SE15	77	F4
Torridge Rd., Th.Hth.	94	H5
Torridon Rd. SE6	78	D7
Torridon Rd. SE13	78	E7
Torrington Ave. N12	31	G5
Torrington Clo. N12	31	G4
Torrington Clo., Esher	98	B6
Torrington Dr., Har.	45	H4
Torrington Dr., Loug.	27	F4
Torrington Gdns. N11	32	C6
Torrington Gdns., Grnf.	55	F1
Torrington Gdns., Loug.	27	F4
Torrington Pk. N12	31	F5
Torrington Pl. E1	17	J2
Torrington Pl. E1	68	D1
Torrington Pl. WC1	11	G1
Torrington Pl. WC1	58	D5
Torrington Rd. E18	42	G3
Torrington Rd., Dag.	53	F1
Torrington Rd., Esher	98	B6
Torrington Rd., Grnf.	55	F1
Torrington Sq. WC1	7	J6
Torrington Sq. WC1	58	D4
Torrington Sq., Croy.	95	A7
Tavistock Gro.		
Torrington Way, Mord.	93	D7
Torver Rd., Har.	37	B4
Torver Way, Orp.	104	G2
Torwood Rd. SW15	74	G5
Tothill St. SW1	15	H4
Tothill St. SW1	67	D2
Totnes Rd., Well.	71	B7
Totnes Wk. N2	39	G4
Tottenhall Rd. N13	32	G6
Tottenham Ct. Rd. W1	7	G6
Tottenham Ct. Rd. W1	58	C4
Tottenham Grn. E. N15	41	C4
Tottenham La. N8	40	E5
Tottenham Ms. W1	11	G1
Tottenham Rd. N1	50	B6
Tottenham St. W1	11	G2
Tottenham St. W1	58	C5
Totterdown St. SW17	84	J4
Totteridge Common N20	30	G2
Totteridge Grn. N20	31	D2
Totteridge La. N20	31	D2
Totteridge Village N20	31	B1
Totternhoe Clo., Har.	37	F5
Totton Rd., Th.Hth.	94	G3
Toulmin St. SE1	16	J4
Toulmin St. SE1	67	J2
Toulon St. SE5	20	J7
Toulon St. SE5	67	J7
Tournay Rd. SW6	66	C7
Toussaint Wk. SE16	17	J5
Tovil Clo. SE20	95	E2
Towcester Rd. E3	60	B4
Tower Bri. E1	17	F2
Tower Bri. E1	68	C1
Tower Bri. SE1	17	F2
Tower Bri. SE1	68	C1
Tower Bri. App. E1	17	F1
Tower Bri. App. E1	68	C1
Tower Bri. Rd. SE1	17	D6
Tower Bri. Rd. SE1	68	B3
Tower Clo. NW3	48	G5
Lyndhurst Rd.		
Tower Clo. SE20	86	E7
Tower Clo., Ilf.	35	E6
Tower Clo., Orp.	104	J2
Tower Ct. WC2	12	A4
Tower Gdns. Rd. N17	40	J1
Tower Hamlets Rd. E7	51	F4
Tower Hamlets Rd. E17	42	A3
Tower Hill EC3	13	F6
Tower Hill EC3	59	B7
Tower Ms. E17	42	A4
Tower Pl. EC3	13	E6
Tower Pt., Enf.	25	A4
Tower Ri., Rich.	73	H3
Jocelyn Rd.		
Tower Rd. NW10	47	G7
Tower Rd., Belv.	71	J4
Tower Rd., Bexh.	80	G4
Tower Rd., Orp.	104	J2
Tower Rd., Twick.	82	C3
Tower Royal EC4	13	A5
Tower St. WC2	11	J4
Tower St. WC2	58	D6
Tower Ter. N22	40	F2
Mayes Rd.		
Tower Vw., Croy.	95	G7
Towers Pl., Rich.	73	H5
Eton St.		
Towers Rd., Pnr.	28	E7
Towers Rd., Sthl.	54	G4
Towfield Rd., Felt.	81	F2
Towing Path Wk. N1	58	D1
York Way		
Town, The, Enf.	25	A3
Town Ct. Path N4	49	J1
Town Hall App. Rd. N15	11	G1
Town Hall Ave. W4	65	D5
Town Hall Rd. SW11	75	J3
Town Meadow, Brent.	64	G7
Town Quay, Bark.	61	E1
Town Rd. N9	33	G2
Towncourt La., Orp.	97	G6
Towney Mead, Nthlt.	54	F2
Towner Ct. E15	64	C3
Townley Ct. E15	51	F6
Townley Rd. SE22	77	B5
Townley Rd., Bexh.	80	F6
Townley St. SE17	21	B3
Townmead Rd. SW6	75	E3
Townmead Rd., Rich.	74	B2
Townsend Ave. N14	32	D4
Townsend Ind. Est. NW10	56	C2
Townsend La. NW9	38	D7
Townsend Rd. N15	41	C5
Townsend Rd., Sthl.	54	E1
Townsend St. SE17	21	D1
Townsend St. SE17	68	A4
Townsends Yd. N6	49	A1
Townshend Clo., Sid.	89	B6
Townshend Est. NW8	6	G1
Townshend Est. NW8	57	H2
Townshend Rd. NW8	57	H1
Townshend Rd., Chis.	88	E5
Townshend Rd., Rich.	73	J4
Townshend Ter., Rich.	73	J4
Townson Ave., Nthlt.	54	A3
Townson Way, Nthlt.	54	A2
Townson Ave.		
Towton Rd. SE27	85	J2
Toynbee Clo., Chis.	88	E4
Beechwood Ri.		
Toynbee Rd. SW20	93	B1
Toynbee St. E1	13	F2
Toynbee St. E1	59	C5
Toyne Way N6	39	J6
Gaskell Rd.		
Tracey Ave. NW2	47	J5
Tracy Ct., Stan.	29	F7
Tradescant Rd. SW8	67	E7
Trading Est. Rd. NW10	56	C4
Trafalgar Ave. N17	33	B6
Trafalgar Ave. SE15	21	G4
Trafalgar Ave. SE15	68	C5
Trafalgar Ave., Wor.Pk.	100	A1
Trafalgar Business Cen., Bark.	61	J4
Trafalgar Clo. SE16	68	H4
Greenland Quay		
Trafalgar Gdns. E1	59	G5
Trafalgar Gro. SE10	69	D6
Trafalgar Pl. E11	42	G4
Trafalgar Pl. N18	33	D5
Trafalgar Rd. SE10	69	D6
Trafalgar Rd. SW19	84	E7
Trafalgar Rd., Twick.	82	A2
Trafalgar Sq. WC2	15	J1
Trafalgar Sq. WC2	67	D1
Trafalgar St. SE17	21	B3
Trafalgar St. SE17	68	A5
Trafalgar Ter., Har.	46	B1
Nelson Rd.		
Trafalgar Way E14	69	C1
Trafalgar Way, Croy.	101	F2
Trafford Clo. E15	51	B5
Trafford Clo., Ilf.	35	J6
Trafford Rd., Th.Hth.	94	F5
Tramway Ave. E15	51	E7
Tramway Ave. N9	25	E7
Tramway Path, Mitch.	93	H4
Tranby Pl. E9	50	G5
Homerton High St.		
Tranley Ms. NW3	48	H5
Fleet Rd.		

Tranmere Rd. N9 25 C7
Tranmere Rd. SW18 84 F1
Tranmere Rd., 72 H7
Twick.
Tranquil Pas. SE3 78 F2
Tranquil Vale
Tranquil Vale SE3 78 E2
Transay Wk. N1 50 A6
Marquess Rd.
Transept St. NW1 10 H2
Transept St. NW1 57 H5
Transmere Clo., 97 F6
Orp.
Transom Sq. E14 69 B4
Transport Ave., 64 D5
Brent.
Tranton Rd. SE16 17 J5
Tranton Rd. SE16 68 D3
Traps Hill, Loug. 27 C3
Traps La., N.Mal. 92 E1
Travellers Way, 72 C2
Houns.
Travers Clo. E17 41 G1
Travers Rd. N7 49 G3
Treacy Clo. 28 J2
(Bushey), Wat.
Treadgold St. W11 57 A7
Treadway St. E2 59 E2
Treaty St. N1 58 F1
Trebeck St. W1 15 D1
Trebovir Rd. SW5 66 D5
Treby St. E3 59 J4
Trecastle Way N7 49 D4
Carleton Rd.
Tredegar Ms. E3 59 J3
Tredegar Ter.
Tredegar Rd. E3 59 J2
Tredegar Rd. N11 32 D7
Tredegar Sq. E3 59 J3
Tredegar Ter. E3 59 J3
Trederwen Rd. E8 59 D1
Tredown Rd. SE26 86 F5
Tredwell Clo., 97 B4
Brom.
Tredwell Rd. SE27 85 H4
Tree Clo., Rich. 82 G1
Tree Rd. E16 60 J6
Treen Ave. SW13 74 E3
Treetops Clo. SE2 71 E5
Treeview Clo. SE19 95 B1
Treewall Gdns., 87 H4
Brom.
Trefgarne Rd., Dag. 53 G2
Trefil Wk. N7 49 E4
Trefoil Rd. SW18 75 F5
Tregaron Ave. N8 40 E6
Tregaron Gdns., 92 E4
N.Mal.
Avenue Rd.
Tregarvon Rd. SW11 76 A4
Tregenna Ave., Har. 45 F4
Tregenna Clo. N14 24 C5
Tregenna Ct., Har. 45 G4
Trego Rd. E9 51 A7
Tregothnan Rd. SW9 76 E3
Tregunter Rd. SW10 18 B5
Tregunter Rd. SW10 66 F6
Trehearn Rd., Ilf. 35 G7
Treherne Rd. SW14 74 D3
Treherne Ct. SW9 76 G1
Eythorne Rd.
Treherne Ct. SW17 85 A4
Trehurst St. E5 50 H5
Trelawn Rd. E10 51 C5
Trelawn Rd. SW2 76 G5
Trelawney St. E9 50 F6
Trelawney Rd., Ilf. 35 G7
Trellick Twr. W10 57 C4
Trellis Sq. E3 59 J3
Malmesbury Rd.
Treloar Gdns. SE19 86 A6
Hancock Rd.
Tremadoc Rd. SW4 76 D4
Tremaine Clo. SE4 78 A2
Tremaine Rd. SE20 95 E2
Trematon Pl., Tedd. 82 F7
Tremlett Gro. N19 49 C3
Tremlett Ms. N19 49 C3
Junction Rd.
Trenance Gdns., 53 A3
Ilf.
Trench Yd. Ct., 93 E6
Mord.
Green La.
Trenchard Ave., 45 B4
Ruis.
Trenchard Clo., 29 D6
Stan.
Trenchard Ct., 93 E6
Mord.
Trenchard St. SE10 69 D5
Trenchold St. SW8 20 A6
Trenchold St. SW8 67 E6

Trenholme Clo. SE20 86 E7
Trenholme Rd. SE20 86 E7
Trenholme Ter. SE20 86 E7
Trenmar Gdns. 56 H3
NW10
Trent Ave. W5 64 F3
Trent Gdns. N14 24 B6
Trent Rd. SW2 76 F5
Trent Rd., Buck.H. 34 H1
Trent Way, Wor.Pk. 99 J3
Trentbridge Clo., 35 J6
Ilf.
Trentham St. SW18 84 D1
Trentwood Side, 24 F3
Enf.
Treport St. SW18 75 E7
Tresco Clo., Brom. 87 E6
Tresco Gdns., Ilf. 53 A2
Tresco Rd. SE15 77 E4
Trescoe Gdns., Har. 36 E7
Tresham Cres. NW8 6 G5
Tresham Cres. NW8 57 H4
Tresham Rd., Bark. 52 J7
Tresham Wk. E9 50 F5
Churchill Wk.
Tressell Clo. N1 49 H7
Sebbon St.
Tressillian Cres. SE4 78 A3
Tressillian Rd. SE4 77 J4
Trestis Clo., Hayes 54 E5
Jollys La.
Treswell Rd., Dag. 62 E1
Tretawn Gdns. NW7 30 E4
Tretawn Pk. NW7 30 E4
Trevanion Rd. W14 66 B4
Treve Ave., Har. 36 J7
Trevelyan Ave. E12 52 C4
Trevelyan Cres., 37 G7
Har.
Trevelyan Gdns. 56 J1
NW10
Trevelyan Rd. E15 51 F4
Trevelyan Rd. SW17 84 H5
Treveris St. SE1 16 H2
Treverton St. W10 57 B4
Treville St. SW15 74 H7
Treviso Rd. SE23 86 G2
Farren Rd.
Trevithick St. SE8 69 A6
Trevone Gdns., Pnr. 36 E6
Trevor Clo., Barn. 23 G6
Trevor Clo., Brom. 96 F7
Trevor Clo., Har. 29 C7
Kenton La.
Trevor Clo., Islw. 73 C5
Trevor Clo., Nthlt. 54 J6
Trevor Gdns., Edg. 38 D1
Trevor Gdns., 54 C2
Nthlt.
Trevor Pl. SW7 14 H4
Trevor Pl. SW7 66 H2
Trevor Rd. SW19 84 B7
Trevor Rd., Edg. 38 D1
Trevor Rd., 34 G7
Wdf.Grn.
Trevor Sq. SW7 14 J4
Trevor Sq. SW7 66 H3
Trevor St. SW7 14 H4
Trevor St. SW7 66 H2
Trevose Rd. E17 42 D1
Trevose Way, Wat. 28 C3
Trewenna Dr., 98 G5
Chess.
Trewince Rd. SW20 92 J1
Trewint St. SW18 84 F2
Trewsbury Rd. SE26 86 G5
Triandra Way, Hayes 54 D5
Triangle, The N13 32 G4
Triangle, The, 90 J1
Hmptn.
High St.
Triangle, The, 92 C2
Kings.T.
Kenley Rd.
Triangle Ct. E16 61 A5
Tollgate Rd.
Triangle Pas., 23 F4
Barn.
Station Rd.
Triangle Pl. SW4 76 D4
Triangle Rd. E8 59 E1
Trident Gdns., 54 D3
Nthlt.
Jetstar Way
Trident St. SE16 68 G4
Trident Way, Sthl. 63 B3
Trigon Rd. SW8 20 D7
Trigon Rd. SW8 67 F7
Trilby Rd. SE23 86 G2
Trimmer Wk., Brent. 64 H6
Netley Rd.
Trinder Gdns. N19 49 E1
Trinder Rd.

Trinder Rd. N19 49 E1
Trinder Rd., Barn. 22 J5
Tring Ave. W5 64 J1
Tring Ave., Sthl. 54 F6
Tring Ave., Wem. 47 A6
Tring Clo., Ilf. 43 G5
Trinidad St. E14 59 J7
Trinity Ave. N2 39 G3
Trinity Ave., Enf. 25 C6
Trinity Ch. Pas. 65 H6
SW13
Trinity Ch. Rd. 65 H6
SW13
Trinity Ch. Sq. SE1 17 A6
Trinity Ch. Sq. SE1 67 J3
Trinity Clo. E11 51 E2
Trinity Clo. NW3 48 G4
Hampstead High St.
Trinity Clo. SE13 78 D4
Wisteria Rd.
Trinity Clo., Brom. 104 B1
Trinity Clo., 72 E4
Houns.
Trinity Cotts., 73 J3
Rich.
Trinity Rd.
Trinity Ct. N1 50 B7
Downham Rd.
Trinity Ct. SE7 70 A4
Charlton La.
Trinity Cres. SW17 84 J2
Trinity Gdns. E16 60 F5
Trinity Gdns. SW9 76 F4
Trinity Gro. SE10 78 C1
Trinity Ms. W10 57 A6
Cambridge Gdns.
Trinity Pl., Bexh. 80 F4
Trinity Ri. SW2 85 G1
Trinity Rd. N2 39 G3
Trinity Rd. N22 32 E7
Whittington Rd.
Trinity Rd. SW17 84 J2
Trinity Rd. SW18 75 G5
Trinity Rd. SW19 84 D6
Trinity Rd., Ilf. 43 F3
Trinity Rd., Rich. 73 J3
Trinity Rd., Sthl. 63 E1
Trinity Sq. EC3 13 E6
Trinity St. E16 60 G5
Vincent St.
Trinity Sq. EC3 59 B7
Trinity St. E16 60 G5
Trinity St. SE1 17 A4
Trinity St. SE1 67 J2
Trinity St., Enf. 24 J2
Trinity Wk. NW3 48 F6
Trinity Way E4 33 J6
Trinity Way W3 56 E7
Trio Pl. SE1 17 A4
Tristan Ct. SE8 78 E3
Tristram Clo. E17 42 D3
Tristram Rd., Brom. 87 F4
Triton Sq. NW1 7 F5
Triton Sq. NW1 58 C4
Tritton Ave., Croy. 101 E4
Tritton Rd. SE21 86 A3
Triumph Ho., Bark. 62 A3
Triumph Rd. E6 61 C6
Trojan Way, Croy. 101 F3
Troon St. E1 59 H6
White Horse Rd.
Trosley Rd., Belv. 71 G6
Trossachs Rd. SE22 77 B5
Trothy Rd. SE1 21 J2
Trott Rd. N10 31 J7
Trott St. SW11 75 G1
Trotwood, Chig. 35 G6
Troughton Rd. SE7 69 H5
Troutbeck Rd. SE14 77 H1
Trouville Rd. SW4 76 G6
Trowbridge Est. E9 50 J6
Trowbridge Rd. E9 50 J6
Trowlock Ave., 82 F6
Tedd.
Trowlock Way, 82 G6
Tedd.
Troy Ct. SE18 70 E4
Troy Rd. SE19 86 A6
Troy Town SE15 77 D3
Truesdale Rd. E6 61 C6
Trulock Ct. N17 33 D7
Trulock Rd. N17 33 D7
Truman Clo., Edg. 30 B7
Pavilion Way
Truman's Rd. N16 50 B5
Trump St. EC2 13 A4
Trumpers Way W7 64 B2
Trumpington Rd. E7 51 F4
Trundle St. SE1 16 J3
Trundlers Way 29 B1
(Bushey), Wat.
Trundleys Rd. SE8 68 G5
Trundleys Ter. SE8 68 G4
Truro Gdns., Ilf. 43 B7

Truro Rd. E17 41 J4
Truro Rd. N22 32 E7
Truro St. NW5 49 A6
Truslove Rd. SE27 85 G5
Trussley Rd. W6 65 J3
Trust Wk. SE21 85 H1
Peabody Hill
Tryfan Clo., Ilf. 43 A5
Tryon St. SW3 18 J3
Tryon St. SW3 66 J5
Trystings Clo., 98 D6
Esher
Tuam Rd. SE18 70 G6
Tubbenden Clo., 104 I12
Orp.
Tubbenden Dr., Orp. 104 G4
Tubbenden La., Orp. 104 G4
Tubbenden La. S., 104 G5
Orp.
Tubbs Rd. NW10 56 F2
Tudor Ave., Hmptn. 81 G6
Tudor Ave., Wor.Pk. 99 H3
Tudor Clo. N6 40 C7
Tudor Clo. NW3 48 H5
Tudor Clo. NW7 30 G6
Tudor Clo. NW9 47 C2
Tudor Clo. SW2 76 F6
Elm Pk.
Tudor Clo., Chess. 98 H5
Tudor Clo., Chig. 35 D4
Tudor Clo., Chis. 97 C1
Tudor Clo., Pnr. 36 A5
Tudor Clo., Sutt. 100 B6
Tudor Clo., Wall. 101 C7
Tudor Clo., 34 H5
Wdf.Grn.
Tudor Ct. E17 41 J7
Tudor Ct., Felt. 81 C4
Tudor Ct. N., Wem. 47 A5
Tudor Ct. S., Wem. 47 A5
Tudor Cres., Enf. 24 J1
Tudor Cres., Ilf. 35 E6
Tudor Dr., Kings.T. 82 G6
Tudor Dr., Mord. 93 A6
Tudor Est. NW10 56 B3
Tudor Gdns. NW9 47 C2
Tudor Gdns. SW13 74 E3
Treen Ave.
Tudor Gdns. W3 56 A5
Tudor Gdns., Twick. 82 C1
Tudor Gdns., 103 C3
W.Wick.
Tudor Gro. E9 50 F7
Tudor Pl. W1 11 H3
Tudor Pl., Mitch. 84 H7
Tudor Rd. E4 34 B6
Tudor Rd. E6 60 J1
Tudor Rd. E9 59 E1
Tudor Rd. N9 25 E7
Tudor Rd. SE19 86 C7
Tudor Rd. SE25 95 E5
Tudor Rd., Bark. 61 J1
Tudor Rd., Barn. 23 D3
Tudor Rd., Beck. 96 B3
Tudor Rd., Hmptn. 81 G7
Tudor Rd., Har. 37 A2
Tudor Rd., Houns. 73 A4
Tudor Rd., Kings.T. 83 A7
Tudor Rd., Pnr. 36 C2
Tudor Rd., Sthl. 54 E7
Tudor St. EC4 12 F5
Tudor St. EC4 58 G7
Tudor Wk., Bex. 80 E6
Tudor Way N14 32 D1
Tudor Way W3 65 A2
Tudor Way, Orp. 97 G6
Tudor Well Clo., 29 E5
Stan.
Tudway Rd. SE3 78 H3
Tufnell Pk. Rd. N7 49 D4
Tufnell Pk. Rd. N19 49 C4
Tufter Rd., Chig. 35 J5
Tufton Gdns., 90 H2
W.Mol.
Tufton Rd. E4 34 A4
Tufton St. SW1 16 B6
Tufton St. SW1 67 D3
Tugela Rd., Croy. 95 A6
Tugela St. SE6 86 J2
Tuilerie St. E2 9 H1
Tuilerie St. E2 102 G1
Tulip Clo., Croy.
Tulip Clo., Hmptn. 81 F6
Partridge Rd.
Tulip Ct., Pnr. 36 C3
Tulse Clo., Beck. 96 C3
Tulse Hill SW2 76 G6
Tulse Hill Est. SW2 76 G6
Tulsemere Rd. SE21 85 J2
Tumbling Bay, Walt. 90 A6
Tummons Gdns. 95 B2
SE25
Tuncombe Rd. N18 33 B4
Tunis Rd. W12 65 H1

Tunley Rd. NW10 56 E1
Tunley Rd. SW17 85 A1
Tunmarsh La. E13 60 H3
Tunnanleys E6 61 D6
  Horse Leaze
Tunnel Ave. SE10 69 D2
Tunnel Gdns. N11 32 C7
Tunnel Rd. SE18 68 F2
  Church St.
Tunstall Clo. Orp 104 H4
Tunstall Rd. SW9 76 E4
Tunstall Rd., Croy. 102 B1
Tunstall Wk. 64 H6
  Brent.
  Ealing Rd.
Tunstock Way, Belv. 71 E3
Tunworth Clo. NW9 38 C6
Tunworth Cres. 74 F6
  SW15
Turenne Clo. SW18 75 F4
Turin Rd. N9 25 F7
Turin St. E2 9 H4
Turin St. E2 59 D3
Turkey Oak Clo. 95 B1
  SE19
Turk's Head Yd. EC1 12 G1
Turks Row SW3 19 A3
Turks Row SW3 66 J5
Turle Rd. N4 49 F1
Turle Rd. SW16 94 E2
Turlewray Clo. N4 49 F1
Turley Clo. E15 60 E1
Turnagain La. EC4 12 G3
Turnage Rd., Dag. 53 E1
Turnberry Ct., Wat. 28 C3
Turnberry Quay E14 69 B3
  Pepper St.
Turnberry Way, 104 G1
  Orp.
Turnchapel Ms. SW4 76 B3
  Cedars Rd.
Turner Ave. N15 41 B4
Turner Ave., Mitch. 93 J1
Turner Ave., Twick. 81 J3
Turner Clo. NW11 39 E6
Turner Dr. NW11 39 E6
Turner Rd. E17 42 C3
Turner Rd., Edg. 37 H2
Turner Rd., N.Mal. 92 D7
Turner St. E1 59 E5
Turner St. E16 60 F6
Turners Meadow 95 J1
  Way, Beck.
Turners Rd. E3 59 J5
Turners Way, Croy. 101 G2
Turners Wd. NW11 48 F1
Turneville Rd. W14 66 C6
Turney Rd. SE21 76 J7
Turnham Grn. Ter. 65 E4
  W4
Turnham Grn. Ter. 65 E4
  Ms. W4
  Turnham Grn. Ter.
Turnham Rd. SE4 77 H5
Turnmill St. EC1 8 F6
Turnmill St. EC1 58 G4
Turnpike Clo. SE8 68 J7
  Amersham Vale
Turnpike Ho. EC1 8 H4
Turnpike La. N8 40 F4
Turnpike La., Sutt. 100 F5
Turnpike Link, 102 B2
  Croy.
Turnpin La. SE10 69 C6
Turnston Clo. NW9 38 E2
  Kestrel Clo.
Turnstone Clo. E13 60 G3
Turpentine La. SW1 19 E4
Turpin Way, Wall. 101 B1
Turpington Clo., 97 B6
  Brom.
Turpington La., 97 B7
  Brom.
Turpins La., 35 C5
  Wdf.Grn.
Turquand St. SE17 21 A2
Turret Gro. SW4 76 C3
Turton Rd., Wem. 46 H5
Turville St. E2 9 G5
Tuscan Rd. SE18 70 G5
Tuskar St. SE10 69 E5
Tustin St. SE15 68 F6
Tuttlebee La., 34 G2
  Buck.H.
Tweedale Ct. E15 51 C5
Tweedale Rd., Cars. 100 G1
Tweedmouth Rd. E13 60 H2
Tweedy Rd., Brom. 96 G1
Tweezer's All. WC2 12 E5
Twelvetrees Cres. 60 C4
  E3
Twentyman Clo., 34 G5
  Wdf.Grn.

Twickenham Bri., 73 F5
  Rich.
Twickenham Bri., 73 F5
  Twick.
Twickenham Clo., 101 F3
  Croy.
Twickenham Gdns., 46 D5
  Grnf.
Twickenham Gdns., 29 B7
  Har.
Twickenham Rd. E11 51 D2
Twickenham Rd., 81 F3
  Felt.
Twickenham Rd., 73 D5
  Islw.
Twickenham Rd., 73 F5
  Rich.
Twickenham Rd., 82 D4
  Tedd.
Twickenham Trd. 73 C6
  Est., Twick.
Twilley St. SW18 75 E7
Twine Ct. E1 59 F7
Twineham Grn. N12 31 D4
  Tillingham Way
Twining Ave., 81 J3
  Twick.
Twinn Rd. NW7 31 B6
Twisden Rd. NW5 49 B4
Twybridge Way 47 C7
  NW10
Twyford Abbey Rd. 55 J3
  NW10
Twyford Ave. N2 39 J3
Twyford Ave. W3 56 A7
Twyford Cres. W3 65 A1
Twyford Pl. WC2 12 C3
Twyford Rd., Cars. 100 G1
Twyford Rd., Har. 45 H1
Twyford Rd., Ilf. 52 F5
Twyford St. N1 58 F1
Tyas Rd. E16 60 F4
Tybenham Rd. SW19 93 C3
Tyberry Rd., Enf. 25 E3
Tyburn La., Har. 37 B7
Tyburn Way W1 11 A5
Tycehurst Hill, 27 C4
  Loug.
Tye La., Orp. 104 F5
Tyers Est. SE1 17 D3
Tyers Est. SE1 68 B2
Tyers Gate SE1 17 D4
Tyers St. SE11 20 C4
Tyers St. SE11 67 F5
Tyers Ter. SE11 20 C4
Tyers Ter. SE11 67 F5
Tyeshurst Clo. SE2 71 E5
Tylecroft Rd. SW16 94 E2
Tylehurst Gdns., 52 F5
  Ilf.
Tyler Clo. E2 9 F1
Tyler Clo. E2 59 C2
Tyler St. SE10 69 E5
Tylers Clo., Loug. 27 B7
Tyler's Ct. W1 11 A4
Tylers Gate, Har. 37 H6
Tylers Path, Cars. 100 J4
  Rochester Rd.
Tylney Ave. SE19 86 C5
Tylney Rd. E7 51 J4
Tylney Rd., Brom. 97 A2
Tynan Clo., Felt. 81 A1
  Sandycombe Rd.
Tyndale Ct. E14 69 B5
Tyndale La. N1 49 H7
  Upper St.
Tyndale Ter. N1 49 H7
  Tyndale La.
Tyndall Rd. E10 51 C2
Tyndall Rd., Well. 79 J3
Tyne St. E1 13 G3
Tyneham Rd. SW11 76 A2
Tynemouth Rd. N15 41 C4
Tynemouth Rd., 85 A7
  Mitch.
Tynemouth St. SW6 75 F2
Type St. E2 59 G2
Tyrawley Rd. SW6 75 E1
Tyrell Clo., Har. 46 B4
Tyrell Ct., Cars. 100 J4
Tyrell Sq., Mitch. 93 H1
Tyron Way, Sid. 88 H4
Tyrone Rd. E6 61 C2
Tyrrel Way NW9 38 F7
Tyrrell Ave., Well. 80 A5
Tyrrell Rd. SE22 77 E4
Tyrwhitt Rd. SE4 78 A3
Tysoe St. EC1 8 E4
Tyson Rd. SE23 77 F7
Tyssen Pas. E8 50 C6
  Tyssen St.
Tyssen Rd. N16 50 C3
Tyssen St. E8 50 C6

Tyssen St. N1 9 E2
Tytherton Rd. N19 49 D3

U

Uamvar St. E14 60 B5
Uckfield Gro., Mitch. 94 A1
Udall St. SW1
Udney Pk. Rd., 82 D5
  Tedd.
Uffington Rd. NW10 55 G1
Uffington Rd. SE27 85 G4
Ufford Clo., Har. 28 H7
  Ufford Rd.
Ufford Rd., Har. 28 H7
Ufford St. SE1 16 F3
Ufford St. SE1 67 G2
Ufton Gro. N1 50 A7
Ufton Rd. N1 50 A7
Ujima Ct. SW16 85 H2
  Sunnyhill Rd.
Ullathorne Rd. SW16 85 C4
Ulleswater Rd. N14 32 E4
Ullin St. E14 60 C5
  St. Leonards Rd.
Ullswater Clo. SW15 83 D4
Ullswater Clo., 87 E7
  Brom.
Ullswater Cres. 83 D4
  SW15
Ullswater Rd. SE27 85 H2
Ullswater Rd. SW13 65 G7
Ulster Gdns. N13 32 J4
Ulster Pl. NW1 7 D6
Ulster Ter. NW1 7 D5
Ulundi Rd. SE3 69 E6
Ulva Rd. SW15 75 A5
  Ravenna Rd.
Ulverscroft Rd. 77 C5
  SE22
Ulverston Rd. E17 42 D2
Ulverstone Rd. SE27 85 H2
Ulysses Rd. NW6 48 C5
Umbria St. SW15 74 G6
Umfreville Rd. N4 40 H6
Undercliff Rd. SE13 78 A3
Underhill, Barn. 23 D5
Underhill Pas. NW1 58 B1
  Camden High St.
Underhill Rd. SE22 77 D5
Underhill St. NW1 58 B1
  Camden High St.
Underne Ave. N14 32 B2
Undershaft EC3 13 D4
Undershaft EC3 59 B6
Undershaw Rd., 87 F3
  Brom.
Underwood, Croy. 103 C5
Underwood, The 88 C2
  SE9
Underwood Rd. E1 9 H6
Underwood Rd. E1 59 D4
Underwood Rd. E4 34 B5
Underwood Rd., 34 J7
  Wdf.Grn.
Underwood Row N1 9 A3
Underwood Row N1 58 J3
Underwood St. N1 9 A3
Underwood St. N1 58 J3
Undine Rd. E14 69 B4
Undine St. SW17 84 J5
Uneeda Dr., Grnf. 55 A1
Union Cotts. E15 51 E7
  Hay Clo.
Union Ct. EC2 13 D3
Union Ct., Rich. 73 H5
  Eton St.
Union Dr. E1 59 H4
  Solebay St.
Union Gro. SW8 76 D2
Union Rd. N11 32 D6
Union Rd. SW4 76 D2
Union Rd. SW8 76 D2
Union Rd., Brom. 97 A5
Union Rd., Croy. 94 J7
Union Rd., Nthlt. 54 G2
Union Rd., Wem. 46 H6
Union Sq. N1 58 J1
Union St. E15 60 C1
Union St. SE1 16 H2
Union St. SE1 67 H1
Union St., Barn. 23 B4
Union St., Kings.T. 91 G2
Union Wk. E2 9 E3
Unity Clo. NW10 47 G6
Unity Way SE18 70 J3
University Clo. NW7 30 F7
University Pl., 71 H7
  Erith
  Belmont Rd.
University Rd. SW19 84 G6
University St. WC1 7 G6
University St. WC1 58 C4

Unwin Clo. SE15 21 H6
Unwin Clo. SE15 68 D6
Unwin Rd. SW7 14 E5
Unwin Rd., Islw. 73 B3
Upbrook Ms. W2 10 D4
Upcerne Rd. SW10 80 F7
Upchurch Clo. SE20 86 E7
Upcroft Ave., Edg. 88 E7
Updale Rd., Sid. 88 J4
Upfield, Croy. 102 E2
Upfield Rd. W7 55 L4
Upgrove Manor Way 76 G7
  SW2
  Trinity Ri.
Uphall Rd., Ilf. 52 E5
Upham Pk. Rd. W4 65 E4
Uphill Dr. NW7 30 E5
Uphill Dr. NW9 38 C5
Uphill Gro. NW7 30 E4
Uphill Rd. NW7 30 E4
Upland Rd. E13 60 F4
  Sutton Rd.
Upland Rd. SE22 77 D7
Upland Rd., Bexh. 80 F3
Upland Rd., S.Croy. 102 A5
Upland Rd., Sutt. 100 G6
Uplands, Beck. 96 A2
Uplands, The, 27 C3
  Loug.
Uplands, The, Ruis. 45 A1
Uplands Clo. SW14 74 B5
  Monroe Dr.
Uplands End, 35 B7
  Wdf.Grn.
Uplands Pk. Rd., 24 G3
  Enf.
Uplands Rd. E17 41 G2
  Blackhorse La.
Uplands Rd. N8 40 F5
Uplands Rd., Barn. 24 A7
Uplands Rd., Rom. 44 D3
Uplands Rd., 35 B7
  Wdf.Grn.
Uplands Trd. Est. 41 G3
  E17
Uplands Way N21 24 G5
Upney La., Bark. 52 H6
Upnor Way SE17 21 E3
Uppark Dr., Ilf. 43 F6
Upper Abbey Rd., 71 F4
  Belv.
Upper Addison Gdns. 66 B2
  W14
Upper Bardsey Wk. 49 J6
  N1
  Marquess Est.
Upper Belgrave St. 15 C5
  SW1
Upper Belgrave St. 67 A3
  SW1
Upper Berkeley St. 10 J4
  W1
Upper Berkeley St. 57 J6
  W1
Upper Beulah Hill 95 B1
  SE19
Upper Brighton Rd., 91 G6
  Surb.
Upper Brockley Rd. 77 J2
  SE4
Upper Brook St. W1 11 B6
Upper Brook St. W1 58 A7
Upper Butts, Brent. 64 F6
Upper Caldy Wk. N1 49 J6
  Marquess Est.
Upper Camelford Wk. 57 B6
  W11
  Lancaster Rd.
Upper Cavendish 39 D3
  Ave. N3
Upper Cheyne Row 18 G6
  SW3
Upper Cheyne Row 66 H6
  SW3
Upper Clapton Rd. 50 E1
  E5
Upper Clarendon Wk. 57 B6
  W11
  Lancaster Rd.
Upper Dengie Wk. N1 58 J1
  Popham Rd.
Upper Elmers End 95 H4
  Rd., Beck.
Upper Fm. Rd., 90 F4
  W.Mol.
Upper Fosters NW4 38 J5
  New Brent St.
Upper Grn. E., 93 J2
  Mitch.
Upper Grn. W., 93 J2
  Mitch.
Upper Grosvenor St. 11 B6
  W1

Upper Grosvenor St. W1	58	A7
Upper Grotto Rd., Twick.	82	C2
Upper Grd. SE1	**16**	**E1**
Upper Grd. SE1	67	G1
Upper Gro. SE25	95	B4
Upper Gro. Rd., Belv.	71	F6
Upper Gulland Wk. N1	49	J6
Marquess Est.		
Upper Ham Rd., Rich.	82	G4
Upper Handa Wk. N1	50	A6
Marquess Est.		
Upper Harley St. NW1	**7**	**C6**
Upper Harley St. NW1	58	A4
Upper Hawkwell Wk. N1	58	J1
Popham Rd.		
Upper Hitch, Wat.	28	E1
Upper Holly Hill Rd., Belv.	71	H5
Upper James St. W1	**11**	**G5**
Upper John St. W1	**11**	**G5**
Upper Lismore Wk. N1	49	J6
Marquess Est.		
Upper Mall W6	65	G5
Upper Marsh SE1	**16**	**D5**
Upper Marsh SE1	67	F2
Upper Montagu St. W1	**10**	**J1**
Upper Montagu St. W1	57	J5
Upper Mulgrave Rd., Sutt.	100	B7
Upper N. St. E14	60	A5
Upper Palace Rd., E.Mol.	90	J3
Upper Pk., Loug.	27	A4
Upper Pk. Rd. N11	32	B5
Upper Pk. Rd. NW3	48	J6
Upper Pk. Rd., Belv.	71	H4
Upper Pk. Rd., Brom.	96	H1
Upper Pk. Rd., Kings.T.	83	A6
Upper Phillimore Gdns. W8	66	D2
Upper Ramsey Wk. N1	50	A6
Marquess Est.		
Upper Rawreth Wk. N1	58	J1
Popham Rd.		
Upper Richmond Rd. SW15	74	F4
Upper Richmond Rd. W. SW14	74	D4
Upper Richmond Rd. W., Rich.	74	A4
Upper Rd. E13	60	G3
Upper Rd., Wall.	101	D5
Upper St. Martin's La. WC2	**12**	**A5**
Upper St. Martin's La. WC2	58	E7
Upper Selsdon Rd., S.Croy.	102	B7
Upper Sheppey Wk. N1	49	J7
Marquess Est.		
Upper Sheridan Rd., Belv.	71	G4
Coleman Rd.		
Upper Shirley Rd., Croy.	102	F2
Upper St. N1	49	H6
Upper Sunbury Rd., Hmptn.	90	E1
Upper Sutton La., Houns.	63	G7
Upper Tachbrook St. SW1	**19**	**G1**
Upper Tachbrook St. SW1	67	C4
Upper Tail, Wat.	28	E3
Upper Talbot Wk. W11	57	B6
Lancaster Rd.		
Upper Teddington Rd., Kings.T.	82	F7
Upper Ter. NW3	48	F3
Upper Thames St. EC4	**12**	**H5**
Upper Thames St. EC4	58	J7
Upper Tollington Pk. N4	40	G7

Upper Tooting Pk. SW17	84	J2
Upper Tooting Rd. SW17	84	J4
Upper Town Rd., Grnf.	54	H4
Upper Tulse Hill SW2	76	F7
Upper Vernon Rd., Sutt.	100	G5
Upper Walthamstow Rd. E17	42	D4
Upper Wickham La., Well.	80	B3
Upper Wimpole St. W1	**11**	**C1**
Upper Wimpole St. W1	58	A5
Upper Woburn Pl. WC1	**7**	**J4**
Upper Woburn Pl. WC1	58	D3
Upperton Rd., Sid.	88	J5
Upperton Rd. E. E13	60	J3
Inniskilling Rd.		
Upperton Rd. W. E13	60	J3
Uppingham Ave., Stan.	37	E1
Upsdell Ave. N13	32	G6
Upstall St. SE5	76	H1
Upton Ave. E7	51	G7
Upton Clo., Bex.	80	F6
Upton Dene, Sutt.	100	E7
Upton Gdns., Har.	37	E5
Upton La. E7	51	H6
Upton Pk. Rd. E7	51	H7
Upton Rd. N18	33	D5
Upton Rd. SE18	70	F6
Upton Rd., Bex.	80	F6
Upton Rd., Bexh.	80	E4
Upton Rd., Houns.	72	G3
Upton Rd., Th.Hth.	95	A2
Upton Rd., S., Bex.	80	F6
Upway N12	31	H7
Upwood Rd. SE12	78	G6
Upwood Rd. SW16	94	E1
Urlwin St. SE5	**20**	**J6**
Urlwin St. SE5	67	J6
Urlwin Wk. SW9	76	H1
Urmston Dr. SW19	84	B1
Ursula St. SW11	75	H1
Urswick Gdns., Dag.	53	E7
Urswick Rd.		
Urswick Rd. E9	50	F5
Urswick Rd., Dag.	53	D7
Usborne Ms. SW8	**20**	**D7**
Usborne Ms. SW8	67	F7
Usher Rd. E3	59	J2
Usk Rd. SW11	75	F4
Usk St. E2	59	G3
Utopia Village NW1	58	A1
Chalcot Rd.		
Uvedale Rd., Dag.	53	G3
Uvedale Rd., Enf.	25	A5
Uverdale Rd. SW10	66	F7
Uxbridge Gdns. Felt.	81	D2
Marlborough Rd.		
Uxbridge Rd. W3	65	A1
Uxbridge Rd. W5	55	J7
Uxbridge Rd. W7	64	C1
Uxbridge Rd. W12	65	G1
Uxbridge Rd. W13	64	E1
Uxbridge Rd., Felt.	81	C1
Uxbridge Rd., Hmptn.	81	G4
Uxbridge Rd., Har.	29	A7
Uxbridge Rd., Hayes	54	A6
Uxbridge Rd., Kings.T.	91	G4
Uxbridge Rd., Pnr.	36	C2
Uxbridge Rd., Sthl.	63	G1
Uxbridge Rd., Stan.	29	C6
Uxbridge St. W8	66	D1
Uxendon Cres., Wem.	46	H1
Uxendon Hill, Wem.	46	J1

V

Valan Leas, Brom.	96	E3
Valance Ave. E4	34	E1
Vale, The N10	40	A1
Vale, The N14	24	D7
Vale, The NW11	48	A3
Vale, The SW3	**18**	**E5**
Vale, The SW3	66	G6
Vale, The W3	65	D1
Vale, The, Croy.	102	G2
Vale, The, Felt.	72	B6
Vale, The, Houns.	63	E6
Vale, The, Ruis.	45	C4

Vale, The, Sun.	81	A6
Ashridge Way		
Vale, The, Wdf.Grn.	34	G7
Vale Ave., Borwd.	22	B5
Vale Clo. W9	**6**	**C4**
Vale Clo., Orp.	104	D4
Vale Ct. W9	**6**	**C4**
Vale Cres. SW15	83	E3
Vale Cft., Pnr.	36	E5
Vale Dr., Barn.	23	C4
Vale End SE22	77	B4
Grove Vale		
Vale Gro. N4	40	J7
Vale Gro. W3	65	D1
The Vale		
Vale La. W3	56	A5
Vale of Health NW3	48	G3
East Heath Rd.		
Vale Ri. NW11	48	C1
Vale Rd. E7	51	H6
Vale Rd. N4	40	J7
Vale Rd., Brom.	97	D2
Vale Rd., Epsom	99	F4
Vale Rd., Mitch.	94	D3
Vale Rd., Sutt.	100	E4
Vale Rd., Wor.Pk.	99	F3
Vale Rd. N., Surb.	98	H2
Vale Rd. S., Surb.	98	H2
Vale Row N5	49	H3
Gillespie Rd.		
Vale Royal N7	49	E7
Vale St. SE27	86	A3
Vale Ter. N4	40	J6
Valence Ave., Dag.	53	D1
Valence Circ., Dag.	53	D3
Valence Wd. Rd., Dag.	53	D3
Valencia Rd., Stan.	29	F4
Valentia Pl. SW9	76	G4
Brixton Sta. Rd.		
Valentine Ave., Bex.	89	E2
Valentine Ct. SE23	86	G2
Valentine Pl. SE1	**16**	**G3**
Valentine Pl. SE1	67	H2
Valentine Rd. E9	50	G6
Valentine Rd., Har.	45	J3
Valentine Row SE1	**16**	**G4**
Valentines Rd., Ilf.	52	E1
Valerian Way E15	60	E3
Valeswood Rd., Brom.	87	F5
Valetta Gro. E13	60	G2
Valetta Rd. W3	65	E2
Valette St. E9	50	E6
Valiant Clo., Nthlt.	54	D3
Ruislip Rd.		
Valiant Clo., Rom.	44	G2
Valiant Ho. SE7	69	J5
Valiant Way E6	61	C5
Vallance Rd. E1	**13**	**J1**
Vallance Rd. E1	59	D4
Vallance Rd. E2	**9**	**J5**
Vallance Rd. E2	59	D3
Vallance Rd. N22	40	C2
Vallentin Rd. E17	42	C4
Valley Ave. N12	31	G4
Valley Clo., Loug.	27	C6
Valley Clo., Pnr.	36	B2
Alandale Dr.		
Valley Dr. NW9	38	A6
Valley Flds. Cres., Enf.	24	G2
Valley Gdns. SW19	84	G7
Valley Gdns., Wem.	46	J7
Valley Gro. SE7	69	J5
Valley Hill, Loug.	27	B7
Valley Link Est., Enf.	25	H6
Valley Ms., Twick.	82	D2
Cross Deep		
Valley Rd. SW16	85	F5
Valley Rd., Belv.	71	H4
Valley Rd., Brom.	96	E2
Valley Side E4	34	A2
Valley Vw., Barn.	23	B6
Valley Wk., Croy.	102	F2
Valleyfield Rd. SW16	85	F5
Valliere Rd. NW10	56	G3
Valliers Wd. Rd., Sid.	88	G1
Vallis Way W13	55	D5
Vallis Way, Chess.	98	G4
Valmar Rd. SE5	76	H2
Valnay St. SW17	84	J5
Valognes Ave. E17	41	H1
Valonia Gdns. SW18	75	C6
Vambery Rd. SE18	70	F6
Van Dyck Ave., N.Mal.	92	D7

Vanbrough Cres., Nthlt.	54	C1
Vanbrugh Clo. E16	61	A5
Fulmer Rd.		
Vanbrugh Dr., Walt.	90	C7
Vanbrugh Flds. SE3	69	F6
Vanbrugh Hill SE3	69	F6
Vanbrugh Hill SE10	69	F6
Vanbrugh Pk. SE3	69	F7
Vanbrugh Pk. Rd. SE3	69	F7
Vanbrugh Pk. Rd. W. SE3	69	F7
Vanbrugh Rd. W4	65	D3
Vanbrugh Ter. SE3	78	F1
Vanburgh Clo., Orp.	104	H1
Vancouver Rd. SE23	86	H2
Vancouver Rd., Edg.	38	B1
Vancouver Rd., Hayes	54	B4
Vancouver Rd., Rich.	82	F4
Vanderbilt Rd. SW18	84	E1
Vandome Clo. E16	60	H6
Vandon Pas. SW1	**15**	**G5**
Vandon St. SW1	**15**	**G5**
Vandon St. SW1	67	C3
Vandy St. EC2	**9**	**D6**
Vandyke Clo. SW15	75	A6
Vandyke Cross SE9	79	B5
Vane Clo. NW3	48	G4
Vane Clo., Har.	37	J6
Vane St. SW1	**19**	**G1**
Vanessa Clo., Belv.	71	G5
Vanguard Clo., Croy.	101	H1
Vanguard Clo., Rom.	44	H2
Vanguard St. SE8	78	A1
Vanguard Way, Wall.	101	E7
Vanoc Gdns., Brom.	87	G4
Vansittart Rd. E7	51	F4
Vansittart St. SE14	68	H7
Vanston Pl. SW6	66	D7
Vant Rd. SW17	84	J5
Varcoe Rd. SE16	68	E5
Varden Clo. W3	56	D6
Varden St. E1	59	E6
Vardens Rd. SW11	75	G4
Vardon Clo. N3	39	B1
Claremont Pk.		
Varley Par. NW9	38	E4
Varley Rd. E16	60	H6
Varley Way, Mitch.	93	G2
Varna Rd. SW6	66	B7
Varna Rd., Hmptn.	90	H1
Varndell St. NW1	**7**	**F3**
Varndell St. NW1	58	C3
Vartry Rd. N15	41	A6
Vassall Rd. SW9	67	G7
Vauban Est. SE16	**17**	**G6**
Vauban Est. SE16	68	C3
Vauban St. SE16	**17**	**G6**
Vauban St. SE16	68	C3
Vaughan Ave. NW4	38	G5
Vaughan Ave. W6	65	F4
Vaughan Gdns., Ilf.	43	C7
Vaughan Rd. E15	51	F6
Vaughan Rd. SE5	76	J3
Vaughan Rd., Har.	36	J7
Vaughan Rd., T.Ditt.	91	E7
Vaughan Rd., Well.	79	J2
Vaughan Way E1	**13**	**H6**
Vaughan Way E1	59	D7
Vaughan Williams Clo. SE8	69	A7
Watson's St.		
Vauxhall Bri. SE1	**20**	**A4**
Vauxhall Bri. SE1	67	E5
Vauxhall Bri. SW1	**20**	**A4**
Vauxhall Bri. SW1	67	E5
Vauxhall Bri. Rd. SW1	**19**	**G1**
Vauxhall Bri. Rd. SW1	67	C3
Vauxhall Gdns., S.Croy.	101	J6
Vauxhall Gdns. Est. SE11	**20**	**D4**
Vauxhall Gdns. Est. SE11	67	F5
Vauxhall Gro. SW8	**20**	**B5**
Vauxhall Gro. SW8	67	F6
Vauxhall St. SE11	**20**	**D4**
Vauxhall St. SE11	67	F5
Vauxhall Wk. SE11	**20**	**C3**
Vauxhall Wk. SE11	67	F5
Vawdrey Clo. E1	59	F4
Veals Mead, Mitch.	93	H1
Vectis Gdns. SW17	85	B6
Vectis Rd.		
Vectis Rd. SW17	85	B6

Name	Page	Grid
Veda Rd. SE13	78	A4
Velde Way SE22	77	B5
East Dulwich Gro.		
Velletri Ho. E2	59	G2
Mace St.		
Vellicoe Rd. E13	60	G4
Jutland Rd.		
Vellum Dr., Cars.	101	A3
Venables Clo., Dag.	53	H4
Venables Ct. NW9	6	F6
Venables St. NW8	67	C1
Vencourt Pl. W6	65	G4
Venetia Rd. N4	40	H6
Venetia Rd. W5	64	G2
Venetian Rd. SE5	76	J2
Venn St. SW4	76	C4
Venner Rd. SE26	86	F6
Ventnor Ave., Stan.	37	E1
Ventnor Dr. N20	31	E3
Ventnor Gdns., Bark.	52	H6
Ventnor Rd. SE14	68	G7
Ventnor Rd., Sutt.	100	E7
Venture Clo., Bex.	80	E7
Venue St. E14	60	C5
Venus Rd. SE18	70	C3
Vera Ave. N21	24	G5
Vera Lynn Clo. E7	51	G4
Dames Rd.		
Vera Rd. SW6	75	B1
Verbena Gdns. W6	65	G5
Verdant La. SE6	87	E1
Verdayne Ave., Croy.	102	G1
Verdun Rd. SE18	71	A6
Verdun Rd. SW13	65	G6
Vere Rd., Loug.	27	F4
Vere St. W1	**11**	**D4**
Vere St. W1	58	B6
Vereker Dr., Sun.	90	A3
Vereker Rd. W14	66	B5
Verity Clo. W11	57	B6
Vermont Rd. SE19	86	A6
Vermont Rd. SW18	75	E6
Vermont Rd., Sutt.	100	E3
Verney Gdns., Dag.	53	E4
Verney Rd. SE16	**21**	**J5**
Verney Rd. SE16	68	D6
Verney Rd., Dag.	53	E4
Verney St. NW10	47	D3
Verney Way SE16	68	E5
Vernham Rd. SE18	70	F6
Vernon Ave. E12	52	C4
Vernon Ave. SW20	93	A2
Vernon Ave., Wdf.Grn.	34	H7
Vernon Clo., Epsom	99	C6
Vernon Ct., Stan.	37	E1
Vernon Dr.		
Vernon Cres., Barn.	24	A6
Vernon Dr., Stan.	37	D1
Vernon Ms. E17	41	J4
Vernon Rd.		
Vernon Ms. W14	66	B4
Vernon St.		
Vernon Pl. WC1	**12**	**B2**
Vernon Pl. WC1	58	E5
Vernon Ri. WC1	**8**	**D3**
Vernon Ri. WC1	58	F3
Vernon Ri., Grnf.	46	A5
Vernon Rd. E3	59	J2
Vernon Rd. E11	51	E1
Vernon Rd. E15	51	E7
Vernon Rd. E17	41	J4
Vernon Rd. N8	40	G3
Vernon Rd. SW14	74	D3
Vernon Rd., Ilf.	52	J1
Vernon Rd., Sutt.	100	F5
Vernon Sq. WC1	**8**	**D3**
Vernon St. W14	66	B4
Vernon Yd. W11	57	C7
Portobello Rd.		
Veroan Rd., Bexh.	80	E2
Verona Dr., Surb.	98	H2
Verona Rd. E7	51	G7
Upton La.		
Veronica Gdns. SW16	94	C1
Veronica Rd. SW17	85	B3
Veronique Gdns., Ilf.	43	F5
Verran Rd. SW12	76	B7
Balham Gro.		
Versailles Rd. SE20	86	D7
Verulam Ave. E17	41	J6
Verulam Bldgs. WC1	**12**	**D1**
Verulam Rd., Grnf.	54	G4
Verulam St. WC1	**12**	**E1**
Verwood Rd., Har.	36	J2
Vesey Path E14	60	B6
East India Dock Rd.		
Vespan Rd. W12	65	G2
Vesta Rd. SE4	77	H2
Vestris Rd. SE23	86	G2
Vestry Ms. SE5	77	B1
Vestry Rd. E17	42	B4
Vestry Rd. SE5	77	B1
Vestry St. N1	**9**	**B3**
Vestry St. N1	59	A3
Vevey St. SE6	86	J2
Veysey Gdns., Dag.	53	G3
Oglethorpe Rd.		
Viaduct, The E18	42	G2
Viaduct Pl. E2	59	E3
Viaduct St.		
Viaduct St. E2	59	E3
Vian St. SE13	78	B3
Vibart Gdns. SW2	76	F1
Vibart Wk. N1	58	E1
Outram Pl.		
Vicarage Ave. SE3	69	G7
Vicarage Clo., Erith	71	J6
Vicarage Clo., Nthlt.	54	F1
Vicarage Ct. W8	**14**	**A3**
Vicarage Cres. SW11	75	G1
Vicarage Dr. SW14	74	D5
Vicarage Dr., Bark.	52	F7
Vicarage Fm. Rd., Houns.	72	E2
Vicarage Flds., Walt.	90	C6
Vicarage Gdns. W8	66	D1
Vicarage Gate		
Vicarage Gdns., Mitch.	93	H3
Vicarage Gate W8	**14**	**A3**
Vicarage Gate W8	66	E1
Vicarage Gro. SE5	77	A1
Vicarage La. E6	61	C3
Vicarage La. E15	51	E7
Vicarage La., Chig.	35	F2
Vicarage La., Ilf.	52	G1
Vicarage Pk. SE18	70	F5
Vicarage Path N8	40	D7
Vicarage Rd. E10	42	A7
Vicarage Rd. E15	51	F7
Vicarage Rd. N17	33	D7
Vicarage Rd. NW4	38	G6
Vicarage Rd. SE18	70	F5
Vicarage Rd. SW14	74	D5
Vicarage Rd., Bex.	89	H1
Vicarage Rd., Croy.	101	G3
Vicarage Rd., Dag.	53	H7
Vicarage Rd., Kings.T.	91	G2
Vicarage Rd. (Hampton Wick), Kings.T.	91	F1
Vicarage Rd., Sutt.	100	E4
Vicarage Rd., Tedd.	82	D5
Vicarage Rd., Twick.	82	B2
Vicarage Rd. (Whitton), Twick.	72	J6
Vicarage Rd., Wdf.Grn.	35	B7
Vicarage Way NW10	47	D3
Vicarage Way, Har.	36	G7
Vicars Bri. Clo., Wem.	55	H2
Vicars Clo. E9	59	F1
Victoria Pk. Rd.		
Vicars Clo. E15	60	G1
Vicars Clo., Enf.	25	B2
Vicars Hill SE13	78	B4
Vicars Moor La. N21	24	G7
Vicars Oak Rd. SE19	86	B6
Vicars Rd. NW5	49	A5
Vicars Wk., Dag.	53	B3
Viceroy Clo. N2	39	H4
Market Pl.		
Viceroy Ct. NW8	6	H1
Viceroy Rd. SW8	76	E1
Vickers Way, Houns.	72	E5
Victor Gro., Wem.	46	H7
Victor Rd. NW10	56	H2
Victor Rd. SE20	86	G7
Victor Rd., Har.	36	J3
Victor Rd., Tedd.	82	B4
Victor Vill. N9	33	A3
Victoria Ave. E6	61	A1
Victoria Ave. EC2	**13**	**E2**
Victoria Ave. N3	39	C1
Victoria Ave., Barn.	23	G4
Victoria Rd.		
Victoria Ave., Houns.	72	F5
Victoria Ave., Surb.	91	G6
Victoria Ave., Wall.	101	A3
Victoria Ave., Wem.	47	B6
Victoria Ave., W.Mol.	90	G3
Victoria Clo., Barn.	23	G4
Victoria Clo., W.Mol.	90	G3
Victoria Ave.		
Victoria Cotts., Rich.	73	J1
Victoria Ct., Wem.	17	A8
Victoria Cres. N15	41	B5
Victoria Cres. SE19	86	B6
Victoria Cres. SW19	84	C7
Victoria Dock Rd. E16	60	G7
Victoria Dr. SW19	75	B7
Victoria Embk. EC4	**12**	**E5**
Victoria Embk. EC4	58	G7
Victoria Embk. SW1	**16**	**B3**
Victoria Embk. SW1	67	E2
Victoria Embk. WC2	**12**	**D6**
Victoria Embk. WC2	58	F7
Victoria Gdns. W11	66	D1
Victoria Gdns., Houns.	72	E1
Victoria Gro. N12	31	G5
Victoria Gro. W8	**14**	**C5**
Victoria Gro. W8	66	F3
Victoria Ind. Est. NW10	56	E3
Victoria La., Barn.	23	C4
Victoria Ms. NW6	57	D1
Victoria Ms. SW4	76	B4
Victoria Ri.		
Victoria Pk. E9	59	H1
Victoria Pk. Rd. E9	59	F1
Victoria Pk. Sq. E2	59	F3
Victoria Pas. NW8	**6**	**E5**
Victoria Pl., Rich.	73	G5
Victoria Pt. E13	60	G2
Victoria Rd.		
Victoria Ri. SW4	76	B3
Victoria Rd. E4	34	E1
Victoria Rd. E11	51	E4
High Rd. Leytonstone		
Victoria Rd. E13	60	G2
Victoria Rd. E17	42	C2
Victoria Rd. E18	42	H2
Victoria Rd. N4	40	F7
Victoria Rd. N9	33	C3
Victoria Rd. N15	41	D4
Victoria Rd. N18	33	C4
Victoria Rd. N22	40	C1
Victoria Rd. NW4	38	J4
Victoria Rd. NW6	57	C2
Victoria Rd. NW7	30	F5
Victoria Rd. NW10	56	E4
Victoria Rd. SW14	74	D3
Victoria Rd. W3	56	D5
Victoria Rd. W5	55	E5
Victoria Rd. W8	**14**	**C4**
Victoria Rd. W8	66	F2
Victoria Rd., Bark.	52	E6
Victoria Rd., Barn.	23	G4
Victoria Rd., Bexh.	80	G4
Victoria Rd., Brom.	97	A5
Victoria Rd., Buck.H.	35	A2
Victoria Rd., Chis.	88	D5
Victoria Rd., Dag.	53	H5
Victoria Rd., Felt.	81	B1
Victoria Rd., Kings.T.	91	J2
Victoria Rd., Mitch.	84	H7
Victoria Rd., Ruis.	45	A1
Victoria Rd., Sid.	88	J3
Victoria Rd., Sthl.	63	F3
Victoria Rd., Surb.	91	G6
Victoria Rd., Sutt.	100	G5
Victoria Rd., Tedd.	82	D6
Victoria Rd., Twick.	73	E7
Victoria Rd. (Bushey), Wat.	28	H1
Victoria Sq. SW1	**15**	**E5**
Victoria Sta. SW1	**19**	**E1**
Victoria Sta. SW1	67	B4
Victoria Steps, Brent.	64	J6
Kew Bri. Rd.		
Victoria St. E15	51	E7
Victoria St. SW1	**15**	**F6**
Victoria St. SW1	67	C3
Victoria St., Barn.	71	F5
Victoria Ter. N4	49	G1
Victoria Ter., Har.	46	B1
Victoria Vill., Rich.	73	J3
Victoria Way SE7	69	H5
Victorian Gro. N16	50	H4
Victorian Rd. N16	50	B3
Victors Dr., Hmptn.	81	E6
Victors Way, Barn.	23	C3
Victory Ave., Mord.	93	F5
Victory Business Cen., Islw.	73	C4
Victory Pl. SE17	**21**	**A1**
Victory Pl. SE17	67	J4
Victory Pl. SE19	86	B6
Westow St.		
Victory Rd. SW19	84	F7
Victory Wk. SE8	78	A1
Ship St.		
Victory Way SE16	68	H2
Victory Way, Houns.	63	C5
Victory Way, Rom.	44	H2
Vienna Clo., Ilf.	43	B2
Coburg Gdns.		
View, The SE2	71	E5
View Clo. N6	39	J7
View Clo., Chig.	35	G5
View Clo., Har.	37	A4
View Rd. N6	39	J7
Viewfield Clo., Har.	37	H7
Viewfield Rd. SW18	75	C6
Viewfield Rd., Bex.	89	C1
Viewland Rd. SE18	70	J5
Viga Rd. N21	24	G6
Vigilant Clo. SE26	86	D4
Vignoles Rd., Rom.	44	G7
Vigo St. W1	**11**	**F6**
Vigo St. W1	58	C7
Viking Clo. E3	59	H2
Selwyn Rd.		
Viking Ct. SW6	66	D6
Viking Rd., Sthl.	54	E7
Viking Way, Belv.	71	J3
Villa Rd. SW9	76	G3
Villa St. SE17	**21**	**C4**
Villa St. SE17	68	A5
Villacourt Rd. SE18	71	A7
Village, The SE7	69	J6
Village Arc. E4	34	D1
Station Rd.		
Village Clo. E4	34	C5
Village Heights, Wdf.Grn.	34	F5
Village Ms. NW9	47	D2
Village Rd. N3	39	B7
Village Rd., Enf.	25	A7
Village Row, Sutt.	100	D7
Village Way NW10	47	D4
Village Way SE21	77	A6
Village Way, Beck.	96	A3
Village Way, Pnr.	36	E7
Village Way E., Har.	36	G7
Villas Rd. SE18	70	F4
Villiers Ave., Surb.	91	J5
Villiers Ave., Twick.	81	F1
Villiers Clo. E10	51	A2
Villiers Clo., Surb.	91	J4
Villiers Ct. N20	23	F7
Buckingham Ave.		
Villiers Path, Surb.	91	H5
Villiers Rd. NW2	47	G6
Villiers Rd., Beck.	95	G2
Villiers Rd., Islw.	73	B2
Villiers Rd., Kings.T.	91	J4
Villiers Rd., Sthl.	63	F1
Villiers St. WC2	**16**	**B1**
Villiers St. WC2	67	E1
Vincam Clo., Twick.	72	G7
Vince St. EC1	**9**	**C4**
Vince St. EC1	59	A3
Vincent Ave., Surb.	99	B1
Vincent Clo. SE16	68	H2
Vincent Clo., Barn.	23	E3
Vincent Clo., Brom.	96	H4
Vincent Clo., Ilf.	35	F6
Vincent Clo., Sid.	88	H1
Vincent Gdns. NW2	47	F3
Vincent Rd. E4	34	D6
Vincent Rd. N15	40	J4
Vincent Rd. N22	40	G2
Vincent Rd. SE18	70	E4
Vincent Rd. W3	65	C3
Vincent Rd., Croy.	95	B7
Vincent Rd., Dag.	53	E7
Vincent Rd., Houns.	72	D2
Vincent Rd., Islw.	73	A1
Vincent Rd., Kings.T.	92	A3
Vincent Rd., Wem.	46	J7
Vincent Row, Hmptn.	81	J6
Vincent Sq. SW1	**19**	**H1**
Vincent Sq. SW1	67	C4
Vincent St. E16	60	F5
Vincent St. SW1	**19**	**H1**
Vincent St. SW1	67	D4
Vincent Ter. N1	**8**	**G1**

Vincent Ter. N1	58	H2
Vine Clo., Surb.	91	J6
Vine Clo., Sutt.	100	F3
Vine Ct. E1	**13**	**J2**
Vine Ct., Har.	37	H6
Vine Gdns., Ilf.	52	F5
Vine Hill EC1	**8**	**E6**
Vine La. SE1	**17**	**E2**
Vine Pl. W5	64	H1
The Common		
Vine Pl., Houns.	72	H4
Vine Rd. E15	51	F7
Vine Rd. SW13	74	F3
Vine Rd., E.Mol.	90	J4
Vine Rd., Orp.	104	J6
Vine Sq. W14	66	C5
Vine St. EC3	**13**	**F4**
Vine St. W1	**11**	**G6**
Vine St., Rom.	44	J4
Vine St. Bri. EC1	**8**	**F6**
Vine St. Bri. EC1	58	G4
Vine Yd. SE1	**17**	**A4**
Vinegar All. E17	42	B4
Vinegar St. E1	68	E1
Reardon Path		
Vinegar Yd. SE1	**17**	**D3**
Viner Clo., Walt.	90	C6
Vineries, The N14	24	C5
Vineries, The, Enf.	25	B3
Vineries Bank NW7	30	H5
Vineries Clo., Dag.	53	G6
Heathway		
Vines Ave. N3	39	E1
Viney Rd. SE13	78	B3
Vineyard, The,	73	H5
Rich.		
Vineyard Ave. NW7	31	B7
Vineyard Clo. SE6	87	A1
Vineyard Hill Rd.	84	C4
SW19		
Vineyard Pas., Rich.	73	H5
Paradise Rd.		
Vineyard Path SW14	74	D3
Vineyard Rd., Felt.	81	A3
Vineyard Row,	91	F1
Kings.T.		
Vineyard Wk. EC1	**8**	**E5**
Vining St. SW9	76	G4
Vintners Pl. EC4	**13**	**A5**
Viola Ave. SE2	71	B4
Viola Ave., Felt.	72	C6
Viola Sq. W12	56	F7
Violet Clo., Wall.	101	A1
Violet Gdns., Croy.	101	H5
Violet Hill NW8	**6**	**C2**
Violet Hill NW8	57	F2
Violet La., Croy.	101	H6
Violet Rd. E3	60	B4
Violet Rd. E17	42	A6
Violet Rd. E18	42	H2
Violet St. E2	59	E4
Three Colts La.		
Virgil Pl. W1	**10**	**J2**
Virgil St. SE1	**16**	**D5**
Virgil St. SE1	67	F3
Virginia Gdns., Ilf.	92	C4
N.Mal.		
Willow Rd.		
Virginia Rd. E2	**9**	**F4**
Virginia Rd. E2	59	C3
Virginia Rd.,	94	H1
Th.Hth.		
Virginia St. E1	**13**	**J6**
Virginia St. E1	59	D7
Virginia Wk. SW2	76	F6
Beechdale Rd.		
Viscount Dr. E6	61	C5
Viscount Gro.,	54	D3
Nthlt.		
Wayfarer Rd.		
Viscount St. EC1	**12**	**J1**
Vista, The SE9	79	A6
Vista, The, Sid.	88	J5
Langdon Shaw		
Vista Ave., Enf.	25	G2
Vista Dr., Ilf.	43	A5
Vista Way, Har.	37	H6
Vivian Ave. NW4	38	G5
Vivian Ave., Wem.	47	A5
Vivian Clo., Wat.	28	A1
Vivian Gdns., Wat.	28	A1
Vivian Gdns., Wem.	47	A5
Vivian Rd. E3	59	H2
Vivian Sq. SE15	77	E3
Scylla Rd.		
Vivian Way N2	39	G5
Vivien Clo., Chess.	98	H7
Vivienne Clo.,	73	G6
Twick.		
Voce Rd. SE18	70	G7
Voewood Clo.,	92	F6
N.Mal.		
Volta Way, Croy.	101	F1
Voltaire Rd. SW4	76	D3
Voluntary Pl. E11	42	G6
Vorley Rd. N19	49	C2
Voss Ct. SW16	85	E6
Voss St. E2	**9**	**J4**
Voss St. E2	59	D3
Vulcan Clo., Wall.	101	F7
De Havilland Rd.		
Vulcan Gate, Enf.	24	G3
Vulcan Rd. SE4	77	J2
Vulcan Ter. SE4	77	J2
Vulcan Way N7	49	F6
Vyne, The, Bexh.	80	H3
Vyner Rd. W3	56	D7
Vyner St. E2	59	E1
Vyse Clo., Barn.	22	J4

W

Wadding St. SE17	**21**	**B2**
Wadding St. SE17	68	A4
Waddington Rd. E15	51	D5
Waddington St. E15	51	D6
Waddington Way	85	J7
SE19		
Waddon Clo., Croy.	101	G3
Waddon Ct. Rd.,	101	G4
Croy.		
Waddon Marsh Way,	101	F1
Croy.		
Waddon New Rd.,	101	H3
Croy.		
Waddon Pk. Ave.,	101	G3
Croy.		
Waddon Rd., Croy.	101	G3
Waddon Way, Croy.	101	G6
Wade Rd. E16	60	J6
Leyes Rd.		
Wades Gro. N21	24	G7
Wades Hill N21	24	G6
Wades La., Tedd.	82	D5
High St.		
Wades Ms. N21	24	G7
Wades Hill		
Wades Pl. E14	60	B7
Wadeson St. E2	59	E2
Wadeville Ave.,	44	F6
Rom.		
Wadeville Clo.,	71	G5
Belv.		
Wadham Ave. E17	34	B7
Wadham Gdns. NW3	48	H7
Wadham Gdns., Grnf.	46	A7
Wadham Rd. E17	42	B1
Wadham Rd. SW15	78	F6
Wadhurst Clo. SE20	95	E2
Wadhurst Rd. SW8	76	C1
Wadhurst Rd. W4	65	D3
Wadley Rd. E11	42	E7
Wadsworth Clo.,	25	G5
Enf.		
Falcon Rd.		
Wadsworth Clo.,	55	F2
Grnf.		
Wadsworth Rd.,	55	E2
Grnf.		
Wager St. E3	59	J4
Waghorn Rd. E13	60	J1
Waghorn Rd., Har.	37	G3
Waghorn St. SE15	77	D3
Wagner St. SE15	68	F7
Wagtail Clo. NW9	38	E2
Swan Dr.		
Waights Ct.,	91	H1
Kings.T.		
Wainfleet Ave.,	44	J2
Rom.		
Wainford Clo. SW19	84	A1
Windlesham Gro.		
Wainwright Gro.,	73	A4
Islw.		
Waite Davies Rd.	78	F7
SE12		
Waite St. SE15	**21**	**F5**
Waite St. SE15	68	C6
Waithman St. EC4	**12**	**G4**
SE19		
Wakefield Gdns.	86	B7
SE19		
Wakefield Gdns.,	43	B6
Ilf.		
Wakefield Ms. WC1	**8**	**B4**
Wakefield Rd. N11	32	D5
Wakefield Rd. N15	41	C5
Wakefield Rd.,	73	G5
Rich.		
Wakefield St. E6	61	A1
Wakefield St. N18	33	D5
Wakefield St. WC1	**8**	**B4**
Wakefield St. WC1	58	E3
Wakeham St. N1	50	A6
Wakehams Hill, Pnr.	36	F3
Wakehurst Rd. SW11	75	H5
Wakelin Rd. E15	60	E2
Wakeling Rd. W7	55	C5
Templeman Rd.		
Wakeling St. E14	59	H6
Wakeman Rd. NW10	56	J3
Wakemans Hill Ave.	38	D5
NW9		
Wakering Rd., Bark.	52	F6
Wakerley Clo. E6	61	C6
Truesdale Rd.		
Wakley St. EC1	**8**	**G3**
Wakley St. EC1	58	H3
Walberswick St. SW8	67	E7
Walbrook EC4	**13**	**B5**
Walbrook EC4	59	A7
Walbrook Ho. N9	33	F2
Walburgh St. E1	59	E6
Bigland St.		
Walcorde Ave. SE17	21	A2
Walcot Rd., Enf.	25	J2
Walcot Sq. SE11	**20**	**F1**
Walcot Sq. SE11	67	G4
Walcott St. SW1	**19**	**G1**
Waldeck Gro. SE27	85	H3
Waldeck Rd. N15	40	H4
Waldeck Rd. SW14	74	C3
Lwr. Richmond Rd.		
Waldeck Rd. W4	65	A6
Waldeck Rd. W13	55	E6
Waldegrave Ave.,	82	C5
Tedd.		
Waldegrave Rd.		
Waldegrave Gdns.,	82	C2
Twick.		
Waldegrave Pk.,	82	C4
Twick.		
Waldegrave Rd. N8	40	G3
Waldegrave Rd.	86	C7
SE19		
Waldegrave Rd. W5	55	J7
Waldegrave Rd.,	97	B4
Brom.		
Waldegrave Rd.,	53	C2
Dag.		
Waldegrave Rd.,	82	C4
Tedd.		
Waldegrave Rd.,	82	C4
Twick.		
Waldegrove, Croy.	102	C3
Waldemar Ave. SW6	75	B7
Waldemar Ave. W13	64	F1
Waldemar Rd. SW19	84	D5
Walden Ave. N13	32	J4
Walden Ave., Chis.	88	C4
Walden Clo., Belv.	71	F5
Walden Gdns.,	94	F4
Th.Hth.		
Walden Rd. N17	41	A1
Walden Rd., Chis.	88	C6
Walden St. E1	59	E6
Walden Way NW7	31	A6
Walden Way, Ilf.	35	H7
Waldenshaw Rd.	86	F1
SE23		
Waldo Clo. SW4	76	C5
Waldo Pl., Mitch.	84	H7
Waldo Rd. NW10	56	G3
Waldo Rd., Brom.	97	A3
Waldram Cres. SE23	86	F1
Waldram Pk. Rd.	86	G1
SE23		
Waldram Pl. SE23	86	F1
Waldrist Way, Erith	71	F2
Waldron Gdns.,	96	D3
Brom.		
Waldron Ms. SW3	**18**	**F5**
Waldron Rd. SW18	84	F3
Waldron Rd., Har.	46	B1
Waldronhyrst,	101	H4
S.Croy.		
Waldrons, The,	101	H4
Croy.		
Waleran Clo., Stan.	29	C6
Chenduit Way		
Walerand Rd. SE13	78	C2
Wales Ave., Cars.	100	H5
Wales Fm. Rd. W3	56	D5
Waley St. E1	59	H5
Walfield Ave. N20	23	E7
Walford Rd. N16	50	B4
Walfrey Gdns., Dag.	53	E7
Walham Gro. SW6	66	D7
Walham Ri. SW19	84	B6
Walham Yd. SW6	66	D7
Walham Gro.		
Walkden Rd., Chis.	88	D5
Walker Clo. N11	32	C4
Walker Clo. SE18	70	F4
Walker Clo. W7	64	B1
Walker Clo., Hmptn.	81	F6
Fearnley Cres.		
Walkers Ct. E8	50	D6
Wilton Way		
Walkers Ct. W1	**11**	**H5**
Walkers Pl. SW15	75	B3
Felsham Rd.		
Walkerscroft Mead	85	J1
SE21		
Walkford Way SE15	68	C7
Daniel Gdns.		
Walks, The N2	39	G3
Wall End Rd. E6	52	D7
Wall St. N1	50	A6
Wallace Clo. SE28	62	D7
Haldane Rd.		
Wallace Cres.,	100	J5
Cars.		
Wallace Rd. N1	49	J6
Wallbutton Rd. SE4	77	H2
Wallcote Ave. NW2	48	A1
Waller Dr., Nthwd.	36	A2
Waller Rd. SE14	77	G1
Wallers Clo., Dag.	62	E1
Wallers Clo.,	35	C6
Wdf.Grn.		
Waller's Hoppit,	27	B2
Loug.		
Wallflower St. W12	56	F7
Wallgrave Rd. SW5	**18**	**A1**
Wallgrave Rd. SW5	66	E4
Wallingford Ave.	57	A5
W10		
Wallington Rd.,	43	J7
Ilf.		
Wallis All. SE1	**17**	**A4**
Wallis Clo. SW11	75	G3
Wallis Rd. E9	50	J6
Wallis Rd., Sthl.	54	H6
Walliss Cotts. SW2	76	E7
Wallorton Gdns.	74	D4
SW14		
Wallwood Rd. E11	51	D1
Wallwood St. E14	59	J5
Walm La. NW2	47	J6
Walmar Clo., Barn.	23	G1
Walmer Clo. E4	34	B2
Walmer Clo., Rom.	44	H2
Walmer Gdns. W13	64	D2
Walmer Ho. N9	33	C1
Walmer Pl. W1	**10**	**J1**
Walmer Rd. W10	57	B7
Walmer Rd. W11	57	B7
Walmer St. W1	**10**	**J1**
Walmer Ter. SE18	70	F4
Walmgate Rd., Grnf.	55	E1
Walmington Fold	31	D6
N12		
Walney Wk. N1	49	J6
Clephane Rd.		
Walnut Clo. SE8	68	J6
Clyde St.		
Walnut Clo., Cars.	100	J5
Walnut Clo., Ilf.	43	F4
Civic Way		
Walnut Ct. W5	64	H2
Walnut Gdns. E15	51	E4
Burgess Rd.		
Walnut Gro., Enf.	25	A5
Walnut Ms., Sutt.	100	F7
Walnut Tree Ave ,	93	H3
Mitch.		
Dearn Gdns.		
Walnut Tree Clo.	74	F1
SW13		
Walnut Tree Clo.,	97	F1
Chis.		
Walnut Tree Rd.	69	E5
SE10		
Walnut Tree Rd.	64	H6
Brent.		
Walnut Tree Rd.,	53	D2
Dag.		
Walnut Tree Rd.,	63	F6
Houns.		
Walnut Tree Wk.	**20**	**E1**
SE11		
Walnut Tree Wk.	67	G4
SE11		
Walnut Way, Buck.H.	35	A3
Walnut Way, Ruis.	45	C6
Walpole Ave., Rich.	73	J2
Walpole Clo. W13	64	F2
Walpole Clo., Pnr.	28	G6
Walpole Cres.,	82	C5
Tedd.		
Walpole Gdns. W4	65	C5
Walpole Gdns.,	82	B2
Twick.		
Walpole Pk. W5	64	F1
Walpole Pl., Tedd.	82	C5
Walpole Rd. E6	51	J7
Walpole Rd. E17	41	H4
Walpole Rd. E18	42	F1
Walpole Rd. N17	40	J3
Walpole Rd. N17	40	J2
Walpole Rd. SW19	84	G6

Walpole Rd., Brom. 97 A5
Walpole Rd., Croy. 102 A2
Walpole Rd., Surb. 91 H7
Walpole Rd., Tedd. 82 C5
Walpole Rd., Twick. 82 B2
Walpole St. SW3 18 J3
Walpole St. SW3 66 J5
Wal... ... .
Walsham Clo. N16 41 D7
  Braydon Rd.
Walsham Clo. SE28 82 D7
Walsham Rd. SE14 77 G2
Walsham Rd., Felt. 72 B7
Walsingham Gdns., 99 E4
  Epsom
Walsingham Pk., 97 G2
  Chis.
Walsingham Rd. E5 50 D3
Walsingham Rd. 64 D1
  W13
Walsingham Rd., 25 A4
  Enf.
Walsingham Rd., 93 J6
  Mitch.
Walsingham Wk., 71 G6
  Belv.
Walter St. E2 59 G3
Walter St., Kings.T. 91 H1
  Sopwith Way
Walter Ter. E1 59 G6
Walter Wk., Edg. 30 C6
Walters Ho. SE17 20 G6
Walters Rd. SE25 95 B4
Walters Way SE23 77 G6
Walters Yd., Brom. 96 G2
Walterton Rd. W9 57 C4
Waltham Ave. NW9 38 A6
Waltham Dr., Edg. 38 A2
Waltham Pk. Way 42 A1
  E17
Waltham Rd., Cars. 93 G7
Waltham Rd., Sthl. 63 E3
Waltham Rd., 35 B6
  Wdf.Grn.
Waltham Way E4 33 J4
Walthamstow Ave. 33 H5
  E4
Walthamstow 42 C2
  Business Cen. E17
Waltheof Ave. N17 41 A1
Waltheof Gdns. N17 41 A1
Walton Ave., Har. 45 F5
Walton Ave., N.Mal. 92 F4
Walton Ave., Sutt. 100 B3
Walton Clo. E5 50 G3
  Orient Way
Walton Clo. NW2 47 H2
Walton Clo. SW8 20 B7
Walton Clo. SW8 67 E7
Walton Clo., Har. 37 A4
Walton Cres., Har. 45 F4
Walton Dr. NW10 47 D6
  Mitchellbrook Way
Walton Dr., Har. 37 A4
Walton Gdns. W3 56 B5
Walton Gdns., Wem. 46 H2
Walton Pl. SW3 14 J5
Walton Pl. SW3 66 J3
Walton Rd. E12 52 D4
Walton Rd. E13 60 J2
Walton Rd. N15 41 C4
Walton Rd., E.Mol. 90 E4
Walton Rd., Har. 37 A4
Walton Rd., Sid. 89 C2
Walton Rd., Walt. 90 C5
Walton Rd., W.Mol. 90 E4
Walton St. SW3 18 H1
Walton St. SW3 66 H4
Walton St., Enf. 25 A1
Walton Way W3 56 B5
Walton Way, Mitch. 94 C4
Walworth Pl. SE17 21 A4
Walworth Pl. SE17 67 J5
Walworth Rd. SE1 20 J2
Walworth Rd. SE1 67 H3
Walworth Rd. SE17 20 J2
Walworth Rd. SE17 67 J4
Walwyn Ave., Brom. 97 A3
Wanborough Dr. 83 H1
  SW15
Wandle Bank SW19 84 G7
Wandle Bank, Croy. 101 E3
Wandle Ct., Epsom 99 C4
Wandle Ct. Gdns., 101 E3
  Croy.
Wandle Rd. SW17 84 H2
Wandle Rd., Croy. 101 J3
Wandle Rd. 101 E3
  (Waddon), Croy.
Wandle Rd., Mord. 93 F4
Wandle Rd., Wall. 101 B2
Wandle Side, Croy. 101 F3

Wandle Side, Wall. 101 B3
Wandle Way SW18 84 E1
Wandle Way, Mitch. 93 J5
Wandon Rd. SW6 66 E7
Wandsworth Bri. 75 E3
  SW6
Wandsworth Bri. 75 E3
  SW18
Wandsworth Bri. Rd. 75 E1
  SW6
Wandsworth 66 F3
  Business Cen., Grnf.
Wandsworth 75 J7
  Common SW12
Wandsworth 75 F5
  Common (North Side)
  SW18
Wandsworth 75 F5
  Common (West Side)
  SW18
Wandsworth High St. 75 D5
  SW18
Wandsworth Plain 75 D5
  SW18
Wandsworth Rd. 20 A5
  SW8
Wandsworth Rd. 76 B3
  SW8
Wangey Rd., Rom. 44 D7
Wanless Rd. SE24 76 J3
Wanley Rd. SE5 77 A4
Wanlip Rd. E13 60 H4
Wannock Gdns., Ilf. 35 E7
Wansbeck Rd. E9 50 J7
Wansdown Pl. SW6 18 A7
Wansey St. SE17 21 A2
Wansey St. SE17 67 J4
Wansford Pk., 22 D4
  Borwd.
Wansford Rd., 42 J1
  Wdf.Grn.
Wanstead Clo., 96 J2
  Brom.
Wanstead La., Ilf. 43 B6
Wanstead Pk. Ave. 52 A2
  E12
Wanstead Pk. Rd., 43 B6
  Ilf.
Wanstead Pl. E11 42 G6
Wanstead Rd., Brom. 96 J2
Wansunt Rd., Bex. 89 J1
Wantage Rd. SE12 78 F5
Wantz Rd., Dag. 53 H4
Wapping Dock St. E1 68 E1
  Cinnamon St.
Wapping High St. E1 17 J2
Wapping High St. E1 68 D1
Wapping La. E1 59 E7
Wapping Wall E1 68 F1
Warbank La., 83 F7
  Kings.T.
Warbeck Rd. W12 65 H2
Warberry Rd. N22 40 F2
Warboys App., 83 B6
  Kings.T.
Warboys Cres. E4 34 C5
Warboys Rd., 83 B6
  Kings.T.
Warburton Clo., 29 A6
  Har.
Warburton Rd. E8 59 E1
Warburton Rd., 81 H1
  Twick.
Warburton Ter. E17 42 B2
Ward Rd. E15 60 D1
Ward Rd. N19 49 C3
Wardalls Gro. SE14 68 F7
Wardell Clo. NW7 30 E7
Wardell Fld. NW9 38 E1
Warden Ave., Har. 45 F1
Warden Rd. NW5 49 A6
Wardens Gro. SE1 16 J2
Wardle St. E9 50 G5
Wardley St. SW18 75 E7
  Garratt La.
Wardo Ave. SW6 75 B1
Wardour Ms. W1 11 G4
Wardour St. W1 11 G3
Wardour St. W1 58 C6
Wardrobe Pl. EC4 12 H5
Wardrobe Ter. EC4 12 H5
Wards Rd., Ilf. 43 G7
Wareham Clo., 72 H4
  Houns.
Waremead Rd., Ilf. 43 E5
Warenford Way, 22 A1
  Borwd.
Warepoint Dr. SE28 70 G2
Warfield Rd. NW10 57 A3
Warfield Rd., 90 H1
  Hmptn.
Warfield Yd. NW10 57 A3
  Warfield Rd.

Wargrave Ave. N15 41 C6
Wargrave Rd., Har. 45 J3
Warham Rd. N4 40 G5
Warham Rd., Har. 37 C2
Warham Rd., 101 H5
  S.Croy.
Warham St. SE5 20 H7
Warham St. SE5 67 H7
Waring Clo., Orp. 104 J6
Waring Dr., Orp. 104 J6
Waring Rd., Sid. 89 C6
Waring St. SE27 85 J4
Warkworth Gdns., 64 D7
  Islw.
Warkworth Rd. N17 33 A7
Warland Rd. SE18 70 G7
Warley Ave., Dag. 44 F7
Warley Ave., Hayes 54 A6
Warley Rd. N9 33 F2
Warley Rd., Hayes 54 A6
Warley Rd., Ilf. 43 D1
Warley Rd., 34 H7
  Wdf.Grn.
Warley St. E2 59 G3
Warlingham Rd., 94 H4
  Th.Hth.
Warlock Rd. W9 57 C4
Warlters Clo. N7 49 E4
  Warlters Rd.
Warlters Rd., The 49 E4
  N7
Warltersville Rd. 40 E7
  N19
Warmington Clo. E5 50 G3
  Orient Way
Warmington Rd. 76 J6
  SE24
Warmington St. E13 60 G4
  Barking Rd.
Warminster Gdns. 95 D2
  SE25
Warminster Rd. 95 D3
  SE25
Warminster Way, 94 B1
  Mitch.
Warndon St. SE16 68 F4
Warneford Rd., Har. 37 G3
Warneford St. E9 59 E1
Warner Ave., Sutt. 100 B2
Warner Clo. E15 51 E5
Warner Clo. NW9 38 F7
Warner Pl. E2 9 J2
Warner Pl. E2 59 D2
Warner Rd. E17 41 H4
Warner Rd. N8 40 D4
Warner Rd. SE5 76 J1
Warner Rd., Brom. 87 F7
Warner St. EC1 8 E6
Warner St. EC1 58 G4
Warner Yd. EC1 8 E6
Warners Clo., 34 G5
  Wdf.Grn.
Warners La., 82 G5
  Kings.T.
Warners Path, 34 G5
  Wdf.Grn.
Warnford Rd., Orp. 104 J5
Warnham Ct. Rd., 100 J7
  Cars.
Warnham Rd. N12 31 G5
Warple Ms. W3 65 E2
Warple Way W3 65 E2
Warren, The E12 52 B4
Warren, The, Hayes 54 A6
Warren, The, Houns. 63 F7
Warren, The, 99 D4
  Wor.Pk.
Warren Ave. E10 51 C3
Warren Ave., Brom. 87 E7
Warren Ave., Orp. 104 J5
Warren Ave., Rich. 74 B4
Warren Ave., 102 G7
  S.Croy.
Warren Clo. N9 25 G7
Warren Clo. SE21 76 J7
  Lairdale Clo.
Warren Clo., Wem. 46 G2
Warren Ct., Chig. 35 G4
Warren Cres. N9 25 C7
Warren Cutting, 83 D7
  Kings.T.
Warren Dr., Grnf. 54 H4
Warren Dr., Ruis. 36 D7
Warren Dr., The E11 42 J7
Warren Dr. N., 99 B1
  Surb.
Warren Dr. S., 99 C1
  Surb.
Warren Flds., Stan. 29 F4
  Valencia Rd.
Warren Footpath, 82 F1
  Twick.

Warren Gdns. E15 51 D5
  Ashton Rd.
Warren Gro., Borwd. 22 D4
Warren Hill, Loug. 26 J5
Warren Ho. E3 60 B3
  Bromley High St.
Warren La. SE18 70 E3
Warren La., Stan. 29 C3
Warren Pk., 83 C6
  Kings.T.
Warren Pk. Rd., 100 G6
  Sutt.
Warren Pl. E1 59 G6
  Pitsea St.
Warren Pond Rd. E4 34 F1
Warren Ri., N.Mal. 92 D1
Warren Rd. E4 34 C2
Warren Rd. E10 51 C3
Warren Rd. E11 42 J6
Warren Rd. NW2 47 F2
Warren Rd. SW19 84 H6
Warren Rd., Bexh. 80 G5
Warren Rd., Brom. 103 G2
Warren Rd., Croy. 102 B1
Warren Rd., Ilf. 43 G5
Warren Rd., 83 C6
  Kings.T.
Warren Rd., Orp. 104 J5
Warren Rd., Sid. 89 C3
Warren Rd., Twick. 72 J6
Warren Rd. 28 J1
  (Bushey), Wat.
Warren St. W1 7 E6
Warren St. W1 58 C4
Warren Ter., Rom. 44 D4
Warren Way NW7 31 B6
Warren Wk. SE7 69 J6
Warrender Rd. N19 49 C3
Warrender Way, 36 A7
  Ruis.
Warrens Shawe La., 30 B2
  Edg.
Warriner Gdns. 75 J1
  SW11
Warrington Cres. W9 6 C6
Warrington Cres. W9 57 F4
Warrington Gdns. W9 6 C6
Warrington Pl. E14 69 C1
  Yabsley St.
Warrington Rd., 101 H3
  Croy.
Warrington Rd., 53 D2
  Dag.
Warrington Rd., 37 B5
  Har.
Warrington Rd., 73 G5
  Rich.
Warrington Sq., 53 D2
  Dag.
Warrington St. E13 60 G4
  Doherty Rd.
Warrior Sq. E12 52 D4
Warsaw Clo., Ruis. 45 B6
  Glebe Ave.
Warsdale Dr. NW9 38 D5
  Mardale Dr.
Warspite Rd. SE18 70 A3
Warton Rd. E15 51 C7
Warwall E6 61 E6
Warwick Ave. W2 10 D1
Warwick Ave. W2 57 F5
Warwick Ave. W9 6 B6
Warwick Ave. W9 57 E4
Warwick Ave., Edg. 30 B3
Warwick Ave., Har. 45 F4
Warwick Clo., Barn. 23 G5
Warwick Clo., Bex. 80 F7
Warwick Clo., 81 J7
  Hmptn.
Warwick Ct. SE15 77 D2
Warwick Ct. WC1 12 D2
Warwick Ct. WC1 10 C1
Warwick Cres. W2 57 F5
Warwick Dene W5 64 H1
Warwick Dr. SW15 74 H3
Warwick Est. W2 10 B2
Warwick Est. W2 57 E5
Warwick Gdns. N4 40 J5
Warwick Gdns. W14 66 C3
Warwick Gdns., Ilf. 52 E1
Warwick Gdns., 91 C5
  T.Ditt.
Warwick Gro. E5 50 E1
Warwick Gro., Surb. 91 J7
Warwick Ho. St. SW1 1 J1
Warwick La. EC4 12 H4
Warwick La. EC4 58 H6
Warwick Pl. W5 64 G2
  Warwick Rd.
Warwick Pl. W9 10 C1
Warwick Pl. W9 57 F5

Warwick Pl. N. SW1 19 F2
Warwick Pl. N. SW1 67 C4
Warwick Rd. E4 34 A5
Warwick Rd. E11 42 H5
Warwick Rd. E12 52 B5
Warwick Rd. E15 51 F6
Warwick Rd. E17 41 J1
Warwick Rd. N11 32 D6
Warwick Rd. N18 33 B4
Warwick Rd. SE20 95 E3
Warwick Rd. SW5 66 D5
Warwick Rd. W5 64 G2
Warwick Rd. W14 66 C4
Warwick Rd., Barn. 23 E4
Warwick Rd., Borwd. 22 D3
Warwick Rd., Houns. 72 B3
Warwick Rd., Kings.T. 91 F1
Warwick Rd., N.Mal. 92 C3
Warwick Rd., Sid. 89 B5
Warwick Rd., Sthl. 63 F3
Warwick Rd., Sutt. 100 F4
Warwick Rd., T.Ditt. 91 C5
Warwick Rd., Th.Hth. 94 G3
Warwick Rd., Twick. 82 B1
Warwick Rd., Well. 80 C3
Warwick Row SW1 15 E5
Warwick Row SW1 67 B3
Warwick Sq. EC4 12 H3
Warwick Sq. SW1 19 F3
Warwick Sq. SW1 67 C5
Warwick Sq. Ms. SW1 19 H2
Warwick St. W1 11 G5
Warwick St. W1 67 C4
Warwick Ter. SE18 70 G6
Warwick Way SW1 19 E3
Warwick Way SW1 67 B5
Warwick Yd. EC1 9 A6
Warwickshire Path SE8 68 J7
Washington Ave. E12 52 B4
Washington Rd. E6 51 J7
St. Stephens Rd.
Washington Rd. E18 42 F2
Washington Rd. SW13 65 G7
Washington Rd., Kings.T. 92 A2
Washington Rd., Wor.Pk. 99 H2
Wastail Clo. NW9 38 E2
Swan Dr.
Wastdale Rd. SE23 86 G1
Wat Tyler Rd. SE3 78 D2
Wat Tyler Rd. SE10 78 C2
Watchfield Ct. W4 65 C5
Watcombe Cotts., Rich. 65 A6
Watcombe Pl. SE25 95 E5
Albert Rd.
Watcombe Rd. SE25 95 E5
Water Gdns., Stan. 29 E6
Water La. E15 51 E6
Water La. NW1 49 B7
Kentish Town Rd
Water La. SE14 68 F7
Water La., Ilf. 52 H3
Water La., Kings.T. 91 G1
Water La., Rich. 73 G5
Water La., Sid. 89 F3
Water La., Twick. 82 D1
Water Rd., Wem. 55 J1
Water St. WC2 12 D5
Water Twr. Hill, Croy. 102 A4
Waterbank Rd. SE6 87 B3
Waterbeach Rd., Dag. 53 C6
Waterbrook La. NW4 38 J5
Watercress Pl. N1 50 B7
Hertford Rd.
Waterdale Rd. SE2 71 A4
Waterden Rd. E15 51 A5
Waterer Ri., Wall. 101 D6
Waterfall Clo. N14 32 C3
Waterfall Cotts. SE19 84 G5
Waterfall Rd. N11 32 B4
Waterfall Rd. N14 32 C3
Waterfall Rd. SW19 84 G6
Waterfall Ter. SW17 84 H4
Waterfield Clo. SE28 71 B1
Waterfield Clo., Belv. 71 G3
Waterfield Gdns. SE25 95 A4
Waterford Rd. SW6 66 E7
Watergardens, The, Kings.T. 83 C6

Watergate EC4 12 G5
Watergate, Wat. 28 D2
Watergate St. SE8 69 A6
Watergate Wk. WC2 12 B6
Waterhall Ave. E4 34 E4
Waterhall Clo. E17 41 G1
Waterhouse Clo. E16 61 A5
Waterhouse Clo. NW3 48 G5
Lyndhurst Rd.
Waterhouse Clo. W6 66 A4
Great Ch. La.
Waterloo Bri. SE1 12 C6
Waterloo Bri. SE1 67 E4
Waterloo Bri. WC2 12 C6
Waterloo Bri. WC2 58 F7
Waterloo Clo. E9 50 F5
Churchill Wk.
Waterloo Est. E2 59 F2
Waterloo Gdns. E2 59 F2
Waterloo Pas. NW6 48 C7
Waterloo Pl. SW1 15 H1
Waterloo Pl. SW1 67 D1
Waterloo Rd. E6 51 J7
Waterloo Rd. E10 42 A7
Waterloo Rd. NW2 47 G1
Waterloo Rd. SE1 16 E3
Waterloo Rd. SE1 67 G1
Waterloo Rd., Ilf. 43 F2
Waterloo Rd., Sutt. 100 G5
Waterloo Ter. N1 49 H7
Waterlow Ct. NW11 39 E7
Heath Clo.
Waterlow Rd. N19 49 C1
Waterman St. SW15 75 A3
Waterman Way E1 68 E1
Waterman's Clo., Kings.T. 82 H7
Woodside Rd.
Watermans Wk. SE16 68 H1
Redriff Rd.
Watermead Rd. SE6 87 B4
Watermead Way N17 41 D3
Watermen's Clo. SE20 86 F7
Watermill Clo., Rich. 82 F3
Watermill La. N18 33 B5
Watermill Way SW19 93 F1
Watermill Way, Felt. 81 F2
Watermint Quay N16 41 D6
Waters Gdns., Dag. 53 G5
Sterry Rd.
Waters Rd. SE6 87 E3
Waters Rd., Kings.T. 92 B2
Waters Sq., Kings.T. 92 B3
Watersedge, Epsom 99 C4
Watersfield Way, Edg. 29 G7
Waterside Clo. SE16 17 J4
Waterside Clo., Bark. 53 A4
Waterside Clo., Nthlt. 54 F3
Waterside Clo., Surb. 98 H2
Culsac Rd.
Waterside Dr., Walt. 90 A5
Waterside Pl. NW1 58 A1
Princess Rd.
Waterside Pt. SW11 66 H7
Waterside Rd., Sthl. 63 G3
Waterside Way SW17 84 F4
Watersmeet Way SE28 62 C6
Waterson St. E2 9 E3
Waterson St. E2 59 B3
Watersplash Clo., Kings.T. 91 H3
Watersplash La., Hayes 63 A4
North Hyde Rd.
Watersplash La., Houns. 63 B5
Waterview Ho. E14 59 H5
Carr St.
Waterworks La. E5 50 G2
Waterworks Rd. SW2 76 F6
Waterworks Yd., Croy. 101 J3
Surrey St.
Watery La. SW20 93 C2
Watery La., Nthlt. 54 C2
Watery La., Sid. 89 B6
Wates Way, Mitch. 93 J6
Wateville Rd. N17 40 J1

Watford Clo. SW11 75 H1
Petworth St.
Watford Rd. E16 60 G5
Watford Rd., Har. 37 D7
Watford Rd., Wem. 46 D2
Watford Way NW4 38 G4
Watford Way NW7 30 E4
Watkin Rd., Wem. 47 B3
Watkinson Rd. N7 49 F6
Watling Ave., Edg. 38 C1
Watling Ct. EC4 13 A4
Watling Gdns. NW2 48 B6
Watling St. EC4 12 J4
Watling St. EC4 58 J6
Watling St., Bexh. 80 H4
Watlings, The, Croy. 95 H6
Watlington Gro. SE26 86 H5
Watney Mkt. E1 59 E6
Commercial Rd.
Watney Rd. SW14 74 C3
Watney St. E1 59 E6
Watneys Rd., Mitch. 94 D5
Watson Ave. E6 52 D7
Watson Ave., Sutt. 100 B3
Watson Clo. N16 50 A5
Matthias Rd.
Watson Clo. SW19 84 H6
Watson St. E13 60 H2
Watsons Ms. W1 10 H2
Watsons Rd. N22 40 F1
Watson's St. SE8 69 A7
Watsons Yd. NW2 47 F2
North Circular Rd.
Wattisfield Rd. E5 50 F3
Watts Gro. E3 60 B5
Watts La., Chis. 97 E1
Watts La., Tedd. 82 D5
Watts Rd., T.Ditt. 91 D7
Watts St. E1 68 E1
Watts Way SW7 14 F5
Wauthier Clo. N13 32 H5
Wavel Ms. N8 40 D4
Wavel Ms. NW6 48 E7
Acol Rd.
Wavel Pl. SE26 86 C4
Sydenham Hill
Wavell Dr., Sid. 79 H6
Wavendon Ave. W4 65 D5
Waveney Ave. SE15 77 E4
Waveney Clo. E1 17 J1
Waverley Ave. E4 33 J4
Waverley Ave. E17 42 D3
Waverley Ave., Surb. 92 B6
Waverley Ave., Sutt. 100 E2
Waverley Ave., Twick. 81 F1
Waverley Ave., Wem. 46 J5
Waverley Clo. E18 42 J1
Waverley Clo., Brom. 97 A5
Waverley Cres. SE18 70 G6
Waverley Gdns. E6 61 B5
Oliver Gdns.
Waverley Gdns. NW10 55 J2
Waverley Gdns., Bark. 61 H2
Waverley Gdns., Ilf. 43 F2
Waverley Gdns., Nthwd. 36 A1
Waverley Gro. N3 39 A3
Waverley Ind. Pk., Har. 37 A3
Waverley Pl. N4 49 H2
Adolphus Rd.
Waverley Pl. NW8 6 E1
Waverley Rd. E17 42 C3
Waverley Rd. E18 42 J1
Waverley Rd. N8 40 E6
Waverley Rd. N17 33 E7
Waverley Rd. SE18 70 F5
Waverley Rd. SE25 95 E4
Waverley Rd., Enf. 24 H4
Waverley Rd., Epsom 99 G6
Waverley Rd., Har. 45 E1
Waverley Rd., Sthl. 54 G7
Waverley Vill. N17 41 C2
Waverley Wk. W2 57 D5
Waverley Way, Cars. 100 H6
Waverton Ho. E3 59 J1
Waverton Rd. SW18 75 F7
Waverton St. W1 15 D1
Waverton St. W1 67 A1
Wavertree Ct. SW2 85 F1
Streatham Hill

Wavertree Rd. E18 42 G2
Wavertree Rd. SW2 85 E1
Waxlow Cres., Sthl. 54 G6
Waxlow Rd. NW10 56 C2
Waxwell Clo., Pnr. 36 D2
Waxwell La., Pnr. 36 D2
Waye Ave., Houns. 72 A1
Wayfarer Rd., Nthlt. 54 D3
Wayfield Link SE9 79 G6
Wayford St. SW11 75 H2
Wayland Ave. E8 50 D5
Waylands Mead, Beck. 96 B1
Wayleave, The SE28 62 B7
Oriole Way
Waylett Pl. SE27 85 H3
Waylett Pl., Wem. 46 G3
Wayman Ct. E8 50 E6
Wayne Clo., Orp. 104 J3
Waynflete Ave., Croy. 101 H3
Waynflete Sq. W10 57 A6
Waynflete St. SW18 84 F2
Wayside NW11 48 B1
Wayside SW14 74 C5
Wayside Clo. N14 24 C6
Wayside Commercial Est., Bark. 62 A2
Wayside Ct., Twick. 73 F6
Wayside Ct., Wem. 47 A3
Oakington Ave.
Wayside Gdns. SE9 88 C4
Wayside Gro.
Wayside Gdns., Dag. 53 G5
Wayside Gro. SE9 88 C4
Wayside Ms., Ilf. 43 D5
Gaysham Ave.
Weald, The, Chis. 88 C6
Weald Clo. SE16 68 E5
Stevenson Cres.
Weald Clo., Brom. 104 B2
Weald La., Har. 37 A2
Weald Ri., Har. 29 C7
Weald Sq. E5 50 E2
Rossington St.
Weald Way, Rom. 44 H6
Wealdstone Rd., Sutt. 100 C2
Wealdwood Gdns., Pnr. 28 H6
Highbanks Rd.
Weale Rd. E4 34 D3
Wear Pl. E2 59 E3
Weardale Gdns., Enf. 25 A1
Weardale Rd. SE13 78 D4
Wearside Rd. SE13 78 B5
Weatherley Clo. E3 59 J5
Weaver St. E1 9 H6
Weaver St. E1 59 D4
Weaver Wk. SE27 85 J4
Weavers Clo., Islw. 73 B4
Weavers Ter. SW6 66 D6
Micklethwaite Rd.
Weavers Way NW1 49 D7
Webb Est. E5 41 B7
Webb Gdns. E13 60 G4
Kelland Rd.
Webb Pl. NW10 56 F3
Old Oak La.
Webb Rd. SE3 69 F6
Webb St. SE1 17 D6
Webb St. SE1 68 B3
Webber Row SE1 16 F4
Webber Row SE1 67 G2
Webber St. SE1 16 G4
Webber St. SE1 67 G2
Webbs Rd. SW11 75 J4
Webbs Rd., Hayes 54 B3
Webbscroft Rd., Dag. 53 G5
Webster Gdns. W5 64 G1
Webster Rd. E11 51 C3
Webster Rd. SE16 17 J6
Webster Rd. SE16 68 D3
Wedderburn Rd. NW3 48 B1
Wedderburn Rd., Bark. 61 G1
Wedgewood Wk. NW6 48 E5
Lymington Rd.
Wedgewood Way SE19 85 J7
Wedgwood Ms. W1 11 J4
Wedlake St. W10 57 B4
Kensal Rd.
Wedmore Ave., Ilf. 43 D1
Wedmore Gdns. N19 49 D2
Wedmore Ms. N19 49 D3
Wedmore St.
Wedmore Rd., Grnf. 55 A3

Wedmore St. N19 49 D3
Weech Rd. NW6 48 D4
Weedington Rd. 49 A5
NW5
Weekley Sq. SW11 75 G3
Thomas Baines Rd.
Weinall Rd. SE12 78 G4
Weighouse St. W1 11 C4
Weighouse St. W1 58 A6
Weighton Rd. SE20 95 F2
Weighton Rd., Har. 37 A1
Weihurst Gdns., 100 G5
Sutt.
Weimar St. SW15 75 B3
Weir Est. SW12 76 C7
Weir Hall Ave. N18 33 A6
Weir Hall Rd. N17 33 A6
Weir Hall Rd. N18 33 A5
Weir Rd. SW12 76 C7
Weir Rd. SW19 84 E3
Weir Rd., Bex. 80 H7
Weir Rd., Walt. 90 A6
Weirdale Ave. N20 31 J2
Weir's Pas. NW1 7 J3
Weir's Pas. NW1 58 D3
Weiss Rd. SW15 75 A3
Welbeck Ave., Brom. 87 G4
Welbeck Ave., Hayes 54 B4
Welbeck Ave., Sid. 89 A1
Welbeck Clo. N12 31 G5
Torrington Pk.
Welbeck Clo., 11 D3
Borwd.
Welbeck Clo., Epsom 99 G7
Welbeck Clo., 92 F5
N.Mal.
Welbeck Rd. E6 61 A3
Welbeck Rd., Barn. 23 G6
Welbeck Rd., Cars. 100 H1
Welbeck Rd., Har. 45 H1
Welbeck Rd., Sutt. 100 G2
Welbeck St. W1 11 C2
Welbeck St. W1 58 A5
Welbeck Way W1 11 D3
Welbeck Way W1 58 B6
Welby St. SE5 76 H1
Weld Pl. N11 32 B5
Weldon Clo., Ruis. 45 B6
Weldon Dr., W.Mol. 90 F4
Welfare Rd. E15 51 E7
Welford Clo. E5 50 G3
Denton Way
Welford Pl. SW19 84 B4
Welham Rd. SW16 85 B6
Welham Rd. SW17 85 A5
Welhouse Rd., Cars. 100 H1
Well App., Barn. 22 J5
Well Clo. SW16 85 F4
Well Clo., Ruis. 45 E3
Parkfield Cres.
Well Cottage Clo. 42 J7
E11
Well Ct. EC4 13 A4
Well Ct. SW16 85 F4
Well Gro. N20 23 F7
Well Hall Rd. SE9 79 B3
Well La. SW14 74 C5
Well Pas. NW3 48 G3
Well Rd. NW3 48 G3
Well Rd., Barn. 22 J5
Well St. E9 50 F7
Well St. E15 51 E6
Well Wk. NW3 48 G4
Wellacre Rd., Har. 37 E6
Wellan Clo., Well. 80 B5
Welland Gdns., 55 C2
Grnf.
Welland Ms. E1 17 J1
Welland St. SE10 69 C6
Wellands Clo., 97 C2
Brom.
Wellbrook Rd., Orp. 104 D4
Wellclose Sq. E1 13 J5
Wellclose Sq. E1 59 D7
Wellclose St. E1 13 J6
Weldon Cres., Har. 37 B6
Weller St. SE1 16 J3
Wellers Ct. NW1 8 A2
Wellesley Ave. W6 65 H3
Wellesley Ct. W9 6 C3
Wellesley Ct. Rd., 102 A2
Croy.
Wellesley Cres., 82 B2
Twick.
Wellesley Gro., 102 A2
Croy.
Wellesley Pl. NW1 7 H4
Wellesley Rd. E11 42 G5
Wellesley Rd. E17 42 A5
Wellesley Rd. N22 40 G2
Wellesley Rd. NW5 49 A5
Wellesley Rd. W4 65 A5

Wedmore St. N19 49 D3
Wellesley Rd., 101 J1
Croy.
Wellesley Rd., Har. 37 B5
Wellesley Rd., Ilf. 52 E2
Wellesley Rd., 100 F6
Sutt.
Wellesley Rd., 82 A3
Twick.
Wellesley St. E1 59 G5
Wellesley Ter. N1 9 A3
Wellesley Ter. N1 58 J3
Wellfield Ave. N10 40 B3
Wellfield Rd. SW16 85 E4
Wellfield Wk. SW16 85 F5
Wellfields Rd., 27 D3
Loug.
Wellfit St. SE24 76 H3
Milkwood Rd.
Wellgarth, Grnf. 46 E6
Wellgarth Rd. NW11 48 E1
Wellhouse La., 22 J4
Barn.
Wellhouse Rd., 95 J4
Beck.
Welling High St., 80 A3
Well.
Welling Way SE9 79 G3
Welling Way, Well. 79 H3
Wellings Ho., Hayes 63 B1
Wellington Ave. E4 34 A2
Wellington Ave. N9 33 E3
Wellington Ave. N15 41 C6
Wellington Ave., 72 G5
Houns.
Wellington Ave., 36 F1
Pnr.
Wellington Ave., 80 A6
Sid.
Wellington Ave., 99 J3
Wor.Pk.
Wellington Bldgs. 19 C4
SW1
Wellington Clo. 77 G1
SE14
Wild Goose Dr.
Wellington Clo. W11 57 D6
Ledbury Rd.
Wellington Clo., 53 J7
Dag.
Wellington Ct. NW8 6 E2
Wellington Cres., 92 C3
N.Mal.
Wellington Dr., 53 J7
Dag.
Wellington Gdns. 69 J5
SE7
Wellington Gdns., 82 A4
Twick.
Wellington Ms. SE22 77 D4
Peckham Rye
Wellington Pk. Ind. 47 G1
Est. NW2
Wellington Pas. E11 42 G5
Wellington Rd.
Wellington Pl. N2 39 H5
Great N. Rd.
Wellington Pl. NW8 6 F3
Wellington Pl. NW8 57 G3
Wellington Rd. E6 61 C1
Wellington Rd. E7 51 F4
Wellington Rd. E10 50 H1
Wellington Rd. E11 42 G5
Wellington Rd. E17 41 H3
Wellington Rd. NW8 6 E1
Wellington Rd. NW8 57 G2
Wellington Rd. 57 A3
NW10
Wellington Rd. 84 D2
SW19
Wellington Rd. W5 64 F3
Wellington Rd., 71 F5
Belv.
Wellington Rd., 80 D5
Bex.
Wellington Rd., 96 J4
Brom.
Wellington Rd., 94 H7
Croy.
Wellington Rd., 25 B4
Enf.
Wellington Rd., 82 A5
Hmptn.
Wellington Rd., 37 B3
Har.
Wellington Rd., 28 F7
Pnr.
Wellington Rd., 82 A4
Twick.
Wellington Rd. N., 72 F3
Houns.
Wellington Rd. S., 72 F4
Houns.
Wellington Row E2 9 G3

Wellington Row E2 59 C3
Wellington Sq. SW3 18 J3
Wellington Sq. SW3 66 J5
Wellington St. SE18 70 D4
Wellington St. WC2 12 B5
Wellington St. WC2 58 E7
Wellington St., 61 F1
Buik.
Axe St.
Wellington Ter. E1 68 E1
Watermann Way
Wellington Ter., 46 A1
Har.
Wellington Way E3 60 A3
Wellmeadow Rd. SE6 78 E7
Wellmeadow Rd. 78 E6
SE13
Wellmeadow Rd. W7 64 D4
Wellow Wk., Cars. 100 G1
Whitland Rd.
Wells, The N14 24 D7
Yeading La.
Wells Dr. NW9 47 D1
Wells Gdns., Dag. 53 H5
Pondfield Rd.
Wells Gdns., Ilf. 43 B7
Wells Ho. Rd. NW10 56 E5
Wells Pk. Rd. SE26 86 D3
Wells Ri. NW8 57 J1
Wells Rd. W12 65 J2
Wells Rd., Brom. 97 C2
Wells Sq. WC1 8 C4
Wells St. W1 11 F2
Wells St. W1 58 C5
Wells Ter. N4 49 G2
Wells Way SE5 21 C5
Wells Way SE5 68 B6
Wells Way SW7 14 E5
Wells Way SW7 66 G3
Wells Yd. N7 49 G5
Holloway Rd.
Wellside Clo., 22 J4
Barn.
Wellsmoor Gdns., 97 D3
Brom.
Wellsprings Cres., 47 B3
Wem.
Wellstead Ave. N9 25 F7
Wellstead Rd. E6 61 D2
Wellwood Rd., Ilf. 53 A1
Welsford St. SE1 21 H3
Welsford St. SE1 68 D5
Welsh Clo. E13 60 G3
Welsh Side Wk. NW9 38 E6
Fryent Gro.
Welshpool Ho. E8 59 D1
Benjamin Clo.
Welshpool St. E8 59 E1
Broadway Mkt.
Weltje Rd. W6 65 G4
Welton Rd. SE18 70 H7
Welwyn St. E2 59 F3
Globe Rd.
Wembley 46 G2
Commercial Cen.,
Wem.
Wembley Hill Rd., 46 J5
Wem.
Wembley Pk. 47 B3
Business Cen., Wem.
Wembley Pk. Dr., 46 J4
Wem.
Wembley Rd., 81 G7
Hmptn.
Wembley Way, Wem. 47 B6
Wemborough Rd., 37 E1
Stan.
Wembury Rd. N6 40 B7
Wemyss Rd. SE3 78 F2
Wendela Ct., Har. 46 B3
Wendell Rd. W12 65 F3
Wendling Rd., Sutt. 100 G1
Wendon St. E3 59 J1
Wendover SE17 21 D3
Wendover Clo., 54 E4
Hayes
Kingsash Dr.
Wendover Dr., 92 F6
N.Mal.
Wendover Rd. NW10 56 F2
Wendover Rd. SE9 79 A3
Wendover Rd., 96 H3
Brom.
Wendover Way, Well. 80 A5
Wendy Clo., Enf. 25 C6
Wendy Way, Wem. 55 H1
Wenlock Ct. N1 9 C2
Wenlock Gdns. NW4 38 G4
Rickard Clo.
Wenlock Rd. N1 8 J2
Wenlock Rd. N1 58 J2

Wenlock Rd., Edg. 30 B7
Wenlock St. N1 9 A2
Wenlock St. N1 58 J2
Wennington Rd. E3 59 G2
Wensley Ave., 34 F7
Wdf.Grn.
Wensley Clo. SE9 79 C6
Wensley Rd. N18 33 F6
Wensleydale Ave., 43 B2
Ilf.
Wensleydale Gdns., 81 H7
Hmptn.
Wensleydale Pas., 90 G1
Hmptn.
Wensleydale Rd., 81 G6
Hmptn.
Wentland Clo. SE6 87 D2
Wentland Rd.
Wentland Rd. SE6 87 D2
Wentworth Ave. N3 31 D7
Wentworth Clo. N3 31 E7
Wentworth Clo., 93 D7
Mord.
Wentworth Clo., 104 H5
Orp.
Wentworth Clo., 98 G2
Surb.
Wentworth Cres. 68 D7
SE15
Wentworth Dr., Pnr. 36 A5
Wentworth Gdns. 32 H4
N13
Wentworth Hill, 46 J1
Wem.
Wentworth Ms. E3 59 J3
Eric St.
Wentworth Pk. N3 31 D7
Wentworth Pl., 29 E6
Stan.
Greenacres Dr.
Wentworth Rd. E12 52 A4
Wentworth Rd. NW11 39 C6
Wentworth Rd., 23 A3
Barn.
Wentworth Rd., 94 G7
Croy.
Wentworth Rd., 63 C4
Sthl.
Wentworth St. E1 13 F3
Wentworth St. E1 59 C6
Wentworth Way, Pnr. 36 D4
Wenvoe Ave., Bexh. 80 H2
Wernbrook St. SE18 70 F6
Werndee Rd. SE25 95 D4
Werneth Hall Rd., 43 C3
Ilf.
Werrington St. NW1 7 G2
Werrington St. NW1 58 C2
Werter Rd. SW15 75 B4
Wesley Ave. NW10 56 D3
Wesley Ave., Houns. 72 E2
Wesley Clo. N7 49 F2
Wesley Clo. SE17 20 H2
Wesley Clo., Har. 45 J2
Wesley Rd. E10 42 C7
Wesley Rd. NW10 56 C1
Hillside
Wesley Rd. SE17 20 H2
Wesley Rd., Hayes 54 A7
Wesley Sq. SW11 57 B6
Bartle Rd.
Wesley St. W1 11 C2
Wesleyan Pl. NW5 49 B4
Gordon Ho. Rd.
Wessex Ave. SW19 93 D2
Wessex Clo., Ilf. 43 H6
Wessex Clo., 92 B1
Kings.T.
Gloucester Rd.
Wessex Dr., Pnr. 28 E7
Wessex Gdns. NW11 48 B1
Wessex La., Grnf. 55 A2
Wessex St. E2 59 F3
Wessex Way NW11 48 B1
West App., Orp. 97 F6
West Arbour St. E1 59 F6
West Ave. E17 42 B4
West Ave. N3 31 D6
West Ave. NW4 39 A5
West Ave., Pnr. 36 F6
West Ave., Sthl. 54 F7
West Ave., Wall. 101 E5
West Ave. Rd. E17 42 A4
West Bank N16 41 B7
West Bank, Bark. 61 E1
Highbridge Rd.
West Bank, Enf. 24 J2
West Barnes La. 92 G5
SW20
West Barnes La., 92 H3
N.Mal.
West Carriage Dr. 10 G6
W2

West Carriage Dr. 57 G7
W2
West Cen. St. WC1 12 A3
West Chantry, Har. 36 H1
Chantry Rd.
West Clo. N9 33 C3
West Clo., Barn. 22 H5
West Clo. 24 A4
(Cockfosters), Barn.
West Clo., Grnf. 54 J2
West Clo., Wem. 46 J1
West Common Rd., 103 G2
Brom.
West Cotts. NW6 48 D5
West Ct. SE18 79 C1
Prince Imperial Rd.
West Ct., Wem. 46 F2
West Cromwell Rd. 66 C4
SW5
West Cromwell Rd. 66 C5
W14
West Cross Route 57 A7
W10
West Cross Route 66 A1
W11
West Cross Way, 64 E6
Brent.
West Dene, Sutt. 100 B6
Park La.
West Dr. SW16 85 C4
West Dr., Har. 29 A6
West Dr. Gdns., 29 A6
Har.
West Eaton Pl. SW1 19 B1
West Eaton Pl. SW1 67 A4
West Eaton Pl. Ms. 15 B6
SW1
West Ella Rd. NW10 47 E7
West End Ave. E10 42 D5
West End Ave., Pnr. 36 D4
West End Ct., Pnr. 36 D4
West End Gdns., 54 C2
Nthlt.
Edward Clo.
West End La. NW6 48 D5
West End La., Barn. 23 A4
West End La., Pnr. 36 D3
West End Rd., 45 C7
Nthlt.
West End Rd., Ruis. 45 A4
West End Rd., Sthl. 63 E1
West Gdns. E1 59 E7
West Gdns. SW17 84 H6
West Gate W5 55 H3
West Grn. Rd. N15 40 H4
West Gro. SE10 78 C1
West Gro., Wdf.Grn. 34 J6
West Halkin St. SW1 15 B5
West Halkin St. SW1 67 A3
West Hall Rd., 74 B1
Rich.
West Hallowes SE9 88 B1
West Ham La. E15 51 D7
West Ham Pk. E7 51 F7
West Hampstead Ms. 48 E6
NW6
West Harding St. 12 F3
EC4
West Heath Ave. 48 D1
NW11
West Heath Clo. NW3 48 D3
West Heath Dr. NW11 48 D1
West Heath Gdns. 48 D2
NW3
West Heath Rd. NW3 48 D2
West Heath Rd. SE2 71 C6
West Hendon Bdy. 38 F6
NW9
West Hill SW15 75 A7
West Hill SW18 75 A7
West Hill, Har. 46 B2
West Hill, Wem. 46 J1
West Hill Ct. N6 49 A3
West Hill Pk. N6 48 J2
Merton La.
West Hill Rd. SW18 75 C6
West Hill Way N20 31 E1
West Holme, Erith 80 J1
West Ho. Clo. SW19 84 B1
West India Ave. E14 69 A1
West India Dock Rd. 59 J6
E14
West Kentish Town 49 A6
Est. NW5
Warden Rd.
West La. SE16 68 E2
West Lo. Ave. W3 65 A1
West Mall W8 66 D1
Palace Gdns. Ter.
West Mead, Epsom 99 G6
West Mead, Ruis. 45 C4
West Ms. N17 33 E6
West Ms. SW1 19 F2

West Oak, Beck. 96 D1
West Pk. SE9 88 B2
West Pk. Ave., 74 A1
Rich.
West Pk. Clo., Rom. 44 D5
West Pk. Rd., Rich. 74 A1
West Pier E1 68 E1
Wapping High St.
West Pl. SW19 83 J5
West Poultry Ave. 12 G2
EC1
West Quarters W12 56 G6
Du Cane Rd.
West Quay Dr., 54 E5
Hayes
West Ridge Gdns., 54 J2
Grnf.
West Rd. E15 60 F1
West Rd. N17 33 E6
West Rd. SW3 19 A4
West Rd. SW3 66 J5
West Rd. SW4 76 D5
West Rd. W5 55 H5
West Rd., Barn. 24 A7
West Rd., Kings.T. 92 C1
West Rd., Rom. 44 D6
(Chadwell Heath)
West Row W10 57 B4
West Sheen Vale, 73 J4
Rich.
West Side Common 83 J6
SW19
West Smithfield EC1 12 G2
West Smithfield EC1 58 H5
West Sq. SE11 16 G6
West Sq. SE11 67 H3
West St. E2 59 E2
Clare St.
West St. E11 51 E3
West St. E17 42 B5
Grove Rd.
West St. WC2 11 J5
West St., Bexh. 80 F4
West St., Brent. 64 F6
West St., Brom. 96 G1
West St., Cars. 100 J3
West St., Croy. 101 J4
West St., Har. 46 A1
West St., Sutt. 100 E5
West St. La., Cars. 100 J4
West Temple Sheen 74 B4
SW14
West Tenter St. E1 13 G4
West Tenter St. E1 59 C6
West Twrs., Pnr. 36 D6
West Vw. NW4 38 J4
West Vw., Loug. 27 C4
West Wk. W5 55 H5
West Wk., Barn. 24 A7
West Wk., Hayes 63 A1
West Warwick Pl. 19 F2
SW1
West Warwick Pl. 67 C4
SW1
West Way N18 33 A4
West Way NW10 47 D4
West Way, Croy. 102 H2
West Way, Edg. 30 B6
West Way, Houns. 63 F7
West Way, Pnr. 36 D4
West Way, W.Wick. 96 D6
West Way Gdns., 102 G2
Croy.
West Woodside, Bex. 80 E7
West World W5 55 H3
Westacott Clo. N19 49 D1
Westall Rd., Loug. 27 E3
Westbank Rd., 81 J6
Hmptn.
Westbeech Rd. N22 40 G3
Westbere Dr., Stan. 29 G4
Westbere Rd. NW2 48 B4
Westbourne Ave. 56 D6
W3
Westbourne Ave., 100 B2
Sutt.
Westbourne Bri. W2 10 C2
Westbourne Bri. W2 57 F5
Westbourne Clo., 54 B7
Hayes
Westbourne Cres. 10 E5
W2
Westbourne Cres. 57 G7
W2
Westbourne Cres. 10 E5
Ms. W2
Westbourne Dr. 86 G2
SE23
Westbourne Gdns. 10 A3
W2
Westbourne Gdns. 57 E6
W2
Westbourne Gro. W2 57 D6

Westbourne Gro. 57 C7
W11
Westbourne Gro. Ms. 57 D6
W11
Westbourne Gro.
Westbourne Gro. 10 A4
Ter. W2
Westbourne Gro. 57 E6
Ter. W2
Westbourne Pk. Ms. 10 A3
W2
Westbourne Pk. Pas. 57 D5
W2
Westbourne Pk. Rd. 57 D5
W2
Westbourne Pk. Rd. 57 B6
W11
Westbourne Pk. 57 D5
Vill. W2
Westbourne Rd. N7 49 F6
Westbourne Rd. 86 G6
SE26
Westbourne Rd., 71 D7
Bexh.
Westbourne Rd., 95 C6
Croy.
Westbourne St. W2 10 E5
Westbourne St. W2 57 G7
Westbourne Ter. W2 10 C3
Westbourne Ter. W2 57 F6
Westbourne Ter. Ms. 10 C3
W2
Westbourne Ter. Ms. 57 F6
W2
Westbourne Ter. Rd. 10 C2
W2
Westbourne Ter. Rd. 57 F5
W2
Westbridge Rd. 75 G1
SW11
Westbrook Ave., 81 F7
Hmptn.
Westbrook Clo., 23 G3
Barn.
Westbrook Cres., 23 G3
Barn.
Westbrook Rd. SE3 78 H1
Westbrook Rd., 63 F7
Houns.
Westbrook Rd., 95 A1
Th.Hth.
Westbrook Sq., 23 G3
Barn.
Westbrooke Cres.
Westbrooke Cres., 80 C3
Well.
Westbrooke Rd., 88 G2
Sid.
Westbrooke Rd., 80 B3
Well.
Westbury Ave. N22 40 H3
Westbury Ave., 98 C6
Esher
Westbury Ave., 54 G4
Sthl.
Westbury Ave., Wem. 46 H7
Westbury Clo., 36 A7
Ruis.
Westbury Gro. N12 31 D6
Westbury La., 34 J2
Buck.H.
Westbury Lo. Clo., 36 D3
Pnr.
Westbury Ms. E17 42 A4
Westbury Rd.
Westbury Pl., Brent. 64 G6
Westbury Rd. E7 51 H5
Westbury Rd. E17 41 J4
Westbury Rd. N11 32 E6
Westbury Rd. N12 31 D6
Westbury Rd. SE20 95 G1
Westbury Rd. W5 55 H6
Westbury Rd., Bark. 61 G1
Westbury Rd., Beck. 95 H3
Westbury Rd., Brom. 97 A1
Westbury Rd., 34 J2
Buck.H.
Westbury Rd., Croy. 95 A6
Westbury Rd., Felt. 81 D1
Westbury Rd., Ilf. 52 D2
Westbury Rd., 92 D4
N.Mal.
Westbury Rd., Wem. 46 H7
Westbury St. SW8 76 C2
Westbury Ter. E7 51 H6
Westchester Dr. NW4 39 A3
Westcombe Ave., 94 E6
Croy.
Westcombe Ct. SE3 69 F7
Westcombe Pk. Rd.
Westcombe Dr., 23 D5
Barn.
Westcombe Hill SE3 69 G6

Westcombe Hill SE10 69 G5
Westcombe Pk. Rd. 69 E6
SE3
Westcombe Ave. 92 F1
SW20
Westcote Rd. SW16 85 C5
Westcott Clo. N15 41 C6
Ermine Rd.
Westcott Clo. 97 B5
Brom.
Ringmer Way
Westcott Cres. W7 55 B6
Westcott Rd. SE17 20 H5
Westcott Rd. SE17 67 H6
Westcourt, Sun. 90 B2
Westcroft Clo. NW2 48 B4
Westcroft Gdns., 93 C3
Mord.
Westcroft Rd., 101 A4
Cars.
Westcroft Rd., 101 A4
Wall.
Westcroft Sq. W6 65 G4
Westcroft Way NW2 48 B4
Westdale Pas. SE18 70 E6
Westdale Rd.
Westdale Rd. SE18 70 E6
Westdean Ave. SE12 87 H1
Westdean Clo. SW18 75 E5
Westdown Rd. E15 51 C4
Westdown Rd. SE6 78 A7
Westel Ho. W5 55 F7
Westerdale Rd. SE10 69 G5
Westerfield Rd. N15 41 C5
Westergate Rd. SE2 71 E6
Westerham Ave. N9 33 A3
Westerham Dr., Sid. 80 B6
Westerham Rd. E10 42 B6
Westerham Rd., 104 A7
Kes.
Westerley Cres. 86 J5
SE26
Western Ave. NW11 39 A6
Western Ave. W3 56 A4
Western Ave. W5 55 J4
Western Ave., Dag. 53 J6
Western Ave., Grnf. 55 B2
Western Ave., 54 F1
Nthlt.
Western Ave., Ruis. 54 E3
Western Ct. N3 31 D6
Huntley Dr.
Western Gdns. W5 56 A7
Western Gateway 60 G7
E16
Western Ho. W5 55 H3
Western La. SW12 76 A7
Western Ms. W9 57 C4
Great Western Rd.
Western Pl. SE16 68 F2
Canon Beck Rd.
Western Rd. E13 60 J1
Western Rd. E17 42 C5
Western Rd. N2 39 J4
Western Rd. N22 40 F2
Western Rd. NW10 56 C4
Western Rd. SW9 76 G3
Western Rd. SW19 93 G1
Western Rd. W5 55 G7
Western Rd., Mitch. 93 H1
Western Rd., Sthl. 63 C4
Western Rd., Sutt. 100 D5
Western Ter. W6 65 G5
Chiswick Mall
Western Trd. Est. 56 B4
NW10
Western Way SE28 70 G3
Western Way, Barn. 23 D6
Westernville Gdns., 43 F7
Ilf.
Westferry Circ. E14 69 A1
Westferry Rd. E14 69 A2
Westfield, Loug. 26 J3
Westfield Clo., 25 H3
Enf.
Westfield Clo., 100 C4
Sutt.
Westfield Dr., Har. 37 G4
Westfield Gdns., 37 G4
Har.
Westfield La., Har. 37 G4
Westfield Pk., Pnr. 28 F7
Westfield Rd. NW7 30 D3
Westfield Rd. W13 64 D1
Westfield Rd., 95 J2
Beck.
Westfield Rd., 80 J2
Bexh.
Westfield Rd., 101 H2
Croy.
Westfield Rd., Dag. 53 E4
Westfield Rd., 93 J2
Mitch.

Name	Page	Grid
Westfield Rd., Surb.	91	G5
Westfield Rd., Sutt.	100	C4
Westfield Rd., Walt.	90	E7
Westfield St. SE18	70	A3
Westfields SW13	74	F3
Westfields Ave. SW13	74	E3
Westfields Rd. W3	90	B0
Westgate Rd. SE25	95	E4
Westgate Rd., Beck.	96	C1
Westgate St. E8	59	E1
Westgate Ter. SW10	**18**	**B4**
Westgate Ter. SW10	66	E5
Westglade Ct., Har.	37	G5
Westgrove La. SE10	78	C1
Westhay Gdns. SW14	74	B5
Westholme NW11	39	E4
Westholme, Orp.	97	H7
Westholme Gdns., Ruis.	45	A1
Westhorne Ave. SE9	79	A5
Westhorne Ave. SE12	78	H6
Westhorpe Gdns. NW4	38	J3
Westhorpe Rd. SW15	74	J3
Westhurst Dr., Chis.	88	E5
Westlake Clo. N13	32	G3
Westlake Clo., Hayes	54	E4
Lochan Clo.		
Westland Dr., Brom.	103	F2
Westland Pl. N1	**9**	**B3**
Westland Pl. N1	59	A3
Westlands Clo., Hayes	63	A4
Granville Rd.		
Westlands Ter. SW12	76	C6
Gaskarth Rd.		
Westlea Rd. W7	64	D3
Westleigh Ave. SW15	74	H5
Westleigh Dr., Brom.	97	B1
Westleigh Gdns. Edg.	38	A1
Westmead SW15	74	H7
Westmead Rd., Sutt.	100	G4
Westmede, Chig.	35	F6
Westmere Dr. NW7	30	D3
Westmill Ct. N4	49	J2
Brownswood Rd.		
Westminster Ave., Th.Hth.	94	H2
Westminster Bri. SE1	**16**	**B4**
Westminster Bri. SE1	67	F2
Westminster Bri. SW1	**16**	**B4**
Westminster Bri. SW1	67	E2
Westminster Bri. Rd. SE1	**16**	**D4**
Westminster Bri. Rd. SE1	67	F2
Westminster Cathedral Piazza SW1	**15**	**F6**
Westminster Clo., Ilf.	43	G2
Westminster Clo., Tedd.	82	D5
Westminster Dr. N13	32	E5
Westminster Gdns. E4	34	E1
Westminster Gdns., Bark.	61	H2
Westminster Gdns., Ilf.	43	F2
Westminster Rd. N9	33	E1
Westminster Rd. W7	64	B1
Westminster Rd., Sutt.	100	G2
Westmoat Clo., Beck.	87	C7
Westmont Rd., Esher	98	B2
Westmoor Gdns. Enf.	25	G2
Westmoor Rd., Enf.	25	G2
Westmoor St. SE7	70	A3
Westmoreland Ave. Well.	79	H3
Westmoreland Pl. SW1	**19**	**E4**
Westmoreland Pl. SW1	67	B5
Westmoreland Pl. W5	55	G5
Mount Ave.		
Westmoreland Rd. NW9	37	J3
Westmoreland Rd. SE17	**21**	**B5**
Westmoreland Rd. SE17	68	A6
Westmoreland Rd. SW13	74	F1
Westmoreland Rd., Brom.	96	E5
Westmoreland St. W1	**11**	**H2**
Westmoreland St. W1	58	A5
Westmoreland Ter. SW1	**19**	**E4**
Westmoreland Ter. SW1	67	B5
Westmoreland Wk. SE17	**21**	**B5**
Westmorland Clo. E12	52	A2
Westmorland Clo., Twick.	73	E6
Westmorland Rd. E17	42	A6
Westmorland Rd., Har.	36	H5
Westmorland Way, Mitch.	94	D4
Westmount Rd. SE9	79	C2
Westoe Rd. N9	33	E2
Weston Ave., T.Ditt.	91	B7
Weston Ave., W.Mol.	90	E3
Weston Ct. N4	49	J3
Queens Dr.		
Weston Dr., Stan.	37	E1
Weston Gdns., Islw.	73	A1
Weston Grn., Dag.	53	F4
Weston Grn., T.Ditt.	98	B1
Weston Grn. Rd., Esher	98	A1
Weston Grn. Rd., T.Ditt.	98	B1
Weston Gro., Brom.	87	F7
Weston Pk. N8	40	E6
Weston Pk., Kings.T.	91	H2
Fairfield W.		
Weston Pk., T.Ditt.	98	B1
Weston Pk. Clo., T.Ditt.	98	B1
Weston Pk.		
Weston Ri. WC1	**8**	**D2**
Weston Ri. WC1	58	F3
Weston Rd. W4	65	C3
Weston Rd., Brom.	87	F7
Weston Rd., Dag.	53	E4
Weston Rd., Enf.	25	A1
Weston Rd., T.Ditt.	98	B1
Weston St. SE1	**17**	**C3**
Weston St. SE1	68	A2
Weston Wk. E8	50	E7
Mare St.		
Westover Hill NW3	48	D2
Westover Rd. SW18	75	F7
Westow Hill SE19	86	B6
Westow St. SE19	86	B6
Westpoint Trd. Est. W3	56	A4
Westpole Ave., Barn.	24	A4
Westport Rd. E13	60	H4
Westport St. E1	59	G6
Westrow SW15	74	J6
Westrow Dr., Bark.	53	A5
Westrow Gdns., Ilf.	52	J2
Westside NW4	38	H2
Westview Clo. NW10	47	F5
Westview Clo. W7	55	B6
Westview Cres. N9	25	B7
Westview Dr., Wdf.Grn.	43	A2
Westville Rd. W12	65	G2
Westville Rd., T.Ditt.	98	D1
Westward Rd. E4	33	H5
Westward Way, Har.	37	H6
Westway NW7	30	G7
Westway SW20	92	H3
Westway W9	57	D5
Westway W10	57	D5
Westway W12	56	B6
Westway, Orp.	97	G5
Westway Clo. SW20	92	H3
Westways, Epsom	99	F4
Westwell Rd. SW16	85	E6
Westwick Gdns. W14	66	A2
Westwick Gdns., Houns.	72	B2
Westwood Ave. SE19	94	J1
Westwood Ave., Har.	45	H4
Westwood Clo. Brom.	97	A3
Westwood Gdns. SW13	74	F3
Westwood Hill SE26	86	D5
Westwood La., Sid.	80	A5
Westwood La., Well.	79	J3
Westwood Pk. SE23	77	E7
Westwood Rd. E16	69	H1
Westwood Rd. SW13	74	F3
Westwood Rd., Ilf.	52	J1
Wetherall Dr., Stan.	37	F1
Wetherby Clo., Nthlt.	45	H6
Wetherby Gdns. SW5	**18**	**C2**
Wetherby Gdns. SW5	66	F4
Wetherby Ms. SW5	**18**	**B3**
Wetherby Pl. SW7	**18**	**C2**
Wetherby Pl. SW7	66	F4
Wetherby Rd., Enf.	24	J1
Wetherby Way, Chess.	98	H7
Wetherden St. E17	41	J7
Wetherell Rd. E9	59	G1
Wetherill Rd. N10	40	A1
Wexford Rd. SW12	75	J7
Wey Ct., Epsom	99	C4
Weybourne St. SW18	84	F2
Weybridge Pt. SW11	75	J2
Weybridge Rd., Th.Hth.	94	G4
Weydown Clo. SW19	84	B1
Weyhill Rd. E1	**13**	**J3**
Weylond Rd., Dag.	53	E3
Weyman Rd. SE3	78	J1
Weymouth Ave. NW7	30	E5
Weymouth Ave. W5	64	F3
Weymouth Ct., Sutt.	100	D7
Weymouth Ms. W1	**11**	**D1**
Weymouth Ms. W1	58	B5
Weymouth St. W1	**11**	**C2**
Weymouth St. W1	58	A5
Weymouth Ter. E2	**9**	**G1**
Weymouth Ter. E2	59	C2
Weymouth Wk. Stan.	29	D6
Whadcote St. N4	49	G2
Seven Sisters Rd.		
Whalebone Ave., Rom.	44	F6
Whalebone Ct. EC2	**13**	**C3**
Whalebone Gro., Rom.	44	F6
Whalebone La. E15	51	E7
West Ham La.		
Whalebone La. N., Rom.	44	E2
Whalebone La. S., Dag.	44	F7
Whalebone La. S., Rom.	44	F6
Wharf La., Twick.	82	D1
Wharf Pl. E2	59	D1
Wharf Rd. E15	60	D1
Wharf Rd. N1	**8**	**J2**
Wharf Rd. N1	58	J2
Wharf Rd., Enf.	25	H6
Wharf Rd. Ind. Est., Enf.	25	H6
Wharf St. E16	60	E5
Wharfdale Ct. E5	50	G4
Rushmore Rd.		
Wharfdale Rd. N1	**8**	**B1**
Wharfdale Rd. N1	58	E2
Wharfedale St. SW10	**18**	**A4**
Wharfside Rd. E16	60	E5
Wharncliffe Dr., Sthl.	64	A1
Wharncliffe Gdns. SE25	95	B2
Wharncliffe Rd. SE25	95	B2
Wharton Clo. NW10	47	E6
Wharton Rd., Brom.	96	H1
Wharton St. WC1	**8**	**D4**
Wharton St. WC1	58	F3
Whateley Rd. SE20	86	G7
Whateley Rd. SE22	77	C5
Whatley Ave. SW20	93	A3
Whatman Rd. SE23	77	G7
Wheatfield Way, Kings.T.	91	H2
Wheatfields, Enf.	25	H2
Wheathill Rd. SE20	95	E2
Wheatlands, Houns.	63	G6
Wheatlands Rd. SW17	85	A3
Stapleton Rd.		
Wheatley Clo. NW4	38	G2
Wheatley Cres., Hayes	54	A7
Wheatley Gdns. N9	33	B2
Wheatley Rd., Islw.	73	C3
Wheatley St. W1	**11**	**C2**
Wheatsheaf Clo., Nthlt.	45	E5
Wheatsheaf La. SW6	65	J7
Wheatsheaf La. SW8	**20**	**A7**
Wheatsheaf La. SW8	67	E7
Wheatsheaf Ter. SW6	66	G7
Bishops Rd.		
Wheatstone Clo., Mitch.	93	H1
Wheatstone Rd. W10	57	B6
Portobello Rd.		
Wheel Fm. Dr., Dag.	53	J3
Wheeler Gdns. N1	58	E1
Outram Pl.		
Wheelers Cross, Bark.	61	G2
Wheelwright St. N7	49	F7
Whelan Way, Wall.	101	D3
Wheler St. E1	**9**	**F6**
Wheler St. E1	59	C4
Whellock Rd. W4	65	E3
Whenman Ave., Bex.	89	J2
Whernside Clo. SE28	62	C7
Whetstone Clo. N20	31	G2
Oakleigh Rd.		
Whetstone Pk. WC2	**12**	**C3**
Whetstone Rd. SE3	78	J2
Whewell Rd. N19	49	E2
Whichcote St. SE1	**16**	**C2**
Whidborne Clo. SE8	78	A2
Cliff Ter.		
Whidborne St. WC1	**8**	**B4**
Whidborne St. WC1	58	E3
Whimbrel Clo. SE28	62	C7
Whinchat Rd. SE28	70	G3
Whinfell Clo. SW16	85	D5
Whinyates Rd. SE9	79	B3
Whipps Cross Rd. E11	42	D5
Whiskin St. EC1	**8**	**G4**
Whiskin St. EC1	58	H3
Whisperwood Clo., Har.	29	B7
Whistler Gdns., Edg.	37	J2
Whistler St. N5	49	H5
Whistler Wk. SW10	**18**	**D7**
Whistlers Ave. SW11	66	G7
Whiston Rd. E2	59	C2
Whitakers Way, Loug.	27	C1
Whitbread Clo. N17	41	D1
Whitbread Rd. SE4	77	H4
Whitburn Rd. SE13	78	B4
Whitby Ave. NW10	56	B3
Whitby Gdns., Sutt.	100	G2
Whitby Rd. SE18	70	C4
Whitby Rd., Har.	45	J3
Whitby Rd., Ruis.	45	B3
Whitby Rd., Sutt.	100	G2
Whitby St. E1	**9**	**F5**
Whitcher Clo. SE14	68	H6
Chubworthy St.		
Whitcher Pl. NW1	49	C7
Rochester Rd.		
Whitchurch Ave., Edg.	29	J7
Whitchurch Clo., Edg.	29	J6
Whitchurch Gdns. Edg.	29	J6
Whitchurch La., Edg.	29	G7
Whitchurch Rd. W11	57	A7
Whitcomb Ct. WC2	58	D7
Whitcomb St.		
Whitcomb St. WC2	**11**	**J6**
Whitcomb St. WC2	58	D7
White Acre NW9	38	E2
White Adder Way E14	69	B4
Spindrift Ave.		
White Bear Pl. NW3	48	G4
New End Sq.		
White Ch. La. E1	**13**	**H3**
White Ch. La. E1	59	D6
White Ch. Pas. E1	**13**	**H3**
White City Clo. W12	56	J7
White City Est. W12	56	H7
White City Rd. W12	56	H7
White Conduit St. N1	**8**	**F1**
White Craig Clo., Pnr.	28	G5
White Gdns., Dag.	53	G6
Sterry Rd.		
White Gate Gdns., Har.	29	C7

<table>
<tr><td>

White Hart La. N17 32 J7
White Hart La. N22 40 G1
White Hart La. NW10 47 F6
Church Rd.
White Hart La. SW13 74 E2
White Hart La., 44 G1
Rom.
White Hart Rd. SE18 70 H4
White Hart Slip, 96 G2
Brom.
White Hart St. SE11 20 F3
White Hart St. SE11 67 G5
White Hart Yd. SE1 17 B2
White Horse Hill, 88 C4
Chis.
White Horse La. E1 59 G4
White Horse Rd. E1 59 H6
White Horse Rd. E6 61 C3
White Horse St. W1 15 E2
White Horse St. W1 67 B1
Who. Dr., 29 F4
Stan.
White Kennet St. E1 13 E3
White Lion Ct. EC3 13 D4
White Lion Hill EC4 12 H5
White Lion Hill EC4 58 H7
White Lion St. N1 8 E2
White Lion St. N1 58 G2
White Lion Yd. W1 11 D5
White Lo. SE19 85 H7
White Lo. Clo. N2 39 G6
White Lo. Clo., 100 F7
Sutt.
White Oak Dr., 96 C2
Beck.
White Orchards N20 23 C7
White Orchards, 29 D5
Stan.
White Post La. E9 50 J7
White Post La. SE13 78 A3
White Post St. SE15 68 F7
White Rd. E15 51 E7
White St., Sthl. 63 D2
White Swan Ms. W4 65 E6
Bennett St.
Whiteadder Way E14 69 B4
Spindrift Ave.
Whitear Wk. E15 51 D8
Whitebarn La., Dag. 62 G1
Whitebeam Ave., 97 D7
Brom.
Whitebeam Clo. SW9 67 F7
Clapham Rd.
Whitebeam Twr. E17 41 H3
Whitebutts Rd., 45 D3
Ruis.
Whitechapel High 13 G3
St. E1
Whitechapel High 59 C6
St. E1
Whitechapel Rd. E1 13 H2
Whitechapel Rd. E1 59 D5
Whitecote Rd., 54 J6
Sthl.
Whitecroft Clo., 96 D4
Beck.
Whitecroft Way, 96 C5
Beck.
Whitecross Pl. EC2 13 C1
Whitecross St. EC1 9 A5
Whitecross St. EC1 58 J4
Whitecross St. EC2 13 A1
Whitecross St. EC2 58 J5
Whitefield Ave. NW2 38 J7
Whitefield Clo. 75 B6
SW15
Whitefoot La., 87 C4
Brom.
Whitefoot Ter., 87 E3
Brom.
Whitefriars Ave., 37 B2
Har.
Whitefriars Dr., Har. 37 A2
Whitefriars Ave.
Whitefriars St. EC4 12 F4
Whitefriars St. EC4 58 G6
Whitehall SW1 16 A1
Whitehall SW1 67 E1
Whitehall Ct. SW1 16 B2
Whitehall Ct. SW1 67 E1
Whitehall Cres., 98 G5
Chess.
Whitehall Gdns. E4 34 D1
Whitehall Gdns. SW1 16 A2
Whitehall Gdns. W3 65 A1
Whitehall Gdns. W4 65 B6
Whitehall La., 34 G2
Buck.H.
Whitehall Pk. N19 49 C1
Whitehall Pk. Rd. 65 B6
W4
Whitehall Pl. SW1 16 A2
Whitehall Pl. SW1 67 E1

</td><td>

Whitehall Pl., Wall. 101 B4
Bernard Rd.
Whitehall Rd. E4 34 E2
Whitehall Rd. W7 64 D2
Whitehall Rd., 97 A5
Brom.
Whitehall Rd., Har. 37 B7
Whitehall Rd., 94 G6
Th.Hth.
Whitehall Rd., 34 F2
Wdf.Grn.
Whitehall St. N17 33 C7
Whitehaven Clo., 96 G4
Brom.
Whitehaven St. NW8 6 G6
Whitehead Clo. N18 33 A5
Whitehead Clo. 75 F7
SW18
Whitehead's Gro. 18 H3
SW3
Whitehead's Gro. 66 H5
SW3
Whitehills Rd., 27 D3
Loug.
Whitehorn Gdns., 102 E2
Croy.
Whitehorse La. SE25 95 A4
Whitehorse Rd. SE1 16 F5
Whitehorse Rd., 94 J7
Croy.
Whitehorse Rd., 95 A4
Th.Hth.
Whitehouse Ave., 22 B3
Borwd.
Whitehouse La., 24 J1
Enf.
Brigadier Hill
Whitehouse Way 32 B2
Whiteledges W13 55 F6
Whitelegg Rd. E13 60 F2
Whiteley Rd. SE19 86 A5
Whiteleys Cotts. 66 C4
W14
Whiteleys Way, 81 G3
Felt.
Whiteoak Gdns., 79 J7
Sid.
Whiteoaks La., 55 A2
Grnf.
Whites Ave., Ilf. 43 H6
Whites Dr., Brom. 96 F7
Whites Grds. SE1 17 E4
Whites Grds. SE1 68 B2
Whites Grds. Est. 17 E3
SE1
White's Row E1 13 F2
White's Row E1 59 C5
White's Sq. SW4 76 D4
Nelson's Row
Whitestile Rd., 64 F5
Brent.
Whitestone La. NW3 48 F3
Heath St.
Whitestone Wk. NW3 48 F3
North End Way
Whitethorn Gdns., 25 A5
Enf.
Whitethorn St. E3 60 A4
Whitewebbs Way, 97 J1
Orp.
Whitfield Pl. W1 7 F6
Whitfield Rd. E6 51 J7
Whitfield Rd. SE3 78 D1
Whitfield Rd., 71 F7
Bexh.
Whitfield St. W1 7 F6
Whitfield St. W1 58 C4
Whitford Gdns., 93 J3
Mitch.
Whitgift Ave., 101 H5
S.Croy.
Whitgift St. SE11 20 C1
Whitgift St. SE11 67 F4
Whitgift St., Croy. 101 J3
High St.
Whiting Ave., Bark. 52 E7
Whitings, Ilf. 43 G5
Whitings Rd., Barn. 22 J5
Whitings Way E6 61 D5
Whitland Rd., Cars. 100 G1
Whitley Rd. N17 41 B2
Whitlock Dr. SW19 75 B7
Whitman Rd. E3 59 H4
Whitmead Clo. 102 B6
S.Croy.
Whitmore Clo. N11 32 B5
Whitmore Gdns. 66 B1
NW10
Whitmore Rd. N1 59 B1
Whitmore Rd., Beck. 95 J3
Whitmore Rd., Har. 36 J7
Whitnell Way SW15 74 J5

</td><td>

Whitney Ave., Ilf. 43 A4
Whitney Rd. E10 42 A7
Whitney Wk., Sid. 89 E6
Whitstable Clo., 95 J1
Beck.
Whitta Rd. E12 52 J4
Whittaker Ave., 73 G5
Rich.
Hill St.
Whittaker Rd. E6 52 A7
Whittaker Rd., 100 C3
Sutt.
Whittaker St. SW1 19 B2
Whittaker St. SW1 67 A4
Whittaker Way SE1 21 J2
Whittell Gdns. SE26 86 F3
Whittingstall Rd. 75 C1
SW6
Whittington Ave. 13 D4
EC3
Whittington Ct. N2 39 J5
Whittington Rd. N22 32 E7
Whittington Way, 36 E5
Pnr.
Whittle Clo., Sthl. 54 H6
Whittle Rd., Houns. 63 C7
Whittlebury Clo., 100 J7
Cars.
Whittlesea Clo., 28 J7
Har.
Whittlesea Rd.
Whittlesea Path, 36 J1
Har.
Whittlesea Rd., 36 J1
Har.
Whittlesey St. SE1 16 F2
Whitton Ave. E., 46 B5
Grnf.
Whitton Ave. W., 46 A5
Grnf.
Whitton Ave. W., 45 H5
Nthlt.
Whitton Clo., Grnf. 46 E6
Whitton Dene, 72 H5
Houns.
Whitton Dene, Islw. 73 A5
Whitton Dr., Grnf. 46 D6
Whitton Manor Rd., 72 J5
Islw.
Whitton Rd., Houns. 72 H4
Whitton Rd., Twick. 73 C6
Whitton Wk. E3 60 A3
Whitton Waye, 72 G6
Houns.
Whitwell Rd. E13 60 G3
Whitworth Pl. SE18 70 E4
Whitworth Rd. SE18 70 D6
Whitworth Rd. SE25 95 B3
Whitworth St. SE10 69 E5
Whorlton Rd. SE15 77 E3
Whymark Ave. N22 40 G3
Whytecroft, Houns. 63 D7
Whyteville Rd. E7 51 H6
Wick La. E3 50 J7
Wick Rd. E9 50 G6
Wick Rd., Tedd. 82 E7
Wick Sq. E9 50 J6
Eastway
Wicker St. E1 59 E6
Burslem St.
Wickers Oake SE19 86 C4
Wickersley Rd. SW11 76 A2
Wicket, The, Croy. 103 A5
Wicket Rd., Grnf. 55 D3
Wickets Way, Ilf. 35 J6
Wickford St. E1 59 F4
Wickford Way E17 41 G4
Wickham Ave., Croy. 102 H2
Wickham Ave., Sutt. 99 J5
Wickham Chase, 103 D1
W.Wick.
Wickham Clo., Enf. 25 E3
Wickham Clo., 92 F5
N.Mal.
Wickham Ct. Rd., 103 C2
W.Wick.
Wickham Cres., 103 C2
W.Wick.
Wickham Gdns. SE4 77 J3
Wickham Ho. E1 59 F5
Jamaica St.
Wickham La. SE2 71 A5
Wickham Ms. SE4 77 J2
Wickham Rd. E4 34 C7
Wickham Rd. SE4 77 J3
Wickham Rd., Beck. 96 B2
Wickham Rd., Croy. 102 F2
Wickham Rd., Har. 37 A2
Wickham St. SE11 20 C3
Wickham St. SE11 67 F5
Wickham St., Well. 79 H1
Wickham Way, Beck. 96 C4
Wickliffe Ave. N3 39 B2

</td><td>

Wickliffe Gdns., 47 B2
Wem.
Wicklow St. WC1 8 C3
Wicklow St. WC1 58 F3
Wicks Clo. SE9 88 A4
Wicksteed Ho., 64 J5
Brent.
Wickwood St. SE5 76 H2
Widdecombe Ave., 45 E2
Har.
Widdenham Rd. N7 49 F4
Widdin St. E15 51 D7
Wide Way, Mitch. 94 D3
Widecombe Gdns., 43 B4
Ilf.
Widecombe Rd. SE9 88 B3
Widecombe Way N2 39 G5
Widegate St. E1 13 E2
Widenham Clo., Pnr. 36 C5
Bridle Rd.
Widgeon Clo. E16 60 H6
Maplin Rd.
Widley Rd. W9 57 D3
Widmore Lo. Rd., 97 A2
Brom.
Widmore Rd., Brom. 96 G2
Wieland Rd., Nthwd. 28 A7
Wigan Ho. E5 50 E1
Warwick Gro.
Wigeon Path SE28 70 G3
Wiggington Ave., 47 B6
Wem.
Wiggins Mead NW9 30 F7
Wigham Ho., Bark. 52 F7
Wightman Rd. N4 40 G4
Wightman Rd. N8 40 G4
Wigley Rd., Felt. 81 D2
Wigmore Pl. W1 11 D3
Wigmore Pl. W1 58 B6
Wigmore Rd., Cars. 100 G2
Wigmore St. W1 11 B4
Wigmore St. W1 58 B6
Wigram Rd. E11 42 J6
Wigram Sq. E17 42 D2
Wigston Rd. E13 60 H4
Wigston's Gdns., Stan. 37 H1
Wigton Pl. SE11 20 F4
Wigton Rd. E17 41 J1
Wilberforce Rd. N4 49 H2
Wilberforce Rd. NW9 38 G6
Wilberforce Way 84 A6
SW19
Wilbraham Pl. SW1 19 A1
Wilbraham Pl. SW1 66 J4
Wilbury Way N18 33 A5
Wilby Ms. W11 66 C1
Wilcox Clo. SW8 20 B7
Wilcox Clo. SW8 67 E7
Wilcox Clo., Borwd. 22 C1
Wilcox Pl. SW1 15 G6
Wilcox Rd. SW8 20 A7
Wilcox Rd. SW8 67 E7
Wilcox Rd., Sutt. 100 E4
Wilcox Rd., Todd. 82 A4
Wild Ct. WC2 12 C3
Wild Ct. WC2 58 F6
Wild Goose Dr. SE14 77 F1
Wild Hatch NW11 39 D6
Wild St. WC2 12 B4
Wild St. WC2 58 E6
Wildcroft Gdns., 29 G6
Edg.
Wildcroft Rd. SW15 74 J7
Wilde Clo. E8 59 D1
Wilde Pl. N13 32 H6
Medesenge Way
Wilde Pl. SW18 75 G7
Heathfield Rd.
Wilder Clo., Ruis. 45 B1
Wilderness, The, 81 H4
Hmptn.
Park Rd.
Wilderness Rd., 88 E7
Chis.
Wilderton Rd. N16 41 B7
Wildfell Rd. SE6 78 B7
Wild's Rents SE1 17 D5
Wild's Rents SE1 68 B3
Wildwood Clo. SE12 78 F7
Wildwood Gro. NW3 48 F1
North End Rd.
Wildwood Ri. NW11 48 F1
Wildwood Rd. NW11 39 E6
Wildwood Ter. NW3 48 F1
Wilford Clo., Enf. 25 A3
Wilford Owen Clo. 84 F1
SW19
Tennyson Rd.
Wilfred St. SW1 15 F5
Wilfred St. SW1 67 C3
Wilfred Turney Est. 65 H3
W6
Sycamore Gdns.

</td></tr>
</table>

Name	Page	Grid
Wilfrid Gdns. W3	56	C5
Wilkes St. E1	**13**	**G1**
Wilkes St. E1	59	C5
Wilkie Way SE22	86	D1
Lordship La.		
Wilkin St. NW5	49	B6
Wilkin St. Ms. NW5	49	B6
Wilkin St.		
Wilkins Clo.,	93	H1
Mitch.		
Wilkinson Rd. E16	60	J6
Wilkinson St. SW8	67	F7
Wilkinson Way W4	65	D2
Southfield Rd.		
Wilks Pl. N1	**9**	**E2**
Will Crooks Gdns.	78	J4
SE9		
Willan Rd. N17	41	A2
Willan Wall E16	60	F7
Victoria Dock Rd.		
Willard St. SW8	76	B3
Willcocks Clo.,	98	H3
Chess.		
Willcott Rd. W3	65	B1
Willenhall Ave.,	23	F6
Barn.		
Willenhall Rd. SE18	70	E5
Orp.		
Willersley Ave.,	104	G3
Sid.		
Willersley Ave.,	88	J1
Sid.		
Willersley Clo.,	88	J1
Sid.		
Willes Rd. NW5	49	B6
Willesden La. NW2	47	J6
Willesden La. NW6	57	C1
Willet Way SE16	68	E5
Egan Way		
Willett Clo.,	54	C3
Nthlt.		
Broomcroft Ave.		
Willett Clo., Orp.	97	H6
Willett Pl.,	94	G5
Th.Hth.		
Willett Rd.		
Willett Rd.,	94	G5
Th.Hth.		
Willett Way, Orp.	97	G5
William Barefoot Dr.	88	C4
SE9		
William Bonney Est.	76	D4
SW4		
William Booth Rd.	95	D1
SE20		
William Carey Way,	37	B6
Har.		
William Clo., Rom.	44	J1
William Dunbar Ho.	57	C2
NW6		
William Ellis Way	**17**	**J6**
SE16		
William IV St. WC2	**12**	**A6**
William IV St. WC2	58	E7
William Gdns. SW15	74	H5
William Guy Gdns.	60	B3
E3		
Talwin St.		
William Margrie Clo.	77	D2
SE15		
Moncrieff St.		
William Ms. SW1	**15**	**A4**
William Morley Clo.	61	A1
E6		
William Morris Clo.	41	J3
E17		
William Pl. E3	59	J2
Roman Rd.		
William Rd. NW1	**7**	**F4**
William Rd. NW1	58	C3
William Rd. SW19	84	B7
William Rd., Sutt.	100	F5
William Saville Ho.	57	C2
NW6		
William St. E10	42	B6
William St. N17	33	C7
William St. SW1	**15**	**A4**
William St. SW1	66	J2
William St., Bark.	52	F7
William St., Cars.	100	H3
Williams Ave. E17	41	J1
Williams Bldgs. E2	59	F4
Williams Clo. N8	40	D6
Coolhurst Rd.		
Williams Gro. N22	40	G1
William's La. SW14	74	C3
Williams La., Mord.	93	F5
Williams Rd. W13	55	D7
Williams Rd., Sthl.	63	E4
Williams Ter.,	101	G6
Croy.		
Williamson Clo.	69	F4
SE10		
Lenthorp Rd.		
Williamson Rd. N4	40	H6
Williamson St. N7	49	E4
Williamson Way	31	B6
NW7		
Willifield Way NW11	39	C4
Willingale Clo.,	27	F2
Loug.		
Willingale Rd.		
Willingale Clo.,	34	J6
Wdf.Grn.		
Willingale Rd., Loug.	27	F1
Willingdon Rd. N22	40	H2
Willingham Ter. NW5	49	C5
Leighton Rd.		
Willingham Way,	92	A3
Sthl.		
Willington Ct. E5	50	H3
Mandeville St.		
Willington Rd. SW9	76	E3
Willis Ave., Sutt.	100	H7
Willis Rd. E15	60	F2
Willis Rd., Croy.	94	J7
Willis Rd., Erith	71	J4
Willis St. E14	60	B6
Willmore End SW19	93	E1
Willoughby Ave.,	101	F4
Croy.		
Willoughby Gro. N17	33	E7
Willoughby La. N17	33	E6
Willoughby Pk. Rd.	33	E7
N17		
Willoughby Rd. N8	40	G3
Willoughby Rd. NW3	48	G4
Willoughby Rd.,	91	J1
Kings.T.		
Willoughby Rd.,	73	G6
Twick.		
Willoughby St. WC1	**12**	**A2**
Willoughby Way SE7	69	H4
Willow Ave. SW13	74	F2
Willow Ave., Sid.	80	A6
Willow Bank SW6	75	B3
Willow Bank, Rich.	82	E3
Willow Bri. Rd. N1	49	J6
Willow Clo. W5	55	G5
Willow Clo., Bex.	80	F6
Willow Clo., Brent.	64	F6
Willow Clo., Brom.	97	C5
Willow Clo.,	35	A3
Buck.H.		
Willow Clo.,	94	G6
Th.Hth.		
Willow Cotts.,	94	C3
Mitch.		
Willow Ct., Edg.	29	H4
Willow Dene, Pnr.	36	D2
Willow Dr., Barn.	23	B4
Willow End N20	31	D2
Willow End, Nthwd.	28	A6
Willow End, Surb.	98	H1
Willow Gdns.,	72	G1
Houns.		
Willow Grn. NW9	38	E1
Clayton Fld.		
Willow Gro. E13	60	G2
Lettsom Wk.		
Willow Gro., Chis.	88	D6
Willow La., Mitch.	93	J6
Willow Mt., Croy.	102	B3
Langton Way		
Willow Pl. SW1	**19**	**G1**
Willow Pl. SW1	67	C4
Willow Rd. NW3	48	G4
Willow Rd. W5	64	H2
Willow Rd., Enf.	25	B3
Willow Rd., N.Mal.	92	C4
Willow Rd., Rom.	44	E6
Willow Rd., Wall.	101	B7
Willow St. E4	26	D7
Willow St. EC2	**9**	**D5**
Willow St. EC2	59	B4
Willow St., Rom.	44	J4
Willow Tree Clo.	84	E1
SW18		
Cargill Rd.		
Willow Tree Clo.,	54	C4
Hayes		
Willow Tree La.,	54	C4
Hayes		
Willow Tree Wk.,	96	H1
Brom.		
Willow Vale W12	65	G1
Willow Vale, Chis.	88	E6
Willow Vw. SW19	93	G1
Willow Wk. E17	41	J5
Willow Wk. N2	39	G2
Central Ave.		
Willow Wk. N15	40	H4
Willow Wk. N21	24	F6
Willow Wk. SE1	**21**	**E1**
Willow Wk. SE1	68	B4
Willow Wk., Orp.	104	E3
Willow Wk., Sutt.	100	C3
Willow Way N3	31	E7
Willow Way SE26	86	E3
Willow Way W11	57	A7
St. Anns Rd.		
Willow Way, Epsom	99	D6
Willow Way, Sun.	90	A4
Willow Way, Twick.	81	H2
Willow Way, Wem	46	D3
Willow Wd. Cres.	95	B6
SE25		
Willowbrook Rd.	81	G8
SE15		
Willowbrook Rd.	68	C6
SE15		
Willowbrook Rd.,	63	G3
Sthl.		
Willowcourt Ave.,	37	E5
Har.		
Willowdene N6	39	J7
Denewood Rd.		
Willowdene Clo.,	72	J7
Twick.		
Willowhayne Dr.,	90	B7
Walt.		
Willowhayne Gdns.,	99	J3
Wor.Pk.		
Willowmead Clo. W5	55	G5
Willows, The,	35	A3
Buck.H.		
Willows, The, Esher	98	B6
Albany Cres.		
Willows Ave., Mord.	93	E5
Willows Clo., Pnr.	36	C2
Willrose Cres. SE2	71	B5
Wills Cres., Houns.	72	H6
Wills Gro. NW7	30	G5
Wilman Gro. E8	50	D7
Wilmar Gdns.,	103	B1
W.Wick.		
Wilmcote Ho. W2	57	D5
Wilmer Clo.,	82	J5
Kings.T.		
Wilmer Cres.,	82	J5
Kings.T.		
Wilmer Gdns. N1	59	B1
Wilmer Lea Clo. E15	51	C7
Wilmer Way N14	32	D5
Wilmington Ave. W4	65	D7
Wilmington Gdns.,	52	G6
Bark.		
Wilmington Sq. WC1	**8**	**E4**
Wilmington Sq. WC1	58	G3
Wilmington St. WC1	**8**	**E4**
Wilmot Clo. N2	39	F2
Wilmot Clo. SE15	68	D7
Wilmot Pl. NW1	49	C7
Wilmot Pl. W7	64	B1
Boston Rd.		
Wilmot Rd. E10	51	B2
Wilmot Rd. N17	41	A3
Wilmot Rd., Cars.	100	J5
Wilmot St. E2	59	E4
Wilmount St. SE18	70	E4
Wilna Rd. SW18	75	F7
Wilsham St. W11	66	A1
Wilshaw St. SE14	78	A1
Wilsmere Dr., Har.	29	B7
Wilsmere Dr.,	45	E6
Nthlt.		
Wilson Ave., Mitch.	84	H7
Wilson Clo., Wem.	37	J7
Wilson Dr., Wem.	37	J7
Wilson Gdns., Har.	36	J7
Wilson Gro. SE16	68	E2
Wilson Rd. E6	61	A3
Wilson Rd. SE5	77	B1
Wilson Rd., Chess.	98	J6
Wilson Rd., Ilf.	43	C7
Wilson St. E17	42	C5
Wilson St. EC2	**13**	**C1**
Wilson St. EC2	59	A5
Wilson St. N21	24	G7
Wilsons Pl. E14	59	J6
Salmon La.		
Wilsons Rd. W6	66	A5
Wilstone Clo.,	54	E4
Hayes		
Kingsash Dr.		
Wilthorne Gdns.,	53	H7
Dag.		
Acre Rd.		
Wilton Ave. W4	65	E5
Wilton Cres. SW1	**15**	**B4**
Wilton Cres. SW1	67	B3
Wilton Cres. SW19	93	C1
Wilton Gdns.,	90	G3
W.Mol.		
Wilton Gro. SW19	93	C1
Wilton Gro., N.Mal.	92	F6
Wilton Ms. SW1	**15**	**C5**
Wilton Ms. SW1	67	A3
Wilton Par., Felt.	81	A2
Highfield Rd.		
Wilton Pk. Ct. SE18	79	D1
Prince Imperial Rd.		
Wilton Pl. SW1	**15**	**B4**
Wilton Pl. SW1	67	A2
Wilton Rd. N10	40	A2
Wilton Rd. SE2	71	C4
Wilton Rd. SW1	**15**	**E6**
Wilton Rd. SW1	67	C4
Wilton Rd. SW19	84	H7
Wilton Rd., Barn.	23	J4
Wilton Rd., Houns.	72	D2
Wilton Rd., Ilf.	52	E3
Ilford La.		
Wilton Row SW1	**15**	**B4**
Wilton Row SW1	67	A2
Wilton Sq. N1	59	A1
Wilton St. SW1	**15**	**D5**
Wilton St. SW1	67	B3
Wilton Ter. SW1	**15**	**B5**
Wilton Ter. SW1	67	A3
Wilton Vill. N1	59	A1
Wilton Way E8	50	D6
Wiltshire Clo. SW3	**18**	**J2**
Wiltshire Gdns. N4	40	J6
Wiltshire Gdns.,	81	J1
Twick.		
Wiltshire Rd. SW9	76	G3
Wiltshire Rd., Th.Hth.	94	G3
Wiltshire Row N1	59	A1
Wilverley Cres.,	92	E6
N.Mal.		
Wimbart Rd. SW2	76	F7
Wimbledon Bri.	84	C6
SW19		
Wimbledon Hill Rd.	84	B6
SW19		
Wimbledon Pk. Est.	84	C1
SW19		
Wimbledon Pk. Rd.	84	C1
SW18		
Wimbledon Pk. Rd.	84	B2
SW19		
Wimbledon Pk. Side	84	A2
SW19		
Wimbledon Rd.	84	F4
SW17		
Wimbledon Sta.	84	C6
SW19		
The Bdy.		
Wimbolt St. E2	**9**	**H3**
Wimbolt St. E2	59	D3
Wimborne Ave.,	54	B6
Hayes		
Wimborne Ave., Orp.	97	J3
Wimborne Ave.,	63	G4
Sthl.		
Wimborne Clo. SE12	78	F5
Wimborne Clo.,	34	J2
Buck.H.		
Wimborne Clo.,	99	J1
Wor.Pk.		
Wimborne Dr. NW9	38	A3
Wimborne Dr., Pnr.	36	D7
Wimborne Gdns.	55	E5
W13		
Wimborne Rd. N9	33	D2
Wimborne Rd. N17	41	B2
Wimborne Way,	95	G4
Beck.		
Wimbourne St. N1	**9**	**B1**
Wimbourne St. N1	59	A2
Wimpole Clo., Brom.	96	J4
Stanley Rd.		
Wimpole Clo.,	91	J2
Kings.T.		
Wimpole Ms. W1	**11**	**D1**
Wimpole Ms. W1	58	B5
Wimpole St. W1	**11**	**D2**
Wimpole St. W1	58	B6
Winans Wk. SW9	76	G2
Wincanton Cres.,	45	G5
Nthlt.		
Wincanton Gdns.,	43	E3
Ilf.		
Wincanton Rd. SW18	75	C7
Winchcomb Gdns.	79	A3
SE9		
Winchcombe Rd.,	100	G2
Cars.		
Winchelsea Ave.,	71	F7
Bexh.		
Winchelsea Clo.	75	A5
SW15		
Winchelsea Rd. E7	51	G4
Winchelsea Rd. N17	41	B3
Winchelsea Rd.	56	D1
NW10		
Winchelsey Ri.,	102	C6
S.Croy.		
Winchendon Rd.	66	C7
SW6		
Winchendon Rd.,	82	A4
Tedd.		

Winchester Ave. NW6 57 B1
Winchester Ave. NW9 37 J3
Winchester Ave., Houns. 63 F6
Winchester Clo. E6 61 B6
Boultwood Rd.
Winchester Clo. SE17 **20 H2**
Winchester Clo. SE17 67 H4
Winchester Clo., Brom. 96 F3
Winchester Clo., Enf. 25 B5
Winchester Clo., Kings.T. 83 B7
Winchester Dr., Pnr. 36 D5
Winchester Ho. SE18 70 A7
Shooter's Hill Rd.
Winchester Ms. NW3 48 G7
Winchester Rd.
Winchester Pk., Brom. 96 F3
Winchester Pl. E8 50 C5
Kingsland High St.
Winchester Pl. N6 49 B1
Cromwell Ave.
Winchester Pl. W3 65 C2
Avenue Rd.
Winchester Rd. E4 34 C7
Winchester Rd. N6 40 B7
Winchester Rd. N9 33 D2
Winchester Rd. NW3 48 G7
Winchester Rd., Bexh. 80 D2
Winchester Rd., Brom. 96 F3
Winchester Rd., Felt. 81 F3
Winchester Rd., Har. 37 H4
Winchester Rd., Ilf. 52 G3
Winchester Rd., Twick. 73 E7
Winchester Sq. SE1 **17 B1**
Winchester St. SW1 **19 E3**
Winchester St. SW1 67 B5
Winchester St. W3 65 C2
Winchester Wk. SE1 **17 B1**
Winchester Wk. SE1 68 A1
Winchfield Clo., Har. 37 F6
Winchfield Rd. SE26 86 H5
Winchilsea Cres., W.Mol. 90 J2
Winchmore Hill Rd. N14 32 D1
Winchmore Hill Rd. N21 24 F7
Winckley Clo., Har. 37 J5
Wincott St. SE11 **20 F2**
Wincott St. SE11 67 G4
Wincrofts Dr. SE9 79 G4
Windborough Rd., Cars. 101 A7
Windermere Ave. N3 39 D3
Windermere Ave. NW6 57 B1
Windermere Ave. SW19 93 E3
Windermere Ave., Har. 37 F7
Windermere Ave., Ruis. 36 C7
Windermere Ave., Wem. 37 F7
Windermere Clo., Orp. 104 E3
Windermere Ct. SW13 65 F6
Windermere Gdns., Ilf. 43 B5
Windermere Gro., Wem. 46 F1
Windermere Ave.
Windermere Ho., Islw. 73 C5
Windermere Rd. N10 40 B1
Windermere Rd. N19 49 C2
Holloway Rd.
Windermere Rd. SW15 83 E4
Windermere Rd. SW16 94 C1
Windermere Rd. W5 64 F3
Windermere Rd., Bexh. 80 J2
Windermere Rd., Croy. 102 C1
Windermere Rd., Sthl. 54 F5
Windermere Rd., W.Wick. 103 E2
Winders Rd. SW11 75 H2

Windfield Clo. SE26 86 G4
Windham Rd., Rich. 73 J3
Winding Way, Dag. 53 C3
Winding Way, Har. 46 B4
Windlass Pl. SE8 68 H4
Windlesham Gro. SW19 84 A1
Windley Clo. SE23 86 F2
Windmill Clo. SE13 78 C2
Windmill Clo., Surb. 98 F1
Windmill Ct. NW2 48 B6
Windmill Dr. SW4 76 B5
Windmill Dr., Kes. 103 J4
Windmill Gdns., Enf. 24 G3
Windmill Gro., Croy. 94 J6
Windmill Hill NW3 48 F3
Windmill Hill, Enf. 24 H3
Windmill La. E15 51 D6
Windmill La., Barn. 22 F6
Windmill La., Grnf. 54 J5
Windmill La., Islw. 64 B4
Windmill La., Sthl. 63 J2
Windmill La., Surb. 91 E6
Windmill La. (Bushey), Wat. 29 A1
Windmill Ms. W4 65 E4
Chiswick Common Rd.
Windmill Pas. W4 65 E4
Chiswick Common Rd.
Windmill Ri., Kings.T. 83 B7
Windmill Rd. N18 33 A4
Windmill Rd. SW18 75 G6
Windmill Rd. SW19 83 J3
Windmill Rd. W4 65 E4
Windmill Rd. W5 64 F4
Windmill Rd., Brent. 64 G5
Windmill Rd., Croy. 94 J7
Windmill Rd., Hmptn. 81 H5
Windmill Rd., Mitch. 94 C5
Windmill Row SE11 **20 E4**
Windmill Rose SE11 67 G5
Windmill St. W1 **11 H2**
Windmill St. W1 58 D5
Windmill St. (Bushey), Wat. 29 B1
Windmill Wk. SE1 **16 F2**
Windmill Wk. SE1 67 G1
Windover Ave. NW9 38 D4
Windrose Clo. SE16 68 G2
Windrush Clo. SW11 75 G4
Maysoule Rd.
Windrush Clo. W4 74 C1
Windrush La. SE23 86 G3
Windsor Ave. E17 41 H2
Windsor Ave. SW19 93 F1
Windsor Ave., Edg. 30 B4
Windsor Ave., N.Mal. 92 C5
Windsor Ave., Sutt. 100 B3
Windsor Ave., W.Mol. 90 G3
Windsor Clo. N3 39 B2
Windsor Clo. SE27 85 J4
Windsor Clo., Borwd. 22 A1
Warrenford Way
Windsor Clo., Brent. 64 E6
Amalgamated Dr.
Windsor Clo., Chis. 88 E5
Windsor Clo., Har. 45 G3
Windsor Clo., Nthwd. 36 A2
Windsor Ct. N14 24 C7
Windsor Ct., Sun. 81 A6
Windsor Rd.
Windsor Cres., Har. 45 G3
Windsor Cres., Wem. 47 B3
Windsor Dr., Barn. 23 J6
Windsor Gdns. W9 57 D5
Windsor Gdns., Croy. 101 E3
Richmond Rd.
Windsor Gro. SE27 85 J4
Windsor Pl. SW1 **15 G6**
Windsor Rd. E4 34 B4
Chivers Rd.
Windsor Rd. E7 51 H5
Windsor Rd. E10 51 B2
Windsor Rd. E11 51 G1
Windsor Rd. N3 39 B2
Windsor Rd. N7 49 E3
Windsor Rd. N13 32 G3
Windsor Rd. N17 41 D2
Windsor Rd. NW2 47 H6
Windsor Rd. W5 55 H7

Windsor Rd., Barn. 23 A6
Windsor Rd., Bexh. 80 E4
Windsor Rd., Dag. 53 E3
Windsor Rd., Har. 37 A1
Windsor Rd., Houns. 72 B2
Windsor Rd., Ilf. 52 E4
Windsor Rd., Kings.T. 82 H7
Windsor Rd., Rich. 73 J2
Windsor Rd., Sthl. 63 F3
Windsor Rd., Sun. 81 A6
Windsor Rd., Tedd. 82 A5
Windsor Rd., Th.Hth. 94 H2
Windsor Rd., Wor.Pk. 99 G2
Windsor St. N1 58 H1
Windsor Ter. N1 **9 A3**
Windsor Ter. N1 58 J3
Windsor Wk. SE5 77 A4
Windsor Way W14 66 A4
Windsors, The, Buck.H. 35 B2
Windspoint Dr. SE15 68 E6
Ethnard Rd.
Windus Rd. N16 50 C1
Windus Wk. N16 50 C1
Alkham Rd.
Windy Ridge, Brom. 97 B1
Windyridge Clo. SW19 84 A5
Wine Clo. E1 59 F7
Wine Office Ct. EC4 **12 F4**
Winefride's Rd. E12 52 C5
Winford Ho. E3 50 J7
Jodrell Rd.
Winforton St. SE10 78 C1
Winfrith Rd. SW18 75 F7
Wingate Cres., Croy. 94 D6
Wingate Rd. W6 65 H3
Wingate Rd., Ilf. 52 E5
Wingate Rd., Sid. 89 C6
Wingate Trd. Est. N17 33 C7
Wingfield Ms. SE15 77 D3
Wingfield St.
Wingfield Rd. E15 51 E4
Wingfield Rd. E17 42 B5
Wingfield Rd., Kings.T. 83 A6
Wingfield St. SE15 77 D3
Wingfield Way, Ruis. 45 B6
Wingford Rd. SW2 76 E6
Wingmore Rd. SE24 76 J3
Wingrave Rd. W6 65 J6
Wingrove Rd. SE6 87 J2
Winifred Gro. SW11 75 J4
Winifred Rd. SW19 93 D1
Winifred Rd., Dag. 53 E2
Winifred Rd., Hmptn. 81 G4
Winifred St. E16 70 C1
Winifred Ter., Enf. 25 C7
Edward Clo.
Winkfield Rd. E13 60 H2
Winkfield Rd. N22 40 G1
Winkley St. E2 59 E2
Winlaton Rd., Brom. 87 D4
Winmill Rd., Dag. 53 F3
Winn Common Rd. SE18 87 H1
Winn Rd. SE12 87 H1
Winnett St. W1 **11 H5**
Winnington Clo. N2 39 G6
Winnington Rd. N2 48 G1
Winns Ave. E17 41 H3
Winns Ter. E17 42 A2
Winscombe Cres. W5 55 G4
Winscombe St. N19 49 B2
Winscombe Way, Stan. 29 D5
Winsford Rd. SE6 86 J3
Winsford Ter. N18 33 A5
Winsham Gro. SW11 76 A5
Winslade Rd. SW2 76 E5
Winslade Way SE26 78 B7
Rushey Grn.
Winsland Ms. W2 **10 E3**
Winsland St. W2 **10 E3**
Winsland St. W2 57 B6
Winsley St. W1 **11 F3**
Winsley St. W1 58 C6
Winslow SE17 **21 D4**
Winslow Clo. NW10 47 D3
Neasden La. N.
Winslow Gro. E4 34 E2
Winslow Rd. W6 65 J6
Winslow Way, Felt. 81 D3
Winsor Ter. E6 61 D5
Winstanley Est. SW11 75 G3
Winstanley Rd. SW11 75 G3

Winstead Gdns., Dag. 53 J5
Winston Ave. NW9 38 E7
Winston Clo., Har. 29 C6
Winston Clo., Rom. 44 H4
Winston Ct., Har. 28 H7
Winston Rd. N16 50 A4
Winston Wk. W4 65 D4
Clement Clo.
Winston Way, Ilf. 52 E3
Winstre Rd., Borwd. 22 A1
Winter Ave. E6 61 B1
Winter Box Wk., Rich. 73 J4
Winterborne Ave., Orp. 104 G3
Winterbourne Rd. SE6 86 J1
Winterbourne Rd., Dag. 53 C2
Winterbourne Rd., Th.Hth. 94 G4
Winterbrook Rd. SE24 76 J6
Winterfold Clo. SW19 84 B2
Wintergreen Clo. E6 61 B5
Yarrow Cres.
Winters Rd., T.Ditt. 91 E7
Winterstoke Gdns. NW7 30 G5
Winterstoke Rd. SE6 86 J1
Winterton Ho. E1 59 E6
Winterton Pl. SW10 **18 D5**
Winterwell Rd. SW2 76 E5
Winthorpe Rd. SW15 75 B4
Winthrop St. E1 59 E5
Winton Ave. N11 32 C7
Winton Clo. N9 25 G7
Winton Gdns., Edg. 29 J7
Winton Rd., Orp. 104 E4
Winton Way SW16 85 G5
Wisbeach Rd., Croy. 95 A5
Wisdons Clo., Dag. 53 H1
Wise La. NW7 30 G5
Wise Rd. E15 60 D1
Wiseman Ct. SE19 86 C5
Wiseman Rd. E10 51 A2
Wiseton Rd. SW17 84 H1
Wishart Rd. SE3 79 A2
Wisley Rd. SW11 76 A5
Wisley Rd., Orp. 89 A7
Wisteria Clo., Orp. 104 E2
Wisteria Rd. SE13 73 D4
Witan St. E2 59 E3
Witham Clo., Loug. 27 B6
Witham Rd. SE20 95 F3
Witham Rd. W13 64 D1
Witham Rd., Dag. 53 G5
Witham Rd., Islw. 73 A1
Witherby Clo., Croy. 102 B5
Witherfield Way SE16 68 E5
Egan Way
Witherington Rd. N5 49 G5
Withers Mead NW9 38 F1
Witherston Way SE9 88 D2
Withy Mead E4 34 D3
Withycombe Rd. SW19 75 A7
Witley Cres., Croy. 103 C6
Witley Gdns., Sthl. 63 F4
Witley Rd. N19 49 C2
Holloway Rd.
Witney Clo., Pnr. 28 F6
Witney Path SE23 86 G3
Inglemere Rd.
Wittenham Way E4 34 D3
Wittersham Rd., Brom. 87 F5
Wivenhoe Clo. SE15 77 E3
Wivenhoe Ct., Houns. 72 F4
Wivenhoe Rd., Bark. 62 A2
Wiverton Rd. SE26 86 F6
Wix Rd., Dag. 62 D1
Wixs La. SW4 76 B3
Woburn Clo. SW19 84 F6
Tintern Clo.
Woburn Pl. WC1 **7 J5**
Woburn Pl. WC1 58 D4
Woburn Rd., Cars. 100 H1
Woburn Rd., Croy. 101 J1
Woburn Sq. WC1 **7 J6**
Woburn Sq. WC1 58 D4
Woburn Wk. WC1 **7 J4**
Woffington Clo., Kings.T. 81 F1
Woking Clo. SW15 74 F4
Woldham Rd., Brom. 96 J4
Wolds Dr., Orp. 104 D4
Wolfe Clo., Brom. 96 G6
Wolfe Clo., Hayes 54 B3
Ayles Rd.

Wolfe Cres. SE7 70 A5
Wolfe Cres. SE16 68 G2
Wolferton Rd. E12 52 C4
Wolffe Gdns. E15 51 F6
Wolffram Clo. SE13 78 E5
Wolfington Rd. SE27 85 H4
Wolftencroft Clo. 75 G3
Wollaston Clo. SE1 20 J1
Wolmer Clo., Edg. 88 D1
Wolmer Gdns., Edg. 30 A3
Wolseley Ave. SW19 84 D2
Wolseley Gdns. W4 65 B6
Wolseley Rd. E7 51 H7
Wolseley Rd. N8 40 D6
Wolseley Rd. N22 40 F1
Wolseley Rd. W4 65 C4
Wolseley Rd., Har. 37 B3
Wolseley Rd., Mitch. 94 A7
Wolseley St. SE1 17 G4
Wolseley St. SE1 68 D2
Wolsey Ave. E6 61 D3
Wolsey Ave. E17 41 J3
Wolsey Ave., T.Ditt. 91 C5
Aragon Ave.
Wolsey Clo. SW20 83 H7
Wolsey Clo., Houns. 72 J4
Wolsey Clo., Kings.T. 92 B1
Wolsey Clo., Sthl. 63 J3
Wolsey Clo., Wor.Pk. 99 G4
Wolsey Cres., Mord. 93 B7
Wolsey Dr., Kings.T. 82 H5
Wolsey Gdns., Ilf. 35 E6
Wolsey Gro., Edg. 30 D7
Wolsey Ms. NW5 49 C6
Wolsey Ms., Orp. 104 J5
Osgood Ave.
Wolsey Rd. N1 50 A5
Wolsey Rd., E.Mol. 91 A4
Wolsey Rd., Enf. 25 E2
Wolsey Rd., Hmptn. 81 H6
Wolsey St. E1 59 F5
Sidney St.
Wolsey Way, Chess. 99 A5
Wolstonbury N12 31 D5
Wolvercote Rd. SE2 71 D2
Wolverley St. E2 59 E3
Bethnal Grn. Rd.
Wolverton SE17 21 D3
Wolverton Ave., 92 A1
Kings.T.
Wolverton Gdns. W5 55 J7
Wolverton Gdns. W6 66 A4
Wolverton Rd., Stan. 29 E6
Wolverton Way N14 24 C5
Wolves La. N13 32 G6
Wolves La. N22 32 G7
Womersley Rd. N8 40 F6
Wonford Clo., 92 E1
Kings.T.
Wontner Clo. N1 49 J7
Greenman St.
Wontner Rd. SW17 84 J2
Wood Clo. E2 9 H5
Wood Clo. E2 59 D4
Wood Clo. NW9 38 D7
Wood Clo., Har. 37 A7
Wood Dr., Chis. 88 B6
Wood End Ave., Har. 45 H4
Wood End Clo., Nthlt. 46 A5
Wood End Gdns., 45 J5
Nthlt.
Wood End La., Nthlt. 45 H6
Wood End Rd., Har. 46 A4
Wood End Way, 45 J5
Nthlt.
Wood La. N6 40 B6
Wood La. NW9 38 D7
Wood La. W12 56 J6
Wood La., Dag. 53 C4
Wood La., Islw. 64 B6
Wood La., Stan. 29 D3
Wood La., Wdf.Grn. 34 F4
Wood Lo. Gdns., 88 B7
Brom.
Wood Lo. La., 103 C3
W.Wick.
Wood Pt. E16 60 G5
Fife Rd.
Wood Ride, Barn. 23 G1
Wood Ride, Orp. 97 G4
Wood St. E16 60 H7
Ethel Rd.
Wood St. E17 42 C3
Wood St. EC2 13 A4
Wood St. EC2 58 J6
Wood St. W4 65 E5
Wood St., Barn. 22 J4
Wood St., Kings.T. 91 H1
Wood St., Mitch. 94 A7
Wood Vale N10 40 C5
Wood Vale SE23 86 E1
Wood Vale Est. SE23 77 F6

Wood Way, Orp. 104 D2
Woodall Rd., Enf. 25 G6
Woodbank Rd., 87 F3
Brom.
Woodbastwick Rd. 86 G5
SE26
Woodberry Ave. N21 32 G3
Woodberry Ave., 36 H4
Har.
Woodberry Clo., Sun. 91 A6
Ashridge Way
Woodberry Cres. N10 40 B3
Woodberry Down N4 40 J7
Woodberry Down 40 J7
Est. N4
Woodberry Gdns. 31 F6
N12
Woodberry Gro. N4 40 J7
Woodberry Gro. N12 31 F6
Woodberry Way E4 34 C1
Woodberry Way N12 31 F6
Woodbine Clo., 82 A2
Twick.
Woodbine Gro. SE20 86 E7
Woodbine La. 99 H3
Wor.Pk.
Woodbine Pl. E11 42 G6
Woodbine Rd., Sid. 88 H1
Woodbine Ter. E9 50 F6
Morning La.
Woodbines Ave., 91 G3
Kings.T.
Woodborough Rd. 74 H4
SW15
Woodbourne Ave. 85 D3
SW16
Woodbourne Clo. 85 E3
SW16
Woodbourne Ave.
Woodbourne Dr., 98 C6
Esher
Woodbourne Gdns., 101 B7
Wall.
Woodbridge Clo. N7 49 F2
Woodbridge Clo. 47 G3
NW2
Woodbridge Ct., 35 B7
Wdf.Grn.
Woodbridge Rd., 52 J5
Bark.
Woodbridge St. EC1 8 G5
Woodbridge St. EC1 58 H4
Woodbrook Rd. SE2 71 A6
Woodburn Clo. NW4 39 A5
Woodbury Clo. E11 42 H4
Woodbury Clo., 102 C2
Croy.
Woodbury Hill, 27 B3
Loug.
Woodbury Hollow, 27 B2
Loug.
Woodbury Pk. Rd. 55 E4
W13
Woodbury Rd. E17 42 B4
Woodbury St. SW17 84 H5
Woodchester Sq. W2 10 A1
Woodchester Sq. W2 57 E5
Woodchurch Clo., 88 G3
Sid.
Woodchurch Dr., 88 A7
Brom.
Woodchurch Rd. 48 D7
NW6
Woodclyffe Dr., Chis. 97 D2
Woodcock Ct., Har. 37 H7
Woodcock Dell Ave., 37 G7
Har.
Woodcock Hill, Har. 37 F5
Woodcombe Cres. 86 F1
SE23
Woodcote Ave. NW7 30 J6
Woodcote Ave., 94 H4
Th.Hth.
Woodcote Clo., Enf. 25 F6
Woodcote Clo., 82 J5
Kings.T.
Woodcote Dr., Orp. 104 G1
Woodcote Ms., Wall. 101 B6
Woodcote Pl. SE27 85 H5
Woodcote Rd. E11 42 G7
Woodcote Rd., Wall. 101 B6
Woodcroft N21 32 F1
Woodcroft SE9 88 C3
Woodcroft, Grnf. 46 D6
Woodcroft Ave. NW7 30 E7
Woodcroft Ave., 37 C1
Stan.
Woodcroft Rd., 94 H5
Th.Hth.
Woodedge Clo. E4 34 F1
Woodend SE19 85 J6
Woodend, Sutt. 100 F2
Woodend Gdns., Enf. 24 E4

Woodend Rd. E17 42 C2
Wooder Gdns. E7 51 G4
Wooderson Clo. 95 B4
SE25
Woodfall Ave., Barn. 23 C5
Woodfall Rd. N4 49 G1
Woodfall St. SW3 30 J6
Woodfarrs SE5 77 A4
Woodfield Ave. 85 D3
SW16
Woodfield Ave. W5 55 F4
Woodfield Ave., 101 A6
Cars.
Woodfield Ave., 46 F3
Wem.
Woodfield Clo. SE19 85 J7
Woodfield Clo., Enf. 25 B4
Woodfield Cres. W5 55 G4
Woodfield Dr., Barn. 24 A7
Woodfield Gdns. W9 57 C5
Woodfield Rd.
Woodfield Gdns., 85 J7
N.Mal.
Woodfield Gro. 85 D3
SW16
Woodfield La. SW16 85 D3
Woodfield Pl. W9 57 C4
Woodfield Rd. W5 55 F4
Woodfield Rd. W9 57 C5
Woodfield Rd., 72 B2
Houns.
Woodfield Rd., T.Ditt. 98 C2
Woodfield Way N11 32 D7
Woodford Ave., Ilf. 43 B3
Woodford Bri. Rd., 43 A3
Ilf.
Woodford Ct. W12 66 A2
Shepherds Bush Grn.
Woodford Cres., 36 B2
Pnr.
Woodford New Rd. 42 E4
E17
Woodford New Rd. 42 E4
E18
Woodford New Rd., 34 F7
Wdf.Grn.
Woodford Pl., Wem. 46 H1
Woodford Rd. E7 51 H4
Woodford Rd. E18 42 G4
Woodford Trd. Est., 43 A2
Wdf.Grn.
Woodgate Ave., 98 G5
Chess.
Woodgate Cres., 28 A6
Nthwd.
Woodger Rd. W12 65 J2
Goldhawk Rd.
Woodget Clo. E6 61 B6
Remington Rd.
Woodgrange Ave. 31 G6
N12
Woodgrange Ave. 65 A1
W5
Woodgrange Ave., 25 D6
Enf.
Woodgrange Ave., 37 F5
Har.
Woodgrange Clo., 37 G5
Har.
Woodgrange Gdns., 25 D6
Enf.
Woodgrange Rd. E7 51 H5
Woodgrange Ter., 25 D6
Enf.
Great Cambridge Rd.
Woodhall Ave. SE21 86 C3
Woodhall Ave., Pnr. 36 E2
Woodhall Dr. SE21 86 C3
Woodhall Dr., Pnr. 36 D1
Woodhall Gate, Pnr. 28 D7
Woodhall La., Wat. 28 D3
Woodhall Rd., Pnr. 28 D7
Woodham Ct. E18 42 H4
Woodham Rd. SE6 87 C3
Woodhatch Clo. E6 61 B5
Leamouth Rd.
Woodhaven Gdns., 43 F3
Ilf.
Brandville Gdns.
Woodhayes Rd. 83 J7
SW19
Woodhead Dr., Orp. 104 H2
Sherlies Ave.
Woodheyes Rd. 47 D5
NW10
Woodhill SE18 70 B4
Woodhill Cres., Har. 37 G6
Woodhouse Ave., 55 C2
Grnf.
Woodhouse Clo., 55 C2
Grnf.

Woodhouse Eaves, 28 A5
Nthwd.
Woodhouse Gro. E12 52 B6
Woodhouse Rd. E11 51 F3
Woodhouse Rd. N12 31 F6
Woodhurst Ave., 97 F6
Orp.
Woodhurst Rd. SE2 71 A5
Woodhurst Rd. W3 56 C7
Woodison St. E3 59 H4
Woodknoll Dr., 97 C1
Chis.
Woodland Clo. NW9 38 C6
Woodland Clo. SE19 86 B6
Woodland Hill
Woodland Clo., 99 E6
Epsom
Woodland Clo., 34 H3
Wdf.Grn.
Woodland Cres. 69 E6
SE10
Woodland Gdns. N10 40 B5
Woodland Gdns., 73 B3
Islw.
Woodland Gro. SE10 69 E5
Woodland Hill SE19 86 B6
Woodland Ri. N10 40 B4
Woodland Ri., Grnf. 46 D6
Woodland Rd. E4 34 C1
Woodland Rd. N11 32 B5
Woodland Rd. SE19 86 C5
Woodland Rd., Loug. 27 B3
Woodland Rd., 94 G4
Th.Hth.
Woodland St. E8 50 C6
Dalston La.
Woodland Ter. SE7 70 B4
Woodland Ter. SE18 70 B4
Woodland Wk. NW3 48 H5
Aspern Rd.
Woodland Wk., 87 E4
Brom.
Woodland Way N21 32 G2
Woodland Way NW7 30 G6
Woodland Way SE2 71 D4
Woodland Way, 102 H1
Croy.
Woodland Way, 85 A7
Mitch.
Woodland Way, 93 C4
Mord.
Woodland Way, 97 F4
Orp.
Woodland Way, 99 B2
Surb.
Woodland Way, 103 B4
W.Wick.
Woodland Way, 34 H3
Wdf.Grn.
Woodlands NW11 39 B6
Woodlands SW20 92 J4
Woodlands, Har. 36 G4
Woodlands, The N14 32 B1
Woodlands, The 78 D7
SE13
Woodlands, The 85 J7
SE19
Woodlands, The, 73 C2
Islw.
Woodlands Ave. E11 51 G1
Woodlands Ave. N3 31 F7
Woodlands Ave. W3 65 B1
Woodlands Ave., 92 C1
N.Mal.
Woodlands Ave., 44 E6
Rom.
Woodlands Ave., 36 C7
Ruis.
Woodlands Ave., 88 H1
Sid.
Woodlands Ave., 99 F2
Wor.Pk.
Woodlands Clo. 39 B5
NW11
Woodlands Clo., 22 B4
Borwd.
Woodlands Clo., 97 C7
Brom.
Woodlands Clo., 98 C7
Esher
Woodlands Dr., Stan. 29 C6
Woodlands Dr., Sun. 90 C2
Woodlands Gro. 73 B2
Islw.
Woodlands Pk. Bex. 89 J4
Woodlands Pk. Rd. 40 H5
N15
Woodlands Pk. Rd. 69 E6
SE10
Woodlands Rd. E11 51 E2
Woodlands Rd. E17 42 C3
Woodlands Rd. N9 33 F1

Name	Page	Grid
Woodlands Rd. SW13	74	F3
Woodlands Rd., Bexh.	80	E3
Woodlands Rd., Brom.	97	B2
Woodlands Rd., Har.	37	C5
Woodlands Rd., Ilf.	52	F3
Woodlands Rd., Islw.	73	A3
Woodlands Rd., Sthl.	63	D1
Woodlands Rd., Surb.	91	G7
Woodlands St. SE13	78	D7
Woodlands Way SW15 *Oakhill Rd.*	75	C5
Woodlawn Clo. SW15	75	C5
Woodlawn Cres., Twick.	81	H2
Woodlawn Dr., Felt.	81	D2
Woodlawn Rd. SW6	66	A7
Woodlea Dr., Brom.	96	E5
Woodlea Rd. N16	50	B3
Woodleigh Ave. N12	31	H6
Woodleigh Gdns. SW16	85	E3
Woodley Clo. SW17 *Arnold Rd.*	84	J7
Woodman La. E4	26	E5
Woodman Path, Chig.	35	H6
Woodman St. E16	70	D1
Woodmans Gro. NW10	47	F5
Woodmans Ms. W12 *Wood La.*	56	J5
Woodmansterne Rd. SW16	85	C7
Woodmere SE9	79	C7
Woodmere Ave., Croy.	95	F7
Woodmere Clo. SW11 *Lavender Hill*	76	A3
Woodmere Clo., Croy.	95	G7
Woodmere Gdns., Croy.	95	F7
Woodmere Way, Beck.	96	D5
Woodnook Rd. SW16	85	B5
Woodpecker Clo. N9	25	E6
Woodpecker Clo. (Bushey), Wat.	28	J1
Woodpecker Rd. SE14	68	H6
Woodpecker Rd. SE28	62	C7
Woodquest Ave. SE24	76	J5
Woodridge Clo., Enf.	24	G1
Woodridings Ave., Pnr.	36	F1
Woodridings Clo., Pnr.	28	F7
Woodriffe Rd. E11	42	D7
Woodrise, Pnr.	36	A5
Woodrow SE18	70	C4
Woodrow Clo., Grnf.	46	E7
Woodrow Ct. N17 *Heybourne Rd.*	33	E7
Woodrush Clo. SE14 *Southerngate Way*	68	H7
Woodrush Way, Rom.	44	D4
Woods, The, Nthwd.	28	A5
Woods Clo. SE19 *Woodland Hill*	86	B6
Woods Ms. W1	**11**	**B5**
Woods Ms. W1	58	A7
Woods Pl. SE1	**17**	**E6**
Woods Rd. SE15	77	E1
Woodseer St. E1	**13**	**G1**
Woodseer St. E1	59	C5
Woodsford SE17	**21**	**B4**
Woodsford Sq. W14	66	B2
Woodshire Rd., Dag.	53	H3
Woodside NW11	39	D5
Woodside SW19	84	C6
Woodside, Buck.H.	34	J2
Woodside Ave. N6	39	J5
Woodside Ave. N10	40	A4
Woodside Ave. N12	31	F4
Woodside Ave. SE25	95	E6
Woodside Ave., Chis.	88	F5
Woodside Ave., Esher	91	B7
Woodside Ave., Wem.	55	H1
Woodside Clo., Stan.	29	E5
Woodside Clo., Surb.	99	C1
Woodside Clo., Wem.	55	H1
Woodside Ct. N12 *Woodside Ave.*	31	F4
Woodside Ct. Rd., Croy.	95	D7
Woodside Cres., Sid.	88	H3
Woodside End, Wem.	55	H1
Woodside Gdns. E4	34	B5
Woodside Gdns. N17	41	B2
Woodside Gra. Rd. N12	31	E4
Woodside Grn. SE25	95	D6
Woodside Gro. N12	31	F3
Woodside La. N12	31	E3
Woodside La., Bex.	80	D6
Woodside Pk. SE25	95	D5
Woodside Pk. Ave. E17	42	D4
Woodside Pk. Rd. N12	31	E4
Woodside Pl., Wem.	55	H1
Woodside Rd. E13	60	J4
Woodside Rd. N22	32	F7
Woodside Rd. SE25	95	E6
Woodside Rd., Brom.	97	B5
Woodside Rd., Kings.T.	41	E7
Woodside Rd., N.Mal.	92	D2
Woodside Rd., Sid.	88	H3
Woodside Rd., Sutt.	100	F3
Woodside Rd., Wdf.Grn.	34	G4
Woodside Way, Croy.	95	E6
Woodside Way, Mitch.	94	B1
Woodsome Rd. NW5	49	A3
Woodspring Rd. SW19	84	B2
Woodstead Gro., Edg.	29	H6
Woodstock Ave. NW11	48	B1
Woodstock Ave. W13	64	D3
Woodstock Ave., Islw.	73	D5
Woodstock Ave., Sthl.	54	F3
Woodstock Ave., Sutt.	93	C7
Woodstock Clo., Bex.	80	F7
Woodstock Clo., Stan.	37	H2
Woodstock Ct. SE12	78	G6
Woodstock Cres. N9	25	E6
Woodstock Gdns., Beck.	96	B1
Woodstock Gdns., Ilf.	53	A2
Woodstock Gro. W12	66	A2
Woodstock La., Surb.	98	F2
Woodstock La. S., Chess.	98	E4
Woodstock La. S., Esher	98	E5
Woodstock Ms. W1	**11**	**C2**
Woodstock Ri., Sutt.	93	C7
Woodstock Rd. E7	51	J7
Woodstock Rd. E17	42	D2
Woodstock Rd. N4	49	G1
Woodstock Rd. NW11	39	C7
Woodstock Rd. W4	65	E3
Woodstock Rd., Cars.	101	A5
Woodstock Rd., Croy.	102	A3
Woodstock Rd., Wem.	46	J7
Woodstock St. E16 *Victoria Dock Rd.*	60	E6
Woodstock St. W1	**11**	**D4**
Woodstock Ter. E14	60	B7
Woodstock Way, Mitch.	94	B2
Woodstone Ave., Epsom	99	G5
Woodsyre SE26	86	C4
Woodthorpe Rd. SW15	74	H4
Woodtree Clo. NW4 *Ashley La.*	38	J2
Woodvale Ave. SE25	95	C3
Woodvale Wk. SE27	85	J5
Woodvale Way NW2 *The Vale*	48	A3
Woodview Ave. E4	34	C4
Woodview Clo. N4	40	H7
Woodview Clo. SW15	83	D4
Woodview Clo., Kings.T.	83	D4
Woodville SE3	78	H1
Woodville Clo. SE12	78	G5
Woodville Clo., Tedd.	82	D4
Woodville Gdns. NW11 *Hendon Way*	39	A7
Woodville Gdns. W5	55	H6
Woodville Gdns., Ilf.	43	E3
Woodville Gro., Well.	80	A3
Woodville Rd. E11	51	H1
Woodville Rd. E17	41	H4
Woodville Rd. E18	42	H2
Woodville Rd. N16	50	B5
Woodville Rd. NW6	57	C2
Woodville Rd. NW11	39	A7
Woodville Rd. W5	55	G6
Woodville Rd., Barn.	23	E3
Woodville Rd., Mord.	93	D4
Woodville Rd., Rich.	82	E3
Woodville Rd., Th.Hth.	94	J4
Woodville St. SE18 *Woodhill*	70	B4
Woodward Ave. NW4	38	G5
Woodward Gdns., Dag. *Woodward Rd.*	53	C7
Woodward Gdns., Stan.	29	C7
Woodward Rd., Dag.	53	B7
Woodwarde Rd. SE22	77	B6
Woodway Cres., Har.	37	D6
Woodwell St. SW18 *Huguenot Pl.*	75	F5
Woodyard Clo. NW5 *Gillies St.*	49	A5
Woodyard La. SE21	77	B7
Woodyates Rd. SE12	78	G6
Wool Rd. SW20	83	H7
Woolacombe Rd. SE3	78	J1
Wooler St. SE17	**21**	**B4**
Wooler St. SE17	68	A5
Woolf Clo. SE28	71	B1
Woollaston Rd. N4	40	H6
Woolmead Ave. NW9	38	G7
Woolmer Gdns. N18	33	D6
Woolmer Rd. N18	33	D5
Woolmore St. E14	60	C7
Woolneigh St. SW6	75	E3
Woolstaplers Way SE16	**21**	**H1**
Woolston Clo. E17 *Riverhead Clo.*	41	G2
Woolstone Rd. SE23	86	H2
Woolwich Ch. St. SE18	70	B3
Woolwich Common SE18	70	D6
Woolwich Garrison SE18 *Repository Rd.*	70	D5
Woolwich High St. SE18	70	D3
Woolwich Ind. Est. SE28 *Hadden Rd.*	70	H3
Woolwich Manor Way E16	61	E7
Woolwich New Rd. SE18	70	E4
Woolwich Rd. SE2	71	D6
Woolwich Rd. SE7	69	H5
Woolwich Rd. SE10	69	H5
Woolwich Rd., Belv.	71	F5
Woolwich Rd., Bexh.	80	G4
Wooster Gdns. E14	60	D6
Woosters Ms., Har.	36	J3
Wootton Gro. N3	39	D1
Wootton St. SE1	**16**	**F2**
Wootton St. SE1	67	G1
Worbeck Rd. SE20	95	E2
Worcester Ave. N17	33	D7
Worcester Clo., Croy.	102	J2
Worcester Clo., Mitch.	94	A2
Worcester Cres. NW7	30	E3
Worcester Cres., Wdf.Grn.	34	J4
Worcester Gdns., Grnf.	45	J6
Worcester Gdns., Ilf.	43	B7
Worcester Gdns., Wor.Pk.	99	E2
Worcester Ms. NW6 *Lymington Rd.*	48	E6
Worcester Pk. Rd., Wor.Pk.	99	C3
Worcester Pl. EC4	**13**	**A5**
Worcester Rd. E12	52	C4
Worcester Rd. E17	41	G2
Worcester Rd. SW19	84	C5
Worcester Rd., Sutt.	100	D7
Wordsworth Ave. E12	52	B7
Wordsworth Ave. E18	42	F3
Wordsworth Ave., Grnf.	55	A3
Wordsworth Dr., Sutt.	99	J4
Wordsworth Rd. N16	50	B5
Wordsworth Rd. SE1	**21**	**F2**
Wordsworth Rd. SE20	86	G7
Wordsworth Rd., Hmptn.	81	F4
Wordsworth Rd., Wall.	101	C6
Wordsworth Rd., Well.	79	H1
Wordsworth Wk. NW11	39	C4
Worfield St. SW11	56	H7
Worgan St. SE11	**20**	**C3**
Worgan St. SE11	67	F5
Worland Rd. E15	51	E7
World Trade Cen. E1	**13**	**G6**
World Trade Cen. E1	59	C7
World's End Est. SW10	**18**	**E7**
World's End Est. SW10	66	F7
Worlds End La. N21	24	F5
Worlds End La., Enf.	24	F4
Worlds End La., Orp.	104	J6
World's End Pas. SW10	**18**	**E7**
World's End Pl. SW10	**18**	**E7**
Worlidge St. W6	65	J5
Worlingham Rd. SE22	77	C4
Wormholt Rd.	65	G1
Wormwood St. EC2	**13**	**D3**
Wormwood St. EC2	59	B6
Wornington Rd. W10	57	B4
Woronow Rd. NW8	57	C1
Worple Ave. SW19	84	A7
Worple Ave., Islw.	73	D5
Worple Clo., Har.	45	F1
Worple Rd. SW19	84	B7
Worple Rd. SW20	92	J2
Worple Rd., Islw.	73	D4
Worple Rd. Ms. SW19	84	C6
Worple St. SW14	74	D3
Worple Way, Har.	45	F1
Worple Way, Rich.	73	H5
Worship St. EC2	**9**	**C6**
Worship St. EC2	59	A4
Worsladde Rd. SW17	84	G4
Worsley Bri. Rd. SE26	86	J4
Worsley Bri. Rd., Beck.	87	A5
Worsley Rd. E11	51	E4
Worsopp Dr. SW4	76	C5
Worth Clo., Orp.	104	H4
Worth Gro. SE17	**21**	**B4**
Worthfield Clo., Epsom	99	D7
Worthing Clo. E15 *Mitre Rd.*	60	E2
Worthing Rd., Houns.	63	F6
Worthington Rd., Surb.	98	J1
Worthy Down Ct. SE18 *Prince Imperial Rd.*	79	D1
Wortley Rd. E6	52	A7
Wortley Rd., Croy.	94	G4
Worton Gdns., Islw.	73	A2
Worton Hall Est., Islw.	73	B4
Worton Pk. Ind. Est., Islw.	74	H3
Worton Rd., Islw.	73	A4
Worton Way, Islw.	73	A2
Wotton Rd. NW2	47	J3
Wotton Rd. SE8	68	J6
Wouldham Rd. E16	60	F6

Wragby Rd. E11 51 E3
Wrampling Pl. N9 33 D2
Croyland Rd.
Wrangthorn Wk., 101 G4
Cory.
Epsom Rd.
Wray Ave., Ilf. 43 D3
Wray Cres. N4 49 C3
Wrayfield Rd., Sutt. 100 A3
Wraysbury Clo., 72 E5
Tnouns.
Dorney Way
Wrekin Rd. SE18 70 F7
Wren Ave. NW2 47 J5
Wren Ave., Sthl. 63 F4
Wren Clo. E16 60 F6
Ibbotson Ave.
Wren Cres. 28 J1
(Bushey), Wat.
Wren Gdns., Dag. 53 D5
Wren Landing E14 69 A1
Cabot Sq.
Wren Path SE28 70 G3
Wren Rd. SE5 77 A1
Wren Rd., Dag. 53 D5
Wren Rd., Sid. 89 C4
Wren St. WC1 8 D5
Wren St. WC1 58 F4
Wrentham Ave. 57 A2
NW10
Wrenthorpe Rd., 87 E4
Brom.
Wrenwood Way, Pnr. 36 B4
Wrexham Rd. E3 60 A2
Wricklemarsh Rd. 78 J1
SE3
Wrigglesworth St. 68 G7
SE14
Wright Rd., Houns. 63 C7
Wrights Clo. SE13 78 D4
Wisteria Rd.
Wrights Clo., Dag. 53 H4
Wrights Grn. SW4 76 D4
Nelson's Row
Wrights La. W8 14 A5
Wrights La. W8 66 E3
Wrights Pl. NW10 47 C6
Mitchell Way
Wrights Rd. E3 59 J2
Wrights Rd. SE25 95 B3
Wrights Row, Wall. 101 B4
Wrights Wk. SW14 74 D3
North Worple Way
Wrigley Clo. E4 34 D5
Wrotham Rd. NW1 49 C7
Agar Pl.
Wrotham Rd. W13 64 E1
Mattock La.
Wrotham Rd., Barn. 23 B2
Wrotham Rd., Well. 80 C1
Wroths Path, Loug. 27 C1
Wrottesley Rd. 56 G2
NW10
Wrottesley Rd. SE18 70 F6
Wroughton Rd. 75 J5
SW11
Wroughton Ter. NW4 38 H4
Wroxall Rd., Dag. 53 C6
Wroxham Gdns. N11 32 C7
Wroxham Rd. SE28 62 D7
Wroxton SE15 77 E2
Wrythe Grn., Cars. 100 J3
Wrythe Grn. Rd., 100 J3
Cars.
Wrythe La., Cars. 93 F7
Wulfstan St. W12 56 F5
Wyatt Clo., Hayes 54 A5
Wyatt Pk. Rd. SW2 85 E2
Wyatt Rd. E7 51 G6
Wyatt Rd. N5 49 J3
Wyatts La. E17 42 C3
Wybert St. NW1 7 F5
Wyborne Way NW10 47 C7
Wyburn Ave., Barn. 23 C2
Wych Elm Pas., 91 J1
Kings.T.
Wyche Gro., S.Croy. 102 A7
Wycherley Clo. SE3 69 F7
Wycherley Cres., 23 E6
Barn.
Wychwood Ave. 29 G6
Edg.
Wychwood Ave., 94 J3
Th.Hth.
Wychwood Clo., Edg. 29 G6
Wychwood End N6 40 C7
Wychwood Gdns., 43 C4
Ilf.
Wychwood Way 86 A6
SE19
Central Hill
Wyclif St. EC1 8 G4

Wycliffe Clo., Well. 79 J1
Wycliffe Rd. SW11 76 A2
Wycliffe Rd. SW19 84 E6
Wycombe Gdns. 48 D2
NW11
Wycombe Pl. SW18 75 F6
Wycombe Rd. N17 41 D1
Wycombe Rd., Ilf. 45 C6
Wycombe Rd., Wem. 56 A1
Wydehurst Rd., 95 D7
Croy.
Wydell Clo., Mord. 93 A6
Wydeville Manor Rd. 87 H4
SE12
Wye Clo., Orp. 97 J7
Wye St. SW11 75 G2
Wyemead Cres. E4 34 E3
Wyevale Clo., Pnr. 36 A3
Wyfields, Ilf. 43 E1
Ravensbourne Gdns.
Wyfold Rd. SW6 75 B1
Wyhill Wk., Dag. 53 H8
Wyke Clo., Islw. 64 C6
Wyke Gdns. W7 64 C3
Wyke Rd. E3 51 A7
Wyke Rd. SW20 92 J2
Wykeham Ave., Dag. 53 C6
Wykeham Grn., Dag. 53 C6
Wykeham Hill, Wem. 46 J1
Wykeham Ri. N20 31 B1
Wykeham Rd. NW4 38 J5
Wykeham Rd., Har. 37 E4
Wyld Way, Wem. 47 H6
Wyldes Clo. NW11 48 F1
Wildwood Rd.
Wyldfield Gdns. N9 33 C2
Latymer Rd.
Wyleu St. SE23 77 H7
Wylie Rd., Sthl. 63 G3
Wyllen Clo. E1 59 F4
Wymering Rd. W9 57 D3
Wymond St. SW15 74 J3
Wynan Rd. E14 69 B5
Wynaud Ct. N22 32 F6
Palmerston Rd.
Wyncham Ave., Sid. 88 H1
Wynchgate N14 32 D1
Wynchgate N21 24 E7
Wynchgate, Har. 29 B7
Wyncroft Clo., Brom. 97 C3
Wyndale Ave. NW9 38 J4
Wyndcliff Rd. SE7 69 H6
Wyndcroft Clo., Enf. 24 H3
Wyndham Clo., Orp. 104 F1
Wyndham Clo., Sutt. 100 D7
Wyndham Cres. N19 49 C3
Wyndham Cres., 72 G6
Houns.
Wyndham Est. SE5 20 J7
Wyndham Est. SE5 67 J7
Wyndham Ms. W1 10 A1
Wyndham Pl. W1 10 A2
Wyndham Pl. W1 57 J5
Wyndham Rd. E6 52 A7
Wyndham Rd. SE5 67 J7
Wyndham Rd. W13 64 E3
Wyndham Rd., Barn. 31 J1
Wyndham Rd., 82 J7
Kings.T.
Wyndham St. W1 10 J1
Wyndham St. W1 57 J5
Wyndham Yd. W1 10 J2
Wyneham Rd. SE24 77 A5
Wynell Rd. SE23 86 G3
Wynford Pl., Belv. 71 G6
Wynford Rd. N1 8 C1
Wynford Rd. N1 58 F2
Wynford Way SE9 88 C3
Wynlie Gdns., Pnr. 36 B2
Wynndale Rd. E18 42 H1
Wynne Rd. SW9 76 G2
Wynns Ave., Sid. 80 A5
Wynnstay Gdns. W8 66 D3
Wynter St. SW11 75 D4
Wynton Gdns. SE25 95 B5
Wynton Pl. W3 56 B6
Wynyard Ter. SE11 20 D3
Wynyard Ter. SE11 67 F5
Wynyatt St. EC1 8 G4
Wyre Gro., Edg. 30 B3
Wyre Gro., Hayes 63 A4
Wyresdale Cres., 55 C3
Grnf.
Wythburn Pl. W1 10 J4
Wythens Wk. SE9 79 E6
Wythenshawe Rd., 53 G3
Dag.
Wythes Clo., Brom. 97 C2
Wythes Rd. E16 70 B1
Wythfield Rd. SE9 79 C6
Wyvenhoe Rd., Har. 45 J3
Wyvil Est. SW8 20 A7
Wyvil Rd. SW8 20 A6

Wyvil Rd. SW8 67 E6
Wyvis St. E14 60 B5

Y

Yabsley St. E14 69 C1
Yalding Rd. SE16 17 H6
Yalding Rd. SE16 68 D3
Yale Clo., Houns. 72 F5
Bramley Way
Yarborough Rd. 93 G1
SW19
Runnymede
Yardley Clo. E4 26 B5
Yardley La. E4 26 B5
Yardley St. WC1 8 E4
Yardley St. WC1 58 G3
Yarmouth Cres. N17 41 E5
Yarmouth Pl. W1 15 D2
Yarnfield Sq. SE15 77 D1
Clayton Rd.
Yarnton Way SE2 71 D7
Yarnton Way, Erith 70 J7
Yarrow Cres. E6 61 B5
Yateley St. SE18 70 A3
Yates Ct. NW2 48 A6
Yeading Ave., Har. 45 E2
Yeading Fork, Hayes 54 C5
Yeading Gdns., 54 B5
Hayes
Yeading La., Hayes 54 B6
Yeading La., Nthlt. 54 C3
Yeames Clo. W13 55 D6
Yeate St. N1 50 A7
Yeatman Rd. N6 39 J6
Yeats Clo. SE13 78 D2
Eliot Pk.
Yeldham Rd. W6 66 A5
Yellow Hammer Ct. 38 E2
NW9
Eagle Dr.
Yelverton Rd. SW11 75 G2
Yenston Clo., Mord. 93 D6
Yeo St. E3 60 B5
Yeoman Clo. SE27 85 H3
Yeoman Clo. E6 72 D7
Yeoman St. SE8 68 H4
Yeomans Acre, Ruis. 36 A6
Yeoman's Ms., Islw. 73 B5
Queensbridge Pk.
Yeoman's Row SW3 14 H6
Yeoman's Row SW3 66 H3
Yeomans Way, Enf. 25 F2
Yeomans St. E1 13 G5
Yeomen Way, Ilf. 35 F6
Yeovil Clo., Orp. 104 H2
Yerbury Rd. N19 49 D3
Yester Dr., Chis. 88 B7
Yester Pk., Chis. 88 C7
Yester Rd., Chis. 88 B7
Yew Clo., Buck.H. 35 A2
Yew Gro. NW2 48 A4
Yew Tree Clo. N21 24 G7
Yew Tree Clo., Well. 80 A1
Yew Tree Clo., 99 E1
Wor.Pk.
Yew Tree Gdns. 44 E5
(Chadwell Heath),
Rom.
Yew Tree Rd. W12 56 F7
Yew Tree Wk., 72 F5
Houns.
Yew Wk., Har. 46 B1
Yewdale Clo., Brom. 87 E6
Yewfield Rd. NW10 47 F6
Yewtree Clo. N22 40 C1
Yewtree Rd., Beck. 95 J3
Yoakley Rd. N16 50 B2
Yoke Clo. N7 49 E6
Ewe Clo.
Yolande Gdns. SE9 79 B5
Yonge Pk. N4 49 G3
York Ave. SW14 74 C5
York Ave., Sid. 88 H2
York Ave., Stan. 37 E1
York Bri. NW1 7 B5
York Bri. NW1 58 A4
York Bldgs. WC2 12 B6
York Clo. E6 61 C6
Boultwood Rd.
York Clo., Mord. 93 E4
York Cres., Borwd. 22 D2
York Cres., Loug. 27 B3
York Gate N14 24 E7
York Gate NW1 7 B6
York Gate NW1 58 A4
York Gro. SE15 77 F1
York Hill SE27 85 H3
York Hill, Loug. 27 B3
York Hill Est. SE27 85 H3
York Ho., Wem. 46 J4
York Ho. Pl. W8 14 A3

York Ho. Pl. W8 66 E2
York Ms. NW5 49 B5
Kentish Town Rd.
York Ms., Ilf. 52 D3
York Par., Brent. 64 G5
York Pl. SW11 75 F2
York Pl. WC2 12 B6
York Pl., Dag. 53 J6
York Pl. Ilf. 52 D3
York Rd.
York Ri. NW5 49 B3
York Ri., Orp. 104 H1
York Rd. E4 34 A5
York Rd. E7 51 G6
York Rd. E10 51 C3
York Rd. E17 41 G5
York Rd. N11 32 D6
York Rd. N18 33 E6
York Rd. N21 25 A7
York Rd. SE1 16 D7
York Rd. SE1 67 F2
York Rd. SW11 75 F4
York Rd. SW18 75 F4
York Rd. SW19 84 F6
York Rd. W3 56 C6
York Rd. W5 64 F3
York Rd., Barn. 23 F5
York Rd., Brent. 64 G5
York Rd., Croy. 94 G7
York Rd., Houns. 72 H3
York Rd., Ilf. 52 D3
York Rd., Kings.T. 82 J7
York Rd., Nthwd. 36 A2
York Rd., Rich. 73 J5
Albert Rd.
York Rd., Sutt. 100 D6
York Rd., Tedd. 82 B4
York Sq. E14 59 H6
York St. W1 10 J2
York St. W1 57 J5
York St., Bark. 61 F1
Abbey Rd.
York St., Mitch. 94 A7
York St., Twick. 82 D1
York Ter., Erith 80 J1
York Ter. E. NW1 7 C6
York Ter. E. NW1 58 A4
York Ter. W. NW1 7 B6
York Ter. W. NW1 58 A4
York Way N1 58 E1
York Way N7 49 D6
York Way N20 31 J3
York Way, Borwd. 22 D2
York Way, Chess. 98 H7
York Way, Felt. 81 F3
York Way Ct. N1 58 E1
Yorkland Ave., Well. 79 J3
Yorkshire Clo. N16 50 B3
Yorkshire Gdns. N18 33 E5
Yorkshire Grey Pl. 48 F4
NW3
Heath St.
Yorkshire Grey Yd. 12 C2
WC1
Yorkshire Rd. E14 59 H6
Yorkshire Rd., 94 E5
Mitch.
Yorkton St. E2 9 H2
Yorkton St. E2 59 D2
Young Rd. E16 60 J6
Young St. W8 14 A4
Young St. W8 66 E2
Youngmans Clo., 24 J1
Enf.
Young's Bldgs. EC1 9 A5
Youngs Rd., Ilf. 43 G5
Yoxley App., Ilf. 43 F6
Yoxley Dr., Ilf. 43 F6
Yukon Rd. SW12 76 B7
Yuletide Clo. NW10 47 E7
Yunus Khan Clo. E17 42 A5

Z

Zampa Rd. SE16 68 F5
Zander Ct. E2 9 J3
Zangwill Rd. SE3 79 A1
Zealand Rd. E3 59 H2
Zennor Rd. SW12 85 C1
Zenoria St. SE22 77 C4
Zermatt Rd., Th.Hth. 94 J4
Zetland St. E14 60 B5
Zion Pl., Th.Hth. 95 A4
Zion Rd., Th.Hth. 95 A5
Zoar St. SE1 16 J1
Zoffany St. N19 49 D2